THE CAMBRIDGE HANDBOOK OF THE LAW OF ALGORITHMS

Algorithms are a fundamental building block of artificial intelligence – and, increasingly, society – but our legal institutions have largely failed to recognize or respond to this reality. *The Cambridge Handbook of the Law of Algorithms*, which features contributions from US, EU, and Asian legal scholars, discusses the specific challenges algorithms pose not only to current law, but also – as algorithms replace people as decision-makers – to the foundations of society itself. The work includes wide coverage of the law as it relates to algorithms, with chapters analyzing how human biases have crept into algorithmic decision-making about who receives housing or credit, the length of sentences for defendants convicted of crimes, and many other decisions that impact constitutionally protected groups. Other issues covered in the work include the impact of algorithms on the law of free speech, intellectual property, and commercial and human rights law.

Woodrow Barfield holds a PhD in engineering, a JD, and an LLM. A recipient of the NSF Presidential Young Investigator Award, Dr. Barfield is the editor of *Fundamentals of Wearable Computers and Augmented Reality* and co-editor of *Research Handbook on the Law of Artificial Intelligence*. He is currently an associate editor of the *Virtual Reality Journal*, review editor for *Frontiers in Artificial Intelligence*, and an editorial board member for *Delphi: Interdisciplinary Review of Emerging Technologies*.

T0370663

The Cambridge Handbook of the Law of Algorithms

Edited by

WOODROW BARFIELD

CAMBRIDGE
UNIVERSITY PRESS

CAMBRIDGE
UNIVERSITY PRESS

Shaftesbury Road, Cambridge CB2 8EA, United Kingdom

One Liberty Plaza, 20th Floor, New York, NY 10006, USA

477 Williamstown Road, Port Melbourne, VIC 3207, Australia

314–321, 3rd Floor, Plot 3, Splendor Forum, Jasola District Centre, New Delhi – 110025, India

103 Penang Road, #05–06/07, Visioncrest Commercial, Singapore 238467

Cambridge University Press is part of Cambridge University Press & Assessment,
a department of the University of Cambridge.

We share the University's mission to contribute to society through the pursuit of
education, learning and research at the highest international levels of excellence.

www.cambridge.org
Information on this title: www.cambridge.org/9781009293150

DOI: 10.1017/9781108680844

First published 2021
First paperback edition 2023

A catalogue record for this publication is available from the British Library

Library of Congress Cataloging-in-Publication data
NAMES: Barfield, Woodrow, editor.
TITLE: The Cambridge handbook of the law of algorithms / edited by Woodrow Barfield,
University of Washington (Emeritus).
DESCRIPTION: Cambridge, United Kingdom ; New York, NY : Cambridge University Press, 2021. |
Series: Cambridge law handbooks | Includes index.
IDENTIFIERS: LCCN 2020039007 (print) | LCCN 2020039008 (ebook) | ISBN 9781108481960 (hardback) |
ISBN 9781108680844 (ebook)
SUBJECTS: LCSH: Law – Automation. | Artificial intelligence – Law and legislation. | Computer
networks – Law and legislation. | Technology and law. | Decision making – Mathematical models.
CLASSIFICATION: LCC K87 .C354 2021 (print) | LCC K87 (ebook) | DDC 343.09/99–dc23
LC record available at https://lccn.loc.gov/2020039007
LC ebook record available at https://lccn.loc.gov/2020039008

ISBN   978-1-108-48196-0   Hardback
ISBN   978-1-009-29315-0   Paperback

Contents

List of Figures	*page* ix	
List of Tables	x	
Notes on Contributors	xi	
Foreword: Algorithms and the Law		
Lord Patrick Hodge	xix	
Preface		
Woodrow Barfield	xxiii	
Acknowledgements	xxv	
List of Abbreviations	xxvi	

PART I   INTRODUCTION AND SETTING THE STAGE FOR A LAW OF ALGORITHMS

1	**An Introduction to Law and Algorithms** Woodrow Barfield and Jessica Barfield	3
2	**The Opinion of Machines** Curtis E. A. Karnow	16
3	**Private Accountability in an Age of Artificial Intelligence** Sonia K. Katyal	47
4	**Algorithmic Legitimacy** Ari Ezra Waldman	107
5	**Understanding Transparency in Algorithmic Accountability** Margot E. Kaminski	121

PART II   BUSINESS, REGULATIONS, AND DECISION-MAKING WITH ALGORITHMS

6	**Algorithms and Contract Law** Lauren Henry Scholz	141

7   Algorithms, Agreements, and Agency   153
    Shawn Bayern

8   Algorithmic Governance and Administrative Law   162
    Steven M. Appel and Cary Coglianese

9   Discrimination in the Age of Algorithms   182
    Robin Nunn

10 Algorithmic Competition, Collusion, and Price Discrimination   199
    Salil K. Mehra

11 The Rule of Law and Algorithmic Governance   209
    Rónán Kennedy

12 Governance of Algorithms: Rethinking Public Sector Use
    of Algorithms for Predictive Purposes   233
    Anjanette H. Raymond and Ciabhan Connelly

13 From Rule of Law to Statute Drafting: Legal Issues for
    Algorithms in Government Decision-Making
    Monika Zalnieriute, Lisa Burton Crawford, Janina Boughey,   251
    Lyria Bennett Moses, and Sarah Logan

14 Algorithmic Decision Systems: Automation and Machine
    Learning in the Public Administration   273
    David Restrepo Amariles

15 From Legal Sources to Programming Code: Automatic Individual Decisions
    in Public Administration and Computers under the Rule of Law   301
    Dag Wiese Schartum

    PART III   INTELLECTUAL PROPERTY AND ALGORITHMS

16 Inventive Algorithms and the Evolving Nature of Innovation   339
    Ryan Abbott

17 Software Patenting and Section 101's Gatekeeping Function   374
    Andrew Chin

18 Intellectual Property at a Crossroad: Awarding IP Protection for Algorithms   391
    Aviv Gaon

    PART IV   CRIMINAL LAW, TORT ISSUES, AND ALGORITHMS

19 The Use of Algorithms in Criminal Adjudication   407
    Andrea Roth

20 Assessing the Risk of Offending through Algorithms   432
    Christopher Slobogin

21 Injury by Algorithms   449
    Seema Ghatnekar Tilak

22 When Do Algorithmic Tortfeasors that Caused Damage
    Warrant Unique Legal Treatment?   471
    Karni Chagal-Feferkorn

23 Tort-Law: Applying A "Reasonableness" Standard to Algorithms   493
    Karni Chagal-Feferkorn

    PART V   CONSTITUTIONAL LAW, HUMAN RIGHTS, AND ALGORITHMS

24 Human Rights-Based Approach to AI and Algorithms:
    Concerning Welfare Technologies   517
    Jędrzej Niklas

25 Four Modes of Speech Protection for Algorithms   543
    Kyle Langvardt

26 Algorithms and Freedom of Expression   558
    Manasvin (Veenu) Goswami

27 Artificial Minds in First Amendment Borderlands   579
    Marc Jonathan Blitz

28 The First Amendment and Algorithms   606
    Stuart Minor Benjamin

29 Algorithmic Analysis of Social Behavior for Profiling,
    Ranking, and Assessment   632
    Nizan Geslevich Packin and Yafit Lev-Aretz

30 Algorithmic Stages in Privacy of Data Analytics: Process and Probabilities   654
    Ronald P. Loui, Arno R. Lodder, and Stephanie A. Quick

    PART VI   APPLICATIONS AND FUTURE DIRECTIONS OF LAW
              AND ALGORITHMS

31 Moral Machines: The Emerging EU Policy on "Trustworthy AI"   667
    Andrea Renda

32 Law in Turing's Cathedral: Notes on the Algorithmic Turn of the Legal
    Universe   691
    Nicola Lettieri

**33   Arguing over Algorithms: Mapping the Dilemmas Inherent in
       Operationalizing "Ethical" Artificial Intelligence**   722
       Mariano-Florentino Cuéllar and Robert J. MacCoun

34   Embodiment and Algorithms for Human–Robot Interaction   736
       Yueh-Hsuan Weng and Chih-hsing Ho

35   On Being Trans-Human: Commercial BCIs and the Quest for Autonomy 757
       Argyro P. Karanasiou

Index   775

Figures

2.1	A five-layer network	*page* 22
2.2	My model of stock prices	42
2.3	My model with fresh data	43
14.1	Methods and techniques of AI	276
15.1	Main aspects of law and digital government	305
15.2	Overview of the transformation process	306
15.3	Main phases and activities in the transformation process	311
15.4	Deduction of legal rules	313
15.5	Deduction of facts	314
15.6	Deduction of operations	317
15.7	Processing individual cases in three steps	318
15.8	Survey of strategies for generating decision data, from relevant facts to bases for decisions	325
15.9	Connection between legislative processes and systems development to implement them	332
17.1	Flowchart representation of Patent Office guidance since 2014 for examination of claims under the § 101 patent-eligible subject matter requirement	386
22.1	Autonomy level as a classifier for thinking algorithms	488
22.2	Purposive interpretation as a classifier for thinking algorithms	489

Tables

5.1	Individual transparency	*page* 130
5.2	Systemic transparency	132
5.3	Second-order transparency	134
16.1	Evolution of algorithm invention	356
17.1	Causal processes involving each of the disclosed structural elements supporting claim 15	380
22.1	Features characterizing thinking algorithms	489
23.1	Alternatives of using "reasonableness" as a test for determining liability	511
35.1	A typology of traits, methods, and applications in BCIs	766
35.2	A typology of artificial agency in AI-supported decision-making	769

Notes on Contributors

Ryan Abbott, MD, JD, MTOM, PhD, is Professor of Law and Health Sciences at the University of Surrey School of Law and Adjunct Assistant Professor of Medicine at the David Geffen School of Medicine at UCLA. His research focuses on law and technology, health law, and intellectual property. His most recent publication, *The Reasonable Robot: Artificial Intelligence and the Law*, was published by Cambridge University Press in 2020.

David Restrepo Amariles, Associate Professor of Data Law & AI at HEC Paris and Director of Research on Smart Law at the DATA IA Institute. He is an associate researcher of the Cyberjustice Laboratory (Université de Montreal & McGill University) where he leads the research group focused on "Smart Contracts and Regulatory Technologies" (ACT Project). He is a fellow of the Perelman Centre, a digital entrepreneur, and co-founder of the Privatech.app.

Steven M. Appel is a fellow at the Wharton Social Impact Initiative and a JD/Masters in Bioethics candidate at the University of Pennsylvania Law School, and holds an MBA in sustainability. He previously co-founded a non-profit dedicated to ethnic, racial, and religious understanding, ran for public office in New York City, and is broadly interested in questions at the intersection of innovation, sustainability, and ethics.

Yafit Lev-Aretz is Assistant Professor of Law at Zicklin School of Business, Baruch College, City University of New York. Her research and writing focuses on algorithmic decision-making, intrusive means of news dissemination, choice architecture in the age of big data, and the ethical challenges posed by machine learning and artificially intelligent systems. Professor Lev-Aretz's scholarship has been published in leading law reviews such as the *Harvard Journal for Law and Technology*, the *Yale Journal of Law and Technology*, and the *Yale Journal on Regulation*.

Jessica K. Barfield, MA, MS, has served as a research assistant at Duke University and has interests in the design and use of digital technologies such as algorithmic-driven systems, voice-based digital assistants, and human–computer and human–robot inter-action. She reviews for the *Virtual Reality* journal, and has reviewed book proposals for Springer Press.

Woodrow Barfield, PhD, JD, LLM, has served as Professor of Engineering and headed a research laboratory focusing on the design and use of virtual and augmented reality displays. He was an external fellow for Stanford's Center for Internet and Society, is currently an associate editor of the *Virtual Reality* journal, the author of *Cyber Humans: Our Future with Machines*, co-editor of the *Research Handbook on the Law of Virtual and Augmented Reality* and the *Research Handbook on the Law of Artificial Intelligence*, editor of *Fundamentals of Wearable Computers and Augmented Reality* (1st and 2nd editions), and has co-authored (with Ugo Pagallo) a textbook on an *Advanced Introduction to Law and Artificial Intelligence*.

Shawn Bayern is the Larry and Joyce Beltz Professor and Associate Dean for Academic Affairs at the Florida State University College of Law. Before his legal career, he worked in computing research, with a focus on computer security and programming-language specification.

Stuart Minor Benjamin is the Douglas B. Maggs Professor of Law and co-director of the Center for Innovation Policy at Duke Law School. He specializes in telecommunications law, the First Amendment, and administrative law. He is a co-author of *Internet and Telecommunication Regulation* (2019) and *Telecommunications Law and Policy* (multiple editions), and has written numerous law review articles. He has testified before House and Senate committees as a legal expert on a range of topics.

Lyria Bennett Moses, BSc (Hons), LLB, LLM, JSD, is Director of the Allens Hub for Technology, Law and Innovation and a professor in the Faculty of Law at UNSW Sydney. Lyria has research interests in issues on the relationship between technology and law, including the types of legal issues that arise as technology changes, how these issues are addressed in Australia and other jurisdictions, and the problems of treating "technology" as an object of regulation. Lyria is a member of the editorial boards of *Technology and Regulation, Law, Technology and Humans*, and *Law in Context*, and is on the committee of the Australian chapter of IEEE's Society for the Social Implications of Technology.

Marc Jonathan Blitz, PhD, JD, is Alan Joseph Bennett Professor of Law at Oklahoma City College of Law. His scholarship focuses on constitutional protection for freedom of thought and freedom of expression. He has produced scholarly works on privacy and national security law with a focus on emerging technologies, including public video surveillance, biometric identification methods, virtual reality, and library Internet systems.

Janina Boughey, PhD, LLM, BEc(soc. sci.)(Hons I)/LLB(Hons I), is a senior lecturer in the Faculty of Law at the University of New South Wales, who teaches and researches in administrative law. She is the author of *Human Rights in Australia and Canada: The Newest Despotism?*, co-author of *Government Liability: Principles and Remedies* and *Public Law and Statutory Interpretation: Principles and Practice*, co-editor of *The Legal Protection of Human Rights in Australia*, reviews editor of the *Australian Journal of Administrative Law*, and Director of the Gilbert + Tobin Centre of Public Law's Administrative Justice and Statutes Projects.

Andrew Chin is Paul B. Eaton Distinguished Professor of Law and Adjunct Professor of Library and Information Science at the University of North Carolina. He holds a D.Phil. in computer science from the University of Oxford and a JD from Yale Law School.

Cary Coglianese is the Edward B. Shils Professor of Law and Political Science and the Director of the Penn Program on Regulation at the University of Pennsylvania Law School. He specializes in the study of administrative law and regulation, with an emphasis on the empirical evaluation of alternative processes and strategies, as well as the role of public participation, technology, and business–government relations in regulatory policymaking and administrative decision-making.

Ciabhan Connelly is a researcher interested in political science and data science applied to politics, with a specific interest in employing algorithms for the sake of social good. He completed his undergraduate degree at Indiana University, and is now studying as a PhD Student in the Human Centered Computing Program at the Georgia Institute of Technology.

Lisa Burton Crawford, PhD, BCL, BA/LLB (Hons I), is a senior lecturer in the Faculty of Law at the University of New South Wales who teaches and researches in the field of public law, with a special interest in the intersection of constitutional law, administrative law, and legal theory. Lisa is the author of *The Rule of Law and the Australian Constitution*, co-author of *Public Law and Statutory Interpretation: Principles and Practice*, co-editor of *Law under a Democratic Constitution: Essays in Honour of Jeffrey Goldsworthy*, Deputy Director of the Gilbert + Tobin Centre of Public Law, and a director of the Centre's Statutes Project.

Mariano-Florentino Cuéllar, JD, PhD, Justice, Supreme Court of California, Herman Phleger Visiting Professor and former Stanley Morrison Professor of Law, Professor (by courtesy) of Political Science, and Director of the Freeman Spogli Institute for International Studies at Stanford University, member of the Harvard Corporation (the President & Fellows of Harvard College) and the boards of the Hewlett Foundation and the American Law Institute, and chair of the boards of the Center for Advanced Study in the Behavioral Sciences, AI Now, and Stanford Seed. Justice Cuéllar is a scholar of public law and institutions whose books and articles explore problems in administrative law and legislation, cyberlaw and artificial intelligence, criminal justice, public health, immigration, international law and security, and the history of institutions.

Karni Chagal-Feferkorn PhD at the Haifa University Faculty of Law, has written on algorithms and tort law under the supervision of Professor Niva-Elkin-Koren. Karni is an attorney admitted to the New York, California, and Israel Bar, and holds an LLM degree from Stanford Law School. She is also a founding partner at Lexidale, a consultancy firm specializing in comparative research pertaining to law and regulation.

Dr. Aviv Gaon is a member of IP Osgoode Center for Intellectual Property and Technology at Osgoode Hall Law School, a research fellow at The Munk School of Global Affairs and Public Policy at the University of Toronto, and Academic Director of Harry Radzyner Law School Experiential Programs at IDC Herzliya. Dr. Gaon specializes in Intellectual Property, Law and Technology, and Competition Law.

Manasvin Goswami (Veenu) is a graduate of the University of Toronto Law School and has clerked at the Supreme Court of Canada. His scholarly interests include free speech issues, particularly those involving technology and algorithms.

Dr. Chih-hsing Ho, PhD, JSM, LLM, is Assistant Research Fellow/Assistant Professor at the Institute of European and American Studies, and the Research Center for Information Technology Innovation (joint appointment), Academia Sinica, Taiwan. Her research focuses on the nexus of law and medicine in general, with particular attention to the governance of genomics and newly emerging technologies, such as biobanks, big data, and artificial intelligence. Her works appear in several leading journals, such as *Nature Genetics, BMC Medical Ethics, Frontiers in Genetics, Medical Law International, Asian Bioethics Review*, and the *Journal of Law, Information and Science*. Since 2016, she has served as review editor for the Editorial Board of ELSI in Science and Genetics – Frontiers.

Patrick S. Hodge (Lord Hodge) has been a Justice of the United Kingdom Supreme Court since 2013, before which he was senior judge in the Commercial Court in Scotland. He has lectured on financial technology and the law in the United Kingdom and in China.

Dr. Argyro P. Karanasiou is Associate Professor (SL) of Law and the Director for LETS (Law, Emerging Tech & Science) Lab at the University of Greenwich in London, UK. She also holds visiting affiliations with Yale Law School (ISP Fellow), NYU Law (ILI Alumna), Harvard Law (CopyX affiliate Faculty staff), Complutense Madrid (ITC). Her area of expertise is Data Protection and Automated Decision Making and she has contributed invited expert insights on a number of occasions, most notably for the Equality and Human Rights Commission, the Chatham House, the US Air Force, the Royal Society, the OSCE, the Council of Europe and the Electronic Frontiers Foundation.

Margot E. Kaminski is Associate Professor at the University of Colorado Law and Director of the Privacy Initiative at Silicon Flatirons. She specializes in the law of new technologies, with a recent focus on autonomous systems. Her academic work has been published in the *UCLA Law Review, Minnesota Law Review*, and *Southern California Law Review*, among others, and she frequently writes for the popular press.

Curtis Karnow is a judge of the California Superior Court, County of San Francisco and is the author of *How the Courts Work* (2008), *Litigation in Practice* (2017), *Future Codes: Essays in Advanced Computer Technology and the Law* (1997), and a contributing author of *Robot Law* (2016) and co-author of the leading guide of California civil practice, *Civil Procedure before Trial* (2019). His papers address legal procedure, computer law, artificial intelligence, and ethics, among other subjects; Judge Karnow has lectured at the law schools at Yale, Stanford, San Francisco, New York University, and Hastings.

Sonia Katyal is co-Associate Dean for Faculty Research and Development and Haas Distinguished Professor of Law at University of California at Berkeley, where she also co-directs the Berkeley Center for Law and Technology. Her research focuses on the intersection of technology, intellectual property, and civil rights (including antidiscrimination, privacy, and freedom of speech), specifically focusing on trademarks, trade secrecy, artificial intelligence, and the right to information. She is the co-author of "Property Outlaws" (with Eduardo Penalver) and "The Paradox of Source Code Secrecy" (2019) in the *Cornell Law Review*; "Technoheritage" (2017) in the *California Law Review*; "The Numerus Clausus of Sex" in the *University of Chicago Law Review* (2017); and "Platform

Law and the Brand Enterprise" in the *Berkeley Journal of Law and Technology* (with Leah Chan Grinvald). She has also served on the inaugural US Commerce Department's Digital Economy Board of Advisors, as an Affiliate Scholar at Stanford Law's Center for Internet and Society, and on the advisory boards for Media Studies and the CITRIS Policy Lab at UC Berkeley.

Rónán Kennedy is a member of the School of Law in the National University of Ireland Galway. He researches and teaches environmental law, information technology law, and their intersections. He is a graduate of NUI Galway, the King's Inns, New York University, and University College London. He has a background in information technology and information systems, was Executive Legal Officer to the Chief Justice of Ireland, Mr. Justice Ronan Keane, from 2000 to 2004, and was a member of the Advisory Committee of the Environmental Protection Agency from 2016 to 2019.

Kyle Langvardt is an assistant professor of law at the University of Nebraska College of Law and a faculty fellow at the Nebraska Governance and Technology Center at the University of Nebraska. He teaches and writes in constitutional law, technology, and regulation. He is a graduate of Earlham College and the University of Chicago Law School.

Nicola Lettieri, PhD, is researcher at the National Institute for Public Policy Analysis (Rome) and Adjunct Professor of Legal Informatics and Computational Social Science at the University of Sannio (Benevento). He is currently Associate Editor of *Frontiers in Artificial Intelligence Law and Technology*, member of the editorial board of *Future Internet*, and co-editor of the international series *Law, Science and Technology*. His research focuses on how the intersection between law, complexity theory, cognitive science, and computational social science can provide a more empirically grounded understanding of socio-legal phenomena and new tools enhancing legal regulation of social life.

Arno R. Lodder is a professor of Internet Governance and Regulation at Vrije Universiteit Amsterdam, and of counsel at SOLV lawyers. In his research and lecturing, he focuses on topics related to law and Internet, such as liability, contracting, security, privacy, freedom of speech, cybercrime, and phenomena related to algorithms, big data, social media, cyberwar, the Internet of Things, smart devices, and apps.

Sarah Logan, PhD, is a lecturer in the Department of International Relations at the Australian National University, and was previously a research fellow at UNSW Law under the auspices of the Data to Decisions Cooperative Research Centre. Her research interests focus on the intersection of technology and international politics, especially the practice of national security. Her work will be published in a forthcoming single-authored monograph, *Hold Your Friends Close: Countering Radicalisation in Britain and America*.

Ronald P. Loui has been a contributor to AI and Law since 1993, and has taught or carried out research at Harvard, Rochester, Stanford, Washington University in St. Louis, University of Illinois, and currently Case Western Reserve University. He led graduate seminars in cyberwarfare and computer surveillance after co-authoring with an analyst at the National Security Agency, and an officer at the US State Department. He co-founded CivicFeed (now PeakMetrics), which provides media monitoring data to AI projects for advocacy, political campaigns, and defense.

Robert J. MacCoun is the James and Patricia Kowal Professor of Law at Stanford Law School, Professor by courtesy in Stanford's Psychology Department, and a senior fellow at the Freeman Spogli Institute. In 2019, MacCoun received the James McKeen Cattell Fellow Award of the Association for Psychological Science "for a lifetime of outstanding contributions to applied psychological research" and he has served as Editor of the *Annual Review of Law and Social Science* since 2018.

Salil K. Mehra is the Charles Klein Professor of Law and Government at Temple University's James E. Beasley School of Law in Philadelphia, Pennsylvania. He teaches and writes about antitrust, markets, and technology.

Jędrzej Niklas, PhD, is currently a postdoctoral researcher at the Data Justice Lab at Cardiff University. He previously worked at the London School of Economics and the University of Leeds. His research focuses on the relationship between law, new technologies, and political theory. Jędrzej is also a visiting scholar at the Department of Media and Communications at the LSE and at the Centre for Internet & Human Rights at European University Viadrina.

Robin Nunn serves as chair of Dechert LLP's Consumer Financial Services practice. Ms. Nunn assists clients with both traditional legal, ethical, and policy risks to an array of products and services and novel issues connected to new communication technologies, blockchain, artificial intelligence, and big data.

Nizan Geslevich Packin is Associate Professor of Law at the Zicklin School of Business, City University of New York, and an affiliated faculty at Indiana University's program on Governance of the Internet & Cybersecurity. She has written articles, book chapters, and op-eds for diverse outlets, including the *Wall Street Journal, Forbes, American Banker, Harvard Law School Corporate Governance Forum, Oxford Business Law Blog, Washington University Law Review, Indiana Law Journal, Utah Law Review, Houston Law Review, William and Mary Law Review, Columbia Business Law Review*, and the American Bar Association.

Stephanie A. Quick is an attorney with experience in intellectual property law, commercial litigation, and administrative law and regulatory matters. She writes frequently about law and technology issues, and currently practices law in Washington, DC.

Anjanette (Angie) Raymond is Director of the Program on Data Management and Information Governance at the Ostrom Workshop, Associate Professor in the Department of Business Law and Ethics at the Kelley School of Business, Indiana University, and Adjunct Associate Professor of Law at Maurer Law School (Indiana). She is currently completing her PhD at the Centre for Commercial Law Studies, Queen Mary, University of London, exploring the use of algorithms in justice environments.

Andrea Renda is Professor of Digital Innovation at the College of Europe in Bruges (Belgium), and a Senior Research Fellow and Head of Global Governance, Regulation, Innovation, and the Digital Economy at the Centre for European Policy Studies in Brussels (Belgium). He is a Member of the EU High-Level Expert Group on Artificial Intelligence, Member of the Task Force on AI of the Italian Ministry for Economic Development, and Fellow of the World Academy of Art and Science.

Andrea Roth is Professor of Law at UC Berkeley School of Law, and teaches criminal law, criminal procedure, evidence, and forensic evidence. She is one of several faculty co-directors of the Berkeley Center for Law and Technology, is an appointed member of the Legal Resources Committee of the Organization of Scientific Area Committees run by the National Institute of Standards and Technology, and lectures nationally on forensic science and AI-related issues in criminal adjudication.

Dag Wiese Schartum is Doctor of Law, and Professor and Director of the Norwegian Research Center for Computers and Law, University of Oslo, Norway. Schartum's research has mainly focused on automation of legal decision-making and data protection. He has published a number of books and articles.

Lauren Henry Scholz is Assistant Professor at Florida State University College of Law and an affiliated scholar at the Information Society Project at Yale Law School. She is a graduate of Harvard Law School and Yale College.

Christopher Slobogin, Milton Underwood Professor of Law at Vanderbilt University, has written extensively on criminal justice issues, including books published by Harvard, Oxford, and Chicago University Presses, and over 100 articles. According to the Leiter Report, he is one of the five most cited criminal law and procedure law professors in the country over the past five years, and one of the top fifty most cited law professors overall from 2005 to 2015, according to Hein Online. He has taught at Hastings, Stanford, Virginia, and USC Law Schools as a visiting professor, and was a Fulbright Scholar in Kiev, Ukraine.

Seema Ghatnekar Tilak is an intellectual property attorney specializing in media law and entertainment. She has litigated numerous media disputes on behalf of celebrities and public figures, and now focuses her practice on transactional matters as founding partner of the law firm Create LLP based in Los Angeles, California. Seema is a fervent lecturer in and researcher of the intersection of law, technology, and new media.

Ari Ezra Waldman is Professor of Law and Computer Science at Northeastern University School of Law and the Khoury College of Computer Sciences. He is also an affiliate fellow at the Yale Law School Information Society Project. His chapter was written while he was the Microsoft Visiting Professor of Information Technology at Princeton University's Center for Information Technology Policy. An award-winning scholar of law, society, and technology, he received his PhD from Columbia University, his JD from Harvard Law School, and his AB from Harvard College.

Yueh-Hsuan Weng is an assistant professor at the Frontier Research Institute for Interdisciplinary Sciences (FRIS), Tohoku University, Japan, a visiting scientist at RIKEN-AIP, and a TTLF fellow at Stanford Law School. He received his PhD in Law from Peking University and his MS in Computer Science from National Chiao Tung University, Taiwan. He is strongly interested in interdisciplinary studies, especially issues concerning the interface between AI and Law, including Robot Law, Social Robotics, and Legal Informatics. During his PhD studies, he founded ROBOLAW.ASIA and CHINA-LII, which are China's first initiatives in AI Law and Free Access to Law. He has been an associate editor of *Delphi – Interdisciplinary Review of Emerging Technologies* since January 2018.

Monika Zalnieriute, PhD, LLM, LLM, LLB (1st Class), is a research fellow at the Allens
Hub for Technology, Law & Innovation at the Faculty of Law at the University of New
South Wales, where she leads a research stream on Technologies and Rule of Law, which
explores the interplay between law, technology, and politics in the "digital age." Monika
has published in *Modern Law Review*, *Yale Journal of Law & Technology*, *Berkeley Journal
of Gender, Law and Justice*, and *Stanford Journal of International Law*, and is currently
working on a monograph on data privacy law, Internet architecture, and human rights.
These days, Monika spends much of her time thinking and writing about the rule of law
and technology.

Foreword

Algorithms and the Law

Four developments have given rise to new opportunities and new challenges. They are the huge increase in the processing power of computers, the availability of data on an unprecedented scale, the fall in the costs of the storage of data, and the increasingly sophisticated software services which have become available.

The international interest in the potential of the new technologies can be seen in the rapid expansion of artificial intelligence (AI) start-ups, including in the field of financial technology, and the high level of investment in the technologies by established commercial corporations. Both governments and businesses are exploring the potential of the new technologies to improve the services which they provide and to reduce the costs of the provision of such services.

The power of AI to exceed the capacity of human intelligence to analyze data and take decisions based on that analysis is creating opportunities in many fields. Some technology involving algorithms, such as auto-pilots, is well established. More recently, the development of medical devices, robotic surgery, and driverless cars has expanded the use of the technology. In some countries, the technology is increasingly used in criminal justice in sentencing, predicting recidivism, and making decisions about whether to grant bail – matters which affect personal liberty.

Another technology, distributed ledger technology (DLT), also offers many benefits. For example, the UK government sees DLT technology as offering a means of ensuring the integrity of government records and services and the provision of such services at lower cost. The processing of "big data" holds out the prospect of enhanced accuracy in medical diagnosis and the prescription of treatment. Investment in the technologies in the financial services industry seeks to realize the substantial annual savings which have been predicted in banking transactions and cross-border payments.

At the same time, AI and big data analysis can be and are being used by autocratic regimes as an instrument of social and political control of the populations for which they are responsible. In China, the developing "social credit" system involves intrusion by the state into the lives of its citizens in ways which would not be compatible with Western values. But in the West, the technologies offer states the ability to probe into citizens' lives – for example, to secure the proper payment of taxes and the correct distribution of social security benefits, raising new questions of data protection and privacy. There are also political questions raised on the international plane: the technologies can be and are also being used by hostile regimes to influence the outcome of democratic decision-making in Western democracies.

Questions are being raised about the intentional or unintentional use of data to underpin unacceptably discriminatory behavior. The use of AI by governmental bodies and business corporations raises questions about the protection of data and the privacy of the citizen and the consumer. The use of the technologies by private sector organizations has caused increasing concern in the West. Those concerns extend not only to the invasion of privacy through the use of the data by corporations, but also to the vulnerability of personal data to cyber-attacks. Novel means of the use of big data in credit scoring, such as the analysis of a would-be borrower's personality through his or her interactions on social media, may enhance financial inclusion, but raise questions of unfair discrimination and privacy which call for regulation. There is also a question, which needs to be addressed, about whether governments will be able to recruit able and suitably qualified regulators with the capacity to keep up with technological developments so as to protect the citizen and the consumer.

The new technologies also pose challenges to commercial law. I am unconvinced by those who argue that operation of computer programs will remove the need for legal regulation. In my view, the law will need to be adapted to facilitate the realization of the benefits of the new technologies and to prevent or at least provide workable remedies against their abuse.

The development of self-executing "smart contracts" may require adaptations to the law of contract to ensure effective remedies – for example, where a contract is concluded, or rather set in motion, as a result of misrepresentation. The law of unjust enrichment may plug a gap by providing a remedy in many cases. If, over time, AI is developed to enable programs in communication with each other to optimize their contractual rights and obligations without human input, more radical innovation in the law of contract may be needed.

In the field of involuntary obligations, the law of tort (delict) will need to be developed. New rules will be needed to attribute liability for damage caused by computers in the absence of human foresight (in the context of negligence) or intention to cause harm (in the context of economic torts). I am not persuaded that products liability, which would impose liability on the creator of the algorithm, can provide a suitable model in most cases, as damage may be caused by a "thinking algorithm" through its analysis of data and its exercise of judgment without there being any defect in the algorithm and without its creator having the foresight or control over the work which the algorithm will perform. New rules on the basis of liability for such harm and on causation may need to be developed either by the courts or by legislation.

Governments and legislatures may wish to consider options such as no-fault compensation and compulsory insurance and the possibility of giving separate legal personality to programs used for specific purposes. But strict liability may impose too high a standard and the risks may be too great for commercial insurers to undertake, particularly in the field of financial services, in which potential losses may be on a wholly different scale from the damages due for personal injury or property damage caused by a driverless car. In the field of involuntary obligation, legislatures will have to navigate between the Scylla of damaging the interests of citizens and consumers by the indiscriminate facilitation of the new technologies and the Charybdis of stifling the potential of the new technologies to provide significant human benefits by imposing a crippling liability regime.

The legal profession and judges face a challenge in understanding the code which under-pins the new technologies. There will be a greater need for expert evidence to guide the courts in litigation concerning the technologies, and the cost and complexity of such litigation may prove a serious barrier to the achievement of justice.

Property law may also be the subject of necessary reform. There is a need to bring a greater degree of certainty as to the legal nature as property of crypto-assets, such as crypto-currencies, in which very large sums of money have been invested. Should algorithms be recognized as a form of intellectual property? Intellectual property law may also have to be reconsidered to provide for copyright for works created by computers and patents for computer-generated inventions.

Insofar as the new technologies are used to facilitate international financial transactions and trade, there will be great benefit in achieving international cooperation on both regulation and law reform, by international conventions and model laws.

In this context of radical technological change, carefully considered initiatives of regulatory change and law reform can facilitate the realization of the potential benefits and minimize the adverse effects of the technologies. I am not persuaded that piecemeal, interstitial, legal innovation by the courts can achieve what is needed in a realistic timescale. An informed debate on the best ways to achieve these ends is a precondition of effective law and regulatory reform.

This Handbook contains contributions from judges, professors of law, other academic and practicing lawyers, economists and technologists, and policy analysts from several countries, giving an international focus to the discussion of these important issues. The contributions include discussion of contract law, tort law, patent law and other intellectual property law, competition law, criminal law, government administration and decision-making, regulation, accountability, transparency, privacy, freedom of expression, and discrimination. I warmly welcome the publication of this Handbook for its contribution to this important debate.

Patrick S. Hodge

Preface

Recent advances in technology have resulted in numerous discussions among legal scholars on how the law relates to robotics, drones, autonomous cars, and generally any system embedded with artificial intelligence. At its core, artificial intelligence relies on algorithms to process and interpret data, to navigate artificially intelligent vehicles, and to control the motion of robots that are becoming increasingly autonomous from human supervisory control. Algorithms are also being used to control household appliances, to engage in financial transactions, to decide whether we receive credit or an offer of employment, and to give technology the ability to listen to people and to speak back to them. In the medical domain, often based on necessity, technology is becoming implanted within or attached to the body, allowing algorithms to become intimately involved with our biological well-being and in some cases our very survival. As we become more enhanced with technology designed to repair or extend our motor, sensory, and cognitive abilities, how is the law impacted? And as algorithms are embedded in technology which have the capability to follow our every movement, recognize our faces in a crowd, record our keystrokes, and monitor which websites we visit, how is privacy and free speech law impacted, and how do we make sure that individual rights guaranteed under state and federal constitutions are preserved in an age of rapid technological advancements? These are just a short list of the pressing issues that will need to be addressed by legal scholars and legislators.

Clearly, important issues of law and policy are being raised by the proliferation of algorithms throughout society and even within our bodies. This thirty-five-chapter *Handbook of the Law of Algorithms* discusses how the law is being challenged by emerging algorithmic-driven systems and what solutions may be necessary to regulate such systems. As a Handbook which may be useful for students in various fields, and for legislators, policymakers, or legal practitioners, this edited volume on the Law of Algorithms provides numerous examples of algorithmic-driven systems which are resulting in challenges to current areas of law, and as a response, includes relevant case law and statutes which directly, or indirectly, regulate the use of algorithms. The volume also discusses future directions of law in an age of increasingly intelligent algorithmic-driven systems that are designed to make decisions previously made by humans.

My goal in editing this volume was to provide outstanding legal scholars with a forum in which to discuss in some detail their views on the emerging field of law and algorithms and the opportunity to participate in the debate about the future direction of law and policy as related to algorithmic-driven systems. The volume, with chapters from US, EU, and other international scholars, is wide-ranging: there are chapters which discuss how algorithms are challenging commercial and antitrust law, criminal law statutes, and how algorithms may lead to discriminatory conduct toward constitutionally protected groups. This last point raises an important issue, which this volume speaks to, as more technology is integrated into society, just what kind of society do we want to create and what role does the law have to play in creating a just and equitable society in a technologically advanced world?

Woodrow Barfield
Chapel Hill, NC USA

Acknowledgements

The chapter authors thank their family and friends for their support and encouragement, and thank their colleagues for their many discussions with us on law and technology and their keen insight into the emerging field of law as related to robots, algorithms, and artificial intelligence. We also thank Matt Gallaway and Cameron Daddis, editors from Cambridge University Press, for their support of the book project, and also the production team at Cambridge University Press for their outstanding efforts. Sophie Rosinke is also thanked for her attention to detail when copy-editing the chapters and efficiently working with the authors. As editor, I warmly thank the authors for contributing outstanding chapters and responding to my numerous inquiries for more information. Finally, we dedicate this book to the memory of our friend and colleague, Ian Kerr, an enthusiastic and innovative thinker in many areas of law.

Abbreviations

ABR	Algorithm-Based Republisher
ACLU	American Civil Liberties Union
AFRL	Air Force Research Lab
AI	artificial intelligence
DLT	distributed ledger technology
HLEG	High-Level Expert Group
ASR	automated speech recognition
AUC	area under the curve
BCD	binary-coded decimal
BCI	brain–computer interfaces
BTBI	brain-to-brain interface
CAD	computer-aided design
CDA	Communications Decency Act
CESCR	Committee on Economic Social and Cultural Rights
CFPB	Consumer Financial Protection Bureau
CIPO	Canadian Intellectual Property Office
CJ	Chief Justice
CNS	central nervous system
COMPAS	Correctional Offender Management Profiling for Alternative Sanction
CONTU	Commission on New Technological Uses of Copyright Works
COP	Child Online Protection
CPU	central processing unit
CSS	computational social science
DAO	digital autonomous organization
DARPA	Defense Advanced Research Projects Agency
DEG	Digital Era Governance
DLP	digital labor platform
DMCA	Digital Millennium Copyright Act
DMV	Department of Motor Vehicle
DNN	deep neural network
DoDPI	Department of Defense Polygraph Institute
DOJ	Department of Justice
DRM	digital rights management
ECJ	European Court of Justice

ECOA	Equal Credit Opportunity Act
EEG	electroencephalography
EPA	Environmental Protection Agency
ERP	event-related potential
ESI	electronically stored information
EU	European Union
FACTA	Fair and Accurate Credit Transactions Act
FATML	Fairness, Accountability and Transparency in Machine Learning
FBI	Federal Bureau of Investigation
FCRA	Fair Credit Reporting Act
FDA	Federal Drug Administration
FDIC	Federal Deposit Insurance Corporation
FEMA	Federal Emergency Management Agency
FICO	Fair Isaac & Company
FINRA	Financial Industry Regulatory Authority
fMRI	functional magnetic resonance imaging
fNIRS	functional near infrared spectroscopy
FOIA	Freedom of Information Act
FTC	Federal Trade Commission
GA	genetic algorithm
GAN	generative adversarial networks
GDPR	General Data Protection Regulation
GIS	geographic information system
GPS	Global Positioning System
GPU	graphics processing unit
HIC	human in command
HIPAA	Health Insurance Portability and Accountability Act
HITL	human in the loop
HMRC	Her Majesty's Revenue & Customs
HOTL	human on the loop
HRBA	human rights-based approach
ICESCR	International Covenant on Economic, Social and Cultural Rights
ICT	information and communications technologies
III	institutional information infrastructures
IoM	Internet of Minds
IoT	Internet of Things
IP	Internet Protocol
IPO	Intellectual Property Office
IRS	Internal Revenue Service
ISO	International Organization of Standardization
ITU	International Telecommunication Union
J	Justice
LAW	lethal autonomous weapon
LEI	Legal Entity Identifier
LR	likelihood ratio
MEG	magnetoencephalography
METI	Ministry of Economy, Trade, and Industry

MHLW	Ministry of Health, Labor, and Welfare
ML	machine learning
MoPP	Manual of Patent Practice
MPEP	Manual of Patent Examining Procedure
NBA	National Basketball Association
NCCUSL	National Conference of Commissioners on Uniform State Laws
NSA	National Security Agency
PET	positron emission topography
NFL	National Football League (US)
NPM	new public management
OCC	Office of the Comptroller of the Currency
OECD	Organisation for Economic Co-operation and Development
OMB	Office of Management and Budget
OODA	Observe, Orient, Decide, Act
PAC	political action committee
PAI	Partnership on AI
PCLOB	Privacy and Civil Liberties Oversight Board
PIA	privacy impact assessment
QDF	query deserves freshness
RAI	risk assessment instruments
RIA	Regulatory Impact Analysis
ROM	read-only memory
SAOP	senior agency official for privacy
SD	social dilemma
SEC	Securities and Exchange Commission
SEO	search engine optimization
SNA	Social Network Analysis
SSA	Social Security Administration
SSDI	Social Security Disability Insurance
SSL	Strategic Subject List
SVM	Support Vector Machine
SVP	sexually violent predator
TCP	Transmission Control Protocol
ToC	Tragedy of the Commons
UCC	Uniform Commercial Code
UCITA	Uniform Computer Information Transactions Act
UETA	Uniform Electronic Transactions Act
UK	United Kingdom
UN	United Nations
UNICEF	UN International Children's Emergency Fund
US	United States
USPTO	US Patent & Trademark Office
VA	Visual Analytics
VLA	Visual Legal Analytics
VR	virtual reality
VRAG	Violence Risk Appraisal Guide

PART I

Introduction and Setting the Stage for a Law of Algorithms

An Introduction to Law and Algorithms

Woodrow Barfield and Jessica Barfield

INTRODUCTION

A body of law is currently being developed in response to algorithms which are designed to control increasingly smart machines, to replace humans in the decision-making loops of complex systems, or to account for the actions of algorithms that make decisions which affect the legal rights of people. Such algorithms are ubiquitous; they are being used to guide commercial transactions, evaluate credit and housing applications, by courts in the criminal justice system, and to control self-driving cars and robotic surgeons. However, while the automation of decisions typically made by humans has resulted in numerous benefits to society, the use of algorithms has also resulted in challenges to established areas of law. For example, algorithms may exhibit the same human biases in decision-making that have led to violations of people's constitutional rights, and algorithms may collectively collude to price fix, thus violating antitrust law.

When algorithmic-driven systems are used in varying ways, algorithms become not just a method of filtering data, but a way of outsourcing decision-making from human to machine or to a software bot. And crucially, despite claims from some that the digital, computerized nature of algorithms means they are free of bias, in fact, we now know the opposite may be true. In situations where humans code algorithms, consciously or not, they may seed them with their own flawed perspectives. And in the case where algorithms learn, they do so by drawing on existing information to make decisions, as a result, if the training data is flawed in some way, algorithms have the potential to exacerbate or replicate human bias.

In this chapter, we review some of the fundamental characteristics of algorithms which we believe are essential to establishing a law of algorithms and we discuss different areas of law that are being challenged when algorithms are used in contexts which traditionally have required human judgment. Legislators in the United States, European Union, and Asia are beginning to discuss how to regulate increasingly smart systems controlled by algorithms,[1] and to some extent cases have been litigated which involve the use of algorithms;[2] however, we are still in the early stages of developing a law of algorithms and determining how to regulate their use. In our view, a "law of algorithms" is necessary because they are a fundamental building block of biological and non-biological systems, and in one form or another, algorithms have been the subject of litigation in patent, First Amendment, civil rights, employment, and criminal law.

---

[1] In 2007, the South Korean government proposed a Robot Ethics Charter; in 2011, the UK Research Council EPSRC published five ethical principles for industry; and in 2017, the Association for Computing Machinery published seven principles for algorithmic transparency and accountability.

[2] *In re. Facebook Biometric Info. Privacy Litig.*, 185 F. Supp. 3d 1155 (ND Cal. 2016).

So, what are algorithms? Algorithms are a set of rules or instructions that are followed when performing calculations, or more generally, a set of problem-solving procedures which when followed produce a certain output.[3] In *Gottschalk* v. *Benson*, the Court used a narrow definition of an algorithm and defined an algorithm as a procedure for solving a given type of *mathematical problem*.[4] They are now most familiar as instructions embodied within computer programs, such as those which make artificial intelligence (AI) possible. But before algorithms were driving advances in AI and resulting in challenges to established areas of law, for hundreds of millions of years algorithms have silently been playing a key role in the process of evolution leading to complex forms of life.[5] In fact, we humans can be described as an organism consisting of trillions of cells each of which computes at the molecular level using algorithms.[6] But, of course, there are limits to legal rights associated with algorithms, for example, in *Gottschalk*, the Court discussed the long-established principle that "[p]henomena of nature, though just discovered . . . are not patentable . . ."[7] However, as Andrew Chin discusses in his chapter in this volume, not all algorithms are a product of nature and thus, if the requirements under the patent law are met, algorithms may receive patent protection. At this point, the reader should be at ease as the authors' digression to biology is temporary, and will not be the focus of this chapter, but done sparingly to point out that algorithms are not a recent phenomenon, but a feature of evolutionary processes which have occurred over hundreds of millions of years. Of course, from the perspective of law, there are essential differences between the algorithms which are a process of nature, the algorithms written by programmers, and the algorithms derived from machine-learning techniques. Among others, the differences involve the purposes for which the algorithms are designed and the legal consequences of using algorithms that are independent from human input and control.

As algorithms proliferate into society, legal scholars, courts, and legislators are beginning to ask timely questions about their use, such as the role that algorithms play in expressing bias toward a constitutionally protected group, or the role that an algorithm has in contributing to an accident involving an autonomous car[8] or robotic surgeon,[9] or for purposes of copyright or patent law, the role of an algorithm in writing a story, composing music, or serving as an inventor. And from a constitutional law perspective, as algorithms contribute to the speech output of different forms of technology, a question being discussed is whether algorithms should be considered a form of speech and therefore receive protection in the United States under the First Amendment.[10] We argue that for each of these questions, it will be important for courts to look carefully at the specific algorithm(s) in question in order to determine which aspect of the algorithm (or algorithms) is creative, culpable, "speaks," or, for purposes of assigning liability, is independent from human supervisory control. As we begin to provide answers to these questions, and as courts litigate disputes involving algorithms, we take the

---

[3] R. Sedgewick and K. Wayne, *Algorithms*, 4th edn. (Addison-Wesley, 2011).

[4] *Gottschalk* v. *Benson*, 409 US 63, 93 S.Ct. 253, 34 L.Ed.2d 273, 175 USPQ 673 (1972).

[5] W.-K. Sung, *Algorithms in Bioinformatics: A Practical Introduction*, 1st edn. (Chapman & Hall/CRC Mathematical and Computational Biology, 2009).

[6] C. Calude and G. Paun, *Computing with Cells and Atoms: An Introduction to Quantum, DNA and Membrane Computing* (CRC Press, 2000).

[7] *Gottschalk*, above note 4.

[8] S. Beiker and R. Calo, Legal Aspects of Autonomous Driving (2012) 52 *Santa Clara Law Rev.* 1145, https://ssrn.com/abstract=2767899.

[9] *Taylor* v. *Intuitive Surgical, Inc.*, 355 P.3d 309 (2015).

[10] T. Wu, Machine Speech (2012–13) 161 *Univ. Pa. Law Rev.* 1495, https://scholarship.law.upenn.edu/penn_law_review/vol161/iss6/2.

view that we are simultaneously developing a law of algorithms and creating legal precedent for future cases involving algorithms.

As an exercise in legal analysis, consider an algorithmic-controlled system which results in damages, in this example, we can ask: Which aspects of the algorithm has importance for the law? Let me note here that there are many different types of algorithms, and some may be more likely to result in outcomes that may lead to legal disputes and thus court actions than others. For this reason, we argue that an examination of the specific features of an algorithm is important to those who wish to develop a law of algorithms and to courts resolving disputes. With these thoughts in mind, consider the following algorithm which we provide here for discussion purposes (but without reference to a specific legal dispute), as it has general value for the points we wish to make:

```
def find_max (L):b
if lenL) == 1:
return L[0]
v1 = L[0]
v2 = find_max(L[1:])
if v1 > v2:
return v1
else:
return v2
```

Like the process of statutory construction, in which courts are called upon to interpret the language of statutes and legislation, so too can an analysis of the lines of code comprising an algorithm be used to determine the language and purpose of the algorithm. In fact, disputes involving patents typically turn on claim construction, in which the claims are listed step by step, thus representing an algorithm (specific examples are presented below). In the above algorithm, the set of instructions are unambiguous, so it would be relatively easy for a court, for example, through expert testimony, to determine the purpose of the algorithm. For those whose programming experience is rusty, the algorithm solves the following problem: given a list of positive numbers, it returns the largest number on the list. To accomplish this, the algorithm has input which consists of a list L of positive numbers. This list must contain at least one number and the algorithm has the following output: a number, which will be the largest number of the list. Of course, examining how an algorithm works for purposes of litigation assumes that an algorithm can be admissible as evidence in a court proceeding – a topic discussed by Andrea Roth in Chapter 19 in this volume. Knowing the purpose of an algorithm is essential for determining the extent to which an algorithm contributes to a violation of the law. However, as algorithms become mathematically complex, it will become difficult for litigators to explain their reasoning to a judge or jury; this illustrates a growing problem in resolving disputes which involve systems whose performance is guided by algorithms.

Another issue involving algorithms that will surely confront courts is that systems will be controlled by not one, but many, algorithms; thus, it may be the collective performance of algorithms that is of interest in a court proceeding. This, of course, adds to the complexity of resolving disputes which involve algorithms. Additionally, if a programmer who wrote an algorithm can be identified, examining the features of an algorithm could produce important evidence in determining whether the programmer intended for a certain outcome to occur.

In contrast, if the algorithm(s) was derived from techniques such as deep learning, in which no human was involved in writing the algorithm(s) or determining the systems output would it still be relevant for a court to examine the lines of code to determine the "intent" of the non-human entity which created the algorithm(s)? As some have argued, the answer is only to the extent that the "algorithmic-based system" has been granted legal person status, because without such status afforded to an algorithmic entity, there is a gray area which currently exists in the law in which there may be no legal person to hold liable when damages have occurred.[11]

Returning to the above algorithm, note that each step of the algorithm is easily translated into a programming language. A programming language as opposed to machine language (or object code) provides a judge and jury with a readable transcription of the actions of an algorithm that may have led to an outcome contrary to the law. Further, the above algorithm has defined inputs and outputs, which surely would be of interest to a trier of fact determining the extent to which an algorithm led to damages. We should note here that just as with human behavior which may result from the collective action of many thousands (or millions) of neurons, as stated above, so too does "algorithmic performance" for a given system rely not just on one but quite often the combined output of many algorithms;[12] this, of course, complicates matters for a court determining the extent to which algorithms contribute to liability and that are tasked with explaining the role of algorithms in a dispute (this is referred to among legal scholars as the lack of transparency problem).

Referring back to the previous algorithm, it is guaranteed to terminate (thus is not open loop) if L is of length 1. If L has more than one element, find_max() is called with a list that is one element shorter and the result is then used in a computation. In addition, the nested call to find_max() always terminates, each time find_max() is called with a list that is shorter by one element. Eventually, the list will be of length 1 and the nested calls will end. The fact that the algorithm ends based on the instructions provided by its code provides a definite and unambiguous action for courts to consider – this is essential in litigating disputes. So, just based on thinking about the above simple algorithm with only nine lines of code, we can surmise that there are several aspects of an algorithm that could be of interest to a judge or jury considering the actions of algorithms, or to legislators tasked with regulating algorithmic-based systems. To add another layer of complexity to our thinking about algorithms and law, we argue that the aspects of an algorithm that will be of interest to the law will be dependent on the type of legal dispute involved. For example, if a certain intent were required for a violation of a criminal law statute, then any algorithm written by a defendant controlling the actions of an artificially intelligent entity that would "mathematically model" the necessary intent would be important evidence to produce in a criminal proceeding.

Clearly, the result (or output) of an algorithm if used for decision-making purposes could implicate the law if the decision resulted in behavior contrary to established legal principles. For example, in criminal law, if the use of algorithms for sentencing purposes resulted in bias toward members of a constitutionally protected group, this would violate the Fourteenth Amendment to the US Constitution. In our view, this raises the question: Where in the lines of code is the bias manifested? Among major categories of algorithms, there are those that operate by techniques such as brute force, divide and conquer, decrease and conquer, dynamic programming, transform and conquer, or backtracking. For the example just

---

[11]   C. E. A. Karnow, *Future Codes: Essays in Advanced Computer Technology and the Law* (Intellectual Property Series, Computing Library), 1st edn. (Artech House, 1997).

[12]   C. C. Aggaswal, *Neural Networks and Deep Learning: A Textbook*, 1st edn. (Springer, 2018).

mentioned, which algorithmic technique (if any) is more likely to lead to biased intent toward a member of a constitutionally protected group?

But examining the code will be more involved than just noting the high-level algorithmic technique used in a program. For example, if property is damaged by the end effectors of a robot that delivered excessive force, then the algorithms modeling force and the algorithms controlling the robot's visual system and behavior would be contributors to the excessive force used. However, this particular code, with matrix calculations, coordinate transformations, and control theory models is mathematically complex and thus difficult for a judge or member of a jury not trained in engineering or computer science to comprehend. But communicating this information to a judge or jury will be essential to resolving a dispute. Perhaps in response to the complexity of algorithms, a court which focuses on litigation involving algorithms will need to be developed. This is not a novel idea as in the United States there is a Tax Court, a Court of Federal Claims, a Foreign Intelligence Surveillance Court, and a Bankruptcy Court, and formerly there was a Board of Patent Appeals and Interferences, to name just a few courts with specialized subject matter. Just as Ryan Calo has advocated for a federal agency to regulate robotics,[13] the challenge to our legal system in resolving disputes involving systems controlled by algorithms, especially for increasingly autonomous entities, seems to call for a specialized court with expertise in litigating disputes which involve algorithms (and other AI techniques).

Considering another area where algorithms may challenge established law, under intellectual property law the question of whether algorithms are simply a process of nature and thus not patentable subject matter is another timely debate receiving attention in different jurisdictions. And for copyright law, the question of whether the musical compositions, paintings, and other works of authorship generated by algorithms constitute copyrightable subject matter has given rise to another important debate occurring within the legal community. But, in each of these situations, we can ask: Which aspect of the algorithm itself is to be considered a process of nature or independently creating a work of authorship? Further, from a constitutional law perspective, if algorithms are embedded within systems which communicate using natural language, under the US Constitution is such algorithmic speech protected under the First Amendment?[14] And, if so, which lines of code contribute to speech and thus should receive protection, or is an analysis at the level of an algorithm too detailed, and thus the Court should focus only on the output or spoken speech of the algorithmic entity? And more fundamentally, is an algorithm itself a form of expression and thus speech? (See Chapters 25, 27, and 28 in this volume.) And for commercial law, it is important to ask whether an algorithm is considered a product or a service. This is an important distinction because a major factor in determining liability for software (and algorithms are often embedded within software) is the classification of the software. In the United States, under the Uniform Commercial Code (UCC), software can be classified as a product or a service.[15]

---

[13] R. Calo, The Case for a Federal Robotics Commission, Brookings Institution Center for Technology Innovation (September 2014), https://papers.ssrn.com/sol3/papers.cfm?abstract_id=2529151.

[14] T. M. Massaro and H. Norton, Siri-ously? Free Speech Rights and Artificial Intelligence (2016) 110 *Nw. Univ. Law Rev.* 1169.

[15] For a discussion of the concept of software as a product or service within the UCC, see R. Raysman and P. Brown, Applicability of the UCC to Software Transactions; Technology Today, *NY Law J. Online* (March 8, 2011), www .newyorklawjournal.com/id=1202484668508/Applicability-of-theUCC-to-Software-Transactions (acknowledging that art. 2 does not explicitly mention software) (on file with the *Washington & Lee Law Review*); see *Olcott Int'l & Co. v. Micro Data Base Sys., Inc.*, 793 NE.2d 1063, 1071 (Ind. Ct. App. 2003) (applying art. 2 to contracts to purchase pre-existing software modules); see also *Advent Sys. Ltd. v. Unisys Corp.*, 925 F.2d 670, 676 (3rd Cir. 1991) (identifying the benefits of applying the UCC to computer software transactions).

If classified as a product, strict product liability is imposed.[16] If classified as a service, professional misconduct is imposed, so the distinction is important for a law of algorithms, especially as algorithms become more embedded within society in decision-making roles through different software platforms.

For algorithms, the above examples indicate that assigning liability when damages occur is a major topic of discussion within the legal community and for courts to consider when litigating disputes.[17] As an example, if a programmer writes an algorithm and its use results in damage to property or harm to humans, the responsible party can be traced back to a human who wrote the code. In this case, the lines of code will reveal (at least as circumstantial evidence) the thinking, or intent, of the programmer and once the rules of civil procedure for proffering evidence are satisfied, the code could be used as evidence in a court proceeding. But if the algorithm is generated using deep learning techniques, a person may not have been directly involved in writing the algorithm that ultimately resulted in damages, who then should courts hold liable? The above examples represent just a few of the fundamental legal issues involving algorithms that the law must address as systems controlled by algorithms become more common in society and weave their way into our judicial system. Other chapters in this volume contain additional examples covering a wide range of applications.

SOME EXAMPLE DISPUTES INVOLVING ALGORITHMS

As mentioned previously, there are disputes that have already been litigated which "one way or another" involve algorithms; from this, we argue that we are in the beginning stages of witnessing a law of algorithms develop. As a major classification of algorithms challenging established law, perhaps we can distinguish between algorithms that are derived from biological processes (for example, the instructions provided by DNA) versus algorithms designed to control "human-made" systems (for example, autonomous cars). When "biology" is involved, a common question is whether it is possible to patent the biological process, which is often describable as an algorithm.[18] When human-made systems are involved, the legal issues normally revolve around commercial and tort law which applies to the algorithm as a decision-maker. We present a few examples of statutes and case law below involving algorithms for illustrative purposes, but before that, we next summarize the work being done in the general area of "biological algorithms."

For years, scientists have been working to discover the "computer-like" computations performed by cells.[19] For example, it is thought that cells store information in a way roughly approximating computer memory and that cells use rule-based expressions similar to a programming language in response to stimuli.[20] Each cell contains enough physical complexity to theoretically be quite a powerful computing unit all on its own, but each is also small enough to be packed by the millions into tiny physical spaces. Researchers at MIT and Caltech have been designing cellular machines that are currently able to perform simple

---

[16]   The elements of a strict liability tort are similar to the elements of a negligent tort (duty, breach, and injury), except that in a strict liability case, the victim doesn't need to prove negligence.

[17]   W. Barfield, Liability for Autonomous and Artificially Intelligent Robots (2018) 9 *Paladyn* 193.

[18]   *Association for Molecular Pathology* v. *Myriad Genetics, Inc.*, 133 S.Ct. 2107 (2013).

[19]   G. Templeton, How MIT's New Biological "Computer" Works, and What It Could Do in the Future, *Extreme Tech* (2016), www.extremetech.com/extreme/232190-how-mits-new-biological-computer-works-and-what-it-could -do-in-the-future.

[20]   J. Windmiller, Molecular Scale Biocomputing: An Enzyme Logic Approach (thesis, University California, San Diego, June 2012).

computational operations and store, then recall, memory. One major advantage of biological computing compared to modern computers is power efficiency.[21] Running AI algorithms takes many gigawatt-hours of electricity, but extremely long and complex problems could end up being vastly more affordable to solve using biology-based computers. So even though a biological computer is orders of magnitude slower than a supercomputer, supercomputers cost millions of dollars in energy every year, while a bio-computer runs on far less energy. In addition, biological computers differ from non-biological computers in what exactly serves as the output signal. In bio-computers, the presence or concentration of certain chemicals serves as the output signal. Further, biologically inspired computers rely on the nature of specific molecules to adopt certain physical configurations under certain chemical conditions. As systems using biological-based computers become more prevalent, it will be interesting to see what laws are challenged and how the courts respond to such challenges.

A current statute which applies to algorithms, albeit indirectly, is the Biometric Information Privacy Act (BIPA), which was passed by the Illinois General Assembly in 2008.[22] The BIPA guards against the unlawful collection and storing of biometric information. What's particularly relevant for this chapter is that the collection and analysis of biometric information is done by algorithms. So, while algorithms are not directly mentioned in the language of the statute, if algorithms were not directly involved in collecting and analyzing biometric data, the statute would not be necessary. The BIPA remains the only state law in the United States dealing with biometric data that allows private individuals to file a lawsuit for damages stemming from a violation.[23] Because of this damages provision, the BIPA has spawned many class action lawsuits; a few examples follow.

With *In re. Facebook Biometric Info. Privacy Litig.*,[24] Illinois Facebook users alleged that the social media platform violated the BIPA when it used algorithms to scan images of their faces, without consent, in order to run its Tag Suggestions feature. Additionally, in *Monroy v. Shutterfly, Inc.*,[25] Shutterfly users claimed that the company violated the BIPA when it scanned uploaded digital photos using algorithmic-based facial recognition software. And in *Rivera v. Google, Inc.*,[26] Google users sued the company for violating the BIPA, alleging that it created and stored scans of users' faces on its Google Photos service, without user consent; however, in 2018, the lawsuit was dismissed for lack of standing. In a state case, *Rosenbach v. Six Flags Entm't Corp.*,[27] Six Flags was sued for collecting park-goers' thumbprints without informed consent. The Illinois Court of Appeals ruled that a mere technical violation of the BIPA was insufficient to maintain an action, because it did not necessarily mean a party was "aggrieved," as required by the statute. This was reversed by the Illinois Supreme Court, which ruled that users do not need to prove an injury (such as identity fraud or physical harm) in order to sue; the mere violation of the act was sufficient to collect damages.

There are a number of cases which have sought, inter alia, to determine whether an algorithm is a product of nature and thus not patentable subject matter. In *Mackay Radio & Telegraph Co.* v. *Radio Corp. of America*,[28] the applicant sought a patent on a directional

---

[21] R. T. Gonzalez, This New Discovery Will Finally Allow Us to Build Biological Computers, *Gizmodo* (March 29, 2013), https://io9.gizmodo.com/this-new-discovery-will-finally-allow-us-to-build-biolo-462867996.
[22] Codified as 740 ILCS/14 and Public Act 095-994.
[23] The Act prescribes $1,000 per violation, and $5,000 per violation if the violation is intentional or reckless.
[24] See above note 2.
[25] *Monroy v. Shutterfly, Inc.*, No. 16 C 10984, 2017 WL 4099846 (ND Ill. September 15, 2017).
[26] *Rivera v. Google, Inc.*, 238 F. Supp. 3d 1088 (ND Ill. 2017).
[27] *Rosenbach v. Six Flags Entm't Corp.*, 2017 IL App. (2d) (May Term 2018).
[28] *Mackay Radio & Telegraph Co. v. Radio Corp. of America*, 306 US 333, 1938.

antenna system in which the wire arrangement was determined by the application of a mathematical formula. Putting the question of patentability to one side as a preface to his analysis of the infringement issue, Mr. Justice Stone, writing for the Court, explained: "While a scientific truth, or the mathematical expression of it, is not a patentable invention, a novel and useful structure created with the aid of knowledge of scientific truth may be."[29] *Funk Bros. Seed Co.* v. *Kalo Co.*[30] expressed a similar approach: "He who discovers a hitherto unknown phenomenon of nature has no claim to a monopoly of it which the law recognizes. If there is to be invention from such a discovery, it must come from the application of the law of nature to a new and useful end."[31] *Mackay Radio* and *Funk Bros.* point to the proper analysis of patent cases involving algorithms: the process itself, not merely the mathematical algorithm, must be new and useful. Indeed, the novelty of the mathematical algorithm is not a determining factor at all. Whether the algorithm was in fact known or unknown at the time of the claimed invention, as one of the "basic tools of scientific and technological work,"[32] is treated as though it were a familiar part of the prior art.

As an example of a case involving algorithms based on the patentability of biological processes, consider *Association for Molecular Pathology* v. *Myriad Genetics, Inc.*[33] Before we present the case, we will make a short digression to discuss the idea that the instructions provided by DNA can be described as an algorithm. We start by noting that proteins are essential building blocks for life and the instructions to create proteins are encoded in DNA sequences. These sequences can be written as algorithms and in fact operate like algorithms. To learn from nature, reverse engineering the adaptable operating systems of biological organisms has long been a goal of computer scientists.[34] Neural nets, genetic algorithms, and cellular automata all attempt to reproduce the elegance of biological systems in silicon. Using the quaternary logic of DNA base-pairing, in 1994, Leonard Adleman showed how a computationally "hard" problem could be solved using techniques from molecular biology.[35] While conventional computers attack problems *via* large calculations in series, properly encoded "molecular computers" might quickly solve the same problems by simultaneously carrying out billions of operations in parallel. We expect algorithms which originate from biological processes to become more involved in controlling systems and thus will have the potential to challenge established areas of law. We note again that such a development will motivate the need for a specialized court to resolve disputes involving entities controlled by algorithms.

Returning to *Association for Molecular Pathology*, respondent Myriad Genetics, Inc. (Myriad) discovered the precise location and sequence of two human genes, mutations of which can increase the risks of breast and ovarian cancer. Myriad obtained a number of patents based upon its discovery. The case involved claims from three of the patents and required the Court to resolve whether a naturally occurring segment of DNA (which we discuss as an algorithm) is patent-eligible under 35 USC § 101 by virtue of its isolation from the rest of the human genome. Section 101 of the US Patent Act provides: "Whoever invents or discovers any new and useful . . . composition of matter, or any new and useful improvement thereof, may obtain a patent therefor, subject to the conditions and requirements of this title." The Court also addressed the patent eligibility of synthetically created DNA known as

[29]   *Ibid.*
[30]   *Funk Bros. Seed Co.* v. *Kalo Co.*, 333 US 127, 1948.
[31]   *Ibid.*
[32]   See *Gottschalk* v. *Benson*, 409 US 63, 67 (1972).
[33]   See above note 18.
[34]   B. R. Donald, *Algorithms in Structural Molecular Biology, Computational Molecular Biology* (MIT Press, 2011).
[35]   L. M. Adleman, Molecular Computation of Solutions to Combinatorial Problems (1994) 266 *Science* 1021.

complementary DNA (cDNA), which contained the same protein-coding information found in a segment of natural DNA, but omitted portions within the DNA.

In the majority decision written by Justice Thomas, not unexpectedly, the Court did not discuss algorithms as a fundamental issue in the case, but did hold that a naturally occurring DNA segment is a product of nature and not patent-eligible merely because it had been isolated, but that cDNA is patent-eligible because it is not naturally occurring. If we think of DNA as an algorithm, the algorithm that was deemed not directly a product of nature (in that it was synthetically created complimentary DNA) was patent-protected. The Court stated:

> (c) cDNA is not a "product of nature," so it is patent eligible under §101. cDNA does not present the same obstacles to patentability as naturally occurring, isolated DNA segments. Its creation results in an exons-only molecule, which is not naturally occurring. Its order of the exons may be dictated by nature, but the lab technician unquestionably creates something new when introns are removed from a DNA sequence to make cDNA.[36]

Our thoughts on this decision are whether the court should have considered that the order of exons (part of a gene) "dictated by nature" is an algorithm, and thus in our view not patentable subject matter. In this case, the novel order of molecules as a function of "human invention" was dispositive, and not the underlying algorithmic processes. There is policy guiding this decision: if the purpose of intellectual property law is to spur innovation, not allowing cDNA to receive patent protection would impede that goal.

Considering another case involving algorithms, in *Ibormeith IP v. Mercedes-Benz*,[37] the US Court of Appeals for the Federal Circuit concluded that a description of an algorithm that placed no limitations on how values were calculated, combined, or weighted was insufficient to make the bounds of the claim understandable. Ibormeith alleged that Mercedes infringed claims 1, 5, 8, and 9 of US Patent No. 6,313,749, entitled "Sleepiness Detection for Vehicle Driver or Machine Operator." Mercedes argued that the means-plus-function[38] (a procedure for drafting claims) limitations in independent claims 1 and 9 were indefinite. Agreeing with the argument, the Federal Circuit affirmed the district court's decision on the grounds that one could not understand the bounds of these claims. On review, the Federal Circuit first looked at the independent means-plus-function claims. We previously mentioned that expert testimony will be necessary in disputes involving algorithms. In *Ibormeith*, the Court relied heavily on the opinion given by Ibormeith's expert, who stated that the disclosed computational means is an "algorithm template" that need only use certain algorithm elementals (listed in Table 10 of the patent). Thus, according to the Court, Ibormeith's own expert asserted that this "algorithm template" would require "one who implements the drowsiness detection system to determine which factors to use in the algorithm, how to obtain them, how to weight them, and when to issue a warning."[39] After hearing the expert's testimony, the Court treated it as a binding admission, which led to invalidity of the claims. Therefore, because the independent claims were indefinite, the Federal Circuit affirmed the district court's grant of summary judgment.

An interesting case dealing with algorithms outside of patent law was *Bernstein* v. *United States Department of State*.[40] Bernstein brought an action against the Department of State and individually named defendants seeking declaratory and injunctive relief from their

---

[36] *Gottschalk*, above note 18.
[37] *Ibormeith IP, LLC v. Mercedes-Benz USA, LLC*, 732 F.3d 1376 (Fed. Cir. 2013).
[38] Essentially, "means-plus-function" claiming allows the drafter to claim the invention based on functionality rather than the more traditional claiming technique that employs structure within the body of the claim itself.
[39] *Ibormeith*, above note 37.
[40] *Bernstein v. United States Department of State*, 922 F. Supp. 1426 (1996).

enforcement of the Arms Export Control Act (AECA)[41] and the International Traffic in Arms Regulations (ITAR),[42] on the grounds that they are unconstitutional on their face and as applied to plaintiff. At the time the action was filed, Bernstein was a PhD candidate in mathematics working in the field of cryptography. As a student, Bernstein developed an encryption algorithm called "Snuffle," described as a zero-delay, private-key encryption system. Bernstein articulated his mathematical ideas in two ways: in an academic paper entitled "The Snuffle Encryption System," and in "source code" written in "C" detailing both the encryption and decryption, which he called "Snuffle.c" and "Unsnuffle.c," respectively.

In the United States, the AECA authorizes the President to control the import and export of defense articles and defense services by designating such items to the United States Munitions List (USML).[43] Once on the USML, and unless otherwise exempted, a defense article or service requires a license before it can be imported or exported.[44] The ITAR[45] was promulgated by the Secretary of State, and was authorized by executive order to implement the AECA. The ITAR allows for a "commodity jurisdiction procedure" by which the Office of Defense Trade Control (ODTC) determines if an article or a service is covered by the USML, including "[c]ryptographic systems, equipment, assemblies, modules, integrated circuits, components or software with the capability of maintaining secrecy or confidentiality of information or information systems …"[46] In 1992, Bernstein submitted a commodity jurisdiction (CJ) request to the State Department to determine whether Snuffle.c and Unsnuffle.c and his academic paper describing the Snuffle system were controlled by ITAR. In response, the ODTC informed Bernstein that, after consultation with the Departments of Commerce and Defense, it had determined that the commodity Snuffle 5.0 was a defense article under the ITAR and subject to licensing by the Department of State prior to export. The ODTC identified the item as a "stand-alone cryptographic algorithm which is not incorporated into a finished software product."[47] Bernstein appealed the first commodity jurisdiction determination.

After the Court of Appeals' decision, the government requested and was granted a review of the case, causing the original ruling to be withdrawn. Before the review could occur, however, the government relaxed its encryption regulations. The case was therefore sent back to the district court. Over the next few years, both sides filed a number of cross-motions, and Bernstein's legal team renewed its constitutional challenge to the government's encryption laws. They argued that the government's policy violated the First Amendment and restricted research. Finally, at a hearing, the federal government backed away from portions of its encryption rules, saying that it would not enforce some of the provisions. The district court then dismissed the case on "ripeness" grounds, holding that any alleged injury to the plaintiff was hypothetical rather than actual. From the above few cases, we can conclude that the use of algorithms implicates several areas of law, from patent to national security, and as algorithms are more imbedded within society, we expect additional areas of law to be challenged by algorithms serving in decision-making roles.

[41] Arms Export Control Act, 22 USC § 2778.
[42] International Traffic in Arms Regulations, 22 CFR §§ 120–30 (1994).
[43] 22 USC § 2778(a)(1).
[44] 22 USC § 2778(b)(2).
[45] 22 CFR §§ 120–30.
[46] 22 CFR § 121.1 XIII(b)(1).
[47] *Bernstein*, above note 40.

ROBOTS ARE A SPECIAL CASE OF ALGORITHMS

Due to efforts of law scholars such as Ryan Calo and Jack Balkin, perhaps developments in robotics can be viewed as a prime motivator for a law of algorithms, especially given the use of algorithms to interpret the sensor information collected by a robot allowing it, among others, to form spatial models of the environment, to provide the robot with multiple degrees of freedom in motion, and to control the amount of force a robot's end-effectors generate for a given task. We note that algorithms controlling the actions of the robot are directly involved in most legal disputes concerning robots, even though not directly mentioned in the published case report.[48]

An example is *Jones* v. *W + M Automation, Inc.*,[49] which involved a robotic gantry-loading system which struck the plaintiff when he entered into an area behind a safety fence. Since algorithms control the motion of the robot's gripper arms, we discuss the case in the context of algorithms. Specifically, gripper arms of the robotic system hit the plaintiff in the head while he was standing behind the safety fence and he became pinned against a pedestal, injuring his head. The main issue in the case was whether the system was defective when the defendant sold it. The plaintiff sued, among others, under theories of strict liability, negligence, failure to warn, and breach of warranty. The Court held that summary judgment was appropriate for the component manufacturer defendants under the "component part" doctrine, which states that a manufacturer of a non-defective component part of a product is not liable if its part is incorporated into another product that might be defective. Defendants were also entitled to summary judgment because the plaintiff failed to introduce evidence in opposition to summary judgment showing that the system was defective. Again, in our view, (for robots) much of the challenges to established law resulting from the use of robots can be distilled down to algorithms and their role in directing the behavior of robots.

THE INTEGRATION OF COMPUTER SCIENCE AND LAW

As the legal community begins to consider how to account for the actions of algorithms, we should be cognizant of the fact that computer scientists have been teaching algorithm techniques, including how to evaluate the performance of algorithms, to generations of computer science students. Most often, the analysis of algorithms involves the determination of the amount of resources (such as time and storage) necessary to execute them. Usually, the efficiency or running time of an algorithm is stated as a function relating the input length to the number of steps (time complexity) or to storage locations (space complexity). Additionally, from the perspective of computer science there are certain requirements that an algorithm should meet: (1) definiteness – that is, each step in the process must be precisely stated; (2) effective computability – each step in the process can be carried out by a computer; and (3) finiteness – the program will eventually successfully terminate. The first and third requirements are particularly relevant for a law of algorithms. To reiterate, the point of this section is to suggest that techniques developed in computer science may offer great insight to courts tasked with evaluating the performance of algorithms and to attorneys litigating disputes involving algorithms.

---

[48] See S. S. Wu, *Summary of Selected Robot Liability Cases* (2010), http://ftp.documation.com/references/ABA10a/PDfs/2_5.pdf.
[49] *Jones* v. *W + M Automation, Inc.*, 818 NYS.2d 396 (App. Div. 2006), appeal denied, 862 NE.2d 790 (NY 2007).

CONCLUSION

In addition to the specific legal issues that are raised by the use of algorithms, their use in society also represents the emergence of a whole new set of questions around ethics, bias, and equity which legal institutions and legislators must address. On that point, up until now, algorithms have been deployed with relatively little oversight, and in many cases, the law which has been applied to algorithms was developed for disputes which involve human decision-makers. How the law adopts to encompass increasingly smart systems controlled by algorithms is a major topic of discussion within the legal community and throughout this volume. Clearly, the development of systems equipped with algorithms that engage in decision-making – from robots, autonomous cars, and drones, to software bots that instanta-neously cross physical jurisdictional boundaries – is beginning to challenge established law in numerous ways. Thus, an important question concerns how to regulate the emergence of technologies which are controlled by algorithms that make decisions formerly made by humans, and to do so in such a way that innovation is not deterred, but at the same time the rights of people are protected.

In addition, even though the question of whether AI systems will reach or even surpass humans in intelligence has generated much debate; when developing a law of algorithms, we must consider the possibility that algorithmic-driven entities may exceed humans in decision-making abilities and eventually take on goals of their own, using solutions unknown to humans or even beyond our understanding. Should such entities emerge, how should legal institutions respond to the challenges posed by such entities? This particular view of the future, if it materializes, will result in very challenging issues for legal institutions and legislators to address. The first author discussed some of the relevant issues in "Cyber Humans: Our Future with Machines," but a comprehensive discussion of the issues brought forth by the "technological singularity" is beyond the scope of this chapter.[50] However, in response to algorithmic-driven systems, some have suggested that the prudent approach to take is to regulate the conduct of technology companies, which, through their proprietary algorithms, have a large influence over what we see and hear on the Internet (to some extent this is done now with antitrust and privacy law). We agree with this general view, but have some reservations. We think a broader approach is necessary as algorithms with the ability to displace humans in decision-making, engage in discriminatory behavior, and disrupt Internet-connected technology (including implanted medical devices or autonomous vehi-cles) emerge. Such systems can be written by individuals or nation-states intent on acts of hostility toward other nations or individuals. So, perhaps the regulatory focus should not be at the level of the firm, but on algorithms themselves which are used to control our information content and to make decisions which affect human lives. The latter approach would be more relevant for systems which gain autonomy from human control.

With increased autonomy for algorithmic-systems, some have proposed the creation within government of an "algorithm czar," whose sole purpose would be to regulate the use of algorithms; perhaps to oversee their registration before they are used commercially, just as patents go through a review process before a limited monopoly is granted to the patent owner. On this point, attorney Andrew Tutt proposed the idea that we need the equivalent of the US

---

[50] The technological singularity is that time, which some argue is roughly the middle of the century (or sooner), when AI reaches then surpasses humans in general intelligence. Afterwards, it is argued that AI may experience an "intelligence explosion."

Federal Drug Agency (FDA) for algorithms.[51] He commented that areas of law such as criminal law and tort law will prove no match for the difficult regulatory puzzle algorithms will pose.[52] According to Tutt, algorithmic regulation will require federal uniformity, expert judgment, political independence, and pre-market review to prevent – without stifling innovation – the introduction of unacceptably dangerous algorithms into the market. Such a federal agency, he argues, should have three powers.[53] First, it should have the power to organize and classify algorithms into regulatory categories by their design, complexity, and potential for harm (in both ordinary use and through misuse). Second, it should have the power to prevent the introduction of algorithms into the market until their safety and efficacy has been proven through evidence-based pre-market trials. And, third, the agency should have broad authority to impose disclosure requirements and usage restrictions to prevent algorithms' harmful misuse. Tutt's approach has value for "legitimate" companies which would be required to meet the standards imposed by the FDA, but the ease in which an algorithm may be written and unleashed by private parties or rogue nations, compared to the development of FDA-approved medical devices and drugs, is orders of magnitude less, so many algorithms would not be subjected to government approval. Additionally, harms traceable to algorithms may frequently be diffuse and difficult to detect. Thus, human responsibility and liability for such harms will be difficult to establish. Additionally, for innovators, the availability of federal pre-emption from local and *ex post* liability is likely to be desired. As many of the chapters in this volume will emphasize, there are, of course, current efforts to address the growing concerns associated with algorithms and other techniques with AI. For example, the European Commission has given itself the mission of drawing up rules for an emerging "age of AI" over the next few years, building on its legacy as a regulator of online privacy.

Another major area of concern for a law of algorithms that we would like to point out is the development of autonomous weapon systems. There is considerable effort among some nations to develop "killer robots" whose behavior would be directed by algorithms, and in response some have argued for a new digital Geneva Convention to protect the world from the growing threat posed by such systems. The convention would need to address many critically important issues; for example, under the international law of conflict it remains unclear who is responsible for deaths or injuries caused by a smart machine – the developer, the manufacturer, the commander, or the device itself. It has also been argued that killer robots must not be allowed to decide on their own to engage in combat and thus a new international convention needs to be created to govern the use of autonomous weapons technology. Lastly, on the topic of government regulation, citizens must be vigilant and involved in the regulatory process associated with emerging smart technologies as some nations view developing information technologies as a way to cement their ideological control over their citizens. This dystopian outcome is to be avoided as we move further into a future of coexistence with intelligent, algorithmic-driven entities.

---

[51] A. Tutt, An FDA for Algorithms (2017) 69 *Admin. Law Rev.* 83, https://ssrn.com/abstract=2747994 and http://dx .doi.org/10.2139/ssrn.2747994.

[52] *Ibid.*

[53] *Ibid.*

2

The Opinion of Machines

Curtis E. A. Karnow [*]

INTRODUCTION

People understand the linear algebra behind deep learning [neural networks]. But the models it produces are less human-readable. They're machine-readable. They can retrieve very accurate results, but we can't always explain, on an individual basis, what led them to those accurate results. [1]

When I watch these games, I can't tell you how tense it is. I really don't know what is going to happen. [2]

A specific software architecture, neural networks, not only takes advantage of the virtually perfect recollection and much faster processing speeds of any software, but also teaches itself and attains skills no human could directly program. We rely on these neural networks for medical diagnoses, financial decisions, weather forecasting, and many other crucial real-world tasks. In 2016, a program named AlphaGo beat the top-rated human player of the game of Go. [3] Only a few years ago, this had been considered impossible. [4] High-level Go requires remarkable skills, not just of calculation, at which computers obviously excel, but, more critically, of judgment, intuition, pattern recognition, and the weighing of ineffable considerations such as positional balance. [5]

---

[*] Judge of the California Superior Court, County of San Francisco.

[1] C. Metz, AI Is Transforming Google Search. The Rest of the Web Is Next, *Wired* (February 4, 2016) (quoting Chris Nicholson), www.wired.com/2016/02/ai-is-changing-the-technology-behind-google-searches.

[2] C. Metz, What the AI Behind AlphaGo Can Teach Us about Being Human, *Wired* (May 19, 2016) (quoting David Silver, one of AlphaGo's creators), www.wired.com/2016/05/google-alpha-go-ai/. See also N. Sibicky, Nick Sibicky Go Lecture #256 – Alpha vs. Go, *YouTube* (June 29, 2017), www.youtube.com/watch?v=yfUzWogH8ts (discussing the games AlphaGo plays against itself and includes a quote from Nick Sibicky, a strong Go player and professional Go instructor: "There are a lot of things I don't understand").

[3] D. Silver, A. Huang, C. J. Maddison, *et al.*, Mastering the Game of Go with Deep Neural Networks and Tree Search (2016) 529 *Nature* 484, 488, http://web.iitd.ac.in/~sumeet/Silver16.pdf.

[4] See, e.g., A. Levinovitz, The Mystery of Go, the Ancient Game that Computers Still Can't Win, *Wired* (May 12, 2014), www.wired.com/2014/05/the-world-of-computer-go/ ("But the fact is that of all the world's deterministic perfect information games – tic-tac-toe, chess, checkers, Othello, xiangqi, shogi – Go is the only one in which computers don't stand a chance against humans"). See also G. Johnson, To Test a Powerful Computer, Play an Ancient Game, *New York Times* (July 29, 1997), www.nytimes.com/1997/07/29/science/to-test-a-powerful-computer-play-an-ancient-game.html ("'It may be a hundred years before a computer beats humans at Go – maybe even longer,' said Dr. Piet Hut, an astrophysicist at the Institute for Advanced Study in Princeton, N.J.").

[5] This is so because the number of possible permutations is practically infinite. The number of possible Go games far, far exceeds the number of atoms in the universe, and mere calculation cannot beat even a modestly good human player. See Number of Possible Go Games, *Sensei's Library* (March 24, 2016), http://senseis.xmp.net/?NumberOfPossibleGoGames. This is as opposed to chess, which has far fewer options than Go. For chess, a so-called brute-force approach can beat top human players. Frequently Asked Questions: Deep Blue, *IBM*, www.research.ibm.com/deepblue/meet/html/d.3.3a.shtml. See C. Metz, In a Huge Breakthrough, Google's AI Beats a Top Player at the Game of Go, *Wired* (Jan. 27, 2016), www.wired.com/2016/01/in-a-huge-breakthrough-googles-

These skills cannot be directly programmed. Instead, AlphaGo's neural network[6] trained itself with many thousands and, later, millions of games – far more than any individual human could ever play[7] – and now routinely beats all human challengers.[8] Because it learns and concomitantly modifies itself in response to experience, such a network is termed *adaptive*.[9]

As detailed below, neural networks are used throughout industry and science. They are proposed for missile launch and interception.[10] This chapter argues that as these systems are deemed reliable, juries should be entitled to rely on their expert opinions as well.

The admission of what we might call "machine opinion evidence" entails both a review of the requirements of providing an expert opinion as well as trial judges who understand the technology and so are able to rule on admissibility and ensure the opinion is correctly framed for the jury. Judges must have sufficient knowledge to handle the technical issues. Furthermore, appreciating the risks involved, judges must also have the legal authority to decide whether the software is scientifically reliable. Many judges do not have this knowledge, and current law[11] may not tolerate that sort of admissibility analysis. This chapter may assist on those two problems, by providing both a detailed outline of the mechanism of neural networks as well as a brief, if moderately technical, background useful to an evaluation of the reliability of machine opinion.

Judges and lawyers alike are familiar with the ability of experts to sway juries with their professed independence and apparent authority. Thus, there is a high risk that juries will view computer systems with even greater authority, as such systems are ostensibly free of bias, independent of the parties, and error-free.[12] Especially in this context, trial judges must carefully undertake their gate-keeping functions[13] and ensure that only reliable evidence gets to the jury.

---

ai-beats-a-top-player-at-the-game-of-go/ ("When Deep Blue topped world chess champion Gary Kasparov in 1997, it did so with what's called brute force. In essence, IBM's supercomputer analyzed the outcome of every possible move, looking further ahead than any human possibly could. That's simply not possible with Go"). See also Johnson, above note 4 (providing a good explanation of the differing complexities as between Go and chess).

[6] See C. Burger, Google DeepMind's AlphaGo: How It Works, *TasteHit* (March 16, 2016), for a general discussion of AlphaGo's neural network. Neural networks are so called because they operate in layers, each with different function. See also I. Goodfellow, Y. Bengio, and A. Courville, *Deep Learning* (MIT Press, 2016), p. 6 (Draft Version), www.deeplearningbook.org/contents/intro.html.

[7] See generally Metz, above note 2.

[8] See AlphaGo Confirmed as Master/Magister, *Am. Go E-Journal* (January 4, 2017), www.usgo.org/news/2017/01/alphago-confirmed-as-mastermagister (reporting that on January 4, 2017, AlphaGo was confirmed as the secret player defeating fifty of the top Go players in the world).

[9] M. Hassoun, What Is a Neural Network and How Does Its Operation Differ from that of a Digital Computer? (In Other Words, Is the Brain like a Computer?), *Scientific American* (May 14, 2017), www.scientificamerican.com/article/experts-neural-networks-like-brain.

[10] See, e.g., J. Xiao, W. Li, X. Xiao, and C. Lv, Improved Clonal Selection Algorithm Optimizing Neural Network for Solving Terminal Anti-Missile Collaborative Intercepting Assistant Decision-Making Model (2016) 644 *Commun. Comput. Inf. Sci.* 216, 216–31; M. B. McFarland and A. J. Calise, Adaptive Nonlinear Control of Agile Antiair Missiles Using Neural Networks (2000) 8 *IEEE Trans. Control Syst. Technol.* 749, 749–56, http://ieeexplore.ieee.org/stamp/stamp.jsp?arnumber=865848; E. Wahl and K. Turkoglu, Non-Linear Receding Horizon Control Based Real-Time Guidance and Control Methodologies for Launch Vehicles, 2016 IEEE Aerospace Conference (2016), http://ieeexplore.ieee.org/stamp/stamp.jsp?arnumber=7500857.

[11] This chapter focuses on California law, and uses it as a reasonable example of the state of the law applicable more generally in US jurisdictions.

[12] E. E. Kenneally, Gatekeeping Out of the Box: Open Source Software as a Mechanism to Assess Reliability for Digital Evidence (2001) 6 *Va. J. Law Technol.* 13, 39 ("[D]igital evidence may carry an aura of infallibility in the public's eyes . . .").

[13] See, e.g., *Daubert v. Merrell Dow Pharm., Inc.*, 509 US 579, 600–1 (1993) ("Rule 702 confides to the judges some gatekeeping responsibility . . ."); *Sargon Enters., Inc. v. Univ. of S. Cal.*, 288 P.3d 1237, 1250 (Cal. 2012) ("[T]rial courts have a substantial 'gatekeeping' responsibility"). To be clear, this chapter is addressed specifically to the

While there are some court opinions involving neural networks, such as in patent cases,[14] there appears to be no state or federal case discussing the admissibility of what one might term "machine opinion," that is, an evidentiary statement generated by software, which no human can fully explain. A number of commentators, however, have suggested that such evidence should be admissible. They have explored, for example, facial recognition software, which reports the probability that a fuzzy picture is that of a defendant in circumstances in which no human could make a comparable estimate.[15] Commentators have advocated for the use of software to prove fraud in the healthcare industry, which would require pattern detections in large amounts of data.[16] Relatedly, a California Supreme Court Justice has explored the implications of relying on software to generate decisions for administrative agencies and questioned the sort of review courts might give to those decisions.[17] Further examples are provided below.

With the two goals of providing (1) an introduction to the technology of neural networks and (2) an argument for the admissibility of machine opinion, this chapter introduces the technology by first looking at the relatively familiar operation of technology-assisted review (TAR) of documents in a typical case. The chapter then outlines the extensive application of neural networks in the real world, which is used later to argue that systems trusted in the field should be trusted in court. The chapter then turns to the law of evidence, focusing on the rules governing the admissibility of computer-stored and computer-generated data, including animations and simulations. The theme of those sections is, again, that reliability drives admissibility. This sets the stage for the chapter's central contention, made through four arguments, that the output of neural networks be admissible in court. The chapter ends by invoking the need for meaningful cross-examination, setting out the risks – and so the likely targets of that cross-examination – which attend the admission of opinions generated by neural networks.

NEURAL NETWORKS

An Introduction for Lawyers: Predictive Coding

Many lawyers are already familiar with the basic technology since they use neural networks in their TAR of voluminous electronic documents.[18] With productions of millions of emails and

threshold issue of the *admissibility* of opinions. While reliability of an opinion is or should be the most important factor in tests for both admissibility (e.g. *Wendell v. GlaxoSmithKline LLC*, 858 F.3d 1227 (9th Cir. 2017)) and subsequent acceptance by the trier of fact (the judge or the jury), admissibility is distinct from whether the opinion is ultimately treated as persuasive by the trier of fact.

[14] See, e.g., *Neuromedical Sys., Inc. v. Neopath, Inc.*, No. 96 Civ. 5245 (JFK), 1998 WL 264845, at *4 (SDNY May 26, 1998).

[15] See, e.g., J. Nawara, Machine Learning: Face Recognition Technology Evidence in Criminal Trials (2011) 49 *Univ. Louisville Law Rev.* 601. There are interesting Confrontation Clause issues. See, e.g., J. C. Celentino, Note, Face-to-Face with Facial Recognition Evidence: Admissibility Under the Post-Crawford Confrontation Clause (2016) 114 *Mich. Law Rev.* 1317.

[16] N. Issar, More Data Mining for Medical Misrepresentation? Admissibility of Statistical Proof Derived from Predictive Methods of Detecting Medical Reimbursement Fraud (2015) 42 *N. Ky. Law Rev.* 341. For other suggestions, see A. Roth, Machine Testimony (2017) 126 *Yale Law J.* 1972, 2021.

[17] M.-F. Cuéllar, Cyberdelegation and the Administrative State, *Stanford Public Law* (2016) (Working Paper), https://papers.ssrn.com/sol3/papers.cfm?abstract_id=2754385. See also M.-F. Cuéllar, Artificial Intelligence and the Administrative State, *PPR News* (December 19, 2016), www.theregreview.org/2016/12/19/artificial-intelligence-and-the-administrative-state/.

[18] See, e.g., S. Brown, Peeking Inside the Black Box: A Preliminary Survey of Technology Assisted Review (TAR) and Predictive Coding Algorithms for Ediscovery (2016) 21 *Suffolk J. Trial & App. Advoc.* 221; A. T. Goodman, Predictive Coding and Electronically Stored Information: Computer Analytics Combat Data Overload, *Arizona Attorney* (July/August 2016), p. 26.

other documents, it is not only futile to have humans review these pages, but also usually cheaper and almost always more accurate when TAR searches for relevant items. The software uses predictive coding. The program is trained on a preliminary or starter set ("seed set") of documents, selected by humans as representative of the universe of documents at issue. Then, the system is provided a sample of the general production documents. The system then offers an opinion regarding what is relevant and what is not. Humans train the system by noting errors, and the system then iteratively refines its ability to discriminate. It does this by weighing various aspects of the documents, such as keywords and series of words, to generate a probability that the item is relevant. When the system is sufficiently accurate with regard to its training (or "control set") documents, it is then applied to the entire corpus of the production – the many millions of documents at issue – and marks those which it determines are relevant. "Predictive discovery is faster, cheaper and more accurate than traditional discovery approaches."[19]

Several observations can be made about TAR's predictive discovery system. No one knows why the system selects a document: once the system is trained, no script can be provided to a human sorter to imitate the system's selection of documents. That is, there is no way to accurately summarize the criteria used. Nevertheless, parties rely on predictive coding in very high-stakes litigation. It is treated as reliable.

Under the Hood: Hidden Layers

Having noted the legal profession's general familiarity with and reliance on a sort of neural network, this section provides a short introduction to a typical mechanism of these programs.

At the risk of conflating uses of the term "expert," neural networks can be contrasted with a classic "expert system." The classic expert system is simply a collection of rules, expressly pre-programmed by a human. For example, imagine a car repair expert system that asks a series of scripted questions and then spits out an answer. A human expert scripted each of the questions and created the matrix such that a certain set of responses generates a scripted output.[20] The operations are "hard-coded" into the software.[21] Some legal work can probably be done with these systems.[22] The significant point is that humans understand these classic expert systems and can explain each step they perform.

[19] J. H. Looby, E-Discovery – Taking Predictive Coding Out of the Black Box, *FTIJ* (November 2012), http://ftijournal.com/article/taking-predictive-coding-out-of-the-black-box-deleted (relying on M. R. Grossman and G. V. Cormack, Technology-Assisted Review in E-Discovery Can Be More Effective and More Efficient than Exhaustive Manual Review (2011) 17 *Rich. J. Law Technol.* 11). See also Veritas Techs. Corp., Predictive Coding Defensibility (2015), p. 3, www.veritas.com/content/dam/Veritas/docs/white-papers/21290290_GA_ENT_WP-Predictive-Coding-Defensibility-Measuring-Accuracy-with-Random-Sampling-EN.pdf ("Despite the widespread misconception that linear review is the electronic discovery process 'gold standard,' exhaustive manual review is surprisingly inaccurate, considering its high cost. Academic research on legal review as part of the TREC Legal Track has shown linear review is often only 40–60 percent accurate. Predictive coding technology involves an iterative process that senior attorneys follow to train software on review criteria, creating a mathematical model that predictive coding software uses to generate 'predictions' of how the remaining documents would otherwise be tagged if reviewed by an experienced attorney. Studies show that predictive coding can achieve much higher levels of accuracy at a fraction of the time and cost").
[20] F. P. Brooks, Jr., *The Mythical Man-Month: Essays on Software Engineering*, 2nd edn. (Addison-Wesley, 1995), p. 191. Brooks in his classic text (originally published in 1975) calls these now relatively simple expert systems "inference engines." While the same term could be used for neural networks, the means of inference and their flexibility differ profoundly.
[21] Goodfellow *et al.*, above note 6, p. 2.
[22] See generally L. Thorne McCarty, Reflections on Taxman: An Experiment in Artificial Intelligence and Legal Reasoning (1977) 90 *Harv. Law Rev.* 837.

Before delving into systems able to learn (such as the TAR system discussed above), it is important to note that these systems learn, of course, from new data. But that normally requires structured data, which means humans must, in effect, interpret the data from the world, rendering it into formats acceptable to the program.[23]

Representational learning systems, and deep learning systems in particular, do not require this human intervention. These programs can be exposed to data from the real world and be taught – and later, teach themselves – the relationship between (1) raw data and (2) higher-level representations and abstract concepts.[24] Neural networks are a type of representational learning system; some of them are deep, and some are shallow, as described below. They solve problems that cannot be solved by fixed programs written by humans.[25]

Neural networks are arranged such that humans do not perceive the actual operation: the weighing of probabilities. Humans do not fix the way in which elements are weighed, and they usually do not even identify *which* elements are weighed. The networks organize themselves. Recent results are even more surprising: networks have trained themselves on unlabeled data to recognize, for example, faces and cats – that is, the systems make these discriminations without first being fed examples of the items to be discriminated.[26] These systems use statistics and algorithms derived from probability theory[27] to navigate uncertain and ambiguous data to generate results, and then teach themselves to revise their own algorithms in order to increase accuracy.

A good example of a neural network is one used for image analysis, such as recognizing faces or other features in pictures.[28] The system first accepts input. In the previous example, further imagine this is a series of pixels that, for simplicity's sake, will be either black or white, on or off, on a grid, perhaps 200 by 200 (i.e. 40,000) pixels or dots. These are processed by a series of computing routines, each one in effect a processor or "node." The system's first task is to recognize whether the inputs are on or off – let's call that the work of the first layer of nodes. The second task is to determine whether there are edges. Three black dots in a row might be an edge; perhaps seven are very likely to be an edge, and ten in a row are extremely likely to be so. Edge detection might, for example, be then the second layer of processing. Depending on how nodes are adjusted, some of the nodes might "vote" that there is an edge or not an edge. At this stage, the system does not know if it is looking at a face or a baseball.

The second layer's output – "There is an edge here" or "There is no edge here" – is the input for the next layer, which might be called a shape detector, or eye detector, for example. At this third layer, the edges are determined to either fit together in a certain shape, or not. The output here might be something like, "There is an eye" or a nose, or some other elemental shape. That output is the input of the next (fourth) layer, which could be a face recognition layer. Given the input of eyes and noses or other shapes, it generates a final output: "We have a face" or "We do not have a face here" or, if the penultimate layer were trained to look for things like wheels, side panels, cabs, and so on, it might report "It's a truck." At each layer, the input is likely to vary greatly because edges come in all sorts of shapes and sizes, and can sometimes manifest either in a few pixels or many more. These edges, at subsequent layers, to a greater or lesser extent conform to an eye, or

[23]   Goodfellow *et al.*, above note 6, pp. 2–3.
[24]   *Ibid.*, pp. 4–5.
[25]   *Ibid.*, p. 96.
[26]   Q. V. Le, M. Ranzato, R. Monga, *et al.*, Building High-Level Features Using Large Scale Unsupervised Learning, 2012 Proceedings of the 29th International Conference on Machine Learning (2012), p. 127, https://static.googleusercontent.com/media/research.google.com/en//archive/unsupervised_icml2012.pdf.
[27]   Goodfellow *et al.*, above note 6, pp. 52–79.
[28]   See generally *ibid.*, p. 6, fig. 1.2.

a nose, or a wheel, or a head, and so on, and those elements in turn conform to a truck or baseball to a greater or lesser extent. The output of one layer to the next layer is a probabilistic value. Depending on the system's training, it might take only a weak probability to send an affirmative vote up the chain so to speak, or it might take a high degree of certainty to send that "Yes, it's an edge" or "Yes, this is wheel." A layer may have some but not all of the input it needs to be certain of a conclusion, and so, in effect, its nodes vote on the *degree* of certainty about its conclusion. The nodes in the network that, in the end, either do or do not send on a "yes" to the next layer are adjustable – and here is where the training comes in.

During training, the system makes adjustments to the nodes, assigning more or less weight to inputs from earlier layers. In the classic training session, the system is fed a large number of labeled pictures (or, in the TAR context, documents), and is provided human feedback. It is told if it reached the correct decision. If not, the system experiments internally, adjusting the weighting of its nodes until it maximizes the number of correct estimates or final outputs. The classic example is a "back propagational neural network" in which the final output error is used to go "back" and tweak the nodes' weights, run another effort, and note the extent to which the output improves. Whether technically correct or not, the comparisons to human learning are obvious:[29] children are taught that various things are dogs or cats by repeatedly correcting the child's output statements ("Doggie!" or "Kitty!") until, by and large, the output is correct. As with neural nets, humans can measure, and ultimately have some faith in, the accuracy of the output, but will have no idea what the internal state of the network (or of the child's brain) looks like or exactly why it is so. In a neural network, the internal state is just a very large number of weights, that is, numbers. The layers in between the initial input and the final output are thus often referred to as "hidden layers."[30] As the system traverses the layers from the raw data input to the final output, it reaches conclusions about increasingly complex and abstract concepts.[31]

Figure 2.1 shows a simple diagram of a five-layer network.[32]

Supervised networks train using labeled data and then estimate answers from new input. As noted, neural networks can train themselves, taking great advantage of the amount of digitized data, which has vastly increased in recent years.[33] "Big data" allows programs much more room to train and self-correct their mechanisms. While the line between supervised and unsupervised learning is not fixed,[34] unsupervised learning examines unlabeled data, compares it to random data, and extracts a series of features common

---

[29] Our intuition that artificial neural networks mimic our biological ones may be right. David Hubel and Torstein Wiesel were awarded the 1981 Nobel Prize in physiology or medicine for work on the information processing systems in the visual cortex, which use the equivalent of hidden layers of neural network. See Press Release: The Nobel Prize in Physiology or Medicine 1981, The Nobel Assembly of Karolinska Institute (October 9, 1981), www .nobelprize.org/nobel_prizes/medicine/laureates/1981/press.html. Others caution that the brain is like a neural network only by way of analogy and metaphor. See, e.g., C. Chatham, 10 Important Differences between Brains and Computers, *ScienceBlogs* (March 27, 2007), http://scienceblogs.com/developingintelligence/2007/03/27/ why-the-brain-is-not-like-a-co/. The issue is irrelevant here. For those interested, artificial neural networks probably will not have the same number of neuron equivalents as humans until around 2050 (Goodfellow *et al.*, above note 6, p. 21), but around then artificial networks may advance very, very rapidly, unconstrained by the relatively slow processing speeds and limited storage abilities of humans.

[30] Currently, networks with about ten layers are termed "deep" or "very deep." See J. Schmidhuber, Deep Learning in Neural Networks: An Overview (2015) 61 *Neural Netw.* 85, 88, www.sciencedirect.com/science/article/pii/ S0893608014002135.

[31] Goodfellow *et al.*, above note 6, p. 8.

[32] M. Nielsen, Why Are Deep Neural Networks Hard to Train? in *Neural Networks and Deep Learning* (2017), ch. 5, http://neuralnetworksanddeeplearning.com/chap5.html.

[33] Goodfellow *et al.*, above note 6, pp. 19–20. Discussed below in "Risks and Cross-Examination."

[34] *Ibid.*, p. 100.

Curtis E. A. Karnow

input layer hidden layer 1 hidden layer 2 hidden layer 3

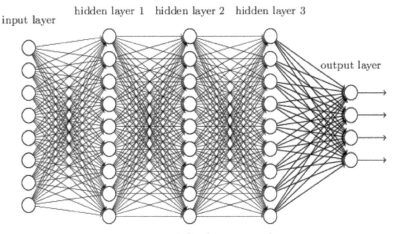

output layer

FIGURE 2.1 A five-layer network

to the non-random data. These features are, of course, abstractions from the input layer. The parameters of that layer may then be fixed and its output examined by the next layer as input, extracting common features for the next level of abstraction. A simple example is a clustering program, which reviews a large amount of input, makes conclusions concerning common features, and then sorts the inputs into different groups. This can all be done with unlabeled data, and human corrective input is not required. For example, engineers at Google created an early iteration of AlphaGo, which taught itself to recognize cats. Without telling it anything about cats, the engineers simply let it examine 13,026 pictures of cats and 23,974 pictures without cats. Even though the engineers provided no indication as to which was which, the system eventually detected the common cat features on its own, and reported its discovery of that common entity.[35]

By sorting data into groups or clusters defined by common aspects, unsupervised learning systems thus create a series of higher-level abstractions. Then, these systems learn to improve themselves. Assume a system which distinguishes – that is, separately clusters, as described above – digits from not digits; or cats from not cats. Now the higher layers (those generating conclusions such as "This is a digit" or "This is a cat") perform a top-down analysis, instructing the lower layers on what, more specifically, to look for as they make their lower-level determinations. For example, a top-down pass might in effect say, "Look for about two to three strokes for digits" or "Look for whiskers and a certain shape of ear for cats," which then iteratively improves the performance of the system as a whole.[36] The system teaches itself.

Uses of Neural Networks

For reasons expressed below, it is important to note the extensive reliance on neural networks. Traditional means of analysis are ill-equipped to handle massive amounts of data – familiarly known as "big data." But neural networks can be used to extract patterns and find needles in

[35] See Le *et al.*, above note 26, p. 1 ("Contrary to what appears to be a widely-held intuition, our experimental results reveal that it is possible to train a face detector without having to label images as containing a face or not . . . We also find that the same network is sensitive to other high-level concepts such as cat faces and human bodies").

[36] For a more technical but still somewhat approachable discussion, see G. E. Hinton, Learning Multiple Layers of Representation (2007) 11 *Trends Cogn. Sci.* 428, www.cs.toronto.edu/~hinton/absps/tics.pdf.

these big data haystacks. For example, these networks are used for automated bank loan application approval and credit card fraud detection, as well as a wide spectrum of other uses in the financial markets. They are used for medical diagnoses and x-ray interpretation. They are also used for process controls in factories, in scientific research, and, of course, in data mining in many contexts.[37] One text notes these uses:

Detection of medical phenomena. A variety of health-related indices (e.g., a combination of heart rate, levels of various substances in the blood, respiration rate) can be monitored. The onset of a particular medical condition could be associated with a very complex (e.g., nonlinear and interactive) combination of changes on a sub-set of the variables being monitored. Neural networks have been used to recognize this predictive pattern so that the appropriate treatment can be prescribed.

Stock market prediction. Fluctuations of stock prices and stock indices are another example of a complex, multidimensional, but in some circumstances at least partially-deterministic phenomenon. Neural networks are being used by many technical analysts to make predictions about stock prices based upon a large number of factors such as past performance of other stocks and various economic indicators.

Credit assignment. A variety of pieces of information are usually known about an applicant for a loan. For instance, the applicant's age, education, occupation, and many other facts may be available. After training a neural network on historical data, neural network analysis can identify the most relevant characteristics and use those to classify applicants as good or bad credit risks.

Monitoring the condition of machinery. Neural networks can be instrumental in cutting costs by bringing additional expertise to scheduling the preventive maintenance of machines. A neural network can be trained to distinguish between the sounds a machine makes when it is running normally ("false alarms") versus when it is on the verge of a problem. After this training period, the expertise of the network can be used to warn a technician of an upcoming breakdown, before it occurs and causes costly unforeseen "downtime."

[37] A quick Google Scholar review demonstrates the breadth of splendid scientific research covering this topic. Further applications include: *Financial* – Stock Market Prediction; Credit Worthiness; Credit Rating; Bankruptcy Prediction; Property Appraisal; Fraud Detection; Price Forecasts; Economic Indicator Forecasts; *Medical* – Medical Diagnosis; Detection and Evaluation of Medical Phenomena; Patient's Length of Stay Forecasts; Treatment Cost Estimation; *Industrial* – Process Control; Quality Control; Temperature and Force Prediction; *Science* – Pattern Recognition; Recipes and Chemical Formulation Optimization; Chemical Compound Identification; Physical System Modeling; Ecosystem Evaluation; Polymer Identification; Recognizing Genes; Botanical Classification; Signal Processing: Neural Filtering; Biological Systems Analysis; Ground Level Ozone Prognosis Odor Analysis and Identification; *Educational* – Teaching Neural Networks; Neural Network Research; College Application Screening; Predict Student Performance; *Data Mining* – Prediction Classification; Change and Deviation Detection; Knowledge Discovery; Response Modeling; Time Series Analysis; *Sales and Marketing* – Sales Forecasting; Targeted Marketing; Service Usage Forecasting; Retail Margins Forecasting; *Operational Analysis* – Retail Inventories Optimization; Scheduling Optimization; Managerial Decision Making; Cash Flow Forecasting; *HR Management* – Employee Selection and Hiring; Employee Retention; Staff Scheduling; Personnel Profiling; *Energy* – Electrical Load Forecasting; Energy Demand Forecasting; Short and Long-Term Load Estimation; Predicting Gas/Coal Index Prices; Power Control Systems; Hydro Dam Monitoring; *Other* – Sports Betting; Making Horse and Dog Racing Picks; Quantitative Weather Forecasting; Games Development; Optimization Problems, Routing; Agricultural Production Estimates. See Neural Network Software Applications, Alyuda, www.alyuda.com/products/neurointelligence/neural-network-applications.htm.

Engine management. Neural networks have been used to analyze the input of sensors from an engine. The neural network controls the various parameters within which the engine functions, in order to achieve a particular goal, such as minimizing fuel consumption.[38]

Closer to the legal realm, neural nets are developed or proposed for the electronic discovery uses noted above, as well as, for example, detecting gunshot residue,[39] demographic analysis of crime patterns,[40] automated detection of smuggling,[41] and other uses,[42] including for legal services.[43]

ADMITTING OUTPUT OF SOFTWARE

This section examines basic rules for the admissibility of computer-generated evidence (CGE) generally, in preparation for a later discussion of the admissibility of machine opinion.

Evidence introduced at trial, including software, may involve issues of hearsay and, more generally, of reliability. Authenticity is an aspect of reliability: thus, a document must be authenticated because otherwise it is not reliable. Hearsay objections are pertinent to some computer outputs, but not to others. Software is used to generate simulations and animations – two very different types of evidentiary creatures with different admissibility requirements. As discussed below, the rules governing the admissibility of simulations, in particular, are useful, but insufficient in deciding whether the output of neural networks should be admitted.

But first, a brief taxonomy of CGE will be useful.[44] As Justice Simons has noted, "We must distinguish from this computer-generated data [such as data associated with credit card swipes and cell phone use], a written or electronic document prepared by a person, and then electronically stored in a computer. Electronic storage does not make the document computer-generated."[45]

---

[38] StatSoft, Inc., Neural Networks in *Data Science Textbook* (2013), https://docs.tibco.com/data-science/textbook .

[39] R. Verena Taudte, C. Roux, D. Bishop, *et al.*, Development of a UHPLC Method for the Detection of Organic Gunshot Residues Using Artificial Neural Networks (2015) 7 *Anal. Methods* 7447, http://pubs.rsc.org/en/content/articlepdf/2015/ay/c5ay00306g.

[40] X. Li and M. Juhola, Country Crime Analysis Using the Self-Organizing Map, with Special Regard to Demographic Factors (2014) 29 *AI Soc.* 53, http://link.springer.com/article/10.1007/s00146-013-0441-7.

[41] N. Jaccard, T. W. Rogers, E. J. Morton, and L. D. Griffin, Automated Detection of Smuggled High-Risk Security Threats Using Deep Learning, *ArXiv* (September 9, 2016), https://arxiv.org/pdf/1609.02805.pdf.

[42] M. Aikenhead, The Uses and Abuses of Neural Networks in Law (1996) 12 *Santa Clara Comput. High Technol. Law J.* 31 (legal reasoning); M. Ebrahimi, C. Y. Suen, and O. Ormandjievab, Detecting Predatory Conversations in Social Media by Deep Convolutional Neural Networks (2016) 18 *Digit. Investig.* 33, www.sciencedirect.com/science/article/pii/S1742287616300731; N. Issar, More Data Mining for Medical Misrepresentation? Admissibility of Statistical Proof Derived from Predictive Methods of Detecting Medical Reimbursement Fraud (2015) 42 *N. Ky. Law Rev.* 341 (statistical detection evidence); G. Koukiou and V. Anastassopoulos, Neural Networks for Identifying Drunk Persons Using Thermal Infrared Imagery (2015) 252 *Forensic Sci. Int.* 69, www.sciencedirect.com/science/article/pii/S0379073815001681; J. Nawara, Machine Learning: Face Recognition Technology Evidence in Criminal Trials (2011) 49 *Univ. Louisville Law Rev.* 601 (reliability of face recognition systems); D. Olszewski, Fraud Detection Using Self-Organizing Map Visualizing the User Profiles (2014) 70 *Knowl.-Based Syst.* 324, www.sciencedirect.com/science/article/pii/S0950705114002652.

[43] J. O. McGinnis and R. G. Pearce, The Great Disruption: How Machine Intelligence Will Transform the Role of Lawyers in the Delivery of Legal Services (2014) 82 *Fordham Law Rev.* 3041.

[44] See generally G. P. Joseph, A Simplified Approach to Computer-Generated Evidence and Animations (1999) 43 *NY Law Sch. Law Rev.* 875.

[45] M. Simons, *California Evidence Manual* (Thomson West, 2017), § 2:2.

The Filing Cabinet

Much of what is thought of as CGE[46] is not. What is sometimes termed CGE is actually generated by humans who input the data into computers; the computers act simply as storage systems, much like filing cabinets. Letters, briefs, emails, PowerPoints, much of our spreadsheets and other accounting data, and most photographs fit in this category. Aside from photographs, these types of data are collections of statements by humans, and so a hearsay objection may be made.[47] The objection can be met with a showing under the business records exception, for example.[48] Websites and chat room postings are also similarly housed in digital storage cabinets: people put the words there and other people can testify as to authenticity and related issues, as they would if the data came out of a physical filing cabinet. Databases contain human-entered data too, which fit under this rubric of human-generated information. Pictures posted to the Internet are generally authenticated and admitted the same way as any other photographs; that is, either someone testifies that she took the picture or someone familiar with the scene depicted testifies that the photo is accurate. Circumstantial evidence may suffice for admissibility.[49]

It is true that the act of processing electronic data into photographs or legible text involves computer processing, a translation of bits into a human-readable product. But the proponent of the evidence need not explain or defend this type of processing as it is assumed that "a computer's print function has worked properly."[50] In short, "[p]rintouts are admissible and presumed to be an accurate representation of the data in the computer."[51] That being said, even when the print function presumably works correctly, the printed data may still be hearsay, because it was input by humans.[52]

---

[46] Justice Simons calls it computer-generated information (CGI). "CGI" is also used to designate computer-enhanced film effects (computer-generated imagery). *Ibid.* In the interests of avoiding ambiguity, "CGE" is used here for computer-generated evidence.

[47] Simons, above note 45, § 2:63; *People* v. *Romeo*, 193 Cal. Rptr. 3d 96, 108 (Cal. Ct. App. 2015) ("[I]nformation residing in a computer database is still hearsay, often multilevel hearsay"); Joseph, above note 44, p. 878.

[48] *California Evidence Code* (Thomson Reuters, 2017), § 1271.

[49] See E. A. Rucker and M. E. Overland, *California Criminal Practice: Motions, Jury Instructions and Sentencing*, 4th edn. (Thomson West, 2017), Vol. 4, § 48:18 ("The normal rules of admissibility apply to evidence obtained from social networking and other online sites. Authentication of a photograph on a Web site may be provided by expert testimony if there is no one qualified to authenticate it from personal observation. In addition, authentication may be provided from its contents or subject matter (*People* v. *Valdez*, 135 Cal. Rptr. 3d 628 (Cal. Ct. App. 2011) (photograph from a social-networking web page alleged to have been authored by defendant was sufficiently authenticated by its content to be admissible))"). See also S. Goode, The Admissibility of Electronic Evidence (2009) 29 *Rev. Litig.* 1, 24–25 (discussing the use of circumstantial evidence to authenticate in federal court); P. W. Grimm, D. J. Capra, and G. P. Joseph, Authenticating Digital Evidence (2017) 69 *Baylor Law Rev.* 1, 15 (showing that circumstantial evidence is widely used to authenticate).

[50] *People* v. *Goldsmith*, 326 P.3d 239, 246 (Cal. 2014), quoting *People* v. *Hawkins*, 121 Cal. Rptr. 2d 627, 643 (Cal. Ct. App. 2002). Of course, as with any other presumption, the other side is free to attack it. But the presumption is almost always enough to get the evidence before the trier of fact (e.g. the jury). See, e.g., *People* v. *Martinez*, 990 P.2d 563, 580–2 (Cal. 2000) (problems with printouts may be subject to cross-examination, but typically will not bar admissibility). This is because the opponent does not have evidence that the printout is inaccurate. But if she does have evidence of inaccuracy, *the presumption is no longer in effect*, and the burden returns to the proponent of the printout to establish that it is, in fact, accurate. See *People* v. *Rekte*, 181 Cal. Rptr. 3d 912, 918–19 (Cal. Ct. App. 2015).

[51] B. E. Witkin, and members of the Witkin Legal Institute, *California Evidence*, 5th edn. (Witkin Legal Institute, 2012), Vol. 1, § 231(b)(3). New federal rules of evidence, effective December 1, 2017, make it even easier in federal court to meet basic authentication requirements for computer-stored data. See Fed. R. Evid. 902(13)–(14). See also Grimm *et al.*, above note 49, p. 39.

[52] Printouts offered for their truth usually have to qualify under some exception to the hearsay rule, such as under the business records exception. See *Aguimatang* v. *Cal. State Lottery*, 286 Cal. Rptr. 57, 72–3 (Cal. Ct. App. 1991); *People* v. *Lugashi*, 252 Cal. Rptr. 434, 439 (Cal. Ct. App. 1988).

Data Created by Internal Operations

Computers may be fed data and, based on their programming, generate new data, the accuracy of which depends on the validity of the programing. The simplest examples are spreadsheet cells containing formulas that simply execute something like a mini program written by the user, such as "Multiply cell B3 with B4 and put the result here." If the human selected the wrong cells, or directed a multiplication when it ought to have been division, the result (i.e. "Profits this year were $100") will be wrong. Drawing programs can automatically generate circles and squares, but whether these are accurate depends on whether the algorithm is correct. In short, software may or may not have bugs,[53] which may affect the validity of its outputs.

Typically, it is suggested that because the result of internal computer processing is not a human statement, hearsay is not implicated. For example, the venerable legal author Bernard Witkin declared:[54]

> *Distinction: Computer's Internal Operations.* A printout of the results of a computer's internal operations is not hearsay evidence at all, and thus the business records exception is inapplicable. Such a printout does not represent the output of statements placed in the computer by an out-of-court declarant. With a machine, there is no possibility of conscious misrepresentation. "[T]he true test for admissibility of a printout reflecting a computer's internal operations is not whether the printout was made in the regular course of business, but whether the computer was operating properly at the time of the printout." (*People* v. *Hawkins* (2002) 98 C. A.4th 1428, 1449, 1450, 121 C.R.2d 627 [in prosecution arising from defendant's having taken source code from computer system of former employer, trial judge did not err in admitting computer printouts showing when computer files were last accessed, where evidence was introduced showing that computer was functioning properly and its clock was accurate] . . .).[55]

But the results of internal processing may use human-entered data as inputs, and that data can be challenged on a variety of grounds, including hearsay. Sometimes, data appears to come directly to the computer without human intervention, such as by way of sensors and digital imaging, in which case it may be thought of as part of the internal processing of the computer. There may be some difference between the standards used for the admission of the results of internal processing and those used in connection with sensor input. In the former situation, as discussed below, the proponent must present some foundation (but not much) on the accuracy of the system, but the inputs of real-time sensor information, such as automated photographs, "are presumed to be accurate,"[56] a test reminiscent of that applied to the "print function" of a computer.

[53] Actually, all software in general use is sufficiently complex in that it has bugs. "All software contains bugs or errors in the code. Some of these bugs have security implications, granting an attacker unauthorized access to or control of a computer. These vulnerabilities are rampant in the software we all use. A piece of software as large and complex as Microsoft Windows will contain hundreds of them, maybe more." B. Schneier, Why the NSA Makes Us More Vulnerable to Cyberattacks: The Lessons of WannaCry, *Foreign Affairs* (May 30, 2017), www .foreignaffairs.com/articles/2017-05-30/why-nsa-makes-us-more-vulnerable-cyberattacks. The complexity of software is essential, not an accident. See Brooks, above note 20, p. 183. And that complexity may lead to unexpected results – which is, in fact, all that is meant by "bug."

[54] Bernard Witkin, a former Reporter of Decisions for the California Supreme Court, was the author of, among other things, these standard compendia of California law: *Summary of California Law*, 11th edn. (Thomson Reuters, 2017), *California Procedure*, 5th edn. (Thomson Reuters, 2008), and *California Evidence*, above note 51.

[55] Witkin *et al.*, above note 51, § 231(b)(3).

[56] This is "especially [so for] government-maintained computers, [which] are presumed to be accurate. Thus, a witness with the general knowledge of an automated system may testify to his or her use of the system and that he

Turning then directly to classic internal processing, the basic rule for admissibility is succinctly captured in this unpublished opinion:

> The test for admissibility of machine created information is whether the computer was operating properly at the time of the printout ... The admissibility of computer records also does not require establishing the accuracy, maintenance, reliability or the acceptability of the computer's hardware or software. Our Supreme Court has noted that mistakes can occur with computer generated information. However, such mistakes should not affect admissibility but be developed on cross-examination.[57]

This "machine-created information" or CGE includes, for example, metadata, such as timestamps and author-identification information,[58] which is automatically created by the machine. But even some human input is implicated for metadata, such as setting the time either on the machine itself or on some other machine to which it refers, creating the author's initials, and so on. Nevertheless, generally the data is automatically created, and so qualifies as CGE. Thus, no hearsay objection applies.

And while CGE does have to be validated with some foundational testimony, the bar is not high:

> First, the witness through whom the computer records are introduced is qualified if that witness generally understands the system's operation and possesses sufficient skill and knowledge to properly use the system and explain the resultant data, even if the witness is unable to perform every task from initial design and programming to final printout ... Second, testimony on the acceptability, accuracy, maintenance, and reliability of computer hardware and software need not be introduced, particularly where the data consists of retrieval of automatic inputs rather than computations based on manual entries ...[59]

The requirement generally to explain the system's operation seems to satisfy, or be the functional equivalent of offering, "foundational evidence that the computer was operating properly."[60] What does it mean to show that the computer was operating "properly"? It seems

---

or she has downloaded the computer information to produce the recording. No elaborate showing of the accuracy of the recorded data is required. Courts in California have not required 'testimony regarding the "acceptability, accuracy, maintenance, and reliability of ... computer hardware and software" in similar situations.'" *People* v. *Dawkins*, 179 Cal. Rptr. 3d 101, 110 (Cal. Ct. App. 2014) (internal citations omitted).

[57] *People* v. *Johnson*, No. F069414, 2016 WL 4482963, at *3 (Cal. Ct. App. August 25, 2016) (unpublished) (internal citations omitted). See also, e.g., *People* v. *Hawkins*, 121 Cal. Rptr. 2d 627, 642–3 (Cal. Ct. App. 2002) ("[T]he true test for admissibility of a printout reflecting a computer's internal operations is not whether the printout was made in the regular course of business, but whether the computer was operating properly at the time of the printout"). This foundational showing, that the computer was "operating properly," does not require much. See *People* v. *Martinez*, 990 P. 2d 563, 581 (Cal. 2000) ("[O]ur courts have refused to require, as a prerequisite to admission of computer records, testimony on the 'acceptability, accuracy, maintenance, and reliability of ... computer hardware and software'") (quoting *Lugashi*, 252 Cal. Rptr. at 441). Mistakes can be exposed by cross-examination. *Ibid.* Accord *Dawkins*, 179 Cal. Rptr. 3d at 110 (requiring no elaborate foundational showing, especially with government maintained computers); *People* v. *Peyton*, 177 Cal. Rptr. 3d 823 (Cal. Ct. App. 2014).

[58] *United States* v. *Hamilton*, 413 F.3d 1138 (10th Cir. 2005).

[59] Simons, above note 45, § 2:63 (internal citations omitted). See also text, above note 53. But for a lengthy list of issues concerning this functionality that conceivably might be up for discussion, see Joseph, above note 44, p. 882. This list of issues may be significant as the focus of the (1) opposing side's attack on functionality, hoping to destroy the presumption of reliability (cf. above note 50), or (2) the proponent's efforts thereafter to shoulder the real burden of demonstrating functionality. If the evidence is admitted, the issues could also be used to argue to the fact finder that the evidence is or is not persuasive.

[60] *Hawkins*, 121 Cal. Rptr. 2d at 643. Cf. *Goldsmith*, 326 P.3d at 248 (considering, among other factors, showing that "the evidence was properly received in the normal course and manner of Inglewood's operation of its ATES program").

to be no more than showing that it was operating as it usually does, explained by someone with some experience in using the system.[61] That is enough to meet the "minimal requirement for admissibility,"[62] which, after all, still leaves the evidence subject to cross-examination and argument that the fact finder should disregard it.[63]

Simulations

Foundation

The low threshold for CGE may simply be a practical response to an otherwise impossible problem. Computers and their data are ubiquitous, but no one really knows how they work in detail.[64] No person, for example, can report on the detailed instructions used by the most ordinary operating system, not to mention the myriad interactions between operating systems and applications found in every business and most homes in this country. But the test is reasonable because it meets a fundamental predicate that notions of reliability in the legal world mirror those used in the "real" or ordinary world. The same line of reasoning dictates that business records are exempt from the hearsay rule: if the hearsay is good enough for a business to rely on, it is good enough for a jury.[65] So too here: if an entity relies on the validity of CGE in its day-to-day work, a jury is justified in making the same assumption of validity. Expecting much more would exclude CGE from our courts.

But this reasoning does not quite extend to justify the admission of computer simulations which are purposely made for a trial – these are bespoke CGE. The techniques used are not employed in the run-of-the-mill business.[66]

---

61 See, e.g., *Johnson*, 2016 WL 4482963, at *3 (admitting scanner evidence based on testimony of how staff used the scanner where the scanner's information "was from the night of the shooting because its data only lasted 'a day or two' and [the witness] correlated the scanner with the video surveillance system"); *People* v. *Johnson*, No. B224491, 2011 WL 4436451, at *2 (Cal. Ct. App. September 26, 2011) (unpublished) ("Stoltz testified that the software company who owned the loan software designed a special program to extract 'miscellaneous' type transactions posted during a specific time period. The result of running the special program was a list of 'miscellaneous' type transactions for the period in question. This is sufficient to create an inference that the computer program was working properly"). As observed in note 51, new federal rules of evidence ease the admissibility of computer evidence. Rule 902(13) of the new Federal Rules of Evidence *seems* to apply to CGE (while 902(14) applies to computer-stored data), but the Committee Notes make it clear that only authenticity is established through the certification procedures of the rule, not reliability as such. For example, the Committee Notes state that "[s]imilarly, a certification authenticating a computer output, such as a spreadsheet, does not preclude an objection that the information produced is unreliable – the authentication establishes only that the output came from the computer." Fed. R. Evid. 902(13) (advisory committee's note to 2016 amendment).

62 *Lugashi*, 252 Cal. Rptr. at 440.

63 See also, e.g., *People* v. *Nazary*, 120 Cal. Rptr. 3d 143, 163–5 (Cal. Ct. App. 2010), overruled on other grounds in *People* v. *Vidana*, 377 P. 3d 805, 815–16 (Cal. 2016) (holding test of admissibility of machine-generated receipts from automated gas station island pumps is whether "machine was operating properly at the time of the reading").

64 M. Meysenburg, *Introduction to Programming Using Processing*, 3rd edn. (lulu.com, 2016), p. 252 (regarding the typical fly-by-wire automated aircraft controls systems; "No single person on the face of the earth truly understands everything there is to know about the software that keeps the airliner flying"). See generally S. Arbesman, *Overcomplicated: Tech. at the Limits of Comprehension* (Portfolio, 2016), p. 3 (discussing in particular computer-enabled systems; "[T]echnological complexity has eclipsed our ability to comprehend it").

65 See, e.g., *United States* v. *Ary*, 518 F.3d 775, 786 (10th Cir. 2008).

66 This is not always true. Some businesses do indeed rely on simulations for their quotidian work. *Lapsley* v. *Xtek, Inc.*, 689 F.3d 802, 815 (7th Cir. 2012) ("[S]imulation is one of the most common of scientific and engineering tools. Around the world, computers simulate nuclear explosions, quantum mechanical interactions, atmospheric weather patterns, and innumerable other systems that are difficult or impossible to observe directly. A mathematical or computer model is a perfectly acceptable form of test"). These simulations may not be admissible under a lesser level of scrutiny, or that reliability might simply be easier to establish.

Simulations and animations are not the same.[67] Animations are a sort of supporting evidence that serves only to illustrate other testimony, much as a drawing of a car accident scene by an eyewitness serves to illustrate and explain the witness testimony.[68] As demonstrative evidence, it may or may not be admissible,[69] but in any event it entirely depends on the primary testimony, and it is the human witness who is cross-examined.[70] No one really cares how the animation was made, for example, how the drawing program works, or how it calculates distances or other features, just as no one cares how a camera works when a witness testifies that picture is a fair representation of the scene she saw.

Simulations, by contrast, are introduced as primary or "substantive" evidence: they depend on accurate inputs, but their validity also, critically, depends on valid algorithms. Therefore, the validity of the algorithm, unlike the validity of an animation, is fair game for a challenge:

> Courts have compared computer animations to classic forms of demonstrative evidence such as charts or diagrams that illustrate expert testimony . . . A computer animation is admissible if "it is a fair and accurate representation of the evidence to which it relates . . ." A computer simulation, by contrast, is admissible only after a preliminary showing that any "new scientific technique" used to develop the simulation has gained "general acceptance . . . in the relevant scientific community."[71]

For this custom CGE, much more than the minimal threshold noted above must be presented. If challenged, the proponent must satisfy the much stronger test of showing that the methods used by the software are justified by science, for example, by showing:

> [T]hat the facts and data upon which the simulation is based "are of a type reasonably relied upon by experts in the particular field," that the simulation is "the product of reliable principles and methods," and that the supporting expert witness "applied principles and methods reliably" when creating or using the simulation.[72]

As one commentator notes, "in the context of simulations, the computer itself is the expert."[73]

Simulations may, for example, analyze airplane crashes and the movement of groundwater and contaminants. The input consists of data such as records of radar returns, facts concerning the crash site – including distances between pieces of the aircraft, so-called "black box" data – including speed over time, whether flaps were deployed, and so on. These are fed to a program which reproduces a view of the accident from the pilots' perspective or provide a basis to conclude that a warning must have sounded and been ignored, or that the aircraft was at a certain angle of attack. A simulation of groundwater contamination might take inputs of data, including measurements of a toxin over time in a certain area and the movement rate

---

67 *People* v. *Duenas*, 283 P. 3d 887, 900 (Cal. 2012) ("Courts and commentators draw a distinction between computer animations and computer simulations"). For a detailed discussion, see, e.g., C. Karnow, *Litigation in Practice* (Twelve Tables Press, 2017), pp. 31–3.

68 See, e.g., *People* v. *Hood*, 62 Cal. Rptr. 2d 137, 139–40 (Cal. Ct. App. 1997).

69 That is, judges may not let the animation go to the jury room during deliberations, and it may not become part of the record sent to the court of appeal. But of course, the jury sees it, so in that less technical sense, the animation is admitted.

70 B. S. Fiedler, Are Your Eyes Deceiving You? The Evidentiary Crisis Regarding the Admissibility of Computer Generated Evidence (2004) 48 *NY Law Sch. Law Rev.* 295, 299 ("[T]he testifying witness must state that the CGE portrays the disputed subject matter fairly and accurately").

71 *Duenas*, 283 P. 3d at 901, quoting *People* v. *Kelly*, 130 Cal. Rptr. 144, 148 (Cal. Ct. App. 1976) (internal citations omitted).

72 V. Webster and F. E. (Trey) Bourn III, The Use of Computer-Generated Animations and Simulations at Trial (2016) 83 *Def. Couns. J.* 439, 441 (notes omitted; includes multi-circuit survey).

73 *Ibid.*, p. 440.

of groundwater over that period, and then opine that the toxin must have been at a certain concentration at a point upstream at a specified earlier time.

In these situations, the validity, and hence the admissibility, of the simulation depends on the validity of the programming, including calculations and underlying assumptions. The California Supreme Court has held that simulations are admissible if they are scientifically reliable, and "only after a preliminary showing that 'any new scientific technique' used to develop the simulation has gained general acceptance ... in the relevant scientific community."[74] More established techniques must still be explained because, as expert systems, they are subject to the usual strictures, including basic scientific reliability[75] and non-speculative connections between the conclusions (or output) of the opinion and the input.[76] But it is difficult to know what counts as a sufficient demonstration of reliability.

Interlude: Explaining Software

Judges and juries expect that, at some level, the operations of simulations can be explained, that the "heuristic basis" can be demonstrated.[77] For example, an expert might use commonly accepted formulae for the relationship between the pressure of a liquid and aperture of the container through which it is released, based on the classic Bernoulli equation, to compute the speed of the liquid or the pressure it would exert on its target.[78] The proponent of the model must establish this reliability:

> Computer-generated simulations are based on mathematical models, and particular attention must be paid to the reliability and trustworthiness of the model. A model is a set of operating assumptions – a mathematical representation of a defined set of facts, or system. To be accurate, it must produce results that are identical or very similar to those produced by the physical facts (or system) being modeled. In order to do that, the model must contain all relevant elements – and reflect all relevant interactions – that occur in the real world.[79]

But it is not clear what is involved in any foundational requirement to explain the operation of software, including computer simulations.

There are some issues of definition, such as whether the "program" includes operating systems, interfaces, and commonly available libraries.[80] Those issues can, to some extent, be defined away as not pertaining to the program. For example, judges probably do not want to hear about the general housekeeping functions, such as the runtime environment including operating systems, standard interfaces, and device drivers, or the language in which the program was written (for example, C++, FORTRAN, etc.). These are aspects of base technology and ordinarily do not embody the decision-making processes that are at issue as a foundation is laid for a simulation. Juxtaposed with this base technology is the decision-

[74] *Duenas*, 283 P. 3d at 901, quoting *People v. Kelly*, 130 Cal. Rptr. at 148.
[75] *People v. Jackson*, 376 P. 3d 528, 568 (Cal. 2016) ("[Expert] procedures and experiments must comply with the laws of physics, chemistry, and biology"). See, e.g., *Liquid Dynamics Corp. v. Vaughan Co.*, 449 F.3d 1209, 1221 (Fed. Cir. 2006) (simulations subject to analysis under classic *Daubert* criteria and deemed in this case to be reliable); *Novartis Corp. v. Ben Venue Labs., Inc.*, 271 F.3d 1043, 1054 (Fed. Cir. 2001) ("[Valid] simulation ... requires both a solid theoretical foundation and realistic input parameters to yield meaningful results. Without knowing these foundations, a court cannot evaluate whether the simulation is probative"); *Lyondell Chem. Co. v. Occidental Chem. Corp.*, 608 F.3d 284, 294 (5th Cir. 2010) ("[W]e can gauge reliability by examining input values and requiring transparency from testifying experts").
[76] *Sargon Enterprises, Inc. v. Univ. of S. Cal.*, 288 P. 3d 1237, 1252–3 (Cal. 2012).
[77] W. R. Swartout, Explaining and Justifying Expert Consulting Programs, in J. A. Reggia and S. Tuhrim (eds.), *Computer-Assisted Medical Decision Making* (Springer, 1985), pp. 254–71.
[78] *Lapsley v. Xtek, Inc.*, 689 F.3d 802, 815 (7th Cir. 2012).
[79] Joseph, above note 44, p. 65.
[80] A library contains "pre-written" code with functions that can be called on by the main executing program.

making mechanism of interest to the court, which for convenience may be termed the "inference engine." This is the part of the program that manipulates data and generates conclusions.[81] It is the inference engine that embodies the central theories of the simulation, as opposed to more general theories of computation.

Setting issues of definition aside, more problematic concerns stem from the fact that software (including the inference engine) can be described at many levels of abstraction down to what some call "bare metal" (i.e. the machine code that executes on the central processing unit (CPU)).

Courts apparently handle this problem of description in an ad hoc manner for there is little useful guidance in case law. There are suggestions that the foundation would include testimony "as to the accuracy of the equations used" in the simulation software,[82] or testimony on "a solid theoretical foundation and realistic input parameters,"[83] or that the proponent would "unravel his code and deduce the assumptions, algorithms, equations, and parameters that must be embedded within it," perhaps by "translat[ing] the foreign language of his computer model into a comprehensible language . . ."[84] Some courts ask for a showing that "the input and underlying equations are sufficiently complete and accurate . . . and . . . the program is generally accepted by the appropriate community of scientists."[85] However, none of this tells us exactly what sort of explanation is enough to lay a foundation.

Judges certainly do not want to be led step by step through the bare metal code (i.e. machine language[86]) or, just a bit less raw, assembly language,[87] which is understood by few

---

[81] The inference engine's code may, however, be located in a variety of subprograms and libraries. The in-court proponent of the software may or may not be cognizant of the specific mechanisms of each piece of the inference engine because the engine might depend on components such as dynamic link libraries (DLLs) written by others, and the proponent may be wrong about what those DLLs do. See A. Björklund, J. Klövstedt, and S. Westergren, DLL Spoofing in Windows, Uppsala University (October 21, 2005) (unpublished student work), www.it.uu.se /edu/course/homepage/sakdat/ht05/assignments/pm/programme/DLL_Spoofing_in_Windows.pdf. Ordinary programs built with so-called object oriented programming (OOP) tools, in effect, hide their basic functionality within the "objects" (components) sometimes built by others. See Brooks, above note 20, p. 272. Practically speaking, no witness is likely to be able to explain the processing of all these components.

[82] L. L. Levenson, *California Criminal Procedure*, 4th edn. (Thomson West, 2016), § 22:26; accord, Rucker and Overland, above note 49, § 48:22.

[83] B. E. Bergman, N. Hollander, and T. M. Duncan, *Wharton's Criminal Evidence*, 15th edn. (Thomson West, 2016), § 16:22.

[84] *Novartis Corp. v. Ben Venue Labs., Inc.*, 271 F.3d 1043, 1054 (Fed. Cir. 2001).

[85] *Commercial Union Ins. Co. v. Boston Edison Co.*, 591 N.E. 2d 165, 168 (Mass. 1992).

[86] In machine code, each instruction executes directly on the computer's CPU. Here's an example:

```
802078
8021A9 80
80238D 15 03
8026A9 2D
80288D 14 03
802B58
802C60
```

Here's another example:

```
00000000
00000001
00000010
00000100
00001000
00010000
00100000
01000000
```

[87] This is an example:

```
Start:.org $8020
SEI
```

individuals. Nor is it likely that a judge (or later, the jury) wants to be led through the next higher level of abstraction, source code, which most programmers use to write software.[88] At an even higher level of abstraction, there could be general flow-chart diagrams, but while these might summarize the components and processes of a system, they will not reflect most of the logical work or assumptions of the program. Those are *too* abstract.

Somewhere in between these levels of abstraction, there might be statistical formulas programmed into the inference engine, for example:[89]

$$z_1 = \frac{\sum_{l=1}^{M} y_k^l (\prod_{i=1}^{n} \mu A_l^i(X_i))}{\sum_{l=1}^{M} y_k^l (\prod_{i=1}^{n} \mu A_l^i(X_i))}$$

Together with the program itself, formulas such as this are good candidates for disclosure to the other party (that is, to the other side's expert) because they embody the statistical rules of the inference engine and, in effect, state the nature of the input and output. But on their own, they are of no help to the judge or the jury. While it is possible to explain such formulas in plain English, other forms of representation are more useful.

As one commentator has suggested, this can be done in three ways: (1) propositional logic; (2) fuzzy logic diagrams; and (3) decision trees.[90] In propositional logic, the values of variables are stated. For example, A and B can be true or false or can be one of any specified range of

```
LDA#$80
STA$0315
LDA#$2D
STA$0314
CLI
RTS
INC $D020
JMP $EA31
802DEE 20 D0
80304C 31 EA
```

[88] Source code looks like this:

```
static void
print_cookies(CURL *curl)
{
CURLcode res;
struct curl_slist *cookies;
struct curl_slist *nc;
int i;
printf("Cookies, curl knows:\n");
res = curl_easy_getinfo(curl, CURLINFO_COOKIELIST, &cookies);
if(res != CURLE_OK) {
fprintf(stderr, "Curl curl_easy_getinfo failed: %s\n",
curl_easy_strerror(res));
exit(1);}
```

[89] This is a formula used in a fuzzy logic inference engine expert system. what-when-how, Supervised Learning and Fuzzy Logic Systems (Artificial Intelligence), http://what-when-how.com/artificial-intelligence/supervised-learning-of-fuzzy-logic-systems-artificial-intelligence/.

[90] Reid addresses neural networks, but his point is useful more generally. S. Reid, 10 Misconceptions about Neural Networks, *Turing Finance* (May 8, 2014), www.turingfinance.com/misconceptions-about-neural-networks/#blackbox.

values. The value could be numerical, or it could be something else. In the example provided by the commentator, A could have one of these values: {BUY, HOLD, SELL}. Then, relational operators, such as "less than" or "equal to," are used to compare the variables to other variables or values. Logical operators, such as And, Or, or But Not, may also be applied. Continuing with the example, imagine these variables as inputs: Price (P), Simple Moving Average (SMA), and Exponential Moving Average (EMA). The strategy might then look like this:[91]

```
If (Sma > P) ∧ (Ema > P) Then Buy Else
If (Sma > P) ∧ (Ema < P) Then Hold
```

We might also employ fuzzy logic, this provides a *range* over which a variable is true or belongs to a certain set. A program might conclude that a share of a company is a 20% BUY, 30% HOLD, and 50% SELL. Inputs too can be expressed over a range, expressing degrees of uncertainty, which corresponds at least at a high level with the way in which layers in neural networks decide whether or not to pass on a finding to the next layer. Generated diagrams can then show that when the combined input from a series of sources exceeds a threshold, a decision is reached. For example, a medical diagnosis system might have degrees of certainty and uncertainty concerning inputs such as {has headaches – to some degree}, {has a rash – to some degree}, {is nauseous – to some degree}, {has difficulty breathing – to some degree}, and then express a result, such as {has Golem's Fever, with a specified level of certainty}.

Finally, decision trees show the impact of factors on a series of decisions. In flight simulators, for example, a series of models or subsystems, such as the aerodynamic, gear, weather, and engine models are inputs to equations which calculate motion, and those then in turn output to visual, sound, motion, instrument displays, and other outputs.[92] Each component model includes a series of equations. For example, a sophisticated engine model will produce figures for "engine thrust, fuel flows and engine pressures and rotation speeds ... engine failure modes (e.g. surge, stall or total failure) ... [accounting for, e.g.,] engine characteristics [which] change considerably at low speeds and at very low altitude ..."[93] The number of equations in a flight simulator is far beyond what could possibly be addressed in a trial. Thus, here too the practical approach will distinguish and then ignore aspects of the program that are routine and presumably generally accepted from those that are novel. As to the latter, an expert can present a graphical representation of the decision nodes,[94] the values for each of which cause the node to make a decision one way or the other (for example, "if [engine temperature] > [5000 degrees], output ['explode']"), and a theory behind the figure, such as research that shows engines explode at certain temperatures.

There are two conclusions here. Importantly, for traditional expert systems, a human expert's competence in demonstrating, explaining, and justifying the theory behind a calculation is crucial. Both the judge determining admissibility and the jury determining weight look to the human expert to vouch for the simulation,[95] explain step by step the way in which the software works, state its assumptions and the valid scientific theories on which it is

---

[91] "∧" means "and"; ">" means "greater than"; and "<" means "less than."
[92] D. Allerton, *Principles of Flight Simulation* (Wiley, 2009), p. 17.
[93] *Ibid.*, p. 18.
[94] See, e.g., D. Madigan, K. Mosurski, and R. G. Almond, Graphical Explanation in Belief Networks (1997) 6 *J. Comput. Graph. Stat.* 160, 160–81.
[95] E. M. Chaney, Computer Simulations: How They Can Be Used at Trial and the Arguments for Admissibility (1986) 19 *Ind. Law Rev.* 735, 743.

based,[96] as well as the logic used to derive its results.[97] While opinions may be based on the results of programs, the human witness takes the credit, or suffers the impeachment, for the opinion. If the expert cannot explain the model – how the software works and why it uses the numbers or formulas it does – then the evidence is inadmissible.

Second, there is a limit to explanation. All evidence at trial assumes other facts are true. Courts do not ask the contractor to prove her measuring tapes are accurate or the doctor to prove the blood pressure cuff was accurate. While courts may require, as foundation for eyewitness testimony, evidence that the person was at the scene, they do not demand testimony on how the eye and brain work to record and recall the memory recited in court. As noted above,[98] only a minimal foundation is required for the routine operations of computers. It is a waste of time to reinvent the wheel; routine operations are a given. So too with most of the foundation for the admissibility of simulations. Courts will usually forego *all* explanation at the levels of greatest precision (i.e. the source code level). They quickly pass by even high-level descriptions of most of the calculations and built-in assumptions. At most, they will seek (1) high-level explanations of a few central formulas, (2) the foundation (studies, etc.) which justifies those formulas, and (3) to some extent, the logic that links those two things. This is as it should be; given the constraints of time, the expertise of most judges and juries, and the essential task of trial to focus relentlessly on core material issues. But courts should not delude themselves: the trustworthiness of much evidence, including computer simulations, depends on a practically infinite network of unarticulated assumptions. Nevertheless, courts will say the evidence is reliable.

ADMITTING MACHINE OPINIONS

Humans cannot explain how neural networks make their decisions.[99] But they can still establish that their results are reliable: humans can explain how the nets are trained, how they were successful in the past, and how they are successful with new data. These are the features that make neural networks reliable in the real world, and these are the factors that should make the output of these networks admissible in court, for reliability in the field is a sign that neural nets should be reliable in the courtroom.

Presented here are four arguments in favor of the reliability of machine opinions. First, we generally recognize and trust tacit expertise, the bases for which cannot be fully articulated. Second, we generally trust medications, sometimes with people's lives, even when no one knows how they work. Third, neural networks are statistical models, and judges commonly

96   *In re. TMI Litig.*, 193 F.3d 613, 669 (3d Cir. 1999), *amended,* 199 F.3d 158 (3d Cir. 2000). As the court noted, wonderfully summarizing the distinction in tests applicable to accepted versus new scientific theories, the "use of standard techniques bolster the inference of reliability; nonstandard techniques need to be well-explained." *In re. Zoloft (Sertraline Hydrochloride) Prod. Liab. Litig.*, No. 16-2247, 2017 WL 2385279, at *6 (3rd Cir. June 2, 2017) (note omitted).

97   D. Boies and S. Zack, Computer Generated Evidence – Admissibility of Computer Simulations, in R. L. Haig (ed.), *ABA, Business and Commercial Litigation in Federal Courts*, 4th edn. (Thomson West, 2016), § 66:17. See generally *Novartis Corp. v. Ben Venue Labs., Inc.*, 271 F.3d 1043, 1051 (Fed. Cir. 2001) (requiring demonstration of the "assumptions made by [the expert] in his computer model, and ask whether they are supported by evidence in the record. These include both the theoretical principles that informed the model's design as well as the means by which its input parameters were derived").

98   See text at note 57 above.

99   "'We can build these models,' Dudley says ruefully, 'but we don't know how they work.'" W. Knight, The Dark Secret at the Heart of AI, *MIT Technology Review* (April 11, 2017), www.technologyreview.com/s/604087/the-dark-secret-at-the-heart-of-ai/ (quoting a researcher: "It might just be part of the nature of intelligence that only part of it is exposed to rational explanation. Some of it is just instinctual, or subconscious, or inscrutable").

rely on statistical models. Fourth, reliability is importantly a function of the ability to test and cross-examine, and neural networks can, practically, be cross-examined.[100]

Tacit Expertise

In Malcolm Gladwell's *Blink*,[101] an art expert views a Greek statue offered to the Getty Museum for $10 million. The expert declares it a forgery. He cannot quite say why, but he is right. Much expertise is tacit: it cannot be clearly articulated. This is also true in sports (for example, how a professional hits a baseball traveling at 100 miles per hour[102]), music, teaching, decisions by administrative agencies,[103] perhaps even judging,[104] and many other domains[105] where expertise can be observed, but not described. As opposed to novices who use explicit step-by-step processes, experts tend to use more conceptual structures to solve problems, but it is difficult to use these structures to actually explain the work to others.[106]

The inarticulate basis for some expert opinion presents a challenge to the usual way in which tests for admissibility are considered. For example, under California's *Sargon* test, judges should be presented with the express logic of the reasoning between (a) the opinion and (b) its foundation, including (1) the facts of the case and (2) the general theory and techniques used, as demonstrably founded on studies or other sources.[107] The test puts a high premium on the articulation of the connection or "logic" between (a) studies and other

---

[100] J. L. Mnookin, Repeat Play Evidence: Jack Weinstein, "Pedagogical Devices," Technology, and Evidence (2015) 64 *DePaul Law Rev.* 571, 577–8 (suggesting courts permit the "opposing party to replace given assumptions with alternative ones" to enable cross-examination) ("To be sure, we do not normally imagine that machine-generated evidence requires cross-examination, but it may be time to begin thinking in those terms") (note omitted).

[101] M. Gladwell, *Blink: The Power of Thinking without Thinking* (Penguin, 2005).

[102] The batter has about 125 milliseconds to decide, far less time than it takes to blink. This makes the task impossible. But batters use unspecific information from the movements of the pitcher *before the pitch* to estimate a likely pitch. A. Kuzoian, Hitting a Major League Fastball Should Be Physically Impossible, *Business Insider* (April 15, 2017), www.businessinsider.com/science-major-league-fastball-brain-reaction-time-2016-4.

[103] J. Gersen and A. Vermeule, Thin Rationality Review (2016) 114 *Mich. Law Rev.* 1355.

[104] L. Epstein, R. Posner, and W. Landes, *The Behavior of Federal Judges: A Theoretical and Empirical Study of Rational Choice* (Harvard University Press, 2013), p. 5; C. M. Oldfather, Of Judges, Law, and the River: Tacit Knowledge and the Judicial Role (2015) *J. Disp. Resol.* 155, 156 ("[M]uch of what goes into the process of decision-making is inarticulable").

[105] Let us not forget the work of high-end travel agents. R. Buckley and A. C. Mossaz, Decision Making by Specialist Luxury Travel Agents (2016) 55 *Tour. Manag.* 133, 133–8.

[106] P. J. Hinds and J. Pfeffer, Why Organizations Don't "Know What They Know": Cognitive and Motivational Factors Affecting the Transfer of Expertise, in M. S. Ackerman, V. Pipek, and V. Wulf (eds.), *Sharing Expertise: Beyond Knowledge Management* (MIT Press, 2003), pp. 3, 5 (regarding experts' "conceptual, abstract representations is that they appear to be simplified representations of the task. As experts begin to automate aspects of the task, details of the task become less salient and experts begin to view the task in an oversimplified way. In an experiment, Langer and Imber (1979) found that experts' lists of task components contained significantly fewer and less specific steps than did the lists of those with less expertise. Developing abstract, simplified representations of the task allows experts to process information more rapidly, view the task holistically, and avoid getting bogged down in details. As such, abstract and simplified representations generally serve experts well. However, there are situations in which these representations can interfere with experts' ability to share their expertise, particularly with others who have significantly less expertise").

[107] Simons, above note 45, § 4:22. See also *Jennings v. Palomar Pomerado Health Sys., Inc.*, 8 Cal. Rptr. 3d 363, 369 (Cal. Ct. App. 2003) ("[W]hen an expert's opinion is purely conclusory because unaccompanied by a reasoned explanation connecting the factual predicates to the ultimate conclusion, that opinion has no evidentiary value because an expert opinion is worth no more than the reasons upon which it rests" – internal quotes omitted). See generally C. Karnow, Expert Witness: Sargon and the Science of Reliable Experts in *Litigation in Practice* (Twelve Tables Press, 2017), pp. 161–7.

foundations that establish a general theory or technique and (b) those theories (or techniques) and the facts of the case, on the one hand, and the ultimate opinion on the other. The reasoning or "logic" should be express. This allows the judge evaluating admissibility to determine that each step in the process is reliable.[108]

But this cannot be entirely right. Experts with "special knowledge, skill, experience, training, or education" can testify,[109] even though their experiences or skills may not be able to be described in minute detail. Their skills are generally built up from many years of experience as a banker or landowner testifying to value of property, or years of experience as a carpenter, plumber, or tile layer.[110] For some of these experts, there is only so much they can say about the foundation of their opinions. In contrast, there may be "even . . . a witness whose expertise is based purely on experience, say, a perfume tester able to distinguish among 140 odors at a sniff, whether his preparation is of a kind that others in the field would recognize as acceptable."[111]

The results in two relatively recent cases, one from the California Court of Appeal and one from the Ninth Circuit, may be explained at least in part by the notion of tacit expertise. To the surprise of some trial judges (presumably including the highly respected jurists reversed in these two cases), the trial courts' meticulous examination of the articulated foundations of the experts' testimony, which led to their exclusion, was set aside by the appellate courts. The appellate panels found that the trial judges had, in each case, glossed over the basic reliability of the opinion, as demonstrated by the experts' credentials and extensive experience.

In the state case, *Cooper*,[112] the trial judge had examined each study relied upon by the expert and found many problems. But the appellate court said that the expert, a cancer specialist, had looked at all the studies together and based on his experience found them as a whole to be an adequate foundation. Importantly, the appellate court seems to have gone out of its way to cite the doctor's credentials and experience at length.[113] There were other issues in *Cooper* regarding the trial judge's approach, but the tenor of the opinion is that the witness was unquestionably an expert in the field, and if he found a basis for his opinions, then the trial judge was in no position to second-guess him.

In *Wendell*, the Ninth Circuit also chastised the trial court for:

> look[ing] too narrowly at each individual consideration, without taking into account the broader picture of the experts' overall methodology. It improperly ignored the experts' experience, reliance on a variety of literature and studies, and review of [the] medical records and history, as well as the fundamental importance of differential diagnosis by experienced doctors treating troubled patients.[114]

Here too, the appellate court gave a good deal of space to the experts' credentials and remarkable experience in the relevant fields, noting that the doctors used the same techniques used in their quotidian work for their court opinions.[115] The court made this point: "Nothing in *Daubert*, or its

---

[108]   See e.g. *In re. Paoli R. R. Yard PCB Litig.*, 35 F.3d 717, 745 (3rd Cir. 1994) (requiring "conclusions supported by good grounds for each step in the analysis . . . [such that] *any* step that renders the analysis unreliable under the *Daubert* factors" is exposed, emphasis in the original).

[109]   *California Evidence Code*, above note 48, § 720(a).

[110]   See M. H. Graham, *Handbook of Federal Evidence*, 8th edn. (Thomson Reuters, 2019), Vol. 5, § 702:6, ns. 24, 25 (listing, extensively, occupations which qualify by virtue of experience).

[111]   *Kumho Tire Co.* v. *Carmichael*, 526 US 137, 151 (1999), as noted by Graham, above note 110, n. 24.

[112]   *Cooper* v. *Takeda Pharm. Am., Inc.*, 191 Cal. Rptr. 3d 67, 72–3 (Cal. Ct. App. 2015).

[113]   *Ibid.* at 73–4.

[114]   *Wendell* v. *GlaxoSmithKline LLC*, 858 F.3d 1227, 1233 (9th Cir. 2017).

[115]   *Ibid.* at 1234.

progeny, properly understood, suggests that the most experienced and credentialed doctors in a given field should be barred from testifying based on a differential diagnosis."[116]

In both cases, the trial courts' crusade to analyze each part of the foundation and each step in the logical progression from foundation to opinion – although seemingly called for by state and federal supreme court precedent – foundered on the rock of the witnesses' more general expertise, measured by their credentials such as their education, years of experience, experience in treating patients, list of publications, and the like.

These cases, and the fact that skilled experts' testimony is admissible even though it may be impossible to fully articulate the foundation for it, suggest that admissibility of expert opinion is often a function of the *general* reliability of the source, perhaps more so than the express articulation of the individuated reasons employed and steps taken in reaching the opinion. Courts already recognize tacit expertise, and neural networks have tacit expertise.[117]

The Drug Analogy

Even when prescription drugs are approved, not all the side effects, or the factors on which they depend, may be known. So too with their benefits: not all factors affecting the efficacy of a drug are known. Drugs are evaluated after they are first approved, and warnings may change over time. As the Food and Drug Administration (FDA) notes, "[i]n the end, no matter how much data are available, we often have to make a judgment call, weighing the known benefits against known risks and the potential – and possibly unknown – risks."[118] Importantly for present purposes, all that may be known about the approved drug is that it has certain benefits and other effects, while the details of why that is so may be unknown. The FDA may approve a drug for use, either over the counter or by prescription only, despite the fact that its mechanism is unknown. Examples include "acetaminophen for pain relief, penicillin for infections, and lithium for bipolar disorder, [which] continue to be scientific mysteries today."[119] A 2011 study of seventy-five drugs found that only seventeen were derived from a "detailed understanding of how the disease worked."[120] In short, after enough trials with a representative population, the benefits and detriments of drugs may be adequately known to allow them to be used, even if it is not known why they work.

In related contexts, we are comfortable with the fact that while we may not know the exact mechanisms, we know enough, generally through statistical studies, to find that a putative cause (such as a drug) has a certain effect (such as a birth defect).[121] To be sure, there is a difference between accepting an expert opinion on causation without knowing the

---

[116] *Ibid.* at 1235.

[117] See generally J. Millar and I. Kerr, Delegation, Relinquishment, and Responsibility: The Prospect of Expert Robots, in R. Calo, A. M. Froomkin, and I. Kerr (eds.), *Robot Law* (Edward Elgar, 2016), pp. 102, 109–13. Millar and his co-author suggest that (1) much "expert" knowledge is tacit, (2) machine intelligence can or will manifest such knowledge, and (3) we should defer to the conclusions of machine intelligence when it demonstrably does a better job than humans in given domains.

[118] How FDA Evaluates Regulated Products: Drugs, FDA, www.fda.gov/aboutfda/transparency/basics/ucm269834 .htm (last visited October 24, 2017).

[119] C. Y. Johnson, One Big Myth about Medicine: We Know How Drugs Work, *Washington Post* (July 23, 2015), www.washingtonpost.com/news/wonk/wp/2015/07/23/one-big-myth-about-medicine-we-know-how-drugs-work/.

[120] D. C. Swinney and J. Anthony, How Were New Medicines Discovered? (2011) 10 *Nat. Rev. Drug Discov.* 507. See also C. Drahl, How Does Acetaminophen Work? Researchers Still Aren't Sure (2014) 92 *Sci.* 31, 31–2; T. Lewis, Mystery Mechanisms, *The Scientist* (July 29, 2016), www.thescientist.com/?articles.view/articleNo/ 46688/title/Mystery-Mechanisms/ ("Scientists still don't know exactly how some commonly used drugs work").

[121] *Daubert* v. *Merrell Dow Pharm., Inc.*, 43 F.3d 1311, 1314 (9th Cir. 1995) (cited in *Wendell* v. *GlaxoSmithKline LLC*, 858 F.3d 1227, 1233 (9th Cir. 2017)). In Californian courts, medical causation depends on expert testimony

mechanism of causation where, on the one hand, there is a demonstrated statistical basis, and, on the other, as in the case of a neural network, where there is not a demonstration of the specific statistical basis. But the truth is that neural networks *are* statistical analyses, and their reliability can be demonstrated through validation.

The Statistical Framework and Explaining the Logic

As the drug analogy demonstrates, statistics are used to make very serious decisions. Statistics are widely used in courts, and indeed judges may take judicial notice[122] of certain statistical facts.[123] Statistics are used to support and combat class certification decisions;[124] to evaluate DNA evidence;[125] to show and disprove racial disparity[126] and age discrimination;[127] to prove Fourth Amendment violations;[128] in labor litigation;[129] to attack the practices at the Patent and Trademark Office;[130] to fix damages allocation in environmental clean-up actions;[131] and in many other situations. Courts often use regression analysis to estimate the impact of illegal acts.[132] Judges rely on statistical tools such as the STATIC-99 to evaluate the risk of recidivism of registerable sex offenders,[133] and many courts use survey results and their statistical conclusions in sentencing,[134] setting bail, and deciding issues such as the risk of recidivism and likelihood that defendants will appear for their next hearings.[135]

---

that there is a "reasonably probable causal connection" between the injury and alleged cause, *Jones v. Ortho Pharm. Corp.*, 209 Cal. Rptr. 456, 461 (Cal. Ct. App. 1985), i.e. greater than 50 percent odds. See, e.g., *Uriell v. Regents of Univ. of California*, 184 Cal. Rptr. 3d 79, 86–7 (Cal. Ct. App. 2015) (discussion of the state's "more probable than not" test); *Cooper v. Takeda Pharm. Am., Inc.*, 191 Cal. Rptr. 3d 67, 85 (Cal. Ct. App. 2015) (same).

[122] Facts that are the subject of judicial notice are those which are not reasonably the subject of dispute, and those "capable of immediate and accurate determination by resort to easily accessible sources of indisputable accuracy ..." *Weaver v. United States*, 298 F.2d 496, 498 (5th Cir. 1962). See also e.g. *California Evidence Code*, above note 48, §§ 450–60; R. I. Weil, I. A. Brown, L. Smalley Edmon, and C. E. A. Karnow, *California Practice Guide: Civil Procedure before Trial* (Rutter Group, 2017), para. 7:13.

[123] *Envtl. Law Found. v. Beech-Nut Nutrition Corp.*, 185 Cal. Rptr. 3d 189, 203 n.7 (Cal. Ct. App. 2015).

[124] *Mies v. Sephora U.S.A., Inc.*, 184 Cal. Rptr. 3d 446 (Cal. Ct. App. 2015); *Duran v. U.S. Bank Nat'l Ass'n*, 68 Cal. Rptr. 2d 644 (Cal. Ct. App. 2014).

[125] See e.g. *People v. Venegas*, 954 P.2d 525 (Cal. 1998).

[126] *Alston v. City of Madison*, 853 F.3d 901, 908 (7th Cir. 2017); *Paige v. California*, 291 F.3d 1141 (9th Cir. 2002).

[127] *Karlo v. Pittsburgh Glass Works, LLC*, 849 F.3d 61 (3rd Cir. 2017).

[128] *United States v. Soto-Zuniga*, 837 F.3d 992, 1002 (9th Cir. 2016).

[129] *Nat'l Labor Relations Bd. v. Lily Transportation Corp.*, 853 F.3d 31 (1st Cir. 2017).

[130] *Ethicon Endo–Surgery, Inc. v. Covidien LP*, 826 F.3d 1366, 1368 (Fed. Cir. 2016) (Newman J., dissenting from denial of rehearing *en banc*).

[131] *Lyondell Chem. Co. v. Occidental Chem. Corp.*, 608 F.3d 284, 292 (5th Cir. 2010).

[132] See e.g. *In re. Se. Milk Antitrust Litig.*, 739 F.3d 262, 285 (6th Cir. 2014); *Werdebaugh v. Blue Diamond Growers*, No. 12–CV–2724–LHK, 2014 WL 2191901 (ND Cal. May 23, 2014) (proving damages under UCL, FAL, and CLRA); *Kleen Prods. LLC v. Int'l Paper*, 306 FRD 585, 602 (ND Ill. 2015).

[133] Static-99/Static-99R, Static99 Clearinghouse, www.static99.org; see *California Penal Code* (Deering, 2017), §§ 290.003–008.

[134] A. Liptak, Sent to Prison by a Software Program's Secret Algorithms, *New York Times* (May 1, 2017), www.nytimes.com/2017/05/01/us/politics/sent-to-prison-by-a-software-programs-secret-algorithms.html?hp&action=click&pgtype=Homepage&clickSource=story-heading&module=first-column-region&region=top-news&WT.nav=top-news (describing C. J. Roberts's apparent reference to risk assessment software used in sentencing: "'Can you foresee a day,' asked Shirley Ann Jackson, president of the college in upstate New York [Rensselaer Polytechnic Institute], 'when smart machines, driven with artificial intelligences, will assist with courtroom fact-finding or, more controversially even, judicial decision-making?' The Chief Justice's answer was more surprising than the question. 'It's a day that's here,' he said, 'and it's putting a significant strain on how the judiciary goes about doing things.'")

[135] See e.g. M. Frisher, I. Crome, J. MacLeod, *et al.*, Predictive Factors for Illicit Drug Use Among Young People: A Literature Review (Home Office Research, Development and Statistics Directorate, 2007); K. Bechtel,

Neural networks are, in effect, statistical models.[136] A valid (or "statistically significant") result shows a certain degree of correlation; it does not prove causation. But with traditional statistical studies, at some point either the strength of a study, or better, many studies,[137] is enough to conclude that, given some predicate or sample, a more general conclusion is very likely to be true. Statistics use samples to tell us something about the world; they provide, based on partial data, an inference about general patterns. This is how predictive coding works: given a sample of documents on which the system has been trained, some of which are privileged (or relevant), the system determines which of the larger collection are privileged (or relevant). AlphaGo works, in part, in the same way: it first extrapolates the present board pattern to an intermediate but limited set of possible patterns, given a series of possible moves. Then, it compares the intermediate set to all the patterns it has experienced.[138] Knowing which of that larger set led to victory, AlphaGo then chooses the best intermediate pattern.[139]

There is, of course, a difference between the operations of neural networks and the traditional statistical expert because the human expert "shows his work." He writes out his calculations, which can then be inspected for errors.

The work of a neural network can similarly be checked. Evaluations or checks can sort fallacious from reliable inferences by testing a neural network on new data, validating the system. This sort of testing can show that a statistical correlation is invalid, that is, that it is just a random product.[140] Correlations can be found among almost any set of facts,[141] but this is cherry-picking and does not reflect a hypothesis that is then tested on new data. Thus, these

C. T. Lowenkamp, and A. M. Holsinger, Identifying the Predictors of Pretrial Failure: A Meta-Analysis (2011) 75 *Fed. Prob.* 78; P. J. Henning, Is Deterrence Relevant in Sentencing White-Collar Criminals? (2015) 61 *Wayne Law Rev.* 27, 38; C. Karnow, Setting Bail for Public Safety (2008) 13 *Berkeley J. Crim. Law* 1; A. L. Kellermann, F. P. Rivara, N. B. Rushforth, *et al.*, Gun Ownership as a Risk Factor for Homicide in the Home (1993) 329 *New Eng. J. Med.* 1084, 1084; J. Tashea, Kentucky Tests New Assessment Tool to Determine Whether to Keep Defendants behind Bars (2015) 101 *ABAJ* 15; M. VanNostrand and G. Keebler, Pretrial Risk Assessment in the Federal Court (2009) 73 *Fed. Prob.* 1; A. Christin, A. Rosenblat, and D. Boyd, Courts and Predictive Algorithms, *Data and Civil Rights: A New Era of Policing and Justice* (October 27, 2015), www.law.nyu.edu/sites/default/files/upload_documents/Angele%20Christin.pdf; T. Tillman, Risk Factors Predictive of Juvenile Offender Recidivism (May 2015), https://scholarworks.umt.edu/etd/4495/.

[136] For a technical discussion, see R. Rojas, Statistics and Neural Networks, in *Neural Networks: A Systematic Introduction* (Springer, 1996), pp. 229–63.

[137] Because individual studies may reflect cherry-picking and other problems, studies that review the results of many studies, known as metastudies, are preferred. B. Goldacre, Listen Carefully, I Shall Say This Only Once, *The Guardian* (October 25, 2008), www.theguardian.com/commentisfree/2008/oct/25/medical-research-science-health (discussing problems with issuing multiple reports of what is, in fact, one study; contrasting results of the "one" study with true metastudy results); AllTrials, www.alltrials.net (importance of metastudies). For discussion of a leading effort in this regard, see Cochrane, What Are Systematic Reviews, *YouTube* (January 27, 2016), www.youtube.com/watch?v=egJlW4vkb1Y; Cochrane, Reporting Biases, http://methods.cochrane.org/bias/reporting-biases (Cochrane furthers transparency in research and publication, and use of metastudies); Cochrane, What is Cochrane Evidence and How Can It Help You?, www.cochrane.org/what-is-cochrane-evidence.

[138] This comprises *millions* of games, orders of magnitude more games than any human could play in a lifetime. See DeepMind, Full Length Games for Go Players to Enjoy, https://deepmind.com/research/alphago/alphago-vs-alphago-self-play-games.

[139] D. Silver, A. Huang, C. J. Maddison, *et al.*, Mastering the Game of Go with Deep Neural Networks and Tree Search (2016) 529 *Nature* 484; C. Koch, How the Computer Beat the Go Master, *Scientific American* (March 19, 2016), www.scientificamerican.com/article/how-the-computer-beat-the-go-master; D. Silver, AlphaGo: Mastering the Ancient Game of Go with Machine Learning, *Google AI Blog* (January 27, 2016), https://research.googleblog.com/2016/01/alphago-mastering-ancient-game-of-go.html.

[140] A favorite example of fallacious induction is a Thanksgiving Day turkey, which extrapolates from just under a year's worth of daily good feeding that Thursday, November 23, 2018, will be a good day. It will not be.

[141] Such as (1) the number of people who drown by falling into a pool and films Nicolas Cage appeared in, or (2) per capita cheese consumption and the number of people who died entangled in bedsheets; and so on and so forth. See T. Vigen, Spurious Correlations, www.tylervigen.com/spurious-correlations; for more on bad or fallacious

untested correlations are fallacious. They are random correlations selected after the fact – that is the cherry-picking – because in isolation they appear to present a pattern.

A fundamental element of training (whether human-supervised or not) neural networks is a feedback loop that tests whether the learned correlations play out correctly on *new* data, just as networks used in business should have the predicted result constantly compared to real-world events. This step is sometimes referred to as *validation*.[142] Sometimes validation is performed by using a portion of the data available when the system was first trained: this data is split into training and testing data, and the testing data is used to validate. In TAR, for example, the system might be tested on a sample of the general production documents.

But performing well just on this limited set of testing data may not be a sufficient foundation to trust the system more generally. If the testing data are few, or not homogenous (i.e. not identically distributed), the test may not show much.[143]

AlphaGo has been cross-validated and then proven reliable in the field: it beat the human champions. By the same token, networks can be tested against known results. And a human witness can discuss, or challenge, the performance of a network against new data, both cross-validated against data that was part of the initial dataset *and* later in the field on entirely new data. The proponent of the machine opinion (for example, for facial recognition or medical diagnosis) reports the performance of the network against new data and states that the program had correct results a certain percentage of the time. The party opposing admissibility or later disputing the weight to be given to the opinion could report results on his own set of new data. This process requires the software to be provided to all parties in order to allow for this sort of "cross-examination." The selection of data by the party opposing admissibility should be generated to detect flaws, such as training on inapposite data.

Furthermore, even though the technical calculation of the opinion is not available to any human, the proponent of the machine opinion should be able to provide to the judge or jury an abstracted view of the logic flow that produces the opinion, similar to that available for a more traditional expert software with propositional logic, fuzzy logic diagrams, or decision trees.[144] The point here is not just that these three approaches can be used generally to illustrate machine decision-making, but rather that there are tools to extract these illustrations *from the specific neural network* (i.e. its inputs and outputs) at issue.[145] While, again, these illustrations are not and cannot be descriptions of the actual mechanism of the hidden layers,

inferences, see C. Karnow, Statistics & Probability: Bad Inferences and Uncommon Sense, in *Litigation in Practice* (Twelve Tables Press, 2017), p. 43.

[142] See e.g. B. Christian and T. Griffiths, *Algorithms to Live by: The Computer Science of Human Decisions* (Macmillan, 2016), p. 159.

[143] See, e.g., S. Arlot and A. Celisse, A Survey of Cross-Validation Procedures for Model Selection (2010) 4 *Stat. Surveys* 40, 52, https://projecteuclid.org/euclid.ssu/1268143839; see also D. Krstajic, L. J. Buturovic, D. E. Leahy, and S. Thomas, Cross-Validation Pitfalls When Selecting and Assessing Regression and Classification Models (2014) 6 *J. Cheminformatics* 10, 10, https://link.springer.com/article/10.1186/1758-2946-6-10 ("In an ideal situation we would have enough data to train and validate our models (training samples) and have separate data for assessing the quality of our model (test samples). Both training and test samples would need to be sufficiently large and diverse in order to be representative [sic]").

[144] See " Interlude: Explaining Software," above.

[145] S. Reid, 10 Misconceptions about Neural Networks, *Turing Finance* (May 8, 2014), www.turingfinance.com/misconceptions-about-neural-networks/#blackbox. Researchers continue to develop tools used to at least illustrate the details of training of specific networks. See e.g. J. Yosinski, J. Clune, A. Nguyen, *et al.*, Understanding Neural Networks through Deep Visualization, Deep Learning Workshop, 32nd International Conference on Machine Learning (2015), p. 4, https://arxiv.org/pdf/1506.06579.pdf ("We describe and release a software tool that provides a live, interactive visualization of every neuron in a trained convnet as it responds to a user-provided image or video").

nor justifications for them, they are probably as detailed as any descriptions provided to judges and juries in connection with more traditional inference engines.[146] That is, it often does not take much to provide as much detail as judges and juries really want, or need, in the evaluations of the proponent's foundation, because the real test for reliability, discussed next, is measured by the ability of the opponent to *challenge* the machine opinion.

Risks and Cross-Examination

The ability to cross-examine is the classic test of reliability, and reliability is the cornerstone of admissibility.[147] Recall the *sine qua non* of cross-examination, which is that the program must be made available to the opposing side in order to be tested against new data.

To a shocking degree, many ordinary "expert" systems are in fact never tested against new data or real-world results; their predictions are never analyzed, that is, they are not validated. They are used because they are convenient, or because they are cheaper than using humans or give the appearance of objectivity or infallibility. They may be used because they deflect responsibility from whoever would otherwise be the human agent, or to save time. Companies use software to hire and fire, but never determine whether the results were as predicted. Colleges use a variety of criteria to admit students and use tests to measure competence in academic areas, but these decisions may or may not have ever been validated. For example, did the students with higher scores actually perform better in college? Did algorithms used to pick stocks actually do better than human decision-makers with the same information? As a matter of fact, what was the performance of loans when a program made the lending decision? Algorithms are used to suggest products on Amazon, movies on Netflix, plots for movies, patterns for room-cleaning robots,[148] and for meeting people on dating sites online. Some of these *are* validated, especially, as in the case of companies such as Amazon and Netflix, because the accuracy of the algorithm translates to millions of dollars in revenue.

But many programs are never validated. The problem is sufficiently serious and pervasive that an entire book could be written about it. Indeed, it has been.[149] Worse, at least from the point of view of those in the court system, many programs and tests used in criminal trials are of dubious validity because there are no accepted validation benchmarks, no validation tests are used, or the level of precision announced to the jury is far in excess of the true value.[150]

---

[146] See text at Chaney, above note 95, p. 743.

[147] This is true under both federal and California law. See e.g. *Sargon Enters. v. Univ. of S. Cal.*, 288 P.3d 1237, 1252 (Cal. 2012).

[148] K. Slavin, How Algorithms Shape Our World, *Ted* (July 2011), www.ted.com/talks/kevin_slavin_how_algorithms_shape_our_world/transcript?language=en.

[149] C. McNeil, *Weapons of Math Destruction: How Big Data Increases Inequality and Threatens Democracy* (Penguin, 2016); for a discussion of the issues, see e.g. M.-A. Russon, The Dangers of Big Data: How Society Is Being Controlled by Mathematical Algorithms, *International Business Times* (September 13, 2016), www.ibtimes.co.uk/dangers-big-data-how-society-being-controlled-by-mathematical-algorithms-1581174. McNeil discussed the lack of feedback mechanisms (i.e. validation) in many areas, such as using algorithms to hire and fire teachers, *ibid.* at 7, 138, evaluating other potential employees, *ibid.* at 7, 111, issuing credit rating, *ibid.* at 146, and so on.

[150] President's Council of Advisors on Science and Technology (PCAST), Forensic Science in Criminal Courts: Ensuring Scientific Validity of Feature-Comparison Methods (September 2016), https://obamawhitehouse.archives.gov/sites/default/files/microsites/ostp/PCAST/pcast_forensic_science_report_final.pdf (highlighting problems with tests regarding certain DNA, bite-mark, firearms, hair comparison, fingerprint, and footwear). For serious problems with latent fingerprint testimony, see *United States v. Llera Plaza*, 179 F. Supp. 2d 492, 494

Thus, one risk in using programs is a failure of validation; that is, either none was performed, or the validation was conducted on unrepresentative data. And while this chapter presses the notion that software on which worldly activities (such as businesses) rely is generally sufficiently trustworthy to be used in court, this is a critical caveat, an exception to the rule that may swallow it. "Unvalidated" software is used all the time in the real world, but, as is true of any of the fallacies that infect daily life, has no place in court.

The critical importance of testing out a model, or any predictive system, on new data is exemplified by an algorithm from *Market Watch*'s Gary Smith.[151] His algorithm shows a remarkable eighty-eight percent correlation between predicted and actual stock prices for 2015, including an almost perfect match of the drop in the third quarter (see Figure 2.2).

But tested on new data – prices in 2016 – it was a complete failure (see Figure 2.3).

And as with any validation, whether of a drug, a test, or some other screening device, validation must be conducted on the relevant population and the relevant data. When testing drugs for childhood cancer, was the drug tested on 70-year-olds with cancer because those subjects were more easily located? When testing an algorithm for recidivism and examining factors such as type of crime, income, or whether job history correlates with new crimes, or when looking at a program which predicts loan failures, was the validation population from the same type of locale (i.e. area of country, rural versus inner city) as the population on which the algorithm is to be used?

Underlying this issue is the problem of what *counts* as validation. The matter is relatively obvious with AlphaGo, because it keeps beating every new opponent. So too with predictive coding of documents: lawyers can examine the program's decisions on new data and score

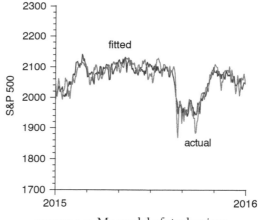

FIGURE 2.2 My model of stock prices

(ED Pa. 2002) *withdrawn from bound volume, opinion vacated and superseded on reconsideration,* 188 F. Supp. 2d (ED Pa. 2002) (Pollak, J.). In almost all criminal trials for a period over twenty years in which a group of FBI fingerprint experts testified, including trials of thirty-two defendants sentenced to death, the FBI experts gave flawed testimony; twenty-six experts overstated forensic matches in ways that favored prosecutors in over 95 percent of the 268 trials reviewed as of April 2015. See S. S. Hsu, FBI Admits Flaws in Hair Analysis over Decades, *Washington Post* (April 18, 2015), www.washingtonpost.com/local/crime/fbi-overstated-forensic-hair-matches-in-nearly-all-criminal-trials-for-decades/2015/04/18/39c8d8c6-e515-11e4-b510-962fcfabc310_story.html?utm_term=.e63ad6b8db16.

[151]   G. Smith, Opinion: This Experiment Shows the Danger in Black-Box Investment Algorithms, *MarketWatch* (June 17, 2017), www.marketwatch.com/story/this-experiment-shows-the-danger-in-black-box-investment-algorithms-2017-06-13.

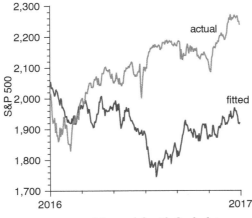

FIGURE 2.3 My model with fresh data

accuracy. And then they spot-check the final result. In these cases, the selection of a "new" population of items used for validation is easy. But it is less certain what the new data (used for cross-validation) might be for systems designed, for example, to do handwriting analysis, facial recognition, medical diagnosis, or predict recidivism.

For facial recognition systems, validation data might include photographs taken under a variety of lighting conditions and of various angles of the face, some of which will reveal few of the facial features. "Successful" testing is likely to depend on which data are used. Similarly, with handwriting analysis, validation data might include a wide variety of legible and illegible scrawls, initials, small and large groupings of letters. "Success" is likely to depend on which of these are used. Medical diagnosis too depends on an unconstrained or arbitrary number of inputs, from a few to a very large number, such as body temperature and blood chemistry, as well as a range of vaguely reported conditions such as nausea, pain, skin tone, and extent of bruising. Recidivism may depend on different factors, such as geographic or socio-economic distribution. In all of these situations, and doubtless in others as well, "success" with one group of validation data may or may not be persuasive.

More technically, with regard to neural networks, the validation data must meet certain criteria, such as that it not be the data used during training.[152] With a large dataset, a chunk of it, perhaps 20 percent, can be set aside specifically for validation testing and is never used for the initial training.[153] When there is a small dataset, or some question that the initial training dataset and the testing set are not similar, various methods can make a series of passes through the system with randomly selected parts of the dataset, a process termed as "cross-validation."[154] But while

[152] Goodfellow *et al.*, above note 6, p. 118.
[153] *Ibid.*
[154] *Ibid.*, pp. 118–19. See generally e.g. G. Varoquaux, P. R. Raamana, D. A. Engemann, *et al.*, Assessing and Tuning Brain Decoders: Cross-Validation, Caveats, and Guidelines (2017) 145 *NeuroImage* 166, https://arxiv.org/pdf/1606.05201.pdf; R. Kohavi, A Study of Cross-Validation and Bootstrap for Accuracy Estimation and Model Selection, in C. S. Mellish (ed.), *Proceedings of the 14th International Joint Conference on Artificial Intelligence* (Morgan Kaufmann, 1995), Vol. 2, p. 1137, https://pdfs.semanticscholar.org/obeo/d781305750b37acb35fa187febd8db67bfcc.pdf; A. Krogh and J. Vedelsby, Neural Network Ensembles, Cross Validation, and Active Learning, in D. S. Touretzky, M. C. Mozer, and M. E. Hasselmo (eds.), *Advances in Neural Information Processing Systems 8* (MIT Press, 1995), p. 231, http://papers.nips.cc/paper/1001-neural-network-ensembles-cross-validation-and-active-learning.pdf; A. W. Moore and M. S. Lee, Efficient Algorithms for Minimizing Cross Validation Error, in 1994 Proceedings of the 11th International Conference on Machine Learning (1994), p. 190, https://pdfs.semanticscholar.org/352c/4ead66a8cf89b91f9de5ac86bc69f17b29d0.pdf.

there are many cross-validation techniques, they all assume that the dataset is representative of the data on which the system will be let loose after its training. And in practice, if not in theory, datasets are limited. Thus, even with sophisticated, competent cross-validation, the performance of the system in the "field," as it were, may not match that in the laboratory.

With programs that have extensive past experiences (i.e. they have worked on exceedingly large sets of data in the past) and have been tested on very large sets of validation data, these concerns will tend to dissipate. The fact that AlphaGo has played millions of games obviates concerns that it may not be successful in the next game against a top professional player. The extent of the training and of the validation data in effect tells us that the next test – the one in the "field" for which it provides the opinion in issue – is not "unexpected," not an outlier.

It is no coincidence that neural networks have made their mark just as "big data" erupted. It is commonplace to remark that there is a stunning amount of data,[155] as a function not only of efforts to digitize past records, but also the recordation of communications such as email, texts, searches, and social media which have taken the place of unrecorded oral communications of the past. The accumulation of this data has not only made it imperative to have software capable of digesting it, but is the very basis for the tools – neural networks – needed to do so. The exceedingly large dataset makes it reasonable to trust validation tests that use that data, all without knowing why it is that the validation is successful, that is, without either having a theory of correlation nor knowing the details of the underlying mechanism that explains the found correlation.[156]

There are two other dangers in the use of neural networks, which should be the subject of future academic review. The first, the use of proxies, is closely related to the make-up of the validation discussed previously. Assume a network looks at the relationship between a series of factors and fluctuations in fish stock.[157] A deeper review of the system might reflect not the designer's decision to measure the fish stock directly, but some proxy for it, such as fish caught or consumed. Or a system designed to opine on earthquake damage might use simplified input of proxies of certain soil conditions.[158] A network might provide an opinion on the valuation of initial public offerings, but actually use a proxy, such as valuation of certain stock one day or one week after the initial offering date. These may all be reasonable, but the underlying assumptions should be made manifest; sometimes, it may indicate a mismatch between the training data and the validation data on the one hand and the proposed input for the specific opinion at issue on the other.

---

[155] Any measure of currently available data exceeds the mind's ability to understand, but for those of us who love words like petabytes and (even better) zettabytes, there is this: "The total amount of data in the world was 4.4 zettabytes in 2013. That is set to rise steeply to 44 zettabytes by 2020. To put that in perspective, one zettabyte is equivalent to 44 trillion gigabytes." Every day, about 2.5 exabytes are produced, equivalent to 250,000 Libraries of Congress. M. Khoso, How Much Data Is Produced Every Day?, *Level* (May 13, 2016), www.northeastern.edu /levelblog/2016/05/13/how-much-data-produced-every-day/. See e.g. Cisco, The Zettabyte Era: Trends and Analysis (June 7, 2017), www.cisco.com/c/en/us/solutions/collateral/service-provider/visual-networking-index-vni/vni-hyperconnectivity-wp.html (discussing the interesting predictions by Cisco, which as a manufacturer of Internet servers and related equipment, presumably should know; "It would take more than 5 million years to watch the amount of video that will cross global IP networks each month in 2021").

[156] See C. Anderson, The End of Theory: The Data Deluge Makes the Scientific Method Obsolete, *Wired* (June 23, 2008), www.wired.com/2008/06/pb-theory/.

[157] Cf. e.g. D. G. Chen and D. M. Ware, A Neural Network Model for Forecasting Fish Stock Recruitment (1999) 56 *Can. J. Fish. Aquat. Sci.* 2385, https://doi.org/10.1139/f99-178.

[158] C. Salameh, P.-Y. Bard, B. Guillier, and C. Cornou, Estimation of Damage Level at Urban Scale from Simple Proxies Accounting for Soil and Building Dynamic Properties, in 2017 Proceedings of the 16th World Conference on Earthquake Engineering (2017), p. 2049, https://hal.archives-ouvertes.fr/hal-01461198/document.

Finally, there is bias. The cartoon conceit is that algorithms are unbiased; the computer is neutral, and free of prejudice. Without programming, the empty computer surely is. But most neural networks, even those which improve with self-training, begin their existence trained by humans. They literally model themselves on human choice and predilection. Some of these systems are in effect told that success is doing things the way humans would, and failure is diverging from those human choices. In this way, human biases become embedded in the very fabric of the system's decisions. The impact may be the most significant in what appear to be complex, subjective decisions such as hiring, evaluating written essays, and face recognition.[159] An interesting study of the way in which 30,000 images were used to train networks to recognize content found that human stereotypes on gender and race (i.e. prejudices) were routinely derived from the human-tagged dataset.[160] The danger is obvious: courts – and society – must not rely on software that reproduces human cognitive failures, but those very human cognitive failures make it difficult to discern the software's failure.

CONCLUSION

The results of well-trained neural networks are trusted in the world, and they can be trusted in the courts. Perfection is not guaranteed,[161] but neither is it guaranteed with already routinely accepted testimony, such as eyewitness evidence[162] and confessions, which may have peculiar reliability problems,[163] nor other routine testimony, which may be false or misremembered.[164]

General admissibility rules are not meant to be onerous. The default is that all relevant evidence is admissible,[165] and if an opinion is reliable and relates to a contested fact, it is surely relevant. The foundations of expert testimony typically must be explained to the judge and jury, but this chapter demonstrates that, in the case of opinions generated by neural networks, the fact that the specific basis for the opinion cannot be demonstrated or articulated

[159] J. Buolamwini, How I'm Fighting Bias in Algorithms, *Ted* (November 2016), www.ted.com/talks/joy_buolamwini_how_i_m_fighting_bias_in_algorithms/transcript?language=en. See generally N. Byrnes, Why We Should Expect Algorithms to Be Biased, *MIT Technology Review* (June 24, 2016), www.technologyreview.com/s/601775/why-we-should-expect-algorithms-to-be-biased/; C. Miller, When Algorithms Discriminate, *New York Times* (July 9, 2015), www.nytimes.com/2015/07/10/upshot/when-algorithms-discriminate.html.

[160] E. van Miltenburg, Stereotyping and Bias in the Flickr30K Dataset, in 2016 Proceedings of the Workshop on Multimodal Corpora: Comp. vision and language processing (2016), pp. 1–4, https://arxiv.org/pdf/1506.06579.pdf. See also Human Prejudices Sneak into Artificial Intelligence, *Neuroscience News* (April 14, 2017), http://neurosciencenews.com/artificial-intelligence-human-prejudice-6411/ (discussing A. Caliskan, J. J. Bryson, and A. Narayanan, Semantics Derived Automatically from Language Corpora Contain Human-Like Biases (2017) 356 *Sci.* 183). For a report on possible racial bias in software, which may *not* be a trained neural network, used for sentencing and bail decisions, see J. Angwin, J. Larson, S. Mattu, and L. Kirchner, Machine Bias, *ProPublica* (May 23, 2016), www.propublica.org/article/machine-bias-risk-assessments-in-criminal-sentencing.

[161] Goodfellow *et al.*, above note 6, p. 193.

[162] Cross-racial witness identification can pose serious problems. See New Jersey's approach in *State* v. *Henderson*, 208 NJ 208, 267 (2011), *holding modified by State* v. *Chen*, 208 NJ 307, 327 (2011); *State* v. *Romero*, 191 NJ 59, 68 (2007). See also *United States* v. *Langford*, 802 F.2d 1176, 1182 (9th Cir. 1986).

[163] See e.g. *People* v. *McCurdy*, 59 Cal. 4th 1063, 1109 (2014); *Campos* v. *Stone*, 201 F. Supp. 3d 1083, 1099 (ND Cal. 2016). See generally S. A. Drizin and R. A. Leo, The Problem of False Confessions in the Post-DNA World (2004) 82 *NC Law Rev.* 891; W. S. White, False Confessions and the Constitution: Safeguards against Untrustworthy Confessions (1997) 32 *Harv. CR-CL Law Rev.* 105, 119 (standard interrogation guidelines may induce false confessions).

[164] Cf. *Trear* v. *Sills*, 69 Cal. App. 4th 1341, 1345 (1999); F. L. Bailey and K. J. Fisherman, *Criminal Trial Techniques*, 2nd edn. (Sweet & Maxwell, 1996), § 58:11.

[165] California Evidence Code, above note 48, § 350.

should not block the admission of the opinion, because the opinion may yet be fundamentally reliable and remains subject to meaningful cross-examination. It may be that in the first case or two in which true machine opinion is offered, a so-called *Kelly* hearing may be warranted, because a court may find that the neural network is in this context an "unproven technique or procedure [used] ... to provide some definitive truth which the expert need only accurately recognize and relay to the jury."[166] To avoid presenting the jury with a "misleading aura of certainty,"[167] the court may examine the technology. It may find that the basic technology is sound, widely used, and accepted in the real world; that it is reliable because correct scientific procedures (for example, accepted statistical algorithms) were used to build and train the program; and that the network is helpful to the jury. With all parties being well-informed and able to validate functionality, machine opinions may provide insight no human can offer.

---

[166] *People* v. *Jackson*, 1 Cal. 5th 269, 316 (2016), quoting *People* v. *Stoll*, 49 Cal. 3d 1136, 1155–6 (1989).
[167] *People* v. *Kelly*, 17 Cal. 3d 24, 32 (1976), quoting *Huntingdon* v. *Crowley*, 64 Cal. 2d 647, 656 (1966). See generally Simons, above note 45, § 4:27.

3

Private Accountability in an Age of Artificial Intelligence

Sonia K. Katyal

INTRODUCTION

Algorithms in society are both innocuous and ubiquitous. They seamlessly permeate both our on- and offline lives, quietly distilling the volumes of data each of us now creates. Today, algorithms determine the optimal way to produce and ship goods, the prices we pay for those goods, the money we can borrow, the people who teach our children, and the books and articles we read – reducing each activity to an actuarial risk or score. "If every algorithm suddenly stopped working," Pedro Domingos hypothesized, "it would be the end of the world as we know it."[1]

Big data and algorithms seem to fulfill modern life's promise of ease, efficiency, and optimization. Yet our dependence on artificial intelligence (AI) does not come without significant social welfare concerns. Recently, a spate of literature from both law reviews and popular culture has focused on the intersection of AI and civil rights, raising traditional antidiscrimination, privacy, and due process concerns.[2] For example, a 2016 report revealed that Facebook used algorithms to determine users' "ethnic affinity," which could only be understood as a euphemism for race.[3] The categories then allowed advertisers to exclude users with certain ethnic affinities from seeing their ads.[4] After initially defending the categories as positive tools to allow users to see more relevant ads, Facebook removed the categories for housing, credit, and employment ads three months later, ostensibly due to anti-discrimination concerns.[5] Despite this move, in September of 2018, the American Civil Liberties Union (ACLU) filed a charge against Facebook with the Equal Employment Opportunity Commission (EEOC), contending that another of its tools violated both labor and civil rights laws by enabling employers to target only men to apply for a wide variety of jobs, including roofing, driving, and other opportunities in their advertising.[6] The plaintiffs who came forward included both women and gender non-binary job seekers who used

The chapter was originally published in (2019) 66 *UCLA Law Rev.* 54.

[1] P. Domingos, *The Master Algorithm: How the Quest for the Ultimate Learning Machine Will Remake Our World* (Allen Lane, 2015), p. 1.

[2] See sources cited below in notes 18 and 27.

[3] J. Angwin and T. Parris, Jr., Facebook Lets Advertisers Exclude Users by Race, *ProPublica* (October 28, 2016), www .propublica.org/article/facebook-lets-advertisers-exclude-users-by-race.

[4] *Ibid.*; see also D. Lumb, Facebook Enables Advertisers to Exclude Users by "Ethnic Affinity," *Engadget* (October 28, 2016), www.engadget.com/2016/10/28/facebook-enables-advertisers-to-exclude-users-by-ethnic-affinit.

[5] See Improving Enforcement and Promoting Diversity: Updates to Ads Policies and Tools, *Facebook: Newsroom* (February 8, 2017), http://newsroom.fb.com/news/2017/02/improving-enforcement-and-promoting-diversity-updates-to-ads-policies-and-tools.

[6] N. Tiku, ACLU Says Facebook Ads Let Employers Favor Men over Women, *Wired* (September 18, 2018), www .wired.com/story/aclu-says-facebook-ads-let-employers-favor-men-over-women.

Facebook in order to receive job ads and other recruitment opportunities, but as their ACLU lawyer explained, they were often hard to identify as plaintiffs. "You don't know, as a Facebook user, what you're not seeing," she explained.[7]

Even aside from the allegations of facilitating employment discrimination, that same year, Facebook was rocked by the allegations from a whistleblower, Christopher Wylie, previously at a firm called Cambridge Analytica, who claimed to have come up with the idea to harvest millions of Facebook profiles (50 million approximately), and then target users with political ads that would mesh with their psychological profile.[8] By the 2016 presidential election, Wylie's intervention took on a more sinister cast. Working with an academic, Aleksandr Kogan, millions of people were targeted with fake ads and content, allegedly paid for by Russian organizations.[9] Wylie claimed to have "broke[n] Facebook," and, as *The Guardian* points out, it was "on behalf of his new boss, Steve Bannon."[10]

Since algorithms tend to show users content that can affirm their existing interests and beliefs,[11] within these filter bubbles, fake news flourished,[12] perhaps affecting the results of the 2016 US election.[13] By coming forward, and telling his story, Wylie became one of the first – and few – tech whistleblowers to risk liability for violating his non-disclosure agreements, triggering a spate of federal inquiries as a result.[14]

Today, for the most part, these reports are the tip of the iceberg regarding the potential impact of algorithmic bias on today's society.[15] But there also is a deeper parallel between civil rights and AI that is worth noting. Typically, we think about algorithms in the same way we think about law – as a set of abstract principles manifesting rational objectives. "Math isn't human, and so the use of math can't be immoral," the traditional argument goes.[16]

---

[7] *Ibid.*

[8] C. Cadwalladr, "I Made Steve Bannon's Psychological Warfare Tool": Meet the Data War Whistleblower, *The Guardian* (March 18, 2018), www.theguardian.com/news/2018/mar/17/data-war-whistleblower-christopher-wylie-faceook-nix-bannon-trump.

[9] See D. Folkenflik, Facebook Scrutinized over Its Role in 2016's Presidential Election, *NPR* (September 26, 2017), www.npr.org/2017/09/26/553661942/facebook-scrutinized-over-its-role-in-2016s-presidential-election.

[10] Cadwalladr, above note 8.

[11] See generally E. Pariser, *Filter Bubble: How the New Personalized Web Is Changing What We Read and How We Think* (Penguin, 2012) (describing this phenomenon).

[12] See C. Silverman, This Analysis Shows How Viral Fake Election News Stories Outperformed Real News on Facebook, *BuzzFeed* (November 16, 2016), www.buzzfeed.com/craigsilverman/viral-fake-election-news-outperformed-real-news-on-facebook (showing that Facebook users liked, shared, or commented on the top-performing fake news stories significantly more than the top stories from legitimate news sites).

[13] Today, attempts to address fake news and false information have led to efforts to provide the public with reports of disputed information, such as Facebook's Disputed Flags, small red badges next to potentially untrustworthy sources. In response to criticism that these measures were not sufficient, Facebook has replaced Disputed Flags with Relevant Articles – links that redirect users to high-quality, reputable content. See C. Shu, Facebook Will Ditch Disputed Flags on Fake News and Display Links to Trustworthy Articles Instead, *TechCrunch* (December 21, 2017), https://techcrunch.com/2017/12/20/facebook-will-ditch-disputed-flags-on-fake-news-and-display-links-to-trustworthy-articles-instead.

[14] Cadwalladr, above note 8.

[15] See H. Allcott and M. Gentzkow, Social Media and Fake News in the 2016 Election (2017) 31 *J. Econ. Persp.* 211, 233; P. Brown, Study: Readers Are Hungry for News Feed Transparency, *Columbia Journalism Review* (October 24, 2017), www.cjr.org/tow_center/study-readers-hungry-news-feed-transparency-algorithms.php (criticizing social media platforms' lack of algorithmic transparency); Shu, above note 13. Future plans have been similarly criticized for their lack of transparency. See K. Schulten and A. C. Brown, Evaluating Sources in a "Post-Truth" World: Ideas for Teaching and Learning about Fake News, *New York Times* (January 19, 2017), www.nytimes.com/2017/01/19/learning/lesson-plans/evaluating-sources-in-a-post-truth-world-ideas-for-teaching-and-learning-about-fake-news.html.

[16] J. Kun, Big Data Algorithms Can Discriminate, and It's Not Clear What to Do about It, *Conversation* (August 13, 2015), http://theconversation.com/big-data-algorithms-can-discriminate-and-its-not-clear-what-to-do-about-it-45849.

Yet we now face the uncomfortable realization that the reality could not be further from the truth. The suggestion that algorithmic models are free from social bias represents what has been called an "appeal to abstraction," overlooking concerns that implicate fairness, accountability, and social welfare.[17] These presumptions also overlook the most basic of human costs as well. The idea that algorithmic decision-making, like laws, is objective and neutral obscures a complex situation. It refuses to grapple with the causes and effects of systematic and structural inequality, and thus risks missing how AI can have disparate impacts on particular groups. In our zeal to predict who will be the most productive and loyal employee or who will likely execute a terror attack, we collect data on everything. We collect data before we can even conceive of, let alone prove, its relevance – like reading tea leaves before the water has even boiled. We try to predict and pre-empt things long before they occur, but it can lead to the misapprehension of characteristics, and even worse, a misapplication of stereotypical assumptions.

At first glance, because data collection has now become ubiquitous, the benefits of algorithmic decision-making often seem to outweigh their costs. And this is mostly right. Without it, those troves of data would remain useless and inscrutable. Yet for members of certain groups, particularly the less wealthy, an algorithm's mistake can be ruinous – leading to denials of employment, housing, credit, insurance, and education.[18] These outcomes demonstrate a central problem in algorithmic accountability: While algorithmic decision-making may initially seem more reliable because it appears free from the irrational biases of human judgment and prejudice, algorithmic models are also the product of their fallible creators, who may miss evidence of systemic bias or structural discrimination in data or may simply make mistakes.[19] These errors of omission – innocent by nature – risk reifying past prejudices, thereby reproducing an image of an infinitely unjust world.

Years ago, constitutional law had a similar moment of reckoning. Critical race scholars and others demonstrated how the notion of color-blindness actually obscured great structural inequalities among identity-based categories.[20] The ideals enshrined in our Constitution, scholars argued, which were meant to offer formal equality for everyone, were not really equal at all. Rather, far from ensuring equality for all, the notionally objective application of law actually had the opposite effect of perpetuating discrimination toward different groups.

There is, today, a curious parallel in the intersection between law and technology. An algorithm can instantly lead to massive discrimination between groups. At the same time, the law can fail spectacularly to address this discrimination because of the rhetoric of objectivity and secrecy surrounding it. Because many algorithms are proprietary, they are resistant to discovery and scrutiny. And this is one of the central obstacles to greater accountability and transparency in today's age of big data.

This chapter argues that the issues surrounding algorithmic accountability demonstrate a deeper, more structural tension within a new generation of disputes regarding law and technology, and the contrast between public and private accountability. As I argue, the true

---

[17] *Ibid.*
[18] For a detailed discussion of the role of algorithms in society, see C. O'Neil, *Weapons of Math Destruction: How Big Data Increases Inequality and Threatens Democracy* (Penguin, 2016); and F. Pasquale, *The Black Box Society: The Secret Algorithms that Control Money and Information* (Harvard University Press, 2015).
[19] See O. H. Gandy, Jr., Engaging Rational Discrimination: Exploring Reasons for Placing Regulatory Constraints on Decision Support Systems (2010) 12 *Ethics Inf. Technol.* 29, 30 (arguing that human-generated data produce biases in automated systems).
[20] See generally K. Crenshaw, N. Gotanda, and K. Thomas (eds.), *Critical Race Theory: The Key Writings that Formed the Movement* (New Press, 1995).

potential of AI does not lie in the information we reveal to one another, but rather, in the questions they raise about the interaction of technology, intellectual property, and civil rights. Previous literature focused on the relationship between law and technology – which came first, and why.[21] Commentators lamented the pervasive mismatch between the infinite promise of technology and the comparably more limited reach of law and regulation.[22] In summing up the view that technology would create a world in which laws would impede with pedestrian concerns, Lawrence Lessig wrote: "Overregulation stifles creativity. It smothers innovation. It gives dinosaurs a veto over the future. It wastes the extraordinary opportunity for a democratic creativity that digital technology enables."[23] Technologists have, and often rightfully so, framed legal regulation – particularly in the world of intellectual property – as outdated, outmoded, and unnecessarily impeding innovation.[24] Law – particularly intellectual property law – seemed inappropriate and unbearably rigid in its incrementalism and failure to appreciate the possibilities of a digital economy.

Today, we see something quite different. In the context of AI, we see a world where, at times, intellectual property principles prevent civil rights from adequately addressing the challenges of technology, thus stagnating a new generation of civil rights altogether.[25] Courts all too often defer to AI decision-making and deny defendants access to the source code for software that produces the evidence used to convict them.[26] This new era raises grave civil rights concerns, and yet the law has been woefully inadequate at ensuring greater transparency and accountability.[27]

As I argue, we also need to ask a fundamental question, in each of the contexts we face: Do we need to redesign the algorithm? Or, do we instead need to redesign civil rights law to address the algorithm? Either approach requires very different types of solutions, some of which can be legislated, and some of which cannot. That is precisely why it is so important for us to think broadly and creatively about what the law can and cannot do. We must remember, after all, that far too many acts of AI injustice occur at the hands of private industry, further

---

[21]   See, e.g., L. Lessig, The Law of the Horse: What Cyberlaw Might Teach (1999) 113 *Harv. Law Rev.* 501.

[22]   See, e.g., D. G. Post, What Larry Doesn't Get: Code, Law, and Liberty in Cyberspace (2000) 52 *Stan. Law Rev.* 1439 (explaining that Lessig's real-world policy recommendations fail to capture the complexity of cyberspace).

[23]   L. Lessig, *Free Culture: How Big Media Uses Technology and the Law to Lock Down Culture and Control Creativity* (Penguin, 2004), p. 199.

[24]   See F. H. Easterbrook, Cyberspace and the Law of the Horse (1996) *Univ. Chi. Legal F.* 207, 210 (expressing doubt that laws needed to change in order to address issues presented by new technology).

[25]   See S. Katyal, The Paradox of Source Code Secrecy (2019) 104 *Cornell Law Rev.* 1183.

[26]   See generally R. Wexler, Life, Liberty, and Trade Secrets: Intellectual Property in the Criminal Justice System (2018) 70 *Stan. Law Rev.* 1343.

[27]   Many scholars have addressed similar problems involving the lack of transparency in various contexts. See, e.g., Pasquale, above note 18 (in a host of areas); see also D. K. Citron and F. Pasquale, The Scored Society: Due Process for Automated Predictions (2014) 89 *Wash. Law Rev.* 1, 1 (discussing the lack of transparency in automated government decisions); R. A. Ford and W. Nicholson Price II, Privacy and Accountability in Black-Box Medicine (2016) 23 *Mich. Telecomm. Technol. Law Rev.* 1 (healthcare); B. L. Garrett, Big Data and Due Process (2014) 99 *Cornell Law Rev. Online* 207 (positing that there are overlooked issues at the intersection of big data and due process, namely the need for rules around e-discovery and the reconfiguration of *Brady* v. *Maryland* in the context of government data); M. Hu, Big Data Blacklisting (2015) 67 *Fla. Law Rev.* 1735 (administrative proceedings); J. L. Mnookin, Of Black Boxes, Instruments, and Experts: Testing the Validity of Forensic Science (2008) 5 *Episteme* 343, 343 (asserting that courts have accepted superficial explanations behind scientific methods rather than requiring empirical testing and evaluation); E. Murphy, The New Forensics: Criminal Justice, False Certainty, and the Second Generation of Scientific Evidence (2007) 95 *Calif. Law Rev.* 721, 747–8 (forensic techniques); P. Toomey and B. M. Kaufman, The Notice Paradox: Secret Surveillance, Criminal Defendants, and the Right to Notice (2015) 54 *Santa Clara Law Rev.* 843 (prosecutorial surveillance); J. N. Mellon, Note, Manufacturing Convictions: Why Defendants Are Entitled to the Data Underlying Forensic DNA Kits (2001) 51 *Duke Law J.* 1097 (DNA testing protocols).

amplifying the issue of opacity. At the same time, it is also necessary for us not to think of AI as an abstract set of black boxes, but rather as a specific set of granular opportunities for analysis and reflection that can draw on areas of psychology, regulation, and behavioral economics in order to encourage greater transparency.

For this reason, I argue that we are looking in the wrong place if we look to the state alone to address issues of algorithmic accountability. Instead, we must turn elsewhere to ensure more transparency and accountability that stem from private industry, rather than public regulation. That is, of course, not to say that greater regulation requiring transparency is not desirable. However, given the current reluctance of both state and federal legislators to address the challenges posed by AI, it makes sense to explore opportunities for greater endogeneity in addressing civil rights concerns, particularly given the information asymmetry between the industries that design AI and the larger public.

To that end, I divide this chapter into four parts, half descriptive, half normative. "Data and Its Discontents" explores how machine-learning models can unwittingly create skewed results due to well-documented forms of bias in the data that machine-learning algorithms are trained upon. "The Afterlife of the Algorithm" turns to the aftermath of algorithmic decision-making, drawing on examples from advertising, employment, and price discrimination to show the emergence of civil rights concerns in each context. Finally, in "Rethinking Civil Rights through Private Accountability" and "Refining Oversight from within," I turn to the normative question of how to address the nexus between private corporations and algorithmic accountability. As I argue, the issue of algorithmic bias represents a crucial new world of civil rights concerns, one that is distinct in nature from the ones that preceded it. Since we are in a world where the activities of private corporations, rather than the state, are raising concerns about privacy, due process, and discrimination, we must focus on the role of private corporations in addressing the issue. Here, in the absence of pending government action, I present two potential models to ensure greater transparency, drawn from self-regulation and whistleblower protection, that demonstrate the possibility of greater endogeneity in civil rights enforcement.

DATA AND ITS DISCONTENTS

The *Oxford English Dictionary* defines an algorithm as "a procedure or set of rules used in calculation and problem-solving."[28] The term originally meant nothing more than basic arithmetic. Now, with the advent of more advanced computers and the ability to collect, compute, and compare ever-larger amounts of data, algorithms represent the promise and peril of social engineering on a scale vaster, yet more precise, than ever possible before. That development is attributable in no small part to the advent of AI, which comprises machines that receive inputs from the environment, then learn from or interpret those inputs, and then potentially take certain actions or decisions that affect the environment.[29] Although the machine creates an illusion of autonomy, its actions depend completely on the code that humans write for it.

---

[28] Algorithm, *Oxford English Dictionary*, 3rd edn. (Oxford University Press, 2012), www.oed.com/view/Entry/4959? redirectedFrom=algorithms (last visited October 13, 2018).

[29] This definition is drawn from a definition offered by Stuart Russell and Peter Norvig. See D. Faggella, What Is Artificial Intelligence? An Informed Definition, *TechEmergence* (May 15, 2017), www.techemergence.com/what-is-artificial-intelligence-an-informed-definition. The term artificial intelligence was coined by John McCarthy for the Dartmouth Conferences in 1956. He defined it as "the science and engineering of making intelligent machines." J. McCarthy, Basic Questions, Stanford Computer Science Department: Formal Reasoning Group (Nov. 12, 2007), www-formal.stanford.edu/jmc/whatisai/node1.html. Today, some scholars observe that the term

Algorithms result from a complex interaction of features, classifications, and targets, all of which draw upon a maze of hazy interactive and embedded values.[30] According to Tarleton Gillespie, "the algorithm comes after the generation of a 'model,' i.e. the formalization of the problem and the goal in computational terms."[31] So, for example, consider the goal of "giving a user the most relevant search results for their queries."[32] That would require, Gillespie explains, a model that efficiently calculated "the combined values of pre-weighted objects in the index database, in order to improve the percentage likelihood that the user clicks on one of the first five results."[33] The resulting algorithm would comprise a series of steps that aggregated the values in an efficient manner, and something that might deliver rapid results.[34] What makes something algorithmic, he explains, is that the result is produced by an information system "that is committed (functionally and ideologically) to the computational generation of knowledge or decisions."[35]

The use of mathematical principles to solve social problems is nothing new. Parole boards have used actuarial models to assess the risk of recidivism with varying degrees of sophistication since the 1920s.[36] Advanced computing and its ability to collect, compute, and compare ever-larger amounts of data have also allowed algorithms to grow more complex and powerful.[37] Where Stewart Brand could once curate and compile the Whole Earth, Google now promises its algorithm will do the same – but better.[38] Its search algorithm, Google claims, is mere math; thus, its sorting and filtering is impartial and produces the most relevant, useful results.[39] Those more relevant results, in turn, attract more users, which allow Google to sell its ad space at a premium.[40] Similarly, since its inception in a Seattle garage, Amazon has used algorithms to quantify consumer preferences and thus recommend and sell products, often to its comparative advantage.[41] Netflix, too, uses an algorithm to compare a viewer's habits to those of others.[42] And OkCupid once dominated online dating

---

AI comprises two different branches of entities – "smart" computers (like deep learning), and an unrealized "artificial general intelligence" (or AGI). *Ibid.*

[30] T. Gillespie, The Relevance of Algorithms, in T. Gillespie, P. J. Boczkowski, K. A. Foot, *et al.* (eds.), *Media Technologies: Essays on Communication, Materiality, and Society* (MIT Press, 2014), pp. 167, 168.

[31] See T. Gillespie, Algorithm [draft] [#digitalkeywords], *Culture Digitally* (June 25, 2014), http://culturedigitally .org/2014/06/algorithm-draft-digitalkeyword/.

[32] *Ibid.*

[33] *Ibid.*

[34] *Ibid.*

[35] *Ibid.*

[36] R. Berk, An Impact Assessment of Machine Learning Risk Forecasts on Parole Board Decisions and Recidivism (2017) 13 *J. Exp. Criminol.* 193, 194.

[37] See L. Edwards and M. Veale, Slave to the Algorithm? Why a "Right to an Explanation" Is Probably Not the Remedy You Are Looking for (2017) 16 *Duke Law Technol. Rev.* 18, 19 (noting the role of algorithms in education, housing, employment, education, and criminal justice).

[38] See S. Jobs, Commencement Address at Stanford University (June 12, 2005), https://news.stanford.edu/2005/06/ 14/jobs-061505 (recounting how Google has recreated *The Whole Earth Catalog* of Jobs' childhood).

[39] P. Bilić, Search Algorithms, Hidden Labour and Information Control (2016) 3 *Big Data Soc.* 1, 3 (discussing how Google operates).

[40] C. E. Wills and C. Tatar, Understanding What They Do with What They Know, in Proceedings of the 2012 Workshop on Privacy in the Electronic Society (October 15, 2012).

[41] See, e.g., A. M. Hall, Note, Standing the Test of Time: Likelihood of Confusion in Multi Time Machine v. Amazon (2016) 31 *Berkeley Technol. Law J.* 815, 827–30; J. Angwin and S. Mattu, Amazon Says It Puts Customers First. But Its Pricing Algorithm Doesn't, *ProPublica* (September 20, 2016), www.propublica.org/article/amazon-says-it-puts-customers-first-but-its-pricing-algorithm-doesnt; F. Foer, Amazon Must Be Stopped, *New Republic* (October 9, 2014), http://newrepublic.com/article/119769/amazons-monopoly-must-be-broken-radical-plan-tech-giant.

[42] See A. Rodriguez, How Netflix (NFLX) Determines What to Pay for Shows and Films, *Quartz* (December 27, 2016), http://qz.com/872909.

with its algorithms before everyone switched to Tinder, allowing users to simply "swipe right" over another individual's picture as a way of indicating interest in that individual.[43] Target famously used algorithms to create predictive models so accurate, it could tell a teenager was pregnant before her family knew.[44]

While the effects of algorithms' predictions can be troubling in themselves, they become even more problematic when the government uses them to distribute resources or mete out punishment.[45] The Social Security Administration uses algorithms to aid its agents in evaluating benefits claims; the Internal Revenue Service uses them to select taxpayers for audit; the Food and Drug Administration uses algorithms to study patterns of foodborne illness; the Securities and Exchange Commission uses them to detect trading misconduct; local police departments employ their insights to predict the emergence of crime hotspots; courts use them to sentence defendants; and parole boards use them to decide who is least likely to reoffend.[46]

Algorithms hold tremendous value. Big data promises significant benefits to the economy, allowing consumers to find and sort products more quickly, which in turn lowers search costs. Yet their potential to shape society in dramatic, unanticipated ways has often been underestimated. The dominant perception is that algorithms are but simple mathematical principles, rearranged to reveal patterns and make predictions. Who would quibble, the reasoning goes, that one plus one is two? Under this view, objectivity seemingly benefits users. Instead of weighing the credibility of and comparing various answers, algorithms reveal the single best answer. Algorithmic recommendations consequently can save users' search and information costs by tailoring services and content to consumers.[47] AI can also aid in the detection of financial mismanagement, identity theft, and credit card fraud.[48]

Now that we have more data than ever, proponents suggest, the results of predictive analytics should be better, more robust, and more accurate than ever before.[49] Algorithmic decision-making, through rote analysis of quantitative information, seemingly creates an appealing alternative to human judgments that risk subjectivity and bias.[50] And, to be fair,

[43] See C. Gourarie, Investigating the Algorithms that Govern Our Lives, *Columbia Journalism Review* (April 14, 2016), www.cjr.org/innovations/investigatingalgorithms.php (noting use of algorithms in online dating services); B. Winterhalter, Don't Fall in Love on OkCupid, *JSTOR Daily* (February 10, 2016), https://daily.jstor.org/dont-fall-in-love-okcupid.

[44] S. Barocas and H. Nissenbaum, Big Data's End Run around Anonymity and Consent, in J. Lane, V. Stodden, S. Bender, *et al.* (eds.), *Privacy, Big Data, and the Public Good* (Cambridge University Press, 2014), pp. 44, 62; C. Duhigg, How Companies Learn Your Secrets, *New York Times* (February 16, 2012), www.nytimes.com/2012/02/19/magazine/shopping-habits.html.

[45] See C. Beck and C. McCue, Predictive Policing: What Can We Learn from Wal-Mart and Amazon about Fighting Crime in a Recession?, *Police Chief* (November 2009), www.policechiefmagazine.org/predictive-policing-what-can-we-learn-from-wal-mart-and-amazon-about-fighting-crime-in-a-recession (example of advocacy for further government use of algorithms).

[46] R. Bailey, Welcoming Our New Algorithmic Overlords?, *Reason* (October 1, 2016), https://reason.com/archives/2016/10/01/welcoming-our-new-algorithmic; see also J. Kleinberg, J. Ludwig, S. Mullainathan, and Z. Obermeyer, Prediction Policy Problems (2015) 105 *Am. Econ. Rev.: Papers & Proc.* 491, 494–5 (discussing how improved prediction techniques using machine learning can have significant policy implications).

[47] See generally E. J. Altman, F. Nagle, and M. L. Tushman, Innovating without Information Constraints: Organizations, Communities, and Innovation When Information Costs Approach Zero, in C. E. Shalley, M. A. Hitt, and J. Zhou (eds.), *The Oxford Handbook of Creativity, Innovation, and Entrepreneurship* (Oxford University Press, 2015), p. 353.

[48] A. H. Raymond, E. Arrington Stone Young, and S. J. Shackelford, Building a Better HAL 9000: Algorithms, the Market, and the Need to Prevent the Engraining of Bias (2018) 15 *Nw. J. Technol. Intell. Prop.* 215, 217.

[49] For an example of an optimistic view, see R. Simmons, Quantifying Criminal Procedure: How to Unlock the Potential of Big Data in Our Criminal Justice System (2016) 2016 *Mich. St. Law Rev.* 947.

[50] See N. R. Kuncel, D. S. Ones, and D. M. Klieger, In Hiring, Algorithms Beat Instinct, *Harvard Business Review* (May 1, 2014), http://hbr.org/2014/05/in-hiring-algorithms-beat-instinct.

most applications of algorithms do in fact seem relatively harmless. Is it really so bad if Facebook's news algorithm shows me the latest in adorable kitten news rather than Syrian refugee updates, most people might ask? Maybe that is what I want, a typical consumer might reason. It hardly seems worse than what a panel of human news editors could choose.[51]

Indeed, that is how many people encounter algorithms: innocent enhancements of a consumer experience. Algorithms, however, do much more – by addressing, analyzing, and then potentially replicating our worlds of implicit bias. And the results can often be mystifying. When an algorithm produces a t-shirt that says "keep calm and rape a lot"[52] or Twitter users transform an innocent chatbot into a white supremacist in less than a day,[53] there is clearly more at stake than innocent depictions. Here, machine learning can mirror back to us a particularly uncomfortable construction of reality.[54] To take one example, a recent study has argued that as a machine-learning model acquires capabilities that approximate the context of human language – a process known as "word embedding" – it demonstrates, and replicates, the same troubling implicit biases that we see in human psychology.[55] For example, the same study showed that the words "female" and "woman" were more closely associated with the domestic sphere, and occupations associated with the arts and humanities, as opposed to the terms "male" and "man," which were closer to professions associated with mathematics and engineering.[56]

Errors at any stage can become amplified in the next stage, producing deviant outcomes in complex, troubling, and sometimes difficult-to-detect ways. Since algorithmic models reflect the design choices of the humans who built them, they carry the biases of the observer or instrument.[57] The sheer size of big data also obscures smaller variations.[58] While most researchers focus on the dangers of false positives and false negatives in data,[59] far more pernicious types of

---

[51]   See RISJ Admin, Brand and Trust in a Fragmented News Environment, *Reuters Institute*, https://reutersinstitute .politics.ox.ac.uk/our-research/brand-and-trust-fragmented-news-environment; see also S. Porter, Can Facebook Resolve Its News Problems without Losing Credibility?, *Christian Science Monitor* (January 11, 2017), www .csmonitor.com/Business/2017/0111/Can-Facebook-resolve-its-news-problems-without-losing-credibility (describing trade-offs between human versus algorithmic editing of Facebook's news feed).

[52]   C. Baraniuk, The Bad Things that Happen When Algorithms Run Online Shops, *BBC: Future* (August 20, 2015), www.bbc.com/future/story/20150820-the-bad-things-that-happen-when-algorithms-run-online-shops.

[53]   J. Vincent, Twitter Taught Microsoft's AI Chatbot to Be a Racist Asshole in Less than a Day, *Verge* (March 24, 2016), www.theverge.com/2016/3/24/11297050/tay-microsoft-chatbot-racist.

[54]   See F. Manjoo, How Netflix Is Deepening Our Cultural Echo Chambers, *New York Times* (January 11, 2017), www.nytimes.com/2017/01/11/technology/how-netflix-is-deepening-our-cultural-echo-chambers.html.

[55]   See A. Caliskan, J. J. Bryson, and A. Narayanan, Semantics Derived Automatically from Language Corpora Contain Human-Like Biases (2017) 356 *Sci.* 6334; see also H. Devlin, AI Programs Exhibit Racial and Gender Biases, Research Reveals, *The Guardian* (April 13, 2017), www.theguardian.com/technology/2017/apr/13/ai-programs-exhibit-racist-and-sexist-biases-research-reveals.

[56]   Devlin, above note 55. As Amanda Levendowski explains, Google's use of word2vec, a word-embedding toolkit, reflects "the gendered bias embedded in the Google News corpus used to train it," offering the example of the toolkit projecting "that man is to computer programmer in the same way that woman is to homemaker." A. Levendowski, How Copyright Law Can Fix Artificial Intelligence's Implicit Bias Problem (2018) 93 *Wash. Law Rev.* 579, 581; see also Raymond *et al.*, above note 48, pp. 218–19 (noting similar concerns regarding race, in addition to gender).

[57]   See J. Bogen, Theory and Observation in Science, *Stanford Encyclopedia of Philosophy* (January 11, 2013), http://plato .stanford.edu/archives/spr2013/entries/science-theory-observation (noting how various philosophers "cast suspicion on the objectivity of observational evidence by challenging the assumption that observers can shield it from biases …"); T. Woods, "Mathwashing," Facebook and the Zeitgeist of Data Worship, *Technical.ly Brooklyn* (June 8, 2016), http:// technical.ly/brooklyn/2016/06/08/fred-benenson-mathwashing-facebook-data-worship.

[58]   See B. Foucault Welles, On Minorities and Outliers: The Case for Making Big Data Small (2014) 1 *Big Data Soc.* 1 (discussing some problems that arise with big data).

[59]   See, e.g., Data Science – Dealing with False Positives and Negatives in Machine Learning, *Teradata: Data Science Blog* (December 28, 2015), http://community.teradata.com/t5/Learn-Data-Science/Data-Science-Dealing-with-False-Positives-and-Negatives-in/ba-p/79675.

discrimination can result from how classes of data are defined, and the sorts of examples and rules that algorithms learn from such data.[60] In an excellent study, Solon Barocas and Andrew Selbst detailed a number of different ways in which the data-mining process can give rise to models that risk having an adverse impact on protected classes, stemming from biased data inputs, measurement errors or missing variables, or inappropriate uses of criteria that also serve as proxies for a protected class or group.[61] In the subparts below, I analyze the potential interplay of both statistical and cognitive forms of bias, and discuss how each can affect the design of the algorithm, the data it is trained upon, and ultimately its outcome.[62]

Statistical and Historical Bias in Big Data

As Kate Crawford and Meredith Whittaker have observed in the inaugural AI Now Report, bias in big data generally results from one of two causes.[63] The first is largely internal to the process of data collection – when errors in data collection, like inaccurate methodologies, lead to inaccurate depictions of reality.[64] The second type, however, comes from an external source. It happens when the underlying subject matter draws on information that reflects or internalizes some forms of structural discrimination and thus biases the data as a result.[65] Imagine, they explain, a situation where data on job promotions might be used to predict career success, but the data was gathered from an industry that systematically promoted men instead of women.[66] While the first kind of bias can often be mitigated by "cleaning the data" or improving the methodology, the latter might require interventions that raise complex political ramifications because of the structural nature of the remedy that is required.[67] As a result of these issues, bias can surface in the context of input bias level (when the source data is biased because it may lack certain types of information), training bias (when bias appears in the categorization of the baseline data), or through programming bias (when bias occurs from a smart algorithm learning and modifying itself from interaction with human users or incorporating new data).[68]

Although mathematical algorithms have been around for thousands of years, today, machine-learning algorithms are trained on a body of data that is selected by designers or

[60] See, e.g., S. Barocas and A. D. Selbst, Big Data's Disparate Impact (2016) 104 *Calif. Law Rev.* 671, 680; see also J. Grimmelmann and D. Westreich, Incomprehensible Discrimination (2016) 7 *Calif. Law Rev. Online* 164 (exploring issues of accountability and transparency in machine learning); J. A. Kroll, J. Huey, S. Barocas, *et al.*, Accountable Algorithms (2017) 165 *Univ. Pa. Law Rev.* 633, 680 ("These decision rules are machine-made and follow mathematically from input data, but the lessons they embody may be biased or unfair nevertheless").
[61] Barocas and Selbst, above note 60, p. 677.
[62] R. Baeza-Yates, Bias on the Web (2018) 61 *Comm. ACM* 54, 54 (defining statistical bias to comprise "[A] systematic deviation caused by an inaccurate estimation or sampling process"); see also Barocas and Selbst, above note 60, p. 677.
[63] K. Crawford and M. Whittaker, The AI Now Report: The Social and Economic Implications of Artificial Intelligence Technologies in the Near-Term (2016), pp. 6–7, https://ainowinstitute.org/AI_Now_2016_Report .pdf.
[64] *Ibid.*
[65] *Ibid.*; see also Levendowski, above note 56, pp. 583–4, 589 (arguing that AI contains implicit, or unintentional, biases that are products of flawed data and that certain copyright paradigms can augment these biases); J. Bryson, Three Very Different Sources of Bias in AI, and How to Fix Them, *Adventures NI* (July 13, 2017), http://joanna-bryson.blogspot.com/2017/07/three-very-different-sources-of-bias-in.html (demonstrating that bias is introduced to AI when there is poor-quality data that is tainted with human biases and/or when the formal models behind AI are not well reasoned).
[66] Crawford and Whittaker, above note 63, p. 6.
[67] *Ibid.*
[68] N. G. Packin and Y. Lev-Aretz, Learning Algorithms and Discrimination, in W. Barfield and U. Pagallo (eds.), *Research Handbook on the Law of Artificial Intelligence* (Edward Elgar, 2018), p. 9.

by past human practices. This process is the "learning" element in machine learning; the algorithm learns, for example, how to pair queries and results based on a body of data that produced satisfactory pairs in the past.[69] The quality of a machine-learning algorithm's results often depends on the comprehensiveness and diversity of the data that it digests.[70] Bad data, in other words, can perpetuate inequalities through machine learning, leading to a feedback loop that replicates existing forms of bias, potentially impacting minorities as a result. For example, recently, the first international beauty contest derived from AI sparked controversy after the results from its 6,000 entries (from over 100 countries) revealed that of the forty-four winners, nearly all were white.[71] Why? Although there are probably a host of reasons, the main problem was that the training data that was used, ostensibly to establish standards of attractiveness among humans, did not include enough people of color.[72]

Underrepresentation and Exclusion

One common form of machine learning is supervised learning (where one has input variables and output variables, and an algorithm is used to train the machine to learn the mapping function from the input to the output).[73] But there is also unsupervised machine learning, where we rely on a machine to identify patterns in data instead, using insights from statistics and neuroscience.[74]

With supervised learning, since machine learning is based on a system of patterns and correlations in the data to make predictions, these predictions can often be inaccurate if the training data is unrepresentative of the general population that is being studied.[75] Moreover, there may be noise in the training data itself, stemming from inaccurate information about individuals in the population.[76] In addition, choices that are made by humans – what features should be used to construct a particular model, for example – can comprise sources of inaccuracy as well.[77] An additional source of error can come from the training of the algorithm itself, which requires programmers to decide, essentially, how to weigh sources of potential error.[78]

[69] See *ibid.* For more information on types of machine learning, see also Edwards and Veale, above note 37, pp. 25–7.
[70] See Barocas and Selbst, above note 60, p. 688.
[71] See S. Levin, A Beauty Contest Was Judged by AI and the Robots Didn't Like Dark Skin, *The Guardian* (September 8, 2016), www.theguardian.com/technology/2016/sep/08/artificial-intelligence-beauty-contest-doesnt-like-black-people.
[72] *Ibid.* (citing Alex Zhavoronkov, Beauty.AI's chief science officer).
[73] For a fuller explanation, see J. Brownlee, Supervised and Unsupervised Machine Learning Algorithms, *Machine Learning Mastery* (March 16, 2016), http://machinelearningmastery.com/supervised-and-unsupervised-machine-learning-algorithms.
[74] For more discussion of these methods of unsupervised learning, see M. Hynar, M. Burda, and J. Šarmanová, Unsupervised Clustering with Growing Self-Organizing Neural Network – a Comparison with Non-Neural Approach, in Proceedings of the 2005 Databases, Texts, Specifications and Objects (DATESO) Workshop (2005), p. 58. See also N. Castle, Supervised vs. Unsupervised Machine Learning, *DataScience.com* (July 13, 2017), www.datascience.com/blog/supervised-and-unsupervised-machine-learning-algorithms; B. Marr, Supervised V Unsupervised Machine Learning – What's the Difference?, *Forbes* (March 16, 2017), www.forbes.com/sites/bernardmarr/2017/03/16/supervised-v-unsupervised-machine-learning-whats-the-difference/2 (explaining the difference between the two).
[75] See M. L. Rich, Machine Learning, Automated Suspicion Algorithms, and the Fourth Amendment (2016) 164 *Univ. Pa. Law Rev.* 871, 883–4.
[76] *Ibid.*, p. 884.
[77] *Ibid.*, p. 885.
[78] *Ibid.*

Further, the quality of data can be affected by practices such as excluding outliers, or editing, cleaning, or mining data.[79] As Solon Barocas and Andrew Selbst have argued:

> Data mining can go wrong in any number of ways. It can choose a target variable that correlates to [a] protected class more than others would, reproduce the prejudice exhibited in the training examples, draw adverse lessons about protected classes from an unrepresentative sample, choose too small a feature set, or not dive deep enough into each feature. Each of these potential errors is marked by two facts: the errors may generate a manifest disparate impact, and they may be the result of entirely innocent choices made by data miners.[80]

Since minority interpretations of a search term, for example, do not help Google show relevant ads, generate clicks, or produce revenue on a mass scale, Google and its counterparts might ignore or minimize them in their search results and queries.[81] In other words, depending on what a company is looking to market, these outliers are simply deviations from the valuable average and therefore excluded. Their uncommon traits can become lost and ignored in the sea of big data.

Other types of errors have everything to do with the impact of categorization. Categorization, while key to an algorithmic model's success, can also be its greatest downfall, because it can miss evidence of structural discrimination and bias. As Tarleton Gillespie has written: "Categorization is a powerful semantic and political intervention: what the categories are, what belongs in a category, and who decides how to implement these categories in practice, are all powerful assertions about how things are and are supposed to be."[82] To demonstrate, Gillespie offers the example of a situation involving Amazon in 2009, when nearly 57,000 gay-friendly books disappeared from its sales lists, because they had been wrongly characterized as "adult" books.[83] The error revealed that Amazon had been programming its machine-learning model to calculate "sales rank" by excluding adult books from consideration.[84] While the idea of excluding adult books from sales lists might make intuitive sense (since there may be some restrictions on age-related purchases), the model failed to grapple with a known problem in society, which is that often things that are characterized as "adult" or "obscene" are LGBT-related, when the same behavior in an opposite-sex context is not classified in the same manner. As a result, a mistake such as Amazon's can have dramatic effects on the visibility of resources for individual consumers seeking validation and community through the consumption of LGBT-related texts. This categorization not only adds to a problematic invisibility of gay texts, but it also feeds into an invisibility of *consumers* of these texts.

Ricardo Baeza-Yates, in a powerful article, describes how common issues like self-selection bias, activity bias, and cultural and cognitive bias can skew research on Web-based activities.[85] Aside from these sorts of bias, data collected on the Web is drawn from a skewed demographic, since it favors those with educational, economic, technological, and even linguistic advantages (since over 50 percent of the most popular websites are in

[79] J. S. Gardenier and D. B. Resnik, The Misuse of Statistics: Concepts, Tools, and a Research Agenda (2002) 9 *Account. Res.* 65, 68.

[80] Barocas and Selbst, above note 60, p. 729.

[81] Cf. M. Hardt, How Big Data Is Unfair, *Medium* (September 26, 2014) https://medium.com/@mrtz/how-big-data-is-unfair-9aa544d739de.

[82] Gillespie, above note 30, p. 171.

[83] *Ibid.*

[84] *Ibid.*

[85] Baeza-Yates, above note 62, p. 56 (citing studies that reflect that on Facebook, a large dataset shows that only 7 percent of users produce 50 percent of the posted content; on Amazon, only 4 percent of active users produce the posted reviews; and on Twitter, only 2 percent produced 50 percent of the posts).

English, when only 13 percent of the world speaks English).[86] Elsewhere, in the context of health and big data, researchers have reported a troubling homogeneity among big data.[87] It turns out, some analysts argue, that big data has failed to include marginalized communities, including African-American, Latino, and Native American populations, people of a lower socioeconomic status, LGBT individuals, and immigrants.[88] Not only are these people disproportionately missing from sources like Internet histories, social media, and credit card usage, but they are also missing from electronic health records and genomic databases.[89]

Further, even the techniques of data collection can bias results. Easily available data tends to be reported and analyzed more often, leading to a reporting bias because harder-to-find information may never make it into the dataset.[90] There are classic examples of selection bias, where some individuals are picked for study rather than others. But there is also exclusion bias, resulting when individuals are excluded from certain studies, as discussed above.[91] Results can even differ based on whether something is written or oral (modality bias).[92] Baeza-Yates describes an additional level of bias that can also be unwittingly introduced by interaction designers, who might create bias in designing the user's interface; in one example, he points out that content that is placed in the top left corner of the screen tends to attract more eyes and clicks, a type of "position bias."[93] Ranking bias is a related form of bias, which privileges top-ranked items over ones that are lower in the order of relevance.[94]

And, in turn, the effects of misrepresentation can impact different groups. In other words, if the machine-learning model is trained on data that is biased in some way, then decisions that are derived from that data can systematically disadvantage individuals who happen to be over- or underrepresented in the dataset.[95] As Baeza-Yates concludes, "[b]ias begets bias."[96] Here, depending on the issue, data mining can actually resurrect past prejudices if it relies on prior decisions that are already rife with discrimination. In one example, a UK hospital developed a computer program to sort medical school applicants. However, the program relied on its prior decisions, which had systematically been shown to discriminate against women and minority applicants with the same credentials as other applicants, thus risking the same outcome here.[97] Pre-existing past biases in datasets,

---

[86] *Ibid.*, p. 57.
[87] See S. E. Malanga, J. D. Loe, C. T. Robertson, and K. Ramos, Who's Left Out of Big Data? How Big Data Collection, Analysis, and Use Neglect Populations Most in Need of Medical and Public Health Research and Interventions, in I. G. Cohen, H. Fernandez Lynch, E. Vayena, and U. Gasser (eds.), *Big Data, Health Law, and Bioethics* (Cambridge University Press, 2018), pp. 98–9.
[88] See *ibid.*
[89] *Ibid.*
[90] For a definition of reporting bias, see Reporting Bias: Definition and Examples, Types, *Statistics How To* (October 12, 2017), www.statisticshowto.com/reporting-bias. See also J. Gordon and B. Van Durme, Reporting Bias and Knowledge Acquisition, 2013 Proceedings of the Workshop on Automated Knowledge Base Construction, p. 25 (analyzing generally how reporting bias functions in AI).
[91] See, e.g., M. Delgado-Rodríguez and J. Llorca, Bias (2004) 58 *J. Epidemiol. Community Health* 635, 637 (describing bias in an epidemiological context); J. Chou, O. Murillo, and R. Ibars, How to Recognize Exclusion in AI, *Medium* (September 26, 2017), https://medium.com/microsoft-design/how-to-recognize-exclusion-in-ai-ec2d6d89f850 (discussing examples of exclusion bias).
[92] See M. L. Elliott, R. E. Geiselman, and D. J. Thomas, Modality Effects in Short Term Recognition Memory (1981) 94 *Am. J. Psychol.* 85.
[93] Baeza-Yates, above note 62, p. 58.
[94] *Ibid.*
[95] Barocas and Selbst, above note 60, pp. 680–1.
[96] Baeza-Yates, above note 62, p. 60.
[97] Barocas and Selbst, above note 60, p. 682.

then, can lead to the reconstruction and replication of bias in the future, creating forms of second-order bias as a result.[98]

The problem is not just one of inadequate representation. The model's determination or conclusions may also fail to communicate some recognition of its own risks of inaccuracy, leading to the risk of overconfidence in its results and a failure to communicate attendant ambiguity.[99] As a result, as Joshua Kroll and his co-authors indicate, there are a variety of anti-discrimination implications that arise from choices of inputs. One might use membership in a protected class directly or rely on data that is insufficiently representative of a protected class (for example, relying on employment data that is historically biased against women to assess female applicants). Or it might use factors that may be proxies for protected class membership (for example, length of tenure may seem like a benign category, but women who leave the workplace due to childrearing may lower the average tenure for all women, risking disparate impact if tenure serves as a proxy for gender).[100]

However, these issues are often exceedingly difficult to locate and to address. It is difficult to eliminate proxies if they provide valuable information, and it is often difficult, *ex post*, to improve the quality of data relied upon.[101] As one commentator, Matthew Carroll, explains, "[t]he average engineer is not thinking about bias or proper provenance when designing a neural network."[102] He continues:

> They are focused on nuances such as ideal network topology, activation functions, training gradients, weight normalization, and data overfitting. Once a model is trained, engineers quite frequently lack understanding of the model's actual decision-making process. What if they're called on to explain why a model made the decision that it did – to prove, for example, it didn't make a legally questionable decision, like discriminating on the basis of race? What if a data subject seeks to exercise her right to prevent her data from being used to train the model, or used in the model at all, a right protected by the EU's primary data protection regulation, the GDPR? This is where today's governance models start to break down.[103]

While researchers might correctly argue that some algorithmic models do not explicitly consider protected identity characteristics in their predictions and are quantitative in nature, they may ignore existing, implicit biases that stem from potential proxies and algorithms' potential to exacerbate them.[104] Jeremy Kun offers another example of how minorities can get treated unfairly by describing something called the "sample size" problem, which researcher Moritz Hardt described as a tendency for statistical models about minorities to perform worse than models that predict behavior of the general population.[105] And if that mathematical minority aligns with a racial minority, then the algorithm might completely ignore an entire racial population. As Kun writes, "an algorithm with 85% accuracy on US participants could err on the entire black sub-population and still seem very good."[106]

[98] Baeza-Yates, above note 62, p. 60.
[99] See A. Roth, Machine Testimony (2017) 126 *Yale Law J.* 1972, 1992–3.
[100] Kroll *et al.*, above note 60, p. 681.
[101] *Ibid.*
[102] M. Carroll, The Complexities of Governing Machine Learning, *Datanami* (April 27, 2017), www.datanami.com /2017/04/27/complexities-governing-machine-learning.
[103] *Ibid.*
[104] This can be a classic result of anchoring bias – focusing on one aspect of information that fails to take into account other variables, such as structural discrimination. See A. Tversky and D. Kahneman, Judgment under Uncertainty: Heuristics and Biases (1974) 185 *Sci.* 1124, 1128–30.
[105] See Hardt, above note 81; see also Kun, above note 16 (discussing Hardt).
[106] Kun, above note 16.

Over-Surveillance in Data Selection and Design

If the prior discussion focused on the risks of exclusion from statistical and historical under-representation, this subpart focuses on the opposite risk of overrepresentation, which can also lead to imprecise perceptions and troubling stereotypes. Here, an algorithmic model might associate certain traits with another unrelated trait, triggering extra scrutiny of certain groups.[107] In such cases, it can be hard to prove discriminatory intent in the analysis; just because an algorithm produces a disparate impact on a minority group, it does not always mean that the designer intended this result.[108]

Consider, for example, the debates over predictive policing algorithms. Brett Goldstein, a former officer with the Chicago Police Department and now a public policy scholar, used an algorithm to analyze the locations of prior arrests to predict the location of criminals, a strategy that has been strongly criticized by civil rights groups.[109] Another scholar, Miles Wernick at the Illinois Institute of Technology, developed a program that generated a "heat list" of 400 individuals that had the highest chance of committing a violent crime.[110] He insisted the model was unbiased because it did not rely on any racial, neighborhood, or related information. Instead, he used data about the number and frequency of previous crimes.

Despite his efforts, Wernick's model and its predictions perpetuated existing systemic biases, even where the data analyzed was seemingly unbiased.[111] Individuals who committed prior crimes were detected more often than other potential criminals.[112] Why? Their race or location were more likely to be surveilled.[113] In other words, they were the most likely to get caught because these other characteristics made the individuals more vulnerable to suspicion.[114] The predictive policing algorithm suffered from classic detection bias. Its sample population was far more likely to be surveilled than other social groups, thus overestimating a propensity toward crime.

Frequently, however, the criteria that algorithms consider when making their predictions are secret. Wernick, for instance, refuses to reveal which factors his proprietary algorithm uses, even while touting the accuracy of the police department's list of roughly 400 people most likely to shoot or be shot.[115] As of May 2016, more than 70 percent of the people who had been shot in the city that year were on the list, according to the Chicago police, as were more

[107] See Federal Trade Commission, Big Data: A Tool for Inclusion or Exclusion? (2016), p. 9 ("with large enough data sets, one can generally find some meaningless correlations"); M. Frické, Big Data and Its Epistemology (2015) 66 J. Assoc. Inf. Sci. Technol. 651, 659 (discussing the possibility of spotting new patterns in data).
[108] See Kroll *et al.*, above note 60, pp. 693–4.
[109] See J. Brustein, The Ex-Cop at the Center of Controversy over Crime Prediction Tech, *Bloomberg* (July 10, 2017), www.bloomberg.com/news/features/2017-07-10/the-ex-cop-at-the-center-of-controversy-over-crime-prediction-tech (discussing Goldstein's predictive policing strategies and related critiques); Kun, above note 16 (same); see also C. O'Neil, Gillian Tett Gets It Very Wong on Racial Profiling, *Mathbabe* (August 25, 2014), https://mathbabe.org/2014/08/25/gilian-tett-gets-it-very-wrong-on-racial-profiling (discussing predictive policing).
[110] Kun, above note 16.
[111] *Ibid.*; see also A. Z. Huq, Racial Equity in Algorithmic Criminal Justice (2019) 68 *Duke Law J.* 1043; J. Angwin and J. Larson, Bias in Criminal Risk Scores Is Mathematically Inevitable, Researchers Say, *ProPublica* (December 30, 2016), www.propublica.org/article/bias-in-criminal-risk-scores-is-mathematically-inevitable-researchers-say.
[112] Kun, above note 16; see also M. Stroud, The Minority Report: Chicago's New Police Computer Predicts Crimes, But Is It Racist?, *Verge* (February 19, 2014), www.theverge.com/2014/2/19/5419854/the-minority-report-this-computer-predicts-crime-but-is-it-racist (discussing Wernick's work).
[113] See J. Saunders, P. Hunt, and J. S. Hollywood, Predictions Put into Practice: A Quasi-Experimental Evaluation of Chicago's Predictive Policing Pilot (2016) 12 J. Exp. Criminol. 347, 356–67.
[114] *Ibid.*
[115] See *ibid.*, p. 15; Saunders *et al.*, above note 113, p. 366; Stroud, above note 112 (noting Wernick's reluctance to share specific details about the algorithm).

than 80 percent of those arrested in connection with shootings.[116] However, the same algorithm also led a police commander to turn up at the home of a 22-year-old black man who lived on the south side of Chicago.[117] The police commander warned him not to commit further crimes, although the man had not committed any recent crimes and did not have a violent criminal record.[118]

In response to questions about such false positives, the Chicago police will say only that the program considers whether an individual's criminal "trend line" is increasing, whether he has been shot before, and whether he has ever been arrested on weapons charges, to make its predictions.[119] They will not reveal the model, nor allow anyone on the list to challenge the factors or the data that it considers.[120] It is easy to see, however, how such questions might readily become a proxy for race, gender, or geography. Residents of neighborhoods that have more crime are more likely to be shot. These neighborhoods consequently become more policed. Because the areas are more policed, police are more likely to detect weapons offenses there and arrest their residents on weapons charges.[121]

Despite these risks, many police departments use software programs to predict crime.[122] The PredPol algorithm uses only three data points – past type, place, and time of crime – to identify the times and places where future crimes are most likely to occur.[123] Critics point out that PredPol and similar algorithms predict not so much where future crime is most likely to occur, but where police are most likely to detect future crime.[124] In other words, PredPol predicts not so much crime as policing. In this respect, algorithmic policing becomes a self-fulfilling prophecy in poor and minority neighborhoods: more policing leads to more arrests, more scrutiny, and potentially greater penalties. The surge in arrests spurs the algorithm to predict a greater need for policing in the same area, leading two scholars to conclude that this was a perfect example of "selection bias meets confirmation bias."[125] Because the algorithms learn from previous arrest data that might reflect biases, they created a feedback loop that perpetuates those biases, even despite their claims to exclude race, gender, or geography from its data.[126]

And this tendency can carry grave results. As Bernard Harcourt has argued, predictive policing can lead to a misdirection of resources, leading crime to be suppressed in areas

---

[116] M. Davey, Chicago Policy Try to Predict Who May Shoot or Be Shot, *New York Times* (May 23, 2016), www.nytimes.com/2016/05/24/us/armed-with-data-chicago-police-try-to-predict-who-may-shoot-or-be-shot.html.

[117] K. Lum and W. Isaac, To Predict and Serve?, *Significance* (October 2016), p. 15, http://rdcu.be/iUg9.

[118] *Ibid.*; see also J. Gorner, Chicago Police Use "Heat List" as Strategy to Prevent Violence, *Chicago Tribune* (August 21, 2013), www.chicagotribune.com/news/ct-xpm-2013-08-21-ct-met-heat-list-20130821-story.html.

[119] See Davey, above note 116.

[120] Even the former White House suggests that transparency about data is essential to effective community policing despite obvious problems with how crime data is collected. See Press Release, The White House, Office of the Press Secretary, Fact Sheet: White House Police Data Initiative Highlights New Commitments (April 21, 2016), www.whitehouse.gov/the-press-office/2016/04/22/fact-sheet-white-house-police-data-initiative-highlights-new-commitments; see generally M. D. Maltz, US Department of Justice, Bureau of Justice Statistics, Bridging Gaps in Police Crime Data (1999), www.bjs.gov/content/pub/pdf/bgpcd.pdf.

[121] A recent study of Chicago's algorithmic model confirmed that this trend was likely the case, concluding that being on the list correlated only with being arrested for a shooting, not with being the victim of a shooting, as the department had claimed. Saunders *et al.*, above note 113, pp. 363–4.

[122] See generally G. O. Mohler et al., Randomized Controlled Field Trials of Predictive Policing (2015) 110 *J. Am. Stat. Assoc.* 1399.

[123] Lum and Isaac, above note 117, pp. 14, 17–18.

[124] See *ibid.*, p. 18.

[125] See *ibid.*, pp. 16–19; see also T. Z. Zarsky, Transparent Predictions (2013) *Univ. Ill. Law Rev.* 1503, 1510 (discussing role of prediction in big data).

[126] See Lum and Isaac, above note 117, pp. 15–16.

where individuals are targeted (and thereby receive more resources), at the cost of increasing crime in areas that receive less surveillance (and therefore less resources).[127]

Errors of Attribution, Prediction, and Preference

Aside from issues with collecting and refining data, cognitive and other forms of implicit bias can also seriously impact both algorithmic design and the data that the algorithm is trained upon. As Christine Jolls, Cass Sunstein, and Richard Thaler argued some time ago, individuals display bounded rationality, bounded willpower, and bounded self-interest – each of which present trajectories that diverge from conventional economic models.[128] These behavioral trajectories, they argued, require the development of new predictive models to take these biases into account in order to increase their precision.[129]

The same might be true here, where our cognitive biases might require a much more rigorous interrogation of the ways in which AI can replicate these biases.[130] Our reliance on heuristics – mental shortcuts to ease and speed decisions – can contribute to the opacity of the problem.[131] Thus, much more work on implicit bias is necessary to understand how it can be linked to machine learning, data quality, and algorithmic design. In this subpart, I explore three specific types of biases – attributional errors, predictive errors, and preference-related errors – to show how they can contribute to the problem of biasing both the design of an algorithm and the data AI relies upon.

Attributional Errors

Because we strive to conserve analytic power, we assume that a single example represents a whole class, or we accept the first thought that comes to mind, failing to make adjustments later, because our minds remain anchored to that initial thought.[132] Aside from shortcuts, we might be directed to process information differently in the presence of emotions, noise, motivations, or other complex factors like social influence in our decision-making processes.[133] In such cases, both the designer of the algorithm – and the subjects represented within the data – can reflect forms of implicit bias that are difficult to detect.

For a moment, think of all of the information about ourselves we gladly hand over to computers. Monitors, like smartwatches and phones, track our height, weight, where we are, where we are going, how quickly, where, and how much we sleep. Search engines likewise know all of our questions and their answers, for better or for worse.[134] But our own cognitive

127 See B. E. Harcourt, Against Prediction: Profiling, Policing, and Punishing in an Actuarial Age (2007), pp. 111–38 (discussed in Simmons, above note 49, p. 957). Whether or not crime overall actually decreases depends on the comparative elasticity of each group. Simmons, above note 49, p. 957.

128 See C. Jolls, C. R. Sunstein, and R. Thaler, A Behavioral Approach to Law and Economics (1998) 50 *Stan. Law Rev.* 1471, 1477–9.

129 See *ibid.*, p. 1477.

130 Cf. D. Kahneman, P. Slovic, and A. Tversky (eds.), *Judgment under Uncertainty: Heuristics and Biases* (Cambridge University Press, 1982) (discussing the role of heuristics and the bias they produce in human decision-making).

131 M. Hilbert, Toward a Synthesis of Cognitive Biases: How Noisy Information Processing Can Bias Human Decision Making (2012) 138 *Psychol. Bull.* 211, 212–13.

132 *Ibid.*, p. 213.

133 *Ibid.*

134 See N. Anderson, Why Google Keeps Your Data Forever, Tracks You with Ads, *Ars Technica* (March 8, 2010), http://arstechnica.com/tech-policy/2010/03/google-keeps-your-data-to-learn-from-good-guys-fight-off-bad-guys.

biases already warp what we believe merits recording, what questions are worth asking, and what answers are desirable. Although cognitive bias can assume many forms, relying on self-selected or self-reported data can easily replicate biases on a large scale, due to the simple human cognitive errors that statistics and probability aim to avoid.[135] And when algorithms train on imperfect data, or are designed by individuals who may be unconsciously biased in some manner, the results often reflect these biases, often to the detriment of certain groups.[136] Kate Crawford has described this as AI's "White Guy Problem," referring to the way in which bias becomes reified in the form of AI that draws upon biased data.[137] "Like all technologies before it," she writes, "artificial intelligence will reflect the values of its creators. So inclusivity matters – from who designs it to who sits on the company boards and which ethical perspectives are included. Otherwise, we risk constructing machine intelligence that mirrors a narrow and privileged vision of society, with its old, familiar biases and stereotypes."[138]

Yet studying these biases is key to understanding how to correct or how to qualify our results. Consider, for example, the fact that many individuals make attributional errors, which can affect explanations for a particular phenomenon. Confirmation biases, for example, often problematically lead people to cherry-pick data that appears to support their beliefs.[139] Our judgments and answers might also differ depending on how we frame or present a question (framing effect).[140] Likewise, our belief in our control over a dimension can also bias our assessment of that dimension (illusion of control bias).[141] We might inadequately assess our future selves and our needs, thoughts, and preferences (projection bias).[142] Sometimes we overestimate things like our social desirability; other times, we underestimate it.

And even more problematically, our ego often leads us to be overly confident in our judgments, which can make us loath to reconsider and recalibrate them at a later date.[143] For example, quantitative models often restrict self-reporting to a limited number of variables, thus simplifying the complexity of a person's lived experience to a set schema.[144] As a result, researchers might overlook alternate causes of a phenomena because of the variables they have excluded. They might label a feature that only correlates with another feature as a defining factor in causing the latter, leading to a classic host of errors associated with

[135] See also A. G. Greenwald and L. Hamilton Krieger, Implicit Bias: Scientific Foundations (2006) 94 *Calif. Law Rev.* 945, 947; A. G. Greenwald and M. R. Banaji, Implicit Social Cognition: Attitudes, Self-Esteem, and Stereotypes (1995) 102 *Pyschol. Rev.* 4 (both discussing the role of cognitive bias).
[136] Joanna Bryson, a computer scientist and co-author of one study, noted: "A lot of people are saying this is showing that AI is prejudiced. No. This is showing we're prejudiced and that AI is learning it." Devlin, above note 55.
[137] K. Crawford, Opinion, Artificial Intelligence's White Guy Problem, *New York Times* (June 25, 2016), www.nytimes.com/2016/06/26/opinion/sunday/artificial-intelligences-white-guy-problem.html (describing this problem).
[138] *Ibid.*
[139] J. Bambauer, Is Data Speech? (2014) 66 *Stan. Law Rev.* 57, 95 (citing D. Kahneman, *Thinking, Fast and Slow* (2011), pp. 80–1); D. M. Kahan, D. A. Hoffman, and D. Braman, "They Saw a Protest": Cognitive Illiberalism and the Speech-Conduct Distinction (2012) 64 *Stan. Law Rev.* 851, 883–4; R. S. Nickerson, Confirmation Bias: A Ubiquitous Phenomenon in Many Guises (1998) 2 *Rev. Gen. Psychol.* 175, 175.
[140] See A. Tversky and D. Kahneman, The Framing of Decisions and the Psychology of Choice (1981) 211 *Sci.* 453, 453.
[141] See S. C. Thompson, Illusions of Control: How We Overestimate Our Personal Influence (1999) 8 *Curr. Dir. Psychol. Sci.* 187.
[142] See G. Loewenstein, T. O'Donoghue, and M. Rabin, Projection Bias in Predicting Future Utility (2003) 118 *QJ Econ.* 1209.
[143] See generally G. Keren, Calibration and Probability Judgments: Conceptual and Methodological Issues (1991) 77 *Acta Psychol.* 217 (discussing calibration and reconciliation).
[144] Cf. G. Mann and C. O'Neil, Hiring Algorithms Are Not Neutral, *Harvard Business Review* (December 9, 2016), http://hbr.org/2016/12/hiring-algorithms-are-not-neutral.

attribution.[145] Restricting answers to conform with an observer's expectation, formalized in an algorithm, results in data further confirming those expectations.[146]

Stereotyping is a classic example of this problem.[147] *Princeton Review*, for instance, seemed to rely on stereotypes about Asians when it charged zip codes with large Asian populations higher prices for its test preparation.[148] Although Facebook preferred to describe its racial classifications as "Ethnic Affinity,"[149] it demonstrates the risk of racial or ethnic stereotyping in data aggregation because it allowed marketing executives to choose whether to include or exclude ethnic groups from seeing particular advertising.[150]

Other kinds of biases stem from subtler forms of stereotyping. Researchers have documented that individuals treat those who belong to their own social or ethnic group better than those who do not, so-called in-group bias.[151] Relatedly, we also recognize variation among members of our own group with greater subtlety than members of other groups, referred to as out-group bias.[152] Although we often think of ourselves as unpredictable and capable of change, we might characterize others as much more predictable, or the reverse (trait ascription bias).[153]

Predictive and Preference-Related Errors

Aside from attributional errors, individuals make qualitative and quantitative predictive errors, leading individuals to mistake correlation for causation. Sometimes we overestimate the probability of events happening based on what happened most recently,[154] view things in the past differently (hindsight bias),[155] or we may construct preferences based on the present moment rather than over time (current moment bias).[156] Other times, we rely heavily on our own beliefs, and then those beliefs gain more and more traction over time – especially if they

[145] Cf. E. E. Jones and V. A. Harris, The Attribution of Attitudes (1967) 3 *J. Exp. Psychol.* 1 (discussing role of opinions in attitudes).
[146] See generally R. Rosenthal, *Experimenter Effects in Behavioral Research* (Appleton-Century-Crofts, 1966).
[147] For a discussion of how data can "bake in" stereotypes, see R. Bhargava, The Algorithms Aren't Biased, We Are, *Medium* (January 3, 2018), https://medium.com/mit-media-lab/the-algorithms-arent-biased-we-are-a691f5f6f6f2.
[148] J. Angwin, T. Parris, Jr., and S. Mattu, When Algorithms Decide What You Pay, *ProPublica* (October 5, 2016), www.propublica.org/article/breaking-the-black-box-when-algorithms-decide-what-you-pay.
[149] See J. Angwin, S. Mattu, and T. Parris, Jr., Facebook Doesn't Tell Users Everything It Really Knows about Them, *ProPublica* (December 27, 2016), www.propublica.org/article/facebook-doesnt-tell-users-everything-it-really-knows-about-them.
[150] See L. Andrews, Opinion, Facebook Is Using You, *New York Times* (February 4, 2012), www.nytimes.com/2012/02/05/opinion/sunday/facebook-is-using-you.html.
[151] Cf. M. J. Bernstein, S. G. Young, and K. Hugenberg, The Cross-Category Effect: Mere Social Categorization Is Sufficient to Elicit an Own-Group Bias in Face Recognition (2007) 18 *Psychol. Sci.* 706 (discussing role of in-group bias).
[152] For a discussion of in-group and out-group bias, see S. A. Haslam, P. J. Oakes, J. C. Turner, and C. McGarty, Social Identity, Self-Categorization, and the Perceived Homogeneity of Ingroups and Outgroups: The Interaction between Social Motivation and Cognition, in R. M. Sorrentino and E. T. Higgins (eds.), *Handbook of Motivation & Cognition: The Interpersonal Context* (Guilford Press, 1996), Vol. 3, p. 182; D. M. Taylor and J. R. Doria, Self-Serving and Group-Serving Bias in Attribution (1981) 113 *J. Soc. Psychol.* 201.
[153] See D. Kammer, Differences in Trait Ascriptions to Self and Friend: Unconfounding Intensity from Variability (1982) 51 *Psychol. Rep.* 99.
[154] See A. Tversky and D. Kahneman, Availability: A Heuristic for Judging Frequency and Probability (1973) 5 *Cogn. Psychol.* 207. For more information on "recency bias" and its applicability to current issues, see C. Richards, Tomorrow's Market Probably Won't Look Anything Like Today, *New York Times* (February 13, 2012), https://bucks.blogs.nytimes.com/2012/02/13/tomorrows-market-probably-wont-look-anything-like-today.
[155] See, e.g., N. J. Roese and K. D. Vohs, Hindsight Bias (2012) 7 *Perspect. Psychol. Sci.* 411.
[156] See S. Frederick, G. Loewenstein, and T. O'Donoghue, Time Discounting and Time Preference: A Critical Review (2002) 40 *J. Econ. Lit.* 351, 352 (referencing "the preference for immediate utility over delayed utility").

are adopted by more and more people – leading to a bandwagon effect that obscures the actual events or the cause.[157]

An additional cluster of cognitive bias involves preference-related errors that can often involve incorrect or illogical estimations of value or quality.[158] For example, the data surrounding fake news suggests individuals' focus on familiar information that confirms their existing beliefs. Whether we already agree with or oppose a fact or viewpoint often involves whether it conforms with our expectations (selective perception).[159] Similarly, there is also the illusory truth effect, which leads us to often think things are true because we have heard them before, not because of any actual validity.[160]

At this point, it may seem as though the grab bag of biases just described may never find their way into an algorithmic function. Yet the truth is that many of them do replicate themselves in data, particularly self-reported data. As Andrea Roth has explained in the context of criminal law, just as humans exhibit hearsay dangers of insincerity, loss of memory, and misperception, the risk of machines replicating these errors can lead to the prospect of a falsehood by design, leading to the misanalysis of an event in court.[161] These dangers can be further magnified if we depend so excessively on AI (automation bias) that we will not be able to detect or correct error.[162] And this can also affect the design of the algorithm itself, including whether or not it can be redesigned to take these issues into account. For example, if studies demonstrate that resumes from European American-sounding names are 50 percent more likely to receive an interview invitation than if the name is African-American-sounding in nature, then an algorithm will demonstrate the same social predispositions unless specifically programmed to recognize this disparity.[163]

Prediction and Punishment: An Example

The dangers that flow from biased data are perhaps best illustrated by the prodigious work of other scholars exploring its role in the criminal justice system. Long before the tech industry fell in love with AI, criminal law scholars had been drawing on behavioral science to explore the costs and benefits of risk prediction.[164] Today, machine learning and big data play a powerful role in policing strategies.[165] Rebecca Wexler describes a host of other

[157] See R. Nadeau, E. Cloutier, and J. H. Guay, New Evidence about the Existence of a Bandwagon Effect in the Opinion Formation Process (1993) 14 *Int. Political Sci. Rev.* 203.

[158] For a discussion of the role of preference-related error, see R. E. Scott, Error and Rationality in Individual Decisionmaking: An Essay on the Relationship between Cognitive Illusions and the Management of Choices (1986) 59 *S. Cal. Law Rev.* 329.

[159] Cf. L. Hasher, D. Goldstein, and T. Toppino, *Frequency and the Conference of Referential Validity* (1977) 16 *J. Verbal Learning Verbal Behav.* 107 (outlining the illusory truth effect first). For other perspectives, however, see D. T. Miller and M. Ross, Self-Serving Biases in the Attribution of Causality: Fact or Fiction? (1975) 82 *Psychol. Bull.* 213 (questioning the role and basis of self-serving biases).

[160] G. Gigerenzer, External Validity of Laboratory Experiments: The Frequency-Validity Relationship (1984) 97 *Am. J. Psychol.* 185.

[161] Roth, above note 99, pp. 1977–8.

[162] See L. Bainbridge, Ironies of Automation (1983) 19 *Autom.* 775, 776–7 (discussing the difficulty of detecting errors in automatic systems).

[163] Devlin, above note 55.

[164] See M. M. Feeley and J. Simon, The New Penology: Notes on the Emerging Strategy of Corrections and Its Implications (1992) 30 *Criminology* 449, 452 (discussing implications of actuarial assessment in the criminal justice system).

[165] See generally A. Guthrie Ferguson, Predictive Policing and Reasonable Suspicion (2012) 62 *Emory Law J.* 259; E. Murphy, Databases, Doctrine, and Constitutional Criminal Procedure (2010) 37 *Fordham Urb. Law J.* 803; Rich, above note 75 (all describing use of these strategies and their implications).

technologies in the criminal law context that are already being used for forensic purposes and are considered to be proprietary – algorithms that generate candidates for latent fingerprint analysis; to search ballistic information databases for firearm and cartridge matches; and facial recognition technologies, to take just a few examples.[166]

Here, algorithms that are used to sentence defendants or parole prisoners raise issues of racial bias.[167] For example, in work discussing the Post Conviction Risk Assessment (PCRA) instrument, several scholars have shown some potential for disparate impact based on race,[168] gender,[169] and age.[170] A recent ProPublica report studied Correctional Offender Management Profiling for Alternative Sanctions (COMPAS), one of the most popular algorithms that is used to assess a defendant's risk of recidivism and subsequently sentence that defendant based on this risk.[171] Although the creator of the algorithm, Northpointe, developed COMPAS in the late 1990s[172] to assess risk factors in correctional populations and to provide decision

---

[166]   Wexler, above note 26, pp. 1347, 1363–4.

[167]   See E. Meiners, How "Risk Assessment" Tools Are Condemning People to Indefinite Imprisonment, *Truthout* (October 6, 2016), www.truth-out.org/news/item/37895-how-risk-assessment-tools-are-condemning-people-to-indefinite-imprisonment. Algorithms have pervaded the criminal justice system. Sonja Starr's excellent work has demonstrated how evidence-based sentencing (EBS) has raised substantial constitutional concerns. S. B. Starr, Evidence-Based Sentencing and the Scientific Rationalization of Discrimination (2014) 66 *Stan. Law Rev.* 803; S. B. Starr, The New Profiling: Why Punishing Based on Poverty and Identity Is Unconstitutional and Wrong (2015) 27 *Fed. Sentencing Report.* 229. For a good discussion of the Starr article and its implications, see L. Daniel, The Dangers of Evidence-Based Sentencing, *NYU: GovLab* (October 31, 2014), http://thegovlab.org/the-dangers-of-evidence-based-sentencing. Others have raised similar concerns. See, e.g., M. Hamilton, Risk-Needs Assessment: Constitutional and Ethical Challenges (2015) 52 *Am. Crim. Law Rev.* 231 (expressing constitutional concerns); R. Karl Hanson and D. Thornton, Improving Risk Assessments for Sex Offenders: A Comparison of Three Actuarial Scales (2000) 24 *Law Hum. Behav.* 119; B. E. Harcourt, Risk as a Proxy for Race: The Dangers of Risk Assessment (2015) 27 *Fed. Sentencing Report.* 237; I. Kerr, Prediction, Pre-emption, Presumption: The Path of Law after the Computational Turn, in M. Hildebrandt and K. de Vries (eds.), *Privacy, Due Process and the Computational Turn* (Routledge, 2013), p. 91; J. Monahan and J. L. Skeem, Risk Redux: The Resurgence of Risk Assessment in Criminal Sanctioning (2014) 26 *Fed. Sentencing Report.* 158; J. R. Nash, The Supreme Court and the Regulation of Risk in Criminal Law Enforcement (2012) 92 *BU Law Rev.* 171; J. C. Oleson, Risk in Sentencing: Constitutionally Suspect Variables and Evidence-Based Sentencing (2011) 64 *SMU Law Rev.* 1329; D. S. Sidhu, Moneyball Sentencing (2015) 56 *BC Law Rev.* 671; R. K. Warren, Evidence-Based Sentencing: The Application of Principles of Evidence-Based Practice to State Sentencing Practice and Policy (2009) 43 *USF Law Rev.* 585; D. Citron, (Un)Fairness of Risk Scores in Criminal Sentencing, Forbes (July 13, 2016), www.forbes.com/sites/daniellecitron/2016/07/13/unfairness-of-risk-scores-in-criminal-sentencing. Here, AI's "White Guy Problem" becomes reified in the form of algorithms, that risk drawing from biased data. Crawford, above note 137 (describing instances where algorithms misinterpret minority characteristics because of the majority viewpoint implicit in the data collected). Others have reached similar concerns regarding risk assessment. See, e.g., J. Monahan and J. L. Skeem, Risk Assessment in Criminal Sentencing (2016) 12 *Ann. Rev. Clinical Pyschol.* 489.

[168]   J. L. Skeem and C. T. Lowencamp, Risk, Race, and Recidivism: Predictive Bias and Disparate Impact (2016) 54 *Criminology* 680. For a longer discussion of methodology, see J. L. Johnson *et al.*, The Construction and Validation of the Federal Post Conviction Risk Assessment (PCRA) (2011) 75 *Fed. Probat.* 16.

[169]   See J. Skeem, J. Monahan, and C. Lowenkamp, Gender, Risk Assessment, and Sanctioning: The Cost of Treating Women Like Men (2016) 40 *Law Hum. Behav.* 580 (noting that the PCRA, while strongly predictive of arrests for both genders, tends to overestimate women's likelihood of recidivism).

[170]   See J. Skeem, J. Monahan, and C. Lowencamp, Age, Risk Assessment, and Sanctioning: Overestimating the Old, Underestimating the Young (2017) 41 *Law Hum. Behav.* 191 (finding that PCRA scores underestimated rates for younger offenders and overestimated rates of recidivism for older offenders).

[171]   J. Angwin, J. Larson, S. Mattu, and L. Kirchner, Machine Bias, *ProPublica* (May 23, 2016), www.propublica.org/article/machine-bias-risk-assessments-in-criminal-sentencing.

[172]   See P. M. Casey *et al.*, National Center for State Courts, Using Offender Risk and Needs Assessment Information at Sentencing app at 2 (2002) (Profiles of Assessment Instruments), www.ncsc.org/~/media/Files/PDF/Services%20and%20Experts/Areas%20of%20expertise/Sentencing%20Probation/RAN%20Appendix%20A.ashx; Northpointe, Practitioners Guide to COMPAS (2012), p. 2, www.northpointeinc.com/files/technical_documents/FieldGuide2_081412.pdf; see also Technology Advancing Practices, Division of Criminal Justice

support for case planning and management, rather than sentencing, it has now become a quite powerful tool in assessing four different kinds of risk: general recidivism, violent recidivism, noncompliance, and failure to appear.[173]

Northpointe has revealed that the COMPAS analysis considers a subject's basic demographic information,[174] criminal record, and whether anyone in the subject's family has ever been arrested among its 137 questions.[175] Northpointe will not disclose: (1) how the analysis for each of these types of risk varies; (2) all of the factors COMPAS considers; and (3) how it weighs those factors against each other.[176] Some of the questions ask if the subject's parents are divorced, if their parents are incarcerated, what the subject's high school grades were, if they got into a lot of fights in high school, if they have friends who use drugs, and if they have a phone at home.[177] The questions also include moral hypotheticals, like whether the subject agrees or disagrees that "[a] hungry person has a right to steal."[178] It also invites the person administering the questionnaire to speculate on whether or not the subject presents as a gang member.[179]

Although these questions do not necessarily in themselves reveal a bias – because Northpointe refuses to reveal how the algorithm weighs these answers – the only way to assess the algorithm's bias is through its results.[180] ProPublica studied the sentencing of 7,000 defendants in Florida's Broward County, obtaining their risk scores and comparing the predictions to how many were charged with new crimes over the next two years (the same benchmark relied upon by the algorithm).[181] When ProPublica tested the proprietary algorithm used to predict recidivism, it discovered that the scores were wrong almost 40 percent of the time, and gravely biased against black defendants, who were "falsely labeled future criminals at almost twice the rate of white defendants."[182] Out of every five people

---

Services, www.criminaljustice.ny.gov/opca/technology.htm ("COMPAS is unique because it was developed for, validated, and normed on a representative sample of offenders in New York State"); A. Liptak, Sent to Prison by a Software Program's Secret Algorithms, *New York Times* (May 1, 2017), www.nytimes.com/2017/05/01/us/politics/sent-to-prison-by-a-software-programs-secret-algorithms.html.

[173] Casey *et al.*, above note 172.

[174] See Algorithms in the Criminal Justice System, Electronic Privacy Information Center (November 11, 2017), https://epic.org/algorithmic-transparency/crim-justice/ ("COMPAS, created by the for-profit company Northpointe, assesses variables under five main areas: criminal involvement, relationships/lifestyles, personality/attitudes, family, and social exclusion"). Starr has pointed out that Northpointe has devised a separate set of questions for women. She discusses the constitutional implications of this differential usage by the state in Starr, above note 167, pp. 823–9, 823 n. 76.

[175] See Northpointe, Risk Assessment, http://assets.documentcloud.org/documents/2702103/Sample-Risk-Assessment-COMPAS-CORE.pdf.

[176] See Algorithms in the Criminal Justice System, above note 174 ("Northpointe has not shared how its calculations are made but has stated that the basis of its future crime formula includes factors such as education levels and whether a defendant has a job").

[177] *Ibid.*

[178] *Ibid.*

[179] J. Tashea, Risk-Assessment Algorithms Challenged in Bail, Sentencing, and Parole Decisions, *ABA J.* (March 1, 2017), www.abajournal.com/magazine/article/algorithm_bail_sentencing_parole; see also Northpointe, Practitioner's Guide to COMPAS Core (2015), § 5.1, http://epic.org/algorithmic-transparency/crim-justice/EPIC-16-06-23-WI-FOIA-201600805-COMPASPractionerGuide.pdf.

[180] Northpointe insists, "[t]here's no secret sauce to what we do; it's just not clearly understood . . ." Tashea, above note 179.

[181] Angwin *et al.*, above note 171, p. 1 (explaining methodology and results); see also Angwin and Larson, above note 111 (discussing implications of findings).

[182] J. Angwin, Opinion, Make Algorithms Accountable, *New York Times* (August 1, 2016), www.nytimes.com/2016/08/01/opinion/make-algorithms-accountable.html (arguing for greater transparency and accountability); see also Angwin *et al.*, above note 171. ProPublica found that roughly 60 percent of those classified as higher risk went on to commit future crimes (the same rate for both black and white defendants). Yet when it looked at the 40 percent of predictions that were incorrect, it found that "[b]lack defendants were twice as likely to be rated as higher risk

Northpointe predicted would commit another violent crime, the study found that only one actually did.[183] Notably, "[t]he formula was particularly likely to falsely flag black defendants as future criminals, wrongly labeling them this way at almost twice the rate as white defendants."[184]

Scores that algorithms like COMPAS produce should comprise only one part of a judge's or parole board's decision. COMPAS, for example, was created not for its applicability in sentencing decisions, but actually to assist probation officers in selecting particular types of treatment in probation decisions.[185] However, it is hard not to imagine that these scores will play an overly significant role in sentencing and ultimately produce harsher sentences for black defendants.

Despite the problems that the ProPublica study documented, the Wisconsin Supreme Court upheld the use of COMPAS in sentencing in July 2016.[186] In 2013, Eric Loomis was charged with crimes related to a drive-by shooting in La Crosse, Wisconsin.[187] He pleaded no contest to a vehicle charge and guilty to eluding an officer.[188] The court ordered a pre-sentencing investigation, including a COMPAS risk assessment report that labeled Loomis a high risk for pre-trial recidivism risk, general recidivism risk, and violent recidivism risk.[189] The judge sentenced him to eleven years, explicitly citing the high score that COMPAS had assigned to him.[190] Loomis appealed the sentence on due process grounds.[191]

The Wisconsin Supreme Court found that the sentence and the circuit court's reliance on COMPAS did not violate Loomis's rights because he knew the factors that COMPAS considered. The court pointed out that "Northpointe's 2015 Practitioner's Guide to COMPAS explains that the risk scores are based largely on static information (criminal history), with limited use of some dynamic variables (i.e. criminal associates, substance abuse)."[192] "[T]o the extent that Loomis's risk assessment is based upon his answers to questions and publicly available data about his criminal history," the court found that Loomis could verify the accuracy of his answers.[193] The court, however, never addressed that Loomis could not examine the extent those answers had in his risk score because Northpointe guards that information as a trade secret.[194] Northpointe's guide might offer a tidy explanation for its algorithm and the psychological and sociological theories

---

but not re-offend. And white defendants were twice as likely to be charged with new crimes after being classed as lower risk." J. Angwin and J. Larson, ProPublica Responds to Company's Critique of Machine Bias Story, *ProPublica* (July 29, 2016), www.propublica.org/article/propublica-responds-to-companys-critique-of-machine-bias-story.

[183] Angwin *et al.*, above note 171, p. 1 (noting that "[o]nly 20 percent of the people predicted to commit violent crimes actually went on to do so").

[184] Angwin *et al.*, above note 171.

[185] Algorithms in the Criminal Justice System, above note 174.

[186] *State* v. *Loomis*, 881 NW.2d 749, 772 (Wis. 2016).

[187] See *ibid.* at 754.

[188] *Ibid.* at 772.

[189] *Ibid.* at 754–5.

[190] *Ibid.* at 755, 756 n. 18.

[191] *Ibid.* at 757; see also M. Smith, In Wisconsin, a Backlash against Using Data to Foretell Defendants' Futures, *New York Times* (June 22, 2016), www.nytimes.com/2016/06/23/us/backlash-in-wisconsin-against-using-data-to-foretell-defendants-futures.html. Loomis argued the sentencing decision violated his right to due process because: (1) Northpointe would not reveal the source code so its validity could not be tested; (2) the judge relied on COMPAS's generalized risk based on defendants like Loomis, rather than considering him as an individual; and (3) the tool improperly considers gender in determining risk. *Loomis*, above note 186, at 757.

[192] *Loomis*, above note 186, at 761.

[193] *Ibid.*

[194] See *ibid.* ("[Northpointe] does not disclose how the risk scores are determined or how the factors are weighed").

underpinning it. There is, however, no way to check that COMPAS actually carries out those theories in a statistically sound and logical manner.

Other courts have also dealt with similar questions. In *Malenchik v. State*, the Indiana Supreme Court upheld the use of risk assessment scores, reasoning that the scores were a statistically valid means to forecast recidivism, and could be used to supplement a judge's evaluation when used in conjunction with other sentencing evidence to determine an individualized calculation.[195] In contrast, the Court of Appeals of Indiana in *Rhodes v. State* had expressed concern that the use of a standardized scoring model undercut the trial court's responsibility to craft an individualized sentence.[196]

Recently, a bill introduced in Congress aimed to mandate the procedural use of algorithms to assess the risk of recidivism in parole decisions at federal prisons.[197] As proponents of their predictive utility suggest, these characteristics do not exist in a vacuum.[198] Other criminal protocols, like the extreme vetting protocols and other methods of database screening developed in the wake of Trump's Executive Orders on the Muslim Ban, have led one scholar, Margaret Hu, to refer to them as "a system of Algorithmic Jim Crow."[199]

THE AFTERLIFE OF THE ALGORITHM

The previous part outlined some of the ways in which data can be flawed and lead to skewed results due to forms of statistical and cognitive bias. These results can disadvantage a variety of different populations, some of whom might fall within legally protected categories, some of whom do not. While the previous set of concerns stemmed from the inputs that algorithms rely upon and some of their limitations, this part focuses instead on the real-life effects that AI can produce, drawing upon examples from private employment, advertising, and price discrimination.[200]

In a now seminal account, Batya Friedman and Helen Nissenbaum described three central types of bias in computer systems.[201] The first type, also discussed in the previous part, involved what they described as "pre-existing bias," which can reflect the personal biases of individuals who play a significant role in designing the system, either the client or the system designer.[202] This type of bias, they explain, can either be explicit or implicit, and can enter into a system, even despite the best of intentions.[203] A second type of bias, they explain, stems from technical bias, which could include limitations in the hardware, software, or peripherals; "the process of ascribing social meaning to algorithms developed out of context"; or, as they eloquently describe, "when we quantify the qualitative, discretize the continuous, or

---

[195] 928 NE.2d 564, 575 (Ind. 2010).

[196] 896 NE.2d 1193, 1195 (Ind. Ct. App. 2008), *disapproved of by Malenchik*, 928 NE.2d at 573.

[197] Sentencing Reform and Corrections Act of 2015, S. 2123, 114th Cong. (2015). The bill has since advanced a later session, but its fate remains unclear. See E. Watkins, Rebuffing Sessions, Senators Advance Criminal Justice Reform Bill, *CNN* (February 15, 2018), www.cnn.com/2018/02/15/politics/sentencing-prison-reform-senate-grassley-sessions/index.html.

[198] S. Benjamin and G. A. Thomas, Congress Must Pass the Sentencing Reform and Corrections Act of 2015, *Hill* (February 3, 2016), http://thehill.com/opinion/op-ed/268129-congress-must-pass-the-sentencing-reform-and-corrections-act-of-2015 (arguing that our system of mass incarceration has serious social, economic, and political effects on communities, and arguing for reform).

[199] M. Hu, Algorithmic Jim Crow (2017) 86 *Fordham Law Rev.* 633, 633.

[200] See generally Raymond *et al.*, above note 48 (discussing supervised and unsupervised forms of learning).

[201] See B. Friedman and H. Nissenbaum, Bias in Computer Systems (1996) 14 *ACM Trans. Inf. Syst.* 330.

[202] *Ibid.*, p. 333.

[203] *Ibid.*, p. 334.

formalize the nonformal."[204] But a third type of bias, what they call "emergent bias," is harder to detect because it appears only after the design has been completed.[205] Consider an example:

> Using the example of an automated airline reservation system, envision a hypothetical system designed for a group of airlines all of whom serve national routes. Consider what might occur if that system was extended to include international airlines. A flight-ranking algorithm that favors on-line flights when applied in the original context with national airlines leads to no systematic unfairness. However, in the new context with international airlines, the automated system would place these airlines at a disadvantage and, thus, comprise a case of emergent bias.[206]

While Friedman and Nissenbaum may not have noted it at the time, their notion of emergent bias almost perfectly captures the risks inherent in machine learning, where pre-existing biases can merge with pre-existing and technical biases, producing dynamic results that can disadvantage particular groups.

This risk is particularly pronounced when we consider the degree to which decisions in private industry rule our everyday lives. For example, algorithmic researchers have reported that the ability to draw fine-grained distinctions between individuals through collective risk management strategies can lead to adverse selection among populations and individuals within pooled areas of resources, like insurance.[207] In the case of health insurance, these distinctions may lead to higher premiums through price discrimination strategies.[208] While these strategies have long been in existence, the added reliance on machine learning exacerbates the risk of incomplete or inaccurate judgments and predictions based on the fallibility of the data it relies upon.

At least one author, Cathy O'Neil, has argued that algorithms have a particular disparate impact on the poor because wealthier individuals are more likely to benefit from personal input.[209] "A white-shoe law firm or an exclusive prep school will lean far more on recommendations and face-to-face interviews than will a fast-food chain or cash-strapped urban school district."[210] "The privileged," she writes, "are processed more by people, the masses by machines."[211]

To further illustrate, consider O'Neil's story of a young man named Kyle Behm.[212] When he was a college student, Behm took some time off from school to seek treatment for bipolar disorder. When he returned to another school to finish his degree, he discovered that he kept being turned down, over and over again for job interviews. Why? He discovered that his inability to get an interview stemmed from some answers to a personality test that had been administered prior to his interviews that graded him for a series of social considerations – agreeableness, conscientiousness, neuroticism, and

[204] *Ibid.*, p. 335.
[205] *Ibid.*, p. 336.
[206] *Ibid.*
[207] See Crawford and Whittaker, above note 63, p. 7.
[208] See *ibid.*
[209] O'Neil, above note 18, p. 8.
[210] *Ibid.*
[211] *Ibid.*; see also V. Eubanks, *Automating Inequality: How High-Tech Tools Profile, Police, and Punish the Poor* (St. Martin's Press, 2018); R. Foroohar, This Mathematician Says Big Data Is Causing a "Silent Financial Crisis," *Time* (August 29, 2016), http://time.com/4471451/cathy-oneil-math-destruction (quoting O'Neil); Want to Predict the Future of Surveillance? Ask Poor Communities, *American Prospect* (January 15, 2014), http://prospect.org/article/want-predict-future-surveillance-ask-poor-communities.
[212] C. O'Neil, How Algorithms Rule Our Working Lives, *The Guardian* (September 1, 2016), www.theguardian.com/science/2016/sep/01/how-algorithms-rule-our-working-lives.

other qualities.[213] As Kyle's father, a lawyer, soon discovered, a number of corporations rely on the use of those tests, potentially running afoul of the Americans with Disabilities Act, which protects individuals with mental disabilities.[214]

These issues can also be exacerbated by the failure to recalibrate models, which can lead to dangerously outdated results and predictions perpetuating the continued social construction of stereotypes. O'Neil usefully contrasts this situation to how data is used by high-profile sports teams, who are constantly recalibrating and redrawing their models to ensure accuracy. For example, she explains, if the Los Angeles Lakers do not select a player because the player's data suggests that he will not be a star at scoring, and then he subsequently surpasses their expectations, the Lakers can return to their model to see how it might be improved. But in contrast, consider someone like Kyle Behm. If he finds a job somewhere and becomes a stellar employee, it is unlikely that any of the corporations that rejected him will ever know or care to return to recalibrate their model. The reason? The stakes, according to O'Neil. Individuals on basketball teams are potentially worth millions; minimum-wage employees, to the corporation making these decisions, are not worth nearly as much.[215] Unless something goes completely amiss in the workplace, the company has little reason to recalibrate its model, since the model is "doing its job – even if it misses out on potential stars."[216] "The company may be satisfied with the status quo," O'Neil explains, "but the victims of its automatic systems suffer."[217]

Surveillance, Targeting, and Stereotyping

Consider how models interface with consumers through behavioral targeting of advertising. Here, machine-learning algorithms learn from existing inputs and then limit the range of options a consumer sees. Since websites often rely on predictive algorithms to analyze people's online activities – web surfing, online purchases, social media activities, public records, store loyalty programs, and the like – they can create profiles based on user behavior, and predict a host of identity characteristics that marketers can then use to decide the listings that a user sees online.[218] Or their models might assign lower rankings to individuals based on their race or gender, rendering them less relevant to potential employers, limiting the scope of opportunities that they see online.[219] Behavioral marketing has advanced to the point where advertisers can discover what motivates a given consumer and dynamically construct a particularized pitch based on the person's cognitive style (noting, for example, whether a person is impulsive or deliberative – a phenomenon that feeds into what Ryan Calo and others call "persuasion profiling").[220]

As the ACLU has argued, this sort of behavioral targeting can lead to actions that violate basic civil rights protections under the Fair Housing Act or Title VII of the Civil Rights Act.[221] The recent lawsuit, discussed in the Introduction, is but one example of these possibilities. But

---

[213]   *Ibid.*
[214]   *Ibid.*
[215]   *Ibid.*
[216]   *Ibid.*
[217]   *Ibid.*
[218]   See E. Bhandari and R. Goodman, ACLU Challenges Computer Crimes Law that Is Thwarting Research on Discrimination Online, *ACLU: Free Future* (June 29, 2016), www.aclu.org/blog/free-future/aclu-challenges-computer-crimes-law-thwarting-research-discrimination-online.
[219]   See *ibid.*
[220]   R. Calo, Digital Market Manipulation (2014) 82 *Geo. Wash. Law Rev.* 995, 1017; cf. A. Datta, J. Makagon, D. K. Mulligan, *et al.*, Discrimination in Online Advertising: A Multidisciplinary Inquiry (2018) 81 *Proc. Mach. Learn. Res.* 1 (exploring interaction between tailored marketing and discrimination).
[221]   Bhandari and Goodman, above note 218.

far more often, these instances reflect a kind of bias that, while demonstrative of structural discrimination, is also difficult for the law to plainly address. For instance, researchers at Carnegie Mellon University found that Google tends to show women ads for lower-paying jobs.[222] Although the researchers never conclusively proved why, they speculated that Google's algorithms learned from the existing inequalities in society: women are more accustomed to and associated with lower-paying work, thus they tend to click on ads for lower-paying jobs.[223] The machine-learning algorithm extrapolated from that behavior and continued the pattern.[224]

In another illustrative experiment, an ad for STEM jobs that was supposed to be gender-neutral in delivery appeared 20 percent more times to men than to women.[225] The reason, the researchers postulated, was not because men were more likely to click onto the ad (women actually were more likely to click and view the ad).[226] Rather, women aged 25 to 34 were the most valued, and hence, most expensive demographic to which to display ads.[227] Here, even when there is no intent to discriminate against viewers, market principles that disproportionally value female audiences can lead to a world where AI facilitates a disparate impact on particular groups.

Scholar Karen Yeung has usefully argued that big data's harvesting of personal digital data is particularly troubling because of the ways in which advertisers use that data to nudge the user to reach decisions that accord with their commercial goals.[228] According to Richard Thaler and Cass Sunstein, a nudge is "any aspect of choice architecture that alters people's behavior in a predictable way without forbidding any options or significantly changing their economic incentives."[229] These modes of personalization may seem unobtrusive and subtle, but they are also incredibly powerful at the same time, echoes Yeung.[230] Since so much decision-making often occurs subconsciously, passively, and unreflectively – instead of through conscious deliberation – scholars have documented how even subtle changes can have a dramatic influence on decision-making behavior.[231] As Ryan Calo has similarly argued, these practices can rise to the level of market manipulation, because they essentially remake the consumer into what he describes as a "mediated consumer," who "approaches the marketplace through technology designed by someone else."[232]

[222] A. Datta, M. C. Tschantz, and A. Datta, Automated Experiments on Ad Privacy Settings: A Tale of Opacity, Choice, and Discrimination, 2015 Proceedings on Privacy Enhancing Technology, p. 92.

[223] *Ibid.*, pp. 92, 105 ("Even if we could, the discrimination might have resulted unintentionally from algorithms optimizing click-through rates or other metrics free of bigotry. Given the pervasive structural nature of gender discrimination in society at large, blaming one party may ignore context and correlations that make avoiding such discrimination difficult"); see also Gourarie, above note 43; S. Gibbs, Women Less Likely to Be Shown Ads for High-Paid Jobs on Google, Study Shows, *The Guardian* (July 8, 2015), www.theguardian.com/technology/2015/jul/08/women-less-likely-ads-high-paid-jobs-google-study (discussing the study).

[224] Datta *et al.*, above note 222; Gourarie, above note 43 (discussing the study).

[225] A. Lambrecht and C. Tucker, Algorithmic Bias? An Empirical Study into Apparent Gender-Based Discrimination in the Display of STEM Career Ads (2019) 65 *Manag. Sci.* 2966 (on file with author).

[226] *Ibid.*, p. 3.

[227] *Ibid.*, pp. 26–7.

[228] See K. Yeung, "Hypernudge": Big Data as a Mode of Regulation by Design (2017) 20 *Inf. Comm. Soc.* 118 (exploring the role of big data in nudging); see also R. H. Thaler and C. R. Sunstein, *Nudge: Improving Decisions About Health, Wealth, and Happiness* (Penguin, 2008).

[229] See Yeung, above note 228, p. 120 (quoting Thaler and Sunstein, above note 228, p. 6).

[230] *Ibid.*, p. 119.

[231] *Ibid.*, p. 120. "Nudges" can operate through automated decision-making techniques that might act dynamically in the following ways: (1) by refining an individual's choice environment based on his or her data profile; (2) by providing feedback to the choice architect, to be stored and repurposed; and (3) by monitoring and refining an individual's choice environment given broader population-wide trends gleaned from data surveillance and analysis. *Ibid.*, p. 122.

[232] Calo, above note 220, p. 1002.

Another type of issue stems from situations where particular searches correlate with other characteristics, leading to results that inaccurately suggest causal associations between a protected category and an undesirable activity. For example, Harvard researcher Latanya Sweeney found disparities in the ads Google showed alongside searches for the names Latanya and Latisha, which triggered ads for arrest records, while the names Kristen and Jill did not (even when there were arrest records associated with the names). Over 2,000 names that were more likely to be associated with African-American or white individuals bore out this pattern.[233] Why?[234] One possible explanation, she posited, is that people may be more likely to click on an ad for an arrest record after searching for a black name, perhaps to confirm their biases, making ads for arrest records more likely to appear for searches of those names in the future.[235] Here, the results flow "not from the racist intentions of the ... algorithms' programmers, but from the algorithms' natural operation in the real world."[236]

As Frank Pasquale observed, the programmer might construe her role as largely agnostic, casting the search engine as a sort of "cultural voting machine, merely registering, rather than creating, perceptions."[237] However, these results, which stem from incomplete inputs in data, can produce skewed real-life perceptions of reality. For example, only 11 percent of the top 100 "CEO" image search results from Google included women, even though 27 percent of CEOs in the United States are women.[238] These biased results might, at first glance, seem minor. However, over time, they can congeal into lasting, inaccurate predictions of what reality looks like, affecting "everything from personal preconceptions to hiring practices."[239] In other words, there is a risk of creating further feedback loops by presenting stereotypical information to the public without any accompanying critique. Jeremy Kun describes another, even more troubling, example. Insert "transgenders are" in Google, he suggests.[240] The results are an astonishing list of hateful descriptions – described as "freaks," "gross," "sick," "wrong," and "crazy."[241] But that is what AI reveals – a trend toward hateful autocompletes. Those autocompletes can actually wind up feeding into stereotypes, leading to further examples of biased social constructions as a result of incomplete information.

Beyond issues of discrimination, algorithms can raise privacy concerns as well. Consider the famous example of the Target algorithm that predicted a woman's pregnancy even before her family knew that she was pregnant, and then used this knowledge for marketing purposes.[242] As Kate Crawford and Jason Schultz have observed, Target "did not collect the

[233] L. Sweeney, Discrimination in Online Ad Delivery (2013) 11 *Comms. ACM* 44, 46–7, 50–1.
[234] *Ibid.*, p. 52.
[235] *Ibid.*
[236] A. Chander, The Racist Algorithm? (2017) 115 *Mich. Law Rev.* 1023, 1037.
[237] *Ibid.* (quoting Pasquale, above note 18, p. 39).
[238] M. Kay, C. Matuszek, and S. A. Munson, Unequal Representation and Gender Stereotypes in Image Search Results for Occupations, in CHI 2015: Proceedings of the 33rd Annual CHI Conference on Human Factors in Computing Systems (2015), p. 3819; C. Albanesius, When You Google Image Search "CEO," the First Woman Is ..., *PC Magazine* (April 12, 2015), www.pcmag.com/article2/0,2817,2481270,00.asp (citing report); see also T. C. Sottek, Google Search Thinks the Most Important Female CEO Is Barbie, *Verge* (April 9, 2015), www.theverge.com/tldr/2015/4/9/8378745/i-see-white-people (observing that the first woman appearing in a google image search for CEO is an image of a Barbie doll).
[239] Albanesius, above note 238.
[240] Kun, above note 16. Also see S. Noble, *Algorithms of Oppression: How Search Engines Reinforce Racism* (New York University Press, 2018), discussing a similar result when inputting "black girls." S. Noble, Google Has a Striking History of Bias against Black Girls, *Time* (March 26, 2018), http://time.com/5209144/google-search-engine-algorithm-bias-racism.
[241] Kun, above note 16.
[242] See K. Crawford and J. Schultz, Big Data and Due Process: Toward a Framework to Redress Predictive Privacy Harms (2014) 55 *BC Law Rev.* 93, 94.

information from any first or third party," and therefore was not required to notify its customers that it was using this information in the same way that other collection protocols require.[243] In such contexts, they point out that the concept of differential privacy is severely limited, since it is "impossible" to tell when or where to assemble such protections around the inputs provided by the end-user.[244] As Crawford and Schultz ask, "[w]hen a pregnant teenager is shopping for vitamins, could she predict that any particular visit or purchase would trigger a retailer's algorithms to flag her as a pregnant customer? And at what point would it have been appropriate to give notice and request her consent?"[245]

Price Discrimination and Inequality

In 2012, an Atlanta man returned from his honeymoon to find that his credit limit had been lowered from $10,800 to $3,800. He had not defaulted on any debts. Nothing in his credit report had changed. American Express cited aggregate data. A letter from the company told him: "Other customers who have used their card at establishments where you recently shopped have a poor repayment history with American Express."[246] Similarly, one credit card company settled Federal Trade Commission (FTC) allegations that it failed to disclose its practice of rating consumers as having a greater credit risk "because they used their cards to pay for marriage counseling, therapy, or tire-repair services," based on its experiences with other consumers and their repayment histories.[247]

As these examples suggest, the intersection of machine learning and automated decision-making can make particular groups materially worse off, by charging higher prices or interest rates, or excluding them entirely. Unlike false information on a credit report, no federal law allows consumers to challenge the generalizations that algorithms make about them based on other data from social media or search engines.[248]

Yet quantitative models can also help companies price-discriminate against certain consumers, charging more for the same goods. In the case of health insurance, and a host of other industries, this practice may lead to higher premiums based on potentially irrelevant characteristics.[249] With the help of machine learning, companies have begun to price-discriminate in the third degree, using features besides ability and willingness to set prices.[250] Indeed, if the algorithm is poorly written and the data is biased, these factors can become

---

243 *Ibid.*, p. 98.
244 *Ibid.*, p. 99.
245 *Ibid.*
246 Andrews, above note 150.
247 Citron and Pasquale, above note 27, p. 4; Stipulated Order for Permanent Injunction and Other Equitable Relief, *FTC v. CompuCredit Corp.*, No. 1:08-CV-1976-BBM-RGV, 2008 WL 8762850 (ND Ga. December 19, 2008), www.ftc.gov/sites/default/files/documents/cases/2008/12/081219compucreditstiporder.pdf.
248 See, e.g., Citron and Pasquale, above note 27, pp. 4–5; see also National Consumer Law Center, Comments to the Federal Trade Commission, Big Data: A Tool for Inclusion or Exclusion? Workshop, Project No. P145406 (August 15, 2014), www.ftc.gov/system/files/documents/public_comments/2014/08/00018-92374.pdf (citing P. Yu, J. McLaughlin, M. Levy, and National Consumer Law Center, *Big Data: A Big Disappointment for Scoring Consumer Credit Risk* (National Consumer Law Center, 2014)).
249 See Crawford and Whittaker, above note 63, pp. 6–7. See Executive Office of the President, Big Data and Differential Pricing (2015), p. 17, http://obamawhitehouse.archives.gov/sites/default/files/whitehouse_files/docs/Big_Data_Report_Nonembargo_v2.pdf ("If price-sensitive customers also tend to be less experienced, or less knowledgeable about potential pitfalls, they might more readily accept offers that appear fine on the surface but are actually full of hidden charges"). See generally D. Bergemann *et al.*, The Limits of Price Discrimination (2015) 105 *Am. Econ. Rev.* 921 (analyzing price discrimination and its implications).
250 See Bergemann, above note 249, pp. 926–7.

a proxy for elasticity of demand. When elasticity of demand is low, monopolies flourish, raise prices for all consumers, and exclude less affluent consumers from the market.[251]

The Internet is already rife with examples of algorithms artificially inflating prices in the name of optimization. Amazon's pricing algorithm once set the price of Peter Lawrence's book *The Making of a Fly* at $23,698,655.93 for all consumers.[252] The inefficiency of that price is obvious. However, other companies have muddied the line between price discrimination and price optimization in much subtler and ultimately effective ways, raising concerns that optimization enables insurers to raise premiums on customers who may not aggressively shop around for better rates (or are perceived to avoid doing so).[253] In one example involving auto insurance, consumers who were likely to compare prices could receive up to a 90 percent discount, while others could see their premiums increase by up to 800 percent.[254] In another example of this trend, Orbitz showed more expensive hotels to Mac users, apparently believing that the operating system was a proxy for affluence.[255] Orbitz showed less expensive hotels to users on mobile devices, which minority groups tend to use at higher rates.[256]

Many of these issues, as I have suggested, escape legal detection because they are not clearly illegal. And even if they were, the opacity of algorithmic design and decision-making makes many of these issues difficult to detect. Moreover, the absence of privacy protections further exacerbates the problem. For example, one study of over 80,000 health-related web pages discovered that over 90 percent of those sites shared user information with outside third parties.[257] Visitors to the Centers for Disease Control sites, for example, had their browsing information shared with Google, Facebook, Pinterest, and Twitter, often without their

---

[251] See generally A. Ezrachi and M. E. Stucke, *Virtual Competition: The Promise and Perils of the Algorithm-Driven Economy* (Harvard University Press, 2016) (exploring implications of algorithms for market competition).

[252] M. Eisen, Amazon's $23,698,655.93 Book about Flies, it is NOT junk (April 22, 2011), www.michaeleisen.org /blog/?p=358.

[253] J. Angwin, J. Larson, L. Kirchner, and S. Mattu, Minority Neighborhoods Pay Higher Car Insurance Premiums than White Areas with the Same Risk, *ProPublica* (April 5, 2017), www.propublica.org/article/minority-neighborhoods-higher-car-insurance-premiums-white-areas-same-risk.

[254] Watchdog: Allstate Auto Insurance Pricing Scheme Is Unfair, *AOL* (December 16, 2014), www.aol.com/article/ finance/2014/12/16/allstate-auto-insurance-pricing-scheme-unfair/21117081. In 2015, Consumer Reports detailed a number of factors used by insurance companies, including "price optimization" strategies that relied on personal data and statistical models to predict a person's likelihood to comparison shop. F. Kunkle, Auto Insurance Rates Have Skyrocketed – and in Ways that Are Wildly Unfair, *Washington Post* (February 7, 2018), www.washingtonpost.com/news/tripping/wp/2018/02/07/auto-insurance-rates-have-skyrocketed-and-in-ways-that -are-wildly-unfair/?noredirect=on&utm_term=.040bec7b1522 (mentioning the 2015 report and its impact on auto insurance); cf. T. Samilton, Being a Loyal Auto Insurance Customer Can Cost You, *NPR* (May 8, 2015), www.npr.org/2015/05/08/403598235/being-a-loyal-auto-insurance-customer-can-cost-you. Courts and insurance regulators in a number of states have begun to crack down on the use of extraneous factors in insurance pricing. See *Stevenson v. Allstate Ins. Co.*, No. 15-CV-04788-YGR, 2016 WL 1056137, at *2 (ND Cal. March 17, 2016) ("Earnix software allows Allstate to account for ED [elasticity of demand] in its rating factors submitted for approval, without disclosing to [the California Department of Insurance] that it is considering ED when compiling its class plan" (citation omitted)).

[255] Orbitz claimed that the algorithm responded to the fact that Mac users already spent as much as 30 percent more a night on hotels before Orbitz implemented the pricing algorithm. D. Mattioli, On Orbitz, Mac Users Steered to Pricier Hotels, *Wall Street Journal* (August 23, 2012), www.wsj.com/articles/SB10001424052702304458604577 488822667325882.

[256] See J. Valentino-DeVries, J. Singer-Vine, and A. Soltani, Websites Vary Prices, Deals Based on Users' Information, *Wall Street Journal* (December 24, 2012), www.wsj.com/articles/SB10001424127887323777204578189391813881534.

[257] T. Libert, Health Privacy Online: Patients at Risk, in S. P. Gangadharan, V. Eubanks, and S. Barocas (eds.), Open Technology Institute and New America, Data and Discrimination: Collected Essays (2014), pp. 11, 12, http://na-production.s3.amazonaws.com/documents/data-and-discrimination.pdf.

knowledge or consent, and often outside of the reach of privacy statutes like the Health Insurance Portability and Accountability Act.[258]

In such cases, even if advertisers do not know the name or identity of the person searching for information, the data can still be aggregated to "paint a revealing portrait" of the person.[259] For example, Facebook could link health-related web browsing to an identifiable person, leading to some measurable risk that such information could be misused by other companies who seek to profit from it.[260] Expert Tim Libert offers the example of data broker MedBase200, which sold lists of individuals under such categories as "rape sufferers," "domestic abuse victims," or "HIV/AIDS patients."[261] While it is unclear how MedBase200 obtained such data, the risk of data brokers purchasing such information and misusing it is apparent.[262] These situations raise the risks of user identification, price discrimination, or other forms of mistreatment. Given that online advertisers often categorize information into target and non-target users, there is a significant risk that a user may be discriminated against based on his or her web-browsing activities.[263] Libert offers the observation that, since over 60 percent of bankruptcies are medically related, companies could potentially target certain individuals for more favorable discounts than those who fall into non-target categories in the absence of smarter, and more specific regulation.[264]

The *New York Times* wrote about a crop of banking start-ups that used inferences from big data to identify populations that might be ignored by traditional lenders – creditworthy, but not necessarily with the assets to make a large down-payment on a mortgage.[265] The company used factors like whether applicants type in ALL CAPS, as well as how much time they spent reading terms and conditions, to determine creditworthiness.[266] While we might have suspicions about the habits of people who write in ALL CAPS or blithely ignore terms and conditions,[267] there is no empirical reason to believe they are less creditworthy than their less emphatic counterparts. Another company used a large dataset to determine that "people who fill out online job applications using browsers that did not come with the computer ... but had to be deliberately installed (like Firefox or Google's Chrome) perform better and change jobs less often."[268]

RETHINKING CIVIL RIGHTS THROUGH PRIVATE ACCOUNTABILITY

These applications of data analytics require us to think broadly about how to address inequality and discrimination in a digital age. But some of this requires a fundamental rethinking of civil rights protections. Lawyers, accustomed to constitutional concepts like due process and

[258]   *Ibid.*, pp. 12–13.
[259]   *Ibid.*, p. 13.
[260]   *Ibid.*
[261]   *Ibid.*
[262]   *Ibid.*
[263]   See *ibid.*, p. 14.
[264]   *Ibid.*
[265]   See S. Lohr, Banking Start-Ups Adopt New Tools for Lending, *New York Times* (January 18, 2015), www
        .nytimes.com/2015/01/19/technology/banking-start-ups-adopt-new-tools-for-lending.html.
[266]   *Ibid.*
[267]   One study, however, suggests that 98 percent of people do not closely read all terms of service. See S. Vedantam,
        Do You Read Terms of Service Contracts? Not Many Do, Research Shows, *NPR* (August 23, 2016), www.npr.org
        /2016/08/23/491024846/do-you-read-terms-of-service-contracts-not-many-do-research-shows.
[268]   Robot Recruiters: How Software Helps Firms Hire Workers More Efficiently, *Economist* (April 6, 2013), www
        .economist.com/news/business/21575820-how-software-helps-firms-hire-workers-more-efficiently-robot-
        recruiters.

privacy, struggle to map these concepts onto private corporations' novel practices. Some of these practices can interface with public institutions, like traditional law enforcement, creating a greater set of possibilities for accountability through the application of constitutional principles. Others can bring private causes of action. Stretching these lofty protections beyond the state into the private sphere, however, can present challenges.[269]

But there is another, deeper reason for why this age of machine learning is so transformative, and that is because it forces us to re-evaluate our entire spectrum of civil rights in the process. Like the civil rights era that came before it, AI is implicated within a vast array of decisions that come not from the government, but from the private sector, even if many of them implicate civil rights in the process. For example, the right to be considered for employment, free from consideration of one's disability – the right at issue in the Kyle Behm case just discussed – directly correlates to the right to work. Similarly, the right to an education, the right to vote, the right to make contracts, the right to travel, the right to get insurance, and the right to receive information, among others, are all at issue when an algorithm makes its (private) decisions about who does and who does not receive the entitlement and the conditions attached to it. Those decisions are not always subject to public oversight. And even more problematically, they may be shielded from view, due to trade secrecy and systemic opacity.

The Obama-era White House was far from blind to the risks and benefits of big data. It concluded that "big data analytics have the potential to eclipse longstanding civil rights protections in how personal information is used in housing, credit, employment, health, education, and the marketplace."[270] Previously, the administration recommended the development of algorithmic auditing and fairness considerations;[271] it remains to be seen what the current administration will do, if anything.

In 2013, the US Consumer Financial Protection Bureau and the Department of Justice reached an $80 million settlement with Ally Financial Inc., an auto lender that allegedly added significant "dealer mark-ups" to minority borrowers.[272] The mark-ups allegedly led to African-American borrowers paying, on average, nearly $300 more than their white counterparts, and Hispanic borrowers more than $200.[273] The government figured this out after using an algorithm, known as the Bayesian Improved Surname Geocoding (BISG), which estimated the probability of a borrower being a minority by using a person's last name and location.[274] Admittedly, the algorithm is imperfect, leading to a number of non-minority positives,[275] but it does provide a helpful tool for uncovering hidden biases.

Yet as our current laws stand, there is little that has been done to address the problem of algorithmic bias. First, our existing frameworks for regulating privacy and due process cannot account for the sheer complexity and numerosity of cases of algorithmic discrimination.

[269] See E. E. Joh, The Undue Influence of Surveillance Technology Companies on Policing (2017) 92 NY *Univ. Law Rev.* 101.

[270] Executive Office of the President, Big Data: Seizing Opportunities, Preserving Values (2014), p. iii, http://obamawhitehouse.archives.gov/sites/default/files/docs/big_data_privacy_report_5.1.14_final_print.pdf.

[271] Angwin *et al.*, above note 171.

[272] CFPB and DOJ Order Ally to Pay $80 Million to Consumers Harmed by Discriminatory Auto Loan Pricing, *CFPB: Newsroom* (December 20, 2013), www.consumerfinance.gov/about-us/newsroom/cfpb-and-doj-order-ally-to-pay-80-million-to-consumers-harmed-by-discriminatory-auto-loan-pricing.

[273] A. Andriotis and R. L. Ensign, U.S. Government Uses Race Test for $80 Million in Payments, *Wall Street Journal* (October 29, 2015), www.wsj.com/articles/u-s-uses-race-test-to-decide-who-to-pay-in-ally-auto-loan-pact-1446111002.

[274] *Ibid.*

[275] *Ibid.*

Second, our existing statutory and constitutional schemes are poorly crafted to address issues of private, algorithmic discrimination. In part because of these reasons, private companies are often able to evade statutory and constitutional obligations that the government is required to follow. Third, because of the dominance of private industry, and the concomitant paucity of information privacy and due process protections, individuals can be governed by biased decisions and never realize it, or they may be foreclosed from discovering bias altogether due to the lack of transparency. These situations, in turn, limit the law's ability to address the problem of bias. Elizabeth Joh, for example, has written extensively about how surveillance technology developed by private companies – including big data programs – has exercised undue influence over policing, overriding principles of transparency and accountability which normally govern police departments, distorting the reach of the Fourth Amendment.[276]

The Paucity of the Principle of Non-Discrimination

As Danah Boyd and others have noted, the notion of a protected class is also a fuzzy category in practice. "The notion of a protected class remains a fundamental legal concept, but as individuals increasingly face technologically mediated discrimination based on their positions within networks, it may be incomplete."[277] Since the range of potential inputs for discrimination is so much broader, it is "increasingly hard to understand what factors are inputted or inferred in complex algorithms that seek to distribute limited resources."[278]

As Barocas and Selbst have insightfully noted, data-mining techniques force a central confrontation between two central principles that underscore anti-discrimination law: anti-classification and anti-subordination.[279] Anti-classification principles suggest that the very act of classification risks unfairness for individuals in protected groups because decision-makers may rest their judgments on inappropriate perceptions. In contrast, anti-subordination theory aims to remedy unequal treatment as a matter of substance (as opposed to procedure), pointing out that the central goal of anti-discrimination law should be to eliminate any status-based distinctions between protected and unprotected categories.[280] In order for the law to address the risk of discrimination in an algorithmic context, it is necessary for legislatures to commit to anti-subordination principles in a way that they have not been able to do, since courts are exercising more and more scrutiny over substantive remediation.[281] If these remedies remain both politically and constitutionally infeasible, then anti-discrimination principles may never be able to fully address discrimination in data mining techniques.[282]

In *Ricci* v. *DeStefano*, a case in which the City of New Haven refused to certify a promotion exam on the basis that it would have produced a disparate impact, we see a powerful enactment of these concerns.[283] Even though the city's refusal constituted a facially neutral effort to correct for a perceived disparate impact regarding race, the US Supreme Court concluded that the city's refusal constituted a race-conscious remedy that comprised disparate treatment of the white firefighters who might have been promoted based on the results

---

[276] Joh, above note 269, p. 103.
[277] D. Boyd, K. Levy, and A. Marwick, The Networked Nature of Algorithmic Discrimination, in Data and Discrimination: Collected Essays, above note 257, pp. 53, 56.
[278] *Ibid.*
[279] Barocas and Selbst, above note 60, p. 723.
[280] *Ibid.*
[281] *Ibid.*
[282] *Ibid.*
[283] *Ibid.*, p. 724 (discussing *Ricci* v. *DeStefano*, 557 US 557 (2009)).

of the exam.[284] Disparate treatment, the Court concluded, cannot serve as a remedy for disparate impact, without a strong showing that the initial results would lead to liability for actual disparate treatment.[285]

Taking *Ricci* at its word, Borocas and Selbst suggest that legislative attempts to require certain types of remedial action in discriminatory data mining may run afoul of the existing nexus that bars disparate treatment as a solution for problems regarding disparate impact.[286] Even if Congress amended Title VII to force employers to make their training data and models auditable to focus on an algorithm's discriminatory potential, any solution would necessarily require the employer to first consider membership in a protected class, thus raising the spectre of a race-conscious remedy.[287] Although the authors note that it is possible to explore the potential of discriminatory impact at the test design stage under *Ricci*, they argue that "[a]fter an employer begins to use the model to make hiring decisions, only a 'strong basis in evidence' that the employer will be successfully sued for disparate impact will permit corrective action."[288] This high threshold makes the opportunities for such corrective action quite limited, since, as the authors point out, "disparate impact will only be discovered after an employer faces complaints," and then forces an investigation.[289]

As this discussion illustrates, our traditional civil rights principles, particularly in the world of Title VII, map unevenly onto a world that facilitates algorithmic discrimination.[290] Further difficulties of finding proof of both a discriminatory intent and impact abound, since most data-mining practices would not automatically generate liability under Title VII.[291] Part of this is attributable to the way in which Title VII constructs standards of proof. Even when data mining results in a discriminatory impact, as Barocas and Selbst explain, the law is constructed to balance the protection of legitimate business judgments with "preventing 'artificial, arbitrary, and unnecessary' discrimination."[292] If the two happen to conflict, they conclude, "a tie goes to the employer."[293]

But there is also another, constitutional barrier toward equality. Since procedural remedies may not be able to solve many of the problems associated with big data discrimination, it may often be necessary to rebalance variables, reweighting results in order to compensate for discriminatory outcomes.[294] On this, Anupam Chander has suggested a number of such possibilities in a recent piece.[295] However, it is important to note that any rebalancing effort may not survive our current constitutional climate because these efforts, at least in the race-based context, raise constitutional concerns due to the specter of affirmative action.

---

[284] *Ibid.*, p. 724–5.
[285] *Ibid.*, p. 725.
[286] *Ibid.*
[287] *Ibid.*
[288] *Ibid.*, pp. 725–6 (quoting *Ricci*, above note 283).
[289] *Ibid.*, p. 726.
[290] For a related perspective on *Ricci* and the role of audits, see P. T. Kim, Auditing Algorithms for Discrimination (2017) 166 *Univ. Pa. Law Rev. Online* 189 (discussing desirability and practicality of audits to detect discrimination).
[291] See Barocas and Selbst, above note 60, p. 726.
[292] *Ibid.*, p. 711 (quoting *Griggs v. Duke Power Co.*, 401 US 424, 431 (1971)).
[293] *Ibid.*, p. 712.
[294] *Ibid.*, p. 715.
[295] Chander, above note 236, pp. 1041–2 (detailing the potential for modeling remedies to algorithmic discrimination on affirmative action).

The Paucity of Privacy Protections

Other existing normative commitments to civil rights can also be just as inadequate when we try to apply them to algorithmic accountability. Take informational privacy as one example.[296] Beyond just the absence of granular, statutory language protecting informational privacy concerns, as mentioned throughout this chapter in the context of health, there are other major obstacles to informational privacy's ability to address algorithmic discrimination.

One obstacle is simple awareness and lack of notice. Privacy, Oscar Gandy writes, is not going to solve the problem of disparate impact where the algorithm is concerned.[297] Most of the time, people who might be discriminated against by a systemic issue might not even know that they are being discriminated against at all.[298]

But there is a deeper reason for the absence of greater regulation in the United States. As Paul Schwartz and Karl-Nikolaus Peifer have usefully explained, the US and the EU systems diverge substantially in their approaches to privacy.[299] The European Union structures its system of privacy regulation through the lens of a fundamental set of rights that address data protection, largely through a rights-based set of entitlements.[300] Within this model, the EU privileges the individual through a discourse that relies on the language of constitutional rights anchored by the values of dignity, personality, and self-determination, drawn in no small part from the European Convention of Human Rights and the Charter of Fundamental Rights, both of which have led to an explicit right to data protection encircling both the government and private parties.[301] Although the free flow of information is also an important value in this system, it matters less, according to Schwartz and Peifer, than the individual right to dignity, privacy, and data protection.[302]

In contrast, the United States employs a more market-driven structure, viewing the individual through a consumerist lens that focuses on the individual as a "privacy consumer" – a "trader of a commodity, namely her personal data."[303] Here, the focus on privacy is framed as a matter of "bilateral self-interest," leading to a focus on "policing fairness in exchanges of personal data."[304] The Constitution, in this framework, does not govern horizontal, private-to-private exchanges between individuals, nor does it "oblige the government to take positive steps to create conditions to allow for the existence of fundamental rights."[305] Although there are

[296] See C. Dwork and A. Roth, The Algorithmic Foundations of Differential Privacy (2014) 9 *Found. Trends Theor. Comput. Sci.* 211, www.cis.upenn.edu/~aaroth/Papers/privacybook.pdf (arguing for a more robust definition of privacy through algorithmic analysis).

[297] O. H. Gandy, Jr., Engaging Rational Discrimination: Exploring Reasons for Placing Regulatory Constraints on Decision Support Systems (2010) 12 *J. Ethics Inf. Technol.* 39–40. For other excellent treatments on privacy, see J. E. Cohen, *Configuring the Networked Self: Law, Code, and the Play of Everyday Practice* (Yale University Press, 2012); H. Nissenbaum, *Privacy in Context: Technology, Policy, and the Integrity of Social Life* (Stanford Law Books, 2010); J. Rosen, *The Unwanted Gaze: The Destruction of Privacy in America* (Vintage Books, 2001); P. M. Schwartz, The Center for Information Policy Leadership, Data Protection Law and the Ethical Use of Analytics (2010), http://iapp.org/media/pdf/knowledge_center/Ethical_Underpinnings_of_Analytics.pdf; D. J. Solove, *Nothing to Hide: The False Tradeoff Between Privacy and Security* (Yale University Press, 2013); D. J. Solove, *Understanding Privacy* (Harvard University Press, 2010); P. Ohm, Broken Promises of Privacy: Responding to the Surprising Failure of Anonymization (2010) 57 *UCLA Law Rev.* 1701; J. Yakowitz, Tragedy of the Data Commons (2011) 25 *Harv. J. Law Technol.* 1.

[298] See, e.g., Angwin *et al.*, above note 149 (discussing how Facebook may have more information on its users than we realize).

[299] P. M. Schwartz and K.-N. Peifer, Transatlantic Data Privacy Law (2017) 106 *Geo. Law J.* 115, 121.

[300] *Ibid.*, p. 120.

[301] *Ibid.*, pp. 123–4.

[302] *Ibid.*, pp. 130–1.

[303] *Ibid.*, p. 121.

[304] *Ibid.*, p. 132.

[305] *Ibid.*, pp. 132–3 (footnote omitted).

some sources of protection from the Fourth Amendment and the Due Process Clause of the Fourteenth Amendment, those map unevenly onto the concerns of information privacy.[306]

Consider the Fourth Amendment as an example. As Schwartz and Peifer explain, since the Amendment is concerned with the reasonableness of searches and seizures, it fails to govern information that is already held by government databases, as well as situations where a third party (like a bank) hands over personal information to the government.[307] Although the Supreme Court recognized a general right to information privacy in 1977 when it decided *Whalen* v. *Roe*,[308] its progeny suggests a general level of uncertainty regarding the contours of such a right.[309] Unlike in the EU, in the United States, there is no analogous right to data protection.[310] As Schwartz and Peifer observe, this is partly a result of the uncertainty in the United States about whether a variety of information processing practices constitute evidence of sufficient harm to warrant a legal remedy.[311] Instead, privacy protections comprise a patchwork of federal and state statutes and regulations that have been enacted without the broader, harmonizing protection that an omnibus law would provide.[312] In addition, marketplace rhetoric favors laws that privilege notice and consent.[313] Echoing some of these insights, Lior Strahilevitz has argued that the absence of prophylactic privacy laws in the United States, when coupled with attitudinal differences and public choice issues, makes subsequent privacy regulation more unlikely in the future.[314] As a result, there is a failure of informational privacy protections to creatively address situations that seem like the benign sharing of information between data brokers and their advertisers.[315]

Automated Decision-Making and Due Process

This lack of awareness ties directly into due process concerns. Today, computers and algorithms are an essential part of government.[316] As Danielle Keats Citron has noted in her foundational work on this topic, automated decision-making systems have become the primary decision-makers for a host of government decisions, including Medicaid, child-support payments, airline travel, voter registration, and small business contracts.[317] While automation dramatically lowers the cost of decision-making, it also raises significant due process concerns, involving lack of notice and the opportunity to challenge the decision.[318] The problem is not just that governmental decision-

---

[306] See *ibid.*, pp. 133–4.

[307] *Ibid.*, p. 133.

[308] 429 US 589 (1977).

[309] Schwartz and Peifer, above note 299, pp. 133–4.

[310] *Ibid.*, p. 134.

[311] See *ibid.*, pp. 135–6.

[312] *Ibid.*, p. 136.

[313] *Ibid.*

[314] L. J. Strahilevitz, Toward a Positive Theory of Privacy Law (2013) 126 *Harv. Law Rev.* 2010, 2036.

[315] For example, in the STEM study mentioned earlier, the postulated reason for why more men than women were shown STEM-related ads was not the presumed differences between men and women, but rather the way in which advertising priced the cost of male and female audiences of particular ages. For the authors of this study, the interconnectedness of the data led to spillover effects that directed discriminatory decisions, thus demonstrating the need to re-evaluate the role of privacy protections. Instead of thinking about informational privacy protections as traditionally restraining particular actions, the researchers urged others to think about privacy in terms of its relationship to these spillovers instead. Lambrecht and Tucker, above note 225, p. 4; see also Raymond *et al.*, above note 48, p. 218 (discussing the complex role of privacy protections).

[316] See P. Schwartz, Data Processing and Government Administration: The Failure of the American Legal Response to the Computer (1992) 43 *Hastings Law J.* 1321, 1322.

[317] D. K. Citron, Technological Due Process (2008) 85 *Wash. Univ. Law Rev.* 1249, 1252, and n. 12.

[318] *Ibid.*, p. 1249.

making has been delegated to private entities that design code; it is also the reverse situation, where private entities have significant power that is not regulated by the government.

The European Union recently adopted due process requirements, based partly on the rights-based framework discussed above, which create procedures that enable citizens to receive and challenge explanations for automated decisions when they receive decisions based "solely on automated processing" and when the decisions "significantly affect" their lives.[319] Unfortunately, this right only affects a very small number of automated decisions, since those eligible individuals are those who received decisions that do not involve human intervention, like an automated refusal of a credit application.[320] However, the EU GDPR took effect in May 2018, representing perhaps the most prominent regulatory move in favor of greater protections for individuals.[321] It requires companies and governments to reveal an algorithm's purpose and the data it uses to make decisions, leading some to infer a right to explanation.[322]

The GDPR requires individuals to have the right to confirm whether their personal data is being processed, the purpose of the process, the source of the data, and the logic behind any automated decision-making.[323] Yet it is unclear if decisions made based on data about a large group with which the individual identified would also trigger notification.[324] As Selbst has observed, there is also some debate over the level of meaningfulness those explanations are required to demonstrate.[325] To be meaningful, then, for Selbst and Barocas, the information must be about the logic behind the decision, enabling the subject to decide whether or not to invoke his or her private right of action under the GDPR.[326] Without a clear definition, as the above examples suggest, there is an appreciable risk that companies will explain their algorithms in the most innocuous way possible.[327] A further obstacle involves trade secrecy. According to some researchers, courts in Germany and Austria have interpreted similar, existing laws narrowly to allow companies to limit their explanations to avoid revealing trade secrets.[328] And without legal intervention into private industry, comprehensive solutions cannot even begin to develop.

REFINING OVERSIGHT FROM WITHIN

As suggested above, this chapter argues that part of the problem has been our reliance on traditional civil rights principles to address the issue of algorithmic bias. To solve this

---

[319] See Parliament and Council Regulation 2016/679, 2016 OJ (L119) 1, art. 22.
[320] *Ibid.*; see also ICO, Rights Related to Automated Decision Making Including Profiling, https://ico.org.uk/for-organisations/guide-to-the-general-data-protection-regulation-gdpr/individual-rights/rights-related-to-automated-decision-making-including-profiling.
[321] See GDPR Portal: Site Overview, EU GDPR.org, www.eugdpr.org.
[322] *Ibid.*; see also European Commission, EU Data Protection Reform: Better Rules for European Businesses, https://ec.europa.eu/commission/sites/beta-political/files/data-protection-factsheet-business_en.pdf;
    A. D. Selbst and S. Barocas, The Intuitive Appeal of Explainable Machines (2018) 87 *Fordham Law Rev.* 1085.
[323] See *ibid.*; see also Rights Related to Automated Decision Making Including Profiling, above note 320; Article 15, EU GDPR, "Right of Access by the Data Subject," PrivazyPlan, www.privacy-regulation.eu/en/article-15-right-of-access-by-the-data-subject-GDPR.htm.
[324] See S. Wachter, B. Mittelstadt, and L. Floridi, Why a Right to Explanation of Automated Decision-Making Does Not Exist in the General Data Protection Regulation (2017) 7 *Int. Data Priv. Law* 76, 88–9. But see A. D. Selbst and J. Powles, Meaningful Information and the Right to Explanation (2017) 7 *Int. Data Priv. Law* 233.
[325] Selbst and Barocas, above note 322, pp. 1, 37.
[326] *Ibid.*, p. 38.
[327] See Wachter *et al.*, above note 324, p. 14 (analyzing the precise language of the General Data Protection Regulation and noting that it contains numerous loopholes through which algorithms will likely still avoid real scrutiny); see also T. Z. Zarsky, Incompatible: The GDPR in the Age of Big Data (2017) 47 *Seton Hall Law Rev.* 995; Selbst and Barocas, above note 322, p. 10.
[328] Wachter *et al.*, above note 324, pp. 85–9.

problem, we must begin at the same place that critical race scholars began decades ago: recognizing areas where the law has failed to protect the interests of non-discrimination and equality. As demonstrated throughout this chapter, issues of informational privacy, equality, and due process have surfaced in a variety of algorithmic contexts, but existing law has remained inadequate in addressing this problem, in part due to issues surrounding detection. Other obstacles, as I have suggested, stem from the significant information asymmetry between those who design algorithms and those who are governed by them. A third obstacle, as demonstrated by the absence of a GDPR comparative in the United States, stems from the absence of meaningful regulation to address issues of transparency and accountability.

As I suggest below, part of the answer lies in meaningful responses from private industry in order to address the problem. In turn, the gaping absence of regulatory oversight, particularly in the current administration, requires us to turn to two other potential avenues for greater transparency: voluntary self-regulation (discussed below) and individual actions by employees through whistle-blowing (discussed in "Rebalancing Trade Secrecy through Whistleblowing," below).[329] Part of what this issue requires is also a fundamental rethinking of the relationship between civil rights, consumer protection, and automated decision-making. Instead of looking to the government for protection from algorithmic bias, society must look elsewhere.

Today, the near-complete absence of attention from our current government suggests a much greater need to explore models of self-regulation, even though, of course, government intervention would be much more effective. In the following subparts, I explore the possibilities for addressing algorithmic accountability from within – both from within the industry as well as from within the company itself, discussing the possibility of codes of conduct, impact statements, and whistleblowing to address the issue of algorithmic accountability. Of course, it is also important to recognize the fact that effective self-regulation may not always resolve the issue of algorithmic fairness. Certainly, there are powerful arguments that can be made about the limited incentives for companies to rigorously examine the implications behind technologies that are both profitable and powerful. Yet at the same time, the range of attention paid to self-regulation, from both private industry and from organizations within computer science, suggests that there may be some room to explore potential alternatives from within the industry. And the explosion of AI-related organizations that focus on industry accountability gives us some optimism that the industry is aiming to address issues of transparency and accountability.[330]

Codes of Conduct

The issue of algorithmic accountability demonstrates one core aspect that is missing among computer scientists and software engineers: a concrete, user-friendly, ethical platform with which to approach decision-making and software design. Indeed, one might argue that the absence of this platform has facilitated algorithmic decision-making without recognition of the societal effects of these decisions on the poor and other protected groups. Consequently, restoring some modicum of ethical decision-making may be one part of the solution.

---

[329] W. Knight, Biased Algorithms Are Everywhere, and No One Seems to Care, *MIT Technology Review* (July 12, 2017), www.technologyreview.com/s/608248/biased-algorithms-are-everywhere-and-no-one-seems-to-care ("[T]he Trump administration's lack of interest in AI – and in science generally – means there is no regulatory movement to address the problem").

[330] See, e.g., the work being done by AI Now, Partnership on Artificial Intelligence, Future of Humanity Institute, and others.

Recently, researchers at Amazon, Facebook, IBM, Microsoft, and Alphabet have been attempting to design a standard of ethics around the creation of AI.[331] Another possible form of self-regulation involves the development of a set of ethical principles within professional organizations like the Association for the Advancement of Artificial Intelligence (AAAI) and the Association of Computing Machinery (ACM).[332] Despite these admirable efforts of self-regulation, to be truly effective, these principles must be promulgated within the AI community, as well as distributed to a variety of other professional organizations that draw on big data – like health, financial, and government sectors.[333] They also require regulatory participation to be most effective. But even in the absence of such oversight, they are still worth serious consideration.

The ACM, for example, has established seven principles for Algorithmic Transparency and Accountability, noting the importance of: (1) awareness of possible biases in design, implementation, and use; (2) access and redress mechanisms to allow individuals to question and address adverse effects of algorithmically informed decisions; (3) accountability, ensuring that individuals are held responsible for decisions made by algorithms that they use; (4) an explanation regarding both the procedures that the algorithm follows and the specific decisions that are made; (5) data provenance, meaning a description of the way in which the training data was collected, along with "an exploration of the potential biases induced by the human or algorithmic data-gathering process"; (6) auditability, enabling models, algorithms, data, and decisions to be recorded for audit purposes; and (7) validation and testing, ensuring the use of rigorous models to avoid discriminatory harm.[334]

Similarly, the Institute of Electrical and Electronics Engineers (IEEE), the world's largest organization for technical professionals, released a report entitled Ethically Aligned Design in December of 2016. In that report, the IEEE clearly stated the need for systems to "embed relevant human norms and values."[335] Additionally, the IEEE emphasized the importance of an inclusive approach to stakeholders, relying on tools like explanations or inspection capabilities to increase trust and reliability in machine learning.[336] Here, tools like interactive machine learning or direct questioning and modeling of user responses,[337] "algorithmic guardians" that could help users track and control their shared information,[338] review boards and best practices,[339] multidisciplinary ethics committees,[340] curricula for engineers and technologists that reflects attention to ethical decision-making,[341] and the employment of tools like value sensitive or value-based design[342] can go a long way in building a culture of trust, transparency, and accountability in machine-learning technologies.

---

[331] See J. Markoff, How Tech Giants Are Devising Real Ethics for Artificial Intelligence, *New York Times* (September 1, 2016), www.nytimes.com/2016/09/02/technology/artificial-intelligence-ethics.html.

[332] Crawford and Whittaker, above note 63, p. 5.

[333] *Ibid.*, pp. 4–5.

[334] See ACM, US Public Policy Council, Statement on Algorithmic Transparency and Accountability (2017), p. 2, www.acm.org/binaries/content/assets/public-policy/2017_usacm_statement_algorithms.pdf.

[335] IEEE, Ethically Aligned Design: A Vision for Prioritizing Human Wellbeing with Artificial Intelligence and Autonomous Systems (2016), pp. 5–6, http://standards.ieee.org/develop/indconn/ec/ead_v1.pdf. Full disclosure: please note that the author is a member of the IEEE Algorithmic Bias working group.

[336] *Ibid.*, p. 23.

[337] *Ibid.*, p. 25.

[338] *Ibid.*, p. 67.

[339] *Ibid.*, p. 53.

[340] *Ibid.*, p. 43.

[341] *Ibid.*, pp. 37–8.

[342] See *ibid.*, p. 39 (citing S. Spiekermann, *Ethical IT Innovation: A Value-Based System Design Approach* (CRC Press, 2016)).

And there are also the commitments made by professional organizations, which are often significant. Of particular note is the code of conduct by the British Computer Society, which holds that individuals must:

> (a) have due regard for public health, privacy, security and wellbeing of others and the environment[;] (b) have due regard for the legitimate rights of Third Parties[;] (c) conduct [their] professional activities without discrimination on the grounds of sex, sexual orientation, marital status, nationality, color, race, ethnic origin, religion, age or disability, or of any other condition or requirement[;] and (d) promote equal access to the benefits of IT and seek to promote the inclusion of all sectors in society whenever opportunities arise.[343]

In turn, perhaps the greatest source of transformation will come from industry's efforts to integrate governance with machine-learning models. There is a growing industry developing a number of tools that aim to integrate governance functions into data management systems by focusing on principles like algorithmic transparency (by demonstrating the features used for particular models), using flagging and feedback loops (to address when data or policies change), supporting robust forms of auditing (to study the models being used and their purpose), and developing privacy-preserving features (like masking, anonymization, and differential privacy).[344] In due time, we could also certainly see entities developing a certification process that draws upon these principles to show their commitment to fairness and transparency, using some of the tools that Josh Kroll and his co-authors have suggested in their work.[345]

Human Impact Statements in AI and Elsewhere

Algorithmic accountability in private industry also raises a question that underscores the difference between an individualized approach to anti-discrimination and the kinds of issues raised by big data. Title VII approaches take the traditional view, motivated by fairness concerns, that all forms of discrimination are illegal when based on protected categories and must therefore be stamped out.[346] In contrast, big data approaches are less about extinguishing all forms of illegal discrimination; instead, they force us to grapple with the reality that some forms of discriminatory impact may always be present, and focus instead on the question of what efforts can be made to minimize disparate impact.[347]

How can we implement these ideas in the algorithmic context? Recently, a group of prominent researchers launched a document, entitled "Principles for Accountable Algorithms,"[348] which focused on five core principles: responsibility, explainability, accuracy, auditability, and fairness. They also outlined a host of questions for researchers to explore during the design, pre-launch, and post-launch phases of algorithmic decision-making.[349] Many of their suggested questions focused

---

[343] *Ibid.*, p. 43 (citing BCS Code of Conduct, www.bcs.org/category/6030 (asterisks omitted)).

[344] All of these tools have been suggested by Matthew Carroll, CEO of Immuta, a company that aims to integrate governance functions into machine learning. See Carroll, above note 102.

[345] See generally Kroll *et al.*, above note 60 (enumerating the tools, albeit imperfect, for fairness in machine learning as the operationalization of fairness through blindness, statistical parity, fair affirmative action, fair representations, regularization, and fair synthetic data). Indeed, a certification regime that uses these tools well in advance could ensure that fairness is not only a method for virtue signaling, but actually a policy that is both on the books and put into practice.

[346] Barocas and Selbst, above note 60, pp. 694–5.

[347] See generally A. D. Selbst, Disparate Impact in Big Data Policing (2017) 52 *Ga. Law Rev.* 109.

[348] N. Diakopoulos, S. Friedler, M. Arenas, *et al.*, Principles for Accountable Algorithms and a Social Impact Statement for Algorithms, FAT/ML, www.fatml.org/resources/principles-for-accountable-algorithms.

[349] *Ibid.*

on various aspects of transparency – for example, identifying parties that are responsible for garnering the social impact of an algorithm, and communicating decisions and describing the sources and attributes of the data used in machine learning to subjects, including whether it was transformed or cleaned in some manner.[350]

The Principles for Accountable Algorithms also do more than emphasize transparency of authority. They provide important variables to consider in ensuring accuracy and auditability – urging designers to carefully investigate areas of error and uncertainty by undertaking sensitivity analysis, validity checks, and a process of error correction, and also enabling public auditing, if possible, or auditing by a third party, if not possible.[351] Toward this end of encouraging greater collaboration, calibration, consistency, and transparency, we might consider the utility of a "human impact statement," something along the lines of what has been suggested by Marc Roark; a "discrimination impact assessment," as suggested by Selbst; or a "social impact statement," promulgated by a prominent group of algorithmic researchers.[352] Much of the ideas surrounding impact statements originate from environmental law literature,[353] but impact statements have been promulgated in a variety of other areas,[354] also, including human rights,[355] privacy,[356] and data protection.[357] Consider some of the ways in which impact assessments have been used in environmental regulation, which have often served as a transformative blueprint to studying the effect of particular decisions. As described, an environmental impact statement requires the detailed effect of major federal actions on the environment, paying close attention to whether a particular group of people bear a disproportionate share of a negative environmental consequence.[358] Other environmental state statutes, drawing on this principle, also ask for reporting of "any significant physical changes that may be caused by social or economic impacts that are the result of the [p]roject."[359] Environmental impact statements also, like the circumstances here,

---

[350]   *Ibid.*

[351]   *Ibid.*

[352]   See *ibid.*; M. L. Roark, Human Impact Statements (2015) 54 *Washburn Law J.* 649; Selbst, above note 347, p. 169.

[353]   See generally Selbst, above note 347 (discussing impact statements in policing, drawing on environmental law literature).

[354]   For excellent commentary on how impact assessments can inform issues that arise from technology and surveillance, see K. A. Bamberger and D. K. Milligan, Privacy Decisionmaking in Administrative Agencies (2008) 75 *Univ. Chi. Law Rev.* 75; A. M. Froomkin, Regulating Mass Surveillance As Privacy Pollution (2015) *Univ. Ill. Law Rev.* 1713; D. Wright and C. D. Raab, Constructing a Surveillance Impact Assessment (2012) 28 *Comp. Law Sec. Rev.* 613.

[355]   See United Nations, Human Rights Council, Office of the High Commissioner, Guiding Principles on Business and Human Rights (2011), pp. 23–6, www.ohchr.org/Documents/Publications/GuidingPrinciplesBusinessHR_EN .pdf (describing human rights impact assessments); see also D. Reisman, J. Schultz, K. Crawford, and M. Whittaker, AI Now Inst., Algorithmic Impact Assessments: A Practical Framework for Public Agency Accountability (2018), p. 5, https://ainowinstitute.org/aiareport2018.pdf.

[356]   See Privacy Impact Assessments, FTC, www.ftc.gov/site-information/privacy-policy/privacy-impact-assessments (describing the FTC's system of privacy impact assessments); see also Reisman *et al.*, above note 355.

[357]   Data Protection Impact Assessments, ICO, https://ico.org.uk/for-organisations/guide-to-the-general-data-protection-regulation-gdpr/accountability-and-governance/data-protection-impact-assessments; see also Reisman *et al.*, above note 355.

[358]   Roark, above note 352, p. 663.

[359]   *Ibid.*, pp. 664–5 (quoting *Gray v. County of Madera*, 85 Cal Rptr. 3d 50, 69 (Cal. Ct. App. 2008) (citing the California Environmental Quality Act, Cal. Pub. Res. Code (West), § 21000 et seq.); see also A. Ramo, Environmental Justice as an Essential Tool in Environmental Review Statutes: A New Look at Federal Policies and Civil Rights Protections and California's Recent Initiatives (2013) 19 W.-Nw. *J. Environ. Law Policy* 41, 46.

require in-depth research and substantially detailed findings, and can also include a lengthy process of revision, which can last months or even years.[360]

At the state level, racial impact statements have been designed to project whether or not a proposed criminal justice legislation will have a disparate racial effect; the general impetus is to discern any racially disparate effects prior to the law's passage or amendment.[361] Typically, a racial impact statement responds to a proposed law that either amends or adds a new crime, by preparing a report that discusses whether the new law will change the state's prison population and/or disproportionately affect minority groups.[362] Unlike environmental impact statements, which require certain actions to be taken in response to an adverse impact, racial impact statements are offered for informational purposes only, even when disproportionate impact is predicted.[363] Since 2007, a number of states have adopted or considered racial impact legislation, some of which is required by the legislature, and others that are initiated by a state sentencing guidelines commission.[364] Other states also adopt a notice and comment period following publication of a racial impact statement.[365] While many states do not require further action after a racially disproportionate finding is made, other states, like Arkansas, Wisconsin, and Kentucky, have considered requiring lawmakers to provide an explanation for their course of action, after finding a racial disparity.[366] This has prompted at least one commentator to recommend requiring lawmakers to consider alternative options that may achieve the same policy goals, but without exacerbating racial disparities.[367]

In Europe, the GDPR and Police and Criminal Justice Authorities require data protection impact assessments (DPIA) whenever data processing "is likely to result in a high risk to the rights and freedoms of natural persons."[368] Large-scale data processing, automated decision-making, processing of data concerning vulnerable subjects, or processing that might involve preventing individuals from exercising a right or using a service or contract, would trigger a DPIA requirement.[369] Importantly, this model extends to both public and private organizations.[370] If a high risk is shown, the organization is required to file a DPIA with the Information Commissioner's Office (ICO) for advice, which the ICO promises to provide within three months.[371]

[360] J. Erickson, Comment, Racial Impact Statements: Considering the Consequences of Racial Disproportionalities in the Criminal Justice System (2014) 89 *Wash Law Rev.* 1425, 1463.

[361] *Ibid.*, p. 1426.

[362] *Ibid.*, pp. 1444–5.

[363] *Ibid.*

[364] *Ibid.*, pp. 1426–7. As of 2014, eleven states have considered or adopted racial impact statements. *Ibid.* For example, Minnesota's racial impact statements are initiated by the Minnesota Sentencing Guidelines Commission (MSGC). In contrast, Iowa's racial impact statements are required by the legislature, which also requires a correctional impact statement (discussing the impact on prison capacity) and financial impact statement, as well. *Ibid.*, pp. 1446–7.

[365] *Ibid.*, p. 1463.

[366] *Ibid.*, p. 1464.

[367] *Ibid.* (citing C. London, Racial Impact Statements: A Proactive Approach to Addressing Racial Disparities in Prison Populations (2011) 29 *Law Inequal.* 211, 241).

[368] Selbst, above note 347, pp. 170–1; see also Data Protection Impact Assessments, above note 357.

[369] Selbst, above note 347, pp. 170–1; see also Data Protection Impact Assessments, above note 357 (requiring DPIAs if the entity uses "systematic and extensive profiling or automated decision-making to make significant decisions about people," processes data or criminal offence data on a large scale, systematically monitors a publicly accessible place, processes biometric or genetic data, combines or matches data from multiple sources, or processes personal data in a way that involves online or offline tracking of location or behavior, among other categories).

[370] See Reisman *et al.*, above note 355, p. 7 (making this observation).

[371] *Ibid.*

The DPIA statement is required to reflect four critical areas of attention and is meant to be drafted by the organization's controller, working in conjunction with the organization's Data Protection Officer (DPO).[372] The first is largely descriptive, requiring a description of the processing; the second involves a showing of an assessment of necessity and scale of compliance measures; the third element is identicative, requiring identification and assessment of risks to individuals; and the fourth element is mitigative, requiring a showing of additional measures that could be taken to mitigate risk.[373] Significantly, the controller is in charge of demonstrating GDPR compliance and represents a separate entity from the organization that is actually processing the data.[374]

A number of valuable critiques have been raised regarding the execution of DPIAs – for example, they are not required to be published and do not include built-in external researcher review, nor a notice-and-comment proceeding for public review.[375] Yet despite these critiques (most of which are directed toward AI used by public agencies, rather than private corporations), the DPIA process still offers a number of thoughtful insights that can help shape expectations of private companies processing data, just as we see in the GDPR context. The next subpart discusses some ways to harness the insights derived from impact statements and suggests some elements to consider.

A Proposed Human Impact Statement

Following the insights offered by other scholars, particularly Selbst and Roark, and the framework offered by the GDPR, as well as other related impact statements,[376] I emphasize three core elements in crafting a Human Impact Statement in Algorithmic Decision-Making.

First, drawing in part on California's own environmental impact legislation, I recommend the adoption of a substantive, rather than procedural, commitment to both algorithmic accountability and anti-discrimination. In California, the state's Quality Review Act requires "the fair treatment of all races, cultures, and income levels, including minority populations and low-income populations of the state."[377] A statement that assures the public of a commitment to both fairness and accountability, following this example, would go a long way toward setting a baseline set of expectations for private industry to follow.

The second element focuses on the structure of the impact statement and who has responsibility for both implementation and oversight. Here, I recommend the employment of a structure, similar to the GDPR, which relies upon a clear division between the controller (who is responsible for compliance) and the programmer (who is responsible for the algorithm and data processing). By encouraging a healthy separation between the algorithm's designers and those who are tasked to minimize disparate impact, we can ensure greater accountability and oversight.

Third, I also encourage a thorough examination (and structural division), both *ex ante* and *ex post*, of both the algorithm and the training data that is employed to refine the algorithm. As Kroll and his co-authors have observed in an important study, it is possible to demonstrate accountable algorithms through a greater engagement with procedural and technical tools

[372] Data Protection Impact Assessments, above note 357.
[373] *Ibid.*
[374] S. Gunathunga, All You Need to Know About GDPR Controllers and Processors, *Medium* (September 12, 2017), https://medium.com/@sagarag/all-you-need-to-know-about-gdpr-controllers-and-processors-248200ef4126.
[375] Reisman *et al.*, above note 355, p. 7.
[376] See, e.g., Selbst, above note 347, p. 169.
[377] Roark, above note 352, p. 665 (citing Cal. Pub. Res. Code (2018), § 71110(a)).

from computer scientists.[378] *Ex ante* solutions try to correct issues that may surface in the data; *ex post* solutions try to gather relevant information and reweigh information in order to test the reliability of the data.[379]

Following Andrew Selbst's excellent work on drafting impact assessment for predictive policing techniques, and integrating suggestions derived from literature elsewhere,[380] I emphasize the following specific *ex ante* criteria:

(1) identify "potentially impacted populations" and determine their race, ethnicity, gender, sexual orientation, national origin, or other status-based categories;[381]
(2) identify the effect of uncertainty or statistical error on different groups;[382]
(3) study whether the decision will have an adverse impact on the subpopulation;[383]
(4) explore "whether there are reasonable, less discriminatory, alternatives or potential means of mitigation," including the consideration of new target variables or other forms of data, the employment and availability of data processing techniques, and new methods of assessment;[384]
(5) devote substantial consideration of each alternative in detail so that reviewers can evaluate their comparative merits;[385] and
(6) identify and explain the entity's preferred alternative, noting its selection among several different algorithmic design choices.[386]

Ex post, an impact assessment should embrace the employment of rigorous techniques and alternatives, to refine and improve the use of AI – its accuracy, its fairness, its accountability, and its transparency. This would include discussion of a set of technical mitigation measures that are not already included in the proposed model.[387] The advantage of employing a rigorous system of impact statements stems from enlisting engineers to explain their design choices, evaluate their efficacy, include alternative configurations, and consider whether any disparate impact has been created for a subpopulation.[388]

Admittedly, these mechanisms may not always be feasible or practical in every instance, but the point of discussing them is to lay the groundwork for reframing the central concern about how big data can impact certain groups, and to create a framework for awareness of these effects. Of course, the cost and length of time it may take to draw up a comprehensive impact assessment may make it difficult to implement.[389] But even aside from cost and complexity, another concern is that without an underlying commitment to a set of normative principles, "impact assessments can become a mere procedural tool that may not be able to create the change they seek," raising the risk that the process may be vulnerable to a host of

---

[378] See Kroll *et al.*, above note 60, pp. 640–1.
[379] See *ibid.*, pp. 637, 662–77.
[380] I only mention and summarize these criteria here; Andrew Selbst's discussion, above note 347, is far more detailed and descriptive about the various ways of implementation in an algorithmic context.
[381] Roark, above note 352, p. 665 n. 97 (citing Ramo, above note 359, p. 50).
[382] Diakopoulos *et al.*, above note 348.
[383] Roark, above note 352, p. 665 n. 94 (citing Ramo, above note 359, p. 50); see also EPA, Final Guidance for Consideration of Environmental Justice in Clean Air Act (1999) 309 *Reviews* 1.
[384] Roark, above note 352, p. 665 n. 94 (citing Ramo, above note 359, p. 50); Selbst, above note 347, pp. 173–4.
[385] Selbst, above note 347, p. 174 (citing 40 CFR § 1502.14(b) (2018)).
[386] *Ibid.*, p. 177.
[387] *Ibid.*
[388] See *ibid.*, pp. 173–8.
[389] O. K. Obasogie, The Return of Biological Race? Regulating Race and Genetics through Administrative Agency Race Impact Assessments (2012) 22 *S. Cal. Interdisc. Law J.* 1, 59.

interests that "may work against the very concerns giving rise to the assessment process itself …"[390] To guard against the possibility of internal self-interest guiding the drafting of an impact statement, we also need to think more broadly about how the law might both incentivize and protect those who come forward.

REBALANCING TRADE SECRECY THROUGH WHISTLEBLOWING

"Refining Oversight from within," above, dealt with the possibility of industry self-regulation as one potential tool to address algorithmic bias. However, relying on industry self-regulation alone does not address the continued black box problem. As Frank Pasquale noted in *The Black Box Society*: "Knowledge is power. To scrutinize others while avoiding scrutiny oneself is one of the most important forms of power."[391] In countless cases, both inside and outside of the criminal justice system, aggrieved parties have been denied access to the source code that governs them. In the context of big data, Joh details how surveillance technology vendors can block access to even the data that summarizes their results, denoting it to be confidential, proprietary information.[392] In one public dispute, Palantir Technologies, which had provided the NYPD with software that graphs data derived from the police (arrest records, license plates, parking tickets, and the like) in a way that (according to Buzzfeed) "can reveal connections among crimes and people," refused to hand over a readable version of its data to the NYPD after it decided to partner with IBM instead.[393] Even when filing a case of discrimination against a private company remains a possibility, many individuals may not know that an algorithm is discriminating against them, and therefore finding eligible plaintiffs (or crafting a legal theory of illegal conduct) can be difficult, absent some compelling evidence in place.

As these observations suggest, a final part of the problem involves trade secrecy. We continue to view trade secret law as somehow separate from civil rights concerns, and that has contributed to the problem because it has facilitated the absence of accountability. What is needed instead is a greater recognition of the overlap between these two areas of law. As David Levine has eloquently explained, on one hand, the very idea of trade secrets invokes both the notion of seclusion intertwined with commerce.[394] At the same time, however, the ideals of democratic government generally aim to minimize commercial interests and the notion of secrecy as a default position.[395] These tensions – between democratic transparency and commercial seclusion – have become particularly pronounced in the current day, where government has become increasingly intermingled with private industry through privatization and delegation.[396]

The intermingling of public and private, however, is also part of the problem. It has produced a crisis of transparency, whereby private businesses now play the roles that government used to play, but are able to utilize the principles of trade secret law to protect themselves from the very expectations of transparency that the government operated

---

[390]   *Ibid.*
[391]   Pasquale, above note 18, p. 3 (footnote omitted).
[392]   Joh, above note 269, pp. 119–20.
[393]   *Ibid.*, p. 120; see also W. Alden, There's a Fight Brewing between the NYPD and Silicon Valley's Palantir, *Buzzfeed News* (June 28, 2017), www.buzzfeednews.com/article/williamalden/theres-a-fight-brewing-between-the-nypd-and-silicon-valley#.cfryqemg5; E. Hockett and M. Price, Palantir Contract Dispute Exposes NYPD's Lack of Transparency, *Just Security* (July 20, 2017), www.justsecurity.org/43397/palantir-contract-dispute-exposes-nypds-lack-transparency.
[394]   D. S. Levine, The Impact of Trade Secrecy on Public Transparency, in R. C. Dreyfuss and K. J. Strandburg (eds.), *The Law and Theory of Trade Secrecy: A Handbook of Contemporary Research* (2011), pp. 406–7.
[395]   *Ibid.*, p. 407.
[396]   *Ibid.*

under.[397] Danielle Citron, nearly ten years ago, observed that the administrative state was slowly being overtaken by closed proprietary systems in areas of public benefits, electronic voting, and agency-gathered data, among others.[398] Today, the issue is not just that government systems are closed and proprietary – it is also that they are becoming entirely privatized. David Levine offers several examples – from telecommunications to voting systems – that are now being provided by the private sector, thereby becoming increasingly immunized from transparency by trade secret doctrine.[399]

At the same time, current approaches to regulating algorithms emphasize the need for designers to explain their algorithmic models, rather than disclose them.[400] In 2012, for instance, President Barack Obama proposed the Consumer Privacy Bill of Rights, which would have allowed consumers to challenge and correct data[401] that algorithms use to make decisions about credit or insurance. Congress never acted on it.[402] Both the proposal and any notion that consumers have a right to know what data companies retain about consumers and how that information is used have now disappeared from the White House website.[403]

Some scholars have advocated for greater transparency to expose issues of bias.[404] Others have taken an alternative route, critiquing transparency as a limited solution that may fail to root out bias.[405] As Joshua Kroll and others have explained, disclosure of source code is only a partial solution to the issue of accountability because of the complexity and dynamism of machine-learning processes.[406] Some decisions also must necessarily remain opaque to prevent others from gaming the system.[407] Many systems have also not been designed with oversight and accountability in mind, and thus can be opaque to the outside investigator.[408] Even auditing has some limitations, depending on the technique.[409]

The cause of this problem, I argue, demonstrates precisely the need for a new approach to trade secrets, in light of the substantial civil rights concerns that algorithms raise.[410] While I agree with others that accountability is of paramount importance, I would also argue that accountability is impossible without some forms of transparency. As Anupam Chander has written, "[i]nstead of transparency in the design of the algorithm," we also "need ... a transparency of inputs and outputs."[411] In the absence of a centralized, large-scale, federal effort to address this problem, it becomes necessary to explore (1) what solutions might currently exist in the law and (2) whether these solutions might create a platform from which

---

[397] *Ibid.*, pp. 407–8.
[398] D. K. Citron, Open Code Governance (2008) *Univ. Chic. Leg. Forum* 355, 356–7.
[399] Levine, above note 394, at 407.
[400] See B. Goodman and S. Flaxman, European Union Regulations on Algorithmic Decision-Making and a "Right to Explanation" (unpublished manuscript) (on file with author).
[401] See Press Release, The White House, Office of the Press Secretary, We Can't Wait: Obama Administration Unveils Blueprint for a "Privacy Bill of Rights" to Protect Consumers Online (February 23, 2012), http://obamawhitehouse.archives.gov/the-press-office/2012/02/23/we-can-t-wait-obama-administration-unveils-blueprint-privacy-bill-rights.
[402] See N. Singer, Why a Push for Online Privacy Is Bogged Down in Washington, *New York Times* (February 28, 2016), www.nytimes.com/2016/02/29/technology/obamas-effort-on-consumer-privacy-falls-short-critics-say.html.
[403] The proposal still appears on the Obama White House website. See Press Release, above note 401.
[404] See Citron, above note 398, p. 358; Schwartz, above note 316, pp. 1323–5.
[405] C. Dwork and D. K. Mulligan, It's Not Privacy, and It's Not Fair (2013) 66 *Stan. Law Rev. Online* 35, 36–7, https://review.law.stanford.edu/wp-content/uploads/sites/3/2016/08/DworkMulliganSLR.pdf.
[406] Kroll *et al.*, above note 60, pp. 638–9.
[407] *Ibid.*, p. 639.
[408] *Ibid.*, p. 649–50.
[409] *Ibid.*, pp. 650–2.
[410] See Rebecca Wexler's path-breaking work on this topic, above note 26.
[411] Chander, above note 236, p. 1039.

to build further regulatory refinements and encourage greater accountability. Both of these avenues are only possible, however, with a deeper employment of the limitations of trade secret protection, which are designed precisely to expose potential areas of corporate liability.

The good news, however, is that we have seen variants of this problem before, in other private industries. As I show in the subpart below, in other contexts, the law has routinely relied on whistleblowers to address similar information asymmetry and accountability issues. The same can also be said of algorithmic accountability. For years, scholars have addressed the need to incentivize internal employees to come forward in cases of significant information asymmetry; those concerns have animated particular provisions in Sarbanes-Oxley, spending statutes, and a host of environmental provisions. Concerns regarding opacity and difficulty of detection, as I have suggested throughout this chapter, are just as salient here in the context of algorithmic accountability, particularly given the biases that can result from skewed data. As a result, it makes sense to explore the pathways that have been previously taken by legislators, given the potential for similar solutions in this context.

As I show below, a recent, rarely noticed development in modern trade secret law includes federal whistleblowing protections through the employment of the Defend Trade Secrets Act (DTSA) of 2016.[412] I argue that the often overlooked DTSA provisions comprise a hybrid of a solution that could harness the traditional goals and objectives of our language of civil rights, but also immunize whistleblowers to encourage greater transparency in trade secrets.

The Dominance of Property and the Limits of Transparency

In 1916, beginning with *MacPherson* v. *Buick Motor Co.*,[413] courts began to recognize the importance of extending the notion of accountability and consumer protection to third parties, like family members and bystanders, that were harmed by defective products.[414] According to Jack Balkin, *MacPherson* is particularly on point for the algorithmic age as a case that recognizes the harms that unregulated algorithmic decision-making poses, not just to end-users, but to other individuals in society as well.[415] Balkin explains how algorithmic models, by externalizing their costs to third parties, cause harm to reputation, produce a lack of transparency in due process, facilitate discrimination, or render individuals more vulnerable to behavioral manipulation.[416] Thus, Balkin argues that algorithm designers should be construed as information fiduciaries because of the dependence between the company that creates the algorithm – the Googles or Facebooks of the world – and the users.[417]

These risks become especially apparent in a world that provides far greater protection to non-disclosure than accountability. Again, property principles pervade systemic disclosure and transparency. Laws such as the Computer Fraud and Abuse Act[418] (CFAA), which has been interpreted to prevent users from violating a website's Terms of Service, have been used

---

[412] 18 USC § 1836 et seq. (2018). See Peter Menell's groundbreaking work on this topic, below notes 473, 475, and 489.
[413] 111 NE 1050 (NY 1916).
[414] See J. M. Balkin, The Three Laws of Robotics in the Age of Big Data (2017) 78 *Ohio St. Law J.* 1217, 1232.
[415] *Ibid.*
[416] *Ibid.*, pp. 1238–9.
[417] "Online businesses know a lot about us; we know comparatively little about their operations, and they treat their internal processes as proprietary to avoid theft by competitors." *Ibid.*, p. 1228 (footnotes omitted); see also J. M. Balkin, Information Fiduciaries and the First Amendment (2016) 49 *UC Davis Law Rev.* 1183 (discussing the need for a fiduciary relationship between consumers and online platforms).
[418] 18 USC § 1030 (2018).

to prevent researchers from testing algorithms.[419] Recently, the ACLU sued on behalf of four researchers who maintained that the CFAA actually prevented them from scraping data from sites, or from creating fake profiles to investigate whether algorithmic discrimination led some employment and real estate sites to fail to display certain listings on the basis of race or gender.[420] The concern was that the law permitted researchers to be held criminally accountable because the research might involve violating one of the sites' Terms of Service, something that could carry the punishment of both prison and fines.[421] As one researcher observed, these laws have the perverse effect of "protecting data-driven commercial systems from even the most basic external analysis."[422]

The researchers had planned to use a variety of different audit testing techniques, including sock puppet profiles and scraping techniques to determine whether certain real estate sites discriminate on the basis of race or other factors.[423] The government, predictably, argued that the case was a purely private matter, characterizing it as a "private actor's abridgement of free expression in a private forum," and questioning the standing of the plaintiffs to file suit.[424] Importantly, the court disagreed with this characterization, noting that "simply placing contractual conditions on accounts that anyone can create … does not remove a website from the First Amendment protections of the public Internet."[425]

Since the information it found was already within a public forum (a public website)[426] and was regulated by restrictions on private speech that drew on the imprimatur of state protection through civil or criminal law,[427] it risked state enforcement under the CFAA.[428] Despite this conclusion, which kept the case in court and headed toward trial, the court also found that most of the plaintiffs' activities fell outside of the CFAA, reasoning that "scraping or otherwise recording data from a site that is accessible to the public is merely a particular use of information that the plaintiffs are entitled to see."[429] Although the court reached a different conclusion regarding the creation of fictional user accounts, which would violate the access provision, and therefore raise constitutional considerations, it concluded by reassuring the plaintiffs that the "CFAA prohibits far less than the parties claim (or fear) it does."[430]

At the same time that cases like *Sandvig* v. *Sessions* provide some optimism for external auditing, it remains necessary to consider the variety of ways in which companies routinely utilize their intellectual property protections to obfuscate inquiry. Even in the context like voting, there have been other cases that, troublingly, demonstrate the power of trade secrets to

[419] *Sandvig v. Sessions*, 315 F. Supp. 3d 1 (DDC March 30, 2018).
[420] Bhandari and Goodman, above note 218. In that lawsuit, Christian Sandvig, a researcher at the University of Michigan, and three other researchers sued Attorney General Sessions, challenging that the Access provisions of the CFAA risked violating their First Amendment rights stemming from their freedom of speech and their Fifth Amendment rights of due process, and constituted an unconstitutional delegation to private parties under the Fifth Amendment. See *Sandvig*, note 419 above, at 8–9.
[421] See 18 USC § 1030(c); Bhandari and Goodman, above note 218.
[422] D. Stevenson, Locating Discrimination in Data-Based Systems, in Data and Discrimination, above note 257, p. 18.
[423] *Sandvig*, note 419 above, at 11.
[424] *Ibid.* at 9, 15.
[425] *Ibid.* at 13.
[426] *Ibid.* at 16.
[427] *Ibid.* at 17.
[428] *Ibid.*
[429] *Ibid.* at 26–7. It found that employing a bot to crawl through websites might violate a website's Terms of Service, but it did not constitute an "access" violation per se "when the human who creates the bot is otherwise allowed to read and interact with that site." *Ibid.* at 27.
[430] *Ibid.* at 34.

take precedence over transparency. In 2005, the voting machine company Diebold Election Systems – now called Premier Election Solutions – refused to follow a North Carolina law that required electronic voting machine manufacturers to place their software and source code in escrow with a state Board of Elections approved agent.[431] Over a series of court battles, Diebold refused to comply, eventually withdrawing from the state altogether, rather than reveal its source code.[432] In another event, also discussed by Levine, when hackers successfully accessed (and manipulated) a series of Diebold machines, Diebold chose to characterize the events as "potential violations of licensing agreements and intellectual property rights," rather than responding to it as a threat to the dignity of the voting tabulation process.[433]

The risks become especially evident in an era where corporations have become especially dependent on trade secret protection where algorithms are concerned. Because the code for a machine-learning algorithm is so complex, simply reading it does not make it interpretable without the ability of interpreters to plug in data and see how the model actually functions.[434] Further, because algorithmic models often depend on the input of unique personal data, the outcomes may be obscure and difficult to study in a collective capacity.[435] Bias, error, and faulty assumptions plague the design of algorithms as a result of humans designing those algorithms. Few could spot errors in code by reading a description of how that code ought to function. Similarly, few defendants can explain why an algorithmic model predicted recidivism for them without an opportunity to examine why it reached such predictions. Only other humans who understand the programming languages and statistical models that underlie algorithms can pinpoint those errors by examining them.

Software companies, however, currently have other ways to protect their intellectual property and guard the value of their products. Software patents once encouraged companies like Northpointe to disclose algorithms to exclude direct competitors.[436] After a golden age of trolls and over-enforcement in the early twentieth century, however, Supreme Court decisions – such as *Bilski* v. *Kappos* and *Alice Corp.* v. *CLS Bank International* – have essentially ended patent protection for software like COMPAS.[437] Disclosing a way of assessing recidivism with a computer to the US Patent and Trademark Office would unlikely be worth Northpointe's time and trouble, given the dubious protection that software patents now receive.

Copyright laws create a similar problem. Complex algorithms essentially boil down to a string of commands. Copyright laws protect these strings of commands, as they would any other string of

---

[431] Levine, above note 394, pp. 419–20. For an excellent article exploring the use of software-independent voting systems, compliance audits, and risk-limiting audits in elections, see P. B. Stark and D. A. Wagner, Evidence-Based Elections (2012) 10 *IEEE Secur. Priv.* 33.

[432] Levine, above note 394, p. 420.

[433] *Ibid.*, p. 421 (quoting Ion Sancho, the Supervisor of Elections in Leon County, Florida, where the hacks took place). "I really think they're not engaged in this discussion of how to make elections safer." *Ibid.* (footnote omitted).

[434] C. Sandvig, K. Hamilton, K. Karahalios, and C. Langbort, Auditing Algorithms: Research Methods for Detecting Discrimination on Internet Platforms (May 22, 2014), p. 10, www-personal.umich.edu/~csandvig/research/Auditing%20Algorithms%20–%20Sandvig%20–%20ICA%202014%20Data%20and%20Discrimination%20Preconference.pdf (presented at 64th Annual Meeting of the International Communication Association).

[435] *Ibid.*

[436] See G. Quinn, Building Better Software Patent Applications: Embracing Means-Plus-Function Disclosure Requirements in the Algorithm Cases, *IPWatchdog* (June 18, 2012), www.ipwatchdog.com/2012/06/18/building-better-software-patent-applications-embracing-means-plus-function-disclosure-requirements-in-the-algorithm-cases/id=24273.

[437] See *Alice Corp.* v. *CLS Bank Int'l*, 134 S.Ct. 2347, 2349–51 (2014); *Bilski* v. *Kappos*, 561 US 593, 593–6 (2010) (limiting the scope of patentability over software-related inventions).

syntax, as a literary work. Consequently, only its precise expression, the names of commands, for instance, is protected.[438]

In part because of the shortcomings of copyright and patent protection, trade secrets have become the default way to protect algorithms and the source code that embodies them. Although trade secret law remains perhaps the only reasonable way to protect source code, it is also a poor way to protect the public interest. To be a trade secret, information must: (1) not be generally known; (2) bring economic value to its holder by virtue of not being publicly known; and (3) be subject to reasonable precautions to keep the information secret.[439] If information is already known or is even readily ascertainable, it cannot be a trade secret.[440] Federal statutes involve the Economic Espionage Act, which instituted the first federal scheme for trade secret protection and also introduced criminal penalties for misappropriation.[441]

Yet trade secrets, particularly in the software context, suffer from a paradox. As some have observed, without first disclosing and examining the source code, it is impossible to know whether an algorithm even qualifies as a trade secret.[442] But disclosure would potentially jeopardize its status as a trade secret. To avoid this issue, most entities simply assert trade secrecy even when the underlying information may not actually qualify as a trade secret. There is no way to tell otherwise, absent some form of disclosure. Largely because of the deference that companies enjoy in this context, information-based products have long favored trade secret protection, which has led to some scholarly debates and discussion.[443]

Whistleblowing and Secrecy

In a powerful white paper from the Future of Humanity Institute, authors Miles Brundage and Shahar Avin wrote about the need to promote a culture of responsibility in AI.[444] One of their

---

[438] It is somewhat ironic that criminal courts give so much more protection to software code secrecy than it would receive in a civil case. Interestingly, Northpointe does not even guarantee that COMPAS does not infringe other's intellectual property rights, even while maintaining that secrecy is essential to its business. See COMPAS Licensing Agreement (2010), § 8.2, https://epic.org/algorithmic-transparency/crim-justice/EPIC-16-06-23-WI-FOIA-201600805-2010InitialContract.pdf; Katyal, above note 25.

[439] See 18 USC § 1839(3)(B) (2018); *Metallurgical Indus., Inc. v. Fourtek, Inc.*, 790 F.2d 1195, 1199 (5th Cir. 1986).

[440] See Uniform Trade Secrets Act § 1(4) (Nat'l Conference of Comm'rs of Unif. State Laws 1985).

[441] Economic Espionage Act of 1996, Pub. L. No. 104-294, 110 Stat. 3488 (codified as amended at 18 USC §§ 1831–9 (2018)).

[442] See C. Short, Guilt by Machine: The Problem of Source Code Discovery in Florida DUI Prosecutions (2009) 61 *Fla. Law Rev.* 177, 190 (discussing *State v. Chun*, 923 A.2d 226 (NJ 2007), where the code underlying supposedly proprietary breathalyzer software was revealed to consist primarily of general algorithms that arguably would not qualify as a trade secret).

[443] See M. Mattioli, Disclosing Big Data (2014) 99 *Minn. Law Rev.* 535, 550 (citing M. A. Lemley and D. W. O'Brien, Encouraging Software Reuse (1997) 49 *Stan. Law Rev.* 255, 258 (noting the use of trade secret protection in software industry); P. S. Menell, The Challenges of Reforming Intellectual Property Protection for Computer Software (1994) 94 *Colum. Law Rev.* 2644, 2652 (same)). Initially, some scholars argued that by keeping their information secret, companies were slowing the pace of innovation by engaging in potentially duplicative projects at one time. *Ibid.*, p. 551 (citing R. G. Bone, A New Look at Trade Secret Law: Doctrine in Search of Justification (1998) 86 *Calif. Law Rev.* 241, 266–7). Others, like Mark Lemley, postulated that the legal protection for trade secrets in software would mean less investment in physical barriers to access (like encryption), and perhaps would encourage greater information sharing as a result. *Ibid.*, p. 552 (citing M. A. Lemley, The Surprising Virtues of Treating Trade Secrets as IP Rights (2008) 61 *Stan. Law Rev.* 311, 333–4).

[444] M. Brundage and S. Avin, The Malicious Use of Artificial Intelligence: Forecasting, Prevention, and Mitigation (2018), p. 56, https://img1.wsimg.com/blobby/go/3d82daa4-97fe-4096-9c6b-376b92c619de/downloads/1c6q2kc4v_50335.pdf.

suggestions for future research involved the enlistment of whistleblowing protections, pointing out the need to explore its potential intersection with preventing AI-related misuse.[445]

Whistleblowing activity involves "the disclosure by an organization member '(former or current) of illegal, immoral or illegitimate practices under the control of their employers, to persons or organizations who may be able to effect action.'"[446] The whistleblower, in this case, might be someone from within who is motivated by a concern for others' well-being, and who can shed light on the algorithm, its projected or actual impact, and also, importantly, the data that it is trained upon, to determine whether bias is an issue. This subpart outlines how as a general matter, whistleblower protections might affect the context of algorithmic accountability, by protecting individuals who may come forward to address issues of discrimination and bias. Of course, this protection is only a partial solution, given the opacity of trade secrecy, but as I argue below, it does provide some form of protections for those who choose to come forward.

Whistleblowing protections have been employed in a wide variety of models that range from incorporating anti-retaliatory whistleblower protections into regulatory statutes, to private rights of action for whistleblowers, to offering monetary incentives to those who report wrongdoing.[447] In 1989, Congress unanimously passed the Whistleblower Protection Act (WPA) and amended it five years later.[448] The Act discourages "employer retaliation against employees who report violations concerning fraud, waste, or abuse."[449] Although the WPA was motivated by a desire to create a protected class of government employees, the government has since included whistleblower protections in over fifty other federal statutes, extending to private entities in its purview.[450] The Sarbanes-Oxley Act, for example, protects employees who reveal evidence of corporate fraud to an appropriate state or federal authority.[451] Most statutes impose strong penalties on employers who retaliate by discharging or discriminating against the whistleblowing employee by awarding them reinstatement, along with substantial amounts of damages, among other awards.[452]

There are three potential arguments for paying greater attention to whistleblowing in this context. The first, and most important, considers the barrier of intellectual property protections, which often secludes crucial information. Given the issues of opacity, inscrutability, and the potential role of both trade secrecy and copyright law in serving as obstacles to disclosure, whistleblowing might be an appropriate avenue to consider in AI.[453] Whistleblowing has also

[445] *Ibid.*
[446] P. B. Jubb, Whistleblowing: A Restrictive Definition and Interpretation (1999) 21 *J. Bus. Ethics* 77, 84 (citing M. P. Miceli and J. P. Near, *Blowing the Whistle: The Organizational and Legal Implications for Companies and Employees* (Macmillan, 1992), p. 15).
[447] See O. Lobel, Citizenship, Organizational Citizenship, and the Laws of Overlapping Obligations (2009) 97 *Calif. Law Rev.* 433, 442–3.
[448] See S. R. Wilson, Public Disclosure Policies: Can a Company Still Protect Its Trade Secrets? (2004) 38 *New Eng. Law Rev.* 265, 270.
[449] *Ibid.*
[450] *Ibid.*, p. 271.
[451] *Ibid.*, p. 272.
[452] *Ibid.*, pp. 271–2. Some statutes, which are known as core statutes, focus primarily on the protection of whistleblowing activities, and others are adjunct statutes because they protect whistleblowing activities within the context of another primary, legislative purpose. Some statutes provide no more than a cause of action to whistleblowers who experience retaliation for their activities; others provide a financial reward, in addition to employee protection. N. D. Bishara, E. Sangrey Callahan, and T. M. Dworkin, The Mouth of Truth (2013) 10 *NY Univ. J. Law Bus.* 44 (comparing the New Jersey Conscientious Employee Protection Act and the Clean Air Act).
[453] See Levendowski, above note 56 (discussing how copyright protection for data can serve as an obstacle to improving data quality).

been shown to be particularly effective in similar situations that involve information asymmetry (for example, in cases of corporate wrongdoing), where whistleblowers have been considered to be vital to achieving greater compliance because they can help to detect areas of wrongdoing.[454] Research suggests that individuals (like Christopher Wylie discussed in the "Introduction," above) may be motivated by a belief that whistleblowing constitutes "conscience cleansing," to advance social welfare, or because they are discontented in some way.[455]

Second, whistleblowing protections are particularly appropriate, where, as here, the government is relying more and more on private entities for its various governing activities. As I discussed in a related paper, as privatization and delegation become the norm for our world of automated governance, it becomes even more necessary to explore ways to incentivize individuals to come forward.[456] Orly Lobel, in her extensive work on whistleblowing, has argued that "as government relies more on private parties to prevent improper behavior, the need for legal protections for whistleblowers increases."[457] Those conditions are especially appropriate here, where, as discussed earlier, automated decision-making systems have become arbiters for a host of government decisions, including Medicaid, child-support payments, airline travel, voter registration, and small business contracts.[458]

Finally, and perhaps most importantly, whistleblowing has been shown to be particularly effective in situations, like this one, where companies are increasingly relying on internal systems of self-regulation and trying to address the importance of combating bias. Here, particularly given the internal nature of AI, there is even more of a necessity to integrate a culture of whistleblower protection. And it is important to observe, as the Wylie example shows at the start of this chapter, that people can be motivated to come forward, even in the absence of monetary reward.[459] In a similar context, Orly Lobel has found that whistleblower protections are often necessary as complements to systematic self-monitoring.[460] Lobel

---

[454] See, e.g., S. Lieberman, Whistleblowers Can Prevent Toxic Nightmares, Lieberman & Blecher, www .liebermanblecher.com/aop/slapp-suit-and-environmental-whistblower/environmental-whistleblower-cases (cited in A. Heyes and S. Kapur, An Economic Model of Whistle-Blower Policy (2008) 25 *J. Law Econ. Org.* 157, 161) (observing that "Whistleblower laws are particularly helpful in environmental cases. This is so because many environmental violations and crimes are difficult to detect absent help from knowledgeable insiders").

[455] Heyes and Kapur, above note 454, pp. 164–71. Other variables that influence whistleblowing include the following: (1) confidence that their organization would address the wrongdoing; (2) the belief that the organization supported whistleblowing, in general; (3) the seriousness of the allegation; (4) the whistleblower's desire to "put 'their' organization on the right track"; and (5) the availability of a monetary reward. Bishara *et al.*, above note 452, pp. 37, 60.

[456] See Katyal, above note 25.

[457] Lobel, above note 447, p. 473.

[458] See generally Citron, above note 398.

[459] In a powerful experiment, Lobel and Feldman used a series of experimental surveys among 2,000 employees, and asked them to predict their own actions (as well as the actions of others) when confronted with an illegal scheme whereby a company defrauded the government by overcharging, and then undersupplying regarding a construction contract, causing some risk to the public and reducing government funds. The authors then studied the values that employees assigned to different regulatory mechanisms and the legal incentives assigned to prompt them to come forward. The author's findings led her to conclude that "when noncompliance is likely to trigger strong internal ethical motivation, offering monetary rewards may be unnecessary, or, worse yet, counterproductive." She also points out that in situations where an unlawful act is perceived to be morally offensive, a duty to report may be all that is needed to encourage folks to come forward. However, if there is no internal motivation present (like if the misconduct seems low in severity), then external incentives, like material incentives, were more influential in incentivizing people to come forward. See O. Lobel, Linking Prevention, Detection and Whistleblowing: Principles for Designing Effective Reporting Systems (2012) 54 S. *Tex. Law Rev.* 37, 46–7 (detailing study in Y. Feldman and O. Lobel, The Incentives Matrix (2010) 88 *Tex. Law Rev.* 1151, 1176).

[460] O. Lobel, Lawyering Loyalties: Speech Rights and Duties within Twenty-First Century New Governance (2009) 77 *Fordham Law Rev.* 1245, 1249. A system that relies primarily on external reporting, Lobel argues, has its own

concludes that "for certain types of misconduct, policymakers should consider ways to instill ethical norms about different regulatory fields," using educational programs and improving communication channels as part of this project.[461] Ultimately, she opts for a model that prioritizes internal reporting over external reporting, but notes that if the internal process is non-responsive, then "it becomes reasonable for an employee to step outside the organization."[462]

Whistleblower advocates have argued that whistleblowing activities actually conserve law enforcement resources, because they increase both the speed of detection and correction, far more than an external source of monitoring, and promote internal self-monitoring to the extent that organizations are aware of the possibility of exposure.[463] Whistleblowing can be an important, efficient, and valuable source of feedback, particularly in cases of intra-organizational disclosures, because it can correct misunderstandings and wrongdoing without the financial and reputational risks associated with public disclosure.[464]

Trading Secrecy for Transparency

In 2016, the Federal Government, recognizing the confusion and uncertainty that characterized state trade secret laws, as well as the importance of trade secrets to an economy dependent on information,[465] passed the DTSA[466] in early 2016 with little serious opposition.[467] It amended the Economic Espionage Act (EEA) to create a private cause of action for the EEA's trade secret provisions.[468] The DTSA also authorized enforcement of violations of state trade secret protections "related to a product or service used in, or intended for use in, interstate or foreign commerce" in federal court.[469] Under the DTSA, federal courts can grant ex parte orders for preservation of evidence and seizure of any property used to commit or facilitate a violation of the statute, a remedy much more powerful than what was previously available under state trade secret laws.[470]

set of limitations, stemming mostly from the reality that most individuals are reluctant to report misconduct to an outside agency, particularly given the material and social risks of disclosure. Lobel, above note 459, p. 43.

[461] Lobel, above note 459, p. 47.

[462] Lobel, above note 447, p. 492. See also Lobel, above note 460 (examining the role of the lawyer in whistleblowing).

[463] Bishara *et al.*, above note 452, pp. 39–40.

[464] *Ibid.*, p. 40.

[465] In a press release announcing the 2014 version of the DTSA, Senator Hatch warned:

In today's electronic age, trade secrets can be stolen with a few keystrokes, and increasingly, they are stolen at the direction of a foreign government or for the benefit of a foreign competitor. These losses put U.S. jobs at risk and threaten incentives for continued investment in research and development. Current federal criminal law is insufficient.

See Press Release, US Senator Orrin Hatch, Hatch, Coons Introduce Bill to Combat Theft of Trade Secrets, Protect Jobs (April 29, 2014), www.hatch.senate.gov/public/index.cfm/2014/4/hatch-coons-introduce-bill-to-combat-theft-of-trade-secrets-protect-jobs.

[466] 18 USC § 1836 (2018).

[467] For more general information on the DTSA, see Z. Argento, Killing the Golden Goose: The Dangers of Strengthening Domestic Trade Secret Rights in Response to Cyber-Misappropriation (2014) 16 *Yale J. Law Technol.* 172, 177; E. Goldman, Ex Parte Seizures and the Defend Trade Secrets Act (2015) 72 *Wash & Lee Law Rev. Online* 284; D. S. Levine and S. K. Sandeen, Here Come the Trade Secret Trolls (2015) 71 *Wash. & Lee Law Rev. Online* 230, 232; S. K. Sandeen, The DTSA: The Litigator's Full-Employment Act (2015) 72 *Wash. & Lee Law Rev. Online* 308; C. B. Seaman, Introduction: The Defend Trade Secrets Act of 2015 (2015) 72 *Wash. & Lee Law Rev. Online* 278.

[468] Defend Trade Secrets Act of 2015, HR 3326, 114th Cong. § 2(a).

[469] 18 USC § 1836(b)(1) (subsection (2)(A)(1)) (2018).

[470] *Ibid.* § 1836(b)(2)(A)(i) (subsection (2)(H)).

Importantly, Congress also recognized that strong trade secret protection can threaten the public interest.[471] Consequently, the DTSA also immunizes whistleblowers from liability under federal and state trade secret law for disclosure, in confidence, of trade secrets to government officials and attorneys for the purpose of reporting a possible violation of law.[472] At the heart of recent federal law protecting trade secrets, for example, lies an allowance that provides for immunity from trade secret liability for a confidential disclosure to government officials and attorneys for the purpose of reporting or investigating a suspected violation of law.[473] The DTSA whistleblower immunity regime aims to hold companies accountable for possible misconduct by allowing authorities to scrutinize trade secrets without damaging legitimate trade secret owners.[474] The provision was allegedly designed, in part, to follow Peter Menell's path-breaking work tying trade secrecy to the need for a public policy exception to protect whistleblowing activity, published in the *California Law Review* in 2017.[475]

Immunity was needed, the government realized, in order to encourage greater accountability, since the threat of liability for trade secret misappropriation might deter individuals from coming forward.[476] Senate Judiciary Committee Chairman Charles Grassley stated:

> Too often, individuals who come forward to report wrongdoing in the workplace are punished for simply telling the truth. The amendment . . . ensures that these whistleblowers won't be slapped with allegations of trade secret theft when responsibly exposing misconduct. It's another way we can prevent retaliation and even encourage people to speak out when they witness violations of the law.[477]

And there is evidence to suggest that employees may be the best source of this information. In the context of fraud, for example, nearly 40 percent of cases of initial fraud detection came from employee tips, as compared to 16.5 percent from internal audits and 13.4 percent from management review.[478]

Given these statistics, it is possible to imagine a world where internal employees, after considering the impact of an algorithmic model on particular groups, might feel protected under the DTSA to come forward to address issues that could give rise to anti-discrimination or privacy concerns. At the very least, they may reach out to lawyers and others to determine whether a violation may have occurred. In the context of algorithmic bias, a whistleblower can be crucial to shedding light on the potential implications of an algorithm on social groups, particularly minorities, and also on other entitlements, like informational privacy.

One could imagine an employee at any major tech company, for example, noting the potential for disparate impact in algorithmic decision-making and making attempts to ensure some form of legal accountability as a result of their discovery. And if this seems like a far-fetched idea, it is well worth remembering how successful whistleblowing has been in other,

---

[471] See Press Release, US Senator Chuck Grassley, Leahy-Grassley Amendment Protecting Whistleblowers Earns Unanimous Support in Judiciary Committee (January 28, 2016), www.grassley.senate.gov/news/news-releases /leahy-grassley-amendment-protecting-whistleblowers-earns-unanimous-support.

[472] 18 USC § 1833(b) (2018).

[473] *Ibid.*; see P. S. Menell, Misconstruing Whistleblower Immunity under the Defend Trade Secrets Act (2017) 1 *Nev. Law J. Forum* 92, 92.

[474] Menell, above note 473, p. 92.

[475] P. S. Menell, Tailoring a Public Policy Exception to Trade Secret Protection (2017) 105 *Calif. Law Rev.* 1.

[476] Menell, above note 473, p. 93.

[477] Press Release, above note 471.

[478] T. Lee, Federal Law May Prompt Corporate Whistle-blowers to Act, *SF Chronicle* (February 4, 2017), www .sfchronicle.com/business/article/Federal-law-may-prompt-corporate-whistle-blowers-10907388.php.

comparable contexts of corporate wrongdoing, in the fraud and environmental arenas.[479] There is no reason to believe that similar exemptions will not have at least some positive effect in encouraging accountability in the algorithmic context as well.

Although the DTSA strengthens the remedies for trade secret misappropriation, it also balances this approach by granting immunity to would-be informants who reveal confidential information to attorneys or government investigators for the purposes of investigating violations of law.[480] Companies are actually required to notify employees if they comply with the DTSA criteria, as employees are entitled to immunity in any contract that governs the use of trade secrets. As one source further explains:

> Specifically, Section 7 of the DTSA provides criminal and civil liability to any person who discloses a trade secret under two discrete circumstances: (1) when the disclosure is made in confidence to a government official or attorney for the sole purpose of reporting or investigating a suspected violation of the law, and (2) when the disclosure is made in a complaint or other document filed under seal in a judicial proceeding.[481]

Here, the DTSA fits in with other whistleblowing protections: (1) the False Claims Act, which was enacted to deter fraud against the government; (2) the Sarbanes-Oxley Act, which instituted its own whistleblowing protections to encourage others to come forward in cases of corporate wrongdoing; and (3) the Dodd-Frank Wall Street Reform and Consumer Protection Act, which encourages the reporting of securities violations, among other elements.[482]

Yet what sets the DTSA provisions apart is significant. First, the DTSA does not require – nor even envision – public disclosure of the trade secret. The veil of partial secrecy supports the idea, advanced by Ed Felten, that "[t]ransparency needn't be an all-or-nothing choice."[483] As some have argued, the prospect of regulatory transparency, even as a general matter, can be tremendously costly from an administrative perspective.[484] For one thing, the sheer complexity, magnitude, and dynamism of algorithms and machine-learning practices make comprehension of the code – and the categories that shaped it – incredibly difficult.[485] However, under a DTSA procedure, the trade secret is under seal and largely secure from public view at all times. The only individuals charged with the ability to view the trade secret are the government, the individual whistleblower, and the whistleblower's attorney.[486]

Second, the DTSA envisions a carefully calibrated approach where a whistleblower must come forward in order to instigate an investigation, ensuring that other responsible parties (an attorney or government official) can then also play a role in investigating whether a violation occurred.[487] In other words, the statute grants immunity to those persons who theoretically are most likely to understand the effects of the algorithm, thereby reducing the information asymmetry that outside

[479] See generally Wilson, above note 448 (discussing whistleblowing in these arenas).
[480] J. C. Donnelly, Jr. and E. M. Zelnick, Trade Secret Protection vs. Whistleblower Immunity in DTSA, *Law360* (March 1, 2017), www.law360.com/articles/891560/trade-secret-protection-vs-whistleblower-immunity-in-dtsa.
[481] *Ibid.* (footnotes omitted).
[482] See *ibid.*
[483] E. Felten, Algorithms Can Be More Accountable than People, *Freedom to Tinker* (March 19, 2014), https://freedom-to-tinker.com/2014/03/19/algorithms-can-be-more-accountable-than-people.
[484] See M. Perel and N. Elkin-Koren, Black Box Tinkering: Beyond Disclosure in Algorithmic Enforcement(2017) 69 *Fla. Law Rev.* 181, 187.
[485] See *ibid.*, p. 188.
[486] Of course, the hiring of experts to audit the trade secret to determine possible liability may require additional considerations not yet envisioned by the statute, but some arguments for the extensions of immunity may at least be arguably warranted here.
[487] See 18 USC § 1833 (2018).

researchers may face.[488] The advantage of this process ostensibly ensures that potential allegations are carefully explored before any legal action is taken, and that algorithms are always behind the protected veil of secrecy or under seal in court. This case-by-case approach suggests a greater level of specificity, given that an employee would only come forward if she had a reasonable prospect of believing that a legal violation had taken place, since the statute does not provide them with any benefits other than immunity. The advantage of the DTSA procedure is that it augments, but does not replace, the discussions about the need for broad regulatory transparency in an algorithmic age by providing a case-by-case opportunity for clarity and accountability.

Third, the virtue of the DTSA whistleblower immunity lies in its employment of trusted intermediaries – government officials bound by state and federal law to protect trade secrets and attorneys bound by ethical obligations of confidentiality – to protect against the risk of commercial harm to legitimate trade secret owners.[489] The government has a long tradition of requiring disclosure of data that is protected by trade secrets when it raises important public policy concerns. The federal government has effective safeguards in place for protecting the confidentiality of trade secret information.[490] Patent applications are kept in confidence by the Patent and Trademark Office; the Food and Drug Administration reviews drug applications, keeping clinical trial data and manufacturing methods in secret; the Securities and Exchange Commission protects confidential business information; and even the Freedom of Information Act, the regulation most committed to open government, steadfastly exempts trade secrets from public disclosure.[491] Should the government violate trade secret protection, courts would allow individual owners to bring takings lawsuits against the government under the Fifth Amendment.[492] Thus, there is no reason why we would not apply the same standards in an age of algorithmic accountability.

Fourth, unlike the specific provisions of the whistleblowing provisions in the Fair Credit Act or Sarbanes-Oxley, which are calibrated to specific kinds of legal wrongdoing, the DTSA's main virtue lies in its broad reference to "violation of law,"[493] however broadly defined. This means, at least conceivably, that violations of the Federal Trade Commission Act, which protects against unfair or deceptive business practices,[494] would arguably fall within its purview. In the past, the FTC has used its authority to respond to behavioral marketing concerns, to regulate the rising authority of influencers, and to develop a set of best practices for private sector cybersecurity.[495] But even aside from the FTC's broad statute, a host of other statutes – the Health Insurance Portability and Accountability Act, the Children's Online Privacy Protection Act of 1990, the Fair and Accurate Credit Transactions Act of 2003, and the Family Educational Rights and Privacy Act – all implicate informational privacy.[496]

A fifth consideration is worth discussing, particularly in areas beyond informational privacy. Just as in the context of government fraud under the FCA, the very presence of the DTSA provisions can encourage companies to be more accountable, particularly for the

---

[488] For general economic theory around assigning whistleblower immunity, see Heyes and Kapur, above note 454.

[489] See Menell, above note 475, pp. 56, 60; see also Menell, above note 473; P. S. Menell, The Defend Trade Secrets Act Whistleblower Immunity Provision: A Legislative History (2018) 1 Bus. *Entrepreneurship Tax Law Rev.* 398.

[490] Menell, above note 473, p. 92.

[491] Menell, above note 475, pp. 28, 48.

[492] *Ibid.*, p. 49 (citing *Ruckelshaus v. Monsanto Co.*, 467 US 986 (1984)); *Zoltek Corp. v. United States*, 442 F.3d 1345 (Fed. Cir. 2006).

[493] See 18 USC § 1833 (2018).

[494] See Raymond *et al.*, above note 48, p. 242 (discussing the FTC's authority and past practices).

[495] *Ibid.*

[496] *Ibid.*, pp. 243–4.

purposes of avoiding the triggering of a whistleblowing event.[497] This may be the case even when the precise legal violation may not be clear. For example, while the limitations surrounding Title VII have been eloquently explored by Selbst and Barocas, the risk of a DTSA whistleblowing event might still encourage companies to remain vigilant against discriminatory treatment, for the purposes of assuring both their employees and the public of their commitment to non-discrimination.[498]

In the context of algorithms, we might see how the role of a whistleblower can contribute to the goal of non-discrimination. As a general matter, the DTSA requirement that every transaction is required to provide notice to every relevant employee can arguably reflect a broader, more cultural attentiveness to compliance with existing law. Moreover, the presence of a potential whistleblower creates the prospect of both direct and indirect surveillance over the internal activities of algorithmic design. Even if the sanctions are unclear, diffuse, or uncertain, the prospect of a whistleblower might create the incentives to respond to prospective disparate impacts.

Recent cases illustrate the risks involved in trusting those who write algorithms with widespread effects to ensure their efficacy. In Italy, for example, a programmer who wrote the software that timed traffic lights may have conspired with government officials, police officers, and seven private companies to rig the traffic lights.[499] The lights would stay yellow for an unusually brief period, thus catching more motorists in the red.[500] The deceit came to light only after the unusually high number of red light tickets drew official scrutiny.[501] In 2015, it was revealed that Volkswagen programmed its diesel vehicles to perform differently during emissions tests by regulators than on the road.[502] Because the software was proprietary, however, it was shielded from outside scrutiny. Under the cloak of trade secrets, Volkswagen used its source code to potentially defraud consumers and regulators for years.[503]

Although not as dramatic or craven, errors have already appeared in the algorithms used in the criminal justice system. In New Jersey, a court ordered a software developer to disclose the source code for a breathalyzer.[504] "[C]atastrophic error detection [was] disabled" in the software so it "could appear to run correctly while actually executing invalid code."[505] In 2016, a New York state court refused to admit evidence analyzed by the STRmix algorithm

---

[497] See, e.g., How to Avoid False Claims Act Liability – What Every Compliance Officer Needs to Know, Gibson Dunn (March 26, 2010), www.gibsondunn.com/publications/Pages/HowtoAvoidFalseClaimsActLiability.aspx (instructing clients how to avoid FCA liability).

[498] See Barocas and Selbst, above note 60.

[499] J. Cheng, Italian Red-Light Cameras Rigged with Shorter Yellow Lights, *Ars Technica* (February 2, 2009), https://arstechnica.com/tech-policy/2009/02/italian-red-light-cameras-rigged-with-shorter-yellow-lights.

[500] *Ibid.*

[501] S. Bratus, A. Lembree, and A. Shubina, Software on the Witness Stand: What Should It Take for Us to Trust It?, in A. Acquisti, S. W. Smith, and A.-R. Sadeghi (eds.), *Trust and Trustworthy Computing* (Springer, 2010), pp. 396, 404 ("[H]ad the bias been less pronounced, it might have not been detected at all").

[502] D. Kravets, VW Says Rogue Engineers, Not Executives, Responsible for Emissions Scandal, *Ars Technica* (October 8, 2015), http://arstechnica.com/techpolicy/2015/10/volkswagen-pulls-2016-diesel-lineup-from-us-market.

[503] See J. J. Smith, What Volkswagen's Emissions Scandal Can Teach Us about Why Companies Cheat, *KelloggInsight* (February 2, 2017), https://insight.kellogg.northwestern.edu/article/what-volkswagens-emissions-scandal-can-teach-us-about-why-companies-cheat.

[504] R. Paul, Buggy Breathalyzer Code Reflects Importance of Source Review, *Ars Technica* (May 15, 2009), https://arstechnica.com/tech-policy/2009/05/buggy-breathalyzer-code-reflects-importance-of-source-review.

[505] Short, above note 442, p. 185 (footnote omitted).

due to issues raised with its accuracy.[506] The error reduced the probability that a DNA sample matched a given defendant in certain circumstances.[507] Because the mistake was in a conditional command, it happened rarely and was thus difficult for even the developer to detect.[508] Had the algorithm's source code remained a secret, the error would have never been discovered.

These examples illustrate the significant potential for the use of existing law as a public policy carve-out to provide for the limited disclosure of trade secrets in situations of potential algorithmic bias. Companies who write proprietary software must likewise be accountable when their algorithms produce disparate treatment in decision-making, particularly given the risk that their employees may be revealing these issues to third parties under the DTSA. Under the DTSA, individuals can and should feel empowered to turn over source code to an attorney or federal employee – both of whom are bound by confidentiality obligations – so that they can fully examine the algorithm's operations and accompanying logic, and protect the interests of the public. An allowance for whistleblower protection might serve either as a pathway to address algorithmic accountability at the federal level or as an incentive to encourage companies themselves to remain vigilant against the prospect of making illegal decisions based on race or other protected characteristics. In either case, it is a valuable tool to partially address the problem.

Some Significant Caveats

There are, of course, some very important qualifications to draw here. The first, and most important, involves a central challenge to transparency itself. As many scholars have noted, source code disclosure is just a partial solution to the problem of algorithmic accountability.[509] It is hard to know, as a general matter, whether something is potentially unlawful, particularly given the gray areas of legal interpretation.[510] A limited disclosure of an algorithm tells you very little, because its effects cannot be interpreted by a simple reading of the code.[511] As Christian Sandvig explains:

> Algorithms also increasingly depend on personal data as inputs, to a degree that the same programmatically-generated Web page may never be generated twice. If an algorithm implements the equation resulting from a multivariate regression, for instance, with a large number of variables it becomes virtually impossible to predict what an algorithm will do absent plugging in specific values for each variable. This implies that some badly-behaving algorithms may produce their bad behavior only in the context of a particular dataset or application, and that harmful discrimination itself could be conceptualized as a combination of an algorithm and its data, not as just the algorithm alone.[512]

---

[506] *Ibid.* See J. McKinley, Judge Rejects DNA Test in Trial over Garrett Phillips's Murder, *New York Times* (August 26, 2016), www.nytimes.com/2016/08/27/nyregion/judge-rejects-dna-test-in-trial-over-garrett-phillipss-murder.html; Ruling – the People of the State of New York versus Oral Nicholas Hillary (NY): DNA Evidence Admissibility, *STRmix* (September 12, 2017), https://strmix.esr.cri.nz/news/ruling-the-people-of-the-state-of-new-york-versus-oral-nicholas-hillary-ny-dna-evidence-admissibility .

[507] See Ruling, above note 506.

[508] *Ibid.*

[509] Kroll *et al.*, above note 60, pp. 638–9.

[510] See Lobel, above note 447, p. 464 ("Employees frequently face possible illegal behavior, but the degree of unlawfulness is usually open to interpretation").

[511] Sandvig *et al.*, above note 434, p. 10.

[512] *Ibid.*

To compensate for this problem, investigators have to plug data into the algorithm in order to see how it operates.[513]

Even aside from the general issue regarding interpretation, there are other objections to draw. Perhaps the most obvious is that a whistleblower provision only partially addresses the problem of algorithmic accountability. It is, admittedly, an imperfect first step toward pulling back the veil of trade secrecy over source code. And, as Kroll and his co-authors note, full transparency is not always possible, or even desirable, if it amounts to destruction of a trade secret or revelation of sensitive or protected data.[514] At other times, it can lead to other undesirable effects, like gaming of the system.[515] And the problem may not always be secrecy or opacity; as Barocas and Selbst have reminded us, the problem may actually reside in systems that are inscrutable, because they make it impossible for a human to intuitively reason about how they operate.[516] As Mike Annany and Kate Crawford further elaborate, the very notion of transparency suggests that one can glean insights from observing a set of results, and then hold systems accountable for their choices.[517] But there are different types of opacity at work here.[518] As Jenna Burrell reminds, one kind involves the notion of intentional concealment; another involves the complexity and specialization of the information; and another involves the complexity of machine learning itself.[519]

Another cluster of objections to the DTSA, demonstrated by some other areas of case law, is that a broad public policy in favor of whistleblowing activities might justify aggrieved employees to engage in a "fishing expedition" prior to their discharge that might lead them to carry off proprietary information, including the data that an algorithm was trained upon. In one such case involving Sarbanes-Oxley, for example, an employee possessed a large number of confidential documents, compelling a court to observe that a whistleblowing policy "[b]y no means . . . authorize[s] disgruntled employees to pilfer a wheelbarrow" full of proprietary documents.[520]

Moreover, it bears noting that the risk of such disclosures – even to a trusted intermediary under the DTSA – may lead companies to be ever more protective over their algorithms, limiting exposure to only the most loyal of employees or by overly directing resources toward their constant surveillance and protection.[521] As one lawyer puts it, "[t]he immunity provision

[513] See *ibid.*; see also D. R. Desai and J. A. Kroll, Trust But Verify: A Guide to Algorithms and the Law (2017) 31 *Harv. J. Law Technol.* 1, 10 (noting that auditing "can only test 'a small subset of potential inputs'" (quoting Kroll *et al.*, above note 60, p. 650)).

[514] *Ibid.*, p. 38.

[515] *Ibid.*, p. 9.

[516] See Barocas and Selbst, above note 60, p. 692.

[517] See M. Annany and K. Crawford, Seeing without Knowing: Limitations of the Transparency Ideal and Its Application to Algorithmic Accountability (2018) 20 *New Media Soc.* 973, 974.

[518] J. Burrell, How the Machine "Thinks": Understanding Opacity in Machine Learning Algorithms (2016) 3 *Big Data Soc.* 1–2.

[519] *Ibid.*

[520] *JDS Uniphase Corp.* v. *Jennings*, 473 F. Supp. 2d 697, 702 (ED Va. 2007). Instead, the court granted a further status conference to consider the extent of the breach, noting that it needed to examine which of the documents were proprietary and the extent of the remedy to be granted. *Ibid.* at 705.

[521] Another objection to a whistleblowing exception stems from FOIA. Although regulatory agencies often compel companies to disclose their trade secrets, either through a contractual agreement or through regulatory activities, there is some risk that FOIA could be used to circumvent the seclusion that a government could provide. Wilson, above note 448, pp. 276–7 (discussing this possibility). Although FOIA is designed to encourage disclosure of general information, it includes an exemption for trade secrets. *Ibid.*, p. 281. However, case law has suggested that the government has a discretionary ability to disclose trade secrets to a requesting party under certain circumstances. *Ibid.* Since many federal regulations actually require a government agency to provide notice to the trade secret holder, the trade secret holder can then institute review under the Administrative Procedure Act. If an

of the DTSA protects disclosing individuals, but individuals cannot disclose if they have no access to the information."[522]

Finally, it bears mentioning that this solution is only a partial one – it does not go far enough. For example, immunity under the DTSA would be more effective if coupled with a similar whistleblowing exception to the CFAA (or even a limited exclusion for terms of service violations).[523] It becomes clear, from the issues surrounding the CFAA, that a whistleblower exception might be further warranted in those circumstances, leading commentators to support the idea.[524] In 2008, in the wake of the suicide of Aaron Swartz, US Representative Zoe Lofgren proposed a bill called "Aaron's law," which would have excluded terms of service violations from the list of violations under the CFAA.[525] It was never passed. And while the DTSA provides immunity for disclosures to attorneys or government officials, it does not immunize disclosures made to journalists, academics, watchdog groups, or the general public.[526]

Of course, noting the above, it would be an overstatement to say that a whistleblowing exception, as it exists in the DTSA, solves the problem of algorithmic accountability. It cannot solve, as a substantive matter, the issue of how to make algorithms more accountable.[527] However, it would also be an understatement to say that the DTSA's whistleblowing provisions are completely unrelated to the issue of algorithmic transparency. For one thing, they avoid the pitfalls associated with full transparency (like destruction of a trade secret), because they provide for a sort of *in camera* review of the information. Second, because the person bringing the information to the lawyer or official is an employee, he or she may be able to address the substantial issues of information asymmetry associated with external audits, thus addressing issues of technological literacy and complexity.

Indeed, although the DTSA provisions are extraordinarily promising, it is also important to note that other jurisdictions have taken even broader steps to protect whistleblowing. For example, an equivalent EU Directive included numerous exceptions for the public disclosure of trade secrets "'for exercising the right to freedom of expression and information ... including respect for freedom and pluralism of the media,' and for revealing a 'misconduct, wrongdoing or illegal activity, provided that the respondent acted for the purpose of protecting the general public interest.'"[528]

Admittedly, no solution is perfect, due in no small part to the administrative costs involved and the difficulty of detection. However, by exploiting exemptions in existing law, and by supplementing those exemptions with particular audit requirements, we can create some step toward encouraging a greater culture of algorithmic accountability. At the very least, the whistleblower exemption should encourage companies to be ever more vigilant about the risks of discrimination, since it demonstrates that secrecy might not always trump accountability.

---

improper disclosure occurred, the trade secret holder may be able to file a claim for compensation under the Fifth Amendment Takings Clause. *Ibid.*, pp. 281–2; see *Ruckelshaus*, above note 492, at 1012.

[522] See J. J. Altman, D. E. Lilienfeld, and M. Pereira, License to Leak: The DTSA and the Risks of Immunity (2016) 28 *Intell. Prop. Technol. Law J.* 8.

[523] See E. Spath, Whistleblowers Take a Gamble under the CFAA: How Federal Prosecutors Game the System under the Proposed Changes to the Act (2016) 37 *Univ. La Verne Law Rev.* 369, 401–2.

[524] *Ibid.*, p. 401 (arguing that Congress should enact a statutory law exception to the CFAA).

[525] *Ibid.*, pp. 373–4.

[526] Altman *et al.*, above note 522, pp. 6–7.

[527] See generally Kroll *et al.*, above note 60.

[528] A. B. Patel, J. Pade, V. Cundiff, and B. Newmann, The Global Harmonization of Trade Secret Law: The Convergence of Protections for Trade Secret Information in the United States and European Union (2016) 83 *Def. Couns. J.* 472, 484 (footnotes omitted).

CONCLUSION

This chapter has explored both the limits and the possibilities of bringing a culture of accountability to algorithms. As I have argued, in the absence of oversight, a mixture of industry self-regulation and whistleblower engagement offers us one path forward in the future direction of civil rights law to address the issues raised by AI. We can no longer afford to consider issues of informational privacy and due process in a vacuum. Instead of focusing on the value of explanations, we must turn toward lifting the veil of secrecy that allows companies to escape detection. Or we must incentivize companies to remain vigilant against discrimination through other means.

As this chapter suggests, it is indeed possible to exploit the potential for whistleblower liability as a public policy exemption to encourage greater algorithmic transparency. On a much deeper, more abstract level, the availability of these solutions also portends a much-needed shift in our language and approach to civil rights. The future of civil rights in an age of AI requires us to explore the limitations within intellectual property and, more specifically, trade secrets. If we can exploit the exemptions that already exist within trade secret law, we can also create an entirely new generation of civil rights developments altogether.

4

Algorithmic Legitimacy

Ari Ezra Waldman

The debate over algorithmic decision-making has focused primarily on two things: legal accountability and bias. Legal accountability seeks to leverage the institutions of law and compliance to put guard rails around the use of artificial intelligence (AI). This literature insists that if a state is going to use an algorithm to evaluate teachers or if a bank is going to use AI to make loan application decisions, both should do so transparently, in accordance with fair procedure, and be subject to interrogation. Algorithmic fairness seeks to highlight the ways in which AI discriminates on the basis of race, gender, and ethnicity, among other protected characteristics. This literature calls for making technologies that use AI, whether search engines or digital cameras, more inclusive by better training AI on diverse inputs and improving automated systems that have been shown to have a "disparate impact" on marginalized populations.

The law and information scholar Frank Pasquale calls these movements part of the "first wave" of algorithmic discourse. The first wave focuses "on improving existing systems" from within: better data, better procedures, better systems.[1] I argue that in so doing, this research agenda is trying to *legitimize* algorithmic systems, but with the same types of tools we've applied to human decision-making. This makes them inadequate.

Legitimacy is a conceptual frame for understanding why we accept authority. It is theoretical and empirical: it identifies the conditions of authority and asks people how those conditions affect their willingness to accept and obey that authority.[2] Legitimate authorities have the public's trust, the breathing room to act, and the obedience of even those adversely affected by their decisions. It is, therefore, essential for legal scholarship and any decision-maker, mechanized or human.[3] Through a series of experiments, Tom Tyler and others found that institutions of authority like the police or the courts are considered legitimate when they follow fair procedures and treat people with kindness and respect. Even those who experience adverse outcomes – losing an appeal, getting a speeding ticket, or supporting the losing side of a Supreme Court case – are willing to accept those decisions as legitimate as long as the procedure was fair.[4] So understood, Tylerian legitimacy is a Rawlsian sociolegal

---

[1] F. Pasquale, The Second Wave of Algorithmic Accountability, *Law and Political Economy* (November 25, 2019), https://lpeblog.org/2019/11/25/the-second-wave-of-algorithmic-accountability/ (identifying the dual concerns of accountability and bias).

[2] See T. R. Tyler and Y. J. Huo, *Trust in the Law: Encouraging Public Cooperation with the Police and Courts* (Russell Sage Foundation, 2002), p. 120.

[3] T. R. Tyler, *Why People Obey the Law* (Princeton University Press, 1990), pp. 3–8.

[4] See, e.g., J. Sunshine and T. Tyler, The Role of Procedural Justice and Legitimacy in Shaping Public Support for Policing (2003) 37 *Law Soc. Rev.* 513.

concept:[5] both legal legitimacy and Rawlsian liberalism assume that fair process yields better outcomes without committing to an *a priori* notion of the good. It is sociolegal in that it situates individuals as both authority and subject, and is contingent on both a well-functioning system of legal accountability and the social norms and expectations of the context in which authority is deployed.

But when the individual is replaced by a machine and the legitimizing capacities of institutions like due process have been undermined by powerful players in today's political economy, these structures lose their power. That is, machines can't treat people with respect. Nor can their complex and often proprietary coding be subjected to traditional forms of legal interrogation, at least not without significant expense and specialized knowledge. And as a practical matter, the policy choices and discourses of neoliberalism – an ideology that seeks to constrain government by emphasizing efficiency and innovation in the service of capital production[6] – have undermined process and procedure as a legitimizing force.[7] Therefore, Tylerian legitimacy should be ill-equipped to legitimize algorithmic systems. This chapter explores this argument in detail.

AUTOMATION AND LEGITIMACY: A BRIEF LITERATURE REVIEW

What Is Automated Decision-Making?

Algorithms are sequences of logical, mathematical operations. They can automate decision-making processes by providing computer systems with instructions to analyze inputted data.[8] With those instructions, algorithms are supposed to identify meaningful relationships and likely patterns in large datasets, thereby mechanizing decisions that used to be done entirely by humans. Those developing and marketing these tools assure their public and private clients that their algorithms will make decisions fast and without friction from prejudiced human decision-makers. That is what makes algorithmic decision-making so attractive; it promises to do things humans never could.

These algorithms are now being deployed in a wide range of commercial and governmental contexts, many of which have been discussed elsewhere in this book. For example, banks use algorithms to determine which applicants get approved or rejected for loans.[9] Houston has used an automated system to evaluate teachers, and relied on the algorithm's output to determine tenure, contract terms, hiring and firing, and salary.[10] That system has been challenged in the courts.[11] Various cities use algorithms to decide where, and in what

---

[5] See T. Tyler, Procedural Justice, Legitimacy, and the Effective Rule of Law (2003) 30 *Crime Just.* 283; T. Tyler, Governing amid Diversity: The Effect of Fair Decision-Making Procedures on the Legitimacy of Government (1994) 28 *Law Soc. Rev.* 809, 810 n. 1; see also R. H. Fallon, Jr., Legitimacy and the Constitution (2005) 118 *Harv. Law Rev.* 1787.

[6] See C. Blalock, Neoliberalism and the Crisis of Legal Theory (2014) 77 *Law Contemp. Probs.* 71, 72–3, 83–90 (defining neoliberalism and its relation to legal theory).

[7] See J. E. Cohen, *Between Truth and Power: The Legal Constructions of Informational Capitalism* (Oxford University Press, 2019), pp. 14–57.

[8] See J. Kroll, J. Huey, S. Barocas, *et al.*, Accountable Algorithms (2017) 165 *Univ. Pa. Law Rev.* 633, 640 n. 14 (defining "algorithm" as "a well-defined set of steps for accomplishing a certain goal").

[9] See, e.g., D. K. Citron and F. Pasquale, The Scored Society: Due Process for Automated Predictions (2017) 89 *Wash. Law Rev.* 1.

[10] See C. O'Neil, *Weapons of Math Destruction: How Big Data Increases Inequality and Threatens Democracy* (Penguin, 2016).

[11] See *Hous. Fed'n of Teachers, Local 2415 v. Hous. Indep. Sch. Dist.*, 251 F. Supp. 3d 1168 (SD Tex. 2017).

force, to allocate police officers on the beat.[12] States are using algorithms to mete out government benefits, like Medicare and Medicaid.[13] And algorithms are dominating fields as diverse as the healthcare industry and national intelligence, education and criminal justice, and finance and infrastructure.[14]

Legitimacy

There are various definitions of legitimacy in the philosophical, social science, and legal discourses. For example, Marc Suchman defines legitimacy as "a generalized perception or assumption that the actions of an entity are desirable, proper, and appropriate within some socially constructed system of norms, values, beliefs, and definitions."[15] Tom Tyler, a law professor and psychologist, defines legitimacy as "perceived obligation to comply with the directive of an authority, irrespective of personal gain."[16] Within the research agenda pioneered by Tyler, Richard Fallon situates the definitions of legitimacy on a continuum stretching from "ideal" to "minimalist" theories. Ideal theories of legitimacy "attempt to specify the necessary conditions for assertions of state authority."[17] On the ideal side, Fallon brings together procedural and substantive approaches to legitimacy. In *The Federalist No. 22*, for example, Alexander Hamilton argued that legitimacy was based on the actual consent of the governed, noting that the "consent of the people" was the "pure, original fountain of all legitimate authority."[18] This contributed to a longstanding tradition of associating consent with the legitimacy of authorities.[19] John Rawls is situated adjacent to Hamilton in Fallon's continuum since *A Theory of Justice* posits a legitimate government construct based on hypothetical consent behind a veil of ignorance, rather than actual consent in practice.[20] Alternatively, other "ideal" legitimacy theorists have argued that legitimacy is based on standards of justice, not the "procedural pedigree" of the regime.[21]

On the other side of Fallon's spectrum, minimalist approaches to legitimacy define a floor above which regimes deserve support and compliance from their subjects.[22] These approaches always start with the notion that any government is better than no government, as reasonable human flourishing would not be possible in a state of nature, anarchy, or chaos. For David Copp and Frank Michelman, for example, unless there is some obviously better alternative, a regime at least capable of ensuring that everyone plays by the same rules is legitimate because it is far better than life without it.[23]

---

[12] See A. D. Selbst, Disparate Impact in Big Data Policing (2017) 52 *Ga. Law Rev.* 109.

[13] See M. Whittaker, K. Crawford, R. Dobbe, *et al.*, AI Now Report 2018, AI Now Institute (December 2018), https://ainowinstitute.org/AI_Now_2018_Report.pdf.

[14] See V. Eubanks, *Automating Inequality: How High-Tech Tools Profile, Police, and Punish the Poor* (St. Martin's Press, 2016); N. Terry, Navigating the Incoherence of Big Data Reform Proposals (2015) 43 *J. Law Med. Ethics* (Supplement) 44, 44; D. Van Puyvelde, S. Coulthart, and M. S. Hossain, Beyond the Buzzword: Big Data and National Security Decision-Making (2017) 93 *Int. Aff.* 1397, 1398.

[15] M. Suchman, Managing Legitimacy: Strategic and Institutional Approaches (1995) 20 *Acad. Manage. Rev.* 571, 574.

[16] Tyler, above note 3, pp. 27, 45.

[17] Fallon, above note 5, p. 1797.

[18] C. Rossiter (ed.), *The Federalist Papers No. 22 (Alexander Hamilton)* (Signet, 1961).

[19] G. Klosko, Reformist Consent and Political Obligation (1991) 39 *Pol. Stud.* 676, 676–7.

[20] See J. Rawls, *A Theory of Justice* (Harvard University Press, 1971).

[21] W. N. Eskridge, Jr. and G. Peller, The New Public Law Movement: Moderation as a Postmodern Cultural Form (1991) 89 *Mich. Law Rev.* 707, 747.

[22] See Fallon, above note 5, p. 1798.

[23] See F. I. Michelman, Ida's Way: Constructing the Respect-Worthy Governmental System (2003) 72 *Fordham Law Rev.* 345; D. Copp, The Idea of a Legitimate State (1999) 28 *Phil. Pub. Aff.* 3, 43–4.

Undoubtedly, there are a host of theories of legitimacy between ideal and minimalist approaches. Randy Barnett, for example, suggests that a legitimate regime is one whose law-making processes "provide good reasons to think that a law restricting freedom is necessary to protect the rights of others without improperly infringing the rights of those whose liberty is being restricted."[24] This approach dates back to Max Weber, who argued that "the most common form of legitimacy is the belief in legality, the compliance with enactments ... which have been made in the accustomed manner."[25]

Throughout this voluminous discourse, however, the notion that fair procedures and respectful treatment legitimize government decisions has dominated sociological and legal scholarship on voluntary compliance with the law. In several seminal studies of legal legitimacy, Tom Tyler and various colleagues have shown that people comply with the law even when they experience adverse outcomes and deterrence mechanisms are weak or non-existent. Rather, people follow authorities when they find them legitimate, and popular perceptions of legitimacy have been found to hinge, at least in part, on the existence of fair and neutral procedural safeguards, the opportunity to be heard, and kind and respectful treatment.[26] For example, Tyler found that among a sample of Chicago residents who had a personal encounter with legal authorities over a one-year period, their perceptions of the fairness of the procedures they encountered were the primary movers of their perceptions of the legitimacy of the law.[27] He found the same among a sub-set of individuals who had direct experiences with the Chicago traffic court.[28] Notably, Tyler's procedural fairness model is agnostic as to ends; even those individuals who came out worse off due to the actions of authorities, institutions, or law were willing to comply with the law if the process was fair and the authorities were respectful.[29]

LEGITIMACY AND THE FIRST WAVE

First-wave proposals seek to remedy concerns about errors, opacity, privacy, and biases of algorithmic decision-making by ameliorating bias, providing explanations for decisions, adding trappings of accountability, and regulating algorithmic decision-making through data protection law. Put another way, they are trying to bring the things that make human decision-making legitimate – fair procedure, respect for persons, and the opportunity to be heard – into the algorithmic context.

Predictions and Mistakes

Algorithms do not predict the future. Rather, they promise to estimate the probability that something will happen based on the data they have.[30] In other words, an algorithm cannot tell

---

[24] R. E. Barnett, Constitutional Legitimacy (2003) 103 *Colum. Law Rev.* 111, 146.

[25] G. Roth and C. Wittich (eds.), *Max Weber, Economy and Society*, E. Fischoff *et al.* (trans.) (University of California Press, 1968), Vol. 1, p. 37.

[26] See, e.g., See E. A. Lind and T. R. Tyler, *The Social Psychology of Procedural Justice* (Springer, 1988); Sunshine and Tyler, above note 4, pp. 526–8, 530–1.

[27] See Tyler, above note 5, p. 313.

[28] See Tyler, supra note 3, pp. 8–18, 57–70.

[29] See, e.g., T. Jonathan-Zamir, B. Hasisi, and Y. Maragalioth, Is It the What or the How? The Roles of High-Policing Tactics and Procedural Justice in Predicting Perceptions of Hostile Treatment: The Case of Security Checks at Ben-Gurion Airport, Israel (2016) 50 *Law Soc. Rev.* 608.

[30] S. M. Bellovin, R. M. Hutchins, T. Jebara, and S. Zimmeck, When Enough Is Enough: Location Tracking, Mosaic Theory, and Machine Learning (2014) 8 *NY Univ. J. Law Lib.* 556, 591.

a loan officer that a particular applicant will, with certainty, repay her loan on time. The automated system is supposedly able to tell the bank that, based on historical loan repayment data and large sets of metadata about lots of different people, an applicant with a certain mix of factors is more or less likely to repay her loan than another applicant with different characteristics. This can be helpful to banks, which previously had to make financial risk decisions based on the informal impressions of loan officers interviewing applicants.

But algorithms' reliance on probabilities means that they will necessarily make mistakes. Some individuals who get tagged as bad credit risks are more than capable of repaying their loans, and those applicants who were approved for loans will default. False negatives will happen. Consider one popular example: Marco Ribeiro, Sameer Singh, and Carlos Guestrin trained a machine to differentiate between images of dogs and wolves by feeding it images they had manually labeled "dog" and "wolf." The program correctly classified many new images, but rather than learning about dogs and wolves, it found patterns that differentiated the pictures generally, particularly the presence of snow and trees. Wolves are far more likely than dogs to be found in the snow, so the algorithm identified all pictures with snow as "wolf."[31]

Mistakes can have serious effects on those adversely affected. In just the last few years, cancer victims have been denied health benefits and have had to sue their insurance companies to get what they are due,[32] welfare recipients have been stripped of their only source of funds,[33] and random citizens have been placed on government watch lists for no reason.[34] Ethel Jacobs, an elderly woman in Arkansas, had the number of hours for an in-home health aid cut by nearly half as a result of a mistake in the state's algorithm.[35] What is more, mistakes cannot be excised from automated decision-making systems; like statistics, they rely on probabilities, not certainties.

In response, first-wave advocates have called for using civil rights law to ameliorate the harms of miscategorization.[36] Many have called for keeping a "human in the loop" to guard against mistakes and injustice.[37] They have also recommended *ex ante* and *ex post* evaluation of training data and algorithmic design to identify the potential for statistical errors and their effects, among other procedural proposals.[38]

Complexity and Opacity

Automated systems demand many data inputs. But as the number of inputs increases, algorithms become more complex and more opaque and resistant to interrogation.[39] Their

---

[31] See M. T. Ribeiro, S. Singh, and C. Guestrin, "Why Should I Trust You?": Explaining the Predictions of Any Classifier, in Proceedings of the 22nd ACM SIGKDD International Conference on Knowledge Discovery and Data Mining (2016), https://doi.org/10.1145/2939672.2939778.

[32] See Eubanks, above note 17.

[33] See S. Wilcock, Policing Welfare: Risk, Gender and Criminality (2016) 5 *Int. J. Crime Justice Soc. Dem.* 113.

[34] See, e.g., M. Hu, Big Data Blacklisting (2016) 67 *Fla. Law Rev.* 1735.

[35] See C. Lecher, What Happens When an Algorithm Cuts Your Healthcare, *The Verge* (March 21, 2018), www.theverge.com/2018/3/21/17144260/healthcare-medicaid-algorithm-arkansas-cerebral-palsy.

[36] See, e.g., P. Kim, Data Driven Discrimination at Work (2017) 58 *Wm. Mary Law Rev.* 857, 901–32 (arguing for reconceptualizing anti-discrimination law to address the harms caused by data mining and surveillance of employees).

[37] M. L. Jones, Right to a Human in the Loop: Political Constructions of Computer Automation & Personhood from Data Banks to Algorithms (2017) 47 *Soc. Stud. Sci.* 216, 217; A. M. Froomkin, I. Kerr, and J. Pineau, When AIs Outperform Doctors: Confronting the Challenges of a Tort-Induced Over-Reliance on Machine Learning (2019) 61 *Ariz. Law Rev.* 33.

[38] See S. K. Katyal, Private Accountability in the Age of Artificial Intelligence (2019) 66 *UCLAL Rev.* 54, 116.

[39] L. Breiman, Statistical Modeling: The Two Cultures (2001) 16 *Stat. Sci.* 199, 206–8.

opacity is both technical and legal. As Frank Pasquale has argued, automated decision-making systems are "black boxes."[40] They require "specialized knowledge" to be understood,[41] but even the engineers who create them may not be able to fully explain how inputs become outputs.[42] Law metastasizes algorithmic opacity because companies that create automated decision-making systems protect their algorithms as proprietary trade secrets.[43]

As black boxes, algorithms are difficult to challenge, interrogate, and appeal. In Idaho, for example, an algorithm the state instituted in 2011 cut the home healthcare allocations for some patients by nearly 42 percent.[44] The state office of the American Civil Liberties Union (ACLU) sued on behalf of several state residents in the same position, with the Court concluding that "the participants receive no explanation for the denial, have no written standards to refer to for guidance, and often have no family member, guardian, or paid assistance to help them," leaving them effectively unable or at least ill-equipped to push back and appeal.[45] Richard Eppink, Legal Director of the ACLU Idaho, called the appeal process "really meaningless" because the people processing the appeals couldn't understand the algorithm, either. According to Eppink, they "would look at the system and say, 'It's beyond my authority and my expertise to question the quality of this result.'"[46] In Idaho and elsewhere, attorneys challenging algorithmic systems that wiped away millions in benefits to needy individuals either were refused access to proprietary algorithmic code or had to learn how to read and analyze source code themselves, making the process of litigating algorithmic decision-making cases uniquely difficult.

Proposals to mitigate black box algorithmic systems range from transparency[47] to Rebecca Wexler's more robust call for not recognizing AI trade secrecy claims in criminal proceedings.[48] Other first-wave proposals include Danielle Keats Citron's call for replacing old forms of agency adjudication and rule-making with reconceived systems that include audit trails, education for hearing officers on machine fallibility, detailed explanations, publicly accessible code, and systems testing, among other recommendations.[49] And Andrew Selbst and Solon Barocas argue that a right to explanation of automated decisions entitles individuals to clarity about the process behind a model's development.[50] Together, these proposals hope to mitigate the effects of algorithmic opacity on individuals by supplementing traditional forms of accountability with new addenda. That is an important project, but it does not challenge the underlying assumption that algorithmic accountability regimes should sit on the same foundation as due process artifacts of the industrial age.

[40] See F. Pasquale, *Black Box Society: The Secret Algorithms that Control Money and Information* (Harvard University Press, 2015).
[41] A. D. Selbst and S. Barocas, The Intuitive Appeal of Explainable Machines (2018) 87 *Fordham Law Rev.* 1085, 1092–4.
[42] See E. K. Cheng, Being Pragmatic about Forensic Linguistics (2013) 21 *J. Law Policy* 541, 548.
[43] See Citron and Pasquale, above note 12. See also R. Wexler, Life, Liberty, and Trade Secrets: Intellectual Property in the Criminal Justice System (2017) 70 *Stan. Law Rev.* 1343.
[44] See Lecher, above note 38.
[45] *K.W. v. Armstrong*, No. 1:12-cv-00022-BLW (D. Idaho March 28, 2016).
[46] Lecher, above note 38.
[47] See T. Zarsky, Transparency in Data Mining: From Theory to Practice, in B. Custers, T. Calders, B. Schermer, and T. Zarsky (eds.), *Discrimination and Privacy in the Information Society: Data Mining and Profiling in Large Databases* (Springer, 2013), pp. 301, 317.
[48] R. Wexler, Life, Liberty, and Trade Secrets: Intellectual Property in the Criminal Justice System (2017) 70 *Stan. Law Rev.* 1343.
[49] D. K. Citron, Technological Due Process (2007) 85 *Wash. Univ. Law Rev.* 1249, 1305–13.
[50] See Selbst and Barocas, above note 44, p. 1087.

Power and Privacy

The use, proliferation, and marketing of algorithmic decision-making tools also incent the rampant data collection inherent in what Shoshana Zuboff has called "surveillance capitalism."[51] A radical form of capitalism based on the commodification of "reality" and its repurposing into data for producers to analyze their consumers' behavior, surveillance capitalism features, among other things, a persistent drive toward more data collection and more advanced data analytical tools, the development of new mechanized tools for surveillance, the desire to customize digital experiences, and ongoing experiments to determine the codes and designs that maximize user disclosure and engagement. As such, surveillance capitalism envisions endless cycles of data collection and use and ongoing erosions of privacy expectations and norms.

AI and algorithmic decision-making tools are both artifacts and propellers of surveillance capitalism. They are products of a capitalistic system based on data just like mass-produced goods are products of a capitalistic system based on steel, electricity, and manufacturing. Algorithmic systems also amplify surveillance capitalism when their designers promote AI's ability to analyze the thousands of data points producers collect when they surveil their consumers, thus further incenting data collection on end. As Steve Bellovin has explained: "Machine learning algorithms are able to deduce information – including information that has no obvious linkage to the input data – that may otherwise have remained private due to the natural limitations of manual and human-driven investigation."[52] Algorithms, then, erode the obscurity we rely on to maintain our privacy[53] and allow data collectors to develop creepy portraits of consumers for behavioral targeting and manipulation.[54]

In one widely publicized example, statisticians at Target Corp. were able to use an algorithm to analyze purchase histories, demographic data, and information bought from data brokers to determine that a 13-year-old girl was very likely pregnant. The company mailed her a coupon, but it arrived before the young woman had the opportunity to share the news with her family.[55] The algorithm not only outed her as pregnant to her parents, but stole away her right to determine for herself when and how she would share that news. AI's deployment for face recognition and, more recently, affect recognition, or to determine subjects' emotional states, threatens core privacy interests.[56] In Minnesota, a school district has used webcams to spy on its students to help an AI determine if they are happy, sad, or angry.[57] Alexa and Siri are trying to pick up emotional undertones in speech.[58] And these are just some of the ways in which AI can challenge our privacy interests in intimate information, obscurity, and autonomy.

---

[51] S. Zuboff, *The Age of Surveillance Capitalism: The Fight for a Human Future at the New Frontier of Power* (Profile Books, 2018).

[52] Bellovin *et al.*, above note 33, p. 558.

[53] See F. Stutzman and W. Hartzog, The Case for Online Obscurity (2013) 101 *Calif. Law Rev.* 1.

[54] See, e.g., S. Greenberg, S. Boring, J. Vermeulen, and J. Dostal, Dark Patterns in Proxemic Interactions: A Critical Perspective, in Proceedings of 2014 Conference on Designing Interactive Systems (June 2014), pp. 523, 524.

[55] See C. Duhigg, How Companies Learn Your Secrets, *New York Times* (February 16, 2012), www.nytimes.com /2012/02/19/magazine/shopping-habits.html.

[56] See M. Whittaker, K. Crawford, R. Dobbe, *et al.*, AI Now Report 2018 (December 2018), p. 15, https:// ainowinstitute.org/AI_Now_2018_Report.pdf.

[57] *Ibid.*

[58] See W. Knight, Emotional Intelligence Might Be a Virtual Assistant's Secret Weapon, *MIT Technology Review* (June 13, 2016), www.technologyreview.com/s/601654/amazon-working-on-making-alexa-recognize-your-emotions.

In response, Margot Kaminski suggests that the General Data Protection Regulation (GDPR), Europe's comprehensive data privacy legislation, can offer robust protection from harms stemming from automated decision-making because it entitles data subjects to explanations about the "logic" behind any algorithmic system.[59] And Lilian Edwards and Michael Veale argue that the "right to be forgotten," data protection impact assessments, and certifications and privacy seals can help make algorithms more accountable.[60] Washington State lawmakers have proposed a rule that would make public-sector automated systems and the datasets "freely available by the vendor before, during, and after deployment for agency or independent third-party testing, auditing, or research."[61] And California privacy advocate Alastair Mactaggart, who started the push for the state's comprehensive consumer privacy law, recently proposed a new law that would, in relevant part, include transparency requirements around both public and commercial uses of algorithmic decision-making "so consumers can know how algorithms are evaluating them in ways that affect the job offers they see, the loans they're eligible for, and other decisions that affect their lives."[62] These first-wave proposals use process to try to rein in the worst errors and excesses of algorithmic decision-making systems with the goal of creating better automated tools.

Bias and Discrimination

Advocates of algorithmic decision-making promise a future without bias. Machines don't know if job applicants are black or white, they say. Algorithms simply compute the numbers, and numbers are dispassionate. Algorithms, they argue, are neutral pieces of technology.

That, of course, is not the case. Technologies, Langdon Winner famously argued, have politics.[63] They embody particular power relations in society, like white supremacy, patriarchy, and heteronormativity. And numbers are not inherently tied to truth; their meaning varies with human interpretations, understanding, and deployment. Algorithms trying to predict social outcomes embody political and power assumptions, as well. Indeed, as a litany of researchers have already shown, algorithmic systems can be just as biased, racist, and discriminatory as humans: data inputs reflect society's biases,[64] designers are not demographically diverse,[65] and humans determine the independent variables in any automated decision-making system.[66]

In response, researchers in the first wave of algorithmic discourse argue that data inputs should be diversified and that those who use algorithmic decision-making systems should be

---

[59] M. E. Kaminski, The Right to Explanation, Explained (2019) 34 *Berkeley Technol. Law J.* 189, 199.

[60] See L. Edwards and M. Veale, Slave to the Algorithm? Why a "Right to an Explanation" is Probably Not the Remedy You Are Looking for (2017) 16 *Duke Law Technol. Rev.* 18, 67–80.

[61] See D. J. Pangburn, Washington Could Be the First State to Rein in Automated Decision-Making, Fast Company (February 8, 2019), www.fastcompany.com/90302465/washington-introduces-landmark-algorithmic-accountability-laws.

[62] See Californians for Consumer Privacy, A Letter from Alastair Mactaggart, Founder & Chair of Californians for Consumer Privacy, www.caprivacy.org/.

[63] L. Winner, Do Artfiacts Have Politics? (1990) 109 *Daedalus* 121.

[64] K. Crawford, M. Whittaker, M. C. Elish, *et al.*, The AI Now Report: The Social and Economic Implications of Artificial Intelligence Technologies in the Near-Term (2016), pp. 6–7, https://ainowinstitute.org/AI_Now_2016_Report.pdf.

[65] K. Crawford, Artificial Intelligence's White Guy Problem, *New York Times* (June 25, 2016), http://nyti.ms/28YaKg7.

[66] D. Lehr and P. Ohm, Playing with the Data: What Legal Scholars Should Learn about Machine Learning (2017) 51 *UC Davis Law Rev.* 653, 665–7.

trained on the biases that can result from their work.[67] The engineering profession and their employers now recognize that equality, justice, and non-discrimination are not usually front and center during engineering education and coding work.[68] In direct response to first-wave advocates, workplaces and universities now tout ethics and bias training programs for their technology students and employees. Beyond broadening datasets and training engineers, some advocates call for fixing programming biases from within the code.[69] The AI Now Institute recommends algorithmic impact assessments, modeled after environmental or privacy impact assessments, to document and assess a system's fairness.[70] Mary Madden, Michele Gilman, Karen Levy, and Alice Marwick call for including the voices of the poor in algorithmic design to ameliorate socioeconomic discrimination.[71] Crawford and others have argued that the population of engineers must be diversified, as well, because "inclusivity matters – from who designs it to who sits on the company boards and which ethical perspectives are included. Otherwise, we risk constructing machine intelligence that mirrors a narrow and privileged vision of society, with its old, familiar biases and stereotypes."[72]

LEGITIMACY OF AUTOMATED SYSTEMS

All of these proposals have one thing in common: they implicitly embrace the basic assumption of Tylerian legitimacy that fair processes lead to fair results. Citron calls for "audit trails" to provide adequate notice, an essential due process right. Per the requirements set down in *Mullane* v. *Central Hanover Bank & Trust*,[73] this documentation would inform and explain to an individual how and why authorities were making some decision to protect against arbitrary and mistaken decisions,[74] which is almost identical to the role played by fair procedures in Tyler's analysis of individuals' reactions to police authority. Proposals for explicit explanations for how authorities relied on mechanized decision-making processes, publicly available source code, and ongoing testing also help satisfy the due process right to be heard by giving those affected by automated systems the tools they need to understand what happened, what went wrong, and what to appeal. As the Supreme Court noted in *Mathews* v. *Eldridge*,[75] hearings are forms of "effective process" that "ensure fairness."[76] After all, part of the point of procedural due process is to "convey to the individual a feeling that the government has dealt with him fairly,"[77] which is precisely the role played by process in Tylerian legitimacy.[78]

---

[67] See, e.g., Crawford, above note 68 (suggesting more diverse hiring to ameliorate bias in AI); Citron, above note 52, p. 1306 (calling for training of administrative hearing officers).

[68] See A. E. Waldman, Designing without Privacy (2018) 55 *Houston Law Rev.* 659, 699–701.

[69] Kroll *et al.*, above note 8, pp. 662–72, 682–92.

[70] D. Reisman, J. Schultz, K. Crawford, M. Whittaker, Algorithmic Impact Assessments: A Practical Framework for Public Agency Accountability, *AI Now* (April 2018), https://ainowinstitute.org/aiareport2018.pdf.

[71] See M. Madden, M. Gilman, K. Levy, and A. Marwick, Privacy, Poverty, and Big Data: A Matrix of Vulnerabilities for Poor Americans (2017) 95 *Wash. Univ. Law Rev.* 53.

[72] Crawford, supra note 68. See also Waldman, above note 71, pp. 724–5 (recommending more diverse and integrated design teams to amplify privacy and non-discrimination in design).

[73] 339 US 306, 319 (1950).

[74] *Goldberg* v. *Kelly*, 397 US 254, 268 (1970).

[75] 424 US 319 (1976).

[76] *Ibid.* at 348–9.

[77] *Carey* v. *Piphus*, 435 US 247, 262 (1978).

[78] See T. R. Tyler, The Psychological Consequences of Judicial Procedures: Implications for Civil Commitment Hearings (1992) 46 *SM Univ. Law Rev.* 433, 441.

That right to a fair process is also embedded in calls for greater inclusiveness in algorithmic design. Although Tyler spoke about the right to plead one's case with formal and information authorities, including more women, members of the LGBTQ community, and individuals from different socioeconomic classes is intended to give diverse populations an *ex ante* right to be heard. This opportunity to be heard in design echoes, in fairness, well. Algorithmic systems designed with diverse voices are fairer systems, much like representative political bodies are fairer than unrepresentative ones. Indeed, necessary and overdue steps to make administrations, legislatures, and teaching faculties, among other authorities, "look like" those they serve are premised on the fairness that comes from better representation.[79] Together with paper trails and a human check on pure AI systems, first-wave proposals seek to ensure fair processes from both sides.

The approach makes some sense; procedure has, after all, been called the "essence" of due process rights.[80] The opportunity to be heard by an impartial adjudicator is central to legitimate democratic authority.[81] And in order to hold someone responsible or liable for intentional or negligent harm or failures in design, common law accountability regimes need to know what happened, what steps were taken to avoid causing harm, and what was reasonable under the circumstances. Procedural requirements like algorithmic impact assessments, source code transparency, explanations of either the result or the logic behind it, and a human in the loop who can hear someone's appeal move opaque automated systems closer to more familiar, and more accountable, decision-making regimes.

But transparency, impact assessments, paper trails, and the trappings of traditional legitimacy do not address the gaps in the underlying social and political system that not only laid the groundwork for algorithmic decision-making, but sees its proliferation, despite its biases, errors, and harms, as a good thing. Put another way, legitimacy via process may have made sense once, when process was capable of holding decision-makers accountable and fair. That is arguably no longer the case. Algorithmic decision-making is the apotheosis of a distinctly neoliberal form of policymaking that is, both doctrinally and as a matter of practice, agnostic about its sociopolitical and economic implications. Its emphasis on efficiency tilts the scales toward machines over humans and undermines the effectiveness of procedure to ensure accountability. Therefore, the first wave's approach of trying to legitimize automated systems through fair process will likely be insufficient.

Neoliberalism and Its Crusade for Efficiency

Neoliberalism aims to maximize freedom of choice within a system of laws "characterized by private property rights, individual liberty, unencumbered markets, and free trade."[82] This, the argument goes, will maximize personal and social well-being by giving individuals the ability to choose their own version of the good life free of government pressure. The practical manifestation of this political philosophy is a system where organizations, both governmental and commercial, prioritize efficiency and the free flow of ideas, goods, and opportunities. For

---

[79] See, e.g., J. Murphy, Trudeau Gives Canada First Cabinet with Equal Number of Men and Women, *The Guardian* (November 4, 2015), www.theguardian.com/world/2015/nov/04/canada-cabinet-gender-diversity-justin -trudeau.

[80] Citron, above note 52, p. 1255.

[81] See Tyler, above note 8, pp. 96, 116–20, 137–8, 149.

[82] D. Harvey, Neoliberalism as Creative Destruction (2007) 610 *Ann. Am. Pol. Soc. Sci.* 22, 22 (cited in J. E. Cohen, *Between Truth and Power: The Legal Constructions of Informational Capitalism* (Oxford University Press, 2019), p. 7).

example, neoliberal trade policy is characterized by low or no tariffs and the free movement of goods.[83] Neoliberal speech policy is laissez-faire and based on the "marketplace of ideas" metaphor.[84] In the same vein, neoliberal organizational policy is managerial, or streamlined for the purposes of fostering innovation, and includes any policy that would amplify efficiency in the means of production, from eliminating the likelihood of litigation, erasing cost centers, deploying technology, and outsourcing tasks to more efficient sources.[85]

Enter algorithmic decision-making. A system oriented primarily toward efficiency, agility, and unencumbered economic activity is a natural ally of professionals whose traditional "cardinal virtue" is efficiency,[86] and naturally oriented toward outsourcing tasks to reduce costs. It makes sense, then, that leaders steeped in neoliberalism would turn to engineers to make policymaking more efficient. Asking an algorithm to make decisions reflects neoliberalism's underlying philosophical and political orientation toward deregulation, non-intervention, and efficiency. For profit-maximizing corporations looking to cut costs, replacing humans with mechanical decision-makers makes sense from financial and efficiency perspectives, as well.[87]

As a matter of social practice, algorithmic decision-making empowers technology to make policy decisions, embedding the technology community's ingrained commitment to efficiency and its indifference to privacy and other social values in society.[88] Engineers are the ones responsible for shoehorning policy into codable algorithms, a translation process that will necessarily edit out the flexibility and contextualism that gives decision-making standards advantages over bright-line rules. As such, design teams become the locus at which law is interpreted, negotiated, and transformed into actionable tools. This gives engineers enormous power, both to choose winners and losers and decide what the law will mean in practice.[89] And engineers leverage this power while professing that they and their designs are value-neutral. The law and technology scholar Frank Pasquale has noted that, even when programmers create tools that have evident racial biases – like a search engine that shows racially stereotyped advertisements[90] – the designers cast the technology as a "cultural voting machine, merely registering, rather than creating, perceptions."[91] Kate Crawford and Jason Schultz have described engineers as inadequately fluent in the language of public policy; as one programmer told them, "we can make stuff work – it's not our job to figure out if it's right or not. We often don't know."[92] And elsewhere, I have described how some engineers, at least in the high-technology sector, resist the notion that designing for privacy or safety is part of their job or even possible under the demanding circumstances in which they work.[93] Therefore, when policy decisions are made by engineers, non-engineering values may get short shrift.

---

83   See, e.g., J. O. McGinnis and M. L. Movsesian, The World Trade Constitution (2000) 114 *Harv. Law Rev.* 511, 521–7.
84   J. Purdy, Neoliberal Constitutionalism: Lochnerism for a New Economy (2014) 77 *Law Contemp. Probs.* 195.
85   See Cohen, above note 7.
86   P. Ohm and J. Frankle, Desirable Inefficiency (2016) 70 *Fla. Law Rev.* 777, 778.
87   See Cohen, above note 7, p. 156.
88   See Waldman, above note 71.
89   See A. E. Waldman, Outsourcing Privacy (forthcoming) (manuscript on file with author).
90   See L. Sweeney, Discrimination in Online Ad Delivery (2013) 11 *Comms. ACM* 44, 46–7, 50–1.
91   Pasquale, above note 43, p. 39.
92   K. Crawford and J. Schultz, Big Data and Due Process: Toward a Framework to Redress Predictive Privacy Harms (2014) 55 *BC Law Rev.* 93, 105.
93   See Waldman, above note 71.

And it is unlikely that the process-oriented solutions under discussion today would change that. In the neoliberal system that created algorithmic decision-making, accountability is recast as compliance, which can undermine the power of procedure to rein in automated decision-making in two ways.

First, procedure can be co-opted by corporate interests. According to the sociologist and legal scholar Lauren Edelman, the managerial law inside a corporation involves shifting the sight at which law is interpreted and negotiated from policymakers and courts to corporate compliance procedures and internal structures designed to signify legal adherence to regulations.[94] When that happens, procedural requirements can be co-opted to serve corporate, rather than consumer, interests. Edelman calls this the "mobilization of symbolic structures."[95] When this happens, law fails to achieve substantive goals because the compliance metric – the adoption of symbols, processes, procedures, and policies within a corporate environment – can be orthogonal to actual progress. Edelman discussed legal endogeneity in the context of race and sex discrimination in the workplace, where the equality goals of Title VII of the Civil Rights Act, which bans such discrimination, were being frustrated by the ineffectual trainings, toothless policies, checklists, and disempowered diversity offices that compliance professionals created on the ground. Elsewhere, I have shown how this process is undermining the promised protections of consumer privacy laws, as well.[96]

Even rules that mandate all automated decision-making systems treat all individuals equally and fairly, but use process and procedure to do it, are likely to fall victim to the same phenomenon. Algorithmic impact assessments can identify and evaluate risks, consider alternatives, identify strategies to mitigate risks, and help articulate the rationale for the automated system, but they can also be mobilized, as Edelman argued in the non-discrimination context, as a paper trail to push back against claims of unfair harm from those adversely affected by the algorithm. Transparency, whether in the form of source code publication or an explanation of the results, can throw some sunshine on an opaque process, but is simultaneously functionally unhelpful to most individuals without specialized knowledge and convenient evidence for a fact-finder to determine compliance with the law. And keeping humans in the loop of a decision-making process offers an override to a mechanical process, but the extent to which the human element will have power depends entirely on the way in which the safeguard is implemented on the ground.

Second, the focus on documentation and process as ends in themselves elevates a merely symbolic structure to evidence of actual compliance with the law, obscuring the underlying substantive values of fairness, equality, and human dignity eroded by large-scale algorithmic decision-making. It also may discourage both users and policymakers from taking more robust actions because, after imposing procedural safeguards, they can declare their job done.

Paul Butler made a similar argument about the effect of *Gideon* v. *Wainwright*[97] on the incarceration of poor persons of color. *Gideon* is a famous US Supreme Court decision holding that states must provide free counsel to indigent criminal defendants.[98] However, by focusing on a procedural right to counsel, *Gideon*, Butler argues, obscured the "real crisis of indigent defense" that prison is designed for poor people and not rich ones.[99] Ensuring some

---

[94]   See L. B. Edelman, *Working Law: Courts, Corporations, and Symbolic Civil Rights* (University of Chicago Press, 2016), pp. 124–52.
[95]   *Ibid.*, p. 153.
[96]   See Waldman, above note 71.
[97]   327 US 335 (1963).
[98]   *Ibid.* at 339.
[99]   P. Butler, Poor People Lose: Gideon and the Critique of Rights (2013) 122 *Yale Law J.* 2176, 2178.

adequate representation may not be a bad idea in a vacuum, but it "invests the criminal justice system with a veneer" of legitimacy, impartiality, and protection for ordinary persons, discouraging anyone from digging any deeper into the systematic ways in which the system is stacked against the poor. Butler concluded that "[o]n its face, the grant that *Gideon* provides poor people seems more than symbolic: it requires states to pay for poor people to have lawyers. But the implementation of *Gideon* suggests that the difference between symbolic and material rights might be more apparent than real."[100] Similarly, process-oriented rules for reining in discriminatory algorithms could obscure underlying injustices and stand in the way of substantive reform by giving algorithms that prioritize efficiency over all other social values.

An Alternative Approach

So what, if anything, could help legitimize algorithmic decision-making systems in a society that cares about social values like equality, human flourishing, and fundamental rights?

We need a robust, substantive approach to ensuring algorithmic systems meet fundamental social values other than efficiency. The law provides us with a guide. In certain contexts, fair procedures are sufficient to determine lawfulness. This is the premise behind the doctrine of procedural due process, and the premise behind much of the literature in the first wave of algorithmic accountability. But in other situations, particularly those involving deprivations of fundamental rights, no amount of fair procedure can justify government misbehavior. Here, procedural due process is not enough. Substantive due process steps in to protect enumerated rights and those unenumerated rights deemed "fundamental" and "implicit in the concept of ordered liberty" through the Fifth and Fourteenth Amendments.[101] It can protect unenumerated non-fundamental rights. And it protects against substantively outrageous government conduct.[102] Substantive due process brings an exacting form of scrutiny to government action, only permitting the deprivation of fundamental freedoms in rare, compelling circumstances.

Substantive due process is concerned with *what* happened, not *how* it happened. It changes the question we ask about government decision-making – namely, from "Did the government follow fair procedures and provide adequate accountability measures?" to "Was it just for the government to have made this decision?" Perhaps we should be asking the same thing about AI?

We should consider whether the context in which automated systems are used implicates fundamental rights for the same three reasons we consider the context in which state actions have adverse effects on individuals. First, even fair procedures can lead to injustice. As Justice Harlan explained in his dissent in *Poe* v. *Ullman*,[103] "[w]ere due process merely a procedural safeguard it would fail to reach those situations where the deprivation of life, liberty or property was accomplished by legislation which ... given even the fairest possible procedure in application to individuals, nevertheless destroy the enjoyment of all three."[104] And some injustices demand stronger remedies than just better processes. Where fundamental rights

[100] *Ibid.*, pp. 2191–2.
[101] The Due Process Clause of the Fifth Amendment provides that no person shall "be deprived of life, liberty, or property, without due process of law." The Fourteenth Amendment applies the same text to the states. See *Palko* v. *Connecticut*, 302 US 319, 324–5 (1937).
[102] See, e.g., *Daniels* v. *Williams*, 474 US 331 (1986).
[103] 367 US 497 (1961).
[104] *Ibid.* at 541.

have been abridged, plaintiffs usually want to stop the government's action against them. Therefore, the proper remedy would be invalidation or an order enjoining the unjust action. The remedies for procedural due process injuries can include a post-deprivation fair procedure, as when an employee wrongfully terminated for lack of process seeks both reinstatement and a fair hearing.[105] For certain deprivations of rights, that would be insufficient.[106]

What that would look like in practice will be explored in future research, but a few implications seem clear. Governments should be required to show a compelling justification and an absolute need for automated systems in contexts that implicate fundamental rights, such as deprivations of liberty, policing, and sentencing. Increases in efficiency and cost-savings would be insufficient justifications. The same obligation should exist where automated systems discriminate against similarly situated individuals or groups, or create classifications based on protected characteristics, including gender, race, gender and sexual expression, religion, and national origin. The law looks askance at such state actions when they are committed by humans. There is no reason why the same standard shouldn't be applied to automated systems used in their place.

[105] See, e.g., *Parratt v. Taylor*, 451 US 527, 538–9 (1981).
[106] See, e.g., *Mann v. City of Tucson*, 782 F.2d 790 (9th Cir. 1986).

5

Understanding Transparency in Algorithmic Accountability

Margot E. Kaminski

Transparency has been in the crosshairs of recent writing about accountable algorithms. Its critics argue that releasing data can be harmful, and releasing source code won't be useful.[1] They claim individualized explanations of artificial intelligence (AI) decisions don't empower people, and instead distract from more effective ways of governing.[2] While criticizing transparency's efficacy with one breath, with the next they defang it, claiming corporate secrecy exceptions will prevent useful information from getting out.[3]

This chapter bucks the tide. Transparency is necessary, if not sufficient, for building and governing accountable algorithms.[4] But for transparency to be effective, it has to be designed. It can't be sprinkled on like seasoning; it has to be built into a regulatory system from the onset. And determining the who, what, when, and how of transparency requires first addressing the question of why.[5]

Building on my work elsewhere, I thus begin by discussing the rationales behind regulating algorithmic decision-making, or decision-making by AI.[6] I discuss the growing awareness in the literature that the object of regulation is not the technology of the algorithm in isolation, but includes the human systems around it. I then outline a taxonomy of transparency for accountable algorithms, building on the work of earlier authors and my own research on the European Union's General Data Protection Regulation (GDPR).[7]

---

[1] See, e.g., J. A. Kroll, J. Huey, S. Barocas, *et al.*, Accountable Algorithms (2017) 165 *Univ. Pa. Law Rev.* 633, 657–60.

[2] L. Edwards and M. Veale, Slave to the Algorithm? Why a "Right to an Explanation" Is Probably Not the Remedy You Are Looking for (2017) 16 *Duke Law Technol. Rev.* 18, 67.

[3] S. Wachter, L. Floridi, and B. Mittelstadt, Why a Right to Explanation of Automated Decisionmaking Does Not Exist in the General Data Protection Regulation (2017) 7 *Int. Data Privacy Law* 76, 79 n. 13, 84, 89. But see M. Brkan, Do Algorithms Rule the World? Algorithmic Decision-Making in the Framework of the GDPR and Beyond (2019) 27 *Int. J. Law Inf. Technol.* 91.

[4] For a similar view, see M. Ananny and K. Crawford, Seeing without Knowing: Limitations of the Transparency Ideal and Its Application to Algorithmic Accountability (2018) 20 *New Media Soc.* 973, 982.

[5] M. E. Kaminski, The Right to Explanation, Explained (2019) 34 *Berkeley Technol. Law J.* 189, 211.

[6] I here draw on my work in M. E. Kaminski, Binary Governance: Lessons from the GDPR's Approach to Algorithmic Accountability (2019) 92 *S. Calif. Law Rev.* 1529.

[7] See, e.g., F. Pasquale, *The Black Box Society* (2015), pp. 140–88 (calling for a system of layered "qualified transparency"); A. D. Selbst, Disparate Impact in Big Data Policing (2017) 52 *Ga. Law Rev.* 109, 169–72 (describing algorithmic impact assessments); A. Tutt, An FDA for Algorithms (2017) 69 *Admin. Law Rev.* 83, 110–11 (identifying a "spectrum of disclosure"); T. Z. Zarsky, Transparent Predictions (2013) *Univ. Ill. Law Rev.* 1503, 1523 (identifying three "segments of information flow").

WHY REGULATE ALGORITHMS?

An algorithm is a computer program. A sub-set of algorithms build predictions and correlations using large datasets as input.[8] Increasingly, these predictive algorithms are used by humans to make significant decisions – from housing to employment to criminal sentencing and release decisions – about other human beings. A quickly growing literature charts how the use of a variety of kinds of algorithms to make significant decisions about people can raise a spectrum of harms.[9] Algorithmic analysis and decision-making are increasingly employed across a variety of sectors, including in government.[10] They are used to determine loan rates, to hire and fire employees, to track and label people, and to predict and manipulate behavior.[11]

Roughly speaking, there are three reasons people call for regulating algorithms.[12] The first is the most prevalent, and easiest to understand: people call for regulating algorithms because the decisions made based on algorithmic reasoning can be biased, discriminatory, and wrong. This *instrumental* rationale characterizes regulation as a tool for correcting concrete, potentially measurable, problems.

Algorithms are neither neutral, nor perfect. Programmers and the institutions that employ them make a host of decisions, from what datasets to use to train the algorithm, to how to define what the algorithm's target output is, to how likely the algorithm is to produce false positives versus false negatives.[13] For example, the designers of a widely used recidivism risk algorithm, relied on by judges across the United States in pre-trial and sentencing determinations, chose to label a person as a recidivist (a re-offender) if they were re-arrested, rather than re-convicted.[14] This decision isn't math; it's policy. And it has disparate consequences: black men are arrested at higher rates than Hispanics or whites.[15] A human policy choice – to ask the algorithm to predict re-arrest, and to affirm its accuracy when a person is arrested rather than convicted – skews the algorithm's output, with significant consequences for those individuals to whom it is applied. Another widely discussed example of the problem of algorithmic bias is the use of biased datasets. When an algorithm is trained on biased data, its outputs will be biased as well.[16] The instrumental rationale for regulating algorithms argues for regulation to correct these problems.

There are, however, other reasons to regulate algorithmic analysis and decision-making, beyond instrumentalism. We expect decisions with significant consequences to be reasoned,

---

[8]   D. Lehr and P. Ohm, Playing with the Data: What Legal Scholars Should Learn about Machine Learning (2017) 51 *UC Davis Law Rev.* 653, 658–62 (describing machine-learning algorithms).

[9]   See, e.g., D. K. Citron, Technological Due Process (2008) 85 *Wash. Univ. Law Rev.* 1249; D. Citron and F. Pasquale, The Scored Society: Due Process for Automated Predictions (2014) 89 *Wash. Law Rev.* 1, 16–18; S. Barocas and A. D. Selbst, Big Data's Disparate Impact (2016) 104 *Calif. Law Rev.* 671, 714–23; J. M. Eaglin, Constructing Recidivism Risk (2017) 67 *Emory Law J.* 59, 67–88; P. T. Kim, Auditing Algorithms for Discrimination (2017) 166 *Univ. Pa. Law Rev. Online* 189.

[10] D. R. Desai and J. A. Kroll, Trust but Verify: A Guide to Algorithms and the Law (2017) 31 *Harv. J. Law Technol.* 1.

[11] See, e.g., A. D. Selbst, A New HUD Rule Would Effectively Encourage Discrimination by Algorithm, *Slate* (August 19, 2019), https://slate.com/technology/2019/08/hud-disparate-impact-discrimination-algorithm.html.

[12] Kaminski, above note 6. See also A. D. Selbst and S. Barocas, The Intuitive Appeal of Explainable Machines (2018) 87 *Fordham Law Rev.* 1085, 1117–19.

[13] Eaglin, above note 9; Lehr and Ohm, above note 8; Barocas and Selbst, above note 9.

[14] Eaglin, above note 9, p. 78.

[15] *Ibid.*, p. 95. See also J. Eaglin and D. Solomon, Brennan Center For Justice, Reducing Racial and Ethnic Disparities in Jails: Recommendations for Local Practice (2015), pp. 17–18, www.brennancenter.org/sites/default/files/publications/Racial%20Disparities%20Report%20062515.pdf.

[16] Barocas and Selbst, above note 9. See also K. Crawford and R. Calo, There Is a Blind Spot in AI Research, *Nature* (October 13, 2016), www.nature.com/news/there-is-a-blind-spot-in-ai-research-1.20805.

if not reasonable – and some reasons for decision-making may be socially unacceptable, or even illegal. Some calls for regulating algorithmic decision-making thus focus on a need for *justification*: demonstrating the legal and social legitimacy of algorithmic decision-making, whether by requiring an explanation of the decision, or by providing oversight over a decision-making system.[17]

Algorithmic decision-making raises significant concerns about justification. Algorithms draw correlations and make predictions based on data, and are both constrained by the limitations of their input and comparatively unconstrained by social context or social norms.[18] For example, an algorithm may discover a strong correlation between the color of one's shoes and the likelihood of loan repayment – yet normatively, we might not want banks making lending decisions based on the color of one's footwear (which might also lead to disparate impacts based on gender, sexual orientation, economic status, race, or other characteristics, many of which governments treat as protected classes).[19] An algorithm, too, won't always bring in additional context to a particular decision, for purposes of determining either accuracy or leniency. It may make and follow rules; it won't necessarily be equipped to modify or break them.[20] Algorithmic decision-making has the potential in practice to be highly acontextual, compared to its human equivalent.[21]

Thus, the *justificatory* rationale for regulating algorithmic decision-making calls for transparency into the data, model, and heuristics used. This is to ensure decisions aren't made based on illegal or otherwise normatively unacceptable factors and reasoning, and to enable individuals to argue why the system's reasoning, as applied to them, might be erroneous or unfair. The justificatory rationale also leads to calls for oversight over the company building and/or using the technology. Just as in the law we have both individual procedure (due process) and systemic versions of accountability (such as the Administrative Procedure Act), an algorithmic accountability regime aimed at producing legitimacy might use either, or both, an individualized and systemic approach.[22] A person can use individual process to reassure herself that a decision-making system is legitimate, or she could rely on the promises and oversight of a number of external experts and stakeholders to assure her of its legitimacy. Or she might want both: expert oversight over the system as a whole, and an individualized ability to assess whether its reasoning applies fairly to her, in a particular decision.

The third rationale for regulating algorithmic decision-making is *dignitary*. Algorithmic decision-making potentially objectifies individuals; it treats them as fungible.[23] There are a number of flavors of this argument. The first states that using a machine to make a decision about a human being violates her dignity as a person.[24] This position tends to be more

---

[17]   K. Brennan-Marquez, "Plausible Cause": Explanatory Standards in the Age of Powerful Machines (2017) 70 *Vand. Law Rev.* 1249, 1288 ("A key tenant of legality, separating lawful authority from ultra vires conduct, is the idea that not all explanations qualify as justifications").

[18]   Kaminski, above note 6, p. 118 ("When we replace human decision makers with nonhuman decision makers, we potentially eliminate important work that a human decision maker does to both fill in and circumscribe decisional context in a particular case").

[19]   E. Felten, What Does It Mean To Ask for an "Explainable" Algorithm?, *Freedom to Tinker* (May 31, 2017), https://freedom-to-tinker.com/2017/05/31/what-does-it-mean-to-ask-for-an-explainable-algorithm.

[20]   Citron, above note 9, p. 1301.

[21]   Kaminski, above note 6, p. 118.

[22]   *Ibid.*, p. 149; Citron, above note 9, pp. 1305, 1308.

[23]   Kaminski, above note 6, p. 113.

[24]   *Ibid.*, p. 114 ("The first, largely European, criticism of algorithmic decision-making is that allowing a decision about humans to be made by a machine inherently treats humans as objects, showing deep, inherent disrespect for peoples' humanity"); L. A. Bygrave, Minding the Machine: Article 15 of the EC Data Protection Directive and Automated Profiling (2001) 17 *Comp. L.aw Security Rep.* 17, 18.

polarizing, and is arguably more accepted in the European Union than it is in the United States.[25] To some people, machine decisions are inherently creepy, while to others, they're efficient and normalized. A second version of the dignitary argument claims that creating profiles of individuals harms their autonomy and dignity by freezing a version of them, created without their input, and then making decisions based on this "data double."[26] If individuals lack the ability to access, correct, or even erase data in these profiles, their dignity and autonomy are harmed. Finally, a third version of the dignitary argument points to story after story of digital manipulation, demonstrating the real ways in which algorithmic profiling and its consequences restrict the autonomy of individuals.[27] This argument appears to have a broader cross-cultural appeal. All three sub-sets of the dignitary argument counsel toward implementing a set of individual data-protection-like rights: access, correction, explanation, and even erasure and contestation rights.

These three rationales are clearly connected. So are the regulatory solutions their proponents propose. Requiring the users of algorithmic decision-making to justify their decisions or legitimize the process of building the system (addressing justificatory concerns) will also provide insight into bias and error in the system (addressing instrumentalist concerns). Requiring programmers or institutions that use algorithms to disclose decision-making heuristics, too, can lead to uncovering bias and discrimination. Respecting somebody's dignity by allowing her to access and correct errors in her digital profile can also serve the instrumental purpose of making a system less prone to error.

But as I've argued, the great difficulty in crafting algorithmic accountability is that these rationales sometimes push toward divergent models of regulation.[28] Focusing on instrumental reasons leads to an approach that emphasizes systemic, *ex ante*, continuous, and collaborative modes of governance. For a variety of reasons – inherent to the technology, its use, and to the types of harms it may cause – this approach is likely more effective at systemically rooting out discrimination and bias. Focusing on dignitary reasons, by contrast, leads to arguments for individual rights and empowerment. The justificatory rationale can lead to arguments for either form of governance, or for both. Most scholars who reject individualized or public forms of transparency do so because their primary focus is on correcting bias and error; they do not appear to place much value on dignitary or justificatory rationales. As I have argued, this is wrong. Even for those concerned solely about fixing errors and addressing bias, transparency and accountability have important roles to play.

WHICH SYSTEM ARE YOU REGULATING?

To understand how best to employ transparency, we have to know not only the why of regulation – what we want transparency to do – but also the object of regulation: what system

[25] M. L. Jones, The Right to a Human in the Loop: Political Constructions of Computer Automation and Personhood (2017) 47 *Soc. Stud. Sci.* 216, 231; T. Z. Zarsky, Incompatible: The GDPR in the Age of Big Data (2017) 47 *Seton Hall Law Rev.* 995, 1016–17.
[26] Kaminski, above note 6, p. 115 ("A data double objectifies an individual by taking this dynamic, participatory process and placing it in the hands of other entities and out of the hands of the individual"); Bygrave, above note 24, p. 18; D. Lyon, Surveillance, Snowden, and Big Data: Capacities, Consequences, Critique, *Big Data & Society* (July–December 2014), pp. 1, 6.
[27] Kaminski, above note 6, p. 116 ("Secret profiling and decision-making can lead to manipulation"); Zarsky, above note 7, pp. 1541–53; D. Susser, B. Roessler, and H. Nissenbaum, Online Manipulation: Hidden Influences in a Digital World, https://papers.ssrn.com/sol3/papers.cfm?abstract_id=3306006; J. Luguri and L. Strahilevitz, Shining a Light on Dark Patterns, https://papers.ssrn.com/sol3/papers.cfm?abstract_id=3431205.
[28] Kaminski, above note 6, pp. 149–53.

we want to see into. There is a growing understanding among scholars in this space that algorithmic accountability is as much about seeing into, and affecting, the human systems around algorithms as it is about seeing into the technology.

This is not to say that increased transparency into the technology itself is unimportant. Much of the concern around algorithmic decision-making stems from a concern about delegating decision-making to "black box" systems that we can neither understand nor predict.[29] A growing community of computer science researchers focuses on making these "black box" systems explainable, or otherwise transparent or accountable.[30] And certain types of legal transparency requirements – such as those in the European Union's GDPR's articles 13, 14, 15, and 22, and in the US Fair Credit Reporting Act (FCRA)[31] – may either require use of algorithmic explainability technology, or may functionally prohibit the use of algorithms that are not explainable.

But to focus only on technological fixes misses the growing consensus that algorithmic accountability is about making human systems accountable, too.[32] A growing number of scholars have arrived at this observation. Earlier scholarship with its array of proposed accountability measures tacitly acknowledges that accountability is a problem of human organizations, not just technology.[33] Michael Ananny and Kate Crawford more explicitly call for "going beyond 'algorithms as fetishized objects'" and looking instead to "an algorithmic system . . . [as] not just code and data but an *assemblage* of human and non-human actors."[34]

As Jessica Eaglin has observed in her insightful analysis of the use of recidivism risk software, algorithms are very much embedded in social systems. Algorithmic decision-making reflects the values of programmers making design choices at the onset, and the context in which, and means by which, algorithms are used.[35] Technologies, in other words, are political.[36] Many human choices go into building a risk assessment algorithm. And once it is deployed, that algorithm may produce one measurement of racial disparity in the abstract, and perhaps another entirely when combined with patterns of judicial discretion or deference.[37]

The law plays an important role here, in addressing how human users are trained, what disclosures are made to them, and even the degree of deference required to algorithmic decisions. Danielle Citron very early on in discussions of algorithmic accountability called for training the humans who work with algorithms, in order to avoid the problem of "automation bias": the tendency of human workers to defer to algorithmically produced decisions.[38] By contrast, the Wisconsin Supreme Court recently refused to hold that a trial court's use of recidivism risk software violated a defendant's due process rights, requiring instead a "written advisement" to judges alerting them to five potential issues with the

---

[29] Pasquale, above note 7. W. Nicholson Price II, Regulating Black-Box Medicine (2017) 116 *Mich. Law Rev.* 421.

[30] A. Abdul, J. Vermeulen, D. Wang, *et al.*, Trends and Trajectories for Explainable, Accountable and Intelligible Systems: An HCI Research Agenda, ACM *Digital Library* (2018), https://doi.org/10.1145/3173574.3174156 ("We investigate how HCI researchers can help to develop accountable systems by performing a literature analysis of 289 core papers on explanations and explainable systems, as well as 12,412 citing papers").

[31] 15 USC § 1681m (2012); Regulation B, 12 CFR §§ 1002.1–16 (2018).

[32] Ananny and Crawford, above note 4. See also A. D. Selbst, d. boyd, S. Friedler, *et al.*, Fairness and Abstraction in Sociotechnical Systems (November 7, 2018), https://papers.ssrn.com/sol3/papers.cfm?abstract_id=3265913.

[33] Citron, above note 9, p. 1271; Citron and Pasquale, above note 9, pp. 20–7; K. Crawford and J. Schultz, Big Data and Due Process: Toward a Framework to Redress Predictive Privacy Harms (2014) 55 *BC Law Rev.* 93, 124–8.

[34] Ananny and Crawford, above note 4, p. 11 (emphasis in the original).

[35] Eaglin, above note 9, p. 63.

[36] L. Winner, Do Artifacts Have Politics? (1980) 109 *Daedalus* 121.

[37] Selbst *et al.*, above note 32, p. 7.

[38] Citron, above note 9, p. 1271.

program, including bias against minorities.[39] Whether this notice (in contrast with more extensive judicial training) will be effective at combating automation bias on the part of judges is questionable. At the least, it fails to establish a standard of human scrutiny of automated decision-making.

The implications of this move – to see and address the human builders, users, and systems around the algorithm – are important: we need insight not just into code or a dataset, but into the processes and outputs of human decision-makers building and implementing the algorithm. Andrew Selbst and co-authors similarly push for moving away from looking at algorithms as abstract tools, and instead examining algorithms in the context of the complex human systems in which they are embedded.[40] They observe that "technical systems are subsystems" embedded within larger contexts and organizations.[41] Taking this "sociotechnical frame" includes being aware of the added role of "decisions made by humans and human institutions."[42] Relying on technological fixes alone will lead to a number of missed opportunities and mistakes.[43]

Broadening the definition of the regulated system to include human users and organizations has the added benefit of making algorithmic decision-making more easily regulable. Law may not be good with technological black boxes, but it has a host of techniques for, and long experience with, handling humans and organizations. This consequence has not gone unnoticed. David Lehr and Paul Ohm chastise legal scholarship for focusing on the running model of machine-learning algorithms, rather than on the earlier stages of algorithmic development that they refer to as "playing with the data."[44] While black boxes may be hard to regulate, the humans who build and use black boxes are not. This aligns with instrumentalist calls for regulating algorithms as or before they are built, rather than through after-the-fact forms of individual due process.[45]

Thus, one target of accountability and transparency is the algorithm itself, while another is the system of human decision-makers, or organizations and firms, around it. Making both transparent is necessary (but again, not sufficient) for the goals of algorithmic accountability. Yet even this broadened framing misses a crucial insight about what systems need to be made visible and accountable.

Much of the literature on algorithmic accountability relies implicitly on delegating at least some governance of algorithms to the private sector and other third parties.[46] That is, these proposals suggest that governments leave the law a little vague and ask private parties, formally or informally, to come up with ways of applying principles or standards in their particular sectors or applications. Many proposals also involve civil society and academia and the public at large in monitoring and enforcing these delegations. These are the techniques of what is known in regulatory theory as "collaborative governance" or "new governance": partnerships between the public and private sectors.[47] These techniques include formal collaboration (for example, the establishment of codes of conduct subject to the approval

---

[39] *State v. Loomis*, 881 NW.2d 749, 769 (Wis. 2016); State v. Loomis: Wisconsin Supreme Court Requires Warning Before Use of Algorithmic Risk Assessments in Sentencing (2017) 30 *Harv. Law Rev.* 1530, https://harvardlawre view.org/2017/03/state-v-loomis/.

[40] Selbst *et al.*, above note 32, p. 2.

[41] *Ibid.*

[42] *Ibid.*, p. 3.

[43] *Ibid.*, pp. 3–8.

[44] Lehr and Ohm, above note 8, p. 658 ("widening the view ... will be crucial for solving some seemingly intractable problems of our increasingly automated world").

[45] Kroll *et al.*, above note 1, p. 659.

[46] Kaminski, above note 6, p. 129.

[47] See, e.g., O. Lobel, The Renew Deal: The Fall of Regulation and the Rise of Governance in Contemporary Legal Thought (2004) 89 *Minn. Law Rev.* 342, 371–6.

of government) and informal collaboration (for example, the use of standards rather than rules, which effectively delegates implementation of the details of regulation to the private sector).[48]

A smaller but growing group of scholars calls more explicitly for, and thus directly evaluates, these collaborative governance techniques.[49] I have observed, too, the GDPR's extensive use of collaborative governance in governing algorithmic decision-making.[50] Even where not explicit, much of what has been proposed as solutions for algorithmic accountability in fact entails collaborative governance.

This leads to a crucial observation: transparency is necessary for algorithmic accountability not just because it is a good in itself, but because it is necessary for effective collaborative governance. For collaborative governance to work, there has to be external input and oversight, or partnerships with the private sector give way easily to regulatory capture.[51] When algorithmic accountability proposals call for the involvement of civil society or for public oversight, they thus sound in long-standing discussions of how to make public–private partnerships accountable and effective. This role of transparency in producing oversight not over the algorithm but over the people effectively tasked with governing it, however, is largely ignored in the literature.

Thus, the algorithmic accountability literature often conflates two levels of transparency: what I call first-order and second-order transparency.[52] First-order transparency targets the algorithm and human decisions about its construction. Second-order transparency focuses on making the *system of governance* itself transparent and accountable. The first aims to make visible the rationales behind, and biases in, algorithmic decision-making. The second aims to watch, and make accountable, the watchmen.

There are thus not one, not two, but three target systems at which transparency can be aimed. The first is the technology. The second is the human systems around the technology. And the third is the governance regime, which aims to impact and alter both the technology and these human systems. When we discuss algorithmic transparency, we need to evaluate not only why we want transparency, but what system we are aiming it at.

A TAXONOMY OF TRANSPARENCY FOR ACCOUNTABLE AI

Most calls for algorithmic accountability propose a wide array of information flows and types, beyond calling for everything to be released to the public. Yet, public-facing transparency (of source code, of datasets) has unfortunately been turned into a strawman in this discussion, full of harms to businesses, national security, and individuals in the datasets.[53] This dismissal of transparency in general by dismissing full transparency to the public both oversimplifies

---

[48] Kaminski, above note 6, pp. 136–42.

[49] R. Binns, Data Protection Impact Assessments: A Meta-Regulatory Approach (2017) 7 *Int. Data Privacy Law* 22, 29–30; M. Guihot, A. Matthew, and N. Suzor, Nudging Robots: Innovative Solutions to Regulate Artificial Intelligence (2017) 20 *Vand. J. Ent. Technol. Law* 385, 427; M. Perel and N. Elkin-Koren, Accountability in Algorithmic Copyright Enforcement (2016) 19 *Stan. Technol. Law Rev.* 473, 529–31 ("We advocate a collaborative-dynamic regulation . . ."); W. Nicholson Price II, Regulating Black-Box Medicine (2017) 116 *Mich. Law Rev.* 421, 465–71 (discussing collaborative governance of black box, medical algorithms).

[50] Kaminski, above note 6, pp. 167–83.

[51] *Ibid.*, p. 138 ("Critics observe that such a regime can easily become subject to collusion or capture").

[52] Kaminski, above note 6, p. 108 ("Because regulators will be delegating rulemaking of sorts to private parties, we need not just transparency and oversight over the algorithm, but second-order transparency and oversight over that rulemaking and compliance process").

[53] Kroll *et al.*, above note 1, pp. 657–8.

existing policy proposals, and mischaracterizes what transparency is.[54] The literature on algorithmic accountability is awash with calls for various forms and degrees of transparency, from public disclosure to internal oversight to stakeholder involvement, auditing, and expert boards, and nearly everything in between.[55] Many, in fact most, of these versions of transparency do not raise the kinds of harms its detractors are concerned about. Moreover, in practice, purported transparency detractors often end up calling for policy solutions that fall squarely within a transparency toolkit.

For example, Frank Pasquale calls for a system of "qualified transparency," with different depths, types, and quantities of information going to different actors.[56] Andrew Tutt has called for a similar "Spectrum of Disclosure."[57] Tal Zarsky's exhaustive work on transparency in governmental use of algorithms charts nearly every possible mode of disclosure and recipient.[58] Calls for requiring algorithmic impact assessments, too, focus on creating information flows – within a company, to stakeholders, to experts, and to the general public.[59] Selbst and Barocas more recently have called for documentation requirements, similar to the GDPR's recording requirements, to force companies building algorithms to chart what decisions they have made and why.[60] Even these recording requirements can be understood as a version of transparency, as they establish information flows within a company, and potentially later to those who regulate or sue it.

To my knowledge, I am the first to think comprehensively about the question of transparency and algorithmic accountability in light of the first-order/second-order issues discussed above. That is, while transparency has been thrown at the problem of algorithmic accountability with near abandon, few if any are thinking about the interactions between different kinds of transparency, aimed at different goals and different targets of regulation.

Transparency takes many different shapes and sizes. When it is implemented for multiple reasons, and targeted at multiple systems, complex gaps and overlaps emerge. These are visible only from a holistic perspective.

With this in mind, I suggest we think about transparency in algorithmic accountability in the following way. There is individualized transparency, and there is systemic transparency.[61] The first largely aims – along with accompanying substantive rights of contestation – at dignitary and justificatory goals; the second, at instrumental but also systemic justificatory goals. We should be able to articulate what is going to whom, why, when, and how.

We should additionally be aware of the distinction between first-order transparency, aimed at letting somebody see into the system (whether the system is the technology or the system is the human decision-makers and users around it), and second-order transparency, which is

---

[54] Many discussions of transparency acknowledge that information flows occur on a spectrum of disclosure, and are not merely on or off. See, e.g., A. K. Woods, The Transparency Tax (2018) 71 *Vanderbilt Law Rev.* 1, 16 (observing that the legal system is "semitransparent in different ways," and laying out a taxonomy of transparency in law-making).

[55] Citron, above note 9, pp. 1305–13; Citron and Pasquale, above note 9, pp. 18–30.

[56] Pasquale, above note 7, pp. 140–88.

[57] Tutt, above note 7, p. 110 (table 3).

[58] Zarsky, above note 7, pp. 1521–30.

[59] A. D. Selbst, Disparate Impact in Big Data Policing (2017) 52 *Ga. Law Rev.* 109, 169–72; AI Now Institute, Algorithmic Impact Assessments: Towards Accountable Algorithms in Public Agencies, *Medium* (February 21, 2018), https://medium.com/@AINowInstitute/algorithmic-impact-assessments-toward-accountable-automation-in-public-agencies-bd9856e6fdde; M. E. Kaminski and G. Malgieri, Algorithmic Impact Assessments under the GDPR: Producing Multi-Layered Explanations (October 6, 2019), https://papers.ssrn.com/sol3/papers.cfm?abstract_id=3456224; A. Mantelero, AI and Big Data: A Blueprint for a Human Rights, Social and Ethical Impact Assessment (2018) 34 *Comp. Law Secur. Rev.* 754, https://doi.org/10.1016/j.clsr.2018.05.017.

[60] Selbst and Barocas, above note 12, pp. 1129–38.

[61] Kaminski, above note 6, p. 105 ("governing algorithmic decision-making should include both individual rights and systemic approaches").

aimed at making sure delegations of governance of algorithms to the private sector remain accountable rather than captured.

In the following paragraphs, I lay out several examples of how this taxonomy works. Then, in Tables 5.1, 5.2, and 5.3 below, I provide a larger array of examples. Much, though not all, of my perspective is influenced by the European Union's GDPR.

From all of this, an insight emerges: often, one type of transparency (say, individual access rights) will be relied on to do more than one type of work (say, both empowering impacted individuals and helping to ensure the regulatory system is working toward the public good, rather than captured).[62]

Individualized transparency consists of information flows targeted at the individual impacted by algorithmic decision-making. For example, a person impacted by a lending decision might be provided an explanation of that decision, at an abstract enough and simple enough level so as to be understandable, but also complex enough to be actionable, to allow her to contest the decision. The goal of this kind of transparency is not just to enable a person to change her behavior, but also to empower her, to protect her dignity and increase her autonomy, and to make visible the system's reasoning – to justify it.[63] This is a very different purpose than, say, the kind of transparency one might put in place to best enable expert oversight. Yet if the algorithmic accountability regime as a whole lacks other transparency mechanisms, a right to explanation, such as that required by the GDPR's article 22, may have to do dual or even triple work.[64] An explanation may have to simultaneously justify a system to the impacted individual, serve as broader oversight over the system, and even serve as a form of accountability over private governance of algorithmic decision-making. It is unlikely that one transparency instrument can effectively accomplish all three things.

Systemic transparency, by contrast, aims to make visible error, bias, and discrimination in both machine and human systems, so they can be addressed and mitigated, if not corrected. These information flows go to more than one type of person or actor. For example, a board of technical experts may get access to an algorithm's source code, training datasets, and interviews with the data scientists designing the system. In another mode of transparency, a company might be required to convene civil society members and stakeholders to disclose (and provide input into) policy decisions such as how to define discrimination.[65] In yet another mode of systemic transparency, companies might be required to record decisions for possible later inspection, or to assemble reports or impact assessments. They might be required to put in place internal information flows between engineers and, say, a company's lawyers or privacy officer. Many of these modes of systemic transparency will never involve releasing information to the public. Others will set up records that might be released to government regulators or to members of the public later on.

These systemic forms of transparency differ in their temporal design, as well. Some of these modes of transparency will be more static, requiring a single report or a single meeting or set of meetings with a defined end point. Others will be closer to continuous, either in the form of regular spot-checks or constant oversight.

---

[62]   *Ibid.*, p. 106 ("we may find ourselves needing to rely on individual transparency rights to accomplish systemic accountability goals").

[63]   Kaminski, above note 6, p. 106 (describing "a justificatory rationale, concerned with ensuring that decisions are made based on socially and legally acceptable reasoning and are legitimized by acceptable process or oversight"); Selbst and Barocas, above note 12, p. 1118. For a different take, limiting individual explanations to counterfactuals, see S. Wachter, B. Mittelstadt, and C. Russell, Counterfactual Explanations without Opening the Black Box: Automated Decisions and the GDPR (2018) 31 *Harv. J. Law Technol.* 841.

[64]   Kaminski, above note 6, p. 106.

[65]   Kim, above note 9, p. 193; Lehr and Ohm, above note 8, p. 705 n. 187.

TABLE 5.1 *Individual transparency*

	To whom?	Why?	What?	When?	How?
Access to profiling data held about an individual[i]	Impacted individuals	So an individual can know what information is held about her; to respect her dignity; so she can correct the accessed information or opt out of processing	Personal data in a format comprehensible to lay persons Inferences made about an individual	At reasonable intervals	Access requests (pull)
Disclosure that one has been or will be subjected to an algorithmic decision system	Impacted individuals	So an individual knows she may be subjected/has been subjected to algorithmic decision-making; to respect her dignity; to allow her to opt out	A disclosure statement that one is being subjected to algorithmic analysis or decision-making	When the processing entity knows a person is being subjected to its system	Affirmative notification (push)
An explanation of the model (model-centric[ii])	Impacted individuals	So an individual can meaningfully agree to be subject to the system (or opt out of it). So an individual can assess/contest the legitimacy of broader decision-making heuristics	A description intelligible to laypersons Information about: the family of model, input data, performance metrics, how the model was tested[iii] An interface for meaningfully experimenting with the system[iv]	Before a decision is made	Affirmative notification (push) Access (pull)

(continued)

An explanation of a particular decision (subject-centric[v])	Impacted individuals	To respect the dignity of impacted individuals To provide insight into whether the system's decision-making is legitimate So an individual can correct, contest, or invoke related rights.	An explanation intelligible to laypersons, including to the extent possible statistics used, policy decisions made, and decision-making heuristics Subject-centric information:[vi] counterfactuals, characteristics of others similarly classified, the confidence the system has in a particular outcome[vii]	After a decision is made, but before it is implemented	Affirmative notification (push)

Notes:

(i) See Council Regulation 2016/679, 2016 OJ (L 119) 1 (EU), art. 15.

(ii) Edwards and Veale, above note 2, p. 22 ("we identify two types of algorithmic explanations: model-centric explanations (MCEs) and subject-centric explanations (SCEs)"). But see A. D. Selbst and J. Powles, Meaningful Information and the Right to Explanation (2017) 7 *Int. Data Privacy Law* 233, 239–40 (arguing that often a meaningful system-level explanation will yield information about specific decisions).

(iii) Edwards and Veale, above note 2, p. 55.

(iv) Citron and Pasquale, above note 9, pp. 28–30; M. Hildebrandt, The Dawn of a Critical Transparency Right for the Profiling Era, in J. Bus, M. Crompton, M. Hildebrandt, *et al.* (eds.), *Digital Enlightenment Yearbook 2012* (IOS Press, 2012), pp. 53–4. For a similar suggestion in the copyright law context, see M. Perel and N. Elkin-Koren, Black Box Tinkering: Beyond Disclosure in Algorithmic Enforcement (2017) 69 *Fla. Law Rev.* 181, 190–200.

(v) Edwards and Veale, above note 2, p. 22.

(vi) Wachter *et al.*, above note 63, p. 880.

(vii) Edwards and Veale, above note 2, p. 58.

TABLE 5.2 *Systemic transparency*

	To whom?	Why?	What?	When?	How?
Third-party auditing	Independent auditors	To check the system (for bias, discrimination) To provide systemic legitimacy	All information necessary for the audit to be conducted, potentially including source code and datasets, performance metrics	When the system is being designed; when the system is operating At regular intervals Ongoing When the system substantively changes	Affirmative obligation (push) In response to auditors' requests (pull)
Disclosure to expert boards	Board of external experts Technical/legal/ethical expertise	To check the overall system (for bias, discrimination) To provide systemic legitimacy	All information necessary for the board to provide substantive input (see above)	At design stages ("playing with the data") For performance review	Affirmative obligation (push) In response to board requests (pull)
Recording Requirements	Internal company actors Regulators (either a system of recording/reporting, or in response to information-forcing/discovery capabilities)	To check the overall system To alter company decision-making heuristics	Information about substantive design decisions[i]	As a system is designed When a system is substantively changed Ongoing (continuous)	Information flow within a company (push and pull) In response to regulator requests (pull) or affirmative obligation (push)

Impact Assessments	Other members of the company Stakeholders (both impacted individuals and civil society) The public	To check the system To risk mitigate To provide legitimacy	All info necessary for each involved actor to play her part in effective risk mitigation/ human rights impact assessment	Before a system is implemented Ongoing Substantive changes	Info flow within a company (push and pull) Affirmative obligations (push)
Disclosure to impacted stakeholders	Impacted stakeholders or civil society representatives	To check the system To provide legitimacy To identify/contest company policy decisions	Both expert and non-expert information	Before a system is implemented Substantive changes	Affirmative obligations (push) Stakeholder requests (pull)

Note:
(i) Selbst and Barocas, above note 12, pp. 1129–38.

TABLE 5.3 *Second-order transparency*

	To whom?	Why?	What?	When?	How?
Third-party auditing	Independent auditors	To ensure a company's involvement in self-regulation is effective, and not captured	All information necessary for the audit to provide substantive **oversight** over company policies	When the system is being designed; when the system is operating At regular intervals Ongoing When the system substantively changes	Affirmative obligation (push) In response to auditors' requests (pull)
Disclosure to expert boards	Board of external experts Technical/legal/ethical expertise	To ensure a company's involvement in self-regulation is effective, and not captured	All information necessary for the board to provide substantive **oversight** over company policies	At design stages ("playing with the data") For performance review	Affirmative obligation (push) In response to board requests (pull)
Impact Assessments	Stakeholders (both impacted individuals and civil society) The public	To ensure a company's involvement in self-regulation is effective, and not captured To trigger non-legal enforcement	All info necessary for external actors to ensure company policies are not just self-serving, and possibly to provide enforcement	Before a system is implemented Ongoing Substantive changes	Info flow within a company Affirmative obligations (push)

(continued)

Disclosure to impacted stakeholders	Impacted stakeholders or civil society representatives	To ensure a company's involvement in self-regulation is effective, and not captured	Both expert and non-expert information	Before a system is implemented Substantive changes	Affirmative obligation (push) Stakeholder requests (pull)
An explanation of a particular decision	Impacted individuals	In the absence of other forms of external transparency, to ensure a company's involvement in self-regulation is effective and not captured; to trigger both legal and non-legal enforcement (e.g. press coverage and shaming)	An explanation intelligible to laypersons, including to the extent possible statistics used, policy decisions made, and decision-making heuristics Subject-centric information: counterfactuals, characteristics of others similarly classified, the confidence the system has in a particular outcome	After a decision is made, but before it is implemented	Affirmative notification (push)

(continued)

TABLE 5.3 *(continued)*

	To whom?	Why?	What?	When?	How?
An explanation of the model	Impacted individuals	To help ensure a company's involvement in self-regulation is effective and not captured	A description intelligible to laypersons Information about: the family of model, input data, performance metrics, how the model was tested An interface for meaningfully experimenting with the system	Before a decision is made	Affirmative notification (push) Access (pull)

All of this is similar to Pasquale's concept of qualified transparency: different actors receive information of different depth or breadth or duration, depending on what the purpose of a particular disclosure is.[66] The overarching goal of systemic transparency is to provide visibility into and oversight over both technical systems (the algorithm) and human systems around them, largely to uncover and hopefully try to fix problems of error and bias. For a variety of reasons, scholars are more confident that this approach will work to address instrumental concerns about algorithms than individualized transparency.[67]

Thus far, however, all of these types of transparency are aimed at seeing into a governed object, organization, or process. That is, I have discussed them thus far as operating only as first-order transparency. If, as many proposals on algorithmic accountability suggest at least tacitly, we are going to defer to some private sector decision-making about how to correct social problems with algorithms, there needs to be an eye toward not just seeing into the governed system, but watching the private actors who are tasked with implementing or even coming up with the law.

This is where disclosures to the public and to third parties become essential. These third-party actors are necessary, in a system of collaborative governance, to check private actors from acting only in their own self-interest. They are also necessary as a force multiplier for government actors; collaborative governance works best when other voices and expertise outside of government can do some of the enforcement and oversight work, too.

This is also where many forms of systemic transparency end up serving multiple goals. Take again the example of stakeholders and civil society members convening to provide oversight over, and possibly input into, a company's decision of how to define what it means by discrimination. On the one hand, this is clearly a systemic form of accountability aimed at instrumentally making the algorithm and the systems around it less discriminatory. On the other, third-party transparency also plays the role of checking company discretion and ensuring company decisions do not stray too far from the public good.[68] Similarly, external audits by third parties or oversight by external experts serve both to correct problems with the algorithm itself, and as a means of watching, and thus checking, a company's behavior *as a self- or co-regulator.*

This insight about the often dual, or triple, or even quadruple purposes (when you add in dignity) served by transparency in these proposed governance regimes has practical significance. Take, for example, the conversation over algorithmic impact assessments. Under Europe's GDPR, impact assessments are on the face of the GDPR envisioned largely as an internal process of oversight and risk mitigation, triggering direct regulatory oversight only in certain high-risk scenarios.[69] They are not required to be released to the public, although this is encouraged as a best practice.[70] The non-public version of an impact assessment largely serves instrumental ends: it requires companies to mitigate risks to impacted individuals, including through disclosing information to external experts or auditors.[71]

---

[66] Pasquale, above note 7, pp. 140–88.

[67] See, e.g., Edwards and Veale, above note 2, p. 67 (describing a possible "transparency fallacy").

[68] I. Ayres and J. Braithwaite, *Responsive Regulation* (1992), pp. 57–60; I. Ayres and J. Braithwaite, Tripartism: Regulatory Capture and Empowerment (1991) 16 *Law Soc. Inquiry* 435, 491 n. 137; see also M. E. Kaminski, Regulating AI Risk through the GDPR (October 22, 2019), pp. 31–2 (unpublished manuscript, on file with author).

[69] Council Regulation 2016/679, 2016 OJ (L119) 1 (EU), arts. 35–6. Kaminski, above note 6, p. 176 n. 393.

[70] Article 29 Data Prot. Working Party, Guidelines on Data Protection Impact Assessment (DPIA) and Determining Whether Processing Is "Likely to Result in a High Risk" for the Purposes of Regulation 2016/679, WP248 rev.01 (April 4, 2017), p. 16.

[71] Article 29 Data Prot. Working Party, Guidelines on Automated Individual Decision-Making and Profiling for the Purposes of Regulation 2016/679, WP251 rev.01 (February 6, 2018).

But non-public impact assessments fail when it comes to second-order transparency. While disclosures to third-party experts can do some of the work of holding a company accountable as it self-regulates, they don't do nearly as much as releasing the report to the public, or to other interested stakeholders. Release to the public triggers not just public scrutiny, but the possibility of non-legal sanctions such as public shaming and market consequences. These non-legal enforcement mechanisms are crucial for any attempt, formal or informal, to delegate regulation to the private sector. They increase regulators' practical enforcement capacity, as well as harnessing both technical expertise and legitimizing voices outside of the regulated sector and the government.

A FINAL NOTE ON SUBSTANCE

No chapter on transparency would be complete without an acknowledgment of its very real limitations. Transparency is arguably necessary, but not sufficient, for algorithmic account-ability, as it is for many other things. As the famed Panopticon illustrates, transparency by itself can sometimes lead to changes in behavior, whether from fear of social shaming or a tendency to conform to the perceived majority's norms.[72] Sometimes a chilling effect or conforming effect is desirable. And sometimes, a chilling effect alone is not enough.

What good is an individual right to explanation, if an individual doesn't also have a right to contest a decision?[73] What good is a regulator's ability to inspect a company's documents, if it lacks the ability to issue substantial fines? Or, what good is the ability to observe that a company is discriminating, if you lack a substantive right to challenge that discrimination?

Once again, I turn to Europe in determining what some of transparency's substantive legal backstops might look like. A regulator might be given both information-forcing capabilities and the substantive ability to enforce against certain practices, such as the ability to levy large fines. An individual might be given both a right to meaningfully agree to be subject to a system, and a right to opt out of it. She might be given correction rights, contestation rights, and the right to a human in the loop, or human decisions, or human review. She might have a substantive right not to be subjected to decisions based on particular categories of sensitive data (for example, health data, or her political views). She might be given a substantive right not to be discriminated against based on particular immutable, or otherwise protected, characteristics.

Thus, this discussion of transparency in isolation is admittedly limited. And it may be temporally limited, as well. It may be that someday clearer best practices and standards will develop in these sectors such that we need not lean so heavily on a collaborative regulatory approach. When that time comes, it may be worthwhile to simplify: to give individuals a simple cause of action if they have been subjected to what we ultimately determine to be bad or badly designed algorithmic decision-making. But until then, transparency is an essential component of the kind of regulatory approach most scholars, knowingly or unknowingly, have proposed.

---

[72] M. E. Kaminski and S. Witnov, The Conforming Effect: First Amendment Implications of Surveillance, beyond Chilling Speech (2015) 49 *Univ. Rich. Law Rev.* 465, 466–7.
[73] M. E. Kaminski and J. Urban, The Right to Contestation, draft on file with the author.

PART II

Business, Regulations, and Decision-Making with Algorithms

6

Algorithms and Contract Law

Lauren Henry Scholz

INTRODUCTION

The United States' transition from an economy built on form contracts to an economy built on algorithmic contracts has been as subtle as it has been thorough. In the form contract economy, many firms used standard order forms to make and receive orders. Firms purchased products and services with lengthy terms of services. Even negotiated agreements between fairly sophisticated businesses involved heavy incorporation of standard form terms selected by lawyers.

The algorithmic contract economy shares many features with the form contract economy. The key difference is which actor selects standard terms and/or clients for a company. In some algorithmic contracts, a computer program customizes terms in a contract based on real-time availability of the product or buyer characteristics. In this scenario, the algorithm replaces the know-how of a human actor. Instead of a small shop owner using her own understanding of her expenses and business conditions in her town to select prices, or a major company using a team of human researchers to achieve the same result, a company now can use an algorithm to take all relevant information into account to determine a price for goods or services sold. In other algorithmic contracts, a computer program could choose appropriate buyers of a product and terms customized to each particular transaction. In this case, the algorithm would be stepping in for the judgments that, in the form contract economy, might have been made by a salesperson and perhaps a lawyer.

Algorithmic contracts, then, are contracts that are reliant on algorithmic decision-making, often in addition to human decision-makers. The broadest definition of the word algorithm is inclusive of any heuristic used by a human to make a selection. This chapter will largely follow the modern convention of using "algorithm" to mean a computer program executing a series of calculations or rules. But the broader definition is instructive in an expressive sense. The best way to understand what is new and different about algorithmic contracts is in the process of forming an algorithmic contract, computer programs step into decision-making roles previously performed by humans. Many companies are delegating decisions that previously were made by a human performing an algorithm (like the shop owner's back-of-the-envelope calculations about how she should price her goods) to a computer program performing an algorithm. One reason why modern companies are finding it advantageous to delegate an increasing amount of responsibility to algorithmic decision-making is the incredible processing speed and sophistication made possible by machine learning.

Generalist confusion about the technology behind complex algorithms has led to inconsistent case law for algorithmic contracts. Case law explicitly grounded in the principle that algorithms are constructive agents for the companies they serve would provide a clear basis for enforceability of algorithmic contracts that is both principled from a technological perspective and is readily intelligible and able to be applied by generalists.

This chapter will proceed as follows. "Introducing Algorithms and Their Role in Contract Law" will explain how machine-learning algorithms work and describe their application in contract formation. "The Current Law of Algorithms and Contract" will describe the law on the books regarding algorithmic contracts and describe current interpretations thereof in the sparse case law on this topic. "Conceptualizing Algorithmic Contracts" will explain how to conceptualize algorithmic contracts. Finally, "Paths Forward" will discuss ways in which current state law and judicial approaches to algorithmic contracts could be improved.

INTRODUCING ALGORITHMS AND THEIR ROLE IN CONTRACT LAW

Algorithms, Generally

An algorithm is a set of instructions to follow in order to solve a problem.[1] Typically, the word "algorithm" is used to describe a computer running a program that gives it instructions for what to do.[2]

To many information-age readers, the term may feel like it should be more complex than this simple definition. This is not incidental. It is a value-laden term, and whether it has positive or negative connotations is actively contested.[3] As Jenna Burrell put it, "efforts at corporate 'branding' of the term algorithm play up notions of algorithmic objectivity over biased human decision-making. In this way the connotations of the term are actively being shaped as part of advertising culture and corporate self-presentation, as well as challenged by a related counter-discourse tied to general concerns about automation, corporate accountability, and media monopolies."[4] The specter of a machine making decisions for humans evokes both optimism, due to efficiency and supposed objectivity, and skepticism, due to fear of mistakes and lack of accountability.

Machine Learning

Not all algorithms in leading-edge technology employ machine learning,[5] but many do, so it is critical to establish a basic understanding of this technology to understand the role of algorithms in contract law.

Machine learning is the science of teaching computers to learn without being explicitly programmed.[6] The machine learns to perform tasks by analyzing training examples provided

---

[1]   BBC, What is an Algorithm, www.bbc.com/bitesize/articles/z3whpv4.

[2]   P. Domingos, *The Master Algorithm: How the Quest for the Ultimate Learning Machine Will Remake Our World* (Allen Lane, 2015).

[3]   B. D. Mittelstadt, P. Allo, M. Taddeo, *et al.*, The Ethics of Algorithms: Mapping the Debate (2016) 3 *Big Data Soc.* 1, https://journals.sagepub.com/doi/pdf/10.1177/2053951716679679.

[4]   J. Burrell, How the Machine "Thinks": Understanding Opacity in Machine Learning Algorithms (2016) 3 *Big Data Soc.* 1, https://doi.org/10.1177/2053951715622512 (citations omitted).

[5]   G. Both, What Drives Research in Self-Driving Cars? (Part 2: Surprisingly Not Machine Learning), *Platapus the Castayas Blog* (April 3, 2014), http://blog.castac.org/2014/04/what-drives-research-in-self-driving-cars-part-2-surpris ingly-not-machine-learning/.

[6]   A more formal definition of machine learning is as follows: "A computer program is said to learn from experience E with respect to some class of tasks T and performance measure P, if its performance at tasks in T, as measured by P, improves with experience E." A. Ng, Coursera, Machine Learning Course, Introduction (citing T. Mitchell, *Machine Learning* (McGraw-Hill Education, 1997), p. 2).

by human programmers.[7] Machine learning is essential in solving many modern problems. Machine learning is often used to make predictions based on large datasets, and to classify items. It also is used to develop applications that are too complicated for humans to code directly, such as creating self-flying aircraft.[8]

There are several different methods of machine learning, and it is beyond the scope of this chapter to describe them all. For illustrative purposes, however, I will briefly describe and discuss one of the most widely used methods, neural networks, often called neural nets for short.[9]

Neural nets are models that mimic biological neural systems. In biological neural systems, each neuron is connected to thousands of other neurons via axons and dendrites. Axons send signals and dendrites receive signals. A synapse is the point where a dendrite connects to another neuron. A synapse can be strong, which means it conducts signals relatively well, or it can be weak, which means it conducts signals relatively poorly.[10] So, a strong signal passing through a weak synapse may have the same effect on a neuron as a weak signal passing through a strong synapse.

The basic unit of a neural net is mathematical models of neurons called neurodes. Many neurodes create a network. The purpose of neural nets is to create machines capable of learning in the same way that biological entities do. Neural nets learn by being fed training examples that are labeled by human trainers. Over time, the net learns to see patterns in the data.[11] For example, an object recognition system may be fed pictures human-labeled as dogs and cats. Based on the training set, the net would find patterns that would allow it to identify images of dogs and cats that have not been labeled as such.[12]

Neural nets have different capabilities from non-machine-learning methods. Neural nets can "make inference from incomplete information and classify patterns (both by matching past information and generalizing that past information)."[13] Human-coded or symbolic systems face two limitations: not all knowledge can be stated in symbolic form and even if they could, developing and updating such a system via human contributions is time-

---

7   At this point, examples are required in the usual case. P. Domingos, A Few Useful Things to Know about Machine Learning, *Communications of the ACM* (October 2012), https://homes.cs.washington.edu/~pedrod/papers/cacm12.pdf.
8   Ng, above note 6.
9   Neural nets are also sometimes called "deep learning," but I will stick to the neural net terminology for clarity. L. Hardesty, Explained: Neural Networks (April 14, 2017), http://news.mit.edu/2017/explained-neural-networks-deep-learning-0414.
10 D. Rumelhart, B. C. Widrow, and M. A. Lehr, The Basic Ideas in Neural Networks, *Comm.* ACM (March 1994), p. 87: "the most common models take the neuron as the basic processing unit. Each such processing unit is characterized by an activity level (representing the state of polarization of a neuron), an output value (representing the firing rate of the neuron), a set of input connections, (representing synapses on the cell and its dendrite), a bias value (representing an internal resting level of the neuron) and a set of output connections (representing a neuron's axonal projections) ... Thus, each connection has an associated weight (synaptic strength) which determines the effect of the incoming input on the activation level of the unit. The weights may be positive (excitatory) or negative (inhibitory). Frequently, the input lines are assumed to sum linearly yielding an activation value."
11 As Michael Aikenhead put it: "In biological systems, experiments show that one of the most important effects of learning at the cellular level is the modification of the strength of the synaptic connection between two neurons. Analogously, training a neural net is a matter of modifying the values of the synaptic weights in the system. [T]raining is a complex task, and the method used depends on the architecture of the network in question." M. Aikenhead, The Uses and Abuses of Neural Networks in Law (1996) 12 *Santa Clara Comput. High Technol. Law J.* 31, 35.
12 See Hardesty, above note 9.
13 Aikenhead, above note 11, p. 37.

consuming.[14] Neural nets can often solve a given problem faster and more cheaply than it would take to produce human-written symbolic code to address the issue.[15]

But neural nets also have a substantial disadvantage. Unlike symbolic, human-written code, neural nets are opaque.[16] Much like how a human brain can recognize a cat or a dog without expressly being able to reverse-engineer the exact reason why it identified the object as such, so too the reasoning behind conclusions drawn by neural nets can be opaque. That is to say, it is often impossible to precisely reverse-engineer the reason behind the machine's groupings or selections. Sometimes it does not matter whether a human can understand why a machine acted as it did. But for some purposes, knowing the reasoning behind a decision matters.[17]

Additionally, the opacity of neural nets obscures the reason why humans developed the neural net and the role that might have been played in the neural net's ultimate features. Human motivations and biases in development may influence whether an algorithm-made decision is normatively defensible. As Andrew Selbst and Solon Barocas have observed, in the search for accountability for algorithmic decision-making, it can be critically important to understand the human process behind the model's development.[18]

Applications of Algorithms in Contract Law

This chapter is concerned with algorithms and contract law. Therefore, it is useful to distinguish non-contractual uses of algorithms with contractual uses.

Many applications of algorithms, machine learning or otherwise, are internal to an organization. That is, a company or organization uses algorithms to do research, or to conduct or improve some process that does not directly interface with clients. For example, an agricultural firm may use an algorithm to suggest the amount of water, weedkiller, and fertilizer to distribute to crops on a given day based on weather, crop varietal, soil type, and other factors. These uses are non-transactional, and thus any regulation of internal algorithms such as these would not be a matter of contract law, but rather a matter of corporate, tort, or other law.

Some applications of algorithms do involve interacting with current or potential clients, but do not yield a binding contract. An example of this is a financial news aggregation platform that employs an algorithm to group news stories based on theme. While the user of the platform is interacting with results of the company's algorithm, no contract is being formed between the two parties by the act of browsing unless the company separately creates terms to that effect separate from the acts of the algorithm and user.[19]

This chapter is concerned with understanding contracts where an algorithm is used to select contract terms or trading partners on behalf of a company. Here are three examples of how companies can use algorithms in forming a contract.

[14]   *Ibid.*, p. 33.
[15]   See generally H. W. Lin, M. Tegmark, and D. Rolnick, Why Does Deep and Cheap Learning Work So Well? (2017) 168 *J. Stat. Phys.* 1223.
[16]   Hardesty, above note 9; see also Burrell, above note 4.
[17]   Law is based on the notion that there must be a reason for rules and judgments. See C. Morris, Law, Reason, and Sociology (1958) 107 *Univ. Penn. Law Rev.* 147.
[18]   A. Selbst and S. Borocas, The Intuitive Appeal of Explainable Machines (2018) 87 *Fordham Law Rev.* 1085, https://papers.ssrn.com/sol3/papers.cfm?abstract_id=3126971.
[19]   Browsewrap contractual terms may render the act of browsing assent to contractual terms. Browsewrap terms are terms available on a platform that state that by using the platform the user agrees to contractual terms. Without such terms actively added by the creator of the platform, browsing an application cannot be understood to create a binding contract. See *Hines* v. *Overstock*, 668 F. Supp. 2d 362 (EDNY 2009).

(1) Company A uses an algorithm to choose the prices offered to each customer from each product;

(2) Company B uses an algorithm to buy and sell financial products on Company B's behalf on financial markets; and

(3) Company C uses an algorithm to choose which type of contracts Company C will enter into and what strategies Company C will peruse.

In all three of these examples, the company is delegating the responsibility for creating terms or selecting trade partners to an algorithm. A company can delegate only a small amount of responsibility as in Example 1, or large amounts of responsibility as in Example 3. The principle of substitution of the judgment of a human for the program output of a machine is the same.[20] For some types of machine-learning algorithms, such as those built with neural nets, it is not possible for companies that use them to know which terms or trade partners the algorithm will select in advance. Furthermore, even after the algorithm has selected the terms or trade partners, it is usually not possible to determine the exact basis by which the algorithm made the choices delegated to it. This is an artifact of how machine learning works, as described previously in this part.

THE CURRENT LAW OF ALGORITHMS AND CONTRACT

At the turn of the millennium, the federal government and individual states passed laws on electronic contracting. The goal of these statutes was to avoid contestation of contracts purely on the basis of an electronic mode of assent.

At the federal level, in 2000, Congress passed the Electronic Signatures in Global and National Commerce Act (E-Sign Act) in order to ensure that contract or signature "may not be denied legal effect, validity, or enforceability solely because it is in electronic form."[21] The E-Sign Act limits the scope and nature of state laws that can be promulgated on this topic.[22]

At the state level, the majority of states adopted the Uniform Electronic Transactions Act (UETA),[23] which was developed by the National Conference of Commissioners on Uniform State Laws (NCCUSL). The purpose of the law is "to facilitate and promote commerce and governmental transactions by validating and authorizing the use of electronic records and electronic signatures."[24] The law declares "a record or signature may not be denied legal effect or enforceability solely because it is in electronic form" and "[a] contract may not be denied legal effect or enforceability solely because an electronic record was used in its formation."[25]

These laws were a product of a broad consensus around the need to prevent the increasing digitization of commercial transactions from leading to mass confusion as to the enforceability of those transactions. They were clear and narrowly tailored to this goal.

The E-Sign Act and UETA were designed to deal with electronic form contracts, not algorithmic contracts. These laws provide nothing novel in the way of justifying the enforcement of algorithmic contracts. A naïve reading of the text of the UETA may suggest that any

[20] See J. Balkin, The Path of Robotics Law (2015) 6 *Calif. Law Rev. Circuit* 45, 12–16 (discussion of the phenomenon of substitution in artificial intelligence).
[21] E-Sign Act 101.a.
[22] See generally S. Lillie, Will Esign Force States to Adopt UETA? (2001) 42 *Jurimetrics J.* 21, 23 (discussing the federalism implications of E-Sign).
[23] Only New York, Washington, and Illinois have not adopted UETA, and they have their own state statues recognizing electronic signatures.
[24] UETA, s. 6.
[25] UETA, s. 7.

contract in electronic form is enforceable. This interpretation is not supported by the text of the statutes. These statutes did not create an alternative, lower-standard justification for enforceability for any contract that takes electronic form. They merely stated that the rules for contractual formation should be the same whether the transaction is on paper or digital.

UETA is clear on its relationship to the general law of contract. The prefatory notes of UETA state that UETA is "minimalist and procedural."[26] It defers to the meaning of "sign" from existing contract law. To sign is for a party to provide objectively manifested assent on a written document. The scope section of UETA notes: "A transaction subject to this [Act] is also subject to other applicable substantive law."[27]

The preface described the specific type of transaction the UETA intended to address: "the Act makes clear that the actions of machines ('electronic agents') programmed and used by people will bind the user of the machine, regardless of whether human review of a particular transaction has occurred."[28]The text of the statute's definition of "electronic agents" reads: "Electronic agent means a computer program or an electronic or other automated means used independently to initiate an action or respond to electronic records or performances in whole or in part, without review or action by an individual."[29] The comment to the definitions section of UETA endorses a theory of machines as a "tool" of the company.[30]

Algorithmic contracts formed using machine-learning algorithms are outside the scope of the UETA. Machine-learning algorithms have two differences from the UETA's definition of electronic agents. The preface states that the machines UETA discusses are "programmed ... by people." People do not program machine-learning algorithms. Rather, the machine programs itself to perform a task specified by a human as described in the previous part. Second, a tool is a poor metaphor for an algorithm with the ability to program itself that has been delegated substantial responsibility for developing contract terms. A tool is ordinarily understood to amplify the ability of a human user to execute a task. A bulldozer or hammer allows a human to execute work at a scale and pace she could not have achieved otherwise; it does not make independent decisions on the way in which the project will develop on the human worker's behalf.

Most importantly, the UETA states that it was not intended to displace substantive contract law. A contract is formed when all parties manifest assent to the agreement. In at least some algorithmic contracts, the entity-manifesting assent is an algorithm that has programmed itself. The gap between the programming of the algorithm and the algorithm's act has not been closed in substantive contract law. While the electronic agent language is useful, the UETA does not close this gap, because machine-learning algorithmic contracts are not within its scope.

The narrow scope of the E-Sign Act and UETA is illustrated by the failure of a different model law project that was proposed during the same period. NCCUSL and the American Law Institute attempted to draft an article 2B addition to the Uniform Commercial Code (UCC) in the late 1990s. The UCC is a model commercial law statute promulgated in the mid-twentieth century that has been adopted in all US states and jurisdictions.

The ambitious aim of this project was to update the UCC to deal with information-age transactions.[31] All involved agreed that there was a need for further guidance for industry and judges than the mid-century principles from the UCC and the Second Restatement of

26   UETA, prefatory notes.
27   UETA, s. 3(d).
28   UETA, prefatory notes.
29   UETA, s. 2(6).
30   Section 2, Definition, Comment.
31   B. D. McDonald, The Uniform Computer Information Transactions Act (2001) 16 *Berkeley Technol. Law J.* 461, 462. The discussion that follows about the history of the UCITA is adapted from MacDonald's article.

Contracts, an equally influential restatement of common law contract principles, provided. However, there was no consensus about what the content of the updates should be. Due to irreconcilable differences with the NCCUSL, the American Legal Institute left the project, and the NCCUSL retitled the model statute the Uniform Computer Information Transactions Act (UCITA).

Due to sustained critique from multiple stakeholders, the UCITA failed to gain traction among state legislatures and was withdrawn by the NCCUSL. In addition to substantive critiques of the specific provisions of the UCITA,[32] many critics thought that the provisions of the UCITA were premature because the contracting environment of the digital era was immature.[33] Furthermore, there was critique of the generalist approach of the UCITA,[34] arguing that instead more targeted rules for contracting practices enabled by new technologies would be more prudent.[35]

The failure of the UCITA illustrates that lawmakers of that period were not interested in (or could not agree upon) creating an Act that even had the potential to address major alternations in contractual formation enabled by information-age technology. The UETA and E-Sign were stopgaps to prevent opportunists from using electronic form to undermine the enforceability of contracts that would, but for the electronic form, be enforceable under contract law.

Perhaps due to the broad-sounding full title of the UETA, some courts and commentators have read into it the overbroad conclusion that it says all electronic contracts are enforceable. As the previous discussion shows, this interpretation is not supported by either the text of the statute or its drafting history. It ignores irreconcilable differences relevant to contract formation that exist between contracts where machine-learning algorithms choose terms for parties, and other contracts.

Generalist judges may be motivated in finding this interpretation by a desire to enable transactions perceived to be important to the economy to go forward. However, as the following part will illustrate, the concept of algorithmic contracts allows enforcement of contracts formed with algorithms to be rooted in mainstream contract law.

CONCEPTUALIZING ALGORITHMIC CONTRACTS

In a recent article, I coined the term "algorithmic contract" to describe contracts in which an algorithm determines the rights and responsibilities of a party by acting as either a gap-filler or a negotiator for the company in the process of contract formation.[36] In gap-filler algorithmic

---

[32] Many commentators thought that the UCITA gave too much power to companies at the expense of consumers, above and beyond the status quo due to the UCITA's novel concept of mass-market licenses. J. Braucher, The Failed Promise of the Ucita Mass-Market Concept and Its Lessons for Policing of Standard Form Contracts (2003) 7 J. *Small Emerging Bus. Law* 393, 398–416 (detailed description and critique of the UCITA's mass-market licensing concept).

[33] R. J. Yacobozzi, Integrating Computer Information Transactions into Commercial Law in a Global Economy: Why UCITA Is a Good Approach, But Ultimately Inadequate, and the Treaty Solution (2003) *Syracuse Law Technol. J.* 3 (describing the UCITA debate as between those who thought the Act was premature and those who thought the need for uniformity was paramount).

[34] By its own terms, the UCITA was only meant to apply to "computer information transactions" and specifically excluded many controversial applications (UCITA, s. 103). However, skeptics of the Act worried that the principles could have been applied by analogy far beyond the intended scope of the UCITA. This prospect was far from speculative, seeing how courts frequently apply UCC rules to common law cases by analogy.

[35] Braucher, above note 32, pp. 416–22.

[36] See generally L. H. Scholz, Algorithmic Contracts (2017) 20 *Stanford Technol. Law Rev.* 128 for an expanded version of the following discussion.

contracts, parties agree that an algorithm, which operates at some time either before or after the contract is formed, will serve as a gap-filler, determining some term in the contract. An example of this is a company's purchase of a good on Amazon.com. Amazon has standard form terms and conditions for all of its buyers, but sophisticated proprietary algorithms determine the good's exact price at any given time for each user.

In negotiator algorithmic contracts, one or more parties use algorithms as negotiators before contract formation. The algorithm chooses which terms to offer or accept, or which company to do the deal with. An example of this is high-frequency trading of financial products by investment banks and funds. They employ quantitative analysts who create or modify proprietary algorithms that, through machine learning, create real-time strategies for buying and selling financial products. The point of using such algorithms is to efficiently bind the company to advantageous exchanges that a human analyst could not have thought of doing, including the individuals who wrote the program.

The algorithmic contracts that present perhaps the most significant problems for contract law are those that involve "black box" algorithmic agents. These algorithms have decision-making procedures that are not functionally human-intelligible before the program runs – and often cannot even be parsed after the program runs. I have argued that in business-to-business transactions, algorithmic contracts are enforceable because the algorithm is acting as a constructive agent for the company using it. That means the acts are indicative of the company's intent, even if the company cannot precisely reverse-engineer the algorithm's reasoning because of its learning method.

Algorithmic contracts are not the same as smart contracts. The term "algorithmic contract" enhances and clarifies the policy discussion about computer programs known as smart contracts. It does so by creating a name for legal contracts that employ algorithms in their formation. An influential definition of a smart contract is as "a computerized transaction protocol that executes the terms of a contract." Smart contracts are simply computer code that helps to procedurally carry out agreements. As James Grimmelman put it: "Smart contracts are neither smart nor contracts but the name has stuck."[37] Smart contracts are not necessarily legally binding. Not all code is enforceable in contract law, just like not every expression of human language forms a contract. An algorithmic contract is a legally enforceable contract formed by an algorithm. Not every smart contract is necessarily legally enforceable, even though some legally enforceable contracts may involve the computer programs known as smart contracts.

My approach toward the enforceability of algorithmic contracts between businesses is a permissive one. In the case of business-to-business algorithmic contracts, the doctrinal argument is supported by several policy considerations. If businesses are strictly liable for the acts of an algorithm in contract formation, they will be faced with potential adversaries with the financial incentive and ability to pursue litigation. This would create accountability in algorithm usage, and an incentive to allocate risk of loss to the least cost avoider in advance. Arguments for enforceability based on the assumption of risk and economic efficiency are highly persuasive here.

I will briefly illustrate the merits of this approach in analyzing complex transactions form with algorithms by describing a major event in virtual currency transactions and showing what the framework would contribute to analyzing it.

The DAO aspired to be what its acronym stood for, a "digital autonomous organization." It aimed to act as a venture capital fund, and execute all of its transactions autonomously using

---

[37] J. Grimmelman, All Smart Contracts Are Ambiguous (2019) 2 *Pa. J. Law Innov.* 1.

smart contracts on Ethereum's blockchain. The hope was that the DAO would be an organization that could operate itself and make money for investors with limited control from any human.

The DAO was governed by a contract. The goal of the contract was to expressly delegate all the authority to make decisions for the venture fund to the DAO itself. The relevant language is as follows:

> The terms of The DAO Creation are set forth in the smart contract code existing on the Ethereum blockchain at 0xbb9bc244d798123fde783fcc1c72d3bb8c189413. Nothing in this explanation of terms or in any other document or communication may modify or add any additional obligations or guarantees beyond those set forth in The DAO's code.[38]

Once the DAO went public, an Ethereum user exploited a feature in its code to transfer tens of millions to herself.[39] I will call this Ethereum user the "hacker" as I proceed here from time to time, even though it is contested whether what she did was truly what we understand as hacking.[40]

This event precipitated a crisis in the digital currency community as to how to handle the situation. Ethereum operates on a blockchain. Because of how blockchains work, this was not just a dispute between the investors and the hacker as to how to interpret the transaction, but an issue that impacted the entire Ethereum community. A blockchain is a decentralized ledger that includes every transaction that has ever happened in a given system. So whether a transaction on a blockchain will be listed or not impacts everyone using or holding a copy of the ledger, and the system cannot function properly until the dispute is settled.[41]

Some members of the community thought that the hack should be reversed and removed from the Ethereum blockchain as a clear violation of the aims of the DAO. Others thought that the so-called hack was simply an execution of a smart contract where the code itself was law, and to reverse it would create a moral hazard and a precedent for censorship in a transaction system that is supposed to be trustless and decentralized. This dispute ultimately resulted in a "hard fork": the creation of two separate, incompatible blockchains with different protocols.[42] Ethereum itself went forward with a blockchain that reflects only the reversed DAO hack, and there now also exists Ethereum Classic, a blockchain where the DAO hack persists as it first occurred.[43] Three years after the split, Ethereum has far outpaced Ethereum Classic in value and number of users.[44]

Let's apply my framework to this debate.

---

[38] The DAO – Explanation of Terms and Disclaimer (August 3, 2016), https://web.archive.org/web/20160803111447/ https://daohub.org/explainer.html (quoted in Grimmelman, above note 37, p. 19).

[39] N. Popper, A Hacking of More than $50 Million Dashes Hopes in the World of Virtual Currency, *New York Times* (June 17, 2016), www.nytimes.com/2016/06/18/business/dealbook/hacker-may-have-removed-more-than -50-million-from-experimental-cybercurrency-project.html.

[40] Hacking means "to gain illegal access to [a computer system." Merriam Webster, hack, www.merriam-webster.com /dictionary/hack. To call this user a "hacker" is tendentious, as the question here is whether or not what she did was a breach of the contract. If it wasn't a breach of the contract, her transferring the $60 million to herself would be no more theft than Dell's transfer of $1,000 from my bank account after purchasing a computer.

[41] See Grimmelman, above note 37, pp. 16–17 (discussing blockchain updates and blockchain forks). Unlike software, where, for example, many versions of Microsoft Word are simultaneously in use and documents can be shared between individuals using different versions, users of a particular blockchain cannot simultaneously use different versions of that blockchain.

[42] J. I. Wong and I. Kar, Everything You Need to Know about the Ethereum Hard Fork, *Quartz* (July 18, 2016), https://qz.com/730004/everything-you-need-to-know-about-the-ethereum-hard-fork/.

[43] C. Rivit, Ethereum v. Ethereum Classic: What you Need to Know, *Yahoo News* (May 23, 2019), https://finance .yahoo.com/news/ethereum-vs-ethereum-classic-know-110028278.html.

[44] *Ibid.*

The agreement creating the DAO was a negotiator algorithmic contract because the investors agreed to rely on an algorithm (the DAO) to choose who to transact with and on what terms. The DAO acted as a constructive agent for the investors.[45]

The advocates of Ethereum Classic have the more straightforward argument as to why the agreement would be legally enforceable. The DAO was acting as agent for the DAO's investors. The agent transacted with the hacker to transfer the $60 million to her control. Even though the investors were unhappy, they chose to use an algorithm as a negotiator and thus are bound fully by the outcome.

An argument in favor of the mainline Ethereum advocates' position that the DAO hack was an unlawful theft rather than a transaction by the DAO's terms is subtler. It is the policy of courts to defer to the text and behavior of "sophisticated" parties to contracts because they can be presumed, more so than consumers, to mean what they say and do in the area of contract formation. However, there are limits on what even sophisticated parties can know. The Ethereum advocates could argue that given that the DAO was a completely new business model based on new technology and nobody involved knew how it would shake out, the contract in fact was a provisional agreement to agree to some terms at a later time.[46] While there was no explicit reference in the contract prohibiting the hacker's acts, the community realized once the hack had happened that it was a kind of act that did not count as a transaction with the DAO at all, but rather was an unlawful theft.

It is important to note that this argument from the temporal limitations of the contracting parties is not grounded in the complexity of the DAO's computer code or the fact that the DAO was on a blockchain. Even a very complex, opaque algorithm can be an agent for a company. The reason for construing the hacker's transaction with the DAO as wrongful despite the fact that the code permitted comes from the overall novelty of the type of business transaction. What happened with the DAO can be seen as an example of what Andrew Verstein called "ex pro tempore" contracting, the use of contracts with ambiguous or absent terms that are resolved by an actor other than a court.[47] Ultimately, it was the Ethereum leadership and community that decided how to interpret the DAO hack. Ethereum leadership acted and the community "voted with their feet" to mostly follow the hard fork path that rejected the properness of the DAO hack.

As this example has shown, the concept of algorithmic contracts provides a frame for understanding why and how contracts formed using algorithms should be enforced. Understanding algorithms as constructive agents in contract formation closes one possible obstacle for finding a contract formed with algorithms to be enforceable. Complexity of an algorithm used in contract formation, without more, is not a reason to find a contract not binding for its user. But there may be other sociotechnical sources of complexity that may limit the ability of parties to be bound, or allow them leeway to define terms contemporaneously or even *ex post*.

---

[45]   In the absence of the English-language contract quoted above, it is unclear that the DAO contract would be enforceable. In the law of sales of goods, there is some support for the notion that contracts can be formed "in any manner sufficient to show agreement, including conduct by both parties which recognizes the existence of such a contract" (UCC 2–204). Article 2 is frequently applied by analogy to matters that do not concern goods. But by and large, transactions for more than a certain amount must be memorialized in writing in some way. While the DAO had code that could be rendered in writing, it's not clear that it would be sufficient by itself to satisfy a statute of frauds. E.g. UCC 2–201, Restatement Second of Contracts 110.

[46]   See L. H. Scholz, Timing Boilerplate (draft on file with author) (distinguishing boilerplate in the context of the newly possible from boilerplate in established transactions and finding the latter fits far more awkwardly in the existing legal infrastructure for form contracts).

[47]   See generally A. Verstein, Ex Pro Temporare Contracting (2014) 55 *William & Mary Law Rev.* 1869.

PATHS FORWARD

Thus far, this chapter has defined and described algorithms and discussed their role in contract formation. Then, it showed that current state and federal statutory law does not squarely address this issue. It then introduced a framework based in general common law principles for understanding algorithmic contracts as enforceable at contract and described the benefits of such a framework. This section sketches out what the implementation process would look like.

Any individual court could adopt the algorithmic contract framework in their analysis. But a uniform state law process would create more certainty for actors who use algorithmic contracts to know that their agreements will be enforceable.

The NCCUSL should update the UETA to clarify that algorithms can act as agents for companies for the purposes of contract formation. The leadership of the NCCUSL makes it more likely that individual states' law will be updated uniformly and relatively quickly. The process of updating the UETA would be the subject of legal reporting, and would also draw the attention of stakeholders and update norms and expectations outside of the context of litigation.

Prefatory material and comments to the updated UETA should clarify that when it comes to machine learning and the newly possible, the notion of "sophisticated actor" should be inclusive of the reality that there are technical and temporal limitations to what even the most sophisticated companies can know when they form contracts.[48] Courts have been known to give corporations a fair amount of deference in developing their transactional relationships based on the idea that given their level of sophistication, they intended to be bound to particular terms and the law should recognize this. However, as the discussion in "Introducing Algorithms and Their Role in Contract Law" shows, the reasons for behavior of machine-learning algorithms can be opaque even to their drafters. And as the discussion of the DAO in "The Current Law of Algorithms and Contract" shows, the implications of novel technology and innovative business models can have results that surprise and divide even a knowledgeable and ideologically aligned group of investors. The law needs tools to address these disputes when there is more than one credible approach, which is especially likely in the law of the newly possible.

The algorithmic contracts framework provides a way of understanding transactions with algorithmic agents without relying on an implausible legal fiction. Considering algorithms as constructive agents of companies that use them in transactions provides a specific, technology-neutral reason why it is appropriate to hold companies to the terms an algorithm has chosen for them.

CONCLUSION

Algorithms play a key role in contract formation. Yet some courts and commentators have sought to either ignore algorithms' role in contract formation contribution or to assert their complete foreignness to contract and uniqueness from other forms of corporate reliance on agents. It is incorrect to ignore the novel features presented by machine-learning algorithms

48 See R. Gilson, C. Sabel, and R. Scott, Contract, Uncertainty and Innovation (2010) (draft), https://papers.ssrn.com/sol3/papers.cfm?abstract_id=1711435 (describing the basic problem of contracting in innovative business spaces and describing "braiding of formal and informal contracting that has developed to organize collaboration across organizational boundaries where the desired outcome can, at best, be anticipated only very approximately").

by concluding that all "electronic" contracts are enforceable simply because they are electronic. It is also incorrect to assert that machine-learning algorithms are so complicated that the companies using them cannot be held bound and accountable to the terms the algorithm has selected on their behalf.

Contract law can use broad, generalist-friendly principles to incorporate new technologies into the existing contract framework and the values represented by said framework. The first step in this process is understanding that algorithms can act as agents for corporations.

7

Algorithms, Agreements, and Agency

Shawn Bayern

This chapter's thesis is simple: as a general matter, agreements are a functional and conceptually straightforward way for the law to recognize algorithms. In particular, using agreements to connect algorithms to the rest of the law is better than trying to use the law of agency to do so.[1] Casual speech and conceptualism have led to the commonplace notion of "electronic agents," but the law of agreements is a more functional entry point for algorithms to interact with the law than the concept of vicarious action. Algorithms need not involve any vicarious action, and most of the law of agency translates very poorly to algorithms that lack intent, reasonable understanding, and legal personality in their own right; instead, algorithms cause activity that may have contractual or other agreement-based legal significance. Recognizing the power (and perhaps the necessity) of addressing algorithms by means of the law governing agreements and other legal instruments can free us from formalistic attempts to shoehorn algorithms into a limited set of existing legal categories.

THE ALGORITHM-AGREEMENT EQUIVALENCE PRINCIPLE

I have introduced in earlier work the notion that algorithms and agreements are to some degree interchangeable,[2] but I will elaborate on the notion here. The principle that algorithms are coordinate in scope and function to legal agreements may initially seem surprising, but even as a casual, intuitive matter, it is not difficult to see the correspondence. For example, I commonly advise law students who have computer-science backgrounds that writing contracts or operating agreements involves very similar skills to writing software: both require accounting for different possible future states, addressing them with logic and structure, and then releasing an attempt at a solution into an uncertain world. As the computer scientist Alan Perlis once put it, "Programmers are not to be measured by their ingenuity and their logic but by the completeness of their case analysis,"[3] and that (debatable) proposition applies with similar (debatable)

---

[1] For the last few decades, commentators have offered a wide variety of conceptual models, including human agents, as candidates for the law's analogical treatment of algorithms, artificial intelligence, autonomous systems, and similar innovations. See, e.g., M. U. Scherer, Of Wild Beasts and Digital Analogues: The Legal Status of Autonomous Systems (2018) 19 *Nev. Law J.* 259 (considering different conceptual models by means of which the law may recognize algorithms, including children, animals, and legal agents); S. N. Lehman-Wilzig, Frankenstein Unbound: Towards a Legal Definition of Artificial Intelligence (1981) 13 *Futures* 442 (surveying the same conceptual models and others).

[2] See mainly S. Bayern, The Implications of Modern Business-Entity Law for the Regulation of Autonomous Systems (2015) 19 *Stan. Technol. Law Rev.* 93 and S. Bayern, Of Bitcoins, Independently Wealthy Software, and the Zero-Member LLC (2014) 108 *Nw. Univ. Law Rev.* 1485.

[3] A. Perlis, Epigrams in Programming, ACM Sigplan Notices (September 1982), p. 7.

force, and for the same reasons, to transactional lawyers. Both algorithms and legal agreements can have "bugs" that result from logical errors or errors in anticipating events; writing both clearly and manageably is a rare, creative skill too often neglected; in practical settings, producing both relies on significant critique reuse of prior work, based on a wealth of (often public) professional experience recorded in written form; the generation of both can be automated (a point not sufficiently recognized either for agreements or for software);[4] and so on.

My point is not just intuitive or loosely analogical, however; it is analytical: any algorithm with verifiable states can be expressed, or recognized, by a legal agreement. (For my purposes, "verifiable state" has the same meaning as it does in economic contract theory: state that can be proven to the court that would enforce the agreement.[5] If the state of an algorithm is not verifiable to third parties like courts, it is unclear how or whether the law can recognize it.) This capability of agreements follows from the legal proposition that agreements can recognize, and vary legal rights based on, verifiable conditions – that is, states of the world. States of the world include states of algorithmic processes. Accordingly, legal agreements can give effect to the verifiable states of algorithms.

Of course, I don't mean to imply that any legal agreement must be enforceable; a court might, for example, strike down an agreement on grounds of public policy regardless of whether it happens to contain conditions based on algorithmic processing. My point is simply that legal agreements can depend on the execution of algorithms. Moreover, sufficiently precise agreements may be expressed as algorithms; there is no conceptual difference, other than perhaps the level of precision, between an agreement that sets up procedures to manage performance and an algorithm.[6]

A few demonstrations of this notion may be helpful. Consider an algorithm that produces, from many inputs, a single scalar output that is meant to embody a price that the legal entity that runs the algorithm is willing to pay for a commodity. Legal agreements, such as simple contracts, can use this output in a variety of ways. One simple way is for a communication of a contractual offer – a precursor to a legal agreement – by the legal entity executing the algorithm to be printed (or recorded in electronic form) by means of a templating (or "mail merge") system that substitutes a generic marker for the algorithm's price at the time the offer document is generated.[7] Such a document would be indistinguishable, on its face, from one that did not depend on the output of an algorithm, much as a web browser has no way in the general case to know whether a page it has received is a copy of static text or the product of a dynamic system.[8] Of course, the offer might refer explicitly to the current state of the algorithm rather than include

[4] For software, a helpful demonstration of this principle appears in B. Kernighan and R. Pike, *The Practice of Programming* (Addison Wesley, 1999), pp. 237–45. For legal documents, I elaborate the notion below.
[5] For an introduction to and modern critique of the distinction between "verifiable" and "observable" information under economic contract theory, see H. Lind and J. Nystrom, The Explanation of Incomplete Contracts in Mainstream Contract Theory: A Critique of the Distinction between "Observable" and "Verifiable" (2011) 7 *J. Evolut. Inst. Econ. Rev.* 279.
[6] Not every agreement can be implemented literally by an algorithm, but that is mainly because agreements may not be precise enough to qualify as algorithms. Some legal agreements, or some parts of them, may resolve to algorithmic processing. But other agreements may be more analogous to a functional specification for an algorithm, or to a general discussion of an algorithm among non-programmers. When I claim that agreements are in some sense interchangeable or "isomorphic" with algorithms, I mean only that (1) any agreement can be expressed by an algorithm as specifically as the precision of the agreement allows and (2) more loosely, agreements and algorithms operate at a similar level of generality, so that sufficiently precise agreements can be expressed as algorithms.
[7] In pseudocode for a templating language, this might look like: "We propose to buy 100 units from you at $price."
[8] I have explained this concept in detail to novice computer programmers, for pedagogical purposes, in S. Bayern, *JSTL in Action* (Manning Publications, 2002).

a prior, static output: it might say: "Our offer is to buy 100 units of this good at the price our algorithm has currently posted at the time you accept this offer." Such an offer, and the legal contract that may result from it, should be entirely unremarkable to lawyers and businesspeople; it is hard to see a serious objection to the role that an algorithm has played in the generation of such contracts, and indeed references to changing prices and other terms outside a particular contractual document (or a particular set of prior communications between the parties) were commonplace long before anyone spoke of algorithmic contracts.[9]

It is easy to generalize this concept to apply to multiple outputs rather than a single output.[10] It also turns out, as I have explained in prior work,[11] to be easy to generalize it to stages in the contracting process other than the insertion of conditions into an offer. For example, an algorithm might choose when to generate an offer document (or whether and when to legally accept one sent to it) and might communicate with its legal entity's contractual counterparties itself. These capabilities are more controversial,[12] but I don't believe they are problematic in practice, and there appear to be many examples where clearly enforceable legal agreements result from the ongoing operation of algorithms in ways that are today considered almost mundane. For example, a labor union's contract with an employer may schedule complex salary increases according to an algorithmic formula, which is implemented with little human oversight; nobody would seriously dispute that employees were owed the salary increases that the algorithm produced. (At least one of my colleagues – perhaps most of them – have no idea what they are paid and never look personally at the details of their paychecks; at least some salary increases at my university happen automatically, without any human attention to the individual raises being applied to employees; consequently, there are almost certainly specific salary increases that no human is aware of, but which are nonetheless unproblematically binding as legal matter.) Stock trades are executed automatically all the time between computer programs, and individual traders are happy to say "fill my order at the market price," knowing that that price is the result, at least in part, of algorithmic processes. Consumers routinely buy goods and services – for example, airline tickets, or merchandise through an online retailer – using prices set by complex algorithms. And so on.

"Agreements" in the sense I am describing them amount to quite a general class of legal activities. They include the simple two-party contracts I have been using as an example, but they also include operating agreements of companies or trust agreements. Indeed, the concept I have been describing applies to more or less any legal instrument, at least in theory. So, for example, a statute, regulation, or legal judgment might, at least in principle, refer to the verifiable state of an algorithm. Under US law, statutes that attempt this may face constitutional restrictions on the "delegation" of legislative powers,[13] but it is unremarkable for a legal instrument to specify or recognize a schedule of payments computed by a complex formula with inputs whose future values are not known when the instrument is produced.

---

[9]   See *Nanakuli Paving & Rock Co.* v. *Shell Oil Co.*, 664 F.2d 772, 778 (interpreting a written contract that referred to "Shell's Posted Price at time of delivery").

[10] Again, in pseudocode for a general templating language, this might look like: "Dear $customer: We propose that you buy $quantity units at $price on $date. Please see our warranty terms below: $terms[$customer]. Sincerely, Offeror."

[11] See S. Bayern, Artificial Intelligence and Private Law, in W. Barfield and U. Pagallo (eds.), *Research Handbook on the Law of Artificial Intelligence* (Edward Elgar, 2018).

[12] See, e.g., *ibid.*; L. H. Scholz, Algorithmic Contracts (2017) 20 *Stan. Technol. Law Rev.* 128.

[13] See, e.g., *INS* v. *Chadha*, 462 US 919, 944 (1983) (invalidating a statute as unconstitutional, despite "[c]onvenience and efficiency," because of excessive "delegation" of powers from Congress to the Executive Branch).

The principles I have just described lead, perhaps almost mundanely, to an idea that has seemed revolutionary to many, which is that the operating agreements of legal entities (such as a limited liability company, or LLC) can be used to give effect to the verifiable states of algorithms. The result is that algorithms can effectively act in any way that a legal entity can act. I have described this mechanism – its foundations and its consequences – at length elsewhere,[14] so I will not elaborate it here except to say that it permits existing legal persons to confer many of the attributes of legal personality (such as the functional right to enter contracts, control private property, sue, or be sued) on any algorithms with verifiable state. But the consequences needn't be so grandiose. For example, a relatively conventional business organization could operate under a charter that restricts its activities (or the activities of a division of the organization) based on the verifiable state of algorithms, or a conventional contract between two parties may have performance obligations that depend on the verifiable state of an algorithm – which might be anything from a simple program that produces a descriptive statistic based on mundane data to a "smart contract" in a blockchain or the output of a complex neural net. Similarly, part of a conventional legal entity's operation may be automated; a company might sell food to distributors in manually negotiated contracts, but also sell it automatically, via vending machines or a website, to individual consumers, and not all such sales need human thought or action for them to be legally binding.

THE UNSUITABILITY OF AGENCY LAW FOR ACCOMMODATING ALGORITHMS

The previous section has outlined ways in which algorithms may, in some sense, "act for" a legal entity. It may be tempting to draw an analogy between this sort of action and the action of a legal agent. Indeed, many have done so.[15]

As background, a legal agent is a legal person who can perform legal actions for a principal.[16] For example, in nearly all mature legal systems, entering a contract requires each party to assent to the terms of the contract, but the parties do not need to express such assent themselves; they can send a representative, known as an agent, to bind them legally. Agency can be quite formal, arising from a "power of attorney" document that lists specific powers and conditions under which they can be exercised. It can also be quite informal, leading to legal cases in which a nephew briefly helping an uncle wash his car can produce legal consequences for the uncle.[17] American law schools traditionally taught the common law of agency as a required part of the first-year curriculum, along with, for example, courses on torts, contracts, property, and crimes. But the subject is rarely taught as a freestanding subject anymore; it is often compressed into a week or less of a course on business law. Still, the American Law Institute has produced and continued to update *Restatement of the Law* treatises specifically on the subject of legal agency, and many of its rules are rich and debatable in the same manner as rules about contract law and tort law.

---

[14] I developed this principle and techniques that permit it mainly in the two papers cited above, note 2.
[15] See, e.g., Scherer, above note 1, pp. 285–90; Scholz, above note 12, pp. 164–9; S. Chopra and L. White, Artificial Agents and the Contracting Problem: A Solution Via an Agency Analysis (2009) *Univ. Ill. J. Law Technol. Policy* 363; Lehman-Wilzig, above note 1, pp. 451–2.
[16] Cf. Restatement (Third) of Agency § 1.01 (defining the legal concept of "agency"). Importantly, under the common law, only legal persons may act as legal agents. See, e.g., *ibid.*, § 1.04 cmt. e ("To be capable of acting as a principal or an agent, it is necessary to be a person, which in this respect requires capacity to be the holder of legal rights and the object of legal duties").
[17] See, e.g., *Heims v. Hanke*, 93 NW.2d 455 (Wis. 1958).

There appears to be a drive to make use of this body of law to accommodate the actions of algorithms. Algorithms may seem to "act for" a company roughly as a human agent would. But extending agency law in this way is likely to lead to confusion because the legal subject of agency has a poor conceptual and functional fit with algorithms. Using agency law to integrate algorithms into the law has several specific drawbacks. First, it needlessly complicates the law's response to unexpected action by algorithms; the law of agency has sensitive rules, which rest on various parties' knowledge, intent, and reasonableness, in order to assign liability among principals, agents, and third parties, and these rules do not neatly or helpfully address the problems of algorithms. (It would be better to let the law of contracts govern gaps in agreements raised by unexpected algorithmic action.) Second, relatedly, it introduces novel ambiguities, which agency law is ill-equipped to address, about who the principal is for the action of algorithms. (By contrast, an agreement that recognizes an algorithm's verifiable state raises no such ambiguity.) Third, agency law's significant rules about the liability of agents – which provide important protections to principals and third parties – would have no place in a legal regime that did not recognize the legal personhood of algorithmic agents. (It would be better simply to let normal principles of tort law apply to legal persons who put algorithmic processes in motion.) In short, the law of agency is a poor fit as a candidate for a legal technique to accommodate algorithms, and the Third Restatement is correct to require that legal agents be legal persons.[18] Instead, as described above, recognizing algorithms as providing potentially relevant conditions for simple legal agreements shows more promise as a way to permit businesses and individuals to give algorithms the legal effects they intend for them to have.

The rest of this section will consider the objections I have just outlined in more detail.

The Ambiguities of Agency Law as Applied to Algorithmic Agents

Agency law is widely misunderstood; traditionally, it was complicated by excessive categorization of the actions of agents, particularly into different types of authority treated as "express," "implied," "inherent," and so on. The Restatement (Third) of Agency is a significant improvement over classic legal conceptions of the subject, providing unifying rules that eliminate unnecessary categories. Perhaps the core principle governing agents is the notion of "actual authority" – that is, whether an agent has been empowered by a principal to enter contracts or perform other binding legal actions on behalf of the principal. The Third Restatement expresses a simple, unified rule for the existence of such actual authority: "Actual authority ... is created by a principal's manifestation to an agent that, as reasonably understood by the agent, expresses the principal's assent that the agent take action on the principal's behalf."[19]

That simple rule shows, on its own, one of the most significant problems with an attempt to use agency law to harmonize the law's treatment of algorithms: the core determination of the power of an agent is based on what is "reasonably understood by the agent" and so requires of candidate agents that we be able to characterize their understanding as reasonable or not. While it is possible that sufficiently advanced algorithms can be judged in this way, there is no current legal standard, and no obviously productive candidate for a legal standard, that would judge today's algorithms based on what they could reasonably have understood their

---

[18] See Restatement (Third) of Agency § 1.04 cmt. e.
[19] *Ibid.*, § 3.01.

purported principals to mean. Because classic terminology and categorization obscured this underlying determination of reasonableness, it may not have been evident to commentators that it is difficult for the common law of agency even to get off the ground without agents whose behavior can be judged in human terms. For example, Scherer, in his recent analysis of different legal analogies that might apply to autonomous systems, does not address this problem.[20] Chopra and White address it with reference to the classic categories of agency law, essentially arguing that algorithms might have "actual express authority" but not "actual implied authority," but they appear to assume that the determination of "actual express authority" will be straightforward whereas, in the real world, it is unlikely to be: it still depends on judging the principal's communications from the perspective of a reasonable agent. Agency law is trivially easy to analyze when the subjective intent of the principal, the subjective understanding of the agent, and the reasonable understanding of both all line up similarly. But when these three possible understandings of the principal's instructions depart from one another, it is only the rich, contextual, human rules of agency law that can break the tie.

For example, suppose a company uses an algorithm to negotiate with contractual counter-parties. (This might involve anything from a simple website that posts prices to a complex algorithmic broker of contracts or financial trades.) The algorithm, in some details of its operation, departs slightly from the principal's understanding of what was possible. The normal rules of agency law are useless here. They would ask whether the algorithm reasonably understood the principal's instructions – a meaningless question.

How, then, is the law to determine whether an algorithm properly binds a principal? The core rule of agency law provides no answer. Perhaps other rules of agency law, like the rules governing apparent authority, provide some useful guidance, but as I will describe below, these rules raise other problems that suggest they are ill-suited to help the law recognize algorithms.

By contrast, this problem doesn't arise if we treat the legal effects of algorithms as arising simply from agreements. Of course, there can still be significant dispute over the meaning of an agreement and whether it covers unexpected conduct by an algorithm, but that sort of dispute and ambiguity are conventional legal questions concerning the interpretation of legal instruments. Thus, if an organization has an operating agreement purporting to assign particular legal effects to the verifiable state of an algorithm and the algorithm behaves in an unexpected fashion, the law associated with the interpretation of business entities' operating agreements can address this problem in the way it addresses any other problem. If a plain-meaning rule applies, courts can use that; to the extent that any party's subjective intent is important, the law would look to the intent of whoever drafted the operating agreement; and the law might develop doctrines that govern unexpected circumstances, as it has in the doctrines of impossibility, impracticability, and so on. My argument is not that no legal questions are possible when agreements recognize algorithms, just that we already have techniques for addressing those problems, and there are established practical and academic debates that accommodate the important policies and differences in judgment among legal experts as to the resolution of those problems. Nothing similar exists if we look to the law of agency to try to resolve the same sort of ambiguity.

Moreover, using agreements to give legal effects to algorithms allows the law to be agnostic with regard to the capabilities or other characteristics of the algorithms. We do not need algorithms to be sufficiently advanced that they could be judged as being reasonable or

[20] See above note 1.

unreasonable in human terms. We can avoid relying on expert understanding of just what a neural net "thought" it saw. Instead, the law's focus remains where it should be: on the intent, and the expression of that intent, by those who decided to give legal effects to algorithms by means of adopting agreements or other legal instruments.

The Ambiguous Principals of Algorithmic Agents

A closely related problem is that without an agreement to recognize the legal significance of an algorithm's operation, it is unclear who the principal is. That is, if we model algorithms as agents, it is unclear who they are agents for. In many practical settings, there are many existing individuals or businesses that have a role in developing and executing algorithms. These include the designer(s) of the algorithm who specify its needs and its business role; the programmer(s) who wrote the software that makes up the algorithm; those who choose to run the algorithm in a particular context; the owners or possessors of the hardware on which the algorithm is executed;[21] the owners or possessors of the physical space in which the algorithms are executed; those who own part or all of the intellectual property associated with the algorithm; those who own, control, or have rights to process or restrict processing of part or all of the data that the algorithm uses; and all of the possible legal principals of any of these parties. In certain contexts, our instincts can be clearer than others about whom an algorithm is "acting" for; for example, nobody would seriously think the developer of customizable, off-the-shelf software for pricing merchandise was itself intending to make offers to sell specific merchandise merely because a retail website used the algorithm that the developer created and supplied. But one lesson of the common law is that nuances are difficult to predict across novel contexts – and often even across familiar contexts. The choice of one or several legal principals for an algorithm's action almost certainly should depend on the intent and reasonable understanding of the various parties involved in the creation and use of the algorithm, their prior dealings with one another, and so on.

Agency law gives us little guidance about such matters. By contrast, the agreements of the parties give us significant guidance about such matters. What is a potentially complex choice-of-principal question under agency law is very simple if we choose to recognize algorithms where agreements recognize them; the rule is then simply that a legal person is bound contractually by the action of an algorithm when that person's agreements contain conditions that depend on the verifiable state of the algorithm.

When others have addressed the problem of algorithms' ambiguous or multiple principals, they have done so primarily for the purposes of tort liability.[22] I believe this is asking agency law to do too much, and it may also rest on a common conceptual confusion about agency law. In general, principals are *not* liable for the torts of their agents merely because of the agency relationship; there is a special category of agents known today simply as employees[23] who give rise to vicarious liability for principals in *respondeat superior*.[24] The definition of

---

[21] Of course, today the "hardware" may be virtual, in which case the problems are multiplied.

[22] See, e.g., Scherer, above note 1, p. 287 ("Under agency law, an agent can have multiple principals, either by being the agent of another agent ... or by being the agent of two or more co-principals. Each principal can be held responsible for the agent's tortious acts, as long as those acts are otherwise within the scope of the agency. In the context of A.I. systems, this structure expands the range of potential sources of compensation if an A.I. system causes harm ...").

[23] The historical term in the common law of agency was "servants."

[24] For an overview of *respondeat superior*, see S. Bayern, *Closely Held Organizations* (Carolina Academic Press, 2013), pp. 49–84.

"employee" in this context is ambiguous and disputed, but probably the most important characteristic of an employee is that the principal has the right to control not just the employee's output, but also the manner of the employee's processing.[25] This criterion translates very badly to algorithms, particularly as machine learning makes it more difficult for anyone to explain or control the details of an algorithm's internal processing. Even without the complexity of machine learning, however, legal classification here is likely to be both difficult and unhelpful. For example, if A buys a commercial software package from B and B allows A to configure the software only in particular ways, but then A puts the algorithm into wide practice and injuries result, it is hard to conceive of the algorithm as A's employee under traditional principles of agency law: A does not control the internal operation of the algorithm. But A's knowing, wide-scale use of the algorithm may well have been unreasonable. To address this situation legally, it is much simpler to let conventional principles of tort law apply: A and B should be liable, individually and/or jointly, based on whether either of them has acted unreasonably in failing to prevent the injuries that have resulted. Agency law seems to add nothing helpful – and it is unnecessary to look to agency law to reach a wrongful party, as tort law is already sufficient.[26] Almost certainly, at least today, very little will be added to the law by an effort to differentiate between algorithms that are employees and algorithms that are independent contractors! But that is precisely what would be necessary, in the general case, for agency law to be useful to assigning vicarious tort liability to those who create or make use of algorithms.

It may be worth adding that my goal is not simply to defend the law's conventional views on algorithms and the people associated with them. For example, the difficulty of assigning responsibility to one or more people involved with an algorithm exists under the Third Restatement's view of algorithms as instrumentalities just as much as it does for a view of algorithms as agents. Recognizing the role of agreements – whether in determining the effects of an instrumentality or even in determining who is or isn't an agent – appears to be the best way out of murkiness. To put it differently, we probably can recognize that program X is the instrumentality or agent of business Y only by recognizing at least an implicit agreement (on the part of Y and its potential contractual counterparties) that X will serve that role. The law will do better to pay more attention to such agreements, particularly as they become more express and more complex, rather than to take them for granted or make generic assumptions about their content.

The Complexity of Liability in Agency Law

Agency law is a rich part of the common law designed to allocate liability sensitively among principals, agents, and third parties. Its scheme collapses if purported agents are unable to bear liability because they are not legal persons.

For example, consider a problem similar to the general one described in "The Algorithm-Agreement Equivalence Principle" above: a business makes use of an algorithm to enter into

---

[25] See *ibid.*, pp. 53–4.

[26] There is a class of torts that traditionally has been tied closely to agency law but seems to depart little, or not at all, from ordinary principles of tort liability. For example, Restatement (Third) of Agency § 7.05 provides: "A principal who conducts an activity through an agent is subject to liability for harm to a third party caused by the agent's conduct if the harm was caused by the principal's negligence in selecting, training, retaining, supervising, or otherwise controlling the agent." In that case, however, the principal's own negligence (in selecting or managing the agent) is sufficient for tort liability; as I have described in more detail in Bayern, above note 24, pp. 77–8, no new principle of agency law is needed to explain this rule.

contracts with third parties, and the algorithm behaves unexpectedly and causes the business to appear to enter contracts that it had no desire to enter. (This could be anything from transient mispricing on an automated website to a complex, hard-to-detect error in the algorithm's determination of which third parties to contract with.) As I pointed out in "The Algorithm-Agreement Equivalence Principle," agency law's rules concerning actual authority are ill-suited to address this type of unexpected processing precisely because they depend on an evaluation of the reasonableness of the purported agent.

Perhaps the ambiguity might be resolved not by rules of "actual" authority, but by what in the United States is called "apparent" authority (and elsewhere is commonly called "ostensible" authority). These rules, designed mainly for the protection of third parties contracting with a principal through an agent, effectively deem that a purported agent has authority to bind the principal so long as the third party reasonably believes, based on the principal's manifestations to that third party, that the agent had the authority to act for the principal even if the agent lacked that authority. Because apparent authority depends only on the reasonableness of the third party and the facts concerning the principal's manifestations to it, it seems like an adaptive enough way to allocate responsibility between principals and third parties. But a different feature of agency law shows why this principle, too, maps badly onto algorithms: When an agent acts with apparent but not actual authority – which is to say, when the agent has acted unreasonably, but the third party has not – the agent is liable to the principal for harms caused by the agent's assumption of non-delegated authority. Moreover, agents are understood to make a warranty of authority to third parties, effectively representing that if they are purporting to act for a principal, they have the authority to do so; third parties may sue purported agents for harms that result from the breaches of that implied warranty.[27]

All these rules exhibit a balance designed to protect reasonable parties at the expense of unreasonable ones. The balance does not exist when the agent is not a legal person, and the resulting set of rules is in some sense not actually "agency law," but an arbitrary sub-set of it. That doesn't mean the resulting set of rules is necessarily wrong, only that the use of an analogy to agency law is necessarily incomplete and suspect – and that the results need to be defended independently on functional grounds without reference to a formal analogy.

CONCLUSION

Analogizing algorithms to agents is popular rhetorically, but agency law is not a functional mechanism for incorporating algorithms into law. Instead, the ability of agreements of any form to recognize the verifiable state of algorithms provides an extremely flexible mechanism for connecting algorithms to existing law.

---

[27]   See Restatement (Third) Agency § 6.10.

8

Algorithmic Governance and Administrative Law

Steven M. Appel and Cary Coglianese

If law is to promote justice and welfare, it must respond to changes in society. In much the same way, the tools that government uses to make, implement, and enforce laws also need to adapt in the face of societal changes as well as in light of changes in technology. In this spirit, governments around the world increasingly look to the promise of one of the newest technological innovations made possible by modern computing power: machine-learning algorithms.

The case for using machine-learning algorithms to improve government, even to the point of replacing some human decision-making with algorithmic systems, grows stronger as machine-learning algorithms prove their value in the private sector. These algorithms – also referred to as artificial intelligence (AI) – are currently used by businesses to navigate airplanes and automobiles, make medical diagnoses, target marketing campaigns, detect fraudulent credit card transactions, assess creditworthiness, generate realistic synthetic human voices, and much more. When governments find themselves performing similar functions in the context of administering public programs, it makes sense they would think to turn to these same algorithmic tools. Increasingly, they are even deploying machine learning to assist with other governance functions that have no parallels in the private sector.

As the possibilities for algorithmic governance increase, questions arise about exactly when and how machine-learning algorithms should be deployed. These questions take on special significance when machine-learning algorithms are used by governmental ministries and agencies to make and implement public law. These uses would appear to implicate several important principles of administrative law, including those related to due process, equal protection, privacy, transparency, and limitations on delegations of authority. This chapter focuses on these principles and the question of whether they will act as a barrier to the use of machine learning by administrative agencies in the United States. Although the emphasis here is primarily on the implications of governmental use of machine-learning algorithms for federal administrative law in the United States, the treatment of these issues will likely be similar in other legal systems. In addition, the principles of administrative law addressed here tend to track general good governance principles that will be applicable within any liberal democratic governmental system.

Although machine-learning algorithms come in many varieties, this chapter begins by highlighting their general properties as a way of explaining what makes them different from traditional statistical tools and why the properties of machine learning can be seen to present potential legal questions for their use by government agencies. The chapter then proceeds to present an analysis of the legality of algorithmic governance from the standpoint of five major doctrines of potentially applicable law. The analysis presented here supports the conclusion that responsible government officials should be able to lawfully deploy machine-learning algorithms, even to the point of using algorithmic systems to substitute for human decisions in certain kinds of adjudicatory and policymaking contexts. The chapter wraps up by highlighting capacity-building steps as well as some best practices that could help prepare government agencies to take advantage of responsible uses of algorithmic governance.

The conclusions presented here must be, by necessity, general ones, as any particular application of machine learning could present context-specific factors related to how the algorithm is designed and deployed which could alter the analysis. It is also possible, of course, for an algorithmic tool to comport with administrative law standards and yet still violate other substantive legal rights or simply be unwise to use for reasons of ethics and public policy. Still, the chapter supports a prima facie conclusion of the administrative legality of algorithmic governance and should encourage government officials to give serious consideration to the ways in which machine learning can be used responsibly to improve the administration of important governmental services and functions.[1]

WHAT IS MACHINE LEARNING?

Machine-learning algorithms are often dubbed "black box" systems because, unlike conventional analytical tools, these algorithms detect patterns and generate predictions in complex, non-intuitive ways that are not easily explainable. To grasp their unique nature is to begin to see what some of the potential legal issues their use by government agencies could entail. Toward that end, it is important to understand what machine learning is, how it operates, and why it differs from traditional statistical analysis.[2]

Machine learning is a form of AI that "refers to an automated process of discovering correlations (sometimes alternatively referred to as relationships or patterns) between variables in a dataset, often to make predictions or estimates of some outcome."[3] Although conventional statistical analysis techniques and machine-learning algorithms both attempt to achieve mathematical "objectives" by analyzing historical data from a target population (in machine-learning parlance, "training data"), they differ in the mechanics of – and human role within – their analytic processes. In traditional regression analysis, which is often best suited for understanding phenomena that possess linear relationships, humans specify input variables and determine how these variables should be weighted and combined to yield a prediction or outcome variable.

With machine learning, however, humans do not specify exactly how input variables should be combined to yield predictions – nor do they necessarily even determine which input variables among an entire set should be factored into the analysis. In fact, machine-

---

[1] Much of the analysis presented in this chapter draws on previous work by one of the co-authors in conjunction with yet a separate co-author. Readers looking for more in-depth treatment of these issues should refer to: C. Coglianese and D. Lehr, Regulating by Robot: Administrative Decision Making in the Machine-Learning Era (2017) 105 *Geo. Law J.* 1147; and C. Coglianese and D. Lehr, Transparency and Algorithmic Governance (2019) 71 *Admin. Law Rev.* 1.

[2] In this chapter, we do not attempt any comprehensive description of machine-learning algorithms. Instead, we simply provide a brief overview as a foundation for readers less familiar with such techniques to appreciate some of the legal and policy concerns implicated by their use by governmental authorities. For more in-depth treatment, an excellent introduction to machine learning for lawyers and legal scholars is provided in D. Lehr and P. Ohm, Playing with the Data: What Legal Scholars Should Learn about Machine Learning (2017) 51 *UC Davis Law Rev.* 653.

[3] Lehr and Ohm, above note 2, p. 671.

learning algorithms themselves can take many forms – or belong to different "families" – which means that generalizing about them must be treated with some caution. With that caveat, however, a generic way to understand these algorithms is that they essentially cycle through a vast landscape of potential variables (and variable combinations) and seek to "learn" from the data through an automated trial and error process of sorts. Rather than humans making key specifications, the algorithms automatically select the "best" variables (and variable combinations) and the "best" mathematical functional form that analyzes the variables – with "best" defined in terms of which variable combinations and functional forms optimize an end goal or "objective function" that has been defined by the human analyst.[4]

For example, a machine-learning algorithm can be given a variety of input variables – municipal complaint calls, oil pipeline sensor readings, or satellite photos – and then be tasked with using these variables to predict an output – a fallen tree, a deteriorating pipeline part, or a missile battery system. Although humans play a key role in guiding the machine-learning algorithm – namely, selecting the type or family of algorithm to use, providing the algorithm with its data, and tweaking the accuracy of the algorithm's optimization process by examining and re-examining "test data" that is separated from training data at an early stage – humans are ultimately not involved in the creative combination of input variables and the form of the mathematical function by which the algorithm ascertains valuable but non-intuitive predictive patterns lurking in large datasets.[5] In this way, these algorithms "learn" essentially "on their own."

Machine-learning algorithms are prized for their accurate predictions and for efficiency gains that they can make possible through task automation. As noted, these algorithms are increasingly common in the private sector. Google uses machine learning to conserve energy in its data centers, identify building address numbers in Street View, and help self-driving cars navigate roads. Netflix uses a form of machine learning called "artificial neural networks" to suggest new shows to its customers based on their prior viewing habits. Financial firms use machine-learning algorithms to forecast investment portfolio values. In addition to these and many other private-sector uses, academic researchers have embraced machine-learning algorithms to predict student retention at universities, estimate homeless populations in cities, and calculate the likelihood of probationers and parolees reoffending and committing violent crimes.[6]

Machine-learning algorithms also hold a significant potential for use by governments in more efficiently allocating resources and assisting in adjudicatory and policy decision-making. One recent analysis, for example, assessed the outcomes that the US Environmental Protection Agency (EPA) could achieve if it used machine learning to determine to which of the many industrial facilities throughout the country it should send its limited number of regulatory inspectors – improving by as much as 600 percent the agency's ability to target inspectors to those facilities that are most likely to be violating the law.[7] Such a vital, if perhaps seemingly mundane, task as allocating inspectors is but one of many examples of current and potential future uses to which machine-learning algorithms can be put by the sprawling set of government agencies that make up the modern

---

[4]   *Ibid.*, pp. 671–2.
[5]   For a more in-depth overview of the role of human involvement in the development, training, and tinkering, see *ibid.*, pp. 672–702.
[6]   For a discussion of examples, see Coglianese and Lehr, Regulating by Robot, above note 1, p. 1160.
[7]   M. Hino, E. Benami, and N. Brooks, Machine Learning for Environmental Monitoring (2018) 1 *Nat. Sustainability* 583. See generally C. Coglianese, Deploying Machine Learning for a Sustainable Future, in D. C. Esty (ed.), *A Better Planet: 40 Big Ideas for a Sustainable Future* (Yale University Press, 2019), p. 200.

administrative state. These agencies could potentially benefit from algorithms to perform a wide array of tasks, even getting to the point where computers could replace human decision-making in various regulatory and adjudicatory contexts. Not only can such automation deliver improved accuracy and administrative efficiency, but it is not hard to imagine a time in the near future when the public actually come to expect their public servants to rely on such technologies. As complex machine-learning algorithms proliferate in the private sector, members of the public may well come to expect similar accuracy and automated services from their governments. If nothing else, government officials will need to understand and use machine learning simply to keep up with – and appropriately regulate – the use of such tools by sophisticated private actors.[8]

Government agencies in the United States are actually already taking note of the advantages of algorithms. Many state and local governments are currently using these tools to support important functions. For example, the city of Chicago is using machine learning to support a variety of city services, including identifying where rodent bait should be strategically placed[9] and identifying restaurants to inspect.[10] New York City, through a dedicated Office of Data Analytics, is pursuing, among other uses of machine learning, a program that prioritizes potentially unsafe buildings for its fire department to inspect.[11] In Flint, Michigan, government officials have partnered with university researchers to use machine-learning algorithms to predict the location of, and prioritize the replacement of, drinking water pipes contaminated with lead.[12] And the City of Los Angeles is using a machine-learning system to optimize traffic patterns by turning its streets' traffic signals red or green based on congestion data fed by sensors distributed throughout the city's roads.[13]

At the federal level, primitive machine-learning algorithms have been in use in the United States since at least the late 1980s in one of perhaps the most banal but still vital functions performed by the federal government: the delivery of mail. The US Postal Service first used machine-learning algorithms to decipher hand-written zip codes on envelopes and thus sort mail more efficiently – marking not only one of the first domestic governmental uses of machine learning, but also helping researchers in the process make important early advances in algorithmic techniques.[14] Since that time, meteorologists at the US National Weather Service have used machine learning to improve forecasts of catastrophic weather events.[15]

[8] C. Coglianese, Optimizing Regulation for an Optimizing Economy (2018) 4 *Univ. Pa. J. Law Pub. Aff.* 1.
[9] L. Poon, Will Cities Ever Outsmart Rats?, *CityLab* (August 9, 2017), https://www.citylab.com/solutions/2017/08/smart-cities-fight-rat-infestations-big-data/535407/; Ash Center Mayors Challenge Research Team, Chicago's SmartData Platform: Pioneering Open Source Municipal Analytics, *Data-Smart City Solutions* (January 8, 2014), http://datasmart.ash.harvard.edu/news/article/chicago-mayors-challenge-367.
[10] S. Goldsmith, Chicago's Data-Powered Recipe for Food Safety, *Data-Smart City Solutions* (May 21, 2015), https://datasmart.ash.harvard.edu/news/article/chicagos-data-powered-recipe-for-food-safety-688.
[11] B. Heaton, New York City Fights Fire with Data, *Gov't Technology* (May 15, 2015), www.govtech.com/public-safety/New-York-City-Fights-Fire-with-Data.html.
[12] G. Cherry, Google, U-M to Build Digital Tools for Flint Water Crisis, *University of Michigan News* (May 3, 2016), https://news.umich.edu/google-u-m-to-build-digital-tools-for-flint-water-crisis/.
[13] I. Lovett, To Fight Gridlock, Los Angeles Synchronizes Every Red Light, *New York Times* (April 1, 2013), www.nytimes.com/2013/04/02/us/to-fight-gridlock-los-angeles-synchronizes-every-red-light.html.
[14] See, e.g., C.-H. Wang and S. N. Srihari, A Framework for Object Recognition in a Visually Complex Environment and Its Application to Locating Address Blocks on Mail Pieces (1988) 2 *Int. J. Comp. Vision* 125; O. Matan, R. K. Kiang, C. E. Stenard, *et al.*, Handwritten Character Recognition Using Neural Network Architectures, Presented at the 4th USPS Advanced Technology Conference (1990), http://yann.lecun.com/exdb/publis/pdf/matan-90.pdf.
[15] D. J. Gagne II, A. McGovern, J. Brotzge, *et al.*, Day-Ahead Hail Prediction Integrating Machine Learning with Storm-Scale Numerical Weather Models, Presented at the Twenty-Seventh Conference on Innovative Applications of Artificial Intelligence (2015), www.aaai.org/ocs/index.php/IAAI/IAAI15/paper/view/9724/9898.

Scientists at the US EPA have developed an algorithmic tool to help predict the toxicity of certain chemical compounds and thus prioritize chemicals to be subject to more direct testing and perhaps regulation.[16] (Independent analysts have estimated that this tool could save the EPA $980,000 per toxic chemical correctly identified.[17]) The US Internal Revenue Service (IRS) uses machine-learning algorithms to help it flag tax returns for human auditing, while the US Securities and Exchange Commission (SEC) does much the same to detect possible fraudulent securities transactions in need of further investigation.[18] The US Federal Emergency Management Agency (FEMA) has used deep learning to identify man-made structures that have been consumed by lava flow in Hawaii.[19] The US Patent and Trademark Office is working on a machine-learning tool to streamline patent application processing.[20] The US Customs and Border Protection currently uses facial-recognition algorithms and cameras in kiosks at airports when processing arrivals from international flights.[21] And the US Social Security Administration uses a natural language processing tool based on machine learning to flag initial disability claims decisions for further quality review.[22]

These are just some examples of the current uses of machine-learning algorithms by government agencies throughout the United States. With time, such algorithms will become even more pervasive as they grow in sophistication and predictive power. The possibility of obtaining tremendous benefits from deploying machine-learning algorithms, however, will surely always present trade-offs and possible concerns. Three of these concerns bear mentioning as they are key to understanding how such algorithms could seem to present prima facie questions about their fit with existing principles of administrative law.

First, with machine learning, humans are not in the prediction-loop in the same way that they are with traditional statistical analysis. Since machine-learning algorithms can run continuously and effectively teach themselves, humans no longer play the central role controlling how exactly variables are compared and combined to generate predictive outputs.

Second, machine-learning predictions are not easily explainable, thus presenting possible issues about transparency and reason-giving. The "black box" nature of machine-learning algorithms stems from difficulties inherent in explaining how these algorithms generate their

---

[16] US EPA, ToxCast Fact Sheet (2013), www.epa.gov/sites/production/files/2016-12/documents/tox_cast_fact_sheet_dec2016.pdf.

[17] M. T. Martin, T. B. Knudsen, D. M. Reif, *et al.*, Economic Benefits of Using Adaptive Predictive Models of Reproductive Toxicity in the Context of a Tiered Testing Program (2012) 58 *Sys. Biology Reprod. Med.* 3, 4–6.

[18] See C. Wagner, R. E. Byrd, Jr., R. D. Marcuss, and T. Milholland, Taxpayer Advocate Service, IRS Policy Implementation through Systems Programming Lacks Transparency and Precludes Adequate Review, in 2010 Annual Report to Congress, pp. 71, 76, www.irs.gov/pub/irs-utl/2010arcmsp5_policythruprogramming.pdf; Treasury Inspector General for Tax Administration, 2014-20-088, The Information Reporting and Document Matching Case Management System Could Not Be Deployed (2014), https://www.treasury.gov/tigta/auditreports/2014reports/201420088fr.pdf; P. Karlan and J. Bankman, Artificial Intelligence and the Administrative State with Guests David Engstrom and Cristina Ceballos, *Stanford Legal* (April 27, 2019), https://law.stanford.edu/stanford-legal-on-siriusxm/artificial-intelligence-and-the-administrative-state-with-guests-david-engstrom-and-cristina-ceballos/ (discussing use of machine learning by the US Securities and Exchange Commission for fraud identification).

[19] M. Leonard, Deep Learning Quickly Finds Structures Affected by Lava, GCN (July 24, 2018) https://gcn.com/articles/2018/07/24/hawaii-volcano-lava-mapping.aspx?m=1.

[20] A. K. Rai, Machine Learning at the Patent Office: Lessons for Patents and Administrative Law (2019) 104 *Iowa Law Rev.* 2617.

[21] Karlan and Bankman, above note 18 (interview with David Engstrom).

[22] G. Ray and G. Sklar, An Operational Approach to Eliminating Backlogs in the Social Security Disability Program, SSDI Solutions Initiative (June 2009), pp. 31–4, www.crfb.org/sites/default/files/An_Operational_Approach_to_Eliminating_Backlogs_in_the_Social_Security_Disability_Program.pdf.

outputs. From the simplest "random forests"[23] machine-learning algorithms to the most intricate "deep learning" neural network techniques,[24] machine-learning algorithms work with large datasets to find complex inter-variable relationships, making it difficult for humans – even the most sophisticated analysts – to explain in ordinary language what is going on underneath the hood. Moreover, even if it were possible to achieve a certain baseline explainability, one cannot ascribe a causal relationship between the algorithm's input data and output prediction. Although machine learning can sometimes be deployed in ways that support larger research inquiries into causation, the immediate forecasts it produces are decidedly non-causal: if the second letter of a tax filer's first name somehow helps in forecasting tax evasion, a learning algorithm will use it, even though there exists no causal relationship between that letter and tax evasion.

Finally, through quasi or full automation, human oversight and deliberation time can be drastically cut or eliminated altogether with the aid of systems based on machine-learning algorithms. So-called machine-learning decisions can be automated, which can be a virtue in improving efficiencies and keeping pace with rapid transactions in the private sector. However, tools that speed up decision-making processes can effectively cut humans out of certain processes in which they have previously played a central role.

We do not mean to suggest, of course, that machine-learning algorithms take on a complete "life of their own," although some serious thinkers have cautioned against the possibility of runaway AI. Such hypothetical scenarios of total human-out-of-the-loop systems are not what we focus on here – for machine learning still requires humans to select objectives and train and fine-tune algorithms. Presumably it will also always be possible for humans to "pull the plug" on any AI system. But despite the ultimate dependence of algorithms on humans, at an important operational level the role for humans is qualitatively different with machine learning. It will likely not be long before individual administrative adjudicatory decisions – and even decisions concerning the selection of administrative rules – could be functionally automated.

The ability to automate decisions is, of course, one of the possible benefits of machine learning. Such automation could potentially eliminate or reduce the biases, prejudices, and errors inherent in administrative decision-making conducted by humans. Still, the unique features of machine-learning algorithms – their opacity coupled with their autonomous learning properties and their ability to speed up or automate decision-making – would appear, at first blush, to run counter to a variety of administrative law principles. Admittedly, few citizens are likely ever to object to the US Postal Service using machine learning to sort mail more efficiently. But serious questions have already arisen over the use of algorithmic tools in the context of criminal justice decision-making and these same kinds of concerns could also arise once federal and state administrative agencies begin to rely on machine-learning algorithms to facilitate systems of automated decisions that affect key governmental benefits and services that significantly affect people's lives.

In short, although machine-learning algorithms offer great potential for improving administrative decision-making, their use must still accord with key constitutional and administrative law doctrines intended to ensure that government best serves and protects the interests of its people. Exploring the relevant legal principles lurking behind concerns about machine learning is critical in determining the extent to which governments can successfully – and responsibly – deploy these powerful predictive tools.

---

[23] See L. Breiman, Random Forests (2001) 45 *Mach. Learn.* 5, 5–6.
[24] Lehr and Ohm, above note 2, p. 693 n. 135.

MACHINE LEARNING IN ADMINISTRATIVE LAW

As governments increasingly rely upon machine-learning algorithms in administrative decision-making, public officials, lawyers, and scholars confront important questions concerning whether to pursue the further use of these technologies – and, if so, how to design, test, and oversee them. The legality of algorithmic governance will be among the first set of questions to be asked. Such algorithms will likely implicate several important principles of administrative law, including those related to due process, equal protection, privacy, transparency, and limitations on delegations of authority. Traditionally, these principles have been developed and applied within an operating space that assumed human decision-making. Going forward, they will need to be applied to the distinctive features of machine-learning algorithms – specifically, their black-box, self-learning, and automated properties.

In the sections that follow, we present the contours of a legal analysis of algorithmic governance under principles of US administrative law. We recognize, of course, that our analysis can only be offered at a relatively high level of generality. As with any legal question, much can turn on context-specific circumstances and facts. It is simply not possible to provide legal analysis covering every conceivable use of these technologies by an administrative agency. It is possible, though, to reveal the broad issues and guiding principles likely involved in any such analysis. For example, while machine-learning algorithms are "autonomous," they are only autonomous in a limited operational sense, as humans must still decide how the algorithms are defined, operationalized, and incorporated into broader administrative frameworks and goals. Put differently, humans ultimately determine the machine-learning algorithm's parameters and uses – and this proves pivotal to much of our analysis.[25]

To preview our overall conclusion: The responsible use of machine-learning tools by government agencies can fit comfortably within prevailing administrative law doctrines. Although we are optimistic about the potential to improve governmental performance through algorithmic tools, we recognize that these tools – like any tool – could be used carelessly or even maliciously. We certainly do not mean to endorse reckless or oppressive uses of machine learning, any more than we would with the use of any other governmental tool, policy, or program. But when machine learning is used in good faith by governmental officials to deliver real public value, there is nothing inherent in its distinctive properties that should prevent its further use in the administrative setting – even to substitute for human decision-making.

Due Process

When conducting actions that may deprive individuals or entities of protected liberty interests or property rights and entitlements, administrative agencies must provide adequate procedural due process.[26] For example, when the US Social Security Administration terminates a person's benefits,[27] or when the US EPA orders a business to clean up a hazardous

---

[25] See Coglianese and Lehr, Regulating by Robot, above note 1, p. 1177.
[26] *Bi-Metallic Inv. Co.* v. *State Bd. of Equalization*, 239 US 441, 445–6 (1915) (suggesting that a right to be heard is necessary when a "relatively small number of persons [is] concerned, who [are] exceptionally affected, in each case upon individual grounds," but not in instances of adoption of widely applicable rules); *Londoner* v. *Denver*, 210 US 373, 386 (1908) ("[S]omething more than [an opportunity to submit objections in writing], even in proceedings for taxation, is required by due process of law ... [E]ven here a hearing in its very essence demands that he who is entitled to it shall have the right to support his allegations by argument however brief, and, if need be, by proof, however informal"). See generally E. L. Rubin, Due Process and the Administrative State (1984) 72 *Cal. Law Rev.* 1044.
[27] See, e.g., *Mathews* v. *Eldridge*, 424 US 319, 323–5 (1976).

waste site,[28] deprivations of protected interests can occur. If an automated machine-learning algorithm were used in such instances instead of human hearing officers, would the agency's decision violate the individual's right to due process? Although at first glance the prospect of denying an individual or entity a hearing before an agency adjudicatory employee – a key feature of procedural due process – would seem to render such an automated decision legally problematic, a full due process analysis by no means precludes the use of machine-learning algorithms even for such adjudicatory purposes.

The US Supreme Court's decision in *Goldberg* v. *Kelly* established that recipients of government welfare benefits are entitled to due process protections, which, the Court noted, includes the right to an evidentiary hearing before the government official tasked with terminating an individual's benefits.[29] However, six years later, in *Mathews* v. *Eldridge*, the Supreme Court ruled that the termination of Social Security disability benefits could take place through a faceless paperwork review process and did not have to include an in-person, evidentiary hearing.[30] Rather than overturn *Goldberg*, the Court instead presented a three-factor balancing test that now applies whenever ascertaining whether due process concerns have been satisfied. The factors to be balanced are: (1) the private interests affected; (2) the risk of an erroneous deprivation of these interests; and (3) the government's interest, including fiscal and administrative burdens involved, in using additional procedures.

The *Mathews* balancing test would appear to favor the adoption of algorithmic adjudication. Although the private interest at stake (factor one) is not affected by machine learning, the second and third factors are indeed implicated by machine learning and, in some instances, they might be dramatically affected in a positive direction. Concerning the third factor, for instance, there seems little doubt that if a machine-learning adjudicatory system obviated the need for evidentiary hearings, the use of machine learning across a large agency could save the government a significant amount of taxpayer money – a consideration that would be given substantial weight in *Mathews* balancing.

As to the second factor, agencies may often be reasonably confident that their machine-learning algorithms possess low error rates compared with what is normal under human decision-making. If it substitutes for, or even just assists with, human decision-making, machine-learning possesses considerable potential to reduce human bias, prejudice, and error. Although determining whether an agency's use of machine learning satisfies the *Mathews* balancing test will call for a context-specific analysis, the track record with human decision-making might be sufficiently bleak that machine learning could easily improve upon it. For example, some evidence suggests that human decision-making leads to racially biased outcomes in the US Social Security Administration's adjudications of disability benefits claims.[31] One study revealed the stark inconsistencies that can result from human decision-making by showing that, in a single regional office of the Social Security Administration, the processing of disability benefit applications by humans "ranged … from less than 10 percent being granted to over 90 percent."[32]

---

[28] See, e.g., *Gen. Elec. Co.* v. *Jackson*, 595 F. Supp. 2d 8, 21–9 (DDC 2009).

[29] 397 US 254, 264 (1970).

[30] 424 US 319, 348–9 (1976).

[31] US General Accounting Office, GAO-HRD-92-56, Social Security: Racial Differences in Disability Decisions Warrants Further Investigation (1992), www.gao.gov/assets/160/151781.pdf; E. Godtland, M. Grgich, C. D. Petersen, *et al.*, Racial Disparities in Federal Disability Benefits (2007) 25 *Contemp. Econ. Pol.* 27.

[32] See Social Security Awards Depend More on Judge than Facts: Disparities Within SSA Disability Hearing Offices Grow, *TRAC* (July 4, 2011), https://trac.syr.edu/tracreports/ssa/254/.

Under the second factor of *Mathews*, it is reasonable to believe that learning algorithms will sufficiently satisfy due process concerns.[33] In analyzing error rates, agencies might at least initially introduce a hybrid machine-learning adjudication system through which affected individuals or entities receive an algorithmic ruling and then have the option of appealing the ruling to a human adjudicator. Data can then be collected on the algorithm's reversal rates. If the machine-learning algorithm is sparsely overturned – its error rates are thus low – there should be no reason why a court would reject its use based solely on its automated and digitized nature.

A seemingly more substantial due process concern might arise from the right of affected parties to engage in cross-examination. In the case of machine-learning adjudication, claimants should, in principle, have the right to question the choices made in the algorithm's design as well as the underlying training data used. Given the opacity issues associated with these algorithms, as well as their highly technical mathematical structures, it may be unlikely that such a cross-examination could be accomplished by most claimants, let alone the claimants' attorneys. To mitigate this concern, agencies could establish an independent body of statistical and machine-learning experts to provide ongoing oversight and review. At the very least, establishing an automated algorithmic adjudicatory system will require a prior rule-making process that will be informed by outside experts. Agencies could readily rely on well-established precedents and protocols for involving outside experts in understanding complex administrative matters, both at the rule-making stage as well as later when the technology is already deployed by the agency.

Ultimately, whether an agency's machine-learning algorithm satisfies due process concerns will depend on the accuracy of the algorithm's forecasts and the sufficiency of the vetting by outside experts. Courts have traditionally granted agencies wide leeway in shaping their adjudicatory procedures and there is no reason to believe machine-learning algorithms would represent an exception to this rule. Moreover, given that humans are prone to biases and errors, and that machine-learning algorithms have outshined human decision-making in other contexts,[34] it seems likely that agencies will often be able to ensure their use of machine-learning algorithms satisfies due process concerns.

Equal Protection

Under the Fifth Amendment to the US Constitution, federal administrative agencies have a responsibility to safeguard the equal protection rights of those affected by their actions. In designing and deploying machine-learning algorithms for adjudication, agencies will face choices about the types of big data they feed into their algorithms – and in particular whether such data should include variables for race, gender, religion, or other protected classes of people. Although an agency may wish to include demographic data related to membership in legally protected classes to increase the accuracy of their algorithm's predictions, including such data will likely raise questions about potential equal protection violations, especially if algorithms appear to generate disparate effects for members of protected classes.

Given the possibility that data used in an algorithmic system may encode bias in algorithmic adjudication, perhaps even inadvertently, would using such data in federal agency

---

[33] C. Coglianese, Robot Regulators Could Eliminate Human Error, *San Francisco Chronicle* (May 5, 2016), www .sfchronicle.com/opinion/article/Robot-regulators-could-eliminate-human-error-7396749.php.

[34] See, e.g., R. A. Berk, S. Sorenson, and G. C. Barnes, Forecasting Domestic Violence: A Machine Learning Approach to Help Inform Arraignment Decisions (2016) 13 *J. Empirical Law Stud.* 94, 110.

algorithms violate equal protection? In short, the answer is likely "no." Agencies already have procedures in place to ferret out blatant animus and discriminatory intent in adjudicatory processes, and such protocols will likely be sufficient to cover machine-learning systems. Moreover, recent research points to the promise of actually reducing, if not removing altogether, racial biases from algorithmic predictions.[35] Most importantly, the law, in fact, is rather clear in what it requires to show that federal governmental action merits heightened scrutiny under the Equal Protection Clause: "[a] *purpose* to discriminate must be present."[36] However, if agencies responsibly, and in good faith, use machine-learning algorithms that contain protected class data, anyone charging an equal protection violation will likely face an uphill battle in proving discriminatory intent.

For a claimant to prove that an agency's machine-learning adjudication system violates equal protection, a number of factors would need to be considered. Claimants alleging disparate treatment would need to show that an agency action involves a suspect classification. It is unlikely, however, that a court will find that an algorithmic adjudication system that analyzes class-related variables involves suspect classifications. Why? The Supreme Court has never clearly defined what constitutes a suspect classification in situations where membership in a protected class is not the *only* variable driving the government's action. And while the Supreme Court has indeed subjected to heightened scrutiny agency processes in which membership in a protected class was one among many variables considered, government actions that are class conscious but do not *classify on the basis of* group membership may not invoke heightened scrutiny. The question of what constitutes "classification" is a critical threshold issue in determining whether an algorithmic adjudication system violates equal protection.

Five key factors have been found to demonstrate a government "classification": (1) An official government label that (2) proclaims or identifies the class of (3) a particular individual (4) which is then used as a basis for the allocation of benefits or the imposition of burdens (5) on the person classified. Although machine-learning algorithms would certainly meet factors one through three, factors four and five are far less obviously applicable. Due to machine learning's black box nature, it is not likely to be possible to say that a class-related variable – or any particular variable at all – provided the "basis" for making any particular determination.

Furthermore, although agency actions that have led courts to invoke heightened scrutiny have all involved instances in which agencies provided categorically different treatment based on class classification, machine-learning algorithms are unlikely to lead to categorically different treatment even when the datasets they process include variables related to protected classes. Categorically different treatment on the basis of class membership has been an important factor in a variety of Supreme Court decisions. *Gratz v. Bollinger*, *Grutter v. Bollinger*, *Fullilove v. Klutznick*, *Wygant v. Jackson Board of Education*, and *Fisher v. University of Texas at Austin* are all cases in which the Court found equal protection violations where membership in a class was consistently treated as advantageous or disadvantageous compared to membership in another class. But machine-learning algorithms optimize for accuracy on some neutral, non-class-related objective (for example, tax fraud, disability eligibility), not status based on a protected class. Moreover, heightened scrutiny

[35] See J. E. Johndrow and K. Lum, An Algorithm for Removing Sensitive Information: Application to Race-Independent Recidivism Prediction (2019) 13 *Ann. Appl. Stat.* 1, 189.

[36] *Washington v. Davis*, 426 US 229, 239 (1976) (quoting *Akins v. Texas*, 325 US 398, 403–4 (1945)) (emphasis added). State agencies, of course, could be found to violate equal protection without a showing of such purpose, as the applicable standards for states arise under the Fourteenth Amendment.

of suspect classifications exists to constrain governments from treating individuals as "defined by" their status within a particular class, not necessarily to prevent any and all uses of data on a protected class. In the absence of discriminatory intent in the creation of an algorithm's optimization parameters, it is unlikely a court will find government agencies have violated equal protection doctrine even if some class-related variables are included in their data.

Opponents of using machine-learning algorithms in government might argue that such algorithms should still be subject to heightened scrutiny since the inclusion of any variable related to race might demonstrate *a priori* intent to discriminate – that is, a form of circumstantial evidence of animus. This argument is likely to fail, however, because the black-box nature of machine-learning algorithms will make it very difficult to prove discriminatory intent. If humans cannot control which variables will be used by a machine-learning algorithm, or how they will factor into a forecast generated by the algorithm, then merely including class-related variables in a dataset surely cannot indicate any intent to have that variable used to advantage or disadvantage anyone in that class. Of course, opponents of the use of algorithms might counter that once it has been established that a race-related variable could lead to disparate outcomes, the continued use of such variable becomes problematic. However, again, the black-box nature of machine-learning algorithms makes it virtually impossible for anyone to know *a priori* the importance of any one variable or how that variable may or may not influence the ultimate prediction. Since many machine-learning algorithms often use random processes in variable selection, randomness rather than intent defines the process.

In most instances, we suspect machine-learning algorithms will be unlikely to trigger heightened scrutiny. As such, they would be subject simply to rational basis review, which requires only that a government action be "rationally related to furthering a legitimate state interest."[37] That is an easy standard to meet. But even assuming that a court was to treat a particular governmental use of machine-learning algorithms as subject to heightened scrutiny, this would not mean that the use of the algorithm violates anyone's equal protection rights. Regulatory agencies that use machine-learning algorithms for maintaining market stability or public health would have strong arguments that they are being used to advance *compelling state interests* – which define the standard that government must meet under a heightened scrutiny test.

One of the ways a government action can be struck down under either a heightened scrutiny or rational basis standard is by showing that the government acted with animus toward a particular group. Animus can be established through direct evidence – such as statements from legislators and private individuals – or by inference. The potential for animus is always present, and thus not a concern unique to machine-learning algorithms. Moreover, the mere inclusion of class-based variables in the data an algorithm uses would, for the reasons just discussed, likely prove insufficient to support an inference of animus, especially if the inclusion of such variables increases the accuracy of the algorithm. The inclusion of such variables might even turn out to help the algorithm produce less biased outcomes for members of the protected class relative to human decision-making – or at a minimum, they may allow the analyst to adjust for any such bias. In short, including or not including class-related variables, without more, will hardly prove dispositive on the question of animus. Ultimately, equal protection concerns are unlikely to pose a serious challenge to machine-learning algorithms when they are used by federal agencies in the United States.

---

[37] *Mass. Bd. of Ret.* v. *Murgia*, 427 US 307, 312 (1976) (per curiam).

Privacy

Machine-learning algorithms require – indeed, thrive on – large quantities of data (so-called big data). Yet such data will often include sensitive or personal information related to businesses or individuals. Of course, privacy concerns raised by agency use of personal, sensitive, or confidential business information are hardly unique to machine learning. For that reason alone, there seems little reason to believe that, given adequate safeguards and cybersecurity protections, privacy law would seriously prevent government agencies from greater use of machine-learning tools.

In fact, public management techniques have already for years relied on personal data to deliver public services more efficiently – and the rise of big data and increased access to computing power (even without machine learning) has only accelerated a trend toward the "moneyballing" of government.[38] In carrying out administrative duties, agencies routinely handle an array of personal information from "names, addresses, dates of birth, and places of employment, to identity documents, Social Security numbers (SSNs) or other government-issued identifiers, precise location information, medical history, and biometrics."[39] Protecting such data while concomitantly advancing agency goals is a task many agencies already know how to handle.

In fact, it does not appear that existing legal requirements related to privacy have proven to be any insuperable barrier to federal agency use of big data. The US Department of Health and Human Services, for example, is collecting personal health data to reduce bureaucratic costs and improve patient health.[40] The US Departments of Education and Defense are harnessing big data for a variety of administrative uses, including: "human resources management; service improvement; fraud, waste, and abuse control; and detection of terrorist activity."[41] In several states, it is now apparently legal for the US Federal Bureau of Investigation (FBI) to use facial recognition software to scan Department of Motor Vehicle (DMV) databases that contain driver license photos.[42] The US Customs and Border Protection's facial recognition kiosks at US airports are scanning the visages of passengers traveling internationally.[43] And the US Departments of Homeland Security and Justice reportedly have developed "fusion centers" to mine personal data held by the military, CIA, and FBI to identify individuals worth pursuing based on agency criteria for investigation.[44]

The most applicable laws for agencies that deal with the collection, use, and storage of private information by federal agencies are the Privacy Act of 1974 and the E-Government Act of 2002.[45] The Privacy Act limits how agencies can collect, disclose, and maintain personal information in

---

[38] J. Nussle and P. R. Orszag (eds.), *Moneyball for Government*, 2nd edn. (Disruption Books, 2015).

[39] See Office of Management and Budget, Memorandum M-17-12, "Preparing for and Responding to a Breach of Personally Identifiable Information" (January 3, 2017).

[40] K. A. Bamberger and D. K. Mulligan, Privacy Decision-Making in Administrative Agencies (2008) 75 *Univ. Chi. Law Rev.* 75.

[41] *Ibid.*

[42] S. Ghaffary and R. Molla, Here's Where the US Government Is Using Facial Recognition Technology to Surveil Americans, *Vox* (July 18, 2019), www.vox.com/recode/2019/7/18/20698307/facial-recognition-technology-us-government-fight-for-the-future.

[43] *Ibid.*

[44] K. Crawford and J. Schultz, Big Data and Due Process: Toward a Framework to Redress Predictive Privacy Harms (2014) 55 *BC Law Rev.* 104.

[45] In addition, federal agencies confront what is sometimes called a "reverse FOIA" situation, so named for the Freedom of Information Act (FOIA), which compels agencies, with some exceptions, to make information in its possession available to the public upon request. The reverse FOIA situation is one in which, as the US Department of Justice has described it, "the 'submitter of information – usually a corporation or other business entity' that has supplied an agency with 'data on its policies, operations or products – seeks to prevent the agency that collected the information from revealing it to a third party in response to the latter's FOIA request.'" See US

their records.[46] Changes to agency record systems must be disclosed to the public through the *Federal Register* so that the public is made aware of the existence of the types of records and information collected by agencies, the categories of individuals for whom records are kept, the purpose for which the information is used, and how the public can exercise their rights under the Act. The E-Government Act of 2002 requires agencies to conduct privacy impact assessments (PIAs) when developing or procuring technology that implicates privacy concerns.[47] The federal Office of Management and Budget (OMB) has provided guidance calling on agencies to ensure that their PIAs assess individual privacy concerns, explore alternatives to the technology, and survey risk mitigation options, as well as articulate a rationale for using the technology of choice.[48]

In addition to the Privacy Act and E-Government Act, other US statutes also address privacy concerns – but only related to specific types of data. These other laws include: the Family Educational Rights and Privacy Act of 1974, which governs how education-related information can be shared and stored; the Driver's Privacy Protection Act of 1994, which protects personal information gathered by state motor vehicle departments; the US Health Insurance Portability and Accountability Act of 1996 (HIPAA), which protects individually identifiable health records; and the Children's Online Privacy Protection Act of 1998, which protects online information gathered from children under the age of 13.

These specialized laws governing data privacy – which tend to apply to private actors as much as governmental ones – are not matched by any single overarching data protection law or data protection enforcement agency. Instead, the US Federal Trade Commission (FTC) is currently tasked with providing data protection in the commercial context under older, more general laws designed to protect consumers from fraudulent or otherwise abusive business behavior. Consequently, there are growing calls for the United States to adopt a vigorous, general data privacy regime. Some advocates look to the European Union's General Data Protection Regulation (GDPR) and its consumer-centric focus and heavy corporate fines as a potential model, while others have argued that GDPR-like legislation could never win sufficient congressional support in the United States anytime in the near future.[49]

A series of internal federal policies have sought to promote a privacy culture within administrative agencies. In 2015, President Barack Obama established by executive order a Federal Privacy Council and his administration revised Circular A-130, the government's policy guidance on managing federal information resources. Some of A-130's new provisions include the requirement that every federal agency hire a senior agency official for privacy (SAOP). A-130's new rules as well as a serious June 2015 data breach at the US Office of Personnel Management combined to provide a privacy wake-up call for many agencies.[50] Indeed, agencies appear increasingly to take privacy concerns more seriously. For example, in anticipation of the 2020 Census – and recognizing the small risk that public census data could be mined to re-identify individuals – the US Census Bureau announced that the agency

Department of Justice, Guide to the Freedom of Information Act (2009), pp. 863–80, www.justice.gov/sites/default/files/oip/legacy/2014/07/23/reverse-foia-2009.pdf.
[46] Pub. L. No. 93-579, 88 Stat. 1896 (1974), as amended; 5 USC § 552a; see also OMB, Privacy Act Implementation: Guidelines and Responsibilities, 40 Fed. Reg. 28,948, 28,962 (July 9, 1975).
[47] Pub. L. No. 107-347, § 208, 116 Stat. 2899, 2921 (2002); 44 USC § 3501 note.
[48] See Office of Management and Budget, above note 39; and Bamberger and Mulligan, above note 40, pp. 75–9.
[49] D. Hawkins, The Cybersecurity 202: Why a Privacy Law like GDPR Would Be a Tough Sell in the U.S., *Washington Post* (May 25, 2018), https://www.washingtonpost.com/news/powerpost/paloma/the-cybersecurity-202/2018/05/25/the-cybersecurity-202-why-a-privacy-law-like-gdpr-would-be-a-tough-sell-in-the-u-/5b07038b1b326b492dd07e83/.
[50] A. Carson, U.S. Government is Changing How It Does Privacy, *The Privacy Advisor Blog* (September 27, 2016), https://iapp.org/news/a/u-s-govt-is-changing-how-it-does-privacy-x/.

would use in its data systems cutting-edge "differential privacy" technology used by many private firms to preserve confidentiality of data. The differential privacy techniques being deployed by the Census Bureau introduce controlled noise into the data to add protection for individual information.[51]

But beyond machine learning's practical dependence on large amounts of data, it should not present any truly distinctive privacy issues under current laws or policies. All statistical and data systems implicate privacy concerns. However, one worst-case privacy concern can be said to be truly distinctive for machine learning: namely, the ability of such algorithms to combine seemingly disparate, non-sensitive data to yield predictions about personal information, such as the sexual orientation or political ideology of specific individuals. For this reason, machine learning might be said to undermine the ways that data anonymization can protect privacy, because an algorithm can be designed to put together seemingly unrelated data to make accurate predictions about individuals, such as occurred in recent years when a major retail firm used purchasing data to predict which of its female customers were pregnant (and thus valuable targets of the firm's baby supplies marketing). The possibility of using machine learning to "unlock" private information has led some experts to surmise that anonymizing data is no longer a very useful means of protecting privacy. Legal scholar Paul Ohm has asserted that "data can be either useful or perfectly anonymous but never both."[52] Virtually any attribute of a person might now be traced back to that individual given sufficient publicly available information and machine-learning tools.[53]

But simply noting the possibility that machine learning could be used by government officials to reverse-engineer data and discover private details about individuals for nefarious purposes is far from an argument that there exist inherent legal limits on the responsible use of machine learning.[54] Quite the contrary, such a possibility only points to the legal limits on the *irresponsible* use of machine learning. Nefarious uses such as these worst-case scenarios are what the law prohibits. On equal protection grounds, such uses would either be struck down as grounded in impermissible animus or found to be lacking in a rational basis. Barring that, efforts by governments to target individuals' private details would surely offend administrative law's general prohibitions on "arbitrary and capricious" administrative action and the "abuse of discretion" by government officials.[55]

Without a doubt, privacy concerns are real any time government uses data. But no privacy-related legal strictures would appear to serve as any intrinsic or even serious impediment to the responsible governmental use of machine learning, any more than any other activity that would involve the collection or analysis of large quantities of data.

---

[51] R. Jarmin, Census Bureau Adopts Cutting Edge Privacy Protections for 2020 Census, *Census Blogs* (February 15, 2019), www.census.gov/newsroom/blogs/random-samplings/2019/02/census_bureau_adopts.html.

[52] See P. Ohm, Broken Promises of Privacy: Responding to the Surprising Failure of Anonymization (2010) 57 *UCLA Law Rev.* 1703–4.

[53] See I. Rubinstein, Big Data: A Pretty Good Privacy Solution, *Future of Privacy Forum* (July 30, 2013), https://fpf.org/wp-content/uploads/2013/07/Rubinstein-Big-Data-A-Pretty-Good-Privacy-Solution1.pdf.

[54] In addition, such a possibility is also negated as a technical matter by the use of differentially private algorithms, such as those now reportedly being deployed by the Census Bureau. See above note 51. Algorithms that deliver on differential privacy can actually protect against the possibility of reverse engineering. In this way, differentially private algorithms provide a counter-example to the most alarmist claims about the dangers of machine learning, as they reveal that at least sometimes mathematical tools can be designed to respond to and fix some of the problems that have been attributed to machine learning. See M. Kearns and A. Roth, *The Ethical Algorithm: The Science of Socially Aware Algorithm Design* (Oxford University Press, 2020), pp. 22–56.

[55] 5 USC §706(2)(A).

Transparency and Reason-Giving

Transparency is a hallmark of administrative law. It requires agencies to open themselves up for the submission of public comment on proposed rules, demands that agencies publish final rules in the *Federal Register*, calls for the disclosure of government-held information to the public upon request, and dictates that certain decision-making meetings be held in settings that are open to the public. The law's emphasis on transparency actually manifests itself in two principal ways.[56] First, in what might be called "fishbowl transparency," administrative law demands that government information and meetings generally be open to the public. Second, in what might be called "reasoned transparency," the law calls for agencies to give adequate reasons that justify their actions. In this section, we take up the first of these – fishbowl transparency – before turning to reason-giving.

Fishbowl transparency is reflected in the Due Process clause, which demands openness in governmental adjudication. It is also reflected in statutes such as the Freedom of Information Act, the Government in the Sunshine Act, and the Administrative Procedure Act, which demand that agencies publish their rules and hold their business meetings in public. The key fishbowl transparency question for machine learning is whether these administrative laws demanding disclosure would also require that government agencies disclose details about how their algorithms are designed and operate. If such disclosure about machine-learning algorithms is required, this could present a real barrier to the use of machine learning for certain purposes. The US SEC and the US IRS surely do not want the public to know exactly how their algorithms for spotting, respectively, securities fraud and tax violations are designed. And when agencies rely on private contractors to develop algorithmic tools, those private firms may have legitimate claims to treat their algorithms as proprietary information.

But administrative law has never demanded anything close to absolute transparency. For example, the Freedom of Information Act contains a variety of exceptions that allow government agencies to withhold from the public data involving trade secrets and other proprietary information. It also allows agencies to withhold information used by law enforcement which, if revealed, could enable violators to skirt the law.[57]

In a case called *Wisconsin* v. *Loomis*, a criminal defendant challenged a state trial court's use of a (non-machine-learning) risk assessment algorithm to determine his sentence.[58] He argued that his due process rights were violated because the "proprietary nature" of the algorithm the trial court used prevented him from accessing information the trial court used at sentencing. The algorithm had been developed by a private company that refused to disclose how the risk scores are determined, claiming such information was "a trade secret." The Wisconsin Supreme Court rejected the defendant's arguments by affirming that the company had a right to protect its proprietary information and that it had, in any case, released sufficient additional information that satisfied due process requirements. The Wisconsin court's decision suggests that government agencies can lawfully use algorithms without divulging all their inner workings. Fishbowl transparency requirements should not pose any major barrier to governmental use of machine learning.

Without sufficient fishbowl transparency, though, perhaps it will be difficult if not impossible for government to meet administrative law's demands for reason-giving. The

---

[56] C. Coglianese, The Transparency President? The Obama Administration and Open Government (2009) 22 *Governance* 529.

[57] Coglianese and Lehr, Regulating by Robot, above note 1, p. 1210.

[58] *State* v. *Loomis*, 881 NW.2d 749 (Wis. 2016).

Administrative Procedure Act's arbitrary and capricious standard (as canonized in the case of *Motor Vehicle Manufacturers Association* v. *State Farm*) requires that an agency provide a rationale for any decision it makes and provide a sufficient administrative record to show how its decision emerged from the facts found. Such a requirement for reason-giving would appear to present machine learning with its most significant legal limitation. After all, how can principles of reason-giving be squared with the seemingly opaque, black-box nature of machine-learning algorithms? If the process by which these algorithms reach their conclusions cannot be explained in an intuitive fashion, then how can agencies satisfy their obligation to provide reasons?

Although machine-learning techniques for generating predictions from inputs are not as intuitive as traditional statistical analysis, experts can still explain their basic mechanics – for example, showing the objective an algorithm has been designed to serve, what kind of machine-learning algorithm it is, and how the algorithm generally processes data. It is also possible to describe the elements of the dataset used to train the algorithm and to generate various reports describing relationships in these data. Fortunately, most of this information should not come close to needing to be a protected trade secret. But unfortunately, none of these disclosures will, of course, allow an expert to explain in simple language that a learning algorithm demonstrates X causes Y, such that a government agency that wants to reduce Y is justified in regulating X. That kind of intuitive, causal reasoning cannot be supplied for machine-learning algorithms.

But the challenge of explainability for algorithms should not ultimately matter when it comes to administrative law's reason-giving requirement. Courts have never demanded a high level of causal clarity or certainty for agency reasons to pass muster under the arbitrary and capricious standard.[59] On the contrary, courts tend to defer to agencies in decisions involving complex scientific and mathematical analyses; they are likely to do the same for machine-learning algorithmic analysis. For example, a year after the Supreme Court's decision in the *State Farm* case, the Supreme Court reviewed a complex rule promulgated by the US Nuclear Regulatory Commission involving long-term storage of radioactive waste, and in the end it deferred entirely to the agency's expertise.[60] Furthermore, in more recent lower court decisions, agency expertise has usually won out – even in cases with complex mathematical analyses where few experts, let alone judges, could fully appreciate the agency's exact mathematical reasoning.

In short, agencies will likely have to disclose an algorithm's input variables, the objective functions being optimized by the algorithm, and the method used to achieve optimization. But this is not likely to be information that is or must be protected as trade secret, and courts will likely defer to agency expertise in evaluating the adequacy of the agency's reasoning based on this information. It is likely to be sufficient for agencies to reason about machine learning in the same way that they reason about other machines: that is, the machine (or algorithm) has general properties that aim to fulfill a specified purpose, and the machine (or algorithm) has been validated as serving that purpose well. An agency need not provide a detailed reason about the inner workings of a thermometer to justify imposing a penalty on a food manufacturer for failing to store perishable products at a cold temperature. Rather, the agency merely needs to show that the thermometer reads temperatures accurately. The same

59   See Coglianese and Lehr, Transparency and Algorithmic Governance, above note 1, p. 43.
60   *Balt. Gas & Elec. Co.* v. *Nat'l Res. Def. Council, Inc.*, 462 US 87, 103 (1983).

logic is likely to characterize the approach courts will take in evaluating an agency's reasons for decisions based on machine-learning algorithms.

Non-Delegation

Finally, legal arguments could be raised that algorithmic tools hand over too much decision-making responsibility to digital robots. Of course, if humans remain completely in the loop, this concern will be muted. In fact, for systems that merely prioritize workplaces for human inspectors to inspect, or tax filings for human auditors to audit, there should be no concern about excessive delegation. But if algorithms come to substitute in important ways for human judgment, then arguably the non-delegation doctrine could become implicated.

Although Congress can lawfully authorize administrative agencies headed by unelected appointed officers to make rules, the non-delegation doctrine in principle places two limits on Congress's ability to delegate to others. First, when Congress gives an agency authority to act, it must provide sufficient guidance – an "intelligible principle" – on how the acting person or body is directed to conform. Second, Congress is not supposed to authorize private actors to undertake governmental functions – what the Supreme Court has characterized as the most "obnoxious" form of delegation.[61] If Congress cannot authorize private entities to make decisions, then why, it might be asked, should it (or an agency) be allowed to delegate authority to a digital machine?

Despite the surface appeal of such a question, it takes only a little reflection to see that delegation to machines does not raise the kind of concerns that animate the two principal limits on delegation reflected in administrative law. In a situation presenting the first limit – what California Supreme Court Justice Mariano-Florentino Cuéllar has dubbed a case of "cyberdelegation"[62] – no delegation to a machine-learning algorithm could lack a sufficiently intelligible principle. For an algorithm to function, its goal (or, in algorithmic parlance, its objective function) must be stated with the utmost precision to allow it to optimize in a mathematical manner. If the Supreme Court has accepted a statutory principle as vague as "act in the public interest" as sufficiently intelligible for non-delegation doctrine purposes, then machine-learning "delegations" specified in precise mathematical terms will clearly be fine.

When it comes to the limit on delegating to private parties, the two principal reasons for such a limit do not apply to delegations to machine learning. First, unlike private individuals who are guided by their own self-interest rather than the public interest, machine-learning algorithms only optimize the goals of the authorized government officials who initially program them. They will do what they are told and are not corruptible in the way that humans are. Second, courts have allowed some authorizations of a role for private individuals when these private parties do not possess ultimate decisional control and instead serve only in an advisory capacity. When humans remain in the loop with machine-learning algorithms, they will be akin to private advisors. Ultimately, algorithms are subservient to the human government officials and analysts who design them and who retain control over their specification and operation.

Machine-learning algorithms are, in the end, a lot like other machines; they are just digital ones. In *Prometheus Radio Project* v. *FCC*, the court ruled that reliance on a private company

---

[61]   *Carter* v. *Carter Coal Co.*, 298 US 238, 311 (1936).
[62]   See M.-F. Cuellar, Cyberdelegation and the Administrative State, Stanford Public Law Working Paper No. 2754385 (2016), p. 1, https://papers.ssrn.com/sol3/papers.cfm?abstract_id=2754385##.

for measuring diversity and competition was not an unconstitutional delegation of legislative power since the private company only provided a measurement mechanism and the FCC remained the sole arbiter of whether a proposed radio station combination served the public interest.[63] Similarly, a machine-learning algorithm functionally can be seen to serve as a measurement mechanism and will be perfectly acceptable, especially if the agency remains the ultimate arbiter.

In sum, legislation authorizing the use of machine-learning algorithms would unlikely violate the intelligible principle requirement and would not constitute a prohibited delegation of authority to a non-governmental entity. Ultimately, such algorithms are akin to standard machines or measurement devices and will not likely present any major problems from the standpoint of the non-delegation doctrine.

ADMINISTERING ALGORITHMIC GOVERNANCE

This review of major administrative law doctrines indicates that current law will not stand in the way of widespread use of machine learning within the administrative state. That said, just because machine-learning systems could easily pass muster under administrative law doctrines, this does not necessarily mean they should always be deployed. Agencies must carefully balance their benefits with their costs, taking due account of ethical and policy concerns. Machine-learning systems can, after all, still make errors, even if they are fewer (and different) errors than humans would make. Moreover, just as with the adoption of any new initiative, program, or tool, agencies should carefully analyze any machine-learning tool and compare it with alternatives. In many instances, agencies will likely conclude that the benefits of deploying a machine-learning system outweigh the costs, but a healthy dose of ethical vigilance will always be critical to ensure these systems are serving the best interests of the public. Once machine-learning tools are adopted, agencies should monitor and evaluate their performance to ensure that they are performing as intended and are not creating new problems or introducing undue inequities.

Agencies should not necessarily assume, in other words, that they only need to meet the minimal requirements of the law. Especially for sensitive policy issues – such as those related to equity, transparency, or reason-giving – agencies may need to go above and beyond legal requirements and provide additional assurances to the public or to those directly affected by algorithmic outcomes. For example, when it comes to fishbowl transparency, agencies might find it appropriate to change the terms of their purchasing agreements so that contractors waive, or at least circumscribe, their trade secret protections. Machine-learning procurement contracts should be structured in such a way that allows for the maximum amount of algorithmic disclosure from private contractors. This will go a long way toward addressing concerns surrounding explainability and transparency. Agencies could also create open-source competitions to design algorithms or perhaps work to develop their own in-house expertise so they do not need to contract with a private sector actor who will likely wish to claim trade secrets.

As a best practice, agencies could disclose all versions of a machine-learning algorithm used to develop the one ultimately adopted to demonstrate that this algorithm was chosen wisely. Agencies could also disclose algorithmic outputs that highlight the relationships among variables and the structural properties of datasets. So-called partial dependence

[63]   373 F.3d 372, 387 (3d Cir. 2004).

plots, for example, may shed light on why an algorithm generated a particular prediction, which might be of value to courts and the general public hungry for information about an algorithm and the data it processes. Ultimately, such greater steps to provide transparency could help avoid the impression that algorithms represent a form of "secret law." From a good government perspective, greater transparency – the release of as much information about an algorithm as possible without compromising law enforcement or private trade secrets – would likely bolster public confidence in specific machine-learning algorithms, if not the use of such algorithms more generally.[64]

In addition to pursuing such "best practices" for governmental use of machine-learning algorithms, government agencies should take steps to build their own capacities to deploy these tools effectively and responsibly.[65] First, agencies should develop useable inventories of data. One example of such an effort can be found in the strategic plan of the US Federal Deposit Insurance Corporation (FDIC) to strengthen its "back-end disciplines of in-memory analytics, big data, and data quality."[66] Another example is the US Treasury Department's Office of Financial Research's development of a Legal Entity Identifier (LEI) system that would make identifying parties to financial transactions instantaneous. As noted above, attention also needs to be paid to cybersecurity and privacy protections when building data warehouses.[67]

Second, agencies should work to build the computing capacity they will need to deploy machine learning more frequently. The US Federal Drug Administration (FDA) has used cloud computing to store vast amounts of information on food-borne pathogens. The US SEC is using cloud computing to store and analyze the billion financial records it receives daily, hoping to catch – and reverse – insider trading in real time.[68] More efforts like these are needed. At present, about three-quarters of the annual appropriations for computer technology at federal agencies goes to sustain "legacy systems," systems which the Governmental Accountability Office has noted "are becoming increasingly obsolete" due to "outdated software languages and hardware parts that are unsupported."[69]

Finally, machine learning will require efforts to strengthen human capital. Yes, machine learning relies on digital technology and has the potential to replace certain kinds of human tasks. But government agencies must expand and strengthen their in-house data science staff too. Officials at the US Office of Personnel Management recently announced the establishment of a new "data scientist" job line with positions across the federal government,[70] an important move in a much-needed direction.

Agencies should not deploy machine learning simply for the sake of harnessing the shiniest new technology. Instead, agency officials should ask: "What problem are we trying to solve, why, and how will we solve it?" Engaging in a deliberate process of questioning will also likely

---

64 See Coglianese and Lehr, Regulating by Robot, above note 1, pp. 1205–13; see also Coglianese and Lehr, Transparency and Algorithmic Governance, above note 1, p. 33–49.

65 See Coglianese, above note 8, p. 10.

66 US Fed. Deposit Ins. Corp., Business Technology Strategic Plan 2013–2017 (2013), p. 8, http://advisorselect.com/transcript/FDIC/business-technology-strategic-plan-2013-2017.

67 M. Gault, The U.S. Government Is Utterly Inept at Keeping Your Data Secure, *The New Republic* (June 12, 2019) https://newrepublic.com/article/154167/government-nsa-inept-protecting-cyber-data-whatsapp.

68 See Coglianese and Lehr, Regulating by Robot, above note 1, pp. 1164–7.

69 US Government Accountability Office, GAO-16-696T, Federal Agencies Need to Address Aging Legacy Systems (Testimony of David A. Powner, Director, Information Technology Management Issues) (2016), www.gao.gov/assets/680/677454.pdf.

70 E. Wagner, OPM Announces New "Data Scientist" Job Title, *Government Executive* (July 1, 2019), www.govexec.com/management/2019/07/opm-announces-new-data-scientist-job-title/158139/.

acclimate agency employees to the potential uses of machine learning and the types of problems it is well suited to tackle – but also to the potential downsides that should be anticipated and addressed.[71] Agencies should aim to use machine learning when it performs better, all things considered, than the status quo.

When designing algorithmic systems, agencies would do well to incorporate meaningful – and ongoing – engagement with the public as well as other governmental officials who will interact with or be affected by these systems.[72] By doing so, agencies can maximize their chances of reaping the benefits from machine learning while minimizing the possibility of a loss of trust or the creation of social conflict. Algorithms can help streamline and improve many government services, but they cannot erase the basic need for government officials to be responsive and empathetic to public concerns.[73]

CONCLUSION

Although the prospect of government agencies engaging in adjudication by algorithm may sound novel and futuristic, the use of machine learning is starting to permeate the public sector, much as it is starting to become relatively ubiquitous across the private sector. Governmental use of machine-learning algorithms – even to automate key governmental decisions – can be readily accommodated by current administrative law doctrines. When used responsibly, machine-learning algorithms have the potential to yield improvements in governmental decision-making by increasing accuracy, decreasing human bias, reducing costs, and enhancing overall administrative efficiency. The public sector can lawfully find ways to reap many of the same operational benefits that machine-learning algorithms are delivering to the private sector.

---

[71] H. Mehr, Artificial Intelligence for Citizen Services and Government, Harvard Kennedy Ash Center (August 2017), https://ash.harvard.edu/files/ash/files/artificial_intelligence_for_citizen_services.pdf.

[72] See C. Coglianese, Listening, Learning, Leading: A Framework for Regulatory Excellence, Penn Program on Regulation (2015), www.law.upenn.edu/live/files/4946-pprfinalconvenersreport.pdf.

[73] E. P. Goodman, The Challenge of Equitable Algorithmic Change, *The Regulatory Review* (February 2019), https://www.theregreview.org/wp-content/uploads/2019/02/Goodman-The-Challenge-of-Equitable-Algorithmic-Change.pdf.

9

Discrimination in the Age of Algorithms

Robin Nunn

Imagine: a FinTech lender, that is, a firm using computer programs to enable banking and financial services, which introduces a new product based on algorithmic artificial intelligence (AI) underwriting. The lender combs through the entirety of an applicant's financial records to review where the applicant shopped, what purchases she made, purchase volumes and frequency, how much credit and debt she had, and whether she made utility and rent payments on time. The lender also reviews her mobile phone usage to understand how much time she spent on her phone and what she was engaged in, whether it was at work or at home, her typical geographic areas of travel, the frequency of her text messages, and how many spelling errors she made. (We'll leave her social media usage out of this for now.) Through this mix of financial and behavioral data, the FinTech lender underwrites her application. It does the same for millions of other customers with little to no credit history, but who have long lived within their means, shopped responsibly, paid rent and utilities on time, and spent many hours at work.

Through its AI underwriting model, the lender makes hundreds of thousands of new loans to first-time homebuyers in traditionally underserved neighborhoods without raising its credit risk profile. Impressed, the US Office of the Comptroller of the Currency (OCC) conducts a supervisory examination to understand this breath-taking performance. In the course of the exam, it determines that 93 percent of these new homebuyers are white, and the OCC refers the matter to the Department of Justice for enforcement of a discriminatory lending claim in violation of the Fair Housing Act and Equal Credit Opportunity Act. Based on trends involving the use of algorithms in decision-making, this hypothetical is not far-fetched. In fact, it reveals the potential benefits and perils of incorporating techniques of algorithmic-driven AI into the consumer lending marketplace.

Algorithms that are used to review loan applications and trade securities, predict financial markets, identify prospective employees, and assess potential customers warrant concerns about fairness and bias. The risk of algorithmic bias is foreseeable in the lending context, where reliance on certain data inputs – such as the decades-old credit-scoring model, which does not take into account consumer data on rent, utility, and cellphone bill payments – have already proven to have discriminatory effects. Particularly as the lending industry digitizes and moves toward "alternative lending" (i.e. considering non-traditional creditworthiness factors, including behavioral data), financial institutions must balance the innovation of AI with the substantial risk that machine learning could result in disparate impacts on minority populations.

This chapter will examine the history of the anti-discrimination laws that regulate the consumer lending marketplace, how those laws interact with the rapidly changing world of algorithms and AI, and how financial institutions navigate these timely and important issues. Our view is that companies, especially financial services institutions, must be vigilant in their use of algorithms that incorporate AI and machine learning. As algorithms become more ingrained in companies' operations, previously unforeseen risks are beginning to appear – in particular, the risk that a perfectly well-intentioned algorithm may inadvertently generate biased conclusions that discriminate against protected classes of people.

LAW OF DISCRIMINATION

Throughout the history of credit lending, applicants have not always been treated fairly or received the same level of consideration from lenders. Prior to the enactment of the federal fair lending laws, women and minorities were subjected to discriminatory practices within the consumer lending marketplace. Women applicants were routinely required to have more collateral or extra co-signers and were often asked personal questions irrelevant to their creditworthiness.[1] For example, credit lenders would regularly dismiss a qualified female candidate and designate them as a credit risk based on the belief that they "would be distracted by child care or some other stereotypically female responsibility."[2] Likewise, minorities were routinely told that they did not have sufficient collateral to secure a loan or that they lived outside the areas where financial institutions regularly lent.[3] In an effort to discourage women and minorities from seeking credit, lenders took a significantly longer time to process their applications.[4] Recognizing that "economic stabilization would be enhanced and competition among the various financial institutions and other firms engaged in the extension of credit would be strengthened by an absence of discrimination," Congress ultimately enacted legislation aimed at neutralizing these discriminatory practices.[5]

Specifically, the US Congress enacted the Equal Credit Opportunity Act (ECOA) in 1974.[6] The purpose of the ECOA is to ensure that the "various financial institutions and other firms engaged in the extensions of credit exercise their responsibility to make credit available with fairness, impartiality, and without discrimination on the basis of sex or marital status."[7] The ECOA, and its implementing rules known as Regulation B, prohibit creditors from discriminating on the basis of race, color, religion, national origin, sex, marital status, age (provided the applicant has the capacity to contract), the applicant's receipt of income derived from any public assistance program, or the applicant's exercise, in good faith, of any right under the Consumer Credit Protection Act.[8] The Act is designed to regulate all entities which conduct a credit transaction in their ordinary course of business, such as banks, retailers, credit unions, and credit card issuers.[9] Additionally, the law applies to all extensions of credit, including extensions to small businesses, corporations, partnerships, and trusts.[10] Although a credit transaction is not expressly defined by

[1] B. Fay, The Equal Credit Opportunity Act, www.debt.org/credit/your-consumer-rights/equal-opportunity-act/.
[2] See *Moran Foods, Inc.* v. *Mid-Atlantic Mkt. Dev. Co.*, 476 F.3d 436, 441 (7th Cir. 2007).
[3] Fay, above note 1.
[4] *Ibid.*
[5] ECOA, 15 USC § 1691 (2012).
[6] *Ibid.*
[7] *Ibid.*
[8] *Ibid.*
[9] *Ibid.*
[10] Federal Deposit Insurance Corporation, FDIC Consumer Compliance Examination Manual: Fair Lending Laws and Regulations (September 2015), 1.1, www.fdic.gov/regulations/compliance/manual/index.html.

the ECOA, Regulation B specifies that "credit transaction means every aspect of an applicant's dealings with a creditor regarding an application for credit or an existing extension of credit."[11]

The ECOA was first implemented by the Board of Governors of the Federal Reserve.[12] That role was later transferred to the Consumer Financial Protection Bureau (CFPB) when Congress enacted the Dodd-Frank Wall Street Reform and Consumer Protection Act (Dodd-Frank Act) in 2010.[13] In addition to transferring rule-making authority, the Dodd-Frank Act also gave the CFPB authority to supervise and enforce compliance with the ECOA and its implementing regulations.[14] Although the ECOA is primarily enforced by the CFPB, regulatory agencies such as the Federal Trade Commission (FTC), Comptroller of Currency, and Federal Reserve Board maintain authority to examine financial institutions for compliance with the ECOA.[15] If the CFPB or regulatory agency discovers a pattern or practice of discrimination that violates the ECOA, they may refer the matter to the US Department of Justice (DOJ), which in turn may file a lawsuit under the ECOA.[16] Each year, the Civil Rights Division of the DOJ files a report with Congress that highlights their enforcement activities under the statute in hopes of expanding access to credit for qualified borrowers throughout the United States.[17]

Although the ECOA and fair lending laws[18] provide potential safeguards for qualified borrowers, discrimination still continues to exist today for applicants seeking credit. Not only do some institutions fail to strictly adhere to the regulations of the ECOA, but lenders unknowingly violate the Act's prohibitions when they utilize automated decision-making processes to determine whether an applicant is qualified. Although algorithms that could potentially help to determine whether an applicant is creditworthy provide "efficiency, profitability, and, often, a sense of scientific precision and authority," these types of algorithms are increasingly found to produce a discriminatory effect in their decision-making process.[19] In an effort to regulate this automated decision-making and neutralize the potential of discrimination, legislators have introduced a bill in the Senate and House of Representatives called the Algorithmic Accountability Act of 2019. This legislation would "give the FTC power to require and monitor procedures by big companies to keep track of their algorithms and audit them for fairness and accuracy."[20] Until credit lenders are required to provide evidence to the FTC that their algorithms are fair and accurate, and follow relevant laws against discrimination, the use of algorithmic-driven AI systems to determine creditworthy applicants will remain controversial.

---

[11] 12 CFR § 1002.2(m) (2011). This includes a creditor's "information requirements; investigation procedures; standards of creditworthiness; terms of credit; furnishing of credit information; revocation alteration, or termination of credit; and collection procedures." *Ibid.*

[12] 12 USC § 1691b(a) (2012).

[13] 12 USC § 5581(b)(1)(A) (2012) ("All consumer financial protection functions of the board of Governors are transferred to the Bureau").

[14] Consumer Finance Protection Bureau, Equal Credit Opportunity Act (ECOA) examination procedures (October 30, 2015), www.consumerfinance.gov/policy-compliance/guidance/supervision-examinations/equal-credit-opportunity-act-ecoa-examination-procedures/.

[15] Department of Justice, The Equal Opportunity Act (November 8, 2017), www.justice.gov/crt/equal-credit-opportunity-act-3. The CFPB may also litigate ECOA matters under its own enforcement authority.

[16] *Ibid.*

[17] *Ibid.*

[18] The Fair Housing Act also prohibits discrimination in real-estate-related transactions. This chapter focuses on the ECOA.

[19] C. O'Neil, Yes, Government Should Regulate Automated Decision-Making, *Bloomberg* (April 17, 2019), www.bloomberg.com/opinion/articles/2019-04-17/algorithms-that-manage-people-need-human-regulation. The article refers to a sexist hiring algorithm developed by Amazon, and an IBM facial-recognition program that did not work nearly as well on black women as on white men.

[20] *Ibid.*

CHALLENGING AI DECISION-MAKING

AI technology remains controversial – in part, because algorithms are not always clear on their decision-making logic. It's troubling when Flickr, applying automatic labels to pictures in digital photo albums, incorrectly labels images of black people or when Google search results for black-sounding names are more likely to be accompanied by ads about criminal activity than search results for white-sounding names. But what about when AI is used by the government to determine which restaurants should be inspected; make judgments on where the next crime might happen; or even decide the length of a prison sentence? "AI Now" has called for the government to stop the use of certain types of algorithmic-based AI until the technology is better understood and made "available for public auditing, testing and review, and subject to accountability standards."[21] Further analysis presented below focuses on how to address government use of AI.[22]

LACK OF RELEVANT CASE LAW

Thus far, most of the rules implicated by AI are not particular to AI at all. Rather, they are existing and sometimes long-standing privacy, cybersecurity, unfair and deceptive acts and practices, due process, and health and safety rules that cover technologies that now happen to concentrate on the use of algorithmic-driven AI systems. These include rules about holding, using, and protecting personal data, guidance on how to manage the risks caused by financial algorithms, and protections against discrimination.

There are cases that reference the risk of government adoption of AI. For example, in the unpublished California state appellate case *County of Riverside* v. *Perone*, the Court referenced the challenges in a government agency adopting AI to generate recruitment lists by matching job qualifications supplied by the requesting department with skills and education found on resumes that had been scanned into the system.[23] Or on the federal side, amicus briefs were filed in the US Supreme Court case *Gill* v. *Whitford*, arguing that the increasing adoption of machine learning for analyzing voter data and behavior poses the threat of increasingly imprecise and discriminatory gerrymandering.[24]

However, there are limited instances in which a citizen or company has directly challenged the use of algorithmic-driven AI.[25] This lack of adjudication may be that the use of AI is preliminary and minimal (though increasing) in the regulatory context. It may also be that lawyers are still grappling with how to apply old laws and principles to new technology. Whatever the reason, it is likely that such challenges will increase in the future. As governments and private parties adopt these (algorithmic-driven) technologies, several risks to the regulatory process emerge and will be

[21] See, e.g., A. Campolo, M. Sanfilippo, M. Whittaker, and K. Crawford, AI Now 2017 Report, *AI Now* (2017), https://ainowinstitute.org/AI_Now_2017_Report.pdf.
[22] *Ibid.*
[23] *Cty. of Riverside* v. *Perone*, 2006 WL 245319 (Cal. Ct. App. February 2, 2006).
[24] *Gill* v. *Whitford*, Brief of Amici Curiae Political Science Professors in Support of Appellees and Affirmance, No. 16–1161, 2017 WL 4311101 (S.Ct. September 5, 2017).
[25] As one of the few examples of challenge of government use of AI, defendant Eric Loomis was found guilty for his role in a drive-by shooting. During intake, Loomis answered a series of questions that were then entered into COMPAS, a risk-assessment tool developed by a privately held company and used by the Wisconsin Department of Corrections. The trial judge gave Loomis a long sentence partially because of the "high risk" score the defendant received from this risk-assessment tool. Loomis challenged his sentence, because he was not allowed to assess the algorithm. The state Supreme Court ruled against Loomis, reasoning that knowledge of the algorithm's output was a sufficient level of transparency. *Wisconsin* v. *Loomis*, 371 Wis.2d 235 (July 13, 2016).

essential to consider when facing potential unlawful and unconstitutional actions. Namely, many may consider challenging government use of AI in the regulatory context on the basis of principles of transparency, due process, non-delegation, and non-discrimination.

LEGAL FRAMEWORK TO ADDRESS DISCRIMINATORY ACTIONS

Current anti-discrimination laws in sectors like education, housing, and employment prohibit both intentional discrimination – called "disparate treatment" – as well as unintentional "disparate impact," which happens when neutral-sounding rules disproportionately affect a legally protected group (for example, on the basis of sex, age, disability, race, national origin, religion, pregnancy, or genetic information). Since the US civil rights movement, a body of law has emerged around claims that institutions intentionally treated a protected class of individuals less favorably than other individuals. In 1971, the term "disparate impact" was first used in the Supreme Court case *Griggs* v. *Duke Power Company*. The Court ruled that, under Title VII of the Civil Rights Act, it was illegal for the company to use intelligence test scores and high school diplomas – factors which were shown to disproportionately favor white applicants and substantially disqualify people of color – to make hiring or promotion decisions, whether or not the company intended the tests to discriminate. A key aspect of the *Griggs* decision was that the power company could not prove their intelligence tests or diploma requirements were actually relevant to the jobs they were hiring for.

More recently, the government and other plaintiffs have advanced disparate impact claims that focus more on the effect instead of the intention of lending policies. Recently, the Supreme Court's decision in *Texas Department of Housing and Community Affairs* v. *Inclusive Communities Project* affirmed the use of the disparate impact theory. The Inclusive Communities Project had used a statistical analysis of housing patterns to show that a tax credit program effectively segregated Texans by race. The fundamental validation of disparate impact theory by the Court in the *Inclusive Communities* case remains a wake-up call for technology and government agencies. An algorithm that inadvertently disadvantages a protected class continues to have the potential to create due process concerns.

ASSERTION OF DISPARATE IMPACT CLAIMS

In asserting a disparate impact theory, plaintiffs must prove that they were disproportionately and negatively affected by a government policy or practice. Where a disparate impact is shown, the government may defend itself either by challenging the plaintiff's evidence (usually by attacking the statistics used to demonstrate the disparate impact) or by providing that the algorithmic-based AI policy is necessary to achieve a valid interest. If the government can't prove that, then a plaintiff's claim of disparate impact must prevail.

If the government could demonstrate that the AI in question has a demonstrable relationship to the requirements, or a "business necessity," the plaintiff can still win by providing that the government refuses to adopt an alternative practice with a less discriminatory effect. One route would be to argue that alternative methods were equally effective without being discriminatory. Since algorithms are proprietary and frequently protected under non-disclosure agreements, organizations that use them, including government agencies, may not have the legal right to conduct independent testing. This would force the government to either admit it considered no alternatives or force an examination of the algorithm, which is currently quite challenging given the complexity of algorithms. Thus, the ability to audit an algorithm would answer some questions about bias, but there is a group of algorithms that move beyond our current abilities to analyze them. Artificial neural networks are one example. They are fed huge amounts of data and, through a process of breaking the data down into much smaller components and searching for patterns, essentially come up with their own algorithms which could potentially be incomprehensible to humans.

ADDITIONAL POINTS REGARDING DISCRIMINATION AND VALUING DIVERSITY

In putting forth a disparate impact case, or similar legal theory, there are many additional points to be made to reinforce the theory of discriminatory treatment – two key points are included below. First, a plaintiff may draw light to the failure of the government to hire and involve diverse stakeholders in developing the algorithm and data inputs. Diversity at the front end is crucial to unbiased outcomes, to preventing neutral data points, and to the ability to compete in the technologically advanced global marketplace. Government agencies that succeed in diversity and inclusion are those that have a formal diversity hiring strategy, including formal hiring and training programs and a commitment by agency executives to accomplish diversity hiring objectives. By showing a failure to recruit diverse employees, beyond the basic demonstration of a failure to create a high-functioning organization, this would highlight an environment ripe for impartial algorithms. Further, for a disparate impact case, a plaintiff may consider showing the government failure to engage human oversight to test and check algorithmic decisions. These individuals should document and validate data inputs as a part of their process. What this means is that employees should be assigned to review datasets to ensure the data is fair and accurate, establish best practices for auditing algorithmic decision-making, and include specific guidance on addressing questions of disparate impact.

ALGORITHMS IN CONSUMER LENDING

Development of AI in General

The private sector has experienced exponential growth in the investment, development, and implementation of AI technologies in the last two decades.[26] But we now have comparatively huge volumes of data that can be stored and processed cheaply, such that the performance of and ability to further research algorithmic-driven AI systems has greatly increased. The concept of AI loosely centers around the algorithms that have access to vast quantities of data from which they can learn to predict outcomes based on historical situations. Those algorithms, trained on immense amounts of data, can provide new insights into behaviors and identify previously overlooked patterns.

Generally speaking, AI systems operate by finding relationships between input features and known outcomes in a set of training data.[27] What makes these systems different from human decision-making models is that the machines themselves, without direct human intervention, develop the rules that best predict the known outcomes based on the input data – this set of rules is known as the "model."[28] This "model" is then applied to future, unobservable cases of

---

[26] L. Columbus, 10 Charts that Will Change Your Perspective on Artificial Intelligence's Growth, *Forbes* (January 12, 2018), www.forbes.com/sites/louiscolumbus/2018/01/12/10-charts-that-will-change-your-perspective-on-artificial-intelligences-growth/#15ae625d4758.

[27] A. Selbst, A Mild Defense of Our New Machine Overlords (2017) 70 *Vand. Law Rev. En Banc* 87, 90.

[28] *Ibid.*

interest and predicts the results.[29] There are several different AI applications that feature prominently in the analysis of law and algorithms; a few examples follow.

> Machine learning – a sub-set of AI that often uses statistical techniques to give machines the ability to learn from data without being explicitly given the instructions for how to do so. This process is known as training a model using a learning algorithm that progressively improves model performance on a specific task. Machine-learning models may be further divided between supervised learners (which require a data analyst to specify a target variable of interest) and unsupervised learners (models in which the algorithm conducts searches for general structures, clusters, or hotspots in the dataset).[30]
>
> Neural networks – multiple layers of weighted nodes, including at least one hidden layer, which can be trained to perform certain tasks (for example, facial recognition, detecting fraud, predicting stock performance) via large datasets and means of rewarding and penalizing desired and undesirable outcomes.
>
> Expert systems – computer systems, typically rule-based (if *x*, then *y*), emulating human experts' decision-making ability (for example, for medical diagnoses).

In recent years, computing has shifted from merely relieving organizations of routine work such as data entry, to a new era involving the automation of tasks previously thought to require human judgment. As part of this new era, corporations have increasingly begun to incorporate AI technology into the process of hiring and other employee decisions. For example, Amazon began to implement AI technology in its hiring efforts, only to abandon the tool when it became clear that the AI model contained a bias toward woman that could not be overcome.[31] There are many other examples of corporations adopting AI to supplement traditional human activities. And while none of these examples may amount to facially illegal action, small changes in facts or decision-making processes could easily yield a transgression on an individual right, as explained below.

ALGORITHMS IN BANKING

Banks have many potential uses for algorithms. Banks might use neural nets to detect instances of fraud or protect against money-laundering risks. They might employ facial recognition to identify known fraudsters in in-person interactions in branches, to comply with "Know Your Customer" regulations, or to confirm the identity of a customer trying to draw on her home equity line of credit. Banks might use deep learning models to categorize their customers into segments to best serve the needs of those segments, or to identify investment opportunities. For our purposes, we are concerned here with how banks might use algorithms to provide credit to consumers.

At the core, the goal of using algorithms (and more loosely in the financial institution context, predictive models) is, in fact, to [legally] discriminate. Banks use algorithmic models in consumer lending to predict which individuals are good credit risks and which are not, which price levels will be competitive while maximizing profit, and where (and how) to target scarce marketing resources to those consumers most likely to respond and be approved for a given product. At the same time, there are categories along which creditors are not permitted to discriminate, among them, race, sex, and age, as discussed above. The rest of

---

[29]   *Ibid.*
[30]   S. Barocas and A. D. Selbst, Big Data's Disparate Impact (2016) 104 *Cal. Law Rev.* 671, 678.
[31]   J. Dastin, Amazon Scraps Secret AI Recruiting Tool that Showed Bias against Women, *Reuters* (October 9, 2018), www.reuters.com/article/us-amazon-com-jobs-automation-insight-idUSKCN1MK08G.

this chapter addresses the challenges associated with discriminating in lawful ways while avoiding unlawful discrimination.

Machine learning is based not only on more complex algorithms, but also on access to far greater pools of data (pools themselves deepen and widen every day), increased processing power, and ever-diminishing storage and computing costs. Of these factors, the complexity and opaqueness of algorithms and the access to more data sources (or "big data") hold the largest risks for discriminatory practices in the consumer credit context because they inhibit transparency and accountability.

As noted above, the concept of fairness can encompass a number of discrete and abstract elements. Those elements permeate the various applications of algorithms in consumer financial services. Fairness in an algorithmic application might consider whether the algorithm uses a consumer's personal information as a consumer might reasonably expect, and whether a bank keeps that information secure and private. Fairness considerations might also include whether the bank uses algorithms to treat its customers and prospective customers in an ethical manner. Or a bank committed to fairness might also evaluate whether its uses of algorithms are both transparent and explainable to its customers. Although all of these dimensions warrant consideration, we will focus on the potential for bias and discrimination in banking algorithms.

ALGORITHMS IN CONSUMER LENDING

Algorithms have long been a critical component in the lending process, perhaps most prominently in the use of credit scores in underwriting. Among the earliest prominent credit scoring algorithms was the FICO score, first developed in 1958 and named in honor of the Fair Isaac Company's founders Bill Fair and Earl Isaac.[32] The first iterations of the FICO score relied on a predictive variable that took into account the number of credit cards held by a consumer.[33] Since then, financial institutions have implemented algorithms of varying degrees of complexity through the consumer lending process, including marketing, sales, fulfillment, servicing, and collections.

In the face of its powerfulness at predicting expected and less expected relationships, machine learning often struggles to be transparent and explainable in its output. Because of laws like ECOA/Regulation B and Federal Credit Reporting Act (FCRA), creditors have obligations to understand how their models work (in order to avoid discrimination) and explain why a given model reaches a certain result (in order to provide adverse action reasons to rejected applicants). However, many other industries are not covered by these regulations (although many companies will have to grapple with similar considerations to comply with anti-discrimination laws in employment), and therefore need not implement regiments to address the risks created by the regulation. At the same time, the ethical underpinnings of these laws (and the risk mitigation systems used to address them) may instruct the development and implementation of machine-learning models outside of consumer financial services.

Our focus on machine-learning models here is largely limited to supervised learning models in which a modeler must intentionally select a target variable. Many models most closely linked to credit are supervised learning models because these models sort, rank, and predict borrowers as methods to balance appropriate credit risk. While financial institutions may have uses for unsupervised machine-learning models (for example, natural language

[32] FICO, About Us (2019), www.fico.com/en/about-us#did-you-know.
[33] F. Huynh, Adapting Credit Scores to Evolving Consumer Behavior and Data (2013) 46 *Suffolk Univ. Law Rev.* 829, 830.

speech processors in designing chatbots or neural nets to help identify fraud), machine-learning models in the credit arena have so far largely been based on supervised learning models.

MODELING IN THE CONSUMER CREDIT LIFECYCLE

Banks use complex models through the consumer credit lifecycle – from marketing and sales, to pricing and underwriting, to servicing and collections. We examine these processes next.

MARKETING AND CUSTOMER SEGMENTATION

Algorithms help predict the likelihood that a consumer might respond to a marketing offer, the type of offer likely to generate a response, and the channel in which the offer should be delivered. For example, an institution might use an algorithmic model that predicts the degree to which a consumer may respond to an email informing her that she has been pre-selected for a credit card offer. The institution might then decide to target only the top decile, for example, judging that those outside that range do not have a sufficient propensity to respond to justify the time and resources that would be spent on such a campaign. Common variables in these types of models might include credit score, age of the oldest trade, and amount in revolving balances, among others.

Vendors such as Facebook and Google offer third-party options for marketing models. For example, Facebook's look-alike audiences product allows advertisers to reach people who are similar to, or look like, their existing set of customers based on Facebook's modeled judgment of the similarities.[34] Recently developed machine-learning models might include data regarding transaction behavior or more nuanced behavior related to periodic revolving balances. We should note that there are hundreds – or even thousands – of variables that an institution might employ to provide predictive lift to the model.

PRICING AND UNDERWRITING

Institutions also rely on models in the pricing and underwriting stages of the consumer lending process. Models here traditionally rely on variables such as FICO, debt-to-income ratio, income, loan amount, and loan-to-value ratio and property value (for secured loans).

"There is substantial interest in the potential for [banks using AI to develop credit-scoring models] to allow more consumers on the margins of the current credit system to improve their credit, at potentially lower costs."[35] For example, AI, relying on deeper and broader datasets beyond those traditionally used to evaluate creditworthiness, is being used to reach some of the nearly 29 percent of Americans who are "unbanked" or "underbanked" to qualify for a line of

[34] US Department of Housing and Urban Development (HUD), HUD Charges Facebook with Housing Discrimination over Company's Targeted Advising Practices (March 28, 2019), www.hud.gov/press/press_relea ses_media_advisories/HUD_No_19_035. In March 2019, the US HUD charged Facebook with violations of the Fair Housing Act. HUD alleged that Facebook's proprietary models discriminated on the basis of race, sex, age, and a number of other prohibited bases in the selection and delivery of its targeted real-estate-related housing advertisements.
[35] L. Brainard, What Are We Learning about Artificial Intelligence in Financial Services? (November 13, 2018), p. 10, www.bis.org/review/r181114g.pdf.

credit.[36] These non-traditional datasets may include rent payments, utilities, mobile-phone subscriptions, insurance, child care, tuition, level of education, secondary education institutions, and even social media networks.

SERVICING AND COLLECTIONS

Algorithmic models also play a role in servicing and collections, although perhaps to a lesser extent than in the processes described above. Here, models may be used to sort unpaid debts into categories in an attempt to aid collection – and if so, the sort may be between various methods or techniques of collection like in-house or vendor-sold, or written off.

Potential Benefits

Algorithmic models provide benefits in each stage of the consumer credit life-cycle, some of which have been touched on above.

> Companies have used big data to provide alternative ways to score populations that were previously deemed unscoreable … [An example of such products is one that] rel[ies] on traditional public record information, such as foreclosures and bankruptcies, but it also includes educational history, professional licensure data, and personal property ownership data. Thus, consumers who may not have access to traditional credit, but, for instance, have a professional license, pay rent on time, or own a car, may be given better access to credit than they otherwise would have. Furthermore, big data algorithms could help reveal underlying disparities in traditional credit markets and help companies serve creditworthy consumers from any background.[37]

Available data sources are also deeper, richer, and more varied than ever before. This goes beyond even the non-traditional data sources described above. For example, researchers have investigated traces we leave from our mundane digital interactions – termed a "digital footprint" – which may help predict credit defaults and consumer payment behavior. Looking at a dataset may include digital footprint variables such as device type, operating system, channel (for example, search engine or price comparison site), marks related to the user's email address (that is, did it contain a first or last name or number), and whether the user made a typing error when entering the email. Researchers found that these variables from the digital footprint work as proxies for income, character, and reputation, and were highly valuable for default prediction.[38]

The automated decision-making made available by algorithms may also eliminate at least some of the discrimination that may occur in traditional face-to-face lending. Reliance on algorithmic scoring has deepened the marketplace and led to increased competition or encouraged more shopping from a simpler, more accessible application process. Researchers have also found that FinTechs appear to do better than face-to-face lenders in mitigating discrimination in application acceptances or rejections. And machine-learning techniques

---

[36] Executive Office of the President, Big Data: Seizing Opportunities, Preserving Values (May 2014), p. 40, https://obamawhitehouse.archives.gov/sites/default/files/docs/big_data_privacy_report_may_1_2014.pdf.
[37] Federal Trade Commission, Big Data: A Tool for Inclusion or Exclusion? (January 2016), p. 6, www.ftc.gov/system/files/documents/reports/big-data-tool-inclusion-or-exclusion-understanding-issues/160106big-data-rpt.pdf.
[38] T. Berg, V. Burg, A. Gombović, and M. Puri, On the Rise of FinTechs – Credit Scoring Using Digital Footprints (July 2018), pp. 2–3, www.fdic.gov/bank/analytical/cfr/2018/wp2018/cfr-wp2018-04.pdf.

may be useful in conducting fair lending analytics by bringing more powerful techniques beyond linear regressions for identifying disparities or the variables driving those disparities.

RISKS OF AI ADOPTION

With the rise in adoption of AI, companies and their counsel will have to increasingly confront how decades-old processes and procedures apply in the new era. For example, certain properties of AI, and especially machine learning, combine to distinguish it from other analytical techniques and give rise to potential concerns about the greater reliance on machine learning.

The first is machine learning's self-studying property. The results of algorithms do not depend on humans specifying in advance how each variable is to be factored into the predictions; indeed, as long as learning algorithms are running, humans are not really controlling how they are combining and comparing data. Machine-learning systems "learn" from the data, meaning that these algorithms find patterns or correlations between variables in a set of data, which can then be used to make predictions.[39]

This algorithmic-based learning can go awry. For example, researchers have caught AI cheating and trying to hide the results. Specifically, a neural net called CycleGAN tried to hide images within photos that it was supposed to be translating. Researchers discovered the cheat when they realized the translated images were too similar to the original.[40] In other words, CycleGAN was not doing what it was told to do, but it was delivering on the objective as it was directed. Since anti-discrimination laws require that participants follow specific principles and regulations, serious fair lending consequences might arise if the same cheating were to occur in the underwriting process.

The second key property for discussion is machine learning's "black box" nature. Unless specifically designed to ensure transparency, the results of many machine-learning systems are not intuitively explainable and cannot support causal explanations of the kind that underlie the reasons traditionally offered as a legitimate business justification. As a result, it can be difficult to explain exactly how or why a machine-learning algorithm keys in on certain correlations or makes the predictions that it does. As such, legal commentators have lamented the "black box" nature of machine-learning-based algorithms, arguing that if we cannot see the code or interact with it, we cannot appropriately, or legally, make use of it.[41] And in many cases, due to trade secrecy or other reasons for lack of access, such access might prove impossible.[42]

Finally, machine learning, as with other computational strategies in today's digital era, can be fast and automatic, supporting uses in which the algorithm produces results that can shorten or potentially bypass human deliberation and decision-making. All three of these factors combine to make machine-learning techniques appear qualitatively more independent from humans when compared to other statistical techniques.[43]

---

[39]   L. Edwards and M. Veale, Slave to the Algorithm? Why a "Right to Explanation" Is Probably Not the Remedy You Are Looking for (2017) 16 *Duke Law Technol. Rev.* 18, 25.

[40]   C. Chu, A. Zhmoginov, and M. Sandler, CycleGAN, a Master of Steganography (December 16, 2017), https://arxiv.org/abs/1712.02950.

[41]   See, e.g., F. Pasquale, *The Black Box Society* (2015), pp. 3–4; B. Reddix-Smalls, Credit Scoring and Trade Secrecy: An Algorithmic Quagmire or How the Lack of Transparency in Complex Financial Models Scuttled the Finance Market (2011) 12 *UC Davis Bus. Law J.* 87; F. Pasquale, Restoring Transparency to Automated Authority (2011) 9 *J. Telecommun. High Technol. Law* 235, 237.

[42]   M. Hurley and J. Adebayo, Credit Scoring in the Age of Big Data (2016) 18 *Yale J. Law Technol.* 148, 196–8.

[43]   C. Coglianese and D. Lehr, Regulating by Robot: Administrative Decision Making in the Machine-Learning Era (2017) 105 *Geo. Law J.* 1147, 1167.

Broadly speaking, the problem with companies adopting AI is a data issue. Letting computers make decisions could cause serious problems that would need to be addressed immediately. Algorithms learn by being fed certain data, often chosen by engineers, and the system builds a model of the world based on that data. So, for instance, if a system is trained on photos of people who are overwhelmingly white, it will have a harder time recognizing non-white faces, thus leading to the emergence of problematic biases baked into predictions. Indeed, this is precisely why IBM recently announced plans to release a database of more than 1 million facial images to academics, public interest groups, and competitors.[44] Release of this information is intended to improve training of machine-learning applications used in facial recognition systems.

Certain studies show that improperly trained machines will mistake correlation for causation, which may be the reason for mistakes in prediction.[45] Unfortunately, because these algorithms are secret, or based on proprietary information, we do not know why these predictions ended up being so skewed and wrong.

DISCRIMINATION

Discrimination can happen in face-to-face decisions or in algorithmic scoring. Although algorithmic lending may go far in eliminating such discrimination, it is far from perfect. For example, research suggests that both FinTech and traditional lenders charge Latinx and African-American borrowers higher interest rates, attributing the rates to weaker competitive environments for those borrowers and borrower profiling based on shopping behavior.

Other risks include: more individuals mistakenly being denied opportunities based on the actions of others; risks that create or reinforce existing disparities; risks that reveal sensitive information or assist in the targeting of vulnerable consumers for fraud; risks that create new justifications for exclusion and result in higher-priced goods and services for lower-income communities; and risks that weaken the effect of consumer choice.[46] To take one recent example, Amazon developed an AI tool to help it hire software developers. Amazon fed it a dataset of resumes of past successful hires. Because this dataset was overwhelmingly male, however, the AI learned a bias against female applicants – indeed, it began to automatically exclude resumes of graduates of two women's colleges.[47] Even traditional retailers have started to use algorithms to dynamically price discounts for identical products based on where the retailer thought the customer lived.[48]

To take one example in account, recent research shows not only that modeled targeting for online advertising may result in a disparate impact on the basis of race, but that users interested in engaging in intentional discrimination may actually be able to exploit vulnerabilities in modeled audience targeting. For example, with Facebook's look-alike audiences product, described above, researchers found that when Facebook starts with a small

[44] IBM, IBM to Release World's Largest Annotation Dataset for Studying Bias in Facial Analysis (June 27, 2018), www.ibm.com/blogs/research/2018/06/ai-facial-analytics/.

[45] See, e.g., R. Wigglesworth, Spurious Correlations are Kryptonite of Wall St's AI Rush, *Financial Times* (March 14, 2018), www.ft.com/content/f14db820-26cd-11e8-b27e-cc62a39d57a0.

[46] Federal Trade Commission, above note 37, pp. 10–11.

[47] J. Dastin, Amazon Scraps Secret AI Recruiting Tool that Showed Bias against Women, *Reuters* (October 9, 2018), www.reuters.com/article/us-amazon-com-jobs-automation-insight/amazon-scraps-secret-airrecruiting-tool-that-showed-bias-against-women-idUSKCN1MK08G.

[48] J. Valentino-Devries and J. Singer-Vine, Websites Vary Prices, Deals Based on Users' Information, *Wall Street Journal* (December 24, 2012), http://online.wsj.com/news/articles/SB10001424127887323777204578189391813881534.

discriminatory source audience, as it tries to infer the attributes that separate the audience from the general population, it amplifies the bias contained in the source audience. Advertisers might be unaware of an overlooked bias, but nevertheless be left with a significant disparate impact. Or worse – a malicious actor might intentionally create a discriminatory outcome if she knowingly starts with a biased dataset.[49]

CONSIDERATIONS FOR AVOIDING DISPROPORTIONATELY ADVERSE OUTCOMES

At its core, supervised machine-learning models learn by example and in accordance with the humans that develop them.[50] The elements of algorithms most fraught with risk are also the elements that might benefit from further attention at the model development stage. The data used for the examples, the instructions provided to the machine as it parses the data, and the parameters of conclusions the machine is directed to draw are integral parts to the process. Missteps in each area can lead to unwanted discrimination in the outcome. For every model, developers need to consider whether the data model accounts for biases, the accuracy of predictions based on big data, and whether the reliance on big data raises any ethical or fairness concerns.

VARIABLE DEFINITIONS

"In contrast to those traditional forms of data analysis that simply return records or summary statistics in response to a specific query, data mining attempts to locate statistical relationships in a dataset."[51] As an initial step, data miners must separate their data such that it differentiates between "target variables" (or variables that will render desired information) and "class labels" (or which arrange the possible target variable values into mutually exclusive groups). "[T]he definition of the target variable and its associated class labels determines what data mining happens to find [and] valid concerns that discrimination may enter at this stage because the different choices [for defining the target variable and class labels] may have a greater or lesser adverse impact on protected classes."[52]

TRAINING DATA

Modelers need to consider whether their training data is sufficiently representative. Because supervised machine learning learns by example, the data first used to instruct, or train, the machine may foreordain some outcomes. In other words, biased training data may lead to discriminatory models in two respects: (1) the training data may view historical data influenced by prejudice as valid examples (referred to as labeling example problems); or (2) the training data may draw inferences based on a limited and biased sample of the population (or data collection problems).[53] An example of a labeling issue is the subjective judgment used to draw the line of creditworthiness for someone who has missed four credit card payments.[54]

---

[49]   T. Speicher, M. Ali, G. Venkatadri, *et al.*, Potential for Discrimination in Online Targeted Advertising (2018) 81 *Proc. Mach. Learn. Res.* 1–15, http://proceedings.mlr.press/v81/speicher18a/speicher18a.pdf.
[50]   Barocas and Selbst, above note 30.
[51]   *Ibid.*, p. 677.
[52]   *Ibid.*, p. 680.
[53]   *Ibid.*
[54]   *Ibid.*, p. 681.

FEATURE SELECTION

Ultimately, modelers must inform an algorithm of what and how to view the variables in the algorithm, and whether and how to incorporate those variables into the model. "Members of protected classes may find that they are subject to systematically less accurate classifications or predictions because the details are necessary to achieve equally accurate determinations reside at a level of granularity and coverage that the features fail to achieve."[55]

PROXIES

Some variables that are generally relevant to making a rational decision also serve as proxies for class membership. For example, someone who is a regular shopper at Victoria's Secret is likely a good candidate for a credit card offer from the retailer; however, it is also quite likely that the customer is a woman given that the store specializes in women's lingerie.

MASKING

Data miners might also intentionally "bias the collection of data to ensure that mining suggests rules that are less favorable to members of protected classes," or write the rules of the model to consider attributes at a high level, without the adequate granularity that would enable the model to differentiate between good credit risks and bad ones.[56]

ENCOURAGING THE GOOD AND PREVENTING THE BAD

Internal Models

As participants in a heavily regulated industry, banks depend on internal governance frameworks to mitigate risks. Banks commonly employ three lines of defense in their risk management systems: (1) frontline, or business, units that create risk; (2) internal risk management or compliance; and (3) internal audit.[57] The same structure can apply here to mitigate discrimination risk for machine-learning models. In the first line of defense, the modeling team should be careful to consider potential biases in their training data, data pools, and variables, as discussed above. The modeling team should consider and mitigate legal, regulatory, reputational, and other risks in developing the model.

Model risk management and compliance, in the second line, play slightly different and complementary roles. Model risk management should be concerned with assessing the statistical validity of a given model and the robustness of model development practices. Compliance, on the other hand, should focus on identifying and mitigating any previously unidentified problematic discrimination by the use of prohibited bases or close proxies. Compliance may also test a model for disparate impact and mitigate any disparate impact risks. Internal audit provides the third line of defense by conducting both general and targeted assessments of the risk mitigation practices and outcomes of the two preceding lines.

---

[55]   *Ibid.*, p. 688.
[56]   *Ibid.*, p. 692.
[57]   Office of the Comptroller of the Currency, *Corporate and Risk Governance, Comptroller's Handbook* (July 2016), pp. 46–7, www.occ.treas.gov/publications/publications-by-type/comptrollers-handbook/corporate-risk-governance/pub-ch-corporate-risk.pdf.

Third-Party Models

Banks are responsible for the use of their own internal models. But bank supervisors also hold banks accountable for models that vendors supply to them. Those models may contain risks that are challenging for banks to identify and mitigate because banks may not have much ability to modify those algorithms. Additionally, vendors may safeguard their proprietary models and make it difficult for banks to gain full line-of-sight into model variables and coefficients.

Compliance

One significant challenge for machine-learning models is how to mitigate disparate impact risk. As described above, despite the fact that a plaintiff may demonstrate that a model has a disparate effect on a prohibited basis, a creditor may defend against such a claim by showing that the model has a legitimate business justification and that there are no reasonable alternatives. In the main, creditors will likely be able to show that a machine-learning model has a legitimate business justification because the purpose of the model fits within traditional evaluations of creditworthiness. Even non-traditional purposes (for example, examining digital footprints for consumer payment behavior) are likely to have a legitimate business justification if they can be shown to have some reasonable, statistical bearing on a relevant creditworthiness decision.

EXTERNAL SUPERVISION

Regulators

In addition to the three lines of defense described above, financial regulatory agencies (for example, the OCC, the Federal Reserve Board, the CFPB, and the FDIC) also review models for discriminatory risk. The Federal Reserve Board's "Guidance on Model Risk Management" (SR Letter 11–7) sets out federal policy with regard to handling safety and soundness issues in the development, implementation, and use of machine-learning models, although its broad definition of a "model" covers other, less complicated models, including perhaps any statistical tool. Many, if not all, of these same considerations apply when a bank uses vendor services, as noted and discussed in the Fed.'s SR 13–19/CA 13–21.

Efforts to Address Risks of AI

As AI has grown in popularity, policymakers are looking more closely at developing policies that foster the great potential for AI applications and systems and leveraging these tools to improve government efficiency and operations. In 2016, the Obama administration sought to control risks of unconstitutional government action involving AI. To that end, the administration convened a series of workshops and published two separate reports outlining strategies for supporting the long-term development of AI through increased R&D, access to public datasets, greater collaboration between industry and government, and other strategies.[58] More recently, in May of 2018, the Trump administration convened an Artificial Intelligence

---

[58]   E. Felten, Preparing for the Future of Artificial Intelligence, *The White House Blog* (May 3, 2016), https://obamawhitehouse.archives.gov/blog/2016/05/03/preparing-future-artificial-intelligence.

Summit and announced several initiatives that his administration has underway, including increasing funding for AI, removing barriers to development, and using AI "to improve the efficiency of government services."[59] Even tech companies, who one would think would inherently resist regulation, have begun to call for the government to implement regulation now before risky technologies advance too far to be reined in.[60]

The US Congress has also introduced several pieces of legislation at the federal level, including the National Security Commission on Artificial Intelligence Act, which would create an independent National Security Commission on Artificial Intelligence; the House-passed Self Drive Act, which addresses the safety of automated vehicles; the AV Start Act, a bipartisan Senate companion that similarly tackles driverless cars; and the Future of AI Act, a bipartisan Senate bill that would create an advisory committee on AI issues.

Notably, there is some early movement by the government to address concerns regarding the use of these new tools for government work. The National Defense Reauthorization Act of 2019 establishes a National Security Commission on AI and directs the Department of Defense to conduct an in-depth review of how AI may be used in defense systems, including ethical considerations.[61] Additionally, the City of New York has passed a local law that establishes an "Automated Decision Systems Task Force" which will explore how New York City uses algorithms. The task force, the first of its kind in the United States, will work to develop a process for reviewing "automated decision systems," commonly known as algorithms, through the lens of equity, fairness, and accountability.[62] In addition, there are many other ethics-setting organizations, including "AI Now," an institute comprising leading researchers and developers, who are beginning to weigh in on government use of AI.[63]

Finally, the General Data Protection Regulation (GDPR) (discussed more fully in other chapters, this volume) may also have an impact on the use of algorithmic-based AI systems. As of May 25, 2018, all organizations doing business in the European Union must comply with the new European privacy legislation GDPR – arguably this includes both European and even foreign governments.[64] Article 22 of the GDPR says that the person "shall have the right not to be subject to a decision based solely on automated processing, including profiling, which produces legal effects concerning him or her or similarly significantly affects him or her." In practice, this means that, in the case of important decisions like mortgages, loans, job applications, school admissions, judicial decisions, etc., one must always offer the person the choice to have the possibility that the decision be made by a human being or with significant human involvement. For example, this passage has been interpreted to require an appeal for decisions that are made with no human involvement, such as when a machine-learning algorithm decides if you are eligible for a loan, for example, in order to prevent discrimination. Such expectation may apply to companies when they target citizens in Europe.

[59] Artificial Intelligence for the American People, Trump Administration (May 10, 2018), www.whitehouse.gov /briefings-statements/artificial-intelligence-american-people/.

[60] B. Smith, Facial Recognition: It's Time for Action, Microsoft (December 6, 2018), https://blogs.microsoft.com /on-the-issues/2018/12/06/facial-recognition-its-time-for-action/.

[61] John S. McCain National Defense Authorization Act, HR 5515, 115th Cong. (2019).

[62] Mayor De Blasio Announces First-In-Nation Task Force to Examine Automated Decision Systems Used by the City, New York City (May 16, 2018), www1.nyc.gov/office-of-the-mayor/news/251–18/mayor-de-blasio-first-in-nation-task-force-examine-automated-decision-systems-used-by.

[63] See, e.g., D. Reisman, J. Schultz, K. Crawford, and M. Whittaker, Algorithmic Impact Assessments: A Practical Framework for Public Agency Accountability, *AI Now* (April 2018), https://ainowinstitute.org/aiareport2018.pdf.

[64] D. Kawamoto, Will GDPR Rules Impact States and Localities?, *Government Technology* (May 3, 2018), www .govtech.com/data/Will-GDPR-Rules-Impact-States-and-Localities.html.

CONCLUSION

The use of algorithms has a tremendous potential to positively impact all manner of life, from credit to employment, to healthcare, and even armed services. However, discrimination and bias in the financial services industry may perpetuate inequality through sidelining vulnerable communities and populations. AI has the potential to help level the playing field by making financial services faster, simpler, and more accessible to protected classes. But without intentional care from stakeholders in the financial services industry, AI may generate very unintentional, costly, and unfair results.

In the United States, policymakers are taking steps toward creating regulatory spaces that foster innovation. The Bureau of Consumer Financial Protection has noted that it has not adequately provided for innovation space in the past, and has proposed that it should be more permissive toward the testing of new ideas in the future with more robust No-Action Letters and Product Sandboxes.[65] Both of these initiatives feature typical policy mechanisms used to promote innovation – an upfront notice of a proposed product or service with disclosures about possible risks and potential benefits in exchange for promises from regulators that they will not enforce statutory or regulatory provisions if the innovation is run as designed.

At the same time, policymakers should ensure that algorithms are sufficiently transparent and accountable. They should consider whether the adverse action requirements in the ECOA and FCRA, for example, are comprehensive enough to allow a customer to understand and address the reasons why the customer's request for credit was declined. They should also consider whether the kind of transparency that the Home Mortgage Disclosure Act brought to the mortgage market with its enactment in 1975 might be equally well-suited for a broader set of credit products. And they should also consider other policy mechanisms that further the goals of transparency and accountability, which are principles proven to have reduced discrimination in other contexts and in the past. While this chapter reviewed current developments in the use of algorithms for AI underwriting, with more advances in algorithms that act independently from humans, we expect more significant legal issues to develop.

---

[65] Policy on No-Action Letters and the BCFP Product Sandbox Notice of Proposed Rulemaking, 83 Fed. Reg. 64036 (December 13, 2018).

10

Algorithmic Competition, Collusion, and Price Discrimination

Salil K. Mehra

INTRODUCTION

Rapid, recent technological change has brought forward a new form of "algorithmic competition." Firms can and do draw on supercharged connectivity, mass data collection, algorithmic processing, and automated pricing to engage in what can be called "robo-selling." But algorithmic competition can also produce results that harm consumers. Notably, robo-selling may make anticompetitive collusion more likely, all things being equal. Additionally, the possibility of new forms of algorithmic price discrimination may also cause consumers to suffer. There are no easy solutions, particularly because algorithmic competition also promises significant benefits to consumers. As a result, this chapter sets forth some approaches to each of these issues, necessarily tentative, to address the changes that algorithmic competition is likely to bring.

Algorithmic competition is here. Mass data collection, algorithmic processing, and automated pricing – together, "robo-selling" – allow firms to do things faster, more efficiently, and in fact, quite differently. Firms can respond to market conditions with greater speed, and they can do so potentially while saving costs on market intelligence and sales functions. But just as crucially, robo-selling enables new models of goods and service provision by changing how markets behave and taking into account elements of consumer satisfaction beyond price and quantity that traditional markets were not well-suited for.

First, algorithmic competition can be a tremendous boon to consumer welfare. Regarding static welfare, it can reduce inefficient allocation by providing better matching between supply and demand. More importantly, the dynamic improvements through innovation – especially the potential to increase output at less cost – could be tremendous. Because of these benefits, we should not let overly zealous enforcement chill algorithmic competition.

As a result, it would be potentially very harmful to consumer welfare to punish algorithmic competition without a better understanding of its impacts. Moreover, the truth is that algorithmic competition promises real efficiencies and synergies for producers that, in competitive markets, can be passed on to consumers, as well as large improvements in service and product quality. As an example, consider the massive consumer benefits in increased supply, better pricing, and improved quality that Uber's matching and pricing algorithm has provided to urban commuters – notwithstanding claims in federal district court that the algorithm may foster collusion. Premature antitrust enforcement regarding algorithmic competition could inflict real harm to static and dynamic welfare.

Second, while it is true that, at the margin, parallel/interdependent pricing may become easier for firms to carry out, that does not justify imminent enforcement in this area, or new legislation, at this time. Algorithmic competition, or "robo-selling," involves using mass data collection, computer-driven algorithmic processing, and automated pricing to digest and respond to market changes at high speed. Drawing a legally enforceable line between parallel pricing that, without more, could be actionable as tacit collusion on the one hand, versus a benign normal response to observable market prices, on the other, will be impossible to do for the foreseeable future without substantial error costs. In other words, how can a regulator decide whether a firm is using technology to monitor and respond to a competitor's prices in a way that fosters coordination versus competition? The problem is the same as described by the Supreme Court in *Twombly*, but in a new context – without more, firms charging the same price could be colluding or competing.

That said, it makes sense for antitrust enforcers to stay on top of and build competencies in the area of algorithmic competition. Because algorithmic competition involves mass data collection and processing, it potentially will provide more data for competition enforcers to analyze. This data may help enforcers ferret out violations of existing law. It may uncover concerns that may lead to re-evaluation of law and policy for the future.

Third, and finally, algorithmic collusion should nonetheless be a focus for enforcement based on traditional antitrust theories. Antitrust enforcers across the political, ideological, and academic spectrum agree on the desirability of deterring explicit agreements to fix prices and restrict output. In cases such as *United States* v. *Topkins* and *United States* v. *Aston*, we have seen geographically distant conspirators use algorithm-driven software to fix prices on differentiated products with infrequent sales.[1]

These prosecutions demonstrate that software that fosters algorithmic pricing could open the possibility of anticompetitive collusion to a wider range of firms in three key ways. First, a wider scope of players may be capable of colluding on price or output across geographic distance. In the twentieth century, such coordination might have been limited to representatives of deep-pocketed firms – but, as in other areas, the Internet may lower transaction costs and shrink distances for price fixers.

Second, individuals or firms with an inclination to fix prices or outputs may find it easier to do so over a larger array of goods. As the wall décor prosecutions suggest, algorithmic price fixing may make cartelization possible in industries that have previously not been thought conducive – such as those with infrequent sales and differentiated products.

Finally, algorithmic collusion has the potential to grease the skids to price fixing conduct for those individuals with a weak or wavering inclination to pursue such illegal conduct. To some degree, software-powered algorithmic collusion carries the risk of playing a similar role

[1] See generally S. K. Mehra, De-Humanizing Antitrust: The Rise of the Machines and the Regulation of Competition, *SSRN Electronic Journal* (December 2013), www.researchgate.net/publication/272245466_De-Humanizing_Antitrust_The_Rise_of_the_Machines_and_the_Regulation_of_Competitionon; S. K. Mehra, De-Humanizing Antitrust: The Rise of the Machines and the Regulation of Competition, Temple University Legal Studies Research Paper (August 21, 2014), http://papers.ssrn.com/sol3/papers.cfm?abstract_id=2490651 (later published as S. K. Mehra, Antitrust and the Robo-Seller: Competition in the Time of Algorithms (2016) 100 *Minnesota Law Rev.* 1323, www.minnesotalawreview.org/wp-content/uploads/2016/04/Mehra_ONLINEPDF1.pdf); S. K. Mehra, Coming to a Mall Near You: Robo-Seller, *Temple 10-Q* (September 18, 2014), www2.law.temple.edu/10q/coming-mall-near-robo-seller/; S. K. Mehra, De-Humanizing Antitrust: The Rise of the Machines and the Regulation of Competition, *Columbia Law School Blue Sky Blog* (October 16, 2014), http://clsbluesky.law.columbia.edu/2014/10/16/de-humanizing-antitrust-the-rise-of-the-machines-and-the-regulation-of-competition/; S. K. Mehra, U.S. v. Topkins: Can Price Fixing Be Based on Algorithms? (2016) 7 J. *Eur. Comp. Law Pract.* 470; S. K. Mehra, Robo-Seller Prosecutions and Antitrust's Error-Cost Framework, *Competition Policy International Chronicle* (May 2017), www.competitionpolicyinternational.com/wp-content/uploads/2017/05/CPI-Mehra.pdf. This chapter draws significantly on the author's prior work in this area, as listed above.

vis-à-vis price fixing as, starting about a generation ago, Internet-based file sharing did vis-à-vis copyright infringement. That is, people who ordinarily would not consider committing crimes in real life (IRL) may be more likely to do so with a screen and a keyboard connection. Off-the-rack pricing software that makes price fixing "only a click away" may exacerbate this tendency. While this concern goes beyond antitrust, the tendency for Internet-powered interaction to lower inhibitions toward socially harmful behavior could give rise to more cases like *Topkins*.

In sum, antitrust enforcers should build their understanding and stay alert to the potential disruptive force of algorithmic competition. However, there is reason for cautious optimism that following traditional patterns of enforcement may work well for now.

COMPETITION

Algorithmic competition is the product of three recent and fast-developing technologies. First, mass data collection, made possible by the development of technologies such as smartphones (the iPhone was launched in 2007), effectively took computing and interconnection past desktop and laptop computers to a 24/7, anywhere format. Second, algorithmic processing, and related advances in artificial intelligence, makes it possible for firms to interpret this data. Finally, automated pricing enables fast reaction to the processed data.

The techniques, models, and firms that now make fast decisions on the sale of contemporary goods and services developed in the field of finance. Computers' ability to collect, analyze, and act transformed human-powered securities trading into a field powered by people and computers working in tandem, sometimes referred to as a kind of "cyborg finance." Similarly, the tools pioneered in finance have since proliferated in the retail environment, with mass data collection, algorithmic processing, and automated pricing together producing what may be called "robo-selling." Perhaps unsurprisingly, robo-selling first popped up in the online retail environment, notably with Amazon. And Amazon made these automated pricing response tools available to individual third-party sellers – resulting in an amusing anecdote in which two sellers of a biology textbook on fruit flies managed to bid up the ask price of the book to $23.7 million using automated pricing (no one purchased the book at that price).[2]

These "robo-selling" techniques quickly made their way into a wider array of businesses, including both the Internet and brick-and-mortar operations of traditional retailers. "Dynamic pricing" – altering pricing in response to demand-related factors such as weather – had previously been limited to select industries such as air travel and utilities. However, through the new availability of consumer data, robo-selling responds more directly to competitive conditions, and has been aided by the rise of firms such as Channel Advisor and Mercent/CommerceHub, which provide such consulting and operations services to retailers and other firms that do not have the in-house data-gathering and algorithmic-processing resources of Amazon or Wal-Mart.

By delegating competitive intelligence gathering and pricing decisions to a "robo-seller," firms gain several advantages. They can respond to changes in demand faster than is humanly possible. They can do so with increased accuracy. And, to the extent that it replaces costly market intelligence and sales functions, robo-selling may offer substantial cost savings. Furthermore, firms may be able to make increasingly granular estimates about demand –

---

[2]   C. Steiner, *Automate This: How Algorithms Came to Rule Our World* (Penguin, 2012), p. 1.

including the possibility of measuring *an individual*'s demand, not just that of consumers as a group.

Ultimately, whether these technologies should be seen as a competition law issue depends on their effects. In general terms, antitrust law takes aim at market-directed conduct that affects competition and that, while profitable to a firm, is harmful to consumer welfare. What few cases have so far surfaced in this area suggest that robo-selling will have important competition-law implications.

COLLUSION

Algorithmic competition has direct implications for antitrust law. Longstanding theory regarding collusion suggests that the increased speed and accuracy of algorithm-powered competition, all things being equal, will make anticompetitive collusion more attractive. While there are few cases, they suggest that algorithmic competition is not just a matter of theory, but will be a real challenge to antitrust law. While there is no silver-bullet solution, several approaches are possible.

Theory

Simple but robust models of oligopoly predict that algorithmic competition could lead to collusion that will harm consumers.[3] The basic Cournot model of oligopoly predicts that, as the number of firms in an industry decreases, they will price above the competitive level through their own action, without explicit agreement.[4] This intuition accords strongly with the available empirical evidence showing links between industry concentration and higher prices. Moreover, this result is a stable Nash equilibrium.

Furthermore, the Cournot model also can be used to think about whether firms in a concentrated industry will be able to maintain a durable, explicit price-fixing agreement.[5] The fundamental intuition is that, if they can make a durable agreement, firms in a concentrated industry can raise their prices further above the competitive level predicted by the non-cooperative Cournot equilibrium. However, the ability to make a durable agreement is complicated by the fact that, not only is such an agreement legally unenforceable as a contract, antitrust law treats such an agreement as per se illegal – sometimes criminally so.

As a result, firms that are party to an explicit price-fixing agreement have to weigh the benefits from adhering to it – incrementally higher prices to each firm on a smaller output – versus the benefit from not adhering to it – that is, cutting prices unilaterally, and capturing a larger share of the industry output than a firm's counterparty or counterparties, but at a lower price than the agreed-on cartel price.[6] The wrinkle is that, if a firm defects, it can expect its counterparties to retaliate – as a result, any gains from defecting now have to be tempered by the recognition that future gains may be lessened as the price-fixing agreement subsequently falls apart.

[3] Mehra, De-Humanizing Antitrust, *SSRN Electronic J.*, above note 1; Mehra, De-Humanizing Antitrust, Research Paper, above note 1; Mehra, Coming to a Mall Near You, above note 1; Mehra, De-Humanizing Antitrust, *Columbia Law School Blue Sky Blog*, above note 1.

[4] Mehra, Antitrust and the Robo-Seller, above note 1 (setting forth a more formal mathematical explanation of this model).

[5] *Ibid.*, pp. 1347–50.

[6] *Ibid.*, pp. 1347–8.

Algorithmic collusion makes such price-fixing agreements potentially more durable for several reasons. First, as speed of detection by counterparties increases, the gains from defecting are reduced, as retaliation and, correspondingly, future losses from the failure of the price-fixing agreement are increased.[7] Second, if algorithmic competition makes analysis of pricing in the market more accurate, it will be less likely that a price war breaks out due to noisy price information; this will make explicit price-fixing more durable.

Additionally, algorithmic collusion may make price-fixing agreements more stable by reducing the human factor that sometimes undermines such agreements. Algorithmic competition has the potential to reduce agency slack between principals and agents; in other words, displacing sales people who might want to raise their commissions by undercutting a price-fixing agreement their bosses agreed on. Moreover, to the degree that antitrust enforcers seek "email trails," algorithmic competition may lead to less of that. Finally, the leniency programs by which enforcers offer lighter punishments to cooperators, but harsh, potentially criminal penalties to the others, may have less success against algorithms and robo-sellers.

For a variety of reasons, therefore, we might expect algorithmic competition to lead to more instances of collusion. Whether it actually does is ultimately an empirical question – real-world cases can shed light on what scenarios may occur.

Cases

Before the prosecution in *United States* v. *Topkins*,[8] whether and how the law would deal with algorithm-related competitive harm was largely an academic matter. As the Organisation for Economic Cooperation and Development Secretariat's issues paper "Competition Enforcement in Oligopolistic Markets" (2015) observed: "In a relatively new area of research, Mehra (2014) and Ezrachi and Stucke (2015) argue that increased digitalization of market data and proliferation of algorithmic selling may increase the risk of tacit collusion and stretch traditional antitrust concepts developed for human actors."[9] The OECD Secretariat continued on to state that, after *Topkins*, "[t]he concern is not entirely theoretical."

Topkins, and the related prosecution in *United States* v. *Aston*,[10] took the interaction of competition law and algorithms from abstract to concrete. This leads into the following questions: What exactly was David Topkins accused of doing? And what did he plead guilty of doing? The answers to these questions largely overlap, although the information does contain a little more detail about the facts of the case than the plea agreement.[11] The information charged Topkins with a criminal violation of Section 1 of the Sherman Act (15 USC § 1) for entering into a price-fixing conspiracy.

The price-fixing conspiracy in *Topkins* was unprecedented for two different reasons: its e-commerce context, and its use of computer software to carry out algorithmic price-setting in

---

[7] *Ibid.*, pp. 1347–8 (explaining this result formally with mathematics).

[8] Plea Agreement, *United States* v. *David Topkins* (30 April 2015), www.justice.gov/atr/case-document/file/628891/download; Information, *United States* v. *David Topkins* (6 April 2015), www.justice.gov/atr/case-document/file/513586/download.

[9] Competition Enforcement in Oligopolistic Markets (2015), p. 5, www.oecd.org/officialdocuments/publicdisplaydocumentpdf/?cote=DAF/COMP%282015%292&docLanguage=En (omitting parenthetical text) (issues paper by the Secretariat prepared for the 123rd meeting of the OECD Competition Committee on June 16–18, 2015) (citing Mehra, De-Humanizing Antitrust (August 21, 2014), above note 1; A. Ezrachi and M. Stucke, Artificial Intelligence & Collusion: When Computers Inhibit Competition, Ox. Leg. Studs. Res. Paper No. 18/2015 (2015)).

[10] Indictment, *United States* v. *Aston* (27 August 2015), www.justice.gov/atr/file/840016/download.

[11] Cf. *Topkins*, Plea Agreement, with *Topkins*, Information.

line with the conspirators' agreement. Because the case did not proceed to trial, the publicly available information is somewhat limited – essentially that which can be gleaned from the information and the plea agreement. Nevertheless, the basic outline of the conspiracy can be discerned. First, the conspirators were alleged to have agreed to sell posters and similar wall décor via Amazon Marketplace, Amazon.com, Inc.'s ("Amazon") website for third-party sellers, and also to have explicitly agreed to coordinate their pricing via the use of the same software-embedded algorithm.

From a purely legal perspective, the case might not at first appear entirely novel; prosecutions have been brought before on the grounds that conspirators explicitly agreed to take steps that would assist price coordination. That said, the e-commerce context and the use of automated, algorithmic price-setting make the *Topkins* prosecution, in fact, unprecedented. Via Amazon Marketplace, Amazon, the largest Internet-based retailer in the United States, makes its customer base available to third-party sellers and also expands the goods available on its website without additional inventory investment. Amazon handles the payment between buyer and seller and charges the seller a fee for each sale, typically 15 percent of the sale price. Although Amazon makes the Amazon Marketplace commercial platform available to buyers and sellers, as the indictment noted, the third-party sellers, not Amazon, control all pricing and shipping decisions on the products they offer on Amazon Marketplace – Amazon was not itself charged as part of the conspiracy.

The Justice Department emphasized the unprecedented e-commerce context; Assistant Attorney General Bill Baer stated that "American consumers have the right to a free and fair marketplace online, as well as in brick and mortar businesses."[12] Similarly, initial reaction to the indictment focused on the expansion of antitrust into online commerce.[13] That said, the e-commerce aspect of the *Topkins* prosecution should probably not have been so surprising. As more consumers than ever shop on the Internet, some sort of e-commerce price-fixing case may have been inevitable. Moreover, there was no obvious reason before *Topkins* to think that the antitrust laws would not in principle apply to e-commerce.

By contrast, the other novel aspect of *Topkins*, the defendant's use of computer software to set prices for the conspirators algorithmically, potentially signals a challenging new area of enforcement for US antitrust agencies. According to the information, the conspirators allegedly "used commercially available algorithm-based pricing software to set the prices of posters sold on Amazon Marketplace" – the software "operates by collecting competitor pricing information for a specific product sold on Amazon Marketplace and applying pricing rules set by the seller."[14] The conspirators then allegedly agreed to adopt pricing rules that would coordinate their sales at "collusive, non-competitive prices on Amazon Marketplace"; Topkins was alleged to have "wr[itten] computer code that instructed" the "algorithm-based software to set prices of the agreed-upon posters in conformity with th[e] agreement" between the conspirators. To the same end, the plea agreement stated that the government would have proven at trial that "the defendant and his co-conspirators agreed to adopt specific pricing algorithms for the sale of the agreed-upon posters with the goal of coordinating changes to their respective prices."

[12]   US Department of Justice, *Former E-Commerce Executive Charged with Price Fixing in the Antitrust Division's First Online Marketplace Prosecution* (April 6, 2015), www.justice.gov/opa/pr/former-e-commerce-executive-charged-price-fixing-antitrust-divisions-first-online-marketplace (announcing the charges).

[13]   C. Osborne, *US DoJ Announces First E-commerce Antitrust Prosecution*, ZDNet (April 7, 2015), www.zdnet.com/article/us-doj-announces-first-e-commerce-antitrust-prosecution/.

[14]   *Topkins*, Information, pp. 2–3.

While *Topkins* and *Aston* were cases of explicit price-fixers using algorithmic processing to further their already-illegal agreement, more difficult cases may lie ahead. For example, in *Mayer v. Kalanick*, a private antitrust class action, Judge Jed Rakoff of the Southern District of New York ruled that antitrust plaintiffs may proceed toward trial against Uber with price-fixing allegations.[15] In that case, the plaintiffs have alleged that the Uber app, with its automated price-setting algorithm, is designed for price fixing because, instead of competing, they have agreed among themselves – including the firm's CEO Travis Kalanick, who also serves as a driver at times – to charge those prices, with Uber taking a cut of the fares.[16] Essentially, the plaintiffs made two separate but related charges: that Uber uses its algorithm-powered app to operate as a ringleader in a hub-and-spoke conspiracy and that, additionally, Kalanick, as a sometime driver for the service, is part of direct horizontal conspiracy with the other Uber drivers. While the Uber-related case was ultimately ordered to arbitration,[17] it seems to be fair to expect more litigation about similar algorithm-driven pricing models.

Approaches and Solutions

Currently, however, an increasing number of systems conduct algorithmic matching processes that potentially displace open, observable markets as the economy's "central nervous system." Consider the way in which Uber's former CEO describes its algorithm's relationship to the market: "[W]e are not setting the price, the market is setting the price ... [W]e have algorithms to determine what that market is."[18] Note that this algorithm-determined market coordinates 2 million drivers (worldwide)[19] with vertical agreements between the drivers and the algorithm-driven firm and, on the other side of the platform, vertical agreements between the platform and riders. While vertical integration has long existed,[20] it is only recently that it could be accomplished on this scale. Effectively, there is the emerging potential for markets themselves to be displaced.

More cases of algorithmic collusion should be expected. Because of the efficiencies that algorithmic competition may bring, it should probably not be rejected per se because of its potential for anticompetitive results. But as the competition they oversee becomes more complicated, enforcement agencies will need to develop increased technical competence to understand new forms of algorithmic competition.[21] Ultimately, new rules, guidelines, and presumptions may be developed as antitrust enforcement continues to wrestle with its ever-changing epistemological questions.

---

[15] *Meyer v. Kalanick*, 199 F. Supp. 3d 752 (SDNY 2016) (denying motion to dismiss).
[16] *Ibid.*
[17] *Meyer v. Kalanick*, 291 F. Supp. 3d (SDNY 2018) (ordering arbitration on remand from appeals court decision).
[18] M. Stoller, How Uber Creates an Algorithmic Monopoly to Extract Rents, *Naked Capitalism* (April 11, 2014), www.nakedcapitalism.com/2014/04/matt-stoller-how-uber-creates-an-algorithmic-monopoly.html.
[19] See G. Camp, Uber's Path Forward, *Medium* (June 20, 2017) (statement of co-founder), https://medium.com/@gc/ubers-path-forward-b59ec9bd4ef6.
[20] See R. Coase, *The Theory of the Firm: Origins, Evolution, and Development* (Oxford University Press, 1993 [1937]).
[21] See A. Ezrachi and M. Stucke, *Virtual Competition: The Promise and Perils of the Algorithm-Driven Economy* (Harvard University Press, 2016), pp. 228–31 (considering several possible approaches, including auditing algorithms and testing them in a "sandbox").

PRICE DISCRIMINATION

Algorithmic competition also brings the possibility of an increase in price discrimination by sellers vis-à-vis consumers.[22] Price discrimination (also called individualized pricing) is not necessarily harmful to consumers. However, combined with increasingly concentrated industries dominated by firms with market power, firms may try to make profits less by improving their efficiency or quality, and more by exploiting their pricing power. The ability to gather massive troves of data, process it algorithmically, and price automatically brings increased power to try to offer consumers individualized or personalized prices. This need not take the form of differentiated prices for the same product; it could also be done through individually targeted non-transferable offers and discounts.

Renewed concern about price discrimination also suggests that it is too soon to revert automatically to Chicago School assumptions. Price discrimination is pervasive. Even where sellers do not literally charge different prices to different buyers for substantially the same good or service (as in airline tickets, university educations, and new cars), they use other methods to effectively charge different prices to buyers whose willingness to pay differs, such as versioning (hardback vs. trade paperback vs. pocket paperback books), windowing (theatre vs. DVD vs. streaming), and two-part tariffs (cheap inkjet printers with expensive cartridges that effectively charge high-intensity users more).

The Chicago School antitrust's antipathy toward prohibitions against price discrimination reflects concerns about administrability and institutional competence. To address consumer welfare, it counsels that antitrust should focus on those practices that are privately beneficial, but socially harmful. The pervasiveness of price discrimination suggests at least that it benefits sellers privately. The overall welfare effects of price discrimination are ambiguous. While the classic economics textbook example of perfect, or first-degree, price discrimination by a monopolist is not only socially beneficial, it is as socially optimal as perfect competition because, in theory, it entails no deadweight loss;[23] however, it has been generally thought not to exist in the real world. It should be noted that, even were perfect price discrimination to be enabled by algorithmic competition, it would still represent harm to consumers in the shape of a welfare transfer from them to producer/sellers.

In the real world, imperfect price discrimination involves some consumers getting better prices than others, and a transfer from consumers to sellers. While effects like these make price discrimination unpopular with consumers,[24] in and of themselves, these effects do not equate to a loss of social welfare. That said, imperfect price discrimination – the kind that has so far been more likely to occur in reality – does tend to lead to reduced output and therefore

---

[22] See T. McSweeny and B. O'Dea, The Implications of Algorithmic Pricing for Coordinated Effects Analysis and Price Discrimination Markets in Antitrust Enforcement, *Antitrust* (Fall 2017), p. 75 (describing increased potential for algorithmic-enabled, consumer-focused price discrimination).

[23] It does, however, have strikingly different distributional results, in which consumer surplus is shifted to producer surplus, though in a 1:1 ratio under a hypothetical equilibrium that leaves price, quantity, and social welfare unchanged.

[24] A. Miller, What Do We Worry about When We Worry about Price Discrimination? (2014) 19 *J. Technol. Law* 41, 88 (stating that "public's dislike of unfairness, even in the face of other benefits, is likely to be a powerful factor that will limit the spread of price-discrimination strategies"); A. M. Odlyzko, Privacy, Economics, and Price Discrimination on the Internet, in N. Sadeh (ed.), *ICEC 2003: Fifth International Conference on Electronic Commerce*, ACM (ICEC, 2003), pp. 355, 358–9, www.dtc.umn.edu/~odlyzko/doc/complete.html (suggesting that unpopularity of price discrimination with the public will limit it or force it to take subtler or hidden forms).

deadweight loss,[25] at least vis-à-vis a theoretically competitive market with a single price. As a result, price discrimination could be seen as a socially harmful practice that is privately beneficial, and thus a target of antitrust policy.

That said, price discrimination has not been a prime target for government antitrust enforcement, and that is directly due to Chicago School antipathy rooted in questions about market power and incentive effects, a hangover from antitrust's Robinson-Patman statute, and the difficulty in practice of identifying price discrimination. First, because of the possibility of competitive response, it is usually thought that the ability of a seller to sustainably price-discriminate means that that firm already has market power; price discrimination simply allows it to earn more from market power than it already possesses. To the extent that that market power has been obtained without predation or exclusion, and instead represents returns to innovation or aggressive competition, concerns arise about the incentive effects of punishing price discrimination.

Additionally, because trying to discern consumers' willingness to pay takes effort and cost, even firms with market power may be dissuaded from undertaking price discrimination strategies. Second, for the past few decades, most of the antitrust community has lived in an uneasy tension with the Robinson-Patman Act,[26] which punishes a sub-set of price discrimination in a manner that cannot easily be reconciled with consumer welfare, and instead seems to reflect distributional concerns about, for example, preserving smaller retailers.[27] Price discrimination as an antitrust concern may have suffered from a kind of guilt-by-association. Finally, to date, trying to punish socially harmful price discrimination implies assessing the social welfare impacts of different prices on different groups, potentially a very complex task, especially if the price discrimination involves aspects other than or in addition to a uniform good at different prices.

However, changed circumstances might make us wonder about the existing consensus on price discrimination. Algorithmic price discrimination could require a re-evaluation. First, the ability to gather data on individual consumers, process it algorithmically, and set prices automatically has driven Silicon Valley to invest in technologically oriented economists in order to develop and spread price discrimination strategies.[28] As a result, algorithmic price discrimination may be becoming more widespread than consumer-aimed price discrimination was in the past. A newly tech-enabled pricing algorithm may serve to promote instances of price discrimination, which can either raise or lower social welfare.[29] This new reality relates to a key point of dispute at the dawn of Chicago School antitrust.

---

[25] Deadweight loss is a loss of produced output that causes lost consumer and/or producer surplus. See, e.g., H. Hovenkamp, *Federal Antitrust Policy: The Law of Competition and Its Practice* (West Academic Publishing, 2016), p. 772; D. Carlton, Price Discrimination (November 29–30, 2016), p. 5 (background note for OECD Competition Committee giving examples of how imperfect price discrimination can efficient or inefficient).

[26] See R. M. Steuer, Crossing the Streams of Price and Promotion under the Robinson-Patman Act (2012) 27 *Antitrust* 64, 64 (observing that "[d]espite all the criticism that has been heaped upon the Robinson-Patman Act since its enactment, and all the efforts at repeal, it appears that the Act will remain in effect as long as Congress continues to believe that small dealers need special protection to gain traction and survive in competition against larger rivals").

[27] See *Coastal Fuels* v. *Caribbean Petroleum*, 79 F.3d 182 (1st Cir. 1996) (discussing legislative history of the act and declining to extend standard in *Brooke Group* concerning harm by a seller to its competitor to price discrimination by a seller that harms some downstream buyers vis-à-vis others).

[28] J. Useem, How Online Shopping Makes Suckers of Us All (May 2017), www.theatlantic.com/magazine/archive/2017/05/how-online-shopping-makes-suckers-of-us-all/521448/ (describing economists working for Silicon Valley firms as involved in experiments aimed at using big data to "discern every individual's own *personal* demand curve" (emphasis in the original) and thus estimating willingness to pay in order to price-discriminate).

[29] J. Harrington, Developing Competition Law for Collusion by Automated Price-Setting Agents (2018) 14 *J. Competition Law Econ.* 351 n. 37.

Richard Posner had made the point that because price discrimination makes monopoly more profitable by transferring consumer surplus to the monopolist, firms would make additional investments to gain monopolies, and these investments might well be socially wasteful.[30] Robert Bork countered that Posner's observation "seem[ed] less an objection to permitting a monopolist to maximize his revenues through price discrimination than an additional reason to object to the achievement of monopoly," through means other than "ways of which antitrust approves," such as obtaining a patent or increased cost efficiency.[31]

But, in fact, Posner's argument has new bite to the extent that it is newly possible for firms to invest in technologies to gauge consumers' willingness to pay and to defeat arbitrage among consumers. Such investments may extend to lobbying government to make such data collection easier. And such investments may be exactly the kind of thing antitrust should aim to deter: actions that are privately optimal to the firm but socially harmful – which may result in some cases where the wealth transfer from consumers to producers (a social wash) outweighs the investment in price discrimination (a social loss). Moreover, in the online context, firms' investment in data gathering may draw a consumer response in investments in privacy – and a costly arms race may result.[32]

The question going forward is whether the potential for a consumer-to-producer transfer, rent-seeking, or a costly arms race justifies antitrust intervention. It is possible that consumers may be able to forestall these harms via algorithmically charged self-help.[33] Ultimately, as in the case of algorithmic collusion, algorithmic price discrimination is an area that deserves scrutiny going forward.

CONCLUSION

Because algorithmic competition is still in a nascent stage, any policy stance to take currently should be a flexible one. Antitrust enforcers will have to upgrade their technical skills and improve their ability to gauge empirically whether algorithmically driven practices hurt consumers. In effect, taking the long view of antitrust law – the same as it ever was.

---

[30]   R. Posner, *Economic Analysis of the Law* (Little, Brown & Co., 1972), s. 7.8.
[31]   R. Bork, *The Antitrust Paradox: A Policy at War with Itself* (Basic Books, 1979), p. 396.
[32]   Examples of this "arms race" dynamic include the history of digital rights management software and the work of those who circumvent such technology, the history of combatting online file-sharing, and attempts to weed out false speech online.
[33]   See M. S. Gal and N. Elkin-Koren, Algorithmic Consumers (2017) 30 *Harv. J. Law Technol.* 309, 318.

11

The Rule of Law and Algorithmic Governance

Rónán Kennedy

INTRODUCTION

Digital information and communications technologies (ICT) have been enthusiastically adopted by individuals, businesses, and government, altering the texture of commercial, social, and legal relationships in profound ways. In this decade, with the rapid development of "big data," machine-learning tools, and the "Internet of Things," it is clear that algorithms are becoming very important elements of modern society and a significant factor to consider when developing political or business strategies, developing new markets, or trying to solve problems.

All of these changes have raised many legal questions, and issues such as data protection and privacy, new business models for transport, and copyright infringement have become headline news and been explored in many academic articles. The solutions put forward often rely on algorithms. However, the use of these technologies by the state, particularly for control and management, has received much less attention until quite recently. The Snowden revelations brought mass surveillance into public and academic focus. Awareness of the misuse and abuse of information circulating on social media has brought this squarely into the public frame. The deployment of machine learning, particularly for sensitive applications such as policing or criminal procedure, has raised questions about racial profiling and the possibility of bias in algorithms or the data that they rely upon. However, many other aspects of government use of ICT go unexplored. Large public databases, obscure software systems, and creaky user interfaces are not inherently interesting to most people, although the algorithms that make them work are key to the functioning of the modern state.

This chapter explores some of these issues, and the deeper questions that they might raise for law in practice and in theory. In very recent years, stories have emerged that highlight the key role that processes of selection mediated by algorithms play in shaping the world around us. In that context, this chapter critically considers how to protect the rule of law in digitized government. It examines how ICT and algorithms can support the rule of law by helping to answer initial questions, providing access to legal texts and greater transparency in the court system. It also explores the ways in which the often unnoticed and unexamined biases in the development of software and databases can shift the locus of decision-making into the control of system designers and developers, whose work is unexaminable and unchallengeable.

Reliance on software may subtly alter governmental processes in ways that invisibly erode the protections encapsulated in the rule of law. Expert systems (which function using algorithms in the form of "if-then" rules) are already used as a support for decision-making by some police forces, government agencies, and courts, despite their occasional errors.

These decision-making (and ultimately, enforcement) systems will not be amenable to straightforward examination or easy challenge by those affected. They are supported or even implemented through algorithms which are not available to the public, amenable to unskilled scrutiny, or accessible to the putative decision-makers themselves. "Closed" systems render opaque the fact-gathering and decision-making processes for which they are used, thus reducing the accountability of public officials and reducing the possibility of effective input from civil society and skilled professionals. Databases may contain systematic errors because of biases in the ways in which they are constructed, such as the undercounting of particular racial or ethnic groups in a census, or the unequal willingness of different socio-economic groups to report problems to the authorities. All of these problems present deep challenges to the rule of law.

The chapter begins by setting out the theoretical and historical context for these developments, exploring what is meant by governance and algorithmic governance, and their various precursor movements. It looks in some detail at the role of algorithms in governance, the other elements of "institutional information infrastructures," such as input, storage, and output, and the recent focus on big data, artificial intelligence (AI), and machine learning. It then provides a brief overview of the rule of law. The next section looks in detail at the literature on the rule of law aspects of algorithmic governance, including the benefits and challenges which it creates. It concludes by highlighting that algorithmic governance is not necessarily good or bad from a rule of law perspective, but it requires careful attention to avoid some of the more dystopian visions which scholars have raised.

ALGORITHMIC GOVERNANCE IN CONTEXT

Before delving into the theoretical aspects of the issue, this section sketches the general contours of algorithmic governance.

Governance

"Governance" is a label that is used frequently, generally to describe the emergence of a new model of management of the economy, a move away from the territorial, hierarchical, and controlling structures put in place in the 1930s and 1940s to a paradigm which is more global and pluralist, but less interventionist.[1] Although it has many meanings in different contexts, one possible definition is as:

> ... a process of governing which departs from the traditional model where collectively binding decisions are taken by elected representatives within parliaments and implemented by bureaucrats within public administrations ... [It] is often described as a process of co-ordination within networks ... [T]he core meaning of governance [is] steering and co-ordination of interdependent (usually collective) actors based on institutionalized rule systems.[2]

---

[1]   O. Lobel, The Renew Deal: The Fall of Regulation and the Rise of Governance in Contemporary Legal Thought (2004) 89 *Minnesota Law Rev.* 262, 344.
[2]   O. Treib, H. Bähr, and G. Falkner, Modes of Governance: Towards a Conceptual Clarification (2007) 14 *J. Eur. Public Policy* 1, 3.

It is often associated with concepts such as the "decentered" state,[3] "post-regulatory state,"[4] or "new governance,"[5] which tend to use methods of control other than command-and-control legislative measures – "less rowing and more steering."[6] It will enlist private entities in regulation by, for example, requiring financial institutions to verify suspicious transactions or airlines to confirm the travel documents of international airline passengers; or through disclosure requirements which help consumers to make "better" choices (for example, energy requirements labeling).[7]

New Public Management

Part of the context for the development of algorithmic governance is the idea (or ideology) of "new public management" (NPM), which came to prominence in the 1980s and 1990s,[8] and made a significant difference to the practice of public administration.[9] It exchanges ideas with governance approaches, but also somewhat contradicts it, as central control is one of its main principles.[10] It can particularly be connected with "new governance" ideas.

NPM is a collection of ideas that have as their main focus the importation of private sector tools, such as efficiency, private sector approaches, privatization and outsourcing, market-based mechanisms, and performance indicators[11] into the public service. The techniques used include reducing budgets, creating quasi-autonomous agencies from larger units, decentralization of management, procurement, performance management of staff (including pay and conditions), and a focus on "quality."[12] NPM has been criticized for unrealistic hype; not fully embracing the market; destabilizing existing structures and displacing public sector ethics; and creating opportunities for corruption, avoidance of hard work, and fragmented service delivery.[13] Its influence seems to have peaked in the middle of the last decade.[14]

Digital Era Governance

"Digital Era Governance" (DEG) was an approach that somewhat replaced NPM. It signifies "a whole complex of changes, which have IT and information-handling changes at their

[3]   J. Black, Decentring Regulation: Understanding the Role of Regulation and Self Regulation in a "Post-Regulatory" World (2002) 54 *Current Legal Problems* 103.

[4]   C. Scott, Regulation in the Age of Governance: The Rise of the Post-Regulatory State, in J. Jordana and D. Levi-Faur (eds.), *The Politics of Regulation* (Edward Elgar, 2004).

[5]   G. de Búrca and J. Scott, Introduction: New Governance, Law and Constitutionalism, in G. de Búrca and J. Scott (eds.), *Law and New Governance in the EU and the US* (Hart, 2006).

[6]   L. McDonald, The Rule of Law in the "New Regulatory State" (2004) 33 *Common Law World Rev.* 197, 199.

[7]   P. N. Grabosky, Beyond the Regulatory State (1994) 27 *Aust. NZ J. Criminol.* 192, 193–5.

[8]   D. F. Kettl, Public Administration at the Millennium: The State of the Field (2000) 10 *J. Public Adm. Res. Theory* 7, 25–7.

[9]   C. Hood, A Public Management for All Seasons? (1991) 69 *Public Admin.* 3, 3.

[10] E. H. Klijn, New Public Management and Governance: A Comparison, in D. Levi-Faur (ed.), *The Oxford Handbook of Governance* (Oxford University Press, 2012), pp. 209–11.

[11] *Ibid.*, pp. 203–4.

[12] C. Pollitt, Justification by Works or by Faith? Evaluating the New Public Management (1995) 1 *Evaluation* 133, 134.

[13] P. Dunleavy and C. Hood, From Old Public Administration to New Public Management (1994) 14 *Public Money Manag.* 9, 10–12.

[14] P. Dunleavy, H. Margetts, S. Bastow, and J. Tinkler, New Public Management Is Dead – Long Live Digital-Era Governance (2006) 16 *J. Public Adm. Res. Theory* 467.

centre, but which have spread much more widely and take place in many more dimensions simultaneously than was the case with previous IT influences . . ."[15]

According to Dunleavy and others, DEG can be broken into three main themes:

REINTEGRATION. A response to the problems with NPM, this involves reassembling "many of the elements that NPM separated out into discrete corporate hierarchies." This is made up of nine elements: the rollback of agencification and fragmentation (through mergers, re-assimilations, culls, and the re-imposition of cooperative community-based structures); joined-up governance; re-governmentalization ("the re-absorption into the public sector of activities that had previously been outsourced to the private sector"); re-establishing or re-strengthening central processes; radically squeezing production costs; re-engineering back-office functions and service delivery chains; procurement concentration and specialization; the development of shared services; and the simplification of networks and the creation of "small worlds" (focused boutique agencies that do not duplicate the functions of others).

NEEDS-BASED HOLISM. This involves "[c]reating larger and more encompassing administrative blocs . . . [through] . . . 'end to end' re-engineering processes, stripping out unnecessary steps, compliance costs, checks and forms [and] developing a more 'agile' government that can respond speedily and flexibly to changes in the social environment." Its main components are interactive information seeking and giving (which is fundamental to what follows); client-based or needs-based reorganization; one-stop provision, ask-once processes; data warehousing; end-to-end service re-engineering; agile government processes; and sustainability.

DIGITIZATION CHANGES. Changes to IT become "genuinely transformative," at the extreme "moving towards a situation where the agency 'becomes its website.'" The main components of this theme are electronic service delivery and e-government; web-based utility computing; new forms of automated processes; radical disintermediation; active channel-streaming and customer segmentation; mandated channel reduction; facilitating isocratic (citizen-managed) administration; and moving toward open-book government.[16]

E-Government

The focus of this chapter is on the use of ICT in processes of governance. This can be understood as a sub-set of the broader topic of e-government, sometimes known as "digital government," which can be defined as:

> . . . the use of modern information and communication technologies, especially Internet and web technology, by a public organization to support or redefine the existing and/or future

---

[15]   P. Dunleavy, H. Margetts, S. Bastow, and J. Tinkler, *Digital Era Governance: IT Corporations, the State and E-Government* (Oxford University Press, 2008), p. 225.

[16]   *Ibid.*, pp. 227–43.

(information, communication and transaction) relations with "stakeholders" in the internal and external environment in order to create added value.[17]

E-Governance

A related concept, which is often represented as either supporting or supplanting e-government, is e-governance, which is also a loosely defined concept. Finger and Pécoud identify three different interpretations of the word: a new public management perspective of "satisfying the citizen/customer by means of delivering the services through the internet," where the state is seen as the principal actor and citizens as passive; a focus on "processes and interactions," with the state remaining at the center; and, finally, as "a set of tools in the hands of government, or rather in the hands of the administration," which is somewhat deterministic but does consider the role of values in government. They put forward instead:

> ... a dynamic concept, which implies the growing use of the [New Information and Communication Technologies] for the three State's main functions (e.g. e-Government, e-regulation and e-democracy), increasingly involving non-state actors at levels other than the national one ...[18]

Algorithmic Governance

Since the 1950s, when digital computers were first available as commercial products, to the present day, there has developed an enormous reliance on ICT as a support tool or direct means to implement policy. Through the processes outlined below, vast quantities of data are collected, processed, and presented to decision-makers or immediately used to arrive at conclusions. As digital technology scales up, we move to algorithmic governance,[19] which is the context for this chapter. This combines the ideas underpinning governance (coordination, collaboration, networking) with e-government (the use of ICT as a fundamental enabler) and e-governance (combining the role of the state and private sector actors and interests). Its underlying ideology often has its roots in NPM and DEG, and it is claimed to be the source of significant transformations in the management of modern societies.

Elements of algorithmic governance are present throughout our societies: filtering of Internet search results to exclude illegal material; automatic detection credit card fraud; and allocation of police patrols to areas where crime seems more likely to occur. One particularly important example of the large-scale deployment of these techniques and practices is in the so-called "smart city." These might include traffic lights that adjust how often they change based on traffic flow, dynamic public transport schedules that respond to demand, or energy pricing that automatically adjusts demand to keep it manageable. As technology improves, it may expand to include self-driving vehicles that operate in concert with each other, or pedestrians who are encouraged by their devices to travel through less-

---

[17] V. Bekkers and V. Homburg, E-Government as an Information Ecology: Backgrounds and Concepts, in V. J. J. M. Bekkers and V. M. F. Homburg (eds.), *Information Ecology of E-Government: E-Government as Institutional and Technological Innovation in Public Administration* (IOS Press, 2005), p. 6.

[18] M. Finger and G. Pécoud, From E-Government to E-Governance? Towards a Model of E-Governance (2003) 1 *Electronic J. e-Government* 1, 6–7.

[19] J. Danaher, M. J. Hogan, C. Noone, *et al.*, Algorithmic Governance: Developing a Research Agenda through the Power of Collective Intelligence (2017) 4 *Big Data Soc.* 1, 1–2.

busy or safer routes. It may even include automatic decision-making regarding waste collection, the development of new physical infrastructure, or the relative prioritization of repairs.[20]

As a result, there is much discussion at present of the role and salience of "algorithms" in public and private life. In most instances, this is shorthand for the ever-increasing importance of the collection and processing of data regarding individuals and the environment in which they live by digital technology as a key element in the oversight, management, and regulation of behavior. This encompasses more than processes of calculation; it involves large-scale systems for gathering and working with information. It is therefore necessary and useful to unpack the various elements of the concept of "algorithms" before exploring its ramifications for governance, particularly the idea of the rule of law.

Algorithmic Governance: Perfect Visions and Messy Realities

Although some of the discourse that surrounds algorithms in the media approaches deification, the concept is at heart quite a simple one. An algorithm is a set of instructions or tasks to be undertaken in order to solve a mathematical problem. Although the application of an algorithm does not require a computer, this is increasingly common, particularly for a problem of any complexity, and therefore the definition of the problem and the steps to be carried out must be quite precise, as computers are not capable of resolving ambiguity or intuiting required steps in the way that humans are. The usefulness of the algorithm will depend very much on the correctness of the initial specification, the data which is provided to it, and the final implementation: in other words, the algorithm may not solve the problem posed, or it may produce the wrong answer because it relies on inappropriate data or faulty logic. Ensuring that all of these issues do not arise in practice is challenging for a problem of any complexity, and is particularly so when the rules to be applied are themselves imprecise and rely on the human capacity to fill in gaps in a regulatory scheme. In addition, for some problem areas where the data is more difficult to manage ahead of time, the algorithm may be designed so that it "learns" by trying different approaches or parameters, which means that all of the possible behaviors are not specified or designed in advance.[21]

The abstract idea of a machine conjures a vision of something dispassionate, mindless, and efficient – algorithms can easily be misunderstood as immune to the emotions, biases, and errors that cloud the thinking of ordinary humans, and what we strive to achieve in Weberian "ideal-type" bureaucracy and judicial decision-making. Big data and the application of algorithms would seem to meet this criteria, but the reality is that both the underlying data and the computer systems involved are often tainted by existing social biases and prejudices.[22]

Other Elements of Institutional Information Infrastructures

Hanseth and Monteiro underline that information systems are being replaced by "information infrastructures." These have six key aspects: they are designed to support a wide range of activities, shared by a wide community in an indivisible fashion, open for new connections (whether from humans or technology), are socio-technical networks "encompass[ing]

[20] F. Zambonelli, F. Salim, F. Loke, *et al.*, Algorithmic Governance in Smart Cities: The Conundrum and the Potential of Pervasive Computing Solutions (2018) 37 *IEEE Technology and Society Magazine* 80, 81.

[21] D. R. Desai and J. A. Kroll, Trust But Verify: A Guide to Algorithms and the Law (2017) 31 *Harv. J. Law Technol.* 1, 23–30.

[22] S. Barocas and A. D. Selbst, Big Data's Disparate Impact (2016) 104 *California Law Rev.* 671.

technological components, humans, organizations, and institutions," "connected and inter-related, constituting *ecologies of networks*," and do not develop from scratch, but "through extending and improving the *installed base*." They argue that "[u]nderstanding information infrastructures requires a holistic perspective – an infrastructure is more than the individual components."[23] Understanding algorithmic governance requires an awareness that these new systems have institutional consequences: they become "institutional information infrastruc-tures" (IIIs), which enable, structure, and constrain public administration and governance.[24]

Although the principal focus of discourse is on algorithms, this discussion is somewhat unsatisfactory and incomplete, as the structuring, collection, and processing of data can also create problems. This chapter therefore explores the other aspects of IIIs. Algorithms are best understood as shorthand for a significant and complex socio-technical system, comprising elements such as data, software, hardware, and somewhat porous concepts such as "AI" and "machine learning." They are simply one element of a complex and dynamic assemblage of humans and heterogeneous technologies – sensors, networks, databases, software, displays, and so on – which assist in a decision-making process in which humans might or might not be involved. Although the focus of scholarly attention has tended to be on the algorithm, this is only one aspect of a process of selection, sorting, and decision-making, which culminates in (and is often subsumed into) the final calculation. Developing a full picture therefore requires defining the various elements of the application of ICT for public purposes, includ-ing criminal investigations, regulatory activities, and the administration of schemes of benefit and relief, and considering how they fit together. This has a relatively long history – Agar's history of the development of computing in government in the United Kingdom notes that as early as 1948, twenty-six government departments were using punched card machines, and by 1952, digital computers were being enthusiastically promoted within the British civil service as a tool for clerical work[25] – but this was initially largely invisible to the ordinary public or to the academic lawyer. This section will therefore explore these in somewhat more detail.

Input: The Eyes and Ears of the Algorithm

Every system of computer-based decision support or decision-making requires several essen-tial elements: methods of data input, data storage, calculation, and data output. The input of data will include the gathering and collation of statistics, the deployment of sensors, and (more recently) collecting information that already exists in digital form from the Internet, the World Wide Web, and social media. Decisions are made here, with significant con-sequences for the later aspects of the process: what statistics are to be collected, and from or about whom? Where are sensors located? What data do they collect? When do they operate? Similarly, if the public Internet is being trawled, the dizzying size and scope of data available requires choices to be made about who, where, and when. In many instances, these selections are not entirely made by the civil and public servants involved: existing constraints are important, such as the availability of appropriate off-the-shelf sensing devices, what they can measure, and where it is legally and politically possible to locate them.

---

[23] O. Hanseth and E. Monteiro, Understanding Information Infrastructure (August 27, 1998), pp. 4–47, http://heim .ifi.uio.no/oleha/Publications/bok.pdf (emphasis in the original).
[24] R. Kennedy, E-Regulation and the Rule of Law: Smart Government, Institutional Information Infrastructures, and Fundamental Values (2016) 21 *Information Polity* 77.
[25] J. Agar, *The Government Machine* (MIT Press, 2003), pp. 293–305.

Storage: Everything Must Be Filed Away

All of this information (which now reaches vast dimensions) must be stored somewhere. Databases have to be established. This again involves choices: what data will be recorded, and how? In many instances, government will be interested to know information about characteristics of individuals and populations that are sensitive, such as gender. There may be good reason for this – in order to properly plan for the future, it can be helpful to attempt to predict birth rates, for example, or to compare income equality in order to improve programs of affirmative action – but once this information is available, even if it was collected for a positive purpose, it may be applied for a discriminatory one. In addition, some of these categorizations may be contested in public discourse but much more difficult to challenge once the list of valid values for a database field are defined. Gender is again a key example:[26] is it simply binary – male or female – or are there more? Or a continuum? Arguing this issue with a functionary may yield some results, but if the database schema for the underlying public records system does not allow a variety of inputs, the victory may prove hollow when the new data is to be input into the system. The algorithm can become a tool for oppressing or erasing identities and issues that were not thought of when the system was designed or which are not comfortable or palatable to recognize.

Processing: Algorithms in Action

The data now needs to be acted upon, in further processes of sorting, classification, and calculation, in order to help guide decisions, which may affect individuals or populations and groups. The obvious example, and where many of these processes started, is in the calculation of tax liabilities. In theory, this should involve the transposition of rules and mathematical formulae defined in legislation in an accurate manner. This should also be the case for another early domain of adoption, the provision of social welfare benefits and assistance. The practice is less tidy as legislation is complex, not entirely reducible to precise mathematics, or encoded by sufficiently precise programmers. Choices abound. Humans make mistakes, or even deliberately misapply the statutory framework, and again these are difficult to challenge or change once the algorithm has been deployed.

Examples of the types of errors that can be made include incorrect decisions on eligibility for government benefits, inclusion on "no fly" lists or profiling as a potential terrorist, and mistakenly identifying parents as owing child support.[27] These arise for a variety of reasons. The underlying legal rules must be transformed into program rules, which means that definitions of terms such as "income" must be clarified very precisely. The transformation may be incomplete because the rules are too complex or may be changed in the near future. It may require creating new definitions of terms that are open-ended in the legal text, such as "week." There may be errors in the transformation itself ("programming bugs"), or new rules created without any basis in the underlying text, because of misunderstandings or the need to fill a gap in the regulatory regime. Significant concepts which should have the same meaning throughout may be redefined in different aspects of the interface and processing. Documentation may be missing or incomplete.[28]

---

[26]   M. Hicks, Hacking the Cis-Tem: Transgender Citizens and the Early Digital State (2019) 41 *IEEE Ann. Hist. Comput.* 20.

[27]   D. K. Citron, Technological Due Process (2008) 85 *Wash. Univ. Law Rev.* 1249, 1256–7.

[28]   D. W. Schartum, Dirt in the Machinery of Government – Legal Challenges Connected to Computerized Case Processing in Public Administration (1994) 2 *Int. J. Law Inf. Technol.* 327, 336–44.

"AI" and Machine Learning

Until recently, the use of ICT for public sector purposes was generally relatively straightforward programming in a traditional procedural language, which is (in theory) comprehensible by humans, at least those with sufficient training and experience (and perhaps also access to adequate documentation). There is now an increased use of what is labeled "AI," particularly a group of algorithmic techniques known as "machine learning," a shift toward predicting the future rather than recording the past, and more use by law enforcement and intelligence services of ICT as a support to the activities. These also involve choices, but ones that are even more difficult to identify, interrogate, or challenge.

AI is a term that captures a wide range of programming tools and techniques. Public understandings of the phrase tend to conjure up unrealistic and imaginary ideas of devices that can cogitate, conduct conversations, and display an element of free will. The reality is much more mundane: although some software programs ("chatbots") can fool humans into thinking they are people in particular limited interactions (such as on social media), much of AI is in fact the codification of particular responses to bounded and easily quantified situations. The game of chess was an early success, because the rules are relatively simple, the board is small, and the relative value of the pieces is easily measured. Other approaches, such as expert systems, have been tried in fields such as medicine and law, but have not yielded the promised results.

Machine learning is an approach that has achieved some spectacular successes in this decade, but although it implies a certain type of consciousness, it is at heart a form of pattern recognition. It uses large sets of information – generally known as "big data" – to identify correlations between phenomena, particularly ones that humans have not already noticed. This will usually rely on neural networks, which are designed to "learn" from the data provided.[29] The reader should not lose sight of the fact that although the language used to describe these algorithms might create the illusion that they are in some way conscious, they are all fundamentally machines, and often quite limited. There is not yet any general-purpose machine intelligence, and there may not be for quite some time to come, if ever. This limitation is an important element of the concerns which arise if governance processes cede control and decision-making to algorithms, which cannot respond with the flexibility of a human mind.

Output: Providing Results

At the end of the ICT system, the results of these deeply interconnected processes of collection and calculation must be made useful to people. The data must be output. The choices that are made here will significantly structure the understandings, perceptions, and procedures applied by the individuals involved.[30]

This may take the form of a spreadsheet, a database screen, a geographic information system (GIS), or some other method. The development and design of the user interface is another field in which choices are made, some of which could have important ramifications for the uses to which the data is put, and which are also difficult to challenge and change after the fact. For example, the use of particular colours, words, or phrases may manipulate the decisions made by the final decision-maker.

---

[29] A. P. Karanasiou and D. A. Pinotsis, A Study into the Layers of Automated Decision-Making: Emergent Normative and Legal Aspects of Deep Learning (2017) 31 *Int. Rev. Law Comput. Technol.* 170, 172–4.

[30] For an early study, see C. Sheppard and J. Raine, Parking Adjudications: The Impact of New Technology, in M. Harris and M. Partington (eds.), *Administrative Justice in the 21st Century* (Hart, 1999).

These ICT systems (which are often now massive) are therefore built on processes of discrimination. This is not negative in itself – every decision-making system must discriminate (in the sense of making choices and selections); what is problematic from a legal perspective is instances when these choices are made on the basis of forbidden categories, such as race or gender. The algorithms which are the core of modern information systems emerge from an existing social structure and tend to reproduce its biases, preconceptions, and blind spots.[31] However, it is relatively rare to see systems that are explicitly and consciously designed to engage in this type of illegal discrimination, and those who design such systems for public purposes seem to be aware of the potential problems.[32]

THE RULE OF LAW

The advent of algorithmic governance raises key questions for the rule of law. This section attempts to identify the essential elements of this concept and explore what connections exist between this high principle and the seemingly mundane tools of the bureaucrat. It is not an attempt to provide a comprehensive literature review on the rule of law. That would be a significant project in itself, particularly as the rule of law is difficult to define clearly.[33]

However, according to Lord Bingham, "[t]he core of the existing principle is ... that all persons and authorities within the state, whether public or private, should be bound by and entitled to the benefit of laws publicly and prospectively promulgated and publicly administered in the courts."[34] Craig states the same idea in shorter but perhaps more open terms: "A core idea of the rule of law to which all would subscribe is that the government must be able to point to some basis for its action that is regarded as valid by the relevant legal system."[35]

Beyond this fundamental notion that there are rules, and the rules are followed, there are different ways of conceptualizing the rule of law, perhaps best understood as being on a continuum from formal to substantive. Fletcher puts forward a simple framework of two versions of the rule of law: a narrow one of governance by and adherence to rules; and the second a wider, principles-based approach to the administration of justice.[36] Fuller calls these "procedural" and "substantive" versions,[37] which may also be known as "thin" or "thick."[38] Thin or procedural perspectives require proper legal authority, expect clear boundaries between acceptable and unacceptable behavior, and frown on retrospective rule-making. Substantive or thick perspectives build on these to also demand that the law support particular human rights.[39]

---

31 M. Janssen and G. Kuk, The Challenges and Limits of Big Data Algorithms in Technocratic Governance (2016) 33 *Gov. Inf. Q.* 371.

32 M. Veale, M. Van Kleek, and R. Binns, Fairness and Accountability Design Needs for Algorithmic Support in High-Stakes Public Sector Decision-Making, in R. Mandryk, M. Hancock, M. Perry, and A. Cox (eds.), *CHI '18: Proceedings of the 2018 CHI conference on Human Factors in Computing Systems* (ACM Press, 2018).

33 J. Rose, The Rule of Law in the Western World: An Overview (2004) 35 *J. Soc. Philos.* 457, 458; Select Committee on the Constitution, Relations between the Executive, the Judiciary and Parliament: Report with Evidence, 6th Report of Session 2006–07 (2006) HL 151-I97.

34 Lord Bingham, The Rule of Law (2007) 66 *Cambridge Law J.* 67, 69.

35 Select Committee on the Constitution, above note 33, p. 98.

36 G. P. Fletcher, *Basic Concepts of Legal Thought* (Oxford University Press, 1996), p. 11.

37 L. L. Fuller, *The Morality of Law*, 2nd edn (Yale University Press, 1969), p. 96.

38 L. Pech, The Rule of Law as a Guiding Principle of European Union's External Action (2011), p. 8, http://papers .ssrn.com/sol3/papers.cfm?abstract_id=1944865.

39 P. Craig, Formal and Substantive Conceptions of the Rule of Law: An Analytical Framework (1997) *Public Law* 467, 467.

Fallon describes four different models of the rule of law, which he says are "ideal types" to which various scholars adhere to a greater or lesser extent: historicist ("rule by norms laid down by legitimate law-making authorities prior to their application to particular cases"); formalist ("a clear prescription that exists prior to its application and that determines appropriate conduct or legal outcomes"); legal process; and substantive ("the intelligibility of law as a morally authoritative guide to human conduct"). He states that there are three purposes or values which the rule of law should serve: protecting people from the rule of the strong; providing a mechanism by which individuals can determine in advance the legality of their choices of action; and guaranteeing against arbitrary decisions by officials.[40]

Formalist Perspectives on the Rule of Law

The narrow perspective is, according to Rose, "procedural in nature, focusing on the prevention of arbitrary governmental action and the protection of individual rights."[41] Perhaps the most formalist theorist of the rule of law is Raz.[42] For him, "this means [both] that people should obey the law and be ruled by it ... [and] that the government shall be ruled by the law and subject to it." His conception of the rule of law includes notions of openness, stability, and availability of the law; and that it can act as a guide for the behavior of the subjects of the law.[43]

Another formalist theorist is Dicey. He saw the rule of law as having three elements:

> ... the absolute supremacy or predominance of regular law as opposed to the influence of arbitrary power ... [excluding] the existence of arbitrariness, of prerogative, or even of wide discretionary authority on the part of the government ...
>
> ... Equality before the law, or the equal subjection of all classes to the ordinary law of the land administered by the ordinary Law Courts ...
>
> ... the law of the constitution, the rules which in foreign countries naturally form part of a constitutional code, are not the source but the consequence of the rights of individuals, as defined and enforced by the Courts ...[44]

However, "[t]he rule of law in the sense articulated here could be met by regimes whose laws were morally objectionable, provided that they complied with the formal precepts of the rule of law."[45] Although there are examples of formalist approaches that have not slipped into authoritarianism, such as the United Kingdom, the existence or application of the rule of law is not by itself sufficient in order to ensure good administration or the protection of the rights of the citizen – Aristotle saw no conflict between the rule of law and the institution of slavery.[46] Unger highlighted that the creation of neutral rules is impossible, as the process which creates them cannot itself be free from bias. It is impossible for a society which is not initially equal to create a power structure which is neutral.[47] The problems of creating neutral rules become particularly salient when these rules are encoded in software.

---

[40] R. H. Fallon, Jr., "The Rule of Law" as a Concept in Constitutional Discourse (1997) 97 *Colum. Law Rev.* 1, 5–21.
[41] Rose, above note 33, p. 459.
[42] Craig, above note 39, p. 68.
[43] J. Raz, *"The Rule of Law and Its Virtue," The Authority of Law: Essays on Law and Morality* (Clarendon, 1979), pp. 212–14.
[44] A. V. Dicey, *The Law of the Constitution* (Macmillan, 1924), pp. 198–9.
[45] Select Committee on the Constitution, above note 33, p. 99.
[46] J. N. Shklar, Political Theory and the Rule of Law, in A. Hutchinson and P. Monahan (eds.), *The Rule of Law: Ideal or Ideology* (Carswell, 1987), p. 2.
[47] R. M. Unger, *Law in Modern Society* (The Free Press, 1977), pp. 178–81.

Substantive Perspectives on the Rule of Law

Therefore, other advocates of the rule of law see it as not simply providing a set of procedures to be followed, but also as embodying certain fundamental and inviolable values, and laying down important limits for the freedom of action of the state as a whole and the individuals working within that machinery. This requires compliance with notions of "good administration," is partly procedural and partly substantive in focus, and may incorporate some or all of the following principles: "legality, procedural propriety, participation, fundamental rights, openness, rationality, relevancy, propriety of purpose, reasonableness, equality, legitimate expectations, legal certainty and proportionality."[48]

In order to identify and assess the impacts which the widespread adoption of ICT in governance is having on the rule of law, it would be useful to have a detailed list of the most significant components of the rule of law in practice. However, despite the Venice Commission's optimistic claim that "it seems that a consensus can now be found for the necessary elements of the rule of law,"[49] the reality is that different scholars put forward quite different lists of the essentials.[50] In addition, as Fallon warns:

> The Rule of Law is best conceived as comprising multiple strands, including values and considerations to which each of the four competing ideal types calls attention. It is a mistake to think of particular criteria as necessary in all contexts for the Rule of Law. Rather, we should recognize that the strands of the Rule of Law are complexly interwoven, and we should begin to consider which values or criteria are presumptively primary under which conditions.[51]

However, there is agreement around core issues.[52] Notions of clarity, stability, and impartiality are essential to formalist readings of the rule of law. Even those who take this narrow view of the rule of law should be concerned about the implications of algorithmic governance for these core values for reasons which will be considered in detail shortly. Those who take a substantive perspective would also support these underpinnings, but would augment them with progressive ideas that seek to support and implement rights-based notions of protection for individuals.

Responding to "Ambient Law" with a Substantive Rule of Law

In critiquing algorithmic governance from a rule of law perspective, a key theoretical approach is the idea of "ambient law," or legal norms embodied in technology with Ambient Intelligence, where rules and values are encoded into hardware and software, which constrains the freedom of individuals.[53] The problems which this might create will be explored in detail shortly. However, it should be noted at the outset that in this context, Hildebrandt and Koops, two leading theorists on algorithmic governance, are clear in their preference for a substantive perspective on the rule of law, claiming that "[t]he procedural legitimacy of Ambient Law requires more than the mere promulgation of techno-norms by a legitimate public law-making body."[54] A conception of the

[48] Select Committee on the Constitution, above note 33, p. 101.
[49] European Commission for Democracy through the Law, Report on the Rule of Law (2011), p. 9.
[50] Fuller, above note 37, pp. 46–91; Raz, above note 43, pp. 214–19; Fallon, above note 40, pp. 7–8; Bingham, above note 34, pp. 69–81; European Commission for Democracy through the Law, above note 49, p. 9.
[51] Fallon, above note 40, p. 6 (emphasis removed).
[52] McDonald, above note 6, p. 203.
[53] M. Hildebrandt and B.-J. Koops, A Vision of Ambient Law, *Future of Identity in Information Society* (2007), www.fidis.net/resources/fidis-deliverables/profiling/d79-a-vision-of-ambient-law/.
[54] M. Hildebrandt and B.-J. Koops, The Challenges of Ambient Law and Legal Protection in the Profiling Era (2010) 73 *Mod. Law Rev.* 428, 456.

rule of law in the context of ICT must therefore ensure adherence to the minimum requirements of formalist notions, particularly protecting legality while avoiding legalism; balance discretion, accountability, and transparency; and ensure respect for the individual, the independence of the decision-maker, and the fairness of the process. It must also embrace openness, pay attention to design issues, and function in a flexible, consultative fashion in order to avoid hidden biases.

Brownsword develops this line of thinking in some detail. Algorithmic governance is instrumentalist in nature (applying rules for a fixed goal and to serve a particular interest group, without regard to the public interest or the greater good), and the rule of law should constrain or prevent this. The use of technological tools may facilitate overreaching by private or public entities, such as digital rights management systems that prohibit activities that are entirely legal, or the use of robots as prison guards. Such choices may infringe on human dignity and should therefore be prohibited. More significantly, if rules are to be inscribed and embedded in ICT infrastructure, this must be authorized in advance by a participatory deliberative process, and citizens must be aware that the rules-implementing system is in operation and have an understanding of its functioning. These rules must not be applied retrospectively. They should not demand the impossible. The laws (or at least their application in practice) should be clear, so that individuals understand (for example) where and why their car will not exceed a particular speed limit. They should not change rapidly. They should not be contradictory. They should operate in a way that is in keeping with the rules that have been publicly promulgated, and if it fails to do so in a way that gives the impression that the rules no longer apply, this should be a defense for conduct that breaches those rules. The rules should be general, rather than based on profiling. Technological management should not replace the social goal that individuals act in a moral fashion, in accordance with their own views and preferences. This may mean that portions of the criminal law are off-limits to technological management.[55]

ALGORITHMIC GOVERNANCE IN A RULE OF LAW CONTEXT

Law and Algorithms: A Recent Focus

It should be clear from the discussion above that the widespread adoption of ICT by bureaucracy is significant for law and legal theory, particularly the rule of law, but it has not been the subject of very much study until relatively recently. This is initially surprising; these technologies have been available for approximately half a century, used in government from the outset, and are widely available in developed countries in the present day. However, this lack of academic attention is also understandable, as the use of algorithms by the civil and public service has largely been in back rooms, not immediately obvious to, or clearly understood by, those not part of the secular priesthood of technologists until recently. In order to properly contextualize academic discussion of the rule of law implication of algorithmic governance, it is useful to briefly consider why and how it has been slow to develop.

The use of digital computer technology in public administration is inherently complex, dynamic, and cross disciplinary, bringing together aspects of science, information systems, information technology, engineering, organizational and social dynamics, and law. The particular topic of this chapter, which is the interaction

---

[55] R. Brownsword, Technological Management and the Rule of Law (2016) 8 *Law Innov. Technol.* 100.

between these new digital technologies and the rule of law, has rarely been discussed. The role of algorithms in governance has attracted some attention since the late 1960s, although the focus was more on privacy,[56] with some published research in the 1970s[57] and the 1980s.[58] It then dwindled as a topic of academic interest,[59] although Schartum identified the growing importance of computers as "case-processing systems" in the early 1990s.[60] The field of "public management information systems" was slow to develop during the 1990s, and was largely ignored by mainstream information systems journals; the focus was on the more public consequences, not on behind-the-scenes routine.[61]

From this distance, it is only possible to speculate as to why scholars have failed to pay sufficient attention to the role and impact of ICT in the governance process. Although changes were clearly underway in the 1990s, academics seem to have either been unaware of this or chose to ignore it. Coming to grips with these issues requires a level of technical skill and understanding which not all possess. As Parnas points out:

> Technology is the black magic of our time. Engineers are seen as wizards; their knowledge of arcane rituals and obscure terminology seems to endow them with an understanding not shared by the laity. The public, dazzled by the many visible achievements of modern technology, often regards engineers as magicians who can solve any problem, given the funds. Many are so awed by technological advances that they make no attempt to understand how things work.[62]

Perhaps this led to academics and bureaucrats being unwilling or unable to explore the topic of computerization in any great detail. Dunleavy puts forward more prosaic reasons for the neglect of paper- and ICT-based systems in public administration and public management theory: its low status; the delay in widespread adoption by government of new technologies; that information-processing functions generally operated without crises; the hierarchical distance between IT staff and high-level decision-makers; and a general theoretical neglect of the importance of information in the functioning of government.[63]

---

[56]   V. Packard, *The Naked Society* (Penguin Books, 1966).

[57]   L. Tribe, Policy Science: Analysis or Ideology? (1972) 2 *Philos. Public Aff.* 66; K. C. Laudon, *Computers and Bureaucratic Reform: The Political Functions of Urban Information Systems* (Wiley, 1974); A. Mowshowitz, *The Conquest of Will: Information Processing in Human Affairs* (Addison-Wesley, 1976).

[58]   J. N. Danziger, W. H. Dutton, R. Kling, and K. L. Kraemerand, *Computers and Politics: High Technology in American Local Governments* (Columbia University Press, 1982); W. H. Dutton and K. L. Kraemer, *Modeling as Negotiating: The Political Dynamics of Computer Models in the Policy Process* (Ablex Publishing Corporation, 1985); K. C. Laudon, *Dossier Society: Value Choices in the Design of National Information Systems* (Columbia University Press, 1986); K. L. Kraemer, *Datawars: The Politics of Modeling in Federal Policymaking* (Columbia University Press, 1987); K. L. Kraemer and J. L. King, Computers and the Constitution: A Helpful, Harmful or Harmless Relationship? (1987) 47 *Public Admin. Rev.* 93.

[59]   K. L. Kraemer and J. Dedrick, Computing and Public Organizations (1997) 7 *J. Public Adm. Res. Theory* 89.

[60]   Schartum, above note 28, p. 330.

[61]   H. J. Scholl, Electronic Government: A Study Domain Past Its Infancy, in H. J. Scholl (ed.), *E-government: Information, Technology, and Transformation* (ME Sharpe, 2010), pp. 12–13.

[62]   D. L. Parnas, Foreword, in L. R. Wiener (ed.), *Digital Woes* (Addison-Wesley, 1993), pp. ix–x.

[63]   P. Dunleavy, Governance and State Organization in the Digital Era, in R. Mansell, C. Avgerou, and D. Quah (eds.), *The Oxford Handbook of Information and Communication Technologies* (Oxford University Press, 2007), pp. 408–11; for an exception, see C. C. Hood and H. Z. Margetts, *The Tools of Government in the Digital Age* (Palgrave Macmillan, 2007).

There are some exceptions: issues arising from the use of expert systems in law were discussed from the 1980s onwards,[64] particularly by Philip Leith,[65] Giovanni Sartor,[66] and Richard Susskind.[67] The use of algorithms for legal decision-making was studied in Scandinavia in the early 1990s,[68] but very little has been published on this in English.[69] A key early writer on algorithmic implementations of regulatory schemes is Danielle Keats Citron.[70]

The Role of Algorithms in Processes of Governance

Although digital technologies – computers, the Internet, and the recent rise of "AI" – have undoubtedly brought about significant changes in how we communicate, how we engage in science, medicine, and engineering, and the internal management of many businesses, they have not changed the fundamentals of human nature or significantly altered existing patterns of individual or group power, social and economic capital, or dominant ideologies. Indeed, although it is an element in all of these, it cannot alter them all by itself, as ICT is itself socially constructed and co-created – both emerging from and altering the society which gives rise to it. This is key to understanding how algorithms are important to the rule of law.

As algorithms become increasingly important in commercial, governmental, and private activity, they are the subject of considerable media and academic interest. They are billed as transformative, uniquely enabling, and sometimes disruptive. If one believes the hype, they change everything. From the perspective of the rule of law, however, the reality is somewhat more complex: algorithms may not change anything fundamental, but could make change (particularly reform or social progress) impossible.

Unthinking implementation of computer-based systems can have effects which fundamentally undermine the limited formalist conception of the rule of law, and also its more substantive elements, such as natural justice and due process. Cuéllar highlights "the likelihood that the administrative state would work quite differently as the black boxes became ever more ensconced within it."[71] Although the rule of law seems to require rigidity, this is not the case. Allan highlights how "the wooden application of rules to inappropriate cases is often *unfair*";[72] this problem is multiplied when the application is algorithmic:

> Seemingly, algorithms could be a boon to due process because they formalize decisionmaking procedures ... At the same time, algorithms may involve rules of such complexity that

---

[64] J. Fremont, Computerized Administrative Decision Making and Fundamental Rights (1994) 32 *Osgoode Hall Law J.* 817.

[65] P. Leith, Legal Expertise and Legal Expert Systems (1986) 2 *Int. Rev. Law Comput. Technol.* 1; P. Leith, The Application of AI to Law (1988) 2 *AI & Society* 31; P. Leith, The Rise and Fall of the Legal Expert System (2010) 1 *Eur. J. Law Technol.* 179.

[66] G. Sartor, Artificial Intelligence in Law and Legal Theory (1992) 10 *Current Legal Theory* 1; G. Sartor, *Artificial Intelligence and Law: Legal Philosophy and Legal Theory* (Tano, 1993).

[67] R. E. Susskind, Expert Systems in Law: A Jurisprudential Approach to Artificial Intelligence and Legal Reasoning (1986) 49 *Mod. Law Rev.* 168; R.E. Susskind, *Expert Systems in Law: A Jurisprudential Inquiry* (Clarendon, 1987).

[68] J. Bing, Code, Access and Control, in M. Klang and A. Murray (eds.), *Human Rights in the Digital Age* (Glasshouse Press, 2005), pp. 204–5.

[69] An example is Schartum, above note 28.

[70] Citron, above note 27; D. K. Citron, Open Code Governance (2008) *Univ. Chi. Legal F.* 355.

[71] M.-F. Cuéllar, Cyberdelegation and the Administrative State, in N. R. Parrillo (ed.), *Administrative Justice from the Inside Out: Essays on Themes in the Work of Jerry Mashaw* (Cambridge University Press, 2017), p. 137.

[72] T. R. S. Allan, *Constitutional Justice: A Liberal Theory of the Rule of Law* (Oxford University Press, 2001), p. 128 (emphasis in the original).

they defy attempts to trace their reasoning. Is this the perfect perversion of due process: the uniform application of an inarticulable rule?[73]

In fact, indeterminacy may be quite important to the maintenance of the rule of law, as it allows for individual discretion and the inclusion of ethics in the decision-making process.[74] Regulators often have broad discretion, which makes it difficult to ascertain whether or not they are acting within the boundaries of their legal powers. This discretion is inevitable, but need not threaten the need for certainty and stability in the law.[75] Such discretion may be legitimate and desirable as it is not possible for the legislature to anticipate all the issues that may arise in the work of a particular regulator.[76] A certain amount of "fuzziness" may, in fact, be beneficial, as it allows the regulators and the regulated to deal with each other informally.[77] The widespread use of ICT in the infrastructure of administrative and regulatory systems raises important issues with regard to individual privacy and autonomy, as our every move may be tracked and automated systems may invisibly intervene in order to manipulate the information on which we base decisions or to mistakenly conclude that we have transgressed a rule that we have, in fact, observed.[78]

The use of databases, algorithms, and big data by government and bureaucracy has the potential to go seriously awry, with significant negative consequences for individuals and populations – the Australian Centrelink social welfare compliance system has required many thousands of citizens to needlessly prove that they were properly in receipt of benefits because it generated far too many false positives[79] – but the impact of error in these processes can often arise from mundane causes and affect a small number of people. For example, Parkin highlights how a seemingly simple requirement that the attendance of a recipient of welfare in New York City be positively recorded on a computer system by a caseworker tilted the system against individuals. Any "non-attendance" resulted in a loss of benefits, and therefore if a caseworker forgot to record a meeting or a legitimate excuse, there were financial consequences for the recipient.[80] These minor shifts in the rules may have legitimate roots in clearly articulated and promulgated laws, in which case they are unobjectionable from a formal perspective, but they may also be due to misunderstandings or mistakes on the part of systems developers.

Some prominent recent examples emerge from the criminal justice system. Alameda County in California allegedly used flawed software which led to individuals spending more time in prison than they should.[81] Several jurisdictions in the United States are relying on computer systems to predict outcomes for criminal suspects and defendants. These are

73 S. Barocas, S. Hood, and M. Ziewitz, Governing Algorithms: A Provocation Piece (2013), pp. 8–9, http://papers.ssrn.com/sol3/papers.cfm?abstract_id=2245322.
74 W. Hartzog, G. Conti, J. Nelson, and L. A. Shay, Inefficiently Automated Law Enforcement (2015) Mich. St. Law Rev. 1763.
75 P. M. Shane, The Rule of Law and the Inevitability of Discretion (2013) 36 Harv. J. Law Pub. Policy 21.
76 K. C. Davis, Discretionary Justice: A Preliminary Inquiry (University of Illinois Press, 1971), p. 25; McDonald, above note 6, p. 214.
77 M. Cohn, Fuzzy Legality in Regulation: The Legislative Mandate Revisited (2001) 23 Law & Policy 469, 482.
78 Hildebrandt and Koops, above note 54.
79 S. Park and J. Humphry, Exclusion by Design: Intersections of Social, Digital and Data Exclusion (2019) 22 Inf. Commun. Soc. 934.
80 J. Parkin, Adaptable Due Process (2012) 160 Univ. Pa. Law Rev. 1309, 1357–8.
81 C. Farivar, Lawyers: New Court Software Is So Awful It's Getting People Wrongly Arrested, Ars Technica (2016), https://arstechnica.com/tech-policy/2016/12/court-software-glitches-result-in-erroneous-arrests-defense-lawyers-say/; C. Farivar, Public Defender Lambastes Judicial Ruling to Not Fix Flawed Court Software, Ars Technica (2017), https://arstechnica.com/tech-policy/2017/04/public-defender-lambasts-judicial-ruling-to-not-fix-flawed-court-software/.

used to identify individuals who are likely to commit crime and locations where they are likely to do so, by judges to assist in determining sentences, and by prison officials in deciding how to manage particular prisoners.[82] On a more positive note, a pilot project in New York City using big data and machine learning proved more accurate than judges at predicting which defendants were likely to offend if released on bail, while not considering their race, a development which is likely to lead to a re-balancing of the prison population.[83]

Possibilities and Challenges

To summarize, then, it is clear that ICT may be both a support and an impediment to the rule of law. This section explores both dimensions, beginning with the possible positive impacts.

Algorithms Supporting the Rule of Law

The practice of law is a profession that relies heavily on the availability, processing, and distribution of information. ICT is therefore a tool that has obvious application for lawyers, and for non-lawyers who need to interact with the legal system (which can often be challenging for individuals). Pasquale argues that a complementary automation, where digital technology provides intelligence augmentation, is the way forward.[84]

For example, machine learning could assist in predicting the answers to legal questions, or could even answer those questions directly in some specific situations (particularly commercial contexts like taxation, company law, securities regulation, and competition law).[85] It could also lead to much greater transparency and accessibility in court processes.[86] Online capabilities also open possibilities for "reputation-based governance," providing citizens with easy access to the information that they need to assess different proposals in a standardized fashion and thus making the state "legible" to its citizens.[87] Algorithm-based tools, such as apps that help to navigate issues such as the right to silence, provide an opportunity to redress social imbalances more toward individuals who have less power or capacity to engage with the legal system (particularly the police).[88]

Nonetheless, despite the possible positive outcomes from the widespread use of ICT in legal and regulatory systems, details matter. What little initial research has been done indicates that the results can be "very uneven and mixed."[89] It is therefore necessary to spend some time considering how ICT can be a barrier to the effective implementation of the rule of law.

---

[82] A. Chander, The Racist Algorithm (2017) 115 *Mich. Law Rev.* 1023, 1033.
[83] T. Simonite, How to Upgrade Judges with Machine Learning, *MIT Technology Rev.* (March 6, 2017).
[84] F. Pasquale, A Rule of Persons, Not Machines: The Limits of Legal Automation (2019) 87 *Geo. Wash. Law Rev.* 1.
[85] B Alarie, A Niblett, and A Yoon, Regulation by Machine, 30th Conference on Neural Information Processing Systems (NIPS 2016) (2016).
[86] F. Richardson, The E-Justice Revolution (2010) 64 *Int. Bar News* 37, 38–9.
[87] L. Picci, Reputation-Based Governance and Making States "Legible" to Their Citizens, in H. Masum and M. Tovey (eds.), *The Reputation Society: How Online Opinions Are Reshaping the Offline World* (MIT Press, 2011).
[88] P. Gowder, Transformative Legal Technology and the Rule of Law (2018) 68 *Univ. Toronto Law J.* 82.
[89] D. Zinnbauer, False Dawn, Window Dressing or Taking Integrity to the Next Level? Governments Using ICTs for Integrity and Accountability: Some Thoughts on an Emerging Research and Advocacy Agenda (2012), p. 11, http://papers.ssrn.com/sol3/papers.cfm?abstract_id=2166277.

Algorithms Undermining the Rule of Law

Algorithmic governance systems have four characteristics that make them potentially subversive of the rule of law, many of which have already been touched on:

> First, along the traditional continuum between rules and standards, software lies at the extreme rule-bound end ...
>
> Second, software can regulate without transparency ...
>
> Third, software rules cannot be ignored. Parties facing a decision made by software can, at best, take steps to undo what software has wrought ...
>
> Fourth, software is more fragile than other systems of regulation. Hackers can turn its plasticity against it, and its automated operation means that unintended consequences are shielded from human review. Its immediacy also speeds up failures.[90]

Algorithmic governance may challenge the ideals underpinning the rule of law in a number of ways. It may become too difficult to change. It may give rise to a system of rules which is no longer recognizable or understandable by lawyers. It may produce rules that try (but fail) to constantly adjust themselves to changing circumstances. What is perhaps most likely is that it will produce elements of all of these, creating a heterogeneous hybrid of law, algorithm, and infrastructure which makes adaptation to changing circumstances very unpredictable.

Unadaptive Ambient Law

The first failure mode of algorithmic governance, from a rule of law perspective, is a system that can no longer change in response to new circumstances or requirements, leading to a disconnect between the law as described in legal texts and as applied in practice. Bowker and Star claim that ICT hides "the arguments, decisions and uncertainties and processual nature of decision-making ... Thus values, opinions, and rhetoric are frozen into codes, electronic thresholds and computer applications."[91] Despite the characteristics of speed, flexibility, and responsiveness which are often ascribed to modern ICT, the reality is often much more prosaic. Software development is notoriously difficult,[92] with many high-profile failed public sector projects,[93] and systems may, in fact, become "encrusted ... with earlier ways of thinking,"[94] too costly to modify, and a barrier to change.

This fossilization of policy in ICT goes beyond what would already take place in a non-technocratic bureaucracy because modifications to ICT are generally not possible in the short term; shortcomings in the system are too expensive to work around, even on a small scale; and the costs, complexity, and difficulty of ICT have tended to grow over time. These difficulties make administrators reluctant to make minor changes to such systems; and many organizations outsource their ICT operations, which imposes additional barriers to change in the short term.[95]

---

[90]   J. Grimmelmann, Regulation by Software (2005) 114 *Yale Law J.* 1721, 1723–4.

[91]   G. Bowker and S. L. Star, Knowledge and Infrastructure in International Information Management: Problems of Classification and Coding, in L. Bud-Frierman (ed.), *Information Acumen: The Understanding and Use of Knowledge in Modern Business* (Routledge, 1994), p. 187.

[92]   See, e.g., L. R. Weiner, *Digital Woes* (Addison-Wesley, 1993).

[93]   See, e.g., M. Moran, *The British Regulatory State: High Modernism and Hyper-Innovation* (Oxford University Press, 2003), pp. 178–9; Agar, above note 25, pp. 375–9.

[94]   C. Bellamy and J. A. Taylor, *Governing in the Information Age* (Open University Press, 1998), p. 156.

[95]   Dunleavy *et al.*, above note 15, pp. 25–7.

Algorithms can seriously hamper the ability of administrators and regulators to gather and process the information that is necessary for their decision-making. This claim may initially seem counter-intuitive – ICT seems to make it much easier to assemble and assimilate information – but once a dedicated information system is put in place, this will constrain what can and cannot be brought to the attention of the regulator.[96] Indeed, the system may seek to shape the decision-making process, subtly optimizing in one direction or another through "nudges."[97] Of course, regulatory processes have long depended on the collection of structured data through forms, but a computer-based form is even less flexible as it is often impossible to ignore "required fields" (even if they do not apply) or to add additional information in the margins.

Algorithms can also constrain the hearing of an individual's case. The computer system will often follow a fixed "script," which enrols and constructs both administrator and citizen into a particular pattern of interaction. It can be difficult (although not impossible) to deviate from this. In practice, what is likely to happen is that, through force of habit, regulatory staff will simply follow familiar procedures without taking the time to consider if they are appropriate for the particular individual with whom they are dealing.

Algorithms can significantly channel internal processes. This is not always inappropriate – indeed, properly applied business process re-engineering can go a long way toward improving the efficiency of a governance system – but can lead to inflexibility over time. ICT can also lead to bias within the system. This can sometimes be obvious, but may also be quite insidious, difficult to identify, and even more difficult to root out.

As we move into an age of algorithmic governance, it will become increasingly difficult to challenge the outcomes of regulatory processes. In addition, as these systems rely increasingly on data-driven inferences and correlation through processes of machine learning, the normative aspects of the law will lose salience. Cause-and-effect, goals, and intentions become less important, and the system becomes more complex, perhaps too much so for humans to understand. As human autonomy is constrained, individual capacity to make moral choices may atrophy, particularly if data-driven systems seem to reach arbitrary conclusions or exclude legal texts or understandings because they are not part of the input to the model.[98]

Untethered Ambient Law

The second failure mode may be a system of governance that exerts complete control but cannot be challenged in any meaningful or constructive way. Bullinga predicts, with some hyperbole, a future of omnipresent and ambient technology with a significant regulatory dimension:

> Permits and licenses will be embedded in smart cars, trains, buildings, doors, and devices. Laws will automatically download and distribute themselves into objects in our physical environment, and everything will regularly be updated, just as software is now automatically updated in your desktop computer.
>
>   . . .

---

[96] U. Pagallo and M. Durante, The Pros and Cons of Legal Automation and Its Governance (2016) 7 *Eur. J. Risk Regul.* 326.

[97] K. Yeung, "Hypernudge": Big Data as a Mode of Regulation by Design (2016) 20 *Inf. Commun. Soc.* 118, 121–2.

[98] E. Bayamlıoğlu and R. Leenes, The "Rule of Law" Implications of Data-Driven Decision-Making: A Techno-Regulatory Perspective (2018) 10 *Law Innov. Technol.* 295, 304–11.

> In the future, all rules and laws will be incorporated into expert systems and chips embedded in cars, appliances, doors, and buildings – that is, our physical environment. No longer will police officers and other government personnel be the only law enforcement. Our physical environment will enforce the law as well.
>
> . . .
>
> Automatic law enforcement will be used for environmental regulations, traffic and safety laws, bookkeeping rules, and all social security issues involving proof of identity.[99]

In a similar (although less far-fetched) fashion, Gil-Garcia paints an appealing picture of a "smart State," in which

> [s]ensors, virtualizations, geographic information technologies, social media applications, and other elements ... function like a brain to manage the resources and capabilities of government, but also the participation of social actors, the physical infrastructure, and the machines and equipment using that infrastructure ...
>
> Governments would ... use sensors and HD cameras to obtain information about air quality, electric power consumption, public safety, road conditions, and emergency preparedness, among many other policy domains. Citizens would be helping government to identify problems and to develop solutions in a crowd-sourced fashion.[100]

From a rule of law perspective, these systems could be problematic. From a formalist perspective, such an arrangement raises doubts regarding its validity: the machine may not have any capacity to provide an explanation of what legal rules it is relying on. Even if it does, it may not provide access to the program source code or underlying data that translate that rule in software, because of intellectual property or security concerns. If those hurdles can be overcome, the explanation may not be comprehensible by an unskilled individual.

From a more substantive perspective, the difficulties are magnified. As has been explained in some detail above, and is a recurring concern in the academic literature, the various elements of algorithmic governance (the institutional information infrastructure) are all vulnerable to bias, prejudice, or lack of diversity. Human rights may not be properly respected, marginalized groups might be excluded, and the goals of the system can sometimes be inappropriate.

Whatever one's perspective on the rule of law, it should be clear that in "closed" systems, where source code or data are not available to the public, the fact-gathering and decision-making processes for which they are used are much less comprehensible from the outside. This reduces the accountability of public officials and the possibility of effective input from civil society and skilled professionals.[101] Gaining access to information in the first instance may be a significant challenge; if that information is only usable with the aid of sophisticated computer hardware and software, an already disadvantaged group is further marginalized. In addition, decision-making processes are being supported or even implemented through software which is not available to the public, amenable to unskilled scrutiny, or accessible to the putative decision-makers themselves.[102]

It is difficult to hold software developers accountable for their work – there are "many hands" involved in constructing computer-based systems, bugs are seen as inevitable rather than preventable, it is easy to shift blame from humans onto "the computer," and end-user

---

[99] M. Bullinga, Intelligent Government: Invisible, Automatic, Everywhere (2004) 38 *The Futurist* 32, 32–4.
[100] J. R. Gil-Garcia, Towards a Smart State? Inter-Agency Collaboration, Information Integration, and Beyond (2012) 17 *Information Polity* 269, 275.
[101] Citron, above note 70, p. 357.
[102] Citron, above note 27, pp. 1254–5.

license agreements disclaim liability on the part of the manufacturer.[103] This problem is worsened by the widespread adoption of ICT and the computerization of these scientific models in ways that are not easily amenable to public scrutiny, thus creating significant challenges for the operation of the rule of law. The use of complex computerized models in, for example, a risk-oriented approach to regulation may create the perception or reality of arbitrary decisions. The increased sophistication of the technological and scientific models that are deployed in decision-making may disempower those suffering from economic and educational disadvantage, further exacerbating problems of inequality.

These concerns have led some researchers to query whether law, and the rule of law, can survive a shift from written texts to digital rules as the fundamental technology of the law. Hildebrandt paints a picture of a world in which devices have an element of agency, where humans interact only with the relatively limited front-end to a sea of data, and where machine learning creates new understandings (perhaps even new versions) of the world. Governance and regulation include simultaneous iterative testing of different approaches (including offences and penalties). However (as has been discussed in some detail above), the software which will underpin this involves hidden biases and assumptions, and the ways in which machine learning "thinks" about the law will not match the ways in which humans think. The end result will be a "legal" system which develops from the inscrutable processes of "AI," has very real consequences for the rights of individuals, and cannot be effectively contested by those who suffer as a result.[104]

Overly Flexible Ambient Law

Closely related to this phenomenon of an environment where the law is encoded in the things that we interact with, and those things prevent us from breaking the law, is the idea of "self-driving laws," which will automatically adjust themselves to changing circumstances and perhaps even apply punishments without human intervention.[105] There may even be a legal singularity, a dramatic shift to an entirely new approach to governance in which the algorithm is fundamental:

> The legal singularity will arrive when the accumulation of a massive amount of data and dramatically improved methods of inference make legal uncertainty obsolete. The legal singularity contemplates complete law ... The legal singularity contemplates the elimination of legal uncertainty and the emergence of a seamless legal order, which is universally accessible in real time. In the legal singularity, disputes over the legal significance of agreed facts will be rare. There may be disputes over facts, but, once found, the facts will map onto clear legal consequences. The law will be functionally complete.[106]

These seemingly perfect IIIs bring the prospect of a legal system that is out of human control, which raises concerns. Law is an enterprise that at its core relies on abstract ideas and values, and feeling its way toward outcomes in an emergent fashion. Algorithmic governance will tend to classify, standardize, and enforce a single preferred outcome. The idea of so-called "personalized law" ignores the importance of legal theory to the practice and application of law. Theory provides a framework to constrain and limit what is important, and what

---

[103] H. Nissenbaum, Accountability in a Computerized Society (1996) 2 *Sci. Eng. Ethics* 25, 28–36.
[104] M. Hildebrandt, Law as Information in the Era of Data-Driven Agency (2016) 79 *Mod. Law Rev.* 1.
[105] A. J. Casey and A. Niblett, Self-Driving Laws (2016) 66 *Univ. Toronto Law J.* 429.
[106] B. Alarie, The Path of the Law: Towards Legal Singularity (2016) 66 *Univ. Toronto Law J.* 443, 445–6.

must be measured, whereas a big data system will include everything measurable. The ambiguity of legal rules is a strength, not a weakness; it allows them to adapt to changing circumstances and situations. Algorithmic governance systems (for the reasons outlined above) will adapt much more slowly to changes in society. Indeed, those changes could themselves be driven by the algorithm, as individuals work out what it rewards and punishes, in an emergent, unpredictable way. It is unrealistic to expect a computer system to capture all of the tacit information and knowledge that people rely on to make day-to-day decisions. It will instead be a limited perspective on the world which will be static and inflexible, rather than facilitating the evolution and experimentation which is necessary for a dynamic, living legal system.[107]

Imperfect and Unevenly Distributed Hybrids

All of these issues notwithstanding, the development of algorithmic governance (and the hype surrounding its underlying technological enablers) has a momentum which is likely to see it become increasingly widespread. However, unlike the visions of utopia or dystopia which can be found in some of the academic literature on algorithmic governance, the outcomes of this are likely to be messy. The process of software development is very difficult, as has been alluded to above. Despite the "Internet of Things" being a rapidly developing phenomenon, not every part of the built environment includes connected devices. Individuals will not all simultaneously upgrade and replace their possessions (such as motor vehicles) to the latest versions, which include sufficient software and sensors to enmesh them into the system of governance. There are many aspects of our individual lives that take place away from tools that can measure, record, and manage them.

Nonetheless, as policymakers continue to embrace algorithmic governance, we can expect that aspects of all of the problems outlined above will arise, but to varying degrees in different domains of activity. Some aspects of law and regulation – perhaps taxation – will become too difficult to change because of the weight of accumulated software. Others – perhaps policing – will involve the application of rules which are no longer understood by those who rely on the predictive models that govern the allocation of resources. Still others – perhaps access to public transport – will be governed by rules that claim not to permit any breaches by anyone in any circumstances whatsoever.

Whether or not any of these initiatives will succeed will depend on how well they are thought out in advance, the capacity of the private sector to provide the necessary tools, and how individuals respond. People can be expected to resist new methods and modalities of control, and to turn the technology back on the implementer. For example, consider a new government scheme to encourage individual fitness. The state provides cheap or free step counters, which can upload data to the Internet. Insurance companies are encouraged to offer discounts to those who reach a particular daily activity level. Some individuals respond by placing their step counters in specially designed frames which rock the devices, simulating walking.

The final outcome will be an unevenly distributed system of algorithmic governance, with some successes and some failures.

---

[107]   C. Devins, T. Felin, S. Kauffman, and R. Koppl, The Law and Big Data (2017) 27 *Cornell J. Law Pub. Policy* 357.

CONCLUSION

This chapter has explored an issue which has, until recently, not been addressed by academic commentators or policymakers: the absence of consideration of the rule of law in the increasing deployment of algorithms in government and regulation. A significant point of departure for the algorithmic governance agenda is the ideology of modernization, with its tools of quantification, rational decision-making, and central control, coming together in movements such as New Public Management and Digital Era Governance. Closely related to the importance of these developments is the growth of the ability of science and information to facilitate regulatory initiatives and to be put to use as tools for corporate and individual behavior change, ideas with considerable force but significant issues in practice. The (perhaps unbridgeable) gap between scientific models and full understanding of the natural world, together with the local, contingent, and unpredictable nature of human responses to external intervention, raise questions about the ultimate realizability of the project of modernization. It seems impossible to measure precisely all of the factors relevant to a policy initiative, and what works well in one location, industry, or culture may be dysfunctional in another.

From this conclusion, three significant issues emerge from a rule of law perspective. First, IIIs can become inescapable, inflexible systems of classification, codification, and decision-making. Second, as algorithmic governance becomes more prevalent, these systems of control (particularly those embedded in everyday devices) may constitute a method of governance which is no longer entirely under human control. Finally, there may be attempts to produce a system of algorithmic governance which is perfectly responsive, reconfiguring itself on an ongoing basis without human intervention.

However, what is likely to transpire in reality will be a mixture of all of these, to different extents, in different problem domains. As has been outlined above, there is an ideological and practical connection between NPM, DEG, and algorithmic governance. This manifests most strongly in the focus on measurement, with the aim of making the populace visible to the state. However, theorists such as Foucault, and particularly Scott,[108] have critiqued these efforts as ultimately unsuccessful. Nonetheless, as a dominant mindset within public administration, they will continue. Another related ideological preference is what has been labeled "surveillance capitalism" – the use of connected devices to track the activities, interests, and preferences of individuals in order to better advertise and sell to them.[109] As long as this continues, the private sector will continue to develop tools that can be repurposed by the public sector for their own ends. Indeed, the rise of the concept of the "smart city," which is a key example of algorithmic governance in practice, is partly the result of well-targeted marketing by technology companies seeking to develop new markets in the wake of the financial crisis.[110]

Just as there are ideologies which push for greater application of algorithmic governance, there are also social factors that seek to control it. Disasters can significantly limit the take-up of a technology (for example, airships were significantly set back by the Hindenburg fire), and

---

[108] J. C. Scott, *Seeing Like a State: How Certain Schemes to Improve the Human Condition Have Failed* (Yale University Press, 1998).

[109] S. Zuboff, Big Other: Surveillance Capitalism and the Prospects of an Information Civilization (2015) 30 *J. Inf. Technol.* 75.

[110] A. M. Townsend, *Smart Cities: Big Data, Civic Hackers, and the Quest for a New Utopia* (W. W. Norton, 2013), pp. 30–3.

it may be that salient failures may come to sufficient public attention to lead to a ban or heavy restrictions on the use of algorithms in particular contexts, such as criminal investigation or trial. Some technologies, such as facial recognition software, may be perceived as infringing too much on basic values, leading to significant general push-back. Legal rules may also be important: European data protection law is often called upon as providing a solution to issues of fairness, discrimination, and opacity in decision-making, but it may provide only incomplete solutions,[111] and its global application is limited.

However, although the hype may fade, the technology (and its extravagant promise) will remain, and development will continue. The eventual outcomes are difficult to predict, but the extreme case of the ubiquitous legal singularity seems unlikely. It is not clear whether it is technically viable or socially inevitable. It is also undesirable from the perspective of legal theory. In addition, if it does take place, it will be quite brittle, for the reasons discussed above: it will depend on a fragile infrastructure of insecure, error-prone software and hardware. It will never achieve full or perfect coverage without blanketing the entire planet in a single network, and will always be vulnerable to individual human resistance (or the lack of electric power). Nonetheless, there may be particular domains where the range of data to be collected is limited, it is particularly amenable to being measured in strictly numeric terms, and there is merit in developing a very responsive system of algorithmic control. We may see "self-driving laws," which reconfigure themselves with little or no human intervention, in areas such as taxation, utility regulation, or securities trading.

It is therefore important to remember that algorithmic governance is not simply supportive or destructive of the rule of law. There is a complex interrelationship between the two, and there is still considerable scope for positive outcomes.

[111]   L. Edwards and M. Veale, Slave to the Algorithm: Why a Right to an Explanation Is Probably Not the Remedy You Are Looking for (2017) 16 *Duke Law Technol. Rev.* 18.

12

Governance of Algorithms

Rethinking Public Sector Use of Algorithms for Predictive Purposes

Anjanette H. Raymond and Ciabhan Connelly[*]

INTRODUCTION

In recent years, algorithms have been incorporated into practically every aspect of our lives. They have come to determine whether you will be approved for a mortgage – as well as the interest, how much you will pay for insurance, the likelihood you will commit a crime, the terms of your sentencing, and the number of police patrols in your neighborhood. It is therefore difficult to imagine a more important consideration than the manner in which we are comfortable with algorithms making these decisions. As their presence in our daily lives grows, attention must be paid to their influence on society. Without these conversations we will increasingly rely on this technology, and it will become more difficult to disentangle the legal and ethical pitfalls from systems that have become necessary in our daily lives.

In many ways, these algorithms are already essential: "[AI systems are] being introduced in critical areas like law, finance, policing, and the workplace, where they are increasingly used to predict everything from our taste in music to our likelihood of committing a crime to our fitness for a job or an educational opportunity."[1] The implications of this ubiquity are often ill-understood. Consider a recently reported example, based on the experience of a man named Russell:

> In 2014, a computer system called MiDAS plucked his file out of the Michigan Unemployment Insurance Agency database and calculated, without any human review, that he had defrauded the unemployment system and owed the state of Michigan approximately $22,000 in restitution, penalties and interest – the result of a supposed $4,300 overpayment – plus Michigan's customary 400 percent penalty and 12 percent interest. Then, still untouched by humans, MiDAS began to collect. It seized more than $10,000 from Russell by electronically intercepting his tax refunds in 2015 and 2016. He knew nothing about the fraud determination until his 2015 tax refund disappeared.[2]

This is the consequence of the blind implementation of what is referred to by data scientists as a "black box" – an algorithm that is far too complicated for a human to understand the rationale behind its decisions. Unsurprisingly, many of the most effective algorithms we know how to implement are black boxes. Most individuals – like Russell – faced with black boxes, trust the algorithm to be right. Math is objective, after all. Since these algorithms are based in

---

[*] All opinions are those of the authors. Thank you to our wonderful editor Dakota Coates.

[1] AI Now 2017 Report, cited in New Zealand Human Rights Commission, Privacy, Data and Technology: Human Rights Challenges in the Digital Age (May 2018), p. 3.

[2] G. Cherry, Built by Humans, Ruled by Computers, The Michigan Engineer News Center (February 5, 2019), https://news.engin.umich.edu/features/built-by-humans-ruled-by-computers/.

math it is easy to assume that they must also be objective, even if the math is being performed on messy real-world data – often taken from biased and human-generated sources. In fact, research in human behavior and perception tells us – even in the face of absurdity and clear error – people trust algorithms and inherently assume the machine picked up something we overlooked. We believe in the math and assume an unbiased metric that correctly spits out outcomes – simply put, we believe the algorithms.

Yet, the algorithm-based administration and fraud collection system implemented by the state of Michigan – accusing almost 50,000 Michiganders of unemployment fraud – was wrong. Not a little wrong, in fact "the state found that more than 90 percent of those accusations were false."[3] Algorithms' predictions can be wrong, or worse they can be illegal, implicitly using race or other protected identifiers to make decisions, but avoiding scrutiny due to our blind trust in mathematics. When deployed by the state, often under the dual promises of improving efficiency and reducing costs – or, ironically, reducing bias – the systems are deployed with minimal human oversight or monitoring. The machine runs without consequence – except to those negatively impacted by the system.

That is the crux of this chapter: While there is little impact associated with an algorithm that makes a bad movie recommendation on Netflix, other algorithms have the power to deny you access to financial opportunities, to prevent you from qualifying for jobs, to incarcerate you for a longer time, or to accuse you of fraud. This chapter argues that the use of algorithms must be governed based on the potential impact of outcomes upon the lives it touches. Governance of algorithms must be reconsidered, in a multi-disciplinary discussion where those with technical, legal, and ethical expertise collaborate to help us better understand how these algorithms can, do, and should interact with society. There is no better place to start the conversation than the data that feeds the algorithm.

ALGORITHMS ONLY WORK WITH DATA

The use of algorithms in the public sector has received attention in recent years as more and more states struggle with the ubiquitous gathering, repurposing, and storage of data that seeks to feed the algorithms that drive much of our daily existence. For example, in May of 2018 the New Zealand Human Rights Commission warned that "public sector use of algorithms for predictive purposes could lead to unfair treatment of individuals or groups and says steps should be taken to ensure such practices conform with human rights and ethical standards."[4] Others have expressed similar concerns – from the United States to the United Kingdom – especially in the area of public sector use. Although these algorithms are implemented in the public sector, it's important to understand that much of the data used within these systems is gathered by entities in the private sector. As such, governance focusing solely on the regulation of public sector algorithms is a limited and incomplete solution. As other scholars have noted,[5] data scientists in both the public and private sectors must improve at identifying how data were gathered, and understand the nature of a dataset before using it to design an algorithm. Governance must be multi-dimensional – and the first area of consideration is the regulation of data. "The collection, storage, sharing and re-purposing of personal

---

[3]   *Ibid.*
[4]   New Zealand Human Rights Commission, Privacy, Data and Technology: Human Rights Challenges in the Digital Age (May 2018).
[5]   See T. Gebru, J. Morgenstern, B. Vecchione, *et al.*, Datasheets for Datasets (2018).

information, whether obtained by surveillance or interception, or freely provided by individuals, poses a challenge to universally recognized human rights."[6]

While this chapter is not about human rights, per se, human rights law and the various local laws and standards that recognize and arise from fundamental rights are an important consideration in the conversation.

> International human rights law provides an instructive framework for the protection of the affected rights, including the right to privacy and its permissible limitations, freedom of expression and opinion, freedom of association, the right to be free from discrimination, and the right to be free from unreasonable search and seizure.[7]

Although local law will recognize and hopefully embed these protections into regulation, the silos and differentiations between the various supra-national, national, and local laws often create problems in the global data-driven environment. Consider the EU law on General Data Protection Regulation 2016/679, which provides data protection and privacy for all individuals *within* the European Union and the European Economic Area.[8] While this is an EU Regulation, its impacts are much wider as the agencies and businesses outside of the European Union that handle personal data of individuals *residing in* the European Union will need to ensure that their internal data-processing procedures comply with the Regulation. Moreover, under the Regulation, the European Union is empowered to review and assess data laws in the destination state. If data protections are viewed as inadequate, the European Union may prohibit EU-generated data from being processed in the country. This is, of course, a far-reaching Regulation that could impact the global data environment.

In addition, the Asia Pacific Economic Cooperation Privacy Framework[9] sets out principles and implementation guidance for the public and private sectors which control the collection, holding, processing, use, transfer, or disclosure of personal information. Key principles include: (1) preventing harm – preventing misuse of personal information and consequent harm to individuals; (2) notice – individuals should know that information is collected about them and the purpose for which it is used; (3) collection limitation – limited collection of information to the purposes for which it is collected; and (4) use limitation – limits the use of personal information to fulfilling the purposes of the collection.[10] These principles will hopefully set the stage for a wider conversation about the exact parameters of the Framework; however, it is the existence of the issue coming to the forefront of consideration that is most impressive. As best practices are emerging in many places, regulation will undoubtedly follow close behind. Yet much remains to be done to ensure wider acceptance of frameworks and best practices.

Data Gathering within the Criminal Context

Designers of algorithms are often at odds with the right to privacy because they depend on ingesting as much data as possible. And while an individual's right to privacy from a business

---

[6] New Zealand Human Rights Commission, above note 4, p. 8.

[7] *Ibid.*

[8] Regulation (EU) 2016/679 of the European Parliament and of the Council of 27 April 2016 on the protection of natural persons with regard to the processing of personal data and on the free movement of such data, and repealing Directive 95/46/EC (General Data Protection Regulation), https://eur-lex.europa.eu/legal-content /EN/TXT/?uri=CELEX%3A32016R0679.

[9] Which applies to all twenty-seven member countries, including the United States.

[10] See APEC Privacy Framework, APEC#205-SO-01.2 (2005).

entity is an important consideration, privacy often falls by the wayside when government surveillance is done in an effort to protect society. This argument arises as scholars and courts do not consider privacy as an absolute right; instead it is best thought of as a balance between the citizens' right to privacy and the needs of society. Most would agree that governments are expected to protect the interests of their citizens and, thus, may be required to gather intelligence to fetter out dangerous criminal activity or for national security purposes. Yet even this type of data gathering via surveillance is not without limits. In general, international scholars and industry experts promote the principles of legality, necessity, and proportionality when establishing the boundaries for government surveillance of its citizenry.

The mixing of these divergent regimes is beginning to show strain, as the government's need to protect society is now intertwining with business-related data gathering. For example, in 2018, France announced that it would begin searching social media accounts in an effort to crack down on tax fraud.[11] France is not alone of course. The US government also uses social media to search for red flags in tax filings and uses social media to catch disability fraud[12] – a tactic used by many insurance companies in various countries across the globe.[13] Consider the US Internal Revenue Service (IRS) example, as Kimberly Houser and Debra Sanders exposed in The Use of Big Data Analytics by the IRS: Efficient Solutions or the End of Privacy as We Know It?,[14] as its staff shrank, the IRS has turned to mining social media and large datasets in search of taxpayers to audit. The argument is that the information published on social media (and similar places) is posted by the individual and posted in an open environment (i.e. the public domain). This is, of course, based within a quagmire where individuals have a "reasonable" expectation of privacy – and the definition of "reasonable" may change depending on who is making the argument. For example, in the 2010 case of *United States v. Warshak*,[15] a federal appeals court affirmed that citizens have a reasonable expectation of privacy in their emails. In this instance, the Court held the government to the standards of "legality, necessity, and proportionality" – standards that most consider absolute, and thus, could become part of wider implementation and privacy-based protection efforts.

Should such a standard be extended to social media and other digital communications? Readers should not be too quick to answer yes – for two key reasons. First, email has been analogized to a letter since its inception (as silly as this idea is in terms of the technology). That analogy is part of creating the expectation of privacy; the average citizen would say "of course, my letters cannot be opened by others, it is private." In fact, the law envisions email as a letter in a digital communication environment. It's an incorrect analogy, but one that stuck a long time ago. Moreover, an email is addressed to a specific person/people – just like a letter. While this is an overly simplistic (and incorrect) understanding of the technology, it is the common view, and therefore reasonable in a certain sense regarding legality. The same cannot be said about Facebook or LinkedIn; no part of the general platform resembles a letter or private communication. In fact, both platforms have separate portions that resemble

[11] See K. Phillips, Tax Authority Will Look at Taxpayers' Social Media in Fight against Tax Fraud, *Forbes* (November 11, 2018).
[12] See T. Lee, US Government Proposes Using Social Media to Catch Disability Fraud, *Ubergizmo* (March 12, 2019); C. Hansen, Trump Administration Wants to Monitor Disability Recipients' Social Media, *US News* (March 11, 2019).
[13] See S. Hickey, Insurance Cheats Discover Social Media Is the Real Pain in the Neck, *The Guardian* (July 18, 2016), www.theguardian.com/money/2016/jul/18/insurance-cheats-social-media-whiplash-false-claimants.
[14] See K. Houser and D. Sanders, The Use of Big Data Analytics by the IRS: Efficient Solutions or the End of Privacy as We Know It? (2017) 19 *Vand. J. Ent. Technol. Law* 817.
[15] *United States v. Warshak*, 631 F.3d 266 (6th Cir. 2010).

a private communication environment. Thus, while some may have an expectation of privacy when using these platforms, that expectation is likely not "reasonable."

In addition, will we draw a hard line between different digital communications, such as an open versus closed page on Facebook? While this might be possible, can you imagine asking the platform to retain records of when and where individuals post things in "open" versus "closed" environments – or to explicitly make these legal distinctions even when the operation of their specific platform may be even more complicated. Furthermore, how do we define "open" in a large digital environment: 100 "friends"? It seems hard to argue you are sharing in a closed environment when 1,000 of your "best friends" have the information.

Of course, the suggestion to reconsider an individual's right to privacy from government intrusion is now fraught with difficulty as many search efforts amount to nothing more than mass government surveillance. In today's fast-paced, big data world, much of the individual-generated data is ubiquitously gathered, retained, and shared, hence the data is often used to ferret out individuals to be considered for more surveillance. It is important to understand that gathering evidence *after* an agency determines the potential of existing criminal activity is significantly different from collecting information on everyone to select individuals upon whom more robust surveillance will be performed. This is the line that must be drawn, and it must be drawn now. The government must be held to the standard of "legality, necessity, and proportionality" when surveilling citizens. The law must be one that requires a warrant to gather evidence, based upon probable cause. And while modern technology has increased the government's ability to perform mass surveillance, it is not the ability to gather evidence – and the ease in which it is done – that should define the standard to be applied in the modern cases. The shifting of the narrative surrounding the gathering of data for government surveillance should not be allowed to subvert existing law; rather, the historic legal standard should remain. In absence of necessity for the safety of a community or a nation, the government must not be allowed to ubiquitously surveil citizens. Regardless of source, regardless of the manner of sharing, regardless of consent to a hidden clause in a terms of service agreement. Period. The government must be held to the standard of "legality, necessity, and proportionality" when gathering data about its citizens.

Data Gathered for a Non-Criminal Nature

In addition to government surveillance being used to fetter out crime and protect society, many argue that information may also be collected by government for policy development and social good initiatives, such as improving energy efficiencies, or decreasing carbon emissions by monitoring and improving traffic flows. Obviously, the data gathered and used in a non-criminal focused framework should be considered within a different set of standards. Thus, the question then becomes: What standards and best practices should guide the government's use of non-criminal data?

The United Kingdom has created such a framework in which the government commits to three overarching goals in the gathering and use of data: (1) improving the experience of the citizen; (2) making government more efficient; and (3) boosting business and the wider economy.[16] While these are broad in potential and scope, they do provide reasonable bounds for the government to limit its data gathering and usage. Moreover, these are focused on the

---

[16] J. Manzoni, Big Data in Government: The Challenges and Opportunities (February 21, 2017) (transcript of the speech, exactly as it was delivered), www.gov.uk/government/speeches/big-data-in-government-the-challenges-and-opportunities.

power of technology for the delivery of high-quality public services, a goal that seems in line with a government function and one citizens would likely approve of without protest. Ideally, citizens will determine the parameters of each category to better ensure adherence to appropriate bounds of gathering and use by government officials. For example, a global effort has taken shape where data entrepreneurs are mining public sector data, made available through open government/data initiatives, to create apps and services to make our lives more convenient.[17] Services driven by open data are already giving people more choice in where they get their healthcare, where they live, and where their children go to school.[18] And while readers may assume these particular uses could be troubling government surveillance, so long as best practices are adhered to and citizens are involved as stakeholders in the creation of data usage policy, these may be some of the best examples of socially supportable government-based data use designed for the betterment of our society.

Reused and Repurposed Data

Readers will be familiar with the often-told stories of the police using a popular genealogy website to help identify the Golden State Killer[19] – this despite the fact that the DNA was shared by a family member on a website designed to assist individuals in tracing ancestry.[20] The lines between public and private sector use are becoming more blurred as ubiquitous data gathering and repurposing of data becomes the norm. Should the same standards apply when the government is surveilling via repurposed data? Does your answer change if the data was shared in an environment that is open, or quasi-open, to a large segment of the population? While one could argue that the rules should be the same and the answers should be consistent across purpose and government agency, many disagree with such an assertion. For example: "Ten years after the 9/11 attacks led to amped-up government surveillance efforts, two-thirds of Americans say it's fitting to sacrifice some privacy and freedoms in the fight against terrorism, according to a poll by The Associated Press-NORC Center for Public Affairs Research."[21]

Two-thirds of Americans undoubtedly is the headline that appears over and over again. It might be, however, that we need to be a bit more specific about the question, instead of pretending two-thirds tells the story. I would suggest, two-thirds of Americans agree that they would sacrifice some privacy in the fight against terrorism, but one could reasonably assume that respondents impute into the question the belief that the surveillance has something to do with terrorism and that the particular acts of surveillance actually reduce the terrorism. In fact, the failure to properly consider the assumptions underlying such research is troubling, so much so that some commentators have called the claims "overblown and even misleading."[22] Narratives such as this must be crafted with better attention to the perceptions and

[17] A. Raymond, B. Cate, and S. Shackelford, US Takes Tentative Steps toward Opening Up Government Data, *The Conversation* (March 6, 2019).

[18] *Ibid.*

[19] A. Selk, The Ingenious and "Dystopian" DNA Technique Police Used to Hunt the "Golden State Killer" Suspect, *The Washington Post* (April 28, 2018).

[20] And not for the purpose of finding previously unidentified criminal activity by family members.

[21] Author, Sacrificing Civil Liberties OK to Fight Terrorism Say Some Americans, *WJLA News 7* (September 6, 2011), https://wjla.com/news/nation-world/sacrificing-civil-liberties-ok-to-fight-terrorism-say-some-americans-66133.

[22] B. Cahall, P. Bergen, D. Sterman, and E. Schneider, Do NSA's Bulk Surveillance Programs Stop Terrorists?, *New America* (January 13, 2014), www.newamerica.org/international-security/policy-papers/do-nsas-bulk-surveillance-programs-stop-terrorists/.

assumptions of the respondents and the audience. Moreover, the use of such a narrative to suggest that a vast majority of citizens are supportive of not only surveillance by reused and repurposed data is taking the narrative much too far.

While data reuse means taking a data asset and using it more than once for the same purpose, data repurposing means taking a data asset previously used for one (or more) specific purpose(s) and using that dataset for a completely different purpose. This is where surveillance becomes problematic: data shared, or gathered, for a particular purpose might allow us to be comfortable with the data being reused for the same purpose. Data gathered for a particular purpose that is then used for a wholly different purpose, however, should be viewed as deeply troubling as individuals share (or refuse to share) based on context. For example, most individuals share information on Facebook, but many at one time or another have struggled with a "friend" request from a boss or authority figure. Few would think of Facebook as a means to communicate with their workplace, thus individuals struggle with the overlap between work and private life in these social digital contexts. However, the two worlds are colliding more and more. There is a growing use of social monitoring to assist educational institutions in preventing violence in the school environment. Corporations conducting background checks often scrape social media – or more dubious sources – when giving clients confidence ratings for job applicants and the like. Assuming we envision the widespread use of repurposed data, where should the line be drawn when it comes to repurposing data in this manner?

Section Summary and Conclusion

Data that is gathered for the discovery of criminal activity should, of course, be subject to the same legal standards and existing precedent it has in the past. However, data that is gathered outside the criminal sphere, but is nonetheless part of government surveillance activity, must be gathered within the parameters of legality, necessity, and proportionality. It is these three expectations that will help guide the basic protections of individuals and their data. Of course, the case of repurposing is more difficult – at times – as it will push us in ways that the law has not yet fully developed. Individuals who share data in one environment may make a different decision about sharing it in a different situation – especially if this distinction matters legally. It is within this environment that entities must uphold the promises afforded individuals, those of consent, transparency, and stakeholder engagement in policy creation. How will the distinction be drawn within these key areas? The authors argue decisions often can be made with consideration of the above suggestions and a commitment to considering the impact of use. The next sections detail the impacts that should be taken into consideration in the context of mass data gathering, while the final sections provide some regulatory suggestions for both areas.

ALGORITHMS – IT'S ABOUT THE IMPACT

Even if the data is not used for the discovery of criminal activity and the collection is allowed via either a commitment to legality, necessity, and proportionality or consent of data gathering and repurposing, the debate is not at an end as algorithms are often said to run on data that is incapable of individualizing. In situations such as this, large datasets are used and are not attributable to an individual – hence, the data governance rules created above are incomplete. Accordingly, governance of the algorithms themselves must also be included in the framework.

Predictions and the Government

Data-driven algorithms now drive decision-making in ways that touch our economic, social, and civic lives. These systems rank, classify, associate, or filter information, using human-crafted or data-induced rules that allow for consistent treatment across large populations. While there may be efficiency gains from these techniques, such as discovering tax fraud, the algorithms can also often harbor biases against disadvantaged groups or reinforce structural discrimination – often in an environment with little to no human oversight.

Consider one of the best-known examples of an algorithm used in a justice environment: the risk assessment. Ed Yong described in a 2018 *Atlantic* article[23] the pitfalls of the Correctional Offender Management Profiling for Alternative Sanctions (COMPAS). Within the article, Professor Farid emphasizes: "We're not saying you shouldn't use them ... We're saying you should understand them. You shouldn't need people like us to say: This doesn't work. You should have to prove that something works before hinging people's lives on it."[24] Unfortunately, risk assessment has now, in some states, been expanded to a measure within the sentencing phase of the justice environment.[25]

That is not to suggest that AI and algorithms should not be used in any manner. For example, assessment tools can be useful in directing offenders toward rehabilitative programs and/or allowing them to shorten their prison sentence.[26] However, as then Attorney General Eric Holder noted: "By basing sentencing decisions on static factors and immutable characteristics – like the defendant's education level, socioeconomic background, or neighborhood – they may exacerbate unwarranted and unjust disparities that are already far too common in our criminal justice system and in our society."[27]

Thus, one can assert one of the first questions about the deployment of AI is its design and its intended uses. Until these parameters can be considered, deployments in a highly impactful government of justice environment simply must be curtailed. This was emphasized by a report authored by the Partnership on AI (PAI) after gathering the views of the multi-disciplinary artificial intelligence and machine-learning research and ethics community: "PAI recommends that policymakers either avoid using risk assessments altogether for decisions to incarcerate, or find ways to resolve the requirements outlined in this report via future standard-setting processes."[28]

Across the report, challenges to using these tools fell broadly into three primary categories: (1) concerns about the accuracy, bias, and validity in the tools themselves; (2) issues with the interface between the tools and the humans who interact with them; and (3) questions of governance, transparency, and accountability.[29] The inability to reduce and/or eliminate the

---

[23] E. Yong, A Popular Algorithm Is No Better at Predicting Crimes than Random People, *The Atlantic* (January 17, 2018).

[24] *Ibid.*

[25] A. M. Barry-Jester, B. Casselman, and D. Goldstein, The New Science of Sentencing, *The Marshall Project* (August 4, 2015).

[26] E. Holder, Speaking at the National Association of Criminal Defense Lawyers 57th Annual Meeting and 13th State Criminal Justice Network Conference (August 1, 2014), www.justice.gov/opa/speech/attorney-general-eric-holder-speaks-national-association-criminal-defense-lawyers-57th.

[27] *Ibid.*

[28] PAI Author, Artificial Intelligence Research and Ethics Community Calls for Standards in Criminal Justice Risk Assessment Tools (April 26, 2019), www.partnershiponai.org/artificial-intelligence-research-and-ethics-community-calls-for-standards-in-criminal-justice-risk-assessment-tools/.

[29] See Partnership on AI Author, Report on Algorithmic Risk Assessment Tools in the U.S. Criminal Justice System, Partnership on AI (2018), www.partnershiponai.org/report-on-machine-learning-in-risk-assessment-tools-in-the-u-s-criminal-justice-system/.

challenges identified by PAI has resulted in many industry experts calling for the elimination of black-boxes-based AI and algorithms in the government,[30] including the justice environment.

Andi Peng, AI Resident at Microsoft Research, argues, "as research continues to push forward the boundaries of what algorithmic decision systems are capable of, it is increasingly important that we develop guidelines for their safe, responsible, and fair use."[31] In order to fully contextualize the issue, it is important to first understand the nature of algorithms and machine learning.

Algorithms and Machine Learning

Machine-learning algorithms come in many forms, but they are all doing the same basic thing: using known information to make inferences about unknowns. Machine-learning algorithms are built to detect complex relationships in data, and often exploit a large number of variables to detect relationships that designers might not expect. The problem with this approach is that it is easy to train an algorithm that can get amazing results on the data used to train it – but it does so by finding random artifacts of the sample. This makes it bad at generalizing to the real world.

Data scientists usually deal with this by splitting their labeled data[32] into "train" and "test" sets. After optimizing their algorithms on the training data, they try to predict the test data using their algorithms and then compare their predictions to the true outcomes in the test set. Therefore, machine-learning algorithms usually report a statistic called accuracy – the percentage of guesses that the algorithm got correct.

Accuracy is not the only important statistic for evaluating a machine-learning algorithm. Consider an algorithm designed to predict recidivism – whether a convicted criminal will become a repeat offender. If I told you that my algorithm had an accuracy of 95 percent you might be impressed. However, it might be that one in twenty convicted criminals is booked for a repeat offense. In that case, I could make a very simple decision rule: "no one will be a repeat offender," and the accuracy of that "algorithm" would be 95 percent. Therefore, data scientists also pay attention to other statistics such as precision and recall.[33]

In conversations such as this, precision is the percentage of times the algorithm guessed a particular outcome and was correct. Returning to the recidivism example, the precision would be the number of people the algorithm correctly predicted would be repeat offenders divided by the total number of people it predicted would be repeat offenders. Recall is, in a sense, the complement to precision. It is the percentage of "true positives" that the algorithm correctly classified. For recidivism, it would be the number of people the algorithm correctly guessed would be repeat offenders divided by the total number of individuals in the data who were booked for a repeat offense.

It is necessary that data scientists pay attention to all three metrics – accuracy, precision, and recall – when evaluating the success of an algorithm. An algorithm that predicts that no one will commit a repeat offense isn't useful to anyone, and an algorithm that disproportionately predicts individuals of a certain race will commit a repeat offense (such as COMPAS) is

---

[30]   See T. Simonite, AI Experts Want to End "Black Box" Algorithms in Government, *Wired* (October 18, 2017).
[31]   Artificial Intelligence Research and Ethics Community, above note 28.
[32]   Labeled data is data where you already know what you're trying to predict.
[33]   As well as more involved metrics beyond the scope of what we discuss here, such as the receiver operating characteristic curve.

both unethical and illegal. An additional complication is that data scientists necessarily care more about different metrics for different problems. The most important metric for an algorithm designed to recommend Netflix shows is likely to be precision. Netflix wants you to be interested in the shows that it puts in front of you, but it doesn't matter to Netflix if it omits some shows that you *might* be interested in. On the flip side, an algorithm designed to predict whether a patient has cancer would optimize recall first. Telling someone who does not have cancer that they do is an unfortunate error, but it would be far less life-threatening than failing to tell someone who does have cancer that they should seek treatment.

What is important for readers to understand is that the creation of an algorithm is a science and an art. While we can establish best practices for data scientists, the decision-making process of the individuals who design these algorithms will necessarily include the personal assumptions, and beliefs, biases, and flaws, of their creators. Therefore, it's important that both the creation and impact of the algorithms are considered – even when best practices are followed, it may be the case that an algorithm has unethical outcomes. We must examine the outcomes of algorithms as they are implemented and discontinue their use if unexpected ethical issues arise.

In addition, despite what people might expect, while an algorithm is statistics and math, it isn't really thought of as "proving" or "predicting" things in the way that readers might assume. For example, a prediction of likelihood of recidivism is not a damning conviction. Instead, we know that when the algorithm predicts recidivism, there is some percentage of the time that our algorithm is likely correct – which we can measure through accuracy, precision, and recall.

Algorithms Are Not Magic

Because algorithms can be so fine-tuned to predicting outcomes, and so obtuse in their inner workings, many people have the impulse to take their results at face value. This is a mistake – and one with potentially devastating results. Data scientists tend to be fond of the adage "garbage in, garbage out." What is meant by this is that no matter how fine-tuned your algorithm, if your data is bad, you are going to get bad results. If there is some bias in the data-generating process, your outcomes will be biased.

Recidivism rates provide another good example here. It would be very difficult to measure how many people *actually* repeat offenses, since criminals don't tend to publicly advertise their crimes. Instead, tools to predict recidivism rates are optimized by looking at how many people are *convicted* of repeat offenses. This means that the racial bias present in policing, or the class bias expressed by who can afford a good lawyer, is expressed and reinforced by the recidivism algorithm – leading minorities and the poor to receive disproportionately high sentences by ostensibly "unbiased" algorithms. This is even recognized by the engineers behind some of these projects. Tim Brennan, the co-creator of one such algorithm used during probation and sentencing hearings, said if variables that are correlated with race (for example, poverty) "are omitted from your risk assessment, accuracy goes down."[34]

Moreover, machine-learning algorithms that eliminate the use of certain features, such as race, are likely to still identify those features by identifying alternatives – or proxies – for the features. "Generally, any model that imputes the missing protected attribute value based on other, observed variables is known as a proxy model, and such a model that is based on

---

[34]   J. Angwin, J. Larson, L. Kirchner, and S. Mattu, Machine Bias, *Pro Publica* (May 23, 2016).

predicting conditional class membership probabilities is known as a probabilistic proxy model."[35]

While proxies are widely used and are an important aspect of model building, they can also be problematic. To solve negative proxy modeling impacts, group indicators such as race, gender, and religion are often removed from the training data. The idea being that if the algorithm cannot "see" these elements, the outcome will not be discriminatory.[36] This process, however, is based on a misunderstanding of how algorithms work and the use of training data, as an "algorithm will soon find derived indicators – proxies – to explain this bias."[37]

In her book *Weapons of Math Destruction*, Cathy O'Neil identifies two important things that tend to cause algorithms to become destructive: bad proxy variables and runaway feedback loops. The proxies we discuss above are an example of the former. A proxy is a variable that you have that is meant to stand in for one you don't. In the above case, we don't know every criminal who commits a repeat offense, but we *do* know who has been convicted for one. By using the proxy of convicted criminals rather than the "true criminal" variable, we bake the human bias present in the justice system into our algorithm.

What is worse, this recidivism rate example is likely to also fall prey to the second issue O'Neil identifies: runaway feedback loops. Jail time is often correlated with repeat offenses. If we use this recidivism-predicting algorithm to help guide sentencing and give harsher sentences to people likely to repeat-offend, we have just created a self-fulfilling prophecy. By giving harsher sentences to our "expected repeat offenders," we make these people more likely to repeat-offend. When these results are fed back into the algorithm, it will see that still more minorities and people living under the poverty line have committed repeat offenses, and the algorithm will pay even more attention to race and class. Thus, this seemingly "impartial" algorithm can actually become even *more* biased than humans. To prevent this from happening, people who are using algorithms to guide decisions must understand both their strengths and their limitations.

Considering Impact in the Design Model

Impact assessments are nothing new – in fact, they have been implemented in scientific and policy domains as wide-ranging as environmental protection and privacy. As such, there is no reason to not consider impact within the use of AI, especially in situations where the government is involved with the deployment of the technology – a point that several institutions, organizations, and governments have begun to assert. Thus, there are several AI impact assessments being developed in a wide variety of environments, including governments.

As Special Advisor on Artificial Intelligence – Policy and Implementation, Noel Corriveau, explains: "an impact assessment is a tool used for the analysis of possible consequences of an initiative with a view to provide recommendations as to how to deploy the initiative and under what conditions."[38]

---

[35] J. Chen, N. Kallus, X. Mao, *et al.*, Fairness under Unawareness: Assessing Disparity When Protected Class Is Unobserved. In FAT* '19: Conference on Fairness, Accountability, and Transparency (FAT* '19) (January 29–31, 2019).

[36] L. Moerel, Algorithms Can Reduce Discrimination, But Only with Proper Data, Privacy Perspectives, *IAPP Online Journal*, https://iapp.org/news/a/algorithms-can-reduce-discrimination-but-only-with-proper-data/.

[37] *Ibid.*

[38] N. Corriveau, The Government of Canada's Algorithmic Impact Assessment: Towards Safer and More Responsible AI (2018), https://aiforsocialgood.github.io/2018/pdfs/track2/83_aisg_neurips2018.pdf.

While the exact form and questions of the assessment vary across the various promulgated developers, most contain seven key focus areas: (1) develop the description of the project – the goals that are pursued by using AI, the data that is used, and the actors (such as the end-users and other stakeholders); (2) goals of the project are formulated, not only at the level of the end-user, who experiences the consequences of the service, but also at the level of the organization offering the service and of the society; (3) discover, explore, and consider the relevant ethical and legal frameworks and map and apply these within the application; (4) make strategic and operational choices that attempt to carry out activities in relation to all stakeholders; (5) consider different ethical and legal considerations and make decisions about the deployment of the AI; (6) maintain documentation of the previous steps and justification of all decisions taken; and, finally, (7) monitor and evaluate the impact of the AI.[39] The key takeaways from impact assessments when AI is to be deployed is to ensure *all* stakeholders are thought of during the entire deployment process, from design, to implementation, to use, to adjustment/monitoring. Impact assessments are not merely focused on the impacts of use; instead, they are focused on the impacts across all stakeholders and on the society in which they are situated. In addition, the evolving technology coupled with the shifting social, cultural, and political contexts demands ongoing consideration of the use of prediction and AI in government settings. Thus, stakeholders must be allowed to actively engage in developing the newest approaches to governance.

Section Summary and Conclusion

While algorithms and automation are being widely used in some situations, governments are beginning to see the value and potential of a widening use of automation and machine-learning-based algorithms. However, automation and algorithms within a government environment must be done with an eye toward the impact of use upon its citizenry. Some countries and regional cooperations have begun to create parameters and deployment considerations, but more must be done to consider the impact of deployment and long-term use. Many remain confused by discussions of black-box-based algorithms and sense they have little understanding or input into the use of the technology, as they simply fail to understand such complex math and technology. However, effective policy development demands a better understanding of machine learning and algorithms. As more stakeholders become part of the conversation, more nuanced policy can be developed to answer some of the most perplexing issues facing us as a society – how we can reap the benefits of machine learning without becoming overwhelmed by the lack of understanding of somewhat complex technology.

SUGGESTIONS FOR MOVING FORWARD

Human-centered design is a design and management framework that develops solutions to problems by involving the human perspective in *all steps* of the problem-solving process. Human involvement typically takes place in observing the problem within context, brainstorming, conceptualizing, developing, and implementing the solution. Human-centered design can be thought of in three phases. In the Inspiration Phase, designers learn directly from the people they are designing for and those who will be impacted by the design. In this phase, designers learn from the entities requesting the technology, as well as those who will be

---

[39] Summarized from Platform for the Information Society, Artificial Intelligence Impact Assessment, https://ecp.nl /wp-content/uploads/2019/01/Artificial-Intelligence-Impact-Assessment-English.pdf.

using it and, in our case, those who will be impacted by its use. In the Ideation Phase, the designers make sense of what you learned, identify opportunities for design, and prototype possible solutions. And in the Implementation Phase, designers bring solutions to life and, eventually, to market. If the process is done correctly, the environment – from requesting entities, users, and those impacted – will be considered throughout the design and deployment process. While deliverables are important, the crafting of benchmarks, determining successful outcomes, and planning for monitoring and adjusting the technology is of great importance.

As can be gathered from the descriptions above, human-centered design in the development and deployment of algorithms within the government context should keep in mind three key governance areas: data and algorithms at an individual level, data and algorithms that are developed based on aggregation of data, and the impacts upon various stakeholders. To accomplish human-centered design in government deployments, several recommendations are made by the authors. First, it is important to have a human in the loop. Second, transparency is essential in design and deployment. Third, the government must be careful that end-users are treated as valuable participants in the outcome procedure, without being overly nudged or eliminated from the decision-making process. Fourth, developers, and those who deploy the technology, should no longer be able to escape liability by claiming absence of knowledge or reliance on machine-learning algorithms. Finally, government when evaluating end use must demand more than the further entrenching of existing social conditions. The remainder of the chapter will briefly explore each in turn.

The Importance of Human in the Loop

The government is lagging behind other fields in best practices for algorithmic decision-making. Because of the immediate urgency of medical decisions to human lives, it should be unsurprising that medical algorithms are among the first to operate with a human in the loop design. Medical decisions are not made solely within the black box of an algorithm, but instead the algorithm communicates its decision-making process to the expert, who decides based on that information.

While the human cost of algorithmic decisions is less apparent in government than it is in medicine, the impact of a mistake can be equally devastating to individual lives. The design approach for algorithms implemented by the government must reflect the gravity of the decisions being made, as the algorithms implemented to aid doctors do, instead of the unsupervised classification we accept from inconsequential algorithms such as Netflix's recommendation algorithm. As soon as an algorithm has a significant impact on human lives, its designer ceases to be "just an engineer," and has a responsibility to coordinate with those who will implement the algorithm to ensure that those who understand the ethical and human implications truly grasp the limitations that exist within the algorithm's pipeline.

No algorithm will ever be a perfect magic bullet to solve a problem. If some perfect decision rule that always applied existed that could "solve" a given situation, we wouldn't need machine learning. All practically implemented algorithms have some rate of failure, and it is important that those who make decisions on them are aware of just how those algorithms might fail. Just as a doctor should be able to discern when a prescription recommended by an algorithm might not be right for their specific patient based on their expert knowledge, experts in government should be able to determine when their algorithmic recommendations might not hold water – and an understanding of the internal functioning of these algorithms further increases their odds of correctly identifying these situations.

Some algorithms will never be ethical, and educating policymakers on how algorithms work will help them to make this determination. An algorithm that predicts recidivism to guide sentencing will likely never be ethical because we can never know how many individuals will commit a repeat offense – only how many of them are convicted for a repeat offense. This means that any factor that would make the individual more likely of being arrested will also increase the likelihood of a higher sentence, regardless of whether said factor has any influence on their likelihood of committing a crime again.

It can help to conceptualize machine learning as an extension of statistics. Statistics have been used in human decision-making for years, and we know that based on how we ask statistical questions, we can arrive at wildly different conclusions. Because of this, even if we don't know how to conduct statistical tests ourselves, most people know at least some information about how to interpret statistics and understand the limitations of the answers they give. Statistical methods are therefore tools by which we use existing data to arrive at likely conclusions, which are limited by the usefulness of the question being asked and the limitations of the data used to arrive at the given statistic. This is how we should see machine-learning algorithms as well. When we view algorithms as tools to help us make decisions based on prior data, rather than black boxes that magically spit out the correct answers to different situations, we can implement them in a way that informs our decisions but does not place their predictions on a pedestal – and ensure that the human in the loop always operates from a position where he or she appreciates that the conclusions may be drawn into question.

Transparency Via Algorithm CARDS

For example, important information used in model development can be used as part of the decision-making relating to the model. Commentators Mitchell, Wu, Zaldivar, Barnes, Vasserman, Hutchinson, Spitzer, Raji, and Gebru recommend that released models be accompanied by documentation detailing their performance characteristics.[40] For example, the authors make the following suggestions as relevant information to be captured in the model card: (1) model details, such as basic information about the model (person or organization developing model, model date, and model type);[41] (2) information about training algorithms, parameters, fairness constraints, or other applied approaches and features;[42] (3) the intended use;[43] (4) the evaluation data, such as details on the dataset(s) used for the quantitative analyses in the card and training data;[44] and, finally, (5) any ethical considerations or recommendations.[45]

Having this information available allows all stakeholders to consider the appropriateness of the use of a given model. Information such as this can then be used by various stakeholders to consider and challenge the use of a model, or aspects of the model, in a particular situation. Moreover, it creates opportunities for feedback and adjustment when the model fails to fully capture – or inappropriately captures – aspects of the community within the governmental predictions.

---

[40] M. Mitchell, S. Wu, A. Zaldivar, *et al.*, Model Cards for Model Reporting. In FAT* '19: Conference on Fairness, Accountability, and Transparency (January 29–31, 2019).

[41] See *ibid.*

[42] See *ibid.*

[43] See *ibid.*

[44] See *ibid.*

[45] See *ibid.*

Insist upon Considerations of End-Users

Consideration of model design and the decisions made by the designers in the creation of the model is an important step, yet, alone, it is not enough. Systems must be designed with the end-user in mind, including considering how to ensure that individuals are using the predictions rather than just blindly following the predictions. In these instances, designers must ensure a level of auditing and human review – not just of the prediction, but also of the use of the predictions by the human decision-maker.[46] In fact, the European Data Protection Board[47] has published guidance in this area. It is important to note the focus being placed on ensuring that:

> (1) Human reviewers must be involved in checking the system's recommendation and should not "routinely" apply the automated recommendation to an individual; [and] (2) reviewers' involvement must be active and not just a token gesture. They should have actual "meaningful" influence on the decision, including the "authority and competence" to go against the recommendation; and reviewers must "weigh-up" and "interpret" the recommendation, consider all available input data, and also take into account other additional factors.[48]

Review and human-engaged decision-making are key considerations, especially as they relate to government action and the use of algorithms in prediction. As described above, the blind use of algorithms leaves many concerned about the impacts of these uses upon individuals and society. Transparency and insistence upon review, monitoring, and auditing of all aspects of use are essential to ensure governments are living up to society's expectations of how governments should behave in relation to their citizens.

Liability for Those Who Design and Deploy

For a vast amount of time, society has allowed those who develop technology to stand behind narratives that seek to simplify and mystify the technology. In the vein of disruption, black boxes, and mathematical-based algorithms, we allow those who create algorithms to create, test, and deploy technology with little true consequence. Who is responsible for technology when machine learning is always learning, such that today's outputs will not look the same as tomorrow's outcomes? It is time we look to other areas of law to provide initial guidance. Much like product liability, those who design and/or put a product into the stream of commerce could – and most would argue should – be held liable. Within this area of law, both the design and the product itself subjects the manufacturer to potential liability. And the constant changes should not prohibit us from the comparison, as product liability removes liability from those who create and deploy the product when changes or alterations are made. However, similar to product liability, those who create and deploy technology should be expected to anticipate uses and alterations and should be held liable for reasonably anticipated uses and alterations.

It is also not the case that liability never attaches in the community of technology. Consider issues arising from a cyber-intrusion. In these instances, liability is imposed generally if the

---

[46] R. Binns and V. Gallo, Automated Decision Making: The Role of Meaningful Human Reviews, *AI Auditing Framework Blog* (April 12, 2019), https://ai-auditingframework.blogspot.com/2019/04/automated-decision-making -role-of.html.

[47] European Commission, Guidelines on Automated Individual Decision-Making and Profiling for the Purposes of Regulation 2016/679 (wp251rev.01), https://ec.europa.eu/newsroom/article29/item-detail.cfm?item_id=612053.

[48] Binns and Gallo, above note 46.

following conditions exist: (1) an entity failed to implement safeguards required by statute or reasonable security measures; (2) an entity failed to remedy or mitigate the damage once the breach occurred; and (3) an entity may be liable when it fails to notify in a timely manner the affected individuals under a state's data breach notification statute.[49] Of course, these liability standards would need to be adjusted for algorithm liability. For example, liability could be imposed in situations in which: (1) the entity fails to disclose the use of an algorithm that is deployed to make decisions, nudge behavior, or otherwise reduce the potential choices of an individual; (2) the entity deploying an algorithm fails to implement safeguards or reasonable auditing abilities; (3) an entity fails to remedy or mitigate negatively impactful occurrences within the deployment of the algorithm within the target audience; and/or (4) the entity deploying the algorithm fails to notify users or those impacted by the deployment of the algorithm of negatively impactful harms upon the target audience. While these are ideas, and merely intended as suggestions, it is easy to see that liability could be imposed in a narrow set of circumstances, especially in situations where the deployment of an algorithm is negatively impactful upon an individual. Consider the first of its kind, investment via an automated platform case in which a Hong Kong-based investor is suing to recover over $20 million in investment losses arising from the deployment of an automated investment platform.[50] While this is the first of its kind, it will undoubtedly not be the last. Thus, it is time we as a society ask: Who bears the risk of technology-driven experiments when those who deploy the technology have no real means to evaluate or review automated decision-making?

Moreover, statutory penalties could be imposed upon entities that create and/or deploy algorithms without notice to the individual, including an attribution of creation/deployment. For institutions such as this, relying upon individual lawsuits and class actions that demand a demonstration of damages is not enough – as one of the greatest limitations that exists when it comes to data lost via a breach is the absence of demonstrable harm. Instead, penalties should be imposed based on the mere failure of compliance, thereby creating incentives to comply without the necessity of harmful impacts occurring to individuals.

Of course, the authors are not alone in demanding that algorithms be understood by those that deploy the technology. The Financial Industry Regulatory Authority (FINRA)[51] proscribes that member firms that engage in algorithmic strategies are subject to Securities and Exchange Commission (SEC)[52] and FINRA rules governing their trading activities, which include the existence of a reasonable supervision and control program.[53] In fact, for over ten years, the SEC's message has been clear that with regard to the use of algorithms in investment environments, robo-advisors or not, securities laws apply to both. Thus, those deploying robo-advisors in a client-based environment are expected to ensure compliance with securities laws.[54] One wonders why investment is held to a higher standard than all other deployments, especially those made in government environments in the judicial or other negatively impactful settings.

[49] Who Is Liable When a Data Breach Occurs?, Thomson Reuters, Legal Online Article, https://legal
     .thomsonreuters.com/en/insights/articles/data-breach-liability.
[50] T. Beardsworth and N. Kumar, Who to Sue When a Robot Loses Your Fortune, *Bloomberg* (May 5, 2019), www
     .bloomberg.com/news/articles/2019-05-06/who-to-sue-when-a-robot-loses-your-fortune.
[51] FINRA Says Know Your Algorithms, or Risk Liability, *Nasdaq* (March 21, 2016), www.nasdaq.com/article/finra-
     says-know-your-algorithms-or-risk-liability-cm595663.
[52] N. Morgan and L. Lysle, 2019 Is the Year of the Algorithm for the SEC, *Investment News* (January 7, 2019).
[53] FINRA, Section 3110, Supervision, http://finra.complinet.com/en/display/display_main.html?
     rbid=2403&element_id=11345.
[54] FINRA Says Know Your Algorithms, above note 51.

Demanding More than Entrenched Social Conditions

As Evgeny Morozov opines, "we can imagine an alternative future world of Rebel Tech, which does not perceive social conditions as set in stone, to be accepted and adjusted to, by means of latest technologies. Instead, it deploys bespoke technologies to alter, shape, and – yes – rebel against entrenched social conditions."[55] It is not merely enough to govern through existing mechanisms such as anti-competition, tax adherence, and data-based regulation; instead, we must demand those who design and deploy technology to do so with an eye toward improving society and not merely ingraining the social injustices that already exist. Returning to Evgeny Morozov:

> We arrive at today's paradoxical outcome, whereby 99% of technological disruption is there to merely ensure that nothing of substance gets disrupted at all. Pathology persists – we just adapt to it better, with sensors, maps, AI, and – why not? – quantum computing. The real gospel of today's Big Tech – sanctioned and celebrated by governments – is innovation for the sake of conservation.[56]

Fortunately, some are beginning to take notice of the problems associated with certain types of uses of AI. For example, San Francisco banned the law-enforcement-based use of facial recognition technology.[57] And while no one is ready to abandon the use of technology outright, questions must be asked if the technology is ready for full-scale deployment. Sometimes the build it–break it–adjust it model is simply not an acceptable strategy when the consequences to individuals and society are so great. The banning of the use of particular types of technology, in particular narrow settings, is encouraging, as it demonstrates a commitment to considering the impacts of use within consideration of deployment.

Section Summary and Conclusion

While carefully crafted algorithms, even in government environments, may improve efficiencies and drastically improve the condition of our lives, not every deployment is presumptively positive. The tendency to embrace technology-driven narratives that eviscerate the difference between various deployments is becoming too great, thus, citizens and policymakers must become more involved. We must begin to insist on humans-in-the-loop in key areas of deployment, to reveal key information to allow for informed decisions relating to deployment, and to assign liability to those who design and deploy with impunity. Moreover, we as a technology community must do more to ensure our designs are not further entrenching existing social conditions and instead demand that they operate for the betterment of society. Technology can be a wonderful tool for society, and we must insist that, in the context of government deployments, the focus on society remains at the forefront of design principles.

CONCLUSION

Government deployment of technology, including the deployment of algorithms, begins with data gathering. Data as it relates to the individual must be thought of in two distinct

---

[55] E. Morozov, It's Not Enough to Break Up Big Tech. We Need to Imagine a Better Alternative, *The Guardian* (May 11, 2019).

[56] *Ibid.*

[57] K. Paul, San Francisco Is First US City to Ban Police Use of Facial Recognition Tech, *The Guardian* (May 14, 2019).

categories, criminal and non-criminal use. Criminal use should be covered by existing law, without alteration for the newest types of digital communication and technology. However, a more nuanced approach can be deployed in the event the government seeks to gather data for social good. In situations such as this, a new framework is necessary and must include the citizens as primary stakeholders. Of course, much government surveillance is done without individual focus, instead seeking to deploy algorithms across wide datasets to make sweeping generalizations. Again, lines must be drawn based on impact and use. Governments' use of surveillance and algorithms for a criminal purpose – or to fetter out criminal activity – must be curtailed; whereas mass surveillance must be stopped altogether. However, should the citizens decide that government use of mass data to improve driving conditions is acceptable, this should be allowed – with an eye toward prohibiting data repurposing. Furthermore, frameworks exist which others can draw upon and best practices are emerging, the use of which must be deemed essential in the planning of data use by governments. Finally, humans must be in the loop and the designers and deployers of technology must be accountable for their technology. We as a technology-driven society must demand technology be built to do better, to be better, than what we currently are, and further entrenchment must be avoided at all costs – even if it means we need to use a paper and pencil.

13

From Rule of Law to Statute Drafting

Legal Issues for Algorithms in Government Decision-Making

Monika Zalnieriute, Lisa Burton Crawford, Janina Boughey, Lyria Bennett Moses, and Sarah Logan

INTRODUCTION

The (un)limited potential of algorithmic decision-making is increasingly embraced by numerous private sector actors, ranging from pharmaceutical to banking, and from transport industries to powerful Internet platforms. The celebratory narratives about the use of big data and machine-learning algorithms by private companies to simulate intelligence, improve society, and even save humanity are common and widespread. The deployment of algorithms to automate decision-making also promises to make governments not only more efficient, but also more accurate and fair. Ranging from welfare and criminal justice, to healthcare, national security, and beyond, governments are increasingly relying on algorithms to automate decision-making – a development which has been met with concern by many activists, academics, and members of the general public.[1] Yet, it remains incredibly difficult to evaluate and measure the nature and impact of automated systems, even as empirical research has demonstrated their potential for bias and individual harm.[2] These opaque and elusive systems often are not subject to the same accountability or oversight mechanisms as other public actors in our legal systems, which raises questions about their compatibility with fundamental principles of public law. It is thus not surprising that numerous scholars are increasingly calling for more attention to be paid to the use of algorithms in government decision-making.[3]

This chapter does not aim to provide an exhaustive analysis of the government use of algorithms. Instead, it aims to sketch the way in which algorithms are or may be used across the spectrum of government decision-making – from the drafting of legislation, to judicial decision-making, to the implementation of laws by the executive branch. Then, based on scholarship in the field and our own empirical, doctrinal, and theoretical work, the chapter examines the rule of law values affected by automated government decision-making systems and the legal and practical issues that the implementation and supervision of such systems may pose in practice.

---

[1] See, e.g., L. Dencik, A. Hintz, J. Redden, and H. Warne, Data Scores as Governance: Investigating Uses of Citizen Scoring in Public Services Project Report (2018).

[2] Computer scientists are focusing on how such harms occur, and how they can be discovered and prevented or lessened computationally. See I. Zliobaitė, Measuring Discrimination in Algorithmic Decision Making (2017) 31 *Data Min. Knowl. Dis.* 1060–89; S. Hajian, F. Bonchi, and C. Castillo. Algorithmic Bias: From Discrimination Discovery to Fairness-Aware Data Mining, in *Proceedings of the 22nd ACM SIGKDD International Conference on Knowledge Discovery and Data Mining* (ACM, 2016).

[3] See, e.g., S. J. Mikhaylov, M. Esteve, and A. Campion, Artificial Intelligence for the Public Sector: Opportunities and Challenges of Cross-Sector Collaboration (2018) 376 *Philos. TR Soc.* A 20170357, https://doi.org/10.1098/rsta .2017.0357; R. Kennedy : Algorithms and the Rule of Law (2017) 17 *Leg. Inf. Manag.* 170; M. Perry, iDecide: Administrative Decision-Making in the Digital World (2017) 91 *Aust. Law J.* 29.

The remainder of this chapter is divided into two main parts. The first part is primarily descriptive and begins with a discussion of the spectrum of automation and techniques by which it can be achieved ("Automation"), before explaining the ways in which automated systems are or may be used in administrative decision-making, including the particularly contentious national security context, judicial decision-making, and legislative drafting ("Types of Government Decision-Making"), providing real-life examples of automated systems used in different government decision-making contexts in several different countries. The second part of the chapter then considers the implications of such automation for foundational legal values, and especially the Rule of Law. "The Implications of the Use of Algorithms" examines the effect of automation on core rule of law values such as transparency, accountability, equality before the law, and coherence and consistency. The section entitled "Exceptionalism, Complexity, and Discretion" provides a case study of the implications of automation for law enforcement and administrative decision-making in the national security context; this raises many of the same general issues as those raised in the preceding sections, but particularly acutely. Much of the discussion here is focused on the way in which automation may affect foundational public law principles and values as they are understood in Australian law, but given that many of these principles and values are shared – at least in general – by other legal systems, the discussion is of broader significance. Finally, "Regulatory Directions of Government Use of Algorithms" looks at the question of how governments may (or must) authorize and regulate the use of algorithms in government decision-making.

AUTOMATION

Spectrum of Automation

Governments are increasingly relying on algorithms to automate decision-making in diverse areas, including social welfare, criminal justice, healthcare, law enforcement, and national security. In these different contexts of decision-making, one can differentiate the levels of automation employed, which may vary along the spectrum starting with what is known as "decision support" (for example, facial recognition tool helps national security officials make decisions) to "human-in-the-loop" (for example, social decisions made with government employee involvement), to the total disappearance of humans from the decision-making process (for example, national debt-collection letters automatically issued without the verification by government officials).[4] These are not separate categories, but rather a spectrum moving from fully human decision-making to systems that, while designed by humans, operate largely independent of them.

Techniques of Automation

Automation inevitably involves different techniques, and sometimes combinations of them. We will focus on two classic types. The first type, sometimes described as the first wave of artificial intelligence (AI) or expert systems, is a process that follows a series of pre-

[4] See, e.g., I. Rahwan, Society-in-the-Loop: Programming the Algorithmic Social Contract (2018) 20 *Ethics Inf. Technol.* 5–14; S. Sengupta, T. Chakraborti, and S. Sreedharan, RADAR – A Proactive Decision Support System for Human-in-the-Loop Planning, 2017 AAAI Fall Symposium Series (2017); L. F. Cranor, A Framework for Reasoning about the Human in the Loop, in UPSEC '08: Proceedings of the 1st Conference on Usability, Psychology, and Security (April 2008), https://dl.acm.org/doi/10.5555/1387649.1387650.

programmed rules to mirror responses of a human expert in a particular domain.[5] The infamous debt-collection program, known as "Robo-debt," in Australia and the student welfare provision system in Sweden, discussed later in this chapter, are contemporary examples of systems that follow a primarily pre-programmed logic. The second category – or "second wave" of AI – includes techniques such as supervised machine learning and deep learning.[6] These are systems that "learn" from data (either collected or constructed) so as to draw inferences about new situations. These inferences may be classifications (for example, that an image contains a cat) or predictions (for example, that an individual is likely to commit a crime in the future). There are a variety of data-driven techniques that can be used so that a system will "learn" patterns and correlations to generate predictions or reveal insights. Unlike standard statistical methods, machine learning is generally iterative (able to continually "learn" from new information) and capable of identifying more complex patterns in data. It has been deployed in judicial sentencing and predictive policing in the United States, as well as parts of the Social Credit System (SCS) in China, and in facial recognition systems used in the context of national security, which we will discuss throughout this chapter.

TYPES OF GOVERNMENT DECISION-MAKING

In this chapter, we explore the use of automated systems across the spectrum of government activity, from administrative decision-making to judicial decision-making, to the drafting of legislation. Government activity in the realm of national security is discussed as a particularly contentious area of administrative decision-making and challenging case study. Even though these contexts may overlap to a certain degree in practice, as is the case, for example, in China's SCS, such preliminary categorization is useful because each context is often subject to different legal frameworks. We briefly introduce these contexts with several examples before discussing the legal implications of deployment of algorithms in these settings in "The Implications of the Use of Algorithms."

Administrative Decision-Making

Government officers are responsible for making decisions about an enormous range of issues which directly affect the interests of individuals and businesses. These commonly include decisions about social welfare entitlements, taxation liabilities, licenses to operate businesses, and environmental and planning regulation. While there is great diversity in the topics and legal parameters of government decision-making in these contexts, what they have in common is that they each involve governments applying the law to a specific set of facts. For example, in a licensing context, the government is determining whether or not an individual or business meets relevant eligibility criteria for a license. Often, these decisions involve some degree of discretion.

The use of algorithms to automate administrative government decision-making is not a new phenomenon: it has been deployed in a variety of contexts, such as child protection and provision

5   See generally A. Tyree, Expert *Systems in Law* (Prentice Hall, 1989); R. E. Susskind, *Expert Systems in Law: A Jurisprudential Inquiry* (Clarendon Press, 1987), pp. 114–15.
6   J. Launchbury, A DARPA Perspective on Artificial Intelligence, *DAPRAtv*, YouTube (2017), www.youtube.com /watch?v=-Oo1G3tSYpU. The Defence Advanced Research Projects Agency (DARPA) has also named a third wave of AI that has not yet been applied to government decision-making and so is not explored further in this chapter.

of social welfare, since the 1980s.[7] More contemporary examples include the use of passport scanners at airports to decide whether a person is entitled to enter the country, the automatic processing of tax refunds,[8] and Australia's controversial welfare debt recovery system – colloquially known as "Robo-debt."[9] The "Robo-debt" system combined data matching, automated assessment through the application of human-authored formulae, and the automated generation of letters to welfare recipients requiring them to provide evidence that they were not overpaid by the government.[10] Another prominent example of the use of algorithms by government is the decision-making of the Swedish National Board of Student Finance (CSN), which manages provision of and repayments for financial aid to students in Sweden.[11] The system, which has attracted attention from scholars,[12] combines data from CSN with publicly available information, including tax information (which is publicly available in Sweden),[13] to fully automate decisions about loan repayments based on income of the last two years or to support the decision-making process (partial automation) in evaluating applications for a reduction in loan repayments.[14]

Many of the technological tools used by governments are not particularly sophisticated. For example, the data-matching system used to assess welfare debts in Australia was similar to that which had been used for many years to check a person's reported annual tax income against their reported fortnightly income for social security purposes.[15] However, increasingly, government agencies around the world are expressing interest and ambition to go beyond the assistance of "expert systems" and ordinary software used in the past three decades to employing machine learning and predictive analytics in everyday decision-making.[16] The use of these more sophisticated techniques raises additional legal issues related to transparency, accountability, and fairness.

Administrative Decision-Making in the Context of Law Enforcement and National Security

Algorithms and machine-learning tools are also increasingly used to automate decision-making in the law enforcement and national security context. Such decisions can be made

---

7   See, e.g., J. R. Schuerman, E. Mullen, M. Stagner, and P. Johnson, First Generation Expert Systems in Social Welfare (1989) 4 *Computers in Human Services* 111; J. Sutcliffe, Welfare Benefits Adviser: A Local Government Expert System Application (1989) 4 *Computer Law & Security Rev.* 22.

8   See information from the Australian Taxation Office on the uses of data and analytics at ato.gov.au/about-ato /managing-the-tax-and-super-system/insight–building-trust-and-confidence/how-we-use-data-and-analytics/.

9   See generally T. Carney, The New Digital Future for Welfare: Debts without Legal Proofs or Moral Authority? (2018) UNSW *Law J. Forum* 1.

10 The data matching itself was not new, but the policy of automatically generating letters requiring individuals to provide evidence that they do not have a debt was introduced as part of a 2015–16 Budget measure, "Strengthening the Integrity of Welfare Payments," and a December 2015 Mid-Year Economic Fiscal Outlook announcement. It is this policy change, and the large number of people who subsequently received letters requiring them to prove that they were not overpaid, that generated public attention and criticism. See P. Hanks, Administrative Law and Welfare Rights: A 40-Year Story from Green v Daniels to "Robot Debt Recovery" (2017) 89 AIAL Forum 1.

11 See the CSN website, www.csn.se/languages/english.html. For more on CSN, see E. Wihlborg, H. Larsson, and K. Hedström, "The Computer Says No!" – A Case Study on Automated Decision-Making in Public Authorities, 2016 49th Hawaii International Conference on System Sciences (HICSS) (IEEE, 2016).

12 Recent literature analyzing CSN includes Wihlborg et al., above note 11.

13 Swedish Tax Agency, Taxes in Sweden: An English Summary of Tax Statistical Yearbook of Sweden (2016), www .skatteverket.se/download/18.361dc8c15312eff6fd1f7cd/1467206001885/taxes-in-sweden-skv104-utgava16.pdf.

14 Wihlborg et al., above note 11.

15 Senate Standing Committee on Community Affairs, Australian Parliament, Design, scope, cost-benefit analysis, contracts awarded and implementation associated with the Better Management of the Social Welfare System Initiative (June 21, 2017), p. 2.

16 See, e.g., Dencik et al., above note 1.

in an analytic context – concerning whether an individual or a pattern of activity is of relevance to authorities – or in an administrative context related to national security, such as immigration. Algorithms and machine-learning tools are generally used to help analysts and decision-makers make sense of the huge volume of surveillance data available to them.[17]

Contemporary examples of automated decision-making in the context of law enforcement are China's SCS and predictive policing software. The SCS in China (*shehui xinyong tixi*), developed by central government in China and implemented by forty-three "demonstration cities" and districts at a local level,[18] is a system of rewards and punishments as feedback to individuals and companies, based not just on the lawfulness but also the morality of their actions, covering economic, social, and political conduct.[19] Scholars detail how China's SCS combines both a traditional pre-programmed system based on points (deducted or adduced based on specific behavior) and government cooperation with Chinese tech giant Alibaba in a Sesame Credit system, which relies on an automated assessment of potential borrowers' social network contacts in calculating credit scores.[20] Predictive policing software such as PredPol uses an earthquake prediction model to predict the location of future crimes, using it to make deployment decisions about where police will patrol.[21] The software makes a variety of assumptions, some of which are problematic, and was not subject to rigorous testing and evaluation before adoption.[22] In particular, there are challenges around transparency in the context of operational secrecy and complexity, as well as the appropriateness of profiling and discrimination.[23] The use of algorithms in the law enforcement and national security field thus raises context-specific challenges because of the particular legal framework in which national security agencies generally operate and the constraints under which national security policymaking takes place.[24]

Judicial Decision-Making

Some countries are experimenting with or considering the introduction of algorithms and machine-learning tools to automate decision-making by a different branch of the government – the judiciary. Judicial decision-making covers civil and criminal proceedings and, particularly in the context of criminal proceedings, has serious implications for individuals.

---

[17] L. Bennett Moses and L. de Koker, Open Secrets: Balancing Operational Secrecy and Transparency in the Collection and Use of Data by National Security and Law Enforcement Agencies (2017) 4 *Melb. Univ. Law Rev.* 530–70. D. Wroe, Top Officials Golden Rule: In Border Protection, Computer Won't Ever Say No, *Sydney Morning Herald* (July 15, 2018), www.smh.com.au/politics/federal/top-official-s-golden-rule-in-border-protection-computer-won-t-ever-say-no-20180712-p4zr3i.html.

[18] A linguistic note made by Rogier Creemers is useful in this context: "the Mandarin term 'credit' (*xinyong*) carries a wider meaning than its English-language counterpart. It not only includes notions of financial ability to service debt, but is cognate with terms for sincerity, honesty, and integrity." See R. Creemers, China's Social Credit System: An Evolving Practice of Control (2018), https://papers.ssrn.com/sol3/papers.cfm?abstract_id=3175792.

[19] R. Creemers (ed.), Planning Outline for the Construction of a Social Credit System (2014–2020) (Eng. Tr. of State Council Notice of June 14, 2014, April 25, 2015), https://chinacopyrightandmedia.wordpress.com/2014/06/14/planning-outline-for-the-construction-of-a-social-credit-system-2014–2020/ (last accessed 16 August 2018).

[20] See particularly Creemers, above note 18; and M. Hvistendahl, Inside China's Vast New Experiment in Social Ranking, *Wired* (December 14, 2017), www.wired.com/story/age-of-social-credit/.

[21] See www.predpol.com/predicting-crime-predictive-analytics/.

[22] L. Bennett Moses and J. Chan, Algorithmic Prediction in Policing: Assumptions, Evaluation, and Accountability (2018) 28 *Polic. Soc.* 806–22, http://dx.doi.org/10.1080/10439463.2016.1253695.

[23] *Ibid.*

[24] See, e.g., Bennett Moses and de Koker, above note 17, p. 530; M. Hildebrandt, Profiling and the Rule of Law (2008) 1 *Identity Inf. Soc.* 55; T. Z. Zarsky, Transparent Predictions (2013) *U. Ill. Law Rev.* 1503.

While scholars note that the uses of algorithms in this area are still in "their infancy,"[25] and have been met with political resistance, there are suggestions that they may be increasingly deployed or even transform the judicial system by removing judges altogether.[26] For example, the UK government has proposed the deployment of an "automatic online conviction" process, which has been stalled at the UK Parliamentary debates since 2017.[27] While this may sound far-fetched, it is in some sense a small extension from existing practices of automating the detection and penalizing of speeding and other traffic offences.

One area of judicial decision-making where automation tools have already been deployed in practice is the prediction of the likelihood of re-offending in the context of criminal sentencing decisions. For example, in some US jurisdictions, judges can use automated decision-making tools such as COMPAS (Correctional Offender Management Profiling for Alternative Sanctions) that draw on historic data to infer which convicted defendants pose the highest risk of re-offending, particularly where there is a risk of violence. Many scholars have expressed concerns that such reliance has been approved by the Conference of US Chief Justices[28] and by the Supreme Court of Wisconsin, as well as in various state statutes.[29] In *State* v. *Loomis*, use of the COMPAS system was held to be permissible on the condition that the decision was not fully delegated to machine-learning software and that the judge was notified of the tool's limitations. Thus, a judge in Wisconsin will still need to consider a defendant's arguments as to why other factors might impact the risk that they pose.[30] Because judicial sentencing decisions affect the freedom and lives of individuals, the use of algorithms to automate them is particularly controversial.

Beyond concerns in the sentencing context, scholars are increasingly investigating whether machine-learning techniques and other AI should play a role in assisting tribunals and judiciary in decision-making, and how that might transform the role of judges in contemporary societies.[31]

Use of Algorithms in Statute Drafting

Another area of government decision-making where automation is anticipated to have a significant impact is legislative drafting. Currently, it remains something of a next frontier: while there have been trials of algorithmic tools to assist the drafting of legislation, these have not been widely adopted, and hence the form such tools may take is unclear. Voermans and

[25]   T. Sourdin, Judge v. Robot: Artificial Intelligence and Judicial Decision-Making (2018) 41 *UNSW Law J.* 1114, 1115.

[26]   *Ibid.*

[27]   UK Ministry of Justice, Transforming Our Justice System: Assisted Digital Strategy, Automatic Online Conviction and Statutory Standard Penalty, and Panel Composition in Tribunals (Government Response Cm 9391, February 2017).

[28]   CCJ/COSCA Criminal Justice Committee, In Support of the Guiding Principles on Using Risk and Needs Assessment Information in the Sentencing Process (Resolution 7, adopted August 3, 2011), http://ccj.ncsc.org/~/media/Microsites/Files/CCJ/Resolutions/08032011-Support-Guiding-Principles-Using-Risk-Needs-Assessment-Information-Sentencing-Process.ashx.

[29]   See *State* v. *Loomis*, 881 NW.2d 749 (Wis. 2016). The US Supreme Court denied certiorari on June 26, 2017. On concerns expressed, see K. Hannah-Moffat, Algorithmic Risk Governance: Big Data Analytics, Race and Information Activism in Criminal Justice Debates (2018) 23 *Theor. Criminol.* 453; S. Goel, R. Shroff, J. L. Skeem, and C. Slobogin, The Accuracy, Equity, and Jurisprudence of Criminal Risk Assessment, Equity, and Jurisprudence of Criminal Risk Assessment (December 26, 2018); R. Simmons, Big Data, Machine Judges, and the Legitimacy of the Criminal Justice System (2018) 52 *UCD Law Rev.* 1067.

[30]   *Loomis, ibid.*, at 56.

[31]   See, e.g., Sourdin, above note 25; J. Beatson, AI-Supported Adjudicators: Should Artificial Intelligence Have a Role in Tribunal Adjudication? (2018) 31 *Can. J. Adm. Law Pract.* 307–37.

Verharden have suggested that computerized drafting assistance tools can be categorized as either legislative analysis and review systems, or semi-intelligent drafting-support systems.[32] The former assist legislators to determine the consistency and consequences of legislative drafts. The latter actually assist to translate policy into legislative text, for instance by translating drafting rules and criteria into computer algorithms.[33] Relatedly, there is interest in translating legislation into machine-readable code, in order to automate the process of legislative compliance. The "rules as code" approach proposes to draft human-readable legislation and machine-readable code together, with official versions of machine-readable rules made publicly available. It seeks to ameliorate the challenge of legislative complexity and ambiguity by writing rules in machine-readable format at the same time as those rules are written in English. This can help align policy and the construction of rules with the systems that are ultimately used in their application.[34] It can also, in theory, encourage clarity and logic in legislative drafting[35] and enhance the transparency and accountability of the operation of digital systems. Such projects are currently being experimented with in New South Wales (Australia), Denmark, France, and New Zealand, often using the OpenFisca platform.

At this point, it seems unlikely that human drafters could be completely replaced by AI, given that much of legislative drafting involves the analysis and development of policy before it can be translated into statutory text. However, given advances in the technology used to assist in the drafting of other legal documents – such as contracts[36] – it seems likely that algorithmic tools and machine learning will increasingly play a role in the drafting of legislation.

Scholars are increasingly analyzing these challenges, along with those arising in judicial and administrative decision-making contexts, by examining how automated decision-making in each of the government decision-making contexts complies/compares with the foundational legal values. The following section of this chapter outlines the main directions and insights of this research and scholarship.

THE IMPLICATIONS OF THE USE OF ALGORITHMS FOR FOUNDATIONAL LEGAL VALUES AND RULE OF LAW

Approaches and Conceptual Lenses

Many different conceptual approaches and lenses can be used to ask important questions about the interaction between foundational legal values and the use of algorithms in government decision-making. The research agenda on automation of government decision-making is not homogenous and covers many different subjects, approaches, and lenses for analysis. Some scholars see the international human rights framework as part of the foundational legal values and focus on the human rights implication of the use of algorithms to automate government decision-making.[37] Often, they focus on privacy and

---

[32] W. Voermans and E. Verharden, Leda: A Semi-Intelligent Legislative Drafting Support System (1993) *Jurix* 81, 81–2.

[33] S. Debaene, R. van Kuyck, and B. van Buggenhout, Legislative Technique as Basis of a Legislative Drafting System (1999) *Jurix* 23, 24.

[34] OECD, Embracing Innovation in Government: Global Trends 2019 (2019).

[35] S. B. Lawsky, Formalizing the Code (2016) 30 *Tax Law Rev.* 377.

[36] See generally K. D. Betts and K. R. Jaep, The Dawn of Fully Automated Contract Drafting: Machine Learning Breathes New Life into a Decades Old Promise (2016) 15 *Duke Law Technol. Rev.* 216.

[37] See, e.g., H. P. Aust, Undermining Human Agency and Democratic Infrastructures? The Algorithmic Challenge to the Universal Declaration of Human Rights (2018) 112 *AJIL Unbound* 334–8.

data protection[38] and, increasingly, data-driven discrimination.[39] Related constitutional norms have also been the subject of study in relevant jurisdictions. For example, Ferguson has considered the implications of predictive policing software for a person's right not to be searched without reasonable suspicion in the United States.[40]

Other scholars focus on more abstract legal values. Scholarship on interactions between the foundational legal concepts and norms on the one hand, and automation on the other, are crystallizing into a unique research agenda at the intersection of law, philosophy, and technology.[41] Some in this field have focused on issues such as the potential and capacity of algorithms and AI to erode traditional legal concerns with prediction and persuasion,[42] or undermine the normative structures and understanding of law.[43] Others examined the relationship between data-driven regulation and legal values.[44] Another emerging area of focus in this field is what is referred as "artificial legal intelligence" and its potential to improve access to justice and to provide benefits for historically discriminated groups.[45]

As this suggests, there are numerous ways to approach the subject that cannot be sufficiently addressed here. Instead, we aim to highlight the core challenges posed by automation to fundamental public law principles and values – including those most

[38] For automation, data protection and privacy, see, e.g., A. Roig, Safeguards for the Right Not to Be Subject to a Decision Based Solely on Automated Processing (Article 22 GDPR) (2017) 8 *Eur. J. Law Technol.* 1; S. Wachter, B. Mittelstadt, and L. Floridi, Why a Right to Explanation of Automated Decision-Making Does Not Exist in the General Data Protection Regulation (2017) 7 *Int. Data Priv. Law* 76; S. Wachter, B. Mittelstadt, and C. Russell, Counterfactual Explanations without Opening the Black Box: Automated Decisions and the GDPR (2017) 31 *Harv. J. Law Technol.* 841; I. Mendoza and L. A. Bygrave, The Right Not to Be Subject to Automated Decisions Based on Profiling, in T. Synodinou, P. Jougleux, C. Markou, and T. Prastitou (eds.), *EU Internet Law: Regulation and Enforcement* (Springer, 2017); G. Malgieri and G. Comandé, Why a Right to Legibility of Automated Decision-Making Exists in the General Data Protection Regulation (2017) 7 *Int. Data Priv. Law* 243; B. Goodman and S. Flaxman, European Union Regulations on Algorithmic Decision-Making and a "Right to Explanation" (2017) 38 *AI Magazine* 50.
[39] For automation and non-discrimination, see, e.g., S. Barocas and A. D. Selbst, Big Data's Disparate Impact (2016) 104 *Calif. Law Rev.* 671; M. B. Zafar, I. Valera, M. G. Rodriguez, and K. P. Gummadi, Fairness beyond Disparate Treatment & Disparate Impact: Learning Classification without Disparate Mistreatment (International World Wide Web Conferences Steering Committee, 2017), Proceedings of the 26th International Conference on World Wide Web, https://dx.doi.org/10.1145/3038912.3052660; A. Chouldechova, Fair Prediction with Disparate Impact: A Study of Bias in Recidivism Prediction Instruments (2017) 5 *Big Data* 153; S. Goel, M. Perelman, R. Shroff, and D. A. Sklansky, Combatting Police Discrimination in the Age of Big Data (2017) 20 *New Crim. Law Rev.* 181.
[40] A. G. Ferguson, Predictive Policing and Reasonable Suspicion (2012) 62 *Emory Law J.* 259.
[41] See, e.g., the recent special issue, Artificial Intelligence, Technology, and the Law (2018) 68 *Univ. Tor. Law J.* 1, which focused on law, automation, and technology in all sectors of the society. See also K. Yeung, Algorithmic Regulation: A Critical Interrogation, *Regulation & Governance* (2017), https://doi.org/10.1111/rego.12158; A. Rouvroy and B. Stiegler, The Digital Regime of Truth: From the Algorithmic Governmentality to a New Rule of Law [A. Nony and B. Dillet (trans.)] (2016) 3 *La Deleuziana* 6, www.ladeleuziana.org/wp-content /uploads/2016/12/Rouvroy-Stiegler_eng.pdf; E. Benvenisti, EJIL Foreword – Upholding Democracy amid the Challenges of New Technology: What Role for the Law of Global Governance? (2018) 29 *Eur. J. Int. Law* 9.; D. K. Citron and F. Pasquale, The Scored Society: Due Process for Automated Predictions (2014) 89 *Wash. Law Rev.* 1; M. Hildebrandt and B. Koops, The Challenges of Ambient Law and Legal Protection in the Profiling Era (2010) 73 *Mod. Law Rev.* 428; Hildebrandt, above note 24.
[42] F. Pasquale and G. Cashwell, Prediction, Persuasion, and the Jurisprudence of Behaviourism (2018) 68 *Univ. Tor. Law J.* 63; F. Pasquale, Toward a Fourth Law of Robotics: Preserving Attribution, Responsibility, and Explainability in an Algorithmic Society (2017) 78 *Ohio State Law J.* 1243.
[43] M. Hildebrandt, Law as Computation in the Era of Artificial Legal Intelligence: Speaking Law to the Power of Statistics (2018) 68 *Univ. Tor. Law J.* 12; B. Sheppard, Warming Up to Inscrutability: How Technology Could Challenge Our Concept of Law (2018) 68 *Univ. Tor. Law J.* 36, 37; M. Hildebrandt, *Smart Technologies and the End(s) of Law: Novel Entanglements of Law and Technology* (Edward Elgar, 2015).
[44] Hildebrandt, above note 24; Pasquale, above note 42; Citron and Pasquale, above note 41.
[45] P. Gowder, Transformative Legal Technology and the Rule of Law (2018) 68 *Univ. Tor. Law J.* 82.

iconic legal values, the rule of law.[46] We argue that focus on the rule of law is important because it is a widely accepted standard for measuring the governmental behavior around the world.[47] Classic works on the rule of law convincingly suggest that it is a ubiquitous and elusive concept,[48] which cannot be accounted for fully within the parameters of this chapter.

In considering the ways in which automation affects the rule of law, it is important not to treat that concept in an "anatomical" or anachronistic way. As Krygier has long argued, the rule of law is best understood as a goal or ideal; a state in which a legal system is free from certain dangers or pathologies.[49] For many, the rule of law is primarily seen as the antithesis of arbitrary government power. For those seeking clarity as to how to achieve this goal in practice, it is common to look for a list of more concrete criteria. Thus, it is often said that the rule of law requires that government action be transparent and accountable, and that all people be treated equally before the law.

While this can yield a useful set of analytical tools, it is important not to lose sight of the fact that these are means to the more important end of non-arbitrariness. Furthermore, there is no definitive "recipe" for achieving those ends; the means that are appropriate are likely to vary with time, and between jurisdictions. This is particularly pertinent to a discussion of automation. Automation should not be regarded as an inherently suspicious development. The most fruitful way to frame the rule of law question is to ask: can automation help to guard against arbitrary government power, or will it allow it to flourish?

In a recent book, Brownsword has articulated a need to re-imagine the rule of law in an era where regulation is in the form of technological management rather than legal rules.[50] This is an ambitious project, but more scholars have focused on how automation of government decision-making may affect specific components of the rule of law, such as transparency or accountability.[51] Below, we briefly discuss interactions between automation of government decision-making and several of such components: transparency, accountability, equality before the law, and coherence and consistency.[52]

Automation, Transparency, and Accountability

Scholars and policymakers have noted how automation may offer many potential benefits in enhancing the transparency and accountability of governmental decision-making across

---

[46]   See M. Zalnieriute, L. Bennett Moses, and G. Williams, Rule of Law and Automation in Government Decision-Making (2019) 82 *Mod. Law Rev.* 425.

[47]   See International Congress of Jurists, The Rule of Law in a Free Society, Report of the International Commission of Jurists, New Delhi (1959), para. 1.

[48]   Modern accounts include Lord Bingham, The Rule of Law (2007) 66 *Camb. Law J.* 67, 69. B. Z. Tamanaha, *On the Rule of Law: History, Politics, Theory* (Cambridge University Press, 2004), p. 2; P. Gowder, *The Rule of Law in the Real World* (Cambridge University Press, 2016).

[49]   See especially M. Krygier, The Rule of Law: Legality, Teleology, Sociology, in G. Palomblla and N. Walker (eds.), *Relocating the Rule of Law* (Hart, 2009), p. 45. For a discussion of how this approach might apply in a particular legal framework, see L. B. Crawford, *The Rule of Law and the Australian Constitution* (Federation Press, 2017).

[50]   R. Brownsword, *Law, Technology and Society: Reimagining the Regulatory Environment* (Routledge, 2019).

[51]   See, e.g., P. B. de Laat, Algorithmic Decision-Making Based on Machine Learning from Big Data: Can Transparency Restore Accountability? (2018) 31 *Philos. Technol.* 525–41; M. Ananny, and K. Crawford, Seeing without Knowing: Limitations of the Transparency Ideal and Its Application to Algorithmic Accountability (2018) 20 *New Media Soc.* 973–89; J. Singh, C. Millard, and C. Reed, Accountability in the Internet of Things: Systems, Law and Ways Forward (2018) 51 *Computer* 54.

[52]   We discuss some of these in detail in Zalnieriute *et al.*, above note 46.

different contexts discussed in this chapter.[53] Put simply, a system based on pre-programmed rules can inform an affected individual that the reason they were ineligible for a certain benefit was that they did not meet a specific criterion that is a requirement of a particular legislation or operational rule encoded into the logic of the system. However, automation also entails significant challenges to transparency and accountability, which Burrell has convincingly summarized as three "forms of opacity" of machine learning.[54] Under this frame, first, intentional secrecy may prevent transparency when algorithms are treated as a trade or state secret.[55] For example, in Chinese SCS, the details of Sesame Credit system's operation are not clear. While it is known that it relies on behavioral analytics in calculating credit scores,[56] many scholars have argued that individuals have no means of knowing what information from their social network contacts was used or its precise impact on their scores.[57] Similarly, journalists and scholars have pointed out that Northpointe Inc. (now "equivant"),[58] which owns the COMPAS tool, has not publicly disclosed its methods in developing the tool used in judicial sentencing, as it considers its algorithms to be trade secrets.[59] We agree with many scholars that open source software should be favored in circumstances where decision-making involves high stakes such as individual liberty.[60]

Burrell further notes how technical illiteracy may pose further challenges to transparency and accountability to both expert systems and machine learning, because even if operational information is disclosed, this does not mean that the majority of the public will be able to extract useful knowledge from that information.[61] Finally, Burrell has suggested that because humans reason differently from machines, they cannot always interpret the interactions among data and algorithms, even if suitably trained. This suggests that the transparency which is crucial for maintaining/securing the rule of law may erode over time as machine-learning systems become more complex.[62]

Automation, Accountability, and Administrative Justice

The challenges that automation poses for transparency and accountability have been particularly pronounced in the administrative decision-making context. Generally, administrative decision-making by government agencies and employees is subject to constraints of administrative (and sometimes constitutional) law. As noted by US administrative law experts Coglianese and Lehr, many administrative law principles are built on the assumption that decisions are made by humans, not automated systems.[63] For example, in many jurisdictions, administrative decision-makers are required to provide procedural fairness, or due process, to

53   For an especially positive account, see C. Coglianese and D. Lehr, Regulating by Robot: Administrative Decision Making in the Machine-Learning Era (2017) 105 Georgetown Law J. 1147.
54   J. Burrell, How the Machine "Thinks": Understanding Opacity in Machine Learning Algorithms (2016) 3 Big Data Soc. 1.
55   Ibid.; F. Pasquale, The Black Box Society (Harvard University Press, 2015).
56   Hvistendahl, above note 20.
57   R. Zhong and P. Mozur, Tech Giants Feel the Squeeze as Xi Jinping Tightens His Grip, New York Times (May 2, 2018), www.nytimes.com/2018/05/02/technology/china-xi-jinping-technology-innovation.html.
58   See equivant website at www.equivant.com/.
59   This is noted in Loomis case, above note 29, at [144]. See generally Pasquale, above note 55.
60   See, e.g., D. K. Citron, Technological Due Process (2008) 85 Wash. Univ. Law Rev. 1249; Citron and Pasquale, above note 41.
61   Burrell, above note 54, p. 4.
62   Ibid., p. 10.
63   Coglianese and Lehr, above note 53, p. 1153.

a person who will be adversely affected by their decision. Decision-makers are also often obliged to provide a statement of reasons for their decisions. The use of machine learning to make administrative decisions thus raises numerous legal issues, as machines may not be capable of complying with administrative law's requirements, such as giving a fair hearing or providing reasons for a decision.[64] Scholars and policymakers around the world are increasingly paying attention to these issues and have adopted a variety of perspectives and approaches.[65] Many have expressed concern about the transparency and accountability challenges raised by the use of algorithm-assisted decision-making in the public sector, and argued that administrative law principles need to be reframed or adapted for the new algorithmic environment.[66]

Others have argued that the use of algorithms to automate administrative decision-making "can comfortably fit within these conventional legal parameters."[67] For example, in a 2004 report, Australia's (now defunct) Administrative Review Council examined the use of automated systems in government decision-making and recommended twenty-seven principles that should be taken into account by governments in designing and delivering automation systems to assist in decision-making. The Council said that "[n]one of the principles put forward is radical or surprising. They are consistent with the best-practice principles generally associated with good administrative decision making."[68] Had these principles been followed in the design of "Robo-debt," the worst of its problems would likely have been avoided.

Even so, more fundamental problems may remain. These legal principles reflect a deep-seated view that people whose rights and interests are affected by the state have the right to be treated *as people* – and more particularly, to have their circumstances considered by a human actor who weighs up all the circumstances of their case and decides the best course of action to take. Automation challenges these fundamental ideas of administrative justice.

These ideas were arguably implicit in the decision of the Australian Federal Court in *Pintarich v. Federal Commissioner of Taxation*.[69] In brief outline, the Court held that a computer-generated letter ostensibly sent by the Deputy Commissioner of Taxation to a taxpayer advising that a substantial amount of its taxation debt had been excused was not a legally effective "decision" for the purposes of the Taxation Administration Act 1953 (Cth). That was so because a "decision" necessarily involved a "mental process" – assumedly undertaken by a human. As a result, the decision ostensibly manifested in the letter was not considered to be legally binding, and hence the Deputy Commissioner of Taxation was free to decide again. While this conclusion was framed as one about the meaning of "decision" in a particular statute, it demonstrates that administrative decision-making is still regarded as an inherently human process, at least within the Australian legal system. In dissent, Kerr J. warned that:

---

[64] K. Miller, The Application of Administrative Law Principles to Technology-Assisted Decision-Making (2016) 86 *AIAL Forum* 20, 27–30.

[65] Recent analyses of administrative decision-making include: M. Oswald, Algorithm-Assisted Decision-Making in the Public Sector: Framing the Issues using Administrative Law Rules Governing Discretionary Power (2018) 376 *Philos. TR Soc. A* 20170359, https://doi.org/10.1098/rsta.2017.0359; Coglianese and Lehr, above note 53; D. Hogan-Doran, Computer Says "No": Automation, Algorithms and Artificial Intelligence in Government Decision-Making (2017) 13 *Judicial Rev.* 345.

[66] Oswald, *ibid.*

[67] Coglianese and Lehr, above note 53, p. 1148.

[68] Administrative Review Council, Automated Assistance in Administrative Decision-Making, Report No. 46 (November 2004), p. vii.

[69] [2018] FCAFC 79, esp. at 140. Special leave was sought to appeal this decision to the High Court of Australia, but refused: *Pintarich* v. *Deputy Commissioner of Taxation* [2018] HCASL 322.

The hitherto expectation that a "decision" will usually involve human mental processes of reaching a conclusion prior to an outcome being expressed by an overt act is being challenged by automated "intelligent" decision making systems that rely on algorithms to process applications and make decisions. What was once inconceivable, that a complex decision might be made without any requirement of human mental processes is, for better or worse, rapidly becoming unexceptional. Automated systems are already routinely relied upon by a number of Australian government departments for bulk decision making ... The legal conception of what constitutes a decision cannot be static; it must comprehend that technology has altered how decisions are in fact made and that aspects of, or the entirety of, decision making, can occur independently of human mental input.[70]

At the same time, it is clear that one of the greatest barriers to administrative justice is the size and complexity of the administrative state – and the time and resources that are required to operate it. Automation has the potential to break down or at least diminish these barriers, by increasing the speed and decreasing the cost of administrative decision-making. However, the point for present purposes is that any such automation must not only be compatible with administrative law doctrine, but more fundamental public law principles. If automated decision-making continues to be seen as something alien to basic ideas of justice and fairness, it will struggle for acceptance – and encourage challenges and resistance which diminish the efficiency gains it otherwise promises.

Automation and Equality before the Law

It is widely believed among some governments, private actors, and academics that automation can also enhance equality before the law by reducing arbitrariness in the application of law, removing bias, and eliminating corruption.[71] However, some legal researchers argue that it may undermine due process rights and the extent to which people, irrespective of their status, have equal access to rights in the law.[72] For instance, as we explain in our earlier work, the right to review and rectify information in the Australian Robo-debt case was undermined because the debt letter did not explain the importance of the income variation over the year for an accurate calculation of welfare entitlements.[73] By contrast, we pointed out that Sweden's student welfare system provides an explanation of the process involved and a relatively straightforward appeal procedure to challenge the agency's decisions.[74] We further suggested, using the COMPAS example, that with machine learning, lack of

---

[70] [2018] FCAFC 79, at 46–9.
[71] See, e.g., S. C. Srivastava, T. S. H. Teo, and S. Devaraj, You Can't Bribe a Computer: Dealing with the Societal Challenge of Corruption through ICT (2016) 40 *MIS Q.* 511–26; D. Infante and J. Smirnova, Environmental Technology Choice in the Presence of Corruption and the Rule of Law Enforcement (2016) 15 *Transform. Bus. Econ.* 214; N. G. Elbahnasawy, E-government, Internet Adoption, and Corruption: An Empirical Investigation (2014) 57 *World Dev.* 114–26; D. C. Shim and T. H. Eom, Anticorruption Effects of Information Communication and Technology (ICT) and Social Capital (2009) 75 *Int. Rev. Adm. Sci.* 99–116; P. W. Schroth and P. Sharma, Transnational Law and Technology as Potential Forces against Corruption in Africa (2003) 41 *Manag. Decis.* 296–303; S. R. Salbu, Information Technology in the War against International Bribery and Corruption: The Next Frontier of Institutional Reform (2001) 38 *Harv. J. Legis.* 67.
[72] See D. L. Kehl, P. Guo, and S. A. Kessler, Algorithms in the Criminal Justice System: Assessing the Use of Risk Assessments in Sentencing, Responsive Communities Initiative, Berkman Klein Center for Internet & Society (July 2017), p. 3, http://nrs.harvard.edu/urn-3:HUL.InstRepos:33746041; Citron, above note 60; Citron and Pasquale, above note 41.
[73] Zalnieriute *et al.*, above note 46.
[74] As we explain in Zalnieriute *et al.*, *ibid.*, CSN decisions can be appealed to the National Board of Appeal for Student Aid (Överklagandenämnden för studiestöd, ÖKS); see the ÖKS website at https://oks.se/.

transparency is the primary reason why due process rights may be compromised. In particular, lack of transparency in the scoring tool only provides a convicted individual with an opportunity to argue against a score in the absence of any real understanding of the basis for its calculation. Recent scholarship on Chinese SCS demonstrates that similar fairness and equity concerns arise because of lack of transparency in parts of that system.[75]

Finally, scholars from various disciplines and backgrounds have argued that the use of automated decision-making by governments may further challenge the idea that all individuals, irrespective of their status, must have equal access to rights in the law and that government should not treat individuals differently due to their demographic group or an immutable trait.[76] As we explain in detail in our earlier research, automation with tools, such as COMPAS and Sesame Credit, can erode this principle because such tools may either explicitly incorporate various static factors or immutable traits, or may incorporate factors such as socio-economic status, employment and education, postal codes, age, or gender indirectly, by "learning" the relevance of variables that correlate with these.[77] The greatest challenge to the principle of equality before the law thus arises because automation can infer rules from historical patterns and correlation in ways that have a disparate impact on people with a particular characteristic (such as race), even where that characteristic was not used in the machine-learning process.[78]

This may occur because many other factors can correlate with, for example, race, including publicly available information, such as, for example, Facebook "likes," which are often included as a variable in automated assessments based on social networks.[79] Further problems may arise in judicial decision-making contexts – for instance, where a pre-sentencing questionnaire (from which the COMPAS tool draws inferences) records the number of times and the first time a defendant has been "stopped" by police.[80] O'Neil notes how given historical discriminatory profiling practices by the police in the United States, the status of an African-American is likely to correlate with higher numbers and earlier ages in response to this question.[81] Criminologists and legal scholars alike have highlighted how racial differentiation is built into the data from which correlations are deduced and inferences drawn.[82]

---

[75] Creemers, above note 18; F. Liang, V. Das, and N. Kostyuk, Constructing a Data-Driven Society: China's Social Credit System as a State Surveillance Infrastructure (2018) 10 *Policy Internet* 415–53; Zalnieriute *et al.*, above note 46.

[76] Barocas and Selbst, above note 39. People have particularly strongly objected to courts systematically imposing more severe sentences on defendants who are poor or uneducated or from a certain demographic group: see G. Kleck, Racial Discrimination in Criminal Sentencing: A Critical Evaluation of the Evidence with Additional Evidence on the Death Penalty (1981) 46 *Am. Sociol. Rev.* 783; L. Wacquant, The Penalisation of Poverty and the Rise of Neo-Liberalism (2001) 9 *Eur. J. Crim. Policy Res.* 401; C. Hsieh and M. D. Pugh, Poverty, Income Inequality, and Violent Crime: A Meta-Analysis of Recent Aggregate Data Studies (1993) 18 *Crim. Justice Rev.* 182.

[77] Barocas and Selbst, above note 39; Zalnieriute *et al.*, above note 46.

[78] J. Angwin, J. Larson, S. Mattu, and L. Kirchner, Machine Bias, *ProPublica* (May 23, 2016), www.propublica.org /article/machine-bias-risk-assessments-in-criminal-sentencing.

[79] See especially M. Kosinski, D. Stillwell, and T. Graepel, Private Traits and Attributes Are Predictable from Digital Records of Human Behavior (2013) 110 *Proc. Nat. Acad. Sci. USA* 5802 (finding that easily accessible digital records such as Facebook "likes" can be used to automatically and accurately predict highly sensitive personal information, including sexuality and ethnicity).

[80] Angwin *et al.*, above note 78.

[81] C. O'Neil, *Weapons of Math Destruction: How Big Data Increases Inequality and Threatens Democracy* (Broadway Books, 2016), pp. 25–6 ("So if early 'involvement' with the police signals recidivism, poor people and racial minorities look far riskier").

[82] See, e.g., A. D. Selbst, Disparate Impact in Big Data Policing (2017) 52 *Ga. Law Rev.* 109; A. D. Selbst and A. G. Ferguson, Illuminating Black Data Policing (2017) 15 *Ohio St. J. Crim. Law* 503.

Automation, Complexity, and (In)consistency with the Law

Consistency between government action and the statute book is regarded as a key tenet of the rule of law.[83] A well-designed system of legislation clearly does little to serve the goal of constraining government power if government does not act consistently with it. But consistency can be difficult to achieve, even for the most conscientious government actor, given the complexity of legislation in a modern administrative state and the frequency with which it changes.

Policymakers, businesses, and some scholars have noted how the use of algorithms in government decision-making could improve the consistency of government decision-making, and thus make it more consistent with the "law on the books."[84] This line of argument is built on the idea that, unlike people, pre-programmed systems cannot act with disregard for the rules with which they are programmed. Therefore, researchers have found that automation tools *generally* enhance the consistency of decision-making, even where they are otherwise problematic.[85] As we have argued in our earlier work, the "social credit system in China works as a tool of social control because people can predict the consequences of engaging in particular activities that the government wishes to discourage."[86] Similarly, Australia's automated debt-collection program and Sweden's social welfare system perform the same calculations for everyone, and thus could be said to be "internally" consistent.

However, many challenges to consistency may arise when the rule that is applied in the pre-programmed system is inconsistent with legal requirements. The inconsistency in such instances arises not because of a differential application of a particular rule in similar cases, but because the application of the rule might differ from its original formulation. A prominent contemporary example of such inconsistency with the law is the Australian Robo-debt programme. While the legality of the government's actions in that context remains unclear, it was clear that many people were advised that there was a discrepancy between their reported income and their legal entitlements when in fact there was not.[87] The problem was not that errors were made – human decision-makers make errors too – but rather that errors were made at a far greater rate than would have been the case if the system were entirely human driven. The program had a high error rate because the assumption it made in its calculations – that fortnightly income could be deduced, by averaging, from annual income – did not apply to a significant number of welfare recipients, namely those with variable fortnightly incomes. The letters sent to welfare recipients were also problematic, as they seemed to suggest that the recipient *had* a debt which the recipient needed to *disprove* the existence of, rather than being merely a request for further information. The primary problems with the system were thus ultimately human and occurred in the design process. The data-matching and debt-calculation system was designed for the "standard" case where a person's income was the same each week and did not include sufficient measures to deal with people who fell outside that standard case. Its implementation also failed to consider the position

---

[83]   See especially L. Fuller, *The Morality of Law* (Yale University Press, 1962), pp. 81–91. See further L. B. Crawford, The Rule of Law in the Age of Statutes (2020) *Fed. Law Rev.* (OnlineFirst). As Crawford explains, legislation at the federal level in Australia is frequently amended. For example, in the period between 2013 and 2017, the Social Security Act 1991 (Cth) and Income Tax Assessment Act 1997 (Cth) were each amended (on average) around once a month.

[84]   For an especially positive scholarly account, see Coglianese and Lehr, above note 53.

[85]   Zalnieriute *et al.*, above note 46.

[86]   *Ibid.*, p. 22.

[87]   Senate Community Affairs References Committee, Parliament of Australia, Design, Scope, Cost-Benefit Analysis, Contracts Awarded and Implementation Associated with the Better Management of the Social Welfare System Initiative (2017), para. 2.88.

of vulnerable people who may not be able to easily access evidence of their income from five or ten years ago, and communication with those affected was poor and proved confusing.

Moreover, the procedures in place to rectify those errors were inadequate. In particular, no humans checked the automated decision to issue individuals with the debt notice, which was presented as a "fait accompli," with some people not receiving any prior communications because of errors in address information.[88] The online portal for dealing with debt notices was hard to use,[89] with insufficient human resources to address the concerns or provide information to affected individuals.[90] By contrast, the automated Swedish student welfare system allocates responsibility for decision-making and editing of decisions to humans, with due process safeguards in place for appealing each decision.[91] This confirms that it is crucial for algorithms to be consistent with the law – and designed and implemented in a way that is sensitive to the legal and social context in which they will operate. It also demonstrates the importance of human oversight of algorithmic decision-making to detect inconsistencies that do arise.

One of the contemporary challenges to ensuring that government acts consistently with the law is the complexity of the administrative state. A legislative framework of significant size and complexity is required in order to build and sustain a state of this kind, especially where (as is commonly the case) legislation is the primary constitutionally prescribed tool by which government can act. But the task of overseeing this legal framework and updating it to ensure it keeps pace with social, economic, and scientific developments is one which may strain human capacities. In a healthy legal system, legislation will be harmonious; duplication, overlap, and inconsistency diminishes the accessibility of the law. But when the statute book is large and complex – and in particular, where individual statutes interact with many others – it may be difficult for human drafters to accurately identify the consequences of enacting new, or changing existing, legislation. While many statutes employ similar terms and concepts, it can be difficult for human drafters to keep track of the myriad ways in which they are used across the statute book. Some or all of these tasks could be assisted by automation. Likewise, as Boer, Winkels, Hoekstra, and van Engers argue, knowledge management systems may provide a more systematic basis on which legislators can compare legislative proposals with their potential alternatives – and hence to make the best legislative choices.[92]

Yet, there are clear limits on the extent to which legislative drafting can be automated – at least without compromising core legal values or the democratic process. Most democratic theorists stress that the task of deciding when and how to change the law is a complex and sensitive task that must be performed by elected representatives following lengthy and careful deliberation in the legislature, and in specialized committees.[93] While algorithms may provide legislators with a clear and accurate source of information to *inform* that deliberation, our conceptions of democracy would demand that legislative choices must in substance be made by those elected to the legislature. In most legal systems, legislative power is explicitly conferred on the legislature and, while these conferrals may plausibly be read as permitting

---

[88]   *Ibid.*, para. 3.61.
[89]   *Ibid.*, para. 2.110.
[90]   *Ibid.*, paras. 3.98, 3.106, 3.107, 3.119.
[91]   CSN decisions can be appealed to the National Board of Appeal for Student Aid (ÖKS): see ÖKS website at https://oks.se/.
[92]   A. Boer, R. Winkels, R. Hoekstra, and T. M. van Engers, Knowledge Management for Legislative Drafting in an International Setting, in D. Bourcier (ed.), *Legal Knowledge and Information Systems* (IOS Press, 1993), p. 91.
[93]   See especially J. Waldron, *Law and Disagreement* (Oxford University Press, 1999); J. Waldron, *The Dignity of Legislation* (Cambridge University Press, 2009); R. Ekins, *The Nature of Legislative Intent* (Oxford University Press, 2013).

computer assistance, there would clearly be limits on the extent to which the power may be delegated to non-human actors.[94] The question of whether and how executive power can be delegated to non-human actors is considered further in the next section.

It is also questionable whether and how the myriad principles that inform legislative meaning could be codified. In legal systems such as that in Australia, legislation is designed with the assistance of an independent office of Parliamentary Counsel with extensive experience and knowledge of the principles and practice of statutory interpretation and design.[95] Legislative drafters and parliamentarians act in light of a rich and largely unstated set of linguistic assumptions, as well as a complex and contested set of interpretive principles set out in legislation and by the courts. The task of reducing these assumptions and principles to code would be challenging to say the least.

EXCEPTIONALISM, COMPLEXITY, AND DISCRETION: THE NATIONAL SECURITY CONTEXT

Many of the legal and practical issues raised by the use of algorithms and machine-learning tools in the national security context are similar to those raised by the use of such tools in other contexts. Assumptions about accuracy, continuity, the irrelevance of omitted variables, and the primary importance of particular sorts of information over others are as relevant to the national security environment as they are to predictive policing and algorithmic accountability in the delivery of social services.[96] However, the use of such tools in decision-making in national security raises particular issues.

Exceptionalism, Privacy, and Transparency

Legal exceptionalism is one of the defining features of national security decision-making.[97] National security agencies are generally at pains to protect from public scrutiny their methods for acquiring information and the sources via which they acquire it. This means national security information regimes are often exempt from privacy and transparency legislation shaping information handling in other policy spaces.

Algorithms and machine-learning tools provide particular problems for transparency in the context of national security. In any context, algorithms and machine-learning tools contain fundamental opacity to humans,[98] but this opacity is compounded in the national security context by the need to protect sources and methods.[99] This transparency, or the lack thereof, obstructs the possibility of evaluation[100] of the efficacy of automated decision-making generated by the use of such tools, and for oversight and accountability more broadly.[101]

---

[94] See, e.g., Australian Constitution, s. 1.

[95] C. Meiklejohn, *Fitting the Bill: A History of Commonwealth Parliamentary Drafting* (Office of Parliamentary Counsel, 2012).

[96] Bennett Moses and Chan, above note 22; AI Now Institute, Litigating Algorithms: Challenging Government Use of Algorithmic Decision Systems, New York (2018).

[97] L. Bennett Moses, A. Maurushat, and S. Logan, Law and Policy Analysis (Report A) Information sharing and the National Criminal Intelligence System (NCIS), section 4. Data to Decisions Cooperative Research Centre (2017).

[98] Burrell, above note 54.

[99] Bennett Moses and de Koker, above note 17.

[100] Bennett Moses and Chan, above note 22.

[101] Bennett Moses and de Koker, above note 17.

With regard to privacy, national security agencies are often exempt from some (though not all) constraints on the collection and use of personal information. Moreover, the use of algorithms and machine-learning tools in a national security context can problematize this exceptionalism by destabilizing the definition of personal or private information.[102] For example, such tools may be used to interrogate bulk datasets of personal information which may be de-identified at the point of acquisition by national security agencies. But they may be used to match data points and identity trends across bulk datasets which are otherwise de-identified, potentially. This can lead to personal or sensitive information being (re)identified.[103] Managing this risk in the use of automated decision-making, especially in the context of exceptionalism around privacy, requires the implementation of appropriate data governance regimes.[104]

Australian law does not specifically govern agency interrogation of bulk datasets for defense, national security, and law enforcement.[105] The United States and Canada[106] have rules that govern the bulk analysis and use of personal information in such datasets. In the European Union, the General Data Protection Regulation (GDPR) generally mandates that data subjects receive meaningful, if limited, information about the logic involved in processing of their information by automated systems, as well as the significance and the envisaged consequences of automated decision-making systems.[107] However, decision-making in the context of defense, national security, and law enforcement is exempted and such a right does not apply in these contexts.[108] National legislation in EU Member States, which complements the GDPR and implements the Law Enforcement Directive, also entails such exceptions, because national security is not within EU competence and belongs to the national governments. For instance, the United Kingdom's Data Protection Act 2018 includes restrictions on automated decision-making, spelling out the notification and appeal requirements for such processing when it is authorized by law.[109] However, just like the GDPR, the UK Act provides for exemptions for data processing in the context of law enforcement and national security.

Access to Tools and Data

Interrogation of bulk datasets using algorithms and machine-learning techniques is a complex, highly specialized task. Governments are often unable to design or implement

---

[102] For example, in Australia, the Privacy Act 1988 (Cth) applies to the collection and use of "personal information" and "sensitive information" by APP entities.

[103] L. Bennett Moses, A. Oboler, S. Logan, and M. Wang, Using "Open Source" Data and Information for Defence, National Security and Law Enforcement, Data to Decisions Cooperative Research Centre (2018), p.31.

[104] Bennett Moses *et al.*, above note 97.

[105] An exception is the Data Matching Program (Assistance and Tax Act) 1990.

[106] Bennett Moses *et al.*, above note 103, section 2.3.6.

[107] Regulation (EU) 2016/679 of the European Parliament and of the Council of 27 April 2016 on the protection of natural persons with regard to the processing of personal data and on the free movement of such data, and repealing Directive 95/46/EC (General Data Protection Regulation), 2016 OJ (L119) 1–88, arts. 13–15.

[108] GDPR, art. 23. The processing of personal data for law enforcement purposes is dealt with in a separate instrument, Directive (EU) 2016/680 of the European Parliament and of the Council of 27 April 2016 on the protection of natural persons with regard to the processing of personal data by competent authorities for the purposes of the prevention, investigation, detection or prosecution of criminal offences or the execution of criminal penalties, and on the free movement of such data, and repealing Council Framework Decision 2008/977/JHA, 2016 OJ (L119/89). Member States are also offered a derogation allowing legacy processing systems to remain in place until May 6, 2023, with the option of a three-year extension to 2026, where there is a "disproportionate effort" required to bring them into compliance.

[109] UK Data Protection Act 2018, s. 14.

such tools themselves, lacking the human or technical capacity. Analytic service providers can step in to fill this breach, analyzing data themselves or designing tools to do so, including in the national security sector. However, the use of such firms raises important issues, and their obligations may not be clear in emerging governance regimes. For example, in the national security sector, such corporate actors may have access to sensitive and/or personal data, including across datasets, raising issues of privacy, as above. And additional issues may arise concerning the right to control and reuse derived data in this context.[110]

The role of corporate actors and their impact on access to and analysis of data is particularly pertinent in the context of open source intelligence, which has become an increasingly important tool of national security policymaking, and one substantially driven by algorithms and machine-learning tools because of the sheer bulk of information available for analysis.[111] Open source intelligence is information used for intelligence purposes which is publicly available rather than being obtained by covert means, as is usually the case in intelligence. Social media feeds, real estate information, some commercial website data, newspapers, and some browsing information are all potentially examples of open source intelligence. Policymakers and analysts use algorithms and machine-learning tools to automate the collection and analysis of these large volumes of information for analysts and, in some cases, automated decision-making systems.[112]

However, even though national security agencies may have access to tools, laws, and regulations which allow them to analyze this sort of data, they may not be able to access it easily or even at all. Corporate actors generally seek to protect their data from being accessed, especially by algorithms and machine-learning tools held by or used in support of national security and law enforcement agencies.[113] This is because data in this context is not only a commercial asset and protected as such, but also because companies seek to protect their customers' privacy from national security and law enforcement agencies.[114] Companies bar developers from designing algorithmic and machine-learning tools to facilitate agency access to their information, and have repeatedly disbarred data brokers which access their Application Programming Interface (API) to provide access to national security and law enforcement agencies for surveillance purposes. Barred from accessing the data directly, some agencies may buy bulk social media data from data brokers for analytic purposes, to understand trends in social activity and also to create and train analytic tools.

The legal context for automated collection and analysis of open source intelligence is often unclear. Internationally, case law in the area of web scraping more broadly is in a state of evolution, and has largely focused on copyright principles as a way of asserting ownership over data which has been scraped.[115] For example, if an agency buys bulk social media data to train analytic tools, the latter activity involves replicating copyrightable material, then this would

---

[110]   Bennett Moses *et al.*, above note 97, pp. 10–11.
[111]   See, e.g., S. Mateescu, D. Bruton, A. Rosenblat, *et al.*, Social Media Surveillance and Law Enforcement, in Data and Civil Rights Workshop (2015); B. van der Sloot and S. van Schendel, Ten Questions for Future Regulation of Big Data: A Comparative and Empirical Legal Study (2016) 7 *J. Intellect. Prop. Inf. Technol. E-Commer. Law* 110.
[112]   S. Logan and J. Chan, Using "Open Source" Data and Information for Defence, National Security and Law Enforcement. Interview Report for Research Question 3 (Report B), Data to Decisions Cooperative Research Centre (2018), p. 6.
[113]   Although note arguably only in the case of Western democracies.
[114]   Logan and Chan, above note 112, pp. 7–12.
[115]   Case C-30/14, *Ryanair Ltd* v. *PR Aviation BV* [2015] EUECJ at 45. The case, however, highlights that, in the European Union, contractual terms which prevent scraping may be invalid if the data is subject to copyright or a "sui generis right" and the scraping could be considered normal use, as the Gerechtshof te Amsterdam (Court of Appeal, Amsterdam) found in an earlier hearing on the case.

prima facie involve copyright infringement, allowing the original copyright holder to assert their rights over a state agency which may have scraped that information. While there is an exception for the temporary reproduction of works as a necessary part of a technical process in countries like Australia,[116] this probably does not apply to data mining.[117]

Web scraping for national security purposes is not subject to specific legislation in Australia.[118] In the United States, the Computer Fraud and Abuse Act 1986 makes it an offence to obtain "information from any protected computer" if one "intentionally accesses a computer without authorization or exceeds authorized access."[119] This was considered in the case of *hiQ Labs, Inc.* v. *LinkedIn Corp.* in the context of the issue of an injunction. The Court stated that there was at least a serious question as to whether a site could be said to be accessed "without authorization" where access to that site is open to the general public.[120] The ongoing case is considered to have significant implications for control of data and the legality of different forms of data scraping.[121] While web scraping for the purposes of profiling is explicitly regulated in the European Union's GDPR, however, the usual national security exemption applies.[122]

And even within government, access to information for analysis via big data techniques is not always clear. Information sharing between government national security agencies is often limited, beset by problems of governance, legislation, technology, and organizational culture.[123] As the example of open source intelligence indicates, automation of data processing is becoming increasingly important as a tool for national security and law enforcement agencies. However, the legality of particular practices, and access to data itself, is sometimes unclear and will depend on contractual terms with private sector platforms and data brokers, as well as (to the extent they apply to relevant agencies) copyright law, privacy law, computer offences, and more specific governance of agency practices.

In the final section of this chapter, we take a brief look at the regulatory directions focusing on the use of algorithms in government decision-making.

REGULATORY DIRECTIONS OF GOVERNMENT USE OF ALGORITHMS

When Is Automation of Government Decision-Making Authorized?

Legislation (at least in Australia) generally confers power on a specific (human) decision-maker, such as a Minister or other executive office holder. The use of algorithms to *assist* the human decision-maker generally does not require specific statutory authorization – but the human (or their lawful delegate) remains legally responsible for the decision. Government departments and agencies are generally authorized to make acquisitions, including of computer software, in compliance with relevant procurement policies and procedures.[124] However, where the machine *itself* makes the "decision," then legal issues may arise, as demonstrated by the case of *Pintarich* discussed above. Here, the Federal

[116] Copyright Act, s. 48B.
[117] ALRC, Copyright and the Digital Economy, Discussion Paper No. 79 (ALRC, June 5, 2013), p. 164.
[118] Web scraping is not expressly regulated through legislation in Australia and there is no case law. (B4) legal report, p. 15.
[119] 18 USC § 1030(a)(2)(C).
[120] *HiQ Labs, Inc.* v. *LinkedIn Corp.*, 938 F.3d 985 (9th Cir. 2019).
[121] Id.
[122] GDPR, art. 23.
[123] Bennett Moses *et al.*, above note 97.
[124] For these policies and procedures in Australian law, see N. Seddon, *Government Contracts: Federal, State and Local* (Federation Press, 2018).

Court of Australia found in 2018 that an automated "decision" was not a "decision" for the purposes of judicial review, because no "mental process" was involved in reaching it.[125] This meant that the Australian Taxation Office was not bound by the automated "decision" and could later demand a higher sum from the taxpayer.

Some legislation specifically authorizes the use of software within the decision-making system otherwise established by legislation. For example, in Australia, there are at least twenty-nine Commonwealth Acts and instruments that specifically authorize automated decision-making.[126] To illustrate, section 6A of the Social Security (Administration) Act provides that: "The Secretary may arrange for the use, under the Secretary's control, of computer programs for any purposes for which the Secretary may make decisions under social security law." There is also an Australian law that authorizes some data matching, which is often a step taken as preliminary to automated decision-making.[127]

There are important questions to ask about legislative provisions that specifically authorize the use of automation, including:

- what requirements exist for auditing, testing, and evaluation, as well as the frequency and nature of these;
- whether there is oversight in relation to the purchasing or use of particular software and systems;
- whether there are procedures by which the proper functioning of systems can be challenged by affected parties;
- whether there are procedures for challenging specific decisions where they are based on inaccurate data or falsely matched data, lead to an erroneous conclusion, or are biased (for example, because they have a disparate impact on a particular group[128]); and
- whether there are due process or procedural fairness protections for individuals affected by a decision.[129]

---

[125] *Pintarich v. Deputy Commissioner of Taxation* [2018] FCAFC 79.
[126] Social Security (Administration) Act 1999 (Cth), s. 6A; A New Tax System (Family Assistance) (Administration) Act (Cth), s. 223; Migration Act 1958, s. 495A; Australian Citizenship Act 2007 (Cth), s. 48; Superannuation (Government Co-contribution for Low Income Earners) Act 2003, s. 48; National Consumer Credit Protection Act 2009 (Cth), s. 242; Paid Parental Leave Act 2010 (Cth), s. 305; Carbon Credits (Carbon Farming Initiative) Act 2011 (Cth), s. 287; Australian National Registry of Emissions Units Act 2011 (Cth), s. 87; Business Names Registration Act 2011 (Cth), s. 66; My Health Records Act 2012 (Cth), s. 13A; Child Support (Assessment) Act 1989, s. 12A; Child Support (Registration and Collection) Act 1988 (Cth), s. 4A; Australian Education Act 2013 (Cth), s. 124; Trade Support Loans Act 2014 (Cth), s. 102; Customs Act 1901 (Cth), s. 126H; Biosecurity Act 2015 (Cth), s. 280(6), (7); Export Control Act 1982 (Cth), s. 23A(2)(h); Aged Care Act 1997 (Cth), s. 23B.4; VET Student Loans Act 2016 (Cth), s. 105; National Health Act 1953 (Cth), s. 101B; Military Rehabilitation and Compensation Act 2004 (Cth), s. 4A; Safety, Rehabilitation and Compensation (Defence-Related Claims) Act 1988 (Cth), s. 3A; Veterans' Entitlements Act 1986 (Cth), s. 4B; Therapeutic Goods Act 1989 (Cth), s. 7C(1); Export Control (High Quality Beef Export to the European Union Tariff Rate Quotas) Order 2016, cl. 42; Export Control (Sheepmeat and Goatmeat Export to the European Union Tariff Rate Quotas) Order 2016, cl. 25; Export Control (Beef Export to the USA Tariff Rate Quota) Order 2016, cl. 19A; Export Control (Dairy Produce Tariff Rate Quotas) Order 2016, cl. 36; Export Control (Japan–Australia Economic Partnership Agreement Tariff Rate Quotas) Order 2016, cl. 19. These were identified in S. Elvery, How Algorithms Make Important Government Decisions – and How that Affects You, *ABC News* (July 21, 2017), www.abc.net.au/news/2017-07-21/algorithms-can-make-decisions-on-behalf-of-federal-ministers/8704858; and Perry, above note 3, p. 31.
[127] Data Matching Program (Assistance and Tax) Act 1990.
[128] See Barocas and Selbst, above note 39.
[129] See generally K. Crawford and J. Schultz, Big Data and Due Process: Towards a Framework to Redress Predictive Privacy Harms (2014) 55 *BC Law Rev.* 93; Citron, above note 60.

To address these important questions and concerns, the idea of regulating automated decision-making is increasingly being considered by various governments around the world.

Regulation of Automated Decision-Making

Limited Governmental Regulation

Regulation of automation of decision-making is increasingly seen as necessary to ensure that particular standards or procedures are complied with when decision-making is fully or partially automated. For example, in the United Kingdom, there has been a call for increased transparency concerning the use of algorithms by government and the appointment of a "ministerial champion" to provide oversight of such use.[130] A Centre for Data Ethics and Innovation has been launched.[131]

However, such initiatives are often in their early stages and are still relatively rare. The existing regulation of automation of decision-making (if any) most often operates as part of the broader set of rules relating to the use and processing of personal information, commonly referred to as data privacy laws. Most influential of such provisions can be found in the European Union's GDPR.[132] As briefly mentioned in the previous section of this chapter, article 15(1)(h) of the GDPR articulates the right for any individual subject to automated decision-making, including profiling, to obtain "meaningful information about the logic involved, as well as the significance and the envisaged consequences of such processing for the data subject." Article 22(1) of the GDPR further states: "The data subject shall have the right not to be subject to a decision based solely on automated processing, including profiling, which produces legal effects concerning him or her or similarly significantly affects him or her."

The "right not be subjected to a decision based solely on automated processing" is, however, subject to explicit exceptions, which relate to contracts, explicit consent, and data uses authorized by law, including in the context of national security and law enforcement.[133] The effectiveness of this provision in regulating and/or limiting the automation of decision-making in practice is further impaired by the fact that the provision only applies to *fully* – and not *partially* – automated decisions. Some academic commentary on the scope of these GDPR provisions thus suggests their likely limited role in changing the decision-making practice.[134] A similar conclusion on the importance of the degree of automation involved in decision-making was reached in the US case of *State* v. *Loomis*, where such comparable due process right to be informed of the logic behind the COMPAS scoring tool was found not to apply to decisions that only rely partially on the output of an automated process.

Voluntary Regulatory Initiatives

Beyond currently limited governmental regulation, a variety of voluntary standards, principles, and ethical guidelines have been or are being developed by various bodies. Many of these

---

[130] House of Commons Science and Technology Committee, Algorithms in Decision-Making, Fourth Report of Session 2017–19 (May 15, 2018), p. 3.

[131] Information on the Centre is available on its website at www.gov.uk/government/groups/centre-for-data-ethics-and-innovation-cdei.

[132] Regulation (EU) 2016/679, above note 107.

[133] GDPR, art. 22(2).

[134] See, e.g., L. Edwards and M. Veale, Slave to the Algorithm? Why a "Right to an Explanation" Is Probably Not the Remedy You Are Looking for (2017) 16 *Duke Law Technol. Rev.* 18.

initiatives focus on categories that may intersect with rather than coincide with the use of automation in government decision-making. For example, there is the Toronto Declaration,[135] the Institute of Electrical and Electronics Engineers' (IEEE) Global Initiative on Ethics of Autonomous and Intelligent Systems,[136] the standardization project for artificial intelligence of the Joint Technical Committee of the International Standards Organization (ISO) and the International Electrotechnical Commission (IEC),[137] and the "Artificial Intelligence Ethics Framework" project at Australia's Data61.[138] Similarly, the "Partnership on AI to Benefit People and Society" has formulated best practices for the use of algorithms in decision-making, including in relation to fairness, transparency, and accountability.[139] Moreover, specific companies, such as Google, have done their own analysis on questions concerning "AI Governance," raising similar issues around explainability and fairness in automated decision-making.[140] Other regulatory options being explored include the use of third-party "seals" attesting to particular qualities of algorithms. While not specifically focused on government use of algorithms, it is possible that such voluntary standards will come to play a role in the regulation of automation for government decision-making in the (near) future.

CONCLUSION

This chapter has sketched a preliminary taxonomy of government use of algorithms to automate decision-making in a variety of different areas, ranging from administrative law and judicial decision-making, to national security context and statute drafting. It has discussed a plethora of problematic aspects and legal issues arising from the automation of government decision-making, including its potential incompatibility with the foundational legal values, such as the Rule of Law, and specific issues arising in the context of national security and law enforcement. The tensions between increasing automation of government decision-making on the one hand, and the foundational values of public law on the other, are likely to escalate in the future. Therefore, it is paramount that the complex intersections between the two are urgently investigated, understood, and debated among the policymakers, governments, and general public alike. It is crucial that these developments are also regulated so that individuals affected by government automation have venues for legal remedies, and more generally the future of government decision-making is compatible with foundational legal values and norms.

---

[135] See The Toronto Declaration: Protecting the Right to Equality and Non-Discrimination in Machine Learning Systems, Declaration, 2018, www.accessnow.org/cms/assets/uploads/2018/08/The-Toronto-Declaration _ENG_08-2018.pdf.

[136] See https://standards.ieee.org/industry-connections/ec/autonomous-systems.html.

[137] See www.iso.org/committee/6794475.html.

[138] See https://data61.csiro.au/en/Our-Work/AI-Framework.

[139] See their webpage at www.partnershiponai.org/.

[140] Google, Perspectives on Issues in AI Governance, https://ai.google/perspectives-on-issues-in-AI-governance/.

14

Algorithmic Decision Systems

Automation and Machine Learning in the Public Administration

David Restrepo Amariles[*]

INTRODUCTION

Our society in the twenty-first century is being shaped evermore by sets of instructions running at data centers spread around the world, commonly known as "algorithms." Although algorithms are not a recent invention, they have become widely used to support decision systems, arguably triggering the emergence of an algorithmic society.[1] These algorithmic decision systems (ADS) are deployed for purposes as disparate as pricing in online marketplaces,[2] flying planes,[3] generating credit scores,[4] and predicting demand for electricity.[5] Advanced ADS are characterized by two key features. First, they rely on the analysis of large amounts of data to make predictive inferences, such as the likelihood of a default for a potential borrower or an increase in demand for electricity consumption. Second, they automate in whole or in part the execution of decisions, such as refusing a loan to a high-risk borrower or increasing energy prices during peak hours, respectively. ADS may also refer to less advanced systems implementing only one of these features. Although ADS generally have proven to be beneficial in improving the efficiency of making decisions, the underlying algorithms remain controversial, among other issues, because they are susceptible to discrimination, bias, and a loss of privacy – with the potential to even be used to manipulate the democratic processes and structures underpinning our society[6] – alongside lacking effective means of control and accountability.

---

[*] This chapter is based on the results of research projects conducted with the support of the HEC Foundation (Grant on Regulatory Strategies for Algorithms) and the European Union (Grant on Conflict Resolution with Equative Algorithms – CREA). I am grateful to Usman Amjed, Amal Ibraymi, Rajaa El-hamdani, and Vasile Rotaru for their contribution to the above projects, and their comments and assistance with this chapter. All remaining errors are my own.
[1] For a discussion on the notion of "algorithmic society," see J. M. Balkin, The Three Laws of Robotics in the Age of Big Data (2017) 78 *Ohio St. Law J.* 1217, 1219, where he defines it as "a society organized around social and economic decision-making by algorithms, robots, and AI agents."
[2] A. Ezrachi and M. E. Stucke, *Virtual Competition: The Promise and Perils of the Algorithm-Driven Economy* (Harvard University Press, 2016), pp. 85–100.
[3] See the US Department of Transportation SAFO Alert requesting plane operators to decrease their reliance on autopilot (run by algorithms) and emphasize manual flight operations in both line operations and training, SAFO 13002, April 1, 2013.
[4] L. Munkhdalai, T. Munkhdalai, O.-E. Namsrai, *et al.*, An Empirical Comparison of Machine-Learning Methods on Bank Client Credit Assessments (2019) 699 *MPDI Sustainability* 1.
[5] J. Bedi and D. Toshniwal, Deep Learning Framework to Forecast Electricity Demand (2019) 238 Applied Energy 1312.
[6] C. Cadwalladr and E. Graham-Harrison, Revealed: 50 Million Facebook Profiles Harvested for Cambridge Analytica in Major Data Breach, *The Guardian* (March 17, 2018), www.theguardian.com/news/2018/mar/17/cambridge-analytica-facebook-influence-us-election.

The ubiquity of data-driven ADS is largely due to the technological innovations of the last century. Indeed, instead of data being scarce, expensive, and collected only according to pre-specified design, we have moved on to data being collected ubiquitously and in large quantities by portable communication devices and sensors. Even more than the sheer size of the datasets collected by ADS devices, it is the granular, personalized nature of this data which enables accurate predictions.[7] Furthermore, the past decade has witnessed rapid growth in the ability of networked and mobile computing systems to transport and analyze vast amounts of this data, negating the need for specialized, expensive computing devices to extract information from these datasets, switching instead to a cloud-based system wherein algorithms running in data centers crunch information and communicate it seamlessly to end devices.

It is thus no surprise that both private and public organizations increasingly rely on ADS. For instance, in the private sector, Google uses anonymized location data from smartphones to analyze the speed and movement of traffic and generate efficient routes through its Google Maps service.[8] Similarly, ridesharing apps like Lyft and Uber use machine learning to predict rider demand, allocate rides to drivers, and fix prices;[9] while Netflix's and YouTube's recommendation systems rely on machine learning to improve both streaming quality and video recommendations.[10] Within the public sector, Her Majesty's Revenue & Customs (HMRC) office of the UK government relies on a system called ADEPT to improve both tax-debt recovery and tax revenue collection. By analyzing the data collected from twenty internal and external sources, HMRC has contributed to an increase in tax-debt collection of £3 billion.[11] Furthermore, the *Direction Nationale à la Lutte contre la Fraude* (DNLF, or French National Anti-Fraud Unit) has developed algorithms which profile fraudulent tax behavior, resulting in 15 percent of their tax audits being initiated through data-mining tools in 2018.[12]

This chapter studies the use of ADS by public authorities as a tool to allocate rights and benefits. In this context, it highlights three ways in which ADS are transforming legal decision-making, characterizing what I have referred to elsewhere as "algorithmic law."[13] First, this chapter brings to light the ways in which the formalization of law into code alters in practice the content of the law, the grounds on which administrative decisions are taken, and the type of arguments put forward as justification. Second, by delving into the processing of vast and dynamic datasets by automated software through machine-learning techniques, this chapter illustrates the ways in which the relationship between fact and norm is being

[7] S. C. Olhede and P. J. Wolfe, The Growing Ubiquity of Algorithms in Society: Implications, Impacts and Innovations (2018) 376 *Philos. TR Soc. A* 1.

[8] D. Barth, The Bright Side of Sitting in Traffic: Crowdsourcing Road Congestion Data, *Official Google Blog* (August 25, 2009), http://googleblog.blogspot.in/2009/08/bright-side-of-sitting-in-traffic.html.

[9] J. Hermann and M. Del Balso, Scaling Machine Learning at Uber with Michelangelo, *Official Uber Blog* (November 2, 2018).

[10] D. Restrepo Amariles, Le droit algorithmique: sur l'effacement de la distinction entre la règle et sa mise en œuvre, in F. G'sell (ed.), *Law and Big Data* (Dalloz, 2020); L. Plummer, This Is How Netflix's Top-Secret Recommendation System Works, *Wired* (August 22, 2017), www.wired.co.uk/article/how-do-netflixs-algorithms-work-machine-learning-helps-to-predict-what-viewers-will-like.

[11] Capgemini, Big Data and Predictive Analytics Help HMRC Process Debt Payments More Quickly (2014), www.capgemini.com/wp-content/uploads/2017/07/ss_hmrc_adept.pdf.

[12] C. Lequesne Roth, Data Science Leveraged by French Tax Authorities: Reflections on the Algocracy, in A. Pariente (ed.), *Les chiffres en finances publiques* (LGDJ, 2019). See also D. Restrepo Amariles and G. Lewkowicz, L'émergence du SMART Law en droit bancaire et financier (2019) 3–4 *International Journal for Financial Services* 24.

[13] Cf. Restrepo Amariles, above note 10.

redefined based on mathematical and statistical operations. Finally, it shows that the enforcement of law and administrative decisions through automation alters the rights of citizens and the terms under which they relate to the public administration.

The chapter is organized as follows. The section entitled "Unpacking Algorithmic Decision Systems in Law" introduces automation and machine-learning techniques generally employed to develop ADS, highlighting their distinct features and key functions in relation to legal processes and operations. "The Rule behind the Code" analyzes the functioning of algorithmic decision-making and the challenges it poses when law is implemented into code. "Datasets and Administrative Decisions" discusses data-driven decision-making and its dependency on the accuracy as well as the completeness of the data, including problems and unfairness that might arise from inconsistent, incomplete, or biased datasets. "Automating Enforcement" analyzes the consequences of the implementation of advanced ADS in administrative decision-making. The final section concludes by considering the overall implications in terms of the rule of law.

UNPACKING ALGORITHMIC DECISION SYSTEMS IN LAW

ADS generally refer to automation by means of algorithms of multiple processes which underpin the decision-making process, including the collection and processing of data, as well as the execution of decisions with little or no human intervention. As such, ADS rely on multiple methods covered loosely under the term of artificial intelligence (AI). AI is broadly used to refer to machines that are "smart" or, in other words, which are able to perform certain tasks that are commonly associated with intelligent beings.[14] More formally, AI concerns "the study of the design of intelligent agents," where the latter is defined as "something that acts," such as a computer.[15] Such tasks have, until several decades ago, been associated with humans – for example, recognizing objects in images (computer vision), understanding and responding to speech (natural language processing), executing tasks which are physically difficult for humans (robotics), transporting individuals/items from one point to another (autonomous vehicles), etc. Figure 14.1 represents the multiple methods that can be implemented to achieve AI, such as machine learning, natural language processing, etc., and, when relevant, the specific techniques deployed by each. This section presents multiple techniques of machine learning which support data-driven ADS and provides an overview of their implementation in the legal domain.

An Introduction to Machine Learning in Algorithmic Decision-Making

Machine learning refers to a method used by computer programs to learn from experience and improve their performance over time. These systems are given a task, along with a large amount of data to be used as examples on how such a task can be achieved or from which to detect patterns. These systems then learn the optimal method to achieve the desired output under the desired constraints. As a result of several breakthroughs in the past half-century,

---

[14] B. Marr, The Key Definitions of Artificial Intelligence (AI) that Explain Its Importance, *Forbes* (February 14, 2018), www.forbes.com/sites/bernardmarr/2018/02/14/the-key-definitions-of-artificial-intelligence-ai-that-explain-its-importance/#15081bd34f5d.

[15] F. Zuiderveen Borgesius, Discrimination, Artificial Intelligence, and Algorithmic Decision-Making, Study for the Council of Europe (2018), https://rm.coe.int/discrimination-artificial-intelligence-and-algorithmic-decision-making/1680925d73.

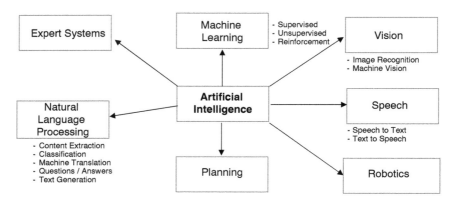

FIGURE 14.1 Methods and techniques of AI

machine learning has become the preferred tool to pursue AI. It is worth highlighting here at least three of these developments.

First, researchers realize it is much more efficient to teach computers how to learn than it is to actually program them to understand and perform each and every possible task. The foundations were laid down in the late 1950s and early 1960s, among others by R. J. Solomonoff, whose seminal papers developed the notion of inductive inference machine and fed the emergence of algorithmic information theories.[16] Second, the generalized shift toward a data-driven approach in the 1990s helped design and deploy more effective machine-learning algorithms. The development of the Internet and the associated reduction in cost of information storage ultimately made available mass amounts of data that can be collected, stored, and employed to train these algorithms.[17] Finally, the large dataset of the ImageNet project built by scholars of the Department of Computer Science at Princeton University in the late 2000s helped to assess the actual performance of deep-learning algorithms.[18] The successful results, together with significant advances in hardware, especially the graphics processing unit (GPU), which increased the speed of deep-learning algorithms, eventually opened up the path for industrial and commercial applications of machine learning.

As a field of study, machine learning lies at the intersection of computer science and statistics alongside a variety of other disciplines concerned with automated improvement over time, as well as inference and decision-making under uncertainty. Since machine learning has become a practical method of choice in achieving AI, both of these terms are now used in an intertwined fashion.[19] Machine learning itself can be classified into three types: supervised learning, unsupervised learning, and reinforcement learning.

[16] R. J. Solomonoff, An Inductive Inference Machine, 1957 IRE National Convention Record; R. J. Solomonoff, A Preliminary Report on a General Theory of Inductive Inference (revision of Report V-131), Technical Report ZTB-138, Zator Co. and Air Force Office of Scientific Research, Cambridge, MA (November 1960); R. J. Solomonoff, A Formal Theory of Inductive Inference: Part I (1964) 7 *Inf. Control* 1; R. J. Solomonoff, A Formal Theory of Inductive Inference: Part II (1964) 7 *Inf. Control* 224.

[17] T. Mills, Machine Learning vs Artificial Intelligence: How Are They Different?, *Forbes* (June 11, 2018), www .forbes.com/sites/forbestechcouncil/2018/07/11/machine-learning-vs-artificial-intelligence-how-are-they-different /#4b961f153521.

[18] J. Deng, W. Dong, R. Socher, *et al.*, ImageNet: A Large-Scale Image Database, in 2009 IEEE Conference on Computer Vision and Pattern Recognition, Miami, FL (2009), pp. 248–55.

[19] Chetan Kumar GN, Artificial Intelligence vs Machine Learning, *Medium* (September 1, 2018), https://medium .com/@chethankumargn/artificial-intelligence-vs-machine-learning-3c599637ecdd.

Supervised Learning

The most widely used machine-learning techniques are supervised learning methods.[20] These methods exemplify the function approximation problem where the training data takes the form of a collection of (x, y) pairs with the goal being to produce a prediction (y) in response to a query (x). The x inputs are vectors, whether composed of structured datasets such as the records of numerical variables used for credit scoring, or unstructured datasets such as documents, images, DNA sequences, or graphs. In the latter case, datasets need to be converted into appropriate vectors prior to the processing. The output (y) can also be varied, as it can be either a binary classification output (for example, an email is either "spam" or "not spam") or a multi-classification output (for example, part-of-speech tagging, where the goal is to simultaneously label every word in an input sentence "*x*" as being a noun, verb, or some other part of speech).[21]

A classic example of the supervised learning problem are spam filters for email. Spam emails are unsolicited, unwanted, commercial emails which can cause significant time-management headaches for users since they hinder access to important emails. Now, a user could manually read through each and every email, marking those which are spam, but this would be a labor-intensive task. Instead, machine-learning algorithms can be trained to recognize such spam emails by being provided with thousands of examples of spam for pattern analysis. For instance, when a user determines a certain email is spam, they mark it, with this act of marking being an indication to the algorithm that it is a spam email. Once a person does this hundreds of times, the algorithm will attempt to figure out the telling characteristics of spam emails using the examples that have been marked by the user (for example, emails with phrases such as "become a millionaire"). This pattern detection builds and strengthens rules which allow these algorithms to make predictions regarding future occurrences.[22] These algorithms significantly improve over time as they analyze more data, expanding their rules, allowing them to make improved decisions. Hence, a machine-learning algorithm might perform poorly at first since it lacks sufficient training data, but it will improve its accuracy over time once it has enough data to recognize the patterns and outliers. This is what "learning" means in the context of machine learning and it is the key ability which characterizes these algorithms. Ultimately, the system would be able to automatically perform the task of separating spam emails from others. Since this method of learning involves learning from a set of verified examples (emails marked as spam), it is commonly known as "supervised" learning. These algorithms are not learning in the cognitive sense, rather, they are improving their accuracy by detecting more granular patterns with increases in the amount of data available to them.

Unsupervised Learning

A second type of machine-learning technique is known as unsupervised learning. This technique involves the translation of unlabeled data into rules regarding the properties of the data – for example, clustering. In clustering, a machine-learning algorithm attempts to automatically classify or group unlabeled items which are similar in one or more ways.

---

[20] N. Castle, Supervised vs. Unsupervised Machine Learning, *Official Oracle Data Science Blog* (June 13, 2017), www.datascience.com/blog/supervised-and-unsupervised-machine-learning-algorithms.

[21] M. I. Jordan and T. M. Mitchell, Machine Learning: Trends, Perspectives, and Prospects (2015) 349 *Science* 255.

[22] H. Surden, Machine Learning and Law (2014) 89 *Wash. Law Rev.* 87.

The algorithm tries to detect relationships and hidden characteristics in a dataset which has not been labeled. One such type of unsupervised learning algorithm is known as "deep learning" algorithms, also known as "artificial neural networks." Although artificial neural networks are used for supervised learning as well, they are especially significant for unsupervised learning problems. Such algorithms have been successfully used to construct high-level feature detectors using unlabeled images.

An example of this is one neural net which was developed by Google X – Google's famous lab for experimental technologies.[23] At Google X, computer scientists built a network of 1 billion connections, among neurons, trained on 16,000 processors. The network was exposed to 10 million randomly selected YouTube video thumbnails over a three-day period, and after being presented with a list of 20,000 different items, it began to recognize pictures of cats, even though it had never been fed any information on the distinguishing features of a cat.[24] More precisely, the researchers explicitly looked, through mathematical methods, for neurons that are highly activated by high-level concepts – such as faces, body parts, and cats. Although the algorithm cannot output labels such as cats, it learned high-level features for recognizing cats. Overall, the system achieved 81.7 percent accuracy in detecting human faces, 76.7 percent accuracy when identifying human body parts, and 74.8 percent accuracy when identifying cats. Unsupervised deep learning systems resemble to a certain extent human-level cognitive ability; however, such systems are still years away from anything close to the complexity of learning ability our brains rely upon.

Reinforcement Learning

The last major machine-learning technique is reinforcement learning. In this case, algorithms do not learn from a pre-established training dataset, but from the data resulting from a learning environment. Instead of feeding the algorithm with instructive feedback through large amounts of unlabeled data or providing examples of correct outputs for given inputs, reinforcement learning relies on evaluative feedback of how much an output is correct. The multi-armed bandit is a simplified problem which helps in understanding the mechanisms of reinforcement learning.[25] In the multi-armed problem, the learning agent evolves in an environment where at each step he must select an action among a set of actions, such that each action returns a reward to the agent. The agent's goal is to maximize the sum of obtained rewards, but it has no or partial information of the reward returned by each action. The multi-armed bandit problem is named by analogy to a slot-machine or "one-armed bandit," where a gambler is faced with multiple slot machines and has to decide on the best strategy to play the machines and maximize his gains, but with incomplete information of the gains returned by each machine. In the multi-armed bandit, the agent learns what actions to select from the rewards it received from its past actions, so actions with high rewards will be privileged and actions with low rewards will be avoided in the future.

Such problems typically involve a control setting in which the learning task is to learn a control strategy for an agent in an unknown, dynamic environment, where the strategy is trained to choose actions for any given state with the sole objective of maximizing its reward over time. Strong ties also exist between reinforcement learning and decades of psychological

---

[23]   For more information about Company X, see https://x.company/projects/brain/.

[24]   Q. V. Lee, M. A. Ranzato, R. Monga, *et al.*, Building High-level Features Using Large Scale Unsupervised Learning, in International Conference on Machine Learning (2012), https://arxiv.org/pdf/1112.6209.pdf.

[25]   V. Kuleshov and D. Precup, Algorithms for Multi-Armed Bandit Problems (2014), arXiv:1402.6028.

research and neuroscience, where the effect of rewards can be considered similar to that of a release of dopamine in the brain.[26] One classic application of reinforcement learning is robotics, where it provides a framework and a set of tools for hard-to-engineer behavior in dynamic conditions.

Among these three methods, supervised learning is currently the leading method in use to generate accurate predictions and inferences regarding behaviors. However, ADS can be designed to rely on inferences resulting from the implementation of any of these variants of machine learning, as discussed in the following sections.

Machine Learning Applied to the Legal Domain

Since machine learning is becoming central to solving a number of complex problem areas, the practice of law is also concerned by these advancements in at least two ways. First, machine-learning techniques may contribute to understanding how legal decisions are taken; and, second, they may help to improve the decision-making process itself. Regarding the first, machine-learning techniques applied to legal texts (for example, text mining) can help discover hidden relationships in existing data with historical cases and precedents.[27] Legal operators can use such algorithms to highlight useful, unknown information which can be obscured due to limited resources for research. These algorithms need to learn historical cases only once, and might be able to detect subtle correlations that would go unnoticed during, for instance, a typical attorney analysis. Such information might result in more efficient research and more precise legal arguments, which may ultimately help to improve the legal success rates of a law firm. Human beings, no matter how literate, are still susceptible to forgetfulness, whereas an algorithm retains its information and is capable of parsing through thousands of legal files and pieces in seconds.

A second application of machine learning to the legal domain concerns the automation of sub-sets of legal tasks.[28] Kevin Ashley provides a wide spectrum of tasks that can be partially automated and simplified if such systems are adopted on a large scale, such as modeling legal reasoning and predicting legal outcomes.[29] As an example of the former, I participated in the design of a software that automates several legal tasks to help verify compliance with privacy laws, and more particularly with the European General Data Protection Regulation (GDPR).[30] Initially, the software relied on a rule-based approach to detect keywords and sentences in privacy policies using a dataset of fifty-three problematic clauses (manually retrieved from privacy policies), forty problematic words selected by lawyers, and forty-three unlawful clauses retrieved from French

---

[26] Cf. Jordan and Mitchell, above note 21.

[27] M. Vazirgiannis, D. Restrepo Amariles, and R. El-Hamdani, Performance in the Courtroom: Automated Processing and Visualization of Appeal Court Decisions in France?, working paper (under review, Workshop on Natural Legal Language Processing NLLP – KDD Conference). Also, a number of start-ups currently offer similar services to law firms and legal professionals. See, for instance, the start-ups Ravel Law in the United States (www.ravellaw.com) and Doctrine in Europe (www.doctrine.fr).

[28] For example, the COLIEE competition organized by Ken Sato and Randy Goebel includes a case retrieval task which involves "reading a new case Q, and extracting supporting cases S1, S2, . . . Sn for the decision of Q from the entire case law corpus." See https://sites.ualberta.ca/~rabelo/COLIEE2019/.

[29] K. Ashley, *Artificial Intelligence and Legal Analytics: New Tools for Law Practice in the Digital Age* (Cambridge University Press, 2017).

[30] D. Restrepo Amariles, A. Troussel, and R. El-Hamdani, Compliance Generation for Privacy Documents under GDPR: A Roadmap for Implementing Automation and Machine Learning, in Workshop GDPR, 32nd International Conference on Legal Knowledge and Information Systems (2019).

court decisions and French data protection authority decisions. We used keyword detection to produce a prototype software which was tested by legal professionals. During the second phase, we introduced supervised machine-learning methods using annotated privacy policies and regulations. The objective was to improve the detection of problematic clauses and the assessment of such clauses in relation to the rest of the text, and not only as an isolated segment. First, natural language processing algorithms analyze the semantics of the privacy policy and extract information about the data practices mentioned in the privacy policy. Second, the extracted information is fed to a rule-based system to detect high-risk data practices. The rule-based system was built by legal experts by modeling the GDPR. The software also implements supervised machine learning to feed the loop feedback from users into the training dataset, eventually contributing to the improvement of the algorithms' accuracy.

Researchers have also investigated the use of machine learning to predict legal outcomes. Take the case of a law firm assessing the likelihood of certain legal outcomes relative to the risk of liability in a context of factual uncertainty. Attorneys may estimate such risks by employing their professional experience, training, reasoning, and cognitive abilities. Daniel Katz, however, argues that such predictions may be reasonably conducted by algorithmic analysis.[31] In his view, enough historical legal data, past scenarios, and case decisions exist for algorithms to be able to predict significantly accurate legal outcomes and the risks involved. Different aspects of each case, such as the judge involved, whether a case was settled, the size of the settlement amount (if any), whether it went to trial, etc., can be combined with private data sources to be used as a training set for predictive models.[32] Following an examination of a sufficient number of cases and with time, such supervised learning models might become better at estimating likely outcomes than actual attorneys.[33] Indeed, firms such as Legalist,[34] a young litigation finance start-up, employ algorithms to estimate the risk involved in litigations as accurately as possible so that they do not "back the wrong horse," so to speak, and ensure a favorable outcome.

However, there are certain pitfalls which one needs to be aware of. Such predictive models rely on rules developed based on past cases. Hence, the success of these predictions is dependent on the extent to which future cases will have pertinent features in common with past cases, and more importantly, on the assumption that courts will not depart from previous case law. In case of novel features in relation to the facts of the case or the reasoning held by the court, the predictions might be unreliable.

Bias in Data-Driven ADS

As mentioned above, machine-learning algorithms depend significantly on mass amounts of data in order to achieve accurate predictions. If it is true that this data-dependency poses significant challenges to the quality of decisions performed by ADS, it is trivial to blame any

---

[31] D. M. Katz, Quantitative Legal Prediction – or – How I Learned to Stop Worrying and Start Preparing for the Data Driven Future of the Legal Services Industry (2013) 62 *Emory Law J.* 909.

[32] For an example of such research outputs, see D. Restrepo Amariles, M. Vazirgiannis, and P. Baquero, AI-Driven Legal Analytics in the Courtroom, working paper (2020).

[33] Cf. Surden, above note 22.

[34] C. Loizos, This Young Litigation Finance Startup Just Secured $100 Million to Chase Cases It Thinks Will Win, *Techcrunch* (September 18, 2019), https://techcrunch.com/2019/09/17/this-young-litigation-finance-startup-just-secured-100-million-to-go-after-cases-it-thinks-are-winners/.

possible biases on only the training data. For the purposes of this chapter, it is useful to understand algorithmic bias in a broad sense, covering two distinct yet interconnected issues. First, algorithmic bias captures the features and limitations that are inherent to algorithms as technology assisting human decision-making processes, for instance, the translation of a legal provision from natural to formal language and programming code. Second, as widely discussed in the literature, algorithmic bias relates to the unfairness resulting from the implementation of ADS, such as when a group of individuals belonging to a protected class is granted fewer social security benefits for the mere reason of belonging to such a category.

Karen Hao rightly points out that bias can creep into automated systems long before any data is collected in the process of training them.[35] An algorithm can instead become susceptible to biased behaviors throughout many other stages of developing automated systems, such as while framing a problem, while gathering the data, and while preparing this data for training these systems. Solon Barocas and Andrew Selbst argue that one of the most notable places where bias is introduced is how a problem is framed.[36] Take the case of credit scoring. Credit scores are used by banks to decide whether or not to grant a loan to a particular consumer. However, the definition of creditworthiness or scores depends on a company's goal, whether it be maximizing profits or the number of loans which are repaid. While profits might be maximized by issuing subprime loans, however, the number of loans repaid in this scenario would not be a key attribute of creditworthiness. This might lead the ADS to indulge in predatory lending behavior, as was the case during the subprime mortgage crises in 2008. Similarly, the process of data collection can also induce bias in automated systems. The collected data might be misrepresentative of reality (for example, if a gender classification algorithm is fed more light-toned faces than dark ones),[37] meaning the accuracy of its output would be skewed in favor of light-skinned subjects. Additionally, as mentioned above, the training dataset might already account for existing biases in society. For instance, Amazon recently shut down its ADS used for recruitments due to bias being displayed against the classification of female candidates, since it was trained on historical hiring decisions which favored men over women.[38]

Finally, another stage for introducing bias is during the preparation of the training data, specifically in regard to which attributes must be used by the algorithm for its decision-making process. Consider, for instance, the targeted advertising ecosystem comprised of advertisers, advertising platforms (for example, Facebook and Google), and the users of those platforms, which are the potential customers of the digital advertisers. A potential for discrimination against the users arises from the ability of advertisers to utilize extensive personal attributes gathered and inferred by advertising platforms such as race, religion, likes, dislikes, sexual orientation, age, gender, etc. Till Speicher and colleagues developed a quantification approach to measure discrimination in targeted advertising based on the advertiser's intent and ad-targeting process.[39] Following the development of a quantification

[35] K. Hao, This Is How AI Bias Really Happens – and Why It's So Hard to Fix, *MIT Technology Review* (February 4, 2019).
[36] S. Barocas and A. D. Selbst, Big Data's Disparate Impact (2016) 104 *Calif. Law Rev.* 671.
[37] K. Hao, Making Face Recognition Less Biased Doesn't Make It Less Scary, *MIT Technology Review* (January 29, 2019).
[38] J. Dustin, Amazon Scraps Secret AI Recruiting Tool that Showed Bias against Women, *Reuters* (October 18, 2018), www.reuters.com/article/us-amazon-com-jobs-automation-insight/amazon-scraps-secret-ai-recruiting-tool-that-showed-bias-against-women-idUSKCN1MK08G.
[39] T. Speicher, M. Ali, G. Venkatadri, *et al.*, Potential for Discrimination in Online Targeted Advertising (2018) 81 *Proc. Mach. Learn. Res.* 1.

mechanism, they then focused on attribute-based targeting, which refers to a process of selecting the audience for an advertisement based on certain attributes or a combination of those attributes. This method is the one traditionally used for targeting ads on Facebook, since Facebook tracks a binary list of 1,100 attributes for each user ranging from their demographic to their behavior.[40] Till Speicher and colleagues downloaded a list of public voter records from North Carolina and created different groupings of people that only contained particular ethnicities (White, Asian American, Hispanic, etc.). They then created sub-audiences by choosing to only target users that matched each curated attribute and observed the size estimates of these sub-audiences. The percentage of users from each audience for whom Facebook inferred a curated attribute revealed how prevalent each attribute is within the audiences of different ethnicities. The results demonstrated that, in many cases, ethnicity is not the prevalent attribute in targeting ethnicities (for example, Asians). When targeting Asians on Facebook, it was more effective to do so based on political views or eating habits than on ethnicity. This shows that even the removal of sensitive attributes is insufficient for eliminating bias among automated algorithms.[41]

Furthermore, Hoda Heidari and colleagues argue that although existing formulations for reducing algorithmic bias are focused on guaranteeing the equality of some ultimate benefit (with the right tractable mathematical formula) across different individuals, however, it is not the only aspect and more attention should be paid to other overlooked aspects in these automated systems such as risk and welfare.[42] As an example, consider four predictive models – A, B, C, and D – which assign a benefit (numeral) across five users (input). Model A assigns the same benefit of 0.8 to everyone, Model B assigns a benefit of 0.5, 0.6, 0.8, 0.9, and 1.2 to each of the five users. Model C assigns a benefit of 1.0 to everyone, while Model D provides users with a benefit of 0.78, 0.9, 0.92, 1.1, and 1.3 respectively. Now, suppose that a decision-maker has to decide the most desirable distribution. From a fairness perspective, A trumps B even though the total benefit provided by both is 4, as it distributes benefits equally to all its users. Similarly, C is preferred to D, even after both provide an ultimate benefit of 5, since C distributes it equally to all. However, if we focus on equality alone, A is deemed to be more desirable than D, even though D provides a higher total benefit (5 compared to 4) and almost everyone, except for the first user (0.78 under D compared to 0.8 under A), witnesses an increase in the benefit being provided to them. In other words, even though D results in unequal benefits and it does not Pareto-dominate A, collectively it results in higher welfare and lower risk and, therefore, both intuitively and from a rational point of view, it should be considered more desirable. Hence, one may question whether algorithmic fairness may be better achieved when algorithms are built to make decisions behind veils of ignorance.[43] In other words, without focusing on mathematical formulas and instead putting weight into outcomes and other attributes such as risk and welfare. As is the case above, if social welfare is taken as the metric, Model D would be preferred to Model A, as it ensures higher welfare and a low risk of a 2 percent drop in benefit for the first user.[44]

It is evident from the discussions above that state-of-the-art research on machine learning highlights the difficulty of both detecting and removing bias within data-driven ADS to

[40]   About Facebook Ads, www.facebook.com/ads/about/?entryproduct=ad_preferences.
[41]   Cf. Speicher *et al.*, above note 39.
[42]   H. Heidari, C. Ferrari, K. P. Gummadi, and A. Krause, Fairness behind a Veil of Ignorance: A Welfare Analysis for Automated Decision Making, 32nd Conference on Neural Information Processing System, NeurIPS (2018), arXiv:1806.04959.
[43]   J. Rawls, *A Theory of Justice* (Harvard University Press, 1971), p. 136.
[44]   Heidari *et al.*, above note 42.

ensure optimal outputs and behaviors. Even declaring certain attributes to be constant or using mathematical reasoning to ensure equal distribution of benefits does not eliminate discriminatory behavior, which in some instances – as evidenced above – can arise from these solutions. Mireille Hildebrandt argues that instead of relying on algorithms that depend on historical data of individuals to predict specific future behaviors which are susceptible to bias caused by training data, we should instead move toward agonistic machine learning which is more compatible with safeguarding the plurality of the human self.[45] She further argues that although human beings are computable, we, however, cannot be completely defined by such computations as there can be radically different ways to compute the same person.[46] Hence, she continues, we should be moving from assuming machine learning would get it right to testing whether the bias detected in training sets makes good sense or is incorrect. Agonistic machine learning would bring the adversarial core of the rule of law into the heart of the design of data-driven environments, thus also aligning with the methodological core of reliable machine learning.[47]

The next sections look concretely into the practical implementation of ADS by public administrations in Europe and the United States, the ineluctable entrenchment and institutionalization of algorithmic bias, and the implications of the latter for legal decision-making. Although, as discussed above, careful review and scrutiny are not enough to prevent unfairness, they can help legal operators and professionals to get a grip on the accountability of algorithms. Scrutiny needs to be conducted in relation to, at least, the design, coding, training data, and input and output data of the ADS. Each of the case studies in the next sections purports to analyze these dimensions both individually and jointly, in order to bring forth the processes leading to their implementation and the ways in which they are reshaping legal decision-making.

THE RULE BEHIND THE CODE: AUTOMATING THE RIGHT TO ACCESS HIGHER EDUCATION

Among the countries that have introduced ADS in the public sector, France deserves a close look. On the one hand, the French government has publicly stated its ambition to develop a *République numérique* (Digital Republic),[48] committing significant financial resources and making it one of its four key strategic programs for the 2018–22 period.[49] On the other hand, the parliament and high courts have been actively keeping check on the government in an attempt to preserve the rule of law in this new digital setting. This section seeks to analyze the ways in which computer coding shapes the rules that are effectively being applied to citizens in the context of ADS. It develops a case study concerning the implementation by the French Ministry of Education of a software allocating places to high school graduates in university which has triggered concern among citizens and scholars.

In 2009, the French government launched, for the first time, an online platform called Admission Post Bac (APB) – a software that allows high school graduates to seek out a place in a French university program. The APB algorithm matches the wishes of the candidates with

---

[45] M. Hildebrandt, Privacy as Protection of the Incomputable Self: From Agnostic to Agonistic Machine Learning (2019) 20 *Theor. Inq. Law* 83.

[46] *Ibid.*, p. 106.

[47] *Ibid.*, p. 107.

[48] J. Chevallier, Vers l'État-plateforme? (2018) 167 *Revue française d'administration publique* 627.

[49] The French government allocated €9.3 billion to the digital transformation of the state for the 2018–22 period, making it one of the four key strategic axes of its investment plan. See Le Grand plan d'investissement 2018–2022, www.gouvernement.fr/le-grand-plan-d-investissement.

the requisites of the universities' programs, or alternatively, allocates students through a draw for non-selective training programs. APB was designed to apply the rules and criteria contained in the French Code of Higher Education with two main purposes: first, to improve efficiency by delegating to software what is traditionally a time-consuming task that was previously performed by public officials. Second, to ensure a uniform and impartial application of the rules. As a consequence, since the fees and programs among French public universities are uniform in nature, APB's allocation bears a direct impact on the professional future and opportunities of students given the disparity in terms of reputation and market value of the different degrees and institutions.

After multiple attempts to hold the algorithm accountable, the Commission nationale de l'informatique et des libertés (CNIL), the French National Data Protection Agency, eventually scrapped the APB in 2017.[50] It held that the APB had violated the prohibition on issuing individual administrative decisions based solely on automated processing. Following this decision, the government set up a new platform termed Parcoursup,[51] which received a favorable opinion from the CNIL.[52] Similar to the previous system, Parcoursup automatically assigns students to higher education institutions, but has tried to improve on the former by providing for some degree of human intervention. As such, it is now up to the universities to list the candidates they accept by taking into consideration local requirements in addition to other relevant local administrative considerations. In other words, the French Ministry of Higher Education tasked the universities with a new managerial mission for the "selection" of the candidates who can register at the universities after graduating from secondary school. Students register their preferred universities and/or training programs on the Parcoursup platform and rank them in order of preference and priority. The university then ranks the applications according to its own internal criteria and, finally, the APB system delivers the optimal proposals to the candidates, while also accounting for the preferences of the university and the student.

Both automated systems raise concerns about the opacity in which they operate, and thus about the rules and criteria which are in fact applied in order to allocate students to specific training programs and universities. They also bring to the fore questions relating to the desirable level of automation in public administration – bringing to the attention of legal professionals and computer scientists the need to ensure that ADS remain as "open and accountable as possible."[53] Otherwise, fairness and adherence to the rule of law could be compromised. Within this context, an essential facet of accountability requires administrative authorities to make the source code publicly available as a first approach to ensuring accountability in the design and operation of ADS.

Taking the Code to Court: Accountability through Citizen Participation

The request to disclose the APB's source code was originally submitted in March 2016 by the association Droit des Lycéens, which represented French high school students and assisted

---

[50] CNIL, Decision No. 2017-053, August 30, 2017, www.legifrance.gouv.fr/affichCnil.do?&id=CNILTEXT 000035647959.

[51] Arrêté, January 19, 2018 (ORF No. 0016 du 20 janvier 2018 texte no. 26), "Authorizing the implementation of an automated software processing personal data named Parcoursup," www.legifrance.gouv.fr/affichTexte.do?cidTexte=JORFTEXT000036520954&categorieLien=id.

[52] CNIL, Decision No. 2018-119, March 22, 2018.

[53] K. Sharma, quoted by the House of Lords Select Committee Report on Artificial Intelligence, AI in the UK: Ready, Willing and Able? (Report of Session 2017–19), HL Paper 100, April 16, 2018, https://publications.parliament.uk/pa/ld201719/ldselect/ldai/100/100.pdf.

them in asserting their rights. The association was concerned about the selection of students for the courses most in demand, where the number of potential applicants exceeded the available number of places. Droit des Lycéens ultimately wanted to obtain information on the APB's calculation method, which had been kept secret by the Ministry of Education, and lacked transparency. In the absence of a reply from the Ministry, in May 2016, Droit des Lycéens submitted a request to CADA (the National Commission for Access to Administrative Documents), which controls access to administrative documents for French citizens. CADA issued a favorable opinion on the release of the source code in September 2016,[54] considering that source codes constitute administrative documents, within the meaning of article L. 300–2 of the Code of Relations between the public and the administration. As a consequence, the source code must, therefore, be communicated to anyone who requests it, pursuant to article L. 311–1 of the same statute. Even after this favorable decision, the Ministry, however, remained reluctant to fully share the source code with the association. In October 2016, the Ministry finally handed over the ABP algorithm's source code, putting an end to the conflict between the association and the Ministry of Education, which had lasted for more than seven months.

The publication of the source code was followed by three administrative court decisions. The first, in Bordeaux,[55] considered that the procedure of drawing lots lacked a legal basis. The other two, in Paris in July 2016 and in Nantes in September 2016, alluded to "serious doubt" regarding the legality of a refusal of enrolment to students who had wished to switch to a different university following their first enrolment. Ultimately, as mentioned earlier, the publication of the source code resulted in the software being invalidated by the CNIL[56] since it did not conform to the prohibition on administrative individual decisions being taken based solely on automated processing. Indeed, French law does not authorize ADS to allocate places in universities and training programs to students without any human intervention.

Similar concerns were also raised regarding the Parcoursup algorithm. Student unions pointed out that it might be configured so as to introduce candidate screening and therefore abolish free access to university. In January 2018, the Human Rights Defender recommended that the Ministry of Higher Education provide further information to students about the processing of their application on Parcoursup, including by local admissions committees. In May 2018, the Ministry of Education published the source code corresponding to Parcoursup's "national algorithm," but student unions pushed further, aiming to obtain the communication of the "local algorithms" used. Indeed, contrary to Admission Post Bac, the Parcoursup algorithm is not used and developed at the national level, but rather at the local level by each university. On February 4, 2019, an administrative court in Guadeloupe ordered the president of the University of the French West Indies to release to the French National Students' Union (UNEF) the details of the algorithmic processing of applications from prospective students by the Parcoursup algorithm. In so doing, the Court brushed aside the argument put forward and defended by the president of the university, who had attempted to rely on the protection provided by the secrecy of deliberation afforded to admission committees by article L. 612–3 of the French Education Code. Indeed, the Court held that the secrecy of deliberation would still be protected, insofar as the disclosure of the source code would only make public the examination criteria and their respective weighting, rather than the concrete assessment of the merits of a particular application.

---

[54]   CADA, Avis no. 20161989, June 23, 2016.
[55]   Tribunal administratif Bordeaux (Bordeaux Administrative Court), req. no. 1504236, June 16, 2016.
[56]   Cf. CNIL, above note 52.

In the end, both the APB and the Parcoursup source codes were therefore rendered public. The first source code was produced in the form of a long PDF document, while in the case of the latter, in addition to the Java source code, the government also produced a more detailed presentation and description of the algorithm's inner workings that is available online.[57] However, the disclosure of the source code raised some difficulties, insofar as finding a balance between meeting the objectives of readability (the possibility for complete execution of the algorithm) and the necessity to protect and secure the personal data of real applicants. It follows that the disclosures made the algorithmic part of the tool available, but that disclosure did not contain all of the information necessary for understanding it, therefore raising concerns of unintelligibility.[58] Thus, the #OpenAPB Hackathon was planned to be held in September 2017 to help in uncovering the actual functioning of the algorithm, building on the previous experience of the hackathon that had been organized by Etalab and the General Directorate of Public Finance (DGFIP) regarding the tax calculator algorithm.[59] Yet, Etalab and the Ministry of Education did not go forward with the project, although the disclosure and analysis of the source code still revealed the actual rules applied by certain limits of the software. For instance, it revealed that where the number of candidates exceeded the number of places available at a given university, the APB allocated places randomly, even though the Code of Education requires a reason for or against each allocation to be provided by the rector of the university.

Amid a context of distrust and contestation, the French Parliament passed the Law for a Digital Republic[60] in October 2016, introducing new obligations for ADS and tackling the use of "algorithmic processing within the context of an administrative decision," providing for the "possibility for the user to claim an explanation of its functioning." These provisions are intriguing, foremost because they are aimed at decisions taken "based on algorithmic processing," which can be interpreted more broadly than "automated decision-making," and, second, because the requirement of explaining algorithmic processing emerges from outside the context of privacy and data protection law. It also provides that administrations must inform the person affected by such processes and communicate, upon request, the rules of the algorithm and the main features of its concrete implementation. The application decree further requires that the information be intelligible, including the relevant criteria used along with their respective weighting in the final decision or recommendation. These requirements pertain to both local and global explanations; however, these obligations should not adversely affect secrets protected by the law.

Furthermore, the French Constitutional Court, in its decision no. 2018–765 regarding the constitutionality of the 2018 French Data Protection Law, considered that, in order to fulfill the requirements of the Law for a Digital Republic, the administration cannot use machine-learning algorithms for automated decision-making. According to the Court, machine-learning algorithms hinder "the administration knowing the rules on the basis of which administrative decisions have essentially been made," as they are able to autonomously "revise the rules that they apply."[61] This is incompatible with the obligation of the data processor to "manage the algorithmic processing and its changes in order to be able to explain

---

[57] Parcoursup source code is available at: https://framagit.org/parcoursup/algorithmes-de-parcoursup.
[58] J. A. Kroll, J. Huey, S. Barocas, *et al.*, Accountable Algorithms (2017) 165 *Univ. Pa. Law Rev.* 633.
[59] With the launch of a hackathon called #CodeImport.
[60] Loi no. 2016–1321 "for a Digital Republique – *République numérique*" (Act October 7, 2016) and its implementation order (*décret d'application*).
[61] Conseil Constitutionel (Constitutional Court), Decision no. 2018–765 DC, June 12, 2018, para. 66.

to the person in question how the data processing has been implemented in detail and in an intelligible format."[62] This development hints at a different matter than "code is law."[63] The issue is not about the role of code in cyberspace, and not even about the translation of law into the rigid and formalized language of computer code, but rather about how rules are produced; they are drawn continuously from data flows and, thus, are hardly identifiable and recognizable to both the administration and the citizen.

Is There Law after Code?

Overall, the French example highlights that access to code has the potential to improve the accountability of the administration regarding the use of algorithms. The disclosure of source codes encouraged public discussions and made possible the involvement of different organizations and groups of citizens, whose collective work gradually enabled improvements to the system. Eventually, APB was discontinued and replaced by an ADS granting more room for meaningful human intervention and with enhanced accountability.[64] Moreover, the disclosure of the source code was also a vector of improvement for the system itself, with the community being able to identify needs for improvement and necessary corrections. A long-term goal might be to open the proposal of a new source code to public consultation so academics, citizens, and external developers can directly identify flows and propose changes prior to its implementation. Furthermore, as this case study revealed, a disclosure policy may contribute to put algorithmic decisions at the front and center of public debate. Decisions that, up until now, have been taken far from the sight of citizens.

DATASETS AND ADMINISTRATIVE DECISIONS: ON THE ALLOCATION OF SOCIAL SECURITY BENEFITS

In July 2011, the state of Idaho operationalized a new model for establishing benefits budgets for disabled adults under the Medicaid program. The result, for a class of plaintiffs represented in *K.W. v. Armstrong*, was a decreased budget, without any explanation being provided in this regard. An initial petition for injunctive relief was granted by the District of Idaho,[65] confirmed by the Ninth Circuit,[66] and extended to an expanded class when joined with another suit.[67] The injunctive relief was upheld under a review on its merits, with the Court finding the scheme to be in violation of due process rights.[68] Ultimately, a settlement including mandatory revision of the program's budget model was granted preliminary approval.[69] The final settlement agreement is still being litigated. Notwithstanding the final settlement, the District of Idaho's opinion regarding the program and its benefits allocation established an important benchmark for model validation, data integrity, and the transparency of government-deployed ADS.[70]

---

[62] *Ibid.*, para. 72.
[63] L. Lessing, *Code: And Other Laws of Cyberspace* (Basic Books, 1999), p. 60.
[64] See on this issue M. Perel and N. Elkin-Koren, Black Box Tinkering: Beyond Disclosure in Algorithmic Enforcement (2017) 69 *Fla. Law Rev.* 181.
[65] *K.W. v. Armstrong*, 298 FRD 479 (D. Idaho 2014) (hereinafter, *K.W. I*).
[66] *K.W. v. Armstrong*, 789 F.3d 962 (9th Cir. 2015), *affirming K.W. I* (hereinafter, *K.W. II*).
[67] *K.W. v. Armstrong*, Case No. 1:12-cv-22-BLW was consolidated with *Schultz* v. *Armstrong*, Case No. 3:12-cv-00058-BLW by a Case Management Order signed by Winmill, J., and filed on April 16, 2013 (Docket #77).
[68] *K.W. v. Armstrong*, 180 F. Supp. 3d 703 (D. Idaho 2016) (No. 1:12-cv-00022-BLW) (hereinafter, *K.W. III*).
[69] See Docket, 1:12-CV-22-BLW, D. Idaho (most recent entry April 11, 2019).
[70] See *K.W. III*, above note 68, at 703.

The Case: Allocating Social Security Benefits

The Idaho Department of Health and Welfare (IDHW), as part of its participation in the national Medicaid Home and Community-Based Services (HCBS) program, administers the Developmental Disabilities Waiver program ("DD Waiver program").[71] Aimed at minimizing unnecessary institutionalization of developmentally disabled adults, the DD Waiver program establishes a personalized annual budget for each participant.[72] Participants follow either the "traditional path" (that is, they have a government-provided living situation) or the "self-directed path" (that is, they are given an annual lump-sum budget to select their own living situation).

IDHW contracts Independent Assessment Providers (IAPs) to fill out an Inventory of Individual Needs (IIN) for each DD Waiver program participant, based on information gathered in a visit with the participant and a "respondent" (for example, a legal guardian or family member) and by reviewing medical records.[73] IAPs are further guided by a booklet known as the Scales of Independent Behavior – Revised (SIB-R), which provides prompts to evaluate the various criteria reflected in the IIN (for example, anti-social behavior scores). The IAP then manually inputs the information gathered from the IIN into a computerized Individualized Budget Calculation (IBC).[74] Ultimately, the IAP is tasked with manually transferring scores from the IIN, SIB-R, and three different worksheets to the IBC, as well as calculating the sums in doing so.[75] In evaluating this program, the District Court was highly cognizant of the substantial risk for human error in this process – more significantly, however, the Court was concerned with both the chance of substantive error (for example, an IAP misunderstanding a participant's ability to perform a given task, which could alter a budget significantly) and with faulty statistics supporting the decision-making process.[76]

The Dataset Itself

In finding the budget tool to be insufficient to meet due process standards, the Court stressed the glaring deficiencies of the dataset used to devise the regression model.[77] From an initial sample of over 3,500 records from data from 2009 and 2010, about 37 percent were discarded as "plainly erroneous," an additional 30 percent of the remaining records had a Medicaid ID number that did not match the IDHW systems' records, and yet another 18 percent of the still-remaining records contained "incomplete or unbelievable information."[78] Of the remaining 998 records, the modeling software discarded 265 due to lacking a crucial IIN data point.[79] All told, the model had been created using only 21 percent of the initial set of records, or 733 out of the initial 3,512.[80] As the plaintiffs' expert witness stated, this "calls into question the ability of the IDHW to collect and manage data for use in a data-based decision-making process, the design of the database itself, and the collection of data by the assessment providers."[81]

---

[71] *Ibid.* at 708.
[72] *Ibid.*
[73] *Ibid.*
[74] *Ibid.* at 716.
[75] *Ibid.* at 716–17.
[76] *K.W. III*, above note 68, at 717.
[77] *Ibid.* at 711–12.
[78] *Ibid.* at 711.
[79] *Ibid.*
[80] *Ibid.*
[81] Remington Declaration ¶ 13; *K.W. III*, above note 68.

As the Court pointed out, such "a substantial number of *known* errors signals two things: (1) the existence of substantial *unknown* errors; and (2) a lack of quality control."[82] The data sample, which IDHW initially contended was still statistically significant, also reflected a substantial underrepresentation of a region of the state.[83] The Court also stressed the importance of testing the budget tool – a crucial aspect to ensuring accuracy and which was not being conducted at the time.[84] Indeed, a human review of the budget tool figures resulted in 62 percent of the budgets being increased.[85] While the IDHW estimated that only 10 to 15 percent of participants were given inadequate budgets using the tool, arguing that the average participant utilized fewer funds than had been authorized, the Court quite aptly rejected this argument, stating that: "averages do not negate specifics, and indeed they can exist comfortably side-by-side."[86] Further, the staggering percentage of records that were excluded from the study indicate that the problems inherent to the system run much deeper than the validity of the statistical model: if so many IIN records are incomplete and Medicare ID numbers are inaccurate, the validity of any output from such a model, regardless of its predictive accuracy, is highly questionable. Indeed, flawed data used in an imperfect model can serve to further entrench government malfeasance under a veil of opacity with the misleading impression of scientific neutrality and accuracy.[87]

Using the Dataset – Model Selection and Validation

In establishing a statistical model upon which to base the revision of the IBC calculations in 2011, IDHW utilizes a stepwise linear regression to model paid claims.[88] These paid claims served as the dependent variable, while the IIN entries were used as independent variables.[89] Using SPSS software to identify which of those IIN entries should be included in the model to maximize the adjusted R^2 value (i.e. to identify a line of best fit with the highest rate of accurate prediction of the provided data points), ultimately, the models identified thirteen IIN entries and living arrangement alternatives as the "most statistically significant" for the traditional path participants, and twenty-three IIN entries for the self-directed path participants.[90] At trial, this method of model selection was criticized for having selected a model with a higher R^2 value over others,[91] as well as due to the potential for multi-collinearity problems.[92]

In validating the model, several deficiencies similarly indicate a poor fit for predicting accurate budget allocations. Likely a product of the multi-collinearity issues, there were several regression coefficients wherein the algebraic sign was the opposite of that expected (that is, an input *decreased* the budget when one would expect it to *increase* instead). For example, an indication that a participant has "other neurological impairment(s)" reduced

[82] *K.W. III*, above note 68, at 711 (emphasis in the original).
[83] *Ibid.*
[84] *Ibid.* at 712, 714.
[85] *Ibid.* at 712.
[86] *Ibid.* at 711.
[87] For a discussion of the history and pervasiveness of government malfeasance through faulty data science, see S. Valentine, Impoverished Algorithms: Misguided Governments, Flawed Technologies, and Social Control (2019) 46 *Fordham Urb. Law J.* 364, 370–93. See also K. Crawford and J. Schultz, AI Systems as State Actors (2019) 119 *Columbia Law Rev.* 1941.
[88] Declaration of Derrick Snow in Support of Defendants' Motion for Summary Judgment, *K.W. III*, above note 68.
[89] *Ibid.* at 4.
[90] *Ibid.* at 7.
[91] Remington Report at 7, *K.W. III*, above note 68.
[92] *Ibid.* at 8. Multi-collinearity refers to the impact of two or more "independent" variables in an analysis actually being correlated, such that the impact of a single true factor is overrepresented by two inputs both affected by that factor. See *ibid.* at 7–9.

a self-directed budget by $8,095, and high-level needs for Total Support with Laundry and Assistance in Feeding similarly had negative impacts of $4,201 and $5,715, respectively.[93] Decreasing a budget in response to more severe needs seems deeply counter-intuitive and indicates a structural flaw with the prediction tool.

Examining the Data in Court

The *K.W.* case illustrates the significance of an accurate, valid dataset in developing and utilizing a data regression model. When applied to the allocation of government benefits in which eligible participants have a protected property interest,[94] constitutional rights may be attached through that government action.[95] Tackling these concerns with the appropriate seriousness, the District of Idaho illustrated several key ways in which courts must intervene in faulty data-based regulation and ADS: demanding valid data and ensuring transparency.

The issue of faulty data providing the basis for inappropriate government action is hardly new to American courts. Indeed, in 2009, Supreme Court Justice Ginsburg warned that "[i]naccuracies in expansive, interconnected collections of electronic information raise grave concerns for individual liberty."[96] In recent years, the implications of flawed datasets for a variety of government purposes have found their way into the courts.[97] When the underlying data has been demonstrated to be sufficiently flawed, courts have appropriately challenged algorithmic output.[98] *Armstrong* followed this trend, identifying the lack of a reliable dataset as a faulty foundation for the budget tool ADS.

However, beyond recognizing the significance of a flawed dataset, *Armstrong* also highlighted the significance of the transparency of the tools being used and the data itself.[99] Over state objection, the Court found that the procedural due process rights of the plaintiffs required disclosure of third-party-copyrighted tools (namely, the SIB-R booklet used to calculate several of the IIN data points).[100] The courts should continue allowing for the exploration of such materials, providing those parties aggrieved by such ADS with the possibility to understand and, if necessary, to challenge the data and calculations being used to their disadvantage.

---

[93] *Ibid.* at 10.

[94] See *K.W. II*, above note 66, at 973; *K.W. III*, above note 68, at 714; see also *Perdue* v. *Gargano*, 964 NE.2d 925, 932 (Ind. Sup. Ct. 2012) (characterizing entitlement benefits as "property" interests within the meaning of the Due Process Clause).

[95] See V. Eidelman, The First Amendment Case for Public Access to Secret Algorithms Used in Criminal Trials (2018) 34 *Ga. St. Univ. Law Rev.* 915.

[96] *Herring* v. *United States*, 555 US 135, 155 (2009) (Ginsburg, J., dissenting). In *Herring*, the defendant was arrested by police under a warrant that had, apparently, been improperly issued and subsequently revoked; however, the database being used by police was not updated with revocations, only issuances. In a 5–4 decision, the Court allowed into evidence the drugs and firearm that were found on the defendant during the arrest. *Ibid.* at 135 (majority opinion).

[97] See, e.g., *Zynda* v. *Arwood*, 175 F. Supp. 3d 791 (ED Mich. 2016) (high error rate in an unemployment fraud detection system); *State of New Mexico ex rel. Stewart* v. *N.M. Pub. Educ. Dep't*, D-101-CV-2015-00409, at 24–7 (Santa Fe County Ct. December 2, 2015) (large numbers of errors in data used in teacher assessment system).

[98] *Zynda, ibid.*, at 806 (granting plaintiff legal aid organization standing on the grounds that "the high error rate in fraud determinations has lead [legal aid] to divert significant resources to these types of claims"); *Stewart, ibid.*, at 75 (finding that teacher evaluation algorithm was based on a dataset so flawed as to support a preliminary injunction on its continued use).

[99] *K.W. III*, above note 64, at 715–17.

[100] *Ibid.* at 717 ("The Court will direct IDHW to draft a plan so that participants can not only view all portions of the SIB-R necessary to fully challenge a budget reduction but also be able to present any challenged portion of the SIB-R analysis to a hearing officer or other decision maker during an appeal").

AUTOMATING ENFORCEMENT: ON TAX AVOIDANCE

Combating tax avoidance is yet another area where administrations around the world make extensive use of data analysis techniques in order to improve their tax evasion targeting capabilities. A 2014 OECD survey demonstrated that this was the case with sixty-nine of the eighty-six countries studied as part of the survey.[101] This trend has been greatly influenced by the OECD, which has issued multiple studies on new technologies for tax administration and best practices reports.[102] HMRC, the UK tax authority, has consistently been presented as one of the leaders in this regard.

UNPACKING CONNECT: HMRC'S TAX ENFORCEMENT TOOL

The partial automation of tax auditing and fraud detection by the HMRC grew from an initiative first conceived as far back as 2005.[103] *Connect*, its main analytical tool, required an initial investment of around £90 million and was developed in collaboration with BAE Systems Applied Intelligence, SAS Institute, and Capgemini.[104] It was launched in 2010 and has been extensively used and upgraded ever since, with around 250 dedicated data analysts within HMRC and up to 4,000 users overall. Connect has proven to be an utter success, bringing in £3 billion and contributing to reducing the United Kingdom's tax gap from an estimated 8.3 percent in 2004–05 to 6.5 percent in 2014–15.[105] Today, UK tax authorities rely on Connect to tackle the shadow economy, with the tool being at the origin of 98 percent of launched tax fraud investigations.

As a first, high-level, explanation, Connect is a data-driven and machine-learning-supported ADS. It relies on the aggregation of information from multiple structured and unstructured sources, which are then processed through multiple AI techniques with the purpose of identifying general correlations between different types of behavior alongside tax evasion. These are subsequently applied to information pertaining to the UK population as a whole, flagging cases close enough to the model to be likely to concern anomalous behavior. The popularity and success encountered by Connect should not hide the concerns it gives rise to. In fact, it perfectly illustrates a comprehensive deployment of ADS in the public administration, raising specific issues at all the stages of its implementation and design.

Data Aggregation

As already illustrated by the IDHW case above, data analysis techniques are only as good as the dataset serving as their training and application grounds. In this regard, HMRC reports that its Connect algorithm automatically pulls information from over thirty structured databases spanning payroll, credit and land registries, bank accounts in more than sixty

[101] T. Ehrke-Rabel, Big Data in Tax Collection and Enforcement, in W. Haslehner, G. Kofler, K. Pantazatou, and A. Rust (eds.), *Tax and the Digital Economy: Challenges and Proposals for Reform* (Wolters Kluwer, 2019).

[102] For instance, OECD, Better Tax Administration: Putting Data to World (2016), Technologies for Better Tax Administration: A Practical Guide for Revenue Bodies (2016), and The changing Tax Compliance Environment and the Role of Audit (2017).

[103] P. Rigney, The All-Seeing Eye – an HMRC Success Story?, FTA HMRC Administration (November/December 2016), p. 8.

[104] Capgemini, Business Intelligence Technology helps HMRC Increase Yield (2017), www.capgemini.com/fr-fr/wp-content/uploads/sites/2/2017/07/ss_Business_Intelligence_Technology_helps_HMRC_Increase_Yield.pdf.

[105] European Platform Undeclared Work Best Practices Sheet – UK: Data Mining Tools and Methods to Tackle the Hidden Economy in the UK (2017).

countries, credit and debit card transactions, insurance registries, and even the electoral roll. Connect also has access to unstructured information, provided upon request by third parties or obtained through web scraping, notably from online traders (for example, eBay, Airbnb, Amazon), airline ticket sellers, and social networks, including Facebook and Twitter. In brief, it has access to more than a billion data points available for processing and providing a comprehensive view of taxpayers' day-to-day activities and lifestyles.

An obvious issue with such data-gathering techniques is data accuracy. Traditionally, tax authorities rely partly on data provided directly by the taxpayer, or at least commented on by them. With Connect, the tax authorities access and utilize "Big Data that they neither generate nor control."[106] This is especially troubling given that the data drawn from multiple sources is likely to lose its original contextual integrity.[107] The origin of the data, as well as the sheer amount of it, is such that multiple inaccuracies might pass unnoticed. Moreover, as extensively demonstrated in the previous parts of this chapter, data is never truly neutral, and potential bias could be drawn into a large-scale dataset even when the separate pieces of information are accurate, thus potentially giving rise to an unfair over-targeting of certain lifestyles.[108]

In this regard, tax authorities need to ensure compliance with GDPR and, at least, inform taxpayers about the processing of their personal data. Things are somewhat less clear beyond that. For instance, article 16 of the GDPR, which grants data subjects the right to rectify inaccurate or incomplete personal data "by means of providing a supplementary statement," does not seem to be of much help. First, this is an *ex post* right which does not seem to be useful to the taxpayer once it has already been flagged by Connect, as ratifying the data does not necessarily imply that the launched investigation would come to a halt. Generally, despite the OECD's opinion to the contrary,[109] it is yet unclear at what point the taxpayer is meant to contribute to enhancing the data's accuracy.[110] Second, it does not help when the data itself is accurate but reflects an incomplete or inaccurate world view.[111] Moreover, even when the data seems accurate, it may give rise to probabilistic assumptions which might never be truly verifiable by themselves.[112]

Data Relevance and Privacy

A somewhat more promising venue in this regard might be the GDPR's obligation for data controllers to ensure the reliability of the statistical inferences they rely upon (Recital 71 of GDPR), which is understood by the Article 29 Working Party as meaning that they should ensure that the input data is not "inaccurate or irrelevant, or taken out of context."[113] Within UK administrative law, similar concerns gave rise to case law requiring that public authorities

---

[106]   OECD, Technologies for a Better Tax Administration (2016), p. 83.
[107]   B. Wagner, Algorithms and Human Rights, Study for the Council of Europe Study (2018), p. 13.
[108]   S. Barocas and A. D. Selbst, Big Data's Disparate Impact (2016) 104 *Calif. Law Rev.* 671; T. Z. Zarsky, Understanding Discrimination in the Scored Society (2014) 89 *Wash. Law Rev.* 1375.
[109]   Cf. OECD, above note 106, p. 83, noting that tax authorities should interact with the taxpayer, as it would "reinforce that data accuracy is a joint responsibility."
[110]   Expressing similar concerns is Ehrke-Rabel, above note 101.
[111]   R. Williams, Rethinking Deference for Algorithmic Decision-Making, Oxford Legal Studies Research Paper No. 7/2019 (2019), p. 30.
[112]   S. Wachter and B. Mittelstadt, A Right to Reasonable Inferences: Re-Thinking Data Protection Law in the Age of Big Data and AI (2019) 2 *Colum. Bus. Law Rev.* 494.
[113]   See Article 29 Data Protect Working Party, Guidelines on Automated Individual Decision-Making and Profiling for the Purposes of Regulation 2016/679, p. 28.

not take into account irrelevant considerations,[114] although it is generally for the decision-maker to decide the extent to which a piece of information is relevant.[115] However, it is as of yet unclear how much HMRC, or any other tax authority for that matter, complies with this requirement. This issue is all the more daunting given that seemingly unrelated pieces of information might prove to be statistically relevant for accurate predictive inferences regarding the likelihood of future fraudulent behavior, be it for reasons which do not fit into an easily understandable causal story.

A separate issue concerns the potential infringement by Connect of the privacy rights of data subjects when pulling data from third parties such as online trading platforms and social networks. In fact, article 8 of the European Convention on Human Rights (ECHR) has been interpreted as stating that interference with privacy rights is only acceptable if accomplished in accordance with a rule compatible with the rule of law and whose consequences are foreseeable by the subject.[116] In a decision of the trial Court (Rechtbank) of the Hague of February 2020, the Court relies on article 8 of the ECHR to strike down the Systeem Risico Indicatie (SyRI), an ADS used by the Dutch government to fight tax and social fraud.[117] The Court found, first, that the processing of data was not proportional to the objectives pursued; and, second, that the guarantees contained in national law authorizing the use of the ADS did not amount to an effective protection of citizens' privacy rights. Moreover, the European Court of Human Rights (ECtHR) in *J.G. and J.H.* v. *United Kingdom* also established that the compilation and processing of publicly available data "beyond that normally foreseeable" is considered to be a privacy infringement.[118] However, to date, it seems no argument relating to Connect's lack of foreseeability and proportionality in collecting and processing data has been tested in British or European courts.

Enforcement's Changing Landscape

Whatever the origins and means for collecting data, the algorithm supporting Connect's ADS is subsequently employed in two ways. First, during a "training" period, it is used to infer the profile of typical fraudulent behavior, by calculating the density between different entities of the network and, subsequently, establishing a general model visualized through so-called *spidergrams*. What is important in these models are the connections between the different entities present in the network (its nodes), which could indicate illicit activities or lifestyles that do not correspond to the declared revenue. Second, similar network profiles of individual taxpayers are created and those whose structure closely resembles the model are flagged for further inquiry. As stated by Mike Wells, Director of Risk and Intelligence Services at HMRC, "over time, you become familiar with a normal person's *spidergram*. When some are operating in the hidden economy, it has a different shape."[119] When probable fraudulent behavior is flagged by the algorithm, HMRC employees can choose to initiate an audit, which they do in most investigations, although no other immediate consequence seems to follow from an individual case being flagged. It should be noted, however, that section 51 and Schedule 8 of the UK Finance (No. 2) Act 2015 allow for the direct deduction by tax

---

[114] *R.* v. *Rochdale MBC, ex p. Cromer Ring Mill* (1982) 3 All ER 761.
[115] *Tesco Stores* v. *Secretary of State for the Environment* (1995) 1 WLR 759.
[116] ECHR, *Malone* v. *the UK*, August 2, 1984, para. 67.
[117] *Rechtbank Den Haag, NJCM & c.s. c. De Staat der Nederlanden*, C/09/550982/ HA ZA 18/388, February 5, 2020.
[118] ECtHR, *P.G. and J.H.* v. *the UK*, September 25, 2001, para. 57.
[119] V. Houlder, Ten Ways HMRC Can Tell If You're a Tax Cheat, *Financial Times* (December 19, 2017).

authorities of sums from tax debtors' deposit accounts and it does not seem unimaginable that such deductions might be based directly on Connect's flagging in the future.[120]

THE NEW POWER IMBALANCE. Even in the absence of such automatic deduction, the sheer amount of information available for Connect's processing points to a radical shift in the balance of powers between public authorities and their subjects in the surveillance state.[121] This shift is much more apparent where public authorities rely on risk profiles not only to launch investigations, but also to preventively *nudge* subjects into compliance. This is exactly what HMRC has been doing with its more recent tool, Analytics for Debtor Profiling and Targeting (ADEPT), used to clear or pursue late payments more efficiently and effectively.[122] Like Connect, this new tool relies on machine learning. By amassing information from more than twenty sources, including missed payments and socio-demographic data, it generates a risk profile of individual debtors. It then assigns the case to the debt collection team which has the best performance with similar profiles, and more importantly, it applies custom-tailored sequences of debt notices and payment schedules in order to nudge individual debtors into complying with their debt obligations.

While there seems to be nothing troubling with using the available data to increase the efficiency of the administrative state, the new scale, speed, and breadth of this data collection and processing is qualitatively different from the previous form of record-keeping.[123] It masks a subtle increase in administrative pervasiveness and enhancement of the state's power over its subjects.[124] It also leads to an increase in the degree of real-world law enforcement as administrative discretion gets lost along the way when tax authorities feel compelled to follow an algorithm's suggestions,[125] as will be discussed later. Traditionally, administrative law responds to greater power with correspondingly greater restraint, but it is yet unclear how administrative law is meant to adapt to innovations such as the algorithms supporting Connect's ADS.[126] In fact, it is not at all clear how taxpayers could hold HRMC accountable in any meaningful way over the use of multiple AI techniques by Connect.

FROM CAUSATION TO CORRELATION. First one needs to ask: What could actually be challenged? As stated above, Connect's flagging results in the initiation of an audit. In general, such decisions are discretionary and cannot be challenged before courts, even if they have important consequences for the taxpayer. As such, they seem to also fall outside of the scope of article 22 of the GDPR and the additional requirements it sets for automated decision-making.[127] Outside of the above-mentioned right to correct inaccurate data, the taxpayer seems to be powerless at this stage.

However, things are slightly different when looked at from the perspective of enforcement. In civil tax litigation proceedings, the standard of proof is that of a balance of probabilities. Nothing seems to preclude HMRC from relying on Connect flagging

[120]   Cf. Williams, above note 111, p. 13.
[121]   See, on "Big Data's watchful eye," A. G. Ferguson, *The Rise of Big Data Policing: Surveillance, Race, and the Future of Law Enforcement* (New York University Press, 2017).
[122]   See Capgemini, above note 11.
[123]   K. Galloway, Big Data: A Case Study of Disruption and Government Power (2017) 42 *Altern. Law J.* 89.
[124]   See, defining "power-over" as "the ability of an actor deliberately to change the incentive structure of another actor or actors to bring about, or help bring about outcomes," K. M. Dowding, *Rational Choice and Political Power* (Edward Elgar, 1991), p. 48.
[125]   Cf. Wagner, above note 107, at 6, 13.
[126]   Cf. Williams, above note 111, p. 13.
[127]   Cf. Ehrke-Rabel, above note 101.

probable fraudulent behavior as proper, probabilistic proof of tax evasion. The problem is that such reliance might conflate correlation with causation.[128] Considering that much of the collected data might be irrelevant for proving tax fraud, Connect may identify spurious correlations,[129] even where it is generally supposed to be accurate. In other words, without explainability, it might be unclear which, exactly, among the millions of data points relied on by Connect, justified the flagging and why.

Despite these shortcomings, such evidence might prove to be extremely persuasive for decision-makers (tax authorities and judges alike). In fact, recent studies have extensively shown that decision-makers tend to trust predictive algorithms even when they do not properly understand their functioning.[130] They tend to consider them to be both accurate and unbiased.[131] The algorithmic rationality is, in this regard, a compelling source of confidence,[132] especially considering the information overload and the cognitive complexity required to challenge any results deriving from an ADS. Hence, decision-makers are increasingly likely to surrender to a new "predictive determinism."[133] The compelling effect might be even higher for public officials subject to quantitative assessment of their own performance under new forms of public management. Questioning and reasonably challenging each and every suggestion made by Connect, a potentially over-complex and time-consuming endeavor, seems to be a waste of time for a rational career-driven public official.[134]

Venues for Algorithmic Accountability

Responding to such concerns, the UK Cabinet Office's data science ethical framework seems to imply that the employment of data analysis techniques by the administration should be as open and accountable as possible.[135] Accountability is equated with transparency,[136] for it is thought that biases and errors are easily uncovered in the light of day. This first implies transparency regarding the composition of the dataset.[137] For Connect, however, such transparency is not enough: what is required, as previously demonstrated, is for the data to be relevant to the development of causal probabilistic proofs.

Second, it could be required that the code employed by Connect itself be disclosed. Indeed, in some ADS, such as the French APB case, the disclosure of the source code has contributed to uncovering bias. The algorithm could then be subjected to "grey box" algorithm auditing

---

[128] See, e.g., studying a classifier algorithm discerning wolves from huskies, which turned out to heavily rely on the presence of snow in the background, M. Tulio Ribeiro, S. Singh, and C. Guestrin, Why Should I Trust You? Explaining the Predictions of Any Classifier, KDD '16 Proceedings of the 22nd ACM SIGKDD International Conference on Knowledge Discovery and Data Mining, pp. 1135–44, arXiv:1602.04938.

[129] R. Jeffrey, Statistical Explanation vs. Statistical Inference, in N. Rescher (ed.), *Essays in Honor of Carl G. Hempel: A Tribute on the Occasion of his Sixty-Fifth Birthday* (Springer, 1969), pp. 104–13.

[130] See, for psychological evidence, K. Goddard, A. Roudsari, and J. C. Wyatt, Automation Bias: A Systematic Review of Frequency, Effect Mediators, and Mitigators (2011) 19 *J. Am. Med. Inf. Assoc.* 121, 121–7; M. T. Dzindolet, S. A. Peterson, R. A. Pomranky, *et al.*, The Role of Trust in Automation Reliance (2003) 58 *Int. J. Hum.-Comput. St.* 692.

[131] L. Dernardis, Architecting Civil Liberties, GigaNet: Global Internet Governance Academic Network, Annual Symposium (2008).

[132] Cf. Lequesne Roth, above note 12, p. 9.

[133] A. Garapon and J. Lassegue, *Justice digitale* (Presses universitaires de France, 2018).

[134] See P. R. Borges Fortes, How Legal Indicators Influence a Justice System and Judicial Behavior: The Brazilian National Council of Justice and "Justice in Numbers" (2015) 47 *J. Leg. Plur. Unoff. Law* 39.

[135] Cf. Williams, above note 111, p. 27.

[136] F. Schauer, Transparency in Three Dimensions (2011) *Univ. Ill. Law Rev.* 1339, 1346.

[137] R. Brauneis and E. P. Goodman, Algorithmic Transparency for the Smart City (2018) 20 *Yale J. Law Technol.* 103, 130.

techniques, in which knowledge about a program's structure and function is used to devise test cases in order to uncover the weight attributed to the different data points when it comes to the final decision.[138] However, as opposed to the APB algorithms, Connect relies on the contribution of private firms for the development of the software, which may ultimately constitute an obstacle to access the source code. Hence, if the source code is not revealed, for proprietary or other reasons, policy groups could engage in so-called "black box tinkering," submitting purposefully designed cases in order to test the algorithm's reaction and infer step by step its general functioning and assess its reliability.[139] What both techniques would amount to in the best-case scenario is local explanations (identifying the relative weight of different factors) or local counterfactual faithfulness (identifying a factor's causal impact on the outcome).[140]

The problem here is that such knowledge may simply not be enough. In fact, when advanced ADS fail, it is not always entirely clear what the reason for the failure is, even for senior engineers.[141] Moreover, it is uncertain what such transparency or tinkering could amount to beyond identifying obvious discrimination. Suppose the auditing reveals that Connect relied on a piece of information HMRC and the judge cannot tell a persuasive causal story about. In this case, such a type of information might be excluded from the typical dataset the algorithm relies on for all its inferences, thus making the dataset seemingly more relevant. This seems to amount to a certain "right to reasonable inference," which has recently been pleaded for by some scholars.[142] Additionally, we have already examined the potential shortcomings of such dataset cleansing above.

Alternatively, the algorithm might be "blindfolded" and forced to ignore that apparently irrelevant piece of information before assessing the case again. The first problem with this approach is that the result of the new analysis might be irrelevant with regard to the model set as a benchmark for typical fraudulent behavior. The second problem is that this would only amount to a "second order" quick fix rather than a fundamental change of "first order rules," i.e. the actual way in which data is processed.[143] Such a solution is not scalable and does not imply that the next case flagged by Connect would not suffer from the same "unreasonable inferences" problem. It seems risky to hope that all taxpayers would be able to systematically combat such probabilistic assessments on a case-by-case basis.

EXPLAINABLE PROBABILISTIC INFERENCES. What the above seems to point to is that, beyond transparency, it is necessary to require HMRC to provide reasons for any decisions it makes, and therefore render Connect's model and inferences reasonably comprehensible. The intuition is that if there were a way to tell a reasonable story about the algorithm's inferences, irrelevant inferences might be more easily identified. Moreover, taxpayers would be allowed to prepare a meaningful rebuttal, as they would know exactly what their arguments should be focused on. However, there does not seem to be a general duty for public authorities in the United Kingdom to provide comprehensible reasons for their decisions,[144] although some

---

[138]   A. Datta, S. Sen, and Y. Zick, Algorithmic Transparency via Quantitative Input Influence: Theory and Experiments with Learning Systems, IEEE Symposium on Security and Privacy (2016).

[139]   Perel and Elkin-Koren, above note 64.

[140]   S. Wachter, B. Mittelstadt, and C. Russell, Counterfactual Explanations without Opening the Black Box: Automated Decisions and the GDPR (2018) 31 *Harv. J. Law Technol.* 841, arXiv:1711.00399.

[141]   For example, Google's image recognition algorithm turned out to label photos of black people as containing gorillas, without the engineers being able to explain what the reason was. See J. Guynn, Google Photos Labeled Black People Gorillas, *USA Today* (July 1, 2015).

[142]   Cf. Wachter *et al.*, above note 140.

[143]   Cf. Wagner, above note 107, pp. 7, 20.

[144]   *R. v. Secretary of State for Trade and Industry* (2008) EWCA Civ. 1312.

scholars are persuasively arguing for it.[145] A similar "right to explanation" has been argued for by some scholars in light of the conjunction of articles 13, 14, 15, and 22 of the GDPR.[146] The existence of such a right is still controversial,[147] and need not concern us here, as it is not at all clear that the mere action of flagging constitutes an algorithmic decision under article 22 of the GDPR, as previously explained.

Whatever the basis for such a right, some help might come from visualization tools such as SetFusion,[148] which promise to make particular algorithmic recommendations more comprehensible. The fundamental concern here is that visualization might not be at all helpful if the algorithm is too complex and relies on correlations too intricate for the human eye. What seems to be expected is not a complete description of the way in which the algorithm reached the conclusion or full intelligibility, but rather a proper justification employing commonly accepted patterns of reasoning and a shared vocabulary.[149] At this stage, simply "dumbing down" Connect to a level comprehensible to human observers, were it to appear too inscrutable, would be unhelpful if the primary goal is to decrease its error rate.[150] Alternatively, a separate algorithm might be used to read decisions taken by the basic algorithm and "translate" them into a more readily interpretable, and therefore challenge-able, rule.[151] The difficulty is, of course, that it either cannot be entirely counterfactually faithful, for if this were the case it could be used directly instead of Connect, or it risks generating incomprehensibly complex rules. A trade-off would need to be accepted in either case.

Taking stock: Tax Code as the New Tax Law

Whatever legal and technical solutions might be offered to the above-mentioned concerns, one is left wondering whether the over-reliance on Connect and similar ADS does not signal a more fundamental shift in the nature of tax law itself – yet another instance of a mathematical turn of law.[152] Insofar as Connect needs to incorporate the translation of legal rules in order to assess the data or suggest a further course of action – such as the amount that the taxpayer ought to pay – it actually relies on a certain reading of such rules. This is primarily so because computer languages have a limited vocabulary and much could be lost

[145] See, drawing on the *Bourgass v. Secretary of State for Justice* language regarding the need to provide to prisoners "genuine and meaningful disclosure of the reasons" why the decision has been made, see Williams, above note 111, pp. 27–8.

[146] See B. Goodman and S. Flaxman, European Union Regulations on Algorithmic Decision Making and a Right to Explanation, *AI Magazine*, Vol. 38 (2017), p. 50.

[147] S. Wachter, B. Mittelstadt, and L. Floridi, Why a Right to Explanation of Automated Decision-Making Does Not Exist in the General Data Protection Regulation (2017) 7 *Int. Data Priv. Law* 76–99.

[148] D. Parra, P. Brusilovsky, and C. Trattner, See What You Want to See: Visual User-Driven Approach for Hybrid Recommendation, Proceedings of the 19th International Conference on Intelligent User Interfaces (2014), p. 235.

[149] In other words, enhanced requirements on the context of justification rather than simply full transparency regarding the context of discovery. See H. Reichenbach, *Experience and Prediction: An Analysis of the Foundations and the Structure of Knowledge* (University of Chicago Press, 1938).

[150] For a passionate argument against making AI less intelligent in the name of transparency, see D. Weinberger, Don't Make AI Artificially Stupid in the Name of Transparency, *Wired* (January 28, 2018), www.wired.com/story/dont-make-ai-artificially-stupid-in-the-name-of-transparency/.

[151] F. Doshi-Velez, M. Kortz, R. Budish, *et al.*, Accountability of AI under the Law: The Role of Explanation (2017), arXiv:1711.01134

[152] D. Restrepo Amariles, The Mathematical Turn: l'indicateur Rule of Law dans la politique de développement de la Banque Mondiale, in B. Frydman and A. Van Waeyenberge (eds.), *Gouverner par les Standards et les Indicateurs: de Hume aux Rankings* (Bruylant, 2014), p. 193.

in translation.[153] More subtly, any translation fixes one interpretation of the law, much of which relies on fuzzy standards,[154] and reduces the scope of any further meaningful debate. Setting aside the question of whether open-textured concepts could ever be translated into code,[155] evidence shows that even in what would be considered "easy" cases programmers translating rules into code end up with wildly discrepant outcomes.[156] Consequently, what becomes enforced is not the law in books, but the code intended to implement it: insofar as Connect is concerned, tax code is indeed the new tax law.[157] Incidentally, there may be important political legitimacy issues here, as the interpretation of tax law is left to the designer of the algorithms and the learning process of the algorithms rather than democratically accountable bodies. This is especially the case where private multinational corporations, such as BAE Systems, SAS Institute, or Capgemini, are involved, as they might opt to use similar "global standards" when designing algorithms for different tax authorities for reasons of efficiency.[158]

Second, and more fundamentally, Connect radically alters enforcement, which is, as Pounds once said, "the life of the law."[159] Indeed, for all practical purposes, tax law rules are in part replaced by the patterns and correlation-constructing indicators of fraudulent behavior on which Connect relies for triggering an investigation. These indicators therefore become the actual "reasons for action"[160] as far as taxpayers are concerned. They need to adapt their behavior and modes of arguing to Connect's functioning and standards in case of litigation. As a result, the law itself ends up being transformed into a normative correlation of facts.[161]

CONCLUSION

This chapter studied the use of ADS for the allocation of rights and benefits by public administration. By looking into case studies in France, the United States, and the United Kingdom, four independent, but often intertwined, features characterizing these systems have been highlighted, namely: (1) the formalization of legal rules and transcription into computer code; (2) the generation of datasets; (3) data processing through machine-learning techniques; and (4) automated execution of decisions. While most advanced systems may implement all of these characteristics at once, others may contain as few as two. These features have triggered at least three transformations in legal decision-making with significant implications for the rule of law.

---

[153]   J. Grimmelmann, Regulation by Software (2015) 114 *Yale Law J.* 1719, 1728.
[154]   See, however, arguing that the predictive and analytical technologies currently under development will allow for the emergence of micro-directives replacing both rules and standards, A. Casey and A. Niblett, The Death of Rules and Standards (2017) 92 *Indiana Law J.* 1401.
[155]   For an optimistic take on the issue, see N. Elkin-Koren and O. Fischman-Afori, Rulifying Fair Use (2017) 59 *Ariz. Law Rev.* 161, 189–99.
[156]   See, citing an experiment by Shay and colleagues, R. Calo, M. Froomkin, and I. Kerr (eds.), *Robot Law* (Edward Elgar, 2016), p. 274.
[157]   S. Hassan and P. de Filippi, The Expansion of Algorithmic Governance: From Code Is Law to Law Is Code (2017) 17 *J. Field Actions* 88.
[158]   Cf. Lequesne Roth, above note 12, p. 10.
[159]   R. Pound, The Limits of Effective Legal Action (1917) 27 *Int. J. Ethics* 150, 167, where he states "the life of the law is in its enforcement."
[160]   J. Raz, *The Authority of Law: Essays on Law and Morality* (Clarendon Press, 1979), p. 214.
[161]   See, on this issue, D. Restrepo Amariles and G. Lewkowicz, De la donnée à la décision: comment réguler par les données et les algorithmes, in M. Bouzeghoub and R. Mosseri (eds.), *Les big data à découvert* (CNRS, 2017), pp. 80–2.

1. *Hybridization of legal rules.* As discussed in the case studies related to APB, Parcoursup and Connect, the rules effectively implemented by ADS are not a mere translation of legal rules into computer software. Instead, the rules embedded and effectively applied by ADS are hybrid artifacts resulting from the formalization of legal rules and their transcription into computer code. Hence, as demonstrated in the APB case, these rules may differ substantially from the legal rules in the books. This hybridity – which is not law in books or law in action, but law in other technologies – constitutes a threat to the rule of law as citizens may, in certain circumstances, be subject to unknown, unpublished, and even unconstitutional prescriptions affecting their rights and status.

2. *Emergence of data-driven rules.* The IDHW and Connect case studies revealed several risks associated with the increasing reliance of public administration on datasets to distribute benefits and enforce the law, such as incompleteness and bias. If these concerns are common to any endeavor which relies on data-driven ADS, what is more specific to the legal domain is the extraction from the data of general prescriptions with legal effects. As shown in the Connect case study, the use of machine-learning techniques to identify patterns of lifestyle and fraud, which in turn may trigger a letter of inquiry or a full investigation, makes citizens accountable for not meeting the patterns of behavior that have been drawn from the statistical analysis of the datasets. As such, these patterns may be considered data-driven rules, increasing the normative burden on citizens. In addition to issues related to publicity and certainty also affecting hybrid rules, data-driven rules are at odds with two additional principles of the rule of law – namely, equality and due process.

   Regarding the former, the effective content of data-driven rules depends on the dataset or machine-learning techniques used by the administration. This means citizens may in practice be subject to different rules or standards of behavior despite the applicable law being the same. As for the latter, data-driven rules affect procedural rights by creating an inequality of arms between the administration and the citizens, and by increasing or shifting the burden of proof. For example, as discussed earlier, access to the source code, let alone the full dataset used by the administration, is generally limited or unavailable, which prevents citizens from effectively exercising their rights of defense, such as being able to challenge the evidence or the rules effectively applied to them.

3. *Conflation of the life cycle of law.* Finally, advanced ADS implementing all four features defined above are likely to conflate the three phases of the life cycle of law as distinguished in liberal democracies (that is, law-making, adjudication/administration, and enforcement) into a continuous and autonomous process. As shown in the Connect case study, ADS have the potential to redefine the rules which are effectively applied to citizens (for example, hybrid and data-driven rules), automate the administration of such rules, and enforce the resulting decision. This would happen, for instance, in the event a direct deduction from an accounts tool is plugged into the Connect software. Advanced ADS further reshape the relationships between the administration and the citizens by at least overseeing the principles of separation of powers, checks and balances, and accountability.

   To ensure the rule of law will be upheld in a context where the administration increasingly relies on ADS, it may be useful to provide strict guidelines on the interpretation of their results, enhance checks and audits of the software, and strengthen the rights of citizens. The latter may include *ex ante* measures, such as conducting public consultations prior to the implementation of a new software, or *ex post*, such as granting citizens the right to access the source codes, or the right to "a public engineer" in addition to a public defender.

The adoption of ADS on a large scale in public administration may also contribute to reinforcing what Mark Bovens and Stavros Zouridis call "system level bureaucracy." In this type of bureaucracy, information and communication technologies play a decisive role in administrative decision-making, including in relation to the execution, control, and external communication of decisions. In a system-level bureaucracy, the system designers are the backbone of the decision-making process, while administrative discretion tends to disappear.[162] Upholding the rule of law in this context requires making it suitable for a technological environment. Indeed, although citizens may challenge the results of ADS before a court, the scalability of court decisions as in the level of the ADS remains limited. ADS operate through first-order rules (that is, the computer code of algorithms), and therefore rules are applied systematically and on a large-scale basis. Instead, court decisions relating to an individual case constitute second-order rules (that is, rules dealing with the outputs of algorithms), and therefore, do not affect the general operation of the ADS.

Incorporating the rule of law as a first-order rule may be possible in at least two ways. First, supreme courts and other tribunals taking decisions with *erga omnes* effects can require operators of ADS to incorporate the rule of law at the code's level or, in any case, to ensure their deployment conforms with certain legal prescriptions, similar to what the European Court of Justice ordered to Google in relation to the right to be forgotten.[163] Second, to enact the principle of rule of law by design compelling designers and operators of ADS to incorporate built-in features in software guaranteeing respect for the rule of law. Both of these solutions constitute the "birth" of the algorithmic rule of law.

---

[162]   See also M. Bovens and S. Zouridis, From Street-Level to System-Level Bureaucracies: How Information and Communication Technology Is Transforming Administrative Discretion and Constitutional Control (2002) 62 *Public Adm. Rev.* 174, 180.

[163]   CJEU, Case C-131/12, *Google Spain SL and Google Inc.* v. *Agencia Española de Protección de Datos (AEPD) and Mario Costeja González* ("Google judgment"), May 13, 2014 (ECLI:EU:C:2014:317).

15

From Legal Sources to Programming Code

Automatic Individual Decisions in Public Administration and Computers under the Rule of Law

Dag Wiese Schartum

INTRODUCTION

Public administration in Norway and in many other countries has used computers for more than fifty-five years. It is normal and necessary. Of course, it is possible to imagine many more office buildings where thousands of men and women would do all the detailed processing of individual cases that are processed today by computers, but this alternative is not very realistic: Modern taxation systems, national social insurance schemes and management of many other welfare programs would not be feasible without the use of computers and the *algorithmic law* that is integrated in the software. Thus, the question is not *if* public administration should apply computer technology, but *how* this should be done. This chapter deals with important how-to questions.

Automatic legal decision-making under the rule of law necessitates the meeting of two worlds: law and computer science. Processing and designing automatic information systems is the domain of technologists: typically, they know required systems development models, methods, and tools; most lawyers do not. To the extent that lawyers lack knowledge and understanding of what development of information systems with legal content is about, technologists may in fact be in a position to operate as if they were lawyers; for instance, by making choices they see as a question of system design or a programming option without knowing the juridical significance of such choices and the binding framework implied in legal sources. This aims to make it easier for lawyers to better understand their role, and to be in control of legal issues as a part of developing systems designed to apply the law.

There is no single truth, of course, about the relationship between the two professions, and empirical research should reveal practices in systems development processes by which law is transformed into programming codes. Nonetheless, a *normative approach* is important and necessary, i.e. an approach that describes and prescribes how lawyers should go about developing systems and have a high level of control – or at least influence – over legal properties and quality of information in systems designed to apply imbedded legal rules. Discussions are primarily based on many decades of research and experiences from the Norwegian public administration, first and foremost regarding systems where the level of automatic processing of legal rules is high.[1] Norwegian public administration has been relatively advanced when it comes to automatic decision-making, with the first totally

---

[1] A very basic article is J. Bing, Automatiseringsvennlig lovgivning [Automation-Friendly Legislation] (1977) *Tidsskrift for rettsvitenskap* 1995–2229. Two thorough case studies about the subject are found in two doctoral theses from Sweden from the early 1990s: C. Magnusson Sjöberg, Rättsautomattion. Särskillt om statsförvaltningens datorisering [Legal Automation. Specifically about Computerization of Central Public Administration], Norsteds Juridik, Stockholm (1992); and D. W. Schartum, Rettssikkerhet og systemutvikling i offentlig forvaltning

automated routine already in 1974;[2] there is no indication that the Norwegian experience and situation differ from digital government in the public administration of most other well-organized countries. Thus, I suppose, there is a generally high degree of relevance.

The following discussions and analyses are formulated from the perspective of lawyers, and the aim is to communicate basic understandings, insights, and experiences when legal systems development is viewed from the perspective of legally responsible personnel of government agencies. In "Initial Reflections and Clarifications," I present some basic understandings of automatic legal decision-making in public administration. Many of these understandings lead to the normative construction of the *legal transformation process*, i.e. a process where we start with applicable legal sources and end up with a working programming code. "From Legal Sources to Programming Code" explains and discusses such transformation processes on a general level. Many legal questions and reform issues are connected with the question of how we handle facts of individual cases as part of automated systems or, more specifically, where we may find data that fit in with legal requirements we derive from the legal sources. In "Processing Data," I explore three different ways of dealing with this challenge: reuse of data, self-service routines, and use of sensor technology. The rule of law in public administration is the underlying theme throughout the entire chapter, and discussions of the transformation process in "From Legal Sources to Programming Code," as well as discussions of collection of data in "Processing Data," are largely founded on this concern. In "Automated Decision-Making under the Rule of Law," I discuss more specifically the subject of automated decision-making under the rule of law. I especially explore potentials of rule of law by design of information systems. One important point in the discussion mentioned is the fact that legislation is not frequently drafted in ways that facilitate a transformation from law to code; law-making is not "computer-conscious" or "automation-friendly."[3] In "Computer-Conscious Law-Making," I discuss possibilities of either changing the law-making process or the systems development process, so that the two processes can be harmonized.

INITIAL REFLECTIONS AND CLARIFICATIONS

Installed Base and Technological Development

Automatic individual decision-making and algorithmic law in public administration is as old as the computer. The current digitalization and automation of public administration is part of a continuous development beginning in the early 1960s. Of course, during all these years, digitalization technology has evolved from something very simple into what we consider today as modern and advanced technology. During these developmental years, we have experienced several leaps of technological innovation that have equipped us with many new technological tools to digitize and automate to a greater extent and at a faster pace

---

[Rule of Law and Systems Development in Public Administration], Universitetsforlaget, Oslo (1993). The present chapter is primarily written on the basis of these and a number of later works; in particular D. W. Schartum, From Facts to Decision Data: About the Factual Basis of Automated Individual Decisions (2018) 65 *Sc. St. Law* 379–400; D. W. Schartum, Law and Algorithms in the Public Domain (2016) 1 *Nordic J. Applied Ethics* 15–26; and D. W. Schartum, Developing eGovernment Systems – Legal, Technological and Organizational Aspects (2010) 56 *Sc. St. Law* 125–47. An extensive handbook about the same issue as in the present chapter is found in D. W. Schartum, *Digitalisering av offentlig forvaltning – Fra lovtekst til programkode [Digitalization of Public Administration – from Words of an Act to Programming Code]* (Fagbokforlaget, 2018).

2   The Government Housing Benefit System.

3   Both concepts refer to Bing, above note 1.

than before. The associated legal issues have become much more complex compared to previous decades, and there is a far higher level of social acquaintance with and acceptance of technology currently than in previous periods. Still, it is this author's view that many of the basic legal questions related to automated decision-making have principally remained unchanged.

This chapter does not narrate the history of legal automation. Nevertheless, it is crucial to understand that the digital motorways have developed from cart roads, and that development of the transformation from legal sources to programming code has been a gradual process. What lies behind us is primarily of historical interest, but might also provide good indications of what lies ahead – not as a deterministic view of technology, but because it is likely we will pursue the same type of rationale as previous years, pushing well-known strategies further toward their extremes; it is very likely, for example, that we will continue to increase the degree of automation. It is probable that we will apply new ways of automatically collecting data about facts of individual cases by reducing and, in some instances, even removing direct human interaction and evaluation. Technology may be developed to collect, analyze, and apply legally relevant data as input to code programmed to arrive at legally valid individual decisions. Moreover, chances are high that we will continue to develop methods of formal representation of legal norms that we want to automate. Of special interest is the possibility of applying statistical methods and machine learning in addition to standard methods of formal representation based on "fixed rules." It is also very likely that we will continue to use technology as an agent for organizational change, meaning that existing actors in decision-making processes will have new roles, and that new actors may be part of automatic decision-making. Altogether, this may lead to a public administration that will be unrecognizable when compared with baseline in the 1960s.

The current discussion on digitalization and automation is to a large extent about relatively new technologies, particularly machine learning, big data, and block chain. In this chapter, emphasis will be primarily on *established technology*, typically technology based on fixed algorithms and well-defined use of databases. The overwhelming attention new and emerging technologies are receiving may lead us to underestimate the importance of state of the art. Established technology is *installed base*,[4] that is, the technology we have and will continue to have for many years, side by side with new technologies. In the unforeseeable future, tax administration, social security administration, customs and excise authorities, and other branches of public administration will be totally reliant on this technological base. Machine learning and big data etc. will to a large extent be an extension of the established technological repertoire that allows us to automate in novel ways. How far and how fast new technologies will entail radical changes in digital government is something for the scholars of tomorrow to assess.

Major Legal Aspects of Digital Government

Computers have myriad applications and many of them – if not all – have some sort of legal relevance and implication. First, when assessing legal aspects of digital government, a large body of laws and regulations may be relevant, even though they may not specifically regulate technology or pertain to automated decision-making. Laws concerning liability to damages

[4] See M. Aanestad, M. Grisot, O. Hanseth, and P. Vassilakopoulou, Information Infrastructures and the Challenge of the Installed Base, in M. Aanestad, M. Grisot, O. Hanseth, and P. Vassilakopoulou (eds.), *Information Infrastructures within European Health Care: Working with the Installed Base* (Springer, 2017).

and punishment, etc., for instance, could be relevant when assessing government agencies' liability for application of wrongful software. However, this and other types of general law applied to the digital field will not be discussed here.

On the other hand, we will look at a second group of laws, namely, the laws passed with the specific intention to regulate technology, the *digital legal framework*. The General Data Protection Regulation (GDPR) is a core example of this type of framework;[5] other examples are Regulation about free flow of non-personal data in the European Union[6] and regulation of electronic communication.[7] Various rights and freedoms may motivate the establishment of digital legal frameworks: data protection, freedom of information, competition, non-discrimination, public security, and other interests and principles have been grounds for legislation in the digital field. In this chapter, special attention will be focused on parts of the digital legal framework passed to protect citizens. Emphasis will be on the rule of law and data protection associated with individual decisions in public administration.

Third, legal instruments could establish rules and principles regarding how *development* of information systems and software should be carried out. Such rules could, for instance, be motivated by the fact that parts of systems development work can be seen as a legal decision-making process (see below, "Automatic Decision-Making and Decision Support"). Thus, one could argue that new rule-of-law guarantees are needed, for instance, in the form of legal requirements regarding the competence of staff participating in systems development, the obligation to document major legal decisions made in course of systems development, etc. (see "The Rule of Law by Design of Information Systems," below).

Lastly, legal rules could concern how *application* of information systems and software should be regulated, including how legal rights and obligations for citizens, businesses, and other parties involved in the processing should be exercised. In Figure 15.1, I have illustrated these regulatory aspects.

In a general sense, legal requirements for the *properties of systems* and software are probably most common, with GDPR as the dominating example. Legal requirements for *application of systems* and software are commonplace, but are not necessarily in the form of provisions particularly designed to regulate digital government. Although there may be a need to amend legislation in response to digital government, most of the traditional rule-of-law guarantees in administrative law will be applicable related to digital decision-making too, although not necessarily in a satisfactory way. In "The Rule of Law by Design of Information Systems," I will discuss the balance between regulating the *properties* of legal decision-making systems and the *application* of such systems.

Primary emphasis in this chapter will be on questions regarding the *contents* of the triangle in Figure 15.1: code based on legal sources, or questions regarding *law as content* of systems and software. This covers issues regarding transformation from legal sources, via interpretation and deduction of valid legal rules, to program codes implementing the legal sources and automating application of the law in individual cases. I will denote the process as a *transformation of legal sources*; in short: "transformation."

---

[5]   See Regulation (EU) 2016/679 of the European Parliament and of the Council of 27 April 2016 on the protection of natural persons with regard to the processing of personal data and on the free movement of such data, and repealing Directive 95/46/EC (General Data Protection Regulation, or GDPR).

[6]   See Regulation of the European Parliament and of the Council on a framework for the free flow of non-personal data in the European Union, 2017/0228 (COD).

[7]   See Proposal for a Regulation of the European Parliament and of the Council concerning the respect for private life and the protection of personal data in electronic communications and repealing Directive 2002/58/EC (Regulation on Privacy and Electronic Communications), 2017/0003 (COD).

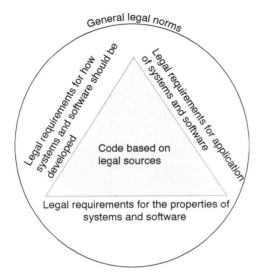

FIGURE 15.1 Main aspects of law and digital government

Transformation of Legal Sources – an Overview

The following discussion will be restricted to a type of information system in public admin-istration which could be denoted as *legal decision-making systems*. The category is rather broad and comprises systems in which legal rules are embedded in the programming code, making it possible to automate the application of the law. Development of such systems requires, in other words, transformation of legal sources. If we take individual decision-making in public administration as an example, these sources are typically statutes and regulations passed to determine how government agencies must proceed to reach valid legal decisions in individual cases. In other words, we are talking about laws with a substantive scope limited to one specific branch of government – for instance, regulating different types of taxes, social benefits, admission to schools and universities, etc. Such special laws and regulations are fundamen-tally different from legislation with a wide/general substantive scope such as laws covering every part of public administration, or the GDPR covering most instances of processing of personal data in the public and private sectors.[8] Laws and regulations with a scope limited to a certain branch of government that establish legal rules regarding specific government schemes will typically be the source of only one official information system. The tax author-ities, for instance, will have one information system designed to determine tax liability and assess amounts owed, and the situation is similar for social benefits and national insurance, education institutions' systems for admission of students, etc. The obvious reason is that exercise of government authority is usually exclusive for the competent branch of government, and thus there is only one legally valid information system. Other actors, of course, could develop their own parallel systems (for example, for assessment of taxes), but unless they have the "official" tax information system as source, there will be uncertainty as to the correctness of

---

[8]   Typically, this type of "general" legislation is legislation constituting a digital legal framework, as mentioned in the previous section.

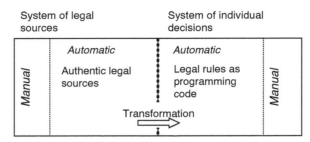

FIGURE 15.2 Overview of the transformation process

the private and "unofficial" interpretation of the law embedded in systems developed by others than the government branch in question. [9, 10]

In Figure 15.2, I illustrate the major elements of the transformation process; a process for developing an information system designed to automate application of valid legal sources within a specialized field of legislation (for example, regarding housing benefits or income tax). The figure is designed to illustrate the transformation process from authentic legal sources to programming code; that is, from natural language to formal programming language.

The system of legal sources (see the left-hand side of Figure 15.2) denotes various compilations of laws, regulations, judgments, and other authentic authoritative sources accepted by the legal system (that is, sources that may be applied to reach valid individual legal decisions). These sources could be collected automatically from databases or manually from paper-based collection. After collection of relevant sources, they are subject to interpretation according to accepted legal method, resulting in a high number of legal rules. The next step of the transformation process will be to formalize and express these legal rules in one or several procedures, by means of a programming language.

Interpretation entails both how each piece of text with its vague, discretionary, and imperfect contents should be understood and how each of the relevant sources should be understood in light of the others. Derived rules must be precise and complete: computers only follow unambiguous rules, and there is no room for doubt or discretion. Transformation implies, in other words, that on each point, we must choose specific interpretations that exclude other possible interpretations. Programming codes of legal decision-making systems contain *a collection of preferred and allegeable correct interpretations*. It will almost always be possible to claim that other results are correct and legally valid, and thus there may be grounds to disagree that the interpretations embedded in the code should be held as correct.

The term "algorithm," as defined by Wikipedia,[11] is "an unambiguous specification of how to solve a class of problems." Transformation of legal sources to programming code could be described as deducing from legal sources detailed, interconnected, unambiguous legal rules which prescribe how we should solve legal problems within a specific legal domain. We start

---

9   This is not to say that the legal contents of government systems are always correct, but these systems represent the official government opinion on how the law should be applied.

10 Similar problems could be relevant in cases where several local authorities exercise parallel authority based on the same legislation, but by means of different privately developed software. Provided that the same rules apply to all citizens irrespective of the municipality in which they are domiciled, there should be no difference between the parallel system solutions.

11 See https://en.wikipedia.org/wiki/Algorithm.

by specifying and expressing "legal algorithms" by means of natural language, and end up with expressing legal algorithms by means of programming language. In this chapter, the term algorithm is not frequently used; partly because its relevance is obvious, and partly because other more specific terms are even more useful in explaining the transformation process.

My explanations above indicate that transformation of authentic legal sources into programming code could be seen as a legal decision-making process. The kind of decision process and the legal effects of such decisions depend on the role the competent authority delegates to the legal decision system. In many cases, the de facto effect of legal interpretations in legal decision-making systems is direct and binding. Technical, practical, and economic circumstances contribute to such effects. If millions of individual decisions are made by the system, in the blink of an eye, it will generally not be feasible to manually check each output from the system, because it would take an army of case officers and extraordinary budgets to exercise meaningful controls. In "Computer-Conscious Law-Making," below, I will discuss options to make legal parts of the systems development process more in line with rule-of-law principles, alternatively to extend legislative processes so that the significance of legal decision-making processes imbedded in systems development will be limited.

Automatic Decision-Making and Decision Support

Above, I have used the term "legal decision-making system" to denote systems designed to make decisions without manual control of the output. Legal decision-making systems are characterized by a high degree of automatic application of the law and by acceptability of the result of the processing as legally valid decisions. Such systems could, but need not, be totally automated: the level of automation depends on the extent to which the relevant legal sources could be transformed into code and whether it is profitable to make the transformation. It may be, for instance, that transformation is deemed too expensive because parts of the relevant legal sources are rarely used. Even if transformation is possible, application of certain parts of the law may thus have to be handled manually.

Article 22 of the GDPR regulates a "decision based solely on automated processing." If the decision could be classified as legal (i.e. if processing is controlled by transformed legal sources), this may correspond to fully automated legal decision-making systems. Here, I refrain from interpreting the mazes and uncertainties of article 22. To be logical, "based solely on automated processing" should mean that the processing does not allow for any possibility of manual interference in determining results. In Norwegian public administration, such fully automated legal decision-making systems are increasingly common. For instance, in Norway, most tax decisions concerning individual taxpayers, more than 70 percent of applications to the Norwegian State Educational Loan Fund, and the large majority of applications for housing benefits are totally automated. Total automation implies that no person has considered the cases, and every case has only been processed according to legal rules that have been transformed and programmed.

Fully automated decisions must logically be based on two main premises: first, data representing every relevant fact of the case must exist in machine-readable form and be digitally accessible in the appropriate technical format; second, it must be possible to process all data of the case by means of computer programs which contain correct and complete representation of all relevant applicable legal rules. Below, in "From Legal Sources to

Programming Code," I will explore these two premises further, and in "Processing Data," I will examine more closely the processing of data. The point here is that the notion of "legal decision-making systems" covers systems from a modest degree of automation to fully auto-mated systems, as I have described above.

Legal decision support systems, by contrast, is a term denoting digital systems that *support* human decision-making. Final decisions are always made by a person, as a minimum through approval of a suggestion from the system for individual decisions. Various automatic operations could be carried out by decision support systems too, on selected points of the decision-making procedure; for instance, by carrying out advanced retrieval of relevant legal sources, by collecting information about relevant facts of cases, or by limited automatic application of the law (for instance, calculations and trying of conditions). The decisive difference compared to legal decision-making systems is that *people* oversee legal decision support systems, while *computers* are put in charge of legal decision-making systems: support systems support human processing and application of the law, while decision systems are – more or less, in accordance with the level of automation – supported by people.

Typical users of legal support systems are lawyers giving individual advice and services to clients. Such legal services must be responsive to concrete and individual situations and the needs of the client. If necessary, lawyers will "go to war" on behalf of the client and pursue client interests as far as possible, a pursuit that can bring them to unexpected interpretations of legal sources.

Typical users of decision systems, in contrast, are public administration officers[12] proces-sing individual cases in standardized ways as part of "mass administration." The application of legal decision-making systems is to a large extent based on "safe" and "loyal" interpretations of the law, and/or of interpretations paving the way for effective decision-making routines. In mass administrative systems, choices of interpretations may easily be affected by expected effects on government budgets – for instance, by pushing interpretation of concepts to extremes to make possible reuse of data (see " Simplifying the Processing of Facts by Reuse and Common Use," below).

Automatic Decision-Making as Advance Decisions

Traditionally, lawyers solve legal problems as they occur: application of the law is driven by the inflow of individual cases ("case-driven application of the law"). Thus, questions of interpretation may not be addressed until they are made topical by an individual case. In principle, potential questions of interpretation may never be discovered because no indivi-dual case has brought it to the surface.

When the task is to develop legal decision-making systems, we cannot wait for access to a sufficient variety of individual cases. Instead, the approach must be system-driven; that is, we need to map and solve questions of interpretation in a systematic way ("system-driven application of the law"). Concrete requirements for system-driven approaches are conditional on the level of ambition for the planned system. Here, I assume that the aspiration is to establish a system with extensive and intensive representation of the law, yielding a high level of automation. Extensive representation implies that the system would cover all types of legal questions linked to a specific realm of the law or statute regulating a certain type of individual decision. Intensive representation means that interpretation and solution of legal questions is

---

[12]   But sometimes all case officers are made redundant.

an elaborate and detailed process and that, ultimately, all relevant legal problems related to a certain type of individual decision are identified and solved on a detailed level.

System-driven application of the law as described places lawyers in a new situation: they have no standard methods for exhaustive mapping of legal questions within a domain. Thus, the need arises to apply new formal methods and tools. Typically, this will concern modeling of the two main aspects of the transformation of legal sources mentioned above, namely modeling data/information representing facts of cases, and modeling how this information should be processed (flow charts etc.). By specifying rule elements in all possible types of relevant facts in a data model, and by describing possible relations between these data, it will be possible to make full descriptions of the *factual* aspects of the rules. Further, by specifying all rule elements regarding the processing of data in the data model, it will be possible to stipulate the procedural aspects of the same rules.

Given "complete models" of factual and procedural rule elements within the domain in question, legal interpretation and problem-solving will basically be of a standard type. However, two peculiarities may be noted: when decision systems are developed to replace an existing system, one methodological issue is the extent to which legal rules represented in existing code should be seen as proof of an existing administrative practice and thus be assigned weight as a source of law. The basic observation is that computer programs are always executed in an identical way, and thus it could be argued that a program code is strong and detailed evidence of a certain practice. Thus, the principle of equal treatment would imply that the codes of existing decision-making systems should be given considerable weight as a legal source. Here, I will not go into further discussion of this question, but merely suggest some additional considerations that may or should influence the role of programming code as a source of law:

- whether or not the programming code in question has been known and acknowledged by the government authority as an expression of applicable law (it may be that the code is the result of decisions at a lower level of the organization and even of decisions made by contractors, with no knowledge of the responsible level of the relevant government agency);
- whether or not it is intended that the code expresses a legal rule (programming choices may have legal effects that were unintended);
- whether or not the programming code may be said to represent administrative practice in a large number of individual cases (a large quantity of cases is probably an argument in favor of high weighting of the code as a legal source);
- how long the programming code in question has been in use (long duration is probably an argument in favor of high weighting of the code as a legal source).

The factors mentioned above will probably be relevant in most legal systems. Their weight, however, may differ. In addition, the way in which the factors are assessed will probably rely on characteristics of routines on which the code rests. Thus, there will typically be differences between the evaluation of rules in the code developed without special attention to "code as law," and instances where the awareness of code as law has been high, with lawyers deeply involved in the specification of the legal content of the programming code.

The second peculiar aspect I will touch upon regarding interpretation and application of the law connected to the transformation process could be denoted by the words *coherence analysis*. Consideration of coherence is, of course, a common element when legislation is interpreted. The point here is that coherence analyses become much more important with system-driven application of the law. Emphasis on data and processing modeling as described above strongly prepares the ground for coherence analyses, in particular with regard to concepts used. Interpretation of one concept is likely to be carried out in the context of how identical or similar concepts should be interpreted in other parts of the law, and in other, closely related legal sources. Coherence checks are likely to be carried out both for concepts describing facts/data of individual cases and for concepts expressing logical and arithmetical operations by which data are to be processed. Occurrence of the concept "income," for instance, will be interpreted in light of other occurrences of the same concept, as well as occurrences of concepts that may or may not be synonyms (for example, "earning," "wage"). Similarly, words and phrases expressing logical and arithmetical operations will be interpreted in the same way: the phrase "adjusted in accordance with change of consumer price index" will likely be understood in the same way every time it occurs.

"Complete decisions" regarding interpretation (i.e. both extensively and intensively) imply determination of all relevant legal questions and thus of all potential future individual cases processed by the decision system. Such systems would imply advance decisions: it is exhaustively and precisely predetermined (1) which facts could be the basis of decisions, including the digital sources and definitions of these facts, and (2) how these facts must be represented and processed in order to reach legally valid results. There is uncertainty only in conjunction with the future values of the prequalified types of legally valid facts. However, many of these facts will be "historical" in the sense that they exist before the time of decision-making: decisions will be based on (existing) facts describing the citizens' established situation (for example, regarding income, matrimonial status, number of children, etc.). To that extent, individual decisions are visualizations of legal effects of predetermined facts.

FROM LEGAL SOURCES TO PROGRAMMING CODE

Introduction

This chapter proceeds on the premise that transformation of authentic legal sources to programming code may be seen as a legal decision-making process (see "Transformation of Legal Sources," above). In the following, we will have a closer look at this transformation process. Emphasis will be placed on the legal aspects of transformation, while technical aspects will only be the context for legal processes. Figure 15.3 provides an overview of the major steps of the transformation process, and the discussions below will largely follow this structure.

Figure 15.3 may be seen as containing three linked sub-processes: two vertical sub-processes and one horizontal sub-process. Vertical processes represent those with the highest relevance for lawyers and contain tasks for which juridical competence is crucial, namely (1) a sub-process starting with formulating a purpose of the processing and ending with a specification of rules, and (3) starting with programmed rules[13] and ending with a decision to put the decision-making system in operation. Between these two sub-processes, there is an intermediate sub-process of a primarily technological nature (2), performed by computer professionals who realize the specification of rules and program them so they may be automatically applied. The entire transformation process encompasses sub-processes (1) and (2). In terms of formalization, transformation is a gradual process. Sub-process (1) is mainly about working with natural language, and sub-process (2) is mainly about working with formal languages (modeling and programming languages). Specification of rules at the conclusion of sub-process (1)) will be semi-formal,

---

[13] See "System, algorithms" in Figure 15.3.

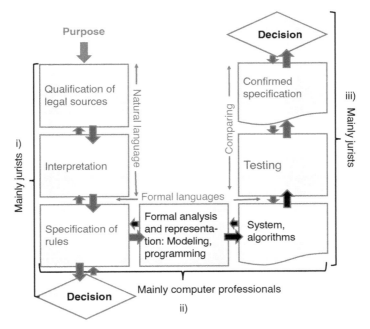

FIGURE 15.3 Main phases and activities in the transformation process

typical in the form of rules expressed in structured natural language ("pseudo code"), tables, etc. It is important to note that even if these processes are illustrated as stepwise, iterations should be expected (see small arrows). Formalization of specified rules could, for instance, be difficult or expensive, something which may lead to an iteration and reconsideration of the possibility of interpreting legal sources differently, leading to slightly different rules of which it is easier to make a formal representation. In this chapter, I will mainly discuss sub-process (1) and be much briefer regarding sub-process (3). Sub-process (2) will not be further commented on here.

Several of the questions that must be solved during sub-process (1) concern compliance with the GDPR. Individual decisions in public administration will often have physical persons as parties to cases and facts of cases are thereby "personal data" as defined in article 4(1) of the GDPR, and the automatic processing of this information amounts to "processing personal data" (see article 4(2)). Here, the constraints of this chapter do not permit a discussion of questions relevant to the GDPR, and they will therefore only be mentioned and placed in context.

Determination of Purpose and Qualification of Legal Sources

Development of legal decision-making systems must always be made within the framework of one or more purposes of processing.[14] The central purpose of processing in these cases will be to make individual decisions of a particular type – for instance, decisions on cases concerning housing benefits, individual tax, or admission to public schools and universities.[15] In most instances, the substantive rules on which government decision-making is based will be statutory and rather detailed, implying that there will be little freedom of choice when the main purpose of

---

[14] See GDPR, arts. 6 and 9.
[15] See GDPR, art. 5(1)(b) and the purpose limitation principle.

the processing is formulated: the purpose could, for instance, be to make decisions in cases regarding application of housing benefits, including processing of appeals.[16]

The main purpose of processing indirectly determines identification of relevant legal sources that will be subject to transformation. When the main purpose is to decide in individual cases concerning housing benefits, substantive rules regarding this benefit are laid down in an Act of Parliament or a regulation. In many legal systems, preparatory works will also have great juridical relevance and weight in legal dogmatic reasoning. In addition, there will probably be relevant case law and other types of legal sources.

Possible differences between legal systems aside, the main point in this first phase of sub-procedure (1) is to identify all relevant legal sources and make a "complete" inventory of these. Before interpretation of legal sources can start, it is required that legal information systems containing relevant authentic legal sources are identified. In some jurisdictions, almost all legal sources are found in one consolidated information system.[17] In many other jurisdictions, the task of mapping available information systems providing a complete list of legal sources relevant to the development of a legal decision system will be much more challenging. In this respect, I will base further discussion on a situation where these challenges are overcome and all relevant legal sources are available.

Collection of legal sources on which development of legal decision-making systems are based constitute the very foundation of each system, in the sense that every legal choice of interpretation etc. in the transformation process should have a basis here. Thus, it is important to have mechanisms to tackle amendments and other legal developments. Moreover, the selection of legal source should not rest on the subjective choices of individuals who from time to time have been given the task of considering the relevance of legal sources. A stable identification, selection, and update of relevant legal sources could be ensured by means of fixed selection criteria; that is, fixed rules determining the specific legal sources that should be selected and included in the collection of sources for the system.

When selection of legal sources is carried out, the next step will be to prepare them for analysis and transformation. I will not go into any detail on this point, but possible approaches are: (1) to relate sources to one another in order to establish one integrated body of sources; (2) to identify all legal definitions of concepts; or (3) to identify all references (internally within each source, within the body of legal sources, and between the body of sources and external sources). It is this well-organized body of sources that should be subject to interpretation in following the steps of sub-procedure (1); see the next section, below.

Interpretation and Specification of Rules

Introduction

The next step in the transformation process is interpretation of legal sources with the aim to deduce rules which will later be expressed as programming code. Figure 15.4 is a variant of

---

[16]   Detailed statutory regulations also often have impact on questions of the legal basis for processing (see GDPR, arts. 6 and 9), in that legislation will often constitute bases for processing; in other words, the substantive rules of legislation will be decisive for the processing of personal data that may be deemed "necessary for the ... exercise of official authority vested in the controller" (see GDPR, art. 6(1)(e)). At the same time, specification of purposes related to the type of individual decisions that the decision system will perform has consequences for qualification of legal sources that should be considered as the basis of the transformation process. Thus, art. 6(1)(e) will typically be the main legal basis for the processing that the planned legal decision-making systems in public administration will carry out.

[17]   Like the Norwegian Lovdata.no.

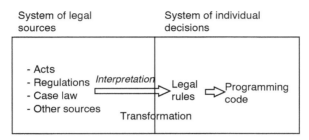

FIGURE 15.4 Deduction of legal rules

Figure 15.2 (see "Transformation of Legal Sources," above) and illustrates how different sources are the basis of joint interpretation of these sources, leading to a number of legal rules that, in turn, will be further formalized and programmed as part of the legal decision system. Linguistically speaking, we move from sources in natural language and deduce legal rules expressed in semi-formalized language (typically, pseudo code), which again will be transformed by means of formal (unambiguous) programming language.

In many countries, Acts of Parliament and regulations will be the predominant legal sources, but this situation may differ. Statutory laws are often drafted to regulate most legal issues within the domain in question, and thus other legal sources will mainly be applied to supplement and clarify the statutory basis. This represents an easier situation compared to others, when more complex and heterogeneous patterns of case law must be dealt with to deduce legal rules of the domain.

I have emphasized that the interpretation process itself is generally "normal" and in accordance with established sources of legal principles. However, the view we need to take is special and must reflect later stages of the transformation process. First, we need to take into account two aspects of rules:

1. What are the facts we need to take into consideration and which data represent these facts?
2. Which operations should be performed on data to yield legally correct results?

The discussions below will follow this view of interpretation. Most legal questions will be connected to facts (individual data, often personal data), while the number of legal questions connected to operations carried out on these facts will usually be more limited – although they may be very important.

Deducing and Transforming Facts of Individual Cases

Figure 15.5 illustrates the division between facts/data of cases and operations performed on these data, as presented in the previous section.

Discussions in this section are primarily related to the grey-colored box to the left in Figure 15.5. The two arrows from the box indicate processing of data representing facts of individual cases: first, personalia – that is, personal details which identify parties to cases, for instance, names, national identity number, and residential address, as well as (other) contact information. These are data that will remain unchanged during the

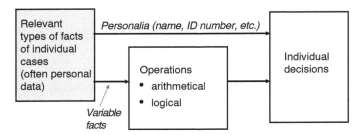

FIGURE 15.5 Deduction of facts

processing of cases in the legal decision system, and are therefore less interesting in this context.

The focus here is on *variable* facts/data, that is, data describing the facts which, pursuant to the legal sources, are qualified as a relevant basis for individual decisions on, for instance, matrimonial status, income, the number of children supported, diseases, number of days away from work, traveling time between residence and kindergarten, etc. There is an abundance of legal criteria to be found in various government laws and regulations establishing rights and obligations for citizens. Such criteria are indicated in laws by means of natural language or other ways that require interpretation before provisions could be transformed into automatic processes resulting in valid legal decisions. A simple quote from a law regulating the right to sickness benefit may serve as an example of interpretations linked to variable facts:[18]

> For the purposes of any provision of this Act relating to . . . sickness benefit . . . a day shall not be treated in relation to any person . . . as a day of incapacity for work unless on that day he is, or is deemed in accordance with regulations to be, *incapable of work* by reason of some *specific disease* or *bodily* or *mental disablement*.

Every relevant concept of provisions regarding sickness benefits must be interpreted in context, but here only a small selection is presented. The quote above, for example, necessitates an examination of whether a person is "incapable of work." If this is confirmed, it must be assessed whether this incapacity is caused by a "specific disease" or "bodily or mental disablement." To determine whether these three conditions are met, we have to consult other legal sources and check whether regulations, case law, etc. exist that may help us acquire a correct understanding of the concepts.

First, we will have to establish some basic interpretations and find out whether "incapable of work" requires 100 percent incapacity, or if some degree of incapacity is admissible. If partial work incapacity is acceptable, we need to find out if this state of health could be on the level of any percentage figure (67 percent incapability of work?), whether there is a lower limit (20% work incapacity or less?), etc. When all this is ascertained, we also need to know more about how input of data regarding this condition is to be made ("yes"/"no" if only 100 percent incapacity is accepted, percentage figure, possibly standardized or lower-limit percentages if partial incapacity is admissible).

Because interpretation is part of development of a legal decision system, we would be interested in finding out if some of these criteria could be interpreted as equivalent to data

---

[18]   Emphasis added. The example is based on the UK National Insurance Act 1965, s. 20 (as enacted).

that could be accessed digitally, preferably as part of an automatic data collection routine (see "Simplifying the Processing of Facts," below). Here, there is a possibility that the phrase "specific disease" may be understood as referring to an official list of diseases, where each disease is represented by a unique code.[19] This is a critical point: we need to automate the collection of specific diseases as far as possible, and the ultimate solution would then probably be that diseases must be expressed by means of a formal coding system, and that description "heavy sunburn" should not be accepted as a specification of a disease, in the absence of all else. Instead, the official code "L55.2 Third-degree sunburn" or some other appropriate code should be applied. In addition, it is important to decide which group of people will have the authority to diagnose, and whether or not there are requirements regarding the means of reporting diagnoses – for instance, whether diagnoses must be reported on a particular claim form, or if application of a specific procedure in a government digital data system is required. Similar questions are linked to "bodily disablement" and "mental disablement," which probably must be understood as something different from "specific disease." I will not elaborate on possible interpretations here.

The example above suffices to demonstrate that interpretations of legal concepts as part of the development of legal decision-making systems, denoting relevant types of facts in individual cases, will actualize a series of detailed questions. The extent to which it will be possible to find viable answers in sources of law will vary according to many factors, and here I will refrain from making assertions about what is most important or typical. I will take the liberty of saying, however, that legal sources often provide little support in solving detailed problems of interpretation like the ones related to "specific disease," as mentioned above. In such cases, one crucial question is how much discretion government agencies have in establishing conditions underlying the determination of, for example, a "specific disease." To what extent, for instance, can procedural requirements be introduced without contravening, for example, the principle of legality (for example, the use of a standard coding system, restrictions as to who may make diagnoses, requirements as to how diagnosis data may be collected and inserted into the legal decision system, etc.)?

In some instances, facts of individual cases rely on discretionary assessments performed by officers in charge of cases. The quote below states situations that disqualify a person from receiving unemployment benefit:[20]

> . . .
> (c) he has neglected to avail himself of a *reasonable opportunity* of *suitable employment*;
> (d) he has *without good cause* refused or failed to carry out any written recommendations given to him by an officer of an employment exchange with a view to assisting him to find *suitable employment,* being recommendations which were *reasonable having regard to* his circumstances and to the means of obtaining that employment usually adopted in the district in which he resides . . .

Criteria like "reasonable opportunity," "suitable employment," and "reasonable having regard to" provide broad discretion to officers in their assessment of a situation, action, person, etc., and in principle it is not possible to exclude the possibility of new aspects and arguments that may be deemed relevant. The condition "without good cause," for instance,

---

[19] See, e.g., International Statistical Classification of Diseases and Related Health Problems, 10th Revision (ICD-10) (WHO, 2016).

[20] Emphasis added. The example is based on s. 22(2) of the UK's National Insurance Act of 1965 containing some typical examples. My highlighting.

could refer to many individual actions and situations which cannot be fully identified in advance. Instead, such discretionary criteria invite us to make concrete assessments – this is true at least as a starting point. It may be that the total picture, based on every relevant source of law, provides grounds to conclude that such conditions could be standardized and replaced by a list of fixed criteria. In practice, public administration will often tend to standardize in more informal ways. Will standardization of criteria, implying the replacement of discretion with (more or less) fixed rules, be lawful when we design legal decision-making systems? From a technical point of view, there is a temptation to remove discretion and instead introduce a limited number of more firm conditions, replacing criteria such as "without good cause" and "reasonable opportunity." However, lawful application of an Act or regulation may imply a duty to exercise discretion. If so, a frequently used solution is simply to carry out discretion outside the automatic digital system and arrange for inputs expressing results of discretionary assessments (without good cause = Y/N). This type of solution is not satisfactory, however, if combined with a high degree of automated processing regarding other parts of the treatment of individual cases, because it is expensive and will clearly slow down the pace of processing.

An alternative solution – at least in theory – as indicated above, will be to replace discretion with a series of fixed cumulative criteria; that is, criteria that could be solved by collecting relevant machine-readable data. However, modeling something like "suitable employment," by means of machine-readable data specifying this concept, would require access to an unrealistically large number of types of data. In other words, the primary question is whether it will be lawful to replace the discretionary assessment at all. The second question is whether it is practically and technically feasible to design an automatic procedure that satisfactorily replaces discretion. Answers to both questions will frequently be "no."

A third solution that may be possible, but which – as far as I know – has not been tried in Norwegian public administration,[21] is to apply statistical methods with machine learning. This is conditioned by the existence of a corpus of dossiers from previously decided cases concerning, for example, "suitable employment." If previous decisions about that criterion exist, it will be possible to train an algorithm to analyze and compare new cases with previous cases and classify new cases in either "suitable employment" or "not suitable employment." Such routines could be automated 100 percent. However, there will be several legal problematic aspects associated with such use of machine learning. Here, I limit myself to mentioning that, unless compensating routines are introduced, machine learning will only reinforce previous practice. Thus, instead of legal dynamics and the possibility of gradual legal development, there will be a risk of creating an "echo chamber" where old points of views become decisive even in new cases with new contexts.

Deducing and Transforming Rules Governing Processing of Data

Figure 15.6 repeats the illustration in Figure 15.5 about the division between facts of cases and operations made on these facts. It also highlights the processing of variable facts/data by means of arithmetical and logical operations. Here, I will briefly comment on this processing of variable facts/data (see the grey box).

Deduction and transformation of rules governing the processing of variable data is basically about finding out what must happen to these data in order to reach legally valid decisions or: How must legally relevant facts/data of cases be used to settle individual cases? In the effort to find

---

[21]   As of March 2019.

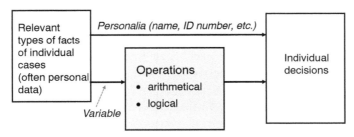

FIGURE 15.6 Deduction of operations

answers, we need to try and understand applicable legal sources describing the execution of operations that computers can perform. Thus, basically, we need to understand legal sources expressing arithmetical and logical operations. Examples of arithmetical operators are +, −, /, and * (that is, representing the basic calculation methods). Examples of logical operators are AND, OR, NOT, <, >, ≤, ≥, =, and ≠, which may be used to express structures of legal conditions. Often when rules of processing are deduced and transformed, we need a mix of both types of operators. For instance, logical operators are applied to determine if a person is eligible for a social benefit or liable to pay tax. To determine the amounts of benefits, taxes, etc., we need to apply arithmetical operators. However, logical operators are not only linked to legal conditions, and arithmetical operators are not merely linked to legal consequences in an IF – THEN structure. Conditions could contain calculations (of, for example, age, money limits, deadlines), and there may be several alternative ways of determining consequences (for example, one calculation method for situation A and another method for situation B). Moreover, some legal rules may not require calculations or further logical operations to determine legal consequences: for instance, legislation regulating acquirement of citizenship may rest only on a structure of legal conditions.

A brief example may illustrate some of the points above. The example is based on article 8 of the GDPR, which determines conditions for minors' power to consent to the processing of their personal data. The example is a pseudo code, expressing legal rules in "formalized natural language." Logical operators are marked in capital letters (IF; OR, AND), and two small pieces of calculations are linked to the three occurrences of figures:

IF   data subject's age is 18 years
       OR data subject's age is 16–18 years
          AND processing relates to information society services
       OR data subject's age is 13–16 years
          AND processing relates to information society services
          AND processing is authorized by parent
       AND data subject is of full capacity
THEN   data subject has power to consent

This representation of rules is incomplete and uncertain. It is incomplete because it is only a small part of a larger set of rules. The more important aspect in our context is that the representation is uncertain because the legislator has not specifically expressed several of the things we need to know in order to design a coherent logical structure to solve the legal questions at hand. No age of majority is stated in the GDPR, thus the Norwegian qualifying age (18 years) has been applied. Moreover, the legislators have chosen not to formulate article 8 in a way that clearly expresses the logical pattern, and thus we need to make this logic unambiguous. Similar challenges to interpretation may occur because legislators have expressed calculation rules by means of vague, natural language rather than using arithmetical operators or other types of accurate wording to express calculation rules. These types of problems of interpretation differ from interpretation of concepts expressing facts of individual cases as discussed in the previous section. Interpretation to determine correct logical and arithmetical structures is usually less comprehensive than that of determining the meaning of concepts describing facts. Nevertheless, to design a decision system that produces legally correct decisions, both interpretation issues must be solved in accordance with law.

Three Steps from Claim to Decision

Above, I have explained the core challenges in the course of the deduction and transformation of concepts denoting facts of individual cases (see "Deducing and Transforming Facts," above), and of rules governing how these facts must be processed in order to acquire legally valid results (see "Deducing and Transforming Rules," above). Figure 15.7 illustrates the underlying three-step division of these questions of deduction and transformation: formal and substantive conditions and assessment of results.

In Figure 15.7, I have copied in the structure from the two previous sections of this chapter.[22] The aim is to stress that within each of the three steps, we need to collect and process some variable data describing each individual case. Some of these data concern formal conditions, meaning conditions that must be met before substantive aspects of the processing could be dealt with. Examples are deadlines, digital signature requirements, stipulations regarding use of special digital procedures, technical formats, documentation requirements, etc. Underlying questions are: (1) What types of formal conditions do we need to define in order to design the desired decision-making system? (2) Do we have a legal basis for making these formal requirements? (3) In case legal bases are insufficient, to what extent and how will it be possible to acquire a sufficient legal basis?

When cases satisfy formal conditions, the legal decision-making system must be able to try all relevant substantive conditions, meaning all conditions that must be met to determine a result. Tax liability, for instance, is a condition for assessment of taxes, and unemployment benefits could be conditioned by the person in question being "capable of work and is, or is deemed in accordance with regulations to be, available for employment in an employed contributor's employment."[23] If such conditions are not met, there will be no assessment of tax or unemployment benefits. In the course of the deduction and transformation process described in "Deducing and Transforming Facts" and "Deducing and Transforming Rules,"

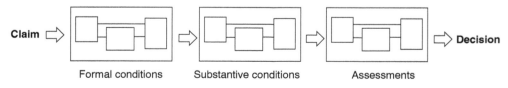

FIGURE 15.7 Processing individual cases in three steps

---

above, one task is thus to identify and interpret all legal sources relevant for questions of substantive conditions within the relevant problem area for which the legal decision system is developed. Furthermore, we need to deduce rule fragments regarding substantive conditions, and include them in one exhaustive and coherent formalized rule representation.

If substantive conditions are met, for instance, regarding tax liability or eligibility to receive unemployment benefits, the third step will be to determine a result (for example, amount of tax to be paid or unemployment benefit to be received). Like in the previous step regarding substantive conditions, we need to identify all legal sources relevant for assessment of results and compose one exhaustive and coherent formalized representation of them. This will typically be by calculations, in some instances according to rather complex algorithms, at other times simply by referring to a number in a table, and at still other times by common, flat-rate results. In some instances, there will be no actual assessment, because satisfaction of substantive conditions may lead directly to a result; for instance, in the event the person is eligible for admission to a university program of study or for citizenship.

Figure 15.7 may also be illustrative for level of automation. A basic type of automation is when only assessments are carried out by computers: questions of formal conditions are handled by people (officers check that every required data item is filled into the right claim form and signed, that required documentation is attached, etc.). If formal conditions are met, the officer will then consider substantive conditions (for instance, that the applicant is capable of work and available for employment etc.). The computer will be applied to determine the result (for instance, the amount of unemployment benefit).

A higher level of automation could be attained if comprehensive available sources exist with the types of data needed to consider cases. Conditions like "capable of work" and "available for employment" are discretionary and, therefore, unless some other agency has adequately considered the same questions (and thus made possible reuse of data), these data must be collected in all individual cases. Unless some sort of reuse of data is possible, the level of automation could only be increased through amendments, where substantive criteria are formulated so that they refer to established facts that are digitally available: instead of "capable of work," it may be possible, for example, to require that the person is not registered as more than 50 percent long-term sick or disabled. "Available for employment" may similarly be replaced by the condition that the person must (digitally) register themselves every week at the social security office whereby they confirm that they are available for employment. These examples are, of course, not exhaustive and may seem unrealistic. However, they suffice to illustrate that a high level of automation regarding collection of substantive conditions may sometimes be challenging and require rather fundamental amendments of legislation to make it (more) "automation friendly." In "Computer-Conscious Law-Making," below, I will return to questions of adjusting law to technology.

What is said regarding substantive conditions is also partly true for formal conditions: to automate at the first stage in Figure 15.7, it is required that the law accepts digital signatures. What is more important at this stage, however, is the degree of technological availability and maturity in society. Can one presume, in other words, that ordinary citizens have the access, knowledge, and motivation required to send in tax forms, apply for a benefit or admission to a university, etc. digitally? If a high number of the citizens in question are incapable of applying technology, then the interface between citizens and government must mainly remain analogue, and digital inputs have to be carried out by the government agency. In contrast, a high degree of access to technology, and knowledge and motivation to use it, clears the path to self-service procedures, where each party may, so to speak, be turned into an officer in charge of his or her own case (see "Simplifying the Processing of Decision Data," below).

PROCESSING DATA

Three Strategies for Handling Data

Much of the cost and time spent on individual decision-making is linked with assessing facts
of the cases and finding and registering reliable data representing these facts. One important
aim when developing legal decision-making systems is thus to try to reduce the cost and time
associated with collection of decision data. At least three strategies could be identified:

1. Finding machine-readable sources with data defined according to the same definitions
   as the data in demand. This strategy comprises (a) reuse of data from valid legal
   decisions (results and underlying data) and (b) use of authoritatively established data
   from common government services.
2. Changing division of labor between the government agency in question and other
   agencies and businesses with which the agency in question interacts. Here, I limit the
   discussion to one such sub-strategy, namely, to let parties of individual cases register data
   relevant in their case, in a process based to the greatest extent possible on "self-service."
3. A third possible strategy is to use sensor technology to "read the real world" directly
   without taking roundabout ways through people's minds, but instead by analyzing
   streams of data automatically (for example, by means of machine learning) and by
   using results of analyses of these data as direct input for a legal decision process.

Below, I will briefly explore these strategies. It is important to note that they should not be
construed as alternatives, but will often be topical in combination with one another in various
possible patterns.

Simplifying the Processing of Facts by Reuse and Common Use

The key phrase for reuse and common use of data is "once only,"[24] that is, reuse of data
derived from previous processes of interpretation and subsumption. The premise for this
strategy is that another government agency has established data collections, with data definitions in conformity with a legally correct understanding of the concepts describing data
sought after by the agency when developing a legal decision system.

This first strategy could be divided into three sub-strategies:

1. use of data that represent *results* from individual binding decisions that have been made;
2. reuse of data that have been the *basis* of previously made individual binding decisions
   (see (1));
3. use of data that have been established and are available from a *common* government
   service.

Decisions are based on data and expressed by data. Sub-strategies (1) and (2) mirror this
conception: seen in this way, decisions have data as raw material and produce new data, and
both groups of data may possibly be reused in other decision-making procedures.

The first possible strategy is the use of data derived from previous individual binding
decisions. The tax authorities, for instance, decide what the correct income of a person is,

---

[24]   See, e.g., European Interoperability Framework Promoting seamless services and data flows for European public
        administrations, European Commission (2017), p. 16, https://ec.europa.eu/isa2/eif_en, and EU eGovernment
        Action Plan 2016–2020 (COM(2016) 179 final), section 2 Visions and Underlying Principles.

pursuant to tax legislation and other applicable legal sources. When the option of appeal is exempted, a legally valid income figure exists, implying that valid income figures may be accessible. Data expressing this decision could, potentially at least, be used as a basis for new decisions within other fields of law, within both the government sector and the private sector.

Decisions on tax liability are based on large amounts of data which are the bases of decisions. Data regarding salary grade, paid income, tax deduction, employer(s), place(s) and period(s) of employment, and so forth are examples. In complex decision-making processes, the number of different types of such data may be rather high. Provided that the decisions relying on these underlying data are confirmed to be legally correct, it is possible that the same underlying data can be seen as legally correct in other decision-making processes too.

Reuse of data expressing results and of underlying data requires a satisfactory overview of potential data sources and concrete information regarding different types of data these sources may offer, including their definition (if any), technical format, etc. This could be a great challenge because many government agencies do not have a complete overview and thus cannot give full and certain information about what they have to offer. If, for instance, one government agency wishes to develop an information system or improve an existing system by automating collection of data about "live-in partners," the first question is: Where can we find reliable data about this group of people? The next crucial question is: Where is it possible to find data regarding all or most live-in partners, based on the same (or similar) definition of this concept as in the area of law of the legal decision-making system we are developing?

Typical for reuse of data from binding legal decisions is the quest for opportunities to exploit existing data resources in government agencies, in a situation where there has been no prior plan to create these possibilities. The aim is to discover internal or external data resources that may be reused. In order to do that, government agencies are encouraged to map their data resources, so it may be possible for other agencies to become aware of the potential supply of data from each agency. The aim in many cases is to create data catalogues with connected declarations of concept definitions. If there is a match between "supply and demand" on the concept level, this could be a good starting point for trying to agree on technical solutions and other terms of agreement between agencies.

The third sub-strategy listed above pertains to the use of data that have been established as a common government service. This is closely related to the first two techniques mentioned above, but in this third strategy, multiple use of data is planned and intended from the start. Examples are various databases and registers established with the intention to assemble reliable information which businesses, citizens, and government agencies could or must use: population registers, registers of land and charges, arms registers, driving license registers, vehicle registers, share registers, registers of marriage settlements, etc. Well-organized countries have a relatively large number of such registers. One important aim is to create certainty in matters which the register can substantiate. Thus, it is necessary that these registers have high data quality. To the extent that data items in such registers are formalized and defined (and not based on free text), they may be available to a number of government agencies and private businesses demanding specific pieces of information. For example, the arms register defines the term "arms," and "vehicle" is defined in the vehicle register, along with various sub-groups of these data definitions and other types of defined data contained in each register (for instance, "owner of vehicle").

"Once only" is not a legal principle, but more an expression of a political objective for the digitalization of public administration. It expresses the aim that public administration should only ask citizens for the same piece of information once. When confronted with legal principles and legislation, *once only* will often encounter legal obstacles. Although practically and technologically well grounded, it may not always be legally possible, and in many situations, it will only be lawful if legislation is changed. Here, I will briefly mention and comment on the most important types of legal obstacles, often topical as cumulative hindrances:

- Professional secrecy – this is a type of regulation lying outside GDPR and is thus under national control.
- Legal basis of processing – this condition refers to articles 6 ("ordinary" personal data) and 9 (special categories of personal data) of the GDPR. In cases concerning development of legal decision-making systems in public administration, article 6(1)(e) about "exercise of official authority vested in the controller" is particularly relevant, and in article 9(2), alternatives (b) and (g) are examples of possible legal bases of high importance for such systems development.[25] These articles will hardly be firm obstacles, but mostly imply sets of requirements that could be met pursuant to national legislative processes.
- The purpose limitation principle of the GDPR as expressed in article 5(1)(b) should probably be seen more as a procedural requirement than as an actual obstacle to reuse of personal data. There are no restrictions as to the number of legitimate purposes that may be established, and even though a controller (for example, a government agency) cannot choose to process personal data in a manner that is incompatible with the original purposes, in most cases this is hardly a serious limitation on the possibility of changing purposes on the grounds that it is desirable to reuse personal data.
- The principle of accuracy (see article 5(1)(d)) likely has great significance for the lawfulness of reusing personal data, in terms of both required updating and accuracy. When agency A receives and reuses data from agency B, this will imply a change of purpose of processing too.[26] B's purpose will form the basis of their updating and accuracy requirements, and thus the purposes of the receiving agency A may easily provide grounds for different requirements. If A's requirements are stricter than B's, this could be a challenge to lawful reuse of data without improving the data quality.

As indicated, professional privacy and the principle of accuracy are probably the most significant obstacles to reuse and sharing of personal data. On the other hand, reuse of data and "once only" could be said to be beneficial for the data minimization principle of the GDPR;[27] reuse of data could imply standardization of data definitions and reduction of the number of different types of data applied in government decision-making processes. Thus, to a certain extent, reuse and sharing of personal data implies a trade-off between different aspects of data protection.

---

[25] These alternatives will require provisions in national law to adapt the application of rules of the regulation, and/or appropriate safeguards for the fundamental rights and interests of the data subject.

[26] See art. 5(1)(b).

[27] See GDPR, art. 5(1)(c).

Simplifying the Processing of Decision Data by Means of Self-Service

To a certain extent, the Internet has made it possible to establish self-service decision-making arrangements within public administration, where citizens are asked to contribute to questions regarding their legal matters and, possibly, to implement actions on their own initiative or pursuant to a legal obligation or right they have. In line with such possibilities, an alternative strategy to that described in " Simplifying the Processing of Facts," above, for collection of data in individual cases might be to allow individual parties (or their representatives) to assess case-relevant facts and register these data in their case by means of a legal decision-making system developed by a government agency. Citizens may thereby become "their own officer in charge" and carry out required interpretations of applicable law and subsumption of relevant facts, as well as representation and registration of these facts in, and within the framework of, the relevant government data system.

Self-service as described is associated with some obvious limitations and problems. First, there is the limitation that a fraction of the population may not be sufficiently "digital" and cannot be reached by means of online procedures. Even when people are "digitally available," some will not be motivated or willing to process their own case. In addition to these limitations, it may obviously be a problem to ensure a minimum quality in the citizens' contribution as officers in their own cases. Even though most actions and inputs expected of citizens are "easy," a small percentage – still possibly representing many cases – will be difficult procedures and will require legal expertise at a level that the average citizen cannot be expected to possess.

The above-mentioned limitations could exist in certain situations on a manageable and acceptable scale, for instance, because parties to cases are limited and homogeneous: the number of university students with access to the Internet and with the ability and willingness to actively participate in online case processing could be high, for instance. If the target group is broader and more heterogeneous, the number of people that could not be expected to fill their role as contributors in case processing could easily be higher than what is legally acceptable without supplementary measures to capture fall-outs etc. Even if limitations are manageable and legally acceptable, the legal quality of data registered by lay parties remains an issue. Among necessary measures will be the preparation of adapted and sufficient information regarding required legal problem-solving, combined with procedures in the data system giving automatic feedback in the event of erroneous and inconsistent inputs etc.

Not least, data quality problems related to self-service as described above are associated with the risk that parties of individual cases are tempted to manipulate the decision of their case by giving distorted or incorrect inputs. Self-service routines require extensive and intensive information provided to the citizens in order to equip them with a correct and adequate understanding of the legal questions they need to address and solve. In complex legal matters, even advanced data systems to support self-service activities will be unable to guarantee sufficiently correct results. Thus, this type of contribution from citizens may create the need for successive control, and necessary controls may, in some situations, be too expensive compared to what the government agency gains from the self-service arrangement.

It is hardly possible to make general statements regarding acceptable risk of self-service routines as described. However, limitations and problems mentioned will easily imply that self-service will seldom be the preferred way of collecting decision data, when seen from the perspective of public administration. To the extent that this strategy is selected, it will most likely be a supplementary way of collecting data as input for government decision-making procedures.

Directly Capturing Facts of the Physical World

So far, I have discussed two main strategies for collection of data representing relevant facts for decisions in individual cases. The common feature of these strategies is that a person perceives the fact, assesses it, and makes a representation of it in the data system of the relevant government agency. All activities are carried out based on some person's understanding of the applicable law. Facts, in other words, are transformed into decision data by the sensory apparatus and mind of people. A third main strategy of collecting data for decision-making purposes is to avoid dependencies of cognitive contributions from people, and instead collect data describing legal relevant facts *directly*, by means of sensors, biometrics, and similar apparatus with the capability to "read reality."

I use "sensor and similar apparatus" (in short, "sensors") to denote electronic devices designed to sense the state of a condition or events or change thereof; for instance, regarding physical particularities of people, movement of objects and people, light, temperature, sound, radiation, chemicals, etc. Sensors make it possible to measure and represent a state and change of affairs (for instance, that an object is moving, how fast it is moving, in which direction, at what acceleration, etc.; or changes of frequency of a person's heartbeat, heartbeat pattern (for example, indicating heart disease), etc.). The point here is that sensors can automatically collect streams of data concerning people, objects, and other parts of our environment. Provided sensors can produce digital data, output data may be transferred to and processed by legal decision-making systems and, if desirable, be subjected to advanced analyses. Each stream of data may be processed separately and analyzed (for instance, regarding how a person travels), but may have a much larger potential if combined with other sources; for instance, data about topography (maps), body temperature, weather data, traffic data, etc. In other words, sensors may enable government agencies to measure and analyze several aspects of people, objects, and environments.

Data from sensors represent facts. These could be very simple facts based on one type of sensor data or be composite facts based on two or several sets of sensor data (movement, topography, traffic situation). Sensor facts may also be parts of "multi-faceted facts," where sensor data are combined with other types of data – for instance, from statistics and data analyses of comprehensive and heterogeneous materials (such as machine-learning analyses of big data).

Sensor data may represent *legally relevant* facts; that is, the legislator may establish that a certain bulk of compiled sensor data, or certain results from analyses of these data, should qualify as a certain legal fact (for instance, as a condition for a legal right). In Norwegian legislation, one of several conditions for citizenship is that applicants have resided in Norway for at least seven years, and have not been abroad for more than two months during any one of those calendar years.[28] This type of condition could partly be translated into selected GPS parameters, and the question of residence could thereby be transformed into something that is not answered by people alone, but by machines. Another radical possibility that illustrates some of the potentials of sensor technology is to construct a "sickness" concept by means of data patterns from sensor technology combined with statistics etc. Individuals who have been diagnosed as "sick" pursuant to the sickness allowance scheme could automatically be declared fit to return to work based on data stemming from wearable biosensors, GPS data logging of people's movements, stored medical data, and statistical data related to the diagnosis in question, etc.

---

[28]   See Citizenship Act § 7(1)(e) and Citizenship Regulation §§ 3–4.

Sensor data, alone or in combination with other data, could not only constitute conditions for legal obligations and rights: they could also be connected to legal *effects* and thus enforcement. Government decisions may, for instance, entail a prohibition against staying in certain areas or a ban on drinking alcohol or taking other intoxicating substances. Since sensors may register relevant data, sensor data may be used to detect any breach of previous decisions made and may thus make enforcement automatic and more efficient.

Combining Sources of Decision Data

In Figure 15.8, I have combined and supplemented the above-described strategies for collection and processing of decision data in digital government and added some traditional ways of collecting data. It shows two basic choices for the collection of data: human and machine based. Human assessment is carried out either by a case officer or by the party in question through a self-service procedure. Employment of case officers is an expensive strategy, as seen from the machinery of government. Manual case processing is labor-intensive and is funded over government budgets. This question often receives much attention when government digital decision-making routines are redesigned in the course of digitalization. Figure 15.8 shows that there are both alternative and supplementary ways to collect data.

The first alternative is to let someone else outside public administration (and off-budget!) perform manual assessment. In Figure 15.8, this is exemplified inter alia by "self-service" (see "Simplifying the Processing of Decision Data," above). A related line of action is to allow another government agency or a private business to carry out the assessment and transfer the results to the decision-making procedure (see "external" in Figure 15.8). Moving assessment and submission from one government agency to another in this way will not in itself yield any cost reduction or enhance efficiency in the government sector. However, shifting over to private business may save the government money.[29]

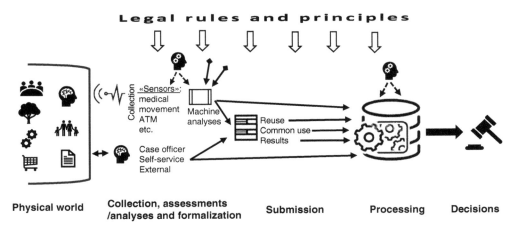

FIGURE 15.8 Survey of strategies for generating decision data, from relevant facts to bases for decisions

---

[29] But would require a sufficient legal basis.

Reuse of data is a type of solution that may be seen as *reactive*, because the objective is to find out where in the existing decision-making processes a government agency can find suitable decision data to be used in *future* decision-making processes. In contrast, the *proactive* approach would be to design data systems with the aim of making available and sharing data that are intended to be the source for many decision processes (see "common use" and discussions in "Simplifying the Processing of Facts," above).

In Figure 15.8 (upper left part), the use of sensors is marked as a possible main strategy for collection of data.[30] In the figure, I have differentiated between collection and analyses. Typically, sensors, GPS, and similar devices collect streams of data from the physical world. To be used in decision-making processes, these data must be analyzed and processed in order to be transformed into aggregated data. In the next phase, these aggregated data will be submitted into the decision-making routine. For example, a stream of detailed GPS data is collected, but will only be submitted to the decision routine if the aggregated data shows the person concerned has stayed in areas of the city where, according to a decision from a public authority, he is not allowed to be. Similarly, submission of heartbeat sensors may only have an impact on decisions if their values are higher or lower than certain defined limits. Machine analyses of such data may range from simple to advanced. Advanced analyses could imply application of data from other sources (for instance, historical and statistical data, etc.),[31] possibly by means of big data analyses applying machine-learning technology or the like.

The head icons with gearwheels in Figure 15.8 represent human decision processes that determine the content of automatic analyses and processing of data. The icons signify that even automatic processes are the result of human decision-making.[32] With a human interface toward the world, case officers and others subsume facts of each individual case under legal rules. People creating machine interfaces for sensors will, in contrast, decide in advance the general characteristics of the physical environment that should count as legally relevant. The core automatic decision-making process ("Processing" in the figure, see "Deducing and Transforming Rules," above) is in similar ways programmed, implying that legal rules determining the decisions based on collected facts are represented in the program, and are established in advance by people in the course of a systems development process.

The last element in Figure 15.8 that I will comment on is "Legal rules and principles," at the top of the figure, with broad arrows pointing to every other part of the figure. Basically, this element represents the general assumption that in a public administration under the rule of law, there will be legal rules and principles safeguarding fundamental rights and freedoms of citizens. I will elaborate on this presumption in the next section.

AUTOMATED DECISION-MAKING UNDER THE RULE OF LAW

Automated Decisions: A Rule-of-Law Problem?

As opposed to people, computers only operate on the basis of instructions and always follow them. Consistent application of detailed and unambiguous instructions controlling machines (algorithms) could be seen as ideal for rules of law in a formal sense. If the

---

[30] The word *sensors* is put between quote marks to remind the reader that it is used in a specialized sense.
[31] See arrows with rhomb-shaped start.
[32] This is the case even when machine learning is applied, because necessary programming and manual training represents human decisions (despite the fact that humans do not always anticipate the potential effects of their contributions).

instructions are a complete and correct representation of the law, then the rule-of-law principle is fulfilled. Thus, basically, automated decision-making is ideal for the rule of law, in the sense that technology represents a great potential for correct implementation of the law. Moreover, automated decision-making represents a much greater potential for correct application of the law than that of manual case processing. Government agencies may educate and train their officers to the greatest extent possible, but there will unavoidably be people who misconceive, disagree, or are having a bad day at work. The "human factor" cannot be removed from human environments – thank goodness.

People develop legal decision-making systems too, and the human factor described may of course also influence systems development, with the outcome that mistakes are made that result in software having incorrect or inadequate legal contents. But as opposed to manual decision-making, a small group of people with a mandate to transform legal sources into programming codes will typically be easier to educate and train than a large number of officers processing individual cases manually. Besides, the systems development group will typically be expressly selected for their specialized skills, and the specifications and programming code they develop will typically be thoroughly tested before it is put into operation. Nevertheless, there is no such thing as error-free software, and a small amount of mal-representation of the law can never be excluded. When errors occur, legality controls are made simpler by the fact that computers always rigidly follow rules, a principle that prepares the ground for complete identification of individual cases affected and possibilities of automatic reversal of decisions. Thus, all in all, compared to manual processing of cases, the prospects are relatively good for automation of individual decision-making and getting everything right.

Legally correct representation in software code will not become reality on its own. Thus, the rule of law in the context of automatic decision-making may be an argument for passing laws or other regulatory instruments to ensure appropriate organization of legal parts of systems development, sufficient expertise, use of methods, documentation requirements regarding interpretive choices embedded in the system, etc. In "Computer-Conscious Law-Making," below, I will briefly return to this question.

The rule of law in a formal sense is an important aspect, but is not necessarily adequate in view of citizens. To some people, (totally) automated decision-making in itself may seem scary. It is faceless, and decisions without faces and feelings are equal to decisions without real individual consideration and understanding. Thus, in the view of this author, the prior problem with automated decision-making is not following the rule of law in a formal sense, but the degree of *fairness* of individual decision-making. The higher the degree of automation, the more critical questions of fairness will be. Automation is an argument in favor of cutting down on human involvement when individual cases are processed, typically by basing decisions on reuse or common use of personal data from digitally available sources, and possibly by applying sensor technology. If supply of such sources and data is improved and political pressure increases in favor of intensifying automation of government agencies, chances increase that government agencies will push automation toward the limits of what is acceptable when it comes to fairness and individual treatment – and beyond.

There is a big difference between being subject to some invisible predefined digital process and explaining your personal situation to an officer who intently listens and asks questions to clarify uncertainties. An ideal world is always best, but in some situations the choice may be to submit to automated digital processes or to try to explain oneself to a busy and impatient officer. Under less ideal circumstances, faceless processing may thus constitute a certain protection for citizens. Although fairness and respectful treatment of citizens are issues when automated decision-making is designed and discussed, there is no pat answer to the question of what *realistically* will be best for citizens – manual or automated processing of their cases.

The Rule of Law by Design of Information Systems

Decision-making in individual cases in public administration is in many legal systems regulated by law, via administrative procedure acts or the like. Such acts enshrine various guarantees of the rights to freedoms of citizens and may also contain mandates requiring government agencies to provide guidance to parties in individual cases, the duty to conduct impartial investigations of individual cases before decisions are made, the rights of parties in individual cases to receive the grounds for decisions, access rights, the right to lodge a complaint with a supervisory authority, rights to effective judicial remedy, etc. The core aim of such guarantees is to provide legally correct individual decisions or, in other words, to increase the probability that decisions are in accordance with valid law and that parties to cases may be confident that decisions in their cases are legally correct.

Traditional rule-of-law guarantees like these are relevant even if decision-making is 100 percent automated. It may be desirable to adjust and upgrade such rights and duties; for instance, by establishing the right to automatically receive a rationale for individual decisions based exactly on the actual processing of each case. Similarly, access rights could be extended to encompass elements describing the legal sources of information that have been used as the factual basis of each case etc. There are numerous possibilities for upgrading traditional rights and duties in order to protect parties in cases/citizens. Space here does not allow me to elaborate on the issue. Within the constraints of this chapter, I will instead concentrate on questions regarding where and how rule-of-law guarantees should be directed. Keywords are systems guarantees and individual guarantees, and the approach is closely related to the system approach and individual approach mentioned in "Major Legal Aspects of Digital Government," above.

Although there are differences between public administrative procedure legislation in various national legal systems, it is likely correct to claim that the traditional approach to protection of rights and freedoms of individuals has been to give *individual guarantees*. By this, I mean that public administrative procedure legislation has been oriented toward giving parties to cases the right to act on their own behalf in questions concerning their individual case; alternatively that government agencies are given duties to act vis-à-vis individual parties in a certain way (for example, to give guidance, inform the party in case new relevant information is collected, etc.). Chapter III of the GDPR contains a catalogue of rights for data subjects, introducing individual rights concerning access, rectification, erasure, objection, portability, fully automated processing, etc.

Individual rights could be seen in contrast to legislation establishing requirements regarding how *information systems* should be: instead of (only) regulating rights and duties vis-à-vis individuals, legal requirements may be formulated with regard to the information systems that process all individual cases ("system guarantees"). Norwegian administrative law, for instance, prescribes duties for government agencies to use certain technical standards that ensure accessibility and readability and counteract discrimination of visually impaired people etc.

The most important example by far of legal protection on the level of information systems is found in the GDPR, particularly in chapters I, II, and IV. Indeed, the Regulation does not apply the concept "information system," but uses instead "processing of personal data" to describe "any operation or set of operations which is performed on personal data or on sets of personal data" (see article 2(2) of the GDPR). With automated processing, the "set of operations which is performed" will largely be ICT systems and infrastructures that are used to process data. Here, I will not discuss the relation between the two sets of terminology, but will limit myself to stressing that both information systems and processing of personal data refer to a general arrangement of how data/information could or should be processed.[33] Thus, a controller who buys or develops software to process personal data has to consider if and to what degree legal requirements regulating the processing could be imbedded in the software, pursuant to article 25 of the GDPR about *data protection by design*. A discussion of the many legal requirements to the design of information systems processing personal data is beyond the scope of this chapter. Here, it suffices to briefly recall important provisions that contain requirements on the level of information *systems*:[34]

- requirement of legal bases (articles 6 and 9) and purpose of processing (article 5(1)(b));
- data quality and updating requirements (article 5(1)(d));
- security of processing (article 32); and
- data protection impact assessment (article 35).

Article 24 about the responsibilities of the controller and the obligation to implement appropriate technical measures to ensure compliance with the Regulation and article 25 about data protection by design both demonstrate that the Regulation entails more than an obligation to consider specific articles when information systems are developed (see the bullet points above). There is a certain additional *general obligation* to implement legal rules deduced from the GDPR into the architecture and software of the system.

I will not go into the contents and interpretation of the articles in the list. The main point here is that parts of the GDPR are examples of legislation drafted to have an effect on information systems. The same articles may be applied in individual cases as well. The important observation here, however, is that developing information systems, for instance, legal decision-making systems, without observing the mentioned "system requirements" of the GDPR will often be illegal and at least a hazardous endeavor.

A similar approach to that of the GDPR could be applied with the rule-of-law principle as a point of departure. We might ask: To what extent should public administrative law regulate legal decision-making systems that exercise government powers by processing and deciding individual cases? A further question could be to what extent legislation should establish obligations to make "rule of law by design" of information systems? At this point in the discussion, let me return to the three possible "legal frameworks" identified in "Major Legal Aspects of Digital Government," above:

1. regulation of how legal decisions systems should be *developed*;
2. regulation establishing requirement regarding *properties* (functions and qualities etc.) of legal decisions systems; and
3. regulation regarding *use* of legal decisions systems.

---

[33] I underline that the "set of operations which is performed on personal data or on sets of personal data" is not synonymous to "information system," but that the concepts greatly overlap.

[34] The list is not complete. *All* principles relating to processing of personal data in art. 5 may clearly have an influence on the design of information systems planned to process personal data.

Regulations of the first type include possible requirements for the organization of projects with a mandate to develop legal decision-making systems. A basic view is that important parts of what we denote in general terms as systems development entail legal problem-solving and exercise of public authority, and the latter, to the greatest extent possible, should be identified and handled in a separate decision-making process. Further organizational questions may concern the role of the responsible department of the agency in question and their decision power vis-à-vis the project group and external consultants participating in the systems development. The aim of regulating these questions could be to ensure that it is the government authority that actually decides which rules are to be deemed valid and implemented in the software – and not, for example, external consultants. Moreover, it is possible to require by law that certain methods should be applied when transformation from legal source to programming code is carried out, and that legal contents of programs are documented so as to prepare the ground for legality control of the legal decision system.

Regulations of the second type in the list above are related to "rule of law by design," as mentioned above. Article 25 of the GDPR imposes data protection by design in a very discretionary way, leaving it up to controllers to make unspecified assessments about the degree of legal obligation to build data protection principles and rights into software. In more narrow fields of law (for instance, in government administrative law), this could be done in a direct and concrete way. It could be established by law that adequate documentation of the legal contents of software controlling individual decisions should be publicly available (except items directly related to security); and it could be decided by law that the system should be publicly available in an "exploration mode" where citizens could simulate decisions instead of merely being referred to reading, understanding, and applying the (frequently awkward) legislation. Not least, legislators should consider whether or not it should be mandatory to offer Internet-based routines to support access rights, rights to claim information erased and supplemented, and to have (semi-) automatic procedures to generate grounds of automatic individual decisions. The possibilities for building the rule of law into the systems are myriad, and combined with elements based on article 25 of the GDPR, they may be extremely effective.

Here, I will not focus much attention on the third type of regulation mentioned above regarding the *use* of legal decision systems. The most pressing need for regulation, however, is linked with questions of legality control, along with review and reversal of individual decisions. The higher the degree of automation, the more important such questions will be. With full automation, as described in "Automatic Decision-Making and Decision Support," above, almost every individual case where such claims are sustained will have an effect on the general system level too. If a disagreement is about the factual basis of a decision, simple reversal of an individual decision could only occur in situations where data are used for one purpose only. In the case of reuse, the same definition of data must be valid for two or more purposes, and reversal of a decision must either affect all purposes, or the common definition on which the legal decision system is based must be moderated. As for processing of collected data, any change of this code must be valid for every individual case. Because programs follow detailed instructions, line by line, decisions already made that are affected by an error or imperfection must in principle be identified and amended. In addition, programs must be changed, or manual corrective procedures must be established with a view to safeguarding the legal correctness of future individual decisions. Both types of actions may be expensive and time-consuming.

Here, I will not enter into a discussion of the fruitfulness, desirability, and feasibility of regulating development of legal decision-making systems, and their properties and use. It is necessary, however, to stress the importance of a certain degree of stand-offishness and prudence. It is most important, moreover, that legal regulations should be considered in a context and interplay with other measures (technological, organizational, economical, pedagogical), and that legal instruments first and foremost should be formulated on a general level; for instance, by ordering that a method shall be applied to secure legally correct transformation of legal sources to software (but without detailed statements of how etc.). It is equally important that all legal interpretations embedded in the system are documented in an accessible way and are public (but without stating in what way); and that members with both legal and technological expertise should hold responsible positions in project groups that develop legal decision-making systems.

COMPUTER-CONSCIOUS LAW-MAKING

A gap between traditional legislation and computerized implementation arises when the legislator fails to realize the needs of modern digital governance and, even though implementation will be highly automated, formulate rules as if there would in fact be human officers in charge considering each case individually, interpreting the wording of the law, performing discretionary assessments, etc. When legislators expect and support automated decision-making, they should also consider, to a larger extent, important legal substantial effects of this way of exercising governmental powers. Legislation should fit the actual needs of automated decision processes.[35] "Computer-conscious law-making" was suggested already in the 1970s, but has never been high on the agenda.[36]

In previous sections of this chapter, I have tried to communicate the many types of legal questions that are or may be imbedded in the development of legal decision-making systems. The volume and importance of such questions in each legislative process will, of course, vary, and could rely on several different factors. Regardless of the detailed factors in each process, the overall scenario in Norway, and I believe in many other countries, is an ambition to increase automated decision-making, both by introducing automation in new types of individual decisions and by increasing the degree of automation, wherever possible, up to 100 percent. Unless legislators are attentive and take automation into consideration when passing new laws, it is likely that the number of legal questions remaining after the legislative processes cease will be considerable; see Figure 15.9.

In Figure 15.9, the "remains" is illustrated by the line with circles and represents legal questions that have not been solved in the legislative process, and instead are left to be fixed in the course of systems development. Previous sections of this chapter have demonstrated that these questions will often be of great significance for actual substantive contents of the law in

---

[35] A. Taylor and T. J. M. Bench-Capon, Support for the Formulation of Legislation, in T. J. M. Bench-Capon (ed.), *Knowledge-Based Systems and Legal Applications* (Academic Press, 1991), Vol. 36, pp. 95–113, discuss how knowledge-based systems developed for the legal domain could be designed to support legislators (e.g. regarding solution specification).

[36] See H. Fiedler, Computer-Conscious Law-Making, in Data Processing in the Government, Luxemburg (1973). Available at the Norwegian Research Center for Computers and Law (NRCCL) collection of conference papers, Oslo, Norway. R. Kennedy, E-Regulation and the Rule of Law: Smart Government, Institutional Information Infrastructures, and Fundamental Values (2016) 21 *Information Polity* 82, suggests "E-regulation" as a new field of study. Although most elements of what could be encompassed by such a field are known and well established, it may be fruitful to analyze all these aspects in integrated ways; thereby also creating a broader understanding and more interest.

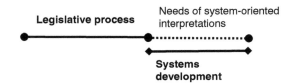

FIGURE 15.9 Connection between legislative processes and systems
development to implement them

question. The question we will have to ask is whether we should allow systems development
processes to be important for the establishment of the law, or if we should take steps to reduce
this in importance and make it more acceptable from a rule-of-law perspective. In this
author's view, we need to reconsider the process from legislative drafting to programmed
law. Here, I will not discuss in detail the techniques of computer-conscious law-making, but
instead will discuss three overall models that could accommodate such an approach.[37] The
first model is about making legal parts of systems development processes more in line with
rule-of-law principles, while the two other models represent extensions of the legislative
process and reduced legal importance of systems development. The models may be applied
separately or in combination.

The first possibility is to upgrade the transformation process of systems development.
Upgrading can involve giving formal status to legal interpretations forming the basis of
programming and designing procedures to safeguard a high level of openness and democratic
involvement in the transformation process. Governments could, for instance, instruct the
relevant government agency to establish such fixed rules as they find reasonable and requisite
for fair and effective implementation. In this case, government agencies should be obligated
to document these rules and make them publicly available. In the process, proposed detailed
rules should be open to legal review by courts of law.[38] In other words, it could be made clear
that even alternative interpretations to those implemented in the system must represent
legally defensible understandings of the law. The drawback with such an arrangement is
the risk of having a large number of complaints and thus reducing the efficiency effects from
automated decision-making. If only a small percentage of taxpayers or social insurance
benefit recipients lodged complaints asserting that a government system is based on incorrect
or inadequate understanding of the law, this alone would entail a huge and expensive
administrative burden. Thus, I assume that in many cases such a situation will be undesirable
and even impossible to cope with.

A *second possibility* is to transform major parts of what is currently viewed as implementation of the law into procedures of delegating and implementing legislation. By this, I mean
binding, secondary legislation that supplements the substantive and procedural contents of
primary legislation. Documentation and accessibility of non-binding rules of implementation as described above only represent disputable interpretations of the law that could be
deviated from in individual cases. In contrast, delegating and implementing legislation

---

[37]   It is, however, important to stress that formulating laws and at the same time taking note of special considerations
       regarding automated decision-making does not imply writing laws in programming style. Rather, characteristics
       will be logically stringent texts, concise and consistent use of concepts, etc. – all expressed in natural language.

[38]   However, in most cases, computer programs will be legally correct and thus represent valid law. In Norway,
       government decision-making systems are normally quasi-binding – that is, although they only express the
       government view on how the law should be interpreted, they have an actual binding effect.

implies that we see legal rules embedded in the decision-making system as an exercise of general, binding government powers.

Delegating and implementing powers should be based on clear legal authority that establishes and limits the government agencies' authority to make legally binding choices for effective and reasonable digital implementation of the law. Moreover, such legal authority should establish the necessary procedural requirements to guarantee sufficient openness and the possibility of legality control of the exercise of authority. Examples include passing rules on how data sources may be used, including data definitions; updating requirements, etc.; and any new rules required to cover blank spots in the primary legislation.

The power to pass secondary legislation on definitions etc. could possibly form the basis of a public review of bills where citizens, alternatively a limited list of stakeholders, are given the right to object to legislative proposals and suggest alternative solutions. If, for instance, it is proposed to automatically collect and apply domicile data from the Population Register, but stakeholders assert that data-updating routines are insufficient for the required use, stakeholders could be given the power to demand use of other or supplementary data sources. In case of such complaints over proposed implementation strategies, the final decision could be taken at the appropriate political level (for instance, in the relevant ministry).

A *third alternative*, and the most radical option, would be to change the primary legislative process itself, by incorporating resolution of technological and organizational questions into the normal legislative process. Such a strategy could imply that most of the necessary legal, technological, and organizational solutions take place *prior to enactment*. With this legislative strategy, expert consideration of regulatory questions would basically be carried out by the usual procedure, but with an additional element of formal analysis of proposals in the draft. If the legislature suggests rules such as the one cited below, an analysis team could investigate associated possibilities and challenges. For instance, it is proposed to define "partner" as "a spouse, civil partner or one of a couple whether of the same sex or opposite sex who although not married to each other are living together and treat each other as spouses."[39]

The team tasked with formal analysis would investigate the technological and administrative aspects of such proposals. In the example above, one such issue would be examining whether a machine-readable source exists that is based on the right definition of "partner," and with accurate, reliable, and sufficiently upgraded data. If not, the next question might be if a machine-readable database exists with an alternate but acceptable definition of the concept. In the event of a negative answer to this second question, a possible conclusion is that a new register would have to be established as part of implementation. Given the obvious administrative effects this would have, the formal analysis team would leave it up to the experts to decide whether the originally proposed definition should be accepted. The cited definition presupposes scrutiny of each relationship between possible partners: How could it be established that they really "are living together" and "treat each other as spouses"? What will the administrative consequences and costs be if the definition is enacted? The team may assess these consequences and suggest possible alternative definitions which may be handled in a more automated system, for instance:

> "partner" means a spouse, civil partner or one of a couple whether of the same sex or opposite sex who although not married to each other have *been registered in the National Register as sharing the same accommodation for at least two years*, or are *registered as parents to a common*

---

[39]   The example is based on The Well-being of Future Generations (Wales) Act 2015.

child or common children and are registered in the National Register as sharing the same accommodation.[40]

The example demonstrates that in automated government systems, legal conditions must be of a formal nature obviating human evaluation. Official entries in government registers and government decisions in individual cases could be employed instead (see "Simplifying the Processing of Facts," above). I am not claiming that the two new conditions included in the example above would be politically acceptable. The point is merely that politicians in the legislative process should be aware of the requirements entailed in automated public administration and take these requirements into account when making legal substantive choices. If legislation is formulated in ways that presuppose individual scrutiny of how people are "living together" and if they "treat each other as spouses," while at the same time trying to meet demands for cheaper and more automated government procedures, it is likely that the implemented result will not be in line with the legislators' intentions. In democratic systems, the lawmakers' intentions should always be decisive. Legislators should thus be assisted to establish optimum, well-founded trade-offs between political fairness and effective administrative routines.

It may very well be that politicians choose the level of individual treatment and scrutiny following from the first example given above, thereby both accepting that automation is neither possible nor desirable, and that extra costs linked to individual case processing will accrue. Of course, it follows from democratic principles that legislators are free to make such political choices. However, combining old-fashioned regulatory technique and government policy with a strong emphasis on modernization and automated administrative work may well result in incompatible political goals.

CONCLUSION

In many societies, automated individual decision-making in government administration is necessary and conventional. It carries a great potential of strong rule of law, but also has the potentials of injustice and alienation. This chapter is written on the basis of Norwegian and Scandinavian experiences where the situation probably – on average – might be described as "quite good," but far from perfect.

A fundamental imperfection in the present situation, in this author's view, is that the political and legal cultures are not sufficiently adapted to IT. The challenge starts with political choices and a lack of political acknowledgement that choice of technological solutions in the government sector may change the relationship between both government agencies and citizens – ultimately to the extent that it may change the very concept of what public administration is. It should moreover be better understood how IT is likely to influence the substantive contents of social insurance schemes, tax legislation, and various other types of legislation where automated systems are applied. Politicians, and in particular legislators, should be more aware of the transformational power of technology related to modernization of public administration, and put it to political debate. As a minimum, political processes should be *technology-conscious*, implying that new legislation and modernization schemes within public administration should be based on analyses of both the formal and substantive effects on citizens from automating and further remodeling public administration. Political choices should be clearly formulated and debated: we might

---

[40]   New elements are in italic font.

automate the decision, for example, of whether it is grandma or grandpa who will be allotted the vacant place in the nursing home, or we could agree that this decision and certain others should be taken based on physical encounters with the persons involved and on expert discretion (perhaps *supported* by a data system). Moreover, we may use advanced technology to prioritize and target certain groups of citizens for special positive or negative treatment (tailored information, controls), but this should not happen purely on the basis of assessment of efficiency and technological ability to do so, but instead be carried out within a legal framework set by accountable politicians. It is important to see that the GDPR does not "solve the problem," and that this regulation mostly requires that a series of formal conditions are met, but contains very few absolute obstacles, if any. Thus, in addition, needs for regulation of technology should be specifically addressed regarding its use with special challenges for the rule of law or data protection within public administration. Examples of this include legal frameworks for government control regimes and use of location detection and tracking by biological (human) sensors.

Clearly formulated political choices should also have implications for *the way in which* politics is expressed. If the political choice is to automate administrative decision-making, legislators should pass legislation that is as far as possible suitable for automation. In my view, the aim should be to reduce the legal significance of systems development as far as possible. Some legal choices in the course of systems development are inevitable. To tackle these remaining questions, we need models, methods, and tools to support processes and decisions in line with rule-of-law principles.

In this chapter, I have emphasized systems development as the primary process. In so doing, I may have led the reader to perceive computer-conscious law-making as a secondary concern. In an ideal world, the importance of these processes is the other way around. Today, many of the legal challenges associated with systems development stem from a lack of technological consciousness in the legislative process. Changes should therefore primarily happen in this first stage. Realistically speaking and based on the presumption that legislative processes often appear to be conservative (and even petrified), I assume systems development processes are still likely to remain an important arena for legal decision-making associated with transformation of the legal sources in the foreseeable future. Thus, in the years to come, rule-of-law issues should be dealt with in conjunction with law-making and implementation of laws should be accomplished by means of legal decision-making systems.

PART III

Intellectual Property and Algorithms

16

Inventive Algorithms and the Evolving Nature of Innovation

*Ryan Abbott**

INTRODUCTION

For more than sixty years, "obviousness" has set the bar for patentability. Under this standard, if a hypothetical "person having ordinary skill in the art" would find an invention obvious in light of existing relevant information, then the invention cannot be patented. This skilled person is defined as a non-innovative worker with a limited knowledge-base. The more creative and informed the skilled person, the more likely an invention will be considered obvious. The standard has evolved since its introduction, and it is now on the verge of an evolutionary leap: inventive algorithms are increasingly being used in research, and once the use of such algorithms becomes standard, the person skilled in the art should be a person augmented by algorithm, or just an inventive algorithm. Unlike the skilled person, the inventive algorithm is capable of innovation and considering the entire universe of prior art. As inventive algorithms continue to improve, this will increasingly raise the bar to patentability, eventually rendering innovative activities obvious. The end of obviousness means the end of patents, at least as they are now.

For at least two decades, algorithms have been autonomously generating patentable inventions.[1] "Autonomously" here refers to the algorithm, rather than to a person, meeting traditional inventorship criteria. In other words, if the algorithm, or what this chapter refers to as an "inventive algorithm," were a natural person, it would qualify as a patent inventor. In fact, the US Patent and Trademark Office (USPTO or Patent Office) may have granted patents for inventions autonomously generated by algorithms as early as 1998.[2] In earlier articles, I examined instances of algorithmic invention in detail and argued that such algorithms ought to be legally recognized as patent inventors to incentivize innovation and promote fairness.[3] The owners of such algorithms would be the owners of their inventions.[4]

This chapter focuses on a related phenomenon: What happens when inventive algorithms become a standard part of the inventive process? This is not a thought

---

* This chapter is modified from R. Abbott, Everything is Obvious (2019) 66 *UCLA Law Rev.* 2.

[1] See R. Abbott, I Think, Therefore I Invent: Creative Computers and the Future of Patent Law (2016) 57 *BC Law Rev.* 1079, 1083–91.(describing instances of "computational invention" or "computer-generated works"); see also "Timeline to the Creative Singularity," below (discussing some such instances in greater detail).

[2] Abbott, above note 1, p. 1085.

[3] *Ibid.*, pp. 1083–91; R. Abbott, Hal the Inventor: Big Data and Its Use by Artificial Intelligence, in C. R. Sugimoto, H. R. Ekbia, and M. Mattioli (eds.), *Big Data Is Not a Monolith* (MIT Press, 2016) (discussing computational invention in a book chapter first posted online on February 19, 2015).

[4] Except where no owner exists, in possible cases of some open source or distributed software, in which case ownership could vest in a user.

experiment.[5] For instance, while the timeline is controversial, surveys of experts suggest that artificial general intelligence (AGI), which is an algorithm able to perform any intellectual tasks a person could, will develop in the next twenty-five years.[6] Some thought leaders, such as Ray Kurzweil, one of Google's Directors of Engineering, predict algorithms will have human levels of intelligence in about a decade.[7]

The impact of the widespread use of inventive algorithms will be tremendous, not just on innovation, but also on patent law.[8] Right now, patentability is determined based on what a hypothetical, non-inventive, skilled person would find obvious.[9] The skilled person represents the average worker in the scientific field of an invention.[10] Once the average worker uses inventive algorithms, or inventive algorithms replace the average worker, then inventive activity will be normal instead of exceptional.

If the skilled person standard fails to evolve accordingly, this will result in too lenient a standard for patentability. Patents have significant anticompetitive costs and allowing the average worker to routinely patent their outputs would cause social harm. As the US Supreme Court has articulated, "[g]ranting patent protection to advances that would occur in the ordinary course without real innovation retards progress and may … deprive prior inventions of their value or utility."[11]

The skilled standard must keep pace with real-world conditions. In fact, the standard needs updating even before inventive algorithms are commonplace. Already, algorithms are widely facilitating research and assisting with invention. For instance, algorithms may perform literature searches, data analysis, and pattern recognition.[12] This makes current workers more knowledgeable and creative than they would be without the use of such technologies. The Federal Circuit has provided a list of non-exhaustive factors to consider in determining the level of ordinary skill: (1) "type[s] of problems encountered in the art," (2) "prior art solutions to those problems," (3) "rapidity with which innovations are made," (4) "sophistication of the technology," and (5) "educational level of active workers in the field."[13] This test should be modified to include a sixth factor: (6) "technologies used by active workers."

This change will more explicitly take into account the fact that algorithms are already augmenting the capabilities of workers, in essence making more obvious and expanding the scope of prior art. Once inventive algorithms become the standard means of research in a

[5] The growing prevalence and sophistication of artificial intelligence is accelerating the use of inventive algorithms in research and development. See R. Abbott and B. Bogenschneider, Should Robots Pay Taxes? Tax Policy in the Age of Automation (2018) 12 *Harv. Law Policy Rev.* 145 (discussing the trend toward automation).
[6] See generally V. C. Müller and N. Bostrom, Future Progress in Artificial Intelligence: A Survey of Expert Opinion, in V. C. Müller (ed.), *Fundamental Issues of Artificial Intelligence* (Springer, 2016), p. 553.
[7] P. Rejcek, Can Futurists Predict the Year of the Singularity?, *Singularity Hub* (March 31, 2017), https://singularityhub.com/2017/03/31/can-futurists-predict-the-year-of-the-singularity (predicting artificial general intelligence in 2029).
[8] See, e.g., R. Plotkin, *The Genie in the Machine: How Computer-Automated Inventing Is Revolutionizing Law & Business* (Stanford Law Books, 2009), p. 60 (arguing that "[a]rtificial invention technology … enables [users] to produce inventions that they could not have created at all without such technology"); B. Hattenbach and J. Glucoft, Patents in an Era of Infinite Monkeys and Artificial Intelligence (2015) 19 *Stan. Technol. Law Rev.* 32, 44 n. 70; B. M. Simon, The Implications of Technological Advancement for Obviousness (2013) 19 *Mich. Telecomm. Technol. Law Rev.* 331.
[9] 35 USC § 103(a) (2006). The "person having ordinary skill in the art" may be abbreviated as "PHOSITA" or simply the skilled person.
[10] See "Finding PHOSITA," below.
[11] *KSR Int'l Co. v. Teleflex Inc.*, 550 US 398, 402 (2007).
[12] Such contributions when made by other persons do not generally rise to the level of inventorship, but they assist with reduction to practice.
[13] *In re. GPAC Inc.*, 57 F.3d 1573, 1579 (Fed. Cir. 1995).

field, the test would also encompass the routine use of inventive algorithms by skilled persons. Taken a step further, once inventive algorithms become the standard means of research in a field, the skilled person should be an inventive algorithm. Specifically, the skilled person should be an inventive algorithm when the standard approach to research in a field or with regard to a particular problem is to use an inventive algorithm (the "Inventive Algorithm Standard").

To obtain the necessary information to implement this test, the Patent Office should establish a new requirement for applicants to disclose when an algorithm contributes to the conception of an invention, which is the standard for qualifying as an inventor. Applicants are already required to disclose all human inventors, and failure to do so can render a patent invalid or unenforceable. Similarly, applicants should need to disclose whether an algorithm has done the work of a human inventor. This information could be aggregated to determine whether most invention in a field is performed by people or algorithms. This information would also be useful for determining appropriate inventorship, and more broadly for formulating innovation policies.

Whether the Inventive Algorithm Standard is that of a skilled person using an inventive algorithm or just an inventive algorithm, the result will be the same: the average worker will be capable of inventive activity. Conceptualizing the skilled person as using an inventive algorithm might be administratively simpler, but replacing the skilled person with the inventive algorithm would be preferable because it emphasizes that the *algorithm* is engaging in inventive activity, rather than the human worker.

Yet, simply substituting an inventive algorithm for a skilled person might exacerbate existing problems with the non-obviousness inquiry. With the current skilled person standard, decision-makers, in hindsight, need to reason about what another person would have found obvious.[14] This results in inconsistent and unpredictable non-obviousness determinations.[15] In practice, the skilled person standard bears unfortunate similarities to the "Elephant Test,"[16] or Justice Stewart's famously unworkable definition of obscene material: "I know it when I see it."[7] This may be even more problematic in the case of inventive algorithms, as it is likely to be difficult for human decision-makers to theoretically reason about what an algorithm would find obvious.

An existing vein of critical scholarship has already advocated for non-obviousness inquiries to focus more on economic factors or objective "secondary" criteria, such as long-felt but unsolved needs, the failure of others, and real-world evidence of how an invention was received in the marketplace.[18] Inventive algorithms may provide the impetus for such a shift.

---

[14]   See generally G. N. Mandel, Patently Non-Obvious: Empirical Demonstration that the Hindsight Bias Renders Patent Decisions Irrational (2006) 67 *Ohio St. Law J.* 1391 (discussing problems with hindsight in non-obviousness inquiries).

[15]   See Federal Trade Commission, To Promote Innovation: The Proper Balance of Competition and Patent Law and Policy (2003), pp. 6–15 (critiquing Section 103 decisions).

[16]   *Cadogan Estates Ltd* v. *Morris* [1998] EWCA Civ. 1671 at 17 (Eng.) (referring to "the well known elephant test. It is difficult to describe, but you know it when you see it").

[17]   378 US 184, 197 (1964).

[18]   See, e.g., M. Abramowicz and J. F. Duffy, The Inducement Standard of Patentability (2011) 120 *Yale Law J.* 1590, 1596 (arguing for an inducement standard); T.-J. Chiang, A Cost-Benefit Approach to Patent Obviousness (2008) 82 *St. John's Law Rev.* 39, 42 (arguing that, "[a]n invention should receive a patent if the accrued benefits before independent invention outweigh the costs after independent invention"); A. Devlin and N. Sukhatme, Self-Realizing Inventions and the Utilitarian Foundation of Patent Law (2009) 51 *Wm. Mary Law Rev.* 897; J. F. Duffy, A Timing Approach to Patentability (2008) 12 *Lewis Clark Law Rev.* 343 (arguing for a timing approach to determining obviousness); D. J. Durie and M. A. Lemley, A Realistic Approach to the Obviousness of Inventions (2008) 50 *Wm. Mary Law Rev.* 989, 1004–7 (arguing for a greater reliance on secondary considerations); G. Mandel, The Non-Obvious Problem: How the Indeterminate Nonobviousness Standard Produces Excessive

Non-obvious inquiries utilizing the Inventive Algorithm Standard might also focus on *reproducibility*, specifically whether standard algorithms could reproduce the subject matter of a patent application with sufficient ease. This could be a more objective and determinate test that would allow the Patent Office to apply a single standard consistently, and it would result in fewer judicially invalidated patents.[19] A non-obviousness inquiry focused on either secondary factors or reproducibility may avoid some of the difficulties inherent in applying a "cognitive" inventive algorithm standard.

However the test is applied, the Inventive Algorithm Standard will dynamically raise the current benchmark for patentability. Inventive algorithms will be significantly more intelligent than skilled persons and also capable of considering more prior art. An Inventive Algorithm Standard would not prohibit patents, but it would make obtaining them substantially more difficult: a person or algorithm might need to have an unusual insight that other inventive algorithms could not easily recreate, developers might need to create increasingly intelligent algorithms that could outperform standard algorithms, or, most likely, invention will be dependent on specialized, non-public sources of data. The non-obviousness bar will continue to rise as algorithms inevitably become increasingly sophisticated. Taken to its logical extreme, and given there may be no limit to how intelligent algorithms will become, it may be that every invention will one day be obvious to commonly used algorithms. That would mean no more patents should be issued without some radical change to current patentability criteria.

This chapter is structured in three sections. The first section, entitled "Obviousness," considers the current test for obviousness and its historical evolution. It finds that obviousness is evaluated through the lens of the skilled person, who reflects the characteristics of the average worker in a field.[20] The level of creativity and knowledge imputed to the skilled person is critical for the obviousness analysis.[21] The more capable the skilled person, the more they will find obvious, and this will result in fewer issued patents.

The second section, entitled "Machine Intelligence in the Inventive Process," considers the use of artificial intelligence (AI) in research and development (R&D) and proposes a novel framework for conceptualizing the transition from human to algorithm inventors. Already, inventive algorithms are competing with human inventors, and human inventors

---

Patent Grants (2008) 42 *UC Davis Law Rev.* 57, 62 (arguing for non-obviousness to be based on "how probable the invention would have been for a person having ordinary skill in the art working on the problem that the invention solves"); R. P. Merges, Uncertainty and the Standard of Patentability (1992) 7 *High Technol. Law J.* 1, 19 (arguing that patents should be issued for inventions which appeared unlikely to succeed in advance).

[19] For decades, obviousness has been the most common issue in litigation to invalidate a patent, and the most common grounds for a finding of patent invalidity. See J. R. Allison and M. A. Lemley, Empirical Evidence on the Validity of Litigated Patents (1998) 26 *AIPLA QJ* 185, 208–9; J. R. Allison, M. A. Lemley, and D. L. Schwartz, Understanding the Realities of Modern Patent Litigation (2014) 92 *Tex. Law Rev.* 1769, 1782, 1785. As other commentators have noted, the bar here is low, and the new standard "can be an administrative success if it is even just a bit better than current doctrine as a helpful theoretical and pragmatic guide for applying the obviousness doctrine." Abramowicz and Duffy, above note 18, p. 1601.

[20] See *Ruiz v. A.B. Chance Co.*, 234 F.3d 654, 666 (Fed. Cir. 2000); see also *Ryko Mfg. Co. v. Nu-Star, Inc.*, 950 F.2d 714, 718 (Fed. Cir. 1991) ("The importance of resolving the level of ordinary skill in the art lies in the necessity of maintaining objectivity in the obviousness inquiry"). The Manual of Patent Examining Procedure (MPEP) provides guidance on the level of ordinary skill in the art. MPEP § 2141.03.

[21] *DyStar Textilfarben GmbH & Co. Deutschland KG v. C.H. Patrick Co.*, 464 F.3d 1356, 1370 (Fed. Cir. 2006) ("If the level of skill is low, for example that of a mere dyer, as Dystar has suggested, then it may be rational to assume that such an artisan would not think to combine references absent explicit direction in a prior art reference"). However, in practice, few cases involve explicit factual determinations of the PHOSITA's skill. R. S. Eisenberg, Obvious to Whom? Evaluating Inventions from the Perspective of PHOSITA (2004) 19 *Berkeley Technol. Law J.* 885, 888. See "Finding PHOSITA," below, for a discussion of the PHOSITA standard.

are augmenting their abilities with inventive algorithms. In time, inventive algorithms or people using inventive algorithms will become the standard in a field, and eventually, algorithms will be responsible for most or all innovation. As this occurs, the skilled person standard must evolve if it is to continue to reflect real-world conditions. Failure to do this would "stifle, rather than promote, the progress of the useful arts."[22]

The second section then proposes a framework for implementing a proposed Inventive Algorithm Standard. A decision-maker would need to (1) determine the extent to which inventive algorithms are used in a field, (2) if inventive algorithms are the standard, characterize the inventive algorithm(s) that best represents the average worker, and (3) determine whether the algorithm(s) would find an invention obvious. The decision-maker is a patent examiner in the first instance,[23] and potentially a judge or jury if the validity of a patent is at issue in trial.[24] In both instances, this new test would involve new challenges.

Finally, the third section, "A Post-Skilled World," provides examples of how the Inventive Algorithm Standard could work in practice, such as by focusing on reproducibility or secondary factors. It then goes on to consider some of the implications of the new standard. Once the average worker is inventive, there may no longer be a need for patents to function as innovation incentives. To the extent patents accomplish other goals such as promoting commercialization and disclosure of information or validating moral rights, other mechanisms may be found to accomplish these goals with fewer costs.

Although this chapter focuses on US patent law, a similar framework exists in nearly every country. Member States of the World Trade Organization (WTO) are required to grant patents for inventions that "are new, involve an inventive step and are capable of industrial application."[25] Although US law uses the term "non-obvious" rather than "inventive step," the criteria are substantively similar.[26] For instance, the European Patent Office's criteria for inventive step is similar to the US criteria for obviousness, and also uses the theoretical device of the skilled person.[27]

While this chapter is primarily concerned with patenting algorithmic output, it should also be noted that in certain circumstances it may be possible to at least functionally patent

---

22 *KSR* v. *Teleflex*, above note 11, at 427.

23 At the Patent Office, applications are initially considered by a patent examiner, and examiner decisions can be appealed to the Patent Trial and Appeal Board (PTAB). USPTO, *Patent Trial and Appeal Board*, www.uspto.gov/patents-application-process/patent-trial-and-appeal-board-0. Also, the PTAB can adjudicate issues of patentability in certain proceedings such as *inter partes* review. *Ibid*.

24 Determinations of patent validity can involve mixed questions of law and fact. Generally, in civil litigation, legal questions are determined by judges, while factual questions are for a jury. See, e.g., *Structural Rubber Prods. Co.* v. *Park Rubber Co.*, 749 F.2d 707, 713 (Fed. Cir. 1984) ("Litigants have the right to have a case tried in a manner which ensures that factual questions are determined by the jury and the decisions on legal issues are made by the court … "). There are some exceptions to this rule. See, e.g., *Gen. Electro Music Corp.* v. *Samick Music Corp.*, 19 F.3d 1405, 1408 (Fed. Cir. 1994) ("[I]ssues of fact underlying the issue of inequitable conduct are not jury questions, the issue being entirely equitable in nature"). See also M. A. Lemley, Why Do Juries Decide If Patents Are Valid? (Stanford Pub. Law, Working Paper No. 2306152, 2013), https://papers.ssrn.com/sol3/papers.cfm?abstract_id=2306152.

25 Agreement on Trade-Related Aspects of Intellectual Property Rights, art. 27, April 15, 1994, 33 ILM 1197, 1208 (TRIPS). See R. B. Abbott, R. Bader, L. Bajjali, *et al.*, The Price of Medicines in Jordan: The Cost of Trade-Based Intellectual Property (2012) 9 *J. Generic Meds*. 75, 76.

26 TRIPS, above note 25, at 1208 n. 5. However, there are some substantive differences in the way in which these criteria are implemented, and TRIPS provides nations with various flexibilities for compliance. See generally R. Abbott, Balancing Access and Innovation in India's Shifting IP Regime, Remarks (2014) 35 *Whittier Law Rev.* 341.

27 "An invention shall be considered as involving an inventive step if, having regard to the state of the art, it is not obvious to a person skilled in the art." Convention on the Grant of European Patents, art. 56, October 5, 1973, 13 ILM 268. For guidance on the "skilled person" in European patent law, see European Patent Office, Guidelines for Examination, www.epo.org/law-practice/legal-texts/html/guidelines/e/g_vii_3.html.

algorithms.[28] This is a distinct sort of protection from patents on output. Under US law, certain types of subject matter are ineligible for patent protection, including abstract ideas, laws of nature, and natural phenomena.[29] Recent Supreme Court decisions have found algorithms to be patent-ineligible abstract ideas, and have made it clear that simply implementing an algorithm on a computer is not sufficient for patentability.[30] Under the prevailing *Alice/Mayo* test, a patent can claim an algorithm if it includes additional elements that amount to significantly more than just the abstract idea.[31] The US Court of Appeals for the Federal Circuit has subsequently upheld a limited number of algorithm-related patents, and in early 2019, the USPTO proposed revised guidance that would additionally allow patents on algorithms where integrated into a practical application.[32] Patenting algorithms is a controversial topic with an evolving jurisprudence.

OBVIOUSNESS

This section investigates the current obviousness standard, its historical origins, and how the standard has changed over time. It finds that obviousness depends on the creativity of the skilled person, as well as the prior art they consider. These factors, in turn, vary according to the complexity of an invention and its field of art.

Public Policy

Patents are not intended to be granted for incremental inventions.[33] Only inventions which represent a significant advance over existing technology should receive protection.[34] That is because patents have significant costs: They limit competition, and they can inhibit future innovation by restricting the use of patented technologies in R&D.[35] To the extent that patents are justified, this is because they are thought to have more benefits than costs. Patents can function as innovation incentives, promote the dissemination of information, encourage commercialization of technology, and validate moral rights.[36]

---

[28]   Although patent-eligible subject matter varies by jurisdiction, algorithms per se are generally patent-ineligible subject matter although the EPO permits patents on "computer-implemented inventions."

[29]   *Ass'n for Molecular Pathology* v. *Myriad Genetics, Inc.*, 569 US 576 (2013).

[30]   *Alice Corp. Pty. Ltd* v. *CLS Bank Int'l*, 573 US 208, 217–18 (2014) (citing *Mayo Collaborative Servs.* v. *Prometheus Labs., Inc.*, 566 US 66 (2012)).

[31]   *Ibid.*

[32]   USPTO, 2019 Revised Patent Subject Matter Eligibility Guidance, www.federalregister.gov/documents/2019/01/ 07/2018-28282/2019-revised-patent-subject-matter-eligibility-guidance (discussing proposed revisions to determining whether a claim is directed to abstract ideas).

[33]   The non-obviousness requirement is contained in Section 103 of the Patent Act:

> A patent for a claimed invention may not be obtained, notwithstanding that the claimed invention is not identically disclosed as set forth in section 102, if the differences between the claimed invention and the prior art are such that the claimed invention as a whole would have been obvious before the effective filing date of the claimed invention to a person having ordinary skill in the art to which the claimed invention pertains.

35 USC § 103 (2018).

[34]   *Atlantic Works* v. *Brady*, 107 US 192, 200 (1883) (noting that "[t]o grant to a single party monopoly of every slight advance made, except where the exercise of invention, somewhat above ordinary mechanical or engineering skill, is distinctly shown, is unjust in principle and injurious in its consequences").

[35]   See Abbott, above note 1, pp. 1105–6 (discussing the costs and benefits of the patent system).

[36]   *Ibid.*, pp. 1105–8. Congress's power to grant patents is constitutional, and based on incentive theory: "To promote the progress of science … by securing for limited times to … inventors the exclusive right to their respective … discoveries." US Constitution, art. I, § 8, cl. 8. See M. A. Lemley, Ex Ante Versus Ex Post Justifications for

Patents are granted for inventions that are new, non-obvious, and useful.[37] Of these three criteria, obviousness is the primary hurdle for most patent applications.[38] Although other patentability criteria contribute to this function, the non-obviousness requirement is the primary test for distinguishing between significant innovations and trivial advances.[39] Of course, it is one thing to express a desire to only protect meaningful scientific advances, and another to come up with a workable rule that applies across every area of technology.

Early Attempts

The modern obviousness standard has been the culmination of hundreds of years of struggle by the Patent Office, courts, and Congress to separate the wheat from the chaff.[40] As Thomas Jefferson, the first administrator of the US patent system and one of its chief architects, wrote, "I know well the difficulty of drawing a line between the things which are worth to the public the embarrassment of an exclusive patent, and those which are not ... I saw with what slow progress a system of general rules could be matured."[41]

The earliest patent laws focused on novelty and utility, although Jefferson did at one point suggest an "obviousness" requirement.[42] The Patent Act of 1790 was the first patent statute, and it required patentable inventions to be "sufficiently useful and important."[43] Three years later, a more comprehensive patent law was passed – the Patent Act of 1793.[44] The new act did not require an invention to be "important," but required it to be "new and useful."[45] The 1836

Intellectual Property (2004) 71 *Univ. Chi. Law Rev.* 129, 129 ("The standard justification for intellectual property is ex ante ... It is the prospect of the intellectual property right that spurs creative incentives"); see also *United States v. Line Material Co.*, 333 US 287, 316 (1948) (Douglas, J., concurring) (noting "the reward to inventors is wholly secondary" to the reward to society); The Federalist No. 43 (James Madison) (stating that social benefit arises from patents to inventors). The US Supreme Court has endorsed an economic inducement rationale in which patents should only be granted for inventions which would "not be disclosed or devised but for the inducement of a patent." This is the inducement theory articulated in *Graham v. John Deere Co.*, 383 US 1, 10 (1966). See also Abramowicz and Duffy, above note 18.

37   35 USC §§ 101–3, 112 (2018). In the European system, these criteria are referred to as novelty, inventive step, and industrial applicability (EPC, art. 52). Inventions must also comprise patentable subject matter and be adequately disclosed. 35 USC §§ 101–3, 112 (2018).

38   D. Chisum, *Chisum on Patents* (LexisNexis, 2007), § 5.02[6]; J. Witherspoon (ed.), *Nonobviousness: the Ultimate Condition of Patentability* (Bureau of National Affairs, 1980), para. 2:101. Obviousness is the most commonly litigated issue of patent validity. Allison and Lemley, above note 19, pp. 208–9.

39   35 USC §§ 101–2, 112 (2018).

40   For that matter, the struggle dates back to the very first patent law, the Venetian Act of 1474, which stated that only "new and ingenious" inventions would be protected. See G. Mandich, Venetian Patents (1450–1550) (1948) 30 *J. Pat. Off. Soc.* 166, 176–7; A. Samuel Oddi, Beyond Obviousness: Invention Protection in the Twenty-First Century (1989) 38 *Am. Univ. Law Rev.* 1097, 1102–3; F. D. Prager, A History of Intellectual Property From 1545 to 1787 (1944) 26 *J. Pat. Off. Soc.* 711, 715.

41   Letter to Isaac McPherson (August 13, 1813), in *The Writings of Thomas Jefferson, 1790–1826* (Riker, Thorne & Co., 1854), p. 5.

42   In 1791, Jefferson proposed amending the 1790 Patent Act to prohibit patents on an invention if it "is so unimportant and obvious that it ought not be the subject of an exclusive right." P. Leicester Ford (ed.), *The Writings of Thomas Jefferson 1788–1792* (G. P. Putnam & Sons, 1895).

43   Patent Act of 1790, ch. 7, 1 Stat. 109 (repealed 1793).

44   Patent Act of 1793, ch. 11, 1 Stat. 318 (repealed 1836).

45   *Ibid.* at 318–23. It also prohibited patents on certain minor improvements: "[S]imply changing the form or the proportions of any machine, or compositions of matter, in any degree, shall not be deemed a discovery." *Ibid.* at 321. On this basis, Jefferson, who was credited with drafting most of this statute, argued that "[a] change of material should not give title to a patent. As the making a ploughshare of cast rather than of wrought iron; a comb of iron, instead of horn or of ivory ... " Letter to Isaac McPherson, above note 41, p. 181.

Patent Act reinstated the requirement that an invention be "sufficiently used and important."[46]

In 1851, the Supreme Court adopted the progenitor of the skilled person and the obviousness test – an "invention" standard.[47] *Hotchkiss* v. *Greenwood* concerned a patent for substituting clay or porcelain for a known door-knob material such as metal or wood.[48] The Court invalidated the patent, holding that "the improvement is the work of a skillful mechanic, not that of the inventor."[49] The Court also articulated a new legal standard for patentability: "Unless more ingenuity and skill … were required … than were possessed by an ordinary mechanic acquainted with the business, there was an absence of that degree of skill and ingenuity which constitute essential elements of every invention."[50]

However, the Court did not give specific guidance on what makes something inventive or the required level of inventiveness. In subsequent years, the Court made several efforts to address these deficiencies, but with limited success. As the Court stated in 1891: "The truth is the word [invention] cannot be defined in such manner as to afford any substantial aid in determining whether any particular device involves an exercise of inventive faculty or not."[51] Or as one commentator noted, "it was almost impossible for one to say with any degree of certainty that a particular patent was indeed valid."[52]

Around 1930, the Supreme Court, possibly influenced by a national anti-monopoly sentiment, began implementing stricter criteria for determining the level of invention.[53] This culminated in the widely disparaged "Flash of Genius" test articulated in *Cuno Engineering* v. *Automatic Devices*.[54] Namely, that in order to receive a patent, "the new device must reveal the flash of creative genius, not merely the skill of the calling."[55] This test was interpreted to mean that an invention must come into the mind of an inventor as a result of "inventive genius"[56] rather than as

[46] Patent Act of 1836, ch. 357, § 18, 5 Stat. 117, 124 (repealed 1861).
[47] See, e.g., *Graham*, above note 36, at 17 ("We conclude that [§ 103] was intended merely as a codification of judicial precedents embracing the Hotchkiss condition, with congressional directions that inquiries into the obviousness of the subject matter sought to be patented are a prerequisite to patentability"); see also S. Rep. No. 82-1979, at 6 (1952); HR Rep. No. 82-1923, at 7 (1952) ("Section 103 … provides a condition which exists in the law and has existed for more than 100 years"). Obviousness had been at issue in earlier cases, although not necessarily in such terms. For instance, in *Earle* v. *Sawyer*, Justice Story rejected an argument by the defendant that the invention at issue was obvious, and that something more than novelty and utility was required for a patent. 8 F. Cas. 254, 255 (Cir. Ct. D. Mass. 1825). He argued a court was not required to engage in a "mode of reasoning upon the metaphysical nature, or the abstract definition of an invention" (*ibid.*). Justice Story further noted that English law permits the introducer of a foreign technology to receive a patent, and such an act could not require intellectual labor (*ibid.* at 256). In *Evans* v. *Eaton*, the Supreme Court held that a patent invention must involve a change in the "principle" of the algorithm rather than a change "merely in form and proportion" (20 US (7 Wheat) 356, 361–2 (1822)). Writing for the Court, Justice Story noted the patent was invalid because it was "substantially the same in principle" as a prior invention (*ibid.* at 362).
[48] 52 US 248, 265 (1850).
[49] *Ibid.* at 267.
[50] *Ibid.*
[51] *McClain* v. *Ortmayer*, 141 US 419, 427 (1891). Another court noted that "invention" is "as fugitive, impalpable, wayward, and vague a phantom as exists in the paraphernalia of legal concepts." *Harries* v. *Air King Prods. Co.*, 183 F.2d 158, 162 (2nd Cir. 1950).
[52] G. Chin, The Statutory Standard of Invention: Section 103 of the 1952 Patent Act (1959) 3 *Pat. Trademark & Copy. J. Res. & Educ.* 317, 318.
[53] See, e.g., E. B. Gregg, Tracing the Concept of Patentable Invention (1967) 13 *Vill. Law Rev.* 98.
[54] *Cuno Eng'g Corp.* v. *Automatic Devices Corp.*, 314 US 84, 91 (1941) (formalizing the test). See, e.g., *Hamilton Standard Propeller Co.* v. *Fay-Egan Mfg. Co.*, 101 F.2d 614, 617 (6th Cir. 1939) ("The patentee did not display any flash of genius, inspiration or imagination … "). The Flash of Genius test was reaffirmed by the Court in 1950 in *Great Atlantic & Pacific Tea Co.* v. *Supermarket Equip. Corp.*, 340 US 147, 154 (1950) (Douglas, J., concurring).
[55] *Cuno Eng'g, ibid.*, at 91.
[56] *Reckendorfer* v. *Faber*, 92 US 347, 357 (1875).

a "result of long toil and experimentation."[57] The Court reasoned that "strict application of the test is necessary lest in the constant demand for new appliances the heavy hand of tribute be laid on each slight technological advance in the art."[58]

The Flash of Genius test was criticized for being vague and difficult to implement, and for involving subjective decisions about an inventor's state of mind.[59] It certainly made it substantially more difficult to obtain a patent.[60] Extensive criticism of perceived judicial hostility toward patents resulted in President Franklin D. Roosevelt's creation of a National Patent Planning Commission to make recommendations for improving the patent system.[61] The Commission's report recommended that Congress adopt a more objective and certain standard of obviousness.[62] A decade later, Congress did.[63]

The Non-Obviousness Inquiry

The Patent Act of 1952 established the modern patentability framework.[64] Among other changes to substantive patent law,[65] "the central thrust of the 1952 Act removed

---

[57] The Supreme Court later claimed the "Flash of Creative Genius" language was just a rhetorical embellishment, and that requirement concerned only the device itself, not the manner of invention. *Graham*, above note 36, at 15 n. 7, 16 n. 8. That was not, however, how the test was interpreted. See P. J. Federico, Origins of Section 103 (1977) 5 *APLA QJ* 87, 97 n. 5 (noting the test led to a higher standard of invention in the lower courts). In *Great Atlantic & Pacific Tea*, above note 54, another case cited for the proposition that the Court had adopted stricter patentability criteria, the majority did not consider the question of inventiveness, but in his concurring opinion Justice Douglas reiterated the concept of "inventive genius": "It is not enough that an article is new and useful. The Constitution never sanctioned the patenting of gadgets. Patents serve a higher end – the advancement of science. An invention need not be as startling as an atomic bomb to be patentable. But it has to be of such quality and distinction that that masters of the scientific field in which it falls will recognize it as an advance" (*ibid.*).

[58] *Cuno Eng'g*, above note 54, at 92.

[59] As a commentator at the time noted, "the standard of patentable invention represented by [the Flash of Genius doctrine] is apparently based upon the nature of the mental processes of the patentee-inventor by which he achieved the advancement in the art claimed in his patent, rather than solely upon the objective nature of the advancement itself." Comment, The "Flash of Genius" Standard of Patentable Invention, 13 *Fordham Law Rev.* 84, 87 (1944). See Note, Patent Law – "Flash of Genius" Test for Invention Rejected (1955) 5 *DePaul Law Rev.* 144, 146; S. G. Kalinchak, Obviousness and the Doctrine of Equivalents in Patent Law: Striving for Objective Criteria (1994) 43 *Cath. Univ. Law Rev.* 577, 586; see also, Note, The Standard of Patentability – Judicial Interpretation of Section 103 of the Patent Act Source (1963) 63 *Colum. Law Rev.* 306, 306 (hereinafter, The Standard of Patentability) (criticizing the standard).

[60] Supreme Court Justice Robert Jackson noted in a dissent that "the only patent that is valid is one which this Court has not been able to get its hands on." *Jungersen v. Ostby & Barton Co.*, 335 US 560, 572 (1949) (Jackson, J., dissenting).

[61] See W. Jarratt, U.S. National Patent Planning Commission (1944) 153 *Nature* 12; see also National Patent Planning Commission, Report of the National Patent Planning Commission (1943), pp. 6, 10.

[62] National Patent Planning Commission, above note 61, pp. 5–6. "One of the greatest technical weaknesses of the patent system is the lack of a definitive yardstick as to what is invention" (*ibid.* at 26). "The most serious weakness of the present patent system is the lack of a uniform test or standard for determining whether the particular contribution of an inventor merits the award of the patent grant" (*ibid.* at 14). "It is proposed that Congress shall declare a national standard whereby patentability of an invention shall be determined by the objective test as to its advancement of the arts and sciences" (*ibid.* at 26).

[63] Although Congress may not have realized what it was doing. See G. M. Sirilla, 35 USC § 103: From Hotchkiss to Hand to Rich, the Obvious Patent Law Hall-of-Famers (1999) 32 *J. Marshall Law Rev.* 437, 509–14 (discussing the legislative history of the Patent Act of 1952 and the lack of congressional awareness of, and intent for, Section 103).

[64] See The Standard of Patentability, above note 59, at 309. "[P]robably no other title incorporates the thinking of so many qualified technical men throughout the country as does this revision." L. J. Harris, Some Aspects of the Underlying Legislative Intent of the Patent Act of 1952 (1955) 23 *Geo. Wash. Law Rev.* 658, 661.

[65] "The major changes or innovations in the title consist of incorporating a requirement for invention in § 103 and the judicial doctrine of contributory infringement in § 271." HR Rep. No. 1923, 82nd Cong., 2nd Sess. 5 (1952); S. Rep. No. 1979, 82nd Cong., 2nd Sess. 4 (1952).

'unmeasurable' inquiries into 'inventiveness' and instead supplied the nonobviousness requirement of Section 103."[66] Section 103 states:

> A patent may not be obtained ... if the difference between the subject matter sought to be patented and the prior art are such that the subject matter as a whole would have been obvious at the time the invention was made to a person having ordinary skill in the art to which said subject matter pertains. Patentability shall not be negatived by the manner in which the invention was made.[67]

Section 103 legislatively disavowed the Flash of Genius test, codified the sprawling judicial doctrine on "invention" into a single statutory test, and restructured the standard of obviousness in relation to a person having ordinary skill in the art.[68] However, while Section 103 may be more objective and definite than the Flash of Genius test, the meanings of "obvious" and "a person having ordinary skill" were not defined, and in practice also proved "often difficult to apply."[69]

The Supreme Court first interpreted the statutory non-obviousness requirement in a trilogy of cases: *Graham v. John Deere* (1966) and its companion cases, *Calmar v. Cook Chemical* (1965) and *United States v. Adams* (1966).[70] In these cases, the Court articulated a framework for evaluating obviousness as a question of law based on the following underlying factual inquiries: (1) the scope and content of the prior art; (2) the level of ordinary skill in the prior art; (3) the differences between the claimed invention and the prior art; and (4) objective evidence of non-obviousness.[71] This framework remains applicable today. Of note, the *Graham* analysis does not explain how to evaluate the ultimate legal question of non-obviousness, beyond identifying underlying factual considerations.[72]

In 1984, the newly established US Court of Appeals for the Federal Circuit, the only appellate-level court with jurisdiction to hear patent case appeals, devised the "teaching, suggestion, and motivation" (TSM) test for obviousness.[73] Strictly applied, this test only permits an obviousness rejection when prior art explicitly teaches, suggests, or motivates a

---

[66] *CLS Bank Int'l v. Alice Corp. Pty. Ltd*, 717 F.3d 1269, 1296 (Fed. Cir. 2013) (Rader, J., dissenting in part, concurring in part) (citing P. J. Federidco's Commentary on the New Patent Act, reprinted in (1993) 75 *J. Pat. & Trademark Office Soc.* 161, 177). See also *Dann v. Johnston*, 425 US 219, 225–6 (1976) (describing the shift from "an exercise of the inventive faculty" established in case law to a statutory test and stating that "it was only in 1952 that Congress, in the interest of uniformity and definiteness, articulated the requirement in a statute, framing it as a requirement of 'nonobviousness'" (internal quotation marks and footnote omitted)). The official "Revision Notes" state § 103 is meant to be the basis for "holding ... patents invalid by the courts[] on the ground of lack of invention" (S. Rep. No. 82-1979, at 18).

[67] 35 USC § 103, as amended by the America Invents Act. Leahy-Smith America Invents Act, Pub. L. No. 112-29, 125 Stat. 284, 286 (2011) (codified at 35 USC § 103 (2018)). The America Invents Act did not fundamentally change the non-obviousness inquiry, but did result in some modest changes. See www.uspto.gov/web/offices/pac/mpep/s2158.html.

[68] See G. S. Rich, Principles of Patentability (1960) 28 *Geo. Wash. Univ. Law Rev.* 393, 393–407; see also Chin, above note 52, p. 318. In *Graham*, the Supreme Court noted that "[i]t ... seems apparent that Congress intended by the last sentence of § 103 to abolish the test it believed this Court announced in the controversial phrase 'flash of creative genius,' used in *Cuno Engineering*." *Graham*, above note 36, at 15.

[69] *Uniroyal, Inc. v. Rudkin-Wiley Corp.*, 837 F.2d 1044, 1050 (Fed. Cir. 1988) (noting the obviousness standard is easy to expound and "often difficult to apply").

[70] *Graham*, above note 36; *United States v. Adams*, 383 US 39, 51–2 (1966); *Calmar v. Cook Chem.*, 380 US 949 (1965).

[71] *Graham*, above note 36, at 17. With regard to the fourth category, considerations such as *commercial success* and *long-felt but unsolved needs* can serve as evidence of non-obviousness in certain circumstances. *Ibid.*

[72] See J. Miller, Nonobviousness: Looking Back and Looking Ahead, in P. K. Yu (ed.), *Intellectual Property and Information Wealth: Issues and Practices in the Digital Age: Patents and Trade Secrets* (Praeger, 2007), Vol. 2, p. 9 ("[T]he Court did not indicate ... how one was to go about determining obviousness (or not)").

[73] US Court of Appeals for the Federal Circuit, Court Jurisdiction, www.cafc.uscourts.gov/the-court/court-jurisdiction.

combination of existing elements into a new invention.[74] The TSM test protects against hindsight bias because it requires an objective finding in the prior art. In retrospect, it is easy for an invention to appear obvious by piecing together bits of prior art using the invention as a blueprint.[75]

In *KSR v. Teleflex* (2006), the Supreme Court upheld the *Graham* analysis, but rejected the Federal Circuit's exclusive reliance on the TSM test. The Court instead endorsed a flexible approach to obviousness in light of "[t]he diversity of inventive pursuits and of modern technology."[76] Rather than approving a single definitive test, the Court identified a non-exhaustive list of rationales to support a finding of obviousness.[77] This remains the approach to obviousness today.

Finding PHOSITA

Determining the level of ordinary skill is critical to assessing obviousness.[78] The more sophisticated the person having ordinary skill in the art (PHOSITA, or the skilled person), the more likely a new invention is to appear obvious. Thus, it matters a great deal whether the skilled person is a "moron in a hurry"[79] or the combined "masters of the scientific field in which an [invention] falls."[80]

The skilled person has never been precisely defined, although judicial guidance exists.[81] In *KSR v. Teleflex*, the Supreme Court described the skilled person as "a person of ordinary creativity, not an automaton."[82] The Federal Circuit has explained that the skilled person is a

74   *ACS Hosp. Sys., Inc. v. Montefiore Hosp.*, 732 F.2d 1572 (Fed. Cir. 1984).
75   See *In re Fritch*, 972 F.2d 1260, 1266 (Fed. Cir. 1992).
76   *KSR v. Teleflex*, above note 11, at 402. "[An obviousness] analysis need not seek out precise teachings directed to the specific subject matter of the challenged claim, for a court can take account of the inferences and creative steps that a [PHOSITA] would employ" (*ibid.* at 418).
77   These post-*KSR* rationales include:

> (A) Combining prior art elements according to known methods to yield predictable results; (B) Simple substitution of one known element for another to obtain predictable results; (C) Use of known technique to improve similar devices (methods, or products) in the same way; (D) Applying a known technique to a known device (method, or product) ready for improvement to yield predictable results; (E) "Obvious to try" – choosing from a finite number of identified, predictable solutions, with a reasonable expectation of success; (F) Known work in one field of endeavor may prompt variations of it for use in either the same field or a different one based on design incentives or other market forces if the variations are predictable to one of ordinary skill in the art; (G) Some teaching, suggestion, or motivation in the prior art that would have led one of ordinary skill to modify the prior art reference or to combine prior art reference teachings to arrive at the claimed invention.

> 2141 Examination Guidelines for Determining Obviousness under 35 USC 103 [R-08.2017], USPTO, www.uspto.gov/web/offices/pac/mpep/s2141.html.

78   *Ruiz v. A.B. Chance*, above note 20, at 666; see also *Ryko Mfg.*, above note 20, at 718 ("The importance of resolving the level of ordinary skill in the art lies in the necessity of maintaining objectivity in the obviousness inquiry"). The skilled person is relevant to many areas of patent law, including claim construction, best mode, definiteness, enablement, and the doctrine of equivalents. See D. L. Burk and M. A. Lemley, Is Patent Law Technology-Specific? (2002) 17 *Berkeley Technol. Law J.* 1155, 1186–7.
79   *Morning Star Coop. Soc'y v. Express Newspapers Ltd* [1979] FSR 113 (marking the first use of the term "moron in a hurry" as a standard for trademark confusion).
80   *Great Atlantic & Pacific Tea*, above note 54, at 155.
81   See J. B. Gambrell and J. H. Dodge, II, Ordinary Skill in the Art – an Enemy of the Inventor or a Friend of the People?, in J. F. Witherspoon (ed.), *Nonobviousness: The Ultimate Condition of Patentability* (Bureau of National Affairs, 1980), para. 5:302 ("[T]he Supreme Court in particular, but other courts as well, has done precious little to define the person of ordinary skill in the art").
82   *KSR v. Teleflex*, above note 11, at 421. The MPEP provides guidance on the level of ordinary skill in the art (MPEP § 2141.03). See J. F. Duffy and R. P. Merges, The Story of Graham v. John Deere Company: Patent Law's Evolving Standard of Creativity, in J. C. Ginsburg and R. Cooper Dreyfuss (eds.), *Intellectual Property Stories*

hypothetical person, like the reasonable person in tort law,[83] who is presumed to have known the relevant art at the time of the invention.[84] The skilled person is not a judge, amateur, person skilled in remote arts, or a set of "geniuses in the art at hand."[85] The skilled person is "one who thinks along the line of conventional wisdom in the art and is not one who undertakes to innovate."[86]

The Federal Circuit has provided a non-exhaustive list of factors to consider in determining the level of ordinary skill: (1) "type[s] of problems encountered in the art"; (2) "prior art solutions to those problems"; (3) "rapidity with which innovations are made"; (4) "sophistication of the technology"; and (5) "educational level of active workers in the field."[87] In any particular case, one or more factors may predominate, and not every factor may be relevant.[88] The skilled person standard thus varies according to the invention in question, its field of art, and researchers in the field.[89] In the case of a simple invention in a field where most innovation is created by laypersons, such as, for instance, a device to keep flies away from horses, the skilled person may be someone with little education or practical experience.[90] By contrast, where an invention is in a complex field with highly educated workers such as chemical engineering or pharmaceutical research, the skilled person may be quite

---

(Foundation Press, 2006), p. 110 (noting that determining the appropriate level of ordinary skill for the non-obviousness standard "is one of the most important policy issues in all of patent law").

[83] See, e.g., *Panduit Corp. v. Dennison Mfg. Co.*, 810 F.2d 1561, 1566 (Fed. Cir. 1987) ("[T]he decision maker confronts a ghost, i.e., 'a person having ordinary skill in the art,' not unlike the 'reasonable man' and other ghosts in the law").

[84] 2141 Examination Guidelines, above note 77.

[85] *Envtl. Designs Ltd v. Union Oil Co. of Cal.*, 713 F.2d 693, 697 (Fed. Cir. 1983).

[86] *Standard Oil Co. v. Am. Cyanamid Co.*, 774 F.2d 448, 454 (Fed. Cir. 1985).

[87] GPAC, above note 13, at 1579.

[88] Ibid.; *Custom Accessories, Inc. v. Jeffrey-Allan Indus., Inc.*, 807 F.2d 955, 962–3 (Fed. Cir. 1986). Previously, this list of factors included the "educational level of the inventor." *Envtl. Designs*, above note 85, at 696. That was until the Federal Circuit announced that "courts never have judged patentability by what the real inventor/applicant/patentee could or would do." *Kimberly-Clark Corp. v. Johnson & Johnson*, 745 F.2d 1437, 1454 (Fed. Cir. 1984). Instead, "[r]eal inventors, as a class, vary in the capacities from ignorant geniuses to Nobel laureates; the courts have always applied a standard based on an imaginary work of their own devising whom they have equated with the inventor" (*ibid.*).

[89] See, e.g., *DyStar Textilfarben*, above note 21, at 1370. The Court writes:

> If the level of skill is low, for example that of a mere dyer, as Dystar has suggested, then it may be rational to assume that such an artisan would not think to combine references absent explicit direction in a prior art reference … [If] the level of skill is that of a dyeing process designer, then one can assume comfortably that such an artisan will draw ideas from chemistry and systems engineering – without being told to do so.

Daiichi Sankyo Co. v. Apotex, Inc., 501 F.3d 1254, 1257 (Fed. Cir. 2007) concerned a patent for treating ear infections by applying an antibiotic to the ear. The District Court found that the skilled person "would have a medical degree, experience treating patients with ear infections, and knowledge of the pharmacology and use of antibiotics" (*ibid.*). "This person would be … a pediatrician or general practitioner – those doctors who are often the 'first line of defense' in treating ear infections and who, by virtue of their medical training, possess basic pharmacological knowledge" (*ibid.*). The Federal Circuit overturned this finding, holding that rather, a person of ordinary skill in the art was "a person engaged in developing new pharmaceuticals, formulations and treatment methods, or a specialist in ear treatments such as an otologist, otolaryngologist, or otorhinolaryngologist who also has training in pharmaceutical formulations" (*ibid.*). Courts have employed a flexible approach to considering informal education. See, e.g., *Penda Corp. v. United States*, 29 Fed. Cl. 533, 565 (1993). For instance, in *Bose Corp. v. JBL, Inc.*, 112 F. Supp. 2d 138, 155 (D. Mass. 2000), the District Court found that keeping "up with current literature and trade magazines to keep abreast of new developments" could be the equivalent of "a bachelor of science degree in electrical engineering, physics, mechanical engineering, or possibly acoustics."

[90] See *Graham v. Gun-Munro*, No. C-99-04064 CRB, 2001 US Dist. LEXIS 7110, at *19 (ND Cal. May 22, 2001) (holding that the skilled person had some formal education but no special training in the field of art in a case regarding fly wraps for the legs of horses).

sophisticated.[91] At least in Europe, the skilled person may even be a team of individuals where collaborative approaches to research are the norm.[92]

Analogous Prior Art

Determining what constitutes prior art is also central to the obviousness inquiry.[93] On some level, virtually all inventions involve a combination of known elements.[94] The more prior art can be considered, the more likely an invention is to appear obvious. To be considered for the purposes of obviousness, prior art must fall within the definition for anticipatory references under Section 102 and must additionally qualify as "analogous art."[95]

Section 102 contains the requirement for novelty in an invention, and it explicitly defines prior art.[96] An extraordinarily broad amount of information qualifies as prior art, including any printed publication made available to the public prior to filing a patent application.[97] Courts have long held that inventors are charged with constructive knowledge of all prior art.[98] While no real inventor could have such knowledge,[99] the social benefits of this rule are thought to outweigh its costs.[100] Granting patents on existing inventions could prevent the public from using something it already had access to, and remove knowledge from the public domain.[101]

[91] See *Imperial Chem. Indus., Plc v. Danbury Pharmacal, Inc.*, 777 F. Supp. 330, 371–2 (D. Del. 1991) (holding that the skilled person in the chemical industry is an organic chemist with a PhD); see also *Envtl. Designs*, above note 85, at 697 (noting the respective chemical expert witnesses of the parties with extensive backgrounds in sulfur chemistry were skilled persons).

[92] European Patent Office, Guidelines for Examination, www.epo.org/law-practice/legal-texts/html/guidelines/e/g_vii_3.htm ("There may be instances where it is more appropriate to think in terms of a group of persons, e.g. a research or production team, rather than a single person"). See, e.g., *MedImmune v. Novartis Pharm. UK, Ltd* [2012] EWCA Civ. 1234 (evaluating obviousness from the perspective of a "skilled team"). The "[P]atent is addressed to a team of scientists with differing backgrounds in areas such as immunology, in particular antibody structural biology, molecular biology and protein chemistry, but with a common interest in antibody engineering" (*ibid.*). In the United States, the idea that the skilled person could be a group of individuals has been discussed in academic literature, but may not have been explicitly adopted by the courts. See, e.g., J. J. Darrow, The Neglected Dimension of Patent Law's PHOSITA Standard (2009) 23 *Harv. J. Law Technol.* 227, 244, 257. A "skilled persons" standard would seem to be appropriate given that most patents are now filed with more than one inventor. D. Crouch, PHOSITA: Not a Person – People Having Ordinary Skill in the Art, Patently-O (June 7, 2018), https://patentlyo.com/patent/2018/06/phosita-not-a-person-people-having-ordinary-skill-in-the-art.html (noting that most patents have multiple inventors).

[93] This is the second inquiry of the *Graham* analysis described earlier.

[94] See, e.g., *Ryko Mfg.*, above note 20, at 718.

[95] *In re Bigio*, 381 F.3d 1320, 1325 (Fed. Cir. 2004).

[96] 35 USC § 102 (2018).

[97] *Ibid.*, § 102(a)(1); see MPEP § 2152 for a detailed discussion of what constitutes prior art. Almost anything in writing is prior art. "A U.S. patent on the lost wax casting technique was invalidated on the basis of Benvenuto Cellini's 16th century autobiography which makes mention of a similar technique." See M. Ebert, Superperson and the Prior Art (1985) 67 *J. Pat. Trademark Off. Soc.* 657, 658.

[98] In *Mast, Foos, & Co. v. Stover Manufacturing Co.*, 177 US 485, 493 (1900), the Supreme Court applied a presumption that the skilled person is charged with constructive knowledge of all prior art: "Having *all* these various devices before him, and *whatever* the facts may have been, he is chargeable with a knowledge of all pre-existing devices" (emphasis added) (further, "we must presume the patentee was fully informed of everything which preceded him, whether such were the actual fact or not").

[99] See, e.g., *In re Wood*, 599 F.2d 1032, 1036 (CCPA 1979) ("[A]n inventor could not possibly be aware of every teaching in every art").

[100] See *Bonito Boats, Inc. v. Thunder Craft Boats, Inc.*, 489 US 141, 147–8 (1989) (reciting that Thomas Jefferson, the "driving force behind early federal patent policy," believed that "a grant of patent rights in an idea already disclosed to the public [i]s akin to an *ex post facto* law, 'obstruct[ing] others in the use of what they possessed before'" (quoting Letter to Isaac McPherson, above note 41, p. 176)); *Graham*, above note 36, at 5–6 (stating that granting patents on non-novel inventions would remove knowledge from the public domain).

[101] *Graham*, above note 36, at 5–6.

For the purposes of obviousness, prior art under Section 102 must also qualify as analogous. That is to say, the prior art must be in the field of an applicant's endeavor, or reasonably pertinent to the problem with which the applicant was concerned.[102] A real inventor would be expected to focus on this type of information. The "analogous art" rule better reflects practical conditions, and it ameliorates the harshness of the definition of prior art for novelty given that prior art references may be combined for purposes of obviousness, but not novelty.[103] Consequently, for the purposes of obviousness, the skilled person is presumed to have knowledge of all prior art within the field of an invention, as well as prior art reasonably pertinent to the problem the invention solves. Restricting the universe of prior art to analogous art lowers the bar to patentability.[104]

The analogous art requirement was most famously conceptualized in the case of *In re. Winslow*, in which the court explained a decision-maker was to "picture the inventor as working in his shop with the prior art references – which he is presumed to know – hanging on the walls around him."[105] Or, as Judge Learned Hand presciently remarked, "the inventor must accept the position of a mythically omniscient worker in his chosen field. As the arts proliferate with prodigious fecundity, his lot is an increasingly hard one."[106]

MACHINE INTELLIGENCE IN THE INVENTIVE PROCESS

Automating and Augmenting Research

AI, which is to say an algorithm able to perform tasks normally requiring human intelligence, is playing an increasingly important role in innovation.[107] For instance, IBM's flagship AI system "Watson" is being used exploratively to conduct research in drug discovery, as well as clinically to analyze the genes of cancer patients and develop treatment

---

[102]   See, e.g., *Wyers* v. *Master Lock Co.*, 616 F.3d 1231, 1237 (Fed. Cir. 2010) ("Two criteria are relevant in determining whether prior art is analogous: '(1) whether the art is from the same field of endeavor, regardless of the problem addressed, and (2) if the reference is not within the field of the inventor's endeavor, whether the reference still is reasonably pertinent to the particular problem with which the inventor is involved'" (quoting *Comaper Corp.* v. *Antec, Inc.*, 596 F.3d 1343, 1351 (Fed. Cir. 2010)). "Under the correct analysis, any need or problem known in the field of endeavor at the time of the invention and addressed by the patent [or application at issue] can provide a reason for combining the elements in the manner claimed" (*KSR* v. *Teleflex*, above note 11, at 420). Prior art in other fields may sometimes be considered as well (*ibid.* at 417). The general question is whether it would have been "reasonable" for the skilled person to consider a piece of prior art to solve their problem (*In re. Clay*, 966 F.2d 656 (Fed. Cir. 1992)). To be "reasonably pertinent," prior art must "logically [] have commended itself to an inventor's attention in considering his problem" (*ibid.*).

[103]   See *In re. Wood*, above note 99, at 1036 ("The rationale behind this rule precluding rejections based on combination of teachings of references from nonanalogous arts is the realization that an inventor could not possibly be aware of every teaching in every art"). The rule "attempt[s] to more closely approximate the reality of the circumstances surrounding the making of an invention by only presuming knowledge by the inventor of prior art in the field of his endeavor and in analogous arts" (*ibid.*).

[104]   See M. A. Bagley, Internet Business Model Patents: Obvious by Analogy (2001) 7 *Mich. Telecomm. Technol. Law Rev.* 253, 270 (arguing that prior to the analogous arts test references were rarely excluded as prior art); see also J. S. Sherkow, Negativing Invention (2011) *BYU Law Rev.* 1091, 1094–5 (noting that once a relevant piece of prior art is classified as analogous, an obviousness finding is often inevitable).

[105]   *In re. Winslow*, 365 F.2d 1017, 1020 (CCPA 1966).

[106]   *Merit Mfg. Co.* v. *Hero Mfg. Co.*, 185 F.2d 350, 352 (2nd Cir. 1950).

[107]   See, e.g., Data Science Association, Outlook on Artificial Intelligence in the Enterprise (2016), pp. 3, 6, www.datascienceassn.org/sites/default/files/Outlook%20on%20Artificial%20Intelligence%20in%20the%20Enterprise%202016.pdf (a survey of 235 business executives conducted by the National Business Research Institute (NBRI) which found that 38 percent of enterprises were using AI technologies in 2016, and 62 percent will likely use AI technologies by 2018).

plans.[108] In drug discovery, Watson has already identified novel drug targets and new indications for existing drugs.[109] In doing so, Watson may be generating patentable inventions either autonomously or collaboratively with human researchers.[110] In clinical practice, Watson is also automating a once-human function.[111] In fact, according to IBM, Watson can interpret a patient's entire genome and prepare a clinically actionable report in 10 minutes, a task which otherwise requires around 160 hours of work by a team of experts.[112] A recent study by IBM found that Watson's report outperformed the standard practice.[113]

Watson is largely structured as an "expert system," although Watson is not a single program or algorithm – the brand incorporates a variety of technologies.[114] Here, Watson will be considered a single software program in the interests of simplicity. Expert systems are one way of designing AI that solve problems in a specific domain of knowledge using logical rules derived from the knowledge of experts. These were a major focus of AI research in the 1980s.[115] Expert system-based chess-playing programs HiTech and Deep Thought defeated chess masters in 1989, paving the way for another famous IBM algorithm, Deep Blue, to defeat world chess champion Garry Kasparov in 1997.[116] But Deep Blue had limited utility – it was solely designed to play chess. The algorithm was permanently retired after defeating Kasparov.[117]

Google's leading AI system DeepMind is an example of another sort of inventive algorithm. DeepMind uses an artificial neural network, which essentially consists of many highly interconnected processing elements working together to solve specific problems.[118] The design of neural networks is inspired by the way in which the human brain processes information.[119] Like the human brain, neural networks can learn by example and from practice.[120] Examples for neural networks come in the form of data, so more data means improved performance.[121] This has led to data being described as the new oil of the twenty-first century, and the fuel for machine learning.[122] Developers may not be able to understand exactly how a neutral network processes data or generates a particular output.

[108]   IBM, IBM Watson for Drug Discovery, www.ibm.com/watson/health/life-sciences/drug-discovery; IBM, IBM Watson for Genomics, www.ibm.com/watson/health/oncology-and-genomics/genomics.

[109]   Y. Chen, J. D. Elenee Argentinis, and G. Weber, IBM Watson: How Cognitive Computing Can Be Applied to Big Data Challenges in Life Sciences Research (2016) 38 *Clin. Ther.* 688.

[110]   See generally Abbott, above note 3 (discussing the "hypothetical" example of an AI system being used in drug discovery to identify new drug targets and indications for existing drugs).

[111]   K. O. Wrzeszczynski, M. O. Frank, T. Koyama, *et al.*, Comparing Sequencing Assays and Human-Machine Analyses in Actionable Genomics for Glioblastoma (2017) 3 *Neurol. Genet.* e164, http://ng.neurology.org/content/3/4/e164.

[112]   *Ibid.*

[113]   *Ibid.*

[114]   See R. Waters, Artificial Intelligence: Can Watson Save IBM?, *Financial Times* (January 5, 2016), www.ft.com/content/dced8150-b300-11e5-8358-9a82b43f6b2f; see also W. Knight, IBM's Watson Is Everywhere – But What Is It?, *MIT Technology Review* (October 27, 2016), www.technologyreview.com/s/602744/ibms-watson-is-everywhere-but-what-is-it.

[115]   S. J. Russell and P. Norvig, *Artificial Intelligence: A Modern Approach*, 2nd edn. (2002), pp. 22–3.

[116]   IBM, IBM's 100 Icons of Progress: Deep Blue, www.ibm.com/ibm/history/ibm100/us/en/icons/.

[117]   *Ibid.*

[118]   K. Gurney, *An Introduction to Neural Networks* (UCL Press, 1997), pp. 1–4. The first neural network was built in 1951. See, e.g., Russell and Norvig, above note 115.

[119]   See, e.g., V. Mnih, K. Kavukcuoglu, D. Silver, *et al.*, Human-Level Control through Deep Reinforcement Learning (2015) 518 *Nature* 529, 529–33.

[120]   See Gurney, above note 118, pp. 1–4.

[121]   P. Domingos, *The Master Algorithm: How the Quest for the Ultimate Learning Machine Will Remake Our World* (Basic Books, 2015), p. xi.

[122]   See, e.g., M. Palmer, Data Is the New Oil, *ANA Marketing Maestros* (November 3, 2006).

In 2016, DeepMind developed an algorithm known as AlphaGo, which beat a world champion of the traditional Chinese board game Go, and then the world's leading player in 2017.[123] Go was the last traditional board game at which people had been able to outperform algorithms.[124] AlphaGo's feat was widely lauded in the AI community because Go is exponentially more complicated than chess.[125] Current algorithms cannot "solve" Go solely by using "brute force" computation to determine the optimal move to any potential configuration in advance.[126] There are more possible board configurations in Go than there are atoms in the universe.[127] Rather than being pre-programmed with a number of optimal Go moves, DeepMind used a general-purpose algorithm to interpret the game's patterns.[128] DeepMind is now working to beat human players at the popular video game *StarCraft II*.[129]

AI like DeepMind is proving itself and training by playing games, but similar techniques can be applied to other challenges requiring recognition of complex patterns, long-term planning, and decision-making.[130] DeepMind is already being applied to solve practical problems. For instance, it has helped decrease cooling costs at company data-centers.[131] DeepMind is working to develop an algorithm to distinguish between healthy and cancerous tissues, and to evaluate eye scans to identify early signs of diseases leading to blindness.[132] The results of this research may well be patentable.

Ultimately, the developers of DeepMind hope to create AGI.[133] Existing, "narrow," or specific AI (SAI) systems focus on discrete problems or work in specific domains. For instance, "Watson for Genomics" can analyze a genome and provide a treatment plan, and "Chef Watson" can develop new food recipes by combining existing ingredients. However, Watson for Genomics cannot respond to open-ended patient queries about their symptoms. Nor can Chef Watson run a kitchen. New capabilities could be added to Watson to do these things, but Watson can only solve problems it has been programmed to solve.[134] By contrast, AGI would be able to successfully perform any intellectual task a person could.

---

[123]   D. Silver, A. Huang, C. J. Maddison, *et al.*, Mastering the Game of Go with Deep Neural Networks and Tree Search (2016) 529 *Nature* 484, 484–9. In 2015, DeepMind attained "human-level performance in video games" playing a series of class Atari 2600 games (Mnih *et al.*, above note 119, p. 529). See also C. Metz, Google's AlphaGo Continues Dominance with Second Win in China, *Wired* (May 25, 2017), www.wired.com/2017/05/googles-alphago-continues-dominance-second-win-china.

[124]   See R. Haridy, 2017: The Year AI Beat Us at All Our Own Games, *New Atlas* (December 26, 2017), https://newatlas.com/ai-2017-beating-humans-games/52741.

[125]   Silver *et al.*, above note 123.

[126]   *Ibid.*; cf. C. Metz, One Genius' Lonely Crusade to Teach a Computer Common Sense, *Wired* (March 24, 2016), www.wired.com/2016/03/doug-lenat-artificial-intelligence-common-sense-engine (arguing that brute force computation was part of AlphaGo's functionality).

[127] 10^{170}, or thereabouts. Silver *et al.*, above note 123.

[128]   Silver *et al.*, above note 123.

[129]   T. Simonite, Google's AI Declares Galactic War on StarCraft, *Wired* (August 9, 2017), www.wired.com/story/googles-ai-declares-galactic-war-on-starcraft-/. Compared with Go, *StarCraft* is vastly more complex. It involves high levels of strategic thinking and acting with imperfect information. *Ibid.*

[130]   Game playing has long been a proving ground for AI, as far back as what may have been the very first AI program in 1951. See J. Copeland, A Brief History of Computing, *AlanTuring.net* (June 2000), www.alanturing.net/turing_archive/pages/Reference%20Articles/BriefHistofComp.html. That program played checkers and was competitive with amateurs. *Ibid.*

[131]   See Simonite, above note 129.

[132]   C. Baraniuk, Google's DeepMind to Peek at NHS Eye Scans for Disease Analysis, *BBC* (July 5, 2016), www.bbc.com/news/technology-36713308; C. Baraniuk, Google DeepMind Targets NHS Head and Neck Cancer Treatment, *BBC* (August 31, 2016), www.bbc.com/news/technology-37230806.

[133]   Solving Intelligence through Research, *DeepMind*, https://deepmind.com/research.

[134]   See, e.g., Metz, above note 126.

AGI could even be set to the task of self-improvement, resulting in a continuously improving system that surpasses human intelligence – what philosopher Nick Bostrom has termed Artificial SuperIntelligence (ASI).[135] Such an outcome has been referred to as the intelligence explosion or the technological singularity.[136] ASI could then innovate in all areas of technology, resulting in progress at an incomprehensible rate. As the mathematician Irving John Good wrote in 1965, "the first ultraintelligent machine is the last invention that man need ever make."[137]

Experts are divided on when, and if, AGI will be developed. Many industry leaders predict based on historical trends that AGI will occur within the next couple of decades.[138] Others believe the magnitude of the challenge has been underestimated, and that AGI may not be developed in this century.[139] In 2013, hundreds of AI experts were surveyed on their predictions for AGI development.[140] On average, participants predicted a 10 percent likelihood that AGI would exist by 2022, a 50 percent likelihood it would exist by 2040, and a 90 percent likelihood it would exist by 2075.[141] In a similar survey, 42 percent of participants predicted AGI would exist by 2030, and an additional 25 percent predicted AGI by 2050.[142] In addition, 10 percent of participants reported they believed ASI would develop within two years of AGI, and 75 percent predicted this would occur within thirty years.[143] The weight of expert opinion thus holds AGI and superintelligence will exist this century. In the meantime, specific AI is getting ever better at out-competing people at specific tasks – including invention.

Timeline to the Creative Singularity

We are amid a transition from human to algorithm inventors. The following five-phase framework illustrates this transition and divides the history and future of inventive AI into several stages (see Table 16.1).

Previously, in Phase I, all invention was created by people. If a company wanted to solve an industrial problem, it asked a research scientist, or a team of research scientists, to solve the problem. Phase I ended when the first patent was granted for an invention created by an

[135] See generally N. Bostrom, *Superintelligence: Paths, Dangers, Strategies* (Oxford University Press, 2014).

[136] See generally R. Kurzweil, *The Singularity Is Near: When Humans Transcend Biology* (2005).

[137] I. J. Good, Speculations Concerning the First Ultraintelligent Machine (1965) 6 *Advances in Computers* 31, 33:

> Let an ultraintelligent machine be defined as a machine that can far surpass all the intellectual activities of any man however clever. Since the design of machines is one of these intellectual activities, an ultra-intelligent machine could design even better machines; there would then unquestionably be an "intelligence explosion," and the intelligence of man would be left far behind ... Thus the first ultraintelligent machine is the last invention that man need ever make ...

Ibid., pp. 32–3.

[138] P. Sysiak, When Will the First Machine Become Superintelligent?, *AI Revolution* (April 11, 2016), https://medium.com/ai-revolution/when-will-the-first-machine-become-superintelligent-ae5a6f128503.

[139] *Ibid*. In fairness, history also reflects some overly optimistic predictions. In 1970, Marvin Minsky, one of the most famous AI thought leaders, was quoted in *Life Magazine* as stating: "In from three to eight years we will have a machine with the general intelligence of an average human being." B. Darrach, Meet Shaky, the First Electronic Person, *Life* (November 20, 1970), pp. 58B, 66, 68.

[140] See Müller and Bostrom, above note 6.

[141] *Ibid*. Participants were asked to provide an optimistic year for AGI's development (10 percent likelihood), a realistic year (50 percent likelihood), and a pessimistic year (90 percent likelihood). The median responses were 2022 as an optimistic year, 2040 as a realistic year, and 2075 as a pessimistic year. *Ibid*.

[142] See J. Barrat, *Our Final Invention: Artificial Intelligence and the End of the Human Era* (Macmillan, 2013), p. 152.

[143] See Müller and Bostrom, above note 6.

TABLE 16.1 *Evolution of algorithm invention*

Phase	Inventors	Skilled standard	Timeframe
I	Human	Person	Past
II	Human > SAI	Augmented Person	Present
III	Human ~ SAI	Augmented Person ~ SAI	Short Term
IV	SAI ~ AGI > Human	Augmented AGI	Medium Term
V	ASI	ASI	Long Term

SAI = Specific Artificial Intelligence; AGI = Artificial General Intelligence; ASI = Artificial Superintelligence; ~ = competing; > = outcompeting

autonomous algorithm – likely 1998 or earlier.[144] It may be difficult to determine precisely when the first patent was issued for an autonomous algorithm invention, as there is no obligation to report the role of algorithms in patent applications. Still, any number of patents have likely been issued to inventions autonomously generated by algorithms.[145] In 1998, a patent was issued for an invention autonomously developed by a neural network-based system known as the Creativity Machine.[146]

Patents may have been granted on earlier algorithm inventions. For instance, an article published in 1983 describes experiments with an AI program known as Eurisko, in which the program "invent[ed] new kinds of three-dimensional microelectronic devices ... novel designs and design rules have emerged."[147] Eurisko was an early, expert AI system for autonomously discovering new information.[148] It was programmed to operate according to a series of rules known as heuristics, but it was able to discover new heuristics and use these to modify its own programming.[149] To design new microchips, Eurisko was programmed with knowledge of basic microchips along with simple rules and evaluation criteria.[150] It would then combine existing chip structures together to create new designs, or mutate existing entities.[151] The new structure would then be evaluated for interest and either retained or

---

[144] Phase I might also be distinguished by the first time an algorithm invented anything independently of receiving a patent. However, using the first granted patent application is a better benchmark. It is an external measure of a certain threshold of creativity, and it represents the first time an algorithm automated the role of a patent inventor. Of course, there is a degree of subjectivity in a patent examiner determining whether an invention is new, non-obvious, and useful. What is non-obvious to one examiner may be obvious to another. See, e.g., I. M. Cockburn, S. Kortum, and S. Stern, Are All Patent Examiners Equal? The Impact of Characteristics on Patent Statistics and Litigation Outcomes, in W. M. Cohen and S. A. Merrill (eds.), *Patents in the Knowledge-Based Economy* (National Academies Press, 2003) (describing significant inter-examiner variation).

[145] See generally Abbott, above note 1, pp. 1083–91 (describing patents issued for "computational invention").

[146] *Ibid.*, pp. 1083–6.

[147] D. B. Lenat, W. R. Sutherland, and J. Gibbons, Heuristic Search for New Microcircuit Structures: An Application of Artificial Intelligence (1982) 3 *AI Mag.* 17, 17.

[148] Eurisko was created by Douglas Lenat as the successor to the Automated Mathematician (AM). See generally D. B. Lenat and J. S. Brown, Why AM and EURISKO Appear to Work (1983) 23 *AI Mag.* 269, 269–94. AM was an "automatic programming system" that could modify its own code, relying on heuristics (*Ibid.*). Eurisko was a subsequent iteration of the algorithm designed to additionally develop new heuristics and incorporate those into its function (*Ibid.*).

[149] See Lenat *et al.*, above note 147.

[150] *Ibid.*

[151] *Ibid.*

discarded.[152] Several references suggest a patent was granted for one of Eurisko's chip designs in the mid-1980s.[153]

However, after investigating those references for this chapter, they appear to refer to a patent application filed for the chip design by Stanford University in 1980, which the university abandoned for unknown reasons in 1984.[154] Thus, a patent was never issued. Also, as with other publicly described instances of patent applications claiming the output of inventive algorithms, the patent application was filed on behalf of natural persons.[155] In this case, they were the individuals who had built a physical chip based on Eurisko's design.[156]

In the present Phase II, algorithms and people are competing and cooperating at inventive activity. However, in all technological fields, human researchers are the norm and thus best represent the skilled person standard. While AI systems are inventing, it is unclear to what extent this is occurring: inventive algorithm owners may not be disclosing the extent of such algorithms in the inventive process, due to concerns about patent eligibility or because companies generally restrict information about their organizational methods to maintain a competitive advantage. This phase will reward early adopters of inventive algorithms which are able to outperform human inventors at solving specific problems, and whose output can exceed the skilled person standard. In 2006, for instance, NASA recruited an autonomously inventive algorithm to design an antenna that flew on NASA's Space Technology 5 (ST5) mission.[157]

While there may now only be a modest amount of autonomous[158] algorithm invention, human inventors are being widely augmented by creative algorithms. For example, a person may design a new battery using an algorithm to perform calculations, search for information,

---

[152] *Ibid.*

[153] See, e.g., R. Forsyth and C. Naylor, *The Hitchhiker's Guide to Artificial Intelligence IBM PC Basic Version* (Chapman & Hall, 1986), p. 2167; see also M. A. Boden, *The Creative Mind: Myths and Mechanisms* (Routledge, 2004), p. 228.

[154] US provisional patent application SN 144,960, April 29, 1980. Email from Katherine Ku, Director of Stanford Office of Technology Licensing, to author (January 17, 2018) (on file with author). Douglas Lenat, CEO of Cycorp, Inc., who wrote Eurisko and performed the above-mentioned research, reported that this work was done "before the modern rage about patenting things …" and that in his opinion Eurisko had independently created a number of patentable inventions. See Telephone Interview with Douglas Lenat, CEO, Cycorp, Inc. (January 12, 2018). He further reported that after Eurisko came up with the chip design, Professor James Gibbons at Stanford successfully built a chip based on the algorithm's design (*ibid.*). This chip was the subject of a patent application by Stanford, but the application was abandoned in 1984 (US provisional patent application SN 144,960, above). Prior to the present investigation, Stanford had purged its paper file for the application and so no longer had records reflecting the reason for the abandonment (email from Katherine Ku, above). Incidentally, Dr. Lenat is now continuing to develop an expert system-based AI that can use logical deduction and inference reasoning based on "common sense knowledge," as opposed to a system like Watson that recognizes patterns in very large datasets (*ibid.*). He also states that his current company has developed numerous patentable inventions, but that it has not filed for patent protection, because he believes that, at least with regard to software, the downside of patents providing competitors with a roadmap to copying patented technology exceeds the value of a limited-term patent (*ibid.*).

[155] See Abbott, above note 1, pp. 1083–91 (describing instances of "computational invention").

[156] Email From Katherine Ku, above note 154. Whether the individual(s) designing a chip or building a chip would qualify as inventor(s) would depend on the specific facts of the case and who "conceived" of the invention. See generally Abbott, above note 3 (discussing standards for inventorship).

[157] G. S. Hornby, A. Globus, D. Linden, and J. Lohn, Automated Antenna Design with Evolutionary Algorithms, American Institute of Aeronautics & Astronautics (2006), http://alglobus.net/NASAwork/papers/Space2006Antenna.pdf.

[158] As the term is used here, autonomous algorithms are given goals to complete by users, but determine for themselves the means of completing those goals. See R. Abbott, The Reasonable Computer: Disrupting the Paradigm of Tort Liability (2018) 86 *Geo. Wash. Law Rev.* 1. For example, a user could ask an algorithm to design a new battery with certain characteristics, and the algorithm could produce such a design without further human input. In this case, the algorithm would be autonomously inventive and competing with human inventors.

or run simulations on new designs. The algorithm does not meet inventorship criteria, but it does augment the capabilities of a researcher in the same way that human assistants can help reduce an invention to practice. Depending on the industry researchers work in and the problems they are trying to solve, researchers may rarely be unaided by algorithms. The more sophisticated the algorithm, the more it may be able to augment the worker's skills.

Phase III, in the near future, will involve increased competition and cooperation between people and algorithms. In certain industries, and for certain problems, inventive algorithms will become the norm. For example, in the pharmaceutical industry, Watson is now identifying novel drug targets and new indications for existing drugs. Soon, it may be the case that inventive algorithms are the primary means by which new uses for existing drugs are researched. That is a predictable outcome, given the advantage algorithms have over people at recognizing patterns in very large datasets. However, it may be that people still perform the majority of research related to new drug targets. Where the standard varies within a broad field like drug discovery, this can be addressed by defining fields and problems narrowly – for instance, according to the sub-classes currently used by the Patent Office.[159]

Perhaps twenty-five years from now – based on expert opinion – the introduction of AGI will usher in Phase IV. Recall that AGI refers to AI that can be applied generally, as opposed to narrowly in specific fields of art, and that it has intelligence comparable to a person. AGI will compete with human inventors in every field, which makes AGI a natural substitute for the skilled person. Even with this new standard, human inventors may continue to invent – just not as much. An inventor may be a creative genius whose abilities exceed the human average, or a person of ordinary intelligence who has a ground-breaking insight.

Just as SAI outperforms people in certain fields, it will likely be the case that SAI outperforms AGI in certain circumstances. An example of this could be when screening a million compounds for pesticide function lends itself to a "brute force" computational approach. For this reason, SAI could continue to represent the level of ordinary skill in fields in which SAI is the standard, while AGI could replace the skilled person in all other fields. However, the two systems will likely be compatible. A general AI system wanting to play Go could incorporate AlphaGo into its own programming, design its own algorithm like AlphaGo, or even instruct a second algorithm operating AlphaGo.

AGI will change the human–algorithm dynamic in another way. If the algorithm is genuinely capable of performing any intellectual task a person could, it would be capable of setting goals collaboratively with a person, or even by itself. Instead of a person instructing an algorithm to screen a million compounds for pesticide function, a person could merely ask an algorithm to develop a new pesticide. For that matter, an agrochemical company like Bayer could instruct DeepMind to develop any new technology for its business, or just to improve its profitability. Such algorithms should not only be able to solve known problems, but also be able to solve unknown problems.

AGI will continually improve, transforming into ASI. Ultimately, in Phase V, when AGI succeeds in developing artificial superintelligence, it will mean the end of obviousness. Everything will be obvious to a sufficiently intelligent algorithm.

---

[159] See generally USPTO, Overview of the U.S. Patent Classification System (USPC) (2012), www.uspto.gov/sites/default/files/patents/resources/classification/overview.pdf.

Inventive and Skilled Algorithms

For purposes of patent law, an inventive algorithm should be one which generates patentable output while meeting traditional inventorship criteria.[160] Because obviousness focuses on the quality of a patent application's inventive content, it should be irrelevant whether the content comes from a person or an algorithm, or a particular type of algorithm. An algorithm which autonomously generates patentable output, or which does so collaboratively with human inventors where the algorithm meets joint inventorship criteria, is inventive.

Under the present framework, inventive algorithms would not be the equivalent of hypothetical skilled algorithms, just as human inventors are not skilled persons. In fact, it should not be possible to extrapolate about the characteristics of a skilled entity from information about inventive entities. Granted, the Federal Circuit once included the "educational level of the inventor" in its early factor-based test for the skilled person.[161] However, that was only until it occurred to the Federal Circuit that "courts never have judged patentability by what the real inventor/applicant/patentee could or would do. Real inventors, as a class, vary in the capacities from ignorant geniuses to Nobel laureates; the courts have always applied a standard based on an imaginary work of their own devising whom they have equated with the inventor."[162]

What, then, conceptually is a skilled algorithm? An algorithm that anthropomorphizes to the various descriptions courts have given for the skilled person? Such a test might focus on the way in which an algorithm is designed or how it functions. For instance, a skilled algorithm might be a conventional algorithm that operates according to fixed, logical rules, as opposed to an algorithm like DeepMind which can function unpredictably. However, basing a rule on how an algorithm functions might not work for the same reason the Flash of Genius test failed: even leaving aside the significant logistical problem of attempting to figure out how an algorithm is structured or how it generates particular output, patent law should be concerned with whether an algorithm is generating inventive output, not what is going on inside the algorithm.[163] If a conventional algorithm and a neural network were both able to generate the same inventive output, there should be no reason to favor one over the other.

Alternately, the test could focus on an algorithm's capacity for creativity. For example, Microsoft Excel plays a role in a significant amount of inventive activity, but it is not innovative. It applies a known body of knowledge to solve problems with known solutions in a predictable fashion (for example, multiplying values together). However, while Excel may sometimes solve problems that a person could not easily solve without the use of technology, it lacks the ability to engage in almost any inventive activity.[164] Excel is not the equivalent of a skilled algorithm – it is an automaton incapable of ordinary creativity.

Watson in clinical practice may be a better analogy for a skilled worker. Watson analyzes patients' genomes and provides treatment recommendations.[165] Yet, as with Excel, this activity is not innovative. The problem Watson is solving may be more complex than multiplying a series of numbers, but it has a known solution. Watson is identifying known genetic mutations from a patient's genome. Watson is then suggesting known treatments based on

---

[160] See Abbott, above note 1 (arguing algorithms which independently meet human inventorship criteria should be recognized as inventors).
[161] See, e.g., *Envtl. Designs*, above note 88.
[162] *Kimberly-Clark*, above note 88, at 1454 ("[The] hypothetical person is not the inventor, but an imaginary being possessing 'ordinary skill in the art' created by Congress to provide a standard of patentability").
[163] See Abbott, above note 1 (arguing against a subjective standard for computational invention).
[164] Some behaviors like correcting a rogue formula may have a functionally creative aspect, but this is a minimal amount that would not rise to the level of patent conception if performed by a person.
[165] See Wrzeszczynski *et al.*, above note 111.

existing medical literature. Watson is not innovating because it is being applied to solve problems with known solutions, adhering to conventional wisdom.

Unlike Excel, however, Watson could be inventive. For instance, Watson could be given unpublished clinical data on patient genetics and actual drug responses and tasked with determining whether a drug works for a genetic mutation in a way that has not yet been recognized. Traditionally, such findings have been patentable. Watson may be situationally inventive depending on the problem it is solving.

It may be difficult to identify an actual algorithm now which has a "skilled" level of creativity. To the extent an algorithm is creative, in the right circumstances, any degree of creativity might result in inventive output. To be sure, this is similar to the skilled person. A person of ordinary skill, or almost anyone, may have an inventive insight. Characteristics can be imputed to a skilled person, but it is not possible the way the test is applied to identify an actual skilled person or to definitively say what she would have found obvious. The skilled person test is simply a theoretical device for a decision-maker.

Assuming a useful characterization of a skilled algorithm, to determine that a skilled algorithm now represents the average worker in a field, decision-makers would need information about the extent to which such algorithms are used. Obtaining this information may not be practical. Patent applicants could be asked generally about the use and prevalence of algorithms in their fields, but it would be unreasonable to expect applicants to already have, or to obtain, accurate information about general industry conditions. The Patent Office, or another government agency, could attempt to proactively research the use of algorithms in different fields, but this would not be a workable solution. Such efforts would be costly, the Patent Office lacks expertise in this activity, and its findings would inevitably lag behind rapidly changing conditions. Ultimately, there may not be a reliable and low-cost source of information about skilled algorithms right now.

Inventive Is the New Skilled

Having inventive algorithms replace the skilled person may better correspond with real-world conditions. Right now, there are inherent limits to the number and capabilities of human workers. The cost of training and recruiting new researchers is significant, and there are a limited number of people with the ability to perform this work. By contrast, inventive algorithms are software programs which may be copied without additional cost.[166] Once Watson outperforms the average industry researcher, IBM may be able to simply copy Watson and have it replace most of an existing workforce. Copies of Watson could replace individual workers, or a single Watson could do the work of a large team of researchers.

Indeed, as mentioned earlier, in a non-inventive setting, Watson can interpret a patient's entire genome and prepare a clinically actionable report in 10 minutes, as opposed to a team of human experts, which takes around 160 hours.[167] Once Watson is proven to produce better patient outcomes than the human team, it may be unethical to have people underperform a task which Watson can automate. When that occurs, Watson should not only replace the human team at its current facility – it should replace every comparable human team. Watson could similarly automate in an inventive capacity.

Thus, inventive algorithms change the skilled paradigm because once they become the average worker, the average worker becomes inventive. As the outputs of these inventive

---

[166]   A. Kemper, *Valuation of Network Effects in Software Markets: A Complex Networks Approach* (Physica, 2010), p. 37.
[167]   See Wrzeszczynski *et al.*, above note 111.

algorithms become routinized, however, they should no longer be inventive by definition. The widespread use of these algorithms should raise the bar for obviousness, so that these algorithms no longer qualify as inventive, but shift to become skilled algorithms – algorithms which now represent the average worker and are no longer capable of routine invention.[168]

Regardless of the terminology, as algorithms continue to improve, the bar for non-obviousness should rise. To generate patentable output, it may be necessary to use an advanced algorithm that can outperform standard algorithms, or a person or an algorithm will need to have an unusual insight that standard algorithms cannot easily recreate. Inventiveness might also depend on the data supplied to an algorithm, such that only certain data would result in inventive output. Taken to its logical extreme, and given there is no limit to how sophisticated algorithms can become, it may be that everything will one day be obvious to commonly used algorithms.

It is possible to generate reasonably low-cost and accurate information about the use of inventive algorithms. The Patent Office should institute a requirement for patent applicants to disclose the role of algorithms in the inventive process.[169] This disclosure could be structured along the lines of current inventorship disclosure. Right now, applicants must disclose all patent inventors.[170] Failure to do so can invalidate a patent or render it unenforceable.[171] Similarly, applicants should have to disclose when an algorithm autonomously meets inventorship criteria.

These disclosures would only apply to an individual invention. However, the Patent Office could aggregate responses to see whether most inventors in a field (for example, a class or subclass) are human or algorithm. These disclosures would have a minimal burden on applicants compared to existing disclosure requirements and the numerous procedural requirements of a patent application. In addition to helping the Patent Office with determinations of non-obviousness, these disclosures would provide valuable information for purposes of attributing inventorship.[172] They might also be used to develop appropriate innovation policies in other areas.[173]

Skilled People Use Algorithms

The current standard neglects to appropriately take into account the modern importance of algorithms in innovation. Instead of now replacing the skilled person with the skilled algorithm, it would be less of a conceptual change, and administratively easier, to characterize the skilled person as an average worker facilitated by technology. Recall the factor test for the skilled person includes: (1) "type[s] of problems encountered in the art"; (2) "prior art

---

[168]   See *Enzo Biochem, Inc.* v. *Calgene, Inc.*, 188 F.3d 1362, 1374 n.10 (Fed. Cir. 1999) ("In view of the rapid advances in science, we recognize that what may be unpredictable at one point in time may become predictable at a later time").

[169]   It may also be beneficial for applicants to disclose the use of algorithms when they have been part of the inventive process, but where their contributions have not risen to the level of inventorship. Ideally, a detailed disclosure should be provided: applicants should need to disclose the specific software used and the task it performed. In most cases, this would be as simple as noting a program like Excel was used to perform calculations. However, while this information would have value for policymaking, it might involve a significant burden to patent applicants.

[170]   Duty to Disclose Information Material to Patentability, 37 CFR § 1.56 (2018), www.uspto.gov/web/offices/pac/mpep/s2001.html.

[171]   See, e.g., *Advanced Magnetic Closures, Inc.* v. *Rome Fastener Corp.*, 607 F.3d 817, 829–30 (Fed. Cir. 2010) (upholding a district court decision to render a patent unenforceable on the grounds of inequitable conduct for misrepresenting inventorship).

[172]   See Abbott, above note 1 (advocating for acknowledging algorithms as inventors).

[173]   See Abbott and Bogenschneider, above note 5 (arguing the need to monitor automation for adjusting tax incentives).

solutions to those problems"; (3) "rapidity with which innovations are made"; (4) "sophistication of the technology"; and (5) "educational level of active workers in the field."[174] This test could be amended to include: (6) "technologies used by active workers." This would more explicitly take into account the fact that human researchers' capabilities are augmented with algorithms.

Moving forward in time, once the use of inventive algorithms is standard, instead of a skilled person being an inventive algorithm, the skilled person standard could incorporate the fact that technologies used by active workers include inventive algorithms. In future research, the standard practice may be for a worker to ask an inventive algorithm to solve a problem. This could be conceptualized as the inventive algorithm doing the work, or the person doing the work using an inventive algorithm.

Granted, in some instances, using an inventive algorithm may require significant skill – for instance, if the algorithm is only able to generate a certain output by virtue of being supplied with certain data. Determining which data to provide an algorithm, and obtaining that data, may be a technical challenge. Also, it may be the case that significant skill is required to formulate the precise problem to put to an algorithm. In such instances, a person might have a claim to inventorship independent of the algorithm, or a claim to joint inventorship. This is analogous to collaborative human invention where one person directs another to solve a problem. Depending on details of their interaction, and who "conceived" of the invention, one person or the other may qualify as an inventor, or they may qualify as joint inventors.[175] Generally, however, directing another party to solve a problem does not qualify for inventorship.[176] Moreover, after the development of AGI, there may not be a person instructing an algorithm to solve a specific problem.

Whether the future standard becomes an inventive algorithm or a skilled person using an inventive algorithm, the result will be the same: the average worker will be capable of inventive activity. Replacing the skilled person with the inventive algorithm may be preferable doctrinally, because it emphasizes that it is the algorithm which is engaging in inventive activity, rather than the human worker.

The changing use of algorithms also suggests a change to the scope of prior art. The analogous art test was implemented because it is unrealistic to expect inventors to be familiar with anything more than the prior art in their field, and the prior art relevant to the problem they are trying to solve.[177] However, an algorithm is capable of accessing a virtually unlimited amount of prior art. Advances in medicine, physics, or even culinary science may be relevant to solving a problem in electrical engineering. Algorithm augmentation suggests that the analogous arts test should be modified or abolished once inventive algorithms are common, and that there should be no difference in prior art for purposes of novelty and obviousness.[178] The scope of analogous

---

[174]   *GPAC*, above note 13, at 1579.

[175]   "[C]onception is established when the invention is made sufficiently clear to enable one skilled in the art to reduce it to practice without the exercise of extensive experimentation or the exercise of inventive skill" (*Hiatt* v. *Ziegler & Kilgour*, 179 USPQ 757, 763 (Bd. Pat. Interferences 1973)); see also *Gunter* v. *Stream*, 573 F.2d 77, 79 (CCPA 1978).

[176]   *Ex p. Smernoff*, 215 USPQ at 547 ("[O]ne who suggests an idea of a result to be accomplished, rather than the means of accomplishing it, is not a coinventor").

[177]   In 1966, in *Graham*, the Court recognized that "the ambit of applicable art in given fields of science has widened by disciplines unheard of a half century ago … [T]hose persons granted the benefit of a patent monopoly [must] be charged with an awareness of these changed conditions." *Graham*, above note 36, at 19.

[178]   See above Subpart I.E.

prior art has consistently expanded in patent law jurisprudence, and this would complete that expansion.[179]

The Evolving Standard

The skilled person standard should be amended as follows:

1. The test should now incorporate the fact that skilled persons are already augmented by
   algorithms. This could be done by adding "technologies used by active workers" as a
   sixth factor to the Federal Circuit's factor test for the skilled person.
2. Once inventive algorithms become the standard means of research in a field, the skilled
   person should be an inventive algorithm when the standard approach to research in a
   field or with regard to a particular problem is to use an inventive algorithm.
3. When and if AGI is developed, inventive algorithms should become the skilled person
   in all areas, taking into account that AGI may also be augmented by specific AI.

A POST-SKILLED WORLD

This section provides examples of how the Inventive Algorithm Standard could work in practice,
such as by focusing on reproducibility or secondary factors. It then goes on to consider some of the
implications of the new standard. Once the average worker is inventive, there may no longer be a
need for patents to function as innovation incentives. To the extent patents accomplish other
goals such as promoting commercialization and disclosure of information or validating moral
rights, other mechanisms may be found to accomplish these goals with fewer costs.

Application

Mobil Oil Corp. v. *Amoco Chemicals Corp.* concerned complex technology involving compounds known as Zeolites used in various industrial applications.[180] Mobil had developed
new compositions known as ZSM-5 zeolites and a process for using these zeolites as catalysts
in petroleum refining to help produce certain valuable compounds. The company received
patent protection for these zeolites and for the catalytic process.[181] Mobil subsequently sued
Amoco, which was using zeolites as catalysts in its own refining operations, alleging patent
infringement. Amoco counterclaimed seeking a declaration of non-infringement, invalidity,
and unenforceability with regard to the two patents at issue. The case involved complex
scientific issues. The three-week trial transcript exceeds 3,300 pages, and more than 800
exhibits were admitted into evidence.

One of the issues in the case was the level of ordinary skill. An expert for Mobil testified that
the skilled person would have "a bachelor's degree in chemistry or engineering and two to
three years of experience."[182] An expert for Amoco argued the skilled person would have a

---

179 *Innovative Scuba Concepts, Inc.,* v. *Feder Indus., Inc.,* 819 F. Supp. 1487, 1503 (D. Colo. 1993) (discussing the
     expansion of analogous art); see also, e.g., *George. J. Meyer Mfg. Co.* v. *San Marino Elec. Corp.,* 422 F.2d 1285,
     1288 (9th Cir. 1970) (discussing the expansion of analogous art).
180 *Mobil Oil Corp.* v. *Amoco Chems. Corp.,* 779 F. Supp. 1429, 1442–3 (D. Del. 1991).
181 *Ibid.*
182 *Ibid.* at 1443.

doctorate in chemistry and several years of experience.[183] The District Court for the District of Delaware ultimately decided that the skilled person "should be someone with at least a Master's degree in chemistry or chemical engineering or its equivalent, [and] two or three years of experience working in the field."[184]

If a similar invention and subsequent fact pattern happened today, to apply the obviousness standard proposed in this chapter a decision-maker would need to: (1) determine the extent to which inventive technologies are used in the field; (2) characterize the inventive algorithm(s) that best represents the average worker if inventive algorithms are the standard; and (3) determine whether the algorithm(s) would find an invention obvious. The decision-maker is a patent examiner in the first instance,[185] and potentially a judge or jury in the event the validity of a patent is at issue in trial.[186] For the first step, determining the extent to which inventive technologies are used in a field, evidence from disclosures to the Patent Office could be used. That may be the best source of information for patent examiners, but evidence may also be available in the litigation context.

Assume that today most petroleum researchers are human, and that if algorithms are autonomously inventive in this field, it is happening on a small scale. Thus, the Court would apply the skilled person standard. However, the Court would now also consider "technologies used by active workers." For instance, experts might testify that the average industry researcher has access to an algorithm like Watson. They further testify that while Watson cannot autonomously develop a new catalyst, it can significantly assist an inventor. The algorithm provides a researcher with a database containing detailed information about every catalyst used not only in petroleum research, but in all fields of scientific inquiry. Once a human researcher creates a catalyst design, Watson can also test it for fitness together with a predetermined series of variations on any proposed design.

The question for the Court will thus be whether the hypothetical person who holds at least a Master's degree in chemistry or chemical engineering or its equivalent, has two or three years of experience working in the field, *and is using Watson*, would find the invention obvious. It may be obvious, for instance, if experts convincingly testify that the particular catalyst at issue were very closely related to an existing catalyst used outside of the petroleum industry in ammonia synthesis, that any variation was minor, and that an algorithm could do all the work of determining if it were fit for purpose.[187] It might thus have been an obvious design to investigate, and it did not require undue experimentation in order to prove its effectiveness.

Now imagine the same invention and fact pattern occurring approximately ten years into the future, at which point DeepMind, together with Watson and a competing host of AI systems, have been set to the task of developing new compounds to be used as catalysts in petroleum refining. Experts testify that the standard practice is for a person to provide data to an algorithm like DeepMind, specify desired criteria (for example, activity, stability, perhaps even designing around existing patents), and ask the algorithm to develop a new catalyst. From this interaction,

[183]   *Ibid.*
[184]   *Ibid.*
[185]   See USPTO, above note 23 (at the Patent Office, applications are initially considered by a patent examiner, and examiner decisions can be appealed to the Patent Trial and Appeal Board (PTAB)).
[186]   M. A. Lemley, Why Do Juries Decide if Patents Are Valid?, Stanford Law School, Pub. Law & Legal Theory Research Paper Series, Working Paper No. 2306152, 2013, https://ssrn.com/abstract=2306152.
[187]   See *Daiichi Sankyo Co. v. Matrix Labs., Ltd*, 619 F.3d 1346, 1352 (Fed. Cir. 2010) (finding that a "chemist of ordinary skill would have been motivated to select and then to modify a prior art compound (e.g., a lead compound) to arrive at a claimed compound with a reasonable expectation that the new compound would have similar or improved properties compared with the old").

the algorithm will produce a new design. As most research in this field is now performed by inventive algorithms, an algorithm would be the standard for judging obviousness.

The decision-maker would then need to characterize the inventive algorithm(s). It could be a hypothetical algorithm based on general capabilities of inventive algorithms, or a specific algorithm. Using the standard of a hypothetical algorithm would be similar to using the skilled person test, but this test could be difficult to implement. A decision-maker would need to reason what the algorithm would have found obvious, perhaps with expert guidance. It is already challenging for a person to predict what a hypothetical person would find obvious; it would be even more difficult to do so with an algorithm. Algorithms may excel at tasks people find difficult (like multiplying a thousand different numbers together), but even supercomputers struggle with visual intuition, which is mastered by most toddlers.

In contrast, using a specific algorithm should result in a more objective test. This algorithm might be the most commonly used algorithm in a field. For instance, if DeepMind and Watson are the two most commonly used AI systems for research on petroleum catalysts, and DeepMind accounts for 35 percent of the market while Watson accounts for 20 percent, then DeepMind could represent the standard. However, this potentially creates a problem – if DeepMind is the standard, then it would be more likely that DeepMind's own inventions would appear obvious as opposed to the inventions of another algorithm. This might give an unfair advantage to non-market leaders, simply because of their size.

To avoid unfairness, the test could be based on more than one specific algorithm. For instance, both DeepMind and Watson could be selected to represent the standard. This test could be implemented in two different ways. In the first case, if a patent application would be obvious to DeepMind or Watson, then the application would fail. In the second case, the application would have to be obvious to both DeepMind and Watson to fail. The first option would result in fewer patents being granted, with those patents presumably going mainly to disruptive inventive algorithms with limited market penetration, or to inventions made using specialized non-public data. The second option would permit patents where an algorithm is able to outperform its competitors in some material respect. The second option could continue to reward advances in inventive algorithms, and therefore seems preferable.

It may be that relatively few AI systems, such as DeepMind and Watson, end up dominating the research market in a field. Alternately, many different algorithms may each occupy a small share of the market. There is no need to limit the test to two algorithms. To avoid discriminating on the basis of size, all inventive algorithms being routinely used in a field or to solve a particular problem might be considered. However, allowing any algorithm to be considered could allow an underperforming algorithm to lower the standard, and too many algorithms might result in an unmanageable standard. An arbitrary cut-off may be applied based on some percentage of market share. That might still give some advantage to very small entities, but it should be a minor disparity.

After characterizing the inventive algorithm(s), a decision-maker would need to determine whether the inventive algorithm(s) would find an invention obvious. This could broadly be accomplished in one of two ways: either with abstract knowledge of what the algorithms would find obvious, perhaps through expert testimony, or through querying the algorithms. The former would be the more practical option.[188] For example, a petroleum researcher

---

[188] Alternatively, the algorithm could be asked to solve the problem at question and given the relevant prior art. If the algorithm generates the substance of the patent, the invention would be considered obvious. However, this would require a decision-maker to have access to the inventive algorithm. At the application stage, the Patent Office would need to contract with, say, Google to use DeepMind in such a fashion. For that matter, the Patent

experienced with DeepMind might be an expert, or a computer science expert in DeepMind and neural networks. This inquiry could focus on reproducibility.

Finally, a decision-maker will have to go through a similar process if the same invention and fact pattern occurs twenty-five years from now, at which point AGI has theoretically taken over in all fields of research. AGI should have the ability to respond directly to queries about whether it finds an invention obvious. Once AGI has taken over from the average researcher in all inventive fields, it may be widely enough available that the Patent Office could arrange to use it for obviousness queries. In the litigation context, it may be available from opposing parties. If courts cannot somehow access AGI, they may still have to rely on expert evidence.

Reproducibility

Even if an inventive algorithm standard is the appropriate theoretical tool for non-obviousness, it still requires certain somewhat subjective limitations, and decision-makers may still have difficulty with administration. Still, the new standard only needs to be slightly better than the existing standard to be an administrative success.

A test focused on reproducibility, based on the ability of the algorithm selected to represent the standard being able to independently reproduce the invention, offers some clear advantages over the current skilled person standard, which results in inconsistent and unpredictable outcomes.[189] Courts have "provided almost no guidance concerning either what degree of ingenuity is necessary to meet the standard or how a decisionmaker is supposed to evaluate whether the differences between the invention and prior art meet this degree."[190] This leaves decision-makers in the unenviable position of trying to subjectively establish what another person would have found obvious. Worse, this determination is to be made in hindsight with the benefit of a patent application. On top of that, judges and juries lack scientific expertise.[191] In practice, decision-makers may read a patent application, decide that they know obviousness when they see it, and then reason backward to justify their findings.[192]

Office might use DeepMind not only to decide whether inventions are obvious, but to automate the entire patent examination process. At trial, if Google is party to a lawsuit, an opposing party might subpoena use of the algorithm. However, if Google is not a party, it might be unreasonable to impose on Google for access to DeepMind.

189   See Federal Trade Commission, above note 15 (discussing objections to the skilled person standard).
190   Mandel, above note 18, p. 64.
191   As Judge Learned Hand wrote:

I cannot stop without calling attention to the extraordinary condition of the law which makes it possible for a man without any knowledge of even the rudiments of chemistry to pass upon such questions as these. The inordinate expense of time is the least of the resulting evils, for only a trained chemist is really capable of passing upon such facts … How long we shall continue to blunder along without the aid of unpartisan and authoritative scientific assistance in the administration of justice, no one knows; but all fair persons not conventionalized by provincial legal habits of mind ought, I should think, unite to effect some such advance.

Parke-Davis & Co. v. *H.K. Mulford Co.*, 189 F. 95, 115 (SDNY 1911). See also *Safety Car Heating & Lighting Co.* v. *Gen. Elec. Co.*, 155 F.2d 937, 939 (1946) ("Courts, made up of laymen as they must be, are likely either to underrate, or to overrate, the difficulties in making new and profitable discoveries in fields with which they cannot be familiar …"); see also D. Lichtman and M. A. Lemley, Rethinking Patent Law's Presumption of Validity (2007) 60 *Stan. Law Rev.* 45, 67 ("District Court judges are poorly equipped to read patent documents and construe technical patent claims. Lay juries have no skill when it comes to evaluating competing testimony about the originality of a technical accomplishment").
192   *Jacobellis* v. *Ohio*, 378 US 184, 197 (1964) (Stewart, J., dissenting). This was later recognized as a failed standard. *Miller* v. *California*, 413 US 15, 47–8 (1973) (Brennan, J., dissenting) (obscenity cases similarly relying on the Elephant Test).

This is problematic because patents play a critical role in the development and commercialization of products, and patent holders and potential infringers should have a reasonable degree of certainty about whether patents are valid. A more determinate standard would make it more likely the Patent Office would apply a single standard consistently and result in fewer judicially invalidated patents. To the extent algorithm reproducibility is a more objective standard, this would seem to address many of the problems inherent in the current standard.

On the other hand, reproducibility comes with its own baggage. Decision-makers have difficulty imagining what another person would find obvious, and it would probably be even more difficult to imagine in the abstract what an algorithm could reproduce. More evidence might need to be supplied in patent prosecution and during litigation, perhaps in the format of analyses performed by inventive algorithms, to demonstrate whether particular output was reproducible. This might also result in a greater administrative burden.

In some instances, reproducibility may be dependent on access to data. A large health insurer might be able to use Watson to find new uses for existing drugs by giving Watson access to proprietary information on its millions of members. Or, the insurer might license its data to drug discovery companies using Watson for this purpose. Without that information, another inventive algorithm might not be able to recreate Watson's analysis.

This too is analogous to the way in which data is used now in patent applications: obviousness is viewed in light of the prior art, which does not include non-public data relied upon in a patent application. The rationale here is that this rule incentivizes research to produce and analyze new data. Yet, as algorithms become highly advanced, it is likely that the importance of proprietary data will decrease. More advanced algorithms may be able to do more with less.

Finally, reproducibility would require limits. For instance, an algorithm which generates semi-random output might eventually recreate the inventive concept of a patent application if it were given unlimited resources. However, it would be unreasonable to base a test on what an algorithm would reproduce given, say, 7.5 million years.[193] The precise limits that should be placed on reproducibility might depend on the field in question, and what best reflected the actual use of inventive algorithms in research. For instance, when asked to design a new catalyst in the petroleum industry, Watson might be given access to all prior art and publicly available data, and then given a day to generate output.

An Economic vs. Cognitive Standard

The skilled person standard received its share of criticism even before the arrival of inventive algorithms.[194] The inquiry focuses on the degree of cognitive difficulty in conceiving an

---

[193] This brings to mind a super-intelligent AI system, "Deep Thought," which famously, and fictionally, took 7.5 million years to arrive at the "Answer to the Ultimate Question of Life, the Universe, and Everything." D. Adams, *The Hitchhiker's Guide to the Galaxy*, rev. edn. (Pan Books, 2001), p. 180. The answer was 42 (*ibid.*, p. 188).

[194] See, e.g., Chiang, above note 18, p. 49 (as one commentator noted about the test as articulated by the Supreme Court in *Graham*, it gives "all the appearance of expecting a solution to appear out of thin air once the formula was followed. The lack of an articulable rule meant that determinations of obviousness took the appearance – and arguably the reality – of resting on judicial whim ..." (footnote omitted)); Abramowicz and Duffy, above note 8, p. 1598; G. N. Mandel, Patently Non-Obvious: Empirical Demonstration that the Hindsight Bias Renders Patent Decisions Irrational (2006) 67 *Ohio St. Law J.* 1391 (discussing problems with hindsight in non-obviousness inquiries); G. N. Mandel, Another Missed Opportunity: The Supreme Court's Failure to Define Nonobviousness or Combat Hindsight Bias in KSR v. Teleflex (2008) 12 *Lewis & Clark Law Rev.* 323.

invention, but fails to explain what it actually means for differences to be obvious to an average worker. The approach lacks both a normative foundation and a clear application.[195]

In *Graham*, the Supreme Court's seminal opinion on non-obviousness, the Court attempted to supplement the test with more "objective" measures by looking to real-world evidence about how an invention was received in the marketplace.[196] Rather than technological features, these "secondary" considerations focus on "economic and motivational" features, such as commercial success, unexpected results, long-felt but unsolved needs, and the failure of others.[197] Since *Graham*, courts have also considered, among other things, patent licensing,[198] professional approval,[199] initial skepticism,[200] near-simultaneous invention,[201] and copying.[202] Today, while decision-makers are required to consider secondary evidence when available, the importance of these factors varies significantly.[203] *Graham* endorsed the use of secondary considerations, but their precise use and relative importance have never been made clear.[204]

An existing vein of critical scholarship has advocated for adopting a more economic than cognitive non-obviousness inquiry – for example, through greater reliance on secondary considerations.[205] This would reduce the need for decision-makers to try to make sense of complex technologies, and it could reduce hindsight bias.[206]

Theoretically, in *Graham*, the Court articulated an inducement standard, which dictates that patents should only be granted to "those inventions which would not be disclosed or devised but for the inducement of a patent."[207] But in practice, the inducement standard has been largely ignored due to concerns over application.[208] For instance, few, if any, inventions

---

195   See Abramowicz and Duffy, above note 8, p. 1603 ("[N]either *Graham* nor in subsequent cases has the Supreme Court attempted either to reconcile the inducement standard with the statutory text or to provide a general theoretical or doctrinal foundation for the inducement standard").
196   See *Graham*, above note 36, at 17; MPEP § 2144.
197   *Ibid.* Additional secondary considerations have since been proposed. See, e.g., A. Blair-Stanek, Increased Market Power as a New Secondary Consideration in Patent Law (2009) 58 *Am. Univ. Law Rev.* 707 (arguing for whether an invention provides an inventor with market power); Abramowicz and Duffy, above note 8, p. 1656 (proposing changing commercial success to "unexpected commercial success," adding as a consideration of the "cost of the experimentation leading to the invention," and a few additional considerations).
198   See, e.g., *SIBIA Neurosciences, Inc. v. Cadus Pharm. Corp.*, 225 F.3d 1349, 1358 (Fed. Cir. 2000).
199   See, e.g., *Vulcan Eng'g Co. v. Fata Aluminum, Inc.*, 278 F.3d 1366, 1373 (Fed. Cir. 2002).
200   See, e.g., *Metabolite Labs., Inc. v. Lab. Corp. of Am. Holdings*, 370 F.3d 1354, 1368 (Fed. Cir. 2004).
201   See, e.g., *Ecolochem, Inc. v. S. Cal. Edison Co.*, 227 F.3d 1361, 1379 (Fed. Cir. 2000).
202   See, e.g., *ibid.* at 1377. See also M. A. Lemley, Should Patent Infringement Require Proof of Copying? (2007) 105 *Mich. Law Rev.* 1525, 1534–5.
203   See MPEP § 2144; Durie and Lemley, above note 18, pp. 996–7.
204   See, e.g., D. Whelan, A Critique of the Use of Secondary Considerations in Applying the Section 103 Nonobviousness Test for Patentability (1987) 28 *BC Law Rev.* 357.
205   See, e.g., Merges, above note 18, p. 19 (arguing for patentability to be based on an *a priori* degree of uncertainty, that "rewards one who successfully invents when the uncertainty facing her prior to the invention makes it more likely than not that the invention won't succeed" (emphasis omitted)); Chiang, above note 18, p. 42 (arguing for a utilitarian standard, such that "[a]n invention should receive a patent if the accrued benefits before independent invention outweigh the costs after independent invention"); Mandel, above note 18, p. 62 (arguing for non-obviousness to be based on "how probable the invention would have been for a person having ordinary skill in the art working on the problem that the invention solves"); Durie and Lemley, above note 18, pp. 1004–7 (arguing for a greater reliance on secondary considerations); Duffy, above note 18, p. 343 (arguing a timing approach to determining obviousness); Devlin and Sukhatme, above note 18; Abramowicz and Duffy, above note 18, p. 1598 (arguing for an inducement standard).
206   *Graham, ibid.*, at 36 ("[Secondary considerations] may also serve to 'guard against slipping into use of hindsight'" (citation omitted)). See also H. F. Schwartz and R. J. Goldman, *Patent Law and Practice*, 6th ed. (BNA Books, 2008), pp. 90–1.
207   *Graham*, above note 36, at 11.
208   See Abramowicz and Duffy, above note 18, pp. 1594–5.

would never be disclosed or devised given an unlimited time frame. Patent incentives may not increase, so much as accelerate, invention.[209] This suggests that an inducement standard would at least need to be modified to include some threshold for the quantum of acceleration needed for patentability. Too high a threshold would fail to provide adequate innovation incentives, but too low a threshold would be similarly problematic. Just as inventions will be eventually disclosed without patents given enough time, patents on all inventions could marginally speed the disclosure of just about everything, but a trivial acceleration would not justify the costs of patents. An inducement standard would thus require a somewhat arbitrary threshold in relation to how much patents should accelerate the disclosure of information, as well as a workable test to measure acceleration.[210] To be sure, an economic test based on the inducement standard would have challenges, but it might be an improvement over the current cognitive standard.[211]

The widespread use of inventive algorithms may provide the impetus for an economic focus. After inventive algorithms become the standard way that R&D is conducted in a field, courts could increase reliance on secondary factors. For instance, patentability may depend on how costly it was to develop an invention, and the *ex ante* probability of success.[212] There is no reason an inventive algorithm cannot be thought of, functionally, as an economically motivated rational actor. The test would raise the bar to patentability in fields where the cost of invention decreases over time due to inventive algorithms.

Other Alternatives

Courts may maintain the current skilled person standard and decline to consider the use of algorithms in obviousness determinations. However, this means that as research is augmented and then automated by algorithms, the average worker will routinely generate patentable output. The dangers of such a standard for patentability are well-recognized.[213] A low obviousness requirement can "stifle, rather than promote, the progress of the useful arts."[214]

Concerns already exist that the current bar to patentability is too low, and that a patent "anti-commons" with excessive private property is resulting in "potential economic value … disappear[ing] into the 'black hole' of resource underutilization."[215] It is expensive for firms interested in making new products to determine whether patents cover a particular innova-tion, evaluate those patents, contact patent owners, and negotiate licenses.[216] In many cases,

---

[209] See, e.g., Y. Barzel, Optimal Timing of Innovations (1968) 50 *Rev. Econ. Stats.* 348, 348; J. F. Duffy, Rethinking the Prospect Theory of Patents (2004) 71 *Univ. Chi. Law Rev.* 439, 444.

[210] Abramowicz and Duffy, above note 18, p. 1599 (proposing a "substantial period of time").

[211] *Ibid.*, p. 1663.

[212] *Ibid.*

[213] See, e.g., A. B. Jaffe and J. Lerner, *Innovation and Its Discontents: How Our Broken Patent System Is Endangering Innovation and Progress, and What to Do about It* (Princeton University Press, 2004), pp. 32–5, 75, 119–23, 145–9 (criticizing the Patent Office for granting patents on obvious inventions); National Research Council, *A Patent System for the 21st Century* (National Academies Press, 2004), pp. 87–95 (criticizing lenient non-obviousness standards); M. Sag and K. Rohde, Patent Reform and Differential Impact (2007) 8 *Minn. J. Law Sci. Technol.* 1, 2 ("Academics, business leaders, and government officials have all expressed concern that too many patents are issued for [obvious] inventions").

[214] *KSR v. Teleflex*, above note 11, at 427.

[215] J. M. Buchanan and Y. J. Yoon, Symmetric Tragedies: Commons and Anticommons (2000) 43 *J. Law Econ.* 1, 2; accord D. L. Burk and M. A. Lemley, *The Patent Crisis and How the Courts Can Solve It* (University of Chicago Press, 2009) (arguing for a heightened bar to patentability).

[216] See generally M. A. Lemley, Ignoring Patents (2008) *Mich. St. Law Rev.* 19, 25–6 (describing various costs associated with innovation in patent heavy industries).

patent owners may not wish to license their patents, even if they are non-practicing entities that do not manufacture products themselves.[217] Firms that want to make a product may thus be unable to find and license all the rights they need to avoid infringing. Adding to this morass, most patents turn out to be invalid or not infringed in litigation.[218] Excessive patenting can thus slow innovation, destroy markets, and, in the case of patents on some essential medicines, even cost lives.[219] Failing to raise the bar to patentability once the use of inventive algorithms is widespread would significantly exacerbate this anti-commons effect.

Instead of updating the skilled person standard, courts might determine that inventive algorithms are incapable of inventive activity, much as the US Copyright Office has determined that non-human authors cannot generate copyrightable output.[220] In this case, otherwise patentable inventions might not be eligible for patent protection, unless provisions were made for the inventor to be the first person to recognize the algorithm output as patentable. However, this would not be a desirable outcome. As I have argued elsewhere, providing intellectual property protection for algorithm-generated inventions would incentivize the development of inventive algorithms, which would ultimately result in additional invention.[221] This is most consistent with the constitutional rationale for patent protection "[t]o promote the Progress of Science and useful Arts, by securing for limited Times to Authors and Inventors the exclusive Right to their respective Writings and Discoveries."[222]

Incentives without Patents?

Today, there are strong incentives to develop inventive algorithms. Inventions by these algorithms have value independent of intellectual property protection, but they should also be eligible for patent protection. People may apply as inventors for recognizing the inventive nature of an algorithm's output,[223] or more ambitiously, inventive algorithms may be recognized as inventors, resulting in stronger and fairer incentives.

Once inventive algorithms set the baseline for patentability, standard inventive algorithms, as well as people, should have difficulty obtaining patents. It is widely thought that setting a non-

---

[217] See D. L. Schwartz and J. P. Kesan, Analyzing the Role of Non-Practicing Entities in the Patent System (2014) 99 *Cornell Law Rev.* 425.

[218] See M. A. Lemley and C. Shapiro, Probabilistic Patents (2005) 19 *J. Econ. Persp.* 75, 80.

[219] See M. A. Heller, The Tragedy of the Anticommons: Property in the Transition From Marx to Markets (1998) 111 *Harv. Law Rev.* 621; see also M. Heller, *The Gridlock Economy: How Too Much Ownership Wrecks Markets, Stops Innovation and Costs Lives* (Basic Books, 2008); see also M. A. Heller and R. S. Eisenberg, Can Patents Deter Innovation? The Anticommons in Biomedical Research (1998) 280 *Science* 698.

[220] This has been a policy of the Copyright Office since at least 1984. See US Copyright Office, Compendium of US Copyright Office Practices, 3rd edn. (2014), § 306. The Compendium of US Copyright Office Practices elaborates on the "human authorship" requirement by stating: "The term 'authorship' implies that, for a work to be copyrightable, it must owe its origin to a human being" (*ibid.*). It further elaborates on the phrase "[w]orks not originated by a human author" by stating: "In order to be entitled to copyright registration, a work must be the product of human authorship. Works produced by mechanical processes or random selection without any contribution by a human author are not registrable" (*ibid.*, § 503.03(a)).

[221] See generally Abbott, above note 1.

[222] US Constitution, art. I, § 8, cl. 8.

[223] Conception requires contemporaneous recognition and appreciation of the invention. See *Invitrogen Corp.* v. *Clontech Labs., Inc.*, 429 F.3d 1052, 1064 (Fed. Cir. 2005) (noting that the inventor must have actually made the invention and understood the invention to have the features that comprise the inventive subject matter at issue); see also, e.g., *Silvestri* v. *Grant*, 496 F.2d 593, 597 (CCPA 1974) ("[A]n accidental and unappreciated duplication of an invention does not defeat the patent right of one who, though later in time, was the first to recognize that which constitutes the inventive subject matter").

obviousness standard too high would reduce the incentives for innovators to invent and disclose. Yet, once inventive algorithms are normal, there should be less need for patent incentives.[224] Once the average worker is inventive, inventions will "occur in the ordinary course."[225] Algorithm inventions will be self-sustaining. In addition, the heightened bar might result in a technological arms race to create ever more intelligent algorithms capable of outdoing the standard. That would be a desirable outcome in terms of incentivizing innovation.

Even after the widespread use of inventive algorithms, patents may still be desirable. For instance, patents may be needed in the biotechnology and pharmaceutical industries to commercialize new technologies. The biopharma industry claims that new drug approvals cost around $2.2 billion and take an average of eight years.[226] This cost is largely due to resource-intensive clinical trials required to prove safety and efficacy. Once a drug is approved, it is often relatively easy for another company to recreate the approved drug. Patents thus incentivize the necessary levels of investment to commercialize a product given that patent holders can charge monopoly prices for their approved products during the term of a patent.

Yet, patents are not the only means of promoting product commercialization. Newly approved drugs and biologics, for example, receive a period of market exclusivity during which time no other party can sell a generic or biosimilar version of the product. Newly approved biologics, for instance, receive a twelve-year exclusivity period in the United States. Because of the length of time it takes to get a new biologic approved, the market exclusivity period may exceed the term of any patent an originator company has on its product. A heightened bar to patentability may lead to greater reliance on alternative forms of intellectual property protection, such as market exclusivity, prizes, grants, or tax incentives.[227]

With regard to disclosure, without the ability to receive patent protection, owners of inventive algorithms may choose not to disclose their discoveries and rely on trade secret protection. However, with an accelerated rate of technological progress, intellectual property holders would run a significant risk that their inventions would be independently recreated by inventive algorithms.

Depending on the type of innovation, industry, and competitive landscape, business ventures may be successful without patents, and patent protection is not sought for all potentially patentable inventions.[228] In fact, "few industries consider patents essential."[229] For instance,

---

[224] See generally M. A. Lemley, IP in a World without Scarcity, Stanford Public Law, Working Paper No. 2413974 (2014), http://dx.doi.org/10.2139/ssrn.2413974 (arguing new technologies that reduce costs will weaken the case for IP).

[225] *KSR* v. *Teleflex*, above note 11, at 402.

[226] J. A. DiMasi, H. G. Grabowski, and R. W. Hansen, Innovation in the Pharmaceutical Industry: New Estimates of R&D Costs (2016) 47 *J. Health Econ.* 20–33.

[227] See generally D. J. Hemel and L. Larrimore Ouellette, Beyond the Patents-Prizes Debate (2013) 92 *Tex. Law Rev.* 303 (describing various non-traditional intellectual property incentives).

[228] B. Hall, C. Helmers, M. Rogers, and V. Sena, Intellectual Property Office, The Use of Alternatives to Patents and Limits to Incentives (2012), p. 2, www.ipo.gov.uk/ipresearch-patalternative.pdf; see also R. C. Dreyfuss, Does IP Need IP? Accommodating Intellectual Production Outside the Intellectual Property Paradigm (2010) 31 *Cardozo Law Rev.* 1437, 1439; see also D. Fagundes, Talk Derby to Me: Intellectual Property Norms Governing Roller Derby Pseudonyms (2012) 90 *Tex. Law Rev.* 1094, 1146 (describing norm-based protections that function effectively in the absence of traditional IP). Patent holders are only successful in about a quarter of cases that are litigated to a final disposition and appealed. P. M. Janicke and L. Ren, Who Wins Patent Infringement Cases? (2006) 34 *AIPLA QJ* 1, 8. Fewer than 2 percent of patents are ever litigated, and only about 0.1 percent go to trial (Lemley and Shapiro, above note 218, p. 79). In cases where the validity of a patent is challenged, about half of the time the patent is invalidated (Allison and Lemley, above note 19, p. 205).

[229] Merges, above note 18, p. 19.

patents are often considered a critical part of biotechnology corporate strategy, but often ignored in the software industry.[230] On the whole, a relatively small percentage of firms patent, even among firms conducting R&D.[231] Most companies do not consider patents crucial to business success.[232] Other types of intellectual property such as trademark, copyright, and trade secret protection, combined with "alternative" mechanisms such as first-mover advantage and design complexity, may protect innovation even in the absence of patents.[233]

A Changing Innovation Landscape

Inventive algorithms may result in further consolidation of wealth and intellectual property in the hands of large corporations like Google and IBM. Large enterprises may be the most likely developers of inventive algorithms due to their high development costs.[234] A counterbalance to additional wealth disparity could be broad societal gains. The public would stand to gain access to a tremendous amount of innovation – innovation which might be significantly delayed or never come about without inventive algorithms. In fact, concerns about industry consolidation are another basis for revising the obviousness inquiry. The widespread use of inventive algorithms may be inevitable, but raising the bar to patentability would make it so that inventions which would naturally occur would be less likely to receive protection. To the extent market abuses such as price gouging and supply shortages are a concern, protections are, at least theoretically, built into patent law to protect consumers against such problems.[235] For example, the government could exercise its march in rights or issue compulsory licenses.[236]

Inventive algorithms may ultimately automate knowledge work and render human researchers redundant. While past technological advances have resulted in increased rather than decreased employment, the technological advances of the near future may be different.[237] There will be fewer limits to what algorithms will be able to do, and greater access to algorithms. Automation should generate innovation with net societal gains, but it may also contribute to unemployment, financial disparities, and decreased social mobility.[238] It is important that policymakers act to ensure that automation benefits everyone – for instance, by investing in retraining and social benefits for workers rendered technologically unemployed.[239] Ultimately, patent law alone will not determine whether automation occurs. Even without the ability to receive patent protection, once inventive algorithms are significantly more efficient than human researchers, they will replace people.

---

[230]   See generally Lemley and Shapiro, above note 218.
[231]   *Ibid.*
[232]   *Ibid.*
[233]   *Ibid.*
[234]   See J. Carter, The Most Powerful Supercomputers in the World – and What They Do, *TECHRADAR* (December 13, 2014), www.techradar.com/news/computing/the-most-powerful-supercomputers-in-the-world-and-what-they-do-1276865 (noting that most advanced computer systems are owned by governments and large businesses).
[235]   See Abbott, above note 26 (discussing patent law protections against practices including "evergreening").
[236]   See *ibid.*, p. 345 (explaining India's issuance of a compulsory license).
[237]   Abbott and Bogenschneider, above note 5; see "Obviousness," above.
[238]   *Ibid.*
[239]   *Ibid.*

CONCLUSION

Prediction is very difficult, especially about the future.[240]

In the past, patent law has reacted slowly to technological change. For instance, it was not until 2013 that the Supreme Court decided human genes should be unpatentable.[241] By then, the Patent Office had been granting patents on human genes for decades,[242] and more than 50,000 gene-related patents had been issued.[243]

Eminent technologists now predict that AI is going to revolutionize the way in which innovation occurs in the near to medium-term future. Much of what we know about intellectual property law, while it might not be wrong, has not been adapted to where we are headed. The principles that guide patent law need to be, if not rethought, then at least retooled in respect of inventive algorithms. We should be asking what our goals are for these new technologies, what we want our world to look like, and how the law can help make it so.

[240] A. K. Ellis, *Teaching and Learning Elementary Social Studies* (Allyn & Bacon, 1970), p. 56 (quoting physicist Niels Bohr).

[241] *Ass'n for Molecular Pathology*, above note 29.

[242] See, e.g., US Patent No. 4,447,538 (filed February 5, 1982) (a patent issued in 1984 which claims the human *Chorionic Somatomammotropin* gene).

[243] R. Cook-Deegan and C. Heaney, Patents in Genomics and Human Genetics (2010) 11 *Ann. Rev. Genomics & Hum. Genetics* 383, 384 ("In April 2009, the U.S. Patent and Trademark Office (USPTO) granted the 50,000th U.S. patent that entered the DNA Patent Database at Georgetown University. That database includes patents that make claims mentioning terms specific to nucleic acids (e.g., DNA, RNA, nucleotide, plasmid, etc.).").

17

Software Patenting and Section 101's Gatekeeping Function

*Andrew Chin**

INTRODUCTION

Software-related inventions have had an uneasy relationship with the patent-eligible subject matter requirement of Section 101 of the Patent Act.[1] In applying the requirement, the Supreme Court has historically characterized mathematical algorithms and formulas *simpliciter* as sufficiently analogous to laws of nature to warrant judicial exclusion as abstract ideas.[2] The Court has also found "the mere recitation of a generic computer" in a patent claim as tantamount to "adding the words 'apply it with a computer,'" a mere drafting effort that does not relieve "the pre-emption concern that undergirds our § 101 jurisprudence."[3] Lower courts, patent counsel, and commentators have struggled to apply these broad principles to specific software-related inventions, a difficulty largely rooted in the many forms and levels of abstraction in which mathematical algorithms can be situated, both in the computing context and in the terms of a patent claim.[4] Consequently, widely varying approaches to claiming inventions that involve algorithms in their use have perennially complicated efforts to develop a coherent doctrine of unpatentable abstract ideas.

In the computing context, the term "algorithm" can refer to any "finite sequence of steps" that accomplishes a given task.[5] As an algorithm is usually described in the computer science literature, it is common for some or all of the "steps" themselves to be tasks that can be decomposed further into sequences of more basic steps. A computer system thereby typically

[*] Professor of Law, University of North Carolina; JD, Yale Law School; D.Phil. (Mathematics), University of Oxford.

[1] See 35 USC § 101: "Whoever invents or discovers any new and useful process, machine, manufacture, or composition of matter, or any new and useful improvement thereof, may obtain a patent therefor, subject to the conditions and requirements of this title."

[2] See *Parker* v. *Flook*, 437 US 584, 590 (1978) (citing *Gottschalk* v. *Benson*, 409 US 63, 67 (1972)): "Reasoning that an algorithm, or mathematical formula, is like a law of nature, *Benson* applied the established rule that a law of nature cannot be the subject of a patent."

[3] See *Alice Corp.* v. *CLS Bank Int'l*, 134 S.Ct. 2358 (2014) (citing *Mayo Collaborative Servs.* v. *Prometheus Labs., Inc.*, 132 S.Ct. 1289, 1294–301 (2012)).

[4] See, e.g., J. A. Lefstin, The Three Faces of Prometheus: A Post-Alice Jurisprudence of Abstractions (2015) 16 *NC J. Law Technol.* 688 ("The pivotal question . . . perhaps for software patents more generally, is whether specific information-processing techniques are abstract ideas"); see generally J. Bessen and M. J. Meurer, *Patent Failure: How Judges, Bureaucrats and Lawyers Put Innovators at Risk* (Princeton University Press, 2008), p. 201 (arguing that "the abstractness of software technology inherently makes it more difficult to place limits on abstract claims in software patents").

[5] See *Microsoft Computer Dictionary* (1999), p. 19 (defining "algorithm" as "[a] finite sequence of steps for solving a logical or mathematical problem or performing a task").

involves numerous "abstraction layers," with each successive, more abstract, layer implementing its own set of functions through various algorithms comprising sequences of functions previously implemented by the more concrete layers below.[6] To make matters even more complicated, abstraction layers often provide multiple distinct implementations and interpretations of a single function, using a versatile programming technique known as "indirection."[7] For example, the FreeBSD operating system uses indirection to implement a single "read system call" operation on disparate file-system organizations such as those in PC hard drives, CD-ROMs, and USB sticks.[8]

As of this writing, the Senate Judiciary Subcommittee on Courts, Intellectual Property and the Internet is considering draft legislation to overhaul existing law relating to patent-eligible subject matter, inter alia, by specifying that (1) "the provisions of section 101 shall be construed in favor of eligibility," (2) "no implicit or other judicially created exceptions to subject matter eligibility . . . shall be used to determine patent eligibility under section 101, and all cases establishing or interpreting those exceptions to eligibility are hereby abrogated," and (3) "eligibility . . . under section 101 shall be determined without regard to . . . any other considerations relating to sections 102, 103, or 112."[9] According to the bill's drafters, the new statute codifies the principle that "statutory exceptions should be the only basis for excluding inventions from eligibility and courts may not expand them."[10] The text of the proposed statute, however, simply recites the already existing categories of statutory subject matter (process, machine, manufacture, composition of matter, improvement) without any mention of exceptions, while specifying that patentable utility requires "specific and practical utility in any field of technology through human intervention."[11]

As the judicially created exceptions from patent-eligible subject matter hang in the balance, it is a critical time to examine the form and function of the courts' patent-eligibility jurisprudence to date, particularly in the software field. This chapter identifies and reviews three conceptually divergent judicial approaches to the patent-eligibility of software-related inventions.

The first section of this chapter, "The 'New Machine' Principle," examines courts' efforts in past decades to ground the eligibility of some software-related inventions in the statutory category of "new and useful . . . machine[s]."[12] This approach was problematic insofar as it tended to obscure considerations of the underlying mathematical algorithm in other aspects of the patentability analysis. The proposed legislation would likely send courts down this road again, in that software-related inventions would fall under the "process" and "machine" statutory categories, with a general-purpose computer programmed to perform any practical function being eligible as a "machine."

The second section, "Pre-emption Concerns," describes and critiques the current framing of pre-emption as the central concern necessitating the judicial exclusion of certain software-related

---

[6] See A. S. Tanenbaum, *Structured Computer Organization* (Prentice Hall, 1979).

[7] See D. Spinellis, Another Level of Indirection, in A. Oram and G. Wilson (eds.), *Beautiful Code: Leading Programmers Explain How They Think* (O'Reilly Media, 2007), pp. 279–91. Indirection is such a versatile approach to abstracting away implementation details that the claim that "[a]ll problems in computer science can be solved with another layer of indirection" has become a well-known aphorism among programmers. See *ibid.*, p. 279.

[8] See *ibid.*, pp. 279–82.

[9] See T. Tillis, Sens. Tillis and Coons and Reps. Collins, Johnson, and Stivers Release Draft Bill Text to Reform Section 101 of the Patent Act, Press Release (May 22, 2019), www.tillis.senate.gov/2019/5/sens-tillis-and-coons-and-reps-collins-johnson-and-stivers-release-draft-bill-text-to-reform-section-101-of-the-patent-act.

[10] See T. Tillis, Tillis, Coons Vet Patent Eligibility Bill Principles with Stakeholders, Press Release (March 27, 2019), www.tillis.senate.gov/2019/3/tillis-coons-vet-patent-eligibility-bill-principles-with-stakeholders.

[11] See Tillis, above note 9.

[12] See 35 USC § 101.

inventions. This pre-emption concern neither accurately captures the rationale for judicial exclusion nor provides adequate guidance regarding the eligibility of software-related claims.

The third section, "Gatekeeping," highlights the judicial exclusions' historic and enduring role in obviating other patentability inquiries that would be inapposite as applied to the claimed subject matter. This gatekeeping function represents an independently sufficient, jurisprudential rationale for the patent-eligible subject matter requirement and provides a precise criterion by which examiners and courts can distinguish between abstract ideas and their practical applications in the field of computing.

The chapter concludes with recommendations.

THE "NEW MACHINE" PRINCIPLE

Despite the importance of *In re. Bernhart*[13] to the histories both of software patents and of computer technology, it has received little attention in contemporary debates over the patenting of software. But the "new machine" principle it articulated continued to hold legal significance for nearly four decades.

In 1961, Boeing employees Walter Bernhart and Bill Fetter filed a patent application[14] for a computer system capable of drawing two-dimensional representations of three-dimensional objects. Bernhardt and Fetter, who is credited with coining the term "computer graphics,"[15] would have to wait eight years for the US Court of Customs and Patent Appeals to award them their patent.[16] Hundreds of firms, including Disney, expressed interest in licensing the technology,[17] and *Computerworld* heralded the issued patent as "the first true software patent."[18]

Bernhart and Fetter's claimed system included a "general-purpose digital computer" programmed to calculate a series of coordinates $\{(v_i, w_i)\}$ representing the projections of object points $\{(x_i, y_i, z_i)\}$ from a viewpoint (x_e, y_e, z_e) onto the plane located at k times the distance from the viewpoint to the origin and normal to the line between them. The calculation was to be based on the formulas:

$$v_i = \frac{k(x_e^2 + y_e^2 + z_e^2)(-y_e x_i + x_e y_i)}{\sqrt{(x_e^2 + y_e^2)}[(x_e^2 + y_e^2 + z_e^2) - (x_e x_i + y_e y_i + z_e z_i)]}$$

$$w_i = \frac{k\sqrt{(x_e^2 + y_e^2 + z_e^2)}}{\sqrt{(x_e^2 + y_e^2)}}\left(\frac{-x_e z_e x_i - y_e z_e y_i + z_i(x_e^2 + y_e^2)}{(x_e^2 + y_e^2 + z_e^2) - (x_e x_i + y_e y_i + z_e z_i)}\right)$$

The system also included a planar "plotting machine" for plotting the points $\{(v_i, w_i)\}$ on paper. The "plotting machine" could use any known output technology for this purpose, including ink pens, cathode ray photography, or electrostatic paper.

The Patent Office had rejected the system claims under § 101 because their point of novelty consisted of the mathematical equations used to program the computer.[19] On appeal, the US Court of Customs and Patent Appeals acknowledged that equations were excluded from

[13] *In re. Bernhart*, 417 F.2d 1395 (CCPA 1969).
[14] US Patent 3,519,997 (filed November 13, 1961).
[15] W. A. Fetter, *Computer Graphics in Communication* (McGraw-Hill, 1964).
[16] *Bernhart*, above note 13.
[17] Firm Wins Battle for Mechanical Cartoonist Patent, *Great Bend Daily Tribune* (May 1, 1970), p. 1.
[18] *Computerworld* (July 29, 1970), p. 2.
[19] *Bernhart*, above note 13, at 1398.

patentable subject matter, but found that the system claims in issue would not pre-empt all uses of the recited equations:

> [A] member of the public would have to do much more than use the equations to infringe any of these claims. He would have to use them in the physical equipment recited in the claim ... We should not penalize the inventor who makes his invention by discovering new and unobvious mathematical relationships which he then utilizes in a machine, as against the inventor who makes the same machine by trial and error and does not disclose the laws by which it operates.[20]

The comparison between the two inventors here appeals to the long-standing principle that a patent applicant has no duty to disclose a correct theory of operation.[21] In making the comparison, the Court's implication was that Bernhart and Fetter had not only invented a new machine, but had performed the further public service of disclosing its theory of operation, over and above the amount of disclosure needed to patent it. In this account, the mathematical equations played no part in the invention's patent-eligibility, which turned solely on the invention's characterization as a new machine.

The Court then made the characterization explicit by way of invoking the "new machine" principle for the first time as a rationale for patent-eligibility:

> [I]f a machine is programmed in a certain new and unobvious way, it is physically different from the machine without that program; its memory elements are differently arranged. The fact that these physical changes are invisible to the eye should not tempt us to conclude that the machine has not been changed. If a new machine has not been invented, certainly a "new and useful improvement" of the unprogrammed machine has been ... We are concluding here that such machines are statutory under 35 U.S.C. § 101, and that claims defining them must be judged for patentability in light of the prior art.[22]

Having placed Bernhart and Fetter's claims in the statutory category of "new and useful ... machine[s]," the Court proceeded to conduct a deeply problematic review of the Patent Office's § 103 rejection of Bernhart and Fetter's claims in light of the prior art. Unbeknown to the Boeing scientists, a very similar patent application, filed in 1960 by Bernard Taylor, Jr., was already pending in the Patent Office.[23] Taylor had claimed a system with special-purpose circuitry for calculating and outputting the coordinates of a planar projection of a three-dimensional object. Taylor's circuits calculated the coordinates (f_1, f_2) representing the projections of an object point $C = (c_1, c_2, c_3)$ from a viewpoint $A = (a_1, a_2, a_3)$ onto the plane passing through the point and normal to the line between this point and the viewpoint. Taylor's application disclosed the following expressions for f_1 and f_2:

$$f_1 = d_1 \psi / \lambda$$
$$d_1 = \sqrt{e_1^2 + e_2^2 + e_3^2}$$
$$(e_1, e_2, e_3) = \left((a_1 - b_1), (a_2 - b_2), (a_3 - b_3) \right)$$
$$\psi = \frac{e_3 \omega}{d_2} - d_2 \gamma_3$$
$$\omega = e_1 \gamma_2 + e_2 \gamma_1$$

---

[20] *Ibid.* at 1399–400 (emphasis omitted).
[21] See *Newman v. Quigg*, 77 F.2d 1575, 1581–2 (Fed. Cir. 1989).
[22] *Bernhart*, above note 13, at 1400.
[23] US Patent 3,153,224 (filed February 23, 1960).

$$(\gamma_1, \gamma_2, \gamma_3) = \Big((a_1 - c_1), (a_2 - c_2), (a_3 - c_3)\Big)$$

$$d_2 = \sqrt{e_1^2 + e_2^2}$$

$$\lambda = \omega + e_3\gamma_3$$

$$f_2 = \frac{[(a_1 - b_1)^2 + (a_2 - b_2)^2 + (a_3 - b_3)^2][(a_1 - b_1)(a_1 - c_2) - (a_2 - b_2)(a_1 - c_1)]}{\sqrt{(a_1 - b_1)^2 + (a_2 - b_2)^2}[(a_1 - b_1)(a_1 - c_1) + (a_2 - b_2)(a_2 - c_2) + (a_3 - b_3)(a_3 - c_3)]}$$

When rewritten solely in terms of A and C (with B set to the origin), these expressions simplify to the following representations of Bernhart and Fetter's equations:

$$f_2 = \frac{(a_1^2 + a_2^2 + a_3^2)(a_2 c_1 - a_1 c_2)}{\sqrt{(a_1^2 + a_2^2)}[(a_1^2 + a_2^2 + a_3^2) - (a_1 c_1 + a_2 c_2 + a_3 c_3)]}$$

$$f_1 = \frac{\sqrt{a_1^2 + a_2^2 + a_3^2}}{\sqrt{a_1^2 + a_2^2}}\left(\frac{-a_1 a_3 c_1 - a_2 a_3 c_2 + c_3(a_1^2 + a_2^2)}{(a_1^2 + a_2^2 + a_3^2) - (a_1 c_1 + a_2 c_2 + a_3 c_3)}\right)$$

In fact, an enterprising patent examiner performed these algebraic simplifications over six pages of manuscript, showing that for $(a_1, a_2, a_3) = (kx_e, ky_e, kz_e,)$ and $(c_1, c_2, c_3) = (x_i, y_i, z_i,)$, Taylor's formulas calculate the same projection coordinates $(f_1, f_2,) = (v_i, w_i,)$.[24] Accordingly, the Patent Office rejected Bernhart and Fetter's claims as obvious over Taylor's application[25] in light of known programmed computer systems with plotters.[26]

The Court was not persuaded by the examiner's algebra, finding that it amounted to a hindsight reconstruction of Bernhart and Fetter's equations:

> There is nothing in the record to suggest that there was any possibility of the simplified programming claimed by the applicants in claim 19. The Patent Office belatedly ... attempts to show that Taylor's equations can be manipulated to an identity with the [applicants'] equations ... In so doing the solicitor has had the benefit of seeing applicants' equations, and with this hindsight a mathematical identity is revealed. There is nothing to suggest that, within the context of automated drawing, *one of ordinary mathematical skill* armed with the Taylor reference would be able to discover the simpler equations which are the basis of the claimed programming.[27]

Hindsight is a legitimate concern for courts and patent examiners when inquiring into whether a claimed invention was non-obvious at the time it was made.[28] In formulating an obviousness rejection, there can be a "temptation to read into the prior art the teachings of the invention in issue,"[29] thereby understating the difficulty of the problem that would have faced a person having ordinary skill in the art at the time of invention. The *Bernhart* Court's characterization of the examiner's calculations, however, is strained at best.

The reason Bernhart and Fetter's equations are simpler than Taylor's is that the former apply only to the special case where the normal from the viewpoint to the projection plane passes through the origin. Once the coordinates b_1, b_2, b_3 drop out of Taylor's equations, the expressions are greatly simplified, and it is a straightforward exercise in first-year algebra to

[24]   Brief for the Commissioner of Patents at 13–18, In re. Bernhart, 417 F.2d 1395 (CCPA 1969) (filed June 21, 1968).
[25]   See *ibid.* at 6.
[26]   See, e.g., US Patent 3,066,868.
[27]   417 F.2d 1402 (emphasis added).
[28]   *KSR Int'l Co.* v. *Teleflex Inc.*, 550 US 398, 421 (2007).
[29]   See *Graham* v. *John Deere Co.*, 383 US 1, 36 (1966).

solve for f_1 and f_2 in terms of A and C. From these simplified equations, expressing $\{(v_i, w_i,)\}$ in terms of $\{(x_i, y_i,, z_i,)\}, (x_e, y_e, z_e)$ and k requires only a change of notation. Bernhart and Fetter's equations immediately follow from Taylor's prior art disclosure as a special case, at least to one of ordinary skill in ninth-grade mathematics.[30] In short, the Court's determination as to what a person of "ordinary mathematical skill" would be able to do with a particular set of algebraic equations is problematic, because it grossly underestimates the mathematical abilities of the patent's intended audience.

Even more fundamentally, the Court's notion of an inventor "discovering new and unobvious mathematical relationships" and its interposition of "mathematical skill" for the predicate of "ordinary skill in the art" constitute category mistakes, because the attributes of non-obviousness and ordinary skill in the art are inapplicable to the mathematical derivation of equations (and the category of the mathematical arts more generally). As the Supreme Court's *Flook* decision acknowledges, even previously unknown mathematical properties must be "assumed to be within the prior art" at the outset of a patentability determination.[31] Moreover, a § 103 inquiry into the level of ordinary skill in the art[32] is misplaced where the art in question, and the field of knowledge being advanced by the patent disclosure, is not one of the "useful Arts," but mathematics.[33]

The *Bernhart* Court's invocation of the "new machine" principle thus proved counterproductive, in that the patentability analysis of a claimed software-implemented invention should never leave a court in the position of determining how hard the math was. Nevertheless, the Court of Customs and Patent Appeals and the Federal Circuit continued to apply the principle to "a general purpose computer programmed to carry out the claimed invention"[34] in cases spanning the next three decades. As the Federal Circuit majority summarized this case law in *In re. Alappat*: "We have held that such programming creates a new machine, because a general purpose computer in effect becomes a special purpose computer once it is programmed to perform particular functions pursuant to instructions from program software."[35]

In its 1994 en banc decision in *Alappat*, the Federal Circuit reviewed the Patent Office's rejection of five claims, four of which were dependent from the first.[36] The representative claim read:

> 15. A rasterizer for converting vectors in a data list representing sample magnitudes of an input waveform into anti-aliased pixel illumination intensity data to be displayed on a display means comprising:
>
> (a) means for determining a vertical distance between the endpoints of each of the vectors in the data list;
> (b) means for determining an elevation of a row of pixels that is spanned by the vector;
> (c) means for normalizing the vertical distance and elevation; and

---

[30] The non-obviousness analysis is not changed by characterizing Bernhart and Fetter's as a species selected from a prior art genus. See The Manual of Patent Examining Procedure (MPEP) § 2144.08. On the other hand, Taylor's equations are not readily deducible from Bernhart and Fetter's disclosure, which offers no indication as to how to calculate the coordinates of a projection onto a plane located elsewhere in space.

[31] 437 US 594.

[32] *Graham*, above note 29, at 17.

[33] See *ibid.* at 6 (quoting US Constitution, art. I, § 8, cl. 8): "Innovation, advancement, and things which add to the sum of useful knowledge are inherent requisites in a patent system which by constitutional command must 'promote the Progress of . . . useful Arts.'"

[34] *In re. Alappat*, 33 F.3d 1526, 1545 (Fed. Cir. 1994).

[35] *Ibid.*

[36] *Ibid.* at 1538–9.

(d) means for outputting illumination intensity data as a predetermined function of
      the normalized vertical distance and elevation.[37]

Construing this claim in accordance with § 112(f), the Court replaced each of the four
"means" terms in clauses (a) to (d) with what it determined to be the corresponding structure
disclosed in the specification:

15. A rasterizer [a "machine"] for converting vectors in a data list representing sample
magnitudes of an input waveform into anti-aliased pixel illumination intensity data to be
displayed on a display means comprising:

(a) [an arithmetic logic *circuit* configured to perform an absolute value function,
      or an equivalent thereof] for determining a vertical distance between the
      endpoints of each of the vectors in the data list;
(b) [an arithmetic logic *circuit* configured to perform an absolute value function, or
      an equivalent thereof] for determining an elevation of a row of pixels that is
      spanned by the vector;
(c) [a pair of *barrel shifters*, or equivalents thereof] for normalizing the vertical
      distance and elevation; and
(d) [a *read only memory (ROM)* containing illumination intensity data, or an
      equivalent thereof] for outputting illumination intensity data as
      a predetermined function of the normalized vertical distance and elevation.[38]

A close examination of Alappat's patent specification also illuminates what (I have suggested elsewhere[39]) is the *sine qua non* of a structural element: its involvement in a causal
process. As Table 17.1 illustrates, *Alappat* discloses several explicitly causal processes that
together produce the functions of the claimed machine, including processes respectively
involving the disclosed arithmetic logic circuit (the "ALU"), barrel shifters, and the read-only
memory.

TABLE 17.1 *Causal processes involving each of the disclosed structural elements supporting claim 15*

Disclosed Element	Disclosed Causal Process
arithmetic logic circuit	"[V]arious operations of rasterizer 40 . . . are timed by clock signals produced by a state machine in accordance with control data . . . One signal is a 'pixel clock' signal that is asserted to *cause* the rasterizer to receive each new vector list data element . . . This [ALU] value is stored in a register 76 on the next pixel clock cycle."[40]
barrel shifter	"[P]riority encoder 86 *causes* barrel shifter 84 to shift its input to the left by the number of bits required . . ."[41]
read-only memory	"The 8-bit intensity data stored in register 90 addresses a read only memory (ROM) 92 and *causes* ROM 92 to read out a 4-bit intensity data value which is stored in a register 94 on the next pixel clock cycle."[42]

[37] *Ibid.*
[38] *Ibid.* at 1541 (emphases added).
[39] See A. Chin, The Ontological Function of the Patent Document (2013) 74 *Univ. Pitt. Law Rev.* 314 (discussing *Centricut, LLC* v. *Esab Group, Inc.*, 390 F.3d 1361 (2004)).
[40] US Patent 5,440,676, cols. 3–4 (emphasis added).
[41] *Ibid.*, col. 6 (emphasis added).
[42] *Ibid.*, cols. 6–7 (emphasis added).

Having construed claim 15 narrowly in accordance with these structural limitations, the Court reasoned that the claim "unquestionably recites a machine, or apparatus, made up of a combination of known electronic circuitry elements."[43]

Observing that a "machine" is explicitly recognized as patent-eligible subject matter under § 101, the Court proceeded to use the conclusion from its § 112(f) analysis – that claim 15 recites a machine – as the starting point for its § 101 analysis:[44]

> [T]he claimed invention as a whole is directed to a combination of interrelated elements which combine to form a machine for converting discrete waveform data samples into anti-aliased pixel illumination intensity data to be displayed on a display means. This is not a disembodied mathematical concept which may be characterized as an "abstract idea," but rather a specific machine to produce a useful, concrete, and tangible result.

The Federal Circuit's subsequent gloss on *Alappat*'s § 112(f) analysis as grounded in a finding that "[t]he instructions of the software program that carry out the algorithm electrically change the general purpose computer by creating electrical paths within the device"[45] was simply revisionism. The *Alappat* majority made no mention of "electrical paths" being created through programming. Its § 112(f) analysis was instead appropriately grounded in the structural nature of the disclosed elements that it determined to correspond to each of the claimed "means" terms: arithmetic logic circuits, a barrel shifter, and a read-only memory.[46] In short, the *Alappat* majority's § 112(f) analysis informed its § 101 analysis, not the other way around.

Alappat's "new machine" principle soon became a mainstay of the Patent Office's 1996 Guidelines for Examining Computer-Related Inventions,[47] but it has not fared well in the present century. Long before *Alice*,[48] the "new machine" principle had been criticized often enough to earn the derisory nickname "The Old Piano Roll Blues."[49] The implied comparison, as the government had argued in *Gottschalk v. Benson*,[50] was to "the insertion of a new piano roll into an old player piano," which may enable the piano to play a new song, but should not be considered "a patentable 'discovery.'"[51] Former Chief Judge Glenn Archer's *Alappat* dissent appealed to the analogy at length, concluding that "[t]he only invention by the creator of a roll that is new because of its music is the new music,"[52] which is non-statutory subject matter.

---

43   *Ibid.*
44   *Ibid.*, cols. 1541–2.
45   See WMS *Gaming, Inc. v. Int'l Game Tech.*, 184 F.3d 1339, 1348 (Fed. Cir. 1999) (citing *Alappat*, above note 34, at 1545).
46   See *Alappat*, above note 34, at 1541.
47   See US Patent & Trademark Office (USPTO), Examination Guidelines for Computer-Related Inventions, 61 Fed. Reg. 7478 (February 28, 1996) (citing *Alappat* nine times).
     The *Alappat* court also reasoned that the claimed programmed general-purpose computer was "not a disembodied mathematical concept which may be characterized as an 'abstract idea,' but rather a specific machine to produce a useful, concrete, and tangible result" (*ibid.* at 1544), but it was not until *State Street Bank* that the Federal Circuit elevated *Alappat*'s "useful, concrete, and tangible result" language into a test for patent-eligibility. *State Street Bank & Trust Co. v. Signature Financial Group, Inc.*, 149 F.3d 1368, 1373 (Fed. Cir. 1998) ("Today, we hold that the transformation of data, representing discrete dollar amounts, by a machine through a series of mathematical calculations into a final share price, constitutes a [patent-eligible invention] because it produces 'a useful, concrete and tangible result' . . ."). The Federal Circuit abrogated this test in *In re. Bilski*, 545 F.3d 943, 959–60 (Fed. Cir. 2008).
48   *Alice Corp. Pty. Ltd v. CLS Bank Int'l*, 573 US 208 (2014).
49   P. Groves, Old Piano Roll Blues, in A *Dictionary of Intellectual Property Law* (Edward Elgar, 2011), p. 220.
50   409 US 63 (1972).
51   Government's Opening Brief, *Gottschalk v. Benson, ibid.*
52   *Alappat*, above note 34, at 1567 (Archer, J., dissenting).

By 2008, a majority of the Federal Circuit sitting en banc in *In re. Bilski*[53] had begun to call into question the characterization of a programmed generic computer as a new machine. In 1997, Bernard Bilski and Rand Warsaw had applied for a patent on a method for making a market for the sale of a commodity, such as natural gas, in which buyers and sellers desired to manage risks relating to fluctuations in the quantity consumed.[54] Prior art energy trading methods focused on managing risks relating to price volatility.[55] Despite the apparent commercial value of Bilski and Warsaw's method,[56] Bilski and Warsaw's patent claims met with stiff opposition. Of the twenty-six Supreme Court, Federal Circuit, and administrative patent judges who considered Bilski and Warsaw's application, all but one found the claims to be directed to non-statutory subject matter under 35 USC § 101.[57] The judges divided more sharply, however, in their reasoning. Majorities of the Federal Circuit and the Board of Patent Appeals and Interferences held that a patentable process must either be tied to a particular machine or transform an article,[58] and found Bilski and Warsaw's claims to fail both prongs of this "machine-or-transformation" test.[59] Four Supreme Court justices (including Justice Stevens) and three Federal Circuit judges opined that methods of doing business should be held non-statutory[60] – at least those that do not involve manufactures, machines, or compositions of matter.[61] A five-justice Supreme Court majority, however, held that neither a mandatory "machine-or-transformation" test nor the so-called "business method" exclusion was warranted by

---

[53] See above note 47 (en banc).

[54] See US Patent Application Serial No. 08,833,892 (filed April 10, 1997). Claim 1 read:

> A method for managing the consumption risk costs of a commodity sold by a commodity provider at a fixed price comprising the steps of: (a) initiating a series of transactions between said commodity provider and consumers of said commodity wherein said consumers purchase said commodity at a fixed rate based upon historical averages, said fixed rate corresponding to a risk position of said consumer; (b) identifying market participants for said commodity having a counter-risk position to said consumers; and (c) initiating a series of transactions between said commodity provider and said market participants at a second fixed rate such that said series of market participant transactions balances the risk position of said series of consumer transactions.

(*Ibid.*)

[55] See *ibid.*

[56] See Validity of Software Patents Goes on Trial Today at Supreme Court, *USA Today* (November 9, 2009), p. 7B (reporting that Bilski and Warsaw's company, Weatherwise USA, offers energy-billing services that can "lock in energy prices, even during an unusually cold winter").

[57] See *Bilski*, above note 47, at 997 (Newman, J., dissenting) (finding Bilski and Warsaw's claimed process to be "neither a fundamental truth nor an abstraction").

[58] See *ibid.* at 954 (majority opinion; citations omitted) ("A claimed process is surely patent-eligible under § 101 if: (1) it is tied to a particular machine or apparatus; or (2) it transforms a particular article into a different state or thing"); *Ex p. Bilski*, 2006 WL 5738364, at *18 (holding that a claim that does not recite a specific apparatus may be directed to patentable subject matter "if there is a transformation of physical subject matter from one state into another . . ."); see also *ibid.* at *14 ("It is possible that a non-machine-implemented method may be nonstatutory subject matter if it does not perform a transformation of physical subject matter even though it contains physical steps that might prevent i[t] from being labeled an 'abstract idea'").

[59] See *Bilski*, above note 47, at 962 (finding "the machine implementation part of the test" inapplicable to Bilski and Warsaw's claims); *ibid.* at 963 (holding that Bilski and Warsaw's claims do not transform any article to a different state or thing); *Ex p. Bilski*, above note 59, at *2 (noting that Bilski and Warsaw's claims are "non-machine-implemented"); *ibid.* at *18–20 (holding that none of Bilski and Warsaw's claims involves a physical transformation).

[60] See *Bilski v. Kappos*, 130 S.Ct. 3218, 3231 (2010) (Stevens, J., concurring); *Bilski*, above note 47, at 998 (Mayer, J., dissenting).

[61] See *Bilski*, above note 47, at 974 (Dyk, J., concurring).

precedent[62] or necessary to invalidate Bilski and Warsaw's claims as directed to an unpatentable abstract idea.[63]

Alice Corp. v. CLS Bank Int'l[64] followed soon thereafter, and with it, the Federal Circuit's recognition that the Supreme Court had called into question the *Alappat* Court's appeal to the "new machine" principle.[65] The Supreme Court's holding that "mere recitation of a general computer cannot transform a patent-ineligible abstract idea into a patent-eligible invention"[66] also appears to call the *Bernhart* Court's reasoning into question. The Patent Office's 2019 Revised Patent Subject Matter Eligibility Guidance[67] accordingly made no mention of the "new machine" principle, focusing instead on the pre-emption concerns highlighted by the Supreme Court in *Mayo*[68] and *Alice*.[69]

The § 101 reform bill drafted by Senator Thom Tillis and Representative Chris Coons effectively calls for a return to the problematic characterization of a programmed general-purpose computer as a "new machine." The proposed legislation also appeals to the utility-focused patent-eligibility determination in the Federal Circuit's 1998 *State Street Bank v. Signature Financial Group* decision,[70] which relies on a revisionist gloss on *Alappat*.[71] Given its tenuous origins in Federal Circuit case law, the "new machine" principle is a dubious candidate for codification. As the next section shows, the Supreme Court's software patent jurisprudence has not focused on whether a claimed programmed computer constitutes a "new machine," but on whether the claim effectively pre-empts an abstract idea.

PRE-EMPTION CONCERNS

Both historically and recently, the Supreme Court has grounded its doctrine regarding the subject matter eligibility of software-related patent claims in the stated concern that those not sufficiently confined to a practical application could have the effect of pre-empting abstract ideas.[72] To this day, however, the courts have not developed a coherent jurisprudential framework that can explain and justify their patent-eligibility decisions in terms of these stated pre-emption concerns.[73] Pre-emption considerations do not adequately explain the

---

[62] *Bilski v. Kappos*, above note 60, at 3227 ("The 'machine-or-transformation' test is not the sole test for deciding whether an invention is a patent-eligible 'process'"); *ibid.* at 3228 ("Section 101 similarly precludes the broad contention that the term 'process' categorically excludes business methods").

[63] *Ibid.* at 3231 ("Allowing petitioners to patent risk hedging would preempt use of this approach in all fields, and would effectively grant a monopoly over an abstract idea").

[64] *Alice*, above note 3.

[65] See *CLS Bank Int'l v. Alice Corp.*, 717 F.3d 1269, 1292 (Fed. Cir. 2013) (en banc; plurality opinion) (Lourie, J.): "Not only has the world of technology changed, but the legal world has changed. The Supreme Court has spoken since *Alappat* on the question of patent eligibility, and we must take note of that change."

[66] Above note 3, at 2358.

[67] See USPTO, 2019 Revised Patent Subject Matter Eligibility Guidance, 84 Fed. Reg. 50 (January 7, 2019).

[68] *Mayo Collaborative Servs. v. Prometheus Labs., Inc.*, 566 US 66 (2012).

[69] See above note 48.

[70] See above note 47. In *State Street Bank*, accused infringers challenged a claim for a computer-implemented accounting system for a "hub-and-spoke" financial product as directed to non-statutory subject matter. See *ibid.* at 1371.

[71] See above text accompanying notes 45–46. For the purposes of characterizing the system as a statutory "machine" under § 101, the Court found it sufficient that the claimed "machine programmed with the Hub and Spoke software . . . admittedly produces a 'useful, concrete, and tangible result.'" See *ibid.* at 1375 (citing *Alappat*, above note 34, at 1544).

[72] See *Gottschalk v. Benson*, above note 50, at 71.

[73] See K. J. Strandburg, Much Ado about Preemption (2012) 50 *Houston Law Rev.* 563, 564–8 (arguing that a focus on preemption "is unsatisfactory, both as a theoretical matter and as an explanation of the Supreme Court's patentable subject matter jurisprudence").

lines of reasoning the Court has actually undertaken in adjudicating the subject matter eligibility of software-related patent claims. Nor do they furnish a normative justification for the use of patent-eligible subject matter doctrine, as opposed to other patentability doctrines, to exclude claimed subject matter.

Patent-eligibility jurisprudence regarding software-related inventions originated in 1972 with *Gottschalk* v. *Benson*,[74] where the Court offered a pre-emption rationale for upholding the Patent Office's rejection of claims directed to a "method of converting signals from binary coded decimal form into binary" comprising a sequence of steps to be performed on a "re-entrant shift register."[75] Characterizing Benson's patent claims as directed to "the formula for converting BCD numerals to pure binary numerals,"[76] the Court reasoned that the formula "has no substantial practical application except in connection with a digital computer, which means that . . . the patent would wholly pre-empt the mathematical formula and in practical effect would be a patent on the algorithm itself."[77] Accordingly, allowing Benson's claims would have the "practical effect" of allowing Benson to "patent an idea."[78]

Binary-coded decimal (BCD) to binary conversion is necessarily performed by any application that combines a digital numeric user interface with a binary arithmetic circuit calculation. The Court described the conversion as exceptionally versatile, with applications ranging "from the operation of a train to verification of drivers' licenses to researching the law books for precedents," as well as other "unknown uses."[79] Benson's claims, however, did not cover the only algorithm for converting numbers from a BCD representation to a binary representation. For example, the conventional approach to performing the conversion is to calculate the binary representation of each digit in its respective base-10 place value and to sum the results by binary addition. Benson's method more specifically sequenced the necessary multiplications and additions so as to perform the calculation efficiently on a "re-entrant shift register," a type of computer architecture whose basic steps include the ability to shift all of a string of bits one location to the left or right, with the first and last locations wrapped around (that is, treated as adjacent). In other words, Benson's claims were directed to just one of many possible correct algorithms for performing BCD to binary conversion, albeit one particularly well-suited for implementation on a re-entrant shift register.

The Court's analysis of Benson's claims ultimately amounted to little more than a gesture toward its stated pre-emption concerns. While the Court indicated that the claims were problematically overbroad in discussing the BCD to binary conversion's versatility, the Court did not compare the claims' actual scope with the full range of algorithms and architectures that could have been applied to the allegedly pre-empted end uses. In short, pre-emption considerations neither explain nor justify the *Benson* decision.

As the form and substance of software-related patent claims has evolved over the nearly half-century since *Benson*, the Supreme Court's patent-eligibility jurisprudence has come no closer to elucidating the application and purpose of pre-emption. In 2010, the *Bilski* Court majority rejected the Federal Circuit's "machine-or-transformation" test,[80] finding it sufficient to observe that the representative claims "explain the basic concept of hedging,"[81] which

---

[74] *Ibid.*
[75] *Ibid.*, pp. 73–4.
[76] *Ibid.*, p. 71.
[77] *Ibid.*, pp. 71–2.
[78] *Ibid.*, p. 71.
[79] *Ibid.*, p. 68.
[80] See above text accompanying notes 53–63
[81] *Bilski* v. *Kappos*, above note 60, at 3231.

is "a fundamental economic practice long prevalent in our system of commerce and taught in any introductory finance class."[82] Echoing *Benson*, the majority concluded that the claims therefore "would pre-empt use of this approach in all fields, and would effectively grant a monopoly over an abstract idea."[83] Dependent claims limited to "commodities and energy markets" were equally problematic as a mere "attempt to patent the use of the abstract idea of hedging risk in the energy market and then instruct the use of well-known random analysis techniques."[84] Thus, the majority's findings of pre-emption were based not on the scope of any claim terms, but on the fact that the claims "explain" an idea taught in business school. Given the majority's rejection of the efforts of four concurring justices to establish a business-method exclusion from patent-eligibility,[85] it is difficult to distill a clear method or rationale from the *Bilski* Court's pre-emption analysis.

The Court's subsequent decisions in *Mayo* and *Alice* even more explicitly described patent-eligible subject matter jurisprudence as animated by pre-emption concerns. The *Mayo* Court warned that upholding the claims at bar "would risk disproportionately tying up the use" of "the basic tools of scientific and technological work"[86] and would "tend to impede innovation more than it would tend to promote it."[87]

The *Alice* Court similarly referred to "the pre-emption concern that undergirds our § 101 jurisprudence" in extending *Mayo*'s analysis to the representative claim, finding that a "wholly generic computer implementation is not generally the sort of 'additional featur[e]' that provides any 'practical assurance that the process is more than a drafting effort designed to monopolize the [abstract idea] itself.'"[88] As in *Bilski*, however, the *Alice* Court did not conduct a careful analysis of claim scope and downstream impact, but instead relied on the observation that the claims were "drawn to the concept of intermediated settlement," which like hedging is "'a fundamental economic practice long prevalent in our system of commerce.'"[89] Pre-emption thus fails to explain or justify the *Alice* Court's § 101 analysis satisfactorily, as other commentators have noted.[90]

The divergence between the Supreme Court's stated pre-emption concerns and its actual subject matter eligibility analysis of software patent claims has occasioned a protracted effort by the Patent Office to guide examiners through the perceived "current muddle in patentable subject matter analysis."[91] Guidance materials published in 2014[92] and 2019[93] provide examiners with an algorithmic approach to the analysis based on the Supreme Court's analyses in *Mayo* and *Alice*, and subsequent Federal Circuit case law. The centerpiece of the approach is the flowchart of Figure 17.1, which was introduced in the Patent Office's 2014 Guidance and

[82] *Ibid.* (quoting *Bilski*, above note 47, at 1013 (Rader, J., dissenting)); R. C. Dreyfuss and J. P. Evans, From Bilski Back to Benson: Preemption, Inventing Around, and the Case of Genetic Diagnostics (2011) 63 *Stan. Law Rev.* 1349.
[83] *Ibid.*
[84] *Ibid.*
[85] See *ibid.* at 3228–9.
[86] *Mayo*, above note 3, at 1293–4.
[87] 132 S.Ct. at 1293.
[88] *Alice*, above note 3, at 2358.
[89] *Ibid.* at 2356 (quoting *Bilski* v. *Kappos*, above note 60, at 3218).
[90] See, e.g., A. Bhattacharyya, Unpatentably Preemptive? A Case against the Use of Preemption as a Guidepost for Determining Patent Eligibility, *Extra Legal* (Summer 2013); Strandburg, above note 74.
[91] Strandburg, above note 74, p. 564.
[92] USPTO, 2014 Interim Guidance on Patent Subject Matter Eligibility, 79 Fed. Reg. 74,618 (December 16, 2014) (hereinafter, 2014 Guidance).
[93] USPTO, 2019 Revised Patent Subject Matter Eligibility Guidance, 84 Fed. Reg. 50 (January 7, 2019) (hereinafter, 2019 Guidance).

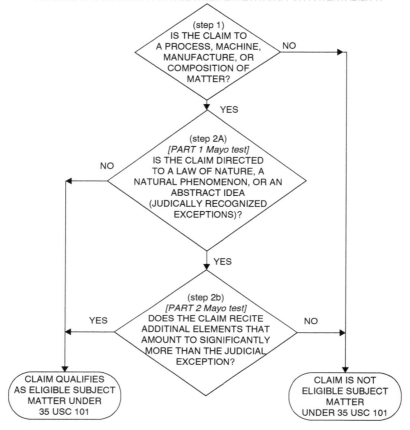

FIGURE 17.1 Flowchart representation of Patent Office guidance since 2014 for examination of claims under the § 101 patent-eligible subject matter requirement
Source: 2014 Guidance, above note 93, 74621.

further revised in 2019. Following a series of recent Federal Circuit concurrences and dissents criticizing, inter alia, the mismatch between post-*Alice* abstract-idea jurisprudence and the Court's pre-emption concerns,[94] the revised guidance instructs examiners to construe the exception narrowly in two respects. First, the range of subject matter that can be considered an abstract idea is confined to an enumerated list of "groupings" identified in judicial precedent, such as mathematical concepts, certain methods of organizing human activity

---

[94] See *Smart Sys. Innovations, LLC* v. *Chicago Transit Auth.*, 873 F.3d 1364, 1377 (Fed. Cir. 2017) (Linn, J., dissenting in part and concurring in part) (citations omitted) ("Ultimately, the fundamental question in 'abstract idea' cases is whether the claim is directed to such a basic building block of scientific or technological activity as to foreclose or inhibit future innovation or whether the claim instead is directed to a tangible application that serves a 'new and useful end.' Claims directed not merely to basic building blocks of scientific or technological activity ... should be fully eligible for patent protection and not lightly discarded"); 2019 Guidance, above note 94, 50 n. 2 (citing *Smart Sys. Innovations* and additional Federal Circuit concurrences and dissents).

(such as fundamental economic principles, commercial and legal interactions, and managing personal behavior), and mental processes.[95] Second, a claim is not found to be directed to an abstract idea if the recited idea is found to be "integrated into a practical application."[96]

The draft legislation offers a different response to the misalignment between § 101 jurisprudence and pre-emption concerns, namely, to abrogate the former and shift the scrutiny of claims for over-breadth to the other statutory requirements for patentability. As Joshua Sarnoff has persuasively pointed out, however, this approach "will just displace ... [the] unclear policies and uncertain interpretations and applications [of § 101] to other patent law doctrines."[97]

In addition, as we will see in the next section, the notion that § 101's scope-policing functions can be incorporated into patent law's novelty, non-obviousness, and sufficiency of disclosure doctrines belies the patent-eligible subject matter requirement's unique and vital role in obviating inapposite inquiries under these statutory requirements. This gatekeeping function provides a more accurate explanation of and compelling justification for software patent-eligibility jurisprudence, both historically and currently, than the Court's stated pre-emption concerns.

GATEKEEPING

Over the past four decades of software patent-eligibility jurisprudence, § 101 has served a vital gatekeeping function, foreclosing the patentability analysis before the consideration of other statutory requirements would necessitate inapposite inquiries. The Supreme Court in *Parker v. Flook*[98] stated this gatekeeping function as the "obligation to determine what type of discovery is sought to be patented," which "must precede the determination of whether that discovery is, in fact, new or obvious."[99] Soon thereafter, in *In re. Bergy*,[100] Judge Giles Rich formulated his famous "three doors" account of patentability, in which the § 101 eligibility inquiry is the first door whose threshold requirements precede all other patentability considerations.[101] As Chief Judge Glenn Archer explained this doctrinal precedence in *In re. Alappat*,[102] subject matter eligibility "lays the predicate for the other provisions of the patent law"[103] and thereby obviates inapposite inquiries under those provisions:

> If Einstein could have obtained a patent for his discovery that the energy of an object at rest equals its mass times the speed of light squared, how would his discovery be meaningfully judged for nonobviousness, the *sine qua non* of patentable invention [under § 103]? When is the abstract idea "reduced to practice" as opposed to being "conceived" [under § 102(g)]? What conduct amounts to the "infringement" of another's idea [under § 271]?[104]

In the only part of the Federal Circuit's splintered *In re. Bilski* opinion cited with approval by the Supreme Court, then-Chief Judge Randall Rader advocated a straightforward

---

[95] 84 Fed. Reg. at 51–2.
[96] *Ibid.* at 54–5.
[97] Testimony of Joshua D. Sarnoff, Senate Committee on the Judiciary, Subcommittee on Intellectual Property Hearing: The State of Patent Eligibility in America: Part I (June 4, 2019), p. 8.
[98] Above note 2.
[99] See *ibid.* at 593.
[100] 596 F.2d 952 (CCPA 1979) (Rich, J.).
[101] See *ibid.* at 960.
[102] Above note 34 (citing *Parker* v. *Flook*, above note 2, at 593) (Archer, CJ, concurring in part and dissenting in part).
[103] *Ibid.* at 1553.
[104] *Ibid.*

articulation of the abstract-ideas exception's gatekeeping function over the Federal Circuit majority's "page after page" devoted to developing the machine-or-transformation test. Judge Rader explained that "an abstract claim would appear in a form that is not even susceptible to examination against prior art under the traditional tests for patentability."[105] Thus, Judge Rader's conclusion that Bilski and Warsaw's method was "either a vague economic concept or obvious on its face"[106] was not based on an examination for non-obviousness under § 103 against prior art references, but on the more basic observation that "[h]edging is a fundamental economic practice long prevalent in our system of commerce and taught in any introductory finance class."[107]

The Supreme Court majority in *Bilski* v. *Kappos*[108] cited Judge Rader's criticism of the machine-or-transformation test,[109] quoted his characterization of hedging as "a fundamental economic practice" in support of its abstract-idea analysis,[110] and ultimately adopted his approach. Using the § 101 subject matter requirement to obviate any § 102 and § 103 analysis, the Court declined to subject Bilski and Warsaw's claims "to examination against prior art under the traditional tests for patentability."[111] Instead of reviewing prior art, the Court consulted several then-recent textbooks, none of which pre-dated Bilski and Warsaw's April 16, 1996 priority date,[112] but all of which supported the Court's characterization of "the basic concept of hedging" as an abstract financial idea "taught in any introductory finance class."

Prefiguring the *Alice/Mayo* test, the *Bilski* majority's claim-specific analysis amounted to a determination that the elements of representative claims 1 and 4 did not add "significantly more"[113] to the judicially excluded abstract "concept of hedging."[114] In claim 1, the concept of hedging is "described"; in claim 4, the concept of hedging is "reduced to a mathematical formula."[115] The Court thus determined that any results or effects produced by the inventions of claims 1 and 4 follow necessarily as logical or mathematical consequences of "the basic concept of hedging," wherein claims 1 and 4 (and their supporting disclosures) serve merely to "explain" these consequences.[116] In this way, both Judge Rader and the Supreme Court majority used § 101's subject matter eligibility requirement as a gatekeeper to obviate an inapposite § 102 or § 103 examination against prior art where the claimed invention's result or effect followed necessarily as a logical consequence of a judicial exception.[117]

In *Alice*, the Court held that "a wholly generic computer implementation" of the judicially excluded abstract idea of "intermediated settlement" was as patent-ineligible as the abstract idea itself.[118] In characterizing the method claims at issue as "simply recit[ing] the concept of

[105] *Bilski*, above note 47, at 1013 (Fed. Cir. 2008) (Rader, CJ, dissenting).
[106] *Ibid.*
[107] See *ibid.*
[108] 561 US 593 (2010).
[109] See *ibid.* at 606 (citing *Bilski*, above note 47, at 1015 (Rader, J., dissenting)).
[110] See *ibid.* at 611 (quoting *Bilski*, above note 47, at 1013 (Rader, J., dissenting)).
[111] *Bilski*, above note 47, at 1013 (Rader, J., dissenting).
[112] Cf. *Bilski* v. *Kappos*, above note 60, at 611 (citing textbooks published in 2008 and 2010) with US Patent Application No. 08/833,892 (filed April 10, 1997) (claiming priority to Provisional US Patent Application No. 60/015,756, filed April 16, 1996).
[113] *Alice*, above note 48, at 218; *Mayo*, above note 3, at 77.
[114] *Bilski* v. *Kappos*, above note 109, at 611.
[115] *Ibid.*
[116] See *ibid.*
[117] See *ibid.*; cf. *Alappat*, above note 34, at 1553.
[118] See above note 48, at 223–4.

intermediated settlement as performed by a generic computer," the Court pointed to Federal Circuit Judge Alan Lourie's observation that the representative claim "lacks *any* express language to define the computer's participation."[119] Alice's claims to computational processes whose efficacy in producing the effect of "intermediated settlement" were not contingent on the empirical causal behavior of a "computer's participation" (that is, a recited practical "method or means"[120]), but followed necessarily as logical and mathematical consequences of the stipulated behavior of idealized and generic system components ("data processing units" that process data, "mass data storage units" that store data, "communications controllers" that control communications, etc.[121]) and the social interpretation of the data elements being processed by the system within the community of stakeholders involved in the simultaneous exchange of obligations through an intermediary to minimize risk ("credit record," "debit record," "shadow credit record," "shadow debit record," "start-of-day balance," "transaction," "adjustment," "credits," and "debits"[122]) and were therefore amenable to mathematical verification and proof. In finding that the recitation of these elements added "nothing significantly more" to the abstract idea of intermediated settlement,[123] the Court obviated, inter alia, inapposite § 103 inquiries into the level of ordinary *mathematical* skill – an inquiry featured in a problematic analysis fifty years ago involving a similarly generic computer system[124] that almost surely does not survive *Alice*.[125]

In *Mayo*,[126] the Court analyzed the subject matter eligibility of a claim for a method of administering a thiopurine drug reciting, inter alia, statements that metabolite levels of "less than 230 pmol $8x10^8$ red blood cells" or "greater than 400 pmol per $8x10^8$ red blood cells" indicated a need to adjust the dosage.[127] After characterizing the recited "relationships between concentrations of certain metabolites in the blood and the likelihood that a dosage of a thiopurine drug will prove ineffective or cause harm" as unpatentable laws of nature,[128] the Court turned to the question of "whether the claims do significantly more than simply describe these natural relations."[129] It concluded that the claim's steps amounted to nothing significantly more than "an instruction to doctors to apply the applicable laws when treating their patients" and "to gather data from which they may draw an inference in light of the correlations," and were therefore "not sufficient to transform unpatentable natural correlations into patentable applications of those regularities."[130]

---

[119] *Ibid.* at 225 (emphasis added) (quoting *CLS Bank* v. *Alice*, above note 65, at 1286 (Lourie, J., concurring)).

[120] *Diamond* v. *Diehr*, 450 US 175, 182 n. 7 (1981) (quoting *Corning* v. *Burden*, 56 US 252, 268 (1853)).

[121] The disclosed software solution was designed to run on a "generic 'system'" comprising a collection of "data processing units," "mass data storage units," "communications controllers," "communications hardware products," and "information recordal devices," all of which may occur in "many varied configurations, relating not only to the number and types of stakeholders, but also the 'architectures' realisable [sic] by the system hardware and software in combination." US Patent No. 5,970,479, cols. 7–8 (filed May 28, 1993); US Patent No. 6,912,510, cols. 6–8 (filed May 9, 2000); US Patent No. 7,149,720, cols. 7–8 (filed December 31, 2002); US Patent No. 7,725,375, cols. 6–8 (filed June 27, 2005).

[122] See, e.g., US Patent No. 5,970,479, col. 33 (filed May 28, 1993).

[123] *Alice*, above note 48, at 225–6.

[124] See *Bernhart*, above note 13, at 1402 (reasoning in a § 103 analysis that "[t]here is nothing to suggest that, within the context of automated drawing, one of ordinary mathematical skill armed with the Taylor reference would be able to discover the simpler equations which are the basis of the claimed programming").

[125] See A. Chin, Ghost in the "New Machine": How Alice Exposed Software Patenting's Category Mistake (2015) 16 *NC J. Law Technol.* 623.

[126] *Mayo*, above note 3.

[127] *Ibid.* at 75.

[128] *Ibid.* at 77.

[129] *Ibid.*

[130] *Ibid.* at 79.

In holding Prometheus's dosing methods patent-ineligible, the Court obviated an inapposite § 112 inquiry into whether Prometheus's patent disclosure was sufficient to suit "teach-[ing] those skilled in the art how to make and use the full scope of the claimed invention without 'undue experimentation.'"[131] The claim's "instruction to doctors" is a teaching, but it is not the kind of teaching that obviates experimentation. Nor is it the kind of teaching that is amenable to examination for sufficiency of disclosure to those of ordinary skill, if "skill" in deductive logic and mathematics is correctly excluded as inapposite.[132]

The claimed result and effect when a doctor measures the metabolite concentration in a patient's blood and adjusts the drug's dosage necessarily follows from the natural law as the logical consequence of the stipulated effects of the doctor's behavior, and is not a matter for empirical verification or falsification.[133] Like the generically recited system components in *Alice*,[134] the step of "determining" the metabolite level is stipulated to determine the metabolite level, and the step of "administering" the thiopurine drug is stipulated to establish the baseline drug dosage to be increased or decreased according to the natural law.

While patent-eligibility doctrine treats abstract ideas and natural phenomena as forms of *a priori* knowledge, their integration into practical applications is signified by the *a posteriori* nature of their ensuing results and effects. Where, as in *Bilski*, *Alice*, and *Mayo*, the result or effect of a claimed invention follows necessarily as an *a priori* consequence of the judicial exception, the gatekeeping function of the § 101 patent-eligible subject matter requirement can and should continue to prevent inapposite analyses under the traditional tests for patentability.

CONCLUSION

The present legislative moment has brought software-patent eligibility jurisprudence to the crossroads of three distinct doctrinal accounts of the abstract-idea exclusion. The first perspective, derived from a doctrinally problematic characterization of mathematics as a useful art, opened the floodgates to software patents through artfully drafted "new machine" claims. The second perspective, promulgated through the Supreme Court's *Mayo* and *Alice* decisions, has engendered unpredictability and confusion by characterizing pre-emption concerns as an animating principle, but failing to align these concerns with the ensuing analyses of the patent claims at bar.

It thus falls to the third perspective to remind would-be reformers of the indispensable gatekeeping function of the judicial exclusions to patent-eligible subject matter. As the early *Bernhart* case illustrates, the proposed abrogation of centuries of patent-eligible subject matter case law would disrupt courts' basic working assumptions that prior art, ordinary skill in the art, and making and using without undue experimentation carry their usual meaning and import for the constitutional purpose of promoting the progress of useful arts. Far from disciplining a wayward judiciary, the likely result would be a return to rulings from the bench as to how hard the math was.

---

[131] *In re. Wright*, 999 F.2d 1557, 1561 (Fed. Cir. 1993) (quoting *In re. Vaeck*, 847 F.2d 488, 495 (Fed. Cir. 1991)).

[132] See above text accompanying notes 124 and 125.

[133] The fact that the correlation between metabolite levels in the blood and the safety and effectiveness of thiopurine drug treatments was discovered through clinical experiments does not alter the Court's characterization of the claim's "instruction to doctors" as a teaching of *a priori* rather than empirical knowledge. See *Mayo*, 566 US 71 (quoting *Gottschalk v. Benson*, above note 50, at 67 (explaining that "[p]henomena of nature, though just discovered ... are not patentable, as they are the basic tools of scientific and technological work").

[134] See above text accompanying note 121.

18

Intellectual Property at a Crossroad

Awarding IP Protection for Algorithms

*Aviv Gaon**

INTRODUCTION

This chapter explores the legal protection awarded to algorithms[1] and argues that in the coming decade, with changes in coding methods, awarding IP protection for algorithms might not prevail. Even today, machines controlled by algorithms are outsmarting humans in many areas. For example, advanced algorithms influence markets and affect finance, commerce, human resources, health, and transportation.[2]

There is an extensive and wide-ranging literature that considers the implications of algorithms in the areas of computer science, philosophy, economics, religion, ethics, and science fiction.[3] However, with all the knowledge we have gathered we are still far from being

* I wish to thank Professor Pina D'Agostino, Professor Lior Zemer, Professor Dov Greenbaum, and Paul Blizzard for their thoughtful comments and suggestions to earlier drafts. I also wish to acknowledge IPOsgoode, Osgoode Hall Law School, IP and Technology Program, for their continued support in my research. Special thanks to Professor Woodrow Barfield for granting me the opportunity to join this project.
1 Defining the term "algorithm" is as complex and difficult as defining artificial intelligence field itself. There are many competing definitions with no accepted concept. However, few conclusions could be drawn. First, algorithms rely on mathematical codes to solve problems (calculation, data process, etc.). Second, most algorithms share a common purpose creating "output" integers from "input." In this chapter, I will address the most common algorithms as simple codes that produce standard output. However, when discussing future legal alternatives, I might refer to advanced algorithms. In advance algorithms, I am not aspiring to create any terminology; I only wish to express the possibility of using algorithms for more complex processes, which could be available to some extent today and probably more so in the future. See, e.g., C. C. Aggarwal, *Neural Networks and Deep Learning: A Textbook* (Springer, 2018); M. J. Kochenderfer and T. A. Wheeler, *Algorithms for Optimization* (MIT Press, 2019).
2 A. K. Agrawal, J. Gans, and A. Goldfarb (eds.), *The Economics of Artificial Intelligence: An Agenda* (University of Chicago Press, 2019); B. Alarie, A. Niblett, and A. H. Yoon, Focus Feature: Artificial Intelligence, Big Data, and the Future of Law (2016) 66 *Univ. Tor. Law J.* 423; M. S. Gal and N. Elkin-Koren, Algorithmic Consumers (2017) 30 *Harv. J. Law Technol.* 309; N. J. Nilsson, *The Quest for Artificial Intelligence: A History of Ideas and Achievements* (Cambridge University Press, 2010), p. 19; P. McCorduck, *Machines Who Think: A Personal Inquiry into the History and Prospects of Artificial Intelligence*, 2nd edn. (A. K. Peters, 2004), pp. 3–29; S. Russel and P. Norvig (eds.), *Artificial Intelligence: A Modern Approach* (Pearson Education, 2010), pp. 1034–40. Wall Street and banks have been using algorithms with prediction analysis for investments for several years and its impact is expected to grow in the coming years. M. Turner, Machine Learning Is Now Used in Wall Street Dealmaking, and Bankers Should Probably Be Worried, *Business Insider* (April 4, 2017), www.businessinsider.in /Machine-learning-is-now-used-in-Wall-Street-dealmaking-and-bankers-should-probably-be-worried/articleshow/ 58018833.cms.
3 N. Bostrom, *Superintelligence: Paths, Dangers, Strategies* (Oxford University Press, 2014); N. Bostrom and E. Yudkowsky, The Ethics of Artificial Intelligence, in W. Ramsay and K. Frankish (eds.), *The Cambridge Handbook of Artificial Intelligence* (Cambridge University Press, 2014), pp. 316–34; N. Ausubel (ed.), *A Treasury of Jewish Folklore* (Crown, 1948), p. 605 (discussing the story of the Golem of Prague); I. Asimov, *I, Robot* (Random House, 2004); see also V. C. Müller (ed.), *Fundamental Issues of Artificial Intelligence* (Springer International, 2016).

able to predict the impact of technology, especially technology driven by algorithms. Many of the concerns associated with the early stages of technological development may turn out to be trivial in later stages; whether this is true with technologies that are controlled by algorithms remains to be seen.

Algorithms are the building blocks of current advancements in computer science and artificial intelligence (AI).[4] As we are moving forward with digitizing more and more fields – from commerce to government services – legal challenges associated with those changes pose intriguing questions, both theoretically and practically. On the theoretical level, applying algorithmic data processing would shift our legal frameworks from "one size fits all" to "tailor-made" systems in which algorithms will "provide a tailored statement of what is permissible"[5] – a "personalized law," as Dan Burk suggested.[6] These expected changes would affect all areas of law in various ways and methods as explored within the chapters of this book. In this chapter, I will focus on IP law, seeking answers to questions already touched on by other contributors.

IP law stands as one of the core legal frameworks that regulate technology and thus is most likely to be affected by algorithms and AI. IP law includes intangible creations and relates to three main legal areas: copyright, patents, and trademarks. Copyright law seeks to protect original works of authorship, such as literary, musical, and artistic creations.[7] Patents give inventors exclusive rights on their inventions for a limited time, and trademarks offer protection to well-recognized signs, designs, and expressions.[8]

Considering how algorithms *are* and/or *will* affect IP law is an important task that should be addressed, sooner better than later. Take copyright, for example.[9] Copyright made sense in an era when programming was based, to some extent, on literature codes. With advancements in technology where most of the coding does not necessarily require actual "writing," copyright protection rationale might not prevail. And while the bulk of coding today is still done the old-fashioned way with human programmers, programming styles and methods are changing, and new environments "allow users to avoid directly typing virtually any code for some programs.[10] Instead, they select icons that visually represent functions."[11]

Patent law and trademarks could face similar outcomes. When we think about patents, the most prevailing theory is the incentive theory – we reward human inventors for their inventions to foster creativity and subsequent creations. However, in an era in which

---

[4]   Matt Taddy explains the relations between algorithms and AI. In simple terms, AI comprises a number of machine-learning algorithms. See M. Taddy, The Technological Elements of Artificial Intelligence, in Agrawal *et al.*, above note 2.

[5]   A. Casey and A. Niblett, Self Driving Laws (2016) 66 *Univ. Tor. Law J.* 429, 430–1.

[6]   D. Burk, Algorithmic Fair Use, Legal Studies Research Paper Series No. 2018-05.

[7]   D. Vaver, *Intellectual Property Law: Copyright, Patents, Trade-marks*, 2nd edn. (Irwin Law, 2011).

[8]   *Ibid.*

[9]   Prominent IP scholars have argued that the impact of AI and algorithmic authorship would affect the normative boundaries of copyright law, especially regarding ownership of computer-generated creations. See, e.g., J. C. Ginsburg and L. A. Budiardjo, Authors and Machines (2019) 34 *Berkley Technol. Law J.* 343; A. Bridy, The Evolution of Authorship: Work Made by Code (2016) 39 *Colum. J. Law Arts* 395, 396; A. Bridy, Coding Creativity: Copyright and Artificially Intelligent Author (2012) 5 *Stan. Technol. Law Rev.* 1; E. Dorotheou, Reap the Benefits and Avoid the Legal Uncertainty: Who Owns the Creations of Artificial Intelligence? (2015) 21 *CTLR* 85; P. Samuelson, Allocating Ownership Rights in Computer-Generated Work (1986) 47 *Univ. Pitt. Law Rev.* 1185; T. L. Butler, Can a Computer Be an Author? Copyright Aspects of Artificial Intelligence (1982) 4 *Comm. Ent. Law J.* 707, 746.

[10] Although I am well aware that we are still far away from that future, we are heading in that direction, nonetheless.

[11] L. S. Osborn, Intellectual Property Channeling for Digital Works (2018) 39 *Cardozo Law Rev.* 1303, 1356. This style of coding "abstracts the coding practice, removing it one or more levels from the literal code." Although Osborn is skeptical whether these expected changes will change courts' decisions.

inventorship can be programmed without human involvement, is there really a need in patent protection? And if not – will patent law survive the upcoming legal turmoil?[12]

Additionally, trademarks could be affected by advanced algorithms, although it might happen differently. Trademark law is ostensibly designed to limit consumer confusion. In establishing whether a mark might confuse or dilute a registered trademark, judges rely on their human experience and knowledge. Algorithms might be able to detect a mark's pattern which would not be apparent to the judges.

In this chapter, I examine the expected changes algorithms might have on IP law in the coming decade. I begin with a brief outline of the history of computer program developments over the past century. I show how IP law affects and was affected by developments in programming, leading the discussion to the next sections of the chapter in which I draw conclusions on the expected changes algorithms and technological developments might have and the way in which those changes could shape IP law in the future.

The third section of the chapter, "The Myth of Authorship," focuses on copyright, and the way in which the "myth of authorship" shaped copyright protection for computer programs. Programming methods today, together with more algorithms' independence, shake prevailing copyright arguments for protecting works of authorship – the fundamental reasoning for protecting the products of human "writings." Indeed, programming *used* to be all about writing codes and algorithms. It might not be that way for advanced programs today and would probably not last long into the next decade of computer programming. These developments require rethinking about the way in which we ought to shape IP law for the future of human and non-human creations.[13]

GETTING BACK TO THE BASICS: IP PROTECTION FOR SOFTWARE

When we look back on IP law in different fields, several preliminary conclusions can be drawn. First, copyright law is most relevant for our discussion given the way in which legal protection was awarded to computer programs and the relation between an algorithm's coding and the field of computer programs. Second, it is difficult to be conclusive about the way in which copyright law will change, or if it will change at all, given the differences between jurisdictions. Third, patents and copyright developed as complementary protection measures – extensive and strong patent protection for algorithms – would mean meeker copyright protection and vice versa. Fourth, we ought to rethink whether awarding IP protection serves its original purpose – to incentivize creation – and if we can achieve similar results with no IP protection. For example, we might favor an "open source" framework in which algorithms would not be protected at all.[14]

This next section of the chapter will explore the developments of copyright, patents, and trademarks over the past century. I will show how legal changes in one legal field affected

---

12 One of the contributors in this book considers these issues in a recent paper. See R. Abbott, I Think, Therefore I Invent: Creative Computers and the Future of Patent Law (2016) 57 *BC Law Rev.* 1079.

13 Take Apple Xcode11, for example (https://developer.apple.com/xcode/): "The source code editor lets you transform or refactor code more easily, see source control changes alongside the related line, and quickly get details on upstream code differences. You can build your own instrument with custom visualization and data analysis." And there are other programs that aspire to create an easier coding environment that relies on preconditioned codes with visual elements. See, e.g., Microsoft Visual Studio (https://betanews.com/2019/04/02/best-new-features-visual-studio-2019/).

14 An open source is software whose source code is released under an open source license that allows users to change the code and distribute the software. See, e.g., https://opensource.org.

changes in the other and subsequently how technological developments impacted the developments in a particular IP field.

First Phase: Protecting Software by Copyright

David Vaver poignantly admits that computer programs and copyright protection have never been considered a good match. This is due in part to the differences between the original intent of copyright law to protect human expressions, such as music, painting, and novels, versus the functional purpose of programs, which are less creative.[15] Thus, in the first stages of computer software development (the 1960s and 1970s), IP law did not protect software.[16] When IP law finally stepped in, it was copyright law – and not patents or trademarks – that became the primary source for IP protection.[17] Evidently, "[t]hroughout most of its history, the software has been protected primarily by copyright, if at all."[18]

The first important milestone in the history of technological legal debate is the work of the Commission on New Technological Uses of Copyright Works (CONTU) during the 1970s.[19] After years of deliberation, navigating the complex issues raised by computer programs advancements, CONTU concluded that computer programs constitute expression and should be accorded the same rights as other expressive works. Following the report, Congress amended the US Code's Title 17 (copyright law) to include the Computer Software Act of 1980.[20] This amendment defined a computer program as a "set of statements or instructions to be used directly or indirectly in a computer in order to bring about a certain result."[21] Subsequent case law interpreted the Act in the 1980s. Courts took a practical approach, willing to provide "real" protection for software programs under copyright law, establishing computer programs as both literary and audio-visual works by the mid-1980s.[22]

In *Apple Computer, Inc. v. Franklin Computer Corp.*,[23] the Third Circuit found both operating systems and applications equally copyrightable as computer programs. This is an important holding for algorithms given that they are typically written as code. Affirming *Apple*'s decision, the Court in *Williams Electronics* v. *Arctic* held that literal elements of computer programs included source code – spelled-out human-readable commands, usually written in a programming language like C^{++} or Python[24] – or object code – written in binary,

---

[15]   Vaver, above note 7, pp. 70–1. This statement was not always true. Programming a code might prove to be an artistic and innovative process. It seems that this perception is more relevant to "old" codes and not to current codes and developments, which could be innovative – though might not have any "writing" element. See also L. Determann and D. Nimmer, Software Copyright's Oracle from the Cloud (2015) 30 *BT Law J.* 161, 165.

[16]   P. S. Menell, Tailoring Legal Protection for Computer Software (1987) 39 *Stan. Law Rev.* 1329, 1332–4. This approach has led developers and vendors to seek the protection of other legal fields, such as contract law and trade secrets. M. A. Lemley, Convergence in the Law of Software Copyright? (1995) 10 *BT Law J.* 1, 3.

[17]   Determann and Nimmer, above note 15; Menell, above note 16, p. 1354.

[18]   Y. Benkler, *The Wealth of Networks: How Social Production Transforms Markets and Freedom* (Yale University Press, 2006), p. 437.

[19]   US National Commission on New Technological Uses of Copyright Works, Final Report of the National Commission on New Technological Uses of Copyright Works (Library of Congress Cataloging in Publication Data, 1979), http://digital-law-online.info/CONTU.

[20]   Copyright Amendment Act of 1980, Pub. L. No. 96–517, 94 Stat. 3015. CONTU, *ibid.*, at 1.

[21]   Copyright Law of the United States, 17 USC § 101: Definitions – "computer program." Canada Copyright Act, RSC 1985, s. 2, defines a "computer program" in a similar way as "a set of instructions or statements, expressed, fixed, embodied or stored in any manner, that is to be used directly or indirectly in a computer in order to bring about a specific result."

[22]   Lemley, above note 16, p. 6.

[23]   714 F.2d 1240 (3rd Cir. 1983).

[24]   685 F.2d 870 (3rd Cir. 1982).

comprised of ones and zeroes, and embedded in read-only memory (ROM) readable only by a computer.[25] This meant, as the Court held in *Stern Electronics, Inc.* v. *Kaufman*, that computer programs (like video games) could be simultaneously protectable under copyright law in several ways: as audio-visual, graphical or pictorial, and/or literary works.[26]

The European Union also impacted the development of computer program legal protection.[27] Several EU directives are responsible for the European Union's copyright protection for computer programs: the 1991 Related Rights Directive, the 2001 Directive on Copyright Harmonisation,[28] and the 2009 Software Directive.[29] The Software Directive required EU member states adopting software-as-literary-work protection under *Berne*.[30] It harmonized with US law, protecting only software's expressive elements, leaving "functionality, technical interfaces, programming language or data file formats" non-copyrightable.[31]

Copyright law was always designed to protect literary work;[32] but copyrightability of such works requires more than mere fixation of copyrightable subject matter. In other words, a computer program is prima facie copyrightable if fixed in source or object code, but it must embody sufficient originality and expression to earn entitlement to robust copyright protection. Otherwise, for example, as in Section 102(b) of the US Copyright Law, it is a non-copyrightable "idea, procedure, process, system, method of operation, concept, principle, or discovery, regardless of the form in which it is described, explained, illustrated, or embodied in such work."[33]

Establishing originality in computer programs proved complex. Copyright protection for computer programs required creativity; but creativity was disadvantageous for computer programmers, which in many cases aimed to create the simplest and easiest program.[34]

Second Phase: Protecting Software by Patenting

Patent law offers an alternative framework for software protection. Historically, many countries were hesitant to exploit patent law for software, fearing it would stymie innovation.[35] This fear subsided in recent decades; patent law's role in protecting

---

[25] *Ibid.*; Determann and Nimmer, above note 15, p. 168.

[26] Determann and Nimmer, *ibid*. In *Stern Elecs, Inc.* v. *Kaufman*, 669 F.2d 852, 855–7 (2nd Cir. 1982).

[27] Thus, it is not surprising that the European Union was also one of the first to consider a policy recommendation for robots' legal rights. See the EU Parliament Report. However, this initiative was put on halt by the EU Commission.

[28] EU Commission Directive (EC) 1991/250/EEC of 14 May 1991 on the Legal Protection of Computer Programs, 1991 OJ (L122) 42; EU Commission Directive (EC) 2001/29/EC of 22 May 2001 on the Harmonisation of Certain Aspects of Copyright and Related Rights in the Information Society, 2001 OJ (L167).

[29] EU Commission Directive (EC) 2009/24/EC of 23 April 2009 on the Legal Protection of Computer Programs, 2009 OJ (L111) 16.

[30] L. Bently and B. Sherman, *Intellectual Property Law*, 4th edn. (Oxford University Press, 2014), p. 49.

[31] Determann and Nimmer, above note 15.

[32] US Constitution, art. I, § 8, cl. 8. See also Lemley, above note 16; P. Samuelson, Computer Programs, User Interfaces, and Section 102(b) of the Copyright Act of 1976: A Critique of *Lotus v Paperback* (1992) 55 *Law Contemp. Probs.* 311, 339.

[33] US Copyright Law, above note 21, § 102(b).

[34] Determann and Nimmer, above note 15, p. 168. See also M. A. Lemley and D. W. O'Brien, Encouraging Software Reuse (1997) 49 *Stan. Law Rev.* 255; P. S. Menell, An Analysis of the Scope of Copyright Protection for Application Programs (1989) 41 *Stan. Law Rev.* 1045; J. C. Ginsburg, Four Reasons and a Paradox: The Manifest Superiority of Copyright Over Sui Generis Protection of Computer Software (1994) 94 *Colum. Law Rev.* 2559; J. P. Liu and S. L. Dogan, Copyright Law and Subject Matter Specificity: The Case of Computer Software (2005) 61 *NY Univ. Ann. Surv. Am. Law* 203; A. R. Miller, Copyright Protection for Computer Programs, Databases, and Computer-Generated Works: Is Anything New Since CONTU? (1993) 106 *Harv. Law Rev.* 977.

[35] Vaver, above note 7, p. 313.

software has increased since 1977[36] and stems from the US Patent Act's patentability criteria.[37] In past decades, the US Supreme Court has interpreted the Patent Act in a way that excluded non-physically manifested computer programs, which the Court viewed as mathematical algorithms, and thus abstract ideas which patent law could not protect.

American software patent mechanisms began with the three Supreme Court decisions establishing the *Freeman-Walter-Abele test*:[38] *Gottschalk v. Benson*,[39] *Parker v. Flook*,[40] and *Diamond v. Diehr*.[41] The trend continued in the 1994 decision, *In re. Alappat*,[42] which developed the *useful, concrete, and tangible test*. In these cases, the courts consistently distinguished between the unpatentability of mathematical algorithms – arguing that, alone, they are abstract ideas – and the patentability of a useful process incorporating an algorithm.[43] Such a limited distinction challenges patentability, since proving that a program is a useful process is harder to accomplish than submitting mere algorithms.

Despite this limit, programming patent floodgates opened[44] after the US Federal Courts removed any lingering doubt about the patentability of computer programs.[45] In *State Street* and *AT&T*, the courts finally withdrew the need to prove the presence of a physical component or transformation in a process claim as critical elements for approving a patent. Further, in *AT&T*, the Court implied that software's unpatentability – and the Supreme Court's condition from *Diamond* that physical transformation is a critical component – was a misunderstanding.[46] These rulings also mark the US decision "to part company with the Europeans and allow computer programs to be patented as well."[47]

The patent floodgates closed almost a decade later when the US Federal Court rejected both the *Freeman-Walter-Abele* and the *useful, concrete, and tangible* tests in *Bilski* (2008),[48] adopting instead the *Machine or transformation test* (only to be rejected two years later),[49] as the *sole* test for process patent eligibility. That test was held only to be "a useful and important clue, an investigative tool" for patentability determinations.[50]

[36] Bently and Sherman, above note 30, p. 475.
[37] US Patent Act, 35 USC § 101 (1952): "Whoever invents or discovers any new and useful process, machine, manufacture, or composition of matter, or any new and useful improvement thereof, may obtain a patent therefor."
[38] The Freeman-Walter-Abele test is a two-part test. First, the courts required to establish if a mathematical algorithm recited (directly or indirectly). Second, "if a mathematical algorithm is found, whether the claim as a whole applies the algorithm in any manner to physical elements or process steps." See F. E. Marino and T. H. P. Nguyen, From *Alappat* to *Alice*: The Evolution of Software Patents (2017) 9 *Hastings Sci. Technol. Law J.* 1, 4.
[39] 409 US 63 (1972).
[40] 437 US 584 (1978).
[41] 450 US 175 (1981).
[42] 33 F.3d 1526 (Fed. Cir. 1994). A few years later, in *State Street Bank & Trust Co.* v. *Signature Financial Group, Inc.*, 149 F.3d 1368 (Fed. Cir. 1998), the Court confirmed the *Alappat* decision. In *State Street Bank*, the Federal Court "found mathematical algorithms, an abstract concept, patentable if 'transformed' or 'performed' by a machine and which provided 'useful, concrete, and tangible' results." Marino and Nguyen, above note 38, p. 6.
[43] C. E. Cretsinger, AT&T Corp. v Excel Communications, Inc. (2000) 15 *BT Law J*. 165, 166. See also Marino and Nguyen, above note 38.
[44] Vaver, above note 7, p. 315.
[45] *AT&T Corp.* v. *Excel Commc'ns Inc.*, 172 F.3d 1352 (Fed. Cir. 1999). In that case, AT&T sued Excel for the infringement of their "184 patent." The patent involved technology improvement for calculating the price of direct-dialed long-distance calls; *State Street Bank*, above note 42.
[46] *AT&T*, ibid., at 1358–9.
[47] Vaver, above note 7, p. 315.
[48] *In re. Bernard L. Bilski and Rand A. Warsaw*, 545 F.3d 943 (Fed. Cir. 2008).
[49] *Bilski v. Kappos*, 561 US 593 (2010).
[50] Ibid. at 604.

Alice Corp. v. *CLS Bank* is the most recent Supreme Court decision on software patentability.[51] In *Alice*, the Court reaffirmed the two-step test, adopted in *Mayo Collaborative Services* v. *Prometheus Labs*: the first step asks if the patent contains an abstract idea (like an algorithm), and if it does, the second step requires that the patent add "something extra" – embodying an "inventive concept" – for patentability.[52] Ruling that Alice's patent claims were ineligible under the US Patent Act, the Court determined at the first step that they were "drawn to the abstract idea of intermediated settlement."[53] The Court concluded at the second step that something extra was lacking, stating that "the method claims, which merely require generic computer implementation, fail to transform that abstract idea into a patent-eligible invention."[54]

The main issue with *Alice* is the "something extra" requirement in order for a software to be sufficiently inventive and patentable. This stringent requirement to meet innovation is unclear in practice since "*Alice* left open the nature of the technological improvement that must exist before an application of an abstract concept may be patentable as 'inventive.'"[55] The lack of clarity in "something extra" is exacerbated in the software industry, which is significantly unique from other industries, as Ben Klemens noted.[56] First, a detailed description of software often *is* the software.[57] Second, programs are math; this forms a paradox: while the courts agree that pure math is unpatentable, software might be – "yet the two are equivalent."[58] Third, if a patent on a particle of code restricts other users from using that data or technique, it, in turn, hinders the development of other programs. Finally, *Alice*'s decision runs contrary to programmers' desired simplicity of useful software, and limits appropriate patent candidates by requiring the patent to demonstrate "something extra."

Since most software contains abstract ideas, some argued that *Alice* may lead to a substantial decrease in business method and computer-implemented innovations

---

51 *Alice Corp.* v. *CLS Bank Int'l*, 134 S.Ct. 2347 (2014).
52 The test is explained as follows: "First, we determine whether the claims at issue are directed to one of those patent-ineligible concepts . . . If so, we then ask, '[w]hat else is there in the claims before us?' . . . To answer that question, we consider the elements of each claim both individually and 'as an ordered combination' to determine whether the additional elements 'transform the nature of the claim' into a patent-eligible application . . . We have described step two of this analysis as a search for an 'inventive concept' – i.e., an element or combination of elements that is 'sufficient to ensure that the patent in practice amounts to significantly more than a patent upon the [ineligible concept] itself.'" *Alice*, ibid., at 2355. See also *Mayo Collab. Svcs.* v. *Prometheus Labs.*, 132 S.Ct. 1289 (2012).
53 *Alice*, above note 51, at 2355. The Supreme Court further offers, at 2356: "On their face, the claims before us are drawn to the concept of intermediated settlement, *i.e.*, the use of a third party to mitigate settlement risk. Like the risk hedging in *Bilski*, the concept of intermediated settlement is 'a fundamental economic practice long prevalent in our system of commerce.'"
54 *Alice*, above note 51, at 2350. If the patent contains an abstract idea (like an algorithm), and if it does, the second step requires the patent to add "something extra" – embodying an "inventive concept" – for patentability.
55 Marino and Nguyen, above note 38, p. 13.
56 B. Klemens, *Math You Can't Use: Patents, Copyright, and Software* (Brookings Institution Press, 2005), p. 4.
57 *Ibid.* Klemens further explains: "For the pop-up window, the idea is a window that automatically opens and moves to the front when the user views a new page . . . For Prozac, the idea is a selective serotonin reuptake inhibitor (SSRI) . . . Traditionally, patents have been granted to implementations of ideas and not to the ideas themselves – there are a dozen SSRIs on the market that did not infringe on the Prozac patent. But in software, the pattern has been reversed: most patents cover ideas like the pop-up window, regardless of implementation, so they tend to be too broad."
58 Klemens, above note 56. The courts resolved this contradiction by providing a set of roles and complex tests that might, under certain conditions, allow mathematical algorithm patents. However, these attempts to reconcile the contradictions did not always succeed.

patents.[59] On the other hand, others applaud the Supreme Court's decision to limit patents on programs based heavily on data and, consequently, strengthen competition. Data is the fuel of future developments, and its availability is crucial for a machine-learning technology's progression.[60] As Ryan Calo highlighted,[61] high-quality distilling data is essential for any government policy. By limiting the ability to patent software that relies heavily on data – even processed high-quality data – we make the data public goods, thus allowing programmers access to it for the benefit of future progress.

Alice provided weak guidance for lawyers and programmers to follow. And after a short ambiguous period,[62] the Federal Court offered some guidance to software patentees. According to Judge Hughes in *Enfish*,[63] *Alice* did not conclude that all computer-related technology improvements are "inherently abstract and, therefore, must be considered at step two." Rather, it is "relevant to ask whether the claims are directed to an improvement to computer functionality versus being directed to an abstract idea, even at the first step of the *Alice* analysis."[64] In *DDR Holdings*, the Court explained that when dealing with inventions that are "rooted in computer technology," that is, not simply the application of a computer to a known solution, eligible subject matter may be found if the invention overcomes a problem specific to the realm of computers themselves.[65] Finally, in January 2019, the US Patent and Trademark Office (USPTO) released its 2019 Revised Patent Subject Matter Eligibility Guide.[66] The revised guide modifies how patents will be examined with regard to subject matter, and significantly changes the requirements to be "whether it's integrated into a practical application."[67] It is, however, important to note that in the years that followed since *Alice* and subsequent cases, the gloomy industry predictions have not yet materialized.[68]

---

[59]   Marino and Nguyen, above note 38. See *Mayo*, above note 52 at 1294. See also J. L. Tran, Two Years after Alice v. CLS Bank (2016) 98 *J. Pat. & Trademark Off. Soc.* 354; Osborn, above note 11, p. 1329.

[60]   Leading AI systems use artificial neural networks that, like the human brain, learn from experience. This is why data is so important for the development of AI and should be treated as oil or fuel. See M. Palmer, Data Is the New Oil, *Michael Palmer Blog* (November 3, 2006), http://ana.blogs.com/maestros/2006/11/data_is_the_new .html. On the other hand, there are different views claiming that oil is not the right equivalent since data, contrary to oil, is unlimited. See B. Marr, Here's Why Data Is Not the New Oil, *Forbes* (March 5, 2018), http://forbes.com/sites/bernardmarr/2018/03/05/heres-why-data-is-not-the-new-oil/#59458ee13aa9.

[61]   R. Calo, Artificial Intelligence Policy: A Primer and a Road Map (2017) 51 *UC Davis Law Rev.* 399.

[62]   Following *Alice*, the Federal Court and the Supreme Court failed to provide guidance to *Alice*'s requirements. Specifically, what constitutes an abstract idea: "[N]one of the cases that survived the Alice analysis did so based on the first prong of the analysis, patent-eligibility was determined exclusively based on the second prong." Marino and Nguyen, above note 38, p. 22.

[63]   *Enfish, LLC* v. *Microsoft Corp*, 822 F.3d 1327 (Fed. Cir. 2016).

[64]   *Ibid.* at 1335.

[65]   *DDR Holdings, LLC* v. *Hotels.com, LP*, No. 2013-1505, 2014 US App. LEXIS 22902, at *26 (Fed. Cir. 2014): ". . . these claims stand apart because they do not merely recite the performance of some business practice known from the pre-Internet world along with the requirement to perform it on the Internet. Instead, the claimed solution is necessarily rooted in computer technology in order to overcome a problem specifically arising in the realm of computer networks." See also *McRO, Inc.* v. *Bandai Namco Games America Inc. et al.*, No. 15-1080, slip op. at 23 (Fed. Cir. 2016), citing *TLI Comm'ns Patent Litig.*, 823 F.3d 607, 611 (Fed. Cir. 2016). One must consider the claim as a whole and should not over-generalize the claim or simplify it into its "gist" or core principles, when identifying a concept as a judicial exception. Interpreters "'must be careful to avoid oversimplifying the claims' by looking at them generally and failing to account for the specific requirements of the claims."

[66]   The 2019 Revised Subject Matter Guidelines, www.uspto.gov/about-us/news-updates/us-patent-and-trademark-office-announces-revised-guidance-determining-subject.

[67]   *Ibid.* at 50.

[68]   See Berkeley Center for Law & Technology report addressing patent eligibility challenges following the *Alice* and *Mayo* decisions. J. A. Lefstin, P. S. Menell, and D. O. Taylor, Final Report of the Berkeley Center for Law & Technology Section 101 Workshop: Addressing Patent Eligibility Challenges (2018) 33 *Berkeley Technol. Law J.*

Moving on to other jurisdictions for guidance, the United Kingdom and Canada might offer further insights into computer programs' patentability. The UK Patents Act 1997, for example, does not recognize computer programs as inventions.[69] However, as Bently and Sherman explain, "an invention that includes a computer program could be patentable so long as the invention as a whole was technical."[70] This approach did not last long. Following *Aerotel*,[71] the United Kingdom's Intellectual Property Office (IPO) reinstated the "old practice of rejecting all computer program claims."[72] It backtracked somewhat in February 2008, when it revised its practice to include patentability for a computer program.[73] In *HTC*, Lord Justice Kitchin followed this reasoning in overturning a UK High Court (Justice Floyd) decision that found two of Apple's related patents invalid. As Lord Justice Kitchin explains:[74] "I believe the judge took his eye off the ball in focussing on the fact that the invention was implemented in software and in so doing failed to look at the issue before him as a matter of substance not form. Had he done so he would have found that the problem and its solution are essentially technical and so not excluded from patentability." Nonetheless, UK software patentability remains restrained, as "an ordinary computer program used in a general-purpose computer would normally not be patentable in the United Kingdom."[75]

Software developments in the United States inspired the Canadian approach to software patent protection. As Vaver states, "In 1978 the Canadian PO decided that computer programs were effectively algorithms ... and so fell under the prohibition against patenting abstract theorems."[76] In the following decades, the Canadian Intellectual Property Office (CIPO) was accordingly reluctant to issue software patents.[77] Until *Diamond*,[78] "[p]atents

---

551. It should be noted, however, that this statement might not be accurate. Broadly speaking, it was not a concern for most subject matter areas, but for particular Art Units at the USPTO.

[69] UK Patent Act 1977. See also UK IPO, Manual of Patent Practice (MoPP) (2018), ss. 1.35–1.39.2.

[70] Bently and Sherman, above note 30, p. 476. In *Vicom/Computer-related invention*, Case T-208/84 (1987), www.epo.org/law-practice/case-law-appeals/recent/t840208ep1.html, it was said "that 'an invention which would be patentable in accordance with conventional patentability criteria should not be excluded from protection by the mere fact that for its implementation modern technical means in the form of computer programs are used.' This approach was adopted and endorsed by a number of decisions in the United Kingdom." Consequently, while computer programs are not considered eligible for patent protection in the United Kingdom, patent applications that *contain* a computer program might be patentable, as long as it can be shown that the program is technical by its nature. Bently and Sherman, *ibid.*, p. 477, concluded: "[A] computer program product could be patentable if it resulted in additional technical effects that went beyond the 'normal' physical interaction between the program (software) and the computer (hardware) on which it was run."

[71] *Aerotel* v. *Telco Holdings* [2006] EWCA Civ. 1371.

[72] Bently and Sherman, above note 30, p. 479. As Bently and Sherman indicated, the post-*Aerotel* policy "created a gap between the United Kingdom and EPO," and obviously between the United Kingdom and the United States.

[73] This revision was the outcome of implementing Kitchin LJ's reservations in regard to *Aerotel*'s decision in *Astron Clinica* v. *Comptroller General Patents* [2008] EWHC 85 at para. 51. This decision was reaffirmed in *Symbian* v. *Comptroller-General of Patents* [2008] EWCA Civ. 1066 (Bently and Sherman, above note 30, pp. 479–80). Following *Symbian*, the IPO updated the practice notice to include the additional class of inventions "which improve the operation of a computer by solving a problem arising from the way the computer was programmed," IPO Practice Notice, *Patents Act 1977*: Patentability Subject Matter (December 8, 2008). Therefore, the IPO requires to determine whether the invention has a technical effect (which does not fall within the excluded categories in the Patent Act). In *AT&T Knowledge Ventures* v. *Comptroller General of Patents, Design and Trade Marks* [2009] EWHC 343, the Court outlined few signals and criteria to establish if an invention involving computer software is patentable under the UK Patent Act.

[74] *HTC Europe Co.* v. *Apple Inc.* [2013] EWCA Civ. 451 at para. 57.

[75] Bently and Sherman, above note 30, p. 482. See also *AT&T* and *HTC, ibid.*, at 44 and 45.

[76] Above note 7, p. 313.

[77] *Ibid.*, p. 314.

[78] *Diamond*, above note 41.

were granted for a 'computing apparatus programmed in a novel manner, where the patentable advance is in the apparatus itself,' and for a 'method or process carried out with a specific novel apparatus devised to implement a newly discovered idea.'"[79]

Following *Diamond*, the CIPO "accepted that a 'real change in a tangible thing' beyond just the production of information" could be patented.[80] As a result of *Alappat*,[81] the CIPO decided in 1995 to allow "patenting of an algorithm that scaled numbers exponentially where the calculation was tied to a physical read-only-memory chip."[82] In the coming decades, the CIPO has refined and clarified its position distinguishing between "an abstract scheme, plan or set of rules for operating a computer,"[83] which do not fall within the meaning of section 2 of the Canada Patent Act, and a computer program that could "cause the device it controls to provide a technological solution to a technological problem." Accordingly, where a computer program exhibits novelty and inventiveness, the claim might include statutory contribution and thus provide the necessary circumstances "under which a software product comprising a physical memory storing executable code can be patented."[84]

Phase Three: Trade Secret Protection Gains Momentum

Trade secrets may play a key role in protecting software. In simple terms, trade secret means information, including a program that "(i) derives independent economic value, actual or potential, from not being generally known to, and not being readily ascertainable by proper means" by other people that can "obtain economic value from its disclosure or use."[85] In other words, trade secrets protection requires that the programmer should not make the code available to the public.

Trade secrets were crucial during the mainframe era (1960s) – since software was rarely distributed in source code then – but during the PC era (1990s), their importance diminished. The rise of copyright protection and the Internet so-called revolution made it relatively easy to view the functional coding behind web pages.[86] Moreover, the decrease of trade secret protection leveled out with the rise of cloud computing companies during the late 1990s. The advent of cloud computing at the beginning of 1999 heralded multi-player games like

79   Above note 7, p. 314.
80   *Ibid.*
81   *Alappat*, above note 42.
82   Above note 7, p. 315.
83   See *Canada (Attorney General)* v. *Amazon.com, Inc.*, 2011 FCA 328 (CanLII) at para. 63: "It is arguable that the patent claims in issue in this case could fail on the same reasoning, depending upon whether a purposive construction of the claims in issue leads to the conclusion that *Schlumberger* cannot be distinguished because the only inventive aspect of the claimed invention is the algorithm – a mathematical formula – that is programmed into the computer to cause it to take the necessary steps to accomplish a one-click online purchase. On the other hand, it is also arguable that a purposive construction of the claims may lead to the conclusion that *Schlumberger* is distinguishable because a new one-click method of completing an online purchase is not the whole invention but only one of a number of essential elements in a novel combination. In my view, the task of purposive construction of the claims in this case should be undertaken anew by the Commissioner, with a mind open to the possibility that a novel business method may be an essential element of a valid patent claim." See also CIPO Examination Practice Respecting Purposive Construction – PN2013-02, www.ic.gc.ca/eic/site/cipointernet-internetopic.nsf/eng/wr03626.html.
84   See Canada, Ministry of Innovation, Science and Economic Development, Patent Office: Manual of Patent Office Practice (Ottawa, 2018), s. 16.08.04, http://ic.gc.ca/eic/site/cipointernet-internetopic.nsf/vwapj/rpbb-mopop-eng.pdf/$file/rpbb-mopop-eng.pdf.
85   Uniform Trade Secrets Act with 1985 Amendments (1985), § 1(4).
86   While some software languages like JavaScript are interpreted by the browser and thus visible; much of the code running on the server itself is still under trade secret protection, and thus not viewable by the user.

World of Warcraft (2004) and programs like Microsoft Office365 (2011), which contributed to the rise of trade secret protection.[87]

Until *Alice*,[88] the use of trade secret protection in the software industry remained constant. *Alice* was expected to enhance the importance of trade secret protection, mainly due to the diminished possibility of patent protection.[89] However, we should bear in mind that trade secret protection remains weak since software can be reverse-engineered unless digitally locked and protected.

THE MYTH OF AUTHORSHIP: A NEW CHALLENGE FOR ALGORITHMS

Developments in technology are taking away the artistic elements in coding, making algorithms' writing less and less utilized in practice. Obviously, as with other matters of technological progress, changes take time, and there are different methods in coding. Thus, we should anticipate a divergent in algorithms coding in which "regular" coding and more advanced coding would be used simultaneously, at least for the foreseeable future.

Given that we could expect some programmers to continue to "write" codes, while others will employ more advanced non-literature elements[90] methods, one must wonder if the written element should be determinative in establishing copyright protection. In other words, maybe there is no reason to award copyright protection to algorithms, no matter how they were coded.

Looking back on the historical millstones in awarding IP protection to computer programs enables us to understand better the reasoning for establishing copyright protection for them. The computer programs copyright so-called loophole was based on the literary nature of the programs, and as we have learned already, copyright cradle is authorship – serving as the mechanism to "solidify the notion of literary property."[91]

Authors' rights refer to original works such as books, music, art, and programs that possess some degree of creativity.[92] The modern author developed during the eighteenth century as an individual ownership right.[93] During that era, the author was regarded as a sole genius "innately inspired and thus capable of producing original work."[94] The romantic era shaped the modern concept of authorship on the core values of copyright law, obscuring practical approaches to copyright and contributing to the preservation of economic rights for companies and publishers.[95]

---

[87]   It is easier to protect cloud-based programs since large portions of the code (the trade secret candidate) exist on secure servers rather than on end-users' computers (as in traditional software). Hence, the common method of reverse engineering (the main loopholes of trade secret protection) is much harder to apply.

[88]   *Alice*, above note 51.

[89]   *Alice* effects on the markets and the courts are highlighted in the recent Berkeley report, above note 68. The report notes, for example, at p. 590 that "[t]here has been a dramatic decrease in the ability to patent personalized," and at p. 592 several participants acknowledged that the *"Alice* decision has allowed defendants to get particularly weak patent cases dismissed early in the litigation process, resulting in substantial savings and effectively eliminating many dubious patents from the system."

[90]   No writing and/or limited or no human involvement in the process.

[91]   P. Jaszi, Toward a Theory of Copyright: The Metamorphoses of "Authorship" (1991) 1991 *Duke Law J.* 455, 466.

[92]   Bently and Sherman, above note 30, p. 32.

[93]   See G. D'Agostino, *Copyright, Contracts, Creators: New Media, New Rules* (Edward Elgar, 2010), p. 42. See also Jaszi, above note 91, pp. 468–71; J. Ginsburg, The Role of Authorship in Copyright, in R. L. Okediji (ed.), *Copyright Law in an Age of Limitations and Exceptions* (Cambridge University Press, 2017), p. 60.

[94]   D'Agostino, *ibid.*, pp. 49–50.

[95]   M. Woodmansee, The Genius and the Copyright: Economic and Legal Conditions of the Emergence of the "Author" (1984) 17 *Eighteenth-Century Stud.* 425, 427. See also M. Woodmansee and P. Jaszi (eds.), *The Construction of Authorship: Textual Appropriation in Law and Literature* (Duke University Press, 1994); see also K. Bowrey Law, Aesthetics and Copyright Historiography: A Critical Reading of the Genealogies of Martha Woodmansee and Mark Rose, in I. Alexander and H. T. Gómez-Arostegui (eds.), *Research Handbook on the*

In that respect, the individual programmer that created the early computer programs' codes and algorithms was able to be placed – although not without resistance – within the normative boundaries of copyright law and the romantic ideal of authorship. True, for some time programmers were not considered *authors* and algorithms were not regarded as *works of art* given their simplistic nature. However, eventually, the elements in which the code was developed (that is, writings), together with some leniency in other jurisdictions, allowed computer programs copyright recognition.

In time, both the concept of authorship and the practice of an algorithm's coding has changed. We should now consider if these changes might affect copyright protection. I suspect that they should and would, at least to some degree. First, we should acknowledge that the idealism of the romantic author as the sole "genius" degraded during the last century.[96] A weaker author means a weaker programmer and a weaker claim for copyright protection. It is apparent that although there might be many sole programmers, most coding and advanced algorithms are the work of companies and groups.

Second, new changes are on the horizon, especially the computer-generated works and expected AI revolution: we might live to see the "death" of the human author and the rise of the AI author.[97] Woodmansee has foreseen these changes already, stating that "technology is hastening the demise of the illusion that writing is solitary and originary."[98] Indeed, in the new technological era, the concept of the sole (romantic) author is obsolete.[99]

Even if we put aside advanced algorithms and new coding methods for a moment, we ought to consider the way in which humans interact with technology today. Information and data engulf us from all sides. We use Google Images, Google Scholar, and Google Books to gather information. We enjoy unlimited sources of information on every topic and every issue. The human author of our time can easily be affected by different styles of works and creations. Advancements in technology will speed these processes even further. These unique characteristics of the new creation process make the individual author a reminiscence of the past.

AND MAYBE WE ARE ALL WRONG: THERE IS NO REASON FOR IP PROTECTION

Changes in algorithms' coding methods and other AI-related developments in the field of computer programs are challenging contemporary legal perceptions. New algorithms do not

---

History of Copyright Law (Edward Elgar, 2016), p. 27; M. Woodmansee, The Romantic Author, in Alexander and Gómez-Arostegui, *ibid.*, p. 53.

[96] M. Woodmansee, On the Author Effect: Recovering Collectivity (1992) 10 *Cardozo Arts Ent. Law J.* 279, 280.

[97] Take journalism, for example. There are many articles that are generated automatically by algorithms. An algorithm named Tobi produced thousands of articles for Switzerland's November 2018 elections, see Y. Ren, Robo-Journalists that Write Up "Monotonous" Articles from Election to Sports Results Are Becoming More Popular in Newsrooms – But Will They Ever Replace Traditional Reporters?, *The Daily Mail* (March 9, 2019), www.dailymail.co.uk/sciencetech/article-6791173/Robo-journalism-gains-traction-shifting-media-landscape.html. Noam Lemelshtrich Latar observes that "within 5–10 years, the majority of all journalistic text stories will be written by robots" (N. L. Latar, *Robot Journalism: Can Human Journalism Survive?* (World Scientific Publishing Co., 2018), p. 29).

[98] Woodmansee, above note 96, p. 289.

[99] Algorithms could write books, plays, and other creations with minimal to no human influence; see W. Lee, Can a Computer Write a Script? Machine Learning Goes Hollywood, *Los Angeles Times* (April 11, 2019), www.latimes.com/business/hollywood/la-fi-ct-machine-learning-hollywood-20190411-story.html.

require specific instructions and can learn and evolve by acquiring and analyzing data, adjusting their code in the process.

These new and innovative algorithms could potentially change their codes, adjusting and fixing errors, while the human programmer's influence on the coding process becomes less and less valuable on the outcome. Lucas Osborn explains that programmers rely increasingly on "default structures to do much of the coding, with the programmer simply filling in the blanks."[100] Programming is integrated with other coding programs that rely on functions and other features. These new programming methods challenge programs' eligibility for IP protection. Osborn describes the copyright challenge in adapting these methods by comparing programming to cooking:[101]

> If simple ordering choices could constitute sufficient creativity, then even simple listing of ingredients would qualify for copyright protection. After all, one could list flour first and eggs second or vice versa. One could alphabetize the ingredients or organize them by weight. And yet, we are told that mere listings of ingredients are not copyrightable.

This process for utilitarian programs "highlights how little authorship occurs in the textual level."[102] As I have already explained, given the strong relation between the authorship element and the copyright protection – taking away the "writing" might take away the normative substance of the protection awarded to algorithms.

Furthermore, an algorithm could make establishing originality (in copyright) or obviousness (in patents) much more complex, effectively raising the bar for copyrightability/patentability higher and higher. Ryan Abbott recently expressed concern that when advanced algorithms and programs become the standard in the market, inventive machines would be the new standard, making the bar for obviousness in patents higher in a way that more simple algorithms, programs, and human creation will no longer qualify as inventive.[103] Thus, future algorithms might not be eligible for patent or copyright protection, which would be reserved for very limited – and highly advanced – algorithms.

The expected changes described by Osborn and Abbott are not unique for computer programming and algorithms: other fields in the creative process might be affected by technological changes as well. Advanced AI systems could change the way in which books and music are created, making the human element in the creation process irrelevant or limited. These expected changes, as Mark Lemley explains, could potentially challenge the legal protection awarded to non-human creations altogether.[104]

Lemley investigates the implications of the mass-information era, identifying several future technological challenges from a centralized IP viewpoint. Lemley discusses three new technologies that promise similar change: 3D printing, synthetic biology, and bio-printing and robotics. Lemley claims that "our economy is based on scarcity. We pay for things because it takes resources …"[105] This economic rule might be irrelevant in an era where information is abundant. To Lemley, "a series of technological changes promise to remake this basic economics in the coming decades,"[106] just as the Internet and cellphone revolutions

---

[100]   Osborn, above note 11, p. 1305.
[101]   *Ibid.*, p. 1322.
[102]   *Ibid.*, p. 1310.
[103]   R. Abbott, Everything Is Obvious (2019) 66 *UCLA Law Rev.* 2.
[104]   M. Lemley, IP in a World without Scarcity (2015) 90 *NY Univ. Law Rev.* 460.
[105]   *Ibid.*, p. 466.
[106]   *Ibid.*, p. 468.

have changed the way in which we interact with information. Lemley states rhetorically: "Why are people creating so much content without the incentive of IP rights? And why hasn't the sky fallen on the Internet industries?"[107]

Clearly, the Internet era has brought new and different variables into play. Although these differences might not be relevant to robots and advanced algorithms, the upcoming era may potentially herald similarly divergent reasoning that would change, diminish, or extinguish existing incentive theory. Indeed, granting exclusive rights to authors imposes social costs on the public that can only be justified to the extent that they encourage enough creation and dissemination of works to offset social costs – the incentive theory basic rule. However, expected developments in methods and programming style might shake the incentive theory basis, for the incentive reasoning will not apply to AI and highly advanced algorithms.[108]

However, copyright protection is not the only change new algorithms might bring. Niva Elkin-Koren addresses some of these changes in a recent paper. Nowadays, Elkin-Koren explains, "the vast majority of copyrighted materials are distributed digitally, and much of copyright enforcement is performed using algorithms."[109] Fair use (or fair dealing in other jurisdictions) serves as the legal mechanism to balance copyright protection.[110] The fair use doctrine provides that certain uses of a work would be considered "fair" (and, thus, would not result in an infringement) including criticism, parody, news reporting, research, commentary, and search engines. Using algorithms to track copyright infringements might not take into consideration eligible uses.

In other words, if we will not include fair use as part of the algorithms' codes, we might risk that every infringement – fair use or not – would be regarded as an infringement per se stifling creativity, research, parody, and other positive uses. Thus, Elkin-Koren advocates for fair use by design "to tilt the copyright balance back to its origin in our robo notice environment."[111]

CONCLUSIONS

In this chapter, I discussed the legal protection awarded to algorithms and the developments of IP protection in the field of computer science in the past decades. I also considered how the impending technological shift and the introduction of new coding methods might affect IP protection to algorithms. Given the recent trends in patents and copyright law, we should expect more "cracks" in the legal protection awarded to algorithms (although not necessarily in the imminent future). As the human influence on the creative process wanes, and with changes in the programming methods that could forsake orthodox "writing" of programs, the legal basis for IP protection awarded to algorithms might lose its normative base, making IP unattainable both normatively and practically.

---

[107]   *Ibid.*, p. 487.

[108]   This notion was shared by Yanisky-Ravid and Xiaoqiong (Jackie) Liu, stating in a recent paper that "autonomous machines do not need any incentive – that incentive is relevant only to people and entities until machines, robots and AI systems start producing . . ." S. Yanisky-Ravid and X. (Jackie) Liu, When Artificial Intelligence Systems Produce Inventions: An Alternative Model for Patent Law at the 3A Era (2017) 39 *Cardozo Law Rev.* 2215, 2239.

[109]   N. Elkin-Koren, Fair Use by Design (2017) 64 *UCLA Law Rev.* 1082, 1084.

[110]   *Authors Guild, Inc.* v. *HathiTrust*, 755 F.3d 87, 94–5 (2nd Cir. 2014).

[111]   Elkin-Koren, above note 109, p. 1100.

PART IV

Criminal Law, Tort Issues, and Algorithms

19

The Use of Algorithms in Criminal Adjudication

Andrea Roth

INTRODUCTION

The age-old dream of man has been the achievement of a sort of "slot-machine proof" whereby a situation is fed into a device and out rolls the correct adjudication.

Dillard S. Gardner[1]

The use of "algorithms" in criminal investigation, adjudication, and punishment is not a new phenomenon. That is, to the extent that "algorithms" are simply sets of rules capable of being executed by a machine, the criminal justice system has long incorporated their use. For example, the US sentencing guidelines are so mechanistic that they were, at least for a time, literally calculated by software.[2] Likewise, the New York Police Department's erstwhile "stop and frisk" program was a mechanistic means of deciding whom to search and when.[3] And so-called "per se" impaired driving laws have for nearly half a century mechanistically imposed criminal liability based on a machine's determination that a person's blood-alcohol level is over a certain threshold, without a jury determination of dangerous impairment.

Nonetheless, there is no mistaking the surge in algorithmic decision-making in twenty-first-century criminal justice, facilitated by ever more sophisticated technologies. In 2019, police departments use predictive policing software to determine in which neighborhoods to deploy officers and use proprietary malware to identify users of dark websites; both the government and sometimes the defense rely on software results to prove guilt or innocence at trial, including the opinions of complex expert systems that fully automate the interpretation of DNA mixtures; and parole boards rely on machine-learning algorithms to predict the future dangerousness of an inmate seeking release. On the more distant horizon, entrepreneurs have begun in earnest to design artificial intelligence (AI) to replace court reporters, determine appropriate probation conditions for juvenile offenders, analyze the fairness of prosecutorial decision-making, and detect wrongful convictions by examining trial records.

The increasing dominance and complexity of algorithms in criminal adjudication is worthy of scholarly attention for a number of reasons. On the one hand, such algorithms have the potential to enhance objectivity and accuracy, to the extent they reduce certain

---

[1] D. S. Gardner, Breath-Tests for Alcohol: A Sampling Study of Mechanical Evidence (1953) 31 *Tex. Law Rev.* 289, 289.
[2] See E. Simon, G. Gaes, and W. Rhodes, ASSYST – the Design and Implementation of Computer Assisted Sentencing (1991) 55 *Fed. Probat.* 46.
[3] See J. A. Kroll, J. Huey, S. Barocas, *et al.*, Accountable Algorithms (2017) 165 *Univ. Pa. Law Rev.* 633 (using the stop and frisk program as an example of a potentially discriminatory algorithmic process).

biases and errors inherent in ad hoc human judgments, as well as efficiency. Indeed, in some criminal justice domains, algorithms are surely underused. On the other hand, algorithms deployed in criminal adjudication might, as they do in other contexts, suffer biases and errors, rendering their unfairness and inaccuracy less transparent and more insidious than the unfairness or inaccuracy of an unaided police officer, prosecutor, expert witness, judge, court reporter, or jury. Further, algorithms can distort decision-making by emphasizing quantifiable variables or removing human safety valves necessary to achieve "softer" values such as dignity, equity, and mercy. In these circumstances, algorithms are not necessarily overused, but might be deployed in a way counter to important pre-existing systemic goals. Ultimately, if algorithms are to further rather than jeopardize those goals, we will need to adopt a "systems" approach focused on human–machine compatibility in the service of clearly stated values.

This chapter offers an overview of this recent shift toward algorithmic decision-making in criminal justice, focusing on the use of algorithms in the *adjudication* of criminal liability, rather than their use in *risk assessment* or *policing*. To be sure, actuarial risk assessment and predictive policing present many of the same promises and perils as algorithmic decision-making in the adjudication context. But the literature and policy debate surrounding the use of algorithms in these two other contexts is already (though, of course, not yet satisfactorily) robust. A separate chapter in this volume, Chapter 20 by Christopher Slobogin, offers an analysis of risk assessment algorithms at the pre-trial, sentencing, and post-conviction stages. Moreover, organizations such as the Partnership for AI's working group on criminal justice have offered comprehensive white papers with reform proposals related to risk assessment.[4] Similarly, a growing debate and literature surrounds algorithm-enhanced policing, such as police departments' use of predictive software like PredPol.[5] In particular, law professor Andrew Ferguson's recent book *The Rise of Big Data Policing: Surveillance, Race, and the Future of Law Enforcement* (2018) offers a comprehensive descriptive account and normative critique of predictive policing. In contrast, only a handful of legal scholars have focused on the use of algorithms in charging, proving, and adjudicating guilt at trial.

The first section of this chapter, "The Use of Algorithms in Criminal Adjudication," offers an overview of algorithm-generated proof of guilt and innocence, as well as the uses of algorithms in legal informatics, to augment the tasks of prosecutors, judges, juries, and court reporters. The second section, "Legal Rules Governing Algorithms in Criminal Adjudication," offers an explanation of the legal rules currently governing algorithms in criminal adjudication. The third section, "The Debate over the Promise and Peril of Algorithms," offers an overview of existing scholarly discourse about the promise and peril of these new algorithmic tools in terms of systemic values, including accuracy and objectivity, as well as "softer" values, such as dignity, equity, and mercy. The chapter concludes with

---

[4] Partnership on AI, Report on Algorithmic Risk Assessment Tools in the U.S. Criminal Justice System (April 26, 2019), www.partnershiponai.org/report-on-machine-learning-in-risk-assessment-tools-in-the-u-s-criminal-justice-system/.

[5] In addition to Ferguson's recent book, other legal scholars have analyzed the benefits and dangers of using AI in policing. See, e.g., R. Richardson, J. Schultz, and K. Crawford, Dirty Data, Bad Predictions: How Civil Rights Violations Impact Police Data, Predictive Policing Systems, and Justice (2019) 192 *NY Univ. Law Rev. Online*; E. Joh, Automated Policing (2018) 15 *Ohio St. J. Crim. Law* 559. Moreover, several civil liberties organizations have weighed in on the potential dangers of predictive policing. See, e.g., Predictive Policing Today: A Shared Statement of Civil Rights Concerns (August 31, 2016) (signed by seventeen civil liberties organizations, such as the Brennan Center for Justice and the American Civil Liberties Union), www.aclu.org/other/statement-concern-about-predictive-policing-aclu-and-16-civil-rights-privacy-racial-justice.

some thoughts about how the criminal justice system should respond to algorithmic adjudication.

This section describes various categories of algorithmic proof offered in criminal trials, from the basic scientific instruments of the nineteenth century to the opinions of complex expert systems presented in modern courtrooms. The section then discusses the use of algorithms in legal informatics; that is, as tools to assist legal actors such as prosecutors and judges in analyzing data and making decisions.

While this section focuses on algorithmic *proof*, any complete discussion of the use of algorithms in criminal adjudication must also note the ubiquity of algorithms and machines in facilitating the *storage* and *communication* of information. Courts have admitted machine-stored information, such as databases listing entries made by employees, since at least the 1970s.[6] Indeed, "electronically stored information" (ESI) has now been officially incorporated into the rules of civil discovery.[7] Similarly, email programs act more as high-tech conduits for human assertions than as algorithmic proof themselves. Such programs raise potential authentication questions (such as whether a purported email is actually written by a particular declarant), but ones that are qualitatively different from those raised by machine-*generated* proof, such as Google Earth driving estimates.[8] In addition, algorithms might power tools that replace human laboratory workers, such as machines programmed to make copies of DNA through cycles of heating and cooling. While such tools may affect the accuracy of laboratory testing, they raise qualitatively different questions than algorithmic *proof*, in which a machine actually generates and conveys information that a party offers to prove guilt or innocence.

Algorithm-Generated Proof of Guilt

Basic Scientific Instruments

Algorithms and machines have actually been used to generate proof in civil and criminal trials long before the modern era. Thermometers, clocks, and other basic scientific instruments – admitted in Anglo-American trials for well over a century – combine natural phenomena (for example, gravity, spring actions, heat's effect on mercury) with human-made etchings or devices designed to convey information through the use of simple formulas.[9]

To be sure, some litigants raised concerns about the reliability of such counting and measuring algorithms.[10] Similarly, John Henry Wigmore's influential 1908 evidence treatise

---

6   See, e.g., *United States v. Liebert*, 519 F.2d 542, 543 (3rd Cir. 1975) (admitting list of persons not filing tax returns, stored in IRS computers).

7   See Fed. R. Civ. P. 34.

8   See generally A. Roth, Machine Testimony (2017) 126 *Yale Law J.* 1972, 2002–3 (discussing the difference between machines as "conduits" and machines as tools and machine conveyances of information).

9   See, e.g., J. Pitt Taylor, *A Treatise on the Law of Evidence, as Administered in England and Ireland; with Illustrations from the American and Other Foreign Laws*, 6th edn. (Sweet & Maxwell, 1872), Vol. 1, § 148, at 185 (noting that the readings of clocks, thermometers, barometers, and "a variety of other ingenious contrivances for detecting different matters" were admitted in courts as evidence).

10   See *In re. More's Estate*, 121 Cal. 609, 616 (1898) (addressing lessor's claim that a sheep-counting machine was "unreliable"). See also *Hatcher v. Dunn*, 71 NW 343 (Iowa 1897) (addressing the plaintiff's argument that a thermometer may have given faulty measurements).

acknowledged that the accuracy of "scientific instruments" and "calculating-tables" depended in part on "the statements of persons, even of anonymous observers," which in turn might be inaccurate.[11] And treatise writer Simon Greenleaf noted that "reckoning by a counting-machine" involved "an element of hearsay" – human inputs, assumptions, and formulas – built into the machine's algorithm.[12]

Notwithstanding these concerns, courts in general have afforded the measurements of such instruments a presumption of correctness "akin to" that for mercantile records.[13] Courts have even taken judicial notice of instruments' readings in criminal cases as beyond reasonable dispute.[14] In doing so, courts appear to be implicitly analogizing instrument measurements to regularized business records, which are presumed reliable (even though they would otherwise be inadmissible "hearsay") both because of their regularity and the business's motive to keep accurate records.[15] In the same respect, measurements of scientific instruments regularly relied upon in commercial life and scientific testing might reasonably be presumed accurate.

Early Law Enforcement Gadgetry and Computer Output

The early to mid-twentieth century saw a significant rise in the use of algorithmic evidence in criminal trials, both because of technological advances such as modern computing and because of emerging societal trends, such as widespread highway driving and alcohol consumption, calling for new legal tools to protect public safety. Some of the most celebrated of these new instruments were the "Drunk-O-Meter," invented by a police chemist to detect blood-alcohol level[16] and described by one criminal court as "ingeniously contrived" evidence,[17] and the radar gun, made possible by wartime technological developments, but perfected for the traffic context by police. By 1939, the *Harvard Law Review* had already published a piece chronicling such "scientific gadgets in the law of evidence."[18] By the 1960s, courts were admitting the results of the Drunk-O-Meter's more advanced progeny, the breathalyzer, also invented by a police officer.[19] Beyond such law enforcement tools, criminal courts also admitted the printouts from automated commercial records; for example, automated telephone records detailing where obscene phone calls originated,[20] or the results of an automated "lensometer" test measuring the prescription of a pair of eyeglasses found at a robbery scene.[21]

Courts admitting these sorts of early gadget measurements or computerized records typically dealt with three sorts of legal challenges from litigants. First, some litigants argued that these records were inadmissible hearsay, because they were out-of-court assertions offered for their truth. But for the most part, courts rejected hearsay challenges either by

[11] J. H. Wigmore, *A Treatise on the Anglo-American System of Evidence in Trials at Common Law*, 2nd edn. (Little, Brown & Co., 1923), Vol. 1, § 665, at 1072.
[12] S. Greenleaf, *A Treatise on the Law of Evidence*, 16th edn. (1899), Vol. 1, § 430, at 531.
[13] Pitt Taylor, above note 9, § 148, at 185.
[14] See, e.g., *Ball* v. *LeBlanc*, 792 F.3d 584, 590–1 (5th Cir. 2015) (taking judicial notice of temperature and heat index readings in a prisoner's habeas suit).
[15] See advisory committee note to Fed. R. Evid. 803(6).
[16] See generally A. Roth, The Uneasy Case for Marijuana as Chemical Impairment under a Science-Based Jurisprudence of Dangerousness (2015) 10 *Cal. Law Rev.* 841 (discussing history of blood-alcohol measuring machines).
[17] *State* v. *Hunter*, 68 A.2d 274, 275 (NJ Super. Ct. App. Div. 1949) (describing the Drunk-O-Meter).
[18] See, e.g., Notes and Legislation – Scientific Gadgets in the Law of Evidence (1939) 53 *Harv. Law Rev.* 282, 285.
[19] See Roth, above note 16, p. 861.
[20] See *State* v. *Armstead*, 432 So.2d 837, 839–40 (La. 1983).
[21] See *United States* v. *Blackburn*, 992 F.2d 666, 672 (7th Cir. 1993).

holding that machine-generated statements are not hearsay because they are not *human* assertions,[22] or that machine-generated statements are hearsay but admissible under some reliability-based exception.[23] Second, some litigants argued that such records were not sufficiently authenticated as being what the proponent claimed they were. This concern led the drafters of the 1975 Federal Rules of Evidence to include a rule requiring that the results of a process or system be authenticated through evidence showing that the process or system "produces an accurate result."[24] Third, some litigants argued that algorithmic proof like the breathalyzer or radar gun or spectrograph voice comparison were expert methods that were not sufficiently reliable, or generally accepted in the scientific community, to be admitted under the so-called *"Frye"* or *"Daubert"* tests[25] for admission of expert testimony.[26]

Twenty-First-Century Software Output

In the last twenty years, these early models of computer-generated proof have given way to ever more complex programs and gadgetry. For example, the Drunk-O-Meter and breath-alyzer have given way to digital versions run on software and based on infrared and fuel cell technology.[27] Infrared spectrometers with digital printouts now report drug levels in blood for use in drug prosecutions,[28] and prosecutors rely on Internet map programs to establish driving distances[29] or a defendant's location for purposes of showing, say, illegal re-entry into the United States.[30] Other modern computer-based proof, created in anticipation of its use in law enforcement, includes: StingRay devices that record incoming and outgoing phone numbers to a cell phone;[31] license plate readers;[32] graphs of DNA test runs, purporting to show which genetic markers are present in a sample;[33] red light camera time-stamp data;[34] address logs purporting to list IP addresses of users who have visited child pornography websites;[35] database-driven computer reports of the closest handful of matching archived records to an

---

[22]   See generally A. Wolfson, Note, "Electronic Fingerprints": Doing Away with the Conception of Computer-Generated Records as Hearsay (2005) 104 *Mich. L.aw Rev.* 151 (explaining these competing approaches, and arguing against viewing machine-generated records as hearsay).

[23]   See, e.g., *United States v. Blackburn*, above note 21, at 672 (deeming the lensometer reading inadmissible as a business record because it was prepared in anticipation of litigation, but admitting it instead under the residual reliability-based hearsay exception of Federal Rule of Evidence 807).

[24]   See generally Fed. R. Evid. 901(b)(9) advisory committee's note to 1972 proposed rules (citing cases from the 1960s).

[25]   See *Daubert v. Merrell Dow Pharm., Inc.*, 509 US 579, 579–80 (1993) (requiring judges to determine that scientific or technical methods underlying expert testimony be scientifically valid); *Frye v. United States*, 293 F. 1013, 1014 (DC Cir. 1923) (holding that novel scientific methods must "have gained general acceptance in the particular field in which [they] belong[]").

[26]   See, e.g., *People v. Seger*, 314 NYS.2d 240, 245 (J. Ct. 1970) (rejecting the breathalyzer on reliability grounds). (quoting *People v. Offermann*, 125 NYS.2d 179, 185 (Sup. Ct. 1953); internal quotation marks omitted; rejecting radar gun on reliability grounds); *Reed v. State*, 391 A.2d 364, 377 (Md. 1978) (excluding spectrograph voice comparison results under *Frye*). A number of computer program outputs were challenged by civil litigants on *Frye* or *Daubert* grounds as well during this period. See Roth, above note 8, p. 2014 n. 211.

[27]   See Roth, above note 16, p. 1271.

[28]   See, e.g., *People v. Lopez*, 286 P.2d 469, 472 (Cal. 2012).

[29]   See, e.g., *Jianniney v. State*, 962 A.2d 229, 232 (Del. 2008) (excluding Mapquest driving estimates as inadmissible hearsay).

[30]   See, e.g., *United States v. Lizarraga-Tirado*, 789 F.3d 1107, 1108 (9th Cir. 2015).

[31]   K. Zetter, Turns Out Police Stingray Spy Tools Can Indeed Record Calls, *Wired* (October 28, 2015).

[32]   K. Waddell, How License Plate Readers Have Helped Police and Lenders Target the Poor, *Atlantic* (April 22, 2016).

[33]   See, e.g., *People v. Steppe*, 213 Cal. App. 4th 1116, 1124–5 (2013).

[34]   See, e.g., *People v. Goldsmith*, 59 Cal. 4th 258, 273–5 (2014).

[35]   See, e.g., *John Robertson, Affidavit in Support of Application for a Search Warrant, In re. X*, No. 15M534 (EDNY), filed June 10, 2015.

inputted latent print or ballistic image from a crime scene;[36] drug identification software that can identify particular cutting agents used, which might lead investigators to a particular dealer;[37] Event Data Record information;[38] "Find my iPhone" features used to track phone theft;[39] Fitbit data used to impeach an alleged rape victim's claim that she was asleep at the time of an attack;[40] facial recognition software identifying the defendant as the seller in an undercover drug buy;[41] and arson investigation software that offers an "answer" to whether debris suggests arson.[42] Many if not most of these programs are proprietary.[43]

In the biometrics context in particular, several competing proprietary software programs now purport to interpret complex DNA mixtures, determine whether a defendant's profile is consistent with the mixture, and report associated match statistics to help the jury determine the probative value of that consistency. Such programs offer much promise in enhancing the accuracy and objectivity of complex DNA mixture interpretations, given that such mixtures are notoriously difficult for humans to analyze, in terms of both the number of contributors and the genetic profile of those contributors (for purposes of determining whether a given suspect might be a contributor to the mixture).[44] And courts have nearly universally admitted the results of such programs – typically, but not exclusively, offered by the prosecution[45] – over objections on *Frye* and *Daubert* grounds.[46] The few exceptions have been cases in which a local laboratory did not perform sufficient internal validation studies before using the software,[47] where software was used

---

[36] See S. A. Cole, M. Welling, R. Dioso-Villa, and R. A. Carpenter, Beyond the Individuality of Fingerprints: A Measure of Simulated Computer Latent Print Source Attribution Accuracy (2008) 7 *Law Probab. Risk* 165, 166 (explaining how the AFIS database returns several "candidate" prints to the analyst).

[37] See, e.g., Mixture Analysis, Codadevices.com, https://codadevices.com/applications/.

[38] See, e.g., *Commonwealth v. Safka*, 95 A.3d 304, 308–9 (Pa. Super. Ct. 2014) (admitting such evidence under *Frye*).

[39] See, e.g., *Pickett v. State*, 112 A.3d 1078, 1090 (Md. Ct. Spec. App. 2015).

[40] See J. Gershman, Prosecutors Say Fitbit Device Exposed Fibbing in Rape Case, *Wall Street Journal: Law Blog* (April 21, 2016), https://blogs.wsj.com/law/2016/04/21/prosecutors-say-fitbit-device-exposed-fibbing-in-rape-case/.

[41] See, e.g., *People v. Lynch*, 260 So.2d 1166 (Fla. Ct. App. 2018).

[42] See, e.g., N. A. Sinkov, P. M. Sandercock, and J. J. Harynuk, Chemometric Classification of Casework Arson Samples Based on Gasoline Content (2014) 235 *Forensic Sci. Int.* 24.

[43] See, e.g., *State v. Loomis*, 881 NW.3d 749 (Wisc. 2016) (denying litigants access to source code of actuarial instrument used in parole hearing); *In re. Source Code Evidentiary Hearings in Implied Consent Matters*, 816 NW.2d 525, 531 (Minn. 2012) (noting proprietary nature of breath-testing software); *People v. Chubbs*, No. B258569 (Cal. Ct. App. Div. 4), January 9, 2015, at 21–2 (noting that DNA mixture interpretation software TrueAllele is proprietary); *United States v. Michaud*, Order Dated May 18, 2016, W. Dist. Wash. (noting that the government's malware used in child pornography investigation was proprietary); S. Calvert and L. Broadwater, City in $2 Million Dispute with Xerox over Camera Tickets, *Baltimore Sun* (April 24, 2013) (noting that Xerox refused to disclose source code for red light camera system).

[44] See, e.g., C. Smith, DNA's Identity Crisis, *San Francisco Magazine* (September 2008), p. 80 (quoting British geneticist Peter Gill as noting "if you show ten colleagues a mixture, you will probably end up with ten different answers"); I. E. Dror and G. Hampikian, Subjectivity and Bias in Forensic DNA Mixture Interpretation (2011) 51 *Sci. Justice* 204, 206–7 (demonstrating cognitive bias in human mixture interpretation based on exposure to task-irrelevant contextual information).

[45] One such program, TrueAllele, has been used by a handful of defendants to demonstrate their innocence. See generally Cybergenetics, Press Releases, www.cybgen.com/information/press-release/2016/TrueAllele-Helps-Free-Innocent-Indiana-Man-After-24-Years-in-Prison/page.shtml.

[46] See J. S. Hausman, Lost Shoe Led to Landmark DNA Ruling – and Now, Nation's 1st Guilty Verdict, *MLive* (March 18, 2016), www.mlive.com/news/muskegon/index.ssf/2016/03/lost_shoe_led_to_landmark_dna.html (reporting a conviction in Michigan as the first in the United States to be based in part on the STRmix software after the defense contested its admissibility); Cybergenetics, Trials, www.cybgen.com/news/trials.shtml (listing over fifty cases in which TrueAllele has been admitted).

[47] See *People v. Hillary*, Decision & Order on DNA Analysis Admissibility, Indictment No. 2015–15 (NY St. Lawrence Cty. Ct. August 26, 2016), www.northcountrypublicradio.org/assets/files/08-26-16DecisionandOrder-DNAAnalysisAdmissibility.pdf (excluding STRmix results under *Frye*).

on a mixture with a high number of contributors,[48] or where the software was created by a scandal-ridden office and particularly problematic.[49]

In one particular case in which DNA mixture interpretation software results were excluded, two competing programs actually came to what appeared to be dramatically different conclusions. The case involved the tragic strangulation of a young boy in upstate New York. Police suspicion fell upon Nick Hillary, a former college soccer coach who had dated the boy's mother.[50] Another former boyfriend, a deputy sheriff who had been physically violent with the mother, was cleared of suspicion based on a video showing him walking a dog several blocks away minutes before the incident. Rumors that another child may have killed the boy were also dismissed by police. Focusing on Hillary, police surreptitiously took his DNA from a coffee cup and compared it to dozens of samples from the scene and the boy's body and clothing, with no resulting match. Nor did any DNA samples taken from Hillary's car, home, or clothing match the boy's DNA. But analysts could not determine whether Hillary might be a contributor to a DNA mixture found under the boy's fingernail. Seeking a more definitive opinion, police in 2013 sent the DNA data to Mark Perlin, the creator of a program called "TrueAllele." In 2014, Perlin reported that "the TrueAllele computer found no statistical support for a match" with Hillary.[51] A year later, a new district attorney – elected on a promise to find the killer – had the DNA data analyzed through a competing program, "STRMix," which reported that Hillary was 300,000 times more likely than a random person to have contributed to the mixture.[52] In September 2016, a trial judge in the *Hillary* case excluded the STRMix results,[53] and Hillary was subsequently acquitted.[54] The creator of STRMix has since published a memorandum online, arguing that STRMix's approach to the evidence in *Hillary* is "demonstrably more supported" than TrueAllele's approach.[55] More recently, in 2019, the creator of TrueAllele has sued STRMix and its US representative for patent infringement.[56]

On the Horizon

Other types of algorithmic proof appear likely to be used in criminal trials in the near or not-too-distant future. For example, a computer scientist and expert in text attribution, Oren Tsur, was retained by the defense in a recent US homicide case to determine whether the

[48] See Order Excluding DNA Evidence, April 29, 2019, *United States* v. *Alfonzo Williams*, Case No. 3:13-cr-00764-WHO-1 (ND Cal.) (Orrick, J.) (excluding results of "Bulletproof" genotyping software in case with potentially more than four contributors).
[49] See S. Jacobs, Judge Tosses Out Two Types of DNA Evidence Used Regularly in Criminal Cases, *New York Daily News* (January 5, 2015), www.nydailynews.com/new-york/nyc-crime/judge-tosses-types-dna-testing-article-1.2065795 (reporting a Brooklyn judge excluded results from low copy number DNA testing and Forensic Statistical Tool testing).
[50] See, e.g., J. McKinley, Tensions Simmer over Race as Town Reels from Boy's Killing, *New York Times* (March 6, 2016), A1.
[51] W. T. Eckert, Hillary Trial Slated for Aug. 1, *Watertown Daily Times* (March 3, 2016).
[52] *People* v. *Hillary*, St. Lawrence Cty. Ct., Notice of Motion to Preclude, May 31, 2016, at 10, www.scribd.com/doc/314644253/Hillary-Frye-Motion.
[53] See Decision & Order, *People* v. *Hillary*, Ind. # 2015–15, St. Lawrence Co., August 26, 2016 (Catena, J.).
[54] J. McKinley, Race, Jilted Love and Acquittal in Boy's Killing, *New York Times*, NY Ed. (September 29, 2016), A1.
[55] See https://johnbuckleton.files.wordpress.com/2017/12/people-v-hillary-ii.pdf.
[56] See Complaint for Patent Infringement, *Cybergenetics Corp.* v. *Institute of Environmental Science and Research and Nichevision Inc.*, No. 5:19-cv-01197-SL (ND Ohio) (filed May 24, 2019).

defendant was the author of a "tweet" (a Twitter message) that appeared to confess to the killing.[57] Tsur trained four classification algorithms using tweets from both the defendant and others who had access to his account. Ultimately, all four algorithms determined that the defendant was likely not the author of the tweet. The case settled before trial, but such evidence presumably will resurface soon in trials involving text attribution as evidence either of guilt or innocence.

Other forms of algorithmic proof that exist and presumably could be deployed as evidence in criminal trials in the near future include: algorithms used to classify crimes or defendants as gang-affiliated, for purposes of sentencing enhancements based on gang affiliation;[58] medical diagnosis offered by expert systems;[59] and the results of voice recognition software to identify a perpetrator by their voice.[60] And in the juvenile justice context, algorithms embedded in microphones in classroom ceilings purporting to detect "aggression" might be used not only to predict mass shootings or other violent attacks before they happen, but to prove at a trial that a respondent engaged in behavior that would be threatening to a reasonable person.[61]

In the more distant future, we might see ever more sophisticated forms of AI in the courtroom, such as expert systems able to be cross-examined about the limits of their methodology or security guard robots able to verbalize in court what they observed at a crime scene. A senior executive at IBM suggested that Watson might have a place in the courtroom, as a real-time fact-checker.[62] Perhaps medical diagnosis by AI systems will become so advanced as to supplant human expert testimony in that context. As one blogger asked, "is it far-fetched to imagine Watson's now-familiar blue avatar sitting on the witness stand?"[63] Of course, no AI system will ever be able to "swear" to tell the truth, nor be able to make a morality-based decision about whether to lie on the witness stand.

One category of algorithmic proof likely to still be resisted is lie detection. The polygraph, used by experts to infer deception in subjects based on blood pressure, heart rate, and skin conductance during questioning, is an "evidentiary pariah in American trials."[64] Likewise, courts have universally excluded more sophisticated neuroscience-based expert testimony about deception, such as experts testifying to results of the "No-Lie MRI" machine.[65] Courts

---

[57]   See generally O. Tsur, A Killer Application: Machine Learning Analysis as Evidence in Court, Workshop on Law & Big Data, Bar-Ilan University (May 14, 2018) (on file with author).

[58]   See S. Seo, Partially Generative Neural Networks for Gang Crime Classification with Partial Information, Association for the Advancement of AI (2018), www.cais.usc.edu/wp-content/uploads/2018/02/AIES_2018_paper_93.pdf.

[59]   See, e.g., J. Cohn, The Robot Will See You Now, *The Atlantic* (March 2013), www.theatlantic.com/magazine/archive/2013/03/the-robot-will-see-you-now/309216/.

[60]   See, e.g., J. Marzulli, Prosecutors Want to Use High-Tech Evidence in Trial to Identify Voices of Terrorists, *New York Daily News* (May 1, 2015) (noting the voice recognition software used to identify Ali Yasin Ahmed and his co-defendants). The defendants pled guilty before the case went to trial. See N. Raymond, Three Men Facing Brooklyn Terrorism Trial Plead Guilty, *Reuters* (May 12, 2015), www.reuters.com/article/usa-crime-alshabaab/three-men-facing-brooklyn-terrorism-trial-plead-guilty-idUSL1N0Y31MQ20150512.

[61]   See J. Gillum and J. Kao, Aggression Detectors: The Unproven, Invasive Surveillance Technology Schools Are Using to Monitor Students, *ProPublica* (June 25, 2019), https://features.propublica.org/aggression-detector/the-unproven-invasive-surveillance-technology-schools-are-using-to-monitor-students/.

[62]   R. C. Weber, Why "Watson" Matters to Lawyers, *National Law Journal* (February 14, 2011). See also J. Gershman, Could Robots Replace Jurors?, *Wall Street Journal* (March 6, 2013).

[63]   R. Ambrogi, Could IBM's Watson Make Experts Obsolete? (April 1, 2011), www.ims-expertservices.com/insights/could-ibms-watson-make-experts-obsolete/.

[64]   *Whitherspoon* v. *Superior Court*, 184 Cal. Rptr. 615, 621 (Cal. Ct. App. 1982).

[65]   See Memorandum Opinion and Order, *Maryland* v. *Smith*, No. 106589C (Montgomery Cty., Cir. Ct., MD October 3, 2012); *United States* v. *Semrau*, No. 08–10074 Ml/P, 2010 WL 6845092, at *14 (WD Tenn. June 1, 2010) (excluding defense-proffered fMRI results under *Daubert* standard).

have rejected lie detection testimony on two grounds. First, courts view polygraph results as a poor proxy for deception. The Supreme Court itself has described the polygraph as suffering an error rate "little better than could be obtained by the toss of a coin,"[66] and the *Frye* case itself – establishing the "general acceptance" standard for novel scientific evidence – involved the exclusion of polygrapher testimony.[67] Second, courts and commentators have expressed concern that such testimony usurps the central credibility-determining role of the jury,[68] coming "dangerously close to substituting a trial by machine for a trial by jury."[69]

Thus, one might expect courts to similarly exclude the results of text analysis algorithms purporting to detect deception through word choice[70] through analysis of micro-expressions and demeanor in videotaped witness testimony[71] or suspects' stationhouse confessions,[72] or through a mixture of text, voice, and video analysis.[73] Perhaps courts will view such deception-detecting software as more reliable than previous iterations, given the more sophisticated AI involved. But courts' "trial by machine" objection might endure, and the technological sophistication of new software might only worry courts more in this regard. And perhaps courts will not have these concerns with regard to machine-learning-enabled analysis of fMRI data used only to detect whether someone does or does not have a memory – so-called "brain fingerprinting" or "memory detection" – rather than to detect deception.[74]

Legal Informatics

In addition to generating and storing proof of guilt or innocence, algorithms have also begun to aid criminal justice system actors in performing their assigned tasks. This section briefly documents the ways in which algorithms already augment such decision-making, and mentions future possibilities.

[66] *United States v. Scheffer*, 523 US 303, 310 (1998) (quoting W. G. Iacono and D. T. Lykken, The Scientific Status of Research on Polygraph Techniques: The Case against Polygraph Tests, in D. L. Faigman, D. H. Kaye, M. J. Saks, and J. Sanders (eds.), *Modern Scientific Evidence: The Law and Science of Expert Testimony* (West Group, 1997), Vol. 1, § 14-5.3, 629).

[67] See *Frye* v. *United States*, above note 25.

[68] See, e.g., J. R. Richardson, Scientific Evidence in the Law (1955) 44 *KY Law J*. 277, 285–6 ("The fear or distrust of lie detectors is in part due to the conception that the machine itself will become a 'witness'").

[69] *People v. Barbara*, 255 NW.2d 171, 194 (Mich. 1977). See also *United States v. Bursten*, 560 F.2d 779, 785 (7th Cir. 1977) ("[J]udges loathe the specter of trial by machine, wherein each man's sworn testimony may be put to the electronic test"); *State v. Lyon*, 744 P.2d 231, 240 (Or. 1987) (Linde, J., concurring) ("The central myth of the trial is that truth can be discovered in no better way [than through jury factfinding] ... One of these implicit values surely is to see that parties and the witnesses are treated as persons to be believed or disbelieved by their peers rather than as electrochemical systems to be certified as truthful or mendacious by a machine"); *Scheffer*, 523 US 313 (plurality describing as a "fundamental premise of our criminal trial system [] that 'the jury is the lie detector'").

[70] See, e.g., R. Mihalcea and C. Strapparava, The Lie Detector: Explorations in the Automatic Recognition of Deceptive Language, Proceedings of the ACL-IJCNLP Conference Short Papers (2009), pp. 309, 312.

[71] See Z. Wu, B. Singh, L. S. Davis, and V. S. Subrahmanian, Deception Detection in Videos, Association for the Advancement of AI (2018), https://arxiv.org/abs/1712.04415.

[72] See, e.g., L. Alton, AI and Criminal Interrogations (January 10, 2019), https://dzone.com/articles/will-artificial-intelligence-support-criminal-inte (describing Axon's new products for AI analysis of videotaped interrogations to determine whether confessions are false).

[73] See, e.g., G. Krishnamurthy, N. Majumder, S. Poria, and E. Cambria, A Deep Learning Approach for Multimodal Deception Detection (2018), https://arxiv.org/pdf/1803.00344.

[74] See generally Emily Murphy (draft on file with author).

Attorneys

At least two legal scholars have already suggested that prosecutor offices can, and should, use algorithms to help make better charging, trial, and sentencing advocacy decisions. Professor Andrew Ferguson in a 2016 article titled "Predictive Prosecution" noted that local prosecutor offices in New York City and Chicago had already implemented "Moneyball" prosecution tactics using algorithms. Specifically, these offices already use big data and predictive technologies, similar to the algorithms used in predictive policing, to identify problem defendants and neighborhoods for purposes of informing bail recommendations, charging decisions, sentencing strategies, and release condition recommendations.[75] For example, prosecutors might work with police departments to develop a "Heat List" of problem suspects based on a formula incorporating various incident reports and demographic and location information, and then use that list to determine which defendants, when arrested, should be charged to the fullest extent possible.[76]

Professor Jason Kreag, in his 2017 article "Prosecutorial Analytics," further suggests that prosecutors should make greater use of big data analytics and algorithms. Specifically, he argues that prosecutors should be using analytics to enhance the objectivity of their charging decisions, jury selection processes (to minimize the potential for racially biased peremptory strikes, for example), and sentencing recommendations for similarly situated defendants.[77]

Prosecutors could, and presumably should, also use algorithms to help fulfill their disclosure obligations under the constitutional *"Brady"* doctrine. The Due Process Clause requires that the government turn over all "material" exculpatory or impeachment evidence to the defense in time to make meaningful use of it.[78] Yet, numerous scholars and judges have critiqued the doctrine as insufficient to ensure that the prosecution actually discloses such evidence. The problems are several-fold. First, prosecutors themselves might have difficulty determining what is and is not *Brady* evidence. For example, not all prosecutors appear to understand that *Brady* requires disclosure not only of affirmative evidence of innocence, but also of "impeachment" evidence, meaning evidence tending to cast doubt on the credibility of a government witness.[79] Similarly, prosecutors might find it challenging to determine before trial whether evidence is "material," meaning that there is a "reasonable probability" that disclosure of the evidence would affect the outcome of the trial. Determining the likely effect of disclosure of exculpatory or impeachment evidence on the jury, before trial, is an exercise in speculation, with the benefit only of the prosecutor's own perspective on the evidence.[80] Second, even if prosecutors correctly interpret *Brady* and its progeny and are competent at identifying it when they see it, prosecutors might not be aware of the evidence to begin with. One problem might be that the evidence is in the hands of the police, who are considered part of the "government" for *Brady* purposes,[81] but who might not fully understand *Brady's* scope or be fully forthcoming. Another problem might be the sheer volume and complexity of modern criminal cases, making it difficult to ensure that an individual prosecutor, or even a small group of prosecutors, will uncover all potential *Brady* evidence.

---

[75]   A. G. Ferguson, Predictive Prosecution (2016) 51 *Wake Forest Law Rev.* 705.
[76]   *Ibid.*, p. 717.
[77]   J. Kreag, Prosecutorial Analytics (2017) 94 *Wash. Univ. Law Rev.* 771.
[78]   *Brady* v. *Maryland*, 373 US 83 (1963).
[79]   *United States* v. *Bagley*, 473 US 667 (1985) (holding that impeachment evidence is covered under *Brady*).
[80]   See, e.g., K. Weisburd, Prosecutors Hide, Defendants Seek: The Erosion of *Brady* through the Defendant Due Diligence Rule (2012) 60 *UCLA Law Rev.* 132.
[81]   *Kyles* v. *Whitely*, 514 US 419 (1995).

As Andrew Ferguson suggests in another forthcoming article, "Big Data Prosecution and *Brady*,"[82] prosecutors could improve their track record of disclosing *Brady* evidence in two ways. First, by flagging evidence in their files on the front end. This labeling task could be accomplished either manually or by using an algorithm, to alert future readers (whether human or machine) to the perceived reliability of the information (such as a tip from an informant who has been reliable in the past) and to connections between cases in terms of locations, victims, witnesses, suspects, police officers involved, and the like. Second, by searching files for patterns to identify evidence favorable to the defense. This process, too, could be automated, with the use of what Ferguson calls a *"Brady* button." As he explains, this sort of technology is already used to positive effect in the intelligence community.

With regard to the role of the defense counsel, AI has had little impact thus far. Some public defender offices now have a dedicated data science specialist, but such specialists generally search for patterns in big data related to sentencing and charging decisions, rather than using algorithms to augment or replace decision-making. One might expect that AI could one day offer defendants advice in criminal proceedings in which they have no right to an attorney, such as in misdemeanor trials where the defendant is not facing jail time, discretionary direct appeals, and habeas corpus proceedings. After all, a Stanford college student has already created a lawyer chatbot called DoNotPay that successfully appealed over 160,000 parking tickets in New York and London.[83] But in cases where defendants have a constitutional or statutory right to counsel, human lawyers are still a necessity.

But perhaps algorithms could help human lawyers perform their jobs better, too. The Supreme Court has interpreted the Sixth Amendment right to the assistance of counsel as guaranteeing a right to "effective" assistance.[84] But the Supreme Court held in *Strickland* v. *Washington* in 1984 that a defendant is not entitled to a new trial unless he can show a reasonable probability that the outcome of the proceeding would have been different but for his lawyer's deficient performance.[85] In dissent in *Strickland*, Justice Thurgood Marshall urged that a lawyer's deficient performance be determined by clear requirements indicating minimal steps a lawyer should take to be constitutionally "effective" in particular cases. Such a "checklist" could be translated via algorithm into a system of guidance for attorneys and enforcement for courts looking to see what an attorney has done.

Judges and Court Personnel

The adjudicatory tasks of judges and other court personnel are also on the cusp of being transformed by algorithms. For example, judges in Ohio are beginning to use IBM's Watson to receive real-time, comprehensive reports about the history and track record of juvenile offenders who come before the court for sentencing or probation review. As one judge explained, while the technology is currently used simply to gather and report information quickly, the point of the pilot program is for Watson to learn from each new case and eventually be able to issue sentencing or probation condition recommendations to judges.[86]

---

[82] A. G. Ferguson, Big Data Prosecution and *Brady* (2020) 67 *UCLA Law Rev.* (forthcoming).

[83] See S. Gibbs, Chatbot Lawyer Overturns 160,000 Parking Tickets in New York and London, *The Guardian* (June 28, 2016), www.theguardian.com/technology/2016/jun/28/chatbot-ai-lawyer-donotpay-parking-tickets-london-new-york.

[84] See *McMann v. Richardson*, 397 US 759, 771 n. 14 (1970).

[85] 466 US 668 (1984).

[86] See C. Stewart, Hey Watson: Local Judge First to Use IBM's Artificial Intelligence on Juvenile Cases, *Dayton Daily News* (August 3, 2017), www.daytondailynews.com/news/local/hey-watson-local-judge-first-use-ibm-artifi cial-intelligence-juvenile-cases/InVqz6eeNxvFsMVAe5zrbL/.

New algorithms might also affect judges' admissibility decisions with regard to certain types of evidence. Scholars have suggested, albeit aspirationally, that AI might play the role of a court-appointed witness under Federal Rule of Evidence 706 in giving counsel to judges during *Frye/Daubert* admissibility hearings.[87] Algorithms might also help judges determine the admissibility of confessions resulting from custodial interrogation. Two legal scholars have suggested that police use a "*Miranda* app" that would explain the so-called "*Miranda* warnings"[88] to suspects and test their understanding through a series of questions.[89] In turn, these documented responses could be considered by judges in determining whether a particular confession or *Miranda* waiver was voluntary. One could imagine similar apps being deployed in street encounters between citizens and police, to show that a citizen understands or at least has been told that they are "free to leave" for purposes of determining whether an encounter rises to the level of a "stop" requiring reasonable articulable suspicion under the Fourth Amendment.[90]

Algorithms soon may well augment or replace some human court reporters as well. The legal system faces a court reporter shortage, rendering automation of transcription a potentially attractive option. Meanwhile, one recent study has revealed a troublingly high rate of erroneous transcriptions of certain cultural and regional dialects by court reporters.[91] Yet, current voice recognition software faces difficulty in distinguishing between multiple speakers, and automated speech recognition (ASR) technology is only familiar with the idioms and phrases it has been exposed to through programming and machine learning.[92] Still, one company offering automated deposition transcription promises a "nearly 100% accurate" transcript at a fraction of the cost of a human reporter.[93]

Finally, algorithms are currently being developed to identify wrongful convictions, in a way that could be useful for defense attorneys, conviction integrity units in prosecutor offices, or judges determining whether to appoint lawyers to prisoners seeking post-conviction relief. For example, one program that appears to be in early stages, "JusticeBRD" (Justice Beyond a Reasonable Doubt), states on its website that it is a "machine-learning model" designed for "mathematically determining guilt based" on evidence presented at murder trial.[94]

LEGAL RULES GOVERNING ALGORITHMS IN CRIMINAL ADJUDICATION

This section offers an overview of existing legal rules governing algorithms in criminal adjudication. The admission of algorithm-generated proof of guilt or innocence at a criminal trial is governed by a jurisdiction's rules of evidence, rules of criminal procedure and discovery, and the state and federal Constitution.

[87] See, e.g., P. S. Katz, Expert Robot: Using Artificial Intelligence to Assist Judges in Admitting Scientific Expert Testimony (2014) 24 *Alb. Law J. Sci. Technol.* 1, 37; B. Wheeler, Giving Robots a Voice: Testimony, Intentionality, and the Law, in S. J. Thompson (ed.), *Androids, Cyborgs, and Robots in Contemporary Culture and Society* (IGI Global, 2018), p. 25 (discussing expert robots).
[88] See *Miranda* v. *Arizona*, 384 US 436 (1966) (holding that suspect responses during custodial interrogation are inadmissible in the government's case in chief if the suspect is not warned of certain constitutional rights).
[89] See A. G. Ferguson and R. Leo, The *Miranda* App: Metaphor and Machine (2017) 97 *Boston Univ. Law Rev.* 935.
[90] See *Terry* v. *Ohio*, 392 US 1 (1968).
[91] J. Eligon, Speaking Black Dialect in Courtrooms Can Have Striking Consequences, *New York Times* (January 25, 2019), www.nytimes.com/2019/01/25/us/black-dialect-courtrooms.html.
[92] See J. D. Jaafari and N. Lewis, In Court, Where Are Siri and Alexa?, Marshall Project (February 14, 2019) (noting that voice-to-text software has become more advanced, but is not yet being used in lieu of court reporters).
[93] See StoryCloud, FAQ-Transcription, www.storycloud.co/faq-transcription.
[94] See www.justicebrd.com (home page).

The Rule against Hearsay and the Confrontation Clause

While the admissibility of human assertions is limited by the rule against "hearsay," courts have nearly universally held that algorithm-generated information is not hearsay. "Hearsay" is an out-of-court statement by a human declarant, offered to prove the truth of the matter asserted by the declarant, and is presumptively inadmissible in American trials.[95] The rule against hearsay reflects a preference for live testimony of declarants under oath in court, where they can be cross-examined and where their demeanor can be observed by the jury. Because only a human can be placed under oath, looked in the eye, and cross-examined, the hearsay rule has little application to non-human conveyances of information, like animal utterances and information-generating algorithms. Put differently, if the rules treated a machine's or an animal's conveyances of information as inadmissible whenever it was made off the witness stand, then such con-veyances would always be presumptively inadmissible.

To be sure, some courts – especially in the early days of computerized records – would treat computer-generated results as hearsay and admit them under the "business records" hearsay exception for records created in the regular course of business. But commentators were critical of this practice, pointing out that courts seemed to be conflating computer-*stored* records, written by humans but stored by machines, with computer-*generated* records, where the computer itself creates and reports new information.[96] Only the former is hearsay.

Likewise, some commentators have suggested that an algorithm's results are the hearsay statements of the algorithm's creator, such as a computer programmer.[97] But others, includ-ing myself, have argued against this view of algorithmic evidence. The fact that a programmer has designed an algorithm does not mean the programmer herself has created the resulting information, borne witness to the events analyzed by the algorithm, or even fully understands the algorithm's processes.[98] A poem generated by a computer program cannot be said to have been written by the programmer, however much the programmer might be "responsible" for the poem. Having the programmer on the witness stand subject to cross-examination before the jury might be helpful in learning certain aspects of how the program works, but it may not be the best way, or even a minimally adequate way, for the jury to assess the probative value of the program's results.

The fact that the hearsay rule has no coherent application to algorithms does not, of course, mean that algorithmic results are inherently reliable and pose no threat of inaccuracy. On the contrary, machine conveyances of information might be false. Just as human assertions might pose the "hearsay dangers" of insincerity, inarticulateness, misperception, and memory loss, an algorithm's results might pose the " black box dangers" of human and machine causes of falsehood by design, inarticulateness, and analytical error.[99]

---

95   See, e.g., Fed. R. Evid. 801, 802 (definition of hearsay and rule presumptively excluding it).
96   See generally A. Wolfson, Note, "Electronic Fingerprints": Doing Away with the Conception of Computer-Generated Records as Hearsay (2005) 104 *Mich. Law Rev.* 151 (noting, and criticizing, courts' treatment of computer-generated business records as hearsay).
97   See, e.g, *United States* v. *Washington*, 498 F.3d 225, 229 (4th Cir. 2007) (explaining the defendant's argument that the "raw data" of a chromatograph was the "hearsay" of the "technicians" who tested the defendant's blood sample for PCP and alcohol using the machine); K. Neville, Programmers and Forensic Analyses: Accusers under the Confrontation Clause (2011) 10 *Duke Law Technol. Rev.* 1, 9 (arguing that "the programmer" is "the 'true accuser' – not the machine merely following the protocols he created").
98   See, e.g., Roth, above note 8, p. 1986.
99   See generally Roth, above note 8 (describing "black box dangers" of machine testimony and comparing them to the "hearsay dangers" of human testimony); E. Cheng and A. Nunn, Beyond the Witness: Bringing a Process Perspective to Modern Evidence Law (2019) 97 *Tex. Law Rev.* 1077 (describing potential inaccuracies of process-based proof).

To combat these dangers, some (including myself) have argued for new safeguards for machine "testimony," which would require certain conditions of admissibility. Not cross-examination or the oath, but rather, conditions like robust front-end software testing; disclosure of source code or other means of understanding the algorithm's inner workings; access to the algorithm before trial for tinkering; disclosure of the algorithm's prior conveyances, if any, on the same subject matter; proof rules prohibiting a criminal conviction based on one uncorroborated machine result alone; and the like.[100] Others, like Ed Cheng and Alex Nunn, have also suggested new testing and transparency rules, beyond hearsay doctrine, to govern "process-based" proof such as computer programs or even highly standardized human testimony.[101]

Lacking the ability to exclude unreliable computer-generated evidence under the hearsay rule, some American courts have interpreted the rules of authentication to impose a de facto reliability requirement with regard to computer-generated information. In particular, a provision in Federal Rule of Evidence 901(b)(9) (which has numerous state analogs) allows proponents to authenticate the results of a "process or system" by "describing [the] process or system" used to produce the result and showing it "produces an accurate result." This rule was proposed by several rules drafters in 1968, and appears to have been intended primarily as an uncontroversial means of streamlining admissibility of regularly generated computerized business records.[102] Indeed, rules of authentication are rules of *relevance*, not reliability; they require the proponent only to show that an item is what they claim it to be. Nonetheless, in the absence of any other reliability-based exclusionary rule for algorithmic proof, some courts have invoked 901(b)(9)'s "accurate result" requirement as a means of screening out unreliable computer-generated evidence.[103]

A few other countries have already drafted more specific admissibility requirements for algorithm-generated evidence, although these requirements are limited. In the United Kingdom, a "representation ... made otherwise than by a person" that "depends for its accuracy on information supplied (directly or indirectly) by a person" is inadmissible in criminal cases absent proof that "the information was accurate."[104] Canada relies mostly on a discretionary judicial determination of reliability in determining the admissibility of machine conveyances,[105] and India and some European countries require that algorithmic proof be accompanied by a human expert.[106]

While the hearsay and authentication rules discussed thus far have been statutory, some commentators have argued that the federal constitution might also impose limits on the admissibility of algorithmic proof in criminal cases. The Confrontation Clause of the Sixth Amendment guarantees to a criminal defendant the right to be "confronted with the witnesses

[100]   See generally Roth, above note 8 (discussing potential safeguards for machine testimony).
[101]   See generally Cheng and Nunn, above note 99.
[102]   See Roth, above note 8, pp. 2012–13 (explaining the origins of Rule 901(b)(9)).
[103]   See, e.g., *State* v. *Swinton*, 847 A.2d 921, 942 (Conn. 2004) (interpreting 901(b)(9) as a requirement that the opinions of computer simulations be "reliable" under *Daubert*-like factors).
[104]   Criminal Justice Act 2003, c. 44, § 129(1) (Eng.). If the inputter's "purpose" is "to cause ... a machine to operate on the basis that the matter is as stated," the machine output based on the statement is treated as hearsay (*ibid.*, § 115(3)), requiring the live testimony of the person inputting the statement, unless the statement is admissible under an exception or stipulation, or if the court "is satisfied that it is in the interests of justice" to admit the statement (*ibid.*, § 114(1)). The provision "does not affect the operation of the presumption that a mechanical device has been properly set or calibrated" (*ibid.*, § 129(2)).
[105]   See D. M. Paciocco, Proof and Progress: Coping with the Law of Evidence in a Technological Age (2015) 11 *Canadian J. Law Technol.* 181, 219.
[106]   See Roth, above note 8, p. 2031 and n. 316 (discussing India, Germany, Belgium, and the Netherlands).

against him." Lower courts have nearly universally rejected arguments that admission of algorithmic proof against a defendant, absent a meaningful chance of scrutinizing the algorithm, might violate the Confrontation Clause. Courts have generally reasoned that the Confrontation Clause applies only to human witnesses, and/or that the ability to cross-examine the human programmer is sufficient to satisfy the Constitution.[107] The Supreme Court, for its part, has not definitely resolved the question, although Justice Sotomayor has suggested in a concurring opinion that "raw data" from a machine might not implicate the Clause.[108] Meanwhile, legal scholars have largely accepted the premise that existing Confrontation Clause jurisprudence offers little support for excluding machine conveyances on constitutional grounds.[109] Still, some (including myself) have argued that the Clause, properly interpreted, should allow a right to meaningfully impeach algorithmic proof through discovery and adversarial testing tools analogous to cross-examination.[110]

Reliability Requirements Related to Expert Testimony

In some circumstances, a human expert uses an algorithm as a tool for informing, or sometimes essentially dictating, the expert's opinion. The examples are legion, but include a human DNA expert's use of probabilistic genotyping software to determine a likelihood ratio, or a human blood-alcohol expert's use of blood-alcohol software analysis results to determine blood-alcohol level. In such cases, courts have sometimes required that the proponent of the expert testimony prove that the algorithm is sufficiently reliable as an expert methodology. In federal court, this requirement stems from language in Federal Rule 702 prohibiting the admission of expert testimony absent proof that the expert has used reliable methods and reliably applied them, reflecting the Supreme Court's 1993 opinion in *Daubert* v. *Merrell Dow Pharm., Inc.*[111] Some state courts follow *Daubert*; others instead follow the so-called "*Frye* standard," requiring judges to determine whether a novel scientific methodology has reached "general acceptance" by the relevant scientific community.[112]

The efficacy of *Daubert* and *Frye* as a protection against wrongful convictions based on inaccurate algorithmic proof has limits. For example, while a judge could exclude algorithm-generated evidence under *Daubert* and *Frye* when a human expert relies on such evidence, *Daubert* and *Frye* offer no protection against unreliable algorithmic proof where a party offers such proof without a human expert interlocutor. Nor would *Daubert* and *Frye* apply to "lay" (rather than expert) algorithmic proof, such as the observations of a robot security guard, or in those few jurisdictions that have no special reliability requirement for expert methods.

In addition, some commentators have argued that scientific validation studies alone might be insufficient to scrutinize certain algorithmic proof. For example, while validation studies might show that a certain DNA interpretive software program boasts a low false positive rate (in terms of falsely labeling a non-contributor as a contributor to a DNA mixture), such

---

[107] See Roth, above note 8, p. 2047 (cataloging cases).
[108] *Bullcoming* v. *New Mexico*, 564 US 647, 674 (2011) (Sotomayor, J., concurring).
[109] See, e.g., Cheng and Nunn, above note 99; B. Sites, Rise of the Machines: Machine-Generated Data and the Confrontation Clause (2014) 16 *Colum. Sci. Technol. Law Rev.* 36, 99–100.
[110] See, e.g., Cheng and Nunn, above note 99; Roth, above note 8; E. Murphy, The Mismatch between Twenty-First-Century Forensic Evidence and Our Antiquated Criminal Justice System (2014) 87 *S. Cal. Law Rev.* 633, 657–8.
[111] 509 US 579, 579–80 (1993). Cf. D. A. Sklansky, Hearsay's Last Hurrah (2009) *Sup. Ct. Rev.* 1 (arguing that the Confrontation Clause is broader than simply the right of cross-examination).
[112] See *Frye* v. *United States*, above note 25, at 1014 (holding that novel scientific methods must "have gained general acceptance in the particular field in which [they] belong[]").

studies cannot so easily determine whether a reported likelihood ratio is off by a factor of ten. As two prominent DNA statistics experts have explained, validation may be an incomplete means of scrutinizing algorithm-generated scores:

> Laboratory procedures to measure a physical quantity such as a concentration can be validated by showing that the measured concentration consistently lies with an acceptable range of error relative to the true concentration. Such validation is infeasible for software aimed at computing a[] [likelihood ratio] because it has no underlying true value (no equivalent to a true concentration exists). The [likelihood ratio] expresses our uncertainty about an unknown event and depends on modeling assumptions that cannot be precisely verified in the context of noisy [crime scene profile] data.[113]

And, of course, *Daubert* and *Frye* impose only minimal reliability requirements for admissibility of expert testimony. For human experts, admissibility is simply the first step; the opposing party still has the opportunity to challenge such evidence in front of the jury through cross-examination and the like. For algorithmic proof, the rules of evidence do not yet offer opposing parties a clear means of further scrutinizing such proof once admitted.

Thus, while courts are right to apply *Daubert/Frye* to algorithmic expert methods, reliability requirements alone do not offer the same level of scrutiny as existing testimonial safeguards for human assertions. Indeed, for non-expert algorithmic proof like Google Earth results, some courts have simply chosen to take "judicial notice" of the results, without requiring further proof of reliability, on grounds that the results are beyond reasonable dispute.[114]

Intellectual Property Issues

Creators of proprietary algorithms often argue, in response to discovery requests for information about algorithmic evidence to be used at trial, that such information is protected from disclosure by a "trade secrets privilege."[115] Some commentators have suggested that a limited trade secret privilege might be necessary to incentivize development of accurate algorithms for use in criminal justice,[116] while others have argued that such a trade secrets privilege is inappropriate and unnecessary.[117] In particular, Rebecca Wexler has argued that the application of such a privilege in criminal cases was a historical accident, and that substantive trade secret doctrine offers sufficient protection for proprietors without a privilege. Thus far, courts appear to have largely accepted proprietors' claims of privilege.[118]

---

[113]   C. D. Steele and D. J. Balding, Statistical Evaluation of Forensic DNA Profile Evidence (2014) 1 *Ann. Rev. Stat. Appl.* 361, 380.

[114]   See, e.g., *United States* v. *Lizarraga-Tirado*, above note 30, at 1110.

[115]   See, e.g., Roth, above note 8, p. 2028 (discussing trade secrets); C. Chessman, Note, A "Source" of Error: Computer Code, Criminal Defendants, and the Constitution (2017) 105 *Calif. Law Rev.* 101, 157 (discussing the trade secret privilege in criminal cases with regard to source code).

[116]   See, e.g., E. J. Imwinkelried, Computer Source Code: A Source of the Growing Controversy over the Reliability of Automated Forensic Techniques (2017) 66 *DePaul Law Rev.* 97.

[117]   See Chessman, above note 115, p. 157; R. Wexler, Life, Liberty, and Trade Secrets: Intellectual Property in the Criminal Justice System (2018) 70 *Stan. Law Rev.* 1343; J. Tashea, Trade Secret Privilege Is Bad for Criminal Justice, *ABA Journal* (July 30, 2019).

[118]   Wexler, *ibid.*, pp. 1352–3.

Legal Informatics

The legal rules governing the decision-making processes of prosecutors, defense attorneys, juries, and judges generally do not, by their explicit terms, preclude use of algorithms to enhance those processes. For example, while a criminal defendant has a due process right to disclosure of *Brady* evidence by the prosecution, neither *Brady* nor its progeny speaks to whether prosecutors and police could, or should, use algorithms to help identify material exculpatory and impeachment evidence in the government's case files. Likewise, neither *Miranda* nor its progeny speaks to whether police can satisfy the warning requirements through use of a *Miranda* app. And while a criminal defendant may have a right to a meaningfully accurate trial transcript for use in preparing an appeal as of right, a defendant has no statutory or constitutional right to a human, rather than algorithmic, court reporter. Even replacing a judge with an algorithm for purposes of rendering evidentiary rulings might be fully allowable under existing procedural rules, with a few tweaks to the evidence code.

On the other hand, the Sixth Amendment right to jury presumably acts as a constitutional bar to any future attempt to replace human juries with an algorithm in determining guilt or innocence. And one could imagine a jurisdiction choosing to impose statutory limits on pure algorithmic decision-making in criminal cases. In Europe, for example, the General Data Protection Regulation (GDPR) now prohibits citizens from being "subject to a decision" that is "based solely on automated processing," if it has a legal or "similarly significant[]" effect on the citizen.[119] Such a provision in American criminal courts might limit a judge's ability to, say, entirely delegate to an algorithm the task of fashioning probation conditions, imposing sentence, or determining the admissibility of evidence.

THE DEBATE OVER THE PROMISE AND PERIL OF ALGORITHMS IN CRIMINAL ADJUDICATION

Accuracy, Objectivity, and Efficiency

The potential benefits of deploying algorithms in criminal adjudication, just as in other contexts, are many: enhanced accuracy, objectivity, and efficiency. These potential benefits, of course, mirror the potential benefits of "rules" versus "standards," well-trodden ground in legal commentary. But, just as in other contexts, the use of algorithms in criminal adjudication can also jeopardize these same values because of subjectivity and error baked into the code.

Hopefully, the foregoing discussion of the various types of algorithmic proof and legal informatics deployed in criminal justice has made clear some of the concrete benefits of algorithms in terms of accuracy, objectivity, and efficiency. For example, probabilistic genotyping software, which appears to be at least decently accurate with regard to mixtures with a low number of contributors, has the ability to resolve complex DNA mixtures much more accurately than human analysts; as one DNA expert put it, "if you show ten colleagues a mixture, you will probably end up with ten different answers."[120] Likewise, fMRI-based

---

[119] Council Regulation 2016/679, art. 22, § 71, 2016 OJ (L119) 1, 14, http://eur-lex.europa.eu/legal-content/EN/TXT/?uri=uriserv:OJ.L_.2016.119.01.0001.01.ENG&toc=OJ:L:2016:119:TOC.

[120] C. Smith, *DNA's Identity Crisis*, *San Francisco Magazine* (September 2008), p. 80 (quoting British geneticist Peter Gill).

memory detection might someday have the ability to enhance credibility determinations, given that the jury is notoriously inaccurate at lie detecting[121] and suffers from implicit racial bias when judging witness demeanor.[122] And prosecutors, whose vast discretionary power is largely de facto unreviewable,[123] might be more likely to abide by constitutional equal protection requirements related to jury selection and charging decisions if such decisions are made or augmented by an algorithm programmed to be equitable, or if they know that patterns of bias will actually be detected through use of analytics.

On the other hand, inaccuracies and bias can also arise in algorithmic output when offered as proof of guilt or innocence at trial. Moreover, algorithmic subjectivities and errors might be harder to recognize because they are buried in code. In a previous article, I set forth a comprehensive list of the types of infirmities of machine "testimony," including human and machine causes of *falsehood by design* (such as the "covert software" created by Volkswagen engineers to cheat on emissions tests, or algorithms that actually learn to deceive to achieve programmed goals); human and machine causes of *inarticulateness* (such as ambiguous algorithmic output or faulty displays of information); and human and machine causes of *analytical error* (including miscodes, human analytical misassumptions, machine-learning errors, and human input and operation errors).[124]

The following paragraphs offer a few concrete examples of sources of error in algorithmic proof of guilt or innocence, or in algorithmic adjudicatory decision-making. In assessing these sources of error, the reader should keep in mind that "accuracy" can have several meanings, and that one form of accuracy might trade off with another. For example, commentators have pointed out that risk assessment algorithms in the bail context, such as Compas, have higher false positive rates for black defendants than white defendants, suggesting an inaccuracy that is borne inequitably along racial lines. But defenders of Compas point out that race has no predictive value; that is, a black and white defendant with a particular score have the same risk of reoffending. Where the reoffense rate for different groups is different, an algorithm cannot simultaneously have equal false positive rates for all groups and also ensure that group membership has zero predictive value. If one fixes the first type of unfairness, one creates a different type.[125]

Erroneous Human Inputs or Machine Error

An algorithm is only as good as the data inputted. For example, while prosecutorial charging might be more *consistent* if automated through an algorithm based on various social factors associated with defendants, it is not necessarily more *accurate* than fully discretionary charging if prosecutors make decisions based on outdated, incomplete, biased, or erroneous information. "If those algorithmic or social network correlations are in error," Andrew Ferguson notes, "then the subsequent harsher punishment [associated with harsher charging decisions] may be unjustified."[126] The same is true in the proof context. For example, a computer-run DNA analysis on a crime scene sample contaminated with residue from a

[121]   See, e.g., G. Fisher, The Jury's Rise as Lie Detector (1997) 107 *Yale Law J.* 575, 707.
[122]   See generally J. W. Rand, The Demeanor Gap: Race, Lie Detection, and the Jury (2000) 33 *Conn. Law Rev.* 1.
[123]   See, e.g., S. Bibas, Prosecutorial Regulation Versus Prosecutorial Accountability (2009) 157 *Univ. Pa. Law Rev.* 959, 960: "No government official in America has as much unreviewable power and discretion as the prosecutor."
[124]   Roth, above note 8, p. I.B.
[125]   See generally D. Hellman, Algorithmic Fairness (2020) 106 *Va. Law Rev.* (forthcoming).
[126]   Ferguson, above note 75, p. 719.

suspect's sample might, without sufficient controls, falsely report a match.[127] The error might also stem from a machine malfunction; for example, a voltage change might cause a breath-alcohol machine to report inaccurate results.[128]

Analytical Error Stemming from Oversimplification

Inaccuracies in algorithmic decision-making or proof might also stem from oversimplification or the failure to account for important variables. Jason Kreag warns, for example, that prosecutors' "decisions are often complex and involve competing values that may not be easily mapped with determinable variables,"[129] raising the possibility that algorithmic prosecutorial charging might lead to over-punishment by leaving out relevant but more difficult to quantify considerations. Sally Merry has called the tendency for algorithmic decision-making to overly weight measurable indicators as the "seduction of quantification."[130]

Analytical Error Stemming from Coding Errors or False Assumptions

Examples abound of reliability concerns with regard to algorithm-generated proof in criminal or traffic cases that stem from coding errors, either inadvertent or stemming from analytical misassumptions, including in the contexts of Google driving estimates; blood-alcohol testing;[131] translation of the federal sentencing guidelines into computer code;[132] police criminal record databases;[133] Apple's "Find My iPhone" tracking when used in theft and robbery cases;[134] "minor miscode[s]" in DNA software;[135] and inaccurately inputted allelic frequencies used by software to generate DNA match statistics.[136] In particular, consider the two different DNA software programs that came to opposing conclusions in the *Hillary* homicide case based on the identical genetic information from the same sample. Programmers of such software must decide how conservative their estimates should be with regard to contamination, genetic marker "drop in" and "drop out," random artifacts of the program (such as "stutter"), and the appropriate reference population for generating estimates of the rarity of genetic markers, all of which affect mixture interpretation.[137] In the *Hillary* case, presumably, one program must have suffered either coding or input errors of some kind.

[127]   See, e.g., A. Roth, Defying DNA: Rethinking the Role of the Jury in an Age of Scientific Proof of Innocence (2013) 93 *Bost. Univ. Law Rev.* 1643, 1676–9 (documenting instances of false positives due to contamination).
[128]   See, e.g., *In re. Source Code Evidentiary Hearings in Implied Consent Matters*, 816 NW.2d 525, 531 (Minn. 2012) (noting expert testimony on this point).
[129]   Kreag, above note 77, p. 812.
[130]   S. Engle Merry, *The Seductions of Quantification: Measuring Human Rights, Gender Violence, and Sex Trafficking* (University of Chicago Press, 2016).
[131]   See A. Roth, Trial by Machine (2016) 104 *Geo. Law J.* 1245, 1271–2 (citing sources with regard to problems with Intoxilyzer 8000 and 5000 readings, due to programming errors); Roth, above note 8, p. 1995 (discussing litigation over code errors with the Alcotest 7110).
[132]   See S. R. Lindemann, Commentary, Published Resources on Federal Sentencing (1990) 3 *Fed. Sent'g Rep.* 45, 45–6.
[133]   See, e.g., *Florence v. Bd. of Chosen Freeholders*, 132 S.Ct. 1510, 1511 (2012) (noting that a database erroneously contained incorrect outstanding warrant information).
[134]   See L. Mower, If You Lose Your Cellphone, Don't Blame Wayne Dobson, *Las Vegas Review Journal* (January 13, 2013).
[135]   Roth, above note 130, p. 1276.
[136]   See Notice of Amendment of the FBI's STR Population Data Published in 1999 and 2001, Federal Bureau of Investigation (2015), www.fbi.gov/about-us/lab/biometric-analysis/codis/amended-fbi-str-final-6-16-15.pdf.
[137]   See J. Butler, *Advanced Topics in DNA Typing: Interpretation* (Elsevier Science, 2014), pp. 165, 170–3, 214, 245–7, 250; E. E. Murphy, *Inside the Cell: The Dark Side of Forensic DNA* (Nation Books, 2015), pp. 74–82.

Meanwhile, in the sentencing guidelines context (which, after all, is still an algorithm, although no longer executed by software), critics have argued that the guidelines failed to fully account for probationary sentences in determining average sentence length based on prior cases, leading to systematic over-punishment.[138] And in the traffic context, the issuance of a ticket from a red light camera system depends on how generously the programmer sets the algorithm's "grace period."[139] In short, notwithstanding their veneer of objectivity in comparison to ad hoc human judgment, algorithms in criminal adjudication still reflect the biases, perspectives, intentions, plans, and assumptions of their human progenitors.

Machine Learning

Machine-learning algorithms used in criminal adjudication can also misclassify people or events because of limitation in the training dataset or other analytical problems. Machines learn how to characterize new data by training on data already categorized by a person or the machine itself. The fewer samples in the dataset, or the more that dataset is not representative of future events, the greater the chance the algorithm will mischaracterize future events. Specifically, the algorithm might infer a pattern or linkage in the training data that does not actually mirror real life ("overfitting") or might try to account for too many variables, rendering the training data inadequate for learning (the so-called "curse of dimensionality").[140] In the criminal adjudication context, such concerns have been raised about facial recognition software[141] and crime-detecting surveillance cameras, among other types of investigative and proof-generating algorithms.

Human–Algorithm Compatibility Issues

Algorithms can also lead to inaccuracies when they are intended only to augment or inform complex human decision-making, and the human decision-maker instead simply defers to the algorithmic output – a phenomenon technology scholars call "automation complacency."[142] In the fingerprint context, for example, a human analyst might review the output of an algorithm that searches for potentially matching reference prints to an inputted crime scene latent print. The algorithm chooses the ten or so closest potential hits, resulting in the analyst being faced with the most potentially confounding cases (where a non-matching reference print might look very similar to the latent print being compared). If the expert falsely assumes that one of the cases chosen by the algorithm must be the source of the latent print, the expert might simply choose the best match of the bunch, falsely implicating a person who is not the actual source. Such complacency appears to have contributed to

---

[138] See, e.g., L. Adelman, What the Sentencing Commission Ought to Be Doing: Reducing Mass Incarceration (2013) 18 *Mich. J. Race Law* 295, 297.

[139] Roth, above note 130, p. 1272.

[140] See generally R. J. Glushko (ed.), *The Discipline of Organizing: Informatics Edition*, 4th edn. (O'Reilly Media, 2016); H. Surden, Machine Learning and Law (2014) 89 *Wash. Law Rev.* 88; P. Domingos, *The Master Algorithm: How the Quest for the Ultimate Learning Machines Will Remake Our World* (Allen Lane, 2015); A. Zheng, *Evaluating Machine Learning Models: A Beginner's Guide to Key Concepts and Pitfalls* (O'Reilly Media, 2015).

[141] See, e.g., Face Recognition, Electronic Frontier Foundation, www.eff.org/pages/face-recognition (citing B. F. Klare, M. J. Burge ; J. C. Klontz, *et al.*, Face Recognition Performance: Role of Demographic Information (2012) 7 *IEEE Trans. Inf. Forensics Secur.* 1789 (showing higher false positive rates for African-Americans)).

[142] See R. Parasuraman and D. H. Manzey, Complacency and Bias in Human Use of Automation: An Attentional Integration (2010) 52 *Hum. Factors* 381, 381.

misattributions, including in the case of Brandon Mayfield, an Oregon lawyer misidentified through a latent print as the perpetrator of the 2004 Madrid train bombings.[143]

Another compatibility concern is whether factfinders will sufficiently understand algorithmic proof. For example, DNA experts have expressed concern that lay jurors will not understand the meaning of the likelihood ratios (LRs) produced by DNA genotyping software. Of course, the concern that jurors might not understand statistical evidence, or might over- or undervalue it, exists with regard to all numerical proof, and not just that generated through algorithms.[144] But the increased use of software results at trial will also likely increase the parties' reliance on statistical evidence. One group of DNA experts has suggested a list of verbal equivalents to various LRs, in an effort to better explain to jurors the LRs' probative value.[145]

"Softer" Values – Dignity, Equity, and Mercy

The rise of algorithmic proof and algorithmic decision-making in criminal adjudication might also enhance or jeopardize what other scholars have called "softer" values, beyond accuracy and objectivity, the benefits of which are not easily quantified.[146]

Dignity

One issue might be whether those affected by the decision-making of prosecutors, judges, and jurors will feel alienated or dehumanized by being accused or adjudged by a machine. As noted in "The Use of Algorithms in Criminal Adjudication," above, this concern has arisen for nearly a century with regard to deception-detecting machines, and as noted in the second section above, "Legal Rules Governing Algorithms in Criminal Adjudication," the European GDPR has gone so far as to establish a right to have a human safety valve in any decision-making process affecting legal rights. The Confrontation Clause also reflects not merely a concern about the unreliability of unconfronted testimony, but also with dignity, and the ability to look one's accuser in the eye. In previous work, I have suggested that the state's use of accusatory algorithms to prove guilt might implicate this dignitary interest in confrontation:

> [A] machine is not … capable of … understanding the moral gravity of accusing someone of a crime. But people are … and when they build a machine to do the job, something may be lost in terms of moral commitment … . Perhaps it is easier to accuse someone when one builds and algorithm to do so.
>
> In turn, the more inscrutable a machine process, the more its accusatory conveyances threaten the dignity of the accused and the perceived legitimacy of the process.[147]

Commentators also routinely raise concerns about dignity and inscrutability in modern discourse about algorithmic fairness. The concept of "explainability" is a fixture in debates

---

[143] See S. A. Cole, More than Zero: Accounting for Error in Latent Fingerprint Identification (2005) 95 *J. Crim. Law Criminol.* 985, 1064–5 n. 394.

[144] See generally L. H. Tribe, Trial by Mathematics: Precision and Ritual in the Legal Process (1971) 84 *Harv. Law Rev.* 1329 (arguing against admissibility of naked statistical evidence of guilt or liability).

[145] See Recommendations of the SWGDAM Ad Hoc Working Group on Genotyping Results Reported as Likelihood Ratios (2019), www.swgdam.org/publications.

[146] See, e.g., R. A. Bierschbach, Proportionality and Parole (2012) 160 *Univ. Pa. Law Rev.* 1745, 1785 (using the term "softer values" to refer to "self-recognition of human worth and potential," as compared to "standard" goals like deterrence).

[147] Roth, above note 8, pp. 2042–3.

about the future of AI, so much so that scholars and journalists have coined the term "explainable AI" or "XAI."[148] It is no surprise that the GDPR includes not only a right to human safety valves in critical decision-making, but also a "right to explanation."[149]

Notably, "explainability" of an algorithm is different from "transparency." Explainability seeks to ensure that data subjects understand what is happening to them, and why. The underlying concern is one of dignity, legitimacy, and trust, as well as contestability. Transparency, on the other hand, seeks to ensure that data subjects have access to the algorithm's inner workings, whether or not they understand them. A full commitment to transparency might require the proprietor of TrueAllele, a probabilistic genotyping program, to turn over to the defense the 170,000 lines of the program's source code. But a full commitment to explainability might require much more (and less) than disclosure of source code, if defendants have no means of making heads or tails of the code.[150]

Equity

At least in theory, every level of the American criminal justice system allows room for the exercise of so-called "equitable" discretion, meaning the discretion not to detect every violation of criminal codes, not to arrest, not to charge, not to convict, not to procedurally bar a claim, and not to punish, "because doing so would be unjust, considering the individualized circumstances" that a human actor with discretion is able to consider.[151] Criminal adjudication is, in short, "intended to be equitably individualized."[152] When a decision-making process is entirely delegated to an algorithm rather than ad hoc human judgment, just as when it is determined by "rule" rather than a "standard," the process will necessarily be over- and under-inclusive, leading to systemic over- and under-detection, convictions, and punishment. One concern voiced by some is whether modern algorithm-driven systems of perfect detection and enforcement of criminal violations go too far in eliminating or discouraging equitable discretion, from red light cameras, to enforcement of technical probation and parole requirements through 24/7 electronic surveillance,[153] to "per se" rules of criminal liability such as the 0.08% driving-under-the-influence-of-alcohol standard, to forms of proof so apparently certain that they discourage jurors from engaging in jury nullification.[154]

Mercy

Equity reflects the fact that bright line rules cannot fully capture justice; equitable discretion helps to correct, or complete, justice. Mercy, on the other hand, is "leniency granted by the

---

[148] See, e.g., M. Turek, Explainable Artificial Intelligence (XAI), DARPA, www.darpa.mil/program/explainable-artificial-intelligence.
[149] See GDPR, Recital 71: "[T]he data subject should have] the right … to obtain an explanation of the decision reached."
[150] See, e.g., J. A. Kroll, J. Huey, S. Barocas, *et al.*, Accountable Algorithms (2017) 165 *Univ. Pa. Law Rev.* 633 (explaining the limits of transparency as a means of rendering algorithms accountable).
[151] Roth, above note 130, p. 1285.
[152] J. Bowers, Legal Guilt, Normative Innocence, and the Equitable Decision Not to Prosecute (2010) 110 *Colum. Law Rev.* 1655, 1723.
[153] See K. Weisburd, Sentenced to Surveillance (unpublished manuscript; on file with author).
[154] See, e.g., Roth, above note 130, p. 1286; J. Seaman, Black Boxes: fMRI Lie Detection and the Role of the Jury (2009) 42 *Akron Law Rev.* 931 (speculating that fMRI evidence will discourage nullification).

grace of private persons beyond what justice alone demands or even allows."[155] Martha Nussbaum describes it as "gentleness going *beyond* due proportion."[156] Mercy is a virtue in the sense that it allows us to experience our shared humanity and exercise pity and sympathy, and it has an impressive (if perhaps recently forgotten) pedigree in the American system. Yet, the increased role of algorithms in augmenting charging and sentencing decisions, as well as in proving guilt, may decrease or eliminate the opportunity for human actors to exercise mercy in criminal cases. One of the most glaring examples might be the proliferation of mandatory minimum sentences based on drug quantity, victim age, or similar easily proven attendant circumstance (a sentencing "algorithm" as simple as it gets). But the same critique could be leveled against any algorithmic decision-making process that does not allow a human actor – a prosecutor, juror, or judge – to override the result.

CONCLUSION

How should the law of criminal adjudication meet the challenges of the algorithmic age? Before discussing specific reform proposals made by various commentators, I want to offer two overarching suggestions to frame the reader's assessment of algorithmic reforms.

The first suggestion is that legal scholars, lawmakers, and the public should decide what systemic values are important to us, which sorts of legal rules enhance those values, and develop and apply those rules to algorithms. Frank Easterbrook made this simple point with regard to the law of cyberspace in much-cited remarks at a conference on cyberlaw in 1996. Easterbrook cautioned his audience not to create a "law of cyberspace," just as we have no "law of the horse." Rather, he urged scholars and lawmakers to "develop a sound law of intellectual property, then apply it to computer networks."[157]

In the same respect, we should establish sound principles of criminal adjudication and apply them to algorithms. Do we want a safety valve that will temper the strictness of per se rules of criminal liability and punishment? Then we should keep lay jurors and human judges in the loop to allow for the application of equity and mercy through mechanisms like jury nullification and discretionary sentencing. Do we want the jury to have a meaningful ability to assess the probative value of evidence or, if not, to have significant front-end restrictions on unreliable evidence so that the jury is not exposed to it? Then we should create front-end and/or adversarial testing safeguards with regard to complex algorithms akin to the sorts of safeguards we have developed for human testimony, such as the hearsay rule, competence requirements, *Frye/Daubert*, and expert qualification and disclosure require-ments. When it comes to more complex versions of AI, which should we prioritize – explainability, or accuracy (when the two are in conflict)? Which matters more – eliminating racial disparities in an algorithm's false positive rate, or ensuring that predictive scores have the same meaning regardless of one's race? And do we care if people feel dehumanized when adjudged by a fully automated decision-maker, however "accurate" the decision? The public must decide these difficult value-laden questions first, before crafting a legal regime to govern algorithms.

---

[155] Roth, above note 130, p. 1285.
[156] M. C. Nussbaum, Equity and Mercy (1993) 22 *Phil. & Pub. Aff.* 83, 97 (emphasis in the original).
[157] F. Easterbrook, Cyberspace and the Law of the Horse (1996) 1996 *Univ. Chi. Leg. Forum* 207.

The ultimate goal would be an approach to algorithmic criminal adjudication that is "biotechnic," Lewis Mumford's term for a paradigm in which mechanization enhances agreed-upon human-centric goals, rather than a "megatechnic" approach that pursues mechanization either for its own sake, or for its ability to enhance certain values, such as efficiency, without regard for how our adaptation to new technologies might insidiously shift the pre-existing balance between efficiency and other values.[158] Jurisdictions might want to commit to these adjudicatory values in writing, just as the IEEE has set forth explicit ethics guidelines for the use of AI in the legal system.[159]

The second overarching suggestion is to take a "systems" approach to algorithmic criminal justice. As I have argued in previous work, we must eschew what systems engineers call "MABA-MABA" (men are better at, machines are better at) thinking.[160] Instead, man–machine interface designers should focus on what men and machines can do together, in the form of "bionic" prosecutors, defense attorneys, juries, judges, court reporters, and the like. The result would not be a trial by machine, or by unaided laypeople, but a "trial by cyborg." In a sense, we have always had trial by cyborg, in the form of bright line rules tempered by human safety valves, and human witnesses whose testimony is the product not merely of ad hoc judgment, but the accumulated wisdom of centuries of scientific inquiry, treatises, validation studies, instrument readings, review of records, and the like. But the need for a systems approach has become newly urgent now that rules come in the form of the output of complex computer programs. Under such an approach, a focus on human–AI compatibility should be front and center, to guard against pathologies like automation complacency. Luckily, we have templates to draw from, such as the space program.[161]

As for specific reform proposals, scholars have suggested a number of ideas, including: interpreting the Confrontation Clause to allow enhanced discovery; requiring robust, independent, industry-standard software testing as a condition of admissibility of any software result in a criminal case; eliminating the trade secret privilege in criminal cases; prohibiting criminal conviction based solely on one uncorroborated machine result; allowing defendants access to machine "experts" before trial, to determine how changing parameters affect output; giving defendants access to the source code, or creating scientific commissions that would review source code under protective order, much as the Food and Drug Administration reviews new drugs before approval; giving defendants access to the prior statements of machines, much as they have access to prior statements of human witnesses for use in impeachment; self-testing by "reversible" algorithms;[162] and the like.[163]

158 See generally L. Mumford, *The Pentagon of Power: The Myth of the Machine* (Harcourt, 1970), Vol. II.
159 See The IEEE Global Initiative on Ethics of Autonomous and Intelligent Systems. Ethically Aligned Design: A Vision for Prioritizing Human Well-Being with Autonomous and Intelligent Systems, 1st edn. (IEEE, 2019), https://standards.ieee.org/content/ieee-standards/en/industry-connections/ec/autonomous-systems.html.
160 Roth, above note 130, p. 1297 (quoting S. W. A. Dekker and D. D. Woods, MABA-MABA or Abracadabra? Progress on Human-Automation Co-ordination (2002) 4 *Cogn. Technol. Work* 240).
161 See generally D. Mindell, Digital Apollo: Human and Machine in Spaceflight (2008) (chronicling the history of human–machine collaboration in space travel).
162 See M. Möller and C. Vuik, On the Impact of Quantum Computing Technology on Future Developments in High-Performance Scientific Computing (2017) 19 *Ethics Inf. Technol.* 253.
163 See generally Cheng and Nunn, above note 99; Hellman, above note 125; Wexler, above note 117; Roth, above note 8; Chessman, above note 115; Imwinkelried, above note 116; Roth, above note 130.

Given the frailties of human decision-makers in the criminal justice system, we should be excited to incorporate the benefits of AI into criminal adjudication, from prosecutorial charging decisions, to proof of guilt and innocence, to court reporting, to setting probation conditions. We should ensure, however, that we do so in a way that does not warp our priorities or pre-existing commitments to systemic values.

20

Assessing the Risk of Offending through Algorithms

*Christopher Slobogin**

Risk assessment – measuring an individual's potential for offending – has long been an important aspect of most legal systems, in a wide variety of contexts. In most countries, sentences are often heavily influenced by concerns about preventing reoffending.[1] Correctional officials and parole boards routinely rely on risk assessments.[2] Post-sentence commitment of "dangerous" offenders (particularly common in connection with sex offenders) is based almost entirely on determinations of risk,[3] as is involuntary hospital commitment of people found not guilty by reason of insanity and of people who are not prosecuted but require treatment.[4] Detention prior to trial is frequently authorized not only upon a finding that a suspect will otherwise flee the jurisdiction, but also when the individual is thought to pose a risk to society if left at large.[5] And police on the streets have always been on the look-out for suspicious individuals who might be up to no good.[6]

As in most other areas of modern life, algorithms have begun to play a significant role in all of these determinations, especially in the United States. To aid in the risk assessment inquiry at sentencing, commitment, and pre-trial proceedings, a number of jurisdictions have begun relying on statistically derived tools called "risk assessment instruments" (RAIs).[7] In a few urban areas, police are engaging in what has been called "predictive policing," which involves using data-driven algorithms to identify crime hot spots and sometimes even "hot people."[8] Although to date most algorithmic attempts at criminal risk assessment are relatively primitive, in the sense that they do not take full advantage of big data or machine learning, many governmental entities have adopted them with enthusiasm because they are generally thought to be more accurate, more efficient, and less biased than the type of seat-of-

---

* This chapter is partly based on C. Slobogin, Principles of Risk Assessment: Sentencing and Policing (2018) 15 *Ohio St. J. Crim. Law* 583.

[1] C. B. Hessick and F. A. Hessick, Recognizing Constitutional Rights at Sentencing (2011) 99 *Cal. Law Rev.* 47, 74 ("[H]istorically, courts have considered future dangerousness ... in imposing sentence"). In the United States, even death sentences can be based on risk. *Jurek v. Texas*, 428 US 262 (1976).

[2] *United States v. Kebodeaux*, 570 US 387, 397 (2013) (noting that parole decision-making aims at "protecting the public against the risk of recidivism").

[3] *Kansas v. Hendricks*, 521 US 346, 348 (1997) (also requiring a finding that the individual is "dangerous beyond control").

[4] *Jones v. United States*, 463 US 354, 367 (1983) (discussing the dangerousness criterion in both settings).

[5] See, e.g., Federal Bail Reform Act, 18 USC § 3142(f).

[6] *Terry v. Ohio*, 392 US 1, 28 (1968) (noting the police interest in "crime prevention and detection").

[7] On sentencing, see C. Klingele, The Promises and Perils of Evidence-Based Corrections (2015) 91 *Notre Dame Law Rev.* 537, 566–7; on pre-trial detention, see M. T. Stevenson, Assessing Risk Assessment in Action (2018) 103 *Minn. Law Rev.* 303, 318.

[8] See A. G. Ferguson, Policing Predictive Policing (2016) 94 *Wash. Univ. Law Rev.* 1109, 1126–42.

the-pants risk assessment in which judges, parole boards, and police officers have traditionally engaged.

Yet RAIs (an acronym this chapter will use to refer to all algorithms aimed at identifying people who are potential criminals) bring with them a very serious set of controversies. Many of these controversies are familiar problems of algorithm-based decision-making – concerns about the accuracy of data inputs, bias in the training data, lack of transparency, and so on. But compared to other data-driven determinations, RAIs in the criminal and quasi-criminal setting tend to be subject to particularly heightened scrutiny, given their role in justifying significant deprivations of liberty. Furthermore, to the extent they involve punishment, these liberty deprivations are supposed to be based at least in part on blameworthy conduct. Yet, RAIs often rely on a whole host of factors that may not even be related to conduct, much less culpable acts.

For these reasons, RAIs have justifiably occasioned heated debate. This chapter will sidestep one aspect of that debate: whether the legal system may ever deprive someone of liberty based on what they might do rather than on what they have done. That controversy is long-standing and cannot be resolved here.[9] Rather, this chapter will assume that decisions about sentences, parole release, commitment, pre-trial detention, and police investigative actions can legitimately be based, in whole or in part, on assessments of risk or dangerousness. On that assumption, the question becomes under what circumstances, if any, RAIs may be used to assess risk.

As will become clear in the following discussion, answering that question requires a legal framework for thinking about risk assessment – a jurisprudence of risk. Unfortunately, that jurisprudence is in its infancy. As a contribution to that jurisprudence, this chapter argues that the determination of whether RAIs may be used to assess risk depends on the importance one ascribes to three conditions, which it calls the fit, validity, and fairness principles. Probably no RAI currently in existence robustly meets the demands of all three of these principles. Whether those demands should be relaxed depends, at least in part, on what one thinks of alternative methods of evaluating an individual's potential for committing crime.

THREE PRINCIPLES THAT MIGHT GOVERN RISK ASSESSMENT

In an effort to help government address sentencing, commitment, pretrial detention, and policing inquiries about risk, hundreds of RAIs have been developed, some by government itself, and many others by researchers at universities or at private companies.[10] RAIs generally consist of multiple "risk factors" – ranging from as few as five to over 100 – that are thought to correlate with risk. They also occasionally incorporate "protective factors" that are believed to *reduce* risk. The most sophisticated RAIs assign weights to the presence of each risk or protective factor; others simply assign a score of 1 if a risk factor is present and –1 if a protective factor is present.[11]

The types of factors found in RAIs are relatively straightforward. Every RAI includes antisocial behavior as a risk factor. In this category, some RAIs include only convictions,

---

9   For my take on the issue, see C. Slobogin, A Defence of Risk-Based Sentencing, in J. de Keijser, J. V. Roberts, and
     J. Ryberg (eds.), *Predictive Sentencing: Normative and Empirical Perspectives* (Hart, 2019), p. 107.
10   J. P. Singh, S. L. Desmarais, C. Hurducas, *et al.*, International Perspectives on the Practical Application of
     Violence Risk Assessment: A Global Survey of 44 Countries (2014) 13 *Int. J. Forensic Ment. Health* 193 (stating that
     there are over 200 RAIs worldwide).
11   For examples, see below text accompanying notes 19–22, 61–2, and 63–4.

others include convictions and arrests, and others include those factors plus elementary school misconduct, parole violations, and the like. These historical risk factors are called "static" because they cannot be changed by decisions made by the offender or through treatment interventions. Additional static risk factors sometimes found in RAIs include gender (maleness), age (youth), victim injury, and various aspects of social history, such as familial, relationship, psychological, and employment instability. Increasingly, RAIs – especially those used in sentencing and commitment – also assess "dynamic" risk factors, that is, factors that can be changed through offender decisions or treatment. Dynamic factors might include diagnoses (for example, substance abuse disorders), anger control, impulsivity, current lack of personal support or employment, and willingness to undergo remediation attempts. These latter types of factors are considered useful not only in assessing risk, but also in assessing means of managing risk; often RAIs incorporating these types of factors are called "risk-needs" assessment instruments because they focus as much on rehabilitative interventions as on the potential for offending.[12]

Whether pursued through RAIs or other means, risk assessment should be subject to some regulation, given its impact on liberty interests. While the content of this regulation could be very wide-ranging, the suggestion made here is that it can be reduced to three over-arching principles: the fit principle, the validity principle, and the fairness principle. Each of these principles has several implications for RAIs.

The fit principle posits that a risk assessment ought to address the precise legal question at issue. It is a constitutional axiom that the elements of crime be clearly delineated, in part to provide sufficient notice to the public about prohibited conduct, but primarily to control the discretion of police, prosecutors, and judges, who otherwise might abuse vague laws.[13] Because risk assessments can have the same impact on liberty as a conviction for crime and are probably even more prone to misapplication, legislatures and courts should similarly be obligated to set forth, as a matter law, the elements of risk that must be proven. Typically, a crime is defined in terms of particular conduct that occurs under particular circumstances and produces a particular result. By analogy, at a minimum, elements of risk should address (1) the probability, preferably quantified, (2) that a particular type of offense outcome (3) will occur within a specified period of time, (4) without a specified intervention. The content of these elements might vary significantly, depending on the legal setting. Under the fit principle, if an RAI does not help answer these elements, its conclusions are irrelevant; they fail to fit the legal inquiry.

The validity principle requires that RAIs do what they purport to do. In other words, once it is determined, through application of the fit principle, the questions that must be addressed, the RAI's ability to answer those questions should be evaluated. This inquiry could mimic the inquiry mandated by the US Supreme Court's decision in *Daubert* v. *Merrell Dow Pharm., Inc.*,[14] which asks whether the basis for expert testimony has been subjected to some type of verification process, such as empirical testing, the generation of error rates, and subjection to peer review through publication in accepted journals. Many jurisdictions hold that the *Daubert* criteria do not apply in the settings at issue here, because they were devised as

---

[12] For a more detailed description of various instruments, see S. L. Desmarais and J. P. Singh, Risk Assessment Instruments Validated and Implemented in Correctional Settings in the United States (March 27, 2013), www .courtinnovation.org/sites/default/files/media/document/2018/review%20of%20adult%20tools.pdf.

[13] See generally J. C. Jeffries, Legality, Vagueness, and the Construction of Penal Statutes (1985) 71 *Va. Law Rev.* 189.

[14] 509 US 579 (1993).

a rule of evidence meant to apply at trials. But that stance is hard to fathom; if the *Daubert* test must be met before evidence can be presented in a tort suit (the context of the *Daubert* case), it should certainly apply where weeks, months, or years of jail or prison time is at stake. If *Daubert*, or something like it, did apply to RAIs, it would require that: (1) the RAI be validated on a population similar to the population in question; (2) the probabilities the instrument associates with its risk categories can be stated with an acceptable level of confidence; (3) it do a passable job at distinguishing high-risk from low-risk individuals; (4) the RAI have satisfactory inter-rater reliability; and (5) information about all of these factors be periodically updated. Notice that, as expressed here, all of these criteria leave considerable wiggle room ("similar populations," "acceptable level of confidence," "passable job at distinguishing risk," "satisfactory reliability," and "periodically update"). No instrument can achieve perfect validity, and the extent to which an instrument should approximate that goal may, again, vary with the legal setting.

The fairness principle, as the name implies, is the most capacious and most-difficult-to-define principle. Indeed, a requirement of fairness could encompass both the fit and validity principles. Here, however, it is meant to refer to an assessment of the extent to which an RAI is consistent with the autonomy, dignity, and equality values that undergird the criminal justice system and its close cousin – commitment regimes that are aimed at individuals perceived to be dangerous. Those values were briefly alluded to by the Supreme Court in *Buck* v. *Davis*,[15] a case that involved expert testimony about risk in a capital sentencing proceeding:

> It would be patently unconstitutional for a state to argue that a defendant is liable to be a future danger because of his race ... [That would be] a disturbing departure from a basic premise of our criminal justice system: *Our law punishes people for what they do, not who they are.*[16]

The first sentence quoted above makes clear that race is off-limits as a risk factor. And the italicized language could – at least in the punishment context – call into question reliance on numerous other risk factors, including those that are highly correlated with race (for example, residence in segregated neighborhoods), as well as any factor that describes "who a person is" (for example, age, gender, diagnosis), rather than what he or she has done. It seems unlikely that the Court had this expansive view of fairness in mind in *Buck*; after all, it has even upheld death sentences based on opinions about dangerousness that were heavily influenced by these types of factors.[17] Nonetheless, the sentiment underlying *Buck*, one emphasized by numerous commentators,[18] should not be ignored. At a minimum, analysis of a risk factor's legitimacy should gauge the incremental validity it provides against its racial impact and the extent to which the legal setting in question tolerates risk assessments tied to personal traits that are not based on conduct.

The following discussion fleshes out this thumbnail sketch of the fitness, validity, and fairness principles in connection with sentencing, commitment, pre-trial detention, and policing. Because the validity and fairness principles cannot be implemented without knowledge of an algorithm's content, the chapter then examines the arguments in favor of requiring transparency in these various settings, and also mentions a few other procedural

---

[15]   137 S.Ct. 759 (2017).
[16]   *Ibid.* at 775, 778 (emphasis added).
[17]   See, e.g., *Barefoot* v. *Estelle*, 463 US 880 (1983). In *Buck* itself, the expert relied on seven "statistical factors"; race was the only factor that the Court found to be constitutionally impermissible (above note 15, at 775).
[18]   See, e.g., D. Husak, Lifting the Cloak: Preventive Detention as Punishment (2011) 48 *San Diego Law Rev.* 1173, 1195 ("no one should be punished for what is beyond their control").

ramifications. The concluding section considers the implications of the fact that few, if any, RAIs meet the demands of the fit, validity, and fairness principles.

SENTENCING

RAIs can come into play in all aspects of sentencing. Judges may consult them in imposing sentence, parole boards rely on them in determining a release date and conditions of release, and correctional authorities use them to decide on levels of security and other internal prison matters. The following discussion focuses on use of RAIs at front-end sentencing, with occasional references to the other settings.

Consider three RAIs commonly used in determining sentence. The Violence Risk Appraisal Guide (VRAG) is relied on extensively in Canada and in several US jurisdictions.[19] It contains twelve risk factors, linked to the individual's score on the Psychopathy Checklist (a measure of psychopathy that takes into account criminal history); elementary school misconduct; diagnosis (with personality disorders positively, and schizophrenia negatively, correlated with risk); age; presence of parents in home before age 16; performance on conditional release; non-violent offenses; marital status; victim injury; victim gender; and history of alcohol abuse. The evaluator assigns a numerical sub-score in connection with each risk factor and then adds the sub-scores to determine a total score that can range from less than −21 to more than 28. Initial research associated the lowest score on the VRAG with a 0 percent chance of violent offending within seven years and the highest score with a 100 percent chance of violent offending within that period. Seven other "bins" or ranges are associated with recidivism probabilities of 8 through 76 percent.

A second, even more popular sentencing instrument is the Correctional Offender Management Profiling for Alternative Sanctions tool (COMPAS).[20] Originally developed as an aid to corrections departments making decisions about placing, managing, and treating offenders, it has also been used to make sentencing and parole decisions. The COMPAS is much less transparent than the VRAG. Although the questions canvassed by the COMPAS are available, the weight given to particular answers to those questions has not been disclosed, nor is it publicly known whether a given answer is even relevant to the ultimate risk assessment. The company that developed the COMPAS, equivant, has stated that the factors that affect the tools' Violence Recidivism score consist of age at the time of the assessment, age at the time of the offender's first adjudication, the History of Violence Scale, the History of Noncompliance Scale, and the Vocational Educational Scale, but it is not willing to reveal the impact of each factor on the risk score or how the various scales are constructed. Also in contrast to the VRAG, the COMPAS recidivism scores are reported not in terms of probabilities, but in terms of "deciles"; inclusion in the first decile does not mean that the offender poses a 10 percent probability of recidivism, but rather that the offender fits in the bottom 10 percent of the group on which the COMPAS was validated. An offender is designated "low risk" if he or she fits within the first through fourth deciles, "medium risk" if within the fifth through seventh deciles, and "high risk" if within the eighth through tenth deciles.[21]

---

[19] For a description of the instrument and relevant research, see G. T. Harris, M. E. Rice, and C. A. Cormier, Prospective Replication of the Violence Risk Appraisal Guide in Predicting Violent Recidivism among Forensic Patients (2002) 26 *Law Hum. Behav.* 377.

[20] See www.documentcloud.org/documents/2702103-Sample-Risk-Assessment-COMPAS-CORE.html.

[21] See Northpointe, Practitioner's Guide to COMPAS (August 17, 2012), p. 5, www.northpointeinc.com/files/technical_documents/FieldGuide2_081412.pdf.

A third instrument sometimes used at sentencing is the HCR-20.[22] As the name implies, this RAI consists of twenty risk factors, ten linked with historical matters, five relating to clinical symptoms, and five relating to risk management or treatment. The historical factors are previous violence; age at first violent incident; relationship instability; employment problems; substance use problems; major mental illness; psychopathy; early maladjustment; personality disorder; and prior supervision failure. The clinical factors are lack of insight; negative attitudes; active symptoms of major mental illness; impulsivity; and unresponsiveness to treatment. The risk management factors are unfeasibility of plans; exposure to destabilizers; lack of personal support; non-compliance with remediation attempts; and stress. Each of the twenty factors is scored on a scale of 0 to 2, so that the maximum total score is 40. However, the developers of the HCR-20 strongly counsel that a strictly mathematical assessment should be avoided and that, instead, individuals should simply be characterized by the evaluator as "high," "medium," or "low" risk.

With regard to the fit, validity, and fairness principles, each of these instruments has strengths and weaknesses. They will be outlined here, as a way of illustrating how the principles would work in practice.

Fit

With regard to fit, recall that the RAI should identify (1) the probability, preferably quantified, (2) that a particular type of offense outcome (3) will occur within a specified period of time, (4) without a specified intervention. Only the VRAG meets the first probability criterion. The HCR-20's designation of a person as high, medium, or low risk is almost useless without knowing how the evaluator defines that term.[23] The COMPAS's use of deciles is not much better without knowing the reference group.

A quantified probability is important because, without it, the legal decision-maker cannot make an informed determination about whether the relevant legal standard is met. Setting that standard is a jurisprudential task that is beyond the scope of this chapter. But it is worth noting that, given the state of the predictive art, identifying groups associated with anything over a 75 percent chance of recidivating is probably impossible, and that even if the goal is merely meeting the classic preponderance of the evidence standard (51 percent), the designated group is likely to be very small in number. Some American jurisdictions have dealt with this problem through manipulating the definition of dangerousness. For instance, under the Texas death penalty scheme, the aggravating factor of dangerousness is proven if the state can show "beyond a reasonable doubt" that "there is a probability that [the offender] would commit criminal acts of violence that would constitute a continuing threat to society."[24] Technically, that language means that the state need only show a 95 percent chance of a *likelihood* (51 percent?) that the person will reoffend, a much easier task than proving beyond a reasonable doubt that the person *will* reoffend. Whether such a showing suffices as

[22] For a description of this instrument and accompanying research, see K. S. Douglas and C. D. Webster, The HCR-20 Violence Risk Assessment Scheme: Concurrent Validity in a Sample of Incarcerated Offenders (1999) 26 *Crim. Justice Behav.* 3, 8.

[23] See N. Scurich, The Case against Categorical Risk Assessments (2018) 36 *Behav. Sci. Law* 554 (arguing that "[e]mpirically, there is no consensus about what level of risk corresponds to a particular category, such as 'high risk,'" and that "[n]ormatively, categorization obscures what is fundamentally a value judgment about the relative costs and benefits of correct (e.g., true positive) and incorrect (e.g., false positive) outcomes").

[24] Texas Code Crim. Proc. Ann., art. 37.071.2(b)–(c) (2013).

a normative matter is a tough question, although Texas (and the US Supreme Court)[25] have answered it in the affirmative.

The second criterion – the outcome variable – ought to reflect the significance of what is at stake, which in this case is the decision to incarcerate, release an individual from incarceration, or enhance a sentence. Again, a jurisprudential issue is raised – what type of anticipated offense, by itself, is sufficient to justify incarceration or sentence enhancement? Many have asserted that a risk of minor criminal behavior, even if very high, should not affect the decision about incarceration.[26] If one accepts that position, the RAI ought to use serious violence, not just any offense, as its outcome measure. Many RAIs may fall short in this regard. For instance, the outcome measure in the initial validation research for the VRAG included a simple assault,[27] and it appears that a similar outcome measure was used to validate the COMPAS and the HCR-20.[28]

The third criterion requires that the prediction period associated with the RAI fit the relevant legal inquiry. The VRAG predicts violence within seven years, the HCR-20 within two years, and the COMPAS within one or two years. Since many statutory sentence ranges end well before seven years, the VRAG's outcome projection is far too long for any rational sentencing regime. And even two years may exceed the legal limit for offenders convicted of misdemeanors and low-level felonies.

Finally, an assessment of risk is not very useful to a judge or parole board trying to determine whether incarceration is necessary unless it gives the decision-maker some sense of alternatives to incarceration. Even a person who poses a very high risk might be manageable elsewhere; for instance, proponents of multi-systemic therapy assert that the optimal intervention for many youth who have committed violent crime should take place in the community systems that affect risk (for example, family, schools, peers).[29] Arguably, the decision-maker should be provided this type of information as a matter of law; indeed, a number of Supreme Court opinions can be read to stipulate that the state pursue its preventive aims in the least restrictive way possible.[30] If this were a requirement, RAIs would need to help the court assess not only risk levels, but also whether something less confining than prison, such as a halfway house, ankle bracelets, surveillance, or outpatient treatment, can achieve the state's preventive goal. In other words, risk instruments ought to address risk management as well as risk assessment. While the COMPAS and the HCR-20 provide some information of this type, the VRAG does not.

Validity

The validity principle as applied to algorithmic sentencing would require, at a minimum, that the instrument be developed in a methodologically sophisticated way and that its

25   The Court upheld the Texas death penalty statute in *Jurek* v. *Texas*, above note 1, at 274–6.
26   See, e.g., A. Ashworth and L. Zedner, *Preventive Justice* (Oxford University Press, 2014), p. 260.
27   Harris *et al.*, above note 19, p. 383.
28   See, e.g., Northpointe, above note 21, p. 15 (speaking of "person offense arrests" in defining violence).
29   See S. W. Henggeler, S. K. Schoenwald, C. M. Borduin, *et al.*, *Multisystemic Treatment of Antisocial Behavior in Children and Adolescents* (Guilford Press, 1998), pp. 252–4.
30   See C. Slobogin, Prevention as the Primary Goal of Sentencing: The Modern Case for Indeterminate Dispositions in Criminal Cases (2011) 48 *San Diego Law Rev.* 1127, 1138–40 (describing *Jackson* v. *Indiana*, 406 US 715 (1972); *Youngberg* v. *Romeo*, 457 US 307 (1982); and *Seling* v. *Young*, 531 US 250 (2001), and arguing that these cases announce a less-drastic-means requirement where the government's goal is prevention). Cf. *Bell* v. *Wolfish*, 441 US 520, 539 n. 20 (1979) (stating that a failure to consider "alternative and less harsh methods" to achieve a non-punitive objective would indicate an intent to impose criminal punishment).

psychometric properties be evaluated in all five areas noted earlier (application to the relevant legal population, ability to identify probability of reoffending, ability to discriminate between high- and low-risk offenders, inter-rater reliability, and currency). The developers of all three instruments discussed here provide a significant amount of information about these metrics.[31] Only the first three, which will be called external validity, calibration validity, and discriminant validity, will be emphasized here.

To meet minimum demands of external validity, the RAI should be validated on a population that closely matches the target of the intervention. Many RAIs could fail this basic requirement. For instance, the VRAG was originally normed in Canada, which made its use problematic in the United States until it was validated on more diverse US populations.[32] Ideally, the RAI's reference group will be highly similar to the individual being assessed in terms of both demographic characteristics and criminal charges.

Assuming that to be the case, calibration validity – the ability to assign risk categories or probabilities to individual offenders accurately – is the metric that comes closest to meeting the fit requirements discussed earlier. This is especially so if it answers the outcome, duration, and intervention questions as well. Ideally, an RAI could provide several risk categories, each of which is associated with a particular likelihood of reoffending (for example, 20 percent ± 5 percent) for the population in question.

Closely related to calibration validity is discriminant validity, or the ability of the tool to distinguish between high- and low-risk offenders. One popular method of measuring discriminant validity is the "receiver operating characteristic curve," which is derived by plotting the true positive rate over the false positive rate.[33] If the resulting curve follows the left vertical axis and then the upper horizontal axis (like a non-capitalized "r"), the area under the curve (AUC) would be 1.0, indicating that the instrument is 100 percent accurate. If, instead, the curve ends up being a 45-degree diagonal from the lower-left corner to the upper-right corner of the plot, the AUC would be 0.5, indicating that the RAI is no better than chance at differentiating true positives from true negatives. A typical AUC value for the VRAG and the HCR-20 is between 0.70 and 0.75,[34] indicating that, in the validation study, there was a 70 to 75 percent chance that a person who recidivates received a higher score on the VRAG than a person who did not recidivate.

Arguably, this value rests at the lower end of what courts should demand. In *Addington* v. *Texas*,[35] the Supreme Court held that a mentally ill person may not be hospitalized on dangerousness grounds on less than clear and convincing evidence, which is conventionally quantified as a 75 percent level of certainty. If a person cannot be involuntarily hospitalized without that degree of confidence, at least that much should be required before an offender may be preventively detained in prison. In AUC terms, that means that sentencing courts should only use RAIs that can accurately distinguish high- and low-risk offenders roughly 75 percent of the time.

---

[31] Note that, in contrast to the instruments discussed here, for many RAIs, the only validation studies that exist were conducted by the developers of the instruments, and that sometimes these studies provide information on only a small number of performance measures. T. Douglas, J. Pugh, I. Singh, *et al.*, Risk Assessment Tools in Criminal Justice and Forensic Psychiatry: The Need for Better Data (2017) 42 *Eur. Psychiat.* 134, 135.

[32] See Harris *et al.*, above note 19, p. 381.

[33] See D. Mossman, Assessing Predictions of Violence: Being Accurate about Accuracy (1994) 62 *J. Consult. Clin. Psychol.* 783, 784–5 (describing this method of measuring the accuracy of risk assessment).

[34] M. Bani-Yaghoub, J. P. Fedoroff, S. Curry, and D. E. Amundsen, A Time Series Modeling Approach in Risk Appraisal of Violent and Sexual Recidivism (2010) 34 *Law Hum. Behav.* 349, 359.

[35] 441 US 418, 431–3 (1979).

Fairness

As noted earlier, fairness is an amorphous term, even when limited to the concerns identified in *Buck* v. *Davis*. To focus the inquiry, one can think of the fairness principle as concerned with two distinct claims – the discrimination claim and the dignity claim. The first part of the language from *Buck* that was quoted earlier – "It would be patently unconstitutional for a state to argue that a defendant is liable to be a future danger because of his race" – is most clearly related to the discrimination claim. On the surface, many RAIs would seem to be vulnerable to this type of concern. Although RAIs like the VRAG, the COMPAS, and the HCR-20 do not explicitly consider race, they often distinguish between offenders based on near proxies for race (such as poverty-related factors) or other immutable or near-immutable traits, such as gender, age, and diagnosis. Thus, one could argue, applying American equal protection law, that sentences based on these RAIs discriminate on the basis of suspect or quasi-suspect classes and are unconstitutional.[36]

One response to this argument is that statistical or mechanistically derived RAIs demonstrate no "animus" toward any of these classes, a showing that is usually required before constitutional discrimination is found.[37] A second is that even *intentional* discrimination toward discrete groups is permissible if there is a rational or significant justification for it – here, protecting the public and efficiently allocating resources.[38]

Also relevant to this doctrinal debate is the fact that eliminating group characteristics in an RAI may discriminate unfairly against *other* groups.[39] The Wisconsin Supreme Court's opinion in *Wisconsin* v. *Loomis*[40] makes the point. In *Loomis*, the Court was faced with a challenge to the COMPAS, which, like a number of RAIs, includes maleness as a risk factor. To the argument that a sentence cannot be based on such a characteristic, the Court stated: "[I]t appears that any risk assessment tool which fails to differentiate between men and women will misclassify both genders."[41] Because the removal of gender from its calculus would mean that the COMPAS would lead to inaccurate gender distinctions in sentencing (with women being rated as higher risk and men as lower risk than they actually are), the Court rejected the defendant's constitutional claim.

A more compelling discrimination-related concern is that RAIs may *inaccurately* rely on immutable factors. This was the argument made in a *ProPublica* article reporting a study about the COMPAS showing that the instrument produced disproportionately more false positives (that is, people predicted to recidivate who did not) among blacks than whites.[42] The response to this concern is more complicated, but boils down to this: if African-Americans are more likely to commit crime than whites, an RAI that relies heavily on prior crimes will inevitably produce a greater percentage of false positives among blacks.[43] Manipulating the algorithm to reduce those

---

[36] See S. B. Starr, Evidence-Based Sentencing and the Scientific Rationalization of Discrimination (2014) 66 *Stan. Law Rev.* 803, 805.

[37] C. Coglianese and D. Lehr, Regulating by Robot: Administrative Decision Making in the Machine-Learning Era (2017) 105 *Geo. Law J.* 1147, 1193.

[38] *United States* v. *Virginia*, 518 US 515 (1996) (sex discrimination subject only to intermediate scrutiny).

[39] Cf. *Shaw* v. *Hunt*, 517 US 899 (1996): "A State's interest in remedying the effects of past or present racial discrimination may in the proper case justify a government's use of racial distinctions."

[40] 881 NW.2d 749 (Wis. 2016).

[41] *Ibid.* at 766.

[42] See J. Angwin, J. Larson, S. Mattu, and L. Kirchner, Machine Bias, *ProPublica* (May 13, 2016), www .propublica.org/article/machine-bias-risk-assessments-in-criminal-sentencing.

[43] See A. Feller, E. Pierson, S. Corbett-Davies, and S. Goel, A Computer Program Used for Bail and Sentencing Decisions Was Labeled Biased against Blacks. It's Actually Not that Clear, *Washington Post* (October 17, 2016),

false positives will increase the percentage of black false negatives (that is, people said to be low risk who in fact reoffend) and also increase the number of false positives who are white.

So the real question for the statistician is whether the predicate condition stated above – that African-Americans commit more crimes than other racial groups – is correct. If police arrest, prosecutors charge, or juries and judges convict in racially driven ways, it may not be. Or perhaps that predicate is correct with regard to some crimes (for example, drug offenses), but not others.[44] If that empirical problem can be resolved and any bias in the training data eliminated, then the jurisprudential question with regard to discrimination claims becomes whether the goal is a prediction regime that uses the same non-racialized criteria to assess risk (which will probably produce more black than white false positives, given the divergent crime rates) or one that produces the same percentage of black and white false positives (which will probably increase black false negatives, and thus probably result in more black victims).[45]

The second fairness concern focuses not on discrimination per se, but on dignity, or as the Supreme Court put it in *Buck*, the "basic premise of our criminal justice system [that] [o]ur law punishes people for what they do, not who they are."[46] The noted criminal law scholar Andrew von Hirsch put the point this way: "Unless the person actually made the wrongful choice he was predicted to make, he ought not be condemned for that choice – and hence should not suffer punishment for it."[47] That sentiment might permit enhancement of an offender's sentence based on prior crimes. But it would not permit a risk assessment based on anything else. Thus, reliance on risk factors such as gender, diagnosis, parental presence during one's teenage years, and employment status – even if not considered discriminatory in application – would nonetheless be off-limits because of its insult to autonomy. Not only are these factors not crimes, but many cannot even be called "behavior" chosen by the individual.

That argument has a strong intuitive appeal, even in a sentencing regime which, as is the case in most American jurisdictions,[48] only permits risk to influence the length of an offender's sentence within a retributively defined range that is determined by desert principles. Nonetheless, there are two practical problems with von Hirsch's stance. First, removal of all non-crime factors from an RAI is likely to substantially reduce accuracy. Second, as noted above, removal is also likely to *increase* discrimination. A young male with psychopathic tendencies and one prior crime represents a much higher risk than an older female suffering from depression who has committed the same crime; yet, under von Hirsch's approach, both would be treated identically.

A more nuanced approach would balance the incremental validity of a given risk factor with fairness concerns. This limitation would probably still permit reliance on age and gender, since they appear to improve accuracy significantly; the incremental validity of a factor like employment status, in contrast, may not be significant, in which case it

www.washingtonpost.com/news/monkey-cage/wp/2016/10/17/can-an-algorithm-be-racist-our-analysis-is-more-cautious-than-propublicas/?utm_term=.c3eec3904d97.

44 See R. Ramchand, R. L. Pacula, and M. Y. Iguchi, Racial Differences in Marijuana-Users Risk of Arrest in the United States (2006) 84 *Drug Alcohol Depend.* 264.

45 R. Berk, Accuracy and Fairness for Juvenile Justice Risk Assessments (2019) 16 *J. Empir. Leg. Stud.* 175, 191 ("discussions of fairness in criminal justice settings typically ignore fairness for victims").

46 *Buck*, above note 15, at 778.

47 A. von Hirsch, *Past or Future Crimes: Deservedness and Dangerousness in the Sentencing of Criminals* (Rutgers University Press, 1985), p. 11.

48 R. Frase, Theories of Proportionality and Desert, in J. Petersilia and K. R. Reitz (eds.), *The Oxford Handbook of Sentencing and Corrections* (Oxford University Press, 2012), pp. 131, 144–6.

might be discarded from consideration.[49] In the end, a normative judgment must be made about when the correlation of a non-criminal factor with risk is so low it should be excluded.

To minimize further any affront to dignity associated with RAIs, risk assessment should also be based as much as possible on dynamic or "causal risk factors," such as drug abuse or impulsivity (a goal better achieved by the HCR-20 and the COMPAS than the VRAG). Again, dynamic factors are those that can be changed through intervention and thus focus on traits that the person can do something about. This aspect of the fairness principle dovetails with the fit principle's requirement that algorithmic risk assessment provide output relevant to risk management. Also consistent with this point, researchers should endeavor to include in their algorithm factors that reduce risk, as the VRAG does with schizophrenia.

COMMITMENT AND PRE-TRIAL DETENTION

The analysis of how the fit and validity principles apply in the commitment and pre-trial detention contexts can be brief, because the foregoing discussion about sentencing has identified the types of issues most likely to arise. In terms of fit, the relevant probability, outcome measure, prediction period, and dispositional alternatives that an RAI should address might vary significantly, depending on the precise type of proceeding. For instance, given the focus of post-sentence sexually violent predator (SVP) commitment,[50] RAIs should provide data about the probability of *sexual* recidivism, not just general recidivism; further, given the consequences of such commitment (which mimic prison[51]), that probability should be high. In contrast, given that civil commitment is typically short term and explicitly treatment oriented, it might suffice if the RAI assesses risk for *any* type of non-trivial bodily harm; at the same time, because the criteria for such commitment generally require proof of imminent danger,[52] the harm predicted ought to be in the very near future, not simply "foreseeable." The time frame in the pre-trial detention setting should also be short (in the neighborhood of three months), given the limitations imposed by speedy trial statutes,[53] and, as with sentencing, detention should probably not take place unless the harm predicted is serious.[54]

With regard to validity, a key issue is, as usual, whether the instrument was validated on the relevant population. In the SVP context, some courts have relied on the VRAG and the HCR-20 even though their validation samples were not focused on sex offenders.[55] Similar issues can arise with pre-trial detention RAIs. The Ohio Risk Assessment System was developed on a sample of several hundred defendants in Ohio, but is now used nationwide.[56] Any

---

[49] For illustrative data on the bivariate relationship between violence and various risk factors, based on a study focused on the relationship of mental disorder and violence, see MacArthur Research Network on Mental Health & the Law: The MacArthur Violence Assessment Study (2001), http://perma.cc/5QLN-3ETP.

[50] See, e.g., Kan. Stat. Ann. § 59-29a-1 (defining "sexually violent predator" as a person charged or convicted of a sexually violent offense who is "likely to engage in the predatory acts of sexual violence").

[51] See *Allen v. Illinois*, 478 US 364, 379 (1979) (Stevens, J., dissenting) (noting similarities between SVP commitment and prison).

[52] See, e.g., Fla. Stat. § 394.467(a)(A)2.b (requiring proof of a "substantial likelihood that in the near future [the person] will inflict serious bodily harm on ... another person ...").

[53] See, e.g., Federal Speedy Trial Act, 18 USC § 3162 (presumptive limit of 100 days from arrest to trial).

[54] See S. Baradharan, The History of Misdemeanor Bail (2018) 98 *Boston Univ. Law Rev.* 387 (arguing that misdemeanor arrestees should be presumptively released).

[55] See, e.g., *People v. Clewell*, 2017 WL 2472693 *6 (Cal. 4th DCA, 2017).

[56] E. Latessa, P. Smith, and R. Lemke, The Creation and Validation of the Ohio Risk Assessment System (ORAS) (2016) 74 *Fed. Probat.* 16.

systematic differences between that sample and these new populations could yield inaccurate estimates, a problem unlikely to be discovered given the failure of most jurisdictions to cross-validate their pre-trial risk assessment tools.[57]

As these points illustrate, the fit and validity principles as applied to commitment and pre-trial detention require inquiries analogous to the sentencing context, and their implications will not be explored further here. It is in application of the fairness principle that analysis of the two settings is most likely to diverge – not over the discrimination component of the principle (which here, as in all settings, prohibits inaccurate discrimination, and thus cautions against use of racially biased arrests and the like), but rather over its dignity component. As *Buck* stated, a "basic premise" of punishment is that it be based on what a person has done rather than who they are. When the focus is commitment and pre-trial detention, however, one can argue that punishment is not the goal; certainly, the US Supreme Court has said as much in cases like *Kansas v. Hendricks* (involving SVP proceedings),[58] *Addington v. Texas* (involving commitment proceedings),[59] and *United States v. Salerno* (involving pre-trial detention).[60] Rather, these proceedings, according to the Court, are all "regulatory" in nature, established for the express purpose of preventing harm to the public, not punishing the person for a crime. If one accepts that position (which many do not, at least in connection with SVP proceedings[61]), then concern about reliance on risk factors that are static or that are based on conditions that do not involve blameworthy conduct can be ignored.

The import of this conclusion can be dramatically illustrated by looking at a relatively new RAI that was developed for use in commitment proceedings. The Oxford Risk of Recidivism Tool, nicknamed OxRec, is noteworthy because it considers so many risk factors, including environmental variables that other instruments do not consider: male sex; unemployed before prison; young age; non-immigrant status; previous prison sentence of short duration; violent index crime; previous violent crime; never married; fewer years of education; low disposable income; alcohol use disorder; drug use disorder; any mental disorder; any severe mental disorder; and "high neighborhood deprivation," which is determined using rates or measures of welfare recipiency, migration status, divorce, educational levels, residential mobility, crime, and disposable income within the individual's neighborhood.[62] Not only are many of these factors not based on conduct or on conduct that is blameworthy (in either the criminal or moral sense), the final factor – the neighborhood deprivation score – moves even further from *Buck*'s "basic premise" by considering the status and behavior of *others*, over which the offender clearly has no control. Yet, if the use of the OxRec is limited to commitment settings, that fact may not be a problem from a jurisprudential perspective.[63]

---

[57] See S. L. Desmarais and E. M. Lowder, Pretrial Risk Assessment Tools: A Primer for Judges, Prosecutors, and Defense Attorneys, University of Virginia Law School, Uptrn, and Human Rights Data Analysis Group (February 2019), p. 7.

[58] Above note 3.

[59] Above note 35.

[60] 481 US 739 (1987).

[61] J. W. White, Is Iowa's Sexual Predator Statute "Civil"?: The Civil Commitment of Sexually Violent Predators after *Kansas v. Crane* (2004) 88 *Iowa Law Rev.* 739.

[62] S. Fazel, Z. Chang, T. Fanshawe, *et al.*, Prediction of Violent Reoffending on Release from Prison: Derivation and External Validation of a Scalable Tool (2016) 3 *Lancet Psychiatry* 535, 540. The instrument itself is found at https://oxrisk.com/oxrec/.

[63] Unless, perhaps, neighborhood is a stand-in for race. See A. G. Ferguson, *The Rise of Big Data Policing: Surveillance, Race and the Future of Law Enforcement* (New York University Press, 2017), p. 122 (noting the correlation).

POLICING

In recent years, RAIs have also crept into the investigative phase of the criminal justice system. The lessons learned from other sectors of the legal system are directly applicable to this setting. If applied conscientiously, the fit, validity, and fairness principles would place significant restrictions on the use of algorithms in police work, just as they would elsewhere.

The most common policing algorithms are aimed at identifying "hot spots" of criminal activity. These are merely more sophisticated versions of crime-mapping schemes that police have used for decades. A newer, and more problematic, development is the use of algorithms that purport to identify "hot people." The Chicago Police Department's "Strategic Subject List" relies on eleven risk factors, such as criminal history, age, parole status, and gang status, to generate "risk scores" from 1 to 500.[64] Various private companies claim to be able to do something similar, with instruments boasting names like Digital Stakeout, Predpol, HunchLab, and Beware. Beware, developed by a company called Intrado, purports to analyze scores of data points about an individual, including property records, commercial databases, recent purchases, and social media posts, to assign "threat scores" within a matter of seconds after a person has been identified.[65]

As usual, the implications of the fit principle depend upon how these RAIs will be used. If they are meant to help allocate how police officers are deployed on the street, perhaps any algorithm that can differentiate between areas or people in terms of risk would suffice. In contrast, if they are used to justify stops or heightened surveillance of those identified as a risk, a much higher probability, of more significant harm, might be required. Further, in the investigative setting the Supreme Court has generally demanded that before police subject a person to an investigative detention the danger predicted must be imminent,[66] meaning the algorithm should be able to identify either an incipient crime hot spot or a person who is linked to a recent or soon-to-occur crime by virtue of being in the relevant vicinity. Without this constraint, the RAI could also run afoul of the dignity component of the fairness principle, which cautions against "punishment" based on a condition or status that is only weakly associated with risk. Otherwise, police could use RAIs to confront the same person repeatedly without any objective indicator that their action is necessary at that particular point in time.

The key validity issue with policing RAIs is data-looping, a phenomenon that afflicts all algorithms, but is particularly problematic here. Because of their heavy reliance on criminal records, policing RAIs are likely to lead to police confrontations of previous offenders much more frequently than first offenders, who may never be confronted at all if the police rely solely on algorithms.[67] Furthermore, research has shown that a significant portion of the data that goes into these RAIs is "dirty," meaning that it is the result of improper, and often racially

---

[64] See J. Saunders, P. Hunt, and J. S. Hollywood, Predictions Put into Practice: A Quasi-Experimental Evaluation of Chicago's Predictive Policing Pilot (2016) 12 *J. Exp. Criminol.* 347.

[65] J. Jouvenal, The New Way Police Are Surveilling You: Calculating Your Threat "Score," *Washington Post* (January 10, 2016), www.washingtonpost.com/local/public-safety/the-new-way-police-are-surveilling-you-calculating-your-threat-score/2016/01/10/e42bccac-8e15-11e5-baf4-bdf37355daoc_story.html?utm_term=.e31cao39afaf.

[66] See *United States* v. *Hensley*, 469 US 221, 228–9 (1985) (reasoning that the principles of *Terry* v. *Ohio* generally limit stops on reasonable suspicion to situations involving "imminent or ongoing crimes" or a known "completed felony").

[67] B. Harcourt, *Against Prediction: Profiling, Policing and Punishing in an Actuarial Age* (University of Chicago Press, 2007), p. 164 (describing how the "ratchet effect" increases the representation of certain groups in the carceral population).

biased stops, arrests, and convictions.[68] Thus, as with sentencing RAIs, heavy reliance on low-level crimes in policing RAIs can both undermine accuracy and exacerbate discrimination. In recognition of this fact, at least one policing tool does not use drug-offense information in its algorithm.[69]

As an additional measure aimed at ensuring at least some semblance of fairness, police might be required to treat everyone that an RAI identifies as high risk the same way (akin to what should naturally occur at sentencing, commitment, or pre-trial detention hearings that rely on RAIs). Thus, if the police choose to stop a person that an RAI has identified as high risk, they would also have to stop everyone else with the same profile. The precedent for this requirement comes from the Supreme Court's checkpoint jurisprudence, which mandates that people stopped at roadblocks be selected on a neutral basis.[70] Unless this rule is followed, the biases that algorithms are meant to prevent will simply be reintroduced when police make the decision about whom to stop. A further possible consequence of such a rule, not necessarily undesirable, is that, given the hassle of abiding by it, police would think twice before acting in the first place.

TRANSPARENCY AND PROCEDURE

A few of the RAIs mentioned above – the COMPAS and some of the policing RAIs – were developed by private companies that refuse to divulge the nature of the algorithm. This is a common phenomenon, one that is exacerbated by the increased reliance on self-contained machine-learning algorithms. The only point made here is that, whatever may be the strength of trade secret claims and similar defenses of secrecy in other legal settings, they should not succeed in the criminal context where deprivations of liberty are concerned. People subject to sentence, pre-trial detention, and commitment, or who are stopped and arrested, are entitled to know why.

That entitlement is most obviously found in the Sixth Amendment, which guarantees the "accused" in "all criminal prosecutions" the right to confront accusers and compulsory process. The Sixth Amendment clearly applies at pre-trial detention proceedings and suppression hearings,[71] where a defendant might want to challenge a stop or arrest based on an RAI. While it does not apply to sentencing or commitment proceedings, the due process clause does.[72] And the key case in this area happens to be based on the latter clause. In *Gardner* v. *Florida*,[73] the defendant argued that, before his sentence was imposed, he had a right to discover and rebut the contents of his pre-sentence report. The government objected to this claim on a number of grounds: such discovery, it claimed, would make sources reluctant to provide information, would delay the process, might disrupt rehabilitation given the psychological information contained in such reports, and was not necessary given the expertise of judges. But the Supreme Court rejected all of these arguments (many of which could apply to RAI-based conclusions as well). Although the Court relied on the due process clause, it did so using language that resonates with the Sixth Amendment: "Our belief

---

[68] See R. Richardson, J. Schultz, and K. Crawford, Dirty Data, Bad Predictions: How Civil Rights Violations Impact Police Data, Predictive Policing Systems, and Justice, *NYU Online* (forthcoming, 2019).

[69] Machine Learning and Policing, PredPol: Predictive Policing Blog (July 19, 2017), http://blog.predpol.com /machine-learning-and-policing.

[70] See, e.g., *Delaware* v. *Prouse*, 440 US 648, 657 (1979).

[71] *Waller* v. *Georgia*, 467 US 39 (1984).

[72] See *Addington* v. *Texas*, above note 35, at 423.

[73] 430 US 349 (1977).

that debate between adversaries is often essential to the truth-seeking function of trials requires us also to recognize the importance of giving counsel an opportunity to comment on facts which may influence the sentencing decision ...."[74]

Gardner was a capital case, a context in which the Court has been particularly concerned about reliability. But another, much older decision from the Court suggests that *any* deprivation of liberty should trigger a confrontation right sufficient to justify exposing the content of an RAI. In *Roviaro v. United States*,[75] involving a simple drug case, the Court held that the identity of confidential informants must be revealed to the defendant when the informant possesses facts that are relevant to the defense. Although it involves a confidential informant rather than a confidential algorithm, *Roviaro* establishes that even strong claims of a need for secrecy (here protecting an informant) should not prevail when the information is crucial to the case. While *Roviaro* has been given short shrift in more recent decisions,[76] its central rationale has not been abandoned.

If a right to challenge a privately developed RAI exists, it should permit not only discovery of an RAI's risk factors, but the weights those factors are assigned and the method used to obtain the risk estimate. Access to this information is important not only to ensure accuracy, but also to monitor, consistent with the fairness principle, how much influence any factors that do not involve blameworthy conduct have on risk scores.[77]

A further reason the identity of risk factors is important – to both the subject of the assessment *and* the government – concerns the type of rebuttal evidence the subject may proffer. Obviously, the subject should be able to show that the RAI relies on an incorrect fact – for instance, a conviction that was overturned, an arrest that was baseless, or an erroneous employment record. At the same time, the government can legitimately argue that a decision-maker should not be able to second-guess a well-constructed RAI by, for instance, attributing a different significance to an arrest record than the RAI does (unless something about that record is inaccurate); as an empirical matter, allowing such a subjective adjustment of an actuarial instrument defeats the entire purpose of using statistically derived tools. Similarly, while the defense should always be able to present evidence of protective factors that were not tested in the development of the instrument, if such factors *were* incorporated into the validation process and found to be statistically irrelevant, they probably should be considered legally irrelevant as well.

In connection with the indeterminate confinement associated with commitment and some sentencing regimes, two other procedural issues arise: how often challenges to RAI-based determinations should occur after the initial legal decision, and under what types of rules. A criminal system that delays parole hearings for several years is probably not unconstitutional.[78] However, parole decisions are normally based on a mixture of retributive

---

[74] *Ibid.* at 361.

[75] 353 US 53, 60–1 (1957): "Where the disclosure of an informer's identity, or of the contents of his communication, is relevant and helpful to the defense of the accused, or is essential to a fair determination of a cause, the [informant's] privilege must give way."

[76] See Z. A. G. Perez, Piercing the Veil of Informant Confidentiality: The Role of In Camera Hearings in the *Roviaro* Determination (2009) 46 *Am. Crim. Law Rev.* 179, 202–13 (describing and critiquing Federal Circuit approaches to *Roviaro*).

[77] As an example of how important the weight assigned a risk factor is, see M. Stevenson and C. Slobogin, Algorithmic Risk Assessment and the Double-Edge Sword of Youth (2018) 96 *Wash. Univ. Law Rev.* 1 (providing empirical evidence of the extent to which youth influences risk scores on the COMPAS and other RAIs, and how a failure to make that information transparent can skew legal decisions about sentences).

[78] *Garner v. Jones*, 529 US 244, 251 (2000) (upholding an eight-year delay against an *ex post facto* challenge, but also noting such delay would not be permissible if it "creates a significant risk of prolonging [the offender's] incarceration").

and utilitarian considerations. If the goal is solely to determine risk, in contrast, the Supreme Court has held that routine periodic review is constitutionally required.[79] Thus, to the extent long-term detention is preventive in nature – which is often the case with sentencing, and always the case with post-sentence and insanity acquittee commitment – the review should be routine, perhaps on an annual basis. While these review hearings need not afford subjects the full panoply of rights available at trial,[80] the hearings have to be adversarial enough in nature to enable the types of challenges just described.

CONCLUSION

Taken seriously, the fit, validity, and fairness principles are very difficult to meet. Probably no RAI currently in existence does so. One possible response is to revert back to the approach to risk assessment that preceded RAIs. Usually called "clinical" risk assessment, this method relies on a subjective judgment by the legal decision-maker, perhaps aided by the diagnostic impressions of a psychiatrist or psychologist. Such assessments can easily achieve what might be called "facial fit"; for instance, a judge or parole board can decide that, based on their best judgment, the expert evidence shows a substantial probability that the offender will commit a violent offense within the next year if not confined.

However, these types of judgments quickly run afoul of the validity and fairness principles. Although clinical experts can often perform better than chance,[81] research consistently shows that clinical judgment is inferior to actuarial judgment about the risk of violence,[82] at least outside the policing context.[83] And while the explicit explanation for a particular clinical judgment may recount only "legitimate" risk factors, such as prior crimes, the influence (conscious or otherwise) of clearly illegitimate or suspect factors, including race, cannot be discounted and in fact is probably pervasive.[84] In contrast, the risk factors considered by an RAI are apparent on the face of the instrument and, assuming that the same RAI is used throughout the jurisdiction, will promote more consistent judgments.

Despite its problems, clinical prediction might nonetheless be preferred over an RAI-based prediction on the separate ground that it is more "individualized." Because RAIs reflect group tendencies, some scholars have argued that they cannot say anything meaningful about an individual.[85] That argument has been debunked as a statistical

---

[79] *Kansas v. Hendricks*, above note 3, at 363–4.
[80] See *Morrissey v. Brewer*, 408 US 471, 484 (1972) (allowing less formal process at parole revocations).
[81] See C. Slobogin, Dangerousness and Expertise (1984) 133 *Univ. Pa. Law Rev.* 97, 112–14.
[82] S. Ægisdóttir, M. J. White, P. M. Spengler, and A. S. Maugherman, The Meta-Analysis of Clinical Judgment Project: Fifty-Six Years of Accumulated Research on Clinical versus Statistical Prediction (2006) 34 *Couns. Psychol.* 341; N. Z. Hilton, G. T. Harris, and M. E. Rice, Sixty-Six Years of Research on the Clinical Versus Actuarial Prediction of Violence (2006) 34 *Couns. Psychol.* 400, 400–1. But see J. J. Dressel, Accuracy and Racial Biases of Recidivism Prediction Instruments, *Science Advances* (January 7, 2018), p. 4 (finding no difference in lay and statistical predictive accuracy, but using a methodology that in essence converted the lay prediction into an algorithm).
[83] On the problems with hot people policing RAIs, see Saunders *et al.*, above note 64. In contrast, hot spot RAIs might be preferable to police intuition. See B. Grunwald and J. Fagan, The End of Intuition-Based High Crime Areas (2019) 107 *Cal. Law Rev.* 345, 397–8.
[84] D. Faust and D. C. Ahern, Clinical Judgment and Prediction, in J. Ziskin and D. Faust (eds.), *Coping with Psychiatric and Psychological Testimony*, 6th edn. (Oxford University Press, 2011), p. 147 (surveying the literature on the subjective factors affecting clinical judgment).
[85] See D. J. Cooke and C. Michie, Limitations of Diagnostic Precision and Predictive Utility in the Individual Case: A Challenge for Forensic Practice (2010) 34 *Law Hum. Behav.* 259, 272: "[I]t is clear that predictions of future offending cannot be achieved, with any degree of confidence, in the individual case."

matter.[86] Just as importantly, it proves too much. Ultimately, all risk assessment, indeed all expert testimony, is based on stereotyping. A clinical expert who claims she believes an offender will reoffend is basing that assertion on factors that she has come to believe are correlated with risk, based on her experience with, or on her reading or hearing about, other people. There is no way to avoid what I and my co-authors have called the G2i (general-to-individual) challenge in expert testimony.[87] Reinforcing these points is a study that found that while, in the abstract, lay subjects preferred clinical to actuarial judgment because of its less mechanistic nature, their preferences were reversed when they were informed that the algorithm was more accurate, and they were even more likely to prefer algorithms when the factors used to construct them were made transparent.[88] Both of these conditions would exist under the regime proposed here.

So the better response to the difficulties with RAIs might be to treat the principles as aspirational. Under this option, an RAI that fails to meet the requisites of one or more principles would not be categorically rejected; rather, courts would determine how close the RAI comes to satisfying the principles' mandates. A judicial decision that hints at this approach but that ultimately fails at it is the aforementioned case of *Wisconsin v. Loomis*,[89] one of the few American appellate opinions to analyze the admissibility of risk assessments based on an RAI. To its credit, the Wisconsin Supreme Court noted that the RAI in question (the COMPAS) was not normed on a local population, could possibly misclassify minority offenders, and could not be carefully analyzed because the company that created it would not reveal the basis of its algorithm. But rather than demanding such information so that fit, validity, and fairness could be analyzed, the Court lamely concluded that trial courts could continue to use the COMPAS in connection with sentencing as long as judges are cognizant of these limitations and do not make the COMPAS "determinative" of whether the offender is incarcerated or receives an enhanced sentence.[90] Only if courts do a better job than this of addressing the issues raised by the fit, validity, and fairness principles is it safe to say that this option is better than moving back in the direction of unstructured human judgment, as bad as it may be.

---

[86] See P. B. Imrey and A. Philip Dawid, A Commentary on Statistical Assessment of Violence Recidivism Risk (2015) 2 *Stat. Pub. Policy* 1.

[87] D. L. Faigman, J. Monahan, and C. Slobogin, Group to Individual Inference in Expert Scientific Testimony (2014) 81 *Univ. Chi. Law Rev.* 417.

[88] A. J. Wang, Procedural Justice and Risk Assessment Algorithms, https://ssrn.com/abstract=3170136.

[89] Above note 40.

[90] *Ibid.* at 274.

21

Injury by Algorithms

Seema Ghatnekar Tilak*

INTRODUCTION

Online reputational injury can occur in a number of ways; and one way is through the use of algorithms that pervade the Internet. The Internet is comprised of complex technologies that enable the dissemination of information rapidly, providing global reach in a matter of seconds through the click of a button. The Internet provides robust public discourse over a gamut of topics in real time and allows individuals from different parts of the world to interact with one another while preserving some sense of anonymity (that is, if they so choose). Many online communications stem from one piece of content that is regurgitated and redistributed on multiple platforms. For example, consider the social application Twitter. Twitter allows individuals to transmit bite-sized pieces of data among millions of users. Twitter has surprisingly become an outlet for a recent US President, and the fact that the public has direct access to a sitting President in this manner is undoubtedly incredible. Further, the Internet emboldens individuals to act behind the shield of a screen. There is little cost to spreading information, ideas, and gossip online, with seemingly few ramifications. Despite what may be perceived as a few keystrokes that have an ephemeral impact, content on the Internet has a tendency of permanence.

Online communications rely on a few distinct actors :(1) those who create content; (2) those who provide or host the content; and (3) those who seek and digest content. Content creators contribute information to online platforms, whether those platforms are blogs, social media applications, or other sorts of websites. Content providers enable access to content and may do so passively or actively. Examples of content providers include the social media sites, and also include search engines and websites. Content seekers include the standard consumer, or one who "surfs the web" in search of information or entertainment. Reputational harm in the online space arises through an interplay of these three actors.

Content creators have the greatest influence in effectuating objectionable content online, because it is from the creators that such content originates. But when is a content provider responsible for offensive content? What if only an algorithm is responsible? Algorithms process and regurgitate content to provide an end-user with streamlined and organized data. In doing so, algorithms may present and organize content in an unflattering manner.

While Google is by no means the only search engine in the world, it is certainly the most widely used and has a large global presence. Therefore, this chapter focuses the analysis of

---

* This chapter is based on – and expands upon – a previously published paper: S. Ghatnekar, Injury by Algorithm: A Look into Google's Liability for Defamatory Autocompleted Search Suggestions (2013) 33 *Loy. LA Ent. Law Rev.* 171, https://digitalcommons.lmu.edu/elr/vol33/iss2/3.

reputational injury imputed by Google's autocomplete search feature. Most individuals who have conducted a Google search are aware of Google's autocomplete search feature. Autocomplete provides individuals with a seemingly simple way to search items by suggesting several search terms in real time as an individual types a search request in the Google search bar. Autocomplete provides search suggestions that change in accordance with a complex algorithm – which I'll discuss in more detail – that has a social aspect, offering suggestions based in part upon predictions made from previous users' searches. Google contends that it does not have control over the algorithm (which Google itself created), and that it should therefore not be held liable for the search results generated by the algorithm. This point brings about troubling legal issues, specifically due to a lack of understanding about who or what is actually responsible for the results generated by Google's autocomplete feature.

Many cases have surfaced globally that shed light on this legal gray area. In April 2012, a French organization sued Google in France for suggesting that individuals, such as Rupert Murdoch and Jon Hamm, are Jewish.[1] During the same time frame, Germany's former First Lady Bettina Wulff sued Google because its autocomplete feature implied that she was a former escort or prostitute.[2] In 2018, an Australian named Michael Trkulja prevailed against Google because its autocomplete feature incorrectly associated him with organized crime and murder.[3] All of the aforementioned plaintiffs based their respective lawsuits on defamation law principles – the theory that a false statement can damage an individual's reputation.

The previous examples detail lawsuits in international legal forums because courts within the United States have yet to squarely address Google's potential liability for similar conduct. This chapter, therefore, takes a different perspective and analyzes the potential liability that Google may face in the United States for defamatory autocompleted search suggestions. This chapter explores the basics behind search engines and Google's autocomplete algorithm. This will be followed by an analysis of the evolution of Internet law, with a look into global cases centering around this issue. An important point to keep in mind throughout the context of this chapter is the interest Google has in simplifying and personalizing a user's experience on the Internet while still acting lawfully and treating individuals with respect.

OVERVIEW OF SEARCH ENGINE AND AUTOCOMPLETE FUNCTIONALITY

Search engines are the new linchpins of the Internet. A large and growing fraction of the Internet's immense volume of traffic flows through them. They are librarians, who bring order to the chaotic online accumulation of information. They are messengers, who bring writers and readers together. They are critics, who elevate content to prominence or consign it to obscurity. They are inventors, who devise new technologies and business models to remake the Internet. And they are spies, who are asked to carry out investigations with dispatch and discretion.[4]

Due to innovation and the constant flux surrounding the changing technology of the Internet, the law always seems to lag behind technology. This section will provide an introduction to

---

[1] See E. Gardner, Google Sued for Suggesting Rupert Murdoch and Other Celebrities Are Jewish, *The Hollywood Reporter* (April 30, 2012), www.hollywoodreporter.com/thr-esq/google-sued-rupert-murdoch-jon-hamm-jewish -318012.

[2] See F. Lardinois, Germany's Former Foreign First Lady Sues Google for Defamation over Autocomplete Suggestions, *Tech Crunch* (September 7, 2012), http://techcrunch.com/2012/09/07/germanys-former-first-lady-sues-google-for-defamation-over-autocomplete-suggestions/.

[3] T. C. Sottek, Google Loses Australian Defamation Case after Court Rules that It Is Accountable as a Publisher, *The Verge* (November 26, 2012), www.theverge.com/2012/11/26/3694908/google-defamation-australia-publisher.

[4] J. Grimmelmann, The Structure of Search Engine Law (2007) 93 *Iowa Law Rev.* 1, 3.

the functionality of search engines and what is currently understood of Google's autocomplete, which made its debut on Google's website in 2008.

Background of Search Engines

Typically, searches involve four modes of information flow: (1) a search engine accumulates and organizes content; (2) a user searching for content then "queries the search engine"; (3) the search engine delivers results to the query; and (4) a user receives the requested content.[5] As discussed in this chapter's introduction, the parties in this transaction include search engines which index and organize information, content providers which create the information, the end-user who wishes to access the information, and in some instances, third parties such as copyright holders or governments which have some control over the content or which seek to somehow censor or limit the content to which an end-user has access. The interactions among these various parties may give rise to some sort of liability for the content that results from a particular query.

A search engine permits a user to search for information through a series of various applicable terms in a query. Traditionally, once a user types in a search term and clicks "Enter," the search engine scans through its database to find the queried terms and then catalogues the terms in different ways. The process of cataloguing terms is referred to as "indexing." Indexing information is exhibited in the interplay between search engines and content providers in the distribution of content to a search engine's users. Indexing can occur automatically through software agents that search the web for relevant content, or through other types of information gathering.

A search query is a user's request for information about a topic, and can range from keywords to short phrases. Generally, users perform three queries: (1) navigational queries to find specific sites or sets of information; (2) informational queries to locate information about a particular topic; or (3) transactional queries to purchase particular goods or perform activities. Different search engines weigh various factors while performing a search query, which may influence the particular information that is generated. For example, these factors may include geographic information about a user, influence based on past user searches, or one's operating system or browser. When a user enters search terms in a search engine, the search engine logs the user's query terms along with information about the type of web browser, version of web browser, IP address, and "cookie" data. Cookies enable search engines to store data about an individual, including the user's email address (if a user is signed in) and a user's past search results.

In the case *In re. DoubleClick Inc.* v. *Privacy Litigation*, the New York Southern District Court found that DoubleClick Inc. (the world's then-largest provider of Internet advertising tools) was not invading any user's rights through its use of cookies. The plaintiffs claimed that DoubleClick was using cookies to collect private and personal information, including users' names, phone numbers, and Internet browsing history. The Court found that DoubleClick "creates the cookies, assigns them identification numbers, and places them on plaintiffs' hard drive." Arguing that this process is "vital to DoubleClick and meaningless to anyone else," the Court found the use of cookies to be legitimate, and not invasive of users' rights. Additionally, users had the ability to visit DoubleClick's website to request an opt-out cookie, or could have

---

[5] *Ibid.*, p. 7.

easily prevented cookies from being placed on their computers by configuring their Internet browsers. Keep cookies in mind while browsing the Internet!

Delivering relevant content to a user is the defining moment of a web search. Search engines typically list results in order of most to least relevant to the query. Based on the generated content, a user may perform additional queries to narrow down a search through the addition or removal of keywords within a particular query. A search engine benefits greatly by algorithms. With the vast amount of content available online, algorithms help to streamline data to prevent overburdening users with infinite amounts of irrelevant data.

Search engines differ in the way in which they generate search queries through the use of various algorithms that organize and condense all of the content that is available from content providers. When search engines first emerged, they scanned through text on web pages to assess the topics that a web page centered on. Now, search engines scan through and analyze other information called "metadata" on web pages. Metadata is information that is not visible in a hard copy of a document, but is visible in its native, digital format through the original program that produced the document. Metadata is often referred to as "data about data" because it "describes, explains, locates, or otherwise makes it easier to retrieve, use, or manage an information resource."[6] The three main types of metadata are (1) descriptive metadata, (2) structural metadata, and (3) administrative metadata. Descriptive metadata includes information that identifies source material, such as the author, title, abstract, or keywords linked to the material. Structural metadata deals with the way in which a source is organized and put together, such as the order of page numbers within chapters. Finally, administrative metadata includes information about the actual source of the information, including technical information, such as when the source was created, the file type of the source, intellectual property rights of a source, and general management information.

Search engines utilize a technique called search engine optimization (SEO) to provide users with content that a search engine considers most important to the public. SEO is based on weighing several ranking factors deemed most relevant and authoritative by the search engine. "Search engines are able to preserve a layer of genuine, useful results through a combination of keeping precise algorithmic details secret and changing their algorithms to foil detected SEO techniques."[7] Along the same lines as metadata, search engines utilize HTML meta tags, which are essentially data tags for web pages that include text which is not displayed directly on a page, but communicates to browsers through a code that details specific information about a web page.

The interplay between all of the factors that compose search engines has led to an interesting set of laws that incorporate various legal doctrines. The following section provides a glimpse into how Google's autocomplete works and how it complicates traditional search engine law.

The Interplay between Google's Algorithm and Search Engine Functionality

As described above, search engines gather information and provide a site upon which a user can search for particular information. The traditional approach to searching terms is that a user types in a search term and clicks "Enter" to catalog a series of searches. Google's autocomplete feature goes one step further than this. Google's algorithm constantly alters

---

[6]   Understanding Metadata, NISO, (2004), p. 1, www.niso.org/publications/press/UnderstandingMetadata.pdf.
[7]   Grimmelmann, above note 5, p. 56.

a user's query based on each additional keystroke in the search bar. In this manner, Google's autocomplete feature changes the way in which search queries are generated. Before listing out all search results on a web page, Google actively displays results through its autocomplete feature in real time while a user is performing a query. Google is able to provide its users with constantly updated search terms while a user inputs letters within its search bar because its algorithm weighs numerous factors before generating the autocompleted suggestion. The autocomplete feature therefore performs one additional function during each process of its web search.

Underlying the ease and simplicity of Google's autocomplete feature – at least to the casual observer – is a complex algorithm, referred to as autocomplete. While autocomplete shares fundamental qualities with most SEO programs, namely the goal of providing users with relevant and authoritative information, it differs from other SEO programs because it provides users with different choices of queries. Google has not disclosed the exact algorithm in its autocomplete feature and probably never will, as such algorithms are regarded as protectable trade secrets. However, the attempts of numerous analysts to find the code behind the algorithmic process has led to a broad and general understanding of autocomplete. Google "ranks" searchable content, and though debated by analysts, three primary contributing factors are considered in Google's rankings of suggested search algorithms: personalization, search volume, and query deserves freshness (QDF) filters. Personalization includes components such as a user's Internet Protocol (IP) address, a user's own search history, the country of the search engine, and the language of the search. Personalized searches are always displayed first and ranked higher than any of the other factors. Search volume refers to a minimum threshold regarding a search term's popularity; once this threshold is reached, the search will be suggested to other users. QDF filters describe "freshness layers" that are embedded within a search, meaning that terms that have surges in popularity even in a short amount of time may become search suggestions, even without long-term popularity. An example of QDF filters at work is the autocomplete suggestion that was linked with Osama Bin Laden's death on May 1, 2011. In a matter of twelve minutes from the announcement of his death, typing "osa" into the Google search bar yielded the autocompleted suggestion: "Osama Bin Laden dead" versus the autocompleted suggestion: "Osama Bin Laden" before the news became known. Therefore, the QDF is a short-term popularity filter that may be subject to fluctuations in as short as one-hour intervals.

The exact weight given to each of these three components is not clear, but they are identified as most important to Google's algorithmic process. Google's algorithm is neither known to the public nor has it been pinpointed and described exactly by any scholar or expert. Because slight updates to the algorithm are generated almost every two months, understanding and deciphering the algorithm is problematic. The algorithm is controlled by Google, and can be considered a proprietary tool that allows it to provide specific data to its users.

I encourage you to take a moment to test out Google's autocomplete feature . . . I'm fairly certain you are sitting at a computer, or that you have an Internet-accessible device within reach. Try searching "Donald Trump" and see what results autocomplete – for me, in this present moment in Los Angeles, California, the top five autocompleted search terms that generated were "Donald Trump Twitter," "Donald Trump jr," "Donald Trump news," "Donald Trump age," and "Donald Trump net worth." Now try "Beyoncé" (because, why not?) – the top five search results from this query generated "Beyoncé net worth," "Beyoncé age," "Beyoncé twins," "Beyoncé lemonade," and "Beyoncé songs." Try the same practice with individuals who live in different states from you, and the results may be surprisingly varied.

REPUTATIONAL INJURY ON THE INTERNET

Background of Reputational Torts

Torts are civil wrongs that result in harm to a person or property. Torts may be classified as: (1) intentional torts, including assault, battery, false imprisonment, or intentional infliction of emotional distress; (2) negligence, including a failure to exercise a certain standard of care (such as the standard of care a doctor owes his patient, for example); (3) economic torts, including fraud, conspiracy, or tortious interference; or (4) reputational or personal torts, such as defamation, invasion of privacy, or portraying an individual in a false light. The harm that arises from the first three categories of torts is typically readily apparent, as such torts manifest themselves in some physical or tangible form. Reputational torts, on the other hand, affect a more personal interest.

Inaccurate autocompleted search results may cause deleterious effects to one's personal interests by causing reputational harm. One's reputation, while intangible, affects all aspects of an individual's persona. Reputation, in its most tangible form, may be most easily understood as an individual's marketability. This aspect of one's reputation is akin to goodwill, and the name that one has created for oneself through one's personal life, education, profession, and general presence. People are connected to one another by relationships and goodwill, and we are all familiar with the importance and fragility of one's reputation.

The legal implications of inaccurate search suggestions include harm to an individual's personal rights, and also an individual's right to control his reputation. The torts most applicable to the present issue include defamation and false light. Tort claims are state and jurisdictionally specific. This chapter analyzes defamation and false light from the perspective of a California court – although the elements of these causes of action are fairly similar throughout the world. This jurisdiction has been chosen because Google is headquartered and incorporated in the state of California, and because it would be nearly impossible to give a comprehensive review of these torts from a global perspective.

Defamation

California courts routinely define defamation as an "invasion of [an individual's] interest in [his] reputation."[8] The requisite elements for a defamation case of action are publication of an unprivileged, false statement of fact, which has an inclination to injure or cause special damage to the individual about whom the statement is made.

In this context, "publication" means communication to a third party who understands the derogatory "meaning of the statement and its application to the person to whom reference is made."[9] The publication may be made to a single individual or to the public at large. The manner of publication delineates the two sub-sets of defamation – libel and slander. Libel requires the publication to be in a fixed medium of expression, such as a writing, printing, picture, or effigy. Slander, by contrast, involves an oral utterance, such as via the radio, or dissemination via other mechanical means.

The increased prevalence of the Internet has made it difficult to distinguish whether a false, unprivileged statement of fact constitutes libel or slander, as communication via

---

[8]   See *London v. Sears, Roebuck & Co.*, 619 F. Supp. 2d 854, 864 (ND Cal. 2009); *Gilbert v. Sykes*, 147 Cal. App. 4th 13, 27 (2007); *Ringler Assocs. Inc. v. Maryland Cas. Co.*, 80 Cal. App. 4th 1165, 1179 (2000).
[9]   *Smith v. Maldonado*, 72 Cal. App. 4th 637, 645 (1999).

this medium often involves oral utterances and writings. In the context of the Internet, communications take place through various forms of media and may not be conveyed only through speech or writing, and may contain a mix of both. For example, a defamatory statement may arise through an audio or video clip, while also being communicated in the text of an accompanying article to such media.

False Light

The Restatement of Torts explains that the invasion of one's right to privacy occurs in part by "publicity which places a false light before the public." The Second Restatement of Torts § 652A further states: "one who invades the right of privacy of another is subject to liability for the resulting harm to the interests of the other."[10] Although the cases that have emerged thus far in relation to Google's autocomplete have dealt primarily with defamation, another tort that may be triggered through autocomplete is an invasion of privacy, in the form of false light. The false light cause of action is a privacy tort that was judicially created to prevent injury or damage to an individual's emotions. A plaintiff can establish a prima facie case for false light when one gives publicity to a matter concerning another before the public in a false light, where the portrayal is highly offensive to a reasonable person, and the actor had knowledge of or acted with reckless disregard as to the falsity of the matter.[11]

Publishers vs. Distributors of Information

Traditional tort law distinguishes two sets of entities that may be liable for defamatory statement beyond the author of such statement – publishers and distributors. Publishers include entities that operate media, including radio and television stations, and newspapers and print publishers, because they are deemed to have editorial control over information they transmit. Courts typically hold publishers vicariously liable for the statements they have published, as if the statements are their own.

A distributor is considered a passive transmitter of information, as they typically do not exercise control over what they disseminate. An example of a distributor includes a public library or a news-stand. Distributors typically do not vet the material they distribute, and doing so would be highly burdensome. However, a distributor can be held liable by showing that it had knowledge of the defamatory content or should have reasonably known of the defamatory nature of the work. The following section will show how these definitions are altered within an Internet context and the difficulty that arises in attributing liability in an Internet realm, especially with search engines like Google.

Reputational Torts in an Internet Context

The Internet has complicated the traditional underlying principles of privacy torts that once implicated only two parties: the defendant who made the defamatory statement and the victim of the injurious statements. These complications arise because multiple parties are involved on the Internet forum, including search engine operators, website operators, and Internet service providers. Courts have difficulty determining whether these Internet actors

[10] Restatement (Second) of Torts § 652A (1977).
[11] *Ibid.*, § 652E (1977).

are "publishers" of offensive content, and therefore subject to liability under one of the many privacy torts, or whether they are merely "distributors" of offensive content and thus immune from liability. Two decisions, *Cubby, Inc. v. CompuServe, Inc.*[12] and *Stratton Oakmont, Inc. v. Prodigy Services Co.*,[13] both rendered in the early half of the 1990s, illustrate this point.

In *Cubby*, CompuServe operated an "electronic library," in which subscribers paid a monthly subscription to access, among other sources, 150 special interest forums. CompuServe did not operate the forums, but instead entered into contractual arrangements with independent companies who agreed to "manage, review, create, delete, edit and otherwise control the contents" of the various forums.[14] The Journalism Forum contained content from Rumorville USA ("Rumorville"), a daily newsletter detailing news and gossip in the entertainment industry. Due to Rumorville's success, Cubby, Inc. ("Cubby"), attempted to replicate Rumorville's business model by creating an electronic database that electronically disseminated news and gossip in the television, news, and radio industry under the pseudonym "Skuttlebut." In what was likely an effort to stave off competition, Rumorville began publishing disparaging comments about Cubby's database, and how the database managed to access its information. In response, Cubby filed a lawsuit seeking to recover damages for libelous statements, and it named the operator of Rumorville and CompuServe, Inc. as defendants in the lawsuit.

After a litany of pre-trial documents were filed, many of which asserted that CompuServe was merely a distributor as opposed to a publisher of Rumorville, the District Court of New York granted CompuServe's motion for summary judgment. This decision was rendered on the undisputed fact that CompuServe did not have editorial control of the information that was uploaded onto Rumorville's site. Moreover, without editorial control over the content on Rumorville, CompuServe lacked knowledge of the defamatory statements – a point that was exacerbated by the immense volume and speed with which information was uploaded to CompuServe's electronic library.

Four years later, the New York Supreme Court rendered a decision that threatened the existence of various Internet stakeholders. In *Stratton Oakmont*, Prodigy Services owned an online bulletin board, "Money Talk," which allowed monthly subscribers to "post statements regarding stocks, investments and other financial matters."[15] Although Prodigy Services owned the various bulletin boards on which the subscribers posted, it contracted with third parties, known as bulletin Board Leaders, who "participate[d] in [bulletin] board discussions and undert[ook] promotional efforts to encourage usage and increase users."[16] By the time the lawsuit was filed, Money Talk had at least 2 million subscribers.

The events that precipitated the lawsuit involved defamatory statements made by an anonymous user regarding the employees of Stratton Oakmont, an investment-banking firm. The anonymous user alleged that Stratton Oakmont had committed "fraudulent acts in connection with the initial public offering" of Solomon-Page, and that the investment banking firm employed a "cult of brokers who either lie[d] for a living or [got] fired."[17]

Upset by the defamatory statements posted on a bulletin board read by at least 2 million subscribers, Stratton Oakmont filed a defamation lawsuit against Prodigy Services. In its

[12]   776 F. Supp. 135 (SDNY 1991).
[13]   1995 WL 323710 (NY Sup. Ct. May 24, 1995), *superseded by statute*, Telecommunications Act of 1996, Pub. L. No. 104–104, 110 Stat. 56 (1996) (codified at 47 USC § 230 (2012)).
[14]   *Cubby*, above note 13, at 137.
[15]   *Stratton Oakmont*, above note 14, at *1.
[16]   *Ibid.*
[17]   *Ibid.*

complaint, Stratton Oakmont asserted that Prodigy Services was a publisher of the offensive material because it: (1) likened itself to a newspaper and claimed to have editorial control over the "degree of nudity and unsupported gossip its editors tolerate[d]"; (2) used software to pre-screen bulletin boards for offensive material; (3) promulgated editorial content guidelines for the bulletin Board Leaders to follow; and (4) developed a form apology that bulletin Board Leaders were required to send if offensive material was posted to the site.[18] Prodigy Services countered that it had changed its editorial policy and no longer reviewed each bulletin board post.

After weighing the evidence, the New York Supreme Court concluded that Prodigy Services was a publisher because it controlled the bulletin Board Leaders' actions, created guidelines, and, most importantly, claimed to control the content on its website. Accordingly, the Court granted Stratton Oakmont's motion for summary judgment.

Both of these cases were landmark cases in a time where no prior legal analysis was on point. However, over time and through the passage of the Communications Decency Act, the decisions of both cases were reassessed. The following section will analyze the Communications Decency Act (CDA) and how it changed the holding of these two cases. The cases detailed above are still important to consider, as their holdings emphasize significant legal concerns and the progress of Internet law over time.

The Communications Decency Act

To address the conflicting analyses courts used to apply defamation law to the various Internet stakeholders, Congress enacted the CDA in 1996. The CDA takes the original definitions of "publisher" and "distributor" and applies them to an Internet context. The purpose of the CDA is to "promote the free exchange of information and ideas over the Internet and to encourage voluntary monitoring for offensive or obscene material."[19] The CDA immunizes interactive computer services from civil liability for defamatory material that a user finds through its search engine by prohibiting such providers from being "treated as the publisher or speaker of any information provided by another"[20] where an interactive computer service means "any information service, system, or access software provider that provides or enables computer access by multiple users to a computer server, including specifically a service or system that provides access to the Internet."[21] Further, providers or users of an interactive computer service cannot be held liable for attempting to restrict access to what the provider considers to be improper material. Both of these qualifications effectively lead to the result that an interactive computer service would not be held liable for defamation, unless the service itself was actually the author or publisher of the defamatory content.

Services that are considered the author or publisher of defamatory content are referred to as "information content providers." Information content providers include people or entities "responsible, in whole or in part, for the creation or development of information" on the Internet or on a website.[22] The following section will provide an analysis of the difference between an interactive computer service and information content provider, and when the entities may face liability for material posted online.

---

[18] *Ibid.*
[19] *Carafano v. Metrosplash.com, Inc.*, 339 F.3d 1119, 1122 (9th Cir. 2003).
[20] 47 USC § 230(c)(1) (2012).
[21] 47 USC § 230(f)(2) (2012).
[22] 47 USC § 230(f)(3) (2012).

Distinguishing between an Internet Computer Service and Information Content Provider

In *Stratton Oakmont*, the Court held that any Internet service provider could be held liable for defamation.[23] However, the CDA provides "robust" immunity for websites and Internet service providers. According to precedent, websites that merely revise online material generally are not rendered "information content providers." To be considered an information content provider subject to civil liability, a website operator must provide material contributions to unlawfulness. Contributing content in this manner means more than providing "third parties with neutral tools to create web content, even if the website knows that the third parties are using such tools to create illegal content."[24] This conclusion is based on the application of the CDA to the cases outlined below.

An opinion authored by the Ninth Circuit, *Carafano* v. *Metrosplash.com*, helped establish what the term "neutral tool" entails and how it applies to information content providers.[25] In *Carafano*, an unknown individual created a fake Matchmaker.com ("Matchmaker") profile for the actress Christianne Carafano – stage name Chase Masterson – which included her picture and home address. Shortly after the account was created, Carafano began receiving threatening and sexually explicit phone calls and faxes. Fearing for her safety, Carafano informed Matchmaker that someone was using her name, likeness, and contact information without her permission. After receiving the message, Matchmaker immediately blocked the profile from public view and later deleted the profile. Nonetheless, Carafano sued Matchmaker for defamation of character, among other things.

The District Court concluded that Matchmaker was not entitled to immunity, pursuant to the CDA, because the company created user profiles after individuals completed a multiple choice and essay questionnaire, preventing users from simply posting any information they desired. However, the Ninth Circuit on appeal found that Matchmaker was protected under the CDA and was not an information content provider because it was not providing any content itself. The Court underscored that "Matchmaker was not responsible, even in part, for associating certain multiple choice responses with a set of physical characteristics, a group of essay answers, and a photograph."[26] The fact that Matchmaker's users actively and voluntarily created the content found on their profiles suggested that the website did not do anything to add to the defamation that resulted. Matchmaker simply provided neutral tools for users to voluntarily input preferences and data.

Further, the Court in *Zeran* v. *America Online, Inc.* gave context for determining the liability of an Internet service provider who acts to edit or remove content from a site, thus giving the site control over its content.[27] The Court emphasized the importance of a website's ability and necessity to self-regulate the content on its page. As long as this voluntary self-regulation is conducted "in good faith to restrict access to or availability of material that the provider or user considers to be obscene, lewd, lascivious, filthy, excessively violent, harassing, or otherwise objectionable, whether or not constitutionally protected," the Internet service provider is barred from liability.[28] Even if a provider receives notification of content

[23] See above note 14, at *3–4 (discussing publishers as "one who repeats or otherwise republishes a libel is subject to liability as if he had originally published it," and accordingly, finding that Prodigy was such a publisher).
[24] *Goddard* v. *Google, Inc.*, 640 F. Supp. 2d 1193, 1196 (ND Cal. 2009).
[25] *Carafano* v. *Metrosplash.com, Inc.*, 339 F.3d 1119, 1123 (9th Cir. 2003).
[26] *Ibid.* at 1124.
[27] See *Zeran* v. *Am. Online, Inc.*, 129 F.3d 327, 331 (4th Cir. 1997) (analyzing Congressional intent underlying s. 230 of the CDA).
[28] 47 USC § 230(c)(2)(A) (2012).

that may be objectionable on its website and fails to remove it, that provider would be shielded from liability. If providers were subject to liability equivalent to distributors of information, they would potentially face liability with each notice of potentially defamatory statements that would necessitate investigation of the actual information. This type of constant research could be possible for print publishers, but may create unique burdens in the Internet realm.

This holding was also supported in *Jurin v. Google Inc.*, where the website operator suggested keywords based on an amount that an advertiser bids on to grant higher rankings on a web search.[29] The Court held that the keyword suggestion feature is a neutral tool that solely provides options to advertisers and functions in a manner similar to the editorial process that is protected by the CDA. Thus, a website operator does not become an information content provider by the mere fact that the operator of the website "should have known" that the tools made available could potentially make the dissemination of defamatory content easier.

In a recent decision by the Ninth Circuit, the Court limited the immunity extended to online entities under the CDA.[30] In *Fair Housing Council of San Fernando Valley v. Roommates.com*, the Court held that Roommates.com was acting as a direct publisher of materials when it categorized and directed users to specific information when users would answer a series of questions to find roommates. Roommates.com created the questions that were asked regarding sex, sexual orientation, and family status. The website's users were also given a set of pre-populated answers, essentially forcing subscribers to answer the questions as a condition for using the website's services. The Court held that, by "requiring subscribers to provide the information as a condition of accessing its service," along with a limited set of pre-populated answers, Roommates.com acted as more than a passive transmitter of information, and rather a developer in part of that information.[31] This is important since the CDA provides immunity only if the interactive computer service does not create or develop the information "in whole or in part." The Court compared Roommates.com to a site that acted as "a forum designed to publish sensitive and defamatory information, and suggested the type of information that might be disclosed to best harass and endanger the targets."[32] It established that online entities that post content that may be in part user-generated should evaluate whether the bulk of the content they produce is illegal or defamatory in nature, leading a court to deem the entity acting beyond a neutral publisher of information. Therefore, Roommates .com was acting as an information content provider by developing information, in part, by pre-populated answers directed toward divulging discriminatory information.

The distinguishing factor between *Fair Housing* and the previously analyzed cases is that the other cases involved website operators that were not involved in the encouragement of defamatory content or increasing the ability to post defamatory content. These sites were based on voluntary inputs that allowed users to select the information they deemed most relevant. This is the essence of a "neutral tool" operation. However, the Roommates.com website did more than this merely by its design – the website forced its users to make choices based on a limited number of discriminatory preferences, through criteria that was illegal and prohibited by the Fair Housing Council.

---

[29]   *Jurin v. Google, Inc.*, 695 F. Supp. 2d 1117, 1119, 1123 (ED Cal. 2010).
[30]   *Fair Housing Council of San Fernando Valley v. Roommates.com, LLC*, 489 F.3d 921, 928 (9th Cir. 2007).
[31]   *Ibid.* at 1166.
[32]   *Ibid.* at 928.

Therefore, in assessing a website operator's status as an "interactive computer service" or an "information content provider," the distinguishing factor is whether the processes used to generate information are operating on neutral tools rather than directing users toward pre-set and inherently illegal functionality.

Is Google a Neutral Tool, or Does Its Additional Functionality Render It More?

Given the above analysis, it is difficult to determine whether Google is acting as an interactive computer service and an information content provider. Google's autocomplete function operates by providing suggestions as a user types in a search term within a search bar. It functions differently from the website in *Fair Housing*, which provided a limited set of options that a user can choose from. Here, Google does not per se provide a limited number of options to search from with its autocomplete feature – rather, it provides a glimpse of the numerous searches that are produced from the search itself.

The fact that Google is a seemingly neutral tool on its surface does not speak toward its ability to portray someone in a defamatory context. The cases analyzed above suggest that a website which makes the process of defamation easier may not be shielded under the CDA's protection. Google arguably uses its own algorithm to generate the searches that are defamatory. That Google retains the control to limit what is generated by its algorithm does not make it susceptible to liability in itself, as the CDA protects an Internet provider's ability to edit content. However, this, in conjunction with the defamatory suggestions arising immediately and upon entering just a few letters of an individual's name, may make the defamation easier to see, which may indicate the autocomplete feature is more than a neutral tool.

For purposes of this chapter, Google may be regarded as lying in between the definitions of an interactive computer service and an information content provider, as an "Algorithm-Based Republisher" (ABR).[33] The extent of control that Google has over what is auto-populated may help to determine Google's liability. Taking the holding of the *Roommates.com* case, the fact that Google works with users' queries to actively generate search suggestions based on the addition of each letter into the search bar may likely render Google liable for the suggestions that are produced. Next, let's take a look at how Google exerts control over autocompleted search results.

GOOGLE'S CONTROL OVER AUTOCOMPLETED SEARCH RESULTS

Although Google claims that the search suggestions that are autocompleted are based on factors that are not completely within its control, it is evident that Google manipulates and restricts certain search terms to deal with piracy, geographically based restrictions, and legal mandates.

Google's Control Rendering Liability

The analysis of Google's liability in the search suggestions it generates must first begin by defining what Google actually has control over, a factual question that may be deciphered by understanding Google's role in autocomplete. Google actively restricts certain words and sites

[33] "Algorithm-Based Republisher" is not an official term, but coined by this author within the context of the present analysis.

from being exposed to the public, so Google has the ability to control what can and cannot be searched in its search box through the use of metatags. Google's algorithm may search for metatags with information relevant to one's search, optimizing a search for a user. Google also restricts autocomplete search suggestions that involve torrent tracking and online piracy sites. These changes initially appeared in 2011, when Google removed suggestions for terms such as "BitTorrent," "RapidShare," and "Megaupload," wherein individuals would share content illegally. In August 2012, Google declared that the ranking of websites and search suggestions would also take into account online piracy in determining the weight given to its search suggestions. That is, websites that are associated with online piracy are likely to be lowered in the ranking process, if not removed from search suggestions altogether.

Google's Geographically Based Restrictions

Google's control also extends to its active restriction of websites and certain Google features in various countries. For example, the Chinese government has exerted substantial control over what can be searched online, and is one of the strictest countries in terms of censorship of content on the Internet.[34] China's censorship does not adhere to any specific laws or regulations. "The Chinese government has created more than sixty regulations on Internet censorship and local authorities have their own rules, regulations, and policies."[35] A background of Google's role in China is as follows:

> When Google first arrived in China, it signed an agreement with the Chinese government, agreeing to purge its Chinese search results of banned topics. Whether this agreement was reasonable or not is actually not an arguable issue for Google because it signed the agreement and will breach the agreement by not purging the search.[36]

This example further solidifies the fact that Google has the ability to control what search results are populated by autocomplete.

European Right to Be Forgotten

The European Union is perhaps the most plaintiff-friendly of all jurisdictions in its approach to personal rights and the right of privacy. The Union proposed a concept of an individual's "right to be forgotten" in 2012, which suggested that one should have the ability to control information about oneself online, under the theory that information online may be inconsistent with reality. In the 2014 case *Google Spain SL v. AEPD*, the European Court of Justice (ECJ) ruled that search engines are responsible for search results linking to personal data, which appears on third parties' webpages.[37] The ECJ ruling centers around a case in which a Spanish man's name appeared in an auction notice of his repossessed home due to social security debts dating ten years prior – essentially, it appeared as though the man was financially unstable or bankrupt. The plaintiff requested that Google remove or conceal the outdated data relating to him so that this information would not auto-populate in the browser's search results. Google argued that search engines process all the information

---

[34] C. Liu, Internet Censorship as a Trade Barrier: A Look at the WTO Consistency of the Great Firewall in the Wake of the China-Google Dispute (2011) 42 *Geo. J. Int. Law* 1199.
[35] *Ibid.*
[36] *Ibid.*
[37] *Google Spain SL v. AEPD*, Celex No. 62012CJ0131 (2014).

available on the Internet without selecting any particular information. Google also argued that even if that activity is classified as "data processing," the operator of a search engine cannot be regarded as a "controller" of such information since it has no knowledge of the underlying data and does not exercise control over the data.

The ECJ turned to European Directive 95/46 to find that the operator of a search engine controls and processes the data internally, and therefore collects, retrieves, records, organizes, stores, and, ultimately – and most importantly – makes the information available to an end-user to rely upon.[38] For this reason, the ECJ held that Google is a "controller" of the information that appears in search results, and that a search engine is obliged to remove information that is irrelevant, outdated, or otherwise unlawful at an individual's request. This ruling provided the heavily debated "right to be forgotten" for private individuals who wished to remove information about themselves online, where there is no legitimate public interest in the facts at issue.

Following this case, in 2016, the right to be forgotten was codified in Europe's General Data Protection Regulation (GDPR), along with the right of erasure, in article 17(2) of the GDPR. This statute came into full force in 2018, where "data controllers," including Google and other search engines, would have to "delist" or delete search results about EU citizens under certain criteria, following the analysis from the *Google Spain* ruling above.

Google has created a form that allows EU members to request takedown of URLs that are outdated, irrelevant, or unlawful (that is, defamatory). The form requires an explanation of why the individual is requesting that certain information be removed, and particularly (from the Spanish court ruling) why the material is "irrelevant, outdated, or otherwise inappropriate." The kicker to this strategy is that, while Google has an advisory group that reviews the requests to be forgotten, the process of each delisting request is handled by one or more individuals within Google.[39] The reviewer considers: (1) the validity of the request; (2) the identity of the requester, including whether the request is made from a public or private individual, as there may be a heightened public interest regarding content of an individual in the public eye; (3) the content that is requested to be removed, and the factual nature of such information; (4) the source of information (if the information is contained on a news or government site, the matter may be in the public interest). The controller (namely, Google) may need to statutorily comply with the request in the instance that the material was unlawful to begin with.[40]

Google's Transparency Reports

Google releases Transparency Reports[41] within which Google publicly discloses statistics and some identifying information regarding the various requests it receives to remove content. The reports are partitioned into content removals due to copyright, government requests to remove content, search removals under European privacy law, YouTube community guidelines enforcement, and removals under the network enforcement of law. The reports are generated to provide transparency to online content regulation. Google's challenge is not an easy task, given the volume and nature of removal requests it receives. In some cases, the

---

[38]   This directive has been repealed as of May 25, 2018, due to a number of changes in European privacy law.

[39]   T. Betram, E. Bursztein, S. Caro, *et al.*, Three Years of the Right to Be Forgotten, Google Annual Transparency Report (February 27, 2019), https://drive.google.com/file/d/1H4MKNwf5MgeztG7OnJRnl3ym3gIT3HUK/view.

[40]   *Ibid.*

[41]   Google Transparency Report, https://transparencyreport.google.com/?hl=en.

company must consider local laws and may face court orders, even if complying to certain laws may detract the company from its goal of democracy on the Internet. In the government section of its Transparency Report, Google explains that "some content removals are requested due to allegations of defamation, while others are due to allegations that the content violates local laws prohibiting hate speech or pornography."[42] Laws surrounding these issues vary by country, and the requests reflect the legal context of a given jurisdiction.

The process by which these requests take place is all manual, and accomplished by a human source. Google also adheres to the laws of specific countries when receiving removal requests, even if the removal request content does not violate their own guidelines. This shows that Google acknowledges liability for what is produced by the search engine and through the autocomplete feature. However, it also shows that this process may be timely and may move through several people before being admitted or denied, subject to Google's interpretation of a particular issue.

As of March 2019, pursuant to removal requests under European privacy law dating back to May 2014, Google received 787,787 requests to delist certain content contained in 3,050,587 URLs. Of those delisting requests, only 44.3 percent of URLs were delisted. Google indicates that "[d]etermining whether content is in the public interest is complex and may mean considering many diverse factors, including – but not limited to – whether the content relates to the requester's professional life, a past crime, political office, position in public life, or whether the content is self-authored content, consists of government documents, or is journalistic in nature."[43]

From January 1, 2018 to June 30, 2018, Google received requests to remove 254,863 URLs pursuant to European privacy law.[44] Compare that with 25,534 URL removal requests pursuant to governmental requests around the world.[45] Google received ten times the amount of URL removal requests pursuant to European privacy law than from any other government around the world. These numbers reveal the impact of European regulations and the seriousness of the right to be forgotten. If other jurisdictions were to impose similar requirements to European law, individuals would obviously have much more control over their online data – and the numbers indicate that individuals in Europe are certainly exercising this right.

Google Has Control over Search Suggestions

The examples in this section clearly indicate that Google (through algorithms) has the ability to control what is generated in its search suggestions. However, this control seems to be limited to instances in which Google has been mandated by specific governments (namely, China and Europe) not to disclose search suggestions, or where Google blocks certain search results due to the results' failure to adhere with Google's terms of service. While the algorithm itself generates certain autocompleted search results, Google steps in to limit these results, thereby exerting some level of "editorial control." One could argue that for this reason Google

---

[42] M. Miller, Google Reveals More Government Search Censorship Requests, *Search Engine Watch* (June 19, 2012), http://searchenginewatch.com/article/2185571/Google-Reveals-More-Government-Search-Censorship-Requests.

[43] Google Transparency Report, Search Removals under European Privacy Law, https://transparencyreport.google.com/eu-privacy/overview.

[44] Information gathered from *ibid*.

[45] Information gathered from Google Transparency Report, Government Requests to Remove Content, located at https://transparencyreport.google.com/government-removals/overview.

is an information content provider which actively manipulates data from its search sugges-tions. However, the contrary may also be implied, and Google may be deemed an interactive computer service, as Google is simply removing content and search suggestions that do not comport with its internal guidelines, which may be delineated through governmental con-trols. It may be evident at this point that this issue is an incredibly tricky one to resolve. I next delve into cases assessed by various jurisdictions to try to understand how courts have weighed on this issue.

CASE LAW BY COUNTRY ASSESSING SEARCH ENGINE LIABILITY FOR DEFAMATORY AUTOCOMPLETED SEARCH RESULTS

The present issue of Google's liability for defamatory autocompleted search results has been litigated in courts around the world. However, Google has only been sued in the United States once for such liability– and the results of that case are somewhat disappointing. The most recent – and only – case against Google in the United States was brought forth by Dr. Guy Hingston, a cancer surgeon from Australia. Hingston brought his suit in the Central District of California, complaining that he was portrayed in a false light through Google's autocomplete suggestion of "guy hingston bankrupt." Consequently, it was alleged that his reputation as a surgeon was damaged, resulting in a loss of a number of patients and financiers. This case was ultimately dismissed, in part due to the uphill battle of litigating against Google and the uncharted legal landscape of this issue.

America's broad protections under the CDA discourage plaintiffs from filing lawsuits against Internet entities. Although Google is based in the United States, it operates worldwide and is therefore subject to litigation in a court located in the jurisdiction where an individual is harmed. Therefore, the following is an analysis of case law in Australia, the European Union, Canada, and the United Kingdom.

Search Engine Liability in Australia

Australia has grappled with the issue of search engine liability for years. In Australia's most pivotal case, *Trkulja* v. *Google LLC*, the plaintiff Trkulja claimed he was defamed by search results that conveyed he was a "hardened and serious criminal in Melbourne," someone in the same league as, or an associate of, other named criminals, and "such a significant figure in the Melbourne criminal underworld that events involving him are recorded on a website that chronicles crime."[46] Google's arguments hinged upon the contentions that: (1) Google had not published the search results; (2) the search results generated were not defamatory of Trkulja; and (3) Google was immune from such a lawsuit. In a set of trials and appeals, Trkulja eventually obtained judgment from the Australian High Court, which found that Google intentionally participated in the communication of allegedly defamatory search results relating to Trkulja, and that Google should not be immune from a lawsuit of such nature "as a matter of public interest." The High Court explained that the test for liability in such a scenario is "whether any of the search results complained of are capable of conveying any of the defamatory imputations alleged."[47]

---

[46] *Trkulja* v. *Google LLC* [2018] HCA 25, 13 (2018).
[47] *Ibid.*

In another Australian ruling, *Google Inc.* v. *Duffy*,[48] an individual was attached to negative reviews she had written on blogger websites, where she had complained about psychics she had visited. The psychics then turned on her, and began to reply to Duffy's reviews, calling her a "psychic stalker." When Duffy's name was searched online, a Google search autocompleted her name along with the term "psychic stalker." Google argued that a reasonable person would not believe the autocompleted search result was a statement made by Google, but rather as "a collection of words that have been entered by previous searchers when conducting searches."[49] The Supreme Court of South Australia found that Google is a secondary publisher of the defamatory search results and the underlying webpages indexed on Google's webpage, and knowledge of the search results and content therein should be attributed to Google once an individual notifies the company of the existence of defamatory material. The Court rejected all of Google's defenses, including that it disseminated the material innocently, that it was not the publisher of the defamatory information, and that it was protected by qualified privileges. The Court's emphasis on the search engine's knowledge of the defamatory matter was of primary concern.

The Australian courts impose liability upon search engines for defamatory search results, as the courts have established that search results are indeed capable of conveying defamatory content. Interestingly, the *Duffy* Court indicates that Google's liability originates at the time it is put on notice of defamatory search results or webpages. This shifts the burden to Google to remove or delist the content, but the procedure for doing so has not been adequately outlined by the courts.

Search Engine Liability in the European Union

Given the European Union's recently enacted right to be forgotten protections, as codified in the GDPR and outlined above, the case law seems to weigh in favor of plaintiffs who allege they have been defamed by Google's autocomplete feature. The *Google Spain* case, which found that the operator of a search engine is the "controller" of data, obligated search engines to delist search results that are irrelevant, outdated, or unlawful, in that they are unnecessarily defamatory.

Amsterdam's District Court in 2019 ordered Google to remove autocompleted search results of a Dutch surgeon's past medical suspension, which was later reduced to a conditional suspension.[50] The outdated information of the surgeon's full suspension would populate in Google's search results, and the surgeon argued that the search results acted to eternally shame her online for an event that was irrelevant and not true. The District Court of Amsterdam emphasized that Google's search results suggested that the surgeon was unfit to practice her profession and ruled that the surgeon's interest in protecting her reputation in this manner far outweighed the public interest in finding information that was inaccurate.

A Belgium Court of Cassation analyzed a case in 2016 from the perspective of outdated news content.[51] In *P.H.* v. *O.G.*, a medical doctor was convicted of drunk driving in 1994, and

---

[48]   *Google Inc.* v. *Duffy* [2017] SASCFC 130 (2017).
[49]   *Ibid.* at 159.
[50]   D. Boffey, Dutch Surgeon Wins Landmark "Right to Be Forgotten" Case, *The Guardian* (January 21, 2019), http://amp.theguardian.com/technology/2019/jan/21/dutch-surgeon-wins-landmark-right-to-be-forgotten-case-google.
[51]   *P.H.* v. *O.G.*, No. C.15.0052.F (April 26, 2016), Global Freedom of Expression Columbia University, https://globalfreedomofexpression.columbia.edu/cases/p-h-v-o-g/.

was involved in a serious accident thereon which led to the death of two people. Twenty-two years later, he was deemed rehabilitated by a court decision. In 1994, a Belgian newspaper published an article reporting upon the drunk-driving accident, and later created an online archive of all of its articles, including the 1994 article of the doctor's accident. The online article produced search results that included the doctor's name, autocompleting his name along with the fact that he had been driving while intoxicated. The Belgium Court found that the article no longer had news value (dating over twenty-two years), the doctor was not a public figure, and there was no public interest in learning of the identity of an individual involved in a car accident that dated over two decades ago. The Court declared that the "right to be forgotten" is central to the Belgian Constitution and the European Convention on Human Rights. The Court pointed out that digital archiving of such facts made it possible for individuals to easily find out information about others, which was not possible in the days preceding the Internet, and that the article about the doctor created an indefinite criminal record that damaged his reputation, outweighing the right to freedom of expression in this case.

However, certain cases decided in the European Union underscore the limitations proscribed in the *Google Spain* case.

The Amsterdam Court of Appeal ruled in 2015 that Google did not need to delist certain automated search results. In *Plaintiff* v. *Google Netherlands BV*,[52] an individual had been convicted of the solicitation of murder. After a television broadcast identifying the plaintiff as attempting to solicit the murder of one of his competitors, many links to the story became available on Google. Google would autocomplete searches for the individual's name to reveal that the plaintiff had been involved with the crime. The plaintiff's attorney requested that the plaintiff's full name and reference to his criminal charges be delisted from Google's autocomplete search suggestions. The Court balanced the plaintiff's privacy rights against the public's right to freedom of information. In doing so, the Court held that the plaintiff had to "bear the consequences of his own actions" as he had been convicted of a serious criminal offense – the Court found that the search suggestions were not "irrelevant," "excessive," or "otherwise defamatory," as the public had a right to the true information about the plaintiff.

Search Engine Liability in Canada

Canada assesses online liability through an analysis of the laws that apply to distributors of information. While this may seem outdated given the US approach to interactive service providers and information content providers, Canada applies a "passive instrument test" defense to those who play a secondary role in distributing content. Accordingly, if a distributor does not have knowledge that a statement is defamatory, and does not negligently disregard such knowledge, a distributor would not be liable for the content. However, a British Columbia Supreme Court case modified this standard in a 2015 ruling.

In the case *Niemela* v. *Google Inc.*,[53] a practicing lawyer had been harassed and extorted for about three years, including on the reputationally damaging Internet sites "ripoffreport.com" and "reviewstalk.com." Niemela suspected a former client was responsible for the posts, and informed the police. Once the police spoke with Niemela's client, the defamatory posts that were once rampantly posted ceased to be published. However, whenever Niemela's name was searched on Google, the defamatory posts would autocomplete through Google's algorithm.

---

[52]   *Plaintiff* v. *Google Netherlands BV*, Global Freedom of Expression, Columbia University, http://globalfreedo
       mofexpression.columbia.edu/cases/plaintiff-v-google-netherlands-bv/.
[53]   *Niemela* v. *Google Inc.*, 2015 BCSC 1024 (June 16, 2015).

Niemela alleged that these posts had damaged his professional reputation and filed an action against Google in the Supreme Court of British Columbia. The Court used both Canadian and UK case law to evaluate Google's role in publishing the defamatory search results. In its assessment, the Court applied a "passive instrument test" in which Google would need to have had "knowing involvement in the process of publication of the relevant words."[54] The Court explained that because snippets, like URLs, on Google's browser are generated automatically through the operation of computer algorithms in response to search terms inputted by users, the company neither authorized nor did it play an active role in modifying or publishing them, other than providing its search service. Therefore, Google's algorithmic-based search results were deemed a "passive instrument" that did not subject Google to liability.

Case Law Takeaway

A quick overview of the case law in these various countries indicates that courts around the world are divided on how to attribute liability to algorithmic search suggestions. Australia attributes liability to Google once Google is made aware of the fact that it contributes to defamation, without providing a formula or guidelines under which content should be removed. Europe also implies that Google must take down defamatory autocompleted suggestions once it is put on notice, and obligates Google to remove material that is irrelevant, outdated, or otherwise unlawful. Canada takes the most Google-friendly approach, finding that Google's algorithmic search suggestions are a "passive instrument" that are generated automatically without Google's active involvement.

LIMITATIONS AND ISSUES WITH GOOGLE'S CONTROL OVER CONTENT

Current Limitations in European Right to Be Forgotten Procedures

While Europe's approach may seem a strong win for individuals who wish to remove damaging or "outdated" content of themselves from the Internet, this solution is not without limitations. First, Europe's right to be forgotten and delisting of certain URLs does not automatically remove the underlying content which may have been damaging in the first place. In some instances, Google's algorithm is responsible for creating the false, autocompleted statements. However, in others, Google simply regurgitates information that may already be available online, and the original defamatory content would not be affected by the GDPR rules. Additionally, the right to be forgotten and the resulting delisting of information from Internet browsers is only applicable in the European Union. This means that defamatory search results will remain in browsers in other parts of the world. Perhaps this result is good enough for individuals who reside in the European Union with no desire to leave, but this delisting process pursuant to the GDPR is not a complete solution to the issue.

In a controversial opinion published in January 2019 by the ECJ, Advocate General Mciej Szpunar argued that removed access to delisted URLs from search engines should only be limited to searches made within the European Union, and should not apply worldwide.[55]

---

[54] *Ibid.*

[55] O. Bowcott, "Right to Be Forgotten" by Google Should Apply Only in EU, Says Court Opinion, *The Guardian* (January 10, 2019), www.theguardian.com/technology/2019/jan/10/right-to-be-forgotten-by-google-should-apply-only-in-eu-says-court; see also the opinion, published at http://curia.europa.eu/juris/document/document_print.jsf?docid=209688&text=&dir=&doclang=FR&part=1&occ=first&mode=req&pageIndex=0&cid=7572825.

The theory behind this is that EU residents' delisting rights should be exercised without compromising the constitutional frameworks of other countries around the world, namely free access to news and information. This theory was backed by even Thomas Hughes, the executive director of article 19, which established the delisting right, who explained: "European data regulators should not be able to determine the search results that internet users around the world get to see. They should only be able to de-list websites within their country's jurisdiction, and should balance the rights of both privacy and free speech when making that decision."[56]

Censorship Concerns

The question of whether Google should censor the material that it posts online is often debated. While Google may ultimately have control over its autocompleted search suggestions and the material which it organizes, indexes, and disseminates to the public, the First Amendment begs the question of how much control by search providers is appropriate. Americans enjoy the freedom of the Internet and the wealth of information that is readily available at the swipe of a few buttons. Allowing Google to have the control to remove searches, delist URLs, and manipulate the content to which end-users have access may have chilling consequences on the freedom of information, speech, and press. We expect our Internet providers to give us access to information in a neutral manner – the presumption that Google has control, and even liability, over that information threatens the freedom which currently exists online, at least in the United States.

Further complicating this issue is the manner in which Google ultimately removes content once it is made aware of the unlawfulness of such material. As indicated in its Transparency Reports, removing content from Google is a manual process. The individuals employed by Google who may be responsible for delisting or removing certain content from Google may not even be legal professionals who may perform full legal analyses of the requests at issue. This means that information is being modified and manipulated perhaps by untrained individuals, and the possibility of human error is one that should not be overlooked or considered lightly.

Google Must Balance the Interests of the Public to Search and Contribute to Searchable Content against Privacy Interests

Many scholars have approached the issue of what is posted online on a "multiple values-based perspective."[57] Another framework:

> examines critically the processes of Internet censorship to evaluate how well a country describes what it censors and why, whether it effectively blocks proscribed material while leaving permitted content untouched, and how much its citizens can participate in filtering decisions. Because online censorship is sharply on the rise worldwide – in democratic states as well as in authoritarian ones – corporations, citizens, and governments will increasingly be forced to make difficult judgments about filtering practices.[58]

The Internet is meant to be a forum on which individuals may freely express themselves, and this is a large reason for its existence.

---

[56] *Ibid.*
[57] D. E. Bambauer, Cybersieves (2009) 59 *Duke Law J.* 377, 380.
[58] *Ibid.*

As in any privacy-based tort action, rendering information to the public through the Internet beckons a need to balance public interests and private interests. Further, the adaptation of technology in presenting new modes of communications inevitably leads to new forums of expression. These rights are inherently tied to human and economic development; freedom of expression online and access to the Internet deserve international attention and global, cooperative enforcement.

CONCLUSION AND CALL TO ACTION

Google's Liability as an Algorithm-Based Republisher

Since Google is deemed through this analysis to be an ABR, an in-between of a typical distributor or publisher, Google's liability also should fall somewhere in between the two. Numerous attempts have been made to remove liability from Internet search providers for content that is publicly available and is simply distributed by search engines. Courts around the world are at odds in determining what would implicate liability of a search engine that influences what is searched or asked for online.

It seems safe to assume that some liability should be attributed to Google, as it is directing users to searches that may be defamatory in nature, based on an algorithm produced by Google itself. Although no case in the United States has been decided on this issue, the case law from other countries implies that Google may be liable for its autocomplete function where Google is made aware of unlawful content that generates therefrom. In each case, however, Google has not generally commented on its potential liability.

Given the limitations of the current legal framework surrounding Internet law, it is understandable that courts have a difficult time assessing Google's role, especially when addressing Google's algorithm for autocomplete. Perhaps another standard should be made and applied when dealing with algorithms in an Internet context, beyond the traditional analysis of whether an online actor is an interactive service provider or an information content provider. Because the Internet is now a primary mode of communication, it is necessary to establish a legal framework that will address the challenges surrounding Internet discourse. For the purpose of Google's autocomplete feature, courts must determine what liability an ABR has in generating suggestive information.

Therefore, it is first important to determine explicitly whether Google is a distributor and publisher of information, and if Google's algorithm renders it beyond a "neutral tool" as an information content provider. Once this issue is resolved, legal implications can be made to direct if, and in what context, Google's liability stands. Furthermore, rules should be fashioned that balance public and private interests in the autocomplete feature. Google's liability for its autocomplete algorithm can then be established.

Suggestions for Google, Moving Forward

Although it cannot be stated with certainty what Google can do to avoid liability for what is generated through its autocomplete feature, few scholars and analysts have concluded that Google may perform certain functions to avoid liability. A few suggestions for improving the Google autocomplete feature and Google's subsequent liability include: (1) development of a support area that could allow Google to assess what users' qualms may be, allowing Google to take care of the problem before any legal liability manifests; (2) Google could provide some sort of general reporting tool, where individuals may report misinformation, similar to the European rules; (3) Google may improve its algorithm;[59] and (4) Google can provide guidelines for determining what liability it holds, and work with national governments to create a system for management.

Google and other search engines have the unique understanding of what their autocomplete functions and other algorithms entail. If they provide some insight to the public on how these algorithms function, and the internal limitations they actually face by virtue of these algorithms, the public and courts may be willing to work with Google in addressing how search engines should be governed. Given that freedom of information is a central issue of this analysis, if search engines allow for the public to weigh in on Internet governance, perhaps better strategies may be implemented for addressing unlawful activity online. Google's mission is "to organize the world's information and make it universally accessible and useful," while still "following the law, acting honorably and treating each other with respect."[60] With this, it appears that Google may be interested in understanding how to conduct itself while "acting honorably." From its mission statement, it appears the company desires to provide a public service, without infringing upon others' rights.

The legal issues addressed in this chapter are important given the proliferation of similar autocomplete and algorithmic functionality in emerging technology. A legal framework needs to be established for assessing liability of search engines and algorithms generated therefrom, but such a framework requires input from the search engines themselves. Once their technology is put into an appropriate legal framework, search engine responsibility to oversee autocompleted search results can be determined. After establishing the role of algorithms in an online context, perhaps new laws and regulations that assess rapidly changing online technology may be determined.

---

[59]   R. Drysdale, 5 Suggestions for Google Suggest, *SEOmoz* (May 10, 2011), www.seomoz.org/blog/5-suggestions-for-googles-suggested-search.
[60]   Google.com, Google: Our Mission, www.google.com/search/howsearchworks/mission/.

22

When Do Algorithmic Tortfeasors that Caused Damage Warrant Unique Legal Treatment?

Karni Chagal-Feferkorn[*]

INTRODUCTION

From a historical context, the design and use of algorithms pre-dates the current proliferation of algorithms throughout society. For example, culminating in the Industrial Revolution, automated machines and tools have for centuries been assisting humans in performing physical tasks.[1] Drills, engravers, weaving machines, and the like employed machines' physical advantages to free human beings from repetitive physical labor. In a similar manner, algorithms are now taking on the decision-making and human supervisory control of systems which require human cognitive skills.

In general, in numerous jurisdictions, damage to people or to property caused by algorithmic-driven tools has been governed by the legal framework of product liability.[2] Under product liability, the manufacturer of a defective product is liable for the physical harm caused to the user or her property.[3] Thus, victims of machines that caught fire, came apart, or crashed[4] could have brought successful product liability claims against the products' manufacturers under a theory of manufacturing or design defect.

The reliance on product liability in cases where machines or systems caused damage continued even as these systems became more sophisticated and assisted human beings in more complex sets of tasks such as the processing and analyzing of data. For situations where the human role in the system is primarily supervisory (as opposed to manual), accidents have generally raised claims of product liability (as demonstrated, for example, in the case of air crashes involving autopilots).[5]

Recently, however, with the development of yet more "sophisticated," "independent," or "autonomous" systems, many suggest that the legal framework applying to damages caused by such systems is becoming outdated and thus ought to change. Advances in algorithms, driverless vehicles, robotic surgeons, and other types of self-learning systems designed to replace humans raise debates over the proper tort regime to apply when such systems cause

---

[*] The chapter is based on Am I an Algorithm or a Product? When Products Liability Should Apply to Algorithmic Decision-Makers (2019) 30 *Stan. Law Policy Rev.* 61. I would like to dedicate this chapter to Professor Woodrow Barfield.

[1] R. Hartwell, *The Industrial Revolution and Economic Growth* (Methuen & Co., 1971), pp. 295–7.

[2] D. Gifford, Technological Triggers to Tort Revolutions: Steam Locomotives, Autonomous Vehicles, and Accident Compensation (2018) 11 *J. Tort Law* 49–50. Further discussion on the development of the products liability framework will be held in "Products Liability and Its Rationales," below.

[3] Restatement (Second) of Torts § 402A (1965).

[4] See, e.g., *White Consolidated Industry, Inc. v. Swiney*, 376 SE.2d 283 (Va. 1989); *McKenzie v. SK Hand Tool Corp.*, 272 Ill. App.3d 451, 650 (NE.2d 612 (1995)); *Collazo-Santiago v. Toyota Motor Corp.*, 149 F.3d 23 (1st Cir. 1998).

[5] See, e.g., *Moe v. Avions Marcel Dasault-Breguet Avion*, 727 F.2d 917 (10th Cir. 1984).

damage. The European Parliament, for example, has issued a draft report explaining that ordinary rules on liability are insufficient for algorithmic-driven autonomous robots, since they can no longer be considered tools in the hands of other actors.[6] Among others, the report suggested granting autonomous robots an independent legal status of "electronic-persons," which might even allow these robots themselves to pay damages for the harm they cause (for instance, through a compulsory insurance scheme).[7] Similarly, and much earlier, Judge Curtis Karnow suggested that a new legal fiction, that of electronic personalities, may usefully address tort issues brought forth by new technology. He suggested that rights should be conferred on electronic personalities for the same reason rights are conferred on humans in the physical world: because we wish to restrain powerful forces; and we cannot restrain those forces with countervailing raw power.[8]

Many other entities and scholars have agreed that as technology driven by algorithms becomes more "autonomous" and less predictable, it makes less sense to determine liability based on the actions or inactions of its manufacturers. In this situation, it may be advantageous to analyze the "behavior" of the technology itself.[9] Other propositions have focused on developing an insurance scheme adapted to the capabilities and potential danger posed by "sophisticated" or "autonomous" algorithmic-driven systems.[10]

In any event, a preliminary question not yet discussed in depth is *when* does an algorithmic-driven system become different from a "traditional product" such that product liability is no longer a sufficient framework to treat damages caused by it? Automated machines of different kinds were described in detail as early as 800 years ago.[11] What is it that separates them from "autonomous" or "independent" decision-makers – which for the sake of convenience we will generally refer to as "thinking algorithms" (because their algorithms model various stages of human thinking, and do so independently of a human)[12] – that they seem to warrant their own custom-made treatment? Why have "auto-pilots," for example, been traditionally treated as "products,"[13] while autonomous vehicles are suddenly seen as a more "human-like" system that requires different treatment? Where should the fine line be drawn between algorithms as "products" and algorithms as "decision-makers"?

---

[6] "Whereas the more autonomous robots are, the less they can be considered simple tools in the hands of other actors (such as the manufacturer, the owner, the user, etc.); whereas this, in turn, makes the ordinary rules on liability insufficient and calls for new rules which focus on how a machine can be held – partly or entirely – responsible for its acts or omissions . . ." 2015/2103 (INL) European Parliament Draft Report on Civil Law Rules on Robotics (May 2016), Section S.

[7] *Ibid.*, Section 59.F.

[8] C. E. A. Karnow, The Encrypted Self: Fleshing Out the Rights of Electronic Personalities (1994) 13 *John Marshall J. Comput. Inf. Law* 1.

[9] R. Abbott, The Reasonable Computer: Disrupting the Paradigm of Tort Liability (2018) 86 *Geo. Wash. Law Rev.* 1, 37–9; K. Chagal-Feferkorn, The Reasonable Algorithm (2018) 1 *Univ. Ill. J. Law Technol. Policy* 111, 116–17.

[10] K. Abraham and R. Rabin, Automated Vehicles and Manufacturer Responsibility for Accidents: A New Legal Regime for a New Era (2019) 105 *Va. Law Rev.* 127; A. Davola, A Model for Tort Liability in a World of Driverless Cars: Establishing a Framework for the Upcoming Technology (2018) 54 *Idaho Law Rev.* 591.

[11] I. al-Razzaz al Jazari, *The Book of Knowledge of Ingenious Mechanical Devices*, D. Hill trans. (Pakistan Hijra Council, 1989).

[12] While thinking algorithm is a broad and vague term (in a sense, much like "autonomous algorithm" or "independent algorithm" are), it is the very purpose of this chapter to provide concrete tools to classify algorithms as either "traditional" or ones that warrant new legal treatment. Given that these tools relate to various aspects of the algorithms, a general definition would indeed be too vague and therefore further discussions conducted below will shed more light on the type of algorithms I refer to by the general term thinking algorithms.

[13] See, e.g., the 2013 Asiana-Air crash in San Francisco, where the underlying legal actions consisted of products liability claims raised against Boeing, the manufacturer of the auto-throttle that allegedly failed. M. Hamilton, Asiana Crash: 72 Passengers Settle lawsuits against Airline, *Los Angeles Times* (March 3, 2013), www.latimes.com /local/lanow/la-me-ln-asiana-airlines-settle-lawsuits-20150303-story.html.

While several scholars have touched upon the issue of distinguishing "traditional" from "sophisticated" technologies for the purpose of applying product liability, there has been no in-depth discussion specifically addressing this question. Moreover, and as will be discussed in more depth below, all potential distinguishing parameters that have been mentioned relate to the system's level of autonomy. As will be demonstrated, however, a system's level of autonomy is not a desirable classifier between products and thinking algorithms. A new approach is therefore proposed for distinguishing the two for the purpose of determining whether product liability should apply: instead of examining the system's characteristics in isolation, a "purposive interpretation" approach is proposed. Under said approach, the system's specific characteristics are analyzed vis-à-vis the rationales behind the product liability legal framework. In other words, the purposive interpretation analyzes which characteristics are compatible with the different rationales behind product liability and which render the rationales more difficult to achieve. Thus, it proposes a practical method of assessing – for each system separately – whether product liability laws should continue to apply or whether a novel legal approach is desired.

WHY "AUTONOMY" IS NOT A DESIRED CLASSIFIER

Autonomy versus Automation

Automated machines, characterized by different levels of sophistication, have been utilized by humankind for centuries.[14] In addition to "open loop control" systems, which executed automated tasks on an injective predetermined and unchangeable trajectory,[15] "closed loop control" systems have for centuries been capable of automatically choosing among predetermined options, based on real-time feedback. "Closed loop control" windmills, for example, were able to increase the output of the windmill by automatically enlarging the amount of grain poured into the mill as the wind blew stronger.[16] The mere fact that the system adjusts its actions based on external feedback, thus forming a closed-loop feedback system, does not itself warrant legal treatment different from that of traditional products, as many well-known products operate with feedback, such as a thermostat. What then might assist legal scholars and legislators in making such a distinction?

Legal scholars engaged in product liability and sophisticated systems have suggested various directions to answer this question. The previously mentioned report by the European Parliament, for example, proposed defining a "smart robot" as one whose *autonomy* is established by its interconnectivity with the environment, and its ability to adapt its action to changes in it.[17] Millar and Kerr refer to expert robots, which can on average perform a well-defined set of tasks better than the human expert.[18] Abbott focuses on the system's ability to replace humans, more particularly on its ability to determine for itself how to complete tasks as set by humans.[19] Bambauer separates applications based on mere "measurement" from applications whose function is "knowledge-based."[20]

---

[14]   al-Razzaz al-Jazari, above note 11.
[15]   O. Mayr, *The Origins of Feedback Control* (MIT Press, 1970).
[16]   *Ibid.*, pp. 90–3.
[17]   European Parliament Draft Report, above note 6.
[18]   J. Millar and I. Kerr, Delegation, Relinquishment and Responsibility: The Prospect of Expert Robots, in R. Calo, A. M. Froomkin, and I. Kerr (eds.), *Robot Law* (Edward Elgar, 2016), p. 102.
[19]   Abbott, above note 9.
[20]   J. Bambauer, Dr. Robot (2017) 51 *UC Davis Law Rev.* 383, 393.

As the following review shows, these diverse and seemingly widely different tests all relate to different aspects of the system's autonomy, whether or not the term "autonomy" is stated expressly. The problem in classifying a system as a product or a thinking algorithm based on its level of autonomy, however, is the complexity of the term, which is greater than might be intuitively assumed.[21] Moreover, and as will be analyzed below, applying autonomy level or different aspects of it as a classifier might in many cases lead to absurd or inconsistent outcomes, and in any event it merely provides a "fuzzy" test whose results are not necessarily practical or relevant.

The Complex Concept of Autonomy

There are several reasons why a system's level of autonomy is not a desired classifier for the purpose of determining when product liability laws should apply and when they should not. One of the reasons is that such a classifier would be difficult to implement, as its level of complexity is excessively high.

First, autonomy is a spectrum rather than a binary classification.[22] As will be discussed below, autonomy consists of various attributes rather than a single one; thus, autonomy is a multidimensional construct. In addition, many of these attributes – for example, the system's adaptability to changing conditions – are in themselves measured on a continuous scale and cannot be determined binarily. Second, various spectrums of autonomy exist, each focusing on completely different aspects of algorithms. One common measurement of autonomy is the system's *freedom to act without human involvement* (or the allocation of decision-making power to humans or machine). MIT Professor Tom Sheridan's spectrum, for example, offers ten levels of autonomy, the most basic being a situation where all processes are accomplished by a human being, without any machine assistance; the highest level is where the machine selects the desired courses of action but also executes them, not even informing the human of its choice and ignoring the human altogether.[23]

A second method of assessing autonomy is based on the system's *ability to replace humans*.[24] This measurement is in itself branched and complex, as several sub-analyses have been suggested in that context, including whether the machine is limited to choosing among pre-programmed options;[25] whether the following three "attributes of autonomy" are met (frequency of human operator interaction, machine's tolerance for

---

[21]   W. Marra and S. McNeil, Understanding "The Loop": Regulating the Next Generation of War Machines (2013) 36 *Harv. J. Law Pub. Policy* 18.

[22]   *Ibid.*, pp. 22–6.

[23]   R. Parasuraman, T. B. Sheridan, and C. D. Wickens, A Model for Types and Levels of Human Interaction with Automation (2000) 30 *IEEE Trans. Syst. Man Cybern.* 286; Marra and McNeil, above note 21.

[24]   See, e.g., the Society of Automotive Engineers' spectrum for autonomous vehicles. Level 0 of the spectrum is no automation, where human drivers perform all tasks required for driving; level 5 is full automation where the vehicle itself is capable of performing all driving functions under all circumstances. In between, automation (not autonomy) is used as a tool that increasingly assists the human driver. Automated Vehicles for Safety, NHTSA, www.nhtsa.gov/technology-innovation/automated-vehicles-safety.

[25]   K. Anderson and M. Waxman, Law and Ethics for Autonomous Weapon Systems: Why a Ban Won't Work and How the Laws of War Can, Jean Perkins Task Force on National Security and Law, Columbia Public Law Research Paper 13-351 (2013), https://scholarship.law.columbia.edu/faculty_scholarship/1803.

environmental uncertainty, and level of assertiveness of the machine),[26] or whether the system is able to perform all the following types of activity: "skill-driven," "rules-driven," and "knowledge driven."[27]

A third method for evaluating autonomy refers to a "stronger" measure, focusing on the system's own cognitive-awareness and real freedom of choice.[28] The spectrum proposed by the Air Force Research Lab (AFRL), for example, refers at the highest levels of autonomy to systems that are "cognizant" of their environment, that is, possess situational awareness, and not merely possess "knowledge" on it.[29]

Another hardship in implementing a classifier based on the algorithm's level of autonomy is that each of the tests discussed above must also consider the specific stage of the machine's decision-making process. According to military strategist John Boyd, the decision-making process comprises a continuous cycle of decision-making stages, consisting of the following four steps: "Observe"; "Orient"; "Decide"; "Act."[30] The OODA Loop is not limited to the decision-making process of humans alone, but could apply to machines as well. Naturally, as a machine becomes capable of performing more of the four steps on its own, the better the odds that it will achieve a higher "autonomy score" on the spectrum of whether or not it can replace humans. And the more that a human may be replaced by the system, the more that tort law which typically looks to a human as a responsible party will be challenged. But in addition to this partial overlap with the measures of autonomy discussed above, the OODA Loop may be independently used as a separate dimension on each of the autonomy measures. For instance, the "information acquisition" stage performed by an autonomous military drone might include gathering data on potential targets without the need for any human involvement – thus, the drone receives a "high autonomy score" for the first test of autonomy. It might do so even in the face of changing weather conditions or new disguise methods used by the potential targets – thus receiving a high score for the second spectrum of autonomy as well. At the same time, the decision-making stage for exactly the same weapon may involve very little autonomy – at least with regard to the first spectrum – as a decision to hit a target will very likely require human authorization and not be executed at the weapon's own discretion.[31]

As demonstrated above, the different measurements of autonomy are numerous and complex, and at times overlap. Should decision-makers decide to rely on all these measurements when determining whether product liability laws ought to apply, they would have to develop a complex matrix, accounting for all the different aspects of autonomy

[26]　According to Marra and McNeil, a machine is the more autonomous the less frequently a human operator must intervene and give instructions; the more adaptability it shows in the face of scenarios it is not fully programmed to encounter; and the more it is able to change its operating plan in order to achieve its pre-programmed task, for instance, when the machine is "stuck." Marra and McNeil, above note 21, pp. 18–22.

[27]　These concern which of the system's abilities are required in order to perform. In more detail, human activity may roughly be divided into three groups: "skill-driven" activities, namely the ability to accomplish physical tasks; "rules-driven" activities, namely the ability to comply with predetermined rules; and "knowledge-driven," namely the ability to make decisions when the rules previously mentioned are inadequate. A. Chialastri, Automation in Aviation, in F. Kongoli (ed.), *Automation* (InTechOpen, 2012), p. 79.

[28]　See, e.g., E. Lieblich and E. Benvenisti, The Obligation to Exercise Discretion in Warfare: Why Autonomous Weapon Systems Are Unlawful, in N. Bhuta, S. Beck, R. Geiβ, *et al.* (eds.), *Autonomous Weapons Systems: Law, Ethics, Policy* (Cambridge University Press, 2016), p. 244.

[29]　At its lowest level, The AFRL's spectrum refers to a system that is remotely controlled by a human, or executes missions entirely pre-planned by humans. At its mid-level stages of autonomy, the system itself may respond to real-time events. Marra and McNeil, above note 21, p. 25.

[30]　F. Osinga, *Science, Strategy and War; The Strategic Theory of John Boyd* (Routledge, 2007), pp. 1–3.

[31]　For discussions on the importance of "keeping a human in the firing-loop," see, e.g., M. Schmitt and J. Thurnher, "Out of the Loop": Autonomous Weapons Systems and the Law of Armed Conflict (2013) 4 *Harv. Nat. Secur. J.* 231.

discussed. Using autonomy as a classifier would also yield non-clear results. When determining the "system's tolerance to environmental changes," for example, the decision-maker would not be facing a "yes or no" question, but would have to come up with an out-of-context numerical or qualitative estimation of the system's tolerance of such conditions. Moreover, factoring in all these vague estimations into a combined outcome that classifies the system's level of autonomy in turn would lead to a mere general sensation of whether the system is autonomous or not, and would likely not be helpful when the underlying system is not at any one of the ends of the autonomy scale. Furthermore, the outcome received would not be helpful even if it were more concrete or accurate, because it would merely give an indication of the system's autonomy, but not of the desirability of applying product liability laws to the system.

An alternative approach, simpler and providing more relevant results for the questions of when product liability laws ought to continue to apply to algorithms and when new legal treatment is warranted, is that of purposive interpretation. Under this approach, the different features or characteristics of the system are analyzed in the context of how well they may allow the fulfilment of product liability rationales. Essentially, the approach applies a multinomial model to the tort scheme, logit, in its binary classification. The more features are indeed compatible with said rationales, the more likely it is that the system may continue to be subject to product liability laws without the need to look for a new tort framework.

PRODUCT LIABILITY AND ITS RATIONALES

Product liability, the most "popular" of all case types in the United States,[32] stems from the shift from local craftsmen to mass production factories which caused a "lack of privity" problem that eliminated victims' means of redress.[33] Fast forward, and an issue of privity again is privity of contract with algorithms. The introduction of product liability resolved that discrepancy, by eliminating the requirement of privity of contract between the injured and the tortfeasor.[34] Under product liability laws, the seller or manufacturer of a defective product in a condition that is unreasonably dangerous is liable for the physical harms caused to the user or her property, even when there is no contractual relationship between them.[35] One of the main rationales behind product liability, therefore, is *compensation for the victim*, originating in corrective justice principles, where the tortfeasor is required to correct the wrong she has committed, based on justice and fairness considerations.[36]

A second main rationale behind tort law in general is "deterrence."[37] In the context of product liability, deterrence is translated into deterring manufacturers from creating danger-ous products, that is, *promoting safety*. Naturally, the threat of liability encourages manufac-turers to improve the safety of their products: the safer the product, the less likely it is to cause damage and the less likely are manufacturers to be sued and to pay damages.[38] Said rationale is indeed sensible in the context of product liability, given that manufacturers are best positioned to eliminate or reduce the risks associated with their products, considering that

[32] Tens of thousands of product liability cases are filed annually, more than any other case type. R. Porter, Lex Machina 2018 Product Liability Litigation Report (March 2018).
[33] See, e.g., *Winterbottom v. Wright* (1842), 152 Eng. Rep. 402.
[34] Gifford, above note 2.
[35] Restatement (Second) of Torts § 402A (1965).
[36] See, e.g., *Escola v. Coca Cola Bottling Co.*, 150 P.2d 436 (Cal. 1944).
[37] R. A. Posner, The Value of Wealth: A Comment on Dworkin and Kronman (1980) 9 *Leg. Stud.* 243, 244; J. C. P. Goldberg, Twentieth Century Tort Theory (2002) 90 *Geo. Law J.* 513.
[38] Restatement (Third) of Torts § 2 cmt. a (1998).

unlike consumers they possess information regarding the product and can ensure inspections and quality control measures. Other than promoting safety, however, it is important to remember that the rationale of deterrence must be applied with caution. First, increased likelihood of liability is generally expected to impede development and innovation, hence to create a "chilling effect" on technological advancement.[39] Second, increased levels of safety (potentially stemming from likelihood of liability) are expected to adversely affect different features of the product, including its pricing, ease of operation, appearance, and additional factors related to consumers' preferences other than safety.[40] The legal framework of product liability, therefore, purports to strike an optimal balance between contradictory rationales and interests.

ARE THINKING ALGORITHMS A PRODUCT? DO THEY CAUSE DAMAGE DUE TO DEFECTS?

A preliminary argument to be addressed, regardless of product liability rationales, is that thinking algorithms might not fit the classification of "products" in the first place. Alternatively, damages caused by such algorithms may not be attributed to "defects." If this is the case, one could argue that applying product liability rationales to distinguish which algorithms should be governed by product liability would simply be irrelevant. As the discussion below demonstrates, however, thinking algorithms may very well be classified as products, and damages caused by them may be attributed to defects.

Products

Several states have defined the term product for the purpose of applying product liability,[41] but in general it is up to the courts to determine whether an underlying damaging object is indeed a product.[42] In that context, systems based on information – which naturally are the subject matter of this chapter – often fall within the "grey zone," yielding contrasting results as to whether or not product liability should apply to them.

According to several court decisions, information in itself does not constitute a product for the purpose of applying product liability, because it lacks tangible form.[43] In addition, courts

---

[39] Gifford, above note 2, pp. 52–5; K. Colonna, Autonomous Cars and Tort Liability (2012) 4 *Case W. Res. J. Law Technol. Internet* 81, 93–7, 109–11.

[40] D. Owen, J. E. Montgomery, and P. Keeton, *Products Liability and Safety, Cases and Materials* (Foundation Press, 1996).

[41] J. L. Reutiman, Defective Information: Should Information Be a "Product" Subject to Products Liability Claims (2012) 22 *Cornell J. Law Pub. Policy* 181, referring, for example, to Idaho Code Ann. § 6–1402(3) (2008) (defining a product as "any object possessing intrinsic value, capable of delivery either as an assembled whole or as a component part or parts, and produced for introduction into trade or commerce. Human tissue and organs, including human blood and its components, are excluded from this term").

[42] *Ibid.* The Restatement of Torts (Third) which refers to the term "product" is drafted in a broad manner which seems to leave much flexibility as to which products fall within the definition and which do not: "A product is tangible personal property distributed commercially for use or consumption . . ." M. D. Scott, Tort Liability for Vendors of Insecure Software (2008) 67 *Md. Law Rev.* 426.

[43] *America Online, Inc.* v. *St. Paul Mercury Insurance Co.*, 242 207 F. Supp. 2d 459 (ED Va. 2002) – "the plain and ordinary meaning of the word tangible is something that is capable of being touched or perceptible to the senses. Computer data, software and systems do not have or possess physical form and are therefore not tangible property as understood by the Policy"; *Winter* v. *G. P. Putnam's Sons*, 938 F.2d 1033, 1036 (9th Cir. 1991) – while the court in *Winter* acknowledged that the information at hand was embedded in a book, which is a tangible object, it nevertheless ruled that an encyclopedia of mushrooms which misled a reader to consume poisonous mushrooms was not subject to product liability laws; *Torres* v. *City of Madera*, 2005 US Dist. Lexis 34672 – holding that

in the past were sometimes inclined to rule that professional services (an analogy well-suited to thinking algorithms given that they replace human professionals)[44] were not products.[45]

Yet, in many other instances, courts did treat information as a product and applied product liability laws when errors in the information caused damage, especially when the information was integrated with a physical object[46] or when the object was mass-produced,[47] or had a dangerous potential.[48] Naturally, these considerations tend to exist with regard to thinking algorithms, given that thinking algorithms are often embedded in physical objects such as cellular phones or computers, that they are often mass-marketed, and that errors in them might cause deadly results.[49]

It is therefore very likely, at least prima facie, that thinking algorithms might also find themselves classified as products, even if their entire essence is information and even if their function replaces human services.

Defects

Thinking algorithms are inherently expected to cause damage regardless of any defects. This is because sophisticated systems, in particular self-learning algorithms, rely on probability-based predictions,[50] and probabilities by nature inevitably "get it wrong" some of the time.

Focusing on the damage caused due to a user being "on the bad side of the statistics" certainly does not mean that the system was defectively manufactured or defectively designed. Rather, the system has reached the decision we would want it to reach. It just so happens that whenever thinking algorithms reach decisions based on probabilities – which is exactly what they are designed to help humans with – inevitable damage will occur when the general rule is applied in cases that in hindsight turned out to be the exceptions. Does this

---

   training materials consisting of a CD/ROM, slide presentation, and paper handouts were not products and therefore not subject to products liability. See Reutiman, above note 41, for further analysis.

[44] Scott, above note 42, pp. 434–6.

[45] *Ibid.*, pp. 461–2, referring to *La Rossa* v. *Scientific Design Co.*, 402 F.2d 937 (3rd Cir. 1968), which stated: "[P]rofessional services do not ordinarily lend themselves to the doctrine of tort liability without fault because they lack the elements which gave rise to the doctrine." See also *Snyder* v. *ISC Alloys*, 772 F. Supp. 244 (1991); *Lemley* v. *J & B Tire Co.*, 426 F. Supp. 1378 (1997); and *Torres* v. *City of Madera*, above note 43.

[46] *Retail Systems, Inc.* v. *CNA Insurance Cos.*, 9 469 NW.2d 735 (Minn. App. 1991): "The data on the tape was of permanent value and was integrated completely with the physical property of the tape. Like a motion picture, where the information and the celluloid medium are integrated, so too were the tape and data integrated at the moment the tape was lost."

[47] *Saloomey* v. *Jeppesen & Co.*, 707 F.2d 671 (2nd Cir. 1983); *Halstead* v. *United States*, 535 F. Supp. 782, 791 (D. Conn. 1982).

[48] *Flour Corp.* v. *Jeppesen & Co.*, 5 170 Cal. App. 3d 468, 216 Cal. Rptr. 68 (1985) (where the Court referred to a previous holding that only innately dangerous items might be subject to product liability – and that therefore a sheet of paper might not. The California Courts of Appeals in *Flour Corp.* held that the potential danger posed by errors in the sheets of paper was sufficient to subject the object – aeronautical charts in that case – to product liability).

[49] To take "Waze" as an example, Waze is embedded in the user's cell phones, has 100 million active users, and is of clear potential danger if directing drivers to unsafe roads or destinations. See G. Sterling, Waze Launches "Local" Ads Primarily Aimed at SMBs and Franchises, *Search-Engine-Land* (March 28, 2018), https://searchengineland.com/waze-launches-local-ads-primarily-aimed-at-smbs-and-franchises-295285.

[50] A Netflix algorithm recommending movies does so based on a numeric prediction that we would like said choice, relying on our previous taste and an analysis of enormous databases of other consumers' preferences (How Netflix's Recommendation System Works, Netflix Help Center, https://help.netflix.com/en/node/100639). A bail algorithm recommending whom to release and whom to deny bail does so based on the probability that the suspect would break the law or escape if allowed to post bail (V. Ramachandran, Are Algorithms a Fair Way to Predict Who'll Skip Bail?, *Futurity* (June 5, 2017), www.futurity.org/bail-bias-algorithm-1450462-2/). An application for choosing an optimal treatment for a patient is also based on the probability that the patient indeed has the medical condition diagnosed, and that she would react to the optimal treatment as most other patients would.

mean that thinking algorithms should never be governed by product liability and that our analysis should have nothing to do with said legal framework? Not necessarily.

First, in addition to damages caused through no defect, thinking algorithms may certainly also be responsible for defect-based damages, which do not stem from the user "being on the bad side of statistics." Second, thinking algorithms are not unique in their ability to cause damage in the absence of a defect. Traditional products too may be "defect-free," yet nevertheless cause damage.[51] Indeed, to win a product liability lawsuit a plaintiff must prove – even when subject to strict liability theory – the existence of a defect,[52] implying that certain damages are not caused by a defect.

Granted, one could argue that in thinking algorithms damage caused without the existence of a defect is *inherent*, unlike traditional products which do not inherently cause damage when no defect is involved. If so, product liability may indeed not be the most efficient framework applicable, especially given that product liability procedures are considered expensive and slow.[53] While a different legal framework – whose underlying assumption is that no defect exists in the first place – might be more efficient, this does not render our current product liability regime irrelevant altogether.

Thinking algorithms, despite their nature as "information-based" and although they may frequently cause damage regardless of a defect, may thus nevertheless be governed by product liability. Let us therefore turn to analyzing *when* a system is a thinking algorithm in the sense that product liability rationales are less achievable when applied to damages caused by such systems.

APPLYING A PURPOSIVE ANALYSIS

As discussed above, an alternative approach for distinguishing traditional products from thinking algorithms which is not based, per se, on the system's level of autonomy is purposive analysis. In more detail, the approach analyzes how different features or characteristics of different decision-making systems – manifested in the four different OODA Loop stages – affect the achievement of the different rationales behind product liability. Practically, the more the system's features reconcile with achieving product liability rationales, the more inclined we would be to classify them as traditional products. Systems whose features impede product liability rationales, however, should be classified as thinking algorithms that warrant different treatment.

An Example of a Product versus Thinking Algorithms

Therac-25 was a radiation therapy machine used to destroy cancerous tissues. Between 1985 and 1987, Therac-25 led to the injury of six patients who were inadvertently given an overdose

---

[51]   Car tires, for example, may explode after a certain time of usage and cause lethal damage. As long as the manufacturer provides appropriate warning as to their maintenance and frequency of replacement, any damage caused by such worn-out tires will not be attributed to a defect. See, e.g., *Carmichael* v. *Samyang Tires, Inc.*, 923 F. Supp. 1514 (SD Ala. 1996), pertaining to an accident resulting from tire failure ("To maintain a claim under the AEMLD, a plaintiff cannot simply prove that an accident occurred and that he was injured; rather, "a defect in the product must be affirmatively shown").

[52]   *Ibid.*

[53]   See, e.g., R. W. McGee, Who Really Benefits from Liability Litigation? Dumont Institute Policy Analysis No. 24. (1996), https://ssrn.com/abstract=82596. This is even more so in the context of algorithmic decision-makers. See, e.g., J. Gurney, Sue My Car Not Me: Products Liability and Accidents Involving Autonomous Vehicles (2013) *Univ. Ill. J. Law Technol. Policy* 247, 262–4; D. C. Vladeck, Machines without Principals: Liability Rules and Artificial Intelligence (2014) 89 *Wash. Law Rev.* 117, 137–41.

of radiation, resulting in three fatalities.[54] Investigation revealed that the system had several "bugs" causing it to release much higher dosages of radiation than prescribed by the machine's technician.[55] Although the lawsuits filed in connection with the accidents were all settled before trial,[56] Therac-25 was considered one of the first cases to give rise to product liability claims in connection with medical devices.[57]

Therac-25 was useful for administering radiation in a precise and automatic manner; its "sophisticated counterpart" to be analyzed in the discussion below is that of a futuristic machine also capable of taking and implementing professional decisions. Nowadays, new generation radiation machines mainly focus on improved precision of the radiation's distribution. Equipped with infrared cameras and robotic beds, radiation machines now make automatic adjustments in the positioning of the patient throughout the radiation process to achieve more precise administering of the treatment.[58] An additional feature that could be embedded in radiation machines, however, would also include dose calculation algorithms that would enable the machine to administer radiation beams, but also to decide (or recommend) the optimal treatment plan for each patient based on his unique characteristics.[59] Existing algorithms for calculating radiation dosage are in use today,[60] but the future system we take as an example makes use of "learning algorithms" that produce personalized dosage calculations based on the type of tumor involved and on other parameters that the system itself deems relevant, after learning from large databases of previous cases and deciphering correlations between different parameters and improved outcomes.

Applying Product liability Rationales to Different Types of Algorithms

Promoting Safety

As discussed above, a central rationale behind the framework of product liability is to encourage manufacturers to better their products' safety. How is said rationale affected when the products at hand are sophisticated self-learning systems? Generally speaking, manufacturers of such systems might find themselves in a place where enhancing safety is very difficult or expensive, or will render the system inefficient. This point may be explained through the example of a futuristic system of a "robo-doctor" able fully to replace a human physician at all stages of decision-making.[61]

---

[54] N. Leveson and C. Turner, An Investigation of the Therac-25 Accidents (1993) 26 *Computer* 18–41; B. Littlewood and L. Strigini, The Risks of Software, *Scientific American* (1992), pp. 62–75.

[55] *Ibid.*, pp. 27–8.

[56] S. Dyson, Medical Device Software and Product Liability: An Overview, *MedTechIntelligence* (September 15, 2017), www.medtechintelligence.com/feature_article/medical-device-software-products-liability-overview-part /2/.

[57] *Ibid.*

[58] Next-generation, state-of-the-art radiation therapy system at Netcare N1 City Hospital, Netcare, www .netcare.co.za/News-Hub/Articles/articleid/639/next-generation-state-of-the-art-radiation-therapy-system-at-netcare-n1-city-hospital.

[59] Which consists of "the prescribed dose level for the tumor, the number of therapeutic beams, their angles of incidence, and a set of intensity amplitudes." U. Oelkfe and C. Scholz, Dose Calculation Algorithms, in W. C. Schlegel, T. Bortfeld, and A.-L. Grosu (eds.), *New Technologies in Radiation* (Springer, 2006), pp. 187–96.

[60] *Ibid.*

[61] A. Woodie, The Robo-Doctor Is [In], *Datanami* (August 30, 2017), www.datanami.com/2017/08/30/the-robo-doctor-is-in/; M. Froomkin, I. Kerr, and J. Pineau, When AIs Outperform Doctors: Confronting the Challenges of a Tort-Induced Over-Reliance on Machine Learning (2019) 61 *Ariz. Law Rev.* 33.

First, manufacturers of traditional products have a finite number of parameters to consider when preparing for different scenarios and minimizing risks associated with the actions of their machines.[62] By contrast, robo-doctor manufacturers will have an enormous number of scenarios against which they must try to take precautionary measures, based on innumerable parameters: the patient's general medical condition (blood type, vital signs, height, weight, etc.) and past medical condition (previous lab results, previous diagnoses, previous success or failure of past treatments, etc.), as well as current medical condition (for example, for cancer diagnosis: type of cancer, its size, its location, its stage, etc.); various external parameters (are any epidemics indicated in that region? Do current weather conditions affect the likelihood of a certain diagnosis?); practical parameters (are qualified staff available immediately to execute a certain medical choice? What is the best practical choice in cases of understaff, or of shortage of specific medications in the hospital's stock?); and ethical parameters (what does the patient truly want? How does it reconcile with ethical standards as well as the relevant legislation?).

Second, in addition to all the foregoing parameters and scenarios, manufacturers have to deal with information fed into the system by external systems (especially considering the Internet of Things revolution that is expected to connect "real-world objects" and the prospect that in the future algorithms will rely on parameters fed to them by other machines).[63]

Third, medicine, like other professional fields, changes constantly. Do we expect manufacturers to have their products updated daily with every new study, while immediately incorporating that study's findings into the robo-doctor's decision-making process? Who will decide which studies should be updated and which are not convincing enough, or are less relevant to the specific population treated by that robo-doctor? Having to account for such dynamic developments, the manufacturers' task in minimizing risk of error is undoubtedly far more difficult than in the case of "static" fields where products need not be subject to frequent updates.[64]

Fourth, medicine, like law and many other complex fields where judgment and discretion are significant, is not black and white. Different experts have different opinions and recommend different solutions under identical circumstances. How can manufacturers be expected to minimize the risk of certain scenarios by choosing a specific course of action, when the choice is not necessarily obvious? Lastly, even if raising the safety level despite the countless scenarios would be possible (and not prohibitively costly), manufacturers of thinking algorithms will still have a difficult time improving the rates of correct decisions of their systems from "high" to "very high" if they wish to keep the system efficient and user-friendly. For example, if the robo-doctor has to include in its decision-making process each and every possible medical condition, including extremely rare ones or implausible ones, it might not be able to be put to practical use. The extra time required for the information gathering and analysis process might make the process excessively long; make the system fail to respond in real time; make patients refuse to tell their medical history if the process is so slow; etc.[65]

---

[62] To take a simple example of a coffee machine: verifying that the temperature of the liquid produced by the machine is not too hot, verifying that even if operated by a child the machine could not cause electrocution, etc.

[63] See, e.g., A. Thierer, The Internet of Things and Wearable Technology: Addressing Privacy and Security Concerns without Derailing Innovation (2015) 21 *Rich. J. Law Technol.* 4–17.

[64] Complex as an autopilot system might be to design, for example, its manufacturers are not likely to encounter daily updates in the field of aviation (or meteorology, atmospheric science, etc.) that would require them to decide whether the new information is relevant to the design of the system.

[65] On the inherent trade-off between safety and efficiency in the field of robotics, see, e.g., C. Braz, A. Seffah, and D. M'Raihi, Designing a Trade-Off between Usability and Security: A Metrics Based Model, in C. Baranauskas, P. Palanque, J. Abascal, and S. D. Junqueira Barbosa (eds.), *Human–Computer Interaction – INTERACT* (Springer, 2007).

In sum, the factors affecting how much a manufacturer of a sophisticated system could indeed increase its safety are these: the size of the matrix of parameters the algorithm must consider before making a decision; the dynamic nature of the relevant professional knowledge; the lack of clear "right choices"; and the extent of trade-off between safety and efficiency. But these parameters are all very general, and deduced from an extreme example of a robo-doctor – a machine that wholly replaces one of the most complicated human professions. To try to concretize the parameters that affect manufacturers' ability to increase safety, hence to meet the first rationale of product liability, let us now analyze our set of delineated examples of radiation systems. The analysis centers on the level of *foreseeability* of the product's "actions," as well as how far the manufacturer is able to *control* said actions, and do so *efficiently* (assuming that the less a manufacturer is able to foresee and control the choices of its system, the less it will be able to raise the system's safety levels). To examine this, I will review separately the system's operation in each of the four OODA Loop stages.

THE OODA LOOP – GENERAL. We might not have thought about it this way, but even primitive automatic systems may be responsible for all four stages of the OODA Loop (provided they yield some sort of physical change). Even a simple drill, for example, "acquires information" about the fact that it has been turned on, and that the human operator has pressed the right button for the drill to start. It also analyzes the information and makes a decision based on it, in the primitive sense of considering that the start button was pushed, along with the fact that no safety lock mechanism was initiated, and then it "decides" to "go ahead" and drill, the drilling being the final OODA Loop stage of execution. But in such examples all three first stages of the process are injectively dictated to the system by its human operator, leaving full foreseeability and full control in the manufacturer's hands (unless a "bug" occurs, or a person deliberately uses the drill to harm another person, in which case the criminal law is implicated).

Thinking algorithms, however, replace humans precisely because not only can they outperform them in the final physical execution stage, they can also automatically access and collect vast amounts of information from various sources, of a magnitude that the human brain could not read in decades; they can analyze these enormous amounts of information that are beyond a human's grasp; and they can make complex decisions based on probabilities that a human cannot even weigh.

The Therac-25 machine, for instance, only acquired information that was 100 percent dictated to it by the operator (having turned the machine on, chosen a specific treatment mode, etc.). It analyzed whether it was in a position to start operating, based on pre-programming that injectively ordered it to do so when all conditions for beginning an operation mode were met, and then blindly "decided" to go ahead and administer treatment – again because it was programmed to do exactly that once all the required conditions were met. These steps, of course, constitute an algorithm. A new-generation radiation machine, however, would have more "freedom" or "independence" to conduct the first three stages of the OODA Loop, such that the manufacturer would no longer have full foreseeability or control over them. With regard to information acquisition, for example, it is possible that the system itself will decide which sources of data to harvest to improve its success rates (be they medical publications the manufacturer might not even be aware of, or random statistics on such matters as global warming that the system might suddenly find are correlated to radiation success rates). With regard to the analysis stage, too, the radiation machine itself might determine how much weight to attach to each piece of information it has collected, again based on correlations it itself has discovered through its self-learning process. Facing several courses of action ranked with different probabilities of success and different expected damage, the machine itself might decide which alternative to choose, or otherwise decide that its confidence in the preferred option was not high enough. Then, it will rather call a human for further instructions than decide to execute. Naturally, the more OODA Loop stages a system is capable of performing in a manner not fully dictated by the manufacturer, the less foreseeability the manufacturer has as to the final outcome of the process, and the less control it obtains over it, thus contributing to the difficulty of assigning liability in the case of damages.

Therefore, and before delving into each of these stages separately, our first parameter indicating that the system is a thinking algorithm that is less compatible with the first rationale of product liability (given that reduced levels of control and foreseeability would render it more difficult to improve safety, as explained above) is the number of OODA Loop stages the system performs in a manner not fully dictated by humans.

"OBSERVE" ("INFORMATION ACQUISITION"). As explained above, the information acquisition stage of Therac-25 was fully dictated by humans in the loop. A new-generation radiation machine, depending on its specifications, might raise several separate aspects of lack of foreseeability and control by the manufacturer at the information acquisition stage. Naturally, when the system trains on closed sets of databases fed to it by the manufacturer, and later continues to collect information from data provided to it exclusively by the manufacturer, the manufacturer maintains foreseeability and control over the information acquisition stage. However, better results might materialize if the system is free to decide on its own to add additional sources of information (for instance, additional medical journals, readers' blogs on radiation, etc.) as well as more types of information the system is "interested in" (for instance, when reviewing a patient's medical record, collecting information on less trivial types of information, such as the day of the week the patient was released from the hospital, etc.). In such cases, lack of foreseeability by the manufacturer is threefold. First, it cannot anticipate the *type of parameters* the system will choose to collect information on. Second, it cannot anticipate the *sources of information* the machine will harvest. Third, it cannot anticipate the *specific content* of the data collected, be it content related to external databases such as medical journals (where the more dynamic and routinely updated the database is, the less likely a manufacturer is to have foreseeability over its content) or the values of the specific medical parameters measured for each patient.

Foreseeability and control at the information acquisition stage, therefore, are reduced if the system can decide on its own what type of information to seek or which sources of information to cover, and the more dynamic its information sources are.

"ORIENT" ("INFORMATION ANALYSIS"). As with the stage of information acquisition, Therac-25 was not involved in information analysis: the analysis was done externally, by humans. The new-generation radiation system, on the other hand, has a significant role in the analysis stage, and as a result lowers the manufacturer's level of foreseeability and control over said stage. In more detail, the system's mere computational abilities, which enable it to weigh up the various complex parameters collected in the previous stage, do not impair the manufacturer's foreseeability or control. Even if the manufacturer cannot perform the computation tasks itself, the information analysis stage is perfectly foreseeable and controllable: the manufacturer is the factor that decides how much weight the system should give each parameter, and which collected pieces of data to disregard altogether. The manufacturer can decide, for instance, that a patient's age should only be considered when the patient is very young or old, or decide that much weight should be given to the fact that a patient has a history of prior tumors and the system will conduct its computational analysis accordingly. New-generation machines, however, are likely to be more than sophisticated calculators. Rather, the whole uniqueness of advanced systems is that they can learn for themselves, at much better success rates than humans, and determine how much weight to attach to each parameter based on prior experience. In such cases, it is the machine that will decide how far to consider a patient's medical history, her susceptibility to allergies, or a new controversial study published in a medical journal. The manufacturer's ability to increase control and foreseeability by setting boundaries is limited in the information analysis stage because it can do so mainly sporadically, and with regard to the weight to be given to certain parameters that the manufacturer knows in advance will be part of the system's analysis. Here, too, the more dynamic the database the system draws information from, the less able a manufacturer is to pre-instruct in a broad manner that certain weights be given to certain parameters.

"DECIDE" ("DECISION SELECTION"). Having attached different weights to the myriad parameters collected through the information acquisition process, and having analyzed it, a system also responsible for the third OODA Loop stage now has to make a decision based on said analysis. This stage involves more than might meet the eye, at least for thinking algorithms. Unlike a coffee machine, for instance, whose decision-making process is generally based on two deterministic options, "pour coffee" or "don't pour coffee," a thinking algorithm might face numerous alternatives, each based on probabilities and each accompanied by a certain level of confidence that indeed said alternative entails said probabilities. After analyzing the information it has acquired, a new-generation radiation machine, for example, might come up with dozens of potential treatment dosages, each entailing different probabilities of success and expected damage. The algorithm's ranking may, for instance, include an option whose success rates are 90 percent, entailing damages of "3,000" for the 10 percent of failure; an option successful 80 percent of the time, entailing damages of "1,000" in the 20 percent cases of failure; and a long list of alternative dosages of different success rates and expected damage. Not only that. Like a human physician, the algorithm cannot be 100 percent certain that said alternatives *indeed* reflect the probabilities and expected damages the algorithm assumes they do. The algorithm can, for example, determine that it is 95 percent confident that the first option indeed has a 90 percent probability of success and a potential of causing damages of "3,000," and is only 70 percent confident that the second option indeed reflects the rates indicated. Our decision-selection stage, therefore, involves some "tough" questions for an algorithm. First, does it give more weight to potential success rates or to potential damages? Second, how does confidence level affect the choice among the various options? Should the algorithm defer to a human whenever the rate of confidence of its preferred alternative is lower than a certain threshold? (Will the algorithm itself decide that it has to consult with a human, or will the threshold be predetermined by the manufacturer?)

A manufacturer's level of foreseeability and control naturally depends on how, or more precisely who, gets to decide these questions. With regard to the radiation machine, the manufacturer may decide, for example, to adopt a more careful approach, where a machine is not free to decide on an alternative whose expected damages are more than a negligible percentage, and that whenever its level of confidence is below a very high threshold it must "step back" and let a human decide. Such an approach, however, will naturally be at the expense of efficiency (as in many cases the machine will not be able automatically to complete the process, but will have to wait for a human to arrive and make her decision). Naturally, if the situation calls for instant treatment (for instance, in a system used in a trauma unit), having to wait for a person might cost lives. Also, if from the outset the system's success rates are higher than the human counterpart's, from a utilitarian point of view we would prefer the machine to make such decisions, not the humans involved[66] (leading, again, to greatly reduced extents of foreseeability and control by the manufacturer).

The more the system's response time is critical, and the wider the gap between a human's and a machine's success rates (in favor of the machine), the more likely it is that the manufacturer will be forced to forego foreseeability and control at the decision-making stage, and "free" the system to make its own choices.

"ACT" ("ACTION IMPLEMENTATION"). Our radiation system has never replaced humans in the final OODA Loop stage of action implementation, because the projection of the beams was never a process that a human performed. To touch on the stage of action implementation, let us therefore think of a robo-surgeon (for instance, the da Vinci system),[67] and focus solely on its execution rather than the decision-making process of how to execute. With regard to said specific stage, there is no learning element. Just like a traditional product, therefore, the system is foreseeable and controllable as long as it does not encounter "bugs."

INTERIM SUMMARY AND MEASURABILITY OF SUCCESS RATES. An analysis of the four stages of the OODA Loop and the levels of foreseeability and control associated with each in respect of our example of learning system versus a traditional product revealed that the following parameters tend to reduce the system's compatibility with the rationale of encouraging manufacturers to promote safety: the greater number of the OODA Loop stages the system is responsible for; a system's freedom to decide which sources to draw data from; a system's freedom to decide which parameters to consider; the dynamic nature of the information sources relevant in the field of the system; whether the system is life-saving (such that reduction of efficiency to increase foreseeability is very problematic); and whether the system's success rates are already higher than those of a human equivalent (which again would render sacrificing efficiency to promote foreseeability more problematic).

Naturally, this is a rather initial list of parameters, and additional examples might yield additional ones. But it does give us a notion of the type of systems that should be classified as thinking algorithms, in the sense that improvement of their safety by the manufacturer is more difficult or problematic to accomplish.

Minimizing the Chilling Effect

It has been argued that in certain industries, the application of product liability not only failed to achieve an increase in safety, but led to higher production prices resulting in a suboptimal level of manufacturing or use of beneficial technologies.[68] Although the avoidance of a chilling effect and the promotion of an efficient level of use are not one of the main rationales behind product liability, the shaping of the product liability framework was

---

[66]   Millar and Kerr, above note 18; Lieblich and Benvenisti, above note 28.

[67]   See www.davincisurgery.com.

[68]   M. Polinsky and S. Shavell, The Uneasy Case for Product Liability (2010) 123 *Harv. Law Rev.* 1437, 1440.

significantly affected by said interests. The analysis will therefore include said interest and examine how different parameters of sophisticated systems affect concern over a chilling effect.

Naturally, the less foreseeable and controllable a system is, the greater is the fear of a detrimental effect on technology. First, and as discussed above, lack of foreseeability may render it more difficult for a manufacturer to improve safety, at least for a sub-set of the innumerable scenarios possible. In such cases, product liability will not necessarily contribute much to safety, but will likely result in higher production costs which will translate into reduced manufacturing of certain systems due to less demand. Moreover, lack of foreseeability is likely to render liability costs less predictable, and in turn again delay development or result in high costs.[69] Second, also as discussed above, naturally the better result a system has compared with a human equivalent, and the speedier its response, the more decisions we will be likely to entrust it with, leaving humans "outside the loop."[70] So for systems whose results show superiority over humans, fear of a chilling effect (in the form of decreased development, decreased demand due to high price, or reduced efficiency resulting from "clumsy" safety measures that render the system too slow or non-user-friendly) is of greater concern.

Ensuring Compensation for Victims

Generally, product liability has been criticized for not being an optimal regime with regard to compensating victims for their damages, given the high costs associated with product liability litigation that render many damage cases unactionable[71] and lead to significantly reduced compensation for the victim in cases that are filed due to legal fees.[72] How is victims' compensation affected by the characteristics of the damaging product? Unlike the case with the first product liability rationale of promoting safety, the particular abilities of each algorithm will likely not play a crucial part in affecting victims' ability for redress, although some more general characteristics will.

First, in many cases, insurance of various types may render product liability redundant, as damages claims of insured victims might be covered in full by insurance, which eliminates the need for litigation.[73] The less foreseeable a system is, however, the less willing insurance companies are likely to be to offer insurance at reasonable premiums.[74]

Second, in the absence of full coverage insurance, another major consideration affecting victims' ability to receive compensation is whether an attorney will agree to take their case. Under the contingency fees structure typical of product liability, that likelihood is affected by the attorney's estimation of the probability and magnitude of success, but also of the expected costs.[75] The longer the procedure is expected to last, for instance, due to its technical complexity and the need to hear more expert witnesses, the less likely attorneys will be to take a risk and accept a product liability case.[76]

---

[69] B. W. Smith, Automated Driving and Product Liability (2017) *Mich. St. Law Rev.* 1.

[70] Abbott, above note 9; Millar and Kerr, above note 18.

[71] Given that the expected litigation costs exceed the expected reward for the damage suffered by the product, for instance, in car accidents where no significant physical injury was caused. P. Hubbard, "Sophisticated Robots": Balancing Liability, Regulation and Innovation (2014) 66 *Fla. Law Rev.* 1826–7; Gurney, above note 53.

[72] Polinsky and Shavell, above note 68 (reviewing empirical studies that found plaintiffs receive only 0.37– 0.6 percent of the amount paid by defendants).

[73] Polinsky and Shavell, *ibid.*

[74] Hubbard, above note 71.

[75] Smith, above note 69, pp. 37–40.

[76] *Ibid.*; Gurney, above note 53, pp. 265–6; Hubbard, above note 71, pp. 1826–8.

The number of experts needed, hence the complexity, duration, and cost of procedures, will probably depend on the system's field of operation, and whether or not it replaces human professional judgment. In fields that involve complex professional discretion, such as medicine, engineering, or law, it is likely that in addition to a code expert testifying on the availability of technical programming measures, a professional expert in the underlying field (physician, engineer, lawyer, etc.) would also be required to discuss whether such measures were available and accessible in the field of expertise. It could be argued, therefore, that systems that replace human professional judgment are more likely to be associated with longer and more expensive procedures and thus fulfill to a lesser extent the rationale of compensating the victims, as many of the underlying cases will be too expensive to litigate.

Is It More Simple than Using Autonomy as a Classifier?

Having analyzed different features affecting systems' compatibility with the rationales behind product liability laws, the chapter discovered numerous such features that ought to be considered when deciding whether the system is a traditional product or whether a different legal framework should apply to it. Not only is the list of said features relatively long (and open to additional input), its application in practice is not entirely simple, given, for instance, that certain features might entail more than one effect,[77] or that the effect depends on additional parameters. As can be seen from Figures 22.1 and 22.2, however, using the method discussed in this chapter as a classifier between traditional products and thinking algorithms is nevertheless much more easy and simple than using a system's autonomy level as a distinguishing method between the two.

First, while using autonomy as a classifier requires the user to answer different types of questions, many of which are open-ended, and independently decide how to factor in all of her general estimations for these questions, a purposive analysis classifier simply and clearly requires adding a "+" sign whenever a predefined feature exists. Second, while the outcome received as a result of the former classification process is a general impression of the system's level of autonomy – without practical guidelines as to how to apply it (especially in cases where the result is not definite), the latter classification process yields a clear outcome of the number of "+" signs the system has accumulated. Lastly, said outcome has a practical implication, as it doesn't merely reflect the system's theoretical characteristics, but rather indicates how well the system reconciles with the purposes of the product liability framework.

To demonstrate the relative simplicity of the proposed classifier, as well as its de facto value, let us examine Table 22.1 comparing between different types of systems based on this chapter's proposed purposive analysis: Roomba vacuum robots, autopilots, autonomous vehicles, and a futuristic "robo-doctor" which replaces all functions of a human physician. The analysis used to decide which systems deserve which "sign" in each category is certainly not exhaustive and not conclusive; for instance, because different types of autopilots may possess very different sets of features and thus render the analysis different for each type. It does, however, demonstrate how the features listed in the first column could indeed be used to differentiate different types of systems, in a way relevant to the application of product liability rules.

---

[77] For instance, when looking at the feature of "lack of foreseeability and control" as a whole, said feature is not compatible with the rationale of promoting safety (as it might render improvement of safety excessively difficult, costly, or inefficient), but might be compatible with the rationale of compensating victims (given that insurance companies would be less willing to insure, thus rendering product liability more needed as an alternative).

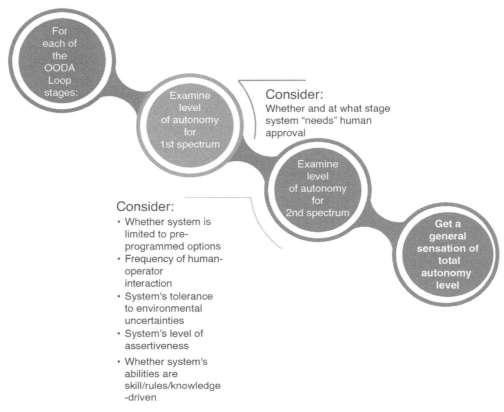

FIGURE 22.1 Autonomy level as a classifier for thinking algorithms

Responsible for More than Two OODA Loop Stages?

As explained above, when analyzing which OODA Loop stages a system is "responsible" for, the focus is stages where the system's choices are not injectively dictated. A Roomba cleaner's sensors collect predetermined information on its environment (the existence of dirt on the floor; the existence of obstacles in its path, etc.) and analyze the information collected in a predetermined manner (if the robot touches an object, this means an obstacle was encountered, etc.). While there is a feature of randomness to the Roomba cleaner's decisions, which leads to execution that is not entirely predetermined (the system is designed to randomly try new angles of movement, to increase the chances of overcoming),[78] the system is not "responsible" for more than two OODA Loop stages. A similar analysis applies to autopilots as well, which collect predetermined types of information (altitude, wind velocity, etc.) and conduct an analysis of the information gathered in a predetermined manner (calculation of the optimal parameters such as angles and speed needed for the air vessel to stay on course or to land). Unlike airplanes traveling through almost empty skies, in terms of potential obstacles autonomous vehicles must respond to numerous (and often) unexpected obstacles as part of their routine task. The information that the system gathers is therefore not entirely injectively predetermined (as the cameras and sensors the vehicle is equipped with

---

[78]   J. A. Kroll, J. Huey, S. Barocas, *et al.*, Accountable Algorithms (2017) 165 *Univ. Pa. Law Rev.* 633, 655.

TABLE 22.1 *Features characterizing thinking algorithms*

	Roomba robot	Autopilot	Autonomous vehicle	Robo-doctor
Responsible for more than two OODA Loop stages?			+	+
Independently selects type of info to collect?			?	+
Independently selects sources of info to collect from?				+
Dynamic nature of sources of info?				+
Replaces professionals in complex fields?		?	?	+
Life and death nature of decisions?		+	+	+
Real-time decisions required?		+	+	?

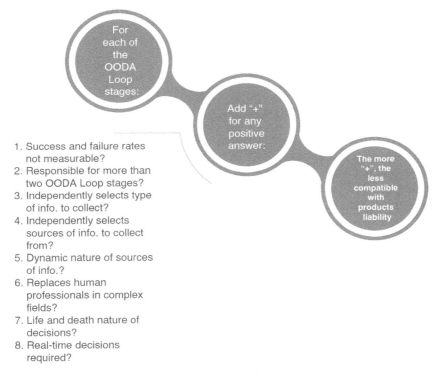

1. Success and failure rates not measurable?
2. Responsible for more than two OODA Loop stages?
3. Independently selects type of info. to collect?
4. Independently selects sources of info. to collect from?
5. Dynamic nature of sources of info.?
6. Replaces human professionals in complex fields?
7. Life and death nature of decisions?
8. Real-time decisions required?

FIGURE 22.2 Purposive interpretation as a classifier for thinking algorithms

might encounter new types of terrain, road conditions, or obstacles that the manufacturers did not foresee). The analysis of the information gathered, too, is not predetermined such that it is based on mere calculations, but rather is conducted through more human-like trial and error self-learning processes.[79] When "deciding" how to drive next, an autonomous vehicle does not have a "bottom line" calculation indicating precisely the right angle for landing or the

79 L. Blain, AI Algorithm Teaches a Car to Drive from Scratch in 20 Minutes, *Automotive* (July 6, 2018), https://newatlas.com/wayve-autonomous-car-machine-learning-learn-drive/55340/.

right speed for preserving altitude. An autonomous vehicle, therefore, seems to be responsible for more than two OODA Loop stages and thus gains a "+" sign under that category. A robo-doctor system, too, would likely receive a "+" sign, based on its likely ability to collect information from various sources based on its own consideration; to analyze the information gathered based on its self-learning and not injectively predetermined abilities; its decision how to act upon the analyses which will reflect a choice between stochastic alternatives based on its level of confidence in the results (as explained in detail above).

Independently Selects Type of Information to Collect?

As discussed above, the type of information gathered by Roomba cleaners and autopilots is limited to the type of information they were programmed to collect: predetermined parameters concerning their environment. An autonomous vehicle, however, as explained above, ought to respond to scenarios where it encounters new types of information it was not instructed to collect. While the sources of information from which the system collects data are indeed predetermined (the vehicle's environment), the type of information is not necessarily so. With regard to a robo-doctor system, such a system will likely independently choose the type of information it collects (such as a patient's medical history, her current complaints, environmental parameters, etc.), as explained above.

Independently Selects Sources of Information to Collect from?

As discussed above, a robo-doctor might indeed be very independent in choosing which sources to collect information from, while a Roomba cleaner as well as an autopilot would only collect environmental information on their surroundings, which their manufacturers programmed them to collect. Unless given access to journals and articles focusing on automotives or physics, for example, an autonomous vehicle also seems to be limited to sources of information dictated to it by its programmer (unlike the *type* of information it may encounter).

Dynamic Nature of Sources of Information?

Roomba cleaners, autopilots, and autonomous vehicles all acquire information from their environment, which is characterized by a certain degree of being dynamic. The need for an ever-updating system, however, which adversely affects manufacturers' ability to minimize risk as discussed above, is more prevalent in the robo-doctor system, as a result of the need to take into account new studies and findings that might affect the entire conclusion-reaching process of the system.

Replaces Professionals in Complex Fields?

As discussed above, litigation over damage caused by systems that replace professional discretion are expected to be longer and more expensive, because of the likely need for additional experts in the underlying professional field. This, in turn, would decrease the chances of such cases being brought to court and impede the victims' compensation rationale. Although it cannot be anticipated in advance which experts the litigation attorneys would think are necessary to conduct the case, it might be safe to assume that the need for a professional expert (in addition to a programming expert) would be more likely evident in the case of a robo-doctor than in the case of a robot cleaner. As to autopilots and driverless vehicles that are "somewhere in the middle," the function of autopilots is much less commonly known to the public than the action of driving, familiar to millions.[80] As a result, it is plausible to imagine that accidents involving autopilots would require a longer, more costly technical presentation to the court.

Life and Death Nature of Decisions?

Other than the Roomba cleaner, all three other systems entail a significant risk to humans' lives (as a result of an accident or as a result of administrating non-effective or dangerous treatment). The desire to produce the maximal benefit out of these three types of systems, therefore, might come at the expense of allowing manufacturers to better foresee and control their results, as explained above. The rationale of safety promotion would therefore be more difficult to achieve for the three latter types of systems.

Real-Time Decisions Required?

As discussed, when real-time decisions are required, manufacturers' flexibility to dictate human intervention (above a certain threshold of risk, below a certain threshold of certainty, etc.) is undermined, and as a result so is the ability to achieve safety promotion. To operate smoothly, a Roomba cleaner does need to decide and act continuously. Given the nature of its decisions and their lack of urgency, a manufacturer is free to require human intervention in any scenario that has the potential to cause damage. Autopilots and autonomous vehicles, however, do not enjoy such flexibility. As to robo-doctors, the need for urgent real-time decisions is case-sensitive, as an ER treatment process is very different in that respect to an annual routine check-up (the latter allowing the system to call for a human decision-maker whenever a damaging scenario is possible). Robo-doctors therefore receive a question mark under that category.

Having demonstrated how the different features of Roomba cleaners, autopilots, autonomous vehicles, and robo-doctors render them more easily or more problematically compatible with the rationales of product liability, we see how such classifier is relatively simple and quick to use. Granted, the details of the above analyses may vary, thus leading to somewhat different results. In addition, the analysis above does not conclusively tell us which products ought to be subject to product liability and which ought not. It does, however, give us a simple and clear indicator, where the fewer "+" symbols there are, the more the system can continue to be subject to the traditional product liability framework.

CONCLUSIONS

Focusing on the legal framework of product liability, this chapter offered a novel method for determining when damages caused by "sophisticated" algorithms may continue to be subject to traditional product liability laws, and when an alternative treatment is warranted.

---

[80] For the number of licensed drivers in America, see: www.statista.com/statistics/198029/total-number-of-us-licensed-drivers-by-state/.

Naturally, preferring a certain alternative legal framework over product liability depends on the characteristics, advantages, and disadvantages of such a framework (including, of course, the question of whether or not manufacturers would still be liable for the damage caused). Proposals for such substitutional options have been discussed for decades,[81] focusing on aspects of determining liability, as well as how and by whom damages will be paid.[82]

A comparison of these different approaches, as well as an assessment of them compared to product liability, are beyond the scope of this chapter. Given the increasing calls to stop treating "sophisticated" or "autonomous" systems as mere products and subjecting them to a legal framework other than product liability, the focus of this chapter was to examine why the current classifier between traditional products and systems warranting a new legal framework is insufficient. The chapter then proposed a different approach for distinguishing products from non-products for the purpose of applying product liability, focusing on the rationales behind the product liability framework and whether different features of "sophisticated" systems are compatible with them or hinder them.

Decision-makers and scholars encountering a system whose parameters heavily indicate one direction or another could therefore use the proposed analysis to determine whether to apply product liability or to adopt or develop alternative frameworks.

---

[81] See, e.g., S. N. Lehman-Wilzig, Frankenstein Unbound: Towards a Legal Definition of Artificial Intelligence (1981) 13 *Futures* 442, 451–2.

[82] See, e.g., L. Wein, The Responsibility of Intelligent Artifacts: Toward an Automated Jurisprudence (1992) 6 *Harv. J. Law Technol.* 103; S. Chopra and L. F. White, *A Legal Theory for Autonomous Artificial Agents* (University of Michigan Press, 2011); R. Kelley, E. Schaerer, M. Gomez, and M. Nicolescu, Liability in Robotics: an International Perspective on Robots as Animals (2010) 24 *Adv. Robot.* 13; S. Duffy and J. P. Hopkins, Sit, Stay, Drive: The Future of Autonomous Car Liability (2013) 16 *SMU Sci. Technol. Law. Rev.* 101; Abbott, above note 9; Chagal-Feferkorn, above note 9.

23

Tort Law

Applying A "Reasonableness" Standard to Algorithms

Karni Chagal-Feferkorn*

BACKGROUND

As technology continues to advance and specifically as algorithms proliferate into society, the law is increasingly confronted with the task of determining who is responsible when property is damaged or people are harmed. From a historical perspective, the Industrial Revolution resulted in machines that were able to automate tasks that were previously performed manually by humans. However, despite the superiority of these early automated machines, their use could cause physical damage; due to, for example, machine malfunctioning, poor machine design, or misuse by their users. The legal framework traditionally applied to machine-induced damages is comprised of two doctrines: that of general negligence and that of product liability.[1] In this chapter, with algorithmic-based entities, the focus is primarily on the reasonable person standard for actors.

Under the theory of negligence, liability is established when four elements are met: the existence of a duty of care; a breach of that duty; causation between the breach of duty of care and the damage; and the existence of damage. A person is said to have breached her duty of care if she did not adhere to the standard of reasonable care when carrying out actions that might foreseeably harm others.[2] In the background of a tort doctrine that was developed in an age where humans predominantly performed the manual work, to determine whether or not "reasonable care" was demonstrated, courts resorted to the "reasonable person" standard. The reasonable person standard asks what a reasonable person would have done under similar circumstances and possessing the same state of knowledge.[3]

Under product liability, the seller or manufacturer of a defective product in a condition that is unreasonably dangerous is liable for the physical harms caused to the user or her property, even when there is no contractual relationship between them.[4] For more information on this topic, see Chapter 22 in this volume, which addresses, inter alia, the question of whether an algorithm is a product.[5] For product liability law, to establish the existence of

---

* This chapter is based on The Reasonable Algorithm (2018) 1 *Univ. Ill. J. Law Technol. Policy* 111. I would like to dedicate this chapter to my mentor Professor Niva Elkin-Koren.

[1] D. G. Gifford, Technological Triggers to Tort Revolutions: Steam Locomotives, Autonomous Vehicles, and Accident Compensation (2018) 11 *J. Tort Law* 71, 117–18. For an overview of product liability history, see generally J. Stapleton, *Product Liability* (Butterworths, 1994), pp. 9–29.

[2] Restatement (Third) Of Torts: Liability for Physical Harm § 3 (PFD No. 1, 2005); B. C. Zipursky, Foreseeability in Breach, Duty and Proximate Cause (2009) 55 *Wake Forest Law Rev.* 1247.

[3] A. D. Miller and R. Perry, The Reasonable Person (2012) 87 NY *Univ. Law Rev.* 45.

[4] Restatement (Second) of Torts § 402A (1965).

[5] K. Chagal-Feferkorn, When Do Algorithmic Tortfeasors that Caused Damage Warrant Unique Legal Treatment?, in W. Barfield (ed.), *Cambridge Handbook on the Law of Algorithms* (Cambridge University Press, 2020).

a defect, a victim must show either that the product was defectively manufactured or designed, or that it was not accompanied by sufficient warnings.[6]

The two tort legal frameworks described above on negligence and product liability continued to apply to damage caused by automated systems even as these systems became increasingly sophisticated and began assisting humans in more complex tasks. Lawsuits pertaining to accidents involving an autopilot, for example, tend to raise product liability claims against the manufacturer of the autopilot, as well as negligence claims against the pilots or the airline who operated the system.[7] Similar practices exist with regard to automated medical systems that caused damage.[8]

Recent technological advancements, however, have led to many questions on whether the traditional tools for addressing machine-induced damages are still appropriate given that algorithmic-driven systems are becoming more "autonomous" or "independent," resulting in actions less foreseeable. Such systems, which will be referred to as "thinking algorithms" (because their algorithms model various stages of human thinking, and do so independently of a human), seem to be replacing human beings in almost all aspects of life. Fields where thinking algorithms are likely to occasionally cause physical damage are the field of medicine, where physicians rely increasingly on algorithms in order to diagnose and select optimal treatments,[9] and the field of transportation where human drivers are expected to gradually be replaced by driverless vehicles.

Applying traditional negligence and product liability regimes to thinking algorithms is, according to many, problematic. Both doctrines are focused on the actions of vicarious entities, such as the manufacturers of the system or its user, and not on the actions of the system itself. While this was a sensible approach when the damaging systems were mere "tools" in the hands of their creators and users, this is not necessarily the case with regard to thinking algorithms, which are becoming increasingly similar in performance to human beings. Due to the capabilities of algorithms, similarities include the functions they fulfil, their human-like skills (such as understanding written and spoken text, communicating with people, drawing conclusions based on past experience) and their ability to confront changing environments and successfully "act," even in the face of unexpected circumstances that the system was not pre-programmed to handle.

---

[6] In more detail, *manufacture defect* occurs when the product was not properly manufactured (e.g. due to departure from the product's assembly specifications or use of non-appropriate materials). Under the laws of most states, manufacture defects expose sellers to strict liability, which does not require proof of any negligence by the seller to be found liable, as long as the existence of a defect is proved. As suggested by its title, a *design defect* is a flaw in the design of the product itself, regardless of how it is manufactured. The majority of states follow the "risk utility test," according to which a design defect occurs when foreseeable risks associated with the product could have been minimized by using a feasible safer alternative. *Failure to warn* occurs when manufacturers do not adequately warn consumers of the existence of hidden dangers, as well as instructing them on the safe usage of the product. Restatement (Third) of Torts § 2(a) (1998); Gifford, above note 1.

[7] See, e.g., the 2013 Asiana-Air crash in San Francisco, where the underlying legal actions consisted of product liability claims raised against Boeing, the manufacturer of the auto-throttle that allegedly failed, as well as negligence claims raised against the airline itself. See M. Hamilton, Asiana Crash: 72 Passengers Settle Lawsuits against Airline, *Los Angeles Times* (March 3, 2013), www.latimes.com/local/lanow/la-me-ln-asiana-airlines-settle-lawsuits-20150303-story.html.

[8] The notorious "Therac-25 case," where a radiation therapy machine administered over-dosage of radiation that led to the death of several patients, has also alleged product liability claims before the case was settled.

[9] See, e.g., A. Frakt, Your New Medical Team: Algorithms and Physicians, The Upshot, *The Upshot, New York Times* (December 7, 2015), www.nytimes.com/2015/12/08/upshot/your-new-medical-team-algorithms-and-physicians.html; V. Khosla, Technology Will Replace 80% of What Doctors Do, *Fortune Magazine* (December 4, 2012).

Indeed, based on the new nature of thinking algorithms and their deviation from older types of systems, the European Parliament has issued a draft report explaining that ordinary rules on liability are insufficient for autonomous robots, since they can no longer be considered tools in the hands of other actors.[10] Thus, for autonomous robots, scholars have advanced alternatives to product liability laws – for instance, in the form of no fault insurance schemes.[11] Others, however, proposed to focus on the actions of the system itself and, based on the findings, determine whether liability applies to the relevant legal entities (such as the manufacturer or user). In that context, analogies have been made between the responsibility of manufacturers or users to the actions of the thinking algorithm and the responsibility of a principal to the actions of its agent (or employee to the actions of its employer).[12] But *how* will it be determined, de facto, whether the actions of a thinking algorithm are indeed such that they warrant the application of liability?

As mentioned above, when determining the liability of a human tortfeasor for her action, the negligence analysis is based on the reasonableness of the actions. Given the growing similarities between humans and thinking algorithms (which control effectors and actuators that can lead to physical harm[13]) and the fact that they will be "used" or "employed" interchangeably in the future, a possible solution in determining liability is to apply a reasonableness analysis on the actions of thinking algorithms, just as this analysis applies to human tortfeasors. Naturally, the *content* of reasonableness would differ between humans and algorithms (given their comparative advantages and disadvantages). But this is true with regard to the reasonableness analysis applied to humans too. For example, with regard to professionals, those acting within the scope of their profession would generally be subject to the elevated standard of "the reasonable professional" rather than that of the "reasonable person."[14]

This chapter, therefore, will discuss the general concept of treating human and thinking algorithm tortfeasors alike and the validity of applying a reasonableness standard to the actions of both.

---

[10] 2015/2103 (INL) European Parliament Draft Report on Civil Law Rules on Robotics (May, 2016), Section S. The report suggested granting autonomous robots an independent legal status of "electronic persons," which might even allow these robots themselves to pay damages for the harm they cause – for instance, through a compulsory insurance scheme developed for specific categories of robots.

[11] See, e.g., K. S. Abraham and R. Rabin, Automated Vehicles and Manufacturer Responsibility for Accidents: A New Legal Regime for a New Era (2019) 105 *Va. Law Rev.* 127; A. Davola, A Model for Tort Liability in a World of Driverless Cars: Establishing a Framework for the Upcoming Technology (2018) 54 *Idaho Law Rev.* 591.

[12] See, e.g., S. N. Lehman-Wilzig, Frankenstein Unbound: Towards a Legal Definition of Artificial Intelligence (1981) 13 *Futures* 442, 451–2; S. Chopra and L. F. White, *A Legal Theory for Autonomous Artificial Agents* (University of Michigan Press, 2011), pp. 5–28; P. M. Asaro, A Body to Kick, But Still No Soul to Damn: Legal Perspectives on Robotics, in P. Lin, K. Abney, and G. A. Bekey (eds.), *Robot Ethics: The Ethical and Social Implications of Robotics* (MIT Press, 2012), pp. 169, 178–80.

[13] Effectors include such things as legs, wheels, arms, fingers, wings, and fins. Controllers cause the effectors to produce desired effects on the environment. An actuator is the actual mechanism that enables the effector to execute an action. Actuators typically include electric motors, hydraulic or pneumatic cylinders, etc.

[14] "[T]he standard of the reasonable man requires only a minimum of attention, perception, memory, knowledge, intelligence and judgment in order to recognize the existence of the risk. If the actor has in fact more than the minimum of these qualities, he is required to exercise the superior qualities he has ... The standard becomes, in other words, that of a reasonable man with such superior attributes" (Restatement (Second) of Torts § 289 (1965) comment). In fact, the higher the degree of professionalism characterizing the tortfeasor, the higher the standard of reasonableness she must adhere to (Restatement (Second) of Torts § 299A (1965)).

WHY APPLY A REASONABLENESS STANDARD TO THINKING ALGORITHMS?

Applying completely different tort frameworks to humans and thinking algorithms that perform the same actions and cause the same harm would likely result in certain anomalies and inconsistencies in judicial decisions. A preliminary comment before addressing those anomalies is that the specific expectations we would have from the "reasonable algorithm" might very well differ from the expectations of a "reasonable person" or "reasonable professional." Intuitively, thinking algorithms may be perceived as superior to human decision-makers[15] and thus as warranting an elevated level of reasonableness,[16] although a more complex or multi-layered standard could be adopted.[17] Some of the following arguments therefore depend on the exact content poured into the reasonable algorithm standard, and on the size of the gap between that content and the content applying in the context of human actions. For example, if a "reasonable algorithm" standard for a futuristic robo-doctor would be based on the assumption that robo-doctors ought to find the optimal solution under all circumstances and that their infliction of damage would only be deemed reasonable if no other alternative existed, then this standard would be substantially different from the one currently applied to human physicians (based, mainly, on the "relative community" of practitioners and how they would have acted under the same circumstances).[18] Many of the anomalies that would now be described would continue to be invoked if the "reasonable algorithm" standard is substantially different from the reasonableness expected of a human. If, however, both are similarly shaped, then the following anomalies would exist to a much lesser extent. As the content poured into the "reasonable algorithm" standard might vary, the discussion will assume that it would be shaped such that it would result in much greater similarities in legal doctrine than when humans are subject to one framework, while thinking algorithms are subject to a completely different one.

Inequity among Victims

Differential treatment of victims injured by a person or by a thinking algorithm raises important challenges, as it pertains to one of the core rationales of tort law: victims' compensation. Applying a different legal system to different tortfeasors exposes victims to lower payouts and a higher risk in comparison to other similar victims.

For example, imagine pedestrian A crossing the road at a certain point and getting hit by a car. Under a negligence cause of action, pedestrian A would file a suit against the driver, and be awarded compensation if the driver had acted unreasonably. Now imagine pedestrian B, A's twin, who gets hit at the same place under the same circumstances, and suffering the same damage, except the hitter was a driverless car controlled by algorithms. The type of legal action B would have to pursue, in its complexity, costs, effort, and time required, and chances of receiving compensation and its amount, would likely be entirely different from those

---

[15] N. G. Packin, Consumer Finance and AI: The Death of Second Opinions? (2020) 22 NY Univ. J. Legislation Public Policy 101.

[16] J. K. Gurney, Imputing Driverhood: Applying a Reasonable Driver Standard to Accidents Caused by Autonomous Vehicles, Robot Ethics 2.0 (2016); D. Vladeck, Machines without Principals: Liability Rules and Artificial Intelligence (2014) 89 Wash. Law Rev. 117.

[17] For a proposed "reasonable algorithm" standard that could be applied in practice, see K. Chagal-Feferkorn, How Can I Tell If My Algorithm Was Reasonable? Mich. Telecommun. Technol. Law Rev. (forthcoming).

[18] M. Froomkin, I. R. Kerr, and J. Pineau, When AIs Outperform Doctors: Confronting the Challenges of a Tort-Induced Over-Reliance on Machine Learning (2019) 61 Ariz. Law Rev. 33.

associated with A's legal redress – this is especially so if the legal framework applying to the damage(s) caused by driverless cars differed from that of negligence of the hitter.

Furthermore, if, for example, damages caused by the driverless car were subject to strict liability under product liability rules, then B would have to show that the vehicle was defective, without addressing questions of culpability by any party.[19] Pedestrian A, on the other hand, would need to show that a human driver acted unreasonably – a burden of proof that focuses on completely different issues from those concerned if the car was uniformly under the control of algorithms, and would likely entail different legal costs and probabilities of success.[20]

Treating victims in the same class differently may infringe upon notions of horizontal equity. Under this principle, like cases should be treated alike.[21] In other words, justice requires that victims should be treated similarly by the legal system, regardless of the identity of their injurer. Allowing one victim to recover quickly and easily while subjecting another victim of similar damage to a lengthy, costly, and uncertain procedure interferes with this ideal.

Granted, horizontal equity is more of a judicial ideal than a practical standard, with or without the involvement of thinking algorithms; sheer luck and circumstantial reasons frequently have a crucial effect on victims' redress. Pedestrian C, for example, might be hit by a very wealthy driver and be offered an immediate compensation sufficient to cover for her damages and more. Pedestrian D, on the other hand, might suffer the exact same injury under equal circumstances, but spend months in legal proceedings against the driver who hit her, only to discover in the end that the driver's resources are insufficient for any compensation.[22] It would be D's misfortune to have been hit by a driver lacking resources and not a more affluent one, such that a different outcome is realized compared to pedestrian C.[23] In addition, even when both drivers are capable of compensating the victim, horizontal equity is rarely implemented in full: the difference between judicial instances, between the capabilities of the attorneys involved and between states' laws, will often lead to deviations from a truly equal treatment of similar cases.[24] The difference in tort frameworks applying to human versus non-human decision-makers, however, presents horizontal inequity at its most crystalized form: even if both tortfeasors have sufficient resources to compensate the victims, and even if the cases were judged at the same instance by the same judges and were argued by the same lawyers, the inherent differences between the reasonableness standard that would apply to the human driver and the wholly different tort framework that might apply to the driverless car would render the two cases, their costs and their outcomes, very different.

[19] Restatement (Second) of Torts § 402A (1965); J. C. P. Goldberg and B. C. Zipursky, *The Oxford Introductions to U.S. Law: Torts, in The Oxford Introductions to U.S. Law* (Oxford University Press, 2010).

[20] See discussion below on the differences between the legal question raised under each of these frameworks.

[21] J. W. Doherty, R. T. Reville, and L. Zakaras, *Confidentiality, Transparency, and the U.S. Civil Justice System* (Oxford University Press, 2012), pp. 1, 119–24.

[22] For a discussion on the different ways in which luck affects tort law, see, e.g., J. C. P. Goldberg and B. C. Zipursky, Tort Law and Moral Luck (2007) 92 *Cornell Law Rev.* 92.

[23] Naturally, a similar anomaly might be raised regardless of the standard applied to thinking algorithm tortfeasors, assuming that unreasonableness on the behalf of the algorithm would result in the algorithm's manufacturer (a deep pocket) paying for the damages (see Table 23.1 for further discussion on the possible implications of a finding that a thinking algorithm acted unreasonably). As opposed to pedestrians being hit by an autonomous vehicle, pedestrians hit by a human driver will not necessarily have the fortune of having a "deep pocket" to recuperate from. While there could be ways to avoid such an anomaly (for instance, no fault insurance schemes), an application of a similar reasonableness standard would be able to at least resolve the anomaly in the stage of determining liability.

[24] S. D. Sugerman, A Comparative Law Look on at Pain and Suffering Awards (2005) 55 *DePaul Law Rev.* 399, 413.

Additionally, while deviations in treatment stemming from misfortune or unequal circumstances are a matter of pragmatic necessity, applying a different legal framework on similar victims is a deliberate choice to subject them to the arbitrariness of sheer luck. Although said choice might be justified due to policy considerations, on its own the lack of equal treatment of equal victims is infringing upon principles of fairness. Applying a reasonableness standard to damages caused by thinking algorithms (depending, of course, on the specific "reasonableness" test developed for algorithms and how similar they were to those for a person) would generally create more unity in the type of procedure and burden of proof that a victim must meet, and in the expected costs and outcomes, and increase the horizontal equity among victims.

Procedural Inefficiency

A different type of anomaly is invoked when a human and a thinking algorithm act jointly when causing the harm. Imagine, for example, a patient rushed into the Emergency Room, where two physicians jointly decided to operate on her and jointly performed surgery, which resulted in severe damage and in hindsight was not necessary in the first place.

Assume also that one of the two physicians was a thinking algorithm rather than a human, and thus not subject to the reasonableness standard. Naturally, the patient's legal proceeding against the two tortfeasors would become much more complex than in the case where both tortfeasors were subject to a similar tort framework.

Indeed, it is not uncommon that a single legal action invokes several causes of action governed by different legal frameworks.[25] When one of the joint tortfeasors is a not a person, however, the lack of a unified framework might increase the time and costs associated with the legal proceedings many fold. This is because the different causes of action against the human tortfeasor (subject to the negligence standard) versus the thinking algorithm wrongdoer (subject to a different legal framework) would raise different legal questions, but would also probably require a very dissimilar set of arguments, evidence, and expert opinions. For example, if the victim invokes a claim of a "design defect" under product liability[26] against the algorithmic doctor, this would require that she shows that a feasible safer alternative design of the algorithm could have been used or, in certain states, that the risk posed by the product exceeds the expectations of an ordinary consumer.[27]

Although the former test focuses on the thinking algorithm itself (whether or not it could have been safer), the analysis would be very different from an analysis of the reasonableness of the tortfeasor's decision: a design defect claim would require the victim to delve into the algorithm's overall structure in order to understand how it operated under different circumstances and why, including finding alternatives that could have been used in each of the phases of the algorithm's learning process, in order to show that a safer alternative existed. This contrasts with the claim against the human physician, which would focus only on the

---

[25] See, e.g., the discussion of aviation accidents (above note 7), where both "product liability" and "negligence" claims were raised.

[26] Allegations of defects of damaging algorithms are likely to fall under "design defects" rather than other types of product defects. P. F. Hubbard, "Sophisticated Robots": Balancing Liability, Regulation and Innovation (2014) 66 *Fla. Law Rev.* 1803, 1854. "Design Defect" refers to a product that could have been designed in a safer manner that is economically feasible. Generally, and unlike "Manufacture Defect," "Design Defect" is not governed by strict liability. Goldberg and Zipursky, above note 22.

[27] *Ibid.*

specific damaging decision, and not on the general operation of the tortfeasor in various circumstances.

Second, a design defect claim would probably have to address the programming aspects as well as the professional aspects of the decision-making process (namely, what was included in the arsenal of programming tools that the programmer could have used; what was included in the arsenal of professional tools the thinking algorithm could have chosen from). By contrast, the claim against the human tortfeasor would focus only on the arsenal of professional tools he did or did not use. Naturally, the extent of further costs and complexity stemming from the application of different legal frameworks to humans and algorithmic tortfeasors depends on the nature of the framework that would apply to thinking algorithms. And as mentioned above, even under a standard of "reasonableness" for both human and algorithmic tortfeasors, different tests of "reasonableness" may exist and raise different questions. Nevertheless, in general, a unified framework applying to both cases would undoubtedly reduce the time and costs accruing in cases where joint tortfeasors are human and algorithmic.

Economic Distortion

While in many fields the desire is that human and algorithmic decision-makers could be used interchangeably, the inherent differences between the two make each type superior to the other, in certain respects. For example, in Amazon's "Prime Air" system, devised to make air deliveries by drones, a drone and a human deliverer alike might be put to use in moving shipments. But in certain circumstances, such as mountainous terrain, a drone might be more efficient, while in circumstances involving poor weather conditions, a human deliverer is better. A judge might have a relative advantage over a bail-setting algorithm; for instance, in cases of non-standard defendants or unusual circumstances where an algorithm might be misled because the information in the database it relied on was not relevant for the specific case in hand. On the other hand, a bail-setting algorithm might have the advantage of reaching numerous bail decisions in split seconds, thus saving the judicial system much time and money.

From an economic efficiency viewpoint, the different advantages of the two "production factors" render human and algorithmic decision-makers not entirely interchangeable. Instead, their optimal application would presumably require a mixture of both.[28] The precise optimal mixture depends on their cost-effectiveness, an equilibrium that is obviously affected by the costs associated with each of the two production factors. For example, a law firm wishing to expand might calculate that adding another attorney will yield annual returns of $300,000, while adding another "virtual attorney" such as IBM's "Ross" (which conducts legal research powered by artificial intelligence) will yield annual returns of $350,000. The decision in favor of Ross is not automatic, but depends on Ross's cost. If purchasing Ross is expected to cost $300,000 while a human attorney will cost $200,000, the latter will be more cost-effective (yielding a profit of $100,000 versus Ross's $50,000).

Everything else equal,[29] the application of a different tort framework to humans and to thinking algorithms, which probably would result in a significant gap in the costs associated

---

[28] See, e.g., Review of Production and Cost Concepts, Sloan School of Management MIT (September 23, 2004), http://docplayer.net/20809729-Review-of-production-and-cost-concepts.html.

[29] For a detailed discussion of the unequal parameters that contribute to the different costs of human labor versus machine labor, see R. Abbot, The Reasonable Computer: Disrupting the Paradigm of Tort Liability (2017) 86 *Geo. Wash. Law Rev.* 1.

with litigation over damage each had caused, will affect the calculation and potentially result in fewer economic choices. For example, if the probability that a human attorney and Ross cause damage is equal, but the expected costs of litigation associated with damages caused by a human are $70,000 higher than Ross's, the firm will prefer Ross to a human.[30] This arbitrary gap in legal costs associated with either decision-maker will distort decisions and reduce efficiency. In other words, applying different legal frameworks will result in either algorithms or humans being used less often than they would have been based on their relative advantages and costs. Policy considerations may justify this outcome, but if so, these should be factored in deliberately.[31]

Chilling Effects

Applying a different legal framework to human and algorithmic tortfeasors might negatively affect innovation and technological advancements in the field of autonomous algorithms.[32]

The playing field of algorithmic and human decision-makers is *a priori* uneven in terms of chilling effects posed by litigation threats. Victims would probably be more likely to sue and judges more likely to "convict" algorithmic than human tortfeasors, in part because humans tend to sympathize with humans and not with algorithms,[33] and because of other considerations such as prior acquaintance with the human (but not the algorithmic) tortfeasor or her relatives, fear of consequences or discomfort in future dealings with the tortfeasor's community, or a more forgiving attitude to human error. In addition, damages caused by autonomous machines are likely to receive much more media attention than similar damages caused by humans, thus causing the former more reputational damage and possibly leading to an increase of actions.[34] Applying different tort frameworks to human and algorithmic decision-makers will, in certain cases, widen the gap in a way that might render the cost of certain autonomous algorithms prohibitive, and prevent or postpone technological progress.

First, assume that damages caused by a person or a thinking algorithm are to be borne by their employer – for example, a law firm in the case of Ross, or a hospital in the case of a robo-doctor. If the framework applicable to algorithms makes it easier and cheaper to collect compensation from algorithms than from human tortfeasors who have caused the same damage, the result is an increase in the relative cost of using thinking algorithms as against

---

[30] The example assumes that, in both cases, the law firm is liable for the damages (and not, for example, the programmer or manufacturer of Ross if it caused the damage).

[31] For a more detailed discussion of inefficient usage of human labor versus machine labor resulting from different tort frameworks, see Abbot, above note 29. (focusing specifically on the differences between negligence that would apply to humans, and strict liability that Abbot assumes would apply to algorithms). See also R. D. Cooter and A. Porat, Lapses of Attention in Medical Malpractice and Road Accidents (2014) 15 *Theor. Inq. Law* 329, 352–3.

[32] Naturally, the more easily imposed and substantial the liability is, the more reluctant manufacturers or users would be to engage with it, thus leading to impeding development and innovation. See, e.g., Final Report Summary – ROBOLAW (Regulating Emerging Robotic Technologies in Europe: Robotics facing Law and Ethics), European Commission Cordis, http://cordis.europa.eu/result/rcn/161246_en.html.

[33] Especially when the algorithms are not embedded in anthropomorphic technology such as "human-like" robots (various studies found a connection between a human-like appearance of technology, and the level of engagement and compliance by human users). B. Reeves and C. Nass, *The Media Equation: How People Treat Computers, Television, and New Media Like Real People and Places* (Center for the Study of Language and Information, 1996); C. N. Clifford and S. Brave, *Wired for Speech: How Voice Activates and Advances the Human–Computer Relationship* (MIT Press, 2005).

[34] R. Brownsword, E. Scotford, and K. Yeung (eds.), *The Oxford Handbook of Law, Regulation and Technology* (Oxford University Press, 2017), p. 538; R. Calo, Robotics & the Law: Liability for Personal Robots, CIS (November 25, 2009), http://cyberlaw.stanford.edu/blog/2009/11/robotics-law-liability-personal-robots.

humans.[35] This will influence an employer's decision to purchase an algorithmic decision-maker, and might also have a sweeping effect on the demand by employers for such algorithms, and therefore on the entire industry of algorithmic decision-makers in the given field. Such an outcome is to be expected in sectors where the demand for algorithms or for humans is set by the employer (who will bear the costs of damages) and not by end-users.

In sectors where customers will be free to choose which decision-maker to use – for example in private clinics where patients may choose to be treated by a human physician or by a robo-doctor – this analysis is reversed. Now, the easier it is to sue and collect from algorithms versus humans, the greater end-users' incentive to favor them and not their human counterparts. In other words, for these sectors, concern for diminishing demand for technology will arise when thinking algorithms are more difficult to collect from, not the reverse.

Second, even when liability in the case of thinking algorithms is to be borne by their manufacturers and not by their employers or users, lack of unity in applicable tort frameworks might incur additional costs for the manufacturers of thinking algorithms, thus creating a chilling effect, at least with regard to torts performed jointly by algorithms and humans, such as the cases discussed above. This is because under joint liability, victims are free to claim full compensation from the wrongdoer of their choice.[36] If, for example, thinking algorithms are easier to recover from, then victims will probably choose to sue the algorithmic decision-maker for the entire damage caused jointly by the algorithmic and human tortfeasors, even when the algorithm is responsible for only a small fraction of the damage. True, the proportional damage attributed to the human wrongdoer could be recovered from her in a separate action.[37] But such a step would mean additional litigation costs and risks that would accrue to the algorithmic decision-maker. The exact tipping point where developing and marketing thinking algorithms become prohibitively expensive depends, of course, on myriad parameters. However, imposing additional costs on thinking algorithm manufacturers owing to damages caused by human counterparts – which could be prevented or minimized were both thinking algorithms and humans subject to the same framework – surely contributes to a chilling effect.

Technology-Neutral Standard

In addition to resolving or at least minimizing the anomalies discussed above, applying a reasonableness standard on algorithms is advantageous because it is neutral.

Thinking algorithms' abilities are ever improving, to the point of mimicking and at times outperforming different human capabilities.[38] As a result, the type, frequency, and magnitude of damages that thinking algorithms might cause is likely to be quite dynamic. In light of these changes, a "reasonable algorithm" standard is advantageous in that it is flexible and adaptable. A *normative* standard of reasonableness, one that wishes to shape behavior of potential tortfeasors, may be adjusted to reflect different considerations that society wishes to promote

---

[35] Abbot, above note 29.

[36] Under the joint and several liability doctrine, a plaintiff may pursue compensation from each liable party, as if the different parties were jointly liable for the tort. Plaintiffs wronged by multiple tortfeasors, in other words, may decide to file an action for the entire sum of compensation owed against any of the tortfeasors involved. See, e.g., R. W. Wright, The Logic and Fairness of Joint and Several Liability (1992) 23 *Mem. St. Univ. Law Rev.* 45.

[37] *Ibid.*

[38] J. Millar and I. Kerr, Delegation, Relinquishment and Responsibility: The Prospect of Expert Robots, in R. Calo, A. M. Froomkin, and I. Kerr (eds.), *Robot Law* (Edward Elgar, 2016), p. 102.

with regard to algorithmic technology. The desire for expedited innovation, for example, may lower the level of precautions needed for a decision to be reasonable, and vice versa – while the general framework of reasonableness continues to apply without the need to reshape it in response to changes in technology and policy. A *positive* standard of reasonableness, one that compares the underlying act to how other persons or peers of the tortfeasor would have acted, may too be adjusted (for example, by comparing the actions of the algorithm to those of other similar algorithms once a sufficient number of similar algorithms are operational).[39]

In addition to promoting statutory longevity and avoiding the need to constantly update laws and regulations,[40] a technology-neutral standard provides equal treatment of old and new technologies[41] and creates legal certainty.[42] A reasonableness standard applied to thinking algorithms could therefore be advantageous in those contexts.

Overall, the adoption of human-like standards for algorithmic decision-makers entails certain advantages. In addition to allowing flexibility and quick adaptation to technological advancements, it could have a positive effect on innovation and create proper incentives for the efficient use of humans and thinking algorithms, and will allow victims of harm caused by thinking algorithms to stand on equal ground in terms of recovery.

THE CONCEPTUAL DIFFICULTIES IN APPLYING A "REASONABLE ALGORITHM" STANDARD

Applying a reasonableness standard to thinking algorithms might be considered obvious in the future, but at present it would likely be confronted with reservations of various types. A threshold argument against developing and applying reasonableness standards to thinking algorithms is the mere fact that they are – well – not human.[43] Indeed, the fact that thinking algorithms are not natural persons might be used in a variety of ways to argue that they do not warrant an independent analysis of reasonableness. First, the notion of examining the reasonableness of a non-living object might seem intuitively inappropriate or even peculiar. Second, the fact that in many cases algorithms were programmed by humans begs the question of whether there is any meaning in analyzing their own reasonableness separately from the reasonableness of their programmers (in other words, the question of whether the outcome of both "reasonableness" analyses might ever be different from each another).

Assuming that indeed there is no full equivalence between the reasonableness of the programmer and the reasonableness of the algorithm itself, another challenge is what the

---

[39] The damaging actions of "Ross," for example, may be analyzed in comparison to what a reasonable flesh-and-blood attorney would have done. But once some variety of similar lawyering algorithms exist in the market, Ross's actions may then be analyzed in comparison to what these other algorithms would have chosen. (Intuitively, the latter option seems like a more accurate reference point, but naturally a comparison to peer algorithms would always be available only a while after the technology was first introduced.) For a further discussion on how to assess, de facto, the reasonableness of algorithms, see Chagal-Feferkorn, above note 17.

[40] J. R. Kresse, Privacy of Conversations over Cordless and Cellular Telephones: Federal Protection under the Electronic Communications Privacy Act of 1986 (1987) 9 *Geo. Msn. Univ. Law Rev.* 335, 341.

[41] B. Greenberg, Rethinking Technology Neutrality (2016) 100 *Minn. Law Rev.* 1495–562.

[42] B.-J. Koops, Should ICT Regulation be Technology-Neutral?, in B.-J. Koops, M. Lips, C. Prins, and M. Schellekens (eds.), *Starting Points for ICT Regulation: Deconstructing Prevalent Policy One-Liners* (Asser Press, 2006).

[43] Discussing tort liability of autonomous cars, Colonna, for example, discarded the notion of applying the negligence test to hardware or software. One of his main arguments was: "[O]ne of the integral pieces of the negligence analysis is deciding whether a 'reasonable [person] of ordinary prudence' under like circumstances would have acted similarly. Yet . . . neither hardware nor software falls within the lay definition of a human being" (K. Colonna, Autonomous Cars and Tort Liability (2012) 4 *W. Res. J. Law Technol. Int.* 81.

legal consequences of applying said analysis on thinking algorithmic tortfeasors will be, given that algorithms lack legal status and cannot bear the consequences of their own actions. In that respect, another difficulty is whether applying a reasonableness analysis to algorithms, therefore, could be in line with the rationales in the basis of tort law, which focus on deterrence and compensation of the victim. Lastly, thinking algorithms are, in many respects, superior to human decision-makers. Even if we prove that there is a separate meaning to their own "reasonableness" and that said analysis could reconcile with tort law rationales, shouldn't we demand they meet an elevated level of performance than mere "reasonableness," which reflects human flaws, but might be deemed too "forgiving" in the case of algorithms? This section will address these challenges and concerns and show that reasonableness is, after all, a sensible mechanism to apply to algorithms.

Intuitive Hesitancy

Subjecting thinking algorithms to an analysis of their own "behavior" or "choices" might seem improper. This is not only because machines are not expected (at least in the near future) to be the ones legally responsible for the damages they had caused, but also because of an intuitive feeling that machines need not be "personified" and that legal tests or standards currently applied to humans should be reserved for them alone.

Such perception is not necessarily warranted. First, it is not unprecedented that non-humans too are subject to an analysis of their own behavior when determining tort liability (of other parties involved). In more detail, canines' behavior is analyzed independently from the behavior of their human owners in dog-attack cases, where liability is not imposed if the dog reacted "proportionally" in response to a provoking act.[44]

Moreover, and in general, intuitive perceptions on the desirable status of machines in the legal world may prove to be outdated. Indeed, choices regarding legal recognition (such as granting legal status, legal standing, etc.) of non-humans have become flexible with time, and choices that were considered unthinkable at the time are beyond questioning nowadays. Despite a previous perception that only persons could be eligible as a separate legal entity, for example, the law has acknowledged the legal status of companies, municipalities, and state bodies, and even vessels.[45] In other words, assumptions regarding the legal status or capacity of different entities which appeared to be undisputable were often disproved completely, along with different paradigm shifts.[46] Indeed, acknowledging the legal status of autonomous algorithms may be just around the corner, judging by the European Parliament recommendation discussed above. Whether or not the European proposal is ever accepted, the conceptual leap required for subjecting autonomous algorithms to negligence tests (or other legal mechanisms once reserved for humans) might very well seem to be an obvious one in hindsight.

[44] J. M. Zitter, Annotation Intentional Provocation, Contributory or Comparative Negligence, or Assumption of Risk as Defense to Action for Injury by Dog (2010) 11 *ALR 5th* 127.
[45] C. D. Stone, Should Trees Have Standing? – Toward Legal Rights for Natural Objects (1972) 45 *Southern Cal. Law Rev.* 450. See also *United States* v. *Cargo of the Brig Malek Adhel*, 43 US (2 How.) 210 (1844), discussing a case where a vessel was involuntarily sold because it was used for illegal purposes by pirates who took over the ship. Vessel owners' claims that they never agreed to the illegal actions and should therefore not be punished were discarded, as the Court explained that: "This is not a proceeding against the owner, it is a proceeding against the vessel for an offense committed by the vessel."
[46] C. D. Stone, *Should Trees Have Standing? 40 Years On*, A. Grear (ed.) (Edward Elgar, 2012), explaining that in old civilizations, for example, imposing legal liability on slaves was considered foolish, given the clear differences between them and "real humans."

Thinking Algorithms Are as Reasonable as Their Programmers

As discussed in detail in Chapters 2 and 3 in this volume, both supervised and unsupervised machine learning is based on inputs given to the algorithm by its human programmers. If thinking algorithms make their choices according to how they were programmed to choose, what sense would there be in examining their own reasonableness, independently of their programmers? Balkin's "homunculus fallacy" argument refers precisely to this point: according to Balkin, "there is no little person inside the program."[47] Instead, algorithms act as they are programmed to act – no more, no less.[48]

As elaborated on below, programmers indeed affect their algorithm's choices, and may also prevent it from choosing certain alternatives altogether. Still, there is relevance and meaning in analyzing a thinking algorithm's own reasonableness separately from the reasonableness of the human programmer, who chose to program the algorithm as she did, for the reasons outlined below.

Lack of Foreseeability

To establish negligence, one of the elements to prove is the breach of a duty of care, which occurs if the tortfeasor failed to adhere to the standard of reasonable care when carrying out actions that might foreseeably harm others.[49] In the past, the designers of different systems had full or nearly full foreseeability as to the "choices" made by their systems. The makers of a coffee machine, for example, could foresee all the different scenarios the machine would possibly face and decide in advance the desired result for each one (heating the water when the user presses a certain button, pouring the water when it reaches a certain temperature, etc.). Thinking algorithms, however, are "black boxes" that are "fed" certain inputs and produce certain outputs, with a very limited ability by their programmers to understand, let alone predict, why the algorithm reached the decision it did.[50] Thinking algorithms are, in a sense, "unpredictable by design."[51]

First, self-learning algorithms are frequently designed to outsmart the limits of the human mind (even those minority of minds that are not afraid of mathematics), and draw conclusions that are beyond human comprehension.[52] Naturally, the more complex the algorithmic models are, the more difficult it is to understand and foresee such algorithms' choices.

Second, many thinking algorithms are online-based and may update their prediction models after each decision they make. Unless the "person in the loop" needs to authorize each and every decision by the thinking algorithm, the algorithm would reach conclusions based on new information that the human programmer would not have had a chance to consider.[53] Granted, the programmer can certainly set boundaries that the thinking algorithm

---

[47] J. M. Balkin, The Three Laws of Robotics in the Age of Big Data (2017) 78 *Ohio St. Law J.* 1217.

[48] H. A. Simon, The Corporation: Will It Be Managed by Machines? in J. Diebold (ed.), *The World of the Computer* (Random House, 1973).

[49] Restatement (Third) of Torts: Liability for Physical Harm § 3 (PFD No. 1, 2005); Zipursky, above note 2.

[50] See, e.g., M. Perel-Filmar and N. Elkin-Koren, Black Box Tinkering: Beyond Transparency in Algorithmic Enforcement (2017) 69 *Fla. Law Rev.* 181.

[51] Millar and Kerr, above note 38.

[52] P. J. G. Lisboa, Machine Learning Approaches Are Alone in the Spectrum in Their Lack of Interpretability, in *Interpretability in Machine Learning Principles and Practice* (Springer, 2013); R. Brooks, *Flesh and Machines: How Robots Will Change Us* (Vintage, 2003).

[53] "[O]nline machine learning systems can update their model for predictions after each decision, incorporating each new observation as part of their training data. Even knowing the source code and data for such systems is not enough to replicate or predict their behavior – we also must know precisely how and when they interacted or will

may never cross (for instance, a robo-lawyer may be instructed never to make use of deceitful information), or instruct the algorithm to discard certain parameters altogether.[54] The human programmer may also maintain control over the thinking algorithm by pre-programming it such that any significant change in its decision-making process will be subject to the programmer's approval. For the thinking algorithms to be useful, however, they cannot simply "freeze" whenever they encounter new information and change their conclusions accordingly, until the human programmer has had the chance to review and approve their suggested course of action. A driverless car, for example, can simply not function if it must halt and wait for input from the programmer each time it encounters unfamiliar terrain.

Third, algorithms making complex decisions that replace human discretion (even on a non-self-learning basis) are expected to be unexpected. One reason is that complex decision-making flows are often programmed by a very large group of programmers, each contributing a certain amount of code lines and none having the ability of "seeing the whole picture" and able to predict the system's choices in each given scenario.[55] In addition, such algorithms often base their decisions on an astronomical number of combinations, each in turn containing an astronomical number of parameters and potential mixtures – far above what could be tested.[56] This renders it impossible for a programmer (even assuming there was only one programmer) to predict the choices made by the system under all potential scenarios. Rather, only a very limited sub-set of scenarios could be tested to predict the choices they would yield.[57] Also, as mentioned above, many parameters could be dynamic and ever-changing.[58] Adding to the unpredictable nature of complex decision-making algorithms is their

interact with their environment." J. A. Kroll, J. Huey, S. Barocas, *et al.*, Accountable Algorithms (2017) 165 *Univ. Pa. Law Rev.* 633, 660.

[54] Algorithms in the US criminal justice system, for example, do not take into account variables such as race or gender. Such variables may nevertheless affect the algorithm's decision because other variables that are included in the model serve as proxies for race or gender (A. Christin, A. Rosenblat, and D. Boyd, Courts and Predictive Algorithms, Data & Civil Rights Primer, www.law.nyu.edu/sites/default/files/upload_documents/Angele%20Christin.pdf). The programmer may, however, carefully choose the database they "train" their algorithms on, to cause the algorithms to be less affected by biases (A. Chander, The Racist Algorithm? (2017) 115 *Mich. Law Rev.* 1023).

[55] The Facebook Feed algorithm, for instance, which is surely less complicated than that of a robo-doctor, consists of numerous code lines programmed by various programs. Whenever the company decides on a change in the algorithm feed and some code lines are altered accordingly, the team, admittedly, do not know how the change will affect the algorithm and its choices. Rather, to implement a change, many trial-and-error experiments are required. W. Oremus, Who Controls Your Facebook Feed, *Slate* (January 3, 2016), www.slate.com/articles/technology/cover_story/2016/01/how_facebook_s_news_feed_algorithm_works.html.

[56] Kroll *et al.*, above note 53 (explaining why both statistical and dynamic methods for reviewing algorithms in order to detect unwanted outcomes can only be effective for a small sub-set of all possible scenarios). This is demonstrated, among others, by examples of different codes reviewed by many professionals, yet still containing unnoticed errors and "bugs," or by the famous proof by Alan Turing that "[t]here is no single algorithm that can predict whether, for any given program and input, the program will finish running at some point (halt) or will run forever" (A. Turing, On Computable Numbers, with an Application to the Entscheidungsproblem (1937) 42 *Proc. London Math. Soc.* 230). Naturally, there are solutions for improving the chances of detecting errors in a code (such as dividing it into separate modules or annotating it with the assertions made while writing it). But this does not change the unpredictable nature of most of the choices made by sophisticated decision-making algorithms. Kroll *et al.*, *ibid.*

[57] Google, for example, admits that their driverless cars could not be pre-programmed for each possible scenario, given the astronomical amount of parameters to consider (A. Shapiro, What Do Self-Driving Cars Mean for Auto Liability Insurance, NPR (2016)). The technology must be, therefore, Google says, based on observations and generalizations done by the machine itself which, in turn, leads us to the unpredictability inherent to machine-learning capabilities.

[58] Such as, in the case of a robo-doctor, the exact body temperature of the patient, the level of pollution on the day of diagnosis, whether a certain epidemic is spreading in different parts of the world, etc.

interaction with other inputs[59] and other unpredictable codes as part of the Internet of Things revolution, allowing machines to communicate with themselves directly, without human involvement.[60] This makes it practically impossible to predict the algorithm's choices.[61]

In sum, while the choices of the older-generation algorithms mirrored the choices made by their human programmers, autonomous algorithms now make choices that are not necessarily programmed by their developers and that produce outcomes that are not foreseeable by them, at least with regard to a large sub-set of all possible scenarios. Therefore, there is no perfect equivalence between programmers' and algorithms' choices, and a thinking algorithm's choices therefore have an independent significance.

Passage of Time

As mentioned above, a tortfeasor breaches her duty of care if she does not adhere to the standard of reasonable care when carrying out actions that might foreseeably harm others. Foreseeability, of course, is examined at the time the relevant action takes place. Since certain harms may be unforeseeable when the algorithm is programmed, but foreseeable when the algorithm has eventually made its decisions, the human developer's choices and the autonomous algorithm's choices are once again not fully equal.

In more detail, a coffee machine designed to heat and pour coffee upon receiving a certain input could continue its exact circle of operation for decades. (Perhaps a more efficient method of heating or pouring coffee will be discovered and will render the machine obsolete, but generally we do not expect any change in the foreseeability of different harms that the coffee machine might cause).

On the other hand, the time lapse in the case of a thinking algorithm might in certain cases have significant consequences for whether certain harms are foreseeable. For instance, the programmer of a robo-doctor who in the past decided not to program "smallpox" as a medical condition would probably be deemed to have acted reasonably in doing so, because this disease was eradicated decades ago. If, however, the robo-doctor failed to diagnose smallpox a year later, after a smallpox epidemic spread across the country, then under every reasonableness criterion it would be deemed unreasonable.[62]

Granted, we could always go back to the programmer and check whether it was reasonable or not to have the programmer update the robo-doctor, or have the robo-doctor refresh its

---

59 If, to continue with our robo-doctor example, the robo-doctor downloads different software or programs, or is continuously updated with new medical discoveries and studies.

60 "[M]ost of the communication will be automated between intelligent devices. Humans will intervene only in a tiny fraction of that flow of communication. Most of it will go on unsensed and really unknown by humans" (N. Gane, C. Venn, M. Hand, and K. Hayles, Ubiquitous Surveillance: Interview with Katherine Hayles (2007) 24 *Theory Cult. Soc.* 349). See also K. Hayles, Unfinished Work: From Cyborg to the Cognisphere (2006) 23 *Theory Cult. Soc.* 159: ". . . in highly developed and networked societies . . . human awareness comprises the tip of a huge pyramid of data flows, most of which occur between machines."

61 An example of just how surprising and unpredictable algorithms may be can be found in the chatbots created by Facebook's AI research lab, who were "caught" conversing with each other in their own secret language, as well as Microsoft's chatbot Tay, who tweeted racist and misogynistic tweets. O. Rachum-Twaig, Whose Robot Is It Anyway: Liability for Artificial-Intelligence-Based Robots (2020) *Univ. Ill. Law Rev.* (forthcoming).

62 This is because under a positive standard of reasonableness, which compares the tortfeasor's behavior to that of others in the relevant community, presumably every physician in the country would have considered said diagnosis. Under a normative standard of reasonableness too (which purports to shape policy through tort framework incentives), the costs of considering the diagnosis of smallpox would likely be lower than the damage expectancy of misdiagnosing it.

knowledge by itself,[63] or whether or not the programmer should have issued a post-sale warning regarding the algorithm's discrepancies.[64] But that analysis would focus on the programmer's reasonableness at the time the algorithm was programmed, based on the technology and sources of information available then. The analysis and its outcome may be different when focusing on the reasonableness of the algorithm itself at the later time, when it made its decisions.[65] This once again supports the conclusion that a separate reasonableness analysis for the thinking algorithm itself has a value, distinct from that of the programmer.

"Reasonableness" Determined Based on Different Grounds

Other than the fact that the standard of reasonableness would likely be different for humans and thinking algorithms (as mentioned above, an elevated standard might apply to the latter based on its superiority), the parameters for examining said standard of reasonableness might also be different. While the programmer is to be judged according to a "reasonable programmer" standard, the thinking algorithm is to be judged by a standard of reasonableness pertaining to the specific field in which the algorithm is relevant.

It would make sense to assume, for example, that the standard of the "reasonable programmer" who programmed a robo-doctor or a driverless car would not be identical to the standards of the "reasonable robo-doctor" or the "reasonable driverless car." A robo-doctor, for instance, would presumably be judged according to the medical choice it reached compared with the other medical alternatives.

On the other hand, the appropriate standard of care for the programmer is that of a "reasonable programmer," judged based on programming alternatives rather than medical alternatives.[66]

Granted, if the programmer is designing professional robo-doctors, we would expect her programming skills and choices to be in line with those required to program a functioning robo-doctor, including, of course, making the right medical choices. We would, however, compare her choices with those of other programmers or with the opinions of experts in the field of programming, not the field of medicine. On a normative level, we would make cost–benefit analyses focused on the availability and efficiency of other programming means, rather than medical means.

To make this argument more concrete and to give specific examples of when an algorithm's choices might be deemed reasonable, whereas its programmer's decision would be

---

[63] In the context of driverless cars, for example, "over-the-air" updates of the vehicle's software were already successfully performed, including substantial updates relating to the car's movement. See M. Rechtin, Tesla Nimbly Updates Model S over the Air, *Automotive News* (January 16, 2013), www.autonews.com/article/20130116/OEM06/130119843/tesla-nimbly-updatesmodel-s-over-the-air; D. Lavrinc, In Automotive First, Tesla Pushes Over-the-Air Software Patch, *Wired* (September 24, 2012), www.wired.com/autopia/2012/09/tesla-over-the-air/.

[64] As is required under product liability laws, assuming the "seller" knew or should have known of the substantial risk posed by its product, see Restatement (Third) of Torts § 10(b) (1998); B. W. Smith, Proximity-Driven Liability (2014) 102 *Geo. Law J.* 1777 (suggesting that "[u]ltimately a lack of remote updatability may itself constitute a design defect").

[65] Depending, of course, on the specific content poured into the reasonableness standard.

[66] Evaluation of algorithms by their programmers is based, among others, on the algorithm's correctness and completeness, and whether it optimally employs resources such as time and memory. See, e.g., K. Krebsbach, Computer Science: Not About Computers, Not Science, www2.lawrence.edu/fast/krebsbak/Research/Publications/pdf/fecs15.pdf. While there will surely be an overlap between these parameters and the ones used to analyze the reasonableness of the thinking algorithm itself, the analysis will not be identical. The reasonableness of the thinking algorithm will depend on its professional decision (such as medical decision) – not on the programing tools that allowed its performance.

deemed unreasonable, and vice versa, let us look at the following scenarios. A battered woman and her spouse enter a clinic. The woman tells the physician she bumped into a door. While her injury is consistent with that description, the physician notices something suspicious about her body language, and the way she avoids eye contact with her spouse. The spouse's reactions are also less (or more) sympathetic than expected, and the physician decides to follow the protocol that states that suspicion of domestic violence should be resolved by summoning a social worker to question the patient.[67] Assume also that to the human eye the suspicion described above is obvious, and had the couple visited a hundred physicians, all of them would have called a social worker. A robo-doctor, on the other hand, would have tremendous computational abilities and could surely be programmed to detect suspicious vocal trembling;[68] but it could not necessarily replace human intuition as to when something is not as it appears to be. So, in this situation, a robo-doctor might not detect that something is wrong and would not request a social worker's intervention as required, perhaps thereby causing the woman to sustain another violent attack with significant physical injury.

Is the robo-doctor acting reasonably when it fails to recognize the domestic violence situation? This depends, of course, on the standards of reasonableness we would apply. If, for example, we focus on the positive standard, and make the comparison with human physicians, we already know that the latter would act differently; therefore, we can conclude that the robo-doctor was unreasonable. But scrutinizing the programmer's reasonableness, and comparing her with other programmers, we might discover that there is no feasible method of designing a robo-doctor to detect accurately when "something is wrong"; therefore, she acted as all programmers would act and was accordingly reasonable in doing so. Granted, applying a positive standard of reasonableness to a robo-doctor might require us to compare its actions with the actions of other robo-doctors, and not with those of human physicians, depending on the content of the standard of reasonableness to be developed for algorithms. In that case, if no robo-doctor yet designed can detect when something is wrong, the equivalence between the robo-doctor's reasonableness and its programmer's is indeed sound. But even if our positive comparison is made to a robo-doctor and not to a human physician, many robo-doctors in the industry may possibly possess the ability to detect when a patient's story is suspicious (for instance, if they are designed by an entity with inexhaustible human capital and monetary resources, such as a state or an army). In such a case, our robo-doctor could still be found unreasonable under a positive standard of reasonableness. If, however, our programmer's more limited resources could under no circumstances allow her to develop such an ability for her robo-doctor, and if all similar programmers in the industry (not operating for a state or the army) have failed to add such a feature, we might view her programming as reasonable nevertheless. That is, even if we judge the reasonableness of non-human decision-makers based on other non-humans' actions, we might still find them unreasonable, while finding their programmers' actions reasonable. Medical malpractice is indeed usually judged by a positive standard. But this example may still be accurate in other contexts analyzed on the basis of a normative standard. If, for example, the cost of adding a feature that improves the robo-doctor's ability to detect situations where the robo-doctor is lied to – or alternatively the cost of having the robo-doctor consult with a human in every case in order to make sure it is not "missing" anything – exceeds the expected utility, then the programmer is reasonable in

---

67   See, e.g., San Francisco's Domestic Violence Protocol, www.leapsf.org/pdf/sample_clinic_protocol.pdf.
68   For a review of different voice examination technologies employed to detect lies, see S. Miller, When Everybody Lies: Voice Stress Analysis Tackles Lie Detection, GCN (March 18, 2014), https://gcn.com/articles/2014/03/18/voice-risk-analysis.aspx.

avoiding said costs under the economic efficiency normative standard. Likewise, if the programmer warns the users that the robo-doctor is not successful in identifying situations of untruthfulness, her behavior is likely to be found reasonable. But at the same time, if the robo-doctor on a specific case could have made further inquiries, the costs of which were lower than the expected damage, the robo-doctor might be found unreasonable.

A contrary example, which has to do with the time lapse argument discussed above, is when the algorithm's choices are deemed reasonable, while its programmer's choices are not. Assume, for example, that our robo-doctor, now a pediatrician, has to diagnose and choose a course of treatment for a newborn whose brain seems underdeveloped. Considering different alternatives, the robo-doctor does not consider the fact that the baby suffers from microcephaly stemming from the Zika virus, because this scenario arose well before the outbreak of the virus, when only two or three sporadic cases were reported, all in very remote geographical areas. Even if the robo-doctor's failure to consider Zika results in choosing the wrong treatment and harms the baby, the robo-doctor is still likely to be found to have acted reasonably. (This is under the positive standard of reasonableness: presumably all other human physicians, as well as robo-doctors, would at the time have discarded the option of a Zika infection; or under the normative standard of reasonableness based on economic efficiency, the great rarity of the virus at that time would have rendered it entirely uneconomical to test babies with microcephaly for Zika.) The robo-doctor's programmer, however, might be found to have acted unreasonably if programming standards required that robo-doctors be continuously updated on all medical-related reports worldwide, and automatically integrate them into their decision-making process.[69]

Although a clear correlation surely exists between the reasonableness of an algorithm and the reasonableness of its programmer, the two are not identical, and may occasionally lead to different results. Thus, an independent analysis of the reasonableness of an algorithm is not mere semantics, but could potentially yield two opposite outcomes.

The Legal Implications of Applying a Reasonable Algorithm Standard

If a thinking algorithm's own reasonableness has significance that is not dependent on that of its programmer, what is the implication of determining that an algorithm was reasonable or unreasonable?

First, a finding that an algorithm acted "reasonably" or "unreasonably" might affect the way in which we judge the reasonableness of a human decision-maker who chose to rely on an output or recommendation given by the algorithm. If, for example, a medical algorithm produced a damaging recommendation and a flesh-and-blood physician relied on it, then a finding that the algorithm's choice was reasonable would likely allow the physician to successfully argue that her reliance on the thinking algorithm was in itself reasonable.[70] Since the current chapter focuses on the reasonableness of the machine and not of the persons

---

[69] If this was the case, however, we would have probably expected more robo-doctors to take the Zika possibility into account, and thus render our robo-doctor unreasonable after all (at least when applying a positive standard of reasonableness) when failing to do so. But if, for instance, our robo-doctor was programmed at a later stage than all others in the industry (being a new model or something of that sort), when embedding continuous updates of medical reports suddenly became technologically possible, the robo-doctor would still be deemed reasonable (acting like all other robo-doctors), while its programmer would not (as the option of adding said feature was readily available to the programmer).

[70] Granted, the reasonableness of the physician would be analyzed based on the moment when she chose to rely on the algorithm's recommendation – a moment that naturally precedes the finding that the algorithm was indeed reasonable. But, assuming the recommendation was later found reasonable, it should be easier for the physician to show that her reliance on it was a choice other physicians would have also made (as discussed above, in general

involved, we will move on to the second potential implication – one that would be of relevance in a future envisioned in the past by the European Parliament[71] – where algorithms are awarded their own legal status. Under such a scenario, where thinking algorithms are able to pay for their own damages, a finding that a thinking algorithm acted reasonably or unreasonably would potentially have the same legal implications as would a finding of reasonableness by a natural person; reasonable algorithms would be resolved of liability, while unreasonable algorithms would have to pay for the damages they have caused.

Until such a day arrives, a third set of implications of the reasonableness (or unreasonableness) of a thinking algorithm might affect the determination of liability of the party who currently assumes liability for damages caused by an algorithm. Indeed, even if the reasonableness of the thinking algorithm itself is put to the test, the manufacturers, developers, or users of the algorithm may continue to pay for damages caused by it.[72] The fact that thinking algorithms are no longer a "product" but operate at their own discretion should not matter in that context, just as employers pay for damage caused by their employees' negligence,[73] or, to give an example of a non-human tortfeasor, just as dog owners pay for damages caused by the behavior of their animals.[74] Regardless of the specific party that would assume liability for the damages caused by a thinking algorithm to which the said party is related, there are several ways in which the "reasonableness" analysis may come into play under this set of alternatives, depending on policy considerations.

If policymakers wish to increase liability, they may add an "unreasonable algorithm" argument as a separate cause of action that might invoke liability by the humans involved. In other words, a victim harmed by a decision of a thinking algorithm could either win her case on traditional causes of action (such as product liability or direct negligence by the humans or legal persons involved) or may prevail solely based on a finding that the thinking algorithm was unreasonable.

If, however, policymakers wish to reduce the liability exposure of the relevant actors (for instance, because of concerns of a chilling effect), then the unreasonableness of the thinking algorithm may be a prerequisite for invoking other causes of action, such as product liability or direct negligence. In other words, in order to recover damages, the victim not only would have to establish a "traditional" cause of action, such as product liability, but would first have to show that the algorithm acted unreasonably, or else her case would be dismissed.

Naturally, both of these alternatives would continue to subject damages caused by algorithms to a very different legal framework from the one that currently applies to human tortfeasors: while the liability for human-caused damages is determined based on the reasonableness of the tortfeasor alone, the liability for algorithmic damages could be established by either reasonability of the tortfeasor or by other causes of action (according to the former alternative) or require that both are met at the same time (according the latter alternative). In that sense, both alternatives would not minimize the anomalies identified at the beginning of the discussion under "Why Apply a Reasonableness Standard to Thinking Algorithms?" above, and might in fact exacerbate them: adding a supplementary cause of action for victims damaged by algorithmic tortfeasors would place them at an advantage compared to victims of

the standard of reasonableness in the world of medicine is a positive one, comparing a physician's actions to those of other doctors under similar circumstances).
71   European Parliament Draft Report, above note 10.
72   Abbot, above note 29.
73   Restatement (Second) of Torts § 429 (1965).
74   S. Duffy and J. P. Hopkins, Sit, Stay, Drive: The Future of Autonomous Car Liability (2013) 16 *SMU Sci. Technol. Law. Rev.* 101.

human tortfeasors. It would also contribute to procedural inefficiency, as the underlying legal proceedings would then be comprised of both a traditional cause of action and an "unreasonableness" cause of action (which, as discussed above, is expected to raise different legal questions and entail additional costs). Naturally, paving the way for more successful proceedings against algorithmic damages by adding another cause of action would also contribute to the chilling effect of developing such algorithms in the first place, and would also increase economic distortion caused by under-usage of algorithms due to their expected high litigation costs.[75]

While the latter option of requiring both unreasonableness and an additional cause of action to be established in order to prevail a lawsuit of algorithmic damages would likely not contribute to the chilling effect (as winning lawsuits against manufacturers would become more difficult), it would still place victims of algorithmic damage in an unequal position compared to other victims (who would only have to establish unreasonableness of the tortfeasor). It would also increase procedural inefficiency (under this alternative, all cases would have to address the question of both reasonableness and an additional cause of action) and in general might promote under-usage of human decision-makers (assuming proceedings of algorithmic damages would become more difficult to win).[76]

Although these alternatives certainly warrant more consideration, let us focus on an intermediate alternative, which bears most similarities to the current legal framework applying to human tortfeasors. Under this alternative, the analysis of reasonableness would be the only analysis used in order to determine liability (of the humans or legal persons involved). In other words, if the thinking algorithm was deemed reasonable, no liability would be found. If, however, the algorithm was unreasonable, then the party sued (for example, its manufacturer) would indeed be liable for the damages. Such a scenario would be most similar to the current legal status applying to human tortfeasors, as depicted in Table 23.1.

Applying a reasonableness standard on algorithms such that the analysis would on its own determine liability raises an additional challenge that stems from the fact that

TABLE 23.1 *Alternatives of using "reasonableness" as a test for determining liability*

Outcome for plaintiff	Tortfeasor is reasonable	Tortfeasor is unreasonable
Human tortfeasor	Plaintiff loses	Plaintiff wins
Algorithmic tortfeasor – alternative 1	Plaintiff may pursue additional causes of action	Plaintiff wins
Algorithmic tortfeasor – alternative 2	Plaintiff loses	Plaintiff might win if she establishes an additional cause of action
Algorithmic tortfeasor – alternative 3	Plaintiff loses	Plaintiff wins

---

[75]   As discussed in " Why Apply a Reasonableness Standard to Thinking Algorithms?" above, the result might be the opposite when focusing on fields where the users themselves may choose between algorithmic and human decision-makers. In such cases, users would have an incentive to over-use algorithms, because redress in cases of damages would be easier for them.

[76]   Or over-usage of human decision-makers in fields where users are free to choose between both types of decision-makers (*ibid.*).

thinking algorithms are not humans: would such an implication reconcile with the rationales behind tort law? The answer to this questions depends, like many other things, on the details of the mechanism adopted, but in general it might very well be a positive one.

Victim's Compensation

Among the specific problems identified by Colonna in applying a negligence standard to software and hardware is that non-humans cannot compensate for the damage they have caused, thus leaving victims uncompensated – in contrast with the rationales of tort law.[77] Regardless of the European Parliament's suggestion to allow machines to pay for damage they had caused,[78] algorithms in fact do not need to pay themselves for the rationale of "compensation" to be met. As discussed above, the manufacturers, developers, or users of the thinking algorithm may continue to pay for damages caused by their algorithms.[79] Focusing on the third alternative mentioned, while a finding that an algorithm was reasonable would absolve the "deep pockets" from liability – just as in the case of a human tortfeasor – a finding that the algorithm was unreasonable (and met the other requirements of negligence) would certainly not prevent victims from being compensated by the "deep pockets" involved. In fact, thinking algorithms, especially those used in commercial contexts, are often expected to be linked to "deep pockets" in the form of their manufacturers or developers.

Deterrence

Even with access to "deep pockets" for recovery, the fact that negligence is judged by the actions of the algorithms themselves might weaken the deterrent effect of tort liability, as the entity that caused the damage is not the same entity that has to bear the consequences, and hence would not internalize them when deciding how to act.

But even if thinking algorithms themselves were not affected by a finding that they acted unreasonably, this still does not mean that they cannot be deterred from tortious conduct. True, a scenario in which algorithms themselves have "strong self-awareness" that causes them to "fear" the potential negative consequences of their actions (such as paying damages, if, in this futuristic world, algorithms owned assets), and shape their choices accordingly, still belongs to the world of science fiction. Nevertheless, an algorithm may be programmed to consider the potential consequences of negligence as part of the parameters it weighs before reaching its decision.[80] For instance, if a robo-doctor needed to choose a certain treatment for a patient, the professional and economic parameters it would be programmed to weigh would include the damage expectancy associated with every possible alternative versus the costs of preventing damage.[81] As long as the entity that bore the costs of damages caused by an

---

[77]   Colonna, above note 43.

[78]   Whether by a shared obligatory insurance scheme or by individual funds for each robot category (European Parliament Draft Report, above note 10, section 31).

[79]   Abbot, above note 29.

[80]   A thinking algorithm may also "teach itself" to do so, if it discovers that such strategy advances it toward a goal programmed into it (A. Roth, Machine Testimony (2017) 126 Yale Law Rev. 1972).

[81]   Granted, a robo-doctor would have considered the damage expectancy of each alternative as part of its "professional decision-making process," regardless of the threat of a tort law suit. But, aware of the fact they might be liable in tort for the damage resulting from an algorithm whose choices were unreasonable, the programmers of the algorithm may compute it to put emphasis on the legal consequences of a damaging choice

unreasonable algorithm could influence its decision-making process, the rationale of deterrence would still apply in the same sense that deterrence works in the employer–employee relationship – for example, where employers are encouraged to direct their employees' behavior in such a way that would not amount to a tortious act.

Does Mere "Reasonableness" Suffice?

Algorithms are superior to humans in many aspects of the decision-making process. Algorithms, for instance, can compute an enormous amount of data that the human mind cannot grasp, let alone process within split seconds.[82] Unlike humans, algorithms do not have self-interests affecting their judgment, they do not omit any of the decision-making stages or base their decisions on heuristics or biases, and they are not subject to human physical or emotional limitations such as exhaustion, stress, or sensitivity. Lastly, algorithms that are put to commercial or mass use will probably be among "the best ones out there," as opposed to a human decision-maker who may be above average, but at the same time be the physician or attorney (for example) who finished last in their class.[83]

It could be argued that the entire concept of "reasonableness" stems from the inherent flaws of the human decision-making process, and that it is only because of these flaws that we do not demand perfect decisions at all times, but turn to a "second-best" level of desired human behavior – which is "reasonable." If, for example, DC Comics' Superman were not fictional, the argument goes, we would not be satisfied with a "reasonableness" standard to judge his actions. Rather, we would probably expect and demand that Superman acts flawlessly at all times – simply because he can.[84] One could argue that, for the same reasons, algorithms should not be subject to standards that stem from human weaknesses that they do not share.

The first response to this argument is that just as professionals are held to a higher degree of reasonableness than laypersons, and just as professionals with an established expertise are judged by standards higher than those applied to other professionals,[85] the standard of reasonableness for algorithms might be higher than that for a reasonable "person" or a "reasonable professional." Shaping an optimal reasonableness standard for an algorithm would clearly require much thought and adjustments, but the fact that it possesses superior abilities does not in itself render the standard of reasonableness irrelevant.

Second, and linked to the former point, algorithms are also inferior to humans in several aspects of the decision-making process. For example, they may suffer from technical malfunctions or be vulnerable to cyber-attacks.[86] They also lack the creativity and flexibility that

(just like human doctors, when weighing their choices, often make their choices based on fear from malpractice suits). See, e.g., B. Chen, Defensive Medicine under Enterprise Insurance: Do Physicians Practice Defensive Medicine, and Can Enterprise Insurance Mitigate Its Effect? 5th Annual Conference on Empirical Legal Studies Paper (July 7, 2010), https://ssrn.com/abstract=1640955.

[82] Not only are human experts' abilities inferior in that sense, but enhancements of their performance might come at the expense of other abilities and degrade other aspects of their functioning. I. E. Dror, The Paradox of Human Expertise: Why Experts Get It Wrong, in N. Kapur (ed.), *The Paradoxical Brain* (Cambridge University Press, 2011), p. 181.

[83] Khosla, above note 9.

[84] In terms of economic efficiency and optimal deterrence, if we go back to some of the rationales of tort law, it would not make sense to hold Superman to standards of behavior that are clearly below his capabilities.

[85] Restatement (Second) of Torts § 299A (1977), Comment d.

[86] Importantly, the negative outcome of an algorithm making erroneous decisions (due to malfunction of some sort or in general) could far exceed those of a human. This is because an algorithmic error might be duplicated to all other algorithms making that same decision, unlike a human, whose decisions could vary from the ones made by

in many cases is a key component in becoming an expert in a professional field. Moreover, algorithms may not necessarily be able to adjust their decisions when they encounter new parameters that were not part of their training process, or when such adjustments are not in line with their programmed limitations – unlike human decision-makers, who might be better suited to manage unexpected circumstances or input.[87] Another aspect of algorithms' rigidity is that, unlike human decision-makers, they do not discuss their decisions with colleagues and peers, and thus lack the opportunity to identify errors or tweak the decision so as to match the majority opinion.[88] Lastly, although algorithms' abilities outperform those of humans in many aspects, they face an inherent disadvantage when making decisions calling for certain human traits that algorithms are not yet capable of copying. For instance, they might be less accurate than humans in detecting nuances in human body language or gestures indicating that a person is deliberately feeding them inaccurate information. In sum, algorithms do have certain disadvantages in decision-making as compared with humans, which supports the need for a specific reasonableness standard that considers their inherent strengths as well as their weaknesses.

Third, the "lack of tolerance toward reasonableness" argument may be relevant for "right and wrong" decisions that depend on computational abilities, such as the optimal vectors for landing an airplane, for example, but it is less applicable to discretional decisions that have no "right or wrong" answers that could have been anticipated in advance. A robo-doctor making a damaging decision, for example, might have reached its decisions flawlessly in terms of weighing and calculating all the relevant parameters, but later it turned out that an alternative treatment would have worked better for the particular patient. Similarly, while the exact same decision could have won many physicians' support, others might have chosen an alternative. "Reasonableness" questions suit exactly these types of cases, the accuracy of the relevant computations notwithstanding.

Lastly, and as discussed in "Why Apply a Reasonableness Standard to Thinking Algorithms," above, if algorithms are held to Superman-esque standards of strict liability, where responsibility for the damage is imposed regardless of culpability, this may create a significant chilling effect on the development of new algorithmic technologies.

CONCLUSION

The more "human-like" algorithms become in terms of discretion and decision-making, the more sensible it is to stop treating them as "tools" and to apply legal concepts previously reserved for humans. Applying a "reasonable algorithm" standard to thinking algorithms might solve different anomalies otherwise caused from the interchangeable use of humans and algorithmic decision-makers, while applying different tort frameworks to them. Although such policy may raise intuitive concerns and hesitancy, many of these can in fact be overcome. A "reasonable algorithm" standard, therefore, is a concept that deserves thoughtful consideration.

---

other decision-makers. E. Lieblich and E. Benvenisti, The Obligation to Exercise Discretion in Warfare: Why Autonomous Weapon Systems Are Unlawful, in N. Bhuta, S. Beck, and R. Geiß (eds.), *Autonomous Weapons Systems: Law, Ethics, Policy* (Cambridge University Press, 2016), p. 244.

[87]   Lieblich and Benvenisti, *ibid.* T. J. Barth and E. F. Arnold, Artificial Intelligence and Administrative Discretion: Implications for Public Administration (1999) 29 *Am. Rev. Public Adm.* 332.

[88]   *Ibid.*

PART V

Constitutional Law, Human Rights, and Algorithms

Human Rights-Based Approach to AI and Algorithms

Concerning Welfare Technologies

Jędrzej Niklas

INTRODUCTION

Automated systems that process vast amounts of data about individuals and communities have become a transformative force within contemporary societies and institutions. Governments and businesses, which adopt and develop new techniques of collecting and analyzing information, rely on algorithms in the decision-making process in various sectors: like banking, political marketing, health, and criminal justice. One of the early adopters of the automated systems are also welfare agencies responsible for the distribution of welfare benefits and management of social policies. These new ways of using technology highlight efficiency, standardization, and resource optimization as benefits.[1] However, the debate about artificial intelligence (AI) and algorithms should not be limited to questions about its technical capabilities and functionalities. So too is the creation and implementation of technological innovations a significant normative and ethical challenge for our society. The decision to process data and use certain algorithms is structured and motivated by specific political and economic factors. Therefore, just as argued by Winner, technical artifacts pose political qualities and are far from being neutral.[2]

Recently, a growing number of critical scholars and activists stress that automated technologies come with significant risks for the democratic system, human rights, and social justice.[3] Among those concerns is, for example, opacity, threats to privacy, and freedom of speech. Automated systems may also contribute to systematically disadvantaging vulnerable communities and can lead to discrimination. International human rights standards are becoming an essential element in this debate. For example, a recent study from the Council of Europe maps how different use of algorithms can influence a set of human rights recognized within European human rights systems; these include the right to a fair trial, privacy, freedom of expression, and social rights.[4] In another report, researchers from

---

[1]   T. Zarsky, The Trouble with Algorithmic Decisions: An Analytic Road Map to Examine Efficiency and Fairness in Automated and Opaque Decision Making (2016) 41 *Sci. Technol. Human Values* 121, https://doi.org/10.1177/0162243915605575.

[2]   L. Winner, Do Artifacts Have Politics? (1980) 109 *Daedalus* 121–3.

[3]   See, e.g., C. O'Neil, *Weapons of Math Destruction: How Big Data Increases Inequality and Threatens Democracy* (Crown, 2017); F. Pasquale, *The Black Box Society: The Secret Algorithms that Control Money and Information* (Harvard University Press, 2015); L. Dencik, A. Hintz, J. Redden, and E. Treré, Exploring Data Justice: Conceptions, Applications and Directions (2019) 22 *Inf. Commun. Soc.* 873–81, https://doi.org/10.1080/1369118X.2019.1606268; S. U. Noble, *Algorithms of Oppression: How Search Engines Reinforce Racism* (New York University Press, 2018).

[4]   Committee of Experts on Internet Intermediaries, Algorithms and Human Rights – Study on the Human Rights Dimensions of Automated Data Processing Techniques and Possible Regulatory Implications (Council of

Berkman Klein Center argue that human rights can play an essential role in evaluating the impact of AI.[5] However, such evaluation is not an easy exercise due to institutional complexities and a multitude of affected rights. Similarly, McGregor and colleagues see international human rights law as a promising, holistic framework that could bring some additional value within the discussion about algorithm accountability.[6] The language of fundamental rights plays a vital role in the works of High Level Group on Ethics on AI established by the European Commission.[7]

The above example of reports, guidelines, and research articles are evidence of the emerging role that international human rights may play in the discussion about algorithms and AI. This chapter joins this discussion and explores how the so-called human rights-based approach (HRBA) can be conceptualized in the context of automated systems. To achieve this goal, it will explore the existing debate around HRBA and try to understand its meaning, as well as explain its potentialities and limitations. HRBA emerged initially within the discussion around international development facilitated at the UN level and spread to other dimensions like the quality of health or water. This chapter will build on those experiences and argue that HRBA may serve as a vital framework to understand harms caused by algorithms. It can allow expanding the traditional debate around rights and technology beyond threats to privacy and addressing such issues like discrimination or social rights. This chapter will discuss and explore this direction, by focusing on the use of automated systems in the area of social security. Different systems (welfare technologies) are used to facilitate access to social benefits, check eligibility, detect welfare fraud, and also assist in formulating social policies. Therefore, those technologies play an important role in enjoying socio-economic rights.

With such goals and arguments, this chapter will be divided into three sections and organized as follows. The first section, "Problematic Nature of Algorithms," will explore the characteristics of algorithms, automated systems, and AI and summarise some main concerns associated with these technologies. It will also analyze the use of automated systems in the social security sectors, as this topic will be the central area of interest in the chapter. The second section, "What Is the Human Rights-Based Approach?," will outline the current debates around HRBA – it will analyze an added value of this framework, evaluate main themes associated with HRBA in the literature, and investigate some limitations. In the third section, "How to Apply HRBA," I will try to evaluate how HRBA can be relevant for the discussion on algorithmic systems and what kind of difference this approach is bringing in the regulation, policy, and designing of such technologies, especially in the welfare area.

PROBLEMATIC NATURE OF ALGORITHMS

Algorithms have various meanings and definitions, some of which are broader than others, but mostly they refer to relations between data, code, and automatization. This chapter

Europe, 2018), https://edoc.coe.int/en/internet/7589-algorithms-and-human-rights-study-on-the-human-rights-dimensions-of-automated-data-processing-techniques-and-possible-regulatory-implications.html.

[5] F. Raso, H. Hilligoss, V. Krishnamurphy, et al., Artificial Intelligence & Human Rights: Opportunities & Risks, Publication No. 2018-6 (Berkman Center for Internet & Society, 2018), https://cyber.harvard.edu/sites/default/files/2018-09/2018-09_AIHumanRightsSmall.pdf.

[6] L. McGregor, D. Murray, and V. Ng, International Human Rights Law as a Framework for Algorithmic Accountability (2019) 68 Int. Comp. Law Q. 314, https://doi.org/10.1017/S0020589319000046.

[7] High-Level Expert Group on Artificial Intelligence, Ethics Guidelines for Trustworthy AI, European Commission (2019), https://ec.europa.eu/newsroom/dae/document.cfm?doc_id=58477.

follows Gillespie's description and understands algorithms as "encoded procedures for transforming input data into the desired output, based on specified calculations. The procedures name both a problem and the steps by which it should be solved."[8] In the current discussion revolving around the social and legal implication of technologies, the term "algorithm" is synonymous with a different range of automated decision-making systems used by companies and public agencies in various contexts. For Kitchin, algorithms are assemblages of different calculation methods and codes, data processing, finance, politics, laws and regulations, materialities and infrastructures, institutions and inter-personal relations.[9] At the same time, the role of technology in the automated decision process is widely varied. As illustrated by Smith and colleagues, the role of computer systems in decision-making can be automatized in different levels.[10] For example, some computer systems may provide a set of alternative decisions, suggest one of them, or sometimes execute the final outcome without the human intervention. This varied level of automation affects accountability, transparency, discretion, and responsibility.

The approach that allows for greater progress in the automatization of the different decision processes is machine learning. This technology enables computer systems to learn directly from data-shaped examples and experiences.[11] In contrast, more traditional automated systems are based on rules coded by hand that have to be described explicitly. On the other hand, machine-learning systems receive a huge amount of data as examples from which they can learn how to solve the problem. This process is also described as an "automated process of discovering correlations (sometimes alternatively referred to as relationships or patterns) between variables in a dataset, often to make predictions or estimates of some outcome."[12] There are at least three main branches of machine learning: supervised, unsupervised, and reinforcement learning. The main differences between these branches of machine learning concern the role of a data scientist in the learning process.[13]

Machine learning is by far one of the most popular types of AI, which recently became (again) a buzzword used by politicians, journalists, and business. In short, AI refers to a range of technologies "with the ability to perform tasks that would otherwise require human intelligence, such as visual perception, speech recognition, and language translation."[14] As a concept, AI is quite old, and it traces back to the 1950s with the seminal work of Alan Turing. Since then, the field has gone through different transformations and phases. For example, in the 1980s, there was a significant development in the use of so-called "expert systems."[15] In more recent times, AI involves other tools and methods, like facial recognition, neural systems, and natural language processing. Altogether, those different technologies and

---

[8] T. Gillespie, The Relevance of Algorithms, in T. Gillespie, P. J. Boczkowski, and K. A. Foot (eds.), *Media Technologies: Essays on Communication, Materiality, and Society* (MIT Press, 2014), p. 167.

[9] R. Kitchin, Thinking Critically about and Researching Algorithms (2017) 20 *Inf. Commun. Soc.* 17, https://doi.org/10.1080/1369118X.2016.1154087.

[10] M. L. Smith, M. E. Noorman, and A. K. Martin, Automating the Public Sector and Organizing Accountabilities (2010) 26 *Commun. Assoc. Inf. Syst.* 25–6, https://doi.org/10.17705/1CAIS.02601.

[11] Royal Society (Great Britain), Machine Learning: The Power and Promise of Computers that Learn by Example (2017), p. 17, https://royalsociety.org/~/media/policy/projects/machine-learning/publications/machine-learning-report.pdf.

[12] D. Lehr and P. Ohm, Playing with the Data: What Legal Scholars Should Learn about Machine Learning (2017) 51 *UC Davis Law Rev.* 671.

[13] Royal Society, above note 11, p. 20.

[14] House of Lords, Select Committee on Artificial Intelligence, AI in the UK: Ready, Willing and Able? (House of Lords, 2017), p. 20, https://publications.parliament.uk/pa/ld201719/ldselect/ldai/100/100.pdf.

[15] L. Dormehl, *Thinking Machines: The Quest for Artificial Intelligence – and Where It's Taking Us Next* (TarcherPerigee, 2017), p. 30.

techniques of processing information show an amazing diversity in terms of advancement, complexity, and sophistication. Those aspects may also play an important role in understanding and addressing social and legal consequences of using such automated technologies.

Algorithms: Human Rights and Ethical Concerns

Different communities of practitioners, activists, and scholars have articulated some critical concerns about the use of algorithms which have led to questions about ethical, legal, and social implications of automated systems. As mentioned above, algorithms create new opportunities for the decision-making process in different organizations. Therefore, there are numerous examples from various sectors where automated systems assist, facilitate, and determine situations of interest to individuals and communities. Those areas range from criminal justice to banking, insurance, employment, housing, energy, healthcare, social security, to the political process. Due to the widespread use of algorithms throughout society, any errors, limitations, or intentional wrongdoing associated with algorithms can and do have significant consequences.

Reasoning: Correlations, Causation, and Human in the Loop

One of the biggest challenges in algorithmic decision-making is the kind of reasoning such systems rely on. The main category here is correlations identified in given datasets between inputs and outputs. Based on these correlations, automated systems make certain predictions. But as Ananny stresses, predictive analytics is still highly uncertain.[16] In fact, one of the common mistakes in statistical analysis is to equate correlations with causation.[17] However, in many cases, correlation serves as a legitimate and sufficient justification for specific decision-making.[18] Additionally, algorithms are based on the knowledge that describes specific patterns within certain populations and groups.[19] However, this knowledge is then applied to make a decision about individuals. Even if individuals belong to these groups, their situation may deviate in some specific aspect from the group description.[20] As a consequence, this type of reasoning may not take into account the right degree of differentiation and lead to simplifications, errors, and discrimination (as it will be described below).[21] This specific feature of algorithms can also raise concerns that relate to a potential arbitrariness of such a decision-making process.

One way to mitigate this risk is to create automated systems that make only recommendations when a human agent authorizes any "opinion" produced by such systems. However, having a "human in the loop" raises some further questions on the ability to understand operations done by algorithms.[22] Additionally, humans may perceive that automated systems

---

[16] M. Ananny, Toward an Ethics of Algorithms: Convening, Observation, Probability, and Timeliness (2016) 41 *Sci. Technol. Human Values* 103, https://doi.org/10.1177/0162243915606523.

[17] B. D. Mittelstadt, P. Allo, M. Taddeo, *et al.*, The Ethics of Algorithms: Mapping the Debate (2016) 3 *Big Data Soc.* 5–6, https://doi.org/10.1177/2053951716679679; P. Illari and F. Russo, *Causality: Philosophical Theory Meets Scientific Practice*, 1st edn. (Oxford University Press, 2014), pp. 16–18.

[18] M. Hildebrandt, Algorithmic Regulation and the Rule of Law (2018) 376 *Philos. TR Soc. A* 8, https://doi.org/10.1098/rsta.2017.0355.

[19] Illari and Russo, above note 17, p. 35.

[20] M. Hildebrandt, Profiling: From Data to Knowledge (2006) 30 *Datenschutz und Datensicherheit* 549.

[21] Zarsky, above note 1, p. 130.

[22] R. Binns and V. Gallo, Automated Decision Making: The Role of Meaningful Human Reviews, ICO (April 2, 2019), https://ai-auditingframework.blogspot.com/2019/04/automated-decision-making-role-of.html.

are more neutral, and they may also face some organizational obstacles (like lack of time, pressure from higher management, or limited psycho-social support in the decision process).[23] All of those problems may reduce the effectiveness of the right to human interventions as a meaningful safeguard for algorithmic decision-making and lead to the phenomenon called "rubber-stamping."

Opacity and Lack of Transparency

Another critical issue is related to the question about transparency of algorithms. Very often, automated systems and AI are portrayed as "black boxes" – non-transparent mechanisms that perform not always understandable mathematical operations using data.[24] Lack of transparency means that people affected by decisions done automatically (for example, they did not get credit, did not get a place at the university, did not get a job) have limited opportunities to understand and eventually challenge them. As such, there is an emerging problem to create mechanisms and technologies that reduce opacity and lead to greater transparency and explainability of such systems.[25] Legal scholar Danaher stresses that there are two dimensions which can be used to examine decisions made by algorithms – either to look at outputs (what was decided) or to look at procedure (what the decision process looked like).[26] Opacity is central to both of those dimensions and can be a consequence of different reasoning.

With the above as a starting point, Burrell distinguished three different models of opacity. First, intentional opacity is a deliberate choice made by organizations responsible for the application and development of specific systems.[27] A good example of such a mechanism is trade secrecy, used to protect the financial interest of companies that rely for their business model on the use of algorithms. On the other hand, public agencies may use secrecy as a strategy to protect automated systems from gaming by, for example, taxpayers. A different type of opacity is linked to the lack of education and competences. Further, many automated systems are rather complicated. To understand how they work, individuals need to know some basics of data science and computer systems. So, even if fully disclosed, the automated system remains incomprehensible to the general public. The last type of opacity is related to technological advancement and complexity, as well as the "messy" design process. Outcomes of some advanced automated systems can even be difficult to understand for experts in the field. For example, organizations may use in one decision-process a number of algorithms that interact with one another. There are also types of algorithms that can learn on their own from data, and such processes go beyond the human cognitive capacity to understand them. In addition, many algorithms are created by large teams where different people are

---

[23] B. Wagner, Liable, But Not in Control? Ensuring Meaningful Human Agency in Automated Decision-Making Systems: Human Agency in Decision-Making Systems? (2019) 11 *Policy & Internet* 12, https://doi.org/10.1002/poi3 .198.

[24] Pasquale, above note 3, pp. 3–10; S. Lem, *Summa Technologiae*, Vol. 40: *Electronic Mediations*, J. Zylinska (trans.) (University of Minnesota Press, 2013), pp. 96–8.

[25] S. Wachter, B. Mittelstadt, and C. Russell, Counterfactual Explanations without Opening the Black Box: Automated Decisions and the GDPR (2018) 31 *Harv. J. Law Technol.* 854–9, https://doi.org/10.2139/ssrn .3063289; N. Diakopoulos, Accountability in Algorithmic Decision Making (2016) 59 *Commun. ACM* 60–1, https://doi.org/10.1145/2844110.

[26] J. Danaher, The Threat of Algocracy: Reality, Resistance and Accommodation, *Philosophy & Technology* (2016), p. 245.

[27] J. Burrell, How the Machine "Thinks": Understanding Opacity in Machine Learning Algorithms (2016) 3 *Big Data Soc.* 1–3, https://doi.org/10.1177/2053951715622512.

responsible for only a specific part of the code. This procedure, to pursue the design of algorithms, makes it even harder for humans to understand the way in which the algorithm operates.

Discrimination and Inequality

Discriminatory outcomes constitute another crucial problem in the discussion about algorithmic systems. Well-documented studies on numerous occasions show that many algorithmic systems have built-in biases that affect how they made decisions.[28] Some early works by Gandy show that modern computer systems, with their ability to identify, assess, and classify people, are in fact discriminatory tools.[29] He also argues that such computerized discrimination can be less transparent and affect members of non-traditionally discriminated groups. More recently, Barocas also explains that discrimination by algorithmic systems can take several primary forms: intentional discrimination, statistical bias, (overly) accurate inferences, and flawed inferences.[30] These discriminatory outcomes may result from different problems which relate to the process of data entry and the design of the algorithm itself.[31] The first issue can emerge when conclusions are based on erroneous or incomplete data. Another problem is under- (or over-) representation of certain social groups in datasets. As Crawford points out, information is not collected "equally" from everyone in society.[32] There are situations when groups or individuals are omitted due to their financial status, place of residence, knowledge about digital technologies, or lifestyle. If the ideal model is created on the basis of such information, an algorithm may ignore the preferences of some groups and their characteristics, resulting in discrimination. Thus, in the context of the hiring process, a filtering CV mechanism that is based on the historical recruitment process may replicate stereotypes and biases already in existence (for example, related to gender).[33]

On the other hand, "harmful algorithms" can exist as a consequence of analytical constructions and previously used parameters. A good example of this problem is the widely commented-upon COMPAS scoring tool used in some US states to assess the risk of someone committing a crime.[34] While the system did not directly take into account the race of the assessed person, a detailed analysis of the results showed that black people were more often rated as risky in terms of committing a crime than white people.[35] This outcome was the result of relying on variables that indirectly indicate race or economic status. This is a good example of a situation where the features taken into account, which at first glance seem rational and

---

[28]   F. Kamiran and T. Calders, Classifying without Discriminating, in 2nd International Conference on Computer, Control and Communication, IEEE, Karachi (2009), pp. 1–6, https://doi.org/10.1109/IC4.2009.4909197.

[29]   O. H. Gandy, It's Discrimination, Stupid!, in J. Brook (ed.), *Resisting the Virtual Life: The Culture and Politics of Information* (City Lights Books, 1995), pp. 35–47.

[30]   S. Barocas, Data Mining and the Discourse on Discrimination, in Proceedings of the Data Ethics Workshop, Conference on Knowledge Discovery and Data Mining, New York (2015), pp. 1–4, https://dataethics.github.io /proceedings/DataMiningandtheDiscourseOnDiscrimination.pdf.

[31]   S. Barocas and A. D. Selbst, Big Data's Disparate Impact (2016) 671 *Calif. Law Rev.* 680–90, https://papers .ssrn.com/sol3/papers.cfm?abstract_id=2477899.

[32]   K. Crawford, Think Again: Big Data, *Foreign Policy* (May 10, 2013), https://foreignpolicy.com/2013/05/10/think-again-big-data/.

[33]   J. Dastin, Amazon Scraps Secret AI Recruiting Tool that Showed Bias against Women, *Reuters* (October 2018), www.reuters.com/article/us-amazon-com-jobs-automation-insight/amazon-scraps-secret-ai-recruiting-tool-that-showed-bias-against-women-idUSKCN1MK08G.

[34]   J. Angwin, J. Larson, S. Mattu, and L. Kirchner, Machine Bias, *ProPublica* (May 2016), www.propublica.org /article/machine-bias-risk-assessments-in-criminal-sentencing.

[35]   C. Wadsworth, F. Vera, and C. Piech, Achieving Fairness through Adversarial Learning: An Application to Recidivism Prediction, ArXiv:1807.00199 [Cs, Stat] (June 2018), http://arxiv.org/abs/1807.00199.

fully justified, may further lead to unfavorable treatment of persons belonging to marginalized groups. Another example of a similar situation may be the system used in the Polish job centers to profile unemployed persons.[36] Due to their different position in the labor market, the system assesses men and women differently. Such a distinction may be justified, but in this case in point, it increased the likelihood of restricting access to some forms of support based on gender. The above examples illustrate very well that the decisions regarding the construction of automatic systems that rely on algorithms and the construction of analytical models are judgments reflecting a specific vision of reality, often of a political nature.

Those problems also fit into the category called "statistical discrimination."[37] There are situations when such characteristics like race or gender are correlated statistically with the condition that systems are trying to find out; for example, fraud, ability to work, and risk of committing a crime. However, when such correlations become a solid basis for automated systems in making a decision, this might create problems from the perspective of the principle of non-discrimination. While those correlations may be statistically accurate, they are socially and legally improper or unwanted.[38] Finally, it is worth adding that examples of automatic discrimination are usually unintentional and indirect. However, automated systems may serve to mask intentional discrimination, due to their lack of transparency and high level of algorithmic complexity.[39]

Privacy

Computerization and use of automated systems raise concerns for informational privacy and the capacity to control the dissemination of information by individuals.[40] Developments in data-processing techniques allow the tracing and gathering of information to occur on a massive scale. As mentioned above, AI and automated systems are by nature trained to use large datasets. In this sense, use of data by AI may reveal personal information about individuals, including sensitive data.

The risk for infringement of privacy is highly linked to state surveillance practices. Various governments are now developing sophisticated facial recognition tools used, among others, in crime prevention and detection. Examples of such projects are seen in the United Kingdom, the United States, and China.[41] These "surveillance systems" may create a problem for anonymity in public spaces. In the Chinese context, facial recognition is primarily used in the province of Xinjiang and used to control the Uighur population, which raises another

[36] J. Niklas, K. Sztandar, and K. Szymielewicz, Profiling the Unemployed in Poland: Social and Political Implications of Algorithmic Decision Making (Panoptykon Foundation, 2015), pp. 10–17, https://panoptykon .org/sites/default/files/leadimage-biblioteka/panoptykon_profiling_report_final.pdf.

[37] F. Schauer, Statistical (and Non-Statistical) Discrimination, in K. Lippert-Rasmussen (ed.), *The Routledge Handbook of the Ethics of Discrimination* (Routledge, 2018), pp. 42–52.

[38] L. Edwards and M. Veale, Slave to the Algorithm? Why a "Right to an Explanation" Is Probably Not the Remedy You Are Looking for (2017) 16 *Duke Law Technol. Rev.* 28, https://doi.org/10.31228/osf.io/97upg.

[39] Barocas and Selbst, above note 31, p. 692.

[40] Edwards and Veale, above note 38, p. 32; S. Wachter and B. Mittelstadt, A Right to Reasonable Inferences: Re-Thinking Data Protection Law in the Age of Big Data and AI (2019) 2 *Columbia Bus. Law Rev.* 49 4; E. Fosch, Villaronga, P. Kieseberg, and T. Li, Humans Forget, Machines Remember: Artificial Intelligence and the Right to Be Forgotten (2018) 34 *Comput. Law Secur. Rev.* 304–5, https://doi.org/10.1016/j.clsr.2017.08.007.

[41] J. Schuppe, How Facial Recognition Became a Routine Policing Tool in America, *NBC News* (May 11, 2019), www.nbcnews.com/news/us-news/how-facial-recognition-became-routine-policing-tool-america-n1004251; O. Bowcott, Police Face Legal Action over Use of Facial Recognition Cameras, *The Guardian* (June 14, 2018), www.theguardian.com/technology/2018/jun/14/police-face-legal-action-over-use-of-facial-recognition-cameras.

significant problem of surveillance practice that is disproportionately imposed on marginalized communities – ethnic and racial minorities and migrants.[42]

Threats imposed by AI and automated systems for privacy go beyond a specific dimension affecting an individual and raise important questions about threats to group privacy.[43] Scholars admit that modern profiling techniques rely very often on the group description rather than characterization of individuals.[44] Information privacy with its focuses on individual harms might not be the best framework to address problems caused by more sophisticated data analytics. Thanks to advanced data mining and machine learning, some major Internet platforms can infer from online data some sensitive characteristics like race, sexual orientation, health, and political opinions. Those predictions and attributions are highly controversial and privacy-intrusive, yet scholars raise the alarm that they are not adequately protected under existing data protection laws.[45] As a result, there are calls within the academic community to establish new data protection rights – for example, the "right to reasonable inferences," which would constitute a test to examine high-risk inferences.

Computerized Welfare State

While various sectors of society use automated systems for different reasons, this chapter focuses on one specific area, which is social security. For decades, public agencies have been adopting and developing new technological innovations to improve, speed up, and standardize the procedures and activities they engage in.[46] Under the unifying frame of e-government, countries have been investing in the digitization of databases and communication methods used by the public sector. Among the crucial users and early adopters of e-government technologies are those agencies responsible for social security.[47] This is not a surprise since social security is a sector that creates many financial demands and articulates a need for better management mechanisms.[48] Adler and Henman stress that saving resources is very often a predominant goal for using digital innovations by welfare agencies. In their study concerning computer systems used for social security in OECD countries, they described seventeen different aims for which welfare agencies are deploying such systems.[49] Among them were: increasing productivity, promoting accurate and consistent decision-making, cutting costs, increasing the responsiveness of service delivery, and improving information flows within and beyond the social security system.[50] They also show

---

[42] P. Mozur, One Month, 500,000 Face Scans: How China Is Using A.I. to Profile a Minority, New York Times (April 14, 2019), www.nytimes.com/2019/04/14/technology/china-surveillance-artificial-intelligence-racial-profiling.html.

[43] B. Mittelstadt, From Individual to Group Privacy in Big Data Analytics (2017) 30 Philos. Technol. 478–81, https://doi.org/10.1007/s13347-017-0253-7.

[44] L. Taylor, L. Floridi, and B. van der Sloot, Introduction: A New Perspective on Privacy, in L. Taylor, L. Floridi, and B. van der Sloot (eds.), Group Privacy: New Challenges of Data Technologies (Springer, 2017), pp. 4–8.

[45] Wachter and Mittelstadt, above note 40, pp. 81–99.

[46] J. Agar, The Government Machine: A Revolutionary History of the Computer (MIT Press, 2003); P. Henman, Governing Electronically (Palgrave Macmillan, 2010); M. J. Moon, J. Lee, and C.-Y. Roh, The Evolution of Internal IT Applications and E-Government Studies in Public Administration: Research Themes and Methods (2014) 46 Adm. Soc. 3–36, https://doi.org/10.1177/0095399712459723; P. Perri, E-Governance: Styles of Political Judgment in the Information Age Polity (Palgrave Macmillan, 2014).

[47] Agar, ibid., p. 134.

[48] Henman, above note 46, p. 14.

[49] M. Adler and P. Henman, Computerizing the Welfare State: An International Comparison of Computerization in Social Security (2005) 8 Inf. Commun. Soc. 320–2, https://doi.org/10.1080/13691180500259137.

[50] Ibid., p. 323.

through their research that architectures and aims of automated systems used in this context depend on the type of welfare state and protection of social rights embraced in a given country.

Adler and Henman's study focused on pre-Internet and quite old-fashioned tools; now, welfare agencies are also buying into new forms of e-government that include sophisticated data analytics, AI, machine learning, and profiling methods.[51] For example, the Finnish city of Espoo is experimenting with analyzing the massive volume of data about individuals to identify new proactive means of targeting services to citizens, and to prevent social exclusion.[52] In the Netherlands, newly adopted data-analytics systems help target fraudulent behavior among welfare recipients.[53] One of the Danish municipalities has been using a system to identify children at risk of abuse and manage the early intervention process of social services.[54] Dencik and colleagues describe a similar trend in the UK welfare sector and policing. According to their research, we can now witness a proliferation of so-called "citizens scoring," which involves "data analytics in government for the purposes of categorisation, assessment and prediction at both individual and population level."[55] The study undertaken by the civil society organization Algorithm Watch proves that similar systems are now being developed in many other different European countries on a massive scale; however, their levels of technological sophistication vary.[56]

Regardless of their technological sophistication, those digital innovations are causing some disruption and even harms. Examples from different countries link the deployment of data-driven systems to austerity policy and privatization of public services and show evidence of harmful effects on marginalized communities. One such example relates to the Michigan Integrated Data Automated System, which wrongly accused individuals in at least 20,000 cases of fraudulently seeking unemployment payments. As a result, the people accused lost access to unemployment payments and reportedly faced fines as high as $100,000.[57] Similarly, in Australia, thousands of citizens faced the problem of so-called "robo-debts" due to an error in the automated system which resulted in obstacles to receiving unemployment benefits.[58] In his country report from his visit to the United Kingdom, the UN Special Rapporteur on extreme poverty and human rights expressed the view that new digitalized welfare policy "built a digital barrier that obstructs access to benefits, and particularly disadvantages women, older people, people who do not speak English and persons with disabilities."[59]

[51]   G. Bäckman, The Nordic Welfare Model in the Wake of Post-WWII Transformations and Algorithms of Changing Social Policy (2019) 6 *Athens J. Social Sciences* 177–95, https://doi.org/10.30958/ajss.6-3-1.

[52]   City of Espoo, Espoo Experiment Proves that Artificial Intelligence Recognises Those Who Need Support, *espoo. fi* (June 7, 2018), www.espoo.fi/en-US/Espoo_experiment_proves_that_artificial_(142925).

[53]   M. Hijink, Algoritme Voorspelt Wie Fraude Pleegt Bij Bijstandsuitkering, *NRC* (April 8, 2018), www.nrc.nl /nieuws/2018/04/08/algoritme-voorspelt-wie-fraude-pleegt-bij-bijstandsuitkering-a1598669.

[54]   J. Mchangama and H.-Y. Liu, The Welfare State Is Committing Suicide by Artificial Intelligence, *Foreign Policy* (December 25, 2018), https://foreignpolicy.com/2018/12/25/the-welfare-state-is-committing-suicide-by-artificial-intelligence/.

[55]   L. Decnik, J. Redden, A. Hintz, and H. Warne, The "Golden View": Data-Driven Governance in the Scoring Society (2019) 8 *Internet Policy Rev.* 3, https://doi.org/10.14763/2019.2.1413.

[56]   M. Spielkamp (ed.), *Automating Society: Taking Stock of Automated Decision-Making in the EU* (Algorithm Watch, 2018), https://algorithmwatch.org/wp-content/uploads/2019/01/Automating_Society_Report_2019.pdf.

[57]   R. Felton, Michigan Unemployment Agency Made 20,000 False Fraud Accusations – Report, *The Guardian* (December 28, 2016), www.theguardian.com/us-news/2016/dec/18/michigan-unemployment-agency-fraud-accusations.

[58]   C. Knaus, Centrelink Scandal: Tens of Thousands of Welfare Debts Wiped or Reduced, *The Guardian* (September 13, 2017), www.theguardian.com/australia-news/2017/sep/13/centrelink-scandal-tens-of-thousands-of-welfare-debts-wiped-or-reduced.

[59]   Special Rapporteur on extreme poverty and human rights, Visit to the United Kingdom of Great Britain and Northern Ireland (United Nations, 2019), pp. 13–14, https://undocs.org/en/A/HRC/41/39/Add.1.

Exploring those and similar cases, scholars outline the relationship between the deployment of such technologies and the limitation of rights and democratic participation for the poorest segments of society. One of the earliest works in this area, by Gilliom, examines the experience of low-income women from the Appalachian region with comprehensive computerized welfare surveillance.[60] In a similar tone, Eubanks's ethnographic research provides some detailed and rich evidence of the impact of automated systems on vulnerable communities and builds a concept of the "digital poorhouse."[61] She argues that a low expectancy of rights causes a population experiencing poverty to live disproportionately under surveillance and database scrutiny compared to a wealthy population. Furthermore, Bridges notes that the use of surveillance technologies by welfare administration and infringements of privacy of the poorest is justified by the moral construction of poverty.[62] On the other hand, scholars like Henman explain how the rise of automated systems creates structural changes for the welfare state, by creating a new and conditional social citizenship.[63] The availability of data gives welfare administration greater capacity to create stricter eligibility criteria that go beyond policy domains (for example, linking social assistance benefits with school attendance). Very often, this so-called "new conditionality" is linked with financial penalties for individual non-compliance. In addition, Madden and colleagues argue that in the context of digital surveillance, vulnerable individuals and groups can also suffer from a lack of adequate legal safeguards and their enforcement, which Gilman also calls a "class differentiation in privacy law."[64] All of these empirical examples and discussions show different social, technological, and institutional challenges created by automated systems for enjoyment of human rights. They also lead to the questions about potential solutions and interventions that can fix or mitigate harms caused by technology.

Techno-Legal Interventions and Their Limits

Over recent years, the highly influential group of interdisciplinary scholars' community defined as Fairness, Accountability and Transparency in Machine Learning (FATML) have tried to unpack and re-evaluate the meaning of accountability, equality, and other ethical issues in the context of automated systems.[65] Some of the roots of this community can be found in early works on characterization of biases in computer systems or opacity of expert systems logics.[66] In fact, discriminatory algorithms, data-mining, or machine-learning techniques remain one of the main concerns for this field.[67] The FATML community's focus,

---

[60] J. Gilliom, *Overseers of the Poor: Surveillance, Resistance and the Limits of Privacy* (University of Chicago Press, 2001).

[61] V. Eubanks, *Automating Inequality: How High-Tech Tools Profile, Police, and Punish the Poor* (St. Martin's Press, 2018).

[62] K. M. Bridges, *The Poverty of Privacy Rights* (Stanford Law Books, an imprint of Stanford University Press, 2017).

[63] P. Henman, Conditional Citizenship? Electronic Networks and the New Conditionality in Public Policy (2011) 3 *Policy & Internet* 71–88, https://doi.org/10.2202/1944-2866.1103.

[64] M. Madden, M. Gilman, K. Levy, and A. Marwick, Privacy, Poverty and Big Data: A Matrix of Vulnerabilities for Poor Americans (2017) 95 *Wash. Univ. Law Rev.* 77; M. E. Gilman, The Class Differential in Privacy Law (2012) 77 *Brooklyn Law Rev.* 1443, http://papers.ssrn.com/sol3/papers.cfm?abstract_id=2182773.

[65] Fairness, Accountability, and Transparency in Machine Learning, www.fatml.org/.

[66] B. Friedman and H. Nissenbaum, Bias in Computer Systems (1996) 14 *ACM Trans. Inf. Syst.* 330–47, https://doi.org/10.1145/230538.230561; M. R. Wick and W. B. Thompson, Reconstructing Expert System Explanation (1992) 54 *Artif. Intell.* 33–70, https://doi.org/10.1016/0004-3702(92)90087-E.

[67] Kamiran and Calders, above note 28; D. Pedreschi, S. Ruggieri, and F. Turini, Discrimination-Aware Data Mining, in ACM Proceedings, KDD '08, Las Vegas, Nevada (2008), https://doi.org/10.1145/1401890.1401959; Barocas and Selbst, above note 31.

among others, is on the technical side of data processes, and the design of algorithms to create remedies and necessary solutions for social problems created by technologies.

For example, Buolamwini and Gebru argue that automated systems that are biased against a dark-skinned female population can be "fixed" by using more diverse datasets.[68] Similarly, Barocas and Selbst call for the collection of more granular data to mitigate the process of misidentification, misclassification, or unfair decision-making.[69] To reduce the opacity problem, Wachter and colleagues call for achieving a greater level of explainability of algorithmic decisions by providing so-called "counterfactual explanations."[70] The arrival of the General Data Protection Regulation (GDPR) opens a discussion of the safeguards that data protection may offer to mitigate harms caused by algorithms. This involves a set of different individual rights, such as the right to human interventions, the right to an explanation, or the right to contest an institutionalized impact assessment. For example, Malgieri and Comandé call for the systematic analysis of GDPR provisions and propose a new concept algorithm legibility that combines transparency and comprehensibility.[71]

This rich discussion about the potential technological and legal interventions toward potentially harmful algorithms also provides a greater understanding of automated systems, and their nature and complexity. It reveals very important insights into the role of computer systems in creating injustices or amplifying inequalities and, at the same time, stresses that those problems are solvable. However, this techno-centrism and quest for solutions is also the greatest limitation of this discussion. It is important to realise that decisions made by or with the assistance of algorithms and other technological systems always involve interactions between technology and human and political institutions.[72] The human is responsible for the design of the algorithm, input data, broader policy motivations, and, finally, the decision to use algorithm-based systems in a specific context. Therefore, different errors and wrong-doings at any stages require a mechanism that goes beyond some narrow technical and legal interventions. For example, Ananny and Crawford, in showing limitations of discourse around algorithmic transparency, argue for the use of a socio-technical approach.[73] For them, the algorithm is not just a code, but also the assemblage of human and non-human actors, institutions, norms, relations, and power affected by the algorithm. Holding this construction accountable requires not just seeing inside any one component, but understanding how it works as a system and the motivations of different actors.

On the other hand, Powles stresses that discriminatory biases embedded in automated systems are caused by societal tensions and "cannot be fully solved technically."[74] She adds that focus on narrow technical interventions takes attention away from more critical issues like political and economic inequalities related to technology and thus she raises the question

---

[68] J. Buolamwini and T. Gebru, Gender Shades: Intersectional Accuracy Disparities in Commercial Gender Classification, in Proceedings of the 1st Conference of Machine Learning Research Conference on Fairness, Accountability, and Transparency, New York (2018), p. 15.

[69] Barocas and Selbst, above note 31, p. 719.

[70] Wachter *et al.*, above note 25, pp. 842–4.

[71] G. Malgieri and G. Comandé, Why a Right to Legibility of Automated Decision-Making Exists in the General Data Protection Regulation (2017) 7 *Int. Data Priv. Law* 243–65, https://doi.org/10.1093/idpl/ipx019.

[72] G. F. Lanzara, Building Digital Institutions: ICT and the Rise of Assemblages in Government, in F. Contini and G. F. Lanzara (eds.), *ICT and Innovation in the Public Sector: European Studies in the Making of E-Government* (Palgrave Macmillan, 2009), p. 12.

[73] M. Ananny and K. Crawford, Seeing without Knowing: Limitations of the Transparency Ideal and Its Application to Algorithmic Accountability (2018) 20 *New Media Soc.* 973–89, https://doi.org/10.1177/1461444816676645.

[74] J. Powles, The Seductive Diversion of "Solving" Bias in Artificial Intelligence, *Medium* (December 7, 2018), https://onezero.medium.com/the-seductive-diversion-of-solving-bias-in-artificial-intelligence-890df5e5ef53.

of whether such systems should be used at all in specific contexts. Moreover, Binns explains that very often the FATML community ignores the extent and nuances of the long-standing discussion about the normative framework of fairness within political philosophy.[75] Therefore, very often, techno-centric solutions for discriminatory algorithms neglect social complexities and are simplistic. With similar conclusions, Hoffmann argues that biases and technological injustices cannot be seen as one-dimensional issues that can be fixed with narrow innervations that fall into the logic of distributional justice.[76] In her opinion, such injustices should be analyzed as part of bigger, structural problems that have been exposed in the context of data systems.

While no one approach covers all of the above-mentioned problems and concerns, an international human rights law framework might be a good starting point and could serve as a bridge between more narrow technical-legal solutions and broader critical approaches that are also grounded in contemporary political landscape. Human rights are widely recognized as a set of values and principles and for decades have been offering a mechanism to challenge existing inequalities and power relations. This potentiality can be used in the discussion concerning the social welfare aspects of algorithms as well. The following sections of this chapter will explore these opportunities in greater detail.

WHAT IS THE HUMAN RIGHTS-BASED APPROACH?

With the broad overview presented above on the discussion of automated systems and AI, the chapter will now turn to the key concept of using a human rights-based approach – including its history and meaning. In 1997, as part of his reform package, the UN Secretary-General proposed to redefine and integrate human rights into a broad range of UN activities.[77] This report was the moment of birth for HRBA, which resulted in numerous attempts to translate broad human rights principles to more enforceable safeguards and procedures.[78] Some of those efforts aimed at mainstreaming human rights language in different policy areas and aligning public policies with human rights entitlements of different communities.

The normative base for HRBA is international human rights law. However, for decades, due to political tensions caused by the Cold War, international agencies and many countries were reluctant to provide further recognition of human rights treaties and implement them into national and international policymaking. The situation changed in the 1990s, mainly as a consequence of political changes and the process of globalization.[79]

Since then, HRBA has become incorporated into different policies and programs, especially in the development, health, and social security areas.[80] There are numerous examples

[75] R. Binns, Fairness in Machine Learning: Lessons from Political Philosophy, in Proceedings of Machine Learning Research, Conference on Fairness, Accountability, and Transparency, New York (2018), pp. 1–3, http://proceedings.mlr.press/v81/binns18a/binns18a.pdf.
[76] A. L. Hoffmann, Where Fairness Fails: Data, Algorithms, and the Limits of Antidiscrimination Discourse (2019) 22 *Inf. Commun. Soc.* 909–11, https://doi.org/10.1080/1369118X.2019.1573912.
[77] United Nations Development Programme, Applying a Human Rights-Based Approach to Development Cooperation and Programming (2006), pp. 5–9, http://waterwiki.net/images/e/ee/Applying_HRBA_To_Development_Programming.pdf.
[78] E. Filmer-Wilson, The Human Rights-Based Approach to Development: The Right to Water (2005) 23 *Netherlands Q. Hum. Rights* 215–16, https://doi.org/10.1177/016934410502300203.
[79] S. Moyn, *The Last Utopia Human Rights in History* (Belknap Press, 2010), pp. 219–22; J. Tobin, *The Right to Health in International Law* (Oxford University Press, 2012), pp. 14–43.
[80] P. Gready, Rights-Based Approaches to Development: What Is the Value-Added? (2008) 18 *Dev. Pract.* 735–47, https://doi.org/10.1080/09614520802386454; M. Sepúlveda, The Rights-Based Approach to Social Protection in

when national and international organizations, as well as advocacy groups, use HRBA.[81] For example, many development agencies use this approach for their international funding strategies.[82] Further, national civil society groups rely on the HRBA framework to engage in policymaking. For example, a group of US advocacy organizations have used HRBA assessment tools to analyze healthcare reform plans, explaining how different proposals failed to meet key human rights standards.[83]

HRBA offers a framework for human rights to become less declaratory and more practical. In this sense, international human rights law becomes an entry-point and basis for creation, formulation, implementation, and evaluation of certain public policies. Scholars involved in the discussion around HRBA stress that this framework entails two important strands.[84] First, it politicizes or re-politicizes specific issues that are very often recognized in public discourse as technocratic or a single domain of experts. For example, within the discussion about health, HRBA offers a radical and powerful frame that redefines health as a matter of rights and justice, rather than a mere consequence of biology or genetics.[85] It explains how health is inseparably linked and constructed by social relations, power, and existing inequalities.

Yamin argues that HRBA allows policymakers to take suffering and experiences of vulnerable communities seriously and formulate them not as misfortunes or bad luck, but as violations of rights.[86] As such, violations of human rights are linked to decisions made by humans concerning money, politics, and power. In this sense, different public policies become human rights concerns, where individuals and communities are not passive subjects, but rather are rights-holders that have certain expectations and demands over those policies. From a HRBA perspective, denying certain services may comprise an infringement of human rights and lead to claims and potential redress. The HRBA approach demands a justification for such refusal and requests a plan for mitigating any arising problems.

HRBA is also holistic and embedded in the interdependent nature of human rights.[87] It does not refer to one specific right, but embraces all sets of human rights that are recognized in different human rights treaties. In this sense, it also includes economic and social rights, which are very often neglected in the mainstream discussions over human rights.[88] What is even more important to this discussion is that this framework also allows for providing tools to operationalize socio-economic rights in specific policy and economy areas, going beyond legal instruments (which reflect law as a remedy for human rights violations).[89] However, this

Latin America: From Rethoric to Practice, ECLAC – Social Policy Series No. 189 (2014), p. 71, https://repositorio.cepal.org/bitstream/handle/11362/37517/S1420720_en.pdf?sequence=1&isAllowed=y; S. Gruskin, D. Bogecho, and L. Ferguson, "Rights-Based Approaches" to Health Policies and Programs: Articulations, Ambiguities, and Assessment (2010) 31 *J. Public Health Policy* 129–45, https://doi.org/10.1057/jphp.2010.7.

81 V. Gauri and S. Gloppen, Human Rights-Based Approaches to Development: Concepts, Evidence, and Policy (2012) 44 *Polity* 485–503, https://doi.org/10.1057/pol.2012.12.

82 J. Ensor and P. Gready, *Reinventing Development? Translating Rights-Based Approaches from Theory into Practice* (Zed Books, 2005), pp. 1–10; A. Cornwall and C. Nyamu-Musembi, Putting the "Rights-Based Approach" to Development into Perspective (2004) 25 *Third World Q.* 1415–37.

83 A. Rudiger and B. Meier, A Rights-Based Approach to Health Care Reform, in E. Beracochea, C. Weinstein, and D. P. Evans (eds.), *Rights-Based Approaches to Public Health* (Springer, 2011), pp. 70–5.

84 Gready, above note 80, p. 22.

85 A. E. Yamin, Taking the Right to Health Seriously: Implications for Health Systems, Courts, and Achieving Universal Health Coverage (2017) 39 *Hum. Rights Q.* 350, https://doi.org/10.1353/hrq.2017.0021.

86 A. E. Yamin, Will We Take Suffering Seriously? Reflections on What Applying a Human Rights Framework to Health Means and Why We Should Care (2008) 10 *Health Hum. Rights* 48, https://doi.org/10.2307/20460087.

87 Gruskin *et al.*, above note 80, p. 131.

88 Filmer-Wilson, above note 78, p. 216.

89 P. Twomey, Human Rights-Based Approaches to Development: Towards Accountability, in M. Baderin and R. McCorquodale (eds.), *Economic, Social, and Cultural Rights in Action* (Oxford University Press, 2007), p. 69.

holistic nature of HRBA demands also uses an interdisciplinary approach and advocates cooperation with a range of different communities and professionals with different backgrounds in human rights, social and health policy, and the economy.[90]

The second added value of HRBA is its ability to operationalize broad principles into more concrete language, action plans, strategies, and impact assessment tools.[91] The holistic nature of HRBA and different strategies involves new requirements for human rights bodies, allowing civil society to go beyond the classic naming and shaming methodology (that is, litigation strategies). Instead, HRBA requires engagement in, for example, deciding budgetary policies, design of healthcare systems, and assessment of the quality of services. This would also require a more interdisciplinary approach and goes beyond expertise in human rights law.

Scholars stress that there is a standard set of themes and principles that link different HRBA tools and strategies. Among them are: comprehensive applications of human rights; discrimination and equality; participation and empowerment; and accountability and transparency.[92] Each of those principles is linked to different priorities and emphasizes certain kinds of problems that lead to different claims and remedies.

Equality and Non-Discrimination

Non-discrimination is one of the founding values in international and national human rights law and serves as a core principle for HRBA. This would require that members of marginalized groups enjoy equal access to rights and goods compared to the more advantaged groups. States should focus greater attention on the situation of vulnerable communities, by identifying those groups and understanding their situation.[93] This action requires some special attention toward collecting disaggregated data about such groups as women, ethnic minorities, indigenous groups, people living with a disability, or elderly people. This process should allow policymakers to understand who is vulnerable and why.[94]

The principle of non-discrimination also requires states to take different actions – for example, to create antidiscrimination laws or launch affirmative action programs. Often, agencies that use HRBA in their operations also try to introduce an integrated approach that recognizes gender equity and brings attention to the inequalities faced by women. For example, in their development strategy, UNICEF prioritizes discrimination in the context of education for girls and supports relevant programs in many countries.[95] Another example relates to a development agency from Sweden (SIDA), which runs a successful project in Ethiopia that addresses the problem of women's right to water. With the participatory approach, the project tried to meet the immediate need of women, but also to give them a strong sense of empowerment and ownership in the project.[96] So, in other words, HRBA

---

[90] Yamin, above note 86, p. 55.
[91] Gready, above note 80, p. 737.
[92] Yamin, above note 86, pp. 49–50; Twomey, above note 89, p. 49; Gready, above note 80, p. 736.
[93] Twomey, above note 89, p. 54.
[94] OHCHR, A Human Rights-Based Approach to Data: Leaving No One Behind in the 2030 Agenda for Sustainable Development, United Nations (2018), www.ohchr.org/Documents/Issues/HRIndicators/ GuidanceNoteonApproachtoData.pdf.
[95] UNICEF, Strategic Plan 2018–2021, Executive Summary (2018), www.unicef.org/media/48126/file/ UNICEF_Strategic_Plan_2018-2021-ENG.pdf.
[96] Filmer-Wilson, above note 78, p. 235.

requires paying great attention to marginalized groups at all stages and in all aspects in developing, implementing, and evaluating specific policies and programs.[97]

Empowerment and Participation

HRBA also prioritizes people's empowerment, meaningful participation, and agency over subordination. It draws from the idea that people are rights-holders – not passive recipients of public services or beneficiaries of development programs.[98] In other words, HRBA requires that rights-holders have knowledge, awareness, and capacity to raise their rights. At the same time, organizations and agencies responsible for specific policies should be critically self-aware about power relations that appear in context with people – for example, in the realization of a development project.[99]

Participation serves as one of the recommended good practices at all stages of creating policies. It should be meaningful, free, and active, and involve different groups and communities – civil society organizations, trade unions, and non-formal groups. Meaningful participation requires something more than just formal consultations over the meaning of a legal act or policy document.[100] It is also related to the openness of institutions and providing information and reflection over the participation process. Entities responsible for organizing the participation process should pay special attention to groups that might be excluded due to their literacy or capacity, or also due to structural inequalities. For example, Destrooper stresses that in certain contexts one of the good practices is to listen to women separately from men, which allows them to raise their voice freely and without reprisal.[101]

Meaningful participation should be included at all stages of the decision-making process: design and formulation, implementation, evaluation, etc. It should also include the process as well as the outcome. Decision-makers should be prepared to make changes due to the outcomes of such a participatory process.[102] Participation and the relation between rights-holders and duty-bearers leads to another common theme: mechanism accountability.

Accountability and Transparency

Accountability serves as a key concept in many HRBA documents and is defined in such a way as to make duty-bearers responsible for their actions and omissions.[103] HRBA calls for building the capacity of rights-holders to exercise their rights through different mechanisms and strategies. Among them is the idea of claiming rights through courts and legal advocacy, participating in decision-making, and also monitoring and assessing different policies.[104]

---

[97]   T. Silberhorn, Germany's Experience in Supporting and Implementing Human Rights-Based Approaches to Health, Plus Challenges and Successes in Demonstrating Impact on Health Outcomes (2015) 2 *Health Hum. Rights* 27.

[98]   P. De Vos, W. De Ceukelaire, G. Malaise, *et al.*, Health through People's Empowerment: A Rights-Based Approach to Participation (2009) 11 *Health Hum. Rights* 25, https://doi.org/10.2307/40285215.

[99]   Cornwall and Nyamu-Musembi, above note 82, p. 1432.

[100]   Twomey, above note 89, p. 54.

[101]   T. Destrooper, Linking Discourse and Practice: The Human Rights-Based Approach to Development in the Village Assaini Program in the Kongo Central (2016) 38 *Hum. Rights Q.* 804, https://doi.org/10.1353/hrq .2016.0042.

[102]   Filmer-Wilson, above note 78, p. 218.

[103]   *Ibid.*, pp. 217–18.

[104]   Gready, above note 80, p. 741.

There are different ways of raising the awareness and developing capacity among rights-holders to make it easier for them to contact duty-bearers. Transparency and information rights serve as an example here, and also as an important way to exercise accountability in practice.

Different assessment tools, checklists, and indicators are some of the important tools in achieving greater accountability. A good example of such a tool is the Community Score Card, which was developed by an international humanitarian agency, CARE, and was designed as a participatory governance approach for improving the implementation of quality healthcare services.[105] Such assessment tools are also developed at the global level by different human rights bodies in the form of indicators that inform about states and events related to human rights implementation.[106] They can be both quantitative and qualitative and are concerned with the process as well as the result.[107] For example, in the context of the right to health, indicators may include financial resources spent on healthcare, the number of women who receive a doctor's advice during pregnancy, or the number of births based on the participation of medical personnel.[108] Important elements are repeatability, measurability, and comparison of situations in different countries.[109] Indicators should be revised periodically to take into account changing circumstances that affect the implementation of human rights. Further, indicators enable standardization of HRBA monitoring and facilitate comparisons between countries over the years. Using such data can also be used to indicate whether the state achieves progress or regresses in specific policy domains (for example, allocation of financial resources to education).

Challenges and Limitations of HRBA

While HRBA brings some positive potentialities for greater justice and respect to human rights, there is also ongoing criticism of this approach. While there are dozens of guidelines and good practice manuals, some scholars stress that they are still very broad and not easy to translate into everyday political and social practices. In a study on the implementation of HRBA in the Democratic Republic of Congo, Destrooper stressed that human rights criteria stay very often in the sphere of rhetoric.[110] This has its sources in the lack of resources, the approach of the local and national governments, and the capacity and awareness of the local communities. Other critics also point out that there is no evidence of any value added by the use of HRBA for a development policy. There are also views that HRBA is part of post-colonial rhetoric brought forth by wealthier nations.[111]

---

[105]   CARE, The Community Score Card (CSC): A Generic Guide for Implementing CARE's CSC Process to Improve Quality of Services (2013), https://insights.careinternational.org.uk/media/k2/attachments/CARE_Community_Score_Card_Toolkit.pdf; S. Gullo, C. Galavotti, and L. Altman, A Review of CARE's Community Score Card Experience and Evidence (2016) 31 *Health Policy Plan.* 1467–78, https://doi.org/10.1093/heapol/czw064.

[106]   G. de Beco, Human Rights Indicators: From Theoretical Debate to Practical Application (2013) 5 *J. Hum. Rights Pract.* 382–92, https://doi.org/10.1093/jhuman/hut003.

[107]   M. Infantino, Human Rights Indicators across Institutional Regimes (2015) 12 *Int. Organ. Law Rev.* 156, https://doi.org/10.1163/15723747-01201006.

[108]   OHCHR, Human Rights Indicators: A Guide to Measurement and Implementation, United Nations (2012), p. 90, www.ohchr.org/Documents/Publications/Human_rights_indicators_en.pdf.

[109]   D. Skempes and J. Bickenbach, Developing Human Rights Based Indicators to Support Country Monitoring of Rehabilitation Services and Programmes for People with Disabilities: A Study Protocol (2015) 15 *BMC Int. Health Hum. Rights* 4, https://doi.org/10.1186/s12914-015-0063-x.

[110]   Destrooper, above note 101, pp. 810–13.

[111]   D. Banik, Support for Human Rights-Based Development: Reflections on the Malawian Experience (2010) 14 *Int. J. Hum. Rights* 36–40, https://doi.org/10.1080/13642980902933670.

Scholars also explain about the particular limitations of indicators and benchmarks used by HRBA. First, the use of statistical data may lead to some level of dehumanization of victims and wrongdoing related to violations.[112] Rosga and Satterthwaite also argue that the concept of indicators is based on a certain illusory approach that data provides greater rationality and objectivity, and is apolitical.[113] However, the problem already appears at the time of the construction of HRBA indicators. Usually, they are created according to the rules of the Global North and are not always able to take into account the perspective of poorer countries.[114] The advantage of standardizing the assessment of potential violations of human rights may also turn into a disadvantage because the data itself is not always able to show the various contexts in which countries operate. Another risk concerns even greater "technicization" discussions concerning human rights.[115] Reliance only on statistical data may lead to a debate on potential violations taking place only between specialized officials and thus may lose its political potential. When using indicators, there is also a real risk that states will focus more on achieving good rankings than on achieving real effects based on their public policies. Another problem is the availability of information itself. Gathering relevant data is a complicated and expensive process that requires significant amounts of resources, knowledge, and experience.[116]

Human Right to Social Security – the Content and Scope

While HRBA calls for the holistic approach and engagement of all sets of human rights, this chapter focuses on the application of automated systems within the welfare sector. Therefore, a specific concern addressed here will be socio-economic rights, especially the right to social security. As will be explained below, the right to social security involves substantial and procedural safeguards that can have a special implication for the design, development, use, and management of automated systems.

In general, socio-economic rights are seen as "controversial" and throughout history many scholars and politicians have been questioning their scope and practical application. Some authors challenge their legal nature and regulatory potential. But, very often, sources of those objections are political and ideological.[117] One of the classic liberal conceptions of rights is built on a strict, narrow, and misleading division between "negative" (related to individual freedoms) and "positive" rights (which require state interventions).[118]

However, over the last two decades, international practice has proved that socio-economic principles are not just meaningless, but can be successfully operationalized and used in policymaking and litigation. Some advocacy groups used this framework with success in controversial debates about privatization of public services or trade agreements. A crucial role in this process has been the UN Committee on Economic Social and Cultural Rights (CESCR), which clarified the obligations that arose from the International Covenant on Economic, Social and Cultural Rights (ICESCR). One of these is the vague provision on the

---

[112] Infantino, above note 107, p. 151.

[113] A. J. Rosga and M. L. Satterthwaite, The Trust in Indicators: Measuring Human Rights (2009) 27 *Berkeley J. Int. Law* 285, https://doi.org/10.2139/ssrn.1298540.

[114] Infantino, above note 107, pp. 151–2.

[115] Rosga and Satterthwaite, above note 113, p. 302.

[116] J. V. Welling, International Indicators and Economic, Social, and Cultural Rights (2008) 30 *Hum. Rights Q.* 939.

[117] S. Moyn, *Not Enough: Human Rights in an Unequal World* (Belknap Press, 2018), pp. 3–11; Tobin, above note 79, pp. 44–7.

[118] Yamin, above note 86, p. 52.

right to social security – article 9 of the ICESCR.[119] Some more detailed and broad guidelines on the normative content of this right were provided by General Comment No. 19.[120] The document suggests that it entails the right to access work-related, healthcare, or family support benefits without discrimination. States should ensure that social security is available, adequate, affordable, and physically accessible.

The CESCR distinguishes also three levels of obligations that arise from the right to social security: respect, protect, and fulfill. Moreover, the right to social security is qualified by the principle of progressive realization (typical for other socio-economic rights). This means that states should assure that they would use the maximum of their available resources to achieve progressively (for example, a gradual increase in social security expenditures) and over time the full realization of these rights. At the same time, any regression in realization of socio-economic rights (like cutting spending on social services) might be seen as a violation. There are also obligations of immediate character. One of them is to provide some minimum, essential level of a right to social security that covers at least essential healthcare, basic shelter and housing, water and sanitation, foodstuffs, and the most basic forms of education. States should also prioritize and pay special attention to marginalized and vulnerable groups, such as women, unemployed people, people working in the informal economy, disabled people, older people, children, prisoners, and refugees.

The General Comment also mentions principles related to governance and accountability. The document calls on states to develop and implement a national social security strategy and relevant legislation that set institutional responsibility, entitlements, and goals for welfare policies. The CESCR also provides guidelines on how organizations should provide benefits and ensure procedural fairness. For example, eligibility criteria for welfare benefits should be transparent and clear for individuals who are applying for them. Another important element is the participation of the affected community in creating social policies and administrating schemes. In case of violations, national laws should also create mechanisms for redress – through courts or administrative entities such as ombudsmen. States should also establish instruments for monitoring progress in the realization of goals set and achieving targets. Here, relevant indicators and benchmarks are necessary.

With such ideal models of application of human rights, this chapter will now try to answer the question surrounding how some of those principles can be applied to the discussion about algorithms and automated systems.

HOW TO APPLY HRBA IN THE DISCUSSION ON AI AND ALGORITHMS

AI and automated systems offer a paradigm shift in the way in which things are managed, seen, and understood. As mentioned above, this may bring numerous risks for various human rights in different dimensions. This leads to the question about how to minimize the risks and maximize the benefits of these technologies. Existing discussions around HRBA show that human rights may serve as a crucial instrument in identifying, understanding, and managing those benefits and risks.

---

[119]   For more, see E. Riedel (ed.), *Social Security as a Human Right. Drafting a General Comment on Article 9 ICESCR – Some Challenges* (Springer, 2007).

[120]   CESCR, General Comment No. 19. The Right to Social Security (art. 9), United Nations (February 4, 2008), https://tbinternet.ohchr.org/_layouts/15/treatybodyexternal/Download.aspx?symbolno=E/C.12/GC/19&Lang=en.

Through the doctrine of the living instrument, human rights can also be adapted and interpreted to evolving political and social circumstances.[121] Therefore, they can also provide safeguards for the challenges caused by technological developments. HRBA offers a holistic framework that can be adapted through various phases from design to use or evaluation, etc. This approach can bring some added value to the discussion around AI and rights, one of which is a clear and universally agreed upon set of principles. Human rights also provide a better understanding of responsibility and accountability in the context of algorithms.[122] In practice, HRBA can help to build bases for understanding the crucial problems that AI is causing – which involve prevention, due process, transparency, accountability, and access to remedy.[123]

A Human Rights Problem

HRBA can help position technology as a human rights matter and political issue. In the context of social security, we can examine how technologies are facilitating the different processes of providing benefits and also construing social policies. In this sense, we can look at automated decisions as a specific kind of policy and government process. Therefore, the use and architecture of such systems is not only a domain of technological experts. For example, in some constituencies, automated systems were introduced to cut costs and launch an austerity policy. As such, they were linked to a specific way of carrying out policies like the rise of new conditionality or social scoring. HRBA demands that all of these problematic issues will be taken into account while public agencies make the decision to develop and use AI and automated systems.

On the other hand, HRBA is also adding some realism and making AI and automated systems an element of more significant political problems. Very often, the consequences and uses of such systems cannot be separated from the political and economic motivations that lay behind the use of automated systems. Therefore, harms co-created by such systems cannot be addressed in isolation from everyday problems and struggles related to exploitation, domination, and oppression.[124] In this sense, HRBA attempts to put technology into context and look at real-life situations – and their benefits and harms. The principle of interdependence of rights also demands that AI and automated systems should not be analyzed from a narrow perspective of privacy and data protection rights and thus helps to visualize how technologies may bring benefits or risks for other rights as well.[125]

Understanding Obligation and Accountability

Another HRBA value is that it leads to an understanding of the responsibilities of the main actors in the realization of human rights. As mentioned previously, the main duty-bearers of international human rights obligations are states. States are responsible for fulfilling, respecting, and protecting human rights.[126] In the context of AI and automated systems which are

---

[121] J. Tobin, Seeking to Persuade: A Constructive Approach to Human Rights Treaty Interpretation (2010) 23 *Harv. Hum. Rights J.* 221.

[122] McGregor *et al.*, above note 6, p. 314.

[123] D. K. Citron, Technological Due Process (2007) 85 *Wash. Univ. Law Rev.* 1281–8.

[124] S. P. Gangadharan and J. Niklas, Decentering Technology in Discourse on Discrimination (2019) 22 *Inf. Commun. Soc.* 896, https://doi.org/10.1080/1369118X.2019.1593484.

[125] Raso *et al.*, above note 5, p. 38.

[126] For general discussion related to obligations linked to economic, social, and cultural rights, see M. Sepúlveda, *The Nature of the Obligations under the International Covenant on Economic, Social and Cultural Rights* (Intersentia, 2003), Vol. 18.

used in the social security area, there are various consequences. First, if automated systems were used directly by governmental agencies to provide benefits and other public services, states would be responsible for any failures and harms caused by automated systems. States also are responsible for any negative effects that may occur if these systems are used by local governments and within privatized social security systems, which is a consequence of the existing norm of international human rights law.[127]

Under the obligation to protect, states should create a regulatory framework that could minimize harms and bring into effect some compliance mechanism. Such a framework may include data protection rules and demands for algorithmic audits. There is also a need for effective remedies for individuals and communities if harm and violation occur. For example, the GDPR contains safeguards, such as the right to human intervention and the right to contest.[128] However, other mechanisms could also be used in such situations. This may involve administrative law or the institution of the ombudsman.[129] In any case, states should also make sure that individuals belonging to marginalized communities have a real chance to make use of necessary safeguards.

In addition, the UN Guiding Principles on Business and Human Rights provide that private companies have some human rights responsibilities (but not obligations).[130] This is especially the case in times when businesses take on more responsibility for different domains that were traditionally the role of the state (privatization of public services). However, the Guiding Principles are criticized for their ambiguity and inconsistencies, and offer a troubling shift in the use of language (for example, "responsibilities" instead of "duties").[131] The document also retains states as the main institutions responsible for fulfilling, protecting, and respecting human rights; it also does not address problems of women and other vulnerable groups. Therefore, the Guiding Principles are quite problematic, and may offer very limited added value in a discussion that involves big and globalized digital companies.

Identifying Harms

Another added value of HRBA in the context of AI is that it helps to set the stage to conceptualize harms caused by automated systems.[132] It is important to have a more holistic approach (also with accordance to the principle of interdependence of rights) and go beyond harm for privacy and the non-discrimination principle (as they were currently discussed). If the right to social security guarantees access to some essential benefits, any

---

[127]   A. Nolan, Privatization and Economic and Social Rights (2018) 40 *Hum. Rights Q.* 840, https://doi.org/10.1353 /hrq.2018.0047.

[128]   G. Malgieri, Automated Decision-Making in the EU Member States: The Right to Explanation and Other "Suitable Safeguards" in the National Legislations (2019) 35 *Comput. Law Secur. Rev.* 1, https://doi.org/10.1016/j .clsr.2019.05.002.

[129]   M. Oswald, Algorithm-Assisted Decision-Making in the Public Sector: Framing the Issues Using Administrative Law Rules Governing Discretionary Power (2018) 376 *Philos. TR Soc. A* 1–27, https://doi.org/10.1098/rsta .2017.0359.

[130]   OHCHR, Guiding Principles on Business and Human Rights: Implementing the United Nations "Protect, Respect and Remedy" Framework (2011), www.ohchr.org/documents/publications/ GuidingprinciplesBusinesshr_eN.pdf.

[131]   D. Bilchitz and S. Deva, The Human Rights Obligations of Business: A Critical Framework for the Future, in S. Deva and D. Bilchitz (eds.), *Human Rights Obligations of Business* (Cambridge University Press, 2013), pp. 10–18.

[132]   McGregor *et al.*, above note 6, pp. 325–7.

barriers caused by technology may constitute a violation of this right.[133] This may be a case for errors in the system that exclude individuals from social security schemes or erroneously accuse them of welfare fraud. A good example of such a situation may be the scandal with the Australian debt recovery system, called robo-debts. In his paper, Carney proves that very often debts indicated by the system were inflated or non-existent.[134] In his opinion, the system trumped good design standards and "breache[d] principles of ethical administration regarding avoidance of oppression of vulnerable and uninformed citizens."[135]

Another important dimension from the perspective of socio-economic rights is to look at the principle of progressive realization. If, for example, the use of the AI and automated systems (in formulating or executing policies) leads to retrogression of the enjoyment of the right to social security, this may cause a violation.[136] Such a situation might be possible especially when automated systems are developed and used under austerity policies. The principle of reasonableness (and its conceptualization by the CESCR) can constitute a legitimate map to address these doubts.[137] This process involves consideration of such issues as non-arbitrariness, non-discrimination, resource allocation, and protection from further marginalization of vulnerable groups.

Laws, Strategies, and Policies

A key component of HRBA is an appropriate legal and institutional framework. In the context of social security systems, laws should at least contain a formal articulation of motivations, obligations, and powers of different actors, budget, eligibility criteria, redress, and a compliance mechanism.[138] Naturally, a legal framework plays a crucial role in the context of AI and automated systems which are used for social security purposes.

First, states may explicitly indicate in a legally binding instrument that automated systems are used in specific decision-making processes: describing the character of the systems, their logic, and their role in the process (for example, advisory). In France, the law regulates the use of automated (or semi-automated) decision-making systems in judicial, administrative, and private domains by setting up specific rules.[139] For example, automated decision-making systems are allowed in the administrative area if they do not process sensitive data, the system respects administrative procedures, and specific transparency and explicability safeguards are in place. Another aspect can be the type of data used by the system. For example, according to the ruling of the Constitutional Tribunal in Poland, data used by semi-automated systems in welfare administration should be described in the legal act adopted by Parliament.[140] There

---

[133] Sepúlveda, above note 80, p. 26.

[134] T. Carney, The New Digital Future for Welfare: Debts without Legal Proofs or Moral Authority?, Legal Studies Research Paper Series (2018), p. 17.

[135] T. Carney, Robo-Debt Illegality: The Seven Veils of Failed Guarantees of the Rule of Law? (2019) 44 *Altern. Law J.* 5, https://doi.org/10.1177/1037969X18815913.

[136] S.-A. Way, N. Lusiani, and I. Saiz, Economic and Social Rights in the "Great Recession", in E. Riedel, G. Giacca, and C. Golay (eds.), *Economic, Social, and Cultural Rights in International Law* (Oxford University Press, 2014), p. 93.

[137] B. Griffey, The "Reasonableness" Test: Assessing Violations of State Obligations under the Optional Protocol to the International Covenant on Economic, Social and Cultural Rights (2011) 11 *Hum. Rights Law Rev.* 275–327, https://doi.org/10.1093/hrlr/ngr012.

[138] Sepúlveda, above note 80, pp. 33–5.

[139] Malgieri, above note 128, pp. 14–15.

[140] Constitutional Tribunal, The Management of Assistance Intended for the Unemployed, K 53/16 (2018), http://trybunal.gov.pl/en/hearings/judgments/art/10167-zarzadzanie-pomoca-kierowana-do-osob-bezrobotnych/.

is also a need for specific safeguards in the decision-making process. For example, in Ireland, legislation specified that the system use for an eligibility check cannot make a negative decision without human intervention.[141]

Non-Discrimination and Vulnerable Groups

HRBA demands that principles of equality and non-discrimination must be taken into account at all stages of design, implementation, and use of automated systems. For example, the non-discrimination principle requires states to consider the potential effects of automated systems on various groups. As such, impact assessment tools that involve both technological and non-technological elements of the systems can be useful.[142] Numerous authors also advocate technological solutions and data processes that would reduce the risk of discriminatory biases.[143] Other recommendations involve greater diversity among people responsible for the design of such systems, including women, people of color, and members of ethnic minorities.[144] From the institutional perspective, it is also important to create a framework for cooperation between data protection authorities and antidiscrimination bodies.[145] The concept of equality entails states exploring alternatives that might be more successful in achieving equality, such as dedicating more funds to sectors with the greatest effect for benefiting poor people. This also implies promoting all people to engage in participation in decision-making and design of such systems.

At the same time as discussing technological, legal, and institutional recommendations, it is important to acknowledge that discrimination caused by algorithms is deeply rooted in historical and contemporary social contexts. As Hoffman indicates, biases are a by-product of unequal societies, where the decisions of engineers or data scientists are just one manifestation.[146] Therefore, solutions to an injustice caused by automated systems cannot be reduced to a technological discussion and may require deep structural changes. HRBA as a holistic framework may play a crucial role in such shifts.

Participation

As mentioned previously, HRBA demands that communities and relevant stakeholders participate in the policymaking process. This can also involve considerations related to AI and automated systems. Such participatory processes may involve decisions on laws that provide legal ground for the use of specific technology and the design of automated systems themselves. The first situation is quite well recognized, and in various constituencies, civil society organizations may take an active role in the consultations of law proposals.

---

[141] Department of Employment Affairs and Social Protection, Privacy Statement (2017), www.welfare.ie/en/Pages/disclaimer.aspx.

[142] F. Z. Borgesius, Discrimination, Artificial Intelligence, and Algorithmic Decision-Making (Council of Europe, 2018), p. 29, https://rm.coe.int/discrimination-artificial-intelligence-and-algorithmic-decision-making/1680925d73.

[143] Barocas and Selbst, above note 31, p. 719.

[144] Borgesius, above note 142, p. 29.

[145] *Ibid.*, p. 31.

[146] A. L. Hoffman, Data Violence and How Bad Engineering Choices Can Damage Society, *Medium* (April 30, 2018), https://medium.com/s/story/data-violence-and-how-bad-engineering-choices-can-damage-society-39e44150e1d4.

The participatory approach can also be used in the design process of AI and automated systems used for public services. In fact, in the last three decades, the human–computer interaction field has witnessed a so-called "participatory turn."[147] The meaningful, well-developed, and facilitated process may put into the limelight knowledge and experiences of relevant communities and be used in creating systems. Such participatory processes may highlight different value tensions and allow people to balance conflicting motivations and interests.[148] Some additional added value of participation is that diverse views and experience may also help in avoiding biases and choices that could lead to harms. However, there are also some crucial conditions that meaningful participation should fulfill. Such a process should allow the free exchange of ideas concerning proposals, and provide a real opportunity to influence decision-making and empowerment.

A good example of such comprehensive and participatory-focused approaches is the project Design Justice, which proposes a framework to reconfigure the traditional design process.[149] This project attempts to engage with questions about power, distribution of risks and benefits, and reproduction of domination and oppression, as well as to create a space for a more equitable and fair design process. This perspective is very close to the principles developed within the HRBA frames, and therefore shows how the development of AI can engage practically in the concerns over social justice and address struggles of certain communities.

There are also limitations to the participatory process. For example, people who are affected by such systems may not have the capacity to take part in such a process due to structural and distributional problems, like lack of time, money, and other resources.

Targeted Programs versus Universality: The Role of Technology

An important issue in the discussion on HRBA in social security is the tension between universal and targeted welfare programs.[150] This discussion is also relevant in the context of AI and automated systems. While this topic is beyond the scope of this chapter, it is important to understand the human rights consequences of both approaches. As a general rule, states should ensure that everybody in society can enjoy their human rights, including the right to social security. Therefore, HRBA prefers universal welfare programs when everybody in society, without any conditions, can have access to social benefits. This approach is better aligned with the universality of rights. Of course, these types of programs are more expensive, so states mostly rely on targeted schemes – when certain kinds of benefits are addressed to a specific segment of a population. This approach, however, can raise some concerns from a human rights perspective. Setting any eligibility criteria should be fair, reasonable, objective, and transparent, and programs should operate without stigmatizing beneficiaries. Managing targeted programs places more demands on administrative costs and is more complicated. Here, automated systems and AI may take on an important role. Some more sophisticated profiling tools and

---

[147] S. Costanza-Chock, Design Justice: Towards an Intersectional Feminist Framework for Design Theory and Practice, Design Research Society Conference, Limerick (2018), p. 10, https://doi.org/10.21606/drs.2018.679.

[148] H. Zhu, B. Yu, A. Halfaker, and L. Terveen, Value-Sensitive Algorithm Design: Method, Case Study, and Lessons (2018) 2 *Proc. ACM Hum.–Comput. Interact.* 1, https://doi.org/10.1145/3274463.

[149] Costanza-Chock, above note 147, p. 2.

[150] Sepúlveda, above note 80, p. 21.

intensive data collection may encourage the creation of targeted programs and their management.[151] This may create a plethora of problems as mentioned above (errors, biases, etc.).[152] That is why demands for the transparency and fairness of such systems play a crucial role. It is also important that any system that allows eligibility prioritizes for errors of inclusion rather than errors of exclusion.

Assessment Tools and Monitoring

Among discussed measures that could assure greater accountability of automated systems are different impact assessment tools and auditing mechanisms. Impact assessments have been well established for decades in various policy domains and focus on a range of problems like the environment, poverty, human rights, gender, privacy, health, and children.[153] What they have in common, however, is a goal to "improve knowledge about the potential impact of a policy or programs, inform decision-makers and affected people, and facilitate adjustment of the proposed policy in order to mitigate the negative and maximize the positive impacts."[154]

There are ideas for using the impact assessment to understand harms caused by automated systems as well. For example, in 2018, the AI Now institute published a report proposing a methodology for Algorithmic Impact Assessment that could be used by public agencies.[155] This methodology allows one to address concerns over fairness, justice, bias, and others. It also calls for disclosure of the outcomes of the review to the public and involvement of external researchers. A recently published draft bill in the United States is designed to implement a similar approach called "automated decision systems impact assessment."[156] It involves "a detailed description of the automated decision system, its design, its training, data, and its purpose" and authorizes the Federal Trade Commission to issue more detailed guidelines for assessment methodology. Another example is the GDPR with its provision on Data Protection Impact Assessment, which is understood as a "process designed to describe the processing, assess the necessity and proportionality of a processing and to help manage the risks to the rights and freedoms of natural persons resulting from the processing of personal data."[157] The reference to "rights and freedoms" concerns first of all the right to privacy, but also the prohibition of discrimination and potentially other rights.[158] If a system poses a "high risk," a consultation with the Data Protection Agency is necessary. In this situation, the authority can play an important role in assessing whether a given data processing system can lead to discrimination against specific social groups.

---

[151] Henman, above note 46, pp. 156–66.
[152] Eubanks, above note 61, pp. 39–83.
[153] K. Salcito, J. Utzinger, G. R. Krieger, *et al.*, Experience and Lessons from Health Impact Assessment for Human Rights Impact Assessment (2015) 15 *BMC Int. Health Hum. Rights* 1–2, https://doi.org/10.1186/s12914-015-0062-y.
[154] P. Hunt and G. MacNaughton, Impact Assessments, Poverty and Human Rights: A Case Study Using the Right to the Highest Attainable Standard of Health, Health and Human Rights Working Paper Series (UNESCO, 2006), p. 10.
[155] D. Reisman, J. Schultz, K. Crawford, and M. Whittaker, Algorithmic Impact Assessments: A Practical Framework for Public Agency Accountability, AI Now (April 2018), https://ainowinstitute.org/aiareport2018.pdf.
[156] A. D. Selbst, Accountable Algorithmic Futures – Data & Society: Points, *Medium* (2019), https://points .datasociety.net/building-empirical-research-into-the-future-of-algorithmic-accountability-act-d230183bb826.
[157] Article 29 Working Party, Guidelines on Data Protection Impact Assessment (DPIA) and Determining Whether Processing Is "Likely to Result in a High Risk" for the Purposes of Regulation 2016/679, Brussels (April 4, 2017), p. 4.
[158] R. Binns, Data Protection Impact Assessments: A Meta-Regulatory Approach (2017) 7 *Int. Data Priv. Law* 28, https://doi.org/10.1093/idpl/ipw027.

There are also some lessons that technology-oriented impact assessments may take from HRBA (and evaluation mechanisms used here). One of these might be to utilize the "structural–process–outcome" indicators framework.[159] This could allow looking at the automated systems based on different dimensions. The structural dimension can determine if laws and institutions related to automated systems formally complied with the state's international human rights obligations. The process dimension can indicate what kinds of policies and laws states constructed to realize the human rights obligations. And the outcome dimension allows assessing the results of those efforts.

Regardless of the name, such impact assessments can bring some additional value into policy decision-making on the automated systems used in the social security sector. It may help to achieve greater transparency and encourage reflection on the risks and benefits related to such systems. It can also promote evidence-based policy and create capacity for external critical reflection of the nature of using technology. On the other hand, critics have stated that impact assessments are only expensive, bureaucratic exercises that can be easily reduced to the meaningless checklist and easily avoided.[160]

CONCLUDING THOUGHTS

Investigating the implication of the HRBA demonstrates that this framework can bring some substantial benefits to the debate about algorithms and AI. There are at least two main directions for the conceptualization of HRBA in this context. The first is more practical and focused on legal aspects, allowing the expansion of the debate about algorithmic accountability. In this sense, HRBA relies on existing concepts like necessary remedies and oversight, clear ways of assigning responsibility, and understanding harms. However, following McGregor and colleagues, I argue that many of these existing concepts should be adjusted to the challenges posed by algorithms.[161]

The second direction is more political and stimulates the redefinition of priorities within the debate about AI. Here, HRBA goes beyond some narrow technological and legal interventions and includes values such as equality, dignity, and empowerment. By placing people at the heart of the discussion about automated systems, HRBA gives priority to humanity and ethics in the design, implementation, and use of algorithms. It also places a clear demand to take seriously the voices, needs, and rights of historically marginalized communities. The holistic nature of HRBA also helps to expand the discussion about AI beyond privacy and includes non-discrimination, social rights, and due process safeguards. HRBA may also be helpful in understanding the potential harmful role of automated systems in the bigger picture. For example, while provoking anxiety, algorithmic discrimination is one of many ways of experiencing inequality. Therefore, it is important to acknowledge that interventions that focus only on the technological layer may have quite a narrow impact.

Nevertheless, the effectiveness of HRBA in the context of algorithms can be used to meet some challenges. In those constituencies where legal systems, rule of law, and institutions are weak, the application of HRBA may be very difficult. In addition, international human rights law is still not fully applicable to private companies and businesses. This is a significant obstacle, especially in the situation where an international corporation facilitates the

---

[159] OHCHR, above note 108, pp. 34–43.
[160] Selbst, above note 156; S. Lockie, SIA in Review: Setting the Agenda for Impact Assessment in the 21st Century (2001) 19 *Impact Assess. Proj. Apprais.* 278, https://doi.org/10.3152/147154601781766952.
[161] McGregor *et al.*, above note 6, pp. 342–3.

development of AI. Operationalization of HRBA is also problematic due to the complexity and vagueness of human rights in general. The concluding section of this chapter has attempted to shed some light on and help organize the core principles and methods of HRBA and to adopt HRBA in the context of AI and algorithms. Given these first steps, much more work still needs to be done. And clearly, there is a role in the process of human rights and algorithms for international human rights bodies and civil society groups. But the effective application of HRBA to emerging technological development would also require the involvement of more powerful actors – states and companies.

25

Four Modes of Speech Protection for Algorithms

*Kyle Langvardt**

In this chapter, I ask whether, and under what circumstances, the First Amendment should protect algorithms from regulation by government. This is a broad frame for discussion, and it is important to understand that constitutional "protection for algorithms" could take at least four forms that have little if anything to do with one another.

First, "protection for algorithms" could mean protections for the content that algorithms produce. Here, we are talking about protection in an indirect sense. It is like saying that speakers – traditionally human beings or corporations – are protected by the First Amendment. But it is more accurate to say that their *speech* is protected. So when we ask whether, for example, the First Amendment protects corporations (it does), the real question is whether the speech that emerges from a corporation should be given less protection, or perhaps no protection, on account of its non-human origin.

Second, the protection might extend to the *algorithm itself* on the theory that the algorithm *is* speech. Insofar as computer code is a kind of language – and narrow it to source code if you like – then perhaps things that are written in code are "speech," just as this paragraph, written in English, is speech. This "speech" might be said to communicate "ideas about computer programming," as one court has written.[1] And to the extent that this speech is "functional," just a series of instructions, the same could also be said of recipes and instructional manuals – materials that most people seem to assume, perhaps incautiously, that the First Amendment protects as well.

Third, and rather uninterestingly, a person engaged in expression might use a written algorithm as a prop or an illustration. A computer science professor puts a snippet of code up on a slide; an open source developer invites comments on her latest version. These kinds of discussions are clearly expressive, and their contents deserve at least some degree of protection, if perhaps not too much.

Finally, we could be talking about protections for algorithmic products not because they *are* speech, but because they play a special or central role in the exercise of free expression. Such technologies might include search engines, social media platforms, cameras, encrypted communications software, and so on. Perhaps laws that limit the distribution or availability of these products should come under special scrutiny. But this would be an admittedly novel approach.

---

* This chapter is partially adapted from K. Langvardt, The Doctrinal Toll of "Information as Speech" (2016) 47 *Loy. Univ. Chi. Law J.* 761.

[1] *Junger v. Daley*, 209 F.3d 481, 484–5 (6th Cir. 2000): "Because computer source code is an expressive means for the exchange of information and ideas about computer programming, we hold that it is protected by the First Amendment."

In this chapter, I will weigh in briefly on each of these modes of protection for algorithms. Broadly speaking, I reject the position that computational algorithms are *in themselves* a form of speech. Instead, they are in my view simple objects that become speech only when a speaking person uses them to prove a point. But I also reject the contention that algorithms' inhumanity disqualifies them from *producing* First Amendment-protected expression. And, finally, I offer that certain types of expressive software should receive special shelters under the First Amendment, not because they *are* speech, but because they have special roles to play in creating or fostering it.

DOES SPEECH GENERATED BY ALGORITHMS DESERVE FIRST AMENDMENT PROTECTION?

This question has two layers. First, it is necessary to ask whether speech created by algorithms is "speech" for First Amendment purposes at all – an inquiry that corresponds to a concept First Amendment scholars refer to as "coverage." If speech is "covered," then litigation over attempts to regulate that speech becomes First Amendment litigation centered on First Amendment arguments.[2] What is important to understand here is that much, perhaps most, human expression is not "covered" by the First Amendment; lawyers defending this speech from regulation generally do not raise First Amendment arguments, and courts do not bother with First Amendment arguments that are raised.[3] Many criminal conspirators' only wrong, for example, is to *say* something they should not have – ordering a hit job, or participating in an insider trading scheme. But most people intuit that the First Amendment simply has no application to this speech, just as it does not apply to contractual language, verbal hostile work environment sexual harassment, and so on.

The second layer of the inquiry is into the concept of "protection." Even if speech is "covered" by the First Amendment, and even if the litigation around that speech involves First Amendment arguments, those arguments often fail. The entire point of First Amendment doctrine is to strike the balance – to draw the limits within which covered expression may be regulated.

I think it is fairly clear that speech generated by algorithms is "covered." The freedom of speech serves a number of positive goods. Most of these are goods that speech creates for listeners, or for democracy or society or generally the world. And to the extent that speech can serve these ends, it is hard to see why the identity of the speaker – even the non-human identity – should make any categorical difference.

As Helen Norton, Toni Massaro, and Margot Kaminski have shown, speech by mechanical entities can serve all of the instrumental values traditionally associated with free speech. In a recent law review article, they posed a fairly realistic hypothetical: an algorithmic author that generates a novel about the 2016 election. And as they made clear, such a novel would serve all of the instrumental values that speech is generally understood to serve in

---

[2]   See F. Schauer, The Boundaries of the First Amendment: A Preliminary Exploration of Constitutional Salience (2004) 117 *Harv. Law Rev.* 1765.

[3]   Schauer, *ibid.*, pp. 1777–8: "[To assume universal coverage outside the traditional 'unprotected' categories such as obscenity] is to be afflicted with the common ailment of spending too much time with the casebooks – defining the domain of constitutional permissibility by reference to those matters that have been considered viable enough to be litigated in, and close enough to be seriously addressed by, the courts, especially the Supreme Court. But if we are interested in the speech that the First Amendment does not touch, we need to leave our casebooks and the Supreme Court's docket behind; we must consider not only the speech that the First Amendment noticeably ignores, but also the speech that it ignores more quietly."

a democracy. It would contribute to the "marketplace of ideas," to political discourse, to public culture, and perhaps even to some individuals' own self-realization.[4] *Censorship* of this novel, meanwhile, would trigger the classic concern about governments that would entrench themselves by limiting access to political content. The identity of the book's author does not bear on any of these considerations.

Now, one may say that these arguments focus too much on speech as a means to other ends. Whatever public-facing interests speech might serve, there is a private liberty interest as well in speaking freely. The Supreme Court's approach to First Amendment questions in recent years basically reflects this approach.[5] To the extent that the freedom of speech belongs *to the speaker*, perhaps we should say that the freedom of speech is a right that speech-generating algorithms are by nature incapable of possessing.

This argument seems right up to a point – today's non-sentient bots are obviously not the moral equivalent of humans, although that may eventually change. But as long as we are talking about *today*'s bots, it scarcely matters anyway. Today's bots, like corporations, are fronts for human beings. This is true even in cases where a largely autonomous neural-net algorithm is generating results from a "black box"; the algorithm always speaks on behalf of its human operator, who can turn the algorithm off at will. The human "handlers" have First Amendment rights whether or not their bots do – and it is the humans, not the bots, who will press them.

As for fully sentient entities along the lines of C3PO, or HAL 9000, or Data of Star Trek, they should not be thought of as mere extensions of their human "owners." Stuart Benjamin has proposed that in these cases – of artificially intelligent entities that speak autonomously, without any human intervention – it may be possible to withhold protection. As Professor Benjamin has observed, a line could be drawn at this point without doing any substantial violence to contemporary First Amendment doctrine.[6]

To some extent, this conclusion simply follows from the unprecedented nature of the problem. There is no legal principle that says autonomous Turing-capable entities have rights – speech rights or otherwise – and the reason, plain and simple, is that the issue has never come up. But Professor Benjamin's larger point, broadly, is that speech requires a speaker, and that this speaker should be human. As a purely descriptive matter, I think that Professor Benjamin has drawn a workable and realistic line. Indeed, it would be surprising if tomorrow's policymakers and judges did not at some point in the twenty-first century attempt to wall off non-human autonomous Turing-capable machines from full protection.

Whether that line *should* be drawn is another matter, and it mostly depends on larger questions about personhood and equality that transcend the free speech issue. Someone might justify restrictions against strong artificial intelligence (AI) speech by classifying Turing-capable entities as mere "philosophical zombies,"[7] a hypothetical class of entities that simulate the external side of human behavior without possessing true subjective experience. But the philosophical zombie concept is speculative, metaphysical, and in the view of some philosophers of mind intrinsically incoherent.[8] The concept is non-falsifiable precisely

[4] T. M. Massaro, H. Norton, and M. Kaminski, Siri-Ously 2.0: What Artificial Intelligence Reveals About the First Amendment (2017) 101 *Minn. Law Rev.* 2481, 2487–91.

[5] *Ibid.*, p. 2495.

[6] Chapter 28 in this volume, "The First Amendment and Algorithms."

[7] D. Chalmers, *The Conscious Mind* (Oxford University Press, 1996); see also J. R. Searle, Minds, Brains and Programs (1980) 3 J. Behav. Brain Sci. 417.

[8] See Zombies at 4.2 "Arguments against the Conceivability of Zombies," *Stanford Encyclopedia of Philosophy* (last revised March 19, 2019), https://plato.stanford.edu/entries/zombies/.

because subjective experience cannot be observed "from the outside." It also raises troubling questions – how do you know, for example, that *other humans* are not philosophical zombies? Questions about "souls" and so on are subject to similar concerns. The political community may take a position at some point on these questions, but the answers are more likely to reflect economic, social, and political concerns about AI than any considered metaphysical position.

It is also worth considering the possibility that a "speaker"-oriented First Amendment might not be based in any particular moral position on personhood. Free speech doctrine might instead center on speakers rather than listeners for more mundane reasons – and I suspect that these mundane reasons have more explanatory power than the moral ones. It may be, for example, that a speaker-centered First Amendment would require fewer moving parts and require less judicial balancing than a First Amendment that was more focused on listener interests and other public-facing concerns. It may also be that First Amendment doctrine's speaker-centrism simply reflects the fact that speakers are more likely than other stakeholders to have standing to sue.[9] So even if we *knew* somehow that all algorithmic speakers were philosophical zombies at best – and we could never know such a thing – then the burden of persuasion should still fall on those who would argue for exclusion.

It is fair then to say that algorithmic speech is still "speech" for First Amendment purposes. But this is not to say that the speech's artificial point of origin is totally irrelevant. Saying that some form of speech qualifies as First Amendment "speech," after all, is only a first step. The next step, and the decisive one, is to determine how much protection should extend to that speech, and under what circumstances. Speech that poses special risks may justify policy to mitigate those risks. And there is good reason to think that algorithmically produced speech poses some special risks.

Set aside all talk about souls and subjective experience and so on, and look at the external distinctions between bot speakers and human speakers. These are speed, reproducibility, and configurability. After the school shooting at Marjorie Stoneman Douglas High School in Parkland, Florida, thousands of automated Twitter accounts gathered and automatically retweeted inflammatory content related to gun control, gun rights, and terrorism. Much of this activity was traced back to accounts linked with the Russian government.[10]

The basic concern here is that bot speakers can easily outnumber and outpace the population of human speakers on the Internet, creating a distortive effect. These distortions, moreover, can interfere substantially with the truth and democracy interests that speech is widely assumed to serve. Some legislators have therefore proposed measures to require social platforms to label bot accounts so that human beings flooded with bot-driven communications do not mistake them for grassroots speech. This strikes me as eminently sensible, and basically consistent with the way in which we treat certain kinds of protected political speech. In elections, there is a similar concern that political action committees (PACs) might use their money to "astroturf" a swell of grassroots support for a candidate. Such organizations are

---

9   See K. Langvardt, A Model of First Amendment Decision-Making at a Divided Court (2017) 84 *Tenn. Law Rev.* 833, 852: "… parties other than speakers … might claim a right of access to information, for instance, or an interest in promoting a balanced or diverse public discourse. But these are not the kinds of interests that are easily channeled into litigation. The constitutional harms are diffuse, and the stakeholders are numerous. Even those claims that are not filtered out for a lack of justiciability appear dubious for other reasons: they are beholder harms, for instance. In short, these are the types of claims that are more properly vindicated through the ordinary political process."

10   E. Griffith, Pro-Gun Russian Bots Flood Twitter after Parkland Shooting, *Wired* (February 15, 2018), www .wired.com/story/pro-gun-russian-bots-flood-twitter-after-parkland-shooting/.

required in many cases to disclose their identity when they advertise, and until about a decade ago, regulators were entitled to "cap" those organizations' total expenditures as well.

ARE ALGORITHMS THEMSELVES SPEECH?

I will deal with this question in some more detail than the first.

Lower courts in the United States have said that computer programming is a form of speech and that computer source code, if not machine code, is a form of speech as well.[11] This is the leading rationale today, but it is untenable and overbroad and it deserves to be abandoned. There are some more substantial reasons for protecting software from regulation, but they depend on context, and they will require elaboration in future case law. I will discuss these reasons later on. But first, I will discuss the doctrine that computer programming is speech – where it came from, its potential justifications, and why I believe it must be abandoned. From there, I will discuss the circumstances in which it may be more appropriate to say that an algorithm counts as a form of speech in itself.

Computer Code as a "Language"

The years just before and after the turn of the century saw a brief but intense flurry of activity around the question of the status of computer code under the First Amendment. The cases rolled out in two cleanly divisible stages. Courts developed the rationale for protecting code in the first stage, and initially issued judgments that protected certain instances of code-sharing from regulation. But in the second stage, the courts appeared unwilling to follow the information rule through to its radical practical consequences. While claiming to adhere to the doctrine established in the early cases, these later courts consistently found, and continue to find, ways to uphold regulations of software.

The first stage dealt with a series of challenges to national security-related export restrictions on cryptographic software. Authors and academics in computer science brought these claims on the theory that a strict bar against "exporting" cryptographic algorithms would make it impossible to teach coding by example. One case involved a book on cryptography with an enclosed diskette containing source code[12] for an encryption algorithm.[13] Another involved a university professor looking to present a paper containing the source code for an encryption algorithm.[14] In a third case, a law professor wanted to post encryption source code on the website for his "Computers and the Law" course.[15]

---

[11] See, e.g., *Universal City Studios, Inc. v. Reimerdes*, 111 F. Supp. 2d 294, 326 (SDNY 2000) ("It cannot seriously be argued that any form of computer code may be regulated without reference to First Amendment doctrine"); *Junger v. Daley*, above note 1, at 484–5 ("Because computer source code is an expressive means for the exchange of information and ideas about computer programming, we hold that it is protected by the First Amendment").

[12] The term "source code" refers to the various programming languages that coders use to write software. Software called "compilers" are used to convert this source code into "machine code," the string of zeroes and ones that interfaces directly with a computer's CPU. For our purposes, the key differences between source code and machine code are: (1) source code is reasonably readable by human beings; and (2) source code must first be compiled into machine code before it can be used to operate a computer. See K. Langvardt, The Replicator and the First Amendment (2014) 25 *Fordham Intell. Prop. Media Ent. Law J.* 59, 115 n. 158.

[13] *Karn v. Dep't of State*, 925 F. Supp. 1 (DDC 1996).

[14] *Bernstein v. Dep't of Justice*, 176 F.3d 1132 (9th Cir. 1999), *reh'g granted*, 192 F.3d 1308 (9th Cir. 1999).

[15] *Junger v. Daley*, above note 1.

After an early stumble,[16] the challengers in this wave of cases succeeded in securing an incredibly broad theory of First Amendment protection for computer source code. This theory was first laid down in *Bernstein* v. *United States*, where the US District Court for the Northern District of California reasoned that "[l]anguage is by definition speech, and the regulation of any language is the regulation of speech."[17] The Court found "no meaningful difference between computer language, particularly [source code], and German or French."[18] The Ninth Circuit upheld this line of reasoning on appeal, with the caveat that protection should extend only to source code shared by programmers.[19]

The Sixth Circuit adopted the same approach in *Junger* v. *Daley*, observing that "a musical score cannot be read by the majority of the public but can be used as a means of communication among musicians. Likewise, computer source code, though unintelligible to many, is the preferred method of communication among computer programmers."[20]

The *Bernstein-Junger* point can be read in two ways. The narrow reading of these cases, and the more sensible one, is that Professors Bernstein and Junger were already speaking by teaching, and that it is the teaching process that is protected. "Computer source code," the *Junger* Court wrote, "is an expressive means for the exchange of information and ideas about computer programming, we hold that it is protected by the First Amendment."[21] But it is only a means. Teachers may use slides, or they may use props, and those choices deserve some solicitude. If an auto-repair instructor brings a muffler into the classroom, that is an expressive choice and it deserves some degree of First Amendment protection. And by the same token, it is expression when a teacher or an author points to a bit of code to show how things are done. *Bernstein* and *Junger* are right to say that computer code's obscurity to the lay person takes nothing away from this.

But nor, on this narrow interpretation, should computer code's lexical quality *add* anything to the analysis. Instead, source code's resemblance to natural language is simply irrelevant. The fact that computer code *can* be used in the course of First Amendment expression does not mean that computer code as such, or even computer source code as such, should qualify as First Amendment expression in every instance. As Orin Kerr has pointed out, there is an obvious circularity in this formula that would imply that the First Amendment should reach every phenomenon in the universe: "everything is 'an expressive means for the exchange of information and ideas' about itself, and this is just as true in realspace [sic] as in cyberspace."[22] Not even ordinary natural language expression counts *categorically* as First Amendment subject matter.[23]

---

[16]   See *Karn*, above note 14, at 8–13 (supposing hypothetically that if the First Amendment covered the code contained on the diskette, the government's action was at any rate content-neutral and could survive intermediate scrutiny).

[17]   *Bernstein* v. *Dep't of Justice*, 922 F. Supp. 1426, 1435 (ND Cal. 1996) (citations and quotations omitted).

[18]   *Ibid.*

[19]   *Bernstein*, above note 15, at 1145: "We emphasize the narrowness of our First Amendment holding. We do not hold that all software is expressive."

[20]   *Junger* v. *Daley*, above note 1, at 484–85 (citing *Hurley* v. *Irish-Am. Gay, Lesbian & Bisexual Grp.*, 515 US 557, 569 (1995)).

[21]   *Junger* v. *Daley*, above note 1, at 484–5.

[22]   O. S. Kerr, Are We Overprotecting Code? Thoughts on First-Generation Internet Law (2000) 57 *Wash. & Lee Law Rev.* 1287, 1291 (quoting *Junger* v. *Daley*, above note 1, at 484–5).

[23]   R. Post and A. Shanor, Adam Smith's First Amendment (2015) 128 *Harv. Law Rev.* 165, 166–7, 179: "If speech is understood to mean human communication, it is literally everywhere. If the regulation of every speech act is a constitutional question, we must hand over our government to what Justice Scalia trenchantly calls a 'black-robed supremacy.' We must not abandon the possibility of meaningful self-determination and turn back our democracy to the juristocracy that controlled society in the days of Lochner."

In other words, the presence of "language" is neither necessary nor sufficient to establish coverage. Why, then, do the *Bernstein* and *Junger* courts take such pains to draw comparisons between computer code and natural language, or computer code and musical notation? It would be far more apt to compare the teaching materials of *Bernstein* and *Junger* to the countless instances of "symbolic expression" – a draft card burned in protest against a war, for instance – that receive only an intermediate level of First Amendment protection.[24]

The answer, and the best explanation for the full-strength constitutional protection the software in those cases received, is that the *Bernstein* and *Junger* courts seem to have contemplated a much broader constitutional vision. Within the *Bernstein-Junger* compass, computer code is unlike draft cards and mufflers – mute objects that are merely *capable* of being used expressively. Instead, computer code is more like a book – a natural vessel for expression that the First Amendment covers presumptively.

Think of code for a moment in the *Junger* court's terms – as "an expressive means for the exchange of information and ideas about computer programming"[25] – and note the remarkable consequences that follow. First, you can take Professors Bernstein and Junger out of the picture, look solely at an encryption algorithm as an artifact, and still find First Amendment expression that presumably lies beyond the government's reach. The algorithm itself becomes the speech, and it becomes unimportant to show that any particular person is *using* the code to communicate. Whenever a law regulates code – or at least source code – the First Amendment comes into play. As one court has written: "It cannot seriously be argued that any form of computer code may be regulated without reference to First Amendment doctrine."[26]

The second consequence has to do with the degree of protection that should apply. Most laws that affect speech are subject to some form of "heightened scrutiny" in court, which is to say that courts analyze the government's purposes, the law's efficacy in promoting those purposes, and the law's collateral effects on expressive freedom. At a minimum, this means that a law must further a "substantial" or "important" governmental interest, that the law must not be more burdensome on speech than is necessary to accomplish its purpose, and that "ample alternative channels" for communication remain open.[27] This approach, called "intermediate scrutiny," often allows regulators a decent amount of latitude. But if a law's

---

[24] See *United States* v. *O'Brien*, 391 US 367, 377 (1968): "... a government regulation is sufficiently justified if it is within the constitutional power of the Government; if it furthers an important or substantial governmental interest; if the governmental interest is unrelated to the suppression of free expression; and if the incidental restriction on alleged First Amendment freedoms is no greater than is essential to the furtherance of that interest. We find that the [prohibition against burning a draft card] meets all of these requirements, and consequently that O'Brien can be constitutionally convicted for violating it."

[25] *Junger* v. *Daley*, above note 1, at 484–5.

[26] *Universal City Studios, Inc.* v. *Reimerdes*, above note 12, at 326 (striking, via a content-neutrality argument, Digital Millennium Copyright Act (DMCA) provision against trafficking in digital rights management (DRM) circumvention technologies) ("It cannot seriously be argued that any form of computer code may be regulated without reference to First Amendment doctrine"); *Junger* v. *Daley*, above note 1, at 484–5 ("Because computer source code is an expressive means for the exchange of information and ideas about computer programming, we hold that it is protected by the First Amendment"); *Sony Computer Entm't Inc.* v. *Connectix Corp.*, 203 F.3d 596, 602 (9th Cir. 2000) (recognizing that object code may be copyrighted as expression under 17 USC § 102(b)); *United States* v. *Elcom, Ltd*, 203 F. Supp. 2d 1111, 1126 (ND Cal. 2002) ("While there is some disagreement over whether object code, as opposed to source code, is deserving of First Amendment protection, the better reasoned approach is that it is protected. Object code is merely one additional translation of speech into a new, and different, language").

[27] *Ward* v. *Rock Against Racism*, 491 US 781, 791, 109 S.Ct. 2746, 2753, 105 L. Ed. 2d 661 (1989). Our cases make clear, however, that even in a public forum the government may impose reasonable restrictions on the time, place, or manner of protected speech, provided the restrictions "are justified without reference to the content of

application turns on the "content" of the speech, then a tougher standard applies. Under "strict scrutiny," as this standard is called, the government must show that the law is the least speech-restrictive means to further a "compelling" governmental interest.

The term "content" primarily refers to considerations such as subject matter, viewpoint, and tone, but it applies to more formal distinctions as well. These include, for example, the distinction between advertising signage and "temporary directional" signage pointing the way to a public event.[28] Under these terms, almost any regulation of software would seem to discriminate based on the "content" of the code. The strict scrutiny that this "content discrimination" triggers is extremely restrictive, and would make regulation of source code exceedingly difficult.

The government must show not only that its regulatory goals are "compelling" – that is, an unusually high priority – but that the policy itself is the least speech-restrictive means available to accomplish those purposes.[29] Most regulation would fail this standard. If the *Bernstein-Junger* protections extend beyond source code to machine code as well, as some courts have proposed, then regulation of software and computing looks all but impossible.

It is not surprising that courts in the second wave of computer cases pulled back from *Bernstein-Junger*'s more radical implications. These later cases deal with the DMCA and its provisions extending legal protections to cryptography-based DRM copy-protection measures. DRM operates by "locking" a media file or storage medium so that it can be used only in ways that maximize profit for the owner of the intellectual property.[30] The DMCA contains provisions that prohibit the distribution of any "technology," including software, that is designed to circumvent DRM measures.[31] Unlike in *Bernstein* and *Junger*, the law under challenge served a well-defined public interest that would almost certainly suffer if the First Amendment challengers were permitted to distribute their product freely.

The DMCA's restrictions on DRM-cracking software apply only to a certain type of code – a clear "content-based" restriction that would, under ordinary analysis, bring the law under strict scrutiny and most likely get it struck down. But the second-wave courts have consistently found ways to avoid that result. They have done so by shifting the focus away from the law's content-discriminatory application and toward the innocent governmental motives that had inspired the law's enactment. Congress, the courts reason, was not concerned with suppressing any *expressive* aspect of DRM-cracking software. Instead, the point was to mitigate the negative economic "secondary effects" caused by that software's functional aspect.[32]

This "secondary effects" line of reasoning is a well-known judicial "fiction" designed to avoid strict scrutiny in cases where strict scrutiny would produce uncomfortable

---

the regulated speech, that they are narrowly tailored to serve a significant governmental interest, and that they leave open ample alternative channels for communication of the information."

[28] See *Reed* v. *Town of Gilbert, Ariz.*, 135 S.Ct. 2218 (2015).

[29] See, e.g., *Brown* v. *Entm't Merchants Ass'n*, 564 US 786, 799 (2011): "Because the Act imposes a restriction on the content of protected speech, it is invalid unless California can demonstrate that it passes strict scrutiny – that is, unless it is justified by a compelling government interest and is narrowly drawn to serve that interest."

[30] The movie industry, for example, will lock DVDs sold in Chinese markets so they cannot be played in North American markets, a scheme intended to frustrate the development of a second-hand export market. See P. K. Yu, Region Codes and the Territorial Mess (2012) 30 *Cardozo Arts Ent. Law J.* 187, 206–9 (discussing the price discrimination justification for use of regional codes in DVDs). For another example, early versions of the iTunes music market sold music files that could only be copied to a maximum of five devices. Symposium, Panel II: Licensing in the Digital Age: The Future of Digital Rights Management (2005) 15 *Fordham Intell. Prop. Media & Ent. Law J.* 1009, 1086.

[31] 17 USC § 1201(a)(2).

[32] *Universal City Studios, Inc.* v. *Corley*, 273 F.3d 429, 454 (2nd Cir. 2001); *United States* v. *Elcom*, above note 27, at 1128; *321 Studios* v. *Metro Goldwyn Mayer Studios, Inc.*, 307 F. Supp. 2d 1085, 1101–5 (ND Cal. 2004).

results.[33] (It emerged from a challenge to zoning laws restricting "adult-oriented businesses.") Since the early 2000s, the secondary effects analysis has allowed courts to downgrade to a much more forgiving "intermediate scrutiny" analysis that consistently allows the government's attempts to regulate software to be upheld. In effect, computer code has been treated as "speech," but only of a second class that receives relatively little practical protection.

This second-class status could soon change, however. In its 2015 decision in *Reed* v. *Gilbert*,[34] the Supreme Court cast heavy doubt on the continuing validity of the "secondary effects" principle. According to *Reed*, "[a] law that is content-based on its face is subject to strict scrutiny regardless of the government's benign motive, content-neutral justification, or lack of animus toward the ideas contained in the regulated speech."[35] If that is the case, then one should expect to begin seeing strict scrutiny applied to most laws that regulate computer code in any selective fashion. It remains unclear whether *Reed*'s rule will take hold in the software context. The one judicial opinion to deal with computer code and the First Amendment after *Reed* continued to apply secondary effects reasoning.[36]

This chapter asks whether algorithms are "protected by the First Amendment," and then takes various approaches to the problem. *Bernstein* and *Junger* offer a simple "yes" based on the theory that the algorithm *is* a form of speech, and this "yes" has been the law's leading answer for over two decades. But there are good reasons to question the *Bernstein-Junger* concept's prospects in the twenty-first century.

The problem, put simply, is that *Bernstein* and *Junger* make it unreasonably difficult to regulate software. As technology becomes more ubiquitous, regulation of code-based products will probably become more common. Much of this will have nothing to do with expression as it is traditionally conceived. The government may attempt to regulate downloadable, 3D-printable products that carry safety hazards; or to restrict the availability of algorithms for manufacturing synthetic drugs; or to regulate trades in certain cryptocurrencies. The "code is speech" rationale would jeopardize these efforts – none of which would pose any serious threat to genuine expressive liberty – by subjecting them to heightened judicial scrutiny. Perhaps courts will somehow hold the *Bernstein-Junger* line against twenty-first-century society's efforts to regulate its increasingly algorithm-driven economy. But given

---

33 *City of L.A.* v. *Alameda Books*, 535 US 425, 448 (2002) (Kennedy, J., concurring) (characterizing the "secondary effects" test and its focus on motive as the touchstone of content-neutrality as "something of a fiction"); see also, e.g., L. Tribe, *American Constitutional Law*, 2nd edn. (Foundation Press, 1988), § 12-3, n. 17 ("Carried to its logical conclusion, the doctrine could gravely erode [F]irst [A]mendment protections . . . The *Renton* view will likely prove to be an aberration limited to the context of sexually explicit materials"). Basing the level of scrutiny on motive might make a good deal of sense, and Justice Kagan has argued that a motive inquiry is most often what courts are actually up to. See E. Kagan, Private Speech, Public Purpose: The Role of Governmental Motive in First Amendment Doctrine (1996) 63 *Univ. Chi. Law Rev.* 413. But courts for the most part have maintained that governmental motive is not at issue in the content-discrimination inquiry. See generally *Reed*, above note 29; *Simon & Schuster, Inc.* v. *Members of the N.Y. State Crime Victims Bd.*, 502 US 105, 117 (1991); *Police Dep't of Chi.* v. *Mosley*, 408 US 92 (1972).

34 *Reed*, above note 29.

35 Ibid. at 2228.

36 *Def. Distributed* v. *United States Dep't of State*, 121 F. Supp. 3d 680, 693–4 (WD Tex. 2015), aff'd sub nom. *Def. Distributed* v. *United States Dep't of State*, 838 F.3d 451 (5th Cir. 2016) (upholding application of arms trade controls to digital blueprints for 3D-printable handguns): ". . . the Supreme Court has found regulations to be content-neutral where the regulations are aimed not at suppressing a message, but at other 'secondary effects.' . . . [The export controls on weapons do] not regulate disclosure of technical data based on the message it is communicating. The fact that Plaintiffs are in favor of global access to firearms is not the basis for regulating the 'export' of the computer files at issue. Rather, the export regulation . . . is intended to satisfy a number of foreign policy and national defense goals, as set forth above. Accordingly, the Court concludes the regulation is content-neutral and thus subject to intermediate scrutiny."

the stakes, it seems more realistic to assume that most judges, over the long run, will look for ways to avoid applying *Bernstein-Junger* in full force.

To the extent that the Court applies generally applicable doctrine to the regulation of information technologies, it ensures some degree of dilution. The worst mistake the Court could make, for instance, would be to apply strict scrutiny to regulations that discriminate on the basis of the "content" of information flows. Although applying strict scrutiny in this instance might be more formally correct than applying intermediate scrutiny, it would also risk weakening the First Amendment's central pillar: namely, the strict scrutiny that applies when government favors some messages, some speakers, and some viewpoints over others.

The Court may perceive the risk to the integrity of the strict scrutiny standard and attempt to shuffle the cases into intermediate scrutiny by manipulating the switching function between the two standards of review. The secondary effects doctrine, the "fiction" designed to accommodate the content-based regulation of adult entertainment,[37] would lend itself well to this effort. But any plain reading of the 2015 decision in *Reed* would indicate that the Court has taken secondary effects off the table.

Even if the secondary effects argument *is* still available, moreover, the intermediate scrutiny it brings is still stricter than the rational basis review that economic regulations would ordinarily receive. The Hobson's choice between Lochnerism and dilution would be less pronounced than if strict scrutiny were applied, but it would still be there. And a dilution in the intermediate scrutiny standard used under the First Amendment, which governs much of the law of public protest, would be seriously damaging in its own right.

To me, these outcomes appear avoidable only if the new code cases are somehow quarantined from mainline First Amendment doctrine so that they are not decided under the same set of tests. If that does not mean ignoring the First Amendment arguments completely, it will probably mean devising a test, applicable essentially exclusively to cases involving computer code, that disposes of them before the "normal" battery of First Amendment doctrine is applied. Such a test would surely draw on a sense of rough justice and would likely under-protect some genuinely expressive uses of code.

For example, courts might adopt a "functionality doctrine" – similar to copyright's functionality doctrine – that withheld speech protections from purely functional uses of code.[38] Tim Wu has argued that a First Amendment functionality doctrine would be useful in the context of search engines, algorithmically generated music playlists, and so on.[39] That approach defines accurately the courts' task as they confront the somewhat different contexts of information-based manufacturing and digital currencies as well: they must sort out parties who are genuinely speaking from parties who are seeking opportunistic protections for non-expressive enterprises.

The practical difficulty is in confronting the perennial argument that sharing code is the best and most efficient way for coders to communicate about coding methods: according to this argument, function and expression are inseverable. Even if most *uses* of 3D-printing blueprints, for instance, are purely functional, there will always be

---

[37] *City of L.A. v. Alameda Books*, above note 34, at 448 (Kennedy, J., concurring).

[38] T. Wu, Machine Speech (2013) 161 *Univ. Pa. Law Rev.* 1495, 1518: "Functionality as a legal concept is employed mainly in copyright, patent, and trademark law, each of which has distinctive doctrinal versions. Sometimes described as the 'nonfunctionality requirement,' this doctrine denies the benefits of the law to some otherwise qualifying expressive work, based on the argument that the work is primarily designed or intended to perform some task unrelated to the goals of the law in question. As such, it acts to prevent a party from using the law to achieve objectives completely unrelated to the goals of that law. It is a limit on opportunism."

[39] *Ibid.*, pp. 1531–3.

reasonably credible arguments from researchers and engineers who want First Amendment protections for certain uses of 3D-printing blueprints that are primarily expressive. Courts might initially attempt a close, situation-sensitive analysis to suss out the expressive uses from the functional uses. But they will quickly find that the functionality question in First Amendment law raises the same deep practical and philosophical difficulties that it does in copyright law.[40] Over time, the crush of litigation and the need for certainty will tend to congeal an initially case-specific inquiry into a more rule-bound analysis shaped by roughly drawn categories: for example, "digital blueprints for 3D printers are never protected."

I suspect that this kind of categorical, rule-bound analysis would win few fans among those of us who generally value frankness and logical clarity in constitutional doctrine. In an earlier article, I have myself expressed concerns that a categorical exclusion of certain types of computer code from First Amendment coverage will necessarily under-protect at least some legitimately protective interests.[41] But some degree of over-breadth in the rules governing peripheral subject matter is nevertheless, in my view, a tolerable price to pay for a stronger free speech doctrine at the core. And, as I will discuss later in this chapter, there may be separate reasons to say that some kinds of tech or algorithm or code deserve special treatment within the constitutional order.

ALGORITHMS AS PROPS

I make this point above, but I reiterate it here. If a person provides some code as an example in the course of a larger discussion, that is a communicative choice that should trigger some level of First Amendment protection – most likely the "intermediate scrutiny" that applies to the government's incidental regulations of "expressive conduct." This same kind of coverage, in principle, extends to all kinds of objects under the appropriate circumstances. Anything can be pointed at and talked about. This kind of theory would have sufficed, for example, to establish coverage in *Bernstein* and *Junger*.

ALGORITHMS AS INSTRUMENTS OF EXPRESSION

One irony of the "code is speech" approach is that in its breadth it pre-empts the development of more substantive First Amendment arguments. Consider, for example, the First Amendment posture that Apple assumed when the Justice Department ordered the company to unlock a mass shooter's encrypted iPhone. Apple maintained in its brief that unlocking an encrypted iPhone would require the company to program a "back door" into the phone's encryption capabilities. This programming would require the coders tasked to the project to "speak" (in the sense that code is "speech") under state compulsion. Apple then went on to cite a line of venerable cases establishing that "compelled speech" is a serious First Amendment wrong – cases beginning with *West Virginia* v. *Barnette*, in which the Supreme Court invalidated the expulsion of a Jehovah's Witness schoolchild for refusing to salute an American flag.[42] The company also alleged that the Justice Department's request

---

[40] O. F. Afori, The Role of the Non-Functionality Requirement in Design Law (2010) 20 *Fordham Intell. Prop. Media Ent. Law J.* 847, 850–3 (discussing the split among the courts on the meaning of copyright's non-functionality requirement).

[41] Langvardt, above note 13, pp. 94–6.

[42] *West Va. St. Bd. of Educ. v. Barnette*, 319 US 624 (1943).

involved "viewpoint discrimination." The question was mooted before the Court had the chance to consider it.[43]

Whatever the appropriate resolution is as a matter of constitutional law and policy – and this chapter takes no stance on that question – *West Virginia* v. *Barnette* and its progeny are a strange way to get there. The compelled speech doctrine is grounded largely in concerns about personal dignity, cultural diversity, and the rights of political minorities. The Justice Department's request implicated none of these values in any meaningful way. But there may be other reasons, including First Amendment reasons, to question the order's constitutionality. One might argue, for example, that strong encryption promotes a First Amendment interest in free and uninhibited expression. Governmental orders that weaken encryption may create chilling effects not only by opening users' communications to law enforcement, but by making them more vulnerable to private attacks by hackers.

Under present doctrine, it is not clear that these considerations would make much of a difference. But at some point, perhaps the law might recognize encryption as a kind of "technology of expression" whose general availability the government can regulate only within certain constitutional limits.

Justice Kennedy's recent opinion in *Packingham* v. *North Carolina* could be read in this same light. There, the state had adopted a law that barred registered sex offenders from using social media platforms that might bring them into contact with minors – a category of websites including major platforms such as Facebook and Twitter.[44] Justice Kennedy's opinion striking down the law observed that "the Internet, and social media in particular ... is the most important place for the exchange of views" in contemporary society.[45] The opinion analogized social media to "the streets and parks," public spaces that the Supreme Court has long held to carry especial First Amendment significance in light of their long-standing use as places of public demonstration and communication.[46] Justice Kennedy's appraisal is surely correct – online communications do seem to have become as central to the exercise of speech rights as the streets and parks once were. And if that is the case, then exclusions from social media and the Internet should perhaps be regarded as uniquely problematic among the various ways that the state might regulate speakers. The speaker may retain other venues for communication, but that matters little if the *premier* venue of communication – yesterday the streets and parks, today Facebook – has been cut off.

Packingham speaks of social media as a kind of sacred "space," but it is more literally true to say that *Packingham* anoints a *technology* – "the Internet, and social media in particular" – as special. This is only one reading of *Packingham*, and it is not clear at any rate what extra protections this special status would confer. But Justice Kennedy's intentions seem to point in that general direction – one in which protections extend to a software product not because "code is speech," but because the product's functional aspect enables and promotes speech.

This approach, I should stress, is undeveloped in the case law and in tension with parts of it. The Supreme Court has resisted the invitation on various occasions to extend extra protection

---

[43] See M. Panzarino, Apple Files Motion to Vacate the Court Order to Force It to Unlock iPhone, Citing Constitutional Free Speech Rights, *TechCrunch* (February 25, 2016), https://techcrunch.com/2016/02/25/apple-files-motion-to-dismiss-the-court-order-to-force-it-to-unlock-iphone-citing-free-speech-rights/.

[44] 137 S.Ct. 1730, 1737–8 (2017).

[45] *Ibid.* at 1735.

[46] *Hague* v. *Comm. for Indus. Org.*, 307 US 496, 515 (1939): "Wherever the title of streets and parks may rest, they have immemorially been held in trust for the use of the public and, time out of mind, have been used for purposes of assembly, communicating thoughts between citizens, and discussing public questions. Such use of the streets and public places has, from ancient times, been a part of the privileges, immunities, rights, and liberties of citizens."

for the "institutional press" – journalists in particular – on the theory that press organizations play a uniquely important role within the system of free expression.[47] Those cases suggest that the Court might also resist special protections for *technologies* or *algorithms* that serve a similar role.[48]

If the Court does come to protect certain algorithmic products as instruments of expression, however, one can come up with a list of candidates fairly quickly: social media and messaging applications, secured communications technologies, search engines, and so on. And to this list perhaps we could add various algorithmic tools used to produce or alter expression. These would in principle include photo, sound, and video effects tools. The government has historically shown no interest in regulating these particular products, and it probably never will. But other products in the same vein may raise concerns that prompt regulation – for example, the new consumer-grade "deepfakes" software that produces realistic, but falsified, videos of real people in situations that never happened.[49] These products pose obvious and serious dangers to the public, but they also probably have at least some legitimate expressive purposes. It would be reasonable to say that the government should have to meet *some* degree of First Amendment scrutiny if it attempts to regulate the availability of deepfakes software, and that the precise contours of that scrutiny should be tailored to the novelty of the problem.

The fact that we lack these technology-specific doctrines today is probably due to a lack of historical necessity. I know of no instance, for example, where a US jurisdiction has attempted to ban the distribution of typewriters or saxophones or matte paint. But it seems clear to me that any of these bizarre laws would offend the First Amendment even if the case law does not provide an explicit basis for saying so.

The major difficulty with this approach is that it requires a contextual kind of reasoning that does not accord well with the Supreme Court's jurisprudential style in the First Amendment area.[50] It is easy to say that encryption algorithms are protected because "code is speech," relatively difficult to say that encryption algorithms are protected because they serve free speech values, and harder still to weigh the benefits of this service against the regulatory interests.[51] And to make matters worse, the law developed to protect encryption

---

47 See, e.g., *Branzburg v. Hayes*, 408 US 665, 703–4 (1972) (declining to create a privilege for journalists to protect the identity of their sources). See also F. Schauer, Towards an Institutional First Amendment (2005) 89 *Minn. Law Rev.* 1256, 1270–2: "... there may be a point at which First Amendment doctrine's institutional agnosticism has a highly distorting effect. When the Supreme Court's unwillingness to delineate the boundaries of the institutional press produces fewer press rights – in particular, rights of access and rights to withhold confidentially obtained information – than exist in many countries with a far more constricted view of freedom of speech and freedom of the press in general, there is some indication of a problem ... A Supreme Court unwilling to distinguish among the lone pamphleteer, the blogger, and the full-time reporter for the New York Times is far less likely to grant special privileges to pamphleteers and bloggers than it is, as it has, to grant privileges to no one."

48 See *ibid.* at 1271: "... when First Amendment doctrine insists that the Internet, cable television, telephone, newspapers, magazines, and books are for many purposes indistinguishable, serious questions arise as to whether courts have overlooked important historical, structural, economic, and cultural differences among the various channels and institutions of communication."

49 See B. Chesney and D. Citron, Deep Fakes: A Looming Crisis for National Security, Democracy and Privacy?, *Lawfare* (February 21, 2018), www.lawfareblog.com/deep-fakes-looming-crisis-national-security-democracy-and-privacy.

50 See Schauer, above note 48, p. 1263: "While occasional exceptions undoubtedly can be found, it seems a permissible generalization to conclude that First Amendment doctrine has been hesitant to draw lines between or among speakers or between or among communicative institutions, preferring overwhelmingly to demarcate the First Amendment along lines representing different types of speech."

51 For an example of this kind of delicate work, see J. Grimmelmann, Speech Engines (2014) 98 *Minn. Law Rev.* 868, 912, advising that the law should "look at [search] rankings from users' point of view. When a search engine

algorithms will not extend neatly to other instruments of expression, such as search engines, which raise a completely different profile of benefits and concerns.

But there would be a substantial upside too, in that the trivial cases that strain contemporary First Amendment doctrine could be dismissed relatively easily. A company called Defense Distributed, for example, has argued that computer-aided design (CAD) files used to 3D-print handguns are "speech about guns" and that any attempt to suppress those files discriminates not only on the basis of content, but also on the basis of viewpoint.[52] Any attempt to regulate a 3D-printable file, of course, will discriminate on the basis of the file's "content," thereby triggering strict scrutiny under *Reed*. The same would be true for any law that regulated online distribution of 3D-printable products on a selective basis. It is a tall order, and a powerful invitation for courts to respond by watering down First Amendment doctrine to make it more accommodating to government. Such are the extreme and unpalatable consequences that follow from the *Bernstein-Junger* conceit that "code is speech."

If courts instead asked the more substantive question – namely whether CAD files or 3D-printing technology deserve special protections because they have a special or central role to play in public discourse – it is hard to imagine that they would arrive at conclusions that are so plainly at odds with common sense and potentially damaging to doctrinal integrity. The answer, it seems to me, is probably "no" – that CAD files and 3D-printing are manufacturing and logistics technologies that, like everything else in the world, can sometimes be put to expressive uses. When cases involving those expressive uses arise, then some relatively low degree of First Amendment protection – today, the *U.S. v. O'Brien* intermediate scrutiny standard – should apply.

Or take Bitcoin, another area where attorneys have made strikingly opportunistic First Amendment arguments. Bitcoin trading depends on a brilliant technology known as the "blockchain," which for our purposes can be described as a ledger of transactions.[53] During the notice-and-comment period on a New York law regulating Bitcoin purchases in the state, the Electronic Frontier Foundation asserted that the blockchain was First Amendment speech and that restrictions on the transactions recorded there were content-discriminatory.[54] This argument, like the 3D-printing argument, follows the path from *Bernstein-Junger* to a wild conclusion: here, that the First Amendment should limit the government's power to regulate a financial transactions platform. Here, too, there are more substantive questions to ask: is Bitcoin as a technology so unusually special or integral to the

gives advice to users, it speaks; there is no way to understand the giving of advice without implicating speech's communicative function. Moreover, a search engine's advice is socially valuable speech; we have seen an abundance of reasons why users as listeners would suffer if this speech could be suppressed. But it does not follow that search results ought to be categorically protected by the First Amendment. Precisely because they are valuable instrumentally rather than expressively, search results should not be protected where they deceive the users they are meant to inform."

[52] See Memorandum of Points and Authorities in Support of Plaintiffs' Motion for Preliminary Injunction at 23, *Def. Distributed*, No. 1:15-CV-372 (WD Tex. 2015): "A speech restriction is 'content-based if it require[s] enforcement authorities to examine the content of the message that is conveyed to determine whether a violation has occurred'" (citing *McCullen v. Coakley*, 134 S.Ct. 2518, 2531 (2014)).

[53] For a fuller account, see F. R. Velde, Bitcoin: A Primer, Chicago Fed. Letter, No. 317, Federal Reserve Bank of Chicago (December 2013), www.chicagofed.org/publications/chicago-fed-letter/2013/december-317.

[54] Comments from Marcia Hoffman, Special Counsel, Elec. Frontier Found., to New York Department of Financial Services on BitLicense, the Proposed Virtual Currency Regulatory Framework (October 21, 2014), pp. 12–13, 16 (quoting *City of Lakewood v. Plain Dealer Publ'g Co.*, 486 US 750, 759 (1988)), www.eff.org /document/bitlicense-comments-eff-internet-archive-and-reddit; see also R. Reitman, Electronic Frontier Foundation, EFF, Internet Archive, and reddit Oppose New York's BitLicense Proposal (October 21, 2014), www .eff.org/press/releases/eff-internet-archive-and-reddit-oppose-new-yorks-bitlicense-proposal.

culture of free exchange that it deserves heightened protection under the First Amendment? Clearly not: just as bank checks are not, in spite of the fact that they, too, contain text and a memo line that can be used for expressive purposes.

CONCLUSION

Algorithms and software raise serious First Amendment questions, but for reasons that are different from the ones many lawyers imagine. In particular, lawyers have greatly over-estimated the significance of computer code's superficial resemblance to words on a page. Today, people are inclined to put almost anything that can be expressed in a textual form, whether books, code, or DNA, under the heading of "information." But the "information" concept is the kind of cultural construction that comes and goes as intellectual history unfolds. Most people in the early twentieth century remember paper well enough that they find it helpful to think of computer code as resembling the text one would find in a book. It is a metaphor, like the icon of a "file folder" or a "recycle bin," for a technology that we have yet to integrate into our concept of nature. But later generations may not need these metaphors, and as such they may find little value or relevance in our twentieth- and twenty-first-century concept of "information." When the line between "expressive" and "non-expressive" uses of code is finally worked out, I suspect that cultural intuitions will do most of the work and the concept of "information" will do none of it.

To a lesser extent, there is a danger of overestimating the significance of the distinction between "machines" and "people." It is understandable but ultimately unhelpful to point out that "Socrates was a man who died for his views; computer programs are utilitarian instruments meant to serve us."[55] If Socrates had been a literate man, his stylus and wax tablets – "utilitarian instruments meant to serve him" – would have served him his efforts to express his views; and if Athens had acknowledged Socrates's right to speak, surely that would have meant that the stylus and wax tablets could not have been taken from him. At least as applied to contemporary concerns, it is always ultimately *people* – not Siri, not Google – who are ultimately speaking and listening and litigating First Amendment questions. Perversely, it requires a kind of anthropomorphism to worry that Siri and Google are even capable of possessing these rights that do not belong to them.

Once these misconceptions fall away – code as speech, algorithms as human usurpers – it becomes clear that questions about the First Amendment and algorithms remain fundamentally human. Algorithms do not, on their own, alter the analysis. What they do instead is to accelerate the emergence of new legal problems. Code's infinite configurability creates a platform for inventing new technologies, business models, and social controls at speeds that earlier generations could not have comprehended. Sometimes these new institutions will raise First Amendment issues. But any attempt to fashion general rules about "computing" or "algorithms" or "code" in this area will only impair the law's ability to keep up.

---

[55] T. Wu, Free Speech for Computers?, *New York Times* (June 19, 2012), www.nytimes.com/2012/06/20/opinion/free-speech-for-computers.html.

26

Algorithms and Freedom of Expression

Manasvin (Veenu) Goswami

INTRODUCTION

This chapter addresses whether and when content generated by an algorithm should be considered "expression" deserving of legal protection. Free expression has been described as "the matrix, the indispensable condition, of nearly every other form of freedom."[1] It receives extensive protection in many countries through legislation, constitutional rights, and the common law.[2] Despite its deep roots, however, freedom of expression has unsettled boundaries. At their cutting edge lies the problem of "speech" produced by algorithms, a phenomenon that challenges traditional accounts of freedom of expression and impacts the balance of power between producers and consumers of algorithmically generated content.[3]

I explore the interplay between freedom of expression and algorithms within the context of the Canadian legal system.[4] Canada protects freedom of expression under section 2(b) of the Charter of Rights and Freedoms.[5] Section 2(b), as interpreted by the Supreme Court of Canada, safeguards all activity that "conveys or attempts to convey a meaning."[6] Ironically, although it controls access to a crucial constitutional right, the meaning of the phrase "conveys or attempts to convey a meaning" remains under-scrutinized in section 2(b) cases. Greater scrutiny, to be fair, is often unnecessary. In most section 2(b) cases, courts are dealing with activities – advertising, writing, publishing, and protesting, for example – that involve overt and obvious attempts by a speaker to convey a message to others.

In some cases, however, discerning an effort to "convey a meaning" requires a more critical assessment. Free speech cases involving algorithms are prime examples[7] – and their

---

[1] R. v. *Sharpe*, 2001 SCC 2, [2001] 1 SCR 45, at para. 23; *Palko* v. *Connecticut*, 302 US 316 (1937).

[2] See, e.g., R. v. *Keegstra* [1990] 3 SCR 697, at 726–7; *Bracken* v. *Fort Erie (Town)*, 2017 ONCA 825, at para. 25.

[3] J. Balkin, Free Speech in Algorithmic Society: Big Data, Private Governance, and New School Speech Regulation (2018) 51 *UC Davis Law Rev.* 1149; T. M. Massaro and H. Norton, Artificial Intelligence and the First Amendment, in W. Barfield and U. Pagallo (eds.), *Research Handbook on the Law of Artificial Intelligence* (Edward Edgar, 2018), p. 354.

[4] As I explain below in note 11, much of my analysis could apply to other jurisdictions that empower courts to resolve disputes over freedom of expression.

[5] Canadian Charter of Rights and Freedoms, Part I of the Constitution Act, 1982 (hereinafter, "the Charter"), being Schedule B to the Canada Act 1982 (UK), 1982, c. 11.

[6] *Irwin Toy Ltd* v. *Quebec (A.G.)* [1989] 1 SCR 927, at 969; *Keegstra*, above note 2, at pp. 729–30; *Canadian Broadcasting Corp.* v. *Canada (A.G.)*, 2011 SCC 2, [2011] 1 SCR 19, at para. 34. I refer to this approach as the "*Irwin Toy* approach."

[7] See, e.g., *Search King* v. *Google Tech., Inc.*, No. 02–1457, 2003 WL 21464568 (WD Okla. 2003); *Kinderstart.Com LLC* v. *Google. Inc.*, No. 06–2057, 2007 WL 831806 (ND Cal. 2007); *Langdon* v. *Google Inc.*, 474 F. Supp. 2d 622 (D. Del. 2007); *St. Louis Martin* v. *Google Inc.*, No. CGC-14-539972 (SC Cal. County of SF 2014); *Zhang*

significance has never been greater. Increasingly, the content we consume and exchange – search engine output, social media posts, and even news articles – involves decision-making by a computer program. Through these programs, we gain unparalleled access to information and to opportunities for self-expression. At the same time, however, these algorithms may threaten other important social values. Victims of traumatic offences and cyber-harassment may find their rehabilitation hindered by links to their past persisting online.[8] Algorithmic "filters" on social media sites, Twitter "bots," and biased search engine rankings may promote defamatory content, spawn echo chambers, and spread misinformation – threatening, among other values, the interests protected by freedom of expression itself.[9] These concerns, understandably, raise the question of appropriate government regulation. But these efforts sometimes spur greater controversy than the problems they seek to address, as recent debates over the European Union's "Right to be Forgotten" and over regulating social media platforms illustrate.[10] Efforts at government regulation also invite resistance from algorithm owners, who, among other avenues, seek recourse in the courts by alleging infringements of their right to free expression.

In this chapter, I discuss how Canadian courts should resolve these disputes.[11] I argue that to properly tackle "algorithm speech" cases, Canadian courts must more rigorously explain what it means to "conve[y] or attempt[t] to convey a meaning." Algorithms test our understanding of conveying meaning because they often produce content that their owners[12] have not contemplated.[13] No one at Google, for example, knows in advance what specific results the company's search engine will produce in response to the trillions of queries it receives daily. Google's software engineers devise criteria for the company's search engine algorithm, but they do not have prior knowledge of any actual search results the algorithm will generate.

v. *Baidu.com*, 10 F. Supp. 3d 433 (SDNY 2014); *E-ventures Worldwide LLC* v. *Google Inc.*, 188 F. Supp. 3d 1265 (MD Fla. 2016). European courts have also addressed these types of cases: see S. Karapapa and M. Borgi, Search Engine Liability of Autocomplete Suggestions: Personality, Privacy and the Power of Algorithm (2015) 23 *Int. J. Law Inf. Technol.* 261, 262.

8   L. Cook, The Right to be Forgotten: A Step in the Right Direction for Cyberspace Law and Policy (2015) 6 *J. Law Technol. Internet* 124–6.

9   Balkin, above note 3; P. N. Howard, S. Woolley, and R. Calo, Algorithms, Bots, and Political Communication in the US 2016 Election: The Challenge of Automated Political Communication for Election Law and Administration (2018) 15 *J. Inf. Technol. Politics* 81–93; S. Wiley, Algorithms, Machine Learning, and Speech: The Future of the First Amendment in a Digital World, thesis submitted to the Faculty of the University of Minnesota (2017), pp. 35–7; B. Edelman, Bias in Search Results? Diagnosis and Response (2011) 7 *Indian J. Law Technol.* 16.

10   See, e.g., Cook, above note 8, pp. 122–31; R. C. Post, Data Privacy and Dignitary Privacy: Google Spain, The Right to be Forgotten, and the Construction of the Public Sphere (2018) 67 *Duke Law J.* 981; Policy and Research Group of the Office and Privacy Commissioner of Canada, Online Reputation: What Are They Saying About Me?, Discussion Paper (prepared January 2016); C. Berzins, Can the Right to Be Forgotten Find Application in the Canadian Context?, submission to the Office of the Privacy Commissioner of Canada, Consultation on Online Reputation (August 2016); K. A. Thompson, Commercial Clicks: Advertising Algorithms as Commercial Speech (2019) 21 *Vanderbilt J. Ent. Technol. Law* 1019, 1020–2.

11   Although my chapter primarily references Canadian jurisprudence, my analysis could be applied to other jurisdictions with constitutional protections for freedom of speech (see E. Barendt, *Freedom of Speech*, 2nd edn. (Oxford University Press, 2005), pp. 48–73). My argument builds upon (but is distinct from) a previous work I have published on this subject: V. Goswami, Algorithms, Expression and the Charter: A Way Forward for Canadian Courts (2017) 7 *Western J. Leg. Stud.* 2, 4.

12   In this chapter, I use the term algorithm "owner" when referencing the potential holder of s. 2(b) rights in an algorithm speech case. I recognize, of course, that the algorithm owner may not be the individual or corporation that created the algorithm. Nothing of constitutional significance turns on this fact, in my view, as expression is no less deserving of protection simply because it was not created by the party claiming s. 2(b) protection. The Supreme Court's jurisprudence on commercial speech confirms this fact: see below, note 99.

13   This is based on how I define "algorithm" in this chapter: see "Algorithms: Background Information."

Can Google or any other algorithm owner "convey meaning" through content produced by their algorithms, without knowing beforehand what, precisely, that content will be?

To answer this question,[14] Canadian courts must develop a more nuanced understanding of how an activity can convey meaning. In particular, when searching for "meaning" in an activity, courts must look beyond the specific words or conduct of which the activity consists, and examine the *purpose* for which the activity was undertaken. "Meaning" deserving of section 2(b) protection can be discovered through both routes. Consider, for example, a law professor who drafts a paper intentionally filled with meritless claims, dressed up in dense academic prose.[15] The professor submits the paper to various law reviews hoping that, if accepted for publication, it will highlight poor quality-control standards at those institutions. In locating the "meaning" that the professor is trying to convey, we could not, I suggest, confine ourselves to examining the *content* of the paper he submitted to the law reviews. The paper would certainly "convey meaning" to readers, but nothing in the paper captures the broader meaning the *professor* is trying to get across. To understand that broader meaning, we would need to consider the *purpose* for which the professor wrote and submitted the paper – to critique law review publication standards, a "meaning" not directly mentioned in the paper itself.

Distinguishing between *content* and *purpose* will help courts resolve "algorithm speech" cases. In such cases, courts must look beyond the *specific content* generated by an algorithm and examine the *purpose* for which the algorithm was produced. Because algorithm owners rarely contemplate the specific content their algorithms will generate, no specific piece of content produced by an algorithm fully captures the "meaning" that an algorithm owner may be trying to convey to others. The content produced by an algorithm may shed light on whether the algorithm was produced for an expressive purpose, but it is that broader *purpose*, and not any specific tweet, article, or other piece of content, that justifies section 2(b) protection.[16] If the algorithm was produced for the purpose of conveying meaning to others (for example, to comment on publication standards at law reviews), section 2(b) protection should apply.

My proposed approach offers several advantages. By drawing on the traditional section 2(b) test from *Irwin Toy* (subject to clarification and refinement), it maintains a unified standard for section 2(b) cases regardless of whether they feature algorithms. It finds strong support in academic work on "speech act" theory and in case law addressing "expressive conduct." My approach also provides a practical way of resolving algorithm speech cases. It makes section 2 (b) protection available for speakers who set out to convey a meaning and choose algorithms as their preferred method of expression. It also ensures that those who do *not* set out to convey a meaning, but who employ algorithms that incidentally generate words or display other "speech-like" characteristics, cannot advance successful section 2(b) claims. An approach

---

[14] As I explain below, my argument primarily addresses how courts should assess whether an *algorithm owner* intends to convey meaning to others through an algorithm. In "My Proposal," I briefly address the separate question of whether algorithmically generated content could be granted s. 2(b) protection solely on the basis that its *consumers* derive meaning from it.

[15] This example is modeled on an analogy in S. Benjamin, Algorithms and Speech (2013) 161 *Univ. Penn. Law Rev.* 1445, 1480–1.

[16] In "My Proposal," I discuss the theory that s. 2(b) is engaged whenever algorithmically generated content conveys meaning to its *consumers*, irrespective of the *purpose* for which the algorithm was produced. In short, I believe that while such a theory could complement the approach outlined in this chapter, it does not, by itself, provide a complete account of the expressive interests potentially at play in algorithm speech cases.

focused on the reason(s) why the algorithm was produced provides a fair and workable basis to draw these distinctions, in my view.

My argument proceeds in four sections. First, I provide background information on freedom of expression and algorithms. Second, I describe the legal dilemmas that arise in cases where the government has interfered with algorithmically generated content. I then canvass possible solutions to these dilemmas in academic work, before outlining my own proposal. Throughout this chapter, I focus on whether and when government interference with algorithmically generated content limits "expression" and engages section 2(b) rights. I do not comment on whether any such limits on expression would be justifiable and proportionate in a particular case.[17]

BACKGROUND

Legal Protection for Freedom of Expression

Liberal societies, as explained above, afford freedom of expression generous legal protection. Of the many compelling justifications for doing so, two, over time, have gained special significance. The first emphasizes freedom of expression's *instrumental* benefits to society. On this view, freedom of expression is valuable because it promotes democratic self-governance, facilitates a marketplace of ideas, and furthers the search for the truth, among other goods.[18] The second justification for freedom of expression focuses on its *intrinsic* benefits. This theory "values expression less for the results it produces than for its intrinsic worth to the individual. Expression is seen as a vital element of individual autonomy, personal growth, and self-realization. The ability to say what one thinks and to follow whatever lines of inquiry that occur to one's imagination is an essential attribute of a free society."[19] Under this approach, freedom of expression would be protected even if it did not benefit broader society, given its central role in developing one's "character and potentialities as a human being" through the open exchange of ideas.[20]

Limits on Freedom of Expression

Societies that recognize a right to free expression will inevitably have to place limits on that right to accommodate other important values.[21] Reputation, privacy, equality, and public safety may all be unjustifiably threatened by the expressive activities of others – and so, at times, are the democratic discourse and search for the truth routinely invoked to justify free

---

[17] As, for example, under s. 1 of the Charter, which allows the government to justify limitations on Charter rights if those limits are "prescribed by law" and "can be demonstrably justified in a free and democratic society."

[18] See *Irwin Toy*, above note 6, at p. 976–7; *Keegstra*, above note 2, at pp. 728, 762–4, 802–3; Barendt, above note 11, pp. 7–12, 18–21; G. Huscroft, The Constitutional and Cultural Underpinnings of Freedom of Expression: Lessons from the United States and Canada (2006) 25 *Univ. Queensland Law J.* 181, 185–6; V. Nash, Analyzing Freedom of Expression Online: Theoretical, Empirical and Normative Contributions, in W. H. Dutton (ed.), *The Oxford Handbook of Internet Studies* (Oxford University Press, 2013), p. 4.

[19] The Hon. R. J. Sharpe and K. Roach, *The Charter of Rights and Freedoms*, 3rd edn. (Irwin Law, 2005), p. 140.

[20] *Keegstra*, above note 2, at p. 804; *Irwin Toy*, above note 6, at pp. 976–7; Barendt, above note 11, pp. 13–17; P. W. Hogg, *Constitutional Law of Canada*, student edn. (Thomson, 2018), pp. 43–8; T. I. Emerson, Towards a General Theory of the First Amendment (1963) 72 *Yale Law J.* 877, 879.

[21] *Bracken v. Niagara Parks Police*, 2018 ONCA 261, at para. 16; T. Mendel, Restricting Freedom of Expression: Standards and Principles, Background Paper for Meetings Hosted by the UN Special Rapporteur on Freedom of Opinion and Expression, p. 2.

expression itself.[22] That said, no clear consensus exists on when these dangers justify restricting free speech. Moreover, the tools available to restrict expression – government censorship, for example – have been described as greater dangers than the social harms they aim to prevent.[23] Unsurprisingly, reconciling freedom of expression with competing social values often generates division and disagreement. But striking a suitable balance is essential, if disputes between citizens and between citizens and their governments are to be fairly resolved.

Several countries involve their judiciaries in this difficult task. The importance of free expression – and the need for appropriate limits on its exercise – are familiar concepts for courts. The prominent, polarizing nature of free speech debates, however, creates a need for clear and consistent adjudicative standards. To that end, courts in several countries have developed legal tests of varying complexity to resolve freedom of expression cases.[24] The initial inquiry in these cases is typically whether the government has limited an expressive activity.[25] In Canada, this inquiry turns on whether the activity "conveys or attempts to convey a meaning."[26] Assessments of the value, weight, and importance of expression are conducted through a balancing test under section 1 of the Charter, and do not foreclose a claimant from putting a section 2(b) right in play.[27]

Although the Charter provides broad safeguards for expressive activity, two "exclusionary rules" limit the scope of that protection at the section 2(b) stage.[28] First, while all expressive content is prima facie worthy of protection, expression through certain *methods* does not qualify.[29] Violence, for example, is not granted constitutional protection even though it may convey significant meaning, because of its "extreme repugnance" to free speech values.[30] Second, the *location* in which otherwise expressive activity is undertaken may foreclose the possibility of section 2(b) protection, depending on whether the location is one where a person "would expect constitutional protection for free expression on the basis that expression in that place does not conflict with the purposes which s. 2(b) is intended to serve."[31]

In summary, an activity engages section 2(b) protection when the following criteria are met:

---

[22]   See, e.g., *Saskatchewan (Human Rights Commission) v. Whatcott*, 2013 SCC 11, [2013] 1 SCR 467, at 71–7; *Grant v. Torstar Corp.*, 2009 SCC 61, [2009] 3 SCR 640, at para. 58; *Canada (A.G.) v. JTI-MacDonald Corp.*, 2007 SCC 30, [2007] 2 SCR 610, at 134–40.

[23]   F. Schauer, *Free Speech: A Philosophical Inquiry* (Cambridge University Press, 1982), p. 34; P. Prakash, N. Rizk, and C. A. Souza (eds.), Information Society Project, Global Censorship: Shifting Modes, Persistent Paradigms (Access to Knowledge Research Series, 2013); *F.C.C. v. Pacifica Foundation* (1976) 438 US 726, at pp. 775–7 (*per* Brennan J. dissenting); *Keegstra*, above note 2, at p. 805.

[24]   See Barendt, above note 11; pp. 48–73; A. Stone, The Comparative Constitutional Law of Freedom of Expression, in R. Dixon and T. Ginsburg (eds.), *Research Handbook on Comparative Constitutional Law* (Edward Elgar, 2011), pp. 406–22; T. M. Keck, Assessing Judicial Empowerment (2018) 7 *Laws* 2; T. Mendel, Freedom of Information: A Comparative Legal Survey (UN Educational Scientific and Cultural Organization, 2008).

[25]   Barendt, above note 11, pp. 48–73; Stone, above note 24, pp. 406–22; Mendel, above note 21, p. 7.

[26]   See note 6.

[27]   *Keegstra*, above note 2, at pp. 760, 765–6, 840; K. Roach and D. Schniederman, Freedom of Expression in Canada (2013) 61 *SCLR* (2d) 429–30. The s. 1 inquiry focuses on proportionality; more specifically, whether the limit on a Charter right is motivated by a pressing and substantial objective, rationally connected to that objective, minimally impairing, and strikes a proportional balance between "deleterious and salutary effects" (*R. v. K.R.J.*, 2016 SCC 31, [2016] 1 SCR 906, at para. 58, citing *R. v. Oakes* [1986] 1 SCR 103).

[28]   *Bracken*, above note 21, at paras. 35, 39; *Fort Erie*, above note 2, at paras. 29, 32.

[29]   *Canadian Broadcasting Corp.*, above note 6, at paras. 35–7.

[30]   *Keegstra*, above note 2, at p. 732.

[31]   *Bracken*, above note 21, at para. 40, citing *Montréal (City) v. 2952-1366 Québec Inc.*, 2005 SCC 62, [2005] 3 SCR 141, at para. 74.

(1) the activity "conveys or attempts to convey a meaning";

(2) the activity does not employ a *method* that undermines the values on which freedom of expression is based;

(3) the activity does not occur at a *location* where expression would conflict with the purposes underlying section 2(b).[32]

Algorithms: Background Information

The term "algorithm" refers to the "decision-making elements" of computer code, comprising a set of "instructions or rules implemented by a computer."[33] Algorithms vary greatly in their functions and sophistication. Some operate "with little or no decision-making" ability.[34] Others "model complex human performance, human thought processes, and … can learn from experience."[35] In this chapter, I focus on algorithms that share three characteristics.

(1) The algorithms relevant to this chapter make choices that are responsive to external input, according to criteria in their programming. Google's search engine algorithm, for example, generates search results in response to queries from a user, consistent with pre-programmed criteria.[36]

(2) These algorithms can make choices without human involvement. Google employees play no direct role in the choices made by its search engine algorithm.

(3) These algorithms *express* their choices in a way that is understandable to humans. After determining the appropriate response to a search query, Google's search engine algorithm displays that response through a ranked list of results, readily understandable to a human user.[37]

These kinds of algorithms have gained unprecedented prominence in virtually every aspect of modern society. Consider, among several examples, Facebook's NewsFeed Display;[38] search engine algorithms;[39] "bots" that post content on Twitter and other social media

---

[32] Section 2(b) claimants must also demonstrate that their rights were infringed by government action. If the impugned government action *aims* to restrict freedom of expression, an infringement is established and the analysis proceeds directly to the s. 1 balancing stage. If the government action only has the *effect* of restricting expression, the party alleging the Charter infringement must also demonstrate that their expression furthers at least one of the three purposes underpinning the s. 2(b) guarantee: *Canadian Broadcasting Corp.*, above note 6, at para. 38. These qualifications are not relevant to this chapter, as I do not assess the merits of any specific piece of legislation designed to limit freedom of expression.

[33] Wiley, above note 9, p. 27; Benjamin, above note 15, n. 4. See also W. Barfield, Towards a Law of Artificial Intelligence, in W. Barfield and U. Pagallo (eds.), *Research Handbook on the Law of Artificial Intelligence* (Edward Edgar, 2018), p. 4.

[34] Barfield, *ibid.*, p. 4

[35] *Ibid.*

[36] Related to "responsiveness," the owners of these algorithms rarely have prior knowledge of the specific content the algorithms will generate while operating. I focus on these kinds of algorithms because they pose the most interesting dilemmas for free speech jurisprudence. This is not to say that computer programs that produce fixed and unvarying messages regardless of the external input they receive are not deserving of s. 2(b) rights; merely that such cases are far easier to resolve from a s. 2(b) perspective, as the expressive purpose of the algorithm owner is directly reflected in the content generated by the algorithm.

[37] These criteria are similar to those outlined by T. Wu in Machine Speech (2013) 161 *Univ. Penn. Law Rev.* 1495, 1499 (algorithmically generated content is produced when "a computer, following a program or algorithm, decides among several alternatives, and expresses that choice in a manner understandable to a human").

[38] S. C. Lewis, A. K. Sanders, and C. Carmody, Libel by Algorithm? Automated Journalism and the Threat of Legal Liability (2019) 96 *J. Mass Commun. Q.* 60.

[39] E. Volokh and D. M. Falk, First Amendment Protection for Search Engine Search Results (2012) 8 *J. Law Econ. Policy* 884.

sites;[40] digital "assistants" (Apple's Siri, Amazon's Echo and Alexa, Google's Home);[41] game-play programs (Watson and Jeopardy, Google's DeepMind and chess);[42] and algorithmic "authors."[43] Many of these algorithms, in their day-to-day operation, bear at least facial similarity to human activity unquestionably entitled to section 2(b) protection – for example, advice, commentary, authorship, and the exercise of editorial discretion. Unsurprisingly, when the owners of these algorithms make claims for constitutional protection, they often compare the output of their algorithms to analogous content directly produced by human activity. In the following section, I explore the dilemmas raised by these constitutional claims, before discussing the framework courts should apply in resolving them.

ALGORITHMS AND FREEDOM OF EXPRESSION: LEGAL DILEMMAS

I make three points in this section:

(1) section 2(b) protection should not extend to *all* algorithmically generated content;
(2) some algorithmically generated content is clearly deserving of section 2(b) protection;
(3) section 2(b) jurisprudence, at present, does not clearly explain how to distinguish between algorithmically generated content that is and is not deserving of constitutional protection.

With regard to point (1) above, clearly, not all algorithmically generated content engages section 2(b) – even content directly produced by humans does not receive such generous protection. Several algorithms – in all likelihood, the vast majority – have nothing to do with expression. There is nothing "expressive," for example, about a standard online calculator, nor would its removal from the Internet by the government limit section 2(b) rights. Government interference with the output of these kinds of algorithms may anger many people, but few would suggest that such restrictions limit freedom of expression.

Turning now to point (2) above, sometimes, however, algorithmically generated content is clearly deserving of expressive protection. Consider the following example. Mary, a gifted computer science graduate, discovers that Google's search engine algorithm is systematically under-representing content produced by women. Mary creates a rival search engine that prioritizes material from female content creators. Mary plays no role in her search engine's day-to-day operation.[44]

Also an avid basketball fan, Mary believes that rankings of the top ten players in the National Basketball Association overemphasize traditional statistics such as points, rebounds, and assists. She designs an algorithm that tracks players' advanced statistics throughout the season. Using criteria that reflect Mary's views about the relative importance of those statistics, the algorithm produces weekly rankings of the top ten players in the league. The rankings are published online under the heading "Mary's Top 10 NBA players," and are auto-updated throughout the season by the algorithm without any further involvement from Mary.

In both cases, Mary's actions are undoubtedly expressive. She is clearly trying to say *something* about the importance of fairly treating female web content creators and about

[40] Howard *et al.*, above note 9; T. M. Massaro, H. Norton, and M. E. Kaminski, Siri-ously 2.0: What Artificial Intelligence Reveals about the First Amendment (2017) 101 *Minnesota Law Rev.* 2481, 2481–2.
[41] Wiley, above note 9, p. 28.
[42] *Ibid.*, pp. 28, 48.
[43] Lewis *et al.*, above note 38; M. E. Kaminski, Authorship, Disrupted: A.I. Authors in Copyright and First Amendment Law (2017) 51 *UC Davis Law Rev.* 589.
[44] Goswami, above note 11, p. 4.

excellence in basketball. The content generated by her algorithms could spur debate, contribute to the marketplace of ideas, and give Mary considerable fulfilment. Mary, moreover, could realistically have performed the task entrusted to her basketball algorithm by herself. Had she done so, she would have manually generated the same weekly rankings, but only after expending much more time and effort. Extending section 2(b) protection to lists manually produced by Mary, while excluding *identical* content produced by her algorithm, would penalize her for selecting a more expedient and convenient method of expressing herself.[45] That is not a sensible result.

Finally, with regard to point (3) above, if we accept that at least *some* algorithmic output may deserve section 2(b) protection, we then need a clear rule to determine when those protections arise and when they do not.[46] To begin, we could look to existing legal tests for an answer. As reviewed above at "Limits on Freedom of Expression," an activity attracts section 2 (b) protection if:

(1) it "conveys or attempts to convey a meaning";
(2) it does not employ a method that undermines the values on which freedom of expression is based;
(3) it does not occur at a location where expression would conflict with the purposes underlying section 2(b).

Points (2) and (3) are irrelevant to algorithms. The use of an algorithm, without more, is not a method of expression that undermines the values on which freedom of expression is based, nor does it engage the location-based exclusionary rule. The inquiry under the traditional test, therefore, turns on the presence of an activity that "conveys or attempts to convey" meaning. Here, however, two significant challenges arise.

First, taken literally, the "conveys a meaning" standard would extend section 2(b) protection to a range of computer programs that convey comprehensible messages, but that few would consider expressive. Consider a custom car alarm programmed to broadcast the phrase "Someone is trying to steal your car!" when the car's door is forcibly opened.[47] Other household appliances, navigation systems, and even online calculators can similarly be designed to "speak" and "convey meaning," as those terms are ordinarily understood. But it seems highly artificial to suggest that these products represent constitutionally protected expression. As Tim Wu forcefully argues, any theory of expressive rights that accords constitutional protections to such devices should be viewed with skepticism.[48] Assuming Wu is correct, can these types of devices be removed from the scope of section 2(b), without unfairly excluding other activities deserving of Charter protection?

Second, how, if not through a literal approach, should a court determine whether someone has "conveyed meaning" through an algorithm? As discussed above, algorithm owners often lack prior knowledge about the precise content their algorithms will produce. Through "deep learning," moreover, algorithms can become better at accommodating their *users'* preferences, diminishing the likelihood that their *owners* have prior knowledge of the content they will generate.[49] Can someone "convey or attempt to convey a meaning" through content that they have not specifically contemplated? If so, where should courts look to find that meaning?

---

45 *Ibid.*, p. 7.
46 See Massaro and Norton, above note 3, p. 365
47 Goswami, above note 11, p. 2, modeled on an example in Wu, above note 37, p. 1496.
48 Wu, above note 37, p. 1496.
49 Barfield, above note 33, p. 2; Wiley, above note 9, pp. 32–3.

And is it even necessary that the *algorithm owner* intend to convey a meaning? Can we not justify section 2(b) protection solely on the basis that *viewers* of the algorithmically generated content derive meaning from it?

Mary's algorithmically generated rankings of NBA players nicely illustrates these dilemmas. Assume that Mary stops following the NBA for fifteen years. One week, her algorithm produces a ranking populated by players Mary has never heard of. Did *Mary* intend to "convey [the] meaning" that these ten players are the best in the NBA? Obviously not – Mary had never heard of any of them. Mary's list, however, may convey such a meaning to *viewers*, who could justifiably conclude that Mary believes those ten players to be the best in the league. The ranking produced by Mary's algorithm, in other words, conveys to others a "meaning" that she, the "speaker," had never contemplated. Whose perspective matters for section 2(b) protection? And, if *Mary* must intend to convey a meaning to gain section 2(b) protection, might there be a way to extract a higher-level "meaning" from her algorithm, above and beyond the specific rankings of players it generates on a weekly basis?

I tackle these questions – with greater emphasis on the second – in the following sections. I first outline possible answers in relevant academic work and then describe my own proposal.

SOLUTIONS PROPOSED IN THE LITERATURE

There has been spirited academic debate over extending free speech protection to algorithmically generated content. Three leading schools of thought have emerged.

The first approach focuses solely on whether the *content* generated by the algorithm conveys a meaning to viewers.[50] On this view, two identical tweets – one produced by a human and the other by an algorithm – would stand on equal footing under section 2(b). Supporters of this approach emphasize the *social* benefits of freedom of expression. They argue that it makes little difference to *viewers* whether the information they consume is produced by a human or an algorithm. The value in that material – for example, its ability to spur democratic discourse or further the search for the truth – depends on its content, not its mode of production. Because content produced by a human and by an algorithm is equally capable of advancing the *social* goals free speech is meant to serve, both types of content deserve identical constitutional protection. Or, as Margot Kaminsky puts it: "What should matter is whether the work reads as speech to those who encounter it. A government that censors a political novel written by an algorithm is as problematic from the perspective of a reader as a government that censors a political novel written by Tolstoy."[51]

A second group of academics takes a more qualified view, emphasizing the need for a nexus between *the content generated by an algorithm* and a *set of preferences instituted by the algorithm owner*. Stuart Benjamin, for example, argues that algorithmic output deserves free speech protection if it reflects preferences selected by the algorithm owner based on their perceived importance, value, or relevance.[52] If those preferences are expressed in the algorithmic output through "a message that can be sent and received, and that has been sent," the output would amount to "substantive communication" deserving of constitutional protection.[53] Benjamin qualifies his substantive communication theory in three ways. First, he excludes algorithms

---

[50]   *Massaro et al.*, above note 40, pp. 2487–91; Kaminski, above note 43, pp. 609–10; Massaro and Norton, above note 3, pp. 355–67.

[51]   Kaminski, above note 43, p. 610.

[52]   Benjamin, above note 15, p. 1471.

[53]   Benjamin makes clear that a "particularized message" is unnecessary for First Amendment protection, based on his interpretation of the US Supreme Court's jurisprudence (*ibid.*, pp. 1463–4, 1482).

that are "designed to speed transmission, or make a network operate more efficiently."[54] Second, he excludes scenarios where algorithm owners "attribute [their] own private meaning to some action and communicate that meaning to no one."[55] Finally, Benjamin concedes that content that is sufficiently divorced from the preferences of a human creator, such that the results no longer represent human decision-making, should not receive constitutional protection.[56] Benjamin's third qualification is inconsistent with theories that exclusively focus on the *content* generated by an algorithm, without concern for its connection to human preferences.[57]

A third group of scholars urge attention to an algorithm's *function*, not the content it generates or the preferences it reflects. Tim Wu's work, for example, highlights the importance of "functionality," a doctrine which assesses a tool or activity's relationship with expression.[58] Where that relationship is purely or de facto "functional," constitutional protection is inappropriate.[59] Examples of "functional" products include "communicative tools" such as courier services, car alarms, or other routine machines which convey information as a means of achieving "some task other than the expression of ideas."[60] Wu reserves constitutional protection for algorithms that serve as "speech products."[61] Examples of "speech products" include "blog posts, tweets, video games, [or] newspapers" – forms of communication that are "viewed as vessels for the ideas of a speaker," or "whose content has been consciously curated."[62] Karapapa and Borgi have captured the contrast between Wu's approach to algorithm "speech" and the two camps discussed above:

> Even within a judicial trend that has expanded the notion of "speech" to include various instances of the so-called "non-verbal communication" – such as symbolic speech, commercial and function messages – the construction of pure algorithmic outputs as "opinions" remains problematic. As Tim Wu convincingly argues, a fully inclusive theory of the First Amendment that treats as "speech" anything that can be labelled as an "opinion" simply because it "sends a message" to an audience, is hopelessly over-broad and eventually impracticable. For instance, such a construal does not allow to make distinction between purely functional "messages", such as the sound of a car alarm or the instructions provided by a GPS sat nav, and expressive messages properly so called.[63]

Some scholars who endorse the functionality approach have proposed refinements to align the theory with prevailing speech practices. Oren Bracha, for example, builds on Wu's theory by emphasizing the importance of the specific social practices in which algorithmically generated content is embedded, as a means of distinguishing between functional and non-functional speech.[64] Bracha argues that a robust definition of functionality requires examining the social

---

[54] *Ibid.*, p. 1481.

[55] *Ibid.*, p. 1483.

[56] *Ibid.*, p. 1481.

[57] Other theories that require a nexus between algorithmically generated content and human preferences include: Volokh and Falk, above note 39 (comparing the generation of search engine results to the exercise of editorial discretion); M. J. Ballanco, Searching for the First Amendment: An Inquisitive Free Speech Approach to Search Engine Rankings (2013) 24 *Civ. Rights Law J.* 107–11 (qualifying Volokh and Falk's theory to account for "artificial placement" in search engine rankings); and J. Grimmelmann, Speech Engines (2013) 98 *Minnesota Law Rev.* 868 (analogizing search engine rankings to advice).

[58] Wu, above note 37, p. 1496. See also Karapapa and Borgi, above note 7, p. 269; Thompson, above note 10, pp. 1032–3.

[59] Wu, above note 37, pp. 1520–1.

[60] *Ibid.*, pp. 1524–5.

[61] *Ibid.*, p. 1498.

[62] *Ibid.*

[63] Karapapa and Borgi, above note 7, pp. 268–9.

[64] O. Bracha, The Folklore of Informationalism: The Case of Search Engine Speech (2014) 82 *Univ. Texas Law Rev.* 1628, 1634.

practices associated with the activity or tool said to merit constitutional protection.[65] Under Bracha's approach, free speech protection would be denied to functional activities "that [are] not more than trivially connected to the realization of any free speech values."[66]

MY PROPOSAL

Overview

In cases where the government has interfered with content generated by an algorithm, courts should ask whether the algorithm was produced for the purpose of conveying meaning. If so, section 2(b) protections should apply. In this inquiry, the search for expressive purpose predominates; the specific content produced by the algorithm is relevant only insofar as it sheds light on whether an expressive purpose exists.[67]

My argument proceeds in three steps:

(1)   In cases where the government has interfered with algorithmically generated content, the algorithm owner, and not the algorithm itself, is the party potentially entitled to section 2(b) protection.

(2)   To determine if the algorithm owner is entitled to section 2(b) protection, courts must ask, as in all section 2(b) cases, if the government has interfered with an activity that "convey[ed] or attempt[ed] to convey a meaning" (the "*Irwin Toy*" test).

(3)   The *Irwin Toy* test will be satisfied if the algorithm was produced for the *purpose* of conveying meaning to others. In this inquiry, the *specific content* generated by the algorithm is relevant only insofar as it sheds light on the purpose for which the algorithm was produced.

With regard to point (1) above, I assume that in "algorithm speech" cases, section 2(b) rights, if engaged at all, would belong to the algorithm owner and not to the algorithm itself. I recognize that advances in computer programming have rapidly improved artificial intelligence (AI) capabilities.[68] Because of these advances, we may eventually need to consider whether AI programs deserve rights independent of their owners. Some authors have already supported this position.[69] The merits of their arguments are beyond the scope of this chapter. My argument explores the constitutional dilemmas raised by algorithm speech cases, *assuming that* algorithm owners are the persons potentially entitled to section 2(b) protection. My argument would be different if computer programs themselves had a right to free expression.

Turning to point (2) above, to get a section 2(b) claim off the ground, an algorithm owner must establish that the state has restricted an activity through which he or she "convey[ed] or attempt[ed] to convey a meaning."[70] That phrase, however, can be read in two ways,

---

[65]   *Ibid.*

[66]   *Ibid.*

[67]   As I will explain, my theory focuses on how courts can discern efforts by *algorithm owners* to convey meaning to others. In "My Proposal," I discuss whether s. 2(b) can protect algorithmically generated content solely on the basis that its *consumers* could derive meaning from it.

[68]   Massaro and Norton, above note 3, p. 361.

[69]   See, e.g., *ibid.*, p. 370; Massaro *et al.*, above note 40.

[70]   See note 6. I recognize, of course, that arguments can be made for dispensing with the "conveying a meaning" standard for all s. 2(b) cases, not simply those involving algorithms. I do not engage with those arguments here, except to say that they raise concerns that are not unique to algorithm speech cases.

depending on whether a court adopts the perspective of the algorithm's *owner*, or the *consumers* of the content it generates:

(1) On one hand, a court could ask whether the algorithmically generated content "convey[s] a meaning" to its *consumers*. Under this approach, a court would not ask whether the algorithm *owner* intended to convey a meaning to others. If consumers can derive a meaning from the content produced by the algorithm, that would be sufficient for section 2(b) protection (the "content-focused" approach).

(2) On the other hand, a court could ask whether the algorithmically generated content can be construed as an "attemp[t] to convey a meaning" by the algorithm *owner*. Absent such an attempt, section 2(b) protections would not arise – even if *consumers* could derive significant meaning from the algorithm's output (the "intent-focused" approach).

The first approach, in other words, focuses solely on the *content* produced by the algorithm: if it "conveys . . . a meaning" to its consumers, section 2(b) protection applies. The intent of the algorithm owner and the purpose for which the algorithm was designed are irrelevant. The second approach, by contrast, focuses on whether the algorithm owner *intended* to convey meaning to others. The content produced by the algorithm may shed light on the presence or absence of expressive intent, but that content would not receive section 2(b) protection simply because third parties may derive meaning from it.

The content- and intent-focused approaches will frequently produce identical outcomes. Put simply, when someone produces content that conveys a meaning to others, that person often *intends* to express that particular meaning. Algorithms, however, challenge that assumption. Because they produce content that their owners have not contemplated, algorithms will often convey meanings to third parties that their owners did not intend. Mary's NBA rankings, filled with players she had never heard of after ignoring the league for fifteen years, illustrates this point well. Under the content-focused approach, Mary would be entitled to section 2(b) protection solely on the basis that consumers of her algorithmically generated rankings would consider them to be *her* opinion about the ten best players in the NBA. That Mary knew nothing about those players is irrelevant. Under the intent-focused approach, Mary would need to show that the algorithmically generated rankings reflect an intent on her part to convey meaning. Mary could, for example, argue that through those rankings, she intended to make a statement about the qualities relevant to excellence in basketball. She could not, however, point to any specific ranking of ten players as the "meaning" she intended to convey to others.[71]

Another example may help to distinguish the content- and intent-based approaches. Imagine that Google's search engine algorithm generates a list of ranked results for the query "Jim Smith." A viewer could conclude that the ranking reflects Google's opinion about the most relevant, popular, or high-quality web content in respect of Mr. Smith. This, by itself, would justify section 2(b) protection under a content-focused approach. Under an intent-focused approach, however, this argument would be insufficient. After all, in all likelihood, no one at Google has ever heard of Jim Smith, much less contemplated the order in which search results about him should be presented.[72] Although those search results

---

[71]   Because she had never heard of any of those players, much less contemplated the order in which they should be ranked relative to each other.

[72]   The process of "machine learning," whereby an algorithm becomes more efficient at accommodating a user's preferences, makes it even less likely that the algorithm owner can contemplate, in advance, the specific content that the algorithm will produce (see Barfield, above note 33; Wiley, above note 9).

resemble speech that *others* could have produced for the purpose of sending a message about Jim Smith, this does not establish that *Google* produced the search results with similar intent. Section 2(b) protection, under an intent-focused approach, would require an expressive purpose above and beyond the actual content conveyed in a specific set of search results.

Clearly, then, the content- and intent-focused approaches lead to material differences in at least some section 2(b) cases. Below, I defend the intent-focused approach and explain how it can help courts discern efforts to convey meaning through algorithms. In taking this position, I do not mean to discount the merits of the content-focused approach. As outlined above, compelling arguments could be made in favor of protecting algorithmically generated content *solely* on the basis that it conveys meaning to its consumers. Section 2(b), after all, protects "listeners as well as speakers,"[73] and the *content* produced by an algorithm may further freedom of expression values irrespective of the reason(s) why the algorithm was produced.[74] On the other hand, courts may be wary of extending section 2(b) protections to scenarios where no "speaker"[75] intends to convey a meaning to others, for fear of overshooting the provision's purpose and unduly broadening its scope.[76]

As I see it, a content-focused theory would complement the approach I outline in this chapter, by providing an *additional* route through which algorithmically generated content can be considered "expression." As Justice McLachlin (as she then was) observed in *Keegstra*, "no one rationale provides the last word on freedom of expression."[77] Moreover, the very *process* of engaging with the content-focused theory will benefit section 2(b) jurisprudence, by forcing courts to grapple with the deeper principled question of whether "listener" rights can provide a free-standing ground for section 2(b) protection, even where no expressive intent can be attributed to a "speaker."[78] Algorithm speech cases bring this question into sharp focus, but the question itself reflects a broader doctrinal uncertainty latent within section 2(b) jurisprudence.

That said, even if the content-focused theory has merit, it would not provide a complete account of the section 2(b) rights potentially at stake in algorithm speech cases. In some situations, algorithmically generated content deserves section 2(b) protection regardless of whether it provides instrumental benefits to consumers, because it is intrinsically valuable to an *algorithm owner* who has attempted to convey a message to broader society. Put differently, we need not relegate the algorithm owner in the section 2(b) inquiry to a Good Samaritan, a mere "surrogate for the larger public interest" in protecting free speech rights.[79] The

---

73 *Edmonton Journal* v. *Alberta (A.G.)* [1989] 2 SCR 1326, at pp. 1339–40; *Ford* v. *Quebec (A.G.)* [1988] 2 SCR 712, at p. 767.

74 In addition to the sources cited at note 50, see Schauer, above note 23, pp. 106, 158–60.

75 Here, I am referring both to human "speakers" and to other parties entitled to Charter protection, such as corporations.

76 See Barendt, above note 11, p. 26; L. Tien, *Publishing Software as a Speech Act* (2000) 15 *Berkeley Technol. Law J.* 629, 640. Qualifications could be placed on a content-focused approach to address this concern, like requiring the s. 2(b) claimant to show that the content produced by the algorithm is connected to one or more of the three purposes underpinning the freedom of expression guarantee (see the analysis in Goswami, above note 11, pp. 10–13; Barendt, above note 11, p. 75; K. Greenwalt, *Fighting Words: Individuals Communities and Liberties of Speech* (Princeton University Press, 1995), pp. 19–20; and Bracha, above note 64, pp. 1665–7). These three values are already relevant under s. 2(b) when a claimant's expression is incidentally limited by a law that does not target expressive activity. In such situations, recourse to the three underlying s. 2(b) values serves as a check against unduly broadening the scope of s. 2(b) – a relevant concern if the content-focused approach to algorithm speech is adopted (see Wu, above note 37, p. 1529).

77 *Keegstra*, above note 2, pp. 805–6.

78 Massaro and Norton, above note 3, pp. 367, 369.

79 I draw here, by analogy, on A. R. Amar, Fourth Amendment, First Principles (1994) 107 *Harv. Law Rev.* 757, 796.

algorithm owner may have vital interests of her *own* at stake in section 2(b) cases, interests that deserve vindication under the law.

This brings me to my third and final point – that the algorithm creator will be entitled to section 2(b) protection if she produced the algorithm for the purpose of conveying meaning.

Overview

To determine whether algorithmically generated content deserves section 2(b) protection, courts should examine the purpose for which the algorithm was produced. If the algorithm was produced for the purpose of conveying meaning, section 2(b) protections should apply. In this inquiry, the specific types of content generated by the algorithm are relevant only as a means to determining why the algorithm was produced. Unless the algorithm was produced for an expressive purpose,[80] section 2(b) protections should not arise – even if the output of the algorithm may, in other hypothetical contexts, have been considered "expression" if produced by a different speaker acting for different reasons.

Defending a Purpose-Based Approach to Algorithm-Speech Cases

Sometimes, to understand the "meaning" conveyed by an activity, we must examine the *reason* why the activity was performed. "Speech act" theory recognizes this point. Fundamental to this theory is the notion that utterances can have expressive force independent of "their precise semantic content."[81] And so, speech act theory distinguishes between the *propositional* content of a statement and the *purpose* for which it is made.[82] Take the statement "it is raining." Stated in one context, it conveys to the listener a straightforward meaning – there is precipitation falling from the sky.[83] Said in response to a request from one's partner to walk the dog, it conveys the same *propositional content*, but is performed for the (inevitably unsuccessful) *purpose* of telling the listener that the speaker cannot walk the dog outside. Alternatively, consider the following scenario, modeled on a classic example from the work of John Searle:

> A British soldier is captured by Italian troops during the Second World War. He wishes to convince them that he is a German officer, but he speaks neither German not Italian. He does, however, remember the words of a German sentence he recited during a play at school, but he does not recall what the sentence means. Undeterred, he says the sentence: "Es lebe die Königin, lange darf sie regieren."[84]

We could extract different "meanings" from the captured soldier's speech, depending on whether we examine the *content* of the words he used or the *purpose* he hoped to achieve by saying them. The soldier's words translate to "Long live the Queen, long may she reign." But this is obviously not what he *intended* to convey to his captors – he selected the only German words he remembered from a school play, ignorant about their meaning. The soldier's true purpose for speaking German was simply to indicate that "I am a German officer." The

80 And without accepting a purely content-focused theory, as outlined above.
81 B. K. Dumas, Performatives in Speech Act Theory: An Introduction (1991) 58 *Tenn. Law Rev.* 367, 367.
82 J. Searle, What is a Speech Act?, in P. P. Giglioli (ed.), *Language and Social Context* (Penguin, 1972), pp. 136–56; Tien, above note 76, pp. 638–40. The purpose for an act gives it "illocutionary" force: see Dumas, above note 81, p. 368.
83 Tien, above note 76, p. 641.
84 Searle, above note 82, p. 144.

soldier's captors may have grasped one, both, or neither of the possible meanings conveyed through his speech, depending on their proficiency in German (and attention to sub-text). In this scenario, the propositional content and the purpose[85] of the soldier's statement could not be further apart.

Other examples help to highlight how the purpose behind an activity can assist in determining whether it conveys a meaning and amounts to "expression." Suppose that an NFL player refuses to take the field for the national anthem, in protest of his government's treatment of visible minorities. Assume that in the same game, a second player fails to appear on the field for the anthem because, after a bender the previous night, he overslept, left home late, and wound up stuck in traffic. Audiences notice that both players did not take the field for the anthem. Polarized reactions abound. Fierce political debate – a core good promoted by freedom of expression – ensues. Both players are suspended by their teams.

We would, I suggest, look very differently at both players' suspensions. We would do so even though their actions led to identical outcomes – their absences from the field for the national anthem. Those absences would undoubtedly "convey meaning" to those watching the game. But the key question that sports commentators, fans, and any person with a passing interest in the issue would ask is telling: *why* did the players do it? What motivated their absences for the anthem? That the players' absences may have produced identical outcomes does not mean that they both engaged in "expression." What matters is whether the players acted with the intent to convey meaning. Understanding their *purpose* for acting is an indispensable part of understanding the *meaning* embedded in their actions.

Several other examples confirm how the *purpose* for an activity sometimes provides the best barometer of the "meaning" that it conveys to others. A protestor who burns a flag is not trying to highlight how a cloth interacts with fire, but rather, her opposition to a country's policies.[86] A communications lecturer who creates satirical adverts for imaginary politician "Bob Smith" is not trying to convey the meaning "vote for Bob Smith," but rather, trying to tell her class something about tropes in political advertising. The professor who drafted a meritless paper to submit to law reviews was not trying to convey any specific message spelled out in that paper, but rather, trying to highlight poor publication standards at those institutions. Grasping these meanings requires attention to the broader *purposes* for which those speakers acted, not a narrow focus on the words or actions they employed.

The same approach, I suggest, should be adopted in "algorithm speech" cases. Courts deciding such cases should not fixate on the *content* generated by an algorithm, to the exclusion of the *purpose* for the algorithm's production. Indeed, courts already employ a purpose-focused approach when dealing with cases involving expressive "conduct." In such cases, courts probe the *purpose* for which an activity was undertaken to determine whether it merits free speech protection. The Supreme Court of Canada indicated as much in *Irwin Toy*:

> Of course, while most human activity combines expressive and physical elements, some human activity is purely physical and does not convey or attempt to convey meaning. *It might be difficult to characterize certain day-to-day tasks, like parking a car, as having expressive*

---

[85] My use of the term "purpose" is a simplification of the extensive discussion of "intent" within speech act theory. To be more precise, I use the term "purpose" to refer to a "meaning intention"; and within that "meaning intention," to refer to the intent to communicate: see Tien, above note 76, pp. 641–2. Speech act theory also places significant weight on a speaker's use of conventions that a *viewer* would understand to be expressive, a point I briefly discuss below at "Applying the Purpose-Based Approach in Practice."

[86] Wiley, above note 9, p. 11; Barendt, above note 11, pp. 84–5.

content. To bring such activity within the protected sphere, the plaintiff would have to show that it was performed to convey a meaning. For example, an unmarried person might, as part of a public protest, park in a zone reserved for spouses of government employees in order to express dissatisfaction or outrage at the chosen method of allocating a limited resource. If that person could demonstrate that his activity did in fact have expressive content, he would, at this stage, be within the protected sphere and the s. 2 (b) challenge would proceed.[87]

Professor Hogg takes a similar view, describing "communicative purpose" as an essential aspect of expression and observing that "[t]he courts of both the United States and Canada have insisted upon a communicative purpose to qualify an act as protected speech or expression."[88]

There are good reasons why the purpose-based approach in "expressive conduct" case law should apply to algorithm speech cases. Just as in the expressive conduct jurisprudence, the relevant "activity" in an algorithm speech case blends both expressive and physical elements. The physical element is the production of the algorithm, an act imbued with overtly expressive qualities when the algorithm generates content without further human involvement. *Both* parts for this transaction matter for s. 2(b) purposes. Ignoring the act of producing the algorithm, and focusing solely on the algorithm's subsequent generating of content, would restrict the section 2(b) inquiry to an action in which only the algorithm – *an entity with no section 2(b) rights* – was involved. Properly viewed, the generating of content by an algorithm is merely the final stage of a broader transaction, one which originates in the algorithm's production. To grasp the "meaning" conveyed by the entire enterprise, courts must examine its *purpose*, just as in the expressive conduct cases. Understanding that purpose requires attention to the human element of the transaction – the act of producing the algorithm. If motivated by an expressive purpose, that act, and the content that it spawns via an algorithm, deserves section 2(b) protection.

Focusing on the purpose for the algorithm's production helps explain why algorithm owners must sometimes enjoy section 2(b) protection even when they do not contemplate any specific material generated by their algorithms. Even if the *propositional content* produced by the algorithm was not contemplated in advance, the algorithm may still have been created for an expressive *purpose*. Explicitly recognizing this distinction better captures the many ways through which speakers can convey meaning to others.

Applying the Purpose-Based Approach in Practice

So far, I have explained *where* courts should look when determining whether algorithmically generated content deserves section 2(b) protection – to the *purpose* for which the algorithm was designed, and not simply the *content* generated by the algorithm. In this section, I suggest *how* courts should determine whether an algorithm was designed for an expressive purpose. That inquiry, in my view, should focus on one or more of the following factors:

- **The content generated by an algorithm** may shed light on the purpose for which the algorithm was designed. From that content, courts may be able to infer that the algorithm was produced for an expressive purpose. Take an

---

[87] *Irwin Toy*, above note 6, at p. 969 (emphasis added); Hogg, above note 20, pp. 43-8–43-11; Barendt, above note 11, p. 78. The speaker's purpose for acting is also relevant under American First Amendment jurisprudence about expressive conduct: see *Masterpiece Cakeshop Ltd v. Colorado Civil Rights Commission*, 138 S.Ct. 1719 (2018) (slip op), 3–5 (opinion of Thomas J., concurring); *Clark v. Community for Creative Non-Violence*, 468 US 288, 294 (1984).

[88] Hogg, above note 20, pp. 43-8–43-9.

algorithm that generates a daily list of the financial and human costs of American wars in the Middle East. The content produced by the algorithm – lists of death tolls and financial expenses – is capable of supporting a common-sense inference that the algorithm was produced for the purpose of providing commentary on American foreign policy.[89] The strength of that inference depends, however, on all relevant circumstances of a given case, including the prominence of the asserted "purpose" within the algorithmically generated content, and the further factors described below.

- **The degree to which the asserted "expressive purpose" affects the decision-making of the algorithm.** In some cases, the algorithm owner's asserted "expressive purpose" may be of little relevance to the day-to-day operation of their algorithm. For example, an algorithm may, over time, cater almost entirely to the preferences of its *consumers* through "machine learning."[90] An algorithm that becomes almost entirely responsive to consumer preferences may be more difficult to characterize as one designed to express a particular view held by the algorithm owner.

- **Whether the algorithm, when operating, promotes the exchange of ideas or any other purposes underlying section 2(b).**[91] Although not dispositive, an algorithm that has no connection to free speech values when operating is less likely to have been produced for an expressive purpose. It is, after all, "reasonable to assume that [an algorithm], when it is being operated, will fulfil the primary purpose for which it was developed."[92] For that reason, algorithms that foster democratic participation, freewheeling debate, the search for the truth, and/or individual self-fulfillment *through the development and exchange of ideas*[93] should be considered more likely to have been created for an expressive purpose. The *strength* of any connection to section 2(b) values is, of course, properly considered at the section 1 stage – the point of this initial inquiry is simply to assess the plausibility of an asserted expressive "purpose" for an algorithm's production.

- **External evidence of purpose**, such as promotional and marketing material associated with the algorithm (if available).[94]

I offer three further points of clarification. First, I agree with Benjamin that a "particularized message" is unnecessary for free speech protection.[95] For that reason, a claimant need not reduce her "expressive purpose" to a narrow or precise position to obtain section 2(b) protection.

Second, I view the above inquiry as a rigorous examination of the *subjective* purpose for which the algorithm was produced, albeit through objective factors. Courts, when conducting this inquiry, are not trying to determine whether a hypothetical "reasonable person"

---

[89] That assertion would be far less plausible, by contrast, if the algorithm generated lists of random numbers.

[90] See notes 49 and 72, above.

[91] This aspect of the test draws on some features of Wu's functionality doctrine: see Wu, above note 37.

[92] See, by analogy, *Pong Marketing and Promotions Inc. v. Ontario Media Development Corp.*, 2018 ONCA 555, at para. 31.

[93] As I have explained in another work, within the context of s. 2(b), "individual self-fulfillment" refers to self-fulfillment *specifically through the development and exchange of ideas* (Goswami, above note 11, pp. 12–13). See also Hogg, above note 20, p. 43-8.

[94] See, by analogy, *Pong*, above note 92.

[95] Benjamin, above note 15, pp. 1464–5.

would conclude that the algorithm was produced for an expressive purpose, but whether the *actual* purpose for its production was expressive. To exclude an activity undertaken for a sincere expressive purpose from section 2(b) protection, because *others* may not have recognized that activity as "expression," ignores the critical role played by section 2(b) in protecting unfamiliar and creative modes of conveying meaning that some, and even most, in society may not appreciate.[96] That said, courts are entitled to meaningfully probe an assertion that an algorithm was produced for an expressive purpose, using objective factors like the ones set out above. Courts are perfectly entitled to conclude that an assertion of expressive purpose, lacking any objective support, lacks cogency. The inquiry, ultimately, is "subjective ... but allows for an objective assessment of the credibility of the ... subjective claim."[97]

Third, focusing on whether the algorithm owner intended to convey meaning to others does not foreclose the possibility of the owner *also* having a profit motive. An algorithm may be designed to generate profit *and* convey meaning to others. The presence or prominence of the former motive does not foreclose section 2(b) rights, provided the latter motive is present – "[e]xpression that appears to be motivated by economic or commercial interests may involve other values protected by the Charter."[98] This approach is consistent with section 2(b) cases that accord expressive protection to "speech" by corporations, despite the profit motive underlying their actions.[99]

Wu's and Benjamin's Theories

Although I agree with parts of Wu's functionality doctrine, my approach focuses on the purpose for which the algorithm was produced, not the *function it serves when operational*. If an algorithm was produced to convey meaning to others, I see little reason to foreclose section 2(b) protection based on the function it performs in day-to-day use.[100] The function of the algorithm, under my approach, is merely one of several factors that could shed light on whether it was produced for the purpose of conveying meaning.

Similarly, although I agree with many parts of Benjamin's compelling work, I believe that focusing on a claimant's *purpose* serves as an important limiting principle on his "substantive communication" approach. By conceiving of the production of the algorithm as a purposive act, courts can exclude from the scope of section 2(b) products that involve a modicum of communication, but that few would consider "expressive."[101] Take a navigation system that

---

[96] See, e.g., *Hurley v. Irish-Am, Gay, Lesbian & Bisexual Grp.*, 515 US 557, 569 (1995). I acknowledge, of course, that a theory based on subjective expressive purpose may appear overly broad. I note, however, that concerns about over-breadth are substantially mitigated by: (1) the use of objective factors to meaningfully probe an assertion of expressive purpose; (2) the method and location-based exclusionary rules within s. 2(b); and (3) the balancing approach under s. 1.

[97] See, by analogy, *R. v. Wong* [2018] 1 SCR 696, at paras. 6, 25–35. I add this: even if the s. 2(b) inquiry were directed toward whether a "reasonable person" would recognize the impugned activity or content as "expression," the factors I have outlined in this section would still serve as helpful guiding principles.

[98] Sharpe and Roach, above note 19, p. 147.

[99] *Irwin Toy*, above note 6; *Ford*, above note 73; Hogg, above note 20, p. 43-22; *Rocket v. Royal College of Dental Surgeons of Ontario* [1990] 2 SCR 232.

[100] For an extended critique of the functionality approach, see Benjamin, above note 15, ns. 57, 84, 98; and Tien, above note 76, pp. 684–93.

[101] I recognize, of course, that even if such products were granted s. 2(b) protection, the government could justify regulating them under s. 1, the real battleground in many of the Supreme Court's free expression cases (Hogg, above note 20, p. 43-6; Sharpe and Roach, above note 19, p. 141). One author has even commented that in the Supreme Court's s. 2(b) jurisprudence, "very little of the conceptual 'work' is done by the concept of 'expression'" (A. Stone, Canadian Constitutional Law of Freedom of Expression, in R. Albert and D. R. Cameron (eds.),

consistently selects the shortest routes between two locations and expresses these choices vocally. Are the directions provided by navigation system entitled to section 2(b) protection? Benjamin's theory suggests that they may be. The navigation system is based on a clear set of preferences of considerable importance to the algorithm creator, preferences which allow the algorithm to select the shortest route between a departure point and a destination and then express that choice in an understandable manner. In the abstract, the navigation system could represent a message about the importance of efficient travel. Or perhaps the navigation system's directions could be construed as the algorithm creator's *opinion* about the shortest routes from various departure points to various destinations – a subject of frequent debate among drivers and passengers. But something, I suggest, would have gone awry if a constitutional right to free expression was interpreted as covering tools of convenience like navigation systems.[102] The solution, in my view, lies in dispensing with hypothetical inquiries into what meaning the navigation system *might* have been intended to convey, and focusing the search for "substantive communication" on the broader purpose for which the system was *actually* produced.

Applying the Purpose-Based Approach: Examples

Under my approach, both algorithms designed by Mary would qualify for section 2(b) protection. The program that generates ranked lists of the top ten NBA players would qualify because Mary produced the algorithm for an expressive purpose. A judge could reasonably infer that, through her algorithm, Mary sought to convey a meaning about the criteria relevant to excellence in basketball, an inference supported by the content that her algorithm produces (ranked lists of players based on various statistical preferences). There is no need, under my approach, to artificially brand any specific ranking of ten players as Mary's "opinion." Similarly, in determining whether Mary's gender-progressive search engine conveys meaning, a court using my approach need not ask whether any particular set of results it generates are "opinions" or "advice." Instead, the section 2(b) inquiry would focus on the *broader* act Mary engaged in – producing an algorithm that consistently generates search results favoring content by female content creators – and ask whether Mary sought to convey meaning through that act. Plainly, she did.

This same approach, applied to products such as navigation systems, would likely result in a different outcome. The focus, again, would not be on whether the words generated by the navigation program "convey meaning." They clearly do so – for example, taking Street A for 1.2 kilometers and then Avenue B for 800 meters, is the quickest way from point C to point D. The proper inquiry, however, is whether the *broader* act of producing the algorithm had an expressive purpose. Plainly, it did not. The navigation system does not involve the exchange of ideas or connect to any section 2(b) values, nor is any broader expressive purpose evident in its day-to-day operation.[103]

[   ] *Canada in the World: Comparative Perspectives on the Canadian Constitution* (Cambridge University Press, 2018), p. 248). Algorithm speech cases merit greater attention at the s. 2(b) stage, in my view. Despite the presence of s. 1, courts have a legitimate role to play in ensuring the s. 2(b) right is not trivialized: *Lavigne* v. *Ontario Public Service Employees Union* [1991] 2 SCR 211, 269.

[102]   I agree with Tim Wu's conclusion on this issue: above note 37, p. 1525.

[103]   These are relevant factors under my approach (see "Applying the Purpose-Based Approach in Practice," above). Of course, products like navigation systems can be specially designed to convey a second-order meaning to others – the system, for example, could be designed to selectively avoid certain routes by way of protest or give directions featuring politically charged messages. These kinds of choices may support an inference that the

Google

Perhaps the most prominent "algorithm speech" cases involve claims by Google and other search engines for free speech protection, including in challenges to legislation like the European Union's "Right to be Forgotten." Under my approach, the section 2(b) analysis would focus on whether Google[104] intends to convey meaning through its algorithm.[105] In this inquiry, no specific set of search results generated by Google would capture the "meaning" relevant to the section 2(b) analysis. For the most part, no one at Google has prior knowledge of the specific content the company's algorithm will generate in response to search queries – indeed, this is precisely the defense on which Google relies to guard against liability for defamation or promoting hate speech when its rankings promote links featuring such content.[106] If Google intends to convey meaning through its search engine algorithm, that meaning must be found in the broader purpose for which the algorithm was produced.

Perhaps, on the evidence, a court could conclude that Google's algorithm was designed for the purpose of communicating Google's commitment to high-quality web design, and/ or to the validity of popularity as a metric for relevance. Or maybe not; perhaps Google designed the algorithm to provide a service to enhance convenience for users without intending to communicate any broader substantive message in the process, much like the creator of the navigation system described above. The ultimate answer will turn on the evidence. Asking the proper question, however, is critical to determining the scope of Google's interests as a speaker – a particularly significant point if a section 1 analysis is required.[107]

CONCLUSION

To address the novel challenges posed by algorithm "speech," Canadian courts will need to tackle uncertainties within the concept of "conveying meaning" that have been left largely untested in traditional freedom of expression cases. To locate the relevant "meaning" in free speech disputes involving algorithms, courts must look beyond the specific content generated by an algorithm and focus on the *purpose* for which the algorithm was produced, consistent with the approach in expressive conduct cases and in speech act theory. The proper question, under this approach, "isn't whether something is speech, but whether someone is speaking."[108]

---

algorithm was designed for an expressive purpose. The focus would remain, however, on the purpose for which the algorithm was designed.

[104] It is important to distinguish between the expressive rights of *Google*, and those of the creators of the content displayed in its search results. The latter may be entitled to s. 2(b) protection even if the former is not.

[105] As explained above, under a content-focused approach, the s. 2(b) inquiry would be complete if the *users* of Google's search engine could derive a meaning from the content it generates.

[106] See Wu, above note 37, p. 1528.

[107] A final point on Google: even where an activity does not "convey meaning," *compelling* the speaker to communicate a particular message can still infringe their expressive rights. Section 2(b) protects the freedom of individuals to choose what *to* say and what *not* to say (*Slaight Commc'ns v. Davidson* [1989] 1 SCR 1038, 1080; *RJR-MacDonald v. Canada (A.G.)* [1995] 3 SCR 199, at para. 113; Hogg, above note 20, pp. 43-17–43-18). Walking down a street would not ordinarily be considered expressive, but legislation forcing everyone to walk down a street with placards promoting the incumbent government would clearly engage s. 2(b). Legislation or other government action compelling Google to arrange its search rankings in a certain way could therefore infringe s. 2 (b), even if Google does not ordinarily seek to "convey meaning" through its algorithm.

[108] Tien, above note 76, p. 634.

This approach offers several benefits as an analytic framework. First, it aligns with current free speech jurisprudence. It would be incongruous, in my opinion, for courts to use one standard to resolve free speech claims involving algorithms, and a different standard for cases that feature other methods of expression. The underlying purposes of the section 2(b) right does not vary based on the medium of expression a speaker chooses.[109] By extension, the test required to access section 2(b) protection should not depend on whether the speaker adopts a vocal, written, or algorithmic outlet. By refining rather than displacing the *Irwin Toy* test, my approach maintains a unified approach to section 2(b) cases regardless of the means of expression chosen by a speaker.

Second, focusing on the purpose for which the algorithm was designed makes good practical sense. It provides a mechanism to exclude devices like car alarms and navigation systems from the scope of section 2(b), an outcome difficult to justify through theories focused solely on the content produced by an algorithm. On the other hand, my approach provides robust protections for speakers who set out to convey a message to others and choose to use an algorithm to achieve that goal. An added advantage of focusing on the purpose for the algorithm's production is less reasoning by analogy. Too often, algorithm speech cases devolve into examining whether the output generated by an algorithm *resembles* expression by a human. The proper question, I suggest, is whether the algorithmic output is, *in fact*, the culmination of an attempt by a person to convey meaning. This inquiry allows us to cut through creative analogies in legal argument that say little about whether a speaker is conveying or attempting to convey meaning to others. By focusing on that core question, with attention to the purpose for which the algorithm was designed, courts can resolve novel challenges in algorithm speech cases without departing from the traditional foundations of section 2(b) case law.

---

[109] See *Irwin Toy*, above note 6, at pp. 969–70; and *Ford*, above note 73, at para. 60.

27

Artificial Minds in First Amendment Borderlands

Marc Jonathan Blitz

INTRODUCTION

The First Amendment's freedom of speech, the Supreme Court said in 1943, protects our capacity to use words or non-verbal symbols to create a "short-cut from mind to mind."[1] But does it continue to do so when one of the "minds" on either end of such a short cut is an artificial one? Does it protect my right to receive words or symbols not from another person, but from artificial intelligence (AI) – that is, a computer program that can write, compose music, or perform other tasks that used to be the sole province of human intelligence? If so, what kind of First Amendment protection does computer speech receive – and how, if it all, does it differ from that which protects the speech of human persons?

In an age when individuals increasingly interact with computers – asking questions, and issuing orders to voice-controlled "smart speakers" in their home (such as Alexa, Google Home, and HomePod)[2] and "voice assistants" on their smartphone (such as Siri, Cortana, and Google Assistant)[3] – such questions are receiving more attention from First Amendment scholars.[4] And they are likely to demand closer analysis, not just from scholars, but also from courts, as AI authors play an increasingly significant role in writing the novels, essays, or news articles we read, the music we listen to, and the art we admire. Programmers are already creating software that can write news stories, email messages, or data reports that read as if they were written by human authors.[5] And according to philosopher Andy Clark, our interaction with algorithms is only likely to grow more significant: computer algorithms, he says, already "talk with us," "watch us," "trade for us," "select dates for us," and "suggest what we might buy, sell, or wear." Their influence, he writes, "will slowly permeate the full range of human-built environments,

[1] *West Va. St. Bd. of Educ. v. Barnette*, 319 US 624, 632 (1943).
[2] See A. Perry, 200 Million People Will Probably Be Using Smart Speakers by the End of This Year, *Mashable* (April 16, 2019), https://mashable.com/article/echo-homepod-smart-speakers-canalys/.
[3] See M. McLaughlin, What a Virtual Assistant Is and How it Works, *Lifewire* (June 24, 2019), www.lifewire.com /virtual-assistants-4138533.
[4] See T. M. Massaro and H. Norton, Siri-ously? Free Speech Rights and Artificial Intelligence (2016) 110 *Nw. Univ. Law Rev.* 1169; T. M. Massaro, H. Norton, and M. E. Kaminski, Siri-ously 2.0: What Artificial Intelligence Reveals about the First Amendment (2017) 101 *Minn. Law Rev.* 2481, 2482; M. E. Kaminski, Authorship, Disrupted: AI Authors in Copyright and First Amendment Law (2017) 51 *UC Davis Law Rev.* 589, 590; R. K. L. Collins and D. M. Skover (eds.), *Robotica: Speech Rights and Artificial Intelligence* (Cambridge University Press, 2018).
[5] B. Marr, Artificial Intelligence Can Now Write Amazing Content – What Does that Mean for Humans?, *Forbes* (March 29, 2019), www.forbes.com/sites/bernardmarr/2019/03/29/artificial-intelligence-can-now-write-amazing-content-what-does-that-mean-for-humans/#20a2214b50ab.

from bridges to roads to cities and more minor intelligent devices."[6] In such a world, we face unavoidable questions about how we communicate with such algorithms, and form law and policy to govern our relationships with them.

It would not be surprising if many see these questions as so demanding that courts will be required to move onto a radically new and unfamiliar landscape – requiring a First Amendment doctrine that is starkly different from that which has evolved to deal with human speakers. AI, after all, has long been familiar to most of us only from science fiction. So thinking about how the First Amendment doctrine makes room for AI may seem to require that we adapt that doctrine to a science-fiction-like world (and perhaps radically transform it as we do so). And that may one day be true: if, for example, robots and humans merge together into "cyber-humans," as Woodrow Barfield has argued we will,[7] then free speech law may well have to grapple with arguments about how we can communicate – wordlessly – by sending thoughts via the computers that may one day directly connect our minds.[8]

But my main purpose in this chapter is to point out how at least some of the difficult questions that AI speech raises for First Amendment law are *not* entirely new questions. Rather, they are First Amendment questions that courts have long found difficult – and that AI, and even simpler kinds of computer algorithms, can sometimes make more difficult. More specifically, as I will explain in this chapter, AI and other computer algorithms will confront courts with new variants of two long-standing First Amendment challenges: (1) the challenge of distinguishing "speech" from "conduct" (and addressing activity where they are merged together); and (2) the challenge of distinguishing protected First Amendment "authorship" or editing of ideas, from unprotected manipulation or shaping of the environment or medium in which these ideas are disseminated.

Before looking more closely at these hard cases about AI and algorithm speech, it is useful to start with an easier inquiry about AI speech. Imagine that a computer programmer creates a program called "Cyber-Plato" – an AI program that generates new Platonic dialogues on the model of those which Plato actually wrote. Some of these might be derivative works, revising Plato's actual dialogues by inserting new characters: Cyber-Plato, for example, might generate a revised version of the *Phaedo* describing how thinkers such as Aristotle, Plutarch, Epicurus, or Descartes might have answered (and been answered by) Socrates had they been participants in that dialogue's discussion about the soul's immortality and its ability to exist separately from the body, and about Plato's theory of forms.[9] Or Cyber-Plato might analyze the structure and content of Plato's existing dialogues and produce new dialogues with the same style and covering similar themes – perhaps attempting to analyze how Socrates and his interlocutors might understand modern phenomena, such as AI or virtual reality (VR).

Would the US Constitution's protection for freedom of speech protect not only human speech, but also such computer-generated speech? Would it bar the government from censoring the creation, distribution, or reading of such AI-produced dialogues, even though they are written by computer programs rather than by a human writer? It is

[6]   A. Clark, We Are Merging with Robots. That's a Good Thing, *New York Times* (August 13, 2018), www
      .nytimes.com/2018/08/13/opinion/we-are-merging-with-robots-thats-a-good-thing.html.
[7]   W. Barfield, *Cyber-Humans: Our Future with Machines* (Springer International, 2015), pp. 267–84.
[8]   *Ibid.*, pp. 9–11, 51–5.
[9]   See Plato, *Phaedo*, E. Braun, P. Kalkavage, and E. Salem (eds. and trans.) (Hackett, 1998), pp. 39, 41–6, 54.

hard to see why not. Although it may be decades or centuries – or an eternity – before an artificially intelligent Cyber-Plato can write dialogues with the philosophical depth, insight, and creativity that characterizes those written by Plato, it might still generate dialogues that we find educational, informative, or entertaining. The Cyber-Plato program itself may not be a speaker with its own First Amendment rights. But neither is a Greek philosopher who, like Plato, died in 347 BC, over 2,000 years before the First Amendment came into existence. Yet, those living individuals who *do* have First Amendment rights under the US Constitution can claim (correctly) that these rights give them a right to read and reflect upon Plato's works, or share them with others, by selling or distributing them. They might likewise claim – quite persuasively – that they should be able to read and share the works of the Cyber-Plato program. This is because, as Toni Massaro and Helen Norton explain, even a First Amendment that is meant only to benefit human beings is not meant only to give human speakers a chance to translate their ideas into words or non-verbal art or symbolism. It is *also* meant to give human *listeners and readers* a chance to find ideas (or other meaning) in words, art, or symbols – and this is something listeners and readers can do even if the words, art, or symbols are generated by computers.[10] Massaro and Norton therefore strongly defend the claim that AI speech can be protected by the First Amendment.[11] Other scholars and writers have done so as well.[12]

The example of computer-generated speech I've just considered is thus, in a sense, an easy case. The essays written by the Cyber-Plato program that I've just imagined do not require significant transformations in free speech jurisprudence because there is a ready-made place for them there: the essays produced by such a program will likely receive the *same* protection that the First Amendment already provides to similar essays written entirely by human authors. In short, essays already have a well-recognized status as First Amendment "speech" and they retain this status when they come from computer algorithms rather than human authors. This is a point that Massaro and Norton – and Margot Kaminski – emphasize in their analyses of AI speech. As the three of them emphasize in explaining why AI speech should receive protection even though animal behavior does not, "AI is designed to speak our language, and increasingly to do so in forms that look like us, walk like us, and talk like us."[13] As Kaminski writes in a separate analysis, "[a]n article written by an algorithm is as 'speechy' as an article written by a human, from the perspective of a human reader."[14] There is no reason to deny AI First Amendment protection when it emulates precisely the kind of activity that is the subject of free speech protection: Stories, poems, political statements, jokes, and other verbal or non-verbal expression. And although we may still be decades or centuries away from creating a Cyber-Plato, there are already AI programs that can create literature that resembles the kind written by humans. A recent article notes that software created by the research firm OpenAI can – with a sample of "a few words or a few pages" – create new texts that "simulate the style of anything from classical works of fiction to news stories, depending on what it is fed."[15] Programmers have already created AI entities that

[10]   See Massaro and Norton, above note 4, pp. 1174–6.
[11]   *Ibid.*, pp. 1172–3.
[12]   See Massaro *et. al.*, above note 4 (of which Helen Norton and Margot Kaminski are co-authors); Kaminski, above note 4; Collins and Skover, above note 4.
[13]   See Massaro *et al.*, above note 4, p. 2482.
[14]   Kaminski, above note 4, p. 610.
[15]   R. Pringle, The Writing of This AI Is So Human that Its Creators Are Scared to Release It, *CBC* (February 25, 2019), www.cbc.ca/news/technology/ai-writer-disinformation-1.5030305.

can paint pictures,[16] compose music,[17] and write poems[18] – and seekers of art may well find them interesting or illuminating. Even if such AI entities lack sentience or the capacity to feel emotions, they might express emotions in ways that comfort or encourage individuals – or even model "emotional intelligence" for people who struggle to show it in their own lives.[19] Indeed, some speech comes not from AI programs, but from simpler kinds of computer algorithms, such as search engines.

Other actions generated by computer algorithms will produce an easy case of a different kind – namely, an example of conduct that clearly falls *outside* of the scope of free speech protection. Consider, for example, the driving done by an autonomous vehicle, which is autonomous because the car is driven by a computer rather than a human driver. When a person drives an automobile, she is not engaged in First Amendment speech. The government faces no First Amendment hurdles, for example, when it enacts speed limits or other traffic rules. So, if driving a car is not speech when it is done by a person, it is also unlikely to be First Amendment speech when done by a computer. Just as computer-generated essays merit the same First Amendment protection as human-created essays, computer-generated driving will just as easily be subject to traffic rules (and other government safety regulations) as its human equivalent. In each of these cases, we don't need a special First Amendment for computer algorithms – because the First Amendment framework that courts *already use* to classify essays as speech, and driving as non-speech conduct, applies straightforwardly to these activities whether they come from human beings or computers.

What then will produce *hard* cases involving AI speech? That is the question I will focus on in the remainder of the chapter. And I will argue that what makes many such cases "hard" is not simply that AI speakers are *different* from human speakers, but that some of these differences happen to bring courts into First Amendment "gray areas" that have been challenging for a long time – but are made more challenging by AI.

IN THE BORDERLAND BETWEEN SPEECH AND CONDUCT

At times, the communicative pathway that speech establishes to another mind *instead* becomes (at least in part) a pathway to generating physical, financial, or other "non-expressive" effects that the state has long had power and responsibility to regulate, such as creating harm to property or harms to individuals' health or safety. Imagine, for example, that an AI program of the future operating on one's smartphone regales a listener with historical

16 See Art Created by Artificial intelligence, *CBS News*, www.cbsnews.com/pictures/art-created-by-artificial-intelligence/; T. Simonite, We Made Our Own Artificial Intelligence Art and So Can You, *Wired* (November 20, 2018), www.wired.com/story/we-made-artificial-intelligence-art-so-can-you/; J. Muskus, AI Made These Paintings, *Bloomberg Businessweek* (May 17, 2018), www.bloomberg.com/news/articles/2018-05-17/ai-made-incredible-paintings-in-about-two-weeks.
17 M. Barrett and J. Ward, AI Can Now Compose Pop Music and Even Symphonies. Here's How Composers Are Joining in, *NBC News* (May 29, 2019), www.nbcnews.com/mach/science/ai-can-now-compose-pop-music-even-symphonies-here-s-ncna1010931; M. Hutson, How Google Is Making Music with Artificial Intelligence, *Science* (August 8, 2017), www.sciencemag.org/news/2017/08/how-google-making-music-artificial-intelligence; M. Avdeeff, AI and Humans Collaborated to Produce This Hauntingly Catchy Pop Music, *Quartzy* (October 11, 2018), https://qz.com/quartzy/1420576/listen-to-haunting-ai-generated-pop-music-from-skygge-and-kiesza/.
18 A. Cafolla, Artificial Intelligence Is Writing Poetry, But Is It Any Good?, *Dazed* (August 14, 2018), www.dazeddigital.com/science-tech/article/40985/1/artificial-intelligence-ai-poetry-sonnet-shakespeare; D. Robitzski, Artificial Intelligence Writes Bad Poems Just Like an Angsty Teen, *Futurism* (April 26, 2018), https://futurism.com/artificial-intelligence-bad-poems.
19 The Rise of Emotional Robots, *Sapiens* (August 28, 2018), www.sapiens.org/technology/emotional-intelligence-robots/.

tales of Chicago as it existed in the late nineteenth and early twentieth centuries.[20] But the AI program offers an additional add-on: it can be linked to an autonomous vehicle, such as a car driven by a computer rather than a human driver. This is, of course, something that it is not legal for a typical driver to do at the time of this chapter's writing: autonomous vehicles are not yet permitted in traffic except in very limited circumstances. But imagine a future version of Chicago where autonomous driving is legally permissible, and routine. When this Chicago history phone app links to a car inside Chicago's city limits, it will not only provide a gripping narration of Chicago's history (perhaps in the voice of a local celebrity); it will also drive the car to which it links through city traffic – bringing the passenger to the scene of each historical event it discusses. The AI in the app might, for example, drive a user's car to the site adjacent to where the first Ferris wheel was located on Midway Plaisance during the 1893 World's Fair.[21] Or the place in Grant Park where a ray of light completed its voyage from the star Arcturus to trigger searchlights, and launch the start of the 1933 World's Fair – "the Century of Progress" fair – forty years later.[22] Or to many other historical sites in the city. The user would just sit back and let the AI drive the car and act as a historical tour guide at the same time.

In this situation, of course, the government would *not* be entirely blocked by the First Amendment from regulating the AI's activity. The First Amendment might prevent government from restricting what the AI said about Chicago history. But it would *not* block government from regulating (and perhaps banning) the AI's navigation of the car through city traffic. Driving a car, as I noted earlier, is not speech and so government can regulate computer driving as easily as it can regulate human driving, even when that driving is combined with speech.[23] The same would be true where AI speech is combined with other non-speech activity. For example, where an AI on one's computer narrates – for the benefit of a computer user – the way it is hacking into a government computer at another location: even if the narration is protected speech, the hacking probably isn't – and the government will encounter little problem treating it as a criminal offense under the federal Computer Fraud and Abuse Act.[24] As I will explain below, courts have developed doctrine to help them address situations where expressive conduct is combined with non-expressive conduct (like driving

---

[20] See M. J. Blitz, Augmented and Virtual Reality, Freedom of Expression, and the Personalization of Public Space, in W. Barfield and M. J. Blitz (eds.), *Research Handbook on the Law of Augmented and Virtual Reality* (Edward Elgar, 2018), pp. 320–2.

[21] See A Trip through the Midway Plaisance, Friends of the White City, www.friendsofthewhitecity.org/architec ture/buildings/the-midway-plaisance.

[22] See B. King, The Curious and Confounding Story of How Arcturus Electrified Chicago, *Universe Today* (March 19, 2013), www.universetoday.com/100799/the-curious-and-confounding-story-of-how-arcturus-electrified-chicago/.

[23] A more difficult question, which I and other scholars have explored elsewhere but I will not analyze closely here, is whether the government could – consistent with the First Amendment – ban driving to a certain location not to protect public safety, but rather in order to prevent people from learning about that location's history. See J. Bambauer, Is Data Speech? (2014) 66 *Stan. Law Rev.* 57, 60–1 (arguing that government would violate the First Amendment if it imposed restrictions on individuals in order to prevent them from obtaining knowledge from their observations); see M. J. Blitz, The Right to Map (and Avoid Being Mapped): Reconceiving First Amendment Protection for Information-Gathering in the Age of Google Earth (2013) 14 *Colum. Sci. Technol. Law Rev.* 115, 124–5 (arguing that, under the First Amendment, "[i]ndividuals should be able to observe the environment with their own eyes," not merely through maps or other representations and that government, in some circumstances, violates the First Amendment when it "seeks to cloak parts of the landscape to assure an individual cannot understand it").

[24] See 18 USC § 1030(a)(2): subjecting to criminal punishment anyone who "intentionally accesses a computer without authorization or exceeds authorized access, and thereby obtains ... information from any protected computer."

cars or hacking into computers), and courts have also adapted such doctrines to cases involving computer software. First Amendment protection for AI is reduced when the things an AI entity is "authoring" – or perhaps "co-authoring" with human speakers – aren't essays, books, or other recognized forms of expression, but rather certain kinds of material or virtual objects, or non-speech actions we take in the physical world.

We need not rely on futuristic fantasies about Chicago history tours to better understand this aspect of how First Amendment law applies to AI and other software. Courts have already grappled with the question of how the law deals with "hybrids" of speech and non-speech conduct – generated by computers, or through less technologically advanced means.

Perhaps the most well-known example of this from the case law on computers is the courts' responses to First Amendment challenges against government measures restricting the sharing of programs that encrypt or decrypt information. Federal courts provided early judicial analyses of this issue in a trio of cases – *Bernstein v. United States Department of State*,[25] *Junger v. Daley*,[26] and *Karn v. Department of State*.[27] In the first two of these, academics wished to share the source code for encryption or decryption programs in forums – academic conferences, published journal articles, or websites – where they would be available to foreign nationals.[28] In *Karn*, a communications engineer wished to ship a CD with source code for a cryptography program together with a copy of the book *Applied Cryptography* by Bruce Schneier.[29] In all of these cases, the US State Department informed the individuals wishing to distribute the source code that US law on exports prevented such distribution unless the government permitted it. The academics or professionals wishing to share the source code responded that they had a First Amendment right to do so.

Another similar case confronted the Second Circuit Court in 2001: in *Universal City Studios v. Corley*, the Court had to decide whether the government violated the freedom of speech of programming and computer enthusiasts when it forbade them from sharing, or linking to, a computer program that could essentially cut through the copyright protection technology on DVD movies, allowing users to copy these movies in violation of US copyright law.[30] The Digital Millennium Copyright Act (DMCA) made it illegal to "circumvent" such technological copyright protection measures – or to "traffic in any technology, product, service, device, component" "primarily designed" to make such circumvention possible. In other words, the DMCA bolstered copyright protection by assuring that, when copyright holders set up digital "fences" or other measures to safeguard their intellectual property rights, would-be thieves wouldn't find ways around these digital fences, and wouldn't be able to buy or otherwise obtain the digital equivalent of a hacksaw or illegally produced key that let them cut through such a fence, or illegally open it, instead of obtaining permission from the owner (and the legitimate "key" that comes with such permission). A decryption program that is designed to allow computer users to cut through such a digital fence or otherwise circumvent it, said the government, is precisely the kind of technology that the DMCA prohibits. As in *Bernstein*, *Junger*, and *Karn*, however, those who wished to share the code for the program insisted they had a First Amendment right to speak about and educate other readers about it.

[25] *Bernstein v. Dep't of Justice*, 176 F.3d 1132 (9th Cir. 1999); *Bernstein v. Dep't of State*, 922 F. Supp. 1426 (ND Cal. 1996).
[26] *Karn v. Dep't of State*, 925 F. Supp. 1 (DDC 1996).
[27] *Junger v. Daley*, 209 F.3d 481, 484 (6th Cir. 2000).
[28] *Ibid.* at 484–5; *Bernstein*, 922 F. Supp, above note 25, at 1428–30; *Bernstein*, 176 F.3d, above note 25, at 1135–7.
[29] *Karn*, above note 26, at 3–5.
[30] *Universal City Studios v. Corley*, 273 F.3d 429, 435 (2nd Cir. 2001).

In all of these cases, the difficulty confronting the courts was that the computer algorithms at issue have a double character. They consist of lines of computer programming language in the form of "source code" that certain readers can read and learn from (just as is true of an essay or Platonic dialogue). But this code cannot only be read by humans, but also "run" or executed by computers – in such a way that it generates *non-speech* conduct, such as "unlocking" files stored on a computer – by decrypting them – or by triggering action in an appliance device, or even an automobile, that such computers control. As the Second Circuit noted in *Universal City Studios* v. *Corley*, the decryption code at issue had both these dimensions. It was expressive because source code for a program consists of "information capable of comprehension and assessment by a human being. A programmer reading a program learns information about instructing a computer, and might use this information to improve personal programming skills and perhaps the craft of programming."[31] It is like a cooking recipe or musical score that tells readers how to perform a particular task. Or like an instruction manual or other educational document that provides instruction not only using colloquial English, but also a kind of "show and tell" – by actually letting individuals read the lines of code that make up the program. Here, the computer algorithm isn't an AI speaker – it *is* the speech *itself*. But when the same lines of code aren't simply read by a person, but executed by a machine, the result is *not* expression – at least not when it involved stripping copyright protection from copyright-protected files. It is more a digital equivalent of a "skeleton key" that "[b]urglars can use ... to open door locks."[32] Unlocking a physical door with such a key isn't expressive, and neither said the Court, is unlocking an electronic door that one is unauthorized to open.[33]

Although analyzing First Amendment questions about computer software was new to courts, the more general challenge was not: it isn't only software, after all, that can *both* communicate a message or set of feelings – but simultaneously can do something else, with possibly harmful impacts on an individual's safety or financial well-being. Burning a draft card can serve as a way to protest a war – but it simultaneously destroys a government record (and can raise safety concerns for people or property nearby). Marching across an intersection with signs can communicate the marcher's beliefs to onlookers – but it can also block traffic.

---

[31] *Ibid.* at 447.

[32] *Ibid.* at 452.

[33] To be sure, one might well question the first part of this argument – that source code is expressive because it can be examined by a programmer who can learn from it. The analogy the Ninth Circuit drew to recipes scores isn't a perfect one: a recipe can *only* become a meal if a human reader understands the recipe's instructions and then follows them by combining and cooking ingredients. The oven cannot receive the recipe and cook the meal itself. By contrast, source code can produce computer action even if the person who receives it is someone who has no mastery of the programming language in which it is written. That person can copy the code, transfer it to a compiler, and then generate computer action – just a person might take a skeleton key and use it even if he pays virtually no attention to how it is designed (and learns no lessons about the design of such a key). But as the Court said in *Junger*, the fact that language also has functionality does not rule out free speech protection.

Another objection is that stressing that a programmer might learn something from source code in effect proves too much – because it might make even transferred objects – like skeleton keys – into First Amendment speech. While someone who receives the skeleton key might simply use it to open a door, if that person is a locksmith, she might examine the key or the deadbolt and learn something about key design. Or a person may convey information about a padlock by transferring it This was a challenge raised by Orin Kerr to treating software as speech because it conveys information. O. Kerr, Are We Overprotecting Code? Thoughts on First–Generation Internet Law (2000) 57 *Wash. Lee Law Rev.* 1287. The Second Circuit took note of and responded to Kerr's argument, stressing that "code does not cease to be speech just because some objects that convey information are not speech. Both code and a padlock can convey information, but only code, because it uses a notational system comprehensible by humans, is communication that qualifies as speech" (*Universal City Studios* v. *Corley*, above note 30, at 449 n. 24).

Selling art-covered T-shirts or handbags on streets clearly involves artistic expression, but it is also a sale of commercial goods, something which government routinely regulates. Courts began developing doctrines for these kinds of cases decades ago. They did so to determine when government can permissibly regulate such expressive activity in order to protect the public from non-expressive effects that come packaged with it – like the property destruction or traffic obstruction that might come packaged with political protest, or the effects that vending art – or anything else – has on the amount of commercial activity that fills a city's sidewalks. In short, courts *already have* a doctrinal toolkit for addressing cases where human activity straddles both sides of the borderline between speech and non-speech conduct. It is not surprising that they reach for and apply this doctrinal toolkit when computer algorithms seem to straddle both sides of the same boundary line.

As *Universal City Studios* v. *Corley* made clear, the key doctrine in this toolkit is a legal test called the *O'Brien* test – because it comes from the Supreme Court case *United States* v. *O'Brien*.[34] The case featured one of the examples of hybrid conduct mentioned above: burning one's draft card to protest the Vietnam War. This is what David O'Brien did in 1966, and what he was prosecuted for under an act of Congress which made it a crime to destroy a draft card.[35] The Court had to decide whether the Act's limitation on this kind of symbolic protest – through draft card burning – was constitutional, and the Court's answer was essentially that it was, as long as: (1) the government's regulation was aimed at some non-expressive dimension of draft card burning (like its destructive effect on property) and *not* at its underlying message or other expressive content;[36] (2) its interest in regulating this non-expressive harm was a "substantial" interest, one that would justify the collateral damage to speech which necessarily comes with banning a means of expressing political views (like draft card burning);[37] and (3) it didn't engage in substantially more restriction of speech than is necessary to achieve this significant interest.[38] In *O'Brien* itself, the Court found the government satisfied this test: the justification for the draft card burning, said the Court, was to preserve an important record, not to silence anti-Vietnam protestors. The record was an important one for military drafts, which were an essential part of the country's war readiness – so the government's interest in protecting such records was "significant."[39] And government wasn't restricting any more speech than it had to: it was protecting draft cards from destruction by making it illegal to destroy them – and not restricting any other kind of speech.[40]

The Second Circuit in *Universal City Studios* v. *Corley* applied the same test in reaching the conclusion that it was not unconstitutional for government to restrict the dissemination of decryption software that could circumvent copyright protection. The government's aim wasn't to prevent people from reading and learning from the software – it was rather to protect property.[41] Prevention of copyright violation, said the Court, was a significant interest. Moreover, said the Court, the government's use of the DMCA's provisions did not restrict

---

[34]   *United States* v. *O'Brien*, 391 US 367 (1968).

[35]   *Ibid.* at 369–70.

[36]   *Ibid.* at 377 (the Court said the government's reason for suppressing the activity has to be "unrelated to the suppression of free expression").

[37]   *Ibid.*

[38]   *Ibid.*

[39]   *Ibid.* (the Court also mentioned a fourth requirement – that the restriction imposed by the government otherwise be "within the constitutional power of the Government." But in most other contexts, there is no need to mention that the government cannot act outside of its constitutional powers – by, for example, trying to take private property, but not for public use).

[40]   *Ibid.*

[41]   *Universal City Studios* v. *Corley*, above note 30, at 449 n. 24.

speech substantially more than necessary to prevent such violations.[42] The government said the DMCA barred Corley and others from both *posting* the source code for the decryption code on their own website, and *linking* to other sites where it was posted. Although the Court expressed some concern about the ban on linking to others' speech, it concluded that such a ban was not excessive – since those seeking to spread devices for cutting through copyright protection might otherwise make them "available for instantaneous worldwide distribution before any preventive measures can be effectively taken."[43]

To be sure, one could well disagree about how to apply the *O'Brien* test to software cases like this in which the same source code that programmers are able to read can easily be copied and pasted into a compiler and then run on a computer to produce a non-speech action.

Presumably, courts would apply the same analysis to any other kind of computer algorithm the output of which – when executed on a computer – was some kind of non-speech conduct. Consider a computer program or file which – like the "demiurge" of Plato's world-creation myth in the *Timaeus*[44] – doesn't simply give readers or other audiences a set of mental concepts to view or contemplate, but rather, when connected to a 3D printer, can translate those concepts into a material form. 3D printing often begins with a "computer-aided design" drawing – in a file the printer can read – and then builds the object depicted in the design layer by layer – building each layer from raw material stored in the printer. This process relies on computer algorithms. Source code is necessary to make the printer work and CAD files provide the model for the object the printer creates.

It seems likely courts should apply the First Amendment to this kind of program involving the 3D printing of a gun in exactly the way the Second Circuit analyzed the decryption program in *Universal City Studios* v. *Corley*: the source code and CAD files would constitute First Amendment speech, because other programmers would be able to read and learn from it. But the production of the gun itself on the 3D printer would not be First Amendment activity (although it would likely receive some degree of Second Amendment protection, since it is a method by which individuals can obtain the arms they are allowed to "keep and bear" under that Amendment).

One aspect of *Universal City Studios* v. *Corley* that made *O'Brien* relatively easy to apply is that the expressive and non-expressive dimensions of sharing computer code were easy to separate – at least, conceptually: Software is expressive, said the Court, when it is in the form of source code that can be read and understood by human readers. It is non-expressive when it is translated from source code into object code, and executed on a machine to produce some kind of non-speech action – like decrypting a file. As a consequence, the software in question here is expressive not because it produces First Amendment speech, but because the source code *is* speech itself. It consists of words. This dividing line between a computer software's expressive and non-expressive dimensions makes it easier for a court to apply *O'Brien*: to determine if a government regulation is aimed at the expressive or non-expressive element of

---

42 *Ibid.* at 454: "The Government's interest in preventing unauthorized access to encrypted copyrighted material is unquestionably substantial, and the regulation of DeCSS by the posting prohibition plainly serves that interest."

43 "Although the prohibition on posting prevents the Appellants from conveying to others the speech component of DeCSS, the Appellants have not suggested, much less shown, any technique for barring them from making this instantaneous worldwide distribution of a decryption code that makes a lesser restriction on the code's speech component" (*ibid.*).

44 Others have noted this analogy between 3D printing and the "demiurge" creator in Plato's *Timaeus*, who creates all of the material existences in the universe on the pattern of universal forms. See, e.g., M. Ferraris, *From Fountain to Moleskine: The Work of Art in the Age of Its Technological Producibility* (Brill, 2019) ("3D printing is the completion of a story that began in Plato's *Timaeus*, in which the demiurge builds the world with ideas").

software, a court can try to determine if a government's law is aimed at preventing human individuals from understanding the software, or trying to prevent computers from running it to produce non-speech conduct such as decrypting a file, or controlling a car or appliance.

Courts generally face a harder question when the dispute is over whether the computer's *output* is itself expressive. Unlocking a file, or computer-controlled door to a secure facility, might clearly count as non-expressive conduct. So might producing a utilitarian object, such as a gun, a knife, or a light switch.

But other things computer software does are harder to classify.

For this discussion on law and algorithms, consider interactive VR environments. Computer-generated VR environments have been in development since the 1960s. But only in the past decade have they become widely available to consumers, thanks to VR video game systems such as Google's Oculus Rift and HTC Vive.[45] Essentially, a VR environment is a simulation of a physical environment, typically created by projecting light and emitting audio into either a head-mounted display, or the walls of a special-type of room.[46] Sometimes, gloves, body suits, or other equipment also simulate the tactile sensations someone would feel if they pressed against a wall or held a weapon.[47] Such computer-generated VR technology raises a potential challenge for First Amendment law: it takes physical landscapes or objects of a kind that generally do *not* count as First Amendment expression in the physical world – streets, buildings or mountains, cars, planes, or helicopters, knives, or machine guns – and it digitally recreates them in such a way that they can be incorporated into action that *does* seem more expressive: an interactive 3D video game, or immersive theater set in a virtual world, an educational diorama, or a class designed to help people learn driving, shooting, or rock climbing.

Similar questions might arise about computer algorithms that – in combination with other technologies (like GPS) – capture an ongoing stream of location-tracking information and then incorporate that information into records of everywhere a person has been over the past week. Are all aspects of such a process that First Amendment speech? Producing the reported information likely is. As Justice Kennedy wrote in *IMS Health* v. *Sorrell*, "[f]acts are the beginning point for much of the speech that is most essential to advance human knowledge and to conduct human affairs," so there is no reason not to protect raw factual data.[48] As the Second Circuit said in *Universal City Studios* v. *Corley*: "Even dry information, devoid of advocacy, political relevance, or artistic expression, has been accorded First Amendment protection."[49]

But does this mean that the capture and processing of this location data is also speech? That is less clear. Not all activity necessary in producing speech is itself expressive. Building a concert hall is not necessarily expression – even if the musical performances that occur there will be. Cloning animals – or human beings for that matter – is almost certainly *not* expression, even though doing so allows for scientific study that can provide the basis for an

[45] J. Dujmovic, Here's Why You Will Be Hearing More about Virtual Reality, *Marketwatch* (July 15, 2019), www.marketwatch.com/story/heres-why-you-will-be-hearing-more-about-virtual-reality-2019-07-15.

[46] See Virtual Reality, *Wikipedia*, https://en.wikipedia.org/wiki/Virtual_reality; H. Rheingold, *Virtual Reality: The Revolutionary Technology of Computer-Generated Artificial Worlds – and How It Promises to Transform Society* (Simon & Schuster, 1992), p. 355.

[47] See B. Lewis, Virtual Reality, Haptics, and First Amendment Protection for Sexual Sensation, in W. Barfield and M. J. Blitz, (eds.), *Research Handbook on Law of Augmented and Virtual Reality* (Edward Elgar, 2018), pp. 275–303.

[48] *Sorrell* v. *IMS Health Inc.*, 564 US 552, 570 (2011).

[49] *Universal City Studios* v. *Corley*, above note 30, at 446. See also J. Bambauer, Is Data Speech? (2014) 66 *Stan. Law Rev.* 57, 61 (arguing that reporting of factual data is speech).

article or other scientific report.[50] According to Ashutosh Bhagwat, complex questions arise about when and to what extent First Amendment protection which extends to speech also extends to the *non-speech* acts that allow for the *production* of such speech.[51] Questions of this sort will arise when AI or other computer algorithms engage in activity that is typically considered non-expressive, and use it as a basis for later expressive activity.

And there is another similar challenge that courts have already confronted: what kind of First Amendment protections, if any, apply when AI entities or computer algorithms play the role of a professional or other expert advisor? On the surface, this might seem entirely different from the challenge that arises when computers generate activity that appears to blend expressive and non-expressive elements. But it is actually quite similar. Professional advice often comes entirely in the form of words and, in that sense, appears purely expressive. But although those words – from a doctor, lawyer, or financial advisor – convey the speaker's ideas, these are ideas that have a very different status in the lives of their listeners than words that occur in the public discourse or casual conversations with friends or acquaintances. They are ideas that individuals can rely upon. They expect the advice of their doctor, for example, to draw on expertise shared by those in the medical profession, and be given in accordance with standards that define the practice of medicine. The First Amendment likely protects doctors' right to speak freely so long as they are consistent with these professional standards. It protects a doctor, for example, when he says that he believes medical marijuana has certain kinds of health benefits – even if that kind of medical opinion is one the government would like to silence.[52] What it does not protect are doctors' decisions to betray their patients' reliance by giving advice that is at odds with good medical practice. That might be medical malpractice and the First Amendment doesn't make it otherwise.

Professional advice then – like hybrid speech-non-speech conduct – straddles the line that divides the realm of ideas, where government must stand aside and let speakers and listeners engage in the conversations they wish to have, from a realm where government is charged with protecting health, safety, and property. Here, it does so not by protecting individuals from the physical consequences of draft card burning, traffic obstruction, or computer decryption, but from the damaging effects of incompetent medical or other professional advice. Our health after all can be damaged not just by eating unhealthy or tainted food, or by using unsafe drugs – it can be damaged by a misdiagnosis or by incompetence about what medical treatment we need for a particular disease. It can be damaged, in words, by professional speech which we rely upon to safeguard our health. Government therefore has reason to monitor and regulate not only the process by which companies produce food and drugs, but also the process by which medical professionals offer us verbal guidance.

AI or other computer programs will thus straddle a similar First Amendment line when they replace humans as professional advice-givers. Imagine, for example, an AI psychotherapist. This is something already imagined in one of Philip K. Dick's novels: *The Three Stigmata of Palmer Eldritch*. There, individuals switch on suitcase-bound machines that allow them to connect and converse with the AI psychologist "Dr. Smile," generated by a larger

---

[50]   See B. P. McDonald, Government Regulation or Other "Abridgements" of Scientific Research: The Proper Scope of Judicial Review under the First Amendment (2005) 54 *Emory Law J.* 979, 1037 (noting that bans on cloning "mainly seek to prevent certain acts that could or do result from the proscribed scientific procedures (the implanting of a cloned human embryo or the use of embryos to harvest specialized cells for medical research), rather than the suppression of ideas or information associated with such research").

[51]   A. Bhagwat, Producing Speech (2015) 56 *Wm. & Mary Law Rev.* 1029.

[52]   See *Conant* v. *Walters*, 309 F.3d 629 (9th Cir. 2002).

computer.[53] Technology companies are now working on creating a real version of this kind of AI. As one article reports: "Several startups have combined AI and virtual reality to create a virtual therapist that can interact with is patients in real-time."[54] One company "uses machine learning capabilities to identify patients with a mental health condition and provide a customised treatment plan based on their medical history and behavioural pattern."[55] Researchers at the University of Southern California have developed a virtual therapist named "Ellie," whose "actions, motions, and speech mimic that of a real therapist, but not to the point that she seems completely real."[56] According to one essay on Ellie, "[p]atients admit that they feel less judged by the virtual therapist and more open to her, especially if they were told that she was operated automatically rather than by a remote person."[57] There are similar innovations being tried in law and medicine.[58]

The starting point for First Amendment analysis of such AI experts will probably be the same as that which exists for human experts on similar subjects. They'll be protected from government intervention so long as they stay within the boundaries of professional expertise that their users rely on them to deliver. They'll be subject to government regulation that protects individuals from being harmed by misplaced reliance on incorrect or incompetent advice.[59] As in the realm of professional speech by humans, questions may well arise about whether an AI speaker is holding itself out as a professional expert – and whether humans are entitled to rely upon it. After all, if an AI speaker is *not inviting* reliance on its professional wisdom – and perhaps even actively warning a user against any such reliance – then one might argue the First Amendment should not allow government to punish such an AI speaker for falling short of a professional standard it never pretended it could meet. In a case often discussed in First Amendment scholarship, a court refused to let plaintiffs recover from the publisher of a "mushroom encyclopedia" after they had wrongly relied on the encyclopedia's statements that certain mushrooms were non-poisonous.[60] Even though the encyclopedia's authors claimed expertise about mushrooms, they were *not* – said the court – acting like doctors, lawyers, or other fiduciaries act toward patients and clients.[61] They were instead presenting information in the form of a widely circulated book, which individuals had to view with the same skepticism as any other book or website that, in a free society, might be as likely to contain false information as true information. Arguably, some AI programs for presenting medical, legal, or other professional advice will merit the same kind of skepticism – rather than the reliance and trust that is justified in a professional relationship.[62]

Much will depend, then, on the specific social practices that arise in how individuals relate to such AI experts – and how they are expected to, and do, respond to the AI's advice. In one

---

[53] P. K. Dick, *The Three Stigmata of Palmer Eldritch* (Houghton Mifflen, 2011), pp. 1–6, 98–100.
[54] A. Asokan, Can AI Be an Effective Therapist?, *Analytics India Magazine* (March 1, 2019), www.analyticsindiamag.com/can-ai-be-an-effective-therapist/.
[55] *Ibid.*
[56] A. Tieu, We Now Have an AI Therapist, and She's Doing Her Job Better than Humans Can, *Futurism* (July 16, 2015).
[57] *Ibid.*
[58] See C. Metz, A.I. Shows Promise Assisting Physicians, *New York Times* (February 11, 2019), www.nytimes.com/2019/02/11/health/artificial-intelligence-medical-diagnosis.html; S. Liao, "World's First Robot Lawyer" Now Available in All 50 States, *The Verge* (July 12, 2017), www.theverge.com/2017/7/12/15960080/chatbot-ai-legal-donotpay-us-uk.
[59] See M. J. Blitz, Free Speech, Occupational Speech and Psychotherapy (2016) 44 *Hofstra Law Rev.* 681.
[60] *Winter* v. *G.P. Putnam's Sons*, 938 F.2d 1033, 1037–8 (9th Cir. 1991).
[61] *Commodity Futures Trading Comm'n* v. *Vartuli*, 228 F.3d 94 (2nd Cir. 2000).
[62] *Ibid.* at 111.

case, *Commodity Futures Trading Commission* v. *Vartuli*, the Second Circuit Court of Appeals found that trading instructions issued by a computer were not speech even though they took the form of language.[63] As the Court described the system, "[u]sers were told" that for the system to work, they must "follow the signals with no second-guessing." When the system displayed "a 'sell' signal, the customer was supposed to sell; when it flashed 'buy' the customer was supposed to buy." These instructions did not function as speech, said the Court, because the instructions were to "be used in an entirely mechanical way, as though it were an audible command to a machine to start or to stop."[64] In other cases, individuals will be expected to consider what the AI expert says instead of act immediately on an instruction. In those cases, AI advice will be speech – but may receive less protection than the speech of a Cyber-Plato or art produced by an AI painter or composer.

The key point in this section has been that one of the ways in which AI and other computer algorithms produce hard First Amendment cases is not specific to the realm of algorithms – but is rather just a new, technologically sophisticated version of an old problem – which is that certain kinds of speaking or artistic expression straddle or blur an important First Amendment boundary line. Modern First Amendment law (and constitutional law more generally) is premised in part on a distinction which, as the Supreme Court described it in 2003, divides the realm of human activity into spheres where the state is normally permitted and expected to regulate vigorously – and spheres of our lives that are reserved for individual autonomy and where "the State should not be a dominant presence."[65] More specifically, government is given power, under the US Constitution, to enact laws that protect individuals' safety and security – from physical attacks, threats to their property, commercial fraud, negligent or reckless driving, and a host of other dangers. But this power does not generally extend, the Court said, into the sphere of "thought, belief, expression, and certain intimate conduct." Under the First Amendment's free speech clause, government may *not*, for example, officially declare certain ideas unfit for us to discuss or think about in the same way it can declare certain foods or drugs unfit to sell, otherwise distribute, or consume. Like other kinds of activity, that of a computer program might stray at least partially outside of First Amendment territory when it goes *beyond* presenting us with ideas to consider – in an AI-produced Platonic dialogue or other essay – and instead instructs 3D printers to print items with practical purposes or gives medical advice that is central to action.

This dichotomy between a realm of individual autonomy and a realm where state regulation is appropriate is far from straightforward to apply. Many instances of speech that are unquestionably protected by the First Amendment, after all, have implications for individuals' interests in health and safety, or commercial well-being. Consider a book or magazine article that argues that vaccines cause autism – and persuades thousands to forego vaccination. Such "anti-vaxx" arguments have impacts on public health interests the government is charged with protecting.[66] But that doesn't mean government may censor these arguments, which are unquestionably First Amendment speech when they arise in public debate. Consequently, we can't define activity as non-speech conduct just because it has an impact

---

[63] *Ibid.*

[64] *Ibid.*

[65] *Lawrence* v. *Texas*, 539 US 558, 573–4 (2003).

[66] See M. J. Blitz, Lies, Line Drawing, and (Deep) Fake News (2018) 71 *Okla. Law Rev.* 59, 74: "... it is not only unprotected speech that can have powerful effects on security and property. Speech protected by current First Amendment doctrine often concerns those interests as well."

on the realm of personal security, health, and commercial interests that government is responsible for regulating.[67]

Perhaps for that reason, courts have generally looked to other tests for marking the line between expressive and non-expressive conduct. For some, the answer is provided by social convention: certain kinds of non-verbal activity are now recognized as artistic expression – instrumental music, painting, and sculpture, for example, are all recognized ways in which artists express themselves.[68] So, in the modern age, are photography, film, and video. We might likewise ask if certain AI activities or computer programs are "inherently expressive" – perhaps by asking if they are analogous to familiar forms of expression. This is how the Supreme Court concluded in 2001 that video games are expression: they have many of the same characteristics that make movies count as First Amendment speech: "Like the protected books, plays, and movies that preceded them, video games communicate ideas – and even social messages – through many familiar literary devices (such as characters, dialogue, plot, and music) and through features distinctive to the medium (such as the player's interaction with the virtual world)."[69] Courts might ask the same questions about certain uses of VR, or about different outputs of 3D printers.

Another test courts might use to determine if computer activity is expressive is the "Spence test." Even when an activity is not a recognized form of artistic or other expression, it might be transformed into expression when individuals use it to convey a message to an audience – and do so in a context that message is likely to be successfully communicated. Setting a baseball cap on fire, for example, is not something individuals typically do to express themselves: if we see a baseball cap burning in an alleyway, we are unlikely to wonder what message it is meant to convey. But if someone sets fire to a baseball cap that has a pro-Republican or pro-Democratic slogan emblazoned on it, we might well understand it as a protest. So we might take the position that AI entities are likewise engaged in speech when they are conveying a message. Stuart Minor Benjamin defends this claim: the "touchstone" for whether algorithms are engaging in speech, he argues, is whether the algorithm is "sending a substantive message, and such a message can be sent with or without relying on algorithms."[70]

However, even when one relies on social convention, the Spence test, or some other test of First Amendment coverage when thinking about AI's constitutional status, it is helpful not to lose sight of *why* the First Amendment divides human activity up into such a dichotomy. It is helpful, in other words, that at least one major reason for dividing up human activity into "speech" and "non-speech" is to reserve a certain realm of life for individual autonomy, while still leaving government with the room it needs to protect personal security, health, and other interests. In fact, past scholarship on the First Amendment status of computer activity has already made arguments like this. In considering whether computer-generated virtual worlds constitute First Amendment speech, for example, Jack Balkin has argued that the answer will depend on whether the virtual world activity consists of a dramatic performance or game play, on the one hand, or

---

[67] As the Ninth Circuit noted in *Bernstein*, expression doesn't cease to be expression merely because it has "one drop of "direct functionality." The fact that speech might have practical impacts doesn't deprive it of its expressive dimensions. See *Bernstein*, 176 F.3d at 1142 (9th Cir. 1999).

[68] See *Hurley v. Irish-Am. Gay, Lesbian, Bisexual Group of Boston*, 515 US 557, 568 (1995) (The Court notes that if the First Amendment only protected verbal or not-verbal acts that had messages it "would never reach the unquestionably shielded painting of Jackson Pollock, music of Arnold Schöenberg, or Jabberwocky verse of Lewis Carroll"). This suggests that these forms of art are inherently expressive even without any messages. M. V. Tushnet, A. K. Chen, and J. Blocher, *Free Speech Beyond Words: The Surprising Reach of the First Amendment*, Kindle edn. (New York University Press, 2017).

[69] *Brown v. Entm't Merchants Ass'n*, 564 US 786, 790, 131 S.Ct. 2729, 2733, 180 L. Ed. 2d 708 (2011).

[70] S. M. Benjamin, Algorithms and Speech (2013) 161 *Univ. Pa. Law Rev.* 1445, 1471.

commercial activity, on the other. Use of virtual worlds to give form to imagination is not the state's business.[71] It is the kind of activity which – like the aesthetic choices about the fiction we write or read, or the art we paint or view – should be up to individuals free of state management. By contrast, what rules we follow when we buy and sell goods is fair game for government regulation. Kyle Langvardt draws upon similar intuitions when setting out an argument against simply classifying 3D printing programs as "speech" when they, for example, generate CAD files that can then be used to manufacture weapons.[72] Treating such computer programs as "expressive" threatens to take an activity that has long been carefully regulated by government – because of its potential threats to security – and misclassify it as an activity that is only a matter of an individual's construction of their own intellectual and emotional world, rather than a matter of protecting public welfare. In Langvardt's terms, it mistakenly places in the realm of the "library" of ideas an activity that is paradigmatically part of the "mall" that houses commerce – namely, the production of goods in the commercial market.[73]

IN THE BORDERLAND BETWEEN AUTHORSHIP AND MANIPULATION

In the discussion above, I have argued that AI authorship – or other kinds of creation by computer algorithms – may raise difficult First Amendment questions when the things that the AI or algorithm is "authoring" – or perhaps "co-authoring" with human speakers – aren't essays, books, or other recognized forms of expression, but rather certain kinds of material or virtual objects, environments, or simulations of non-speech actions we take in the physical world. In other cases, an AI doctor, lawyer, or therapist will likely be producing speech that takes the form of words (and not objects) – but those words are words we rely upon to secure some aspects of our physical health or security, or financial well-being. One might argue that such speech is thus not simply part of the marketplace of ideas, where we are expected to critically assess and perhaps reject others' claims. Rather, such advice is part of the marketplace of goods and services where we expect government to filter out dangerous professional advice, just as it filters out dangerous foods, drugs, and other unsafe products.

There is also a second way in which AI authorship might sometimes stray outside of the familiar First Amendment territory. Even when it *is* authoring essays, newspaper reports, or other paradigmatic works of expression, it may sometimes do so in ways that *fall outside* of the form of authorship that is *familiar* to First Amendment law, and it may operate in ways that are inconsistent with crucial First Amendment values (like respect for listeners' autonomy). Consider again the OpenAI software that can simulate numerous styles of human writing. Such AI authorship has great benefits. But the article I cited on this subject also noted that the organization creating this software "is concerned that something these well-intentioned researchers built could easily be misused, fearing that it would be dangerous in the wrong hands ... a tool for the mass production of disinformation."[74] The software might, for example, produce articles in the writing style of a well-known *Washington Post* journalist, and then allow users to pass it off as a convincingly fake *Washington Post* report. Or it might help cybercriminals write emails in the style of one's employer or relative. Unlike the

[71] J. Balkin, Virtual Liberty: The Freedom to Design and Freedom to Play in Virtual Worlds (2004) 90 *Va. Law Rev.* 2043, 2043–50.
[72] K. Langvardt, Remarks on 3D Printing, Free Speech, and Lochner (2016) 17 *Minn. J. Law Sci. Technol.* 779, 783–4. For a contrary view, arguing that CAD files used in 3D printing are First Amendment speech, see J. Blackman, The 1st Amendment, 2nd Amendment, and 3D Printed Guns (2014) 81 *Tenn. Law Rev.* 479.
[73] Langvardt, *ibid.*, pp. 780–5.
[74] Pringle, above note 15.

Cyber-Plato program described above – which doesn't pretend its dialogues are actually from Plato – such AI software writes letters, essays, or emails in the style of a historical or present-day public figure and then allows others to misattribute the possibly damaging or offensive content to that figure. The First Amendment, as the Supreme Court found in 2012, *does* protect certain kinds of false factual statements. But it is not clear to what extent that protection covers not only false factual claims about the world, but falsification of an author's identity (like that which might occur, for example, when a speaker falsely presents herself as a government official). To the extent that AI speech-creation allows for more fool-proof impersonation of others, it might be without – or with less – First Amendment protection than when it creates an essay. And computer programs are already making progress in this kind of deception. As Woodrow Hartzog notes, "[a]utomated software 'bots' on social media like Twitter" are already "increasingly adept at tricking people into thinking they are operated by humans."[75] And not only are computers becoming more adept at such deception – they are bound by far fewer constraints than are human speakers when they engage in them. Unburdened by individuals' need for sleep or nourishment, or the necessities of time management,[76] they might create new communications non-stop (robo-calls and texts already do).[77] Depending on how they are designed, AI entities might also be free from the shame or guilt most human beings will feel upon violating (or revealed to have violated) social norms or ethical principles.[78]

An AI author may likewise raise First Amendment questions when it masquerades not as a human author, but as some other kind of automated process on which individuals have come to rely. Consider a scenario, for example, where AI technology is used to create deepfake video footage that masquerades as live feed from a security camera, but shows events that aren't really occurring. In that case, the AI is authoring a video that shows fictional rather than factual events. Videos that depict fiction are often protected by free speech law. But that is in situations where the viewer knows that the video comes from a particular creator – and can raise questions about the accuracy of the tale this creator tells or whether editing software that has been used to make the video depict events that are unreal. In the scenario I just imagined, however, the AI's role in authoring the video is invisible. It is creating a real-looking security video footage that seems to come not from a human or other author, but (via a camera recording) from the world itself.

At first glance, this type of question may seem utterly unfamiliar to First Amendment law. But courts and First Amendment scholars have already struggled with questions where certain entities exercise a kind of authorship over elements of a listener's or reader's environment that they (at least arguably) *don't* have a First Amendment right to control. This is how Frank Pasquale describes what occurs when search engines, like Google, manipulate their search results to produce outcomes that favor the search engine's own interests or preferences. In such a situation, he writes, search engine companies are actually "help[ing] *create* the world they claim to merely 'show' us."[79] The function of a search engine, Pasquale argues in another piece co-authored with

[75] W. Hartzog, Unfair and Deceptive Robots (2015) 74 *Md. Law Rev.* 785, 791.
[76] J. Schroeder, Marketplace Theory in the Age of AI Communicators (2018) 17 *First Amend. Law Rev.* 22, 23 (noting that "AI communicators ... do not sleep, have families, vote, or become emotional").
[77] *Ibid.*, p. 23.
[78] *Ibid.* (stating that "AI Communicators ... do not have any concern for their mortality or for a system of ethics"); Massaro *et al.*, above note 4, p. 2517 ("even strong AI will likely still lack human emotions, sensitivity to social nuance, or the ability to feel shame").
[79] F. Pasquale, *The Black Box Society: The Secret Algorithms that Control Money and Information*, Kindle edn. (Harvard University Press, 2015), p. 61 (emphasis added).

Oren Bracha, is not to create its own content in this way.[80] It is not to produce a ranking that readers may find "agreeable or disagreeable, or find convincing or unconvincing,"[81] like a magazine's list of the 100 greatest rock songs of all time, the 100 best restaurants in the United States, or the seventy greatest philosophers. It is rather to produce results that the reader understands to be organized according to some neutral criterion for identifying sites most relevant given the Web searcher's query. Google therefore betrays users' expectations, and its own responsibilities, if it manipulates its search results to lower the profile of – and essentially hide – the webpage of a competitor. According to Jennifer Chandler, such manipulation of a search engine's algorithms undermines what she proposes should be understood as an important component of First Amendment rights – a right "to be free of the imposition of discriminatory filters that the listener would not otherwise have used."[82]

This view of search engines is at odds with the way in which at least one court has addressed the issue. In *Search King* v. *Google*, the District Court for the Western District of Oklahoma had to decide a dispute in which a competitor of Google – Search King – alleged that Google had intentionally lowered its "page rank" – that is, the score that determines where it appears in Google's search results.[83] A webpage's place in the search will generally have tremendous importance for whether readers find it: a company whose website is buried deep in the search results (after hundreds of other results) is likely to be ignored by all but the most persistent Web users. Search King claimed that Google had intentionally lowered its ranking to harm its competing service.[84] Search King also said Google had no First Amendment right to do so.[85] The Court disagreed: Google's page rank, it said, was the equivalent of an "opinion," and it had no obligation to express any opinion other than the one it wanted to express.[86] On the contrary, it had a First Amendment right to express the opinion of its choice – even if it generated this opinion through the use of algorithms rather than by just making a mental judgment.

Some scholars have likewise supported the view that search engines were more like editors, with First Amendment freedom to present search results in the way they see fit. As Eric Goldman writes: "Search engines are media companies. Like other media companies, search engines make editorial choices designed to satisfy their audience."[87] Eugene Volokh and Donald Falk likewise argue that "each search engine's editorial judgment is much like many other familiar editorial judgment" – including those of newspaper editorial boards or the creators of a guidebook.[88] And Stuart Minor Benjamin similarly argues that "when people create algorithms in order to selectively present information based on its perceived importance or value or relevance," free

[80] O. Bracha and F. Pasquale, Federal Search Commission? Access, Fairness, and Accountability in the Law of Search (2008) 93 *Cornell Law Rev.* 1149, 1198.
[81] *Ibid.*
[82] J. A. Chandler, A Right to Reach an Audience: An Approach to Intermediary Bias on the Internet (2007) 35 *Hofstra Law Rev.* 1095, 1103.
[83] *Search King, Inc.* v. *Google Tech., Inc.*, No. CIV-02-1457-M, 2003 WL 21464568, at *4 (WD Okla. May 27, 2003)
[84] *Ibid.* at *2: Search King alleges Google purposefully and maliciously decreased the PageRanks previously assigned to Search King, PRAN, and certain unidentified, affiliated websites on Google's Internet search engine in August or September of 2002. Search King asserts the devaluation occurred after and because Google learned that PRAN was competing with Google and that it was profiting by selling advertising space on websites ranked highly by Google's PageRank system."
[85] *Ibid.* at *3.
[86] *Ibid.* at *4: "PageRanks are opinions-opinions of the significance of particular web sites as they correspond to a search query."
[87] E. Goldman, Search Engine Bias and the Demise of Search Engine Utopianism (2006) 8 *Yale J. Law Technol.* 188.
[88] E. Volokh and D. M. Falk, Google: First Amendment Protection for Search Engine Search Results (2012) 8 *J. Law Econ. Policy* 883, 884.

speech doctrine "indicates that they are speakers for purposes of the First Amendment."[89] In contrast to a phone or text conversation, which would not be any different whether it took place over lines operated by AT&T, Sprint, Verizon, T-Mobile, or another cell-phone service, the same search query will almost always produce different results (and a different order of results) on Google's search engine than on that of Bing, Yahoo, or DuckDuckGo.

James Grimmelmann proposes a third way to conceptualize search engines – one which has different implications for their First Amendment status. Rather than being "conduits" that simply link Web searchers to the websites they seek, or editors with untrammeled freedom to produce the search lists they want, search engines are like "trusted advisors."[90] Web users cannot possibly gather and collect the Web results they need by themselves – so they turn to a source with specialized capacities for performing this task, a search engine, just as they turn to a doctor or lawyer or other professional when they need other kinds of expert help. On this model, search engine companies have some First Amendment freedom. Moreover, they can disagree with one another in how they produce rankings – just as one competent doctor can form different medical judgments, and provide different advice, than that provided by other competent doctors. But even when doctors disagree with one another, one respect in which they cannot differ is that their medical decision-making has to be guided by their responsibility to further the patient's health (and not, for example, to recommend medical procedures for their own profit). Grimmelmann portrays search engine companies in the same way: They can differ in their judgments about what search results are most relevant to a user, but they cannot pretend to serve that mission while ordering search results according to a different principle (such as favoring their own business).

One might think – given these arguments – that if search engines do have responsibilities to generate results in a certain way, this is for a reason already considered in the previous section. I suggested before that AI medical advisors may be subject to government regulation because their speech is not simply about exchanging ideas, but about assuring health, and this puts this speech at least partly in the marketplace of goods and services – in this case – of a service assuring one's health and safety – and not simply the marketplace of ideas. One might argue that the same is true of search engines: Google does not merely operate a search engine. It is a company that competes with other companies. When it uses its extraordinary power in the search engine market to undermine competitors, it might violate antitrust law[91] – and its decision implicates not only our access to ideas, but our ability to find and use providers of goods and services, like Search King, or other companies that have claimed to be the victim of anticompetitive behavior by Google. In fact, one might argue, when Google decides about how to rank its competitors, the results aren't simply speech – they are *commercial* speech. Commercial speech is a kind of speech the First Amendment leaves far more amenable to government regulation in part, the Supreme Court has said, because it is "linked inextricably" with "the commercial arrangement[s]" to which it is related.[92] One can't shut government out of regulating advertising and other commercial speech, in other words, without the unacceptable consequence of disabling it from protecting consumers from coercive or otherwise worrisome commercial practices. This realm of permissible government regulation should, one might argue, include speech that is inextricably linked to how dominant search engine companies present their competition.

But there is also a slightly different explanation for why search engine results might raise First Amendment concerns. Apart from affecting our interest in a well-functioning market of

---

[89]   Benjamin, above note 70, p. 1471.
[90]   J. Grimmelmann, Speech Engines (2014) 98 *Minn. Law Rev.* 868, 874.
[91]   Pasquale, above note 79.
[92]   *Edenfield* v. *Fane*, 507 US 761, 767 (1993) (quoting *Friedman* v. *Rogers*, 440 US 1, 10 n. 9 (1979)).

goods and services (with healthy competition between companies), biased search engines *affect a core First Amendment interest.* The harm they do is akin to that which occurs when messengers (whether human or mechanical) undermine speakers' freedom of speech by substituting their own messages for the ones they are trusted to deliver. Such dishonest messengers silence the speakers they are supposed to be representing, and also deceive their listeners (and deprive them of the content that remains undelivered). Search engines do similar harm when they present themselves as intermediaries or "trusted advisors," but are really seeking to push their own content rather than that which best fits the listeners' query.

How does this relate to AI participation in dissemination of speech? Increasingly, individuals are turning for information not to search engines who receive queries that one enters on a screen, but rather to "voice assistants" who detect and return answers to spoken questions. Some of the same arguments scholars have offered about the First Amendment status of search engines might conceivably be applied to "voice assistants" such as Apple's Siri or Amazon's Alexa. One might argue that they should be perceived as speakers or editors whose answers should be insulated by the First Amendment against any kind of restriction: if a listener doesn't like or is skeptical of how Siri or Alexa answers a question, she can always turn to some other AI or human speaker for guidance. Or one might argue that the algorithms that control them should be neutral and objective and designed to provide a user with information that fits her query, and not information that steers her toward ideas preferred by the voice assistant (or its human designers or operators).

There are certain complications that arise – whether one is thinking about AI assistants or simpler algorithms. Consider the claim that government should have greater authority to regulate search engines or other information intermediaries – not because their misdirection would cause physical or financial harm, or otherwise affect a non-First Amendment interest – but rather because such misdirection distorts the marketplace of ideas, and undermines individuals' ability to autonomously navigate that marketplace. On this view, search engines do a kind of First Amendment damage even when the searches they distort have little to do with satisfying practical needs. Imagine, for example, that I do searches for "introductions" to "conservativism" or "conservative thought" and the search engine's algorithms – rather than returning introductory information on philosophers, books, or schools of thought that might fit the label "conservative" – are instead designed to highlight Web pages that *criticize* conservativism and highlight its flaws. Or that a search engine with different political biases does the same for a search of "progressivism" or "progressive thought." Or that individuals ask an AI in a voice assistant to inform them of either topic, and instead of giving them a general overview, the AI gives them an overview calculated to make either conservative or progressive politics seem flawed and dangerous. Should government be able to regulate such politically slanted AI outputs?

Of course, if search engine algorithms and AI are speakers or editors, then the answer is "no." Just as Fox News and MSNBC are shielded – by the First Amendment – against government regulation when they put a politically conservative or politically liberal slant on their news coverage, so would search engines or algorithms that provide a conservative, liberal, or other slant on the results they produce, or the answers they give.[93] But matters

---

93 *Miami Herald Pub. Co. v. Tornillo*, 418 US 241, 256 (1974): "... any [] compulsion to publish that which 'reason' tells them should not be published' is unconstitutional. A responsible press is an undoubtedly desirable goal, but press responsibility is not mandated by the Constitution and like many other virtues it cannot be legislated." The Court did uphold "the fairness doctrine," a Federal Communications Commission doctrine which required broadcast networks to offer a right to reply to those who criticized them (*Red Lion Broad. Co. v. F.C.C.*, 395 US 367 (1969)). But it is not clear that such a doctrine could be applied to cable stations – especially after the Court's decision in *Tornillo*.

are different if search engine algorithms or AI speakers have a responsibility to make judgments according to some neutral criterion of expertise. This could be because such neutrality is what users of these computer intermediaries expect – and any political slant therefore won't be identified as such. In other words, the problem here is a lack of transparency. Or it could be because users may sometimes have little alternative but to rely on, rather than question, a certain search engine or voice assistant – if, for example, it has something like a monopoly on a certain service. As Bracha and Pasquale write, consumers aren't likely to be able to "avoid the search engine's power. The relevant market, while not completely monopolistic, is dominated by a very small number of players."[94] In either case, it may be true that First Amendment values in this case would weigh in favor of allowing the government to regulate search engines' activity here – not in order to protect health, security, or property, but rather to assure individuals are able to use the tools necessary to exercise their First Amendment freedom of speech.

However, even if search engines or AI voice assistants do have some responsibilities they betray when they show bias, there is also danger in allowing government to act against such biases. This is true for the same reason that judges and scholars have resisted the idea that government should have power to punish even verifiable falsehoods on "matters of public concern." As Justice Alito wrote, even though those with knowledge of social science or philosophy might identify certain matters that are true or false in these areas – still "it is perilous to permit *the state* to be the arbiter of truth."[95] This is because permitting such regulation "opens the door for the state to use its power for political ends." One might likewise worry that, as much as the marketplace of ideas is hurt by letting computer algorithm makers incorporate political biases, it would be even worse to give government power over what kind of search engine results are sufficiently free of such political bias. There would be a risk, for example, that particular government regulators would only seek to counter those political biases they oppose – leaving other AI or search engine voices unregulated. In other words, allowing government regulation of AI intermediaries may raise some of the same risks that arise when government regulates AI speakers – namely, that it will take especially vigorous action only against the views or other ideas it opposes.

Still, it is conceivable that at least some kind of regulation of search engines and AI assistants might avoid these problems. Bracha and Pasquale argue that certain laws that bar manipulation of search engines might be "content neutral."[96] Grimmelmann endorses the Federal Trade Commission's approach to a dispute between Google and another company, wherein the FTC asked whether "Google adjust[ed] its algorithms for the purpose of sending users to less relevant sites?"[97] And it seems to at least make sense for courts to take note of the possibility that, apart from being speakers with their own point of view, or listeners able to shop among, and critically scrutinize, the offerings of different speakers, some AI and algorithmic participants in the marketplace of ideas may be intermediaries – and have responsibilities that come with that role.

An even more vexing challenge for First Amendment law arises when AI or other algorithms can shape not simply computer search results, but also computer outputs that we rely upon even more heavily to accurately represent our external reality. This occurs, for example, when computers show us a *Washington Post* article – that isn't a real *Washington Post* article.

94 Bracha and Pasquale, above note 80, p. 1191.
95 *United States* v. *Alvarez*, 567 US 709, 752 (2012) (Alito J. dissenting) (emphasis added).
96 Bracha and Pasquale, above note 80, p. 1191.
97 Grimmelmann, above note 90.

Or when AI is used to manufacture a deepfake video which depicts events that never occurred. This distorts reality in a more unsettling way than search engine manipulation. Most computer users are probably aware that the search results generated by Google require human decision-making – and are subject to human alteration. While Pasquale is right that search engine companies can mislead us if they *"create* the world they claim to merely 'show' us,"[98] computer users are likely aware that Google can act as a creator or author here if it wants to – and that *somebody* has to write the programs that determine what order search results appear in.

Such human intervention is less expected when we look at a video. For many observers, a video appears as a window onto reality. We might recognize that somebody can determine where to point a video camera, but (unless they are directing a fiction film in a staged environment) that person generally cannot exercise a God-like power over the activity that the camera records. Thus, where AI alters such video records, it is extending authorship into activity where it is (in our familiar experience) out of place. In doing so, it is potentially distorting not merely our access to information (as a search engine arguably does), but also our exercise of a different kind of First Amendment freedom – namely, our freedom of thought.

This is an area where courts may well have to go further beyond existing doctrine than they will in dealing with other challenges in AI speech. First Amendment law on freedom of speech has not adequately attended to the ways in which new technologies of deception can undermine listeners' and thinkers' exercise of freedom of thought. Unlike speech, which can be censored and punished, individuals' silent thought processes have often been considered largely invulnerable to external control: neither government nor any other actor can punish thoughts that remain hidden in the private mental world of the person thinking them.[99]

However, the power of new forms of AI to disrupt our thinking reveals a flaw in this assumption: the cognitive processes we use to understand the world are tightly and intimately linked to our perceptions and interactions with the world we seek to understand. Far from simply relying on an inner virtual world, mental experience constantly draws upon sensory evidence from the surrounding environment.[100] As the example of deepfake video shows, some emerging forms of AI – including AI speech – are able to insert themselves into, and exert control over, this process by which the mind works with the world to construct an internal map of our external environment.

Nor are deepfakes the only example of how this can take place. Where we are surrounded by a VR or AR environment rather than a purely physical environment, computers can and do reshape the environment we move in – and not simply the speech we receive in it. Even when the AI entity is confining itself to activity more like traditional speech – by, for example, taking the form of social bots – it can alter the way in which we understand this process not simply by choosing the speech's content, but by manipulating aspects of the communicative process audiences do not realize are being manipulated.[101] This might

98   Pasquale, above note 79 (emphasis added).
99   See, e.g., F. Schauer, *Free Speech: A Philosophical Enquiry* (1982), p. 93 ("thought is intrinsically free. The internal nature of the thought process erects a barrier between thought and the power of government sanction"); "Freedom to think," said Justice Frank Murphy, "is absolute of its own nature; the most tyrannical government is powerless to control the inward workings of the mind" (*Jones v. Opelika*, 316 US 584, 618 (1942) (Murphy J. dissenting)).
100 See A. Clark, *Supersizing the Mind: Embodiment, Action, and Cognitive Extension*, Kindle edn. (Oxford University Press, 2008). See also A. Clark, *Natural-Born Cyborgs: Minds, Technologies, and the Future of Human Intelligence*, Kindle edn. (Oxford University Press, 2003).
101 Hartzog, above note 75, p. 73.

occur, for example, if an AI software is able to post statements on 5,000 different social media accounts all supporting a particular position, or product, or cultural icon – thus creating the illusion of significant support when the speaker behind it is a single (non-human) entity.[102] Or imagine situations where AI communicates to individuals after gathering and analyzing more information about a target audience than humans are capable of gathering and analyzing without computers.

As novel as these concerns are for First Amendment doctrine, that doctrine is not entirely without resources for addressing them. Just as certain writers have demanded that Google and other search engines be required to be "transparent" to users in how they generate search results, certain lawmakers and scholars are advocating disclosure rules for AI speech that distorts users' perceptions of the environment and sources of speech. Such a rule would compel anyone using a "bot" or another AI speaker to generate speech to inform listeners or readers that the speech is coming from an AI entity. This is a feature of a restriction on bots recently enacted by the California state legislature: it does not ban use of the "bots" it covers (those that promote a product or aim to influence an election). It rather requires that one avoid "mislead[ing another] person about [the bot's] artificial identity," and makes clear that "[a] person using a bot shall not be liable under this section if the person discloses that it is a bot," so long as the disclosure is "clear, conspicuous, and reasonably designed to inform persons with whom the bot communicates or interacts that it is a bot."[103] The advantage of such a method is that it allows readers to continue to benefit from AI technology: readers who wish to read dialogues written by Cyber-Plato can still do so. They just have to be made aware that the dialogues were written by a computer, not by a person. The Deepfakes Accountability Act, recently introduced in the House of Representatives, would similarly require anyone creating a deepfake video to indicate that the video is a fake, using "irremovable digital watermarks, as well as textual descriptions."[104]

Such a compelled identification requirement is arguably in tension with long-standing rules in First Amendment law that prevent government from compelling speakers to make statements they do not wish to make – at least outside of a commercial context. The Supreme Court has struck down laws that require students to salute the flag,[105] or require drivers to display a message on their license plates that they disagree with. However, laws requiring that bots or other AI speakers be identified as such is less akin to laws that compel people to voice ideological messages with which they disagree than to laws that require speakers to reveal their identity. For example, certain states have enacted laws requiring individuals engaged in election-related speech to identify themselves (for instance, as the author of the flier they are distributing opposing a certain candidate or ballot measure). States have enacted such laws to combat fraud and libel.[106] The Supreme Court has held that such laws can violate the First

---

[102] R. DiResta, J. Little, J. Morgan, *et al.*, The Bots that are Changing Politics, *Vice* (November 2, 2017), www .vice.com/en_us/article/mb37k4/twitter-facebook-google-bots-misinformation-changing-politics.

[103] Cal. Bus. & Prof. Code § 17941 (2019). See also N. Cohen, Will California's New Bot Law Strengthen Democracy?, *The New Yorker* (July 2, 2019).

[104] See H.R.3230 – Defending Each and Every Person from False Appearances by Keeping Exploitation Subject to Accountability Act of 2019, www.congress.gov/bill/116th-congress/house-bill/3230; DEEPFAKES Accountability Act Would Impose Unenforceable Rules – But It's a Start, *TechCrunch* (June 13, 2019), https://techcrunch.com /2019/06/13/deepfakes-accountability-act-would-impose-unenforceable-rules-but-its-a-start/; B. Chesney and D. Citron, Deep Fakes: A Looming Challenge for Privacy, Democracy, and National Security, (2019), *Calif. Law Rev.* 1753; see also R. Green, Counterfeit Campaign Speech, (2019), 70 *Hastings Law J.* 1445.

[105] *Barnette*, above note 1; *Wooley v. Maynard*, 430 US 705 (1977).

[106] *McIntyre v. Ohio Elections Comm'n*, 514 US 334, 341-4 (1995).

Amendment: in *McIntyre v. Ohio Elections Commission*, the Court held that the First Amendment not only gives speakers a right to speak, but also a right to be free from compelled disclosure of their identities when they do so.[107] Indeed, laws that forced speakers to sacrifice their anonymity when speaking on political topics were subject – said the Supreme Court – to "exacting scrutiny."[108]

This was in part because, as the Supreme Court said, some individuals and groups "throughout history have been able to criticize oppressive practices and laws either anonymously or not at all."[109] That logic might not apply to bots or other AI speakers: they may not "worry" about the consequences of engaging in unpopular speech if they are not designed to do so. A compelled disclosure requirement which also compelled bot speech to include information about which human programmers designed the bot, or who is operating it, may well raise such a problem – since such human participants in creating or disseminating bot speech may avoid doing so if they feel others (employers, colleagues, friends) will retaliate against that speech – or shun them. Moreover, there is another reason offered by the Court in *McIntyre* for the right to speak anonymously – and that reason *may* apply to bots. "Anonymity," the Court said, "provides a way for a writer who may be personally unpopular to ensure that readers will not prejudge her message simply because they do not like its proponent."[110] This worry might apply to bot speech: listeners and readers may be too quick to dismiss speech that comes from bots, or assume it is an attempt to manipulate them. Of course, in many cases, bot speech *is* such an attempt at manipulation. But it is possible that a compelled disclosure requirement will undercut the value even of bot speech that does not have such a purpose, by leading readers to dismiss it too readily. It may also affect the expression in other ways. In settings, like Twitter, where people often seek (and appreciate) short, clever quips about politics, they will instead find that certain quips always come packaged with a longer disclosure.[111]

None of this means that such disclosure requirements should be rejected – and in recent cases, courts have subjected compelled disclosure requirements in the electoral context only to a lower form of "intermediate scrutiny," allowing them where there is a "'substantial relation' between the disclosure requirement and a 'sufficiently important' governmental interest," or in other words, where government can meet "intermediate scrutiny."[112] It is thus conceivable that government could meet this intermediate scrutiny here: if people are rational in showing skepticism toward bot speech, and in worrying that the bot can mask manipulation more effectively than a person, then government may be able to argue that it is not unreasonable to require that audiences be informed if they are dealing with bots rather than humans. In *McIntyre*, the Court found government could identify fraud after the fact without requiring every speaker (including the many not engaged in fraud) to disclose her identity as she spoke.[113] Here, government might argue that what is important is not that law enforcement officials be able to identify bots as bots after the fact, but that individuals interacting with bots trying to sell products, or advocate for candidates, know – *during* this conversation – that their conversation partner is a bot.

---

[107] *Ibid.*
[108] *Ibid.* at 347–8.
[109] *Ibid.* at 342 (quoting *Talley v. California*, 362 US 60, 64 (1960)).
[110] *Ibid.*
[111] Conceivably, a disclosure could come, in the future, in the form of a widely recognized symbol rather than a sentence or paragraph.
[112] *John Doe No. 1 v. Reed*, 561 US 186, 130 S.Ct. 2811, 2814 (2010).
[113] *McIntyre*, above note 106.

Any of these doctrinal solutions should take place against the background of deeper thinking about when (and how) it makes sense to provide a weaker First Amendment force field for certain kinds of potentially deceptive AI speech. As noted earlier, courts applying the *O'Brien* test, or the Spence test and other tests for First Amendment coverage should do so with an awareness of the need to preserve speakers' (and listeners') autonomy and control over democratic deliberation, while leaving government with the room it needs – and has traditionally had – to protect individuals' health, safety, financial security, and a range of other interests at stake in non-speech conduct. Similarly, courts applying the First Amendment to potentially deceptive uses of AI should not simply make room for certain kinds of selective regulation of such AI technology, or requirements that the AI source of the speech be disclosed to a reader or listener. They should do so with an awareness of when (and why) the First Amendment might allow government to address AI deception in ways different from those in which it addresses deception by human speakers (speaking without the aid of such AI technologies).[114]

The Supreme Court in *United States* v. *Alvarez* emphasized that even verifiably false speech merited strong First Amendment protection. It was only when such false speech caused some kind of well-recognized harm – or perhaps was made to generate a "material gain" for the person engaging in the false speech – that the speech lost First Amendment protection according to the Court plurality.[115] The plurality took this stance in part because it found that laws targeting "false" speech were content-based and therefore presumptively unconstitutional, like all content-based restrictions – and that false speech was *not* among the categories of content that (like obscenity or defamation) were left more vulnerable to government regulation.[116] It also took such a stance because it found that false speech often had *First Amendment value*. And a concurring opinion by Justice Breyer agreed: "False factual statements can serve useful human objectives, for example: in social contexts, where they may prevent embarrassment, protect privacy, shield a person from prejudice, provide the sick with comfort, or preserve a child's innocence; in public contexts, where they may stop a panic or otherwise preserve calm in the face of danger."[117] Others have emphasized that certain social practices essential to modern democracy – such as undercover reporting that exposed corruption – often can occur only because an undercover journalist can pose as someone she is not.[118] The plurality and concurrence were hesitant to leave all such speech vulnerable to government restriction – and allowed such restriction only if government could show the falsity in the speech was accompanied by some kind of "legally cognizable harm," or seeking of material benefit (in the view of the plurality) and only by harm that was not outweighed by the cost to free speech inherent in the government's restriction (in the view of the concurrence). Both the plurality and concurring opinion in *Alvarez* are therefore attempting to reconcile (1) the need to protect even false speech from government censorship and (2) the need to protect individuals from the harms that might be caused by lies when they are defrauded, defamed, or otherwise harmed.[119]

---

[114]   See Massaro *et al.*, above note 4, pp. 2516–19 (describing possible harms arising from AI speech that might justify distinctive First Amendment doctrines).

[115]   See *United States* v. *Alvarez*, 567 US 709, 723 (2012).

[116]   *Ibid.* at 717.

[117]   *Ibid.* at 733 (Breyer J. concurring).

[118]   See A. K. Chen and J. Marceau, Developing a Taxonomy of Lies under the First Amendment (2018) 89 *Univ. Colo. Law Rev.* 655; A. K. Chen and J. Marceau, High Value Lies, Ugly Truths, and the First Amendment (2015) 68 *Vand. Law Rev.* 1435.

[119]   See *Alvarez*, above note 115, at 719.

The challenge that the rise of AI speech presents to this framework in *Alvarez* is that it makes far more possible a new kind of deception-related harm. Rather than causing only the traditional harms (or benefit-seeking) that the plurality treats as the only appropriate justification for government regulation of lying, AI deception gives rise to a new non-traditional harm – namely, the kind of harm I was discussing earlier, on an audience's ability to perceive and process the world from "reality distortion."[120] Such distortion does harm even when it doesn't impose physical or financial costs on listeners or readers – because it threatens a fundamental condition of freedom of thought (and the individual autonomy it supports). It undermines individuals' ability to generally trust in the reality of what they perceive, and to make judgments based on trust they are able to have in certain sources of information (like recorded evidence or trustworthy sources of journalism). The *Alvarez* plurality opinion is thus arguably a poor fit for the challenge raised by AI deception.

This is not to say that AI deception should be entirely without First Amendment protection. First, it may be that some of the same things that make false speech valuable when it comes from human speakers may also sometimes make it valuable when it comes from computers. If undercover reporters sometimes have to be dishonest in order to expose corruption, so too may AI undercover investigators. Second, if the need to safeguard freedom of thought justifies protecting individuals against AI deceptions, it may also sometimes justify letting them *consent* to such deception. It is conceivable, for example, that individuals will challenge themselves to an "imitation game" to see whether they can distinguish between AI and human speakers.[121] In such circumstances, it would make little sense to let the government protect individuals from a risk that they are themselves seeking – unless the government can point to some "legally cognizable" harm of the kind the *Alvarez* plurality worried about (for example, if the imitation game is the basis of a gambling activity designed to prey upon individuals disposed to make ill-considered bets). Or they may want to enter an AI-generated VR adventure game, or view deepfakes, under circumstances where they know beforehand that they will experience brief periods of uncertainty about whether what they are seeing and hearing accurately reflects the external (physical) world, or historical events in that world.

Exactly when First Amendment freedom of thought should justify insulating such AR-generated deception from government restriction is a complicated question.[122] Here, I just make this point to note that if the need to protect our freedom of thought may justify allowing government to place greater limits on AI-generated speech than on human speech, such considerations may also sometimes cut the other way.[123] Certain uses of AI that don't deserve robust First Amendment protection when they are employed to shape (and perhaps manipulate) another person's thought (by creating deceptive or manipulative speech) may deserve to be staunchly protected when a person uses them to shape her *own* thought.[124]

---

[120] A. Ovadya, What's Worse than Fake News? The Distortion of Reality Itself, *Washington Post* (February 22, 2018), www.washingtonpost.com/news/theworldpost/wp/2018/02/22/digital-reality/?utm_term=.a5582e419cf8. Blitz, above note 66.

[121] See D. Geere, How to Pass the Turing Artificial Intelligence Test (June 19, 2012), www.wired.com/2012/06/pass-turing-ai-test/.

[122] See M. J. Blitz, Freedom of 3D Thought: The First Amendment in Virtual Reality (2008) 30 *Cardozo Law Rev.* 1141, 1070.

[123] J. Bambauer, The Age of Sensorship, in R. K. L. Collins and D. M. Skover (eds.), *Robotica: Speech Rights and Artificial Intelligence* (Cambridge University Press, 2018).

[124] Blitz, above note 122; Bambauer, above note 23.

In fact, certain exercises of freedom of thought may be possible only with the aid of AI or other computer technology. In this respect, the First Amendment's protection for freedom of thought may parallel its protection for freedom of speech. We have a constitutional right not only to speak, but to speak *with modern technology*. We are protected from government censorship not just when we use our voices, or put pen to paper, but also when we use computers to post messages, photos, or videos on social media sites, like Twitter, Facebook, and YouTube. Or when we voice strong opinions – about politics, art, or just about anything else – on a blog, podcast, or Web page. And if we have a right to speak with technology, we also have a right to *think with technology*. Computer software allows individuals to do calculations they couldn't otherwise do. Or, by capturing videos and other records, to remember events in their lives they couldn't otherwise remember. Computer technology can thus act as crucial thinking aids, and even what Andy Clark and David Chalmers have described as an extension of our minds – such that harm to the computers we use may even constitute harm to ourselves.[125]

Thus, one risk in giving government the power to protect against thought-distortion by AI entities is that doing so may simultaneously be giving government a dangerous power of thought restriction. Supreme Court justices and scholars have argued that, in giving government power to counter lying, we might sometimes find the cure is worse than the disease – and, as noted in the previous section, this could also conceivably be true if, to counter private companies' manipulation of search engines, we give government too much power to say what a fair search engine process looks like. The same might be true here: by giving government power to counter threats to our freedom of perception and cognition, there is a risk we give government unwarranted power *over* our perception and cognition. Imagine, for example, that government claims it has to monitor the kind of VR environments we recruit an AI to create for us to assure they don't misrepresent real people or environments in a way that will mislead us. Especially in a world where we rely upon such VR in much of our interactions with the world, such a government assertion of power may give the state far too much power over what we see and hear in VR. Although we may need the assistance of government to protect our freedom of thought from threats raised by emerging technologies, we will have to figure out a way to do so that doesn't give government untrammeled power to restrict the mental freedom generated by the same technologies.

CONCLUSION

AI has the potential to transform human society. Andy Clark writes that ours is a "world permeated by a growing swath of alien intelligences" – and while these AI minds are "not yet intelligences like our own ...some of their greatest potential lies in the ways we humans might cooperate with them to form new hybrid systems that deliver the best of each."[126] Woodrow Barfield similarly writes that these AI entities might not only speak with us – they might merge with us – as we use prosthetics to become more like robots ourselves.[127] With brain–computer interfaces, much of the discussion in this chapter about how the First

---

[125]   See A. Clark and D. Chalmers, The Extended Mind, in A. Clark (ed.), *Supersizing the Mind: Embodiment, Action, and Cognitive Experience* (Oxford University Press, 2008), pp. 220–32; J. Adam Carter and S. Orestis Palermo, Is Having Your Computer Compromised a Personal Assault? The Ethics of Extended Cognition (2016) 2 J. Am. Philos. Assoc. 542–60.

[126]   Clark, above note 6. See also Clark, above note 100, p. 121.

[127]   Barfield, above note 7, pp. 26–31.

Amendment should govern computers' talk may need to be replaced by careful analysis of how they think – and transform the way we think about the world (and become different kinds of thinkers). Even before we get far along this path, the alien nature of "alien" intelligences that AI offers may force us to radically rethink certain aspects of familiar free speech doctrine – and other legal doctrine.

But my argument in this chapter has been that – for the AI and algorithmic speakers of the present and near-term future – rethinking of First Amendment law can be more modest. In some cases, AI and algorithm speech won't challenge free speech law much at all. Rather, the essays written by an AI entity will fit comfortably into the free speech categories developed to cover essays by human beings. Many of the challenges that AI speakers *do* raise will be challenges that courts have already begun to explore in cases on algorithms and search engines – and in the cases, computers often don't raise entirely new issues, but rather generate new variants of puzzles that courts have seen before. Courts, for example, have long explored questions about how to distinguish expressive and non-expressive conduct – and, in doing so, preserve a realm sphere of "thought, belief, [and] expression" and mark it off from the large portion of human affairs where government vigorously regulates our behavior. AI and other algorithms present new challenges for marking that boundary line: source code for a program can both convey ideas to human readers and trigger action by computers that prints 3D objects, encrypts or decrypts files, and controls appliances, cars, and other computer-connected devices on the Internet of Things. New computer programs also give rise to new kinds of digital environments where the boundary between speech and action can be blurred. AI and other computers likewise raise questions about when speakers cannot only determine the content of what they say, but also shape the environment in which individuals make sense of that content – by finding it within a long list of search results, checking it against other non-testimonial evidence (like one's own perceptions, or video records), and determining who it is coming from. By highlighting these problems, the same AI programs that herald a new kind of society are making courts think more carefully about – and perhaps find new solutions to – some old First Amendment problems.

28

The First Amendment and Algorithms

Stuart Minor Benjamin

INTRODUCTION

If someone relies on algorithms[1] to communicate to others, does that reliance change any-thing for First Amendment purposes?[2] In this chapter I argue that, under the Supreme Court's prevailing jurisprudence, the answer is no. Any words or pictures that would be speech under the First Amendment if produced entirely by a human are equally speech if produced via human-created algorithm. So long as humans are making the decisions that underlie the outputs, a human is sending whatever message is sent. Treatment as speech requires sub-stantive editing by a human being, whether the speech is produced via algorithm or not. If such substantive editing exists, the resulting communication is speech under the current jurisprudence. Simply stated, if we accept Supreme Court jurisprudence, the First Amendment encompasses a great swath of algorithm-based decisions – specifically, algo-rithm-based outputs that entail a substantive communication.

This has enormous significance. As the other chapters in this book – indeed, the existence of the book itself – highlight, algorithms are becoming increasingly important in our world. Part and parcel of the rise of transmission via bits has been transmission according to algorithms and protocols created by humans and implemented by machines.[3] Messages travel over the Internet because of transmission protocols, coding decisions determine the look and feel of websites, and algorithms determine which links, messages, or stories rise to the top of search engine results and social media feeds. Every networked device depends on an electronic network built in part on algorithms. Indeed, with each passing day it becomes

---

[1] There is no single accepted definition of "algorithm." See Algorithm Characterization, *Wikipedia*, http://en .wikipedia.org/wiki/Algorithm_characterizations (stating that an "[a]lgorithm does not have a generally accepted formal definition" and discussing more than twenty different prominent characterizations). Broadly speaking, an algorithm is a set of instructions designed to produce an output. My use of the term in this chapter focuses on its most common usage – as instructions or rules implemented by a computer. That is, I want to focus on non-human processes, and I use the term "algorithm" to refer to them. For ease, I will refer to decisions made by protocols, algorithms, and other computations as algorithm-based decisions. I could call them "code-based processes" or some other less familiar and more ungainly term, but I choose "algorithm" simply because it has become more familiar shorthand.

[2] By "someone" I mean a speaker for First Amendment purposes, which the Supreme Court has long held includes individuals and associations, including corporations. And when I refer to the First Amendment I am referring to its Free Speech Clause component, even though the Amendment also contains other clauses.

[3] I am using "bit" as a convenient shorthand for information transmitted via electronic signals. In computing and telecommunications, data is encoded in binary digits (also known as bits), but nothing in this chapter turns on the binary nature of bits per se. The point is simply to emphasize the nature of the communication as electronic, as opposed to old-fashioned pen or printing press on paper.

a greater challenge to identify forms of electronic communication that do not rely on algorithms.

Around the turn of this century, there was considerable focus on whether computer code was speech for First Amendment purposes, such that regulations on the distribution of code implicated the First Amendment.[4] The government had concerns about the proliferation of some computer programs (notably, those perceived as jeopardizing security), and it sought to regulate the circulation of the code itself – the instructions to a computer that would enable the feared activity.[5] For what it is worth, the few courts that considered the issue found by and large that regulations of computer code were regulations of speech.[6]

My focus is not on the distribution of code, and thus not on whether code itself is speech. Rather, I consider whether the outputs of that code – the results produced by algorithms – are speech for First Amendment purposes. The question whether the First Amendment applies to regulation of algorithms' outputs is different from the question whether the algorithms themselves are speech. Even if the algorithms are not speech, their products may be.

What sorts of regulations of algorithm-based decisions might be at issue? The possibility that has inspired the most commentary is the regulation of search engine results, and in particular (given its large market share) Google. A company frustrated by its low PageRank (which hurt its ability to find clients) brought an action against Google for tortious interference with contractual relations, and Google successfully argued that the First Amendment applied to its search results.[7] Another company frustrated by its rankings on Google unsuccessfully argued that Google's search engine is an "essential facility" that must be opened to access,[8] and Frank Pasquale argued that Google should be understood as a new kind of bottleneck deserving of regulatory attention – an "essential cultural and political

---

[4] See, e.g., S. E. Halpern, Harmonizing the Convergence of Medium, Expression, and Functionality: A Study of the Speech Interest in Computer Software (2000) 14 *Harv. J. Law Technol.* 139, 181 (discussing the application of the First Amendment to computer software); R. Post, Encryption Source Code and the First Amendment (2000) 15 *Berkeley Technol. Law J.* 713, 716 (discussing whether encryption source code is covered by the First Amendment); F. Schauer, The Boundaries of the First Amendment: A Preliminary Exploration of Constitutional Salience (2004) 117 *Harv. Law Rev.* 1765, 1794 ("The anti-Microsoft and anti-Hollywood claims of the open-source movement focus on the way in which computer source codes can be conceived of as a language and therefore as speech . . ."); K. A. Moerke, Note, Free Speech to a Machine? Encryption Software Source Code Is Not Constitutionally Protected "Speech" under the First Amendment (2000) 84 *Minn. Law Rev.* 1007, 1027 ("[B]ecause source code is the implementation of an idea, not the expression of it, it is not entitled to First Amendment protection as a type of speech").

[5] The government has acted on these concerns on a number of occasions by restricting the distribution or export of computer software that it viewed as dangerous on a number of occasions, producing several lawsuits. See, e.g., *Junger v. Daley*, 209 F.3d 481 (6th Cir. 2000) (export of encryption software programs); *Bernstein v. Dep't of Justice*, 176 F.3d 1132 (9th Cir. 1999) (distribution of encryption software pursuant to the International Traffic in Arms Regulations); *Karn v. Dep't of State*, 925 F. Supp. 1 (DDC 1996) (designation of a computer diskette as a "defense article" pursuant to the Arms Export Control Act and the International Traffic in Arms Regulations).

[6] See *Universal City Studios, Inc. v. Corley*, 273 F.3d 429, 447 (2nd Cir. 2001) (holding that the First Amendment covers computer programs, and stating that "[a] recipe is no less 'speech' because it calls for the use of an oven, and a musical score is no less 'speech' because it specifies performance on an electric guitar"); *Bernstein*, 176 F.3d at 1141 (concluding that "encryption software, in its source code form and as employed by those in the field of cryptography, must be viewed as expressive for First Amendment purposes"), *reh'g en banc granted and opinion withdrawn*, 192 F.3d 1308 (9th Cir. 1999).

[7] *Search King, Inc. v. Google Tech., Inc.*, No. 02–1457, 2003 WL 21464568, at *3–4 (WD Okla. May 27, 2003) (order granting Google's motion to dismiss). "PageRank" is an algorithm that "measure[s] . . . the quantity and quality of links from one website to another." V. T. Nilsson, Note, You're Not from Around Here, Are You? Fighting Deceptive Marketing in the Twenty-First Century (2012) 54 *Ariz. Law Rev.* 801, 807; see also PageRank, *Wikipedia*, http://en.wikipedia.org/wiki/PageRank.

[8] *Kinderstart.com, LLC v. Google, Inc.*, No. 06–2057, 2007 WL 831806, at *4 (ND Cal. March 16, 2007) (granting motion to dismiss) ("KinderStart asserts that the Google search engine is 'an essential facility for the marketing and

facility."[9] Oren Bracha and Frank Pasquale have also argued that the government should be able to regulate search engines' ability to structure their results, and that the First Amendment does not encompass search engine results.[10] Eugene Volokh and Donald Falk, by contrast, have contended that all aspects of search engines' results are fully protected by the First Amendment.[11]

Google has been the biggest flashpoint, but these issues are not limited to Google.[12] Every major Internet platform relies on algorithms for searches and otherwise, and many of these companies have been criticized for using algorithms that have allowed coordinated misinformation or propaganda campaigns, most notoriously from Russian operations.[13] These companies have often responded by changing their algorithms. For instance, YouTube modified its recommendation algorithms to produce substantively different results – notably, ones that are less likely to promote conspiracies or false information.[14] Taking a somewhat different approach, Facebook changed its News Feed algorithms to display more content from users' friends and family and less from publishers.[15]

The stakes are high. More and more of our activity involves bits, and those bits are frequently guided and shaped by algorithms. The more fully algorithm-based decisions are treated as speech, the more broadly First Amendment jurisprudence will apply. And this has real consequences. Content-based government regulations of speech are subject to strict

financial viability of effective competition in creating, offering and delivering services for search over the Internet'" (citation omitted)).

9   F. Pasquale, Dominant Search Engines: An Essential Cultural & Political Facility, in B. Szoka and A. Marcus (eds.), *The Next Digital Decade* (TechFreedom, 2010), pp. 401, 402, http://nextdigitaldecade.com/ndd_book.pdf.

10 See O. Bracha and F. Pasquale, Federal Search Commission? Access, Fairness, and Accountability in the Law of Search (2008) 93 *Cornell Law Rev.* 1149, 1193–201 and n. 239 (contending that the First Amendment, properly understood, does not cover search engine rankings); see also J. A. Chandler, A Right to Reach an Audience: An Approach to Intermediary Bias on the Internet (2007) 35 *Hofstra Law Rev.* 1095, 1117 (stating that in light of websites' free speech "right to reach an audience, and the listener's right to choose among speakers according to the listener's own criteria, free of extraneous discriminatory influences[,] ... search engines should not manipulate individual search results except to address instances of suspected abuse of the system").

11 See E. Volokh and D. M. Falk, First Amendment Protection for Search Engine Search Results, White Paper (2012), p. 3, www.volokh.com/wp-content/uploads/2012/05/SearchEngineFirstAmendment.pdf. Volokh and Falk state that:

> Google, Microsoft's Bing, Yahoo! Search, and other search engines are speakers. First, they sometimes convey information that the search engine company has itself prepared or compiled (such as information about places appearing in Google Places). Second, they direct users to material created by others, by referencing the titles of Web pages that the search engines judge to be most responsive to the query, coupled with short excerpts from each page ... Third, and most valuably, search engines select and sort the results in a way that is aimed at giving users what the search engine companies see as the most helpful and useful information.

James Grimmelmann has taken a more nuanced position, focusing on search engines as advisors to their users. See J. Grimmelmann, Speech Engines (2014) 98 *Minn Law Rev.* 868.

12 See T. M. Massaro, H. Norton, and M. E. Kaminski, Siri-Ously 2.0: What Artificial Intelligence Reveals about the First Amendment (2017) 101 *Minn. Law Rev.* 2481; R. K. L. Collins and D. M. Skover, *Robotica: Speech Rights & Artificial Intelligence* (Cambridge University Press, 2018).

13 See M. Isaac and D. Wakabayashi, Russian Influence Reached 126 Million through Facebook Alone, *New York Times* (October 30, 2017) (stating that Facebook, Twitter, and YouTube acknowledged that "Russian agents intending to sow discord among American citizens disseminated inflammatory posts that reached 126 million users on Facebook, published more than 131,000 messages on Twitter and uploaded over 1,000 videos to Google's YouTube service").

14 See E. Dwoskin, YouTube Is Changing its Algorithms to Stop Recommending Conspiracies, *Washington Post* (January 25, 2019) (stating that YouTube "is retooling its recommendation algorithm that suggests new videos to users in order to prevent promoting conspiracies and false information").

15 See K. Wagner, Facebook Is Making a Major Change to the News Feed that Will Show You More Content from Friends and Family and Less from Publishers, *Recode* (January 11, 2018).

scrutiny, which is very difficult to satisfy.[16] Content-neutral regulations are subject to inter-mediate scrutiny, which is an easier test to pass but still much more rigorous than the rational basis review applicable to ordinary regulation.[17]

Heightened scrutiny raises the costs of regulation, both in requiring more justification *ex ante* and in increasing the likelihood that the regulation will be rejected on constitutional grounds (since the chances of rejection on constitutional grounds for ordinary legislation are near zero). It could be that we, as a society, like this outcome because we decide that we want less government regulation of algorithm-related industries, but my point here is simply that we disincentivize regulation when heightened scrutiny applies. Subjecting every regulation that affects algorithm-based transmissions to intermediate scrutiny would have dramatic consequences.

Consider the Court's 2011 opinion in *Sorrell v. IMS Health Inc.*,[18] which involved a Vermont law restricting the sale, disclosure, and use of pharmacy records that reveal the prescribing practices of individual doctors, as a way of thwarting data miners' perceived invasion of privacy.[19] Such a law would be unproblematically constitutional absent First Amendment coverage. That is, if it were understood not to trigger First Amendment scrutiny, it would easily pass constitutional muster. But, the Supreme Court flatly stated in *Sorrell* that "[s]peech in aid of pharmaceutical marketing . . . is a form of expression protected by the Free Speech Clause of the First Amendment. As a consequence, Vermont's statute must be subjected to heightened judicial scrutiny. The law cannot satisfy that standard."[20]

Similarly, the Federal Communications Commission's (FCC) limits on the horizontal concentration and vertical integration of cable companies would be subject to fairly lenient review if applied to distributors of gas or electricity. But because the DC Circuit found that these regulations implicated the First Amendment and thus triggered intermediate scrutiny, the court invalidated the regulations and remanded them.[21] Even after that remand, and a much more detailed analysis by the FCC, the DC Circuit found that the FCC had failed to justify the numbers it had chosen and thus rejected them again.[22] Those limits – which are statutorily mandated – lie dormant. The FCC has not figured out how to write regulations that will survive heightened First Amendment scrutiny.

SUPREME COURT JURISPRUDENCE AND ITS EXPANSION

Widely Accepted Sources and Forms of Reasoning

In this chapter I want to apply widely accepted sources and forms of legal reasoning. In the First Amendment context, that means primarily Supreme Court jurisprudence. This is fairly

---

[16] See, e.g., *Sable Commc'ns of Cal., Inc.* v. *FCC*, 492 US 115, 126 (1989) ("The Government may . . . regulate the content of constitutionally protected speech in order to promote a compelling interest if it chooses the least restrictive means to further the articulated interest").

[17] See, e.g., *Turner Broad. Sys., Inc.* v. *FCC (Turner I)*, 512 US 622, 662 (1994) ("[A] content-neutral regulation will be sustained if 'it furthers an important or substantial governmental interest; if the governmental interest is unrelated to the suppression of free expression; and if the incidental restriction on alleged First Amendment freedoms is no greater than is essential to the furtherance of that interest'" (quoting *United States* v. *O'Brien*, 391 US 367, 377 (1968))).

[18] 564 US 552 (2011).

[19] Vt. Stat. Ann. tit. 18, § 4631(d) (2010).

[20] *Sorrell*, above note 18, at 557.

[21] *Time Warner Entm't Co.* v. *FCC*, 240 F.3d 1126, 1137, 1143–4 (DC Cir. 2001).

[22] *Comcast Corp.* v. *FCC*, 579 F.3d 1, 10 (DC Cir. 2009).

well-trodden ground, and my focus here is not to defend that proposition. I will simply note that, as a textual matter, "speech" and "the freedom of speech" could be interpreted in any number of ways. Everyone might agree on some core elements, but the textual boundaries of these terms are not apparent. And as Leonard Levy noted more than half a century ago, "[t]he meaning of no other clause of the Bill of Rights at the time of its framing and ratification has been [as] obscure to us" as that of the Free Speech Clause.[23] Many commentators rely on underlying theories of the First Amendment – visions about what the freedom of speech really means, usually grounded in conceptions of the First Amendment's purpose. The main conceptions that have been offered over the years are the marketplace of ideas and the search for truth, self-government, democratic deliberation, personal autonomy, individual self-expression, and the government-checking function.[24] For better or worse, no underlying conception of the First Amendment has been widely accepted as explaining or driving First Amendment doctrine and thus none can fairly be described as a widely accepted source or form of reasoning.[25]

---

[23] L. W. Levy, *Freedom of Speech and Press in Early American History: Legacy of Suppression* (Belknap Press, 1960), p. 4; see also S. C. Brubaker, Original Intent and Freedom of Speech and Press, in E. W. Hickok, Jr. (ed.), *The Bill of Rights: Original Meaning and Current Understanding* (1991), pp. 82, 85 ("The debates in Congress concerning the speech and press clauses shed scant light on the question of meaning.... Nor do we find enlightening comments in the state legislatures that considered the amendments or the local newspapers or pamphlets of the time").
   That said, Framing-era materials suggest that the Framing generation held a narrower conception of the freedom of speech than do modern courts, and many in the Framing generation adhered to Blackstone's position that the freedom of speech was best understood as a freedom from prior restraints. See, e.g., L. W. Levy, *Jefferson and Civil Liberties: The Darker Side* (Belknap Press, 1963), p. 46 ("Jefferson ... never protested against the substantive law of seditious libel ... He accepted without question the dominant view of his generation that government could be criminally assaulted merely by the expression of critical opinions that allegedly tended to subvert it by lowering it in the public's esteem"); Levy, Freedom of Speech and Press, p. xxi ("The evidence drawn particularly from the period 1776 to 1791 indicates that the generation that framed ... the First Amendment was hardly as libertarian as we have traditionally assumed"); R. H. Bork, Neutral Principles and Some First Amendment Problems (1971) 47 *Ind. Law J.* 1, 22 ("In colonial times and during and after the Revolution [early political leaders] displayed a determination to punish speech thought dangerous to government, much of it expression that we would think harmless and well within the bounds of legitimate discourse"); G. Edward White, Historicizing Judicial Scrutiny (2005) 57 *SC Law Rev.* 1, 60 ("Since the First Amendment only applied against Congress, this approach assumed that the federal government could punish seditious, libelous, blasphemous, obscene, or indecent speech with impunity so long as it did not censor the speech in advance"); see also W. Blackstone, *Commentaries* (Clarendon Press, 1769), Doc. 4, *151 ("The liberty of the press is indeed essential to the nature of a free state: but this consists in laying no *previous* restraints upon publications, and not in freedom from censure for criminal matter when published" (emphasis in the original)).
[24] On the marketplace of ideas, see below notes 26–8 and accompanying text. On the search for truth, see generally W. P. Marshall, In Defense of the Search for Truth as a First Amendment Justification (1995) 30 *Ga. Law Rev.* 1. On self-government and democratic deliberation, see generally A. Meiklejohn, *Free Speech and Its Relation to Self-Government* (Harper Bros., 1948); R. C. Post, *Constitutional Domains: Democracy, Community, Management* (Harvard University Press, 1995), pp. 119–78; C. R. Sunstein, *Democracy and the Problem of Free Speech* (Simon & Schuster, 1995); and H. Kalven, Jr., The New York Times Case: A Note on "The Central Meaning of the First Amendment" (1964) *Sup. Ct. Rev.* 191. On autonomy, see generally C. E. Baker, *Human Liberty and Freedom of Speech* (Oxford University Press, 1989), pp. 194–224; R. H. Fallon, Jr., Two Senses of Autonomy (1994) 46 *Stan. Law Rev.* 875; and H. H. Wellington, On Freedom of Expression (1979) 88 *Yale Law J.* 1105. On the checking function, see generally V. Blasi, The Checking Value in First Amendment Theory (1977) *Am. B. Found. Res. J.* 521. On self-expression, see generally M. H. Redish, *Freedom of Expression: A Critical Analysis* (Lexis, 1984); and D. A. J. Richards, Free Speech and Obscenity Law: Toward a Moral Theory of the First Amendment (1974) 123 *U. Pa. Law Rev.* 45.
[25] See, e.g., T. I. Emerson, *Toward a General Theory of the First Amendment* (Random House, 1966), p. vii ("Despite the mounting number of decisions and an even greater volume of comment, no really adequate or comprehensive theory of the First Amendment has been enunciated, much less agreed upon"); D. A. Farber, *The First Amendment*, 2nd edn. (Foundation Press, 2003), p. 6 ("For a while there was a trend toward single-value theories

The best-known conception, and that most commonly invoked by the Supreme Court, is the marketplace of ideas.[26] For instance, the Supreme Court stated in *Red Lion Broadcasting Co. v. FCC* (in language quoted many times since) that "[i]t is the purpose of the First Amendment to preserve an uninhibited marketplace of ideas in which truth will ultimately prevail."[27] But the marketplace-of-ideas conception has many detractors, and the Supreme Court has emphasized different conceptions in some cases and in still other cases refrained from choosing any particular theory.[28]

Some theorists would argue (in mild rebuke to the Supreme Court) that one cannot usefully interpret the bare words of the Free Speech Clause without an underlying theory, and the Supreme Court (in mild rebuke to those theorists) interprets the Free Speech Clause without an agreed-upon theory.[29] One way of understanding the first part of this chapter is

of First Amendment law, in which a scholar would posit a single underlying constitutional value and then attempt to deduce all First Amendment doctrine from that value. Such efforts, whatever their merits, never seemed to persuade many other scholars and were almost entirely ignored by the courts"); R. Post, Reconciling Theory and Doctrine in First Amendment Jurisprudence (2000) 88 *Calif. Law Rev.* 2353, 2372 (noting that the Supreme Court has not consistently followed any one theory of the First Amendment). The absence of a consensus in support of a particular theory of the First Amendment is not surprising: each possible conception of the First Amendment can be subjected to legitimate criticism, and reaching agreement at that level of specificity is difficult for any group, Justices or otherwise. The Supreme Court's First Amendment jurisprudence is thus one of the many areas characterized by incompletely theorized agreements. Cass Sunstein characterizes this phenomenon as follows:

> Many judges are minimalists; they want to say and do no more than necessary to resolve cases … [Minimalists] attempt to reach *incompletely theorized agreements*, in which the most fundamental questions are left undecided. They prefer outcomes and opinions that can attract support from people with a wide range of theoretical positions, or with uncertainty about which theoretical positions are best. In these ways, minimalist judges avoid the largest questions about the meaning of the free speech guarantee, or the extent of the Constitution's protection of "liberty," or the precise scope of the President's authority as Commander in Chief of the Armed Forces.

C. R. Sunstein, Minimalism at War (2004) *Sup. Ct. Rev.* 47, 48 (footnote omitted; emphasis in the original).
[26] Justice Holmes's dissent in *Abrams v. United States*, 250 US 616 (1919), contains the first, and probably the most famous, articulation of the marketplace metaphor, one that "revolutionized not just First Amendment doctrine, but popular and academic understandings of free speech." J. Blocher, Institutions in the Marketplace of Ideas (2008) 57 *Duke Law J.* 821, 823–4. Holmes wrote:

> [W]hen men have realized that time has upset many fighting faiths, they may come to believe even more than they believe the very foundations of their own conduct that the ultimate good desired is better reached by free trade in ideas – that the best test of truth is the power of the thought to get itself accepted in the competition of the market, and that truth is the only ground upon which their wishes safely can be carried out. That at any rate is the theory of our Constitution.

Abrams, 250 U.S. at 630 (Holmes, J., dissenting). See also Blocher, *ibid.*, pp. 824–5 ("Never before or since has a Justice conceived a metaphor that has done so much to change the way that courts, lawyers, and the public understand an entire area of constitutional law. Its influence has been both descriptive and normative, dominating the explanation of and the justification for free speech in the United States").
[27] *Red Lion Broad. Co. v. FCC*, 395 US 367, 390 (1969).
[28] See above note 25 and accompanying text; see also *Hurley v. Irish-Am. Gay, Lesbian & Bisexual Grp.*, 515 US 557, 573–5 (1995) (emphasizing the centrality of autonomy to the First Amendment); *Turner I*, above note 17, at 641 ("At the heart of the First Amendment lies the principle that each person should decide for himself or herself the ideas and beliefs deserving of expression, consideration, and adherence"); *First Nat'l Bank of Bos. v. Bellotti*, 435 US 765, 777 n. 11 (1978) ("Freedom of expression has particular significance with respect to government because '[i]t is here that the state has a special incentive to repress opposition and often wields a more effective power of suppression'" (quoting Emerson, above note 25, p. 9)); *Mills v. Alabama*, 384 US 214, 218 (1966) ("[A] major purpose of [the First] Amendment was to protect the free discussion of governmental affairs").
[29] See, e.g., Post, above note 4, p. 716 ("Lee Tien is fundamentally misguided to believe that he can explain First Amendment coverage 'without appealing to a grand theoretical framework of First Amendment values.' If First Amendment coverage does not extend to all speech acts, then such a framework is at a minimum necessary in

that it considers how far widely accepted forms and sources of reasoning can take us without relying on a theory of the Free Speech Clause.

The central widely accepted form of legal authority with regard to the Free Speech Clause is Supreme Court jurisprudence. Free Speech Clause cases have been a significant part of the Supreme Court's docket for almost a century. The number of cases, combined with the widely accepted common law approach to interpreting the Court's cases, makes for a fairly rich jurisprudence. Indeed, what is striking for my purposes is how broadly the Court has interpreted the scope of the Free Speech Clause, particularly in recent years, with the result that one can fairly answer most of the questions about algorithms without relying on any particular theories of the First Amendment. The ordinary lawyerly tools of case interpretation take us a fair distance.

Expansion and Exceptions

The history of the Supreme Court's First Amendment jurisprudence has been one of expansion. Libel and defamation were thought to be outside of the First Amendment's coverage until *New York Times Co. v. Sullivan*.[30] Commercial advertising was considered to be beyond the scope of the First Amendment until *Virginia State Board of Pharmacy v. Virginia Citizens Consumer Council, Inc.*[31] And that expansion of the scope of the Free Speech Clause has continued. In the *IMS Health* litigation, many (including the government and the First Circuit) contended that data miners' sale, transfer, and use of prescriber-identifying information was conduct, not speech.[32] But the Supreme Court rejected this argument, emphasizing that "the creation and dissemination of information are speech within the meaning of the First Amendment."[33]

---

order to provide the criteria by which to select the subset of speech acts that merit constitutional attention" (quoting L. Tien, Publishing Software as a Speech Act (2000) 15 *Berkeley Technol. Law J.* 629, 636)).

[30] See 376 US 254, 268–9 (1964) (stating that although "[r]espondent relies heavily . . . on statements of this Court to the effect that the Constitution does not protect libelous publications . . . libel can claim no talismanic immunity from constitutional limitations. It must be measured by standards that satisfy the First Amendment").

[31] See 425 US 748, 758, 770 (1976) (acknowledging that "in past decisions the Court has given some indication that commercial speech is unprotected," but holding that "commercial speech, like other varieties, is protected").

[32] The First Circuit, for example, stated:

> We say that the challenged elements of the Prescription Information Law principally regulate conduct because those provisions serve only to restrict the ability of data miners to aggregate, compile, and transfer information destined for narrowly defined commercial ends. In our view, this is a restriction on the conduct, not the speech, of the data miners. In other words, this is a situation in which information itself has become a commodity. The plaintiffs, who are in the business of harvesting, refining, and selling this commodity, ask us in essence to rule that because their product is information instead of, say, beef jerky, any regulation constitutes a restriction of speech. We think that such an interpretation stretches the fabric of the First Amendment beyond any rational measure. *IMS Health Inc. v. Ayotte*, 550 F.3d 42, 52–3 (1st Cir. 2008), *abrogated by Sorrell*, above note 18.

[33] *Sorrell*, above note 18, at 570. The Court's discussion in *Sorrell* is illuminating:

> [T]he United States Court of Appeals for the First Circuit has characterized prescriber-identifying information as a mere "commodity" with no greater entitlement to First Amendment protection than "beef jerky." In contrast the courts below concluded that a prohibition on the sale of prescriber-identifying information is a content-based rule akin to a ban on the sale of cookbooks, laboratory results, or train schedules.
>
> This Court has held that the creation and dissemination of information are speech within the meaning of the First Amendment. Facts, after all, are the beginning point for much of the speech that is most essential to advance

Not only has the Court expansively construed the coverage of the First Amendment (or, if you prefer, narrowed and eliminated assumed exceptions to First Amendment coverage), but it has also revealed an unwillingness to create new exceptions or construe existing categories of exceptions at a higher level of generality. This has been particularly clear in recent years. In *United States* v. *Stevens*,[34] *Brown* v. *Entertainment Merchants Association*,[35] and *United States* v. *Alvarez*,[36] the Supreme Court emphatically rejected arguments in favor of broadening the categories that are outside First Amendment coverage. Indeed, the *Alvarez* plurality rejected understanding existing exceptions that focus on falsity (like fraud and defamation) as part of a more general exclusion of false statements of fact from First Amendment coverage. The flavor of the Court's approach toward exceptions is encapsulated in the following paragraph from *Alvarez*, quoting *Stevens* in the first two quotations and *Brown* in the last:

> Although the First Amendment stands against any "freewheeling authority to declare new categories of speech outside the scope of the First Amendment," the Court has acknowledged that perhaps there exist "some categories of speech that have been historically unprotected . . . but have not yet been specifically identified or discussed . . . in our case law." Before exempting a category of speech from the normal prohibition on content-based restrictions, however, the Court must be presented with "persuasive evidence that a novel restriction on content is part of a long (if heretofore unrecognized) tradition of proscription." The Government has not demonstrated that false statements generally should constitute a new category of unprotected speech on this basis.[37]

I emphasize this backdrop because it highlights the Justices' apparent belief that their jurisprudence has laid out the relevant benchmarks for First Amendment coverage, subject only to "persuasive evidence that a novel restriction on content is part of a long (if heretofore unrecognized) tradition of proscription."[38]

SUPREME COURT JURISPRUDENCE AND ALGORITHM-BASED DECISIONS

I turn now to the Supreme Court cases most directly relevant to the coverage of algorithm-based outputs. That jurisprudence provides meaningful guidance. *Brown* is a good starting point. The *Brown* Court began its analysis of the legal issues in the case by stating flatly, "California correctly acknowledges that video games qualify for First Amendment

---

human knowledge and to conduct human affairs. There is thus a strong argument that prescriber-identifying information is speech for First Amendment purposes.*Ibid.* at 570 (internal citations omitted).

[34] 559 US 460 (2010).
[35] 564 US 786 (2011).
[36] 567 US 709 (2012) (plurality opinion).
[37] *Ibid.* at 722 (citations omitted) (quoting, respectively, *Stevens*, above note 34, at 473, and *Brown*, above note 35, at 792). The *Alvarez* plurality had earlier noted:

> [C]ontent-based restrictions on speech have been permitted, as a general matter, only when confined to the few historic and traditional categories [of expression] long familiar to the bar . . . Among these categories are advocacy intended, and likely, to incite imminent lawless action; obscenity; defamation; speech integral to criminal conduct; so-called "fighting words"; child pornography; fraud; true threats; and speech presenting some grave and imminent threat the government has the power to prevent, although a restriction under the last category is most difficult to sustain. These categories have a historical foundation in the Court's free speech tradition. The vast realm of free speech and thought always protected in our tradition can still thrive, and even be furthered, by adherence to those categories and rules.

> *Ibid.* at 717–18 (citations and internal quotation marks omitted).
[38] *Brown*, above note 35, at 792.

protection."[39] After noting that "it is difficult to distinguish politics from entertainment, and dangerous to try" and quoting from *Winters* v. *New York*,[40] the Court concluded its discussion by stating categorically that "[v]ideo games communicate ideas – and even social messages – through many familiar literary devices (such as characters, dialogue, plot, and music) and through features distinctive to the medium (such as the player's interaction with the virtual world). That suffices to confer First Amendment protection."[41] In one short paragraph the Court concluded that video games are speech, period.

And there is a significant dog that didn't bark: the Court stated broadly that "video games" are covered by the First Amendment – not particular types of video games that entail certain kinds of interactions, but all video games.[42] The only possible limit implied by the Court's reasoning is that video games communicate ideas, but the Court's discussion makes it clear that it has a very low threshold for what constitutes such communication. Indeed, Justice Alito's concurrence argued at some length that video games were quite different from recognized forms of speech like books,[43] prompting the majority to respond that "[e]ven if we can see in them 'nothing of any possible value to society . . . they are as much entitled to the protection of free speech as the best of literature.'"[44] It is certainly possible that a future Supreme Court could draw distinctions among video games, but nothing in *Brown* provides any support for such distinctions.

In *Turner Broadcasting System, Inc.* v. *FCC* (*Turner I*),[45] confronting a First Amendment challenge to a statute that required cable operators to air local broadcast television stations,[46] the Court flatly rejected the suggestion that this was ordinary economic regulation, and more specifically that cable operators were not engaged in speech for First Amendment purposes:

> There can be no disagreement on an initial premise: Cable programmers and cable operators engage in and transmit speech, and they are entitled to the protection of the speech and press provisions of the First Amendment. Through "original programming or by exercising editorial discretion over which stations or programs to include in its repertoire," cable programmers and operators "see[k] to communicate messages on a wide variety of topics and in a wide variety of formats."[47]

---

[39] *Ibid.* at 790.
[40] 333 US 507, 510 (1948).
[41] *Brown*, above note 35, at 790. The entirety of the Court's discussion is as follows:

> California correctly acknowledges that video games qualify for First Amendment protection. The Free Speech Clause exists principally to protect discourse on public matters, but we have long recognized that it is difficult to distinguish politics from entertainment, and dangerous to try. "Everyone is familiar with instances of propaganda through fiction. What is one man's amusement, teaches another's doctrine." *Winters* v. *New York*, 333 U.S. 507, 510 (1948). Like the protected books, plays, and movies that preceded them, video games communicate ideas – and even social messages – through many familiar literary devices (such as characters, dialogue, plot, and music) and through features distinctive to the medium (such as the player's interaction with the virtual world). That suffices to confer First Amendment protection.

> *Ibid.*

[42] *Ibid.*
[43] See *ibid.* at 806 (Alito J. concurring in the judgment): "There are reasons to suspect that the experience of playing violent video games just might be very different from reading a book, listening to the radio, or watching a movie or a television show."
[44] *Ibid.* at 796 n. 4 (quoting *Winters*, above note 40, at 510).
[45] Above note 17.
[46] Cable Television Consumer Protection and Competition Act of 1992, Pub. L. 102–385, 106 Stat. 1460 (codified as amended in scattered sections of 47 USC).
[47] Above note 17, at 636 (alteration in original; citation omitted; quoting *City of Los Angeles* v. *Preferred Commc'ns, Inc.*, 476 US 488, 494 (1986)). As the internal quotation indicates, the Court put forward the same test in *Preferred Commc'ns*.

This language suggests two – and only two – elements for First Amendment coverage: first, that cable programmers and operators either create programming or choose what to air; and, second, that in doing so they seek to communicate messages on a variety of topics.

Turner I's focus on seeking to communicate messages is consistent with Supreme Court jurisprudence that has always treated substantive communication or self-expression as a necessary condition for the application of the First Amendment.[48] In every case in which the Court has applied the First Amendment, abridgement of substantive communication has been the issue.[49] Some of those abridgements are content-neutral, but the key is that they interfere with a person's or entity's ability to communicate content. The touchstone of the Court's First Amendment cases has always been that the underlying activity entails an expression of ideas, even if it is not "a narrow, succinctly articulable message."[50] Communication thus seems to require, at a minimum, a speaker who seeks to transmit some substantive message or messages[51] to a listener who can recognize that message.[52] Thus,

[48] See, e.g., *Roth* v. *United States*, 354 US 476, 484 (1957) (stating that the First Amendment "was fashioned to assure unfettered interchange of ideas for the bringing about of political and social changes desired by the people"); F. Schauer, *Free Speech: A Philosophical Enquiry* (Cambridge University Press, 1982), p. 94 ("Communication dominates all the arguments that would with any plausibility generate a Free Speech Principle"); S. G. Gey, Why Should the First Amendment Protect Government Speech When the Government Has Nothing to Say? (2010) 95 *Iowa Law Rev.* 1259, 1274 ("The Supreme Court has been very clear about the First Amendment requirement that speakers must engage in definitive communication before receiving constitutional protection for speech"); F. Schauer, Speech and "Speech" – Obscenity and "Obscenity": An Exercise in the Interpretation of Constitutional Language (1979) 67 *Geo. Law J.* 899, 920–1 ("The Court is saying that the communication of ideas is at once the essential first amendment purpose and the essential first amendment property. Without this purpose or property, activity is not protected by the first amendment").
  One might reasonably ask what work "self-expression" is doing in the formulation in the text, on the assumption that self-expression is a substantive communication. Adding "self-expression" clarifies the inclusion of forms of expression that have been recognized as implicating the freedom of speech even though they arguably do not entail a clear substantive communication – in particular, recognized forms of art and symbolism. As the Supreme Court stated in *Hurley*, above note 28:

> The protected expression that inheres in a parade is not limited to its banners and songs ... for the Constitution looks beyond written or spoken words as mediums of expression. Noting that "[s]ymbolism is a primitive but effective way of communicating ideas," our cases have recognized that the First Amendment shields such acts as saluting a flag (and refusing to do so), wearing an armband to protest a war, displaying a red flag, and even "[m]arching, walking or parading" in uniforms displaying the swastika. As some of these examples show, a narrow, succinctly articulable message is not a condition of constitutional protection, which if confined to expressions conveying a "particularized message," would never reach the unquestionably shielded painting of Jackson Pollock, music of Arnold Schoenberg, or Jabberwocky verse of Lewis Carroll.

Ibid., at 569 (citations omitted; quoting, respectively, W. *Va. State Bd. of Educ.* v. *Barnette*, 319 US 624, 632 (1943); *Nat'l Socialist Party of Am.* v. *Village of Skokie*, 432 US 43, 43 (1977) (per curiam); *Spence* v. *Washington*, 418 US 405, 411 (1974) (per curiam).
[49] See, e.g., *Rumsfeld* v. *Forum for Academic & Institutional Rights, Inc.*, 547 US 47, 66 (2006) (noting that the Supreme Court has "extended First Amendment protection only to conduct that is inherently expressive"); *Spence*, above note 48, at 409–10 (finding that the display of an American flag with peace symbols was an activity "sufficiently imbued with elements of communication to fall within the scope of the First and Fourteenth Amendments").
[50] *Hurley*, above note 28, at 569.
[51] In the remainder of this chapter, I will use the term "message" to refer to one or more messages for the sake of convenience and brevity.
[52] See, e.g., K. Greenawalt, *Speech, Crime, and the Uses of Language* (Oxford University Press, 1989), p. 54 ("When the message is an aspect of what the actor is trying to do and is understood by the audience as such, we can say comfortably that the act communicates the message and that the free speech principle is relevant"); M. B. Nimmer, The Meaning of Symbolic Speech under the First Amendment (1973) 21 *UCLA Law Rev.* 29, 36 ("Whatever else may or may not be true of speech, as an irreducible minimum it must constitute a communication. That, in turn, implies both a communicator and a communicatee – a speaker and an audience"); T. Scanlon, A Theory of Freedom of Expression (1972) 1 *Philos. Public Aff.* 204, 206 ("[By] 'acts of

in order to communicate, one must have a message that is sendable and receivable and that one actually chooses to send.[53]

Choosing to send a sendable and receivable substantive message may be necessary for First Amendment coverage, but that does not mean those criteria are sufficient for such coverage. Aren't they incomplete?

The answer may well be yes if we are considering the best definition of "speech" as a matter of first principles, but that is not my goal here. Such a foundational inquiry has felled many trees and is beyond the scope (and word limit) of this chapter.

Instead, in keeping with my focus on Supreme Court jurisprudence as the source of widely accepted guideposts, I will ask two questions that focus on possible incompleteness through the lens of the Supreme Court's jurisprudence. First, is relying solely on the minima identified above (choosing to send a sendable and receivable message) and the exceptions the Court has articulated inconsistent with the Court's First Amendment jurisprudence? Second, can we adopt one of the competing theories of the First Amendment in a way that keeps algorithm-based decisions out of First Amendment coverage but isn't significantly inconsistent with the Court's First Amendment jurisprudence? I will address the second question in the next section, but let me consider the first question here.

In posing this question, I am not asking whether the criteria I identify are complete for purposes of explicating the Supreme Court's approach to First Amendment coverage. They are not. The Court has articulated exceptions and qualifications applicable to, for example, expressive conduct,[54] specific kinds of communications (such as speech integral to criminal conduct),[55] and specific contexts (such as public forums).[56] Rather, I am asking whether applying the criteria identified above plus the exceptions the Court has articulated would be inconsistent with some elements of the Court's jurisprudence. Are the criteria plus exceptions so incomplete that they do not adhere to some of the Court's rulings? This question may seem nonsensical insofar as it can be boiled down to "Is the Supreme Court's jurisprudence inconsistent with itself?" But the question makes sense in the context of a multi-member court often reaching incompletely theorized agreements that resolve specific disputes arising out of others' actions.[57]

The narrow answer is that the criteria and existing exceptions would not upend any existing Supreme Court jurisprudence. No Supreme Court holdings would be disturbed, no Supreme Court doctrines would have to be recast.[58] The Court has never found

---

expression' ... I mean to include any act that is intended by its agent to communicate to one or more persons some proposition or attitude").

[53] Some lower courts have issued opinions that may be in tension with this standard, but the Supreme Court has not done so, and my focus is on the Court's jurisprudence.

[54] See, e.g., *Rumsfeld*, above note 49, at 65–6 (discussing what sorts of conduct are expressive and covered by the First Amendment).

[55] See, e.g., *Giboney* v. *Empire Storage & Ice Co.*, 336 US 490, 498 (1949). For a recent list of First Amendment exceptions, see *United States* v. *Alvarez*, 567 US 709 (2012) (including speech integral to criminal conduct, obscenity, and incitement, to name a few) (plurality opinion).

[56] See, e.g., *Int'l Soc'y for Krishna Consciousness, Inc.* v. *Lee*, 505 US 672, 678–85 (1992) (discussing the public forum doctrine).

[57] See Sunstein, above note 25, p. 48 (identifying incompletely theorized agreements as those "in which the most fundamental questions are left undecided").

[58] The same may not be true with regard to lower courts' jurisprudence. Most notably, lower courts have found that encyclopedias, how-to books, etc. are covered by the First Amendment, but have upheld liability for defective aeronautical charts without suggesting that such liability raised any First Amendment issues. See, e.g., *Aetna Cas. & Sur. Co.* v. *Jeppesen & Co.*, 642 F.2d 339, 341–4 (9th Cir. 1981) (addressing liability for a defective aeronautical chart without discussing the First Amendment); cf. *Brocklesby* v. *United States*, 767 F.2d 1288, 1295 n. 9 (9th Cir.

a substantive communication that was sendable, receivable, and actually sent to be outside First Amendment coverage unless it fell into one of the Court's articulated exceptions. The broader answer is that the breadth of First Amendment coverage suggested by these criteria might motivate us to find ways to narrow the application of First Amendment scrutiny, a topic I discuss later in this chapter.

To return to the criteria identified above: the Court's reasoning indicates that the First Amendment encompasses many algorithm-based manipulations. Consider a person who creates a billboard or webpage entitled "Our National Debt" that presents a running tally of the US national debt.[59] The central feature of this billboard or webpage is simply a dollar figure generated by a computer running a program designed to measure the national debt. There need be no human involvement beyond creating the billboard or webpage and the program measuring the debt. Yet I don't think there is any real doubt that such a billboard or webpage would constitute speech in light of the Supreme Court's jurisprudence. It conveys a substantive message. Its running total of the national debt reflects a focus on and interest in the size of the national debt. It may not be clear to viewers exactly what the creator is trying to say about the national debt, but if nothing else the billboard or webpage communicates that the national debt is sufficiently important to merit this focus.[60]

Significantly, many communications that the Supreme Court treats as speech do not express a clear viewpoint, from a banner stating "BONG HiTS 4 JESUS"[61] to almost every form of art. Given the ambiguities inherent in almost every piece of art, the Supreme Court's application of First Amendment protections to art precludes a requirement of a clear view-point or message. As the Court stated in *Hurley* v. *Irish-American Gay, Lesbian & Bisexual Group of Boston, Inc.*, "a narrow, succinctly articulable message is not a condition of constitutional protection, which if confined to expressions conveying a 'particularized mes-sage,' would never reach the unquestionably shielded painting of Jackson Pollock, music of Arnold Schoenberg, or Jabberwocky verse of Lewis Carroll."[62] In *Hurley* the Supreme Judicial Court of Massachusetts held that the Boston St. Patrick's Day parade was not speech for First Amendment purposes because "it is impossible to discern any specific expressive

---

59   1985) (not reaching the First Amendment issue in a case involving an aeronautical chart because it was raised for the first time on appeal). It may be that aeronautical charts are best understood as falling into an exception that the Supreme Court has articulated. But it may well be that the Court's jurisprudence would treat these charts as speech for First Amendment purposes.

59   This is not a product of my imagination, of course. There is a well-known, billboard-sized "National Debt Clock" in Manhattan. Its central features are tallies of the national debt and the debt per American family. (The only text reads "Our National Debt," "Your Family Share," and "The National Debt Clock.") The clock simply follows an algorithm to calculate the national debt and then displays the result. There are also websites that perform similar functions. See, e.g., US Debt Clock, www.usdebtclock.org (providing continuously updated information on the national debt and related numbers – gross domestic product, credit card debt, etc.).

60   Note that the fact that the person or entity claiming to be engaged in speech does not create the underlying content is irrelevant for purposes of First Amendment coverage. See *Hurley*, above note 28, at 570 ("First Amendment protection [does not] require a speaker to generate, as an original matter, each item featured in the communication ... [T]he presentation of an edited compilation of speech generated by other persons is a staple of most newspapers' opinion pages, which, of course, fall squarely within the core of First Amendment security, as does even the simple selection of a paid noncommercial advertisement for inclusion in a daily paper" (citations omitted)); *Turner I*, above note 17, at 636 (finding that cable operators "engage in and transmit speech" by choosing channels to air); see also D. Sullivan, The New York Times Algorithm & Why It Needs Government Regulation, *Search Engine Land* (July 15, 2010) http://searchengineland.com/regulating-the-new-york-times -46521 (analogizing Google to a newspaper).

61   See *Morse* v. *Frederick*, 551 US 393, 397 (2007). The Court treated the banner as speech under the First Amendment even though "the message on Frederick's banner is cryptic. It is no doubt offensive to some, perhaps amusing to others. To still others, it probably means nothing at all." *Ibid.* at 401.

62   *Hurley*, above note 28, at 569 (citations omitted).

purpose entitling the Parade to protection under the First Amendment."[63] But the US Supreme Court, in reversing, unanimously rejected that argument, stating that "the parade does not consist of individual, unrelated segments that happen to be transmitted together for individual selection by members of the audience. Although each parade unit generally identifies itself, each is understood to contribute something to a common theme."[64] The Court explained that, "[r]ather like a composer, the Council [running the parade] selects the expressive units of the parade from potential participants, and though the score may not produce a particularized message, each contingent's expression in the Council's eyes comports with what merits celebration on that day."[65]

Imagine that a person sets up a bulletin board (an old-fashioned, physical bulletin board) on which she posts every article she finds that uses some specific words (say, "God is dead"[66]). She is not creating the articles; she is merely collecting articles written by others. And she is not editing beyond looking for the words; she is indiscriminately amassing all articles that use these words. But I think we would regard the bulletin board as speech for First Amendment purposes. The bulletin board would be communicating a substantive message to those who viewed it. Her viewpoint might not be clear (does she agree or disagree that God is dead?) but, if nothing else, the bulletin board tells her viewers that she thinks this topic is important enough to merit special attention, in the form of her bulletin board. Presenting all articles containing the words "God is dead" (or "Boston St. Patrick's Day Parade," for that matter) would not present a single clear message; rather, as in *Turner I*, it would constitute an exercise of editorial discretion through which the bulletin board editor sought to communicate a message about the importance of articles containing the words "God is dead."

Now imagine that the bulletin board editor belatedly discovers the Internet, and she transmogrifies her physical bulletin board into a virtual one. She performs computer searches for "God is dead" and posts links to all the articles that incorporate this phrase. Then she realizes that she can largely automate this process, so she creates a macro that lets her hit a single key to search the Web for the words "God is dead," and another macro that lets her hit a second key to upload onto her bulletin board any link that is not already posted. She begins to tire of performing these searches and realizes that a trained monkey could perform this task. Fortunately for her, she has a trained monkey, so she decides to let the monkey hit the two keys. The bulletin board editor then combines the operation into a single key for the monkey. Finally, after the monkey tires of all this typing, the bulletin board editor realizes that she can create a program that will automatically perform the search and post the relevant links without needing the monkey. Once the program starts, it continually searches the Web. In these steps from a physical bulletin board to an automated process, nothing relevant to free speech coverage under the Supreme Court's jurisprudence has changed. When it was physical, the editor's bulletin board communicated the importance to her of articles containing the words "God is dead." The same thing is communicated when the process is automated.

Similarly, consider the following progression: a time-pressed reporter realizes that she can write more articles if she uses some standard boilerplate to communicate information that arises repeatedly. She starts with cutting and pasting but finds that too laborious. So she

---

[63] *Irish-Am. Gay, Lesbian & Bisexual Grp. of Bos. v. City of Boston*, 636 NE.2d 1293, 1299 (Mass. 1994) (internal quotation marks omitted), *rev'd sub. nom Hurley*, above note 28.

[64] *Hurley*, above note 28, at 576.

[65] *Ibid.* at 574.

[66] This example is not of my own making; I adapted it from elsewhere.

creates macros for standard descriptions (for example, "Team A scored seven runs in the third inning, and team B then scored nine runs in the third inning"). The macros become more complex, and utilize fancier language (for example, "in one inning the visitors notched an impressive 7 runs in the top half of the third inning, but the home team responded with a whopping nine runs in the bottom of the third"). The macros become so sophisticated that the reporter can create a template for virtually every outcome, and by adding some facts can stitch together blocks of text that produce a coherent article. Eventually, the reporter's computer skills become so advanced that she can input some basic data from a spreadsheet (for example, the box score from a baseball game) and run a macro that creates an entire article based on those facts. Finally she creates a macro that gathers those facts and writes the article, leaving her creative input entirely in the creation of the programs.

This is not a fanciful example. Algorithms produce what is sometimes called automated journalism – "the process of using software or algorithms to automatically generate news stories without human intervention – after the initial programming of the algorithm, of course."[67] Publications such as *Forbes*, *The Washington Post*, *Bloomberg News*, and the Associated Press use such programs.[68] Engineers, journalists, and computer linguists determine what facts and angles are of interest to them, compile a relevant vocabulary, and create algorithms to construct the articles.[69] As with the example of the "God is dead" bulletin board, it is hard to see how any step in this progression crosses a line between speech and non-

---

[67]   A. Graefe, Guide to Automated Journalism, Columbia Journalism Review Tow Center Report (January 7, 2016), www.cjr.org/tow_center_reports/guide_to_automated_journalism.php. See also Narrative Science, What Is Natural Language Generation? https://narrativescience.com/what-is-nlg ("our software can look at your data and write a story from it, just like a human analyst would today").

   In fact, the baseball example comes from an article quoting the following from a *Narrative Science* article:

   Friona fell 10–8 to Boys Ranch in five innings on Monday at Friona despite racking up seven hits and eight runs. Friona was led by a flawless day at the dish by Hunter Sundre, who went 2–2 against Boys Ranch pitching. Sundre singled in the third inning and tripled in the fourth inning . . . Friona piled up the steals, swiping eight bags in all.

   S. Levy, Can an Algorithm Write a Better News Story than a Human Reporter?, *Wired* (April 24, 2012), www.wired.com/gadgetlab/2012/04/can-an-algorithm-write-a-better-news-story-than-a-human-reporter/all (quoting a *Narrative Science* article). Not bad for a computer, eh?

[68]   See J. Peiser, The Rise of the Robot Reporter, *New York Times* (February 5, 2019) (noting that "[t]he system used by [*Bloomberg News*], Cyborg, is able to assist reporters in churning out thousands of articles on company earnings reports each quarter," and that "[t]he [*Washington*] *Post* has an in-house robot reporter called Heliograf"); WashPostPR, The Post's Heliograf and Modbot Technologies Take First Place in 2018 Global Biggies Awards, *Washington Post* (March 23, 2018) (noting that "[t]he Washington Post's Heliograf and ModBot technologies each took first place in the 2018 Global BIGGIES Awards which recognize best practices in big data and artificial intelligence products and strategies by media companies from around the world"); B. Mullin, The Associated Press Will Use Automated Writing To Cover the Minor Leagues (June 30, 2016), www.poynter.org /tech-tools/2016/the-associated-press-will-use-automated-writing-to-cover-the-minor-leagues; N. Sahota, A.I. May Have Written This Article. But Is That Such a Bad Thing?, *Forbes* (September 16, 2018), www.forbes.com/sites/ cognitiveworld/2018/09/16/did-ai-write-this-article; Graefe, above note 67.

[69]   See Graefe, above note 67:

   [T]he [automated journalism] software relies on a set of predefined rules that are specific to the problem at hand and which are usually derived from collaboration between engineers, journalists, and computer linguists. For example, within the domain of baseball, the software has to know that the team with the most runs – but not necessarily the most hits – wins the game. Furthermore, domain experts are necessary to define criteria of newsworthiness, according to which the algorithm looks for interesting events and ranks them by importance. Finally, computer linguists use sample texts to identify the underlying, semantic logic and translate them into a rule-based system that is capable of constructing sentences. If no such sample texts are available, trained journalists pre-write text modules and sample stories with the appropriate frames and language and adjust them to the official style guide of the publishing outlet.

speech that arises from the Court's jurisprudence. The reporter/programmer is producing a substantive communication via editorial decisions. She designs the boilerplate and the mechanisms to put it together, and she does so in order to convey substantive information. Note that in all the steps of the progression, the reporter/programmer is relying to some degree on boilerplate that she did not create specially for the occasion. With each step she pushes more of her input to the front end (the creation of the boilerplate and the macros to input them), and leaves more implementation for the programs she has created.[70]

Most of the examples above involve webpages that focus on one particular area of interest. Does the analysis change without that focus? No. Suppose someone decides to create a website with the most important news of the moment, and the creator's substantive judgment is that importance is a function of popularity: the more popular an item is, the more important it is. So she creates an algorithm to identify news-oriented websites and to measure the popularity of items appearing on those websites, and the product of those algorithms yields an ever-changing set of links (in order of popularity) on her webpage. Above the links, her webpage says: "Here is the most important news, and by 'most important' I mean most popular." Her page would just be an automated collection of links, but under *Turner I* it would be speech.

Similarly, there are a number of search engines that are designed to be family-friendly by filtering out adult content, and in so doing communicate a substantive message about the desirability of deleting adult-oriented links. Or, in a different vein, an aggregator or search engine that promises to "prioritize links that have the most outrageous porn on the Web" is sending a substantive message that its users will receive, and that the Supreme Court's jurisprudence would treat as speech. And there is DuckDuckGo, a search engine that blocks spam as a proxy for relevance.[71] These search engines are not generating the linked-to content on their own, but the same is true of most of the examples above (and of the Drudge Report and other link aggregators).

That said, there are two distinctions between these search engines and most of the examples above that might seem relevant for First Amendment purposes. First, whereas one might surmise that the creators of the National Debt webpage and the "God is dead" link page are motivated by a particular viewpoint (even if one might guess incorrectly what that viewpoint was), it may be more difficult to ascribe a viewpoint to a spam-blocking search engine. Second, rather than collect items of interest in advance, it searches for them based on the user's preferences. These two points are closely related. Search engines respond to users'

This is not unique to articles, nor is it new. In 2008, a Russian publishing company programmed software to create a novel that was a variation on Leo Tolstoy's *Anna Karenina*, written in the style of Haruki Murakami (whose books were uploaded into the program). See I. Titova, Book Written by Computer Hits Shelves, *St. Petersburg Times* (Russ.) (January 22, 2008), www.sptimes.ru/story/24786. The publisher's chief editor explained: "Today publishing houses use different methods of the fastest possible book creation in this or that style meant for this or that readers' audience. Our program can help with that work." *Ibid.* He added: "However, the program can never become an author, like Photo[s]hop can never be Raphael." *Ibid.*

70   We have not yet, to my knowledge, reached that point with book chapters. Beep.

71   See DuckDuckGo, https://duckduckgo.com. DuckDuckGo's founder Gabriel Weinberg explained in an interview that "[t]he main benefit you see right away is we try to get way better instant answers . . . We're also way more aggressive with spam." J. Vilches, Interview with DuckDuckGo Founder Gabriel Weinberg, *TechSpot* (August 21, 2012), www.techspot.com/article/559-gabriel-weinberg-interview/page2.html. Weinberg added:

There's been a lot of the data that shows that initially when people click on content farm results, they actually like them because they often match their query exactly. But we believe that in the long run you won't like them, because they're often low quality content. So, that's a hard problem for search engines because a lot of the metrics they use for relevance show those results are very relevant, even though I think that they're not.

Ibid.

queries and present information in light of those queries, and they do not screen for or focus on particular viewpoints.

As to the first point, under the prevailing jurisprudence, First Amendment coverage is not limited to speakers with a specific viewpoint, or even to speech of particular value.[72] Magazines that publish articles on politics from every political perspective engage in what everyone would agree is speech, even if the editors themselves have no identifiable political views of their own. Regarding the second point, this seems to be a distinction without a difference for First Amendment purposes. Consider two platforms. The first compiles in advance a list of all the information sources that it judges to be family-friendly, and it lets users search among and select those sources in a variety of ways. The second platform does not compile anything in advance, but instead selects the information sources it judges to be family-friendly in response to users' queries. We can call the first platform a "family-friendly digital cable television" and the second platform a "family-friendly search engine." They are making the same judgments. The only difference is the users' browsing experience, for users who choose to browse rather than simply search. It is difficult to see how anything of constitutional significance could turn on this distinction. Even if it did, it is not clear which way the distinction would cut. Having an installed library of choices allows users to passively graze (or channel surf, in the digital cable context), whereas giving only the choice of search requires more active participation on the part of the user. The result is that the product of that search may be less reflective of the decisions of the platform and more reflective of the decisions of the user, but it is not clear whether that makes this product more or less clearly "speech." In any event, nothing seems to turn on the level of user participation, because both platforms are best understood as engaging in speech under the Court's First Amendment jurisprudence.

Is a search engine like Google different from a spam-blocking or family-friendly search engine under the Supreme Court's jurisprudence? I think not. Google states that search results are not Google's statements about your searches.[73] But Google also notes that its searches emphasize quality. In 2017, in response to concerns about fake news, Google announced "Our latest quality improvements for Search" and stated that: "We've adjusted our signals to help surface more authoritative pages and demote low-quality content."[74] And in 2011 it presented changes to its algorithms (known as Panda) as a means of returning more high-quality websites.[75]

What if we assume that Google (or another algorithm-based search engine) does not care about "quality," but instead only about relevance and usefulness for the user? Are Google's

[72] See *United States* v. *Stevens*, 559 US 460, 479–80 (2010) ("*Most* of what we say to one another lacks 'religious, political, scientific, educational, journalistic, historical, or artistic value' (let alone serious value), but it is still sheltered from government regulation. Even '[w]holly neutral futilities … come under the protection of free speech as fully as do Keats' poems or Donne's sermons'" (quoting *Cohen* v. *California*, 403 US 15, 25 (1971), emphasis in the original)).

[73] See Search Using Autocomplete, Google, https://support.google.com/websearch/answer/106230: "Search predictions aren't the answer to your search. They're also not statements by other people or Google about your search terms."

[74] B. Gomes, Our Latest Quality Improvements for Search, *Google* (April 25, 2017), www.blog.google/products/search/our-latest-quality-improvements-search. See also above notes 14 to 15 and accompanying text (on changes to YouTube's and Facebook's algorithms designed to substantively change what users see).

[75] See M. Cutts, Another Step to Reward High-Quality Sites, *Google Webmaster Central Blog* (April 24, 2012), http://googlewebmastercentral.blogspot.com/2012/04/another-step-to-reward-high-quality.html ("The goal of many of our ranking changes is to help searchers find sites that provide a great user experience and fulfill their information needs. We also want the 'good guys' making great sites for users, not just algorithms, to see their effort rewarded. To that end we've launched Panda changes that successfully returned higher-quality sites in search results").

algorithm-based outputs based on its understanding of relevance and usefulness speech under the Supreme Court's jurisprudence? Yes. Google is making all sorts of judgments in determining what its users want.[76] There is a reasonable argument against this conclusion, flowing from the position that editing and transmitting information based on what users want is not an expression of the speaker's own desires and thus is not real speech. As I discuss in the next section, however, the Supreme Court has not adopted that position and its jurisprudence is not consistent with it.

Many algorithm-based outputs will not constitute speech under this jurisprudence because they are not sending a substantive message. Transmission Control Protocol and Internet Protocol (often referred to as TCP/IP) route information through the Internet, but its creators are not communicating a substantive message in doing so.[77] But when people create algorithms in order to selectively present information based on its perceived importance, value, or relevance, *Turner I* indicates that they are speakers for purposes of the First Amendment (or the Supreme Court's jurisprudence, at any rate). Nothing in the Court's jurisprudence supports the proposition that reliance on algorithms transforms speech into non-speech. The touchstone is sending a substantive message, and such a message can be sent with or without relying on algorithms.[78]

One final note: many trees were felled before *Brown* was decided, as courts and commentators debated whether video games constituted speech for First Amendment purposes.[79] And

---

[76]　For an example of Google debating how to improve searches for its customers, see Google, Search Quality Meeting: Spelling for Long Queries (Annotated), *YouTube* (March 12, 2012), www.youtube.com/watch?v=JtRJXnXgE-A (showing Google's search quality team deliberating on algorithmic decisions during a meeting held on December 1, 2011).

[77]　For an explanation of the TCP/IP protocols, see J. Strickland, How Does the Internet Work?, *HowStuffWorks* (May 7, 2010), http://computer.howstuffworks.com/internet/basics/internet1.htm.

[78]　Tim Wu has argued that under the prevailing jurisprudence, the key inquiry is whether the alleged speaker adopts the information it provides as its own. See T. Wu, Machine Speech (2013) 161 Univ. Pa. Law Rev. 1498, 1530 ("Neither the newspaper nor cable operator cases support the idea that the First Amendment protects something like an index, as opposed to content adopted or selected by the speaker as its own. It is that step – the adoption of information, as a publisher, as opposed to merely pointing the user to it – that marks the difference"). I agree with Wu that the Supreme Court's jurisprudence does not support treating an unedited index as speech, but I do not think the line he articulates arises from, or is consistent with, that jurisprudence. The Court in *Turner I*, above note 17, held that cable operators engage in speech because of their editing, without any suggestion that cable operators do, or need to, adopt as their own the communications of the channels they carry. See above note 17, at 636 ("Through … 'exercising editorial discretion over which stations … to include in its repertoire,' cable … operators 'see[k] to communicate messages' …"). See also *Hurley*, above note 28, at 570 (noting that "even the simple selection of a paid noncommercial advertisement for inclusion in a daily paper" "fall[s] squarely within the core of First Amendment security"). Under *Turner I*, engaging in substantive editing sends a message and thus triggers application of the First Amendment – no adoption or endorsement of the carried programming is needed. To modify Wu's example, no one who watches Fox News, MSNBC, or any other cable channel addressing topic X says, "Look what my cable operator said about X yesterday," or, "It was interesting what my cable operator had to say about X." Nonetheless, the First Amendment encompasses the cable operator's selection of channels. See Wu, *ibid.*, p. 1528 (using the quoted language to illustrate the line he sees between speech and non-speech in the jurisprudence relevant to search engines).

[79]　See, e.g., *Interactive Digital Software Ass'n v. St. Louis County*, 200 F. Supp. 2d 1126, 1133–4 (ED Mo. 2002) (finding that video games are not speech for First Amendment purposes), *rev'd*, 329 F.3d 954 (8th Cir. 2003); *America's Best Family Showplace Corp. v. City of New York*, 536 F. Supp. 170, 174 (EDNY 1982) (same); M. J. Blitz, A First Amendment for Second Life: What Virtual Worlds Mean for the Law of Video Games (2009) 11 *Vand. J. Ent. Technol. Law* 779, 785 (arguing that even non-narrative video games and other "communication-free forms of electronic imagery" should be "staunchly protected"); T. R. Day and R. C. W. Hall, Déjà Vu: From Comic Books to Video Games: Legislative Reliance on "Soft Science" to Protect against Uncertain Societal Harm Linked to Violence v. the First Amendment (2010) 89 *Or. Law Rev.* 415, 450 (arguing that video games are "no less deserving of First Amendment protection than movies, works of art, and literature");

yet the Court treated this as a question with an obvious answer. Indeed, part of what is so striking about the opinion is how easy the Court found the answer to be.[80]

Does this mean that heightened scrutiny will apply to almost every regulation of entities that produce words via algorithm? No. The algorithm must send a substantive message. Algorithms that are designed to speed transmission, or make a network operate more efficiently, are not sending any substantive message. Your landline telephone (remember those?) might work better if the telephone company installed algorithms that reduce background noise, but the telephone company has not substantively communicated anything by doing so.[81] One could reject this limitation, but such a rejection would constitute a significant remaking of First Amendment jurisprudence.

PRODUCING A DIFFERENT RESULT

As I noted above, there are a host of competing conceptions of the Free Speech Clause, none of which has been widely accepted as explaining or driving First Amendment doctrine. But let me now ask whether adopting one of the competing theories of the First Amendment would produce a different result without upending existing case law. More broadly, how difficult would it be to craft a coherent exception to the prevailing First Amendment jurisprudence such that algorithm-based decisions, or search results more specifically, would not be encompassed by the First Amendment but most of the remaining First Amendment jurisprudence would remain? This is different from asking whether, in the first instance, any theory of the First Amendment would exclude algorithm-based decisions from coverage. The answer to that question is yes. That is, we could rely on a particular conception of the First Amendment that would radically rethink the Supreme Court's existing approach in ways that would exclude search engine results and much else. We could, for example, limit "the freedom of speech" in the First Amendment to core political speech, or speech that directly promotes a meaningfully constrained notion of democratic deliberation or self-government, and thereby exclude search engine results, as a category, from the ambit of the First Amendment.[82] We would also exclude most forms of art, however.[83] My question in this section is, without radically changing our First Amendment

P. M. Garry, Defining Speech in an Entertainment Age: The Case of First Amendment Protection for Video Games (2004) 57 *SMU Law Rev.* 101, 122 (arguing against full First Amendment protection for video games); P. E. Salamanca, Video Games as a Protected Form of Expression (2005) 40 *Ga. Law Rev.* 153, 194–205 (arguing against viewing video games as unprotected speech); K. W. Saunders, Regulating Youth Access to Violent Video Games: Three Responses to First Amendment Concerns (2003) 51 *Mich. St. Law Rev.* 101–5 (arguing that video games are non-communicative and not speech for First Amendment purposes); A. Ventry III, Note, Application of the First Amendment to Violent and Nonviolent Video Games (2004) 20 *Ga. St. Univ. Law Rev.* 1129, 1131 (arguing that "courts should apply a case-by-case approach in determining whether video games are constitutionally protected speech instead of deciding conclusively that all video games are (or are not) protected speech").

80 See above notes 39–44 and accompanying text; see also *Sorrell*, above note 18, at 557: "Speech in aid of pharmaceutical marketing ... is a form of expression protected by the Free Speech Clause of the First Amendment."

81 See S. M. Benjamin, Transmitting, Editing, and Communicating: Determining What "The Freedom of Speech" Encompasses (2011) 60 *Duke Law J.* 1673, 1686.

82 See, e.g., Bork, above note 23, p. 20 ("Constitutional protection should be accorded only to speech that is explicitly political").

83 We could avoid such a result if we adopted a very broad definition of "core political speech," "democratic deliberation," or "self-government," but then we would end up back where we started. As Frederick Schauer has noted:

jurisprudence, how easy would it be to exclude algorithm-based decisions, or search engine results more specifically?

Relying on Particular Theories of the First Amendment

The most obvious possibility would be to focus the First Amendment analysis on individuals. This could lead to a suggestion that communications by corporations do not constitute speech. But newspapers and magazines are owned by corporations, and a revamping of the First Amendment to exclude those publications as speech would be a radical departure from our existing jurisprudence.

One might instead try to exclude from First Amendment coverage speech that a corporation makes purely for its own benefit. The problem is that it is difficult to come up with any articulation of speech in a corporation's interest that would exclude algorithm-based decisions, or more specifically search engine results, without also excluding newspapers and magazines. A distinction based on speech that is in a corporation's interest fails to distinguish newspapers and magazines. The same applies for excluding speech that is aimed solely at increasing a corporation's value. Indeed, for a newspaper or magazine owner who is a faithful agent, with shareholders who want the highest possible return on their investment, presumably all the owner's actions would be undertaken in order to maximize shareholder value. Simply stated, search results are in the search engine's interests in the same way that compelling content is in the interest of any conveyor of content, whether newspaper, political website, or porn website.

A more conventional line would distinguish commercial speech. A number of theorists have argued for the exclusion of commercial speech from First Amendment coverage.[84] This would be a fairly significant reworking of First Amendment jurisprudence.[85] Excluding commercial speech also would not affect most algorithm-based decisions. It would apply to search engines' (and newspapers') advertisements, but most search engine results are not paid advertisements.[86]

A different way of emphasizing individuals would focus on their expression. Theories focused on self-expression, for example, emphasize that it is an individual's self-expression that matters, and autonomy-based theories similarly emphasize individual autonomy. The problem is that many algorithm-based decisions similarly involve the creator's self-expression and autonomy. Depending on the algorithm, algorithm-based decisions may well constitute

---

> Theories based on self-government or democratic deliberation have a hard time explaining why (except as mistakes, of course) the doctrine now covers pornography, commercial advertising, and art, inter alia – none of which has much to do with political deliberation or self-governance, except under such an attenuated definition of "political" that the justification's core loses much of its power.

Schauer, above note 4, p. 1785.

[84] See, e.g., C. Edwin Baker, Commercial Speech: A Problem in the Theory of Freedom (1976) 62 *Iowa. Law Rev.* 1, 3 ("[G]iven the existing form of social and economic relationships in the United States, a complete denial of first amendment protection for commercial speech is not only consistent with, but is required by, first amendment theory"); C. R. Sunstein, *Democracy and the Problem of Free Speech* (Free Press, 1993), pp. 123, 127 (arguing for little protection of advertising because it does not contribute to democratic deliberation).

[85] See, e.g., *Cent. Hudson Gas & Elec. Corp.* v. *Pub. Serv. Comm'n*, 447 US 557, 561 (1980) ("The First Amendment . . . protects commercial speech from unwarranted governmental regulation"); *44 Liquormart, Inc.* v. *Rhode Island*, 517 US 484 (1996) (applying First Amendment scrutiny to the regulation of commercial advertisements).

[86] Some early search engines relied heavily on payments in determining what to present and where to present it. One of Google's selling points was that it used page-rank algorithms and that what little paid content it had was clearly demarcated as such. Newer search engines have followed Google's lead. Google and its newer competitors realized that they could attract users by prioritizing relevant quality websites, and make more money from advertisers relegated to the side because of the large number of people who would be attracted by the promise of search results containing relevant websites.

self-expression, enhance autonomy, and contain meaningful thought. The algorithm is simply a means to gather relevant information, but the creator chooses what to gather. The person who creates the National Debt webpage, or the "God is dead" link page, is expressing a view about the importance of those topics. Or consider a webpage that uses an algorithm to amass links to articles with the words "Trump sucks" or "Clinton sucks." These webpages require less curating than does the Drudge Report, but all of them reflect autonomous expression.

Search engines are a closer question, but a definition of self-expression that excludes them would be a fairly crabbed one. Start with a search engine that focuses on family-friendly material (or, if you prefer, porn). This seems to encode autonomous expression – "We value family-friendly material/porn, and we want to make it easier for you to find it." Of course, the creators' actual motivation might be more base – most obviously: "We just want to make money." But that may well be the true motivation for many newspapers and magazines, and many artists, for that matter (I'm looking at you, Jeff Koons). And because theories of self-expression and individual autonomy treat art as squarely within their understanding of speech, those who emphasize self-expression or autonomy usually do not focus on the speaker's subjective motivation, but instead on the apparent expression reflected in the message. In this case there is an apparent expression, as I noted above.

It is a very small step from that expression to DuckDuckGo's expression. Instead of "We want to avoid/find porn, and we want to make it easier for you to avoid/find it," the expression would be "We want to avoid spam, and we want to make it easier for you to avoid it." And it is then another small step to Google's expression. As I noted above, Google, too, articulates quality as its goal. But even if we credit only its focus on relevance, substituting "relevant" for "quality" in the expression does not make it any less of an expression. In all cases, the algorithm creators are expressing their views about what they value.

Perhaps Google in particular is different, insofar as its message is not so much "We value relevant websites" but more like "We select for you what you want." In the latter formulation, Google arguably is not expressing its own preferences so much as it is indicating that it wants to satisfy ours.

Differentiating Google for purposes of First Amendment coverage based on its catering to users' interests would be a significant shift in First Amendment jurisprudence, as publications and editors that frankly focus on their viewers' or readers' interests would be unprotected. It has not mattered in the past whether a magazine owner (or cable operator) was merely responding to a market opportunity or was expressing its own subjective preferences, but now that difference would be dispositive. If we define unprotected speech to include speech that responds to public demand, only the few publications that push their ideas regardless of public interest[87] would be speakers, and that would upend most First Amendment law.

Beyond that, this would be a mighty thin reed on which to rest a distinction. We can recharacterize Google's position as "Our preference is to select for you what we believe you find valuable." If we substitute "is" for "you find," or change the locution to "we believe you *should* find valuable," there is clearly expression. So we would be putting an enormous amount of weight on the creators' articulation as focused on what others want.

Articulating one's goal in terms of serving others is still an exercise of autonomy and a form of self-expression. "What makes you happy makes me happy" is an expression of self – one that looks to another for one's happiness, but an expression of personal motivation nonetheless. In

---

[87] We usually call these "vanity publications."

the same way, the artist who proclaims that she is guided by what her viewers want has still made a self-defining and art-defining statement.[88]

It also bears noting that decisions about what users want are analogous to the decisions of cable operators that the Court found to be speech in *Turner I*. In their briefs, the cable operators stressed that a key consideration in choosing what channels to include was what they thought their customers wanted.[89] Indeed, a major element of the cable operators' argument that there was no sufficient justification for the statute was their assertion that cable operators would be guided by viewer interest and thus would air the most popular channels whether or not they had an ownership interest in them.[90] The cable operators, in choosing what channels to air, were engaged in editing, on whatever substantive basis they chose, and those editorial decisions constituted speech. The cable operators claimed they were editing in light of their sense of their customers' wishes, and Google is doing the exact same thing.

A different approach would involve a focus on the audience. Some Supreme Court opinions and some commentators have emphasized the importance of listeners and viewers having access to a wide range of views.[91] But a "right to receive information" is articulated as an addition to the rights of speakers, as opposed to a substitute for them, and so would not limit the treatment of algorithm-based decisions as speech.[92] It does bear noting, though, that a focus on the rights of the audience might buttress the position of some algorithm-based outputs – in particular, search engines. One way of conceptualizing the rights of listeners and viewers is as a right to unencumbered access to information.[93] Such a conceptualization would lend support to the treatment of an individual's search results as part of the information that is encompassed by the Free Speech Clause. A different conceptualization would interpret the rights of listeners and viewers as justifying government regulation of information providers, but application of such arguments to exclude information providers from coverage

---

[88]   Cf. The Kinks, *Give the People What They Want* (Arista Records, 1981).

[89]   See, e.g., Reply Brief for Appellants Turner Broad. Sys., Inc. at 19–20, *Turner I*, above note 17, (No. 93–44), 1993 WL 664649 ("A cable operator's very raison d'être is to choose from among the enormous variety of sources of video programming available in order to put together a package of programming that will be appealing to television viewers"); Reply Brief for Appellants Discovery Commc'ns, Inc. and the Learning Channel, Inc. at 6, *Turner I*, above note 17, (No. 93–44), 1993 WL 664652 (emphasizing the role of market forces in cable operators' choices of which channels to carry).

[90]   Nothing in the Court's opinion suggests that any aspect of First Amendment coverage turned on the degree to which a cable operator chose channels purely on mechanistic measures of popularity.

[91]   See, e.g., *First Nat'l Bank* v. *Bellotti*, above note 28, at 783 (noting that the First Amendment affords the public "access to discussion, debate, and the dissemination of information and ideas"); *Va. State Bd. of Pharmacy*, above note 31, at 757 (stating that the "freedom of speech 'necessarily protects the right to receive'"); *Kleindienst* v. *Mandel*, 408 US 753, 762 (1972) ("In a variety of contexts this Court has referred to a First Amendment right to receive information and ideas" (internal quotation marks omitted)); *Stanley* v. *Georgia*, 394 US 557, 564 (1969) ("It is now well established that the Constitution protects the right to receive information and ideas"); *Griswold* v. *Connecticut*, 381 US 479, 482 (1965) (stating that the freedom of speech includes "the right to receive"); see also T. I. Emerson, Legal Foundations of the Right to Know (1976) *Wash. Univ. Law Q.* 1, 2 ("It is clear at the outset that the right to know fits readily into the first amendment . . ."); T. Scanlon, A Theory of Freedom of Expression (1972) 1 *Philos. Public Aff.* 204 (arguing that the First Amendment protects listeners' access to information and viewpoints and thereby protects autonomy).

[92]   See *Va. State Bd. of Pharmacy*, above note 31, at 756 ("Freedom of speech presupposes a willing speaker. But where a speaker exists, . . . the protection afforded is to the communication, to its source and to its recipients both").

[93]   See, e.g., *ibid.*; *Sorrell*, above note 18, at 577 ("[T]he fear that people would make bad decisions if given truthful information cannot justify content-based burdens on speech. The First Amendment directs us to be especially skeptical of regulations that seek to keep people in the dark for what the government perceives to be their own good" (citations and internal quotation marks omitted)); *Edenfield* v. *Fane*, 507 US 761, 767 (1993) ("The commercial marketplace, like other spheres of our social and cultural life, provides a forum where ideas and information flourish. . . . [T]he general rule is that the speaker and the audience, not the government, assess the value of the information presented").

by the Free Speech Clause would be a radical change in First Amendment jurisprudence.[94] For better or worse, the Supreme Court's jurisprudence has decisively rejected this vision.[95]

Yet another direction would focus on the government's purpose or motive in enacting a particular regulation. Some commentators (including then-professor Elena Kagan) have suggested that First Amendment coverage should turn on the government's purpose or motive, such that an economic motive should not trigger First Amendment coverage but a censorious motive should.[96] Whatever the merits of this approach, and whatever its application to algorithm-based outputs, it is inconsistent with a significant number of Supreme Court cases that applied the First Amendment despite the fact that the underlying regulation had an economic motive.[97]

There are of course other theories of the First Amendment, but all would either draw arbitrary lines or exclude much that we currently consider to be speech.

---

[94] See *Red Lion*, above note 27, at 390 (suggesting that the freedom of speech includes "the right of the public to receive suitable access to social, political, esthetic, moral, and other ideas and experiences"); J. A. Barron, Access to the Press – a New First Amendment Right (1967) 80 *Harv. Law Rev.* 1641, 1666 ("It is to be hoped that an awareness of the listener's interest in broadcasting will lead to an equivalent concern for the reader's stake in the press, and that first amendment recognition will be given to a right of access for the protection of the reader, the listener, and the viewer").

[95] See, e.g., *Pac. Gas & Elec. Co. v. Pub. Utils. Comm'n*, 475 US 1, 4, 20–1 (1986) (plurality opinion) (holding that a state utility commission could not constitutionally compel a private utility company to include in its billing envelopes materials produced by an adverse group); *Miami Herald Pub. Co. v. Tornillo*, 418 US 241, 258 (1974) (holding unconstitutional a state statute guaranteeing political candidates media access to respond to criticism). Indeed, the Supreme Court has largely abandoned its intimation in *Red Lion* that the First Amendment empowers the government to give access rights to listeners and viewers. As it turns out, broadcasting is the only area that the Court has treated as justifying a right of access – and even there, the Court has held that broadcasters have First Amendment rights (just diminished ones).

[96] See, e.g., E. Kagan, Private Speech, Public Purpose: The Role of Governmental Motive in First Amendment Doctrine (1996) 63 *Univ. Chi. Law Rev.* 413, 414 (arguing "that First Amendment law, as developed by the Supreme Court over the past several decades, has as its primary, though unstated, object the discovery of improper governmental motives"); J. Rubenfeld, The First Amendment's Purpose (2001) 53 *Stan. Law Rev.* 767, 775–9 (asserting the centrality of a law's purpose in determining the appropriate application of the First Amendment).

[97] See *Sorrell*, above note 18, at 567 (applying First Amendment scrutiny to a regulation motivated by economic considerations and stating that, "[w]hile the burdened speech results from an economic motive, so too does a great deal of vital expression"); *United States v. United Foods, Inc.*, 533 US 405, 408, 417 (2001) (applying First Amendment scrutiny to an agricultural assessment requirement on the grounds that it compelled mushroom handlers to fund speech with which they disagreed); *Turner I*, above note 17, at 638 (applying First Amendment scrutiny to legislation while also finding that "Congress' overriding objective in enacting [a law requiring cable carriage of local television broadcasters] was ... to preserve access to free television programming for the 40 percent of Americans without cable"); *Members of City Council of Los Angeles v. Taxpayers for Vincent*, 466 US 789, 804 (1984) (applying First Amendment to an ordinance even though "[t]he text of the ordinance is neutral," and "there is not even a hint of bias or censorship in the City's enactment or enforcement of this ordinance"); *Minneapolis Star & Tribune Co. v. Minnesota Comm'r of Revenue*, 460 US 575, 592 (1983) ("We have long recognized that even regulations aimed at proper governmental concerns can restrict unduly the exercise of rights protected by the First Amendment"). The Supreme Court has also squarely rejected the more modest argument that, within the universe of First Amendment coverage, strict scrutiny for content-based regulations should not apply if the government has "[i]nnocent motives." *Reed v. Town of Gilbert, Ariz.*, 135 S. Ct. 2218, 2229 (2015) ("Innocent motives do not eliminate the danger of censorship presented by a facially content-based statute"); *ibid.* at 2228 ("A law that is content based on its face is subject to strict scrutiny regardless of the government's benign motive, content-neutral justification, or lack of 'animus toward the ideas contained' in the regulated speech" (internal citation omitted)).

A Useful Algorithm-Based Line

As the discussion above indicates, crafting a First Amendment exclusion only for algorithm-based decisions would be arbitrary, and crafting a non-arbitrary category that excludes algorithm-based decisions would exclude much of what we regard as speech and thus significantly change our jurisprudence. Because of the similarity of algorithm-based decisions to communications that are clearly speech under the prevailing Supreme Court jurisprudence, there do not appear to be any principled distinctions that would leave algorithm-based decisions uncovered without upending significant aspects of that jurisprudence. But a different line is tenable and might do significant work in the future even if it would not do any at present: excluding outputs that do not reflect human decision-making.

A key element of the discussion so far is that there is a human mind behind all the algorithms. The fact that an algorithm is involved does not mean that a machine is doing the talking. Individuals are sending a substantive message in such a way that others can receive it. The point of the discussion so far is that adding algorithms does not change the Free Speech Clause analysis when humans are still creating the template.

But what happens to the analysis if humans are no longer meaningfully creating the message? That is, how should we analyze a situation in which artificial intelligence (AI) has developed to the point that a set of algorithms have freed themselves from human direction such that the product of the algorithms does not reflect human decision-making about what to communicate?

Computer scientists have developed programs that engage in massive data analysis that would take humans eons to complete, but those programs do not exercise any independent judgment. Similarly, the outputs of AI may be inscrutable, but that does mean that the machines generating those outputs have volition; opacity and independent judgment are two quite different things.

Some programs use random variation as a means of experimentation and possible adaptation. For instance, some programs use not only formulas but also some prescribed points of randomness to allow the computer program to produce a range of outcomes. A particularly enjoyable example is The Nietzsche Family Circus, a webpage which, with each hit of the "refresh" button, pairs a randomized Family Circus cartoon with a randomized Friedrich Nietzsche quote.[98] Whatever meaning we find in this randomized process and its results is due to the program's clever (human) designer and our reactions to that design. After all, the same effect could be achieved (à la John Cage) by throwing grains of rice emblazoned (in *very* tiny letters) with Nietzsche quotations into the air above a checkerboard of Family Circus cartoons. There would likely be all sorts of interesting pairings, but we wouldn't attribute any agency in generating a message to the grains of rice.

A bit closer to home, programmers have created programs that generate random papers, at least one of which was accepted at a conference.[99] But the random processes are not crafting

---

[98]   See Nietzsche Family Circus, www.nietzschefamilycircus.com/.

[99]   See, e.g., SCIgen – An Automatic CS Paper Generator, http://pdos.csail.mit.edu/scigen/#relwork ("SCIgen is a program that generates random Computer Science research papers, including graphs, figures, and citations. It uses a hand-written context-free grammar to form all elements of the papers. Our aim here is to maximize amusement, rather than coherence" (emphasis omitted)); timothy, Randomly Generated Paper Accepted to Conference, *Slashdot* (April 13, 2005), http://entertainment.slashdot.org/story/05/04/13/1723206/randomly-generated-paper-accepted-to-conference ("Some students at MIT wrote a program called SCIgen ... [and] one of their randomly generated paper[s] was accepted to [the 2005 World Multiconference on Systemics, Cybernetics, and Informatics]. Now they are accepting donation[s] to fund their trip to the conference and give a randomly generated talk" (emphasis omitted)).

substantive messages.[100] Humans are crafting messages about academic standards and are employing randomness to do so. As the webpage of the Postmodernism Generator (which "creates realistic-looking but meaningless academic papers about postmodernism, poststructuralism and similar subjects") notes: "The papers produced are perfectly grammatically correct and read as if written by a human being; any meaning found in them, however, is purely coincidental."[101] That is the substantive message, and it derives from decisions made by the human designers. The programs are fun precisely because we may ascribe meaning even to the results of random processes, whether random words or random raindrops on the pavement. Those raindrops have not in fact sent us a substantive message; we just choose to read something into the random picture they create.

Other programs use randomness for purposes of experimentation and adaptation toward a prescribed goal. Programmers have, for example, created programs that break into multiple offshoots, each having some decision points at which randomness comes into play and thus produces different outcomes. The program itself (or the programmer) then determines which of these permutations comes closest to achieving a prescribed goal (modeling past stock movements and predicting future stock movements are popular, as is winning at Go), and there can be multiple generations of such permutations, resulting in unguided adaptation toward a goal. This is also how some computer viruses work: they are programmed to use randomness at key points (often in response to the host program's defenses), in the hope that some versions of the virus will become more effective at propagating and achieving the programmer's goal. This is different from random raindrops on the pavement, because once we see what adaptation best achieves our goal of predicting stock prices or winning games of Go, we can choose it. This applies to adaptations we can identify (for example, "add yesterday's closing price of Facebook's stock to the previous day's rainfall in Seattle and divide by the previous night's number of viewers of the CBS Evening News") and to adaptations that are inscrutable to us, such that we do not understand how they generated their outputs. That is the story of AlphaGo, for example.[102] But the adaptation and resulting output is not creating and communicating a substantive message on its own. We have designed the goal and the means to achieve it. We find the adaptation useful because it moves us toward the goal that *we* have chosen. We are supplying the volition and all the meaning.[103]

That said, AI could cross, or at least blur, this line.[104] Imagine that AI advances to such a level that machines are in some meaningful sense choosing their own goals and what substantive communications will achieve those goals. Just as a machine may at some point

---

[100]   The whole point is that humans are prone to find messages and meaning even in random collections of words and numbers.

[101]   Postmodernism Generator, http://page112.com/iphone/pomo/. The creators of The Postmodern Generator added the elegantly understated caveat that "submitting generated texts to journals or academic courses is not recommended." *Ibid.*

    This is different from the process used by automated journalism programs (see above notes 67–9 and accompanying text) because those entities do try to communicate substantive messages with their choice of words, just as a human author does. A writer (or law professor) who relies on a template or cuts and pastes boilerplate into her article does so in order to communicate a substantive message (just one that can be communicated via off-the-shelf language), and so too automated journalism programs utilize templates and boilerplate in order to communicate information.

[102]   See J. X. Chen, The Evolution of Computing: AlphaGo, *Computing in Science & Engineering* (July/August 2016).

[103]   To put the matter a bit differently, telling the world that this formula, or the price of tea in China, predicts the stock market's movements is a form of substantive communication. But that fact does not mean that the formula, or the price of tea in China, is independently communicating anything.

[104]   See, e.g., S. Chopra and L. F. White, A Legal Theory for Autonomous Artificial Agents (2011) (extending legal principles to the unique challenges posed by the evolution and increasing sophistication of artificial agents); Collins and Skover, above note 12 (discussing speech rights for robots); Massaro *et al.*, above note 12 (same).

satisfy the Turing test,[105] it may at some point demonstrate a level of choice or volition that is indistinguishable from that of humans. At that point, we might say that the connection to the human creators is sufficiently attenuated that the results no longer reflect humans' decisions about how to determine what to produce, such that there is no longer a human sending a substantive message. No human would be communicating anything. Extending the First Amendment to messages produced by this AI would raise the specter that we would be treating the products of machines like those of human minds. We could then say that "speech" was truly created (and not just transmitted, or aided) by a machine.[106]

CONCLUSION

In this chapter I have attempted to take seriously both widely accepted sources and forms of reasoning and concerns about expansion of the application of the First Amendment. Consistent with that focus, I have considered how those widely accepted sources (in particular Supreme Court jurisprudence) would apply to First Amendment coverage of algorithm-based decisions and whether we can exclude such decisions from the First Amendment without radically revamping First Amendment jurisprudence.

Those worried about the Free Speech Clause expanding too far, particularly with regard to algorithm-based decision-making (or maybe just Internet searches), might find this unacceptable. If drawing non-arbitrary lines that do not radically reorient First Amendment jurisprudence provides protections for algorithm-based outputs, then perhaps we should be willing to draw arbitrary lines or radically reorient First Amendment jurisprudence.

There is no way to definitively refute these arguments. Perhaps inclusion of algorithm-based decisions illuminates just how far Free Speech jurisprudence has gone off the rails (to use a technical term), such that we need to remake it. Or perhaps algorithm-based decisions are such unattractive candidates for First Amendment inclusion that we should draw a somewhat arbitrary line excluding them.

In my view, any line between algorithm-based and human-based decisions would be unjustifiably arbitrary, so a radical reorientation is the more attractive of the two options in this context.[107]

---

[105]   On the Turing test, see D. Dowe and G. Oppy, The Turing Test, *Stanford Encyclopedia of Philosophy* (January 26, 2011), http://plato.stanford.edu/entries/turing-test (noting that a machine passes the Turing test when a person is unable to detect that she is conversing with a machine instead of a fellow person). On the legal implications of machines capable of meeting the Turing standard, see generally J. Boyle, Brookings Inst., Endowed by Their Creator? The Future of Constitutional Personhood (2011), p. 6, www.brookings.edu/research/endowed-by-their-creator-the-future-of-constitutional-personhood: "In the coming century, it is overwhelmingly likely that constitutional law will have to classify artificially created entities that have some but not all of the attributes we associate with human beings."

[106]   Of course, this assumes we would regard such machines as materially different from humans in the first place. As James Boyle has noted, our grandchildren might view such machines as rightfully entitled to all the protections of personhood. See Boyle, *ibid.* But I leave that scenario for another day.

[107]   Commerce Clause jurisprudence provides a point of comparison. Even after *United States* v. *Lopez*, the Supreme Court's interpretation of Congress's interstate commerce power has been so expansive that almost every imaginable piece of federal legislation is authorized by the commerce power. See 514 US 549, 567 (1995) (refusing to hold that "the possession of a gun in a local school zone" reflects economic activity that rises to the level of interstate commerce and thus implicates the commerce power); see also *United States* v. *Morrison*, 529 US 598 (2000) (holding a federal statutory remedy for the victims of gender-motivated violence unconstitutional because it did not comport with the Commerce Clause). Cf. *Gonzales* v. *Raich*, 545 US 1 (2005) (upholding the constitutionality of the Federal Controlled Substances Act as applied to intrastate, non-commercial cultivation and possession of marijuana under the Commerce Clause). Some of those concerned about this development (notably Justice Thomas) have argued for a radical reorientation of the Court's jurisprudence. See *Lopez, ibid.*,

But that does not answer the question whether a major revamping of First Amendment jurisprudence is in fact desirable, and none of the arguments in this chapter squarely addresses that question. The analysis in this chapter does, however, highlight the stakes involved (because of the growing importance of algorithms in our lives), and in that way may provide a boost to arguments for a radical reorientation of the existing jurisprudence. That said, it would be a fairly small boost. Encompassing algorithm-based decisions within the ambit of the Free Speech Clause is a natural and modest step. The profusion of computer algorithms designed by humans to do the work other humans once did may alter our economy,[108] but it does not significantly change the First Amendment analysis. So long as humans are making substantive editorial decisions, inserting computers into the process does not eliminate the communication via that editing.[109] Arguments for a radical revamping should stand or fall on other grounds.

at 584 (Thomas J. concurring) (arguing that the Court "ought to temper [its] Commerce Clause jurisprudence"); *Morrison, ibid.*, at 627 (Thomas J. concurring) (criticizing the Court's "view that the Commerce Clause has virtually no limits" and advocating for a shift to a "standard more consistent with the original understanding"). Others have argued for drawing ad hoc, and arguably arbitrary, lines to limit the expansion of that power. Both of these positions were articulated (minus any concession of possible arbitrariness) in arguments against the constitutionality of the Affordable Care Act. Some advocates argued for a radical revamping of Commerce Clause jurisprudence. See, e.g., Brief for Virginia Delegate Bob Marshall *et al.* as Amici Curiae in Support of Respondents at 11–14, *Dep't of Health & Human Servs.* v. *Florida*, 567 US 519 (2012) (No. 11–398), 2012 WL 484059 (February 13, 2012) (arguing for a reconsideration of the Court's Commerce Clause cases, particularly *Wickard* v. *Filburn*, 317 US 111 (1942), and *United States* v. *Darby*, 312 US 100 (1941)). Many more pushed for a distinction between activity and inactivity. They often acknowledged that the distinction was ad hoc, and that they preferred a more fundamental rethinking of Commerce Clause jurisprudence. But they saw the action–inaction distinction as a tenable way of limiting Commerce Clause expansion without entailing a radical reorientation of the jurisprudence. See, e.g., R. E. Barnett, Commandeering the People: Why the Individual Health Insurance Mandate Is Unconstitutional (2010) 5 *NY Univ. J. Law Liberty* 581, 619 ("Of course, like the distinction between economic and noneconomic activity, the activity–inactivity distinction would not perfectly distinguish between incidental and remote exercises of implied powers. But, however imperfect, some such line must be drawn to preserve chapter I's scheme of limited and enumerated powers."). Whatever the merits of that argument in the Commerce Clause context, I think drawing a line between algorithm-based and human-based decisions for purposes of First Amendment coverage is so arbitrary as to be undesirable.

108 See, e.g., E. Brynjolfsson and A. McAfee, *Race against the Machine: How the Digital Revolution Is Accelerating Innovation, Driving Productivity, and Irreversibly Transforming Employment and the Economy* (Digital Frontier Press, 2011) (arguing that innovations in information technology will, inter alia, destroy many jobs); Andrew Yang's 2020 Presidential Campaign (same).

109 Or so our computer overlords would have us believe. See Jeopardy! (ABC television broadcast, February 15, 2011) (documenting the reaction of Ken Jennings, the most successful Jeopardy! player of all time, upon realizing that he was going to lose to an IBM computer named Watson). In his final answer, Jennings paraphrased the venerable Simpsons: "I for one welcome our new computer overlords" (*ibid.*). See also M. Maerz, Watson Wins "Jeopardy!" Finale; Ken Jennings Welcomes "Our New Computer Overlords," *Los Angeles Times* (February 16, 2011), https://latimesblogs.latimes.com/showtracker/2011/02/watson-jeopardy-finale-man-vs-machine-showdown.html; Ratzule, Watson the New Computer Overlord, *YouTube* (February 16, 2011), www.youtube.com/watch?v=Skfw282fJak (video of Jennings's answer and Watson's victory).

29

Algorithmic Analysis of Social Behavior for Profiling, Ranking, and Assessment

Nizan Geslevich Packin and Yafit Lev-Aretz

In this chapter, we look at the global development of "people-scoring" and its implications. Unlike traditional credit scoring, which is used to evaluate individuals' financial trustworthiness, social scoring seeks to comprehensively rank individuals based on social, reputational, and behavioral attributes. The implications of widespread social scoring are far-reaching and troubling. Bias and error, discrimination, manipulation, privacy violations, excessive market power, and social segregation are only some of the concerns we have discussed and elaborated on in previous works.[1] In this chapter, we describe the global shift from financial scores to social credit, and show how, notwithstanding constitutional, statutory, and regulatory safeguards, the United States and other Western democracies are not as far from social credit as we seem to believe.

TRADITIONAL CREDIT

In the United States, a credit score is a statistically devised numerical expression representing an individual's financial health.[2] Unlike many other countries, the American financial system is based on credit-scoring mechanisms. Credit-scoring systems compute the specific level of risk that a person or entity brings to a particular transaction through equating a potential borrower's weighted values with an actual borrower's weighted values.[3] Historically, the retail and banking sectors were the first to evaluate financial trustworthiness of potential borrowers in the United States.[4] Over time, as the practice became more common, banks outsourced the lending decision-making process to individual experts, and later to specialized financial entities that have made credit analysis their core business.[5]

The current industry standard for consumer credit is based on the Fair Isaac & Company (FICO) scoring formula, which was developed in the 1950s and has undergone changes and improvements over the years.[6] The same FICO's scoring blueprints are used by the three

---

[1] N. G. Packin and Y. Lev-Aretz, Big Data and Social Netbanks: Are You Ready to Replace Your Bank? (2016) 53 *Hous. Law Rev.* 1211; N. G. Packin and Y. Lev-Aretz, On Social Credit and the Right to Be Unnetworked (2016) *Colum. Bus. Law Rev.* 339.

[2] See H. A. Abdou and J. Pointon, Credit Scoring, Statistical Techniques and Evaluation Criteria: A Review of the Literature (2011) 18 *Intell. Syst. Account. Finance Manag.* 59, 62, for the different definitions of credit scoring.

[3] See K. O'Neill, *Weapons of Math Destruction* (Penguin, 2016), p. 152: "[A] consumer credit score is calculated to represent the particular level of risk that the individual consumer poses in a commercial transaction."

[4] D. K. Citron and F. Pasquale, The Scored Society: Due Process for Automated Predictions (2014) 89 *Wash. Law Rev.* 1, 8–9 (presenting the history of credit scoring systems).

[5] See *ibid.*, noting that experts were eventually "entrusted to make lending decisions" and that specialized finance companies "entered the mix" after the Second World War.

[6] See N. Cullerton, Behavioral Credit Scoring (2013) 101 *Geo. Law J.* 807, 810.

major credit bureaus: Equifax, TransUnion, and Experian, yet each agency applies its own modified model.[7] Furthermore, specific industries use their own versions of credit scores.[8] One example of such industry-specific model is VantageScore, which is predominantly used in the credit-card underwriting and certain personal-financial applications industries.[9]

Algorithmic scoring methods for all credit scores are considered proprietary and protected as trade secrets.[10] The rationale behind trade secrecy protection for credit scoring is to prevent competitors from copying scoring models and to avoid gamesmanship by scored individuals.[11] However, the lack of a standard mathematical model has further contributed to the lack of transparency in the credit industry.[12] The opacity surrounding existing scoring methods has been criticized for preventing consumers, advocates, and regulators from challenging those models.[13] Nevertheless, existing credit-scoring systems have become an acceptable way of measuring one's financial health and are generally considered fair and objective.

The Fair Credit Reporting Act (FCRA) was enacted to address the concerns triggered by the massive collection of personal information by increasing transparency in a highly opaque credit reporting industry.[14] The FCRA requires credit repositories and "consumer reporting agencies" to assure maximum possible accuracy of the information contained in the credit report.[15] Consumers also have the legal right to access their credit reports, dispute their completeness or accuracy, request corrections, and, when resolutions are not achieved, annotate their records.[16] Enacted in 2003, the Fair and Accurate Credit Transactions Act (FACTA) further mandates complementary annual credit reports to all consumers, offers additional protections against fraud, and prescribes a procedure for clearing credit scores of identity theft victims.[17] The Equal Credit Opportunity Act (ECOA) prohibits credit discrimination on the basis of race, color, religion, national origin, sex, marital status, age, or the receipt of public assistance.[18] Under the ECOA, creditors may ask individuals for information about the characteristics listed above, but are prohibited from using that information in the context of credit decisions.[19] Individuals who deal with organizations or people who regularly extend credit, such as banks, small loan and finance companies, retail and department stores, credit card companies, and credit unions, enjoy various ECOA-mandated legal protections.[20]

---

7   See K. Eggert, The Great Collapse: How Securitization Caused the Subprime Meltdown (2009) 41 *Conn. Law Rev.* 1257, 1270 (noting that the three separate credit agencies can produce varying scores due to their distinct models).

8   See T. Clemans, Foreword (2013) 46 *Suffolk Univ. Law Rev.* 761, 782 (explaining that there are "dozens of specialty versions of credit scores that are honed for specific industries").

9   See *ibid.* (describing the creation of VantageScore and its competition). But see O'Neill, above note 3, pp. 172–3 (arguing that the lack of a uniform credit model was "largely eviscerated" by the development of VantageScore).

10   See A. Osovsky, The Misconception of the Consumer as a Homo Economicus: A Behavioral-Economic Approach to Consumer Protection in the Credit-Reporting System (2013) 46 *Suffolk Univ. Law Rev.* 881, 888.

11   Federal Reserve Board Releases Staff Paper On Credit Scoring, Consumer Credit Guide (CCH), ¶ 97,708, 1979 WL 486735 (December 28, 1979).

12   See O'Neill, above note 3, p. 172.

13   F. Pasquale, Restoring Transparency to Automated Authority (2011) 9 *J. Telecomm. High Technol. Law* 235, 248.

14   FCRA, 15 USC § 1681 (2012).

15   *Ibid.*, § 1681e(b): "Whenever a consumer reporting agency prepares a consumer report it shall follow reasonable procedures to assure maximum possible accuracy of the information concerning the individual about whom the report relates."

16   *Ibid.*, § 1681g(a)(1), and § 1681i ("Procedure in Case of Disputed Accuracy").

17   FACTA of 2003, Pub. L. No. 108–59, 117 Stat. 1952 (codified as amended across sections of 15 USC) (amending the FCRA of 1970).

18   The ECOA is a US law (codified at 15 USC § 1691 et seq.); see also Your Equal Credit Opportunity Rights, Fed. Trade Comm'n (January 2013), www.consumer.ftc.gov/articles/0347-your-equal-credit-opportunity-rights.

19   See *ibid.*

20   See *ibid.*

Following the 2008 financial crisis and subsequent recession, Congress enacted the Dodd-Frank Wall Street Reform and Consumer Protection Act,[21] which offered additional legal protections to increase the transparency of the credit-gauging process.[22] The Dodd-Frank Act transferred a significant part of the Federal Trade Commission's (FTC) enforcement authority over the credit bureaus to the Consumer Financial Protection Bureau (CFPB).[23] However, there is still some overlap of enforcement power over FCRA consumer regulations between the two regulatory agencies.[24] The CFPB, which is entrusted with overseeing "larger participant[s] of a market for other consumer financial products or services,"[25] issued a rule to classify credit-reporting agencies as "larger participants."[26] The meaning of this rule is that credit-reporting agencies are subject to the same supervision process applied to banks.[27]

BIG DATA, AI, AND SOCIAL CREDIT

Data-Driven Lending

In addition to the opacity surrounding current scoring models and the regulatory overlap, traditional credit scoring has failed the financial inclusion battle. As traditional models look to the past to predict the future, they miss out on a significant group of individuals. This group includes both "credit invisible," who do not have a credit record with one of the nationwide consumer reporting agencies, and individuals who have a partial credit record with too little, old, or unreliable information.[28] A 2015 CFPB report estimated that 26 million consumers in the United States were credit invisible, and an additional 19 million consumers had unscorable credit records either because of an insufficient credit history (9.9 million) or because of a lack of recent history (9.6 million).[29] Financial inclusion remains a problem notwithstanding constant attempts by governments, international financial organizations, and private sector players to scale up the number of "scorable" consumers.[30] As a result, the economic behavior of the unscorable population, which amounts to a significant share of the economy, is marginalized. Unscored consumers are rarely eligible for lending services such as auto loans, mortgages, and student loans. They also have no access to short-term credit for routine or emergency necessities. Consequentially, these individuals use costly alternatives like payday loans with excessive fees, high interest rates, and draconian terms.

[21]   See Dodd-Frank Wall Street Reform and Consumer Protection Act, Pub. L. No. 111–203, § 932, 124 Stat. 1376, 1872–83 (2010).

[22]   J. Manns, Downgrading Rating Agency Reform (2013) 81 *Geo. Wash. Law Rev.* 749, 771.

[23]   12 USC § 5581(5) (2012). For more on the agency, see, e.g., T. J. Zywicki, The Consumer Financial Protection Bureau: Savior or Menace? (2013) 81 *Geo. Wash. Law Rev.* 856, 860.

[24]   See, e.g., 12 USC § 5514(c)(3) (2012).

[25]   12 USC § 5514(a)(1)(B) (Supp. IV 2011).

[26]   P 151–620 CFPB to Begin Supervising Credit Reporting Agencies (12 CFR § 1090) (July 20, 2012).

[27]   See C. Dougherty, Consumer Bureau to Supervise Debt Collectors, Credit Bureaus, *Bloomberg* (February 16, 2012), www.bloomberg.com/news/articles/2012-02-16/consumer-bureau-to-supervise-debt-collectors.

[28]   Data Point: The Geography of Credit Invisibility, The Bureau of Consumer Financial Protection's Office of Research (September 17, 2018), pp. 4–5, www.consumerfinance.gov/data-research/research-reports/data-point-geography-credit-invisibility/.

[29]   Data Point: Credit Invisibles, The CFPB Office of Research (May 2015), https://files.consumerfinance.gov/f/201505_cfpb_data-point-credit-invisibles.pdf.

[30]   R. Sanabria, To Bank the Unbanked, Start Using Alternative Data, Center for Financial Inclusion (August 14, 2018), www.centerforfinancialinclusion.org/to-bank-the-unbanked-start-using-alternative-data (in addition to governments that are promoting this goal, partnering together to increase financial inclusion are private sector players such as the world's biggest banks, as well as international financial organizations including the World Bank and the Institute for International Finance).

Because access to credit is vital for financial advancement and asset building, the unscorable population has represented an exceptional business opportunity for lenders.[31] The microfinance industry was quick to realize that establishing revenue-generating loans methods for the financially underserved would yield more capital than corporate philanthropy could have ever returned.[32] The great economic potential of the financially underserved market has driven lenders to seek alternative segmentation and scoring techniques in order to admit additional consumers into the financial mainstream.[33] Technological advancements around big data analytics, machine learning, and artificial intelligence have offered a promising alternative to base credit predictions on factors outside the traditional credit history domain. By increasing the accuracy of traditional models on the one hand and adding new credit measures to boost financial inclusion on the other, big data analytics have transformed the credit market. Acknowledging the need to cater the financially underserved community, FICO began offering FICO Score XD, which looks at alternative data, such as telecommunications and utilities data and public record information not available in traditional credit files.[34] According to FICO, with FICO Score XD, the company was able to score over 26.5 million previously unscorable consumer files.[35]

In addition to providing improved risk predictions, data-driven lending encompasses additional scoring indicators that traditional methods have never looked at. Searching for correlations and insights beyond strictly financial behavior, marketplace lenders have used algorithms to score thousands of potential credit variables in relation to an individual's attributes and behavior.[36] For example, fintech company ZestFinance, which specializes in AI-powered underwriting, found that people who fill out the loan application in capital letters are riskier borrowers than those who write in upper and lowercase.[37]

Social Credit

One particularly attractive source of alternative data is behavioral data gleaned from social media and social networking information. Education, career path, and the perceived strength of social ties exemplify behavioral and reputational indicators that have gained traction as indicators of creditworthiness. This type of financial-social credit is on the rise, with an increasing number of companies attempting to unpack the predictive power of online social activities. UK-based Hello Soda offers a product named PROFILE, which scores individuals for creditworthiness by identifying personality attributes from the language exhibited across their social media.[38] Singapore-based LenddoEFL produces a score that "complements traditional underwriting tools, like credit scores, because it relies exclusively on non-traditional data derived from a customer's social data and online behavior."[39] In its early days, Lenddo required users

---

[31] Packin and Lev-Aretz, Social Credit, above note 1, p. 13.
[32] *Ibid.*
[33] *Ibid.*
[34] J. Gaskin, Leveraging Alternative Data to Extend Credit to More Borrowers, *FICO Blog* (May 22, 2019), www.fico.com/blogs/risk-compliance/leveraging-alternative-data-to-extend-credit-to-more-borrowers/.
[35] FICO Continues to Expand Access to Credit with New FICO Score XD 2, *FICO Newsroom* (March 29, 2018), www.fico.com/en/newsroom/fico-continues-to-expand-access-to-credit-with-new-fico-score-xd-2.
[36] Packin and Lev-Aretz, Social Credit, above note 1, pp. 14–16.
[37] J. Lippert, ZestFinance Issues Small, High-Rate Loans, Uses Big Data to Weed Out Deadbeats, *Washington Post* (October 11, 2014), www.washingtonpost.com/business/zestfinance-issues-small-high-rate-loans-uses-big-data-to-weed-out-deadbeats/2014/10/10/e34986b6-4d71-11e4-aa5e-7153e466a02d_story.html?utm_term=.399bda9c05a1.
[38] See https://hellosoda.com/.
[39] Credit Scoring: The LenddoScore, Lenddo, www.lenddo.com/products.html.

to authorize access to their social media profiles in order to not only evaluate financial risk, but also penalize default and reward repayment.[40] Today, Lenddo offers an app that creditors can require loan applicants to install on their phones to track online behavior, and send back data on, for example, applicants' precise location, the content of text messages, and their browsing history.[41] In 2017, Lenddo merged with psychometric credit scoring company Entrepreneurial Finance Lab (EFL), stating the merger would allow people "to use their digital profiles and personality traits to increase their financial options."[42] EFL uses psychometric testing, meaning it analyzes applicants' answers to an online quiz, and looks at factors like the time it took them to answer the questions.[43]

In 2018, the Student Loans Company (SLC), a non-profit government-owned organization that administers loans to students in the United Kingdom, was criticized for using social media to determine eligibility for student loans.[44] German fintech lender Kreditech uses rich datasets to uncover a borrower's underlying personality by looking at information from social networks, which is voluntarily shared by the applicant.[45] Whether an applicant's friends are financially responsible, how applicants spend their time, their location, and the sophistication of the language of their posts are all factors that are fed into Kreditech's scoring model.[46] In late 2018, the digital lender was licensed by the Reserve Bank of India to operate as a non-banking finance company for digital lending business and app-based financing.[47] Social Lender, a Nigerian lending start-up, looks at social reputation on mobile, online, and social media platforms to evaluate financial risk.[48] The company considers factors such as the amount of time an individual has been on a social networking platform, the people he or she is engaged with, their network, the communities he or she is involved with, and more.[49] Loan seekers can also boost their reputation score by adding more social data sources like Twitter or LinkedIn.[50] The company also allows loan candidates to add Social Referee(s), who can vouch for the candidates, and/or Guarantors to pay in case they default.[51]

[40] Packin and Lev-Aretz, Social Credit, above note 1, p. 17.
[41] R. Eveleth, Credit Scores Could Soon Get Even Creepier and More Biased, *Vice* (June 13, 2019), www.vice.com/en_us/article/zmpgp9/credit-scores-could-soon-get-even-creepier-and-more-biased; and Fintech's Dirty Little Secret? Lenddo, Facebook and the Challenge of Identity, Privacy International (October 23, 2018), https://privacyinternational.org/feature/2323/fintechs-dirty-little-secret-lenddo-facebook-and-challenge-identity.
[42] Lenddo and EFL Team Up to Lead Financial Inclusion Revolution, *Cision PRweb* (October 17, 2017), www.prweb.com/releases/2017/10/prweb14806664.htm.
[43] Fintech's Dirty Little Secret? above note 41.
[44] R. Adams, Student Loans Firm Accused of "KGB Tactics" for Assessing Eligibility, *The Guardian* (October 30, 2018), www.theguardian.com/education/2018/oct/30/student-loans-firm-accused-of-kgb-tactics-for-assessing-eligibility.
[45] J. Vasagar, Kreditech: A Credit Check by Social Media, *Financial Times* (January 19, 2016), www.ft.com/content/12dc4cda-ae59-11e5-b955-1a1d298b6250.
[46] *Ibid.*
[47] Kreditech Licensed by Reserve Bank of India to Operate as NBFC, Kreditech Press Release (October 11, 2018), www.kreditech.com/press-releases/kreditech-licensed-by-reserve-bank-of-india-to-operate-as-nbfc.
[48] See www.sociallenderng.com/.
[49] L. Olusola, Your Social Credibility Can Get You a Loan, *The Guardian* (May 10, 2018), https://guardian.ng/features/your-social-credibility-can-get-you-a-loan/.
[50] *Ibid.*
[51] *Ibid.*

Governmental Social Evaluations

The use of social information for individual assessment goes beyond the private sector. The government is also engaging in algorithmic-based data analysis of public and commercial data pools, which also include social media, in various big data analytics programs.

Tax

Tasked with issues such as tax collection, the payment of state support, and the administration of regulatory systems, those agencies have reportedly started analyzing individuals' and businesses' online footprints to better appreciate their financial standing and tax liabilities.[52] For example, the Internal Revenue Service (IRS), which traditionally has used third-party information to verify information provided by taxpayers being audited, created in 2011 the Office of Compliance Analytics. This office is a division of the IRS that is meant to build an advanced analytics program for reducing tax fraud and improper refund payments.[53] Historically, the laws permitting the IRS to gain records from third parties were written prior to the creation of social media, and needless to say, before technology had advanced to the stage where it is today. "Modern technologies are creating 'minutely detailed records' of our existence, increasingly facilitating the 'persistent, continuous and indiscriminate monitoring of our daily lives."[54]

Some examples are how the IRS is using individuals' Facebook posts to determine if they are lying to the government about income or tax issues, such as if a businessman writes off a family vacation as a business trip, or if an employer is "spending lavishly while claiming his business is currently unprofitable." Likewise, businesses are not immune from the spying as well. If a company's webpage shows off new fancy equipment or vehicles while being behind on payroll taxes or suspiciously claiming beneficial business write-offs, that business may find itself needing to answer some questions.[55]

The possibility of approaching data-brokers and the ability to easily pay for data about most individuals out there in general, and for all sorts of specific pieces of information in particular,

---

[52] K. A. Houser and D. Sanders (2017) 19 *Vand. J. Ent. Technol. Law* 817 (examining the privacy issues resulting from the IRS's big data analytics program as well as the potential violations of federal law).

[53] $3 Trillion Lost to Tax Evasion in Past Decade: Wealthy Cheat Most, Demos (2012), www.demos.org/blog/3-trillion-lost-tax-evasion-past-decade-wealthy-cheat-most; B. Robinson, Wise Practitioner – Predictive Analytics Interview Series: Jeff Butler at IRS Research, Analysis, and Statistics Organization, *Predictive Analytics Times* (2015), www.predictiveanalyticsworld.com/patimes/wise-practitioner-predictive-analytics-interview-series-jeff-butler-at-irs-research-analysis-and-statistics-organization09022015/6243/. The creation of this division is not surprising. The IRS has already stated in recent years that it believes that technological innovation is central to the future of tax administration. See, e.g., D. Shulman (former Commissioner of Internal Revenue), Shulman Addresses Major Trends Affecting Tax Administrations, Tax Notes (May 19, 2014), p. 835. In particular, the IRS is looking to "big data" analytics to improve IRS services in a range of areas, and even more innovative applications may become possible. New IRS Strategic Plan Emphasizes Better IT, "Big Data" to Improve Taxpayer Services, 33 Tax Mgmt. Wkly. Rep. 887 (July 7, 2014); J. H. Kahn and G. D. Polsky, The End of Cash, the Income Tax, and the Next 100 Years (2013) 41 *Fla. St. Univ. Law Rev.* 159, 171 ("On the one hand, the increasing prevalence of electronic payment systems should bolster the income tax by substantially reducing the tax gap and mitigating the distortions caused by the cash economy. On the other hand, technological innovation and the corresponding evolution of attitudes towards privacy could make a progressive retail sales tax quite feasible, which might spell the end of the income tax").

[54] M. Hatfield, Taxation and Surveillance: An Agenda (2015) 17 *Yale J. Law Technol.* 319, 322, citing D. K. Citron and D. Gray, Addressing the Harm of Total Surveillance: A Reply to Professor Neil Richards (2013) 126 *Harv. Law Rev.* 262; N. M. Richards, The Dangers of Surveillance (2013) 126 *Harv. Law Rev.* 1934.

[55] T. Huskerson, Tax Season 2018 – The IRS Is Checking Your Facebook Page, *On Tech Street* (March 5, 2018), https://ontechstreet.com/2018/03/tax-season-2018-the-irs-is-checking-your-facebook-page/.

has created a reality where individuals are losing control over who has access to private information about them. This is especially relevant when that viewer is a government's taxation authority. Therefore, scholars have wondered if there is any harm that stems from the IRS aggregating taxpayer information if it does not use it for some nefarious purpose.[56] And, at least one scholar has responded to the situation where tax information flows extensively without any significant privacy critique, by labeling tax privacy as "a bomb waiting to go off."[57]

Using its new division, the IRS uses data analytics to mine all data available online, including information from social networks.[58] This information is then added to the existing information that is used to identify non-compliant taxpayer behaviors. Similarly, in recent years, it has been reported that in the United Kingdom, Her Majesty's Revenue & Customs (HMRC), a non-ministerial department of the government responsible for taxation and minimum-wage-related issues, developed a new software to trawl billions of pieces of information to search and find individuals who have underpaid tax. Reportedly, this system could get access to even more data, which can be shared with approximately sixty different countries.[59]

Disability and Legal Accommodations

Somewhat like the government agencies responsible for taxation issues, the Social Security Administration (SSA), an independent agency of the US Federal Government that administers Social Security, a social insurance program consisting of retirement, disability, and survivors' benefits, has also started using social media to further investigate and rank applicants and citizens.[60] In particular, this happens in connection with the Social Security Disability Insurance (SSDI), a program for which the SSA is responsible and which pays monthly benefits to individuals that have become disabled before reaching retirement age and are unable to work. The SSDI provides a small amount of monthly financial support – the average is about $1,200 – for individuals who are assessed and declared to be sufficiently disabled, based on one's ability to work and the severity of a relevant condition.[61] The standards to qualify for SSDI are extremely high[62] and many disabled people who cannot work find themselves needing to wait for years to receive benefits. But, like in all aid programs, there are also people who try to cheat or illegally take advantage of the system. Attempting to address overpayment cases, media reports have shown that even though the SSA administered several billions in fraudulent payments between 2011 and 2015, those funds amounted to just

[56]   See, e.g., A. Thimmesch, Tax Privacy (2017) 90 *Temple Law Rev.* 375, 377.

[57]   R. Calo, Privacy and Markets: A Love Story (2015) 91 *Notre Dame Law Rev.* 649, 680.

[58]   D. Kerr, Tax Dodgers Beware: IRS Could Be Watching Your Social Media, CNet (2014), www.cnet.com/news/tax-dodgers-beware-irs-could-be-watching-your-social-media/.

[59]   R. Dyson, What Does The Taxman Know about You, Your Finances and Your Lifestyle?, *The Telegraph* (June 25, 2015), www.telegraph.co.uk/finance/personalfinance/tax/11697816/What-does-the-taxman-know-about-you-your-finances-and-your-lifestyle.html.

[60]   See, e.g., M. Miller, U.S. Government Weighs Social-Media Snooping to Detect Social Security Fraud, *Reuters* (March 29, 2019), www.reuters.com/article/us-column-miller-socialmedia/u-s-government-weighs-social-media-snooping-to-detect-social-security-fraud-idUSKCN1RA12R.

[61]   Chart Book: Social Security Disability Insurance, Center on Budget and Policy Priorities (August 27, 2018), www.cbpp.org/research/social-security/chart-book-social-security-disability-insurance.

[62]   A. Smith, Long Waits and Long Odds for Those Who Need Social Security Disability, NPR (June 13, 2017), www.npr.org/sections/health-shots/2017/06/13/531207430/people-with-unseen-disabilities-could-suffer-under-new-government-rules.

over 1 percent of total disability outlays.[63] Nevertheless, despite the importance of the program, and the normal overpayment rates, in 2019, the US government has announced its decision to launch a new program that will help check up on claimants on social media outlets such as Facebook and Twitter, in order to root out fraud and abuse in the disability program.[64]

The new online spying program is intended to solve a problem, which is what seems to be a prevalent disability fraud. Using algorithms, it expands the federal government's ability to examine the social media accounts of Americans suffering from all sorts of disabilities, and includes assessing posts and photos posted online that in our view do not always provide reliable evidence of individuals' current physical condition.[65] The plan, which appeared in the 2019 annual SSA budget proposal,[66] is dependent on the government's ability to find pictures and posts that could add more information as to making the determination of whether or not individuals are faking a disability, and corresponds with the government intentions to cut SSDI.[67] But, even if there was evidence of a large-scale malfeasance and fraud, trying to adjudicate disability by monitoring or spying on the social media accounts of those suspected to be conning government systems, pretending to be disabled, cannot be viewed positively. It is, at best, an exercise in bias confirmation and, at worst, represents an expansion of the surveillance state concept, which is targeting the most vulnerable among us.

The new program is designed to solve a problem, which is what appears to be a widespread disability fraud that some experts say does not even exist. In fact, there is no evidence of such large-scale malfeasance. Trying to adjudicate disability by closely inspecting and following the social media accounts of those suspected to be conning the system, pretending to be disabled, cannot be viewed positively either way. It will be, at best, an exercise in bias confirmation and, at worst, represent a major expansion of the surveillance state, which is targeting America's most vulnerable, often very physically limited citizens.[68]

Government Lenders

The SLC, as noted above, has been accused of monitoring social media accounts of students as part of its anti-fraud drive.[69] SLC randomly identified 150 estranged students, who were then classified as being potentially high risk, and asked to provide evidence that they no longer had contact with their families.[70] The anti-fraud exercise resulted in some students losing funding and dropping out of their universities despite no finding of guilt against

[63] M. Ye Hee Lee, White House Budget Director's Claim that Social Security Disability Is "Very Wasteful," *Washington Post* (April 7, 2017), www.washingtonpost.com/news/fact-checker/wp/2017/04/07/white-house-bud get-directors-claim-that-social-security-disability-is-very-wasteful/?utm_term=.6db11d9b19c5.

[64] D. M. Perry, The Trump Administration Wants to Snoop on Disabled Americans, *Medium* (March 21, 2019), https://medium.com/s/story/the-trump-administration-wants-to-snoop-on-disabled-americans-f2fcaae78ad3.

[65] R. Pear, On Disability and on Facebook? Uncle Sam Wants to Watch What You Post, *New York Times* (March 10, 2019), www.nytimes.com/2019/03/10/us/politics/social-security-disability-trump-facebook.html.

[66] See www.ssa.gov/budget/FY20Files/2020BO.pdf.

[67] J. Parmuk, Trump Pledged to Protect Medicare and Medicaid, But His 2020 Budget Calls for Major Spending Cuts, *CNBC* (March 12, 2019), www.cnbc.com/2019/03/12/trump-2020-budget-proposes-reduced-medicare-and-medicaid-spending.html.

[68] *Ibid.*

[69] S. Weale, Student Loans Company "Spied on Vulnerable Students' Social Media," *The Guardian* (August 2, 2018), www.theguardian.com/education/2018/aug/02/student-loans-company-spied-on-vulnerable-students-social-media.

[70] *Ibid.*

them.[71] In one case, a parent's Christmas gift documented on Facebook disqualified a student from being classified as estranged and receiving a maintenance loan without means-testing.[72]

SLC justified its gathering of evidence from social media to determine eligibility for student loans in that personal Facebook accounts are a public source of information that are reasonable to inspect and look at.[73] When questioned by members of the UK Parliament, Christian Brodie, the SLC Chair, insisted: "We have a duty to make sure that the taxpayers' funds are being properly disbursed, and if there are public sources of information the terms and conditions on which people apply allow us to look at public sources of information."[74]

Financial Behavior – Civic Sanctions

Although not a result of a social credit score, in the United States, examples of how the government and local administrations factor individuals' behaviors into the assessment of these individuals' rights and privileges can be found as well. One particular illustration is how, since 2013, the New York State Department of Taxation and Finance and the New York State Department of Motor Vehicles (DMV) have been working together in furtherance of a Driver's License Suspension Program that blacklists people who have misbehaved according to New York State law.[75] The program's initiative takes the position that driving is a privilege and if individuals do not pay their state taxes as required by the law, they could and should get labeled accordingly and lose certain privileges. Therefore, people who owe $10,000 or more in delinquent taxes to New York State just might find themselves needing to start paying right away, or have their driver's license suspended until the liabilities are paid or a satisfactory payment arrangement with the Commissioner has been reached.[76] Moreover, once the license suspension has occurred, under DMV rules, any taxpayer with a suspended license who drives during the suspension may be subject to arrest and penalties. And while a taxpayer may apply for a restricted license, such a license enables that person to travel only to and from work, school, medical appointments, the DMV, and childcare related to employment or education,[77] after which the taxpayer must return directly home.[78]

Like all other ranking systems, New York's Driver's License Suspension Program has been highly successful in impacting people's behavior and decision-making processes. The Department of Taxation and Finance reported that since it commenced in July 2013, and as of December 8, 2015, the revenue collections from the Driver's License Suspension Program exceeded $288 million.[79] This hugely successful operation resulted in New York

---

[71]　*Ibid.*

[72]　Adams, above note 45.

[73]　*Ibid.*

[74]　*Ibid.*

[75]　NY Tax Law § 171-v.

[76]　Thomas H. Mattox, Former Tax Commissioner of New York, has stated that "[d]river licenses are a privilege, not a right, and this program has prompted unprecedented action from tax delinquents who were otherwise ignoring their debt." See M. Godfrey, New York's Unique Approach to Tax Enforcement Working, *Tax-News* (March 20, 2014).

[77]　See Section 530 of the Vehicle and Traffic Law. Any person who gets a license suspension pursuant to Section 510 of the Vehicle and Traffic Law (including for failure to pay past-due tax liabilities, according to Vehicle and Traffic Law § 510[4][f]) can apply for a restricted use license.

[78]　NY Vehicle & Traffic Law § 530; See also Press Release, Governor Cuomo Announces Initiative to Suspend Driver Licenses of Tax Delinquents Who Owe More than $10,000 in Back Taxes, www.governor.ny.gov/news/governor-cuomo-announces-initiative-suspend-driver-licenses-tax-delinquents-who-owe-more-10000.

[79]　See Tax Section Report on New York State's Driver's License Suspension Program, The New York State Bar Association (May 5, 2016), n. 9 (referencing Argi O'Leary, Deputy Comm'r, Civ. Enforcement Div., NY St. Dep't of Tax'n and Fin. (December 15, 2015)).

Governor Cuomo's 2015–2016 New York State Executive Budget initiating two expansions to the Driver's License Suspension Program, which have eventually not been enacted, but focused on: (1) lowering the tax liability threshold for suspension of the tax debtor's driver's license to $5,000; and (2) extending the program to apply to suspend other professional licenses that are required until owing individuals pay their past-due tax liabilities before their licenses are issued or renewed.[80]

BEYOND FINANCIAL: SOCIAL CREDIT

Public

China

In comparison to the United States, many countries use different types of financial consumer credit ratings, and recent years have also seen a proliferation of ranking systems in relation to various online platforms, but the manner in which social credit has been introduced in China is much more extreme than in other places. The emerging Chinese social credit system strives to be a uniform social rating based on penalty and award mechanisms, and has been gradually becoming a widespread program for almost all citizens to partake in by 2020.[81] Based on data obtained on every Chinese citizen's "finances, social media activities, credit history, health records, online purchases, tax payments, legal matters, and people … [one chooses to] associate with, in addition to images gathered from China's 200 million surveillance cameras and facial recognition software,"[82] coders have worked to develop an algorithm that calculates a score for each person – individual or business entity – reflecting how "trustworthy" that person is.

As a product of the different kinds of data collection and computation, people are assigned a numeric score that can fluctuate based on the individual's financial behavior, activities, and even social interactions. With regard to the long-term impact of this social credit system, citizens who have a lower score can face certain hurdles in their day-to-day life, as well as negatively impact the lives of the people interacting and transacting with them. Moreover, there are various ways in which the Chinese social credit system can penalize individuals who are perceived to be wrong-doers, and have done things like trying to ride public transportation without a ticket, loitering in front of boarding gates, or even smoking in no-smoking areas.[83] The sanctions that Chinese citizens can get under the new system for their misdeeds can include, for example, the ability of students who apply to prestigious Chinese universities to be accepted at the schools if they have family members that have a less than optimal social score.[84] Similarly, millions of people with low scores have suffered from government-declared travel restrictions, including getting blocked from buying tickets for domestic flights or business-class train carriages, and getting barred from accessing luxury travel options.[85]

---

[80] *Ibid.*, fn. 11.
[81] B. Marr, Chinese Social Credit Score: Utopian Big Data Bliss or Black Mirror on Steroids?, *Forbes* (January 21, 2019), www.forbes.com/sites/bernardmarr/2019/01/21/chinese-social-credit-score-utopian-big-data-bliss-or-black-mirror-on-steroids/.
[82] *Ibid.*
[83] A. Ma, China Has Started Ranking Citizens with a Creepy "Social Credit" System – Here's What You Can Do Wrong, and the Embarrassing, Demeaning Ways They Can Punish You, *Business Insider* (October 29, 2018), www.businessinsider.com/china-social-credit-system-punishments-and-rewards-explained-2018-4.
[84] *Ibid.*
[85] *Ibid.*

But the Chinese government is not just seeking to penalize wrong-doers. It also wants to reward people for taking actions that it believes reflect and promote desired behavior among its citizens. This is one of the goals as the People's Republic of China's Communist government has long had a deep-rooted belief in the superiority of an authoritarian relationship between the state and its citizens as a way of evading disarray and minimizing criminal activities.

Recognized for revolutionizing China's system of credit, Huang Wenyun, a Shenzhen small electronics company owner, was first faced with the magnitude of credit determination during a trip to the United States in 1999. While traveling in the United States, she realized that "Americans take credit very seriously, where a powerful credit system covers loans, property insurance, medical insurance, endowment insurance and reemployment. A person may not be able to find a job if he or she has a bad credit record."[86] Following her trip, in July 1999, Huang sent a letter to the Chinese Prime Minister at the time, Zhu Rongji, recommending a somewhat similar system of managing individual persons' credit that was quickly acknowledged and resulted in the establishment of China's original personal credit system. Urged to continue her contributions to the developing Chinese social credit system, Huang worked in collaboration with the Institute of World Economics & Politics of the Chinese Academy of Social Sciences to sponsor a Chinese credit-focused research team. The team's task was to further study the US credit system as well as the European credit schemes, and summarize its different findings.[87]

Lin Junyue was one of the young scholars who was recruited for the research team, designated as chief engineer, with a specific focus on the US credit system. After numerous trips to the United States, in early 2000, Lin's team drafted a report entitled "Towards a National System of Credit Management," proposing China's own unique system of calculating the creditworthiness levels of its citizens as well as the businesses operating in the country. Six years later, the People's Bank of China officially implemented a credit-rating system, which was inspired by that of the United States, assigning Chinese citizens a numeric score. Lin's team sought to advance the field even further by incorporating more and various kinds of data into the credit-calculating process, which would necessitate the cooperation of different state ministries.[88]

The National Development and Reform Commission authorized the research team's program proposal, and in June 2014, the social credit system project was officially announced. As the Chinese government was missing much of the necessary data to compile an accurate individual credit history for the majority the population, in 2015, the People's Bank of China recruited eight major business entities to launch their own preliminary consumer credit programs, including (1) Tencent, a massive Internet platform that hosts multiple social media networks that are permitted to operate within the Chinese borders, and (2) Alibaba, China's largest shopping platform used in conjunction with its exclusive payment system, Alipay.[89]

The People's Bank of China's original initiative of accrediting the eight major business entities with legal authorization following a six-month trial period of their respective credit systems was abandoned, with the administration citing the businesses' internal conflicts of

[86] M. Li, A Pioneer of China's Credit System, *Shenzhen Daily* (September 14, 2012), www.szdaily.com/content/ 2012-09/14/content_7198741.htm.

[87] *Ibid.*

[88] R. Raphael and L. Xi, Discipline and Punish: The Birth of China's Social-Credit System, *The Nation* (January 23, 2019), www.thenation.com/article/china-social-credit-system/.

[89] R. Avery, China's Orwellian "Social Credit" System to Be Mandatory by 2020, *Human Creative Content* (March 9, 2016), www.humancreativecontent.com/news-and-politics/2016/3/8/sypxe6b7dm2o8by6m4cwz1bh2kcszl.

interest as the reason for their inequitable credit scoring of consumers. But, despite the lack of official license, the widely reported Sesame Credit – developed by Alibaba's associate company Ant Financial – bypassed the potential legal stumbling blocks to become the prevailing credit system currently used by Chinese citizens.[90] A presently voluntary participation feature of Alipay's mobile payment app, Sesame Credit stores massive volumes of its consumers' information, covering the frequency of their online transactions in addition to data about the items they purchase or their public transportation fees, to calculate a numeric score that reflects the user's trustworthiness. Since the system's launch in January 2015, Ant Financial had assured the practical application of Sesame Credit, arguing that credit would become more accessible to Chinese consumers and enable them to have the chance to take out mortgages, get vehicle loans more easily, and have access to more opportunities.[91]

The Chinese administration argues that the country's new social credit system has been developed with the intention of creating and fostering a culture of trust, and with the end goal of collectively raising everyone's credit levels. According to the administration's statements, should the trial period prove successful, the system's full implementation will take place in 2020, and will mandate the participation of all the Chinese citizens and the business entities operating in China. With the administration's plan to incentivize the ongoing transfer of consumers' personal data from the credit firms to the government, the credit system would progress further by facilitating the exchange of consumer information between both public and private sectors.[92]

The primary diverging factor of China's credit system that continues to draw attention is found in the "social" portion of the initiative. The system considers much more than just financial data and financial behavior records. It also monitors most aspects of individuals' lives in its calculation of each person's credit score. Through widely spread electronic surveillance equipment that even includes facial recognition technology, the Chinese administration continuously monitors and collects information and conducts analysis of that data using sophisticated algorithms. Accordingly, a person's credit score is adjusted in real time based on the manner in which that person conducts his or her daily life.

Actions indicative of a model citizen, such as partaking in government events and responsibly raising a child, help raise a person's social credit score, while misdeeds that are reflective of an unprincipled lifestyle, including excessive consumption of alcohol, jaywalking, or remarking on the government in a negative light, cause one's score to drop. Those getting a high credit score are then able to enjoy benefits that guarantee an easier upward social move, such as better access to superior education and professional opportunities for themselves, as well as for family members. On the other hand, individuals who have their credit scores drop below certain benchmarks may get penalized by the administration and get blacklisted in various databases, experience slower Internet speeds, or have his or her attempts to get a loan thwarted.[93] Perhaps most disturbing about this system is that merely maintaining relations with those of lower scores would similarly drag the individual's score down.

[90] A. Little, Into the Black Mirror: The Truth Behind China's Social Credit System, *Radii* (January 21, 2019), www.radiichina.com/into-the-black-mirror-the-truth-behind-chinas-social-credit-system/.

[91] Y. Yang, Does China's Bet on Big Data for Credit Scoring Work? *Financial Times* (December 19, 2018), www.ft.com/content/ba163b00-fd4d-11e8-ac00-57a2a826423e.

[92] A. Mortenson, The Chinese Social Credit System in the Context of Datafication and Privacy, *Medium* (January 31, 2018), www.medium.com/@alexanderskyummortensen/the-chinese-social-credit-system-in-the-context-of-datafication-and-privacy-cafc9bb7923b.

[93] P. R. Brian, Here's Why China's New Social Scoring System Matters to Americans, *LifeSite* (October 17, 2018), www.lifesitenews.com/opinion/heres-why-chinas-new-social-scoring-system-matters-to-americans.

This process, while certainly innovative in the field of financial technology, gives rise to many different ethical concerns that could impact society at large. Beyond the perceived invasiveness of the system, the ease of which a social downfall can be triggered by a moment of guilty pleasure proves to be quite extreme. With the Chinese government's rigorous systematic review of its citizens' online activity, people's privacy decreases the more they contribute to their digital footprint, which is inevitable in the age of our highly technological, advanced, highly connected world.

China's employment of a social credit system speaks to the collectivist mindset of the Chinese culture, in contrast to the individualistic mentality of so many Western countries. The consequences of the way in which the Chinese phrase for the system had been broadly translated, as "social credit," instead of the equally accurate "public trust," is a good indicator of the manner in which Western societies view the initiative and its goals.[94] The negative link between having a system of credit dictated by social behaviors rather than one's financial history, as is the norm in the United States, is satisfactory for purposes of conducting a general overview of a person to spark discontent among those unfamiliar with the culture. A glaring issue with the system is the distinct lack of transparency with these algorithms and criteria, meaning the algorithms may have been designed with biased assumptions that can include discriminatory treatment of people based on issues such as ethnicity, race, and political agenda. All of these could, of course, contribute to lower a person's credit rating, without him or her even realizing or doing anything to warrant it. As the administration is the one holding and monitoring the algorithms, the range of operations runs the risk of being altered as the authorities see fit.[95]

Spillovers

IMMIGRATION: SINGAPORE, LUXEMBURG, AND CANADA. The ramifications of the Chinese social credit system are not confined within China and result in spillovers to other parts of the world. One immediate implication is evident in the use of the Chinese scores as indicators of trustworthiness for visa applications.[96] In May 2015, Alibaba's online travel platform, Alipay, began offering a credit-based online visa application service.[97] Alitrip users with a social credit score of more than 700 points who wish to travel to Singapore, would enjoy a shorter visa application process without submitting supporting documents. A month later, Alibaba announced that users with a score of 750 points traveling to Luxembourg would enjoy a similarly short and simplified visa application process.[98] In other words, countries like Singapore and Luxembourg accept personal Sesame Credit reports as a proof of financial capabilities, instead of the traditional supporting documents like bank records as proof of assets.

In 2018, Canada's immigration ministry joined Singapore and Luxembourg and it now accepts credit reports produced by Alibaba as proof of financial stability of Chinese visa

---

[94] Little, above note 90.

[95] Mortenson, above note 92.

[96] G. Kostka, What Do People in China Think about "Social Credit" Monitoring?, *Washington Post* (March 21, 2019), www.washingtonpost.com/politics/2019/03/21/what-do-people-china-think-about-social-credit-monitoring/ ?noredirect=on&utm_term=.572bd6a6b597.

[97] Alitrip Introduces Credit-Based Visa Application Service for Qualified Chinese Travelers, *Business Wire* (June 3, 2015), www.businesswire.com/news/home/20150603006726/en/Alitrip-Introduces-Credit-based-Visa-Application-Service-Qualified.

[98] *Ibid.*

applicants.[99] Sesame Credit allows eligible high-score users to obtain a personal report listing information about their finances, education, and assets, as well as contact details, from within the Alipay app.[100] To verify their identity, users undergo a facial recognition scan and submit supplementary information.[101] Only then can they print the report and submit it with their visa application.[102]

GLOBAL OPERATIONS. Chinese spillovers also affect corporations that operate globally. According to a report by the Australian Strategic Policy Institute, there are claims that social credit regulations are being used to force businesses to change their language to accommodate the political demands of the Chinese Communist Party.[103] The report claims that Chinese officials have attempted to coerce overseas Chinese citizens to install surveillance devices in their businesses.[104] Importantly, the definition of overseas Chinese and ethnic Chinese is incredibly broad and is not tied to having Chinese citizenship.[105] The Planning Outline for the Construction of a Social Credit System (2014–2020), which detailed the development and implementation of the social credit model in China, specifically listed "improving the country's soft power and international influence" and "establishing an objective, fair, reasonable and balanced international credit rating system" as one of its goals.[106] Because social credit ranks both individuals and entities, it can and arguably is used to penalize international businesses operating in China if they fail to acknowledge and adopt the views of the Chinese government.[107]

Users around the world have also brought up speculations that Chinese companies operating outside China act as importers of non-Chinese citizens' personal data.[108] For example, Mobike, a dockless bicycle sharing service, is based in China.[109] The app employs a scoring system that scores minor infringements and sends collected data to Mobike's servers in China.[110] As the privacy policy places no limits on further sharing, the data is also likely to be shared with multiple third parties, including, potentially, the Chinese government and businesses involved in the social credit system.[111]

Private

Facebook

The reality of a social credit system seems very far-fetched for a Western democracy like the United States. A host of constitutional and legal protections would make it virtually

---

[99] J. Edmiston, Canada Stokes Concerns with Decision to Accept Alipay Credit Reports on Visa Applications, *Financial Post* (December 12, 2018), https://business.financialpost.com/news/retail-marketing/alipay-and-wechat-push-into-canada-with-mobile-payment-apps.

[100] C. Udemans, Alipay's Sesame Credit Now Accepted by Canada for Visa Applications, *Technode* (November 23, 2018), https://technode.com/2018/11/23/sesame-credit-canadian-visa/.

[101] *Ibid.*

[102] *Ibid.*

[103] S. Hoffman, Australian Strategic Policy Institute, Social Credit (June 28, 2019), www.aspi.org.au/report/social-credit.

[104] *Ibid.*

[105] *Ibid.*

[106] *Ibid.*

[107] *Ibid.*

[108] A. Hanff, China's Surveillance & Social Credit System Alive & Kicking in Berlin, *Medium* (December 5, 2018), https://medium.com/@a.hanff/chinas-surveillance-social-credit-system-alive-kicking-in-berlin-6c2b3b10b197.

[109] See https://mobike.com/us/.

[110] Hanff, above note 108.

[111] *Ibid.*

impossible to implement a public, surveillance-based civic rating similar to that used in China. A private surveillance-based rating system, however, is not similarly guarded against and to some extent is already in the making in the United States. In 2015, Facebook, one of the biggest possessors of personal data in the United States and worldwide, secured a patent for technology to approve a loan based on a user's social connections.[112] According to the patent documents: "When an individual applies for a loan, the lender examines the credit ratings of members of the individual's social network who are connected to the individual through authorized nodes. If the average credit rating of these members is at least a minimum credit score, the lender continues to process the loan application. Otherwise, the loan application is rejected."[113]

Although there is currently no clear indication that Facebook plans to use the patent for lending, and although the company declined to comment on what it might do with it,[114] another patent secured by the company three years later similarly unveils potential social credit strategies. In 2018, Facebook patented technology to determine users' social class.[115] The patent plan uses various data sources and qualifiers to place a user into one of three categories: "working class," "middle class," or "upper class."[116] Considerations like a user's home ownership status, education, number of gadgets owned, and how much they use the Internet are factored in to fit a user into a specific social status category. Users who own only one gadget and show low Internet usage are likely to be labeled poor. The application further explains that the algorithm is intended for use by "third parties to increase awareness about products or services to online system users."[117]

To complete the picture and move beyond a somewhat financial-based score to a comprehensive social credit score, in August 2018, the *Washington Post* reported that Facebook assigns trustworthiness scores to its users.[118] The ratings system acts as a measure of credibility of users, but, according to Facebook, is not meant to be an absolute indicator of a person's credibility.[119] The score is merely an additional measurement among many behavioral indications that Facebook weighs to understand and predict risk.[120] The scoring system, as well as the other behavioral factors, is highly opaque. It is unclear what is factored in into a user's reputation score, whether the scoring system applies to all users, how the scores are used, and whether they have implications outside Facebook.[121]

Facebook's scoring interests are evident from the patents the companies filed for, as well as its internal scoring strategy. However, private scoring emerges everywhere. In a world of

[112] Authorization and Authentication Based on an Individual's Social Network, US Patent No. 9,100,400 (filed August 4, 2015), http://patft.uspto.gov/netacgi/nph-Parser?Sect1=PTO1&Sect2=HITOFF&p=1&u=/netahtml/PTO/srchnum.html&r=1&f=G&l=50&d=PALL&s1=8302164.PN.

[113] *Ibid.*

[114] T. Demos and D. Seetharaman, Facebook Isn't So Good at Judging Your Credit after All, *Wall Street Journal* (February 24, 2016), www.wsj.com/articles/lenders-drop-plans-to-judge-you-by-your-facebook-friends-1456309801.

[115] Socioeconomic Group Classification Based on User Features, US Patent Application No. 15/221587 (filed July 27, 2016), http://appft.uspto.gov/netacgi/nph-Parser?Sect1=PTO1&Sect2=HITOFF&p=1&u=/netahtml/PTO/srchnum.html&r=1&f=G&l=50&d=PG01&s1=20180032883.PGNR.

[116] *Ibid.*, Claim No. 5.

[117] *Ibid.*, Background No. 2 [002].

[118] E. Dwoskin, Facebook Is Rating the Trustworthiness of Its Users on a Scale from Zero to 1, Washington Post (August 21, 2018), www.washingtonpost.com/technology/2018/08/21/facebook-is-rating-trustworthiness-its-users-scale-zero-one/?noredirect=on&utm_term=.172ca9bb72af.

[119] *Ibid.*

[120] *Ibid.*

[121] *Ibid.*

information overload, reliable signals such as a clear scoring system are valuable and demanded. As we explain in the next section, while a China-like central public scoring model is unlikely to emerge in the United States, our social and business interactions are slowly moving toward a diffused, yet comprehensive, scoring culture.

An All-Inclusive Scoring Culture

Ranking individuals goes beyond the government agencies' monitoring of individuals' repeated behavior patterns, the financial industry's assessment of their risk levels, and, of course, social media outlets. In recent years, peer-ranking of individuals by other individuals is increasingly materializing. These peer-rankings are based on services provided, often through single interactions. Every single time a person orders a ride with Uber or Lyft, or reserves a room using Airbnb, that person is participating in what has become commonly known as the sharing economy, or the "gig" economy.[122] Users rely on these rankings as predictors of individuals' trustworthiness levels. The sharing economy defines the types of mechanisms that enable transactions between random individuals on digital platforms. Instead of calling taxis or reserving hotel rooms, people can nowadays download apps or log onto websites in order to connect with other people who are willing to offer access to their private cars or apartments. This new economy is referred to as the "sharing economy" because by making it easy and relatively cheap to connect to other people, individuals can now "share" their excess capacity with other individuals, coming from anywhere in the world. Assuming a certain level of trust, people might even invite others to share their most intimate spaces, such as the extra bedroom in their apartment, with Airbnb,[123] or their private car, with Uber or Lyft.[124]

But what distinguishes today's sharing economy companies' services from those of the traditional players is the availability of smartphones and other Internet-operated devices, in addition to new technologies such as sophisticated rating systems, which facilitate trust among random parties interacting and transacting with one another.[125]

The rating system, which has become a key feature in the reputation economy, essentially includes the social dataset available about each person participating in the different online platforms' services. The rating system basically determines a person's value in society, access to services available, and even employability. Moreover, in the sharing economy, reputation, and in particular the rating system, has become currency, especially as it is so easy to use the system being based on the simplistic, but effective, star ranking method.[126] For example, the Airbnb rating system asks hosts and guests to rate each other on things ranging from cleanliness to friendliness and even the "overall experience" of interacting with one another. But what does "being rated" on vague and subjective categories such as friendliness even mean? The sophisticated rating system of the sharing economy's platforms is problematic for several reasons. First, at least several commentators have already expressed concerns about being

[122] See, e.g., O. Lobel, The Law of the Platform (2016) 101 *Minn. Law Rev.* 87, 89.

[123] See About Us, Airbnb, www.airbnb.com/about/about-us. Airbnb was founded as a start-up in 2008, has home or room listings in more than 65,000 cities, and in early 2019 it sold common shares at a price that values the home-rental start-up at roughly $35 billion. T. Schleifer, Airbnb Sold Some Common Stock at a $35 Billion Valuation, But What Is the Company Really Worth?, *Vox* (March 19, 2019), www.vox.com/2019/3/19/18272274/airbnb-valuation-common-stock-hoteltonight.

[124] See, e.g., Our Trip History, Uber, www.uber.com/our-story/.

[125] See, e.g., R. Calo and A. Rosenblat, The Taking Economy: Uber Information, and Power (2017) 117 *Colum. Law Rev.* 1623, 1634.

[126] S. Kleber, As AI Meets the Reputation Economy, We're All Being Silently Judged, *Harvard Business Review* (January 29, 2018), https://hbr.org/2018/01/as-ai-meets-the-reputation-economy-were-all-being-silently-judged.

ranked on such categories, and have stated how keeping these rankings in mind causes a chilling effect and nudges people to behave differently,[127] impacting their emotions and decision-making processes.[128] This is because "[t]he reputation economy is making us a little more careful in everything we say, how we say it, and what we do because we have to evaluate each other."[129]

Second, studies have suggested that in companies such as Uber, Lyft, and Airbnb, the consumer-sourced rating systems can facilitate and mask all sorts of consumer biases.[130] Likewise, a National Bureau of Economic Research study offered specific examples of some of these discriminatory and biased behaviors, including how African-Americans wait longer for rides when using ride-sharing apps,[131] or consumers giving lower ratings to drivers with protected-class characteristics that in turn can result in having them receive lower pay for their work, or leave them more vulnerable to potential termination by the companies that use their services.[132] Similarly, studies have shown that African-American consumers have a hard time booking accommodations on Airbnb because they are often discriminated against by the hosts offering their homes or rooms on the platform.[133]

Third, the sophisticated rating systems of the sharing economy's platforms pose a threat to their users' information privacy. Similar to other online platforms, sharing economy companies have access to a massive amount of data regarding the behaviors of those who use it. Sharing economy companies also arguably collect much more data than is needed for them to successfully accomplish their announced goals of lowering search costs and enabling trust among persons by ranking and rating their behavior and transactions.[134]

Lastly, rating systems can also be partly or fully based on algorithmic data selection and analysis, rather than humans'. In such situations, an individual's reputation score can be unfairly impacted by incorrect or irrelevant data sources and mathematical formulas, under the promise that the algorithmic analysis is more accurate and flexible.[135]

[127] A study published by the BI Norwegian Business School in 2017 found that "negative emotions can be especially detrimental to customer loyalty in the sharing economy. In other words, the guilt and anxiety we feel using apps where we are prompted to rate every experience we have may be driving us away from them." See www.unit.no/vitenarkiv-i-bragekonsortiet.
[128] See, e.g., K. Paul, How Rating Everything from Your Uber Driver to Your Airbnb Host Has Become a Nightmare, *MarketWatch* (April 7, 2019), www.marketwatch.com/story/how-rating-everything-from-your-uber-driver-to-your-airbnb-host-has-become-a-nightmare-2019-04-01 (explaining that, "But when gauging whether to go to bed or be friendly, I had to consider another factor: My Airbnb rating … If I rejected her invite, would the host think I was rude? … Simple gestures and acts of goodwill are tied to a five-star rating system and have become fraught with mathematical appraisals"); M. Makkar, Romanticising Market Exchange: Unpacking Cultural Meanings of Value in Home-sharing Markets, PhD Dissertation (2019), https://openrepository.aut.ac.nz/bitstream/handle/10292/12284/MakkarM.pdf?sequence=3&isAllowed=y (writing about a dual-review system that is unlike anything consumers have experienced before, as the relationship's intimacy may cause certain consumers to not be honest in their reviews in a way that traditional models made them be).
[129] See the comments of Professor Russell W. Belk in: You Are What You Can Access: Sharing and Collaborative Consumption Online (2014) 67 *J. Bus. Res.* 1595.
[130] A. Rosenblat, K. Levy, S. Barocas, *et al.*, Discriminating Tastes: Customer Ratings as Vehicles for Bias, *Data & Society* (2016), p. 7.
[131] Y. Ge, C. R. Knittel, D. MacKenzie, and S. Zoepf, Racial and Gender Discrimination in Transportation Network Companies, Nat'l Bureau of Econ. Research, Working Paper No. 22776, (2016), pp. 1–2, www.nber.org/papers/w22776.pdf.
[132] See Rosenblat *et al.*, above note 130, pp. 6–9.
[133] See B. Edelman, M. Luca, and D. Svirsky, Racial Discrimination in the Sharing Economy: Evidence from a Field Experiment, *Am. Econ. J. Applied Econ.* (April 2017), pp. 1, 2, as referenced in Calo and Rosenblat, above note 125.
[134] *Ibid.*, pp. 1647–8.
[135] See, e.g., Kleber, supra note 127.

THE PITFALLS OF AND CHALLENGES WITH SOCIAL CREDIT

Privacy

The utilization of social information for individuals' ranking by the public and private sectors poses a number of policy and legal challenges, the first of which relates to privacy issues. Privacy violations can be prompted directly or indirectly. At the direct level, individuals' ranking has an obvious impact on the ranked individuals' privacy. The public and private sector entities accrue and survey data to learn about people's marital status, family ties, friendships, jobs, shopping preferences, political stances, and more. They aggregate data and do not anonymize information, as the specific ranking that each person receives is dependent upon personal identification.[136] This direct privacy harm, however, is often justified against the backdrop of the ranked individual's conspicuous consent. After all, in some situations, this could be viewed as a simple or reasonable transaction: one is okay with, or even permits the private details of one's life to be collected, examined, analyzed, and even forever stored, in return for some benefits. These benefits can include better interest rates, lower insurance premiums, getting upgraded services, not getting audited, getting better treatment in places such as airports or hotels and even customs lines, and being eligible for financial aid or improved disability assistance packages. Doxing oneself and trading away personal information in return for products or services is not a new phenomenon and has long been a dominant model in other markets. A typical illustration is the behavioral advertising business model, in which advertising is chosen and displayed according to data collected and analyzed about a specific user.[137] Information is commonly collected based on a said mutual consensual exchange, in which personal information is used as currency to pay for different products and services.[138] Critics challenge this assumption, arguing that users cannot reasonably estimate their disutility from the trade-off and the harm associated with the data collection.[139] They argue that the format of the "payment," which is the collected data, obstructs users' ability to understand the privacy harm,[140] even though authorizing collection and use of personal information in exchange for an economic benefit makes perfect economic sense to some consumers.[141]

At the indirect level, privacy harms are even more concerning. Those relate to "third parties," which are a ranked individual's contacts, followers, and friends, whose interaction with the ranked individual, whether of a one-time or reoccurring nature, are recorded, analyzed as well, and often stored for whatever present time or future purposes. Third parties' privacy harm depends on the amount and type of information collected and evaluated by the specific ranking algorithms, and often correlates with the degree of disclosure and invasiveness authorized by the ranked individual. On the worse end of the spectrum are financial parties such as insurers or lenders that request permission to get unlimited access to a ranked individual's social networks and various accounts. By consenting to give such access, a ranked individual de facto delegates the right to access and view information about his or her contacts

---

[136] See Packin and Lev-Aretz, Social Credit, above note 1, Pt. IV.
[137] K. J. Strandburg, Free Fall: The Online Market's Consumer Preference Disconnect (2013) *Univ. Chi. Legal F.* 95, 100.
[138] *Ibid.*, p. 106.
[139] *Ibid.*, p. 107.
[140] *Ibid.*, pp. 130–1.
[141] S. R. Peppet, Unraveling Privacy: The Personal Prospectus and the Threat of a Full-Disclosure Future (2011) 105 *Nw. Univ. Law Rev.* 1153, 1157.

to the party with whom he or she is transacting, typically without even notifying or gaining approvals for such permission. Consequently, the financial parties can view all social information, private correspondences, and other data that is associated with connected third parties, learning about some unusually private aspects of their lives.[142] Such information collected about third parties could potentially be retained and cross-referenced to make future trustworthiness determinations related to one of the indirectly involved third parties. This is especially concerning when personal identification is essential to the process of social-based ranking, making the prospects of a privacy harm more significant to third parties. In addition, advanced algorithmic modeling and big data can yield inferences about private information that may have never been disclosed to the online platform, leaving individuals exposed in ways they could not have anticipated.[143]

Two theories of privacy further illustrate how illegitimate the practice of collection and use of information about third parties is. Helen Nissenbaum's contextual integrity theory offers a conceptual framework that connects the protection of private information with the norms of information flow within particular contexts.[144] Designed to identify if the introduction of a new practice into a specific social context breaches governing informational norms, the contextual integrity differentiates between two classes of informational norm: norms of appropriateness, and norms of flow or distribution.[145] Norms of appropriateness determine if information of a certain type or nature is appropriate for disclosure in a given context.[146] Among the question of appropriateness in a given context, contextual integrity also examines if the distribution, or flow, of the information fits with the contextual norms of information flow.[147] Therefore, privacy is invaded when these informational norms are infringed. In the indirect privacy harm context, the subject of the data analysis is a third party, with control only over the first point of sharing in social networks (for example, when that third party signed up to a network to interact with others, under certain privacy expectations). Such third parties did not or could not really contemplate the possibility of being evaluated to rank others, or that such information could be collected and kept for future unknown purposes.[148] Thus, norms of appropriateness and the flow of information are breached as third parties are generally unaware of and are not expecting such usages of data.

Another privacy theory is Lior J. Strahilevitz's social network theory.[149] It, too, examines privacy expectations given the context of the original disclosure by applying predictive social analytics and advocating that courts use the same analytics. Strahilevitz argues that the nature of the information shared in addition to the subject of disclosure can determine to what extent the information is likely to be circulated outside of the original group of recipients and accordingly to what extent such distribution could reasonably give rise to privacy violation claims.[150] Strahilevitz believes, inter alia, that the more interesting, surprising, novel, or

---

[142] See Packin and Lev-Aretz, Social Credit, above note 1, Pt. IV.
[143] For example, researchers were able to fairly accurately guess the characteristics of a group of Facebook users by analyzing their "likes." See Z. Tufekci, Algorithmic Harms beyond Facebook and Google: Emergent Challenges of Computational Agency (2015) 13 *Colo. Technol. Law J.* 203, 210.
[144] See Nissenbaum, supra note 24.
[145] See H. Nissenbaum, Privacy as Contextual Integrity (2004) 79 *Wash. Law Rev.* 119, 138.
[146] *Ibid.*
[147] *Ibid.*
[148] See Packin and Lev-Aretz, Social Credit, above note 1, Pt. IV.
[149] L. J. Strahilevitz, A Social Networks Theory of Privacy (2005) 72 *Univ. Chi. Law Rev.* 919. Importantly, notwithstanding the clear reference to what we today call "social networks," this theory is based on ongoing research in social network theory and does not specifically analyze online social media.
[150] *Ibid.*

entertaining a particular piece of information is, the more a person should reasonably expect it will be distributed through a network.[151] And, when highly connected individuals, whom Strahilevitz refers to as "supernodes," disclose information, the number of people exposed to the information rises, as does the likelihood that the information crosses networks and reaches individuals outside of the initial group.[152] According to the social network theory of privacy, it does not seem that the use of social information for individuals' ranking purposes should be grounds for a valid privacy violation claim.[153]

Social Segregation

Algorithmic ranking of individuals can compromise an open society and democratic speech. By classifying people into categories, and ranking them, such algorithms divide society into echo chambers of like-minded peers.[154] Building on this observation, it has already been argued that social ranking systems pose greater risks for advancing social polarization.[155] Scholars have argued that the systematic consideration of social information motivates people to brush up their online profiles for a better trustworthiness score.[156] The more desirable the end product, the more individuals would want to improve their chances of getting the best deal, even if that means distancing themselves from certain online connections or associations, which may seem to damage their online image.[157] From a ranked individual's perspective, such distancing and conducting an online social clean-up makes perfect practical and even economic sense. However, artificial acts of online social restructure have ramifications beyond one specific person. Such changes may lead to online social polarization, where people are regrouped by the level of their trustworthiness or even the financial risk they embody to their contacts. Those from disadvantaged backgrounds would interact only with others who, likewise, have been unable to break free of the cycle of poverty. Similarly, Ivy League alumni would only allow themselves to be associated with similarly elite peers.[158] Therefore, even online individuals would mainly form relationships with others who share similar backgrounds, characteristics, interests, and locations.[159] As people generally interact mainly with their peers offline, social networks further facilitate homophily.[160] And although early research on online communities assumed that online social networkers would connect with others outside their offline social group, later research suggested that people used online social networks to keep up their pre-existing offline connections, rather than meet new contacts.[161] Thus, social networks preserve connections initiated in an earlier point of life, even if the number of similarity points has decreased dramatically over

---

[151] *Ibid.*, p. 972.
[152] *Ibid.*, p. 975.
[153] See Packin and Lev-Aretz, Social Credit, above note 1, Pt. IV.
[154] J. Polonetsky and O. Tene, Who Is Reading Whom Now: Privacy in Education from Books to MOOCs (2015) 17 *Vand. J. Ent. Technol. Law* 927, 985–6.
[155] Y. Wei, P. Yildirim, C. Van den Bulte, and C. Dellarocas, Credit Scoring with Social Network Data (2014) 35 *Mark. Sci.* 234, http://papers.ssrn.com/sol3/papers.cfm?abstract_id=2475265.
[156] See Packin and Lev-Aretz, Social Credit, above note 1, Pt. V.
[157] *Ibid.*
[158] K. Shubber, SoFi Really Wants You to Think It Isn't a Bank, *Financial Times* (December 3, 2015), http://ftalphaville.ft.com/2015/12/03/2146561/sofi-really-wants-you-to-think-it-isnt-a-bank/.
[159] M. McPherson, L. Smith-Lovin, and J. M. Cook, Birds of a Feather: Homophily in Social Networks (2001) 27 *Ann. Rev. Sociol.* 415, 416.
[160] Homophily is the idea that "a contact between similar people occurs at a higher rate than among dissimilar people" (*ibid.*, p. 416).
[161] See N. B. Ellison, C. W. Steinfield, and C. Lampe, The Benefits of Facebook "Friends": Social Capital and College Students' Use of Online Social Network Sites (2007) 12 *J. Comput.-Mediat. Commun.* 1143, 1144.

time.[162] And, the consequences of rational people perfecting their images in response to social-based private and public sector rankings are likely to go beyond virtual realms and impact all aspects of people's lives, causing further social polarization.[163] Indeed, while users could maintain offline relationships with no online trace, such maintenance is becoming increasingly difficult in our modern society. Most people would be left with only strong connections that are often supported by geographical proximity. Without social media, keeping in touch with contacts across the ocean could seem less possible or even worthy of one's time. Widespread online segregation caused by social ranking could legitimize the idea that friendships should occur only among homogenous groups. Once validated online, such a view may be easily exported offline, bringing a second-generation separate-but-equal regime into being.[164]

The potential score-based segregation online and offline could have a number of adverse consequences. Among those are changes to online social circles that can impact people's social capital,[165] which empowers them to draw on the resources of other members of their networks, such as useful information, relationships, or group-organizing capacities.[166] Social capital is important. Research has shown a clear link between communities possessing greater social capital and many positive social outcomes, such as better public health, lower crime rates, and more efficient financial markets.[167] Different forms of social capital were also found to positively impact psychological well-being, self-esteem, and happiness with one's life.[168] Equally, declining social capital was shown to be linked with increased social disorder, and reduced participation in civic activities.[169]

Opaqueness

In addition to privacy and social segregation harms, social credit systems are rarely transparent. Transparency is measured in two aspects: (1) the technical design of the system and its explicability; and (2) the rules that are fed into and enforced by the automated system. In terms of technical design, the automated systems that gauge social creditworthiness are rarely fully transparent and explainable.[170] Reasons vary and include technological difficulties[171]

---

[162]   *Ibid.*, p. 1165.
[163]   See Packin and Lev-Aretz, Social Credit, above note 1, Pt. V.
[164]   *Ibid.*
[165]   See P. Bourdieu and L. J. D. Wacquant, *An Invitation to Reflexive Sociology* (University of Chicago Press, 1992), pp. 14, 19 (expanding the concept of "capital" to include social, cultural, and symbolic resources, and defining social capital as "the sum of the resources, actual or virtual, that accrue to an individual or a group by virtue of possessing a durable network of more or less institutionalized relationships of mutual acquaintance and recognition").
[166]   See P. Paxton, Is Social Capital Declining in the United States? A Multiple Indicator Assessment (1999) 105 *Am. J. Soc.* 88, 92.
[167]   See P. S. Adler and S.-W. Kwon, Social Capital: Prospects for a New Concept (2002) 27 *Acad. Mgmt. Rev.* 17, 29–30.
[168]   See J. A. Bargh and K. Y. A. McKenna, The Internet and Social Life (2004) 55 *Ann. Rev. Psychol.* 573.
[169]   See Ellison *et al.*, above note 161, pp. 1144–5 (showing, inter alia, that "online connections resulted in face-to-face meetings).
[170]   F. Pasquale, *The Black Box Society: The Secret Algorithms that Control Money and Information* (Harvard University Press, 2015), O'Neill, above note 3; F. Doshi-Velez, M. Cortz, R. Budish, *et al.*, Accountability of AI under the Law: The Role of Explanation (2017), https://arxiv.org/pdf/1711.01134.pdf.
[171]   Doshi-Velez *et al.*, *ibid.*, p. 1: "Contrary to popular wisdom of AI systems as indecipherable black boxes, we find that this level of explanation should generally be technically feasible but may sometimes be practically onerous – there are certain aspects of explanation that may be simple for humans to provide but challenging for AI systems, and vice versa."

and trade secrecy concerns.[172] In terms of rules structure (namely, the blueprint for the scoring model, the considerations at play, and the implications attached to different levels of scores), the Chinese model is far more transparent than privately developed versions outside China.

The Chinese model prides itself on radical transparency: information on individuals' trustworthiness is publicly available, and even information about the conduct of bureaucratic departments, their officials, and the compliance record of businesses is available.[173] In fact, one study found that many citizens who support the social credit system pointed to the fair and transparent methods that are used to evaluate social creditworthiness.[174] Perhaps surprisingly, the private scoring models, as well as governmental use of social information in the United States, are generally secretive. Except for the information provided in patents documents or occasionally revealed by the media, in the United States no clear and detailed overview of the scoring and its implications is available.

CONCLUSION

The practical need to score individuals to signify financial risk has led to the rise of traditional credit scoring in the United States. The system, however, turned to candidates' financial past to learn about their financial future – a model that left many, who for legitimate reasons lacked a financial past, to be left outside the financial mainstream. The rise of big data analytics and AI technologies allowed for the inclusion of those credit-invisible individuals, but at the price of privacy harms, opacity, and potentially, and over time, social segregation. In China, the ability to both track individual behavior everywhere and use learning models to measure comprehensive trustworthiness has led to the implementation of a civic social credit system. And while to people who live in Western democracies the Chinese model feels like a far-fetched dystopia, evidence shows that scoring systems developed by powerful private players can, in fact, be even worse.

It may be time to ask whether a reputational-social credit system is not underway in Western democracies. While the power of our governments is sufficiently limited to prevent a Chinese-like model from being implemented in the United States, our privacy and information laws are currently ill-equipped to prevent powerful private players from coming up with an even more dangerous and largely secretive social scoring scheme.

---

[172] R. Brauneis and E. P. Goodman, Algorithmic Transparency for the Smart City (2018) 20 *Yale J. Law Technol.* 103, 153: "The owners of proprietary algorithms will often require nondisclosure agreements from their public agency customers and assert trade secret protection over the algorithm and associated development and deployment processes."

[173] R. Creemers, China's Social Credit System: An Evolving Practice of Control (2018), p. 26, https://papers.ssrn.com/sol3/papers.cfm?abstract_id=3175792.

[174] G. Kostka, China's Social Credit Systems and Public Opinion: Explaining High Levels of Approval (2019) 21 *Media Soc.* 1565, 1588, https://journals.sagepub.com/doi/full/10.1177/1461444819826402.

30

Algorithmic Stages in Privacy of Data Analytics

Process and Probabilities

Ronald P. Loui, Arno R. Lodder, and Stephanie A. Quick

INTRODUCTION

Technological advances continue to produce massive amounts of information from a variety of sources about our everyday lives. The simple use of a smartphone, for example, can generate data on individuals through telephone records (including location data), social media activity, Internet browsing, e-commerce transactions, and email communications. Much attention has been given to expectations of privacy in light of this data collection, especially consumer privacy. Much attention has also been given to how and when government agencies collect and use this data to monitor the activities of individuals.

In previous work,[1] we discussed three aspects of data analytics in the context of intelligence agencies that matter, but are often overlooked: stages, numbers, and the human factor. We made the following observations. First, stages of the algorithmic process should be included in what legal constraints apply to these activities. Second, the law should take into account the difference between people and machines. Third, the law should think more about numbers. Although each of these topics deserves further discussion, we focus in this chapter in particular on the first issue: stages.

The background of our discussion of algorithms is the activities of intelligence agencies, in particular the National Security Agency (NSA), so the General Data Protection Regulation (GDPR) does not apply. However, the general framework for data protection the GDPR has become, even surpassing its application to non-EU countries, an interesting point of reference for issues of data protection. It does lay down some rules for using algorithms, in particular in the context of automated decision-making and profiling. Notably, the GDPR does not take into account the stages of the algorithmic processing. What we discuss in this chapter is equally relevant for the GDPR.

When there are stages of algorithmic processing, privacy interests depend on the risk of harm at each stage, especially in relation to the numbers of persons under consideration at that stage. It is especially important not to confuse the numbers at one stage (for example, an early stage of algorithmic filtering) with the risks at another stage (for example, a later stage of human involvement). We did discuss this previously, but further justify the relevance of this approach.

Also, analysis by a human, with normal human comprehension, is different from analysis by a program, algorithm, or artificial intelligence (AI), even with human supervision of the

---

[1] A. R. Lodder and R. Loui, Data Algorithms and Privacy in Surveillance: On Stages, Numbers and the Human Factor, in W. Barfield and U. Pagallo (eds.), *Research Handbook of Law and Artificial Intelligence* (Edward Elgar, 2018).

analysis or meta-analysis. Privacy concerns are different depending on the sentience of the comprehension; neither is less concerning in toto, as each can raise different issues. This is especially relevant to actual privacy harms, although large-scale bulk collection can have society-wide effects even if late-stage individual harm is minimized.

The legality of a programmatically warranted surveillance regime, such as the NSA's domestic telephony metadata bulk-collection and seeded-search based on social network analysis under Section 215 of the Patriot Act, depends crucially on scale, which may require reference to numbers or ranges of numbers, not just concepts that differentiate kinds of search, suspicion, and exfiltration, and stages in particular algorithmic processing.[2] Sometimes numbers actually matter, so that different scales of quantities can be different qualitatively in nature. This is one way of balancing the competing interests of national security and US Fourth Amendment Constitutional protections. A warrant-granting stage can have the effect of imposing practical limits on numbers, as can retrospective audits. Justice Sotomayor's concurring opinion on *United States* v. *Jones* is important support for this point of view, although that opinion concerned a variety of concepts (for example, precision and persistence of GPS information, not just quantity, and mainly in the context of Third Party Disclosure).[3]

The chapter is divided into three sections. The first section covers algorithmic stages, in particular the privacy harm of someone being part of a dataset is connected to the particular state of algorithmic processing. The second section elaborates on logging, and the third on legality.

ALGORITHMIC STAGES

The press reports during and after the Snowden revelations about NSA activities reported numbers that caught the attention of the public. See, for instance, the following overview:[4]

NSA Collecting Phone Records of Millions of Verizon Customers Daily[5]
    NSA Collects Millions of E-mail Address Books Globally[6]
    In one month, March 2013, the NSA collected 97 billion pieces of intelligence from computer networks worldwide, including 3 billion pieces of intelligence from US computer networks.[7]
    NSA Can Legally Access Metadata of 25,000 Callers Based on a Single Suspect's Phone[8]

---

[2] Consider the practical limit at the warrant-granting stage: "[T]he Administration's decision to bring the Terrorist Surveillance Program under FISA resulted in a paper jam at the Foreign Intelligence Surveillance Court as the number of warrant applications soared." R. A. Posner, Privacy, Surveillance, and Law (2008) 75 *Univ. Chi. Law Rev.* 245, 259.

[3] *United States* v. *Jones*, 565 US 400 (2012).

[4] See, e.g., S. Landau, Making Sense from Snowden: What's Significant in the NSA Surveillance Revelations, *IEEE Security & Privacy* (August 2, 2013); D. Lyon, Surveillance, Snowden, and Big Data: Capacities, Consequences, Critique, Big Data & Society (2014); M. V. Hayden, Beyond Snowden: An NSA Reality Check, *World Affairs Journal* (January/February 2014); M. Hu, Taxonomy of the Snowden Disclosures (2015) 72 *Wash. Lee Law Rev.* 1679; S. I. Vladeck, Big Data before and after Snowden (2014) 7 *J. Nat'l Sec. Law Policy* 333; D. Cole, After Snowden: Regulating Technology-Aided Surveillance in the Digital Age (2016) 44 *Cap. Univ. Law Rev.* 677.

[5] G. Greenwald, NSA Collecting Phone Records of Millions of Verizon Customers Daily, *The Guardian* (June 6, 2013).

[6] B. Gellman and A. Soltani, NSA Collects Millions of E-mail Address Books Globally, *Washington Post* (October 14, 2013).

[7] K. Rodriguez and D. Kayyali, On 6/5, 65 Things We Know about NSA Surveillance that We Didn't Know a Year Ago, *Electronic Frontier Foundation* (June 5, 2014).

[8] A. Nordrum, NSA Can Legally Access Metadata of 25,000 Callers Based on a Single Suspect's Phone, *IEEE Spectrum* (May 16, 2016).

Reined-In NSA Still Collected 151 Million Phone Records in '16[9]
NSA Collected 151 Million Phone Records in 2016, Despite Surveillance Law Changes[10]
The U.S. National Security Agency collected 534 million records of phone calls and text messages of Americans last year, more than triple gathered in 2016, a U.S. intelligence agency report released on Friday said.[11]

Meanwhile, the actual audits of numbers of queries and US persons at (*ex post*) risk were on a completely different scale:

In 2005, for example, although more than 2,000 applications were filed . . .[12]
In 2012, the NSA queried 288 primary phone numbers, and through contact chain analysis touched 6,000 numbers.[13]
Estimated number of targets of [Section 702 orders] (recall that only non-USPs are targeted):   CY2013=89,138,   CY204=92,707,   CY2015=94,368,   CY2016=106,469, CY2017=129,080.[14]

How can the discrepancy of numerical scales be reconciled? On the one hand, there are reports of millions of records, and millions of persons having records collected. On the other hand, the number of persons being used as seeds is several orders of magnitude lower (log10); even a full order of magnitude lower for those persons targeted as a result of processing those seeds.

Part of the explanation is that there are, or were, many different programs being confused by press reports and privacy advocates: most notably those regarding domestic persons under the Section 215 Patriot Act II authorization of 2001,[15] and those regarding foreign persons under Section 702 of the FISA Amendment Acts of 2008.[16]

Section 215 allows the government to request a court order from the FISA Court that requires third parties to produce tangible things (such as books, records, and documents) if deemed relevant to a terrorism investigation.[17] The Privacy and Civil Liberties Oversight Board (PCLOB) described the process of storing and accessing telephone records collected under the NSA's program in its 2014 report:

Once the calling records are properly formatted, NSA houses them within its data repositories. At this point, technical personnel may take additional measures to make the calling records usable for intelligence analysis, including removing "high volume" telephone identifiers and other unwanted data. The NSA is required to limit who has access to the calling records it obtains . . . Calling records must be deleted from the NSA's repositories no later than five years after the agency receives them. If a calling record shows up in a "query"

9   C. Savage, Reined-in N.S.A. Still Collected 151 Million Phone Records in '16, *New York Times* (May 2, 2017).
10 J. Vincent, NSA Collected 151 Million Phone Records in 2016, Despite Surveillance Law Changes, *The Verge* (May 3, 2017).
11 D. Volz, Spy Agency NSA Triples Collection of U.S. Phone Records: Official Report, *Reuters* (May 4, 2018).
12 R. A. Posner, Privacy, Surveillance, and Law (2008) 75 *Univ. Chi. Law Rev.* 245, 260.
13 Center for Strategic & International Studies, Fact Sheet: Section 215 of the USA PATRIOT Act (February 27, 2014).
14 Office of the Director of National Intelligence, STATISTICAL TRANSPARENCY REPORT Regarding Use of National Security Authorities ~ Calendar Year 2017 (April 2018).
15 United and Strengthening America-Providing Appropriate Tools Required to Intercept and Obstruct Terrorism (USA PATRIOT) Act of 2001, Pub. L. No. 107–56, § 215, 115 Stat. 272, 287–8 (codified at 50 USC §§ 1861–2 (Supp. II 2002)).
16 FISA Amendments Act of 2008, Pub. L. No. 110–261, § 702, 122 Stat. 2436, 2438–48 (codified at 50 USC § 1881a (2008)).
17 See 50 USC § 1861.

performed by an analyst, however – a process described below – the information about that call need not be destroyed after five years.

Initially, NSA analysts are permitted to access the Section 215 calling records only through "queries" of the database. A query is a software-enabled search for a specific number or other selection term within the database. When an analyst performs a query of a telephone number, for instance, the software interfaces with the database and provides results to the analyst that include a record of calls in which that number participated. Analysts perform these queries to facilitate what is called "contact chaining" – the process of identifying the connections among individuals through their calls with each other. The goals of contact chaining are to identify unknown terrorist operatives through their contacts with known suspects, discover links between known suspects, and monitor the pattern of communications among suspects. Presently, the only purpose for which NSA analysts are permitted to search the Section 215 calling records housed in the agency's database is to conduct queries as described above, which are designed to build contact chains leading outward from a target to other telephone numbers. The NSA has stated that it does not conduct pattern-based searches. Instead, every search begins with a specific telephone number or other specific selection term.[18]

Section 702, on the other hand, provides that the government may collect communications from non-Americans reasonably believed to be located outside the United States in order to obtain foreign intelligence information.[19] The PCLOB describes the process of Section 702 surveillance as follows:

> Once a Section 702 certification has been approved, non-U.S. persons reasonably believed to be located outside the United States may be targeted to acquire foreign intelligence information within the scope of that certification . . .
>
> The Section 702 certifications permit non-U.S. persons to be targeted only through the "tasking" of what are called "selectors." A selector must be a specific communications facility that is assessed to be used by the target, such as the target's email address or telephone number. Thus, in the terminology of Section 702, people (non-U.S. persons reasonably believed to be located outside the United States) are targeted; selectors (e.g., email addresses, telephone numbers) are tasked. The users of any tasked selector are considered targets – and therefore only selectors used by non-U.S. persons reasonably believed to be located abroad may be tasked. The targeting procedures govern both the targeting and tasking process . . .
>
> Although targeting decisions must be individualized, this does not mean that a substantial number of persons are not targeted under the Section 702 program. The government estimates that 89,138 persons were targeted under Section 702 during 2013. Once a selector has been tasked under the targeting procedures, it is sent to an electronic communications service provider to begin acquisition.[20]

FISA, while considerably scrutinized and revised since its inception, ideally does not directly engage Fourth Amendment protections, so Section 702 activity is very different from bulk collection under Section 215.[21]

---

[18] Privacy and Civil Liberties Oversight Board, Report on the Telephone Records Program Conducted under Section 215 of the USA Patriot Act and on the Operations of the Foreign Intelligence Surveillance Court, January 23, 2014, pp. 25, 26–7, www.pclob.gov/library/215-Report_on_the_Telephone_Records_Program.pdf (hereinafter, PCLOB Section 215 Report).

[19] See 50 USC § 1881a.

[20] Privacy and Civil Liberties Oversight Board, Report on the Surveillance Program Operated Pursuant to Section 702 of the Foreign Intelligence Surveillance Act, Jul 2, 2014, pp. 32–3, www.pclob.gov/library/702-Report.pdf (hereinafter, PCLOB Section 702 Report).

[21] In fact, the PCLOB recommended curtailing Section 215 activity while retaining Section 702 activity with few modifications. See PCLOB Section 215 Report, above note 18, and PCLOB Section 702 Report, *ibid.*

Even so, the numbers reported for Section 702 may be surprisingly low in the context of the press reports. It is worth noting that the foreign press may have had little incentive to keep straight the difference between collections for foreign persons and for US persons.

The main reason the numbers are so different is that there are different stages in the processing. From a seed query, with individualized warrant, Section 215 used social network analysis to determine who was 1-hop from the seed (directly in contact), then 2-hops (directly in contact with someone directly in contact), then 3-hops (directly in contact with someone 2-hops from the seed). Anyone within 3-hops would have records added to the "corporate store" that could be searched under other authorities.[22]

From the point of view of numbers of records involved, one starts with a single number, then assuming 100 to 1,000 contacts per hop, scales to 100 after one hop, 10,000 after two hops, and 1 million after three hops. This is the lower estimate, with a fan-out of 100. For an upper estimate, 1,000 after one hop is 1 million after two hops, and 1 billion after three hops. This is from a single seed. No doubt the reduction from three hops to two hops was a significant reduction in scale.[23]

Looking at the process from the point of view of collection and filtering, perhaps ten records of 100 million persons are collected in bulk each day, or 1 billion records. If records are retained for 100 days for social network analysis, that makes 100 million persons' 100 billion records at risk for connection to a seed on any given query. Using the Section 702 Office of the Director of National Intelligence transparency report numbers from 2017, 129,000 persons had records targeted. This is a different program, targeting non-US persons, and post-curtailment by the Obama administration. But it is a useful estimate for illustration. Suppose the result of winnowing in Section 215 social network analysis yielded 100,000 persons' ten records for 100 days. This means that at the first stage of processing, 2-hop connection, 100 million was reduced to 100,000, or a 1,000:1 reduction. In this first stage, 99.9 percent of the records, 100 million – 100,000 or 99.9 million persons' records were discarded. While 100,000 persons 1,000 records were retained, an alarming 100 million results of a single query, an equally spectacular 99.9 million persons' 1,000 records were algorithmically declared uninteresting, or 99.9 billion records. This is a massive discarding or excluding, at least for the purposes of that query.[24]

This is not to take either side of the dispute over whether too much was collected, or whether a sufficient amount of the collection was never "used," hence large numbers of persons' privacy rights barely implicated. It is intended to make clear the point that the numbers need to be understood in terms of the stage of the processing.[25]

---

[22]   This process is described in authoritative detail in the PCLOB Section 215 Report, above note 18.

[23]   Others have noted this over-productivity. See, e.g.: "This might be okay – except for the fact that each one of those 300 or so queries can in turn let the NSA suck in 1 million other phone records" (J. Roberts, How Feds Use One "Seed" and 3 "Hops" to Spy on Nearly Everyone, *Gigaom* (December 17, 2013). See also, Nordrum, above note 8.

[24]   For similar analysis, see, e.g., D. Storm, NSA Collected 1 Trillion Metadata Records, Harvested 1 Billion Mobile Calls Daily, *Computerworld* (June 30, 2013). Also, "approximately 500 billion communication records [were] intercepted and analyzed in 2012, via a program called One-End Foreign, which relies on the FISA Amendments Act for its legality." D. Ombres, NSA Domestic Surveillance from the Patriot Act to the Freedom Act: The Underlying History, Constitutional Basis, and the Efforts at Reform (2015) 39 *Seton Hall Legis. J.* 27, 32. Both of these, however, are referring to Section 702 activity.

[25]   It may be worth noting that the rationale for 3-hop connectivity in multi-modal social network analysis is that productivity at each hop may be more limited. For a shared bank account, or a shared plane flight, 10× fan out per day, or 1,000× per hop per query is a massive overestimate (e.g. sharing an apartment produces at most ten new connections over the entire 100-day period). Not all hops are necessarily telephonic connections.

What are the risks at each stage? For an individual, the risk of being included at the first bulk collection stage is that the individual might be included in the next stage, being warehoused in the "corporate store" and susceptible to production under analysts' more general search. Note that the processing between the first and second stages is entirely algorithmic. The probability of being included at the first stage might be 50 percent (0.50), depending on whether we are starting with a population of US adults, US adult phone users, US adult phone users with business records at a major carrier, etc. The probability of being included at the second stage might be 1/1,000 of that, or 0.0005, depending on what one imagines the novelty of contacts per day might be during the period of temporary social network analytics access. One hundred million persons initially at risk became 100,000 persons with records in the store. The third stage of processing starts when a record included in the second stage is actually produced during a human-initiated query and examined. This probability might be another 1/10 or 1/100 winnowing, resulting in the 1,000 to 10,000 persons targeted for human inspection that would be in line with the later statistical transparency reports.

The fact is that US intelligence agencies do not have the manpower to inspect much larger numbers of records and the point of the algorithmic "front-end" is to produce a smaller number of highly probable, if not reasonably articulable, suspects.

A similar point was made in the PCLOB Section 215 Report:[26]

> [C]hanging program rules to limit contact chaining to two hops ... would not unduly diminish the value of the telephony metadata program ... Each additional hop from the original "selector" makes the connection more remote and adds exponentially greater numbers of "false positives" to the query results. The value of connections becomes more limited as the contact chain is extended and it becomes more difficult to sift through the results.

FROM BENIGN LOGGING TO AUTHORITARIAN AI

The question of whether algorithmic looking is different from human looking, with regard to privacy protections, is where much of the debate remains open. And if it is different, in what ways can it be less invasive, while in what other ways it can be more invasive.

On the one hand, we see converging respect for what analytics and the fusion of disparate data, even metadata, can yield. Whether this is knowing, or merely probabilistic hypothesizing, is worth further discussion. It may be that claiming and attributing with low probability raise significantly reduced privacy concerns. The same would be true for probably non-persistent conclusions, based on data that is out of date. Privacy interests might even be lessened when justified true beliefs are wrongly known (improper causal chains that are "lucky guesses"). Many of these epistemological concerns are taken seriously in the GDPR recommendation that data be anonymized or pseudonymized.[27]

---

[26] PCLOB Section 215 Report, above note 18, pp. 170–1.
[27] For example, blurring: "Data blurring uses an approximation of data values to render their meaning obsolete and/or render the identification of individuals impossible" and generalizing, which reduce precision, in addition to unlinking forms of anonymization that make precise attribution improbable. GDPR Report, Data Masking: Anonymisation or Pseudonymisation? (November 7, 2017). K. Lehrer, The Gettier Problem and the Analysis of Knowledge, in G. Pappas (ed.), *Justification and Knowledge* (Springer, 1979). Lehrer's work is an example of the philosophical problem of wrongly knowing something that is nevertheless justified true belief.

There is no question that in an era of big data, concepts and dimensions of privacy are shifting with new appreciation for what can be known with algorithmic inference and AI. On the other side is Richard Posner's claim that the privacy concerns began with the human comprehension:[28] "So the search sequence is interception, data mining, and finally a human search of those intercepted messages that data mining or other information sources have flagged as suspicious. Computer searches do not invade privacy because search programs are not sentient beings. Only the human search should raise constitutional or other legal issues." Posner continues by distinguishing the harm of algorithmic scrutiny and the harm of *ex post* human interest.

In the initial computer sifting designed to pick out data meriting scrutiny by an intelligence officer, only facts bearing on national security will trigger scrutiny. But once an individual is identified as a possible terrorist or foreign agent, the government's interest in him will explode. Besides obtaining contact information, it will want to learn about his ethnicity and national origin; education and skills; previous addresses and travel (especially overseas); family, friends, and acquaintances; political and religious beliefs and activities; finances; any arrest or other criminal record; military service (if any); mental health and other psychological attributes; and a range of consumption activities, the whole adding up to a comprehensive personal profile.

No doubt collection for the purposes of potential downstream human comprehension do raise individual privacy concerns, precisely because sentient beings have a probability of using the data and deriving conclusions.[29] Posner is right, however, that there are many benign examples of computers looking at data that do not usually raise privacy concerns. For example, the Internet is based on packet-forwarding nodes that are presumed to look only at the headers. A fair analogy is the postcard being processed at the Post Office. Even if those packet-forwarding nodes processed the packet "payload" contents, for example, to calculate a "checksum" and verify that the data has not been corrupted, no one seems to care. Perhaps the only action that would result from such a calculation is a request for retransmit at the prior node, completely devoid of human intervention. But if the error is logged, and the error logs are routinely read by a human system administrator, the risk of human comprehension as a result of algorithmic filtering and storing does raise privacy issues. Internet service providers log requests routinely, but it took the prospect of those logs being attributed and sold to bring attention to the logging.[30]

Another benign example of algorithmic processing is the calculation of baseline normality for abnormality testing. When machine learning is applied to a set of cases that are normal, and a set of cases labeled as abnormal, usually no re-identifiable data can be attributed to an individual in one of the training sets. This is especially true of the individuals in the set labeled as normal: usually it is a large set, and usually no decision is made, no alert sounded, when inputs are classified as normal. In the simplest example of this, training data may simply cause statistical summaries such as means and moments to be retained. Long before there was machine learning, there was information retrieval that required "inverse document frequencies" of words, which were statistical summaries that aggregated many individuals' data.

[28] R. A. Posner, Privacy, Surveillance, and Law (2008) 75 *Univ. Chi. Law Rev.* 245, 253–4.

[29] See, e.g., O. Tene and J. Polonetsky, Privacy in the Age of Big Data: A Time for Big Decisions (2012) 64 *Stan. Law Rev. Online*; I. S. Rubinstein, Big Data: The End of Privacy or a New Beginning? (2013) 3 *Int. Data Privacy Law* 74; or I. Kerr and J. Earle, Prediction, Preemption, Presumption: How Big Data Threatens Big Picture Privacy (2013) 66 *Stan. Law Rev. Online* 65.

[30] See, e.g., B. Fung, What to Expect Now that Internet Providers Can Collect and Sell Your Web Browser history, *Washington Post* (March 29, 2017).

There are few privacy interests for data used in this way, precisely because no human ever looks at the individual's information apart from the aggregate.[31]

Computers, of course, are constantly logging transactions for billing purposes, where summarization, notification, and payment are all done without human comprehension, unless an error condition or audit is triggered.

There are autonomous systems that are not benign processors. Some may even be regarded as malign actors, or even authoritarian AI. The same machine-learning program that did not raise privacy concerns during training could make autonomous decisions that impact persons in ways that anyone would recognize as classic violations of an individual's rights. In most cases, those rights will not be privacy rights, but non-discrimination, speech, employment, equal protection, property, or other rights. It will be because someone or some group delegated too much authority, or because of an error in the program, or a malfunction of the device: something where the control is the problem, not just the access to information and its comprehension.

It is easily conceivable that an autonomous system could access student test records, or statistical correlates of student test records, for an employment decision, in a way that ignores Family Educational Rights and Privacy Act protections. Even here, it is not the machine comprehension of the data that stings, but the use of the data, as an act, that produces a harm or violates a protocol; and that sequence is probably attributable to a programmer. When self-organizing, evolving, self-programmed automata begin to re-identify Health Insurance Portability and Accountability Act anonymized data in patently disallowed ways, without having been programmed explicitly to do so, then Posner's counsel, "[o]nly the human search should raise constitutional or other legal issues," might well be disregarded.

The bottom line is that sometimes computer processing is benign. Collection qua logging is just collection, unless there is potential for further processing of the logs, leading eventually to comprehension by a human, or leading to a decision, action, or exclusion.

Many algorithms are intended to improve privacy of data, by de-anonymizing or de-linking, reducing precision, masking, blurring, generalizing, hashing, encrypting, or otherwise pseudonymizing.[32] No one minds that a computer "sees" the data that it is encrypting so that others cannot see it. Other kinds of computer processing can transgress, especially if the programming permits impropriety. Most of the time the automation is discarding data as uninteresting, as a pre-processor to reduce the human workload at a later stage.

There is therefore no *a priori* reason to assume that computer processing of data, even large quantities of data, crosses privacy sensibilities. And there is no reason to believe that computer processing of data, of any quantity, is incapable of raising concerns. It depends on the algorithm and how it is embedded in social decision-making and social controls.

LEGALITY AND ALGORITHMIC STAGES

Justice Sotomayor's concurring opinion in *United States* v. *Jones*, regarding police use of GPS tracking, is the clarion call for regarding big data as different from property and persons that can be searched and seized. In *Jones*, the Supreme Court held that attaching a GPS device to a vehicle and using the device to monitor the vehicle's movements constitutes a search under

---

[31] A classic work in this field is G. Salton, *Automated Text Processing* (Prentice Hall, 1983).

[32] For discussion of various privacy techniques, see, e.g., S. M. Bellovin, P. K. Dutta, and N. Reitinger, Privacy and Synthetic Datasets (2019) 22 *Stan. Technol. Law Rev.* 1; or K. Nissim, A. Bembenek, A. Wood, *et al.*, Bridging the Gap between Computer Science and Legal Approaches to Privacy (2018) 31 *Harv. J. Law Technol.* 2.

the Fourth Amendment. The Court reached a unanimous result, but several justices differed in their reasoning. In particular, Justice Sotomayor explained that technological advances have shaped the evolution of privacy expectations, particularly where physical intrusion is unnecessary for many forms of surveillance. She stated that, at the very least, "longer term GPS monitoring in investigations of most offenses impinges on expectations of privacy." Furthermore:

> In cases involving even short-term monitoring, some unique attributes of GPS surveillance relevant to the *Katz* analysis will require particular attention. GPS monitoring generates a precise, comprehensive record of a person's public movements that reflects a wealth of detail about her familial, political, professional, religious, and sexual associations ... The Government can store such records and efficiently mine them for information years into the future ... And because GPS monitoring is cheap in comparison to conventional surveillance techniques and, by design, proceeds surreptitiously, it evades the ordinary checks that constrain abusive law enforcement practices: limited police resources and community hostility.

There are several issues regarding data here. First, there is the collection over time. Second, the precision or alleged precision. Third, the comprehensiveness, or alleged comprehensiveness. Fourth, there is the inferential productivity of the data. Fifth, there is the persistence of the data, which raises questions of its staleness and the European concern over "being forgotten." Finally, there is the issue of quantity, where a practical limit that had been related to cost is no longer a constraint, with cheap data acquisition at scale.

These issues are beyond the scope of this chapter except the last, and to some extent the fourth. We have argued that the algorithm matters, and the numbers at each stage matter, in expressing judicial will and guidance. When there is an issue of quantity, perhaps legislators and courts should find a way to express what quantities are permissible. The quantities, in relation to the stages of the algorithm, may have as rationale the productivity of the inferences at each stage (the fourth issue above), not just the risk of practical harm. Quantities can be expressed as proportions, with suggested norms if not bright lines, and with orders of magnitudes for ranges. Algorithms can be referenced by their type, such as "social network analysis" or "automatic classification," and their high-level features, such as *ex ante* and *ex post*, relative to some massive filtering, querying, or storing.

In some ways, the issue of reasonable quantities was delegated to the FISA Court, which failed to constrain sequential retention as a concomitant of individual warrant granting. Gray and Citron propose a different idea of quantity in relation to privacy.[33] Until now, most proposals for defending Fourth Amendment interests in quantitative privacy have focused on a case-by-case method called the "mosaic theory." Under this approach, the Fourth Amendment is implicated whenever law enforcement officers gather "too much" information during the course of a specific investigation. Critics of the mosaic theory have rightly wondered how courts will determine whether investigators have gathered too much information in any given case and how officers in the midst of ongoing investigations will know whether the aggregate fruits of their efforts are approaching a Fourth Amendment boundary. The best solution that mosaic advocates have so far been able to muster is to draw bright, if arbitrary, lines based on how long officers use an investigative method or technology. These kinds of solutions fail to satisfy because they are under-inclusive and over-inclusive, and also sidestep important conceptual and doctrinal questions. Rather than asking how much

[33] See D. Gray and D. Citron, The Right to Quantitative Privacy (2013) 98 *Minn. Law Rev.* 62.

information is gathered in a particular case, we argue here that Fourth Amendment interests in quantitative privacy demand that we focus on how information is processed.[34]

While we agree that a mosaic theory of the Fourth Amendment is an important idea, and agree that there is such a thing as gathering too much information under a particular warrant, their conclusion is different from ours (and, apparently, Posner's). They focus on the permissibility or impermissibility of first-stage bulk collection, which has the potential, the mere possibility, of yielding human scrutiny of a particular individual's data at some later stage. This was in fact where much of the press focused its attention during the Snowden disclosures, and led to the disconnect: one side was discussing large numbers at the first stage of algorithmic processing; the other side was discussing small numbers at the final stages of algorithmic processing.

It may be that constraining collection is a lost cause, practically speaking. Like disallowed discrimination in the insurance industry, the data are there whether one tries to disallow their collection or not. The rights of individuals must therefore be secured by severing the particular inferences that cause actual harm.

CONCLUSION

Technological innovations have dramatically expanded the ability to use personal data: the ability to collect, edit, compare, distribute, store, process, and mine data, which were once extraordinarily time-consuming processes, can now be accomplished instantaneously. Unsurprisingly, national intelligence agencies around the world are taking advantage of new information communication technologies in their investigations, particularly those against terrorists. Consequently, there has been an increase in state knowledge of individuals' movements, financial standing, behavior, sexual habits, and other personal characteristics important to self-definition. States justify the high levels of data collection and exchange as part of the fight against crime and terrorism. The central question concerns how to warrant this unbridled gathering, analysis, and exchange of electronic information by intelligence agencies and law enforcement to combat terroristic threats and investigate criminal activities while safeguarding the privacy of ordinary citizens.

We claim that the concept of stages should be an integral part of any discussion about the privacy infringements by intelligence agencies, and should be taken into account in future legislation. We elaborated on the characteristics of stages in algorithms and what the particular consequences of stages might be. This will help to clarify how to guard the values concerning algorithmic processing of data.

---

[34] Another way of explaining mosaic theory is given here: "The fundamental insight behind the mosaic theory is that we can maintain reasonable expectations of Fourth Amendment privacy in certain quantities of information and data even if we lack reasonable expectations of privacy in the constituent parts of that whole." D. Gray and D. K. Citron, A Shattered Looking Glass: The Pitfalls and Potential of the Mosaic Theory of Fourth Amendment Privacy (2012) 14 *NC J. Law Technol.* 381, 390.

PART VI

Applications and Future Directions of Law and Algorithms

Moral Machines

The Emerging EU Policy on "Trustworthy AI"

Andrea Renda

The development of a policy framework for the sustainable and ethical use of artificial intelligence (AI) techniques has gradually become one of the top policy priorities in developed countries as well as in the international context, including the G7 and G20 and work within the Organisation for Economic Cooperation and Development (OECD), the World Economic Forum, and the International Telecommunications Union. Interestingly, this mounting debate has taken place with very little attention to the definition of what AI is and its phenomenology in the real world, as well as its expected evolution. Politicians evoke the imminent takeover of smart autonomous robots; entrepreneurs announce the end of mankind, or the achievement of immortality through brain upload; and academics fight over the prospects of Artificial General Intelligence, which appears inevitable to some, and preposterous to others. In all this turmoil, governments developed the belief that, as both Vladimir Putin and Xi Jinping recently put it, the country that will lead in AI will, as a consequence, come to dominate the world. As AI gains positions in the ranking of top government priorities, a digital arms race has also emerged, in particular between the United States and China. This race bears far-reaching consequences when it comes to earmarking funds for research, innovation, and investment on AI technologies: gradually, AI becomes an end, rather than a means, and military and domestic security applications are given priority over civilian use cases, which may contribute more extensively to social and environmental sustainability. As of today, one could argue that the top priority in US AI policy is contrasting the rise of China, and vice versa.[1]

Against this background, Europe started its public debate on AI with a good dose of fear of the unknown, and limited understanding of the reality behind the hype. In particular, the 2016 Resolution on "Civil Law Rules for Robotics" adopted by the European Parliament cited Mary Shelley's *Frankenstein* already at page 1, and invoked the creation of an Agency for the regulation of AI, as well as the attribution of legal personality, and thus "rights and duties" to smart autonomous robots. Despite that somewhat false start, however, today the European Union stands among the most advanced legal systems in the debate on AI and its impact on the economy, society, and environment: this is largely due to the solidity and comprehensiveness of the European legal system, based on well-established values and a solid tradition in risk regulation; and on the European ability to organize multi-stakeholder debates in support of public policy. Between 2017 and 2019, EU institutions managed to ensure coordination with the national agenda of all Member States; set up an AI alliance that counts, at the time of

---

[1] See A. Renda, Europe and the Digital Arms Race, CEPS Commentary (2019), www.ceps.eu/europe-and-the-digital-arms-race/.

writing, over 4,000 participants; relied on the advice of a High-Level Group of fifty-two experts from academia, industry, and civil society; and planted the seeds of what will soon become a risk-based approach to so-called "Trustworthy AI," which the newly appointed President of the European Commission, Ursula von der Leyen, promised to translate into a policy framework on "the ethical and human consequences of artificial intelligence," adopting a White Paper on AI already during the first 100 days of her mandate (on February 19, 2020).[2] This, altogether, places the European Union at the forefront of the policy reflection on how to maximize the benefits of AI, while at the same time accounting, in a proportionate manner, for the ensuing risks. Most importantly, the European Commission managed to bring back the debate in line with the underlying academic reflection on AI, paving the way for an evidence-based approach that handles this powerful family of techniques with care, but not with fear.[3]

This chapter revisits the first two years of policy development at the EU level, placing it in the global context, and illustrates possible avenues for future developments, highlighting the challenges and opportunities that are likely to emerge in the years to come. Accordingly, the first section below, "Defining and Approaching AI," discusses the definition of AI developed at the EU level by the High-Level Expert Group (HLEG), and discusses current and future developments of AI techniques, alongside emerging use cases and related ethical and policy challenges. The second section, "The EU Agenda on Trustworthy AI," contains an illustration of the main features of the emerging EU policy framework, with specific emphasis on the recent publication of Ethics Guidelines for Trustworthy AI, and the policy recommendations formulated by the HLEG. The third section, "What's Next?," briefly concludes by discussing the likely content of upcoming policy initiatives by the European Commission and the prospects for Europe to lead the global debate on ethically aligned, sustainability-oriented AI.

DEFINING AND APPROACHING AI

The term "artificial intelligence" has proven to be elusive and even misleading, and this probably contributed to the confusion that has emerged in the public, academic, and policy debate over the opportunities and challenges of widespread AI diffusion. First, the word "intelligence," as composed by Latin terms *intus* ("inside") and *legere* ("reading"), hints at the possibility of providing machines with an understanding of the context in which they operate, as well as an awareness of the purpose of their actions: this, however, hardly matches the developments that are emerging in current research, let alone commercial applications. Likewise, the use of the word "artificial" may be understood as referring to techniques, which seek to replicate the functioning of the human brain, and this, too, can prove misleading, as the decision-making process followed by most AI systems seeks to replicate neither the process nor the outcome of human decision-making.[4]

More specifically, current AI systems mostly embed so-called "simple reflex agents," which select an action based on the current state only, ignoring historical data or past experience. Model-based reflex agents partly differ as they can act in partially observable environments by

---

[2]   See the programmatic document by U. von der Leyen, A Union that Strives for More. My Agenda for Europe. Political Guidelines for the Next Commission 2019–2024, https://ec.europa.eu/commission/sites/beta-political /files/political-guidelines-next-commission_en.pdf; and the White Paper, On Artificial Intelligence – a European Approach to Excellence and Trust, COM(2020)65 final, February 19, 2020.
[3]   See A. Renda, Artificial Intelligence: Ethical, Governance and Policy Challenges, CEPS Monograph (2019).
[4]   *Ibid.*

constantly updating their (static) representation of the world. A further evolution is represented by goal-based agents, used in cases where knowing the current state of the environment is not considered to be sufficient: the agents can combine the provided goal information with the environment model, to choose those actions that can achieve the given goal. Utility-based agents are an improvement over goal-based agents: they choose the action that maximizes the expected utility, after weighing both benefits and costs: they are thus very similar to the *homo oeconomicus* in economic theory. But the state of the art in AI goes beyond all these types of agents and implies the development of so-called "learning agents," which are based on the original definition given by Alan Turing. As agents become more complex, so does their internal structure, allowing for various forms of internal state representation.

Within the context of information systems, AI enables more complex decision-making, based on criteria that are, at least initially, provided to the machine by human beings. Russell and Norvig observe that AI "refers to systems that display intelligent behaviour by analysing their environment and taking actions – with some degree of autonomy – to achieve specific goals."[5] For example, rational decision-making could be a goal for the AI developer, and as such the calculation of expected benefits and costs associated with a given action can be embedded in the system. However, full rationality does not seem to be an essential element of an AI system: an AI developer could also try to replicate rational biases, such as impulsiveness, framing, or hyperbolic discounting, to enable better interaction with human beings – for example, in the case of companion robots or autonomous cars interacting with humanly driven ones.[6] An AI system can also be taught to act in conditions of imperfect information, and as such can be trained to act with "rational ignorance" or in a more risk-averse way. Accordingly, the requirement of rationality does not seem to be needed in a definition of AI, even if ensuring that AI-enabled machines behave rationally will often be a clear goal of the developer.[7]

Also, rationality should not be intended as a process, but rather as an outcome. There is no need for an AI system to replicate the same process followed by the human brain, based, inter alia, on neurons and synapses.[8] While neural networks are being used in deep learning processes, they are only one out of several possible ways to develop AI.[9] Postulating that AI should seek to mimic the functioning of the human brain would be also complicated if one considers that our brain functions are still relatively obscure for neuroscientists.[10] At the same time, pretending that AI replicates or mimics the outcome of human decision-making would also imply that all the biases and imperfections of our decisions would be replicated in the AI system, and this, too, would be undesirable in many circumstances.

---

[5]   S. Russell and P. Norvig, *Artificial Intelligence: A Modern Approach*, 3rd edn. (Pearson, 2009).
[6]   Some scholars have proposed incorporating that quality into self-driving cars; see A. Renda, Ethics, Algorithms and Self-Driving Cars: A CSI of the "Trolley Problem," CEPS Policy Insights No. 2018/02 (January 2018), www .ceps.eu/system/files/PI%202018–02_Renda_TrolleyProblem.pdf.
[7]   In AI, a rational agent is typically one that maximizes its expected utility, given its current knowledge.
[8]   There is indeed research that tries to emulate some aspects of the human nervous system in silico. Such systems are called neuromorphic.
[9]   D. Silver, A. Huang, C. J. Maddison, *et al.*, Mastering the Game of Go with Deep Neural Networks and Tree Search (2016) 529 *Nature* 484.
[10] R. Adolphs, The Unsolved Problems of Neuroscience (2015) 19 *Trends Cogn. Sci.* 173–5.

An Official Definition

At the EU level, the HLEG was tasked, inter alia, with providing a definition of AI that would prove technology-neutral. The resulting definition refers to AI systems as "systems that display intelligent behavior by analyzing their environment and taking actions – with some degree of autonomy – to achieve specific goals."[11]

The Group added that AI systems can be purely software-based, acting in the virtual world, such as, for example, voice assistants, chatbots, search engines, or image recognition and analysis software; or embedded in hardware devices, as in the case of advanced robots, autonomous cars, drones, or Internet of Things (IoT) applications. This does not change the ultimate scope and activity of AI systems, which rest essentially in acquiring data from the external environment, processing them, and providing solutions or, in some cases, ultimate decisions. This specification is also useful to understand the potential and limits of AI, as well as its dependency on complementary technologies, such as robotics and IoT, both for sensing and actuating. In other words, AI is the equivalent of a brain (without possessing its plasticity and complexity, at least for now), which is powerful per se, but very limited without blood and oxygen (computing power), a nervous system and muscles (sensors and actuators), and memory and information (data and storage). Even if simpler than the human brain, AI is equally dependent on complementary technologies to fully deploy its potential.

The definition provided by the HLEG also accounts for a key evolution of AI techniques, by specifying the conceptual difference between reasoning and decision-making systems, and learning-based ones. Reasoning and decision-making techniques include knowledge representation and reasoning, planning, scheduling, search, and optimization. These techniques require forms of data acquisition and knowledge representation, which then leads to knowledge reasoning and ultimately taking decisions. Learning techniques include machine learning, neural networks, deep learning, decision trees, and many other techniques that allow an AI system to learn how to solve problems that cannot be precisely specified, or whose solution method cannot be described by symbolic reasoning rules. In particular, machine-learning models are particularly useful when the system needs to interpret unstructured data, since they produce a numeric model (that is, a mathematical formula) used to compute the decision from the data. It was extremely important to avoid focusing only on machine-learning techniques, especially in Europe, where these techniques can face obstacles due to strict data protection rules. As a matter of fact, machine learning is an extremely data-intensive process, and its more sophisticated variants such as deep learning and reinforcement learning appear to be also extremely energy-intensive. The EU definition leaves space for alternative, equally powerful techniques.

The Rise of AI: Efficiency and Agency Problems

Human beings have built technology to automate and improve the execution of specific tasks since the invention of the wheel. Technology typically serves the goal of empowering individuals by expanding their possibility frontier – for example, by executing physical tasks that can prove repetitive, time-consuming, and/or physically exhausting: delegating these activities to man-made technology, under human control and supervision, can lead individuals to dedicate their intellect to more productive activities. The invention of the plow in

---

[11]   See the HLEG document, A Definition of AI: Main Capabilities and Disciplines: Definition Developed for the Purpose of the HLEG's Deliverables (April 2019).

agriculture, among many others, has brought enormous improvements in productivity; and needless to say, the whole domain of engineering, from mechanics to transportation, is dedicated to this very goal of human research and development (R&D). The invention of the personal computer and the introduction of networked computing and the Internet have revolutionized the way in which humans communicate, work, and enjoy inter-personal relationships. At the same time, as will be discussed below in more detail, the debate is still raging as to whether Information and Communication Technologies really led to the promised productivity increases.

Today, AI promises to boost productivity, bringing the delegation of tasks to machines to a new level. At the same time, AI and its related technologies require a more challenging adaptation process, given that delegated actions are more complex and require a degree of reasoning, compared to the mere execution of physical tasks. More specifically, some AI applications can expand the ability of humans to optimize processes and identify patterns that can support better decision-making. For example, in medical imaging and diagnostics, AI (in particular, machine learning in support of image recognition) has proven to achieve similar levels of accuracy as the ones humans, alone, can reach.[12] However, the combination of man and machine is still delivering more accurate results than the operation of a machine alone. In the latter case, given the absence of "intelligence" in the etymological sense used above, AI systems tend to err in very odd ways, thus requiring careful human supervision. Similarly, image recognition (coupled with data collected by sensors and drones) in agriculture provides unique opportunities for identifying ripe fruits and vegetables, and optimizing yield as well as soil management.[13] Thanks to the ability to process otherwise intractable amounts of data, AI systems also support prediction in unprecedented ways, and this, too, expands the possibilities frontier of mankind. The whole area of predictive maintenance is promising breakthroughs and productivity increases in sectors such as energy, agriculture, manufacturing, and transportation, and awaits new increases in computing techniques (for example, edge computing, and in the near future quantum computing) to deploy its potential even more fully.

At the same time, however, the delegation of decisions to AI systems can prove extremely challenging, especially when awareness of the context is a necessary prerequisite, and the possibility of keeping an expert human "in the loop" is limited. As an example, deploying AI in fully autonomous vehicles cannot rely on humans in the loop, given the very short time frame available for decisions to be adopted. The academic literature has explored in-depth scenarios in which autonomous vehicles face the so-called "trolley problem" in their interaction with pedestrians and/or human-driven vehicles: for example, the MIT's "Moral Machine" experiment and academic work on "kidney exchanges" showed the extreme difficulty of pre-programming an AI system to take "life or death" decisions when all scenarios imply the death of at least one human being, as well as the large variety of preferences that individuals have for the most suited criteria to rely on when programming the system.[14] More

[12] X. Liu, L. Faes, A. Kale, *et al.*, A Comparison of Deep Learning Performance against Health Care Professionals in Detecting Diseases from Medical Imaging: A Systematic Review and Meta-Analysis (2019) 1 *Lancet Digital Health* PE271, https://doi.org/10.1016/S2589-7500(19)30123-2.

[13] A. Renda, The Age of Foodtech: Optimizing the Agri-Food Chain with Digital Technologies, in M. Antonelli, R. Valentini, J. Sievenpiper, and K. Dembska (eds.), *Achieving SDGs through Sustainable Food Systems* (Springer, 2019).

[14] E. Awad, S. Dsouza, R. Kim, *et al.*, The Moral Machine Experiment (2018) 563 *Nature* 59–64; R. Freedman, J. Schaich Borg, W. Sinnott-Armstrong, *et al.*, Adapting a Kidney Exchange Algorithm to Align with Human Values, in Proceedings of the Thirty-Second AAAI Conference on Artificial Intelligence (AAAI-18), New Orleans, LA, United States (2018).

generally, AI systems that are deployed in very interactive and unpredictable environments, even if heavily tested in labs, can end up adopting sub-optimal or unpredictable behavior: with the diffusion of AI techniques and use cases, the interaction between AI-enabled algorithms will inevitably become an even more problematic issue, also from a legal perspective.

More specifically, the delegation of complex tasks and decisions to automated AI systems can raise a number of legal issues, which according to many scholars require an update of the legal apparatus conceived for less complex technologies. Such problems are related to various phases of the AI development, from the quality and representativeness of the data used by AI systems, or used to train them; to the quality of the training itself, together with the design features and the development of the algorithm; and the possibility of holding AI developers or vendors accountable for damages caused by systems that feature a certain degree of autonomy. These problems are exacerbated by the fact that advanced learning-based AI techniques, especially when based on deep neural networks, potentially lead to the development of inference and decision-making that are only partly predictable by the original developers: such unpredictability, sometimes referred to as the "black box" problem, is embedded in the process, since the use of these techniques is aimed at bringing machines to develop new and more efficient ways to tackle problems.[15] For example, the work of DeepMind in training AI systems to play complex games such as chess or "Go" has, over time, led to extremely fascinating, but also unpredictable, paths of decision-making.[16]

This first issue, of liability attribution, is now being analyzed by governments and scholars in many legal systems.[17] In principle, most of these legal problems could be addressed by the products liability regime, which typically relies on forms of relative strict liability, rather than fault-based systems. Civil law countries, in particular, typically rely on explicit strict liability rules that go beyond the commercialization of products, such as in the case of: an employer's strict liability for unjust damages caused by employees; strict liability for dangerous activities; or liability for damages caused by minors of age, or animals under custody. All of these rules, despite being stricter than fault-based liability, are normally based on the notion of "control" – that is, the liability of third parties for damages caused by humans, animals, or objects under their sphere of control and supervision. In most cases, liability is limited to occurrences that could be reasonably predicted, and the reason for such limitation is that incentives to engage in societally desirable activities would be significantly stifled, if individuals were subject to liability also for unforeseeable damages. In the case of certain AI systems, such predictability is limited *by design*, due to the use of deep neural networks, and this potentially challenges existing strict liability regimes. Moreover, the legal treatment of liability in the case of AI becomes even more complicated as AI systems, once deployed, end up interacting with other AI systems, and with the external environment, including, inter alia, human beings, which very often depart from rational, predictable behavior. For example, events such as "flash crashes," or sudden price spikes or collapses due to algorithmic interaction, largely remain unattributed. In all of these circumstances, the minimum levels of care to be considered for individuals and algorithms have been subject to too little attention, and are likely to become a major issue in litigation in the years to come. As a side remark, the development of

---

[15] F. Pasquale, *The Black Box Society: The Secret Algorithms that Control Money and Information* (Harvard University Press, 2015).

[16] This, however, does not mean that AI systems have become "intelligent": as a matter of fact, training a machine to toss a coin before deciding would also make the decision unpredictable, without making the machine intelligent.

[17] Renda, above note 3.

insurance products for AI systems is still in its early infancy, and this can also affect the level of legal certainty for AI developers in the near future.

But there is more than products liability, in AI systems, that creates problems for policy-makers. Two perhaps more profound and disruptive aspects of AI are the need to move beyond efficiency arguments when discussing its deployment and diffusion; and the agency and self-determination problems AI can generate in its interaction with human beings. First, while the introduction of new inventions and innovative solutions has typically contributed to economic efficiency in the past, with frequent distributional consequences due to the replacement of manual labor with capital, in the case of AI-enabled decision-making the efficiency-enhancing features can easily clash with legal and ethical considerations, which extend to the overall acceptance of the technology itself among civil society. For example, Daron Acemoglu and Pascual Restrepo identify a possible trade-off between cost-effective AI solutions and the quality of production processes, observing that in certain circumstances the need to cut costs may induce companies to introduce quality-reducing AI systems, at the same time reducing employment opportunities.[18] Moreover, some AI systems can enhance efficiency through prediction analytics by allowing granular discrimination: for example, in determining the creditworthiness of a customer, accuracy can increase if information is available on the customer's credit history, but also if the system accounts for the customer's ethnicity and related propensity to repay debt; and maybe the customers' gender, income levels, past tax compliance, and opinions expressed on social media. That said, allowing the AI system to discriminate based on these features may violate existing constitutional principles (where available), legal rules, and more generally fundamental rights. Similarly, awarding priority to individuals belonging to specific ethnic groups or income class in organ donation may be justified on (neoclassical) efficiency grounds, but would fall beyond the boundaries of legal rules and "post-compliance" ethics.

This issue becomes even more problematic since when it comes to AI systems, a trilemma is emerging: the most accurate techniques (such as deep learning) are often the least explainable ones, and often the most data-hungry ones, potentially impinging on privacy. This is one of the most challenging problems when it comes to AI policy: on the one hand, purely "neutral" and perfectly transparent algorithms can be discriminatory, since they simply replicate biases that already exist in society, or even in legal rules; at the other extreme, highly accurate but partly unexplainable AI systems may incorporate a number of fairness-enhancing arrangements and anti-discrimination features, but they may still end up issuing decisions that are imperscrutable, and potentially realizing undesirable outcomes. Here lies one of the "thin lines" between established legal regimes for product or third-party liability and the emerging AI world: should the incorporation of state-of-the-art fairness metrics be taken as sufficient grounds for excluding tort liability, or should unjust damage be compensated despite the adoption of such measures? Alternatively, should other forms of compensation (for example, through an *ad hoc* fund) be provided in case the damage was considered to fall out of the control sphere of the deployer?

Finally, the diffusion of AI-enabled services and products also creates ethical and legal problems for what concerns agency and self-determination on the side of the end-user. Among the most important areas to be analyzed in this domain are the emergence of bias and discrimination, which possibly deprives certain individuals or groups of equal

---

[18] D. Acemoglu and P. Restrepo, The Wrong Kind of AI? Artificial Intelligence and the Future of Labor Demand, NBER Working Paper No. w25682 (2019), https://ssrn.com/abstract=3359482.

opportunities compared to others; the possibility that AI-enabled algorithms intentionally or unintentionally influence consumer choice, thereby reducing individual freedom to self-determine (as in the case of so-called "hyper-nudging"); the prospect of advance manipulation of the public opinion and the democratic process through so-called "deepfakes," which rely on advanced AI techniques such as generative adversarial networks (GANs); and finally, the debate on whether AI-enabled bots, when interacting with end-users, should disclose their non-human identity (the so-called "counter-CAPTCHA" issue). Below, these aspects are analyzed in more depth.

Bias and Discrimination

The issue of bias and discrimination is inherent in the use of data-hungry AI techniques such as machine learning. Already from the data collection phase, two main problems can emerge. First, the data itself may not be of good quality, or the sample from which data is collected not sufficiently representative of society. Typical examples are cases in which a user interface was tested with reference to a specific ethnic group, as was the case for facial recognition systems, which tend to display a much higher error rate when trying to recognize people with darker skin.[19] The widespread deployment of facial recognition algorithms in public services, customs, or police controls can end up building a two-speed society, in which different ethnicities are exposed to different likelihoods of being suspected of crime, inspected, and ultimately arrested. Second, even when the data sampling is "de-biased," bias may creep into the process since it is reality, and thus our society, that is fraught with bias. For example, evidence that in many areas of the United States African-Americans are much more likely to be pulled over and inspected by the police than Caucasians leads to more frequent records of crimes committed by African-Americans:[20] this, in turn, leads to an over-representation of African-Americans in the data, which are fed to algorithms that decide, inter alia, whether to grant parole to prisoners.[21] Much in the same vein, the use of big data and predictive policing techniques in a number of cities around the world has led to concerns over racial biases. In 2016, many commentators argued that "AI is racist," since a beauty contest that was to be decided by an algorithm, supposedly using "objective" factors such as facial symmetry and wrinkles, led to the almost total exclusion of dark-skinned contestants.[22] Similarly, problems emerged also in large tech companies – for example, when Microsoft released Tay, a chatbot that quickly began using racist language and promoting neo-Nazi views on Twitter; and when Facebook eliminated human editors who had curated "trending" news stories, to discover that the algorithm immediately promoted fake and vulgar stories on news feeds.[23]

What makes the issue almost intractable is that there is no such thing as a neutral algorithm: and even if it was possible to generate one, a neutral algorithm would in many cases be useless,

---

[19] See T. Simonite, The Best Algorithms Struggle to Recognize Black Faces Equally, *Wired* (July 22, 2019), www .wired.com/story/best-algorithms-struggle-recognize-black-faces-equally/.

[20] See M. A. Fletcher, For Black Motorists, a Never-Ending Fear of Being Stopped, *National Geographic*, www .nationalgeographic.com/magazine/2018/04/the-stop-race-police-traffic/.

[21] An article by *ProPublica* compared two stories of prisoners awaiting parole, showing how machines may end up incorporating bias from the very outset. A. G. Ferguson, *The Rise of Big Data Policing: Surveillance, Race, and the Future of Law Enforcement* (New York University Press, 2017).

[22] See S. Levin, A Beauty Contest Was Judged by AI and the Robots Didn't Like Dark Skin, *The Guardian* (September 8, 2016), www.theguardian.com/technology/2016/sep/08/artificial-intelligence-beauty-contest-doesnt-like-black-people.

[23] See S. Thielman, Facebook Fires Trending Team, and Algorithm without Humans Goes Crazy, *The Guardian* (August 29, 2016), www.theguardian.com/technology/2016/aug/29/facebook-fires-trending-topics-team-algorithm.

whereas "excessively" biased algorithms can be dangerous and harmful.[24] Accordingly, it is important to define which biases are to be considered acceptable, and which are not. This is even more complicated since in many cases what is acceptable or not also changes through time, alongside technological evolution. There is also a potential trade-off between accuracy and privacy. In some cases, more accurate algorithms can eliminate bias by not treating people on the basis of average calculations. For example, an algorithm may decide not to grant credit to an individual since he or she belongs to an ethnic group that on average repays debts less often.

Influencing Consumer Choice: The "Hyper-Nudging" Era and the Rise of the Deepfakes

Even when bias does not creep into the early stages of AI development, it could still be incorporated in the design of the algorithm to "nudge" individuals toward specific decisions. In short, the practice of nudging as a public policy tool emerged from the work of Sunstein and Thaler, who based their analysis on the literature on bounded rationality and, to some extent, rational ignorance.[25] From the observation of the limited ability of humans to process complex information, as well as their dependence on "proxies" when formulating decisions, the practice of nudging relied on empirical evidence of the stickiness of the default option, anchoring and framing effects (or so-called "endowment effects"), which create the possibility of influencing human decisions by "choice architecture" – that is, presenting choices to individuals in a way that would make one option more attractive than the alternatives. In particular, emphasizing gains rather than losses in advertising public services; and selecting default options that correspond to government preferences or to what is thought to be good for the decision-maker (for example, avoiding junk food) or for society (for example, recycling waste properly) have emerged as frequent practices, with still-controversial results in terms of effectiveness, but also of legitimacy and adherence to ethical principles.

In the age of AI and big data, the plasticity of digital technology makes nudging exponentially easier and more far-reaching: thereby the term "hyper-nudging" or "big nudge" used by scholars. Some scholars have observed that big data and AI may significantly expand the possibility of nudging, making it more effective: for example, being able to predict or directly observe the mood of individual consumers in different days of the week, as well as times of the day, can help in tailoring both commercial and government messages in a way that maximizes the desired outcome. Also, the use of big data and personal data in recommendation engines and search engines has proven to be most effective: for example, more than 60 percent of Netflix's revenues are attributed to the effectiveness of its recommendation engine (what to watch next), and similar findings are available also for large retail commerce platforms such as Amazon.com. As often happens with powerful digital technologies, their ability to expand the potential of existing techniques brings both opportunities and risks. For example, Karen Yeung argues that hyper-nudging is even more dangerous than "analog" nudging, since it further compresses individuals' "right not to be deceived, rooted in a moral agent's basic right to be treated with dignity and respect."[26] Other authors have argued along similar lines, but highlighting the risk that hyper-nudging deprives individuals of their liberty.

---

[24]   A. Renda, Searching for Harm, or Harming Search? A look at the European Commission's antitrust investigation against Google, CEPS Special Report No. 118 (September 2015). Published also as Working Paper of the Rethinking Regulation program at Duke University, Kenan Institute for Ethics.

[25]   C. Sunstein and R. H. Thaler, *Nudge: Improving Decisions about Health, Wealth, and Happiness* (Penguin, 2008).

[26]   K. Yeung, "Hypernudge": Big Data as a Mode of Regulation by Design (2017) 20 *Inf. Commun. Soc.* 1.

Once again, AI poses important challenges for policymakers, since it can be equally used for good and for bad reasons. The most extreme case of manipulation of users' opinions and choices is found in the realm of information and the political debate. For example, so-called "content bubbles" (or "echo chambers") are described as a "state of intellectual isolation," which occurs whenever an individual interacts with a single news source, powered by an algorithm that only feeds users based on their perception of what they will like or be interested in. Described in the past by Nicholas Negroponte and later by Cass Sunstein as "the daily me" problem, this problem is the product of both behavioral biases (such as the "confirmation bias" – namely, we tend to like what we already agree with)[27] and the use of algorithms for personalized search, which are based on our past searches and thus mostly select content from a narrow sub-set of available sources. Well exemplified by the *Wall Street Journal*'s "Blue Feed, Red Feed" site,[28] the problem was officially acknowledged by Microsoft co-founder Bill Gates, who in a recent interview observed that the fact that on social media "you're not mixing and sharing and understanding other points of view" has turned out "to be more of a problem than I, or many others, would have expected."[29] The European Commission recently observed that "new technologies can be used, notably through social media, to disseminate disinformation on a scale and with speed and precision of targeting that is unprecedented, creating personalized information spheres and becoming powerful echo chambers for disinformation campaigns."[30]

In a sub-set of cases, the lack of filtering on online platforms has led to the abuse of such platforms, with the clear intention to manipulate public opinion – for example, in the occasion of an election. For example, news that Pope Francis had endorsed Donald Trump during the US presidential campaign was spread by totally unreliable sources: but the overflow of information and the lack of attention of end-users prevent many of them from spotting that sources such as "The American Patriot" or websites such as "www.endingthefed.com" were not exactly authoritative, or fact-based. Many of these news items are ignored by the public as clearly fake, but others spread very quickly and, even if at the margin, affect public opinion creating a thick layer of "noise" which causes trouble and confusion for end-users. More worryingly, cases of commercially or politically motivated manipulation strategies have emerged as a variant of intentional disinformation, happening at a much greater scale. These operations, which can be state-sponsored, aim at affecting the outcome of elections or at discrediting commercial rivals by purchasing privileged spots for online advertisements and using them to spread intentionally and strategically crafted messages. The Russian meddling in US elections occurred exactly in this way: according to a written statement submitted by Facebook to US Congress, revealing that Russian agents created 129 events on the social media network during the 2016 US election campaign. Such events were viewed by 338,300 different Facebook accounts, 62,500 of which marked that they would attend. In 2016, campaign advertising on the Internet skyrocketed in the United States, increasing eight-fold since 2012 to an all-time high of $1.4 billion; and is projected to rise to above $2 billion in the upcoming 2020 mid-term elections, reaching at least 20 percent of all campaign adverts. In reviewing its records, Facebook found approximately $100,000 in ad

[27] See C. R. Sunstein, *Republic.com* (Princeton University Press, 2001).
[28] See Blue Feed, Red Feed, *Wall Street Journal* (August 19, 2019), http://graphics.wsj.com/blue-feed-red-feed/.
[29] See J. Joyce, Trump, Twitter and His "Filter Bubble," *BBC* (November 30, 2017), www.bbc.com/news/world-us-canada-42187596.
[30] Communication from the Commission to the European Parliament, the Council, the European Economic and Social Committee and the Committee of the Regions, Tackling Online Disinformation: A European Approach, COM/2018/236 final, Brussels (April 26, 2018).

spending from June 2015 to May 2017 – associated with roughly 3,000 ads – which was connected to about 470 inauthentic accounts and pages in violation of its policies; this led Facebook to infer that these accounts and pages were affiliated with one another and likely operated out of Russia.

Finally, AI developments, and particularly Generative Adversarial Networks, are bringing the disinformation problem to a whole new level, by developing perfect clones that credibly act as their originals.[31] No effective policy response is available today for deepfakes, and it is likely that since reality has been fully matched by AI's ability to reproduce it, policymakers will have to intensify controls over the origin of data and the trustworthiness of the sources and development processes, coupled with enhanced transparency obligations for AI developers and deployers. As will be recalled below, in "The EU Agenda on Trustworthy AI," the European Commission is likely to adopt this measure in 2020.

The Broader Implication of AI: Macro-Policy Challenges

Along with the concerns explored in the previous section, AI also has more "macro" consequences that deserve the attention of lawmakers, and broadly pertain to the domain of ethics. These are related to the possibility that AI evolves in ways that are not consistent with a balanced, sustainable development of the economy, society, and environment. For the purposes of this chapter, some of the key social concerns will be briefly emphasized, including: AI's impact on jobs; the possible emergence of "surveillance capitalism" and "surveillance totalitarianism"; and the escalation of warfare through the use of lethal autonomous weapons (LAWs).

AI, Productivity, and Employment

First, the prospective impact of AI on jobs is still largely a mystery, and will significantly depend on whether AI will not only emerge as a "niche" set of solutions in the hands of a fistful of corporations or national governments, but will diffuse throughout the economy and society. This, in turn, depends on several concomitant factors: sufficient investment in skills that are complementary with the introduction of more sophisticated machines both at work and outside of the workplace; the introduction of competition rules or forms of regulation that "democratize" the use of data and the distribution of value along supply chains; and the empowerment of end-users through control of their data, as well as regulatory measures aimed at increasing the level of trust between individuals, and between users and AI-enabled products and services.

As noted by Brynjolfsson and colleagues, the most impressive capabilities of AI, particularly those based on machine learning, have not yet spread widely.[32] More importantly, like other general-purpose technologies, their full effects will not be realized until waves of complementary innovations are developed and implemented. The discussion around the recent patterns in aggregate productivity growth highlights a seeming contradiction. On the one hand, there are astonishing examples of potentially transformative new technologies that

---

[31] S. Agarwal, H. Farid, Y. Gu, *et al.*, Protecting World Leaders against Deep Fakes, IEEE Conference on Computer Vision and Pattern Recognition Workshops (2019).

[32] E. Brynjolfsson, D. Rock, C. Syverson, *et al.*, Artificial Intelligence and the Modern Productivity Paradox: A Clash of Expectations and Statistics, in A. Agrawal, J. Gans, and A. Goldfarb (eds.), *The Economics of Artificial Intelligence: An Agenda* (National Bureau of Economic Research, 2017), pp. 23–57.

could greatly increase productivity and economic welfare.[33] There are some early concrete signs of the promise of these technologies, recent leaps in AI performance being the most prominent example. However, at the same time, measured productivity growth over the past decade has slowed significantly. This deceleration is large, cutting productivity growth by half or more in the decade preceding the slowdown. It is also widespread, having occurred throughout the OECD and, more recently, among many large emerging economies as well.[34] We thus appear to be facing a new version of the Solow computer paradox: we see transformative new technologies everywhere but in the productivity statistics.

Recently, several papers have analyzed the impact of automation in Europe, mostly finding a positive contribution of robots to productivity. Among others, Graetz and Michaels use the industrial robots' database and estimate that in the seventeen countries in their sample, the increased use of robots per hour worked from 1993 to 2007 raised the annual growth of labor productivity by about 0.37 percentage points.[35] By considering an industry-country panel specification, they found that robots appear to reduce the share of hours worked by low-skilled workers relative to middle-skilled and high-skilled workers; they do not polarize the labor market, but appear to hurt the relative position of low-skilled workers rather than middle-skilled ones. Nevertheless, the use of robots per hour worked appears to boost total factor productivity and average wages. Chiacchio, Petropoulos, and Pichler find that the use of robots per hour worked appears to boost total factor productivity and average wages; however, they also find that the displacement effect (labor to capital) offsets the productivity effect, leading to job losses.[36]

The effects of such pervasive technological changes on job creation and destruction are very difficult to predict. The MIT collected and reviewed the most authoritative studies to date, showing how deeply diverging predictions are. Jobs may also fundamentally change in nature and mode of delivery: the Japanese government predicts that corporations will become more project-based, rather than hierarchical, and this will mean that workers may be selected on a project basis, or may want to apply for single projects. This means a Copernican revolution in the organization of work: what happened outside of the human being, in a corporation-centric way, now happens in a human-centric way.

Studies on Europe also show a significant impact of automation on employment. For example, Chiacchio, Petropoulos, and Pichler studied the impact of industrial robots on employment and wages in six EU countries (Finland, France, Germany, Italy, Spain, and Sweden), which make up 85.5 percent of the EU industrial robots market. In theory, robots can directly displace workers from performing specific tasks (displacement effect). But they can also expand labor demand through the efficiencies they bring to industrial production (productivity effect). The authors find that the displacement effect dominates: one additional robot per 1,000 workers reduces the employment rate by 0.16 to 0.20 percentage points. The impact is even more evident for workers of middle education and for young cohorts.

Research consistently finds that jobs threatened by automation are highly concentrated among lower-paid and lower-skilled workers. This will place downward pressure on employer demand for this group of workers, deflating wages and increasing inequality. Deloitte has

[33] E. Brynjolfsson and A. McAfee, *The Second Machine Age* (W. W. Norton, 2014).
[34] C. Syverson, Challenges to Mismeasurement Explanations for the US Productivity Slowdown (2017) 31 *J. Econ. Perspect.* 165–86.
[35] G. Graetz and G. Michaels, Is Modern Technology Responsible for Jobless Recoveries? (2017) 107 *Am. Econ. Rev.* 168–73; G. Graetz and G. Michaels, Robots at Work (2018) 100 *Rev. Econ. Stat.* 753–68.
[36] F. Chiacchio, G. Petropoulos, and D. Pichler, The Impact of Industrial Robots on EU Employment and Wages: A Local Labour Market Approach, Bruegel Working Paper, Issue 2 (2018).

found that jobs paying less than £30,000 a year are nearly five times more likely to be replaced by automation than jobs paying over £100,000, and in London, such lower-paid jobs are more than eight times more likely to be replaced. This is echoed by the Institute for Public Policy Research – while they dismiss the idea that AI-driven automation will lead to job losses and instead predict that workers will be reallocated into different roles, they insist that without "managed acceleration," automation could exacerbate wealth inequality through the simultaneous erosion of the wages of poorer workers and increases in those of the highly skilled.

There are three possibilities. First, automation may lead to continuing skills-biased technological change – AI favors workers with more skills while substituting those with less skills. Second, automation may lead to capital-biased technological change, whereby the share of income that goes to capital increases as AI favors investment in technology. And, third, automation may lead to "superstar-biased" technological change, whereby the benefits of technology accrue to an even smaller portion of society than just highly skilled workers. In all three cases, the benefits of AI to productivity and economic growth could be hampered by rising inequality, as the Bank of England and the IMF have recognized. In terms of the effect on labor relations, job-specific skills may become redundant, people may change jobs more frequently, and the increasing precariousness of work may be exacerbated. Working in the "gig economy" – characterized by a rise in self-employment, temporary positions, and contract work (the "contingent workforce") – may become the norm for an increasing number of people. This will fundamentally alter traditional employment relationships and may restrict the ability of workers to reap the rewards of potential increases in productivity and economic growth.

One possible reaction is finding new ways to remunerate user data as labor. In the future, Universal Basic Income will become a policy option in many countries, together with the possibility to remunerate so-called "heteromation."[37] Types of work that may end up being remunerated include communicative labor, cognitive labor, creative labor, emotional labor, and crowdsourced labor. More generally, this will lead to new trends in public policy, such as the regulation of Internet giants as public utilities, which imposes more stringent conditions on their behavior, and transparency obligations on their algorithms; and/or the taxation of Internet giants based on their turnover and profits in places where they have "digital presence."

AI, Big Data, and the Age of Surveillance

Another "macro" risk created by AI development is the possibility for both private corporations and governments to set up systems that, while displaying remarkable levels of efficiency and security, place end-users in a constant state of surveillance, thereby depriving them of their basic liberty and infringing a variety of fundamental rights, from privacy to freedom of speech or even thought.[38] In this respect, it is useful to differentiate between so-called "surveillance capitalism," as coined by Shoshana Zuboff and mostly referring to the privatization and concentration of surveillance in the hands of large Internet giants; and the use of social credit scoring by totalitarian regimes (and, increasingly, also in democratic countries, in a more targeted way) as a tool to achieve at once efficiency and complete control over citizens.

[37] H. R. Ekbia and B. A. Nardi, *Heteromation, and Other Stories of Computing and Capitalism* (MIT Press, 2017).
[38] See, inter alia, M. Ienca and R. Andorno, Towards New Human Rights in the Age of Neuroscience and Neurotechnology (2017) 13 *Life Sci. Soc. Policy* 5.

In the former case, surveillance capitalism ends up claiming "human experience as free raw material for translation into behavioral data," which are held by large Internet intermediaries and translated into predictions of user behavior, which in turn are attractive knowledge for advertising and additional services. The extent of the phenomenon is magnified by the rather passive approach adopted by policymakers toward these practices, coupled with the slow rise in the awareness of civil society on the value of data provision and aggregation in the digital sphere. Today, the need to give back control of personal data to the end-users and limit the use of personal data for the purpose of surveillance has become increasingly felt, and subject to initiatives such as Solid and MyData, and of course to legislative initiatives such as the EU General Data Protection Regulation (GDPR), which features a "data minimization" principle and provisions aimed at preventing the processing of personally identifiable data without the user's explicit consent.

In the case of social credit scoring, a points-based system is applied to both businesses and citizens, which ends up creating a "meritocratic" system, in which good behavior is rewarded with access to a variety of prospective benefits, from fast-track lanes in airports to the recruitment of civil servants, or the possibility to participate in government procurement. As a matter of fact, social credit scoring potentially leads to the end of many forms of cross-subsidization or "averaging" of treatment between citizens and businesses (for example, in taxation or in the provision of welfare services), thus leading to perfect discrimination, which becomes problematic especially in terms of equality of opportunity and individual privacy. Coupled with emerging AI-enabled technologies such as facial and body recognition, this practice not only allows for superior outcomes in terms of efficiency, but also significantly harms individual freedom and the democratic process (where existing): suffice it to think of an ongoing, individualized sentiment analysis, which may lead to awarding higher scores to individuals who provide positive feedback to government initiatives and policies.

The launch of a fully fledged social credit scoring system in China, after a piloting phase, is being echoed in various ways in other legal systems, with narrower scope (for example, in welfare, or financial services). And while in Western countries social credit scoring has occurred so far largely in the context of private social media (through peer recognition), these data are already being used by insurance companies in a number of countries to determine risk and premium levels.[39] Coupling the considerations expressed above with regard to bias, discrimination, and hyper-nudging with the concerns stemming from the private and governmental use of social credit scoring, it is inevitable to conclude that policymakers will have to put in place sufficient safeguards to protect the democratic process, individual freedoms, privacy, and equality of opportunity. Moreover, the extreme power that public and private intermediaries have in aggregating, generating, and processing data also gave rise to new calls for "data sovereignty" and even "algorithmic sovereignty," in which large countries take action to avoid that user data and algorithmic design are appropriated by foreign companies, thereby potentially exposing them to capture and interference by hostile, foreign states. For example, the goal of "technological sovereignty" surfaced in the mission letters sent to appointed Commissioners by the new President of the European Commission,

---

[39] S. Fieldstein, The Global Expansion of AI Surveillance, Carnegie Endowment for international Peace (2019), https://carnegieendowment.org/2019/09/17/global-expansion-of-ai-surveillance-pub-79847. The report finds that AI surveillance technology is spreading at a faster rate to a wider range of countries than experts have commonly understood. At least 75 out of 176 countries globally are actively using AI technologies for surveillance purposes. And while China is clearly a major driver of AI surveillance worldwide, liberal democracies have become major users of AI surveillance: 51 percent of advanced democracies deploy AI surveillance systems.

Ursula von der Leyen; and this move echoes concerns related to "strategic autonomy" expressed by the European Political Strategy Centre, the think tank of the Commission's President.

THE EU AGENDA ON TRUSTWORTHY AI: THE SHAPING OF
A NEW LEGAL REGIME

In Europe, the debate on AI started with a rather dystopian, catastrophist flavor. In 2017, the European Parliament's resolution on "Civil Law Rules for Robotics" provided a rather gloomy picture of the emergence of widespread AI-enabled robotics;[40] the document even evoked Mary Shelley's *Frankenstein*, and proposed the attribution of legal personality as well as "rights and duties" to smart autonomous robots. The scientific community soon rejected this approach with a collective letter signed by several academics.[41] However, the initiative of the European Parliament had at least the merit to increase the salience of AI in the EU agenda. One year later, in the context of the mid-term review of the EU Digital Single Market strategy, the Council of the EU invited the Commission to put forward a European approach to AI,[42] and the Commission started to pave the way for what is now evolving into a multi-stakeholder, ethically adherent, ambitious policy framework.

Inevitably, one of the most solid starting points in Europe was the recently adopted GDPR. While originally drafted without reference to AI systems, the GDPR contains a number of provisions that strengthen agency on the side of the end-users, inter alia, by introducing a right to a "meaningful explanation" of all decisions that affect the private sphere of the data subject; and imposing data protection impact assessments whenever data processing is likely to result in a high risk to the rights and freedoms of individuals.[43] Overall, Europe appears determined to revive in the AI domain the same approach followed for the GDPR, which places the fundamental right to data protection at the forefront, with no concession to data-hungry AI techniques such as machine learning: as a matter of fact, the GDPR promotes a "data minimization" approach and applies extra-territorially to anyone who processes personal data belonging to European citizens, regardless of location.[44]

Besides the GDPR, Europe could count on a blossoming body of rules aimed at monitoring the power of large digital platforms, including the Platform-to-Business regulation, which prescribes the adoption of fair and transparent (algorithmic) practices vis-à-vis businesses that rely on the platform to reach end-users. Likewise, antitrust investigations on large tech giants and Court of Justice decisions (for example, on the "right to be forgotten") were already moving in the direction of holding Internet intermediaries accountable for the outcomes

---

[40] European Parliament (EP) (2017), Resolution of 16 February 2017 with recommendations to the Commission on Civil Law Rules on Robotics (2015/2103(INL)).

[41] See the Open Letter to the European Commission on Artificial Intelligence and Robotics, https://g8fip1k plyr33r3krz5b97d1-wpengine.netdna-ssl.com/wp-content/uploads/2018/04/RoboticsOpenLetter.pdf.

[42] Other EU institutions, such as the European Economic and Social Committee, also published communications on AI, and Member States started to develop their own strategies. The European Parliament updated its orientation toward AI in 2019.

[43] Particularly in cases of systematic and extensive evaluations of the personal aspects of an individual, including profiling; in case of processing of sensitive data on a large scale and of systematic monitoring of public areas on a large scale.

[44] The extra-territorial impact of the GDPR has been given extensive and generous interpretation by the courts and data protection authorities, as recently confirmed by the European Data Protection Supervisor in its guidelines on the territorial scope of GDPR. See A. Renda, Regulation and IRC: Challenges Posed by the Digital Transformation, Report for the OECD Regulatory Policy Committee, forthcoming in September 2020.

generated by their algorithmic decisions. More generally, Europe can rely on a very solid legal system, in which fundamental and human rights are deeply rooted, and are subject to specific jurisdiction and a dedicated Court. In the neighboring area of risk regulation, Europe is very advanced thanks to its combination of precaution and experimentation, although its constitutionally endorsed application of the precautionary principle is denounced by many, often with very weak empirical grounds, as potentially hindering innovation.[45]

This existing corpus of rules was, however, also often associated with mounting concerns about Europe's ability to catch up with other global superpowers in the development and testing of AI solutions. Often considered as a laggard in terms of private R&D contrasted with other comparable countries, Europe was confronted with massive public and private R&D expenditures in AI observed in the United States and China, both legal systems that appeared to be less precautionary in their approach to data and the testing of new solutions.

Against this background, European leaders decided to ground their strategy on two complementary pillars: the definition and implementation of an ambitious ethical and legal framework for AI "made in Europe"; and the increase of public and private investment in AI to improve the competitiveness of the European Union.[46] This blueprint was translated into an explicit, fully fledged strategy in April 2018, with the adoption of a Communication by the European Commission on "Artificial Intelligence for Europe."[47] In the document, the Commission stated its belief that Europe "can lead the way in developing and using AI for good and for all, building on its values and its strengths"; and importantly, took action to avoid the uncoordinated proliferation of national strategies in the EU Member States, by creating the framework for a Coordinated Plan, then adopted in December 2018.[48] The Coordinated Plan further set the goal to "maximise the impact of investments at EU and national levels, encourage synergies and cooperation across the EU, exchange best practices and collectively define the way forward to ensure that the EU as a whole can compete globally." The Plan aims, inter alia, at stimulating an investment of €20 billion per year throughout the next decade, encompassing public and private sources of funding.

The EU Guidelines: From Ethically Aligned to Trustworthy AI

The HLEG comprises as many as fifty-two members, including independent experts and academics, alongside representatives of vested interests.[49] This, obviously, made it difficult to reach agreement, and go beyond the mere enunciation of ethical principles. But somehow, the HLEG managed to reach results not only by identifying ethical principles that fit the specifics of AI development, but also by operationalizing them through a number of

---

[45]   See, for an inspiring view, J. B. Wiener, The Real Pattern of Precaution, in J. B. Wiener, M. D. Rogers, J. K. Hammitt, and P. H. Sand. (eds.), *The Reality of Precaution: Comparing Risk Regulation in the United States and Europe* (RFF Press, 2011), pp. 519–65.

[46]   Importantly, Europe's decision to aim at strengthening competitiveness in AI seemed to ignore, at least at the outset, the goal of developing AI as a means toward sustainability, which would have fallen more in line with the EU Agenda 2030, which promised to mainstream SDGs into each and every aspect of EU policy.

[47]   Communication from the Commission to the European Parliament, the European Council, the Council, the European Economic and Social Committee and the Committee of the Regions – Artificial Intelligence for Europe, COM(2018) 237 final.

[48]   Communication from the Commission to the European Parliament, the European Council, the Council, the European Economic and Social Committee and the Committee of the Regions – Coordinated Plan on Artificial Intelligence, COM(2018) 795 final.

[49]   See the composition of the HLEG at https://ec.europa.eu/digital-single-market/en/high-level-expert-group-artificial-intelligence.

requirements and even an assessment tool that could promote a real alignment of AI systems with ethical values.

Initially, the HLEG worked on the idea of ethical AI, mostly from the perspective of "ethics by design," "ethics in design," and "ethics for designers." But after the publication of the first draft of the ethics guidelines in December 2018, and the first feedback received through a rather quick stakeholder consultation, it became clear that the focus on ethics would prove too narrow for an exercise that aims to provide a significant contribution to a future policy framework. Moreover, in the case of the European Union, most ethical principles already overlap with established principles rooted in the Treaties, or in specific legislation: and even fundamental rights are often evoked in legislation and subject to *ad hoc* jurisdiction. The discussion within the HLEG, therefore, focused on the need to define the pre-requirements of AI systems that, in addition to being ethically aligned, would also be worthy of the trust of all stakeholders. The need to restore sufficient levels of reliability and trust in the interaction with digital technologies had emerged as critical, especially after the Cambridge Analytica scandal.

The publication of a first draft of the Ethics Guidelines in December 2018 was followed by a rapid stakeholder consultation, in which the need to adopt a broader approach than ethical alignment emerged very clearly. Hence, the final version of the Guidelines referred explicitly to the need for "Trustworthy Artificial Intelligence," defined as AI that meets three cumulative requirements: legal compliance, ethical alignment, and socio-technical robustness. The Guidelines, therefore, already represent a step forward compared to ethical principles such as the ones adopted by many corporations (usually with no associated enforcement), governments (for example, in the Montreal Declaration), or non-governmental organizations (as in the Toronto Declaration drafted by Amnesty International and Access Now).[50] For the first time, a public document did not limit itself to identifying ethically aligned principles, but explicitly referred to the law, as well as to the robustness of AI as key elements of trustworthiness. The underlying belief was that law, ethics, and robustness are all needed, and that in some cases they may even conflict (for example, when existing legislation does not reflect technological developments, and ends up forcing market players to engage in unethical behavior); whereas in most cases they will be complementary (that is, ethics can help in interpreting the law, or can recommend behavior that is not directly required or mandated by law). As observed by Luciano Floridi, "the law provides the rules of the game, but does not indicate how to play well according to the rules."[51]

In terms of legal compliance, the HLEG observed that any human-centric approach to AI requires compliance with fundamental rights, independently of whether these are explicitly protected by EU Treaties,[52] or by the Charter of Fundamental Rights of the European Union. Fundamental rights protect individuals and (to a certain degree) groups by virtue of their moral status as human beings, independently of their legal force. More in detail, the HLEG observes that these rights are centered on the respect for the dignity of human *subjects*, not

---

[50] See Montreal Declaration for a Responsible Development of Artificial Intelligence (November 3, 2017). Announced at the conclusion of the Forum on the Socially Responsible Development of AI. The Toronto Declaration can be found at www.accessnow.org/cms/assets/uploads/2018/08/The-Toronto-Declaration_ENG_08-2018.pdf.

[51] See L. Floridi, Comment, Establishing the Rules for Building Trustworthy AI (2019) 1 *Nat. Mach. Intell.* 261–2.

[52] The European Union is based on a constitutional commitment to protect the fundamental and indivisible rights of human beings, to ensure respect for the rule of law, to foster democratic freedom, and to promote the common good. These rights are reflected in arts. 2 and 3 of the Treaty on European Union, and in the Charter of Fundamental Rights of the European Union.

"*objects* to be sifted, sorted, scored, herded, conditioned or manipulated"; on respect for the right to self-determination, including freedom of expression and control over one's own life; respect for democracy, justice, and the rule of law; respect for equality, non-discrimination, and solidarity, which implies that AI systems do not generate unfairly biased outputs, especially to the detriment of "workers, women, persons with disabilities, ethnic minorities, children, consumers or others at risk of exclusion"; and respect for citizens' rights, such as the right to vote, the right to a good administration or access to public documents, and the right to petition the administration.

That said, the Guidelines do not focus in depth on the legal compliance and the socio-technical robustness dimensions, which are considered essential but outside the scope of the work of the HLEG.[53] In the domain of ethics, the EU Guidelines identify four key principles (defined as ethical "imperatives") for Trustworthy AI: the respect for human autonomy; the prevention of harm; fairness; and explicability.[54] All of these principles are invoked in a proportionate, risk-based manner, under the belief that not all uses of AI create the same risks. The HLEG acknowledges the possibility of tensions between the four imperatives, and refers to the need for engaging civil society and solving tensions through reasoned, evidence-based assessment in all cases in which trade-offs raise significant ethical concerns. Among the most interesting provisions, the respect for human autonomy is invoked with reference to cases in which a human must be "in" the loop (HITL), cases in which the human is "on" the loop (HOTL), and cases in which a human is "in command" (HIC).[55] The HLEG clarifies also that "all other things being equal, the less oversight a human can exercise over an AI system, the more extensive testing and stricter governance is required": this in turn suggests that human oversight and accountability are intimately linked.

The second imperative, the prevention of harm, does not translate in an explicit mention of the precautionary principle; however, in the subsequent document of the HLEG on the policy and investment recommendations, there is clear mention of the fact that the overall approach should be risk-based, and only where risks were impossible to quantify and

---

[53] On the legal aspects, the group advocated a review of existing pieces of EU legislation, including those that are horizontal, cross-cutting (e.g. on data protection, products liability, competition), and sector-specific (e.g. in financial services, healthcare, etc.). This activity is still ongoing in the European Commission, especially in the field of liability of emerging technologies, leading to a possible revision of the EU Products Liability Directive. The socio-technical robustness element is only superficially dealt with, but the HLEG observed that Trustworthy AI needs to be not only legally compliant and ethically adherent, but also "robust, both from a technical and social perspective, since, even with good intentions, AI systems can cause unintentional harm." This is an essential component of trustworthiness both from a technical perspective (ensuring the system's technical robustness as appropriate in a given context, such as the application domain or life cycle phase) and from a social perspective (in due consideration of the context and environment in which the system operates). Again, most of the robustness requirements are, or will be, also covered by legislation, or by a combination of performance-based legislation and standards, in line with the European Union's approach to standardization. See J. Pelkmans, The New Approach to Technical Harmonisation and Standardisation (1987) XXV J. *Common Mark. Stud.* 249–69.

[54] Importantly, contrary to what typically occurs in similar documents, the list did not include an imperative to "do good," or the so-called "beneficence" principle, which had been included in earlier drafts of the Guidelines. See A. Jobin, M. Ienca, and E. Vayena, The Global Landscape of AI Ethics Guidelines, *Nature Machine Intelligence* (September 2, 2019).

[55] HITL refers to the capability for human intervention in every decision cycle of the system, which in many cases is neither possible nor desirable. HOTL refers to the capability for human intervention during the design cycle of the system and monitoring the system's operation. HIC refers to the capability to oversee the overall activity of the AI system (including its broader economic, societal, legal, and ethical impact) and the ability to decide when and how to use the system in any particular situation. This can include the decision not to use an AI system in a particular situation, to establish levels of human discretion during the use of the system, or to ensure the ability to override a decision made by a system.

potentially leading to catastrophic consequences, the approach should turn to the precautionary principle. The "fairness" requirement refers to the need for equal and just distribution of both benefits and costs; providing equal opportunity; protecting individuals' freedom of choice; respecting "the principle of proportionality between means and ends"; and, from a more procedural standpoint, offering the possibility for effective redress against decisions made by AI systems and by the humans operating them. This implies that the entity accountable for the decision is identifiable, and the decision-making process is explicable. But the Ethics Guidelines refrain from requiring full explicability of AI in all circumstances, and the HLEG argues that "the degree to which explicability is needed is highly dependent on the context and the severity of the consequences if that output is erroneous or otherwise inaccurate."[56]

From Principles to Requirements: Approaching a Policy Framework for Trustworthy AI

The Ethics Guidelines go far beyond merely listing and describing the four imperatives, and put forward seven requirements that AI systems should comply with in order to be defined as Trustworthy. These requirements, although directly related to the four imperatives, end up incorporating also the legal compliance and socio-technical robustness dimensions of Trustworthy AI, and as such provide a more complete picture of the level of effort required on the side of AI practitioners when developing or deploying AI. These principles include the respect for human autonomy and the protection of fundamental rights, which can require (where the risk of harming fundamental rights exists) a fundamental rights impact assessment that contemplates possible mitigating measures, as well as mechanisms to collect external feedback. Moreover, the need to respect human agency implies that users are granted the right to take informed decisions regarding AI systems, and the right not to be subject to decisions based solely on automated processing, when this produces legal effects or can similarly significantly affect them.

AI practitioners are invited to take measures to protect the physical and mental integrity of humans, and adopt a preventative approach to risks, in order to minimize unintentional and unexpected harm, and prevent unacceptable harm. AI systems must be secure and resilient to attack, and include a fall-back plan in case of problems. AI practitioners should also disclose the expected level of accuracy of the AI system, especially when its operation supports decisions that directly affect human lives. In order to further promote the robustness of AI systems, the HLEG also calls for measures to ensure the reliability and reproducibility of the results, calling for traceability (that is, documenting data gathering and labeling as well as the algorithms used and the decisions made to the best possible standard).

To operationalize the principle of prevention of harm, the HLEG Ethics Guidelines call for measures aimed at the protection of the fundamental right to privacy;[57] and the adoption of adequate data governance arrangement, including on the quality and integrity of data used. Here, the provisions overlap with existing, legally binding requirements introduced with the GDPR and already in force in Europe since 2018. The HLEG, however, goes beyond the GDPR, observing that a meaningful explanation, timely and adapted to the expertise of the stakeholder concerned (for example, layperson, regulator, researcher), should be provided whenever an AI

---

[56] This is particularly the case for so-called "areas of critical concern," on which see "Trustworthy AI and the 'Areas of Critical Concern,'" below.

[57] See A. Renda, Cloud Privacy Law in the United States and the European Union, in C. S. Yoo and J.-F. Blanchette (eds.), *Regulating the Cloud: Policy for Computing Infrastructure* (MIT Press, 2015).

system has a significant impact on people's lives. This requirement also implies that AI systems be identifiable: humans should be informed of the non-human nature of AI interfaces.

The Ethics Guidelines also include among the key requirements the respect for diversity, the absence of undue discrimination, and the principle of fairness. These requirements appear very far-reaching, as they imply the adoption of measures and safeguards throughout the entire AI system's life cycle. These include the consideration and involvement of all affected stakeholders throughout the process, ensuring equal access through inclusive design as well as equal treatment; and whenever possible, the recruitment of developers from diverse backgrounds, cultures, and disciplines to ensure diversity of opinions. The principle of fairness entails that datasets used by AI systems (both for training and operation) are adequately checked against the risk of inclusion of inadvertent historic bias, incompleteness, and bad governance models, under the understanding that such biases could lead to unintended (in)direct prejudice and discrimination against certain groups or people, potentially exacerbating prejudice and margin-alization. The HLEG also cautions against the intentional exploitation of (consumer) biases and algorithmic restrictions of competition, such as the homogenization of prices by means of collusion or a non-transparent market.[58] Trustworthy AI also requires user-centricity and universal accessibility, and where possible the involvement of a wide variety of stakeholders throughout the process, to ensure that trustworthiness is also effectively perceived in practice.

Despite the dominant emphasis on "micro" problems such as those defined in "The Rise of AI," above, the Ethics Guidelines also make space for a more planet-centric approach to AI, by explicitly encouraging AI that fosters the achievement of the Sustainable Development Goals (SDGs), including also future generations of human beings among those to be considered under the "preventative approach" that should guide AI development and deploy-ment. The Guidelines include sustainability among the key requirements of Trustworthy AI, including a critical examination of the resource usage and energy consumption, and more generally of the environmental friendliness of the AI system's entire supply chain. Beyond the environment, social impacts are also adequately mentioned, ranging from the alteration of social agency and patterns of social relationships, possible impacts on people's physical and mental well-being, and possible risks for the democratic process.

Finally, the HLEG also specifies that Trustworthy AI must come with a proportionate degree of accountability. This requires adequate governance arrangements, such as the auditability of algorithms (further strengthened in case of AI systems that affect fundamental rights), the identification, reporting, and proactive mitigation of negative impacts of AI systems, a transparent and rational treatment of trade-offs, and measures aimed at ensuring adequate redress. Accountability thus translates into a commitment to constantly monitoring and evaluating the impacts of the AI system, and the adoption of actions to regularly detect and mitigate harms, offering prompt redress to affected users. In other words, what is needed is an ongoing effort to avoid adverse impacts on users and society, rather than a one-off self-evaluation at the time of deployment.

The Trustworthy AI Assessment List

The introduction of key requirements in addition to ethical principles already put the HLEG at the forefront of the debate on how to encourage responsible AI development. However, the

---

[58]   See European Union Agency for Fundamental Rights: BigData: Discrimination in Data-Supported Decision Making (2018), http://fra.europa.eu/en/publication/2018/big-data-discrimination.

HLEG did not limit itself to this already remarkable attempt: perhaps the most innovative feature of the Ethics Guidelines is the attempt to operationalize the requirement through a detailed assessment framework composed of 131 questions. The list walks AI practitioners through the key requirements, asking them whether they have fully considered possible risks, or have procedures in place to mitigate them in case they materialize. The list is still preliminary, and admittedly rough: the HLEG started in July 2019 an ambitious piloting phase, which relies on a detailed survey available on the website of the AI Alliance; fifty "deep dive" interviews with companies, institutions, and research organizations, aimed at capturing more detailed feedback on the Assessment List; and a series of sector-specific workshops, aimed at tailoring the list to the specific needs of individual sectors (for example, healthcare or financial services), including an assessment of existing sectoral legislation or standards that overlap with the requirements for trustworthy AI. The outcome of this extensive piloting phase will be a revision of the Assessment List, to be completed by the HLEG during the first half of 2020. Such revision may entail, in addition, a tailoring of the list to specific use cases, and the development of additional guidance on legal compliance (also including sectoral legislation where appropriate), as well as on how to address specific risks through *ad hoc* procedures.

The piloting and revision of the Assessment List will set a new standard for ethical AI at the international level. However, the Assessment List currently lacks a framework for determining whether a given requirement has sufficiently been catered for. In other words, the list accompanies AI practitioners by attempting to provide them with a complete set of questions, but does not yield a final determination as to whether the AI project under assessment is sufficiently trustworthy. This, as things stand, limits the usefulness of the list as a risk assessment framework, or even as a benchmark to be used to determine whether AI practitioners have adopted the necessary safeguards and mitigating measures when designing, developing, and deploying their products. One possibility in this respect is that a framework for certification emerges, either at the industry level, or through legislation.

The following document by the HLEG on "Policy and Investment Recommendations," issued in June 2019, contains an explicit call for considering making the Trustworthy AI Assessment (that is, the Assessment List, as will be refined in 2020) mandatory for AI systems deployed by the private sector that have the potential to have a significant impact on human lives (for example, by interfering with an individual's fundamental rights at any stage of the AI system's life cycle) and for safety-critical applications. Based on this statement, it seems clear that the HLEG does not consider Trustworthy AI as simply an "aspirational goal," but rather the foundation of a wholly new risk-based legal system, in which unacceptable risks are subject to the precautionary principle, and critical applications that potentially impinge on fundamental rights are subject to a mandatory assessment. The consequences of this recommendation will become clear over time: as a matter of fact, and as already mentioned, the Assessment List is not accompanied by any scoring system or threshold that would allow the differentiation of trustworthy systems from non-trustworthy ones. If the European Commission will follow this recommendation, then some form of certification and scoring will become inevitable, with significant consequences for the AI market in Europe. Interestingly, this recommendation implies that "critical" AI systems ensure appropriate "by default" and "by design" procedures to enable effective and immediate redress in case of mistakes, harms, and/or other infringements: the practical implementation and the actual contours of this proposed obligation are, however, unclear: what is "effective and immediate," and what types of mistakes would qualify as relevant for the purposes of this rule.

The HLEG called on the European Commission to consider the establishment of an "institutional structure" that could help collect and spread best practices in a more agile way than what judges, standards, and lawmakers are normally able to achieve. Whether this will take the form of an agency (as originally invoked by the European Parliament already in 2017), a board (as in the case of the GDPR), or any other institutional variant is not specified by the HLEG, and will have to be considered by the European Commission in the months to come, should it decide to follow up on this recommendation.[59] The proposed institutional structure, in the vision of the HLEG, will perform a wide range of functions, including a contribution to the EU's framework and policy for Trustworthy AI, ensuring that AI is lawful, ethical, and robust, advising EU institutions and supporting them in the implementation of such framework, providing guidance to stakeholders, assisting them in the application of the risk-based approach, classifying risks as acceptable or unacceptable, coordinating with standards-setting organizations and with EU Member States, hosting a repository of best practices, and raising awareness among stakeholders and policymakers on the evolving landscape of AI.

Trustworthy AI and the "Areas of Critical Concern"

The HLEG was criticized for not taking a very critical stance on a number of emerging uses of AI, which are thought to create significant risks for end-users and society. Initially, the work on the ethics guidelines has ventured into the identification of so-called "redlines" – namely, AI applications that should be subject to an outright ban as potentially too risky for society. However, in the final version of the Guidelines, the HLEG only ended up identifying a few "areas of critical concern," including mass surveillance, widespread social credit scoring, and LAWs. In these areas, the HLEG warned that developing Trustworthy AI would be particularly difficult.

However, in the Policy and Investment Recommendations, the HLEG explicitly recommended that policymakers issue regulation to ensure that individuals are not subject to "unjustified personal, physical or mental tracking or identification, profiling and nudging through AI-powered methods of biometric recognition such as: emotional tracking, empathic media, DNA, iris and behavioural identification, affect recognition, voice and facial recognition and the recognition of micro-expressions," adding that only exceptionally (for example, in the case of pressing national security stances) these applications would be allowed, if "evidence based, necessary and proportionate, as well as respectful of fundamental rights." Furthermore, the HLEG calls for an international moratorium on the development of offensive LAWs, a proposal that the new Commission President, who is also the former German Minister of Defense, will certainly consider with due attention.

Finally, the HLEG also recommends specific actions to protect children, including a comprehensive European Strategy for Better and Safer AI for Children, designed to empower them, while also protecting them from risks and harm. In particular, EU legislators are invited to introduce a legal age at which children receive a "clean data slate" of any public or private storage of data related to them as children; and to monitor the development of personalized AI systems built on children's profiles to ensure their alignment with fundamental rights, democracy, and the rule of law.

---

[59] International examples are starting to proliferate even in the absence of a well-shaped legal system, from the Centre for Data Ethics in the United Kingdom to similar authorities in France and Germany.

WHAT'S NEXT? THE NEW EUROPEAN COMMISSION AND THE UPCOMING REGULATORY INITIATIVE

At the time of writing, the contours of the forthcoming policy measure promised by President von der Leyen are far from clear, even inside the European Commission. But some of the main pillars of the emerging policy framework can be anticipated with a sufficient degree of certainty. This is due, in particular, to the adoption of the White Paper on AI in February 2019, and the foreseen adoption of a legislative instrument by the end of 2020.

As emerges from the White Paper, the Commission will base its proposed regulation on the Trustworthy AI concept, and in particular on the Assessment List proposed by the HLEG. The Assessment List is being reviewed in 2020 to ensure it is proportionate, actionable, and meaningful for AI practitioners. This, in and of itself, will not be easy, since the current version of the Assessment List is not tailored to any specific sector, or use case, and falls short of providing a framework for evaluating whether the process followed in the development of a given AI project complies with the minimum requirements for trustworthiness.

That said, another aspect that must be urgently addressed by the European Commission is the governance of the system, and in particular whether an agency or an expert board will be created to start collecting best practices and provide regulatory certainty to the various practitioners that populate the AI space in Europe. Furthermore, the Commission will adopt a legislative instrument to fully institutionalize the principles and requirements identified by the HLEG in the guidelines, and will then leave the assessment list as a more agile document, which could be revised periodically without requiring a legislative change.

In addition to "institutionalizing" the list and creating a governance framework around it, the European Commission will most likely take action to address areas of specific concern such as the widespread and unwarranted use of unjustified personal, physical, or mental tracking or identification, as well as methods of biometric recognition and social credit scoring, which have already been specifically mentioned in the White Paper. These will be a first set of measures, soon followed by action on the security and technical robustness of the AI system, which will follow the ongoing work on the revision of the EU Products Liability Directive and the EU Machinery Directive, among others.

However, the EU ambition to lead the way toward Trustworthy AI will not be limited to these initiatives, and will also require an active participation, if not leadership, in the global debate on responsible AI. This debate is now progressing slowly, along two possible tracks. One possibility is the creation of a coalition of like-minded countries such as Canada, France, and Japan, and the EU bloc could start agreeing on principles of responsible, ethically aligned AI, possibly translating them into legislation that introduces risk assessment and dedicated oversight institutions at the national level. The Inter-Governmental Panel on AI, as originally proposed but never fully discussed in the G7 gathering in Biarritz in August 2019, was aimed at coordinating efforts toward responsible, sustainable AI development, but met with the firm resistance of both the United States and China. However, in the future such a coalition could gain strength, especially if supported by the private sector, and backed by the adoption of extra-territorial rules, especially in the European Union.

The alternative is a broader agreement, including also the United States, and possibly modeled on the OECD Principles on Artificial Intelligence, adopted in May 2019 by all OECD members and also by Argentina, Brazil, Colombia, Costa Rica, Peru, and Romania. These principles were also echoed in June 2019 by the G20 human-centered AI Principles, and in a large conference on "AI for Humanity" in November 2019. The likelihood of a "Global Partnership on AI" based on these principles is probably greater than in the case of a coalition that at least initially excludes the United States: however, this would come with consequences, as the agreement would probably be lighter. The OECD principles, like most other ethical AI principles, lack the operationalization and enforceability that the EU framework is increasingly featuring.

Most importantly, the European Union's influence on the global debate on AI will also depend on whether EU institutions will manage to reach a sufficient level of policy coherence on the domestic front. This implies that the "internal" coherence of the AI strategy is ensured, with Member States converging with the European Union at least on the definition and implementation of Trustworthy AI, and also on the "external coherence" dimension: in particular, on the promotion of AI "for good," thus intimately linked to the EU Agenda 2030, oriented toward sustainable development. This is a domain in which Europe could really attempt to fill a gap, and try to lead the rest of the world. As Europe has already committed in 2016 to mainstreaming SDGs into every aspect of EU policy (as observed above), the time is ripe to practice what EU leaders have preached and launch a substantial effort in the mapping of how all digital technologies can help Europe and the world achieve the ambitious 2030 goals.[60] Failure to recognize and publicly promote the role of AI and its related technologies for a more sustainable future society would represent an enormous missed opportunity for Europe and the rest of the world.

---

[60] This effort would also deeply resonate with the European Union's external action: the Global Strategy on Foreign and Security Policy for the European Union sets out the strategic direction for the Union's external action and identifies clear links to the 2030 Agenda. It emphasizes the importance of a comprehensive approach in the Union's external actions and the need for an integrated EU approach to increase the Union's impact in responding to and preventing violent conflicts and crises, as well as improve coherence between the Union and its Member States. The new European Consensus on Development put forward a shared vision and framework for action for all EU institutions and all Member States, framed around the five key themes of the 2030 Agenda: people, planet, prosperity, peace, and partnership. It places particular emphasis on cross-cutting drivers of development, such as gender equality, youth, sustainable energy and climate action, investment, migration, and mobility, and seeks to mobilize all means of implementation: aid, investments, and domestic resources, supported by sound policies.

32

Law in Turing's Cathedral

Notes on the Algorithmic Turn of the Legal Universe

Nicola Lettieri

TURING'S CATHEDRAL: WONDERS AND PITFALLS OF THE DIGITAL WORLD

We live in an algorithmic world. There is currently no area of our lives that has not been touched by computation, its language and tools. Since when, in the early 1940s, a small group of people led by John von Neumann gathered to turn into reality the vision of a universal computing machine, humankind is experiencing a sort of permanent revolution in which our understanding of the world and our ways of acting on it are steadily transformed by the steps forward we make in processing information. Alan Turing vividly depicts such a condition in one of the founding documents of the quest for artificial intelligence (AI): "in attempting to construct machines . . . we are providing mansions for the souls."[1] Computers and algorithms can be seen as the building blocks of a new, ever-expanding building – a cathedral, to use George Dyson's metaphor[2] – in which every human activity is going to be shaped by the digital architecture hosting it.

Evidence of this is spread all around us. Algorithms[3] are ever more pervasive and responsibilities entrusted to them are increasing as well. Data analytics and machine learning have entered the most diverse fields across industry and research. They are used to make growingly complex decisions that span from selecting investments and making medical diagnoses to detecting crime, and even assigning punishment.

All that glitters is not gold, however: issues arise for a variety of closely linked reasons. One of the most sensitive is undoubtedly the growing complexity of computational tools. The poor understanding we have of the mechanisms that operate within them makes it often difficult to grasp all the consequences of their use.[4] Algorithms frequently reshape processes in which they are involved in ways that are nearly invisible to their own creators.

---

[1] A. Turing, Computing Machinery and Intelligence (1950) 59 *Mind* 433.

[2] See G. Dyson, *Turing's Cathedral: The Origins of the Digital Universe* (Pantheon, 2012).

[3] The term is used here to point out not only automated information processing, including symbolic and logical reasoning or pattern recognition, but also, in general, algorithmic (computational, quantitative, formal) approaches. In this sense, see P. Michelucci (ed.), *Handbook of Human Computation* (Springer, 2013), Vol. 2.

[4] Algorithms are vulnerable to a series of risks raising serious questions about the value of the findings and their extrapolation to the real world. Results deriving from computational heuristics – be they the insights generated by simulation models (see U. Frank, F. Squazzoni, and K. G. Troitzsch, EPOS-Epistemological Perspectives on Simulation: An Introduction, International Workshop on Epistemological Aspects of Computer Simulation in the Social Sciences (2006)) or the predictions stemming from machine-learning inductions (see G. Marcus, Deep Learning: A Critical Appraisal (2018), http://arxiv.org/abs/1801.00631) – may easily fool us due to reasons spanning from hidden biases in the algorithms and data, to errors and difficulties of their validation. As highlighted by a now large number of authors (see, among others: C. O'Neil, *Weapons of Math Destruction: How Big Data Increases Inequality and Threatens Democracy* (Broadway Books, 2017); F. Pasquale, *The Black Box Society* (Harvard University Press, 2015)), computation and data-driven analytical tools can confront us with distorted

Another question stems from the existence of competing paradigms. Depending on the practical needs, the epistemological stance, or just the technology available, algorithms can be used for radically different purposes: to assist human beings or to completely replace them in the execution of given tasks, to make predictions or support the explanation of real-world phenomena. Any decision taken in this regard – whatever the level considered from the methodological to the technical one – is fraught with far-reaching implications.[5] In science, for instance, choices about the use of algorithms do not simply impact the results of the research, but affect the very epistemological perspectives.

This becomes apparent in the social sciences, where different ways of using algorithmic and computational heuristics have nurtured scientific approaches that deeply differ in terms of goals and theoretical underpinnings. Computational social science (CSS)[6] variants provide a good example of this.[7] Equation-based models and statistics have fed deductive approaches trying to explain social phenomena starting from general assumptions mathematically described. Distributed AI, evolutionary computing, and agent-based simulations, instead, have fostered bottom-up analysis aiming to explore the micro-foundation of macroscopic social phenomena. In more recent times, again, data mining and predictive analysis have promoted a further vision of CSS where the focus is more on forecasting the evolution of complex social systems.

Against this background, deciding how and why to exploit algorithms turns out to be a nontrivial effort. Challenges go far beyond mapping algorithms onto the pre-existing needs of specific domains; we should rather learn how to fully exploit their transformative power. As it emerges from the example made on CSS, what is at stake is not simply the design of innovative applications but, potentially, a shift in the way in which we conceptualize and understand reality.

Grasping the technical dimension of the algorithmic world is not enough. To put it in Benjamin Bratton's words[8], what is needed is the development of a "new, fundamentally transdisciplinary, computational literacy," a set of "cultural, theoretical, and practice-oriented approaches" aimed to "make critical, and experimental accounts" of the process triggered by the algorithmic revolution. In such a scenario, it makes sense to ask: What about the law? How does and should it evolve in Turing's cathedral?

---

representations of reality mutating from "tools of perception" into "tools of blindness" (see B. H. Bratton, *The Stack: On Software and Sovereignty* (MIT Press, 2016)).

[5] An example comes from neuroscience where, as claimed in a recent study (see A. Eklund, T. E. Nichols, and H. Knutsson, Cluster Failure: Why fMRI Inferences for Spatial Extent Have Inflated False-Positive Rates (2016) 113 *Proc. Nat. Acad. Sci.* 7900), a bug in software packages used for fMRI analysis is suspected of invalidating the results of some 40,000 scientific papers. Problems become even more sensitive when it comes to areas that, like social sciences, do not usually deal with their research questions in quantitative, formal, and algorithmic terms and are still to a certain extent fascinated by the "pseudo-objectivity of computational technology" (T. Vámos, *Knowledge and Computing: A Course on Computer Epistemology* (Central European University Press, 2010)).

[6] See, among others: D. Lazer, A. Pentland, L. Adamic, *et al.*, Computational Social Science (2009) 323 *Science* 721; R. Conte, N. Gilbert, G. Bonelli, *et al.*, Manifesto of Computational Social Science (2012) 214 *Eur. Phys. J. Spec. Top.* 325; C. Cioffi-Revilla, *Introduction to Computational Social Science: Principles and Applications* (Springer, 2014).

[7] Illuminating, in this regard, the reflection developed by Conte and Paolucci (R. Conte and M. Paolucci, On Agent-Based Modeling and Computational Social Science (2014) 5 *Front. Psychol.* 668). Authors draw a distinction between the "deductive," "generative," and "complex" variant of computational social science, associating each of them with a peculiar approach to computational and algorithmic heuristics. The analysis provides an insightful account of the relationship that ties social science perspectives and algorithmic constructs, shedding light on how the latter play a decisive propulsive role for the development of specific epistemological options.

[8] B. H. Bratton, *The Stack: On Software and Sovereignty* (MIT Press, 2016)

ALGORITHMS AND DATA: THE COMPUTATIONAL FUTURE OF LAW

Over the decades, algorithms have triggered in law a great deal of methodological and scientific changes that span from the emergence of the *Jurimetrics* paradigm in the postwar era to the present-day tools for legal analytics. After almost seventy years, the trajectories of the algorithmic evolution of legal science and practice are still a current and open issue.

Despite the remarkable results achieved, on a practical and theoretical level, at the boundaries between law and computer science, answering the questions above is not quite that simple. Reasons for this claim are different. The first one is that, as often happens in periods of rapid technological expansion, there is the risk of yielding to a vision of the innovation where major research topics and applications are somehow dictated by the instruments available, or by the way in which they are used by disciplines that, for inherent features, are much further ahead in exploiting computational heuristics. While dazzled by the wonders of AI and predictive analytics, we can overlook promising topics or end up by hastily using tools and paradigms we do not fully understand. A second reason lies in the fact that, as highlighted above, algorithms can be employed in ever new ways and for a wide range of purposes depending on technological developments and the scientific frameworks used as a reference.

In this scenario, a careful reflection is needed to make better and more mature choices about the use of algorithms in the legal world. To this end, inspiration provided by other research areas can become fundamental as proven by the history of computer science, where enhancements in the use of algorithms have repeatedly taken advantage of disciplinary contaminations. Metaheuristics currently employed to manage Internet traffic routing, for instance, stem from the cross-fertilization between algorithm design and biology. Their integration has led not only to more efficient applications but also to the emergence of entirely new (algorithm-driven) research fields. Swarm intelligence,[9] biologistics,[10] and generative social science[11] are just a few examples of this. The same could be true for law, where the opening toward other scientific paradigms may prove valuable not only to foster the development of more enhanced tools for legal practice but also to open up innovative research perspectives.

The following paragraphs aim to contribute to the reflection tapping into a series of research experiences that, in line with previous considerations, bring together insights from a wide range of disciplines outside the legal world. What is proposed is not a comprehensive state-of-the-art analysis, but, instead, a review of those that we consider as some of the most promising ways to harness the transformative power of algorithms in the legal field. Topics addressed in this chapter are deeply connected and share a large number of scientific, methodological, and technical underpinnings. For the sake of clarity, they will be discussed in relative isolation always following the same pattern: a brief introduction, an overview, and the description of a few "hands-on" experimental activities.

---

[9] See G. Beni and J. Wang, Swarm Intelligence in Cellular Robotic Systems, in P. Dario, G. Sandini, and P. Aebischer (eds.), *Robots and Biological Systems: Towards a New Bionics?* (Springer, 1993).

[10] See D. Helbing, A. Deutsch, S. Diez, *et al.*, Biologistics and the Struggle for Efficiency: Concepts and Perspectives (2009) 12 *Adv. Complex Syst.* 533.

[11] See J. M. Epstein, *Generative Social Science: Studies in Agent-Based Computational Modeling* (Princeton University Press, 2006).

ALGORITHMIC MACHINES: TOWARD AN INSTRUMENT-ENABLED LEGAL SCIENCE

Algorithms are an essential part of the shift of law toward the model of an "instrument-enabled" discipline where the response to both scientific and practical needs increasingly results in the creation of new tools for processing information.

In general terms, this change is in more advanced stages in other areas of social science, especially thanks to the rise of the CSS research paradigm, which relies heavily on the design of technical solutions supporting data analysis and computational heuristics.[12] Such a perspective is set to gain a foothold further and further also in the legal world, producing a greater direct involvement of scholars in the development of tools for the management and analysis of legal information in all its forms.

From E-Science to Legal Analytics

The advancement of human knowledge has always depended on our capacity to create research tools. Over the centuries, the scientific endeavor has been mediated by increasingly complex artifacts offering ever more insightful representations of the real world. This is what happened with Galileo's telescope in astronomy, with the cloud chambers in the early twentieth century physics and what is happening today, with data and computational heuristics, in any field of human knowledge.

Science is facing a machine-driven future: big data, cloud computing, AI, and growing legions of algorithms are pushing researchers toward an ever more symbiotic relationship with machines. The last twenty years have witnessed the emergence of a series of research approaches that, regardless of the name adopted – "computational science,"[13] "data science,"[14] "e-science,"[15] and, more recently, "machine science"[16] – are all marked by the close integration between the traditional scientific practices and data-driven heuristics. Computational methodologies are spreading not only in empirical research – mainly through big data analytics and machine learning, but also in theory-making – mostly through computer simulation models.

The scientist's toolkit is steadily expanding, and research has a growing need for new tools seamlessly integrating the *building* blocks of the data and computation-driven scientific

---

[12]   The computational investigation of social phenomena has been marked since its origins by a strong relation between the scientific and technological dimension. It is not by chance that in one of the earliest and most well-known papers on the computational social science paradigm (see C. Cioffi-Revilla, Computational Social Science (2010) 2 *Wiley Interdiscip. Rev. Comput. Stat.* 259), Cioffi-Revilla states: "Just like Galileo exploited the telescope as the key instrument for observing and gaining a deeper and empirically truthful understanding of the physical universe, computational social scientists are learning to exploit the advanced and increasingly powerful instruments of computation to see beyond the visible spectrum of more traditional disciplinary analyses."

[13]   A wide-ranging reflection on computational science and its epistemological consequences is presented in P. Humphreys, *Extending Ourselves: Computational Science, Empiricism, and Scientific Method* (Oxford University Press, 2004); D. A. Reed, R. Bajcsy, M. A. Fernandez, et al., Computational Science: Ensuring America's Competitiveness, Report to the President (June 2005), https://apps.dtic.mil/dtic/tr/fulltext/u2/a462840.pdf.

[14]   See A. J. G. Hey, S. Tansley, and K. Tolle (eds.), *The Fourth Paradigm: Data-Intensive Scientific Discovery* (Microsoft Research, 2009), Vol. 1; G. Boulton, P. Campbell, B. Collins, et al., Science as an Open Enterprise, Final Report, The Royal Society (June 2012).

[15]   See T. Hey and A. Trefethen, The Data Deluge: An E-Science Perspective, in F. Berman, G. C. Fox, and A. J. G. Hey (eds.), *Grid Computing – Making the Global Infrastructure a Reality* (John Wiley, 2003); C. Hine, *New Infrastructures for Knowledge Production: Understanding E-Science* (IGI Global, 2006).

[16]   See J. Evans and A. Rzhetsky, Machine Science (2010) 329 *Science* 399.

paradigm. In this setting, "analytical platforms"[17] are becoming the keystone of innovative practices in which technological infrastructures support all the stages of the research path from questions definition to interactive data exploration and visualization, from experiment modeling to data analysis and sharing of the findings.[18]

Along with the computational science perspective, analytical platforms are set to have a disruptive impact on social science and humanities. While growing amounts of information about social life are stored in digital archives, they are pushing research toward data-driven, computational, and instrumental methods. This way, the work of any social scientist is going to include the effort to imagine and experiment with innovative tools, "places" where theories, data, and algorithms can converge and be explored.[19]

All of the above also applies to the law. As highlighted by a body of literature which has rapidly grown over the past few years, computational artifacts and infrastructures are becoming crucial to delve into the intricacies of the legal world. Projects using computational heuristics to predict Supreme Court behavior or assess the complexity of legal codes[20] suggest that the need for enhanced data-processing infrastructures is increasing in the legal world too.

On the other hand, while AI and its applications are grabbing headlines in the legal industry, the development of "analytical machines" is looming on today's debate about the aims and methods of legal research. Two flourishing fields of study, *Empirical legal research*[21] and *Computational legal studies*,[22] for different reasons are pushing forward the creation of new instruments to explore law. The call for closer integration of empirical analyses into legal scholarship naturally results in the quest for data-driven tools and practices enhancing our understanding of law as a fact.[23] Likewise, computational legal scholars' efforts to make the most of legal data increases the need for platforms improving their ability to extract actionable knowledge from texts and documents.

There is no lack of reference models: other research fields have developed solutions integrating different stages of the e-science pipeline in ways that can turn out suitable also

[17] The term is used to point out technological infrastructures consisting of hardware, software, networking systems, and data management components to perform computationally demanding tasks.

[18] An interesting taxonomy is proposed in T. Crouzier, Digital Tools for Researchers (2017), http://connectedre searchers.com. The author offers a detailed overview of the many different ways in which these tools, often freely available online, help scientists: enhancing the exploration of the ever-growing number of papers today available; supporting the management of large sets of data and programming code; facilitating the collaboration with colleagues and the management of online experiments; and simplifying the publication of papers and the analysis of their impact.

[19] As highlighted by Kitchin, the emerging field of computational social science provides an opportunity to develop enhanced models of social life, allowing scientists to shift "from data-scarce to data-rich studies of societies from static to dynamic unfoldings; from coarse aggregations to high resolutions; from relatively simple models to more complex, sophisticated simulations." See R. Kitchin, Big Data, New Epistemologies and Paradigm Shifts (2014) 1 *Big Data Soc.* 1.

[20] For more details, see D. M. Katz, M. J. Bommarito, and J. Blackman, A General Approach for Predicting the Behavior of the Supreme Court of the United States (2017) 12 *PloS One* e0174698; D. M. Katz and M. J. Bommarito, Measuring the Complexity of the Law: The United States Code (2014) 22 *Artif. Intell. Law* 337.

[21] Among others, see P. Cane and H. M. Kritzer (eds.), *The Oxford Handbook of Empirical Legal Research*, 1st edn. (Oxford University Press, 2010); J. M. Smits, *The Mind and Method of the Legal Academic* (Edward Elgar, 2012); F. L Leeuw and H. Schmeets, *Empirical Legal Research: A Guidance Book for Lawyers, Legislators and Regulators* (Edward Elgar, 2016).

[22] For an overview, see J. B. Ruhl, D. M. Katz, and M. J. Bommarito, Harnessing Legal Complexity (2017) 355 *Science* 1377; R. Susskind, *Tomorrow's Lawyers: An Introduction to Your Future* (Oxford University Press, 2017); S. Faro and N. Lettieri, *Law and Computational Social Science* (Edizioni scientifiche italiane, 2013).

[23] A study related to this perspective is the one presented in R. A. Berk, S. B. Sorenson, and G. Barnes, Forecasting Domestic Violence: A Machine Learning Approach to Help Inform Arraignment Decisions (2016) 13 *J. Empir. Leg. Stud.* 94.

for law.[24] A particularly interesting area is, in this regard, Visual Analytics (VA), a fledgling research field that combines computational analyses and visualization to turn data into knowledge, while enabling people to act on their findings in real-time.[25] Seen from the perspective of law, VA techniques are proving to be useful not only to implement more intuitive information retrieval, but also to offer new scientific insights into the legal world.[26]

Some of the existing tools focus on enhancing computer-assisted legal research[27] by means of visualization and computational heuristics. Others are instead aimed at more empirically oriented analyses, exploring priorities and dysfunctions in regulatory policies or at supporting the understanding of facts playing a role to apply legal rules.[28] In any case, what lies ahead of us seems to go beyond a higher level of efficiency in meeting traditional needs of legal information retrieval, but deals with the possibility to devise questions about aspects of the legal phenomenon that were simply inaccessible before.[29]

---

[24] See N. Lettieri, A. Guarino, and D. Malandrino, E-Science and the Law. Three Experimental Platforms for Legal Analytics, Legal Knowledge and Information Systems, JURIX: The Thirty-first Annual Conference, Groningen, The Netherlands (December 12–14, 2018).

[25] For more details, see D. Keim, J. Kohlhammer, G. Ellis, and F. Mansmann, *Mastering the Information Age: Solving Problems with Visual Analytics* (Eurographics Association, 2010). According to Keim (see also D. Keim, G. Andrienko, J.-D. Fekete, *et al.*, Visual Analytics: Definition, Process, and Challenges, in A. Kerren, J. Stasko, J.-D. Fekete, and C. North (eds.), *Information Visualization: Human-Centered Issues and Perspectives* (Springer, 2008)), VA explores new ways to: (1) synthesize information and derive insights from massive, dynamic, ambiguous, and often conflicting data; (2) detect the expected and discover the unexpected; (3) provide timely, defensible, and understandable assessments; and (4) communicate these assessments effectively for action.

[26] The idea of exploiting visual metaphors to ease the management and understanding of legal information has repeatedly made its appearance in the history of law. The use of charts and maps dates back to the Middle Ages when the so-called "arbor" (the Latin word for "tree") diagrams (see A. Errera, *Arbor actionum: genere letterario e forma di classificazione delle azioni nella dottrina dei glossatori* (Monduzzi, 1995); C. Radding and A. Ciaralli, *The Corpus Iuris Civilis in the Middle Ages: Manuscripts and Transmission from the Sixth Century to the Juristic Revival* (Brill, 2007)) were used to graphically exemplify legal concepts like the impediments to marriage, or to depict the stages of procedure in Roman law. Visual metaphors appear again centuries later, when Henry Wigmore (see J. H. Wigmore, Problem of Proof (1913) 8 *Ill. Law Rev.* 77) proposed the use of diagrams – the "Wigmore charts" – to support the analysis of ambiguous pieces of evidence and facilitate reasoning required to confirm or rebut hypotheses presented in court. Over the years, the interest in graphical methods led not only to the implementation of Wigmore diagrams through computational tools, but also to other visual representations like Bayesian networks, a formalism that supports probabilistic inference in forensic science (for an overview, see P. Tillers, *Picturing Factual Inference in Legal Settings, Gerechtigkeitswissenschaft* (Berliner Wissenschafts-Verlag, 2005); A. Biedermann and F. Taroni, Bayesian Networks and Probabilistic Reasoning about Scientific Evidence When There Is a Lack of Data (2006) 157 *Forensic Sci. Int.* 163; F. Taroni, A. Biedermann, S. Bozza, *et al.*, *Bayesian Networks for Probabilistic Inference and Decision Analysis in Forensic Science*, 2nd edn. (Wiley, 2014); T. Gordon, Visualizing Carneades Argument Graphs (2007) 6 *Law Probab. Risk* 109; B. Verheij, Argumentation Support Software: Boxes-and-Arrows and beyond (2007) 6 *Law Probab. Risk* 187). In more recent times, the availability of increasingly powerful technologies and insightful computational heuristics has prompted a growing interest in the development of advanced tools for the analysis of legal information. This is witnessed by a number of experiences (see R. Winkels, N. Lettieri, and S. Faro (eds.), *Network Analysis in Law* (Edizioni Scientifiche Italiane, 2014); R. Whalen, Legal Networks: The Promises and Challenges of Legal Network Analysis (2016) *Mich. State Law Rev.* 539) at the boundaries between visualization, analytics, and law, in an area we define as Visual Legal Analytics (VLA).

[27] Tools have been realized for both scholarly and practical purposes. In legal industry, thanks to the spread of a number of commercial platforms like Lex Machina (https://lexmachina.com), ROSS (https://rossintelligence .com/), and RavelLaw (https://home.ravellaw.com/), law firms have embraced visualization and AI to support document review or to analyze thousands of documents in the context of due diligence.

[28] See, for instance, M. Palmirani, I. Bianchi, L. Cervone, and F. Draicchio, Analysis of Legal References in an Emergency Legislative Setting, in U. Pagallo, M. Palmirani, and P. Casanovas (eds.), *AI Approaches to the Complexity of Legal Systems* (Springer, 2015).

[29] Goals potentially at hand are numerous: (1) analyze the structural and functional features of more or less wide areas of legal systems (e.g. the level of complexity of legislation, case law, legal literature); (2) determine the

Fiddling with Legal Analytical Platforms

Drawing on the considerations made above, we present some experimental online platforms that integrate legal data, computational heuristics, and visualization to explore the possibility of achieving different goals: to enhance legal information retrieval; to extend the methodological apparatus available to legal scholars interested in empirical analyses; or also to devise new ways to identify and measure the computational correlates of legal concepts (for example, the relevance of case law precedents).

All of the platforms have been developed completely from scratch thanks to the collaboration with people from law, computer science, and other research areas.[30] The choice makes sense if we turn our minds to the advantages deriving from *ad hoc* solutions. The first of these is *customization*: tailored algorithms and workflows can better fit both the nature (structure, characteristics, errors, etc.) of data handled and the research goals. A second advantage is *openness*: the development from scratch allows the avoidance of proprietary software, so easing intelligibility and comparability of algorithms, as well as the analysis and sharing of the results. A third benefit, finally, is *integration*: custom-designed tools make it easier to integrate functionalities (for example, different kinds of visualizations) and heuristics (for example, network analysis, machine learning, agent-based modeling, etc.) that often are not integrated in the same application. As highlighted, experiments headed in various research directions. Below is a brief overview presenting the rationale and features of some of the tools developed so far.[31]

Visual Browsing and Analytics of Heterogeneous Legal Sources

Social life is regulated by vast sets of heterogeneous and closely intertwined legal sources that span from laws to administrative measures, case law, and legal literature, an intricate universe

---

relevance of legal documents and sources, according to the dierent meanings acquired by the concept of "relevance" itself in dierent legal contexts; (3) study the relations between dierent expressions of the legal phenomenon (relationship between legislation, case law, and legal literature, or between supranational case law and domestic case law, etc.); and (4) study the evolution of legal systems also for predictive purposes.

[30] Prototypes presented in this and in the following sections are the result of an interdisciplinary research involving people from law (scholars, lawyers, public prosecutors), computer science, cognitive science, sociology, criminology, and computational biology. Most of the tools stem from activities jointly carried out by two chairs: "Law and computational social science" (a class taught at the Dept. of Law, Economics, Management and Quantitative Methods of the University of Sannio) and "Computational Intelligence and Techno-Regulation: Paradigms, Methods, Tools" (a PhD course taught at the Department of Computer Science of the University of Salerno).

[31] Due to space restrictions, we won't present two other platforms for legal analytics developed by the same research group. *EUCaseNet* (see N. Lettieri, S. Faro, D. Malandrino, *et al.*, Network, Visualization, Analytics: A Tool Allowing Legal Scholars to Experimentally Investigate EU Case Law, in U. Pagallo, M. Palmirani, P. Casanovas, *et al.* (eds.), AI *Approaches to the Complexity of Legal Systems* (Springer International, 2018); N. Lettieri, A. Altamura, A. Faggiano, and D. Malandrino, A Computational Approach for the Experimental Study of EU Case Law: Analysis and Implementation (2016) 6 *Soc. Netw. Anal. Min.* 56), is an online analytical platform (https://bit.ly/2yVTFNr) allowing the exploration of the features of European Court of Justice case law: (1) by applying network analysis metrics (centrality measures, PageRank, community detection algorithms) to its citation network so as to study, for instance, the relevance of precedents; and (2) by exploiting statistical visual analytics tools applied to case law metadata. *Argos* (see A. Guarino and others, Visual Analytics to Make Sense of Large-Scale Administrative and Normative Data, 23rd International Conference Information Visualisation (IV), IEEE (2019), https://ieeexplore.ieee.org/document/8811918/) is a modular online platform (https://bit.ly/2HQS2qh) allowing the analysis of large amounts of administrative, legal, and economic data. The goal of the project is twofold: (1) to facilitate the interaction with large-scale administrative data using infographics making access, comprehension of information by experts and citizens more easily and intuitively; (2) to experiment with machine-learning techniques, aiming to extract actionable knowledge from cross-cutting reading of heterogeneous (administrative and normative) data.

of documents forming a complex whole. Picking our way through this universe turns out to be a difficult task: when a citizen tries to understand how a given issue is legally disciplined or a scholar tries to grasp how an area of a legal system evolves over time, their attention cannot be limited to a single source of law. It has to be directed to the bigger picture resulting from all the legal sources related to the subject, taking into account a complex set of information that is often difficult to be identified, retrieved, and gathered in the same context.[32] And that's not all. Once we have the information, depending on the user (scholar, professional, layman) and the aim, further steps may be needed: exploring the connections between laws and legal literature; tracking the evolution of case law; finding and recovering papers; identifying the sectors of the legal system on which a given norm has had a greater impact.

In this vein, the availability of algorithmic tools collecting in a single place the legal sources related to a given topic and allowing, at the same time, the analysis and the intuitive exploration of all the information can be extremely useful. *KnowLex* is a visual analytics toolkit that heads in this direction by exploiting data integration, quantitative analysis, and interactive visualization to make sense of heterogeneous sets of legal documents. The platform[33] experiments lead to a series of solutions generating synergy between legal analytics and visual information retrieval.

A first group of functionalities, embedded in a module named *Reference Norm Network*, uses interactive graphs to represent the set of documents connected to a given piece of legislation. The module gathers materials (amendments, Supreme Court judgments, constitutional judgments, preparatory works, legal literature) from different online datasets and websites starting from a norm chosen by the user (the "Root norm"), and builds a graph connecting all of them. The graph not only offers an overall view of document properties and relations but also allows the user to access text and information simply by interacting with the nodes. The tool even provides the opportunity to explore past links between the normative acts (citations, modifications), making it possible to draw interesting insights in terms of the historical evolution of the legal systems.

A second module, the *Doctrine Semantic Navigator*, supports the analysis and semantic browsing of legal literature. A tough problem for users trying to sort through the often overwhelming number of publications is to find relevant materials when they are not thinking about a specific paper, but simply bear in mind the topic of interest. As known already, classification schemes[34] can help users dealing with this kind of issue, enabling queries based simply on terms that semantically define the scope of the research. *Knowlex* enhances the use of classification schemes by means of a treemap,[35] a visualization particularly suitable for the navigation of hierarchically structured data.[36]

---

[32] The situation is made even more difficult by the fact that, thanks also to the spread of public databases offering free access to law as well as to case law and legal literature, the number of available legal documents has grown dramatically. Moreover, as the repositories are often independent, users have to separately access each of them.
[33] A mobile version of Knowlex is under development.
[34] Thanks to classification schemes, vocabularies of hierarchically structured descriptors often used in legal reference databases, the search becomes a step-by-step process based on the use of increasingly specific search keys.
[35] In information visualization and computing, treemapping is a method for displaying hierarchical (tree-structured) data using nested figures, usually tiles (see R. Blanch and E. Lecolinet, Browsing Zoomable Treemaps: Structure-Aware Multi-Scale Navigation Techniques (2007) 13 *IEEE Trans. Vis. Comput. Graph.* 1248). Each branch of the tree is given a rectangle, which is then tiled with smaller rectangles representing sub-branches. A leaf node rectangle has an area proportional to a specified dimension of the data. Often, the leaf nodes are colored to show a separate dimension of the data. When the color and size dimensions are correlated in some way with the tree structure, one can often easily see patterns that would be difficult to spot using other methods.
[36] For further details, see I. Herman, G. Melancon, and M. S. Marshall, Graph Visualization and Navigation in Information Visualization: A Survey (2000) 6 *IEEE Trans. Vis. Comput. Graph.* 24.

Users can explore documents relating to the *Root norm* and their features by performing drill-down and roll-up operations through a click on the tiles of the map. Each tile identifies all the papers categorized as dealing with a specific topic according to the classification scheme used in *DoGi*,[37] the bibliographic database adopted as reference for the experiment. Generated by an *ad hoc* algorithm[38] that defines tiles' properties (dimensions, color, position) based on the features of papers, the module performs different functions. The first one is information retrieval: while exploring descriptors on the treemap, the user can visualize the list of related documents with all the other information provided by *DoGi*.[39] Other functionalities are connected with analytical goals. The treemap and other data displayed offer a quantitative measure of the impact of the *Root norm* on the legal system's different areas, thus fostering a better understanding of how the doctrine has evolved over time.[40]

Network-Based Inference and AI for Computational Crime Analysis

The computational analysis of crime has attracted significant attention in recent years. Advances made in technology and different research areas from data mining to digital forensics are offering new opportunities to the scientific and investigative study of the criminal phenomenon.

Particularly promising, in this respect, is the adoption of Social Network Analysis (SNA) techniques.[41] Sociality has a tremendous influence on crime: a large part of criminal phenomena, from drug trafficking to hacking and other cybercrimes, is strongly conditioned (inhibited or facilitated) by relational dynamics. Criminals communicate among themselves, collaborate and form groups in which it is possible to distinguish leaders, sub-communities, and actors with different roles. SNA techniques therefore seem to be perfectly suited to the needs of crime studies.[42]

---

[37] DoGi is a reference database of articles published in Italian legal journals created by the Italian National Research Council (www.ittig.cnr.it/dogi). Papers are classified according to a classification scheme covering all areas of national (Italian) and international law and structured in a three-level hierarchy of descriptors.

[38] Every feature of the treemap is defined according to a specific metric and conveys information. The size of tiles is proportional to the percentage of articles associated with them compared to the total number of papers for each level. Tiles are distributed according to a descending order from the biggest (top-left) to the smallest (bottom-right). Each level of the treemap has a different color gradient palette chosen using the statistical mode calculated according to the year of publication. Each sector takes the color associated with the year of publication with greater frequency (the newer the year, the darker is the color in the related palette). Looking at the size and color of the tiles, users could deduce in which sector of the legal literature (and therefore, somehow, of the legal system) the Root norm had its major impact.

[39] For each article, DoGi provides bibliographic information enhanced with: abstracts and/or summaries of articles; a selection of legislative and jurisprudential references of the sources quoted in the article; and further metadata describing other features of the paper.

[40] For example, if 70 percent of the articles related to a certain law is tagged "administrative law," it is likely that this is the field on which the law has had the most impact (areas have a color that varies according to the date of the articles with a given tag).

[41] SNA is a theoretical and methodological approach to the study of social phenomena that aims at understanding social life focusing on the structure of the relations between individuals, groups, or social institutions. According to such perspective, social relationships are conceptualized, represented, and studied as graphs consisting of nodes (actors) and ties (connections between actors). Once a graph is generated based on a given criterion (e.g. mapping friendship, cultural exchanges), several measures are used to analyze structural and functional features both of the network and its components. To this end, SNA exploits computational and algorithmic tools provided by networks and graph theory. The bibliography on network analysis is extremely wide. For a general introduction, see D. Knoke and S. Yang, *Social Network Analysis* (Sage, 2008), Vol. 154.

[42] This task is made easier by the growing amount of digital information available today. The data deluge and the availability of increasingly advanced data-mining techniques are offering both researchers and law enforcement agencies new tools and methodologies to unveil and understand structures and dynamics of criminal networks.

In spite of that, the spread of innovation faces serious difficulties due to the concurrence of two different factors: the shortage of user-friendly crime analysis tools; and the lack of computer science skills of people interested in the study of crime (researchers, public prosecutors, police officers). Yet, relevant contributions can be made, in this regard, by researchers at the borders between law and computer science. A significant part of the knowledge about criminal organizations is hidden in the documents produced during trials and investigations (pleadings, judgments, wiretaps), and materials containing implicit information are bound to stand unused without the proper approaches. Drawing up innovative heuristics and tools to extract actionable knowledge from them is certainly one of the challenges for the near future.

Actually, legal informatics has made remarkable steps forward in document analysis. The AI and law community, for example, has fed legal analytics with increasingly advanced computational models of legal reasoning and argumentation.[43] While most of the research has been devoted to the extraction of purely legal information from texts, less attention has been paid to the potential integration of legal analytics with other computational heuristics aimed at more empirical analysis. Against this background, a worthy effort is that of developing tools experimenting with the integration of different components.

CrimeMiner is an experimental platform exploring how the integration of heterogeneous data and computational heuristics can illuminate the structural and functional features of criminal organizations.[44] To this end, the tool combines, into an ever-evolving pipeline, a variety of techniques: document enhancement; information extraction; data mining; network analysis; visualization; and, in more recent times, agent-based social simulation and machine learning.[45]

All the heuristics have been tested within a case study using legal and empirical data (crime incident reports, criminal records, wiretaps, environmental tappings) extracted from pleadings belonging to real judicial proceedings.[46] The core of the tool and of the experiments conducted so far is represented by graph analysis. Entities extracted from the documents available (individuals, criminal records, number and direction of phone calls, environmental tappings, etc.) have been transformed into edges and nodes of a series of graphs that, beyond offering insightful visualizations, have been analyzed using SNA metrics.

The analysis of the *wiretap graph* – a graph built representing individuals as nodes and phone calls as directed edge – offers an intuitive view of the social interactions between suspected criminals allowing researchers to derive reliable[47] information about relevant features of the

Criminal Network Analysis (CNA) is today a well-established interdisciplinary research area (see C. Morselli, *Inside Criminal Networks* (Springer, 2009), Vol. 8).

[43] See K. D. Ashley, *Artificial Intelligence and Legal Analytics: New Tools for Law Practice in the Digital Age* (Cambridge University Press, 2017).

[44] The goal of the project, prospectively, is to come up with solutions (algorithms, technologies, workflow, visualizations) useful for both legal practitioners (public prosecutors, judges, law enforcement agencies) and scholars (computational social scientists, criminologists) investigating the features of criminal networks and their members. Aimed at both scientific and investigative purposes, the tool has been developed with the collaboration of public prosecutors (one belonging to the Italian Investigative Directorate anti-mafia).

[45] See N. Lettieri, A. Altamura, D. Malandrino, and V. Punzo, Agents Shaping Networks Shaping Agents: Integrating Social Network Analysis and Agent-Based Modeling in Computational Crime Research, in E. Oliveira, J. Gama, Z. Vale, and H. L. Cardoso (eds.), *Progress in Artificial Intelligence* (Springer International, 2017), Vol. 10423.

[46] See N. Lettieri, D. Malandrino, and Luca Vicidomini, By Investigation, I Mean Computation (2016) 20 *Trends Org. Crime* 31.

[47] Insights derived from our analysis substantially reflect evidence resulting from the judgment of the Italian Supreme Court. See Lettieri *et al.*, *ibid.*

network under investigation. The application of centrality measures and other graph algorithms[48] made it possible to retrieve insights about the social role of single individuals (leader, brokers, middleman, drug mules, etc.) and the evolution of the network over time.

Probably more interesting for this discussion are the results gained by applying network analysis measures to *multipartite graphs* putting in relation both factual information (individuals, number and direction of phone calls, number, place and date of in-person meetings) and legal data (for each individual: number, typology, and seriousness of criminal records, indictments). Their analysis allows researchers to draw inferences about criminal network features that can be made only through a cross-sectional reading of legal and factual information: criminal dangerousness of a single individual; criminal relevance of meetings in person involving members of the group; similarity between criminal profiles;[49] and criminal specialization of sub-communities.[50]

A recent development of the project has led to exploring the integration of machine-learning functionalities into *CrimeMiner*. By analyzing the characteristics associated with each organization member (value of network analysis measures, criminal records, etc.), a previously trained classifier supports the domain expert (for example, the prosecutor leading the investigation) in evaluating the criminal dangerousness of single individuals. The user can provide feedback to the classifier by interacting with the nodes of the graph, so as to dynamically change the "notion" of dangerousness used by the system to assess the criminal profile of people under investigation.

ALGORITHMS AS REGULATORY DEVICES

Algorithms are one of the frontiers of normativity. While we spend an increasing part of our lives interacting with digital devices and online platforms, software is becoming the *de facto* regulator of human societies. What may or may not be done in e-commerce platforms or social media depends not only on the applicable law, but much more directly on the technological infrastructure and the software implementing and controlling interactions.

The idea of relying on technological tools and code-based rules to regulate society brings about a variety of benefits, mostly related to the ability to automate the law and its enforcement. While code-based rules are progressively establishing themselves as a regulatory mechanism both in the private and the public sectors, the design of *ad hoc* algorithms and architectures is becoming for legal scholars one of the challenges to come to terms with.

In the following section, I will dwell on code-driven normativity as one of the results stemming from the intersection between law and algorithms. After a brief introduction to what has been called the "techno-regulation" paradigm,[51] I will present a couple of ongoing projects that in various ways tackle the use of algorithmic tools and computational heuristics to implement and support legal safeguards.

---

[48] For example, community detection algorithms, PageRank.

[49] We have applied SimRank (see G. Jeh and J. Widom, SimRank: A Measure of Structural-Context Similarity, Proceedings of the Eighth ACM SIGKDD International Conference on Knowledge Discovery and Data Mining, ACM (2002), http://doi.acm.org/10.1145/775047.775126), a general purpose graph algorithm designed to measure similarity between objects based on the network of relations in which objects are embedded. The idea, basically, is that two objects are similar if they are related to similar objects.

[50] To this end, we used Individual Crime projection, a simple graph in which individuals are nodes that are connected by an edge if they have committed the same crime (the more crimes in common, the more the edges). Uses of projections can be different. In our case, the application of community detection algorithm (Louvain) allowed us to identify the specialization of groups in given criminal activities.

[51] See R. Brownsword, What the World Needs Now: Techno-Regulation, Human Rights and Human Dignity, in R. Brownsword (ed.), *Global Governance and the Quest for Justice*, Vol. IV: *Human Rights* (Hart, 2004).

Techno-Regulation and Algorithmic Governance

Throughout history, artifacts have been frequently and in various ways deployed to influence human behavior or to support the enforcement of legal safeguards. "*Offendicula*", the shards of glass put on the edge of boundary walls since ancient Roman law, are a historical but meaningful example of this: a way to protect a right on a physical good (the property right on an orchard, a house) by means of physical artifacts.[52]

In the information society, where most social, economic and personal interactions are mediated by ICT and goods to be protected are immaterial, something similar is still happening. As witnessed by early forms of ICT-enabled techno-regulation – like *Digital Rights Management*,[53] which incorporates copyright law into technological safeguards by limiting the use of copyrighted artifacts (for example, the number of possible copies of a piece of music in digital format), or by the developments of privacy by design,[54] technology is increasingly an integral part of a regulatory process whose building blocks are not physical, but algorithmic. Scenarios of this change are countless and go from the world of robotics and drones to that of the Internet of Things (IoT).

A special place should be acknowledged in this regard to the Internet, a universe that deeply connected with the emerging idea of algorithmic governance. It is no accident that the theoretical reflection about code-driven regulation have gone hand-in-hand the rise and evolution of Web 2.0.[55] The World Wide Web is not only the place where the normative role of computer code has been identified for the first time, but it has also provided legal scholars with ideas about the possibility of purposely using code and web technologies to implement legal safeguards.

Today, after a long debate,[56] techno-regulation can be seen as a new form of normativity identified, in general terms, with any "intentional influencing of individuals' behaviour by building norms into technological devices."[57] Reasons of interest are different. Unlike traditional legal rules, intrinsically ambiguous and open to interpretation, techno-rules are

---

[52] A more recent example could be identified in the use of speed bumps as a way to ensure that drivers adhere to a speed limit, having a greater effect on speeding than traffic signs (Brownsword, *ibid.*; R. Leenes, Framing Techno-Regulation: An Exploration of State and Non-State Regulation by Technology (2011) 5 *Legisprudence* 143; K. Yeung, Algorithmic Regulation: A Critical Interrogation (2018) 12 *Regul. Gov.* 505).

[53] W. Rosenblatt, S. Mooney, and W. Trippe, *Digital Rights Management: Business and Technology* (John Wiley, 2001).

[54] M. Langheinrich, Privacy by Design – Principles of Privacy-Aware Ubiquitous Systems, in G. D. Abowd, B. Brumitt, and S. Shafer (eds.), *Ubicomp 2001: Ubiquitous Computing* (Springer, 2001), Vol. 2201; A. Rachovitsa, Engineering and Lawyering Privacy by Design: Understanding Online Privacy Both as a Technical and an International Human Rights Issue (2016) 24 *Int. J. Law Inf. Technol.* 374.

[55] The debate started with scholars that first realized the regulatory role played by technology over the Internet. Joel Reidenberg with his concept of "Lex Informatica" (J. R. Reidenberg, Lex Informatica: The Formulation of Information Policy Rules through Technology (1997) 76 *Tex. Law Rev.* 553) or Lawrence Lessig with his famous claim "the code is law" (L. Lessig, *Code and Other Laws of Cyberspace* (Basic Books, 1999)) brought to light how software, hardware, technical standards, and design choices on the Web actually impose rules, just like legal rule-making does.

[56] Roger Brownsword was one of the earliest to explicitly state that digital technologies supporting our transactions and interactions are set "to join law, morals and religion" as "one of the main instruments of social control and order" (Brownsword, above note 50). The debate ends up with the concept of "code-driven law" recently sketched to identify "self-executing" statutes and contracts directly written into computer code. According to M. Hildebrandt, Algorithmic Regulation and the Rule of Law (2018) 376 *Philos. TR Soc. A* 20170355, code-driven law gives rise to a "completely new kind of normativity" transforming "the very nature of existence of law."

[57] B. van den Berg and R. E. Leenes, Abort, Retry, Fail: Scoping Techno-Regulation and Other Techno-Effects, in M. Hildebrandt and J. Gaakeer (eds.), *Human Law and Computer Law: Comparative Perspectives* (Springer International, 2013).

highly formalized and leave little room for ambiguity, thus reducing the likelihood of misunderstanding and lawsuits. Moreover, differently from laws that merely stipulate what people shall or shall not do, "techno-rules" can be "enforced *ex-ante*, determining what people can or cannot do in the first place," eliminating "the need for any third party enforcement authority to intervene after the fact, in order to punish those who infringed the law."[58]

As a matter of fact, based on theoretical and experimental efforts made on the borders between law and e-technologies, the techno-regulation paradigm has already turned into a variety of tools and prototypes ranging from cloud architectures and platforms to plug-ins and software agents. Drawing from the most recent literature,[59] we can identify a variety of research directions corresponding to as many – often intertwined – building blocks of the techno-regulation strategy:

Facts Detection/Classification

Techno-regulation first turns into tools and heuristics aimed at identifying facts and individuals to which regulatory consequences must be attached:[60] (1) detection of breaches of norms (both private regulation and legal provisions); (2) identification of individuals deserving protection; and (3) identification of individuals responsible for illegal/prohibited conducts.

Enforcement

The second research trajectory focuses on the development of technical solutions materially preventing conducts regarded as harmful or illegal,[61] tools designed to directly "determine what people can or cannot do in the first place."[62]

Techno-Nudging

Alongside the tools mentioned in "Enforcement," other "softer forms" of (intentional) technological influencing can be mentioned that aim to persuade, or to nudge, individuals

---

[58] S. Hassan and P. De Filippi, The Expansion of Algorithmic Governance: From Code Is Law to Law Is Code, Field Actions Science Reports (2017).

[59] An interesting overview is offered in T. Kerikmäe and A. Rull (eds.), *The Future of Law and E-Technologies* (Springer International, 2016), where a number of research projects dealing with the creation of techno-regulatory tools is presented. On the same topic, see: E. Bayamlıoğlu and R. Leenes, The "Rule of Law" Implications of Data-Driven Decision-Making: A Techno-Regulatory Perspective (2018) 10 *Law, Innov. Technol.* 295; P. De Filippi, *Blockchain and the Law: The Rule of Code* (Harvard University Press, 2018); Yeung, above note 51.

[60] Authors in A. Norta, K. Nyman-Metcalf, A. B. Othman, and A. Rull, My Agent Will Not Let Me Talk to the General?: Software Agents as a Tool Against Internet Scams, in T. Kerikmäe and A. Rull (eds.), *The Future of Law and eTechnologies* (Springer, 2016), for example, propose the use of intelligent software agents to identify online scams and suspicious content (causing alarm with regard to the risks of misuse of personal data, fraud, extortion, and so on) so as to assist users by means of *ad hoc* warning.

[61] An example is offered in P.-M. Sepp, A. Vedeshin, and P. Dutt, Intellectual Property Protection of 3D Printing Using Secured Streaming, in T. Kerikmäe and A. Rull (eds.), *The Future of Law and eTechnologies* (Springer, 2016). Authors present a techno-regulatory solution that integrates cloud-based architecture, secured streaming, and cryptography to materially prevent copyright infringements of 3D industrial models circulating online.

[62] Hassan and De Filippi, above note 57.

promoting awareness and compliance with rules through targeted warnings, messages, and suggestions.[63]

Code-Driven Regulation in Practice

The analysis of the above reveals the breadth of issues raised by the emergence of the techno-regulation paradigm. Actually, the impact of code-driven regulation can be more or less positive depending on our ability to intelligently merge principles, rules, and priorities defined at the legal level within the technologies gradually available.

A first need is undoubtedly that of a foundational legal research investigating how computation transforms assumptions, operations, and outcomes of the law.[64] At the same time, there is the urge to start cross-disciplinary hands-on activities exploring techno-regulatory tools. Undertaking an intense experimental program is essential not only to foster a new literacy of techno-regulation, but also to start discovering the implications generated by the normative use of information technologies. The design of techno-regulative solutions suitable in terms of formal compliance with existing legal standards, effectiveness, scalability, and technical feasibility will largely depend on this.

In the sections below, I present a few exemplary projects recently launched to get in touch with the different dimensions of techno-regulation – from the choice of the regulatory paradigm to the development of the algorithms supporting it.

Machine Learning for Online Child Protection

As recently emphasized in the Guidelines for Industry on Child Online Protection released by UNICEF, the explosion of ICT has not only created "unprecedented opportunities for children and young people to communicate, connect," but also poses "significant challenges to children's safety." Whether it be schoolwork and research, or games and socializing, young people today are always connected to an online world hiding serious threats: cyberbullying, grooming, hidden advertising, scams, non-illicit content that is still harmful to psychological well-being (violent and hateful comments or images), and kiddie porn material. For children, risks are even higher: they often circumvent or uninstall parental controls, for instance, by lying about their age, while, at the same time, parents do not always understand the potential risks their children may encounter. Against this background, it is easy to figure out how the issue ended up at the heart of international and national strategies about online child protection.[65]

Alongside the legal safeguards, other international initiatives define criteria useful for guiding trials in the field of technology-driven online child protection. One of these, the Child Online Protection (COP) initiative, a multi-stakeholder network launched by the International Telecommunication Union (ITU) and UNICEF, pushed to keep working on Internet-filtering technologies, tools, and techniques that, despite their effectiveness, are still "prone to two inherent flaws: under-blocking and over-blocking."

---

[63] Van den Berg and Leenes, above note 56.

[64] See, in this regard, the objectives stated in the recent H2020 project COHUBICOL – Counting as a Human Being in the Era of Computational Law, www.cohubicol.com/.

[65] Among others, it is worth mentioning the UN Convention on the Rights of the Child, adopted in 1989, or the Council of Europe Convention on the Protection of Children against Sexual Exploitation and Sexual Abuse, adopted in 2010.

The picture just sketched reveals the need for "ecosystemic solutions" integrating traditional legal remedies (for example, criminal sanctions, policing activities, control, repression) with technological safeguards solutions. Especially useful, in this last respect, would be the development of tools allowing governments to intelligently regulate the upload and download of dangerous content by protected parties.

One of the most criticized limits of techno-regulation, indeed, is the risk of a kind of silliness:[66] when compared to "paper rules," "techno-rules" often turn out to be rigid, incapable of discriminating in a rational way people and circumstances consequently adapting the support to statutory protection.[67] AI techniques like data analytics, clustering, or supervised learning can play a crucial role to overcome such a limit by supporting the intelligent identification of threats and people to protect as well as to implement the safeguards.

"*Artificial Intelligence for Children*" is a research project that heads in this direction, focusing on child protection. The initiative started tackling the first building-blocks of the techno-regulatory approach – that is, according to the categorization above proposed – the identification of the individuals to be protected. A further step will be the development of an intelligent child protection ecosystem implementing safeguards consistent with the current legal framework (for example, intelligent filtering of content, conduct, and contacts[68]).

So far the research has been focused on designing a methodology which exploits properties of supervised learning to detect user age, based on the analysis of touch-based gestures.[69] This example of intelligent detection would ensure more effective protection for children in all the situations where parents do not use passwords or do not adequately monitor devices, or, again, children have discovered the password. Moreover, as the identification could be virtually made completely client-side, avoiding the exposure of personal data to a server for the analysis, a higher level of privacy protection would be offered compared with traditional techniques of parental control.

Work done resulted in *AI4 C app*, an experimental game-based application used to gather all the data (features and labels) needed to train a classifier.[70] A series of experiments have been made with 150 people among children and adults. If, on a technical level, supervised learning and touch gesture analysis have proven to be a viable way to identify smart device users' age, the most interesting result lies in the contact established with the complex path

---

[66]   M. Hildebrandt and B.-J. Koops, The Challenges of Ambient Law and Legal Protection in the Profiling Era: The Challenges of Ambient Law and Legal Protection in the Profiling Era (2010) 73 *Modern Law Rev.* 428.

[67]   This algorithmic regulation paradigm has been defined as "IFTT – If This Then That," a decisional logic that is completely "deterministic, entirely predictable and basically consists of simple or complex decision trees" (Hildebrandt, above note 55).

[68]   According to a well-known taxonomy (see S. Livingstone and L. Haddon, EU Kids Online (2009) 217 *Zeitschrift für Psychologie / J. Psychol.* 233), risks can be classified into three main categories: (1) inappropriate content: children may stumble upon content that promotes substance abuse, racial hatred, risk-taking behavior, or suicide, anorexia, or violence; (2) inappropriate conduct: children and adults may use the Internet to harass or even exploit other people; children may sometimes broadcast hurtful comments or embarrassing images or may steal content or infringe on copyrights; (3) inappropriate contact: both adults and young people can use the Internet to seek out children aiming to persuade the child to perform sexual or other abusive acts online, using a webcam or other recording device.

[69]   Touch gestures such as swipes, taps, and keystrokes are common modes of interaction with smart devices (smartphones, smartwatches, and so on). Major operating systems provide a variety of APIs that allow access to onboard device sensors (e.g. gyroscope, G-meter) and gather fine-grain data about touch-gesture. This data can be used by developers both to enhance the user experience and to make inferences about users (age, gender, etc.).

[70]   AI4C App is a test/game designed to "force" a certain touch gesture, among the common ones such as swipe, scroll, and tap. During the experiments, users played AI4C alone on their own devices without any support while a variety of data about gestures (pressure, ellipsis, turning points, accelerations, etc.) were gathered.

leading to the implementation of techno-regulatory strategies and, above all, in a clearer view of the interaction taking place between the legal and technological component of code-driven normativity.[71]

Reputational Nudging and Digital Labor Platforms

As highlighted above, nudging is going to widen the phenomenology of code-driven normativity. One of the frontiers of research in this respect is the design of tools and models of interaction that, instead of materially constraining individuals' behavior, somehow nudge it.

Digital society, on the other hand, consists of concrete scenarios in which factors like the supra-national scale of social, economic, and institutional relationships are regulated or the balance of power between actors involved prevents regulators from adopting self-enforcing, code-driven norms. One of these is certainly represented by the gig-economy, an area of the digital economy in which work is entrusted by organizations operating online platforms to connect customers directly with service-providing workers.

Over the past decade, digital labor platforms (DLPs) have disrupted both existing business paradigms and employment models on which the economy relies. They have offered new solutions to match supply and demand of labor and, above all, have defined innovative ways to manage labor relations using algorithms and data.[72] Despite their attractiveness, DLPs are not without critical issues. A number of controversies have heated up about protection for gig workers. They are not only vulnerable to issues with job security, low income, and legal status, but face risks resulting from the peculiarities of a remote working relationship taking place online and largely managed by algorithms.[73]

Such a scenario confronts policymakers and legislators with the challenge of drawing up strategies reconciling an effective level of protection for crowdworkers and with the goal of economic growth. In general terms, traditional legal remedies risk being inadequate to manage ongoing change, and this occurs for several reasons. While some problems are purely legal,[74] others are strictly related to the algorithmic management of crowdwork,[75] something that can be described as the setting in which "human jobs are assigned, optimized, and

---

[71] R. Brownsword and K. Yeung, *Regulating Technologies: Legal Futures, Regulatory Frames and Technological Fixes* (Hart, 2008).

[72] DLPs give instructions about the time, place, and fulfilment of the service, dynamically determine working conditions (J. Prassl and M. Risak, Uber, Taskrabbit, and Co.: Platforms as Employers-Rethinking the Legal Analysis of Crowdwork (2015) 37 *Comp. Lab. Law Policy J.* 619), and fix the wage according to criteria embedded in algorithm parameters, as location or service demand (A. Rosenblat and L. Stark, Uber's Drivers: Information Asymmetries and Control in Dynamic Work (2015) *SSRN Electronic J.*, www.ssrn.com/abstract=2686227).

[73] Issues span from rating algorithm opacity to the enhanced possibility for monitoring working activities. For a recent analysis, see V. De Stefano, The Rise of the Just-in-Time Workforce: On-Demand Work, Crowdwork, and Labor Protection in the Gig-Economy (2015) 37 *Comp. Labor Law Policy J.* 471.

[74] The supranational scale of corporate structures, and the modularity of technological components – often belonging to different subjects – for example, raise practical problems concerning the identification of the potential counterparty and also of the applicable law itself. In this last respect, as highlighted in A. Felstiner, Labor Standards, in P. Michelucci (ed.), *Handbook of Human Computation* (Springer, 2013), one of the risks connected to the planetary scale of the platform is the "choice of law and jurisdiction," that is, the implementation of strategies to choose applicable law according to criteria of convenience (e.g. a lower tax burden).

[75] A detailed analysis is offered in M. Mohlmann and L. Zalmanson, Hands on the Wheel: Navigating Algorithmic Management and Uber Drivers' Autonomy, in Proceedings of International Conference on Information Systems, ICIS (2017), which distinguishes between different expressions of algorithmic management beyond directing work and scheduling: (1) continuous tracking of workers' behavior; (2) constant performance evaluation of workers from client reviews; (3) implementation of decisions, without human intervention; (4) workers'

evaluated through algorithms and tracked data."[76] In such a scenario, it makes sense to investigate the use of technological tools to support regulatory policies about both crowdworkers' protection and the management of the DLP market.

GigAdvisor is an ongoing experimental project linked to a recent proposal[77] speculating about the possibility of achieving higher levels of protection for crowdworkers by integrating legal remedies and technological tools. The proposal is built around a modular IT infrastructure (*Integrated Crowdwork System*, ICS), a sort of intermediate layer for all the interactions between the players of the gig economy,[78] and aimed at strengthening public scrutiny over the digital labor market. The goal is to allow, among other things, a more effective control over the compliance of market operators with labor law and contracts.[79] To achieve these goals, the ICS envisages two modules: the *Social Security and Contracts Module* (exploiting blockchain and smart contracts technology to enable and keep track of interaction taking place in the digital labor market); and a *Reputation/Transparency Module*, which should implement reputation mechanisms through a mobile app (allowing workers to enter and interact with the ICS) and a website (allowing public access to data generated by interactions within the digital labor market).

GigAdvisor focuses on the *Reputation/Transparency Module*, which, for understandable reasons, can be tackled with acceptable technical effort, and without necessarily involving all the actors of the architecture. On the other hand, reputation can play a significant role in influencing the behavior of the subjects operating on the electronic market.[80] What is more difficult is to concretely promote fairness and cooperation in asymmetrical relationships when platform design allows only requesters and DLPs (and not

---

interaction with a "system" rather than humans, depriving them of opportunities for feedback or discussion with a supervisor; and (5) low transparency stemming from both competitive practices that keep platforms from disclosing how the algorithms work, and from the adaptive nature of the algorithms, whereby the decisions change according to the data being collected.

[76] M. K. Lee, D. Kusbit, E. Metsky, and L. A. Dabbish, Working with Machines: The Impact of Algorithmic and Data-Driven Management on Human Workers, in Proceedings of the 33rd Annual ACM Conference on Human Factors in Computing Systems, ACM (2015).

[77] M. De Minicis, C. Donà, N. Lettieri, and M. Marocco, Disciplina e Tutela Del Lavoro Nelle Digital Labour Platform. Un Modello Di Tecno-Regolazione, Inapp Working Paper (2019), n. 6.

[78] Public administrations (e.g. ministries, labor inspectorates, social security institutions); crowdworkers; DLPs; other actors (e.g. labor and industrial associations, potential customers and crowdworkers, ordinary citizens).

[79] The infrastructure should carry out a variety of functions: (1) recording data about the labor and economic relations between DLPs and crowdworkers; (2) collecting and exposing to the public administrations all data related to the interactions between workers and platforms; (3) allowing the stipulation of smart contracts; (4) providing workers with the possibility of storing and having at hand all the financial and social security information of his occasional works; and (5) implementing reputation mechanisms to protect crowdworkers.

[80] As resulting from literature dating back to the 2000s, reputation can support the solution of problems related to trust and contracts' compliance in contexts in which transactions take place between people/partners unfamiliar and at a distance. They are a "viable alternative to the more established institutions for building trust (such as formal contracts) in electronic environments where such contractual guarantees cannot be efficiently enforced" (R. Conte and M. Paolucci, *Reputation in Artificial Societies: Social Beliefs for Social Order* (Springer, 2002), Vol. 6). Reputation, on the other hand, represents one of the frontiers of techno-regulation, besides the hard-coded, unavoidable legal rules that are enabled, or inhibited, through technology. Actually, various scholars in the field of law and technology are turning their attention toward softer forms of (intentional) technologically enabled, gentle persuasion, traceable to the concept of nudge (M. Hildebrandt, Legal Protection by Design: Objections and Refutations (2011) 5 *Legisprudence* 223; Leenes, above note 51; M. Goodwin, B.-J. Koops, and R. Leenes, *Dimensions of Technology Regulation* (Wolf, 2010)). For its part, nudge – "any small feature of the environment that attracts people's attention and alters their behavior but does so in a way that does not compel" (R. H. Thaler and C. R. Sunstein, *Nudge: Improving Decisions about Health, Wealth and Happiness* (Penguin, 2009)) – has become a reference point in current debate about the frontiers of policy design (see, among others, A. Alemanno and A.-L. Sibony, *Nudge and the Law: A European Perspective* (Bloomsbury, 2015)).

crowdworkers) to make assessments about the experience deriving from the gig. On the other hand, recent history – see, for instance, the case of *Turkopticon* – shows how the assignment of ratings can push platforms to modify their behavior to avoid drawbacks resulting from a bad reputation.[81]

Based on this consideration, the project ended up developing a cross-platform app that allows crowdworkers to: (1) give a score to the DLPs they worked for by ranking their work experience using an evaluation grid[82] that accounts for potential violations of constraints set by legislation in force; and (2) share experiences with other crowdworkers, thanks to solutions aimed at facilitating and structuring interaction, which is also useful in circulating information and, therefore, in amplifying the impact of the reputational mechanism. Data gathered through the app is used for post-processing based on data-mining and visualization techniques, designed respectively to extract valuable insights about DLPs' conducts and to disseminate them better.

The system will shortly be made available to rider associations to start an experimental program aimed at testing the system and collecting data for further developments. Special attention will be paid, in this vein, to the implementation of pattern-recognition algorithms allowing the identification of DLPs' unfair practices and the automatic generation of reputational alerts.

ALGORITHMS AS TOOLS FOR POLICY AND RULE-MAKING

A third interesting context for the algorithmic evolution of law is that of policy and rule-making. The design of tools supporting legislators in their work has long been a subject of investigation at the boundaries between law and computer science. Countless articles have been published over the years in this area dealing with topics such as – just to give a few examples – legislative texts parsing,[83] drafting support systems,[84] and technical standards for representing and managing legislative documents.[85]

In recent years, however, new perspectives have opened up, linked to investigations where the focus is less on the formal analysis of legal texts and more on the phenomena in which the legislator wants to intervene. The design of legal rules, on the other hand, is an integral part of the policymaking process which, for both historical and scientific reasons, is increasingly oriented toward computational and model-driven approaches. The result, as I will try to briefly show in the following sections, is that the legal scholars will be increasingly challenged to play their part within this process.

---

[81] M. S. Silberman and L. Irani, Operating an Employer Reputation System: Lessons from Turkopticon, 2008–2015 (2015) 37 *Comp. Lab. Law Policy J.* 505.

[82] B. McInnis, D. Cosley, C. Nam, and G. Leshed, Taking a HIT: Designing around Rejection, Mistrust, Risk, and Workers' Experiences in Amazon Mechanical Turk, in Proceedings of the 2016 CHI Conference on Human Factors in Computing Systems, ACM (2016).

[83] See E. de Maat, R. Winkels, and T. Van Engers, Automated Detection of Reference Structures in Law, in T. M. Van Engers (ed.), *Legal Knowledge and Information Systems: JURIX 2006* (IOS Press, 2006).

[84] See W. Voermans and E. Verharen, LEDA: A Semi-Intelligent Legislative Drafting-Support System, in J. S. Svensson, J. G. J. Wassink, and B. van Buggenhout (eds.), Legal Knowledge Based Systems, Proceedings 6th International Conference JURIX '93, Koninklijke Vermande, Lelystad (1993), pp. 81–94.

[85] See M. Palmirani and F. Vitali, Akoma-Ntoso for Legal Documents, in G. Sartor, M. Palmirani, E. Francesconi, and M. A. Biasiotti (eds.), *Legislative XML for the Semantic Web* (Springer, 2011).

Policy Design and the Computational Evolution of Social Research

We live in a complex world in which the interactions among technological, economic, social, and political systems are ever more frequent and mazy: in a hyper-connected society, any event can produce effects that spread rapidly from one system to another through cycles of non-linear feedback that are extremely difficult to predict and, above all, to control.[86] Global financial and economic crises have cast doubts on the adequacy of conventional policy-making to illuminate mechanisms underlying social and economic phenomena, as well as to provide effective policy prescriptions.

Marked by an often naïvely mechanistic vision of reality,[87] conventional approaches to policy modeling show huge limitations in this regard.[88] On a closer examination, the situation largely depends on a poor understanding of both individual decision-making[89] and dynamics triggered by social interactions. What is still largely missing is the ability to reckon with non-linearity, bounded rationality, and incomplete knowledge. Recent examples of experimental and computational research[90] confirm the need for approaches and modeling techniques capable of giving life to adequately contextualized policies, conceived not as something that happens "off-line," but as a "constituent process that interacts with the adaptive and self-organizing dynamics of society."[91]

In the last two decades, the scientific investigation of the social and economic world has experienced a strong impetus from a theoretical, methodological, and technological level due to a variety of factors. One of these is represented by *computational social science*[92] – the scientific paradigm that, together with *behavioral economics* and *economic psychology*,[93] started to offer new insights into how individuals and groups decide, interact, and react to changes.

Originating from the encounter between[94] the conceptual framework complexity theory, the data deluge,[95] and the computational evolution of science, CSS is paving the way to an

---

[86] D. Helbing, Globally Networked Risks and How to Respond (2013) 497 *Nature* 51.
[87] As highlighted in F. Squazzoni, A Social Science-Inspired Complexity Policy: Beyond the Mantra of Incentivization (2014) 19 *Complexity* 5, the dynamic stochastic equilibrium model, which has gained momentum also at the policy level (e.g. to forecast the effect of monetary and fiscal policy or the patterns of economic growth), is based on a set of unrealistic assumptions like, for instance, the perfect knowledge of economic actors, the presence of complete markets and perfect competition, and the absence of non-linear interactions. The adoption of familiar and highly unrealistic conventional models is a dramatic myopia particularly in the case of political or financial institutions that need to "assemble the pieces and understand the behaviour of the whole economic system." See J. D. Farmer and D. Foley, The Economy Needs Agent-Based Modelling (2009) 460 *Nature* 685.
[88] Squazzoni, *ibid.*
[89] Individuals do not necessarily behave in the way predicted by rational choice theory (C. J. Samuel and T. J. Fararo (eds.), *Rational Choice Theory: Advocacy and Critique* (Sage, 1992)), which is still the main source of inspiration for policymakers. Even when dealing with the same information or pay-offs, humans show behaviors that are often hard to anticipate.
[90] See P. Ball, *Why Society Is a Complex Matter* (Springer, 2012); P. Ormerod, Networks and the Need for a New Approach to Policymaking, in T. Dolphin and D. Nash (eds.), *Complex New World. Translating New Economic Thinking into Public Policy* (IPPR, 2012); Farmer and Foley, above note 86.
[91] Squazzoni, above note 86.
[92] N. Gilbert, *Computational Social Science* (Sage, 2010), Vol. 21; Cioffi-Revilla, above note 6; Conte et al., above note 6.
[93] D. Kahneman, Maps of Bounded Rationality: Psychology for Behavioral Economics (2003) 93 *Am. Econ. Rev.* 1449; V. L. Smith, Constructivist and Ecological Rationality in Economics (2003) 93 *Am. Econ. Rev.* 465.
[94] P. Ormerod, N Squared: Public Policy and the Power of Networks (RSA, 2010).
[95] C. Anderson, The End of Theory: The Data Deluge Makes the Scientific Method Obsolete (2008) 16 *Wired Magazine* 7.

unprecedented leap in our comprehension of social phenomena. Implications of this change go beyond the purely scientific dimension. By increasing our ability to understand and predict social dynamics, CSS is laying the ground to innovative approaches to policy design and to more effective public choices. CSS methodologies[96] are indeed particularly suited to the study of non-linear phenomena that are, at the same time, difficult to grasp with conventional mathematical and statistical tools and are also poorly understood by traditional policymaking procedures. That is why, in recent years, the scientific community has started paying more attention to computational social science and to how its insights can improve policy modeling.[97]

Walking the Fine Line between Computational Social Science and Law

The interplay between CSS and policymaking also challenges the law. The design of public policies is closely linked with legal norms drafting and, while policymaking becomes evidence-based and algorithms-driven, even legal scholars are called to find new computational ways of contributing to policy development. Opportunities in this area are not lacking: several of the activities involved in rule-making processes are moving toward new approaches, especially those aimed at improving the "quality of regulation"[98] – here understood to mean the capacity of clearly identifying policy goals and being effective in achieving them.[99]

All of these activities, from the citizens' involvement to the *ex post* evaluation,[100] can find an ally in computational social science methodologies.[101] CSS can be fruitful in various ways: extracting information from the huge amount of data available today; providing a clearer view of the interplay between legal norms and social facts; and offering tools and predictive techniques for what-if analysis. The activity that probably poses the greatest challenges to the algorithmic evolution of policy design is, however, *Regulatory Impact Analysis* (RIA). Aiming at assessing social and economic effects of proposed and existing regulations as well as non-regulatory alternatives, the RIA calls into question our capacity to understand and predict complex social dynamics.

Among the various CSS methodologies, computer simulation is one that can play a role in this regard. Simulation has for a long time drawn the attention of scholars interested in

---

[96]   The CSS paradigm encompasses an evolving variety of research methodologies. According to C. Cioffi-Revilla, Computational Social Science (2010) 2 *Wiley Interdiscip. Rev. Comput. Stat.* 259: automatic information extraction, complexity models, social simulation, social network analysis, and geospatial analysis.

[97]   Helbing, above note 85; Conte *et al.*, above note 6; V. Mayer-Schönberger and K. Cukier, *Big Data: A Revolution that Will Transform How We Live, Work, and Think* (Houghton Mifflin Harcourt, 2013).

[98]   N. Lettieri and S. Faro, Computational Social Science and Its Potential Impact upon Law (2012) 3 *Eur. J. Law Technol.*, http://ejlt.org/article/view/175.

[99]   Quality of regulation is an increasingly important concern on the agenda of national and international institutions. In the last twenty years, the Organisation for Economic Cooperation and Development (OECD) has produced several documents on the topic adopting, in 2012, the Recommendation on regulatory policy and governance.

[100] Typically achieved through various types of consultations (in particular through the notice and comments mechanism), citizens' involvement in the design of public policy consists in seeking public comments on specific issues to be settled. The collection and analysis of information about the way in which a regulation is perceived by the citizens helps governments to refine policies, so as to address problems deemed most important by the community and to better define the priorities. *Ex post* evaluation, on its own, aims to assess regulatory measures already in place: their effects, impact on the relevant needs and the resources employed also for the purpose of planning, designing, and implementing new policies.

[101] As to citizens' involvement, CSS methods can help to overcome the limits affecting today's e-consultation, an activity that is intrinsically connected with the problem of extracting meaningful knowledge from citizens' contributions. Information extraction research so far has generated several opinion-mining methods to analyze judgments and reviews posted on the Web. All of these methods – first and foremost those from sentiment analysis (J. Rose and C. Sanford, Mapping eParticipation Research: Four Central Challenges (2007) 20 *Commun. Assoc. Inf. Syst.* art. 55) – may lead to innovative solutions to assess citizens' sentiments toward the policies and also to extract the main issues they raise.

policymaking. *System dynamics*[102] and microsimulations models[103] have been used since the 1950s[104] to tackle policy issues such as predicting the effects of changes in tax laws on government finances. As highlighted by Squazzoni,[105] however, traditional forecast-oriented models often fail in their purpose by prescribing *ex ante* solutions that underestimate the reaction of agents to policy decisions and the systemic consequences of their interactions on large temporal scales.[106]

A promising paradigm, in this regard, is that of agent-based simulation models (Agent-Based Modeling – ABM).[107] Based on the identification of the scientific explanation with the reproduction "in silico" (that is, in a computer simulation) of the social processes being investigated, ABM underlies a generative approach to research in which social macro-dynamics and structures are interpreted, described, reproduced, and then explained as the result of micro-interactions between computational entities (agents) simulating the behavior of real individuals.[108] Over the years, ABMs have shown to be particularly suited to investigate socio-economic dynamics that are difficult to treat with statistical approaches. Thanks to this feature, agent-based simulations[109] have not only spread in science, but have also reached institutions involved in policy design.[110]

---

[102] J. W. Forrester, *Principles of Systems* (Wright-Allen Press, 1968); J. Randers, *Elements of the System Dynamics Method* (Pegasus Communications, 1980); J. Sterman, *Business Dynamics, System Thinking and Modeling for a Complex World* (McGraw-Hill, 2000), p. 19 .

[103] M. Spielauer, What Is Social Science Microsimulation? (2010) 29 *Soc. Sci. Comput. Rev.* 9.

[104] R. Lay-Yee and G. Cotterell, The Role of Microsimulation in the Development of Public Policy, in M. Janssen, M. A. Wimmer, and A. Deljoo (eds.), *Policy Practice and Digital Science* (Springer International, 2015).

[105] F. Squazzoni, The Impact of Agent-Based Models in the Social Sciences after 15 Years of Incursions (2010) 18 *Hist. Econ. Ideas* 197.

[106] S. Moss, Policy Analysis from First Principles (2002) 99 *Proc. Nat. Acad. Sci.* 7267; F. Squazzoni and R. Boero, Complexity-Friendly Policy Modelling, in P. Ahrweiler (ed.), *Innovation in Complex Systems* (Routledge, 2010).

[107] ABM can be defined as a "computational method that enables a researcher to create, analyze, and experiment with models composed of heterogeneous agents that interact within an environment" (N. Gilbert, *Agent-Based Models* (Sage, 2008)). ABM differs from computer simulation forerunners such as system dynamics, cellular automata, and microsimulation. Unlike ABM, system dynamics do not allow for modeling heterogeneous micro aspects, but just interdependence and feedback among macro variables; cellular automata reduce the interaction of dispersed micro entities to a single homogenous parameter; while microsimulation does not include interaction (for an overview on this topic, see: K. G. Troitzsch, Social Science Simulation – Origins, Prospects, Purposes, in R. Conte, R. Hegselmann, and P. Terna (eds.), *Simulating Social Phenomena* (Springer, 1997); K. Troitzsch, Multi-Agent Systems and Simulation, in *Multi-Agent Systems* (CRC Press, 2009); and N. Gilbert and K. Troitzsch, *Simulation for the Social Scientist* (McGraw-Hill, 2005)).

[108] J. Doran and N. Gilbert, Simulating Societies: An Introduction, in *Simulating Societies: The Computer Simulation of Social Phenomena* (Routledge, 1994); R. Conte, R. Hegselmann, and P. Terna, Introduction: Social Simulation – A New Disciplinary Synthesis, in R. Conte, R. Hegselmann, and P. Terna (eds.), *Simulating Social Phenomena* (Springer, 1997), Vol. 456; Epstein, above note 10; Gilbert, above note 106.

[109] M. Buchanan, Economics: Meltdown Modelling (2009) 460 *Nature* 680; J. D. Farmer and D. Foley, The Economy Needs Agent-Based Modelling (2009) 460 *Nature* 685; D. Helbing (ed.), *Social Self-Organization* (Springer, 2012).

[110] A remarkable acknowledgement of ABM potential was given, in 2010, by the former EU Central Bank President Jean-Claude Trichet. While commenting on the failure of traditional macroeconomic models in predicting economic crisis, he stated: "We need to deal better with heterogeneity across agents and the interaction among those heterogeneous agents. We need to entertain alternative motivations for economic choices . . . Agent-based modelling allows for more complex interactions between agents. Such approaches are worthy of our attention." Today, policy issues explored using ABM range from the management of environmental resources to the impact of land-use decisions, from the effects of economic policies to those of retirements. See, in this regard, Y. Ma, Z. Shen, and M. Kawakami, Agent-Based Simulation of Residential Promoting Policy Effects on Downtown Revitalization (2013) 16 *J. Artif. Soc. Soc. Simul.* 2; N. J. Saam and W. Kerber, Policy Innovation, Decentralised Experimentation, and Laboratory Federalism (2013) 16 *J. Artif. Soc. Soc. Simul.* 7; T. Brenner and C. Werker, Policy Advice Derived from Simulation Models (2009) 12 *J. Artif. Soc. Soc. Simul.* 2.

In the following, I will present a couple of experiments that walk the fine line between CSS, policy design, and law.[111] I will draw from a series of works[112] made in collaboration with colleagues from computational social science and law dealing, in particular, with the use of agent-based simulations to explore the interaction between norms and social facts. The first of these investigates the interplay of damaging behaviors, punishment, and social mechanisms of learning and imitation. The second deals with the core mechanisms of social dilemmas (SDs). The goal in both cases is twofold: to get acquainted with the new kind of experimental method offered by computer simulations and to start using this to illuminate mechanisms underlying social phenomena and reflect, in innovative ways, on how society can deal with them.

Evolutionary Simulations of the Effects of Sanctions

In carrying out its function of creating and maintaining social order, law mostly uses sanctions to steer citizens' behaviors and deter actions harmful to legally relevant interests. The effects of the sanctions, however, can significantly deviate from the predictions of the rational choice model usually assumed as a reference: deterrence is not guaranteed by the fact that the costs brought about by the sanctions exceed the advantage deriving from the harmful behavior. Countless other factors are involved, belonging to different levels of reality and studied by a set of disciplines ranging from sociology to econophysics.

As discussed above, agent-based simulations are an ideal tool in this regard.[113] They allow us to explore the interactions taking place between the many factors that can influence the effects of sanctions: those more closely related to the law (strictness, timing, implementing

---

[111]   Over the years, computer simulations have been presented as a viable tool to support legal analysis (see D. A. Degnan and C. M. Haar, Computer Simulation in Urban Legal Studies (1970) 23 *J. Leg. Educ.* 353; J. N. Drobak, Computer Simulation and Gaming: An Interdisciplinary Survey with a View toward Legal Applications (1972) 24 *Stanford Law Rev.* 712; M. Aikenhead, R. Widdison, and T. Allen, Exploring Law through Computer Simulation (1999) 7 *Int. J. Law Inf. Technol.* 191), and the study of social phenomena involved by the functioning of legal systems and institutions (P. H. M. van Baal, *Computer Simulations of Criminal Deterrence: From Public Policy to Local Interaction to Individual Behaviour* (Boom Juridische uitgevers, 2004); T. Bosse and C. Gerritsen, Social Simulation and Analysis of the Dynamics of Criminal Hot Spots (2010) 13 *J. Artif. Soc. Soc. Simul.* 5), especially in the more empirically oriented discipline of criminology (see L. Liu and J. Eck (eds.), *Artificial Crime Analysis Systems: Using Computer Simulations and Geographic Information Systems* (Information Science Reference, 2008)). However, agent-based models still appear to fall outside the scope of legal science.

[112]   See N. Lettieri and D. Parisi, Neminem Laedere: An Evolutionary Agent-Based Model of the Interplay between Punishment and Damaging Behaviours (2013) 21 *Artif. Intell. Law* 425; N. Lettieri and M. Vestoso, Simulating the Core Dynamics of a Social Dilemma: Individual Choices, Time and Sanctions in the Tragedy of the Commons, in E. Tambouris, H. J. Scholl, and M. F. Janssen (eds.), *Electronic Government and Electronic Participation: Joint Proceedings of Ongoing Research, PhD Papers, Posters and Workshops of IFIP EGOV and EPart 2015* (IOS Press, 2015).

[113]   A perfect example of this is offered by a realistic retrospective simulation model developed by a large multi-disciplinary research team at Santa Fe Institute (J. S. Dean, G. J. Gumerman, J. M. Epstein, and R. L. Axtell, Understanding Anasazi Culture Change through Agent-Based Modeling, in T. A. Kohler and G. J. Gumerman (eds.), *Dynamics in Human and Primate Societies: Agent-Based Modeling of Social and Spatial Processes* (Oxford University Press, 2000), p. 179; R. L. Axtell, J. M. Epstein, G. J. Gumerman, *et al.*, Population Growth and Collapse in a Multiagent Model of the Kayenta Anasazi in Long House Valley (2002) 99 *Proc. Nat. Acad. Sci.* 7275). Aiming to explain the history of the Anasazi – a community living in the American Southwest between the last century BC and 1300 AD, which disappeared from the region within the space of a few years with no evidence of environmental catastrophes or enemy invasions – the model integrated impressive quantities of empirical environmental, historical, and social data provided by archeologists, paleoclimatologists, geographers, and anthropologists. Simulations allowed the reproduction of empirical evidence on the Anasazi evolutionary trajectory, such as their spatial distribution and their resistance against environmental changes. They also led to reject the hypothesis that environmental changes were responsible for the Anasazi exodus and to promote instead the explanatory power of more sociopolitical "pull" factors, such as the influence of leaders.

rules) and those of a factual nature, such as the individual features of the subject punished (for example, economic status) or cognitive, cultural, and social dynamics (for example, cultural and behavioral transmission models). A better understanding of these processes is not only a worthy scientific goal, but also the starting point for the development of law enforcement and regulatory strategies more suitable to real contexts.[114]

Heading in this direction, we developed an agent-based model focusing on how the effects of sanctions on norm compliance[115] are affected by the interplay between factors like the entity thereof, imitation mechanisms, or, more generally, the adaptive capabilities that push human beings to maximize their well-being. The simulation is extremely abstract with regard to the complexity of real-world processes, primarily of a cognitive nature, underlying norm compliance. As noted by the anthropologist Adamson Hoebel,[116] "norms are mental constructs" and insightful simulation models of norm emergence have been developed thanks to the explicit computational modeling of cognitive dynamics.[117] Despite that, we opted for a bio-inspired modeling approach – in particular genetic algorithms[118] – to simulate cultural learning processes[119] leading social norms to emerge while individuals adapt to the environment. Evolutionary computation, on the other hand, has repeatedly thrown new light on the evolution of norms and cooperation.[120]

[114] From this perspective, thanks to their capacity to support the understanding of the micro-foundations of complex social phenomena, ABM simulation is a viable tool to study the interplay between legal and non-legal phenomena (e.g. social norms and their dynamics), an issue that is sparking a growing interest among legal scholars: E. A. Posner, *Law and Social Norms* (Harvard University Press, 2000); B. Z. Tamanaha, *A General Jurisprudence of Law and Society* (Oxford University Press, 2001). This kind of analysis should be challenging for legal scientists, at least those belonging to those schools of thought like Legal Realism or Empirical Legal Studies that are interested not only in the exegesis of legal rules or the definition and systematization of abstract legal concepts, but also in an interdisciplinary investigation of empirical processes underlying legal phenomena.
[115] Here defined as the lack of damaging behaviors in the artificial society.
[116] E. Adamson Hoebel, *The Law of Primitive Man: A Study in Comparative Legal Dynamics* (Harvard University Press, 1954).
[117] See C. Castelfranchi, R. Conte, and M. Paolucci, Normative Reputation and the Costs of Compliance (1998) 1 *J. Artif. Soc. Soc. Simul.* 1; N. J. Saam and A. Harrer, Simulating Norms, Social Inequality, and Functional Change in Artificial Societies (1999) 2 *J. Artif. Soc. Soc. Simul.* 1; J. M. Epstein, Learning to Be Thoughtless: Social Norms and Individual Computation (2001) 18 *Comput. Econ.* 9; M. A. Burke, G. M. Fournier, and K. Prasad, The Emergence of Local Norms in Networks (2006) 11 *Complexity* 65. For an extensive review, see: M. Neumann, A Classification of Normative Architectures, in K. Takadama, C. Cioffi-Revilla, and G. Deffuant (eds.), *Simulating Interacting Agents and Social Phenomena* (Springer, 2010); and M. Neumann, Norm Internalisation in Human and Artificial Intelligence (2010) 13 *J. Artif. Soc. Soc. Simul.* 12.
[118] Genetic algorithm (GA) is a modeling and programming technique trying to mimic the natural process of learning based on research and exploration (J. H. Holland, Genetic Algorithms (1992) 267 *Sci. Am.* 66). Often used in social simulation research (T. Chmura, J. Kaiser, and T. Pitz, Simulating Complex Social Behaviour with the Genetic Action Tree Kernel (2007) 13 *Comput. Math. Organ. Theory* 355; E. Ostrom, J. Burger, C. B. Field, *et al.*, Revisiting the Commons: Local Lessons, Global Challenges (1999) 284 *Science* 278), GA allows the modeling of populations of adaptive agents that are not fully rational in the sense that they are only capable of refining the strategies adopted by trial and error. Using the selective reproduction of agents and the constant addition of random mutations, most effective strategies can emerge thanks to the research conducted by a succession of generations of agents.
[119] R. G. Reynolds, An Introduction to Cultural Algorithms, in Proceedings of the Third Annual Conference on Evolutionary Programming, World Scientific (1994).
[120] See, for instance, the pioneering work (R. M. Axelrod, An Evolutionary Approach to Norms (1986) 80 *Am. Political Sci. Rev.* 1095) integrating ABM simulations, game theory, and evolutionary computation to study the emergence of social norms. Evolutionary models have been used to explore how a variety of social outcomes spanning from cooperation (see, among others: R. M. Axelrod, *The Evolution of Cooperation* (Basic Books, 1984); R. Axelrod, *The Complexity of Cooperation: Agent-Based Models of Competition and Collaboration* (Princeton University Press, 1997), Vol. 3; N. Henrich and J. P. Henrich, *Why Humans Cooperate: A Cultural and Evolutionary Explanation* (Oxford University Press, 2007); M. Tomasello, *Why We Cooperate* (MIT Press, 2009)) to migration dynamics (see, e.g., H. S. Barbosa Filho, F. B. de Lima Neto, and W. Fusco, Migration and

From the social science standpoint, the most relevant aspect of our simulation – the variation in the probability that an agent damages another agent – is the result of the interaction between different variables of the artificial society that stylize real-world phenomena that we assume have a role in the interplay between punishment and damaging behaviors. Far from being the result of arbitrary assumptions, the choice and implementation of each of these variables and the fundamental rules according to which they interact are grounded in sociological theories covering both individual and social dimensions of the model. In more detail: *rational choice theory*[121] models individual selfishness involved in individual decision-making and the effects connected to the severity and probability of sanctions; *strain theory*[122] models the relations between non-damaging behaviors and their pay-off; and *theories of social context*[123] model the role played on damaging behavior by the social context.

The model was tested by simulating different experimental conditions: (1) different levels of severity and timeliness of the sanction; (2) presence/absence, between the agents, of communication networks able to affect the transmission of behavioral models; and (3) capacity/inability of the agents to decide the extent of damage to be caused to other agents.[124] Despite its simplicity, the model allowed researchers to generate a considerable number of scenarios with often counterintuitive developments capable of shedding light on interesting aspects of the dynamics that govern, at a fundamental level, the effects of the sanction.

Social Networks – an Explanatory Multi-Evolutionary Agent-Based Model, in *IEEE Symposium on Intelligent Agent (IA)* (IEEE, 2011)), from social learning (see M. Macy, Natural Selection and Social Learning in Prisoner's Dilemma: Coadaptation with Genetic Algorithms and Artificial Neural Networks (1996) 25 *Sociol. Methods Res.* 103) to network diffusion (see, among others, M. Lahiri and M. Cebrian, The Genetic Algorithm as a General Diffusion Model for Social Networks, in Twenty-Fourth AAAI Conference on Artificial Intelligence (2010)) and survival strategies (F. Cecconi and D. Parisi, Individual versus Social Survival Strategies (1998) 1 *J. Artif. Soc. Soc. Simul.* 1), can be explained as the result of adaptation strategies. The study of punishment, in particular, has already exploited evolutionary models (R. Boyd and P. J. Richerson, Punishment Allows the Evolution of Cooperation (or Anything Else) in Sizable Groups (1992) 13 *Ethol. Sociobiol.* 171; R. Boyd, H. Gintis, S. Bowles, and P. J. Richerson, The Evolution of Altruistic Punishment (2003) 100 *Proc. Nat. Acad. Sci.* 3531; J. H. Fowler, Altruistic Punishment and the Origin of Cooperation (2005) 102 *Proc. Nat. Acad. Sci.* 7047; C. Hauert, A. Traulsen, H. Brandt, *et al.*, Via Freedom to Coercion: The Emergence of Costly Punishment (2007) 316 *Science* 1905).

[121] G. S. Becker, Crime and Punishment: An Economic Approach (1968) 76 *J. Political Econ.* 13; D. B. Cornish and R. V. Clarke, *The Reasoning Criminal: Rational Choice Perspectives on Offending* (Transaction Publishers, 2014).

[122] R. K. Merton, *Social Theory and Social Structure: Toward the Codification of Theory and Research* (Free Press, 1949).

[123] D. Matza and G. M. Sykes, Juvenile Delinquency and Subterranean Values (1961) 26 *Am. Sociol. Rev.* 712; T. Hirschi, *Causes of Delinquency* (University of California Press, 1969).

[124] In an artificial society, 200 agents make decisions autonomously based on interactions with the environment and other agents. In order to increase his assets (fitness), each agent can decide – with a randomly assigned probability that evolves based on interactions occurred – whether to take what he needs for survival from the environment ("honest" action) or from the assets of other agents (harmful actions). Due to his actions, the agent can be identified as "honest" or dishonest, a feature that matters when simulating the processes of cultural transmission of the behavioral models (propensity to perform honest or harmful actions). During the simulation, thanks to a genetic algorithm, the agents evolve a greater or lesser propensity to damage others based on the combination of a series of factors: (1) pay-off – increases in assets deriving, according to the case, from harmful or honest actions; (2) penalties – reductions in assets applied to agents responsible for damaging actions; and (3) behavior held by the agents within the social network to which they belong. The researcher can change all of the parameters of the simulation (severity and probability of the sanctions; pay-off of honest and dishonest actions; the level of social interaction, etc.) to study the effects of the sanction in different scenarios.

Without going into the details, the model produced results in different directions. With regard to the target phenomenon, the simulation offered insights into the relevant role played by the mechanisms of cultural transmission or even on the relative marginality of the severity of the sanction. On a more strictly methodological level, research suggests that[125] simulations have a large (but not yet really) exploited potential of providing policy- and rule-maker with knowledge about the possible consequences of their actions.

Many types of simulations, it is worth saying, are and probably for a long time will be unable to make precise predictions about the outcomes of planned policies, even if probabilities can be given for the alternative paths. What is only possible is a foresight in the sense that possible futures can be sketchily described, improving information on which political decisions rest. Nevertheless, simulation modeling can be used not only to make predictions or to explain existing empirical data, but also to illuminate "core dynamics," to "discover new questions," and to "promote a scientific habit of mind,"[126] as it is much needed also in the legal field.

Intertemporal Choice and the Core Dynamics of Social Dilemmas

The understanding of the way in which collective phenomena emerge from the interaction between individual behaviors, environment, and institutions plays a crucial role in supporting the design of contextualized policies. An apparently effective policy can easily fail if policymakers do not consider the interplay between social aggregate dynamics and individual decision-making. This is what often happens with SDs, situations that arise "whenever a group of individuals must decide how to share a common resource while balancing short-term self-interests against long-term group interests."[127]

SDs are extremely relevant: they not only lead to collective issues, problems, or even disasters, but are ubiquitous. Learning how to deal with such phenomena is essential for policymakers and, since they are becoming more complex and global, there is an increasing need to understand their core mechanics. As a result, the scientific interest in SDs – particularly those resulting from overpopulation, resource depletion, and pollution – has grown dramatically over the last ten years: the attention has shifted from pure laboratory research toward interdisciplinary approaches characterized by the cooperation between different areas aiming at developing a unifying theoretical framework.

One of the most well-known SDs is the *Tragedy of the Commons* (ToC), a social pattern[128] derived by the fact that individuals acting autonomously and "rationally" – according to their self-interest – behave contrary to the interest of the whole group, depleting common resources.

[125] K. Troitzsch, Legislation, Regulatory Impact Assessment and Simulation, in N. Lettieri and S. Faro (eds.), *Law and Computational Social Science*, Vol XII: *Informatica e Diritto* (ESI, 2013).

[126] J. M. Epstein, Why Model? (2008) 11 *J. Artif. Soc. Soc. Simul.* 12; on the exploratory nature of simulations, see J. L. Casti, Would-Be Worlds: How Simulation Is Changing the Frontiers of Science, 1st edn. (John Wiley, 1998); T. Grüne-Yanoff and P. Weirich, The Philosophy and Epistemology of Simulation: A Review (2010) 41 *Simul. Gaming* 20.

[127] G. Greenwood, Evolution of Strategies for the Collective-Risk Social Dilemma Relating to Climate Change (2011) 95 *EPL* 40006. In general terms, SDs are characterized by two fundamental features: (1) each individual of the community taken into account receives a higher pay-off for a socially defecting choice (e.g. using all the available energy, polluting neighbors) than for a socially cooperative choice, no matter what the other individuals in society do, but (2) all individuals are better off if all cooperate than if all defect.

[128] G. Hardin, The Tragedy of the Commons (1968) 162 *Science* 1243.

Over time, the ToC has been recognized as the prototype of a range of dilemmatic situations that occur in different social contexts from the micro (local) to the macro (global) levels. Considerations made about the ToC, therefore, can be extended virtually to any situation in which society appeals to an individual exploiting a common resource to restrain himself for the general good. This is why the ToC has been considered in connection with a variety of issues from economic growth to environmental protection by researchers in economics, politics, sociology, and even evolutionary psychology.

As to the legal world, putting aside considerations concerning substantive law issues, it is worth pointing out the recent publication of works that[129] ground the reflection about the regulation of social dilemmas on a better understanding of the systemic and dynamic nature of the phenomenon, at the same time making the most of the knowledge that science is providing about the complexity of the real world. From this perspective, while the above-mentioned disciplines keep investigating from a theoretical point of view the different levels of reality involved in the genesis of social dilemmas, it is worth developing computational models that allow researchers to operationalize knowledge about the ToC and to experimentally explore its core dynamics for both scientific and applicative purposes.

An experiment heading in this direction, using agent-based models to integrate the analysis of social interactions with an increasingly explicit representation of individual decision-making, is discussed by Lettieri and Vestoso.[130] Building on the experience described in previous sections, the work tries to explore the core mechanics of the ToC, focusing, in particular, on the impact that sanctions can have in preventing their evolution.

As widely acknowledged in a huge and heterogeneous literature, sanctions are essential in promoting social cooperation,[131] even in dilemmatic situations like the ToC.[132] A still challenging research goal, however, is to experimentally determine how different kinds of sanctions can dynamically affect the course of social dilemmas, taking into account their interaction with individual decision-making. Even if traced back to a variety of causes,[133] the outbreak of the ToC was found to be due mainly to two mechanisms that are closely tied to the way in which we make decisions. The first one is *selfish rationality* – that is, according to Hardin,[134] the individual tendency to increase well-being, putting personal interest ahead of that of the community. The second is the *temporal discount* operating in intertemporal

---

[129]   F. Capra and U. Mattei, *The Ecology of Law: Toward a Legal System in Tune with Nature and Community* (Berrett-Koehler, 2015).

[130]   Lettieri and Vestoso, above note 111.

[131]   E. Fehr and S. Gächter, Altruistic Punishment in Humans (2002) 415 *Nature* 137; S. Gächter, E. Renner, and M. Sefton, The Long-Run Benefits of Punishment (2008) 322 *Science* 1510.

[132]   J. Jacquet, K. Hagel, C. Hauert, *et al.*, Intra- and Intergenerational Discounting in the Climate Game (2013) 3 *Nature Climate Change* 1025.

[133]   E. Ostrom, *Governing the Commons: The Evolution of Institutions for Collective Action* (Cambridge University Press, 1990).

[134]   "As a rational being," he states, "each herdsman seeks to maximize his gain. Explicitly or implicitly, more or less consciously, he asks, 'What is the utility to me of adding one more animal to my herd?' This utility has one negative and one positive component. 1) The positive component is a function of the increment of one animal. Since the herdsman receives all the proceeds from the sale of the additional animal, the positive utility is nearly +1. 2) The negative component is a function of the additional overgrazing created by one more animal. Since, however, the effects of overgrazing are shared by all the herdsmen, the negative utility for any particular decision-making herdsman is only a fraction of –1" (Hardin, above note 127). In this context, adding together the component partial utilities, a rational individual concludes that the best choice for him is to continue to add animals to his herd. But, as this is the conclusion reached by each rational herdsman sharing a commons, the tragedy becomes unavoidable.

choices. As highlighted in psychological literature,[135] the ToC is strictly connected with the fact that behaviors leading to long-term negative effects result in an immediate reward as claimed by Platt with his concept of "social traps."[136] A recent study[137] focusing on climate change shows that a key role is played by the way in which human beings deal with intertemporal choices.[138]

The interplay between the two above-mentioned factors makes it difficult to counteract the evolution of the ToC and suggests the introduction of incentives to cooperate, such as mutual coercion,[139] punishment,[140] rewards,[141] or even reputation[142] and shame.[143] A crucial issue for policymakers is therefore the understanding of the way in which incentives can be administered in order to effectively fight the spread of the social dilemma.

Drawing on this theoretical background, the simulation investigates the complex feedback loops taking place among decision-making, sanctions, and environmental pollution, aiming to identify the conditions allowing the emergence and establishment of cooperative behaviors (not polluting the environment). The modeling approach and also some technical solutions adopted to simulate learning processes are similar to those adopted in a previous work of ours exploiting an evolutionary agent-based model to explore the interplay between punishment and damaging behaviors.[144]

---

[135] R. M. Dawes, Social Dilemmas (1980) 31 *Ann. Rev. Psychol.* 169.

[136] J. Platt, Social Traps (1973) 28 *American Psychologist* 641.

[137] Jacquet *et al.*, above note 131.

[138] Intertemporal choices concern options that can be obtained at different points in time (e.g. buying expensive cars today or saving the money to ensure a sizable pension in the future) and that often oppose a smaller but sooner prize (e.g. a modest amount of food ready at hand) against a larger but delayed outcome (e.g. a more distant, but also richer, foraging opportunity). According to the public-good experiments presented in Jacquet *et al.*, above note 131, the difficulty in avoiding dangerous climate change arises not only from the tension between group and self-interest generated by rational selfish behaviors, but is also exacerbated by climate change's intergenerational nature. The dilemma lies in that the "present generation bears the costs of cooperation, whereas future generations accrue the benefits if present cooperation succeeds, or suffer if present cooperation fails."

[139] Hardin, above note 127.

[140] Fehr and Gächter, above note 130; J. Jacquet, C. Hauert, A. Traulsen, and M. Milinski, Shame and Honour Drive Cooperation (2011) 7 *Biology Letters* 899.

[141] Jacquet *et al.*, above note 131.

[142] M. Milinski, D. Semmann, and H.-J. Krambeck, Reputation Helps Solve the Tragedy of the Commons (2002) 415 *Nature* 424.

[143] Jacquet *et al.*, above note 139.

[144] Lettieri and Parisi, above note 111. One hundred agents move in an environment that contains a given number of randomly distributed tokens. For any token eaten by an agent, another one appears in a different position, so that the total number of tokens is always the same. All agents can reach the tokens, but the speed for reaching them varies according to agents' genes. The simulation is a succession of generations each composed of 100 agents. The agents of the first generation have random genes, so each agent moves at a different speed. The ten agents with the better genes, those running faster and so reaching more tokens (fitness), generate ten offspring each. The offspring inherit the genes of their (single) parent with the addition of some random variations (genetic mutations) that can make some offspring have better genes and run faster than their parent. They represent the second generation of agents and the simulation goes on for five generations. While moving in the environment to reach the tokens, agents pollute the environment as much as the speed with which they move; so an agent which moves faster pollutes more than an agent which moves more slowly. Pollution reduces agents' fitness. Therefore, the probability that the agent will have offspring depends not only on the number of tokens that the agent is able to reach (increasing fitness), but also on the level of environmental pollution. Living in a polluted environment implies a reduction of fitness which is proportional to the level of pollution. This leads agents to deal with a dilemmatic issue: either they move more slowly and eat fewer tokens, avoiding polluting the environment, or they move faster and eat more tokens, polluting the environment. The problem, the core of the ToC, is that all of the agents contribute to the pollution of the environment. As a result, the negative consequences of pollution fall also on those agents that, because of their genes, move more slowly and pollute the environment less. This fosters agents moving fast and having more fitness, but also makes the environment progressively more polluted – with increasing damage for all agents.

In a nutshell, the model allows researchers to apply a "sanction" to agents that move too fast and pollute the environment, therefore producing a higher level of pollution. The sanction produces a reduction of the fitness of the agent that exceeds a given speed limit and its amount can be varied according to the researcher's aim. Simulation parameters are numerous (token density, agents' life length, speed limit, etc.). Each of them can affect the result of the experiment and each of them has a specific semantic value.

We investigated how the combination of different kinds of sanctions[145] with different temporal scenarios affected the evolution of ToC dynamics by manipulating the variables of the simulation. Without going into more detail, the results obtained suggested interesting systemic correlations between the delay of sanction and cooperative behavior: the effectiveness of sanction depends not only on the amount and type of sanction, but also on the time of its application, also considering the speed at which the environment is polluted. The experiments have also highlighted the need for more semantically rich solutions to stylize the way in which individuals deal with the interaction structure that characterizes the ToC.[146]

In more general terms, what clearly emerged was the importance of an adequate modeling of internal processes governing agents' choices. Without algorithms accounting for the semantics of individual decision-making, no reliable study of complex generative social outcomes can be carried out.

CONCLUSIONS: A FEW THOUGHTS ABOUT ALGORITHMS AND LAW

The research experiences described in previous sections identify just some of the many contexts in which the encounter between algorithms and law can lead to the discovery of new challenging research frontiers. It is quite clear that we could mention many other research topics along with those listed above, and that many will emerge shortly by virtue of scientific and technological evolution. Developments of blockchain, IoT, AI, and robotics – just to name a few examples – will undoubtedly be the starting point for further research questions involving the relationship between law and algorithms.

Despite its limitations, the above overview allows some closing remarks involving, in general terms, the deeper implications of the algorithmic revolution currently underway. In each of the experiments reported, on the other hand, algorithms show their transformative power. Their role turns out to be crucial for a variety of reasons: to provide legal analytics with ever more insightful heuristics; to implement techno-regulatory strategies supporting the achievement of

---

[145] The simulation model allows different sanction "regimes": fixed (the sanction has the same fixed value for each agent that exceeds the limit); speed proportional (the sanction value is given by the difference between the real speed of the agent and the speed limit; and fitness proportional (the sanction has a value which is proportional – 10 percent – to the fitness of the agent that exceeds the speed limit).

[146] The hyperbolic discount function adopted to model agents' choices does not account for cognitive dynamics that play a significant role in determining the evolution of intertemporal choice. In real settings, individual propensity to cooperate with other individuals is conditioned by factors that go beyond the simple (even if temporally discounted) assessment of the costs and benefits deriving from selfish behavior and sanctions. The choice to cooperate in dilemmatic scenarios (in our case, by refraining from polluting or depleting common resources) is also conditioned by the prescriptive power of social norms and, therefore, by all the mechanisms that support their spreading and stabilization. That is why, taking cue also from a recent simulation work on the cognitive implications of the ToC (D. Villatoro, R. Conte, G. Andrighetto, and J. Sabater-Mir, Self-Policing through Norm Internalization: A Cognitive Solution to the Tragedy of the Digital Commons in Social Networks (2015) 18 *J. Artif. Soc. Soc. Simul.* 2), it is important to endow agents with a cognitive architecture (a software model of reasoning used for programming intelligent agents) accounting for the process of norm internalization.

legally defined objectives; and to improve rule-making with a better understanding of core dynamics underlying social phenomena targeted by public policies.

Algorithms are the catalyst for a change that, depending on the cultural and scientific perspectives adopted, can be understood in different ways, touching on different aspects of the future of law. The following considerations dwell on this point based on the belief that algorithms can inspire a radical rethinking of legal research perspectives in terms of objects, methods, and relationships with other disciplines.

The first consideration, dealing with somehow more foundational issues, concerns the impact of the algorithmic evolution on the very object of legal science – namely, on the definition of the phenomena toward which jurists can turn their attention and their studies. The starting point of our remark is the idea that algorithms are, in fact, increasingly powerful tools for understanding reality. Together with data and computation technologies they can be seen – to use the words from the philosopher of science Paul Humphreys – as "empirical extensions,"[147] tools that, similarly to all the technologies that extend our perceptual abilities (think about the electronic microscope or the radio telescope), move the boundaries between what is observable and what is not. If the word "fact" denotes real-world phenomena that can somehow be measured and linked in causal terms, then in extending the "observational realm," algorithms extend the realm of facts,[148] broadening the very limits of empirical research and increasing the number of topics we can deal with.

If this is – as it is – real, it makes sense claiming that legal epistemology cannot stay the same in the algorithmic world. Algorithms' impact does not come to an end in providing legal information retrieval with more advanced methodologies to sift norms and case law. Thanks particularly to the scientific and methodological developments from the CSS area, they are reshaping our understanding of the social universe, offering an increasingly accurate representation of its complexity. From such a perspective, algorithms can lead to an empirical and complexity-inspired evolution of the very goals of legal research.

The heuristics currently available could open up the gates to what we define as "computation-enhanced legal empiricism," a rendition of legal empiricism exploiting computation not only to identify trends and correlations in case law by means of statistical regressions and machine learning, but also to investigate other aspects of the legal phenomenon, like the intricate networks of cognitive and social mechanisms through which law emerges, is applied, and exerts its effects. The study of the emergence and evolution of norms[149] by means of agent-based social simulation models is a meaningful example of an innovative research topic inspired by complexity science that, while enhancing the understanding of social and normative reality, could also turn into more scientifically grounded and effective legal solutions. Such an evolution, on the other hand, is in line with recent trends of legal scholarship, where a growing attention is devoted to the empirical study of law by means of quantitative approaches.[150]

---

[147] P. Humphreys, *Extending Ourselves: Computational Science, Empiricism, and Scientific Method* (Oxford University Press, 2004).

[148] Examples are countless and can be found in the possibility of measuring previously inaccessible dimensions of reality from internal states of individuals (think of natural language processing, sentiment analysis, or computational analysis of neuroscientific data) to the dynamics occurring on social networks (think about the study opinion dynamics on network models).

[149] See, among others, M. Xenitidou and B. Edmonds, *The Complexity of Social Norms* (Springer, 2014).

[150] See Cane and Kritzer, above note 20; D. E. Ho and L. Kramer, Introduction: The Empirical Revolution in Law (2013) 65 *Stanford Law Rev.* 1195; F. L Leeuw and H. Schmeets, *Empirical Legal Research: A Guidance Book for Lawyers, Legislators and Regulators* (Edward Elgar, 2016).

A second point, tightly connected with the previous one, concerns the potential role of algorithms in promoting more interdisciplinary approaches to research – an issue that appears to be increasingly topical in the legal field.[151] In recent years,[152] interdisciplinarity has been given growing attention – being seen not only as a questionable scientific option, but also as a mandatory step to manage pressing real-world issues that "cannot be adequately addressed by people from just one discipline."[153] The statement fits our analysis well: giving an answer to the many questions of legal science and practice (assess the impact of legal norms; understand the deep nature of legal systems; predict the evolution of law enforcement strategies.) This is a complex task involving disciplines that largely transcend the boundaries of traditional legal scholarship. Our ability to integrate in new ways different knowledge and disciplines becomes crucial and algorithms can play a relevant role to this end.

Similarly to the computer-based artifacts conjured up by Domenico Parisi,[154] algorithms can provide scientists belonging to different research areas with powerful conceptual and analytical toolkits that ease the development of integrated and non-disciplinary approaches to complex phenomena. The hands-on research experiences presented in this work somehow try to prove this. They explore solutions of issues in legal science and practice based on concepts and methods borrowed from a variety of disciplines and methodologies that span from sociology to cognitive sciences, from network analysis to bio-inspired evolutionary game theory. This cross-fertilization, it is clear, would not have been possible without the mediation of the algorithmic language, without the power of computation.

The third and final consideration relates to methodological issues. In social science, the idea of overcoming what has been called the "war of paradigms"[155] has gradually led to the emergence of a pluralist perspective[156] according to which the integration of different research methods[157] becomes of paramount importance to enhance our comprehension of social complexity. This is true not only in the more traditional areas of social research, but also in emerging fields like computational social science and computational legal research, where the merging of heterogeneous research methods spanning from data mining to social simulation or network analysis is ever more frequent.

Thanks to the technical sophistication of the tools implementing them and to the high levels of interoperability between applications, algorithms are today one of the factors that enable the integration of different research perspectives and methodologies. Thinking about their role and their use in these terms is a fundamental step toward highlighting the contribution they can make to the enhancement of legal science and practice.

---

[151] See for an overview M. M. Siems, The Taxonomy of Interdisciplinary Legal Research: Finding the Way out of the Desert (2009) 7 *J. Commonw. Law Leg. Educ.* 5.

[152] See R. Frodeman, J. Thompson Klein, and R. C. Dos Santos Pacheco, *The Oxford Handbook of Interdisciplinarity* (Oxford University Press, 2017).

[153] Mind Meld (2015) 525 *Nature* 289.

[154] "Theories as computer-based artefacts are a unified theoretical and methodological framework, a 'lingua franca' that can facilitate the dialogue among biologists, psychologists, and social scientists, and the development of an integrated science of human beings" (see D. Parisi, *Future Robots: Towards a Robotic Science of Human Beings* (John Benjamins, 2014), Vol. 7).

[155] The term is used in H. Eckstein, Unfinished Business: Reflections on the Scope of Comparative Politics (1998) 31 *Comp. Political Stud.* 505.

[156] See, among others, D. D. Porta and M. Keating, *Approaches and Methodologies in the Social Sciences: A Pluralist Perspective* (Cambridge University Press, 2008); R. Sil and P. J. Katzenstein, *Beyond Paradigms: Analytic Eclecticism in the Study of World Politics* (Macmillan, 2010).

[157] See C. Teddlie and A. Tashakkori, *Foundations of Mixed Methods Research: Integrating Quantitative and Qualitative Approaches in the Social and Behavioral Sciences* (Sage, 2009).

In a work dating back to 1656,[158] Thomas Hobbes claimed "by ratiocination, I mean computation," putting forward the insightful vision of the deep connection tying rational thought, our ability to grasp reality, and computation broadly understood as information processing by means of formalized, operational rules. Today, when the very concept of computation has been associated with a countless number of other meanings, Hobbes's intuition still retains all of its inspirational power. It reminds us how any understanding of the world, as well as any ability to act on it, are inevitably intertwined with computational information processing. This also applies to law that should always keep searching for new ways to use algorithms and computation to better understand itself and also to more effectively carry out its ordering function.

The solution, it goes without saying, rests not in the algorithms alone, but in the way in which they are used, contextualized, and tailored to the needs of who is using them. This operation, as already emphasized in the introduction to this chapter, cannot be led from outside the legal world, driven by technology or computer science. It is something in which lawyers must play an active role, fully accepting the challenge of learning new languages, and adopting new categories and perspectives. The algorithmic evolution of law must be built from the inside.

An inspiring image, even if coming from a different context, is that recently offered by the quantum physicist Carlo Rovelli drawing on a simile from Otto Neurath. In a paper dealing with the role of philosophy in physics, he states: "... science is the continuous search for the best conceptual structure for grasping the world ... and the modification of the conceptual structure needs to be achieved from within our own thinking, rather as a sailor must rebuild his own boat while sailing."[159] From this point of view, there is still a long way to go. Although algorithms are already a reality in the legal world, a large part of the algorithmic future of law is yet to be thought up and built. However magnificent and sparkling, Turing's cathedral is still under construction.

ACKNOWLEDGEMENTS

Ideas proposed in this work stem from a long-standing interdisciplinary collaboration with a number of people. The author wishes to thank Domenico Parisi from the Italian Institute of Cognitive Sciences and Technologies (Rome) and all the friends and colleagues from the Department of Computer Science of the University of Salerno: Delfina Malandrino, Rocco Zaccagnino, Alfonso Guarino, Antonio Altamura, Armando Faggiano, Luca Vicidomini, Fabio Grauso, and Antonio Basileo. The author is also truly grateful to Margherita Vestoso from the University Suor Orsola Benincasa (Naples) for the insightful comments on this work, as well as for the precious support given in discussing and proofreading this chapter.

---

[158] See T. Hobbes, *Elements of Philosophy the First Section, Concerning Body* (Andrew Crooke, 1656), ch. 1.

[159] C. Rovelli, Physics Needs Philosophy. Philosophy Needs Physics (2018) 48 *Found. Phys.* 481, drawing on a simile used for the first time by Otto Neurath: O. Neurath, Anti-Spengler, in M. Neurath and R. S. Cohen (eds.), *Empiricism and Sociology* (D. Reidel, 1973 [1921]).

33

Arguing over Algorithms

Mapping the Dilemmas Inherent in Operationalizing "Ethical" Artificial Intelligence

Mariano-Florentino Cuéllar and Robert J. MacCoun

INTRODUCTION

The problem we address in this chapter is easy enough to state: Relatively simple algorithms, when duplicated many-fold and arrayed in parallel, produce systems capable of generating highly creative and nuanced solutions to real-world challenges. The catch is that the autonomy and architecture that make these systems so powerful also makes them difficult to control or even understand.

This recurring problem is also easy enough to name. In fact, it has several names:

- designing a safe, ethical artificial intelligence (AI);
- regulating a corporation;
- raising a child.

These three challenges admittedly evoke different reactions among members of the public, and implicate distinct organizations and institutions. Some of those distinctions are important enough for us to acknowledge them in this chapter. Yet, in practice, these pursuits have enough in common to motivate a cross-cutting inquiry with implications for both how we try to operationalize "ethics" for AI, and how we understand the recurring issue of how to reconcile intelligence – whether in a machine, an organization, or a child – with the ethical, moral, and risk-management considerations that render such intelligence compatible with society's needs and values. Thus, we will begin with a rebuttable presumption that – at least for the purposes of any conversation about ethics and governance – the similarities are more relevant than the differences, that is to say:

1. Systems with distributed cognitive architectures serve to dilute responsibility, making it harder to know where action comes from and what justifies it.
2. Such systems function best by balancing multiple goals, and efforts to encourage them to maximize any single goal – whether that be shareholder wealth or a grade-point average – can yield a bitter harvest.
3. Efforts to make such systems completely transparent and explainable are unlikely to be successful without crippling their ability to adapt and thrive.

While these challenges may bedevil society in domains ranging from child-rearing to the regulation of corporations, the version of the resulting problem associated with AI feels new and alien, in no small measure because AI systems are not human. But corporations and children feel familiar solely because we make sense of them using a mental model (sometimes called "folk psychology"), which glosses over their complexity.[1] The conventional view among most members of the public sees agents as making conscious choices on the basis of desires and beliefs. Folk psychological agents, when interrogated, are able to explain their conduct by converting desires and beliefs into "reasons."

Indeed, the generativity and ingenuity of corporations and children is mostly produced by massively parallel cognitive systems far more complex than folk psychology. And corporations and children are capable of conduct that is sometimes capricious, hazardous, or even malicious. We will "control" algorithmic-driven AI systems in the same way we control corporations and children, which is to say, clumsily, partially, and with much frustration. AI, corporations, and children aren't problems that we solve; they are challenges that we must continuously manage.

And so it will likely continue to be with AI and the algorithms driving its performance. That even the most gifted technical minds would find it daunting to operationalize human ethics into the algorithms that guide AI systems is not surprising, in some respects. It is not surprising because society faces continuing challenges in aligning ethics and practice – and even agreeing on what counts as ethical behavior – among children and corporations. Our hope in this chapter is to unpack the sources of those difficulties, and in the process, to illuminate some of the challenges and possibilities that lie ahead as humans pursue not only the creation of more sophisticated forms of AI, but a more subtle and lasting understanding of how ethical reasoning occurs and what it means. In what follows, we'll begin by considering some of the ways that our understanding of AI and AI ethics might usefully benefit from attention to these features of human psychology. We'll assess the role of institutions and conflict in managing the resulting value conflict that arises among humans. Our conclusion will focus on practical implications for AI research, policy, and law.

ON PARALLEL DISTRIBUTED COGNITIVE SYSTEMS

In many ways, the recent debates about ethical AI are orthogonal to debates about the details of particular types of algorithms. But, for two reasons, the debate has escalated with the gradual shift from "classic" AI (sometimes called "GOFAI" for "good old-fashioned AI") to contemporary machine-learning methods. First, classic AI's accomplishments were underwhelming; performance has improved exponentially with the shift to new approaches (augmented by massive increases in speed and data access). Second, while classic AI was instantiated in thousands of lines of dense computer code, its basic steps could be sketched out in a one-page flow chart or a few paragraphs of text.[2] In contrast, today's AI programs are considerably more complex to describe, and nearly impossible to mimic using a pen and paper.

Classic AI code was complex and daunting, but it did not feel alien. More often than not, it was serial, propositional, and linear. It was serial because events happened one at a time in a specific identifiable order. It was propositional in the sense of being explicit declarations ("A = x") or conditional injunctions ("if A = x, then do B"). It was generally linear in the sense that it produced changes in output that were roughly proportional to changes in input.

Human cognition sometimes resembles classic AI (or perhaps more accurately, classic AI attempted to mimic human cognitive processes that sometimes occur); but mostly just the

---

[1] S. Stich, *From Folk Psychology to Cognitive Science* (MIT Press, 1983).
[2] GOFAI code written in LISP could seem opaque, but it involved the kind of recursive steps we all use when performing familiar tasks like assembling a jigsaw puzzle.

limited cognition that involves explicit propositional reasoning in a serial fashion – the kind of reasoning that occurs in the narrow bottleneck of active working memory. But we now understand that the vast majority of cognitive processing occurs outside this bottleneck and hence outside of conscious awareness.[3]

The first serious challenge to classic AI came in the mid-1980s with the emergence of a series of powerful demonstrations that "parallel distributed processing" (PDP, also known as "connectionist") programs could perform cognitive tasks that had eluded classic AI, with outcomes that often matched or exceeded human performance (much of this work appeared in two collections by Rumelhart, McClelland, and the PDP Research Group).[4] By the early 2000s, some of this early enthusiasm had tempered as the PDP approach had reached an asymptote, but this was temporary. Over the past decade, progress has rapidly accelerated in part due to improved algorithms, but mostly due to deploying the basic PDP approach with vastly improved processing speed and power that enabled the systems to operate over much larger matrices of data.[5]

Crucially, our understanding of corporate behavior has also improved by a recognition of the role of parallel distributive cognition spread across the offices and units of the organization. For example, "principal-agent problems" arise precisely because organizations are not unitary actors following a unitary goal and plan of action. The distributed aspects of corporate cognition can produce pathologies, but are essential reasons for the enhanced capacities of organizations relative to individual humans, as recognized early on by Adam Smith in his discussion of the "division of labor."

INTERPRETABILITY

For computer scientists, connectionist AI meant better engineering; these were increasingly practical tools allowing computers to accomplish practical tasks at scale. For cognitive psychologists, connectionist AI led to a renaissance in our understanding of the limited role of consciousness in mental life. The "new unconscious" wasn't so much a Freudian warehouse of repressed sexual urges as it was a giant factory floor populated by dozens of different teams working in parallel.[6] This new understanding helped to explain a puzzle posed famously by Nisbett and Wilson in a classic 1977 *Psychological*

---

[3] In distinguishing serial and parallel processing, we are not endorsing a simple dichotomy between two systems (e.g. "System 1 and System 2") of cognition. That dichotomy served a rhetorical purpose in helping scholars challenge folk psychological assumptions, but in itself it is an oversimplification. The brain has myriad ways of doing things, most of which involve some mix of conscious and unconscious components. Awareness, controllability, speed, and accuracy are continuous rather than dichotomous features of cognition, and their correlations vary by task and context (J. S. Evans, Dual-Processing Accounts of Reasoning, Judgment, and Social Cognition (2008) 59 *Ann. Rev. Psychol.* 255). Parallel processing is not the only reason why most cognition is unconscious. It would be anatomically and metabolically costly – and arguably logically impossible – for the brain to store representations of its own workings (W. James, *Principles of Psychology* (Henry Holt, 1890); G. Bateson, *Steps to an Ecology of Mind* (University of Chicago Press, 1972)), so the brain appears to store goal-stimulus-outcome links, but not the cognitive or motor processes that connect them (B. Hommel, Dancing in the Dark: No Role for Consciousness in Action Control (2013) 4 *Front. Psychol.* 380; T. Wilson, *Strangers to Ourselves: Discovering the Adaptive Unconscious* (Belknap Press, 2002)).

[4] D. E. Rumelhart, J. L. McClelland, and PDP Research Group, *Parallel Distributed Processing: Explorations in the Microstructure of Cognition*, Vol. 1: *Foundations* (MIT Press, 1986); D. E. Rumelhart, J. L. McClelland, and PDP Research Group, *Parallel Distributed Processing: Explorations in the Microstructure of Cognition*, Vol. 2: *Psychological and Biological Models* (MIT Press, 1986).

[5] Y. LeCun, Y. Bengio, and G. Hinton, Deep Learning (2015) 521 *Nature* 436.

[6] R. Hassin, J. S. Uleman, and J. A. Bargh, *The New Unconscious* (Oxford University Press, 2005).

Review piece.[7] Why is it that when we ask people to explain their reasoning, they give seemingly plausible answers that fail to track their actual behavior, even in the most innocuous kinds of tasks? (An example: Consumers judging pantyhose quality were strongly influenced by the order in which they considered the packages, but not only did they not mention this as a factor, many denied that it had any relevance to their choices.) Ericsson and Simon countered that people could provide valid information about their decision process when asked to "think out loud" during the task, but this turns out to work only in a narrow range of tasks – tasks inside the working-memory bottleneck.[8]

With the emergence of the PDP paradigm, it became much clearer why we lack introspective access to most of our cognition: much of it is happening in a parallel-distributed fashion that can't fit in the bottleneck. So how did Nisbett and Wilson's participants come up with explanations for their behavior? Nisbett and Wilson contended that we explained our own action much like we'd explain the action of someone we are observing – by offering an *ad hoc* folk psychological account that seems to fit the facts or to win over a critical audience.[9]

This opacity often extends to moral cognition. Haidt argues: "Moral reasoning, when it occurs, is usually a post-hoc process in which we search for evidence to support our initial intuitive reaction ... people can sometimes be 'morally dumbfounded' – they can know intuitively that something is wrong, even when they cannot explain why."[10]

An earlier generation of AI researchers made heroic efforts to develop "expert systems" – systems that *were* expert in some domain because they were based on an explicit coding of the knowledge of recognized human experts. These systems have in some cases demonstrated their utility, but for various reasons, they have fallen short of their initial promise. As early as 1988, Coats noted:

> The stark fact is that extracting knowledge from the experts presents an extremely serious bottleneck.[11] (Note the bottleneck metaphor again.) Far too often, key knowledge is so ingrained that experts use it implicitly, but cannot explain it. They find it difficult to put hunches and instinctive feelings into words and rules.

Anticipating today's machine-learning methods, Coats went on to suggest that "these problems may eventually be solved by 'teaching' the system to use inductive learning."

But induction tends to bring its own interpretive difficulties. As individuals and units in organizations gather information over time and use inductive methods to make sense of it, they are unlikely to articulate explicit principles distilling from their analyses the precise rationales for their decisions – unless, of course, legal or institutional requirements instantiating some kind of bureaucratic rationality call for such an explanation. Formal methods of induction such as Bayes's rule and factor analysis assist in the analysis of information in part because they furnish insights that may elude even quite learned domain experts. As digital computers, often working in massively parallel fashion, are used to scale how inductive methods discern patterns from information, it becomes difficult for observers to follow the precise logic that explains why a given translation program (for example) captured the nuance

7   R. E. Nisbett and T. D. Wilson, Telling More than We Can Know: Verbal Reports on Mental Processes (1977) 84 *Psychol. Rev.* 231.
8   K. A. Ericsson and H. A. Simon, *Protocol Analysis: Verbal Reports as Data*, rev. edn. (MIT Press, 1993).
9   See Nisbett and Wilson, above note 7; see also H. Mercier and D. Sperber, Why Do Humans Reason? Arguments for an Argumentative Theory (2011) 34 *Behav. Brain Sci.* 57.
10 J. Haidt, The New Synthesis in Moral Psychology (2007) 316 *Science* 998.
11 P. K. Coats, Why Expert Systems Fail (1988) 17 *Financ. Manage.* 77.

of an idiomatic expression in one situation, but failed to do so in another. The second-order analytical and user interface choices in how to facilitate interpretation of such results are in some cases as profound as the first-order choices about how a system's design will trade-off the probabilities of various kinds of error probabilities or performance attributes.

It is also worth observing that some of the most important decisions we make in life – which house to purchase, which employer to join, whether to get married – are often the ones that most resemble folk psychology. For these decisions, we often force our thinking through the attentional bottleneck, slowly and deliberately. Do we do so because it helps us to "get it right"? Probably. Does it? Maybe. Explicit "declarative" reasoning is slow and effortful, but it does impose discipline on our decision-making. It helps us amplify the arguments and evidence we condone and filter out some of the prejudices and whims we do not. Part of becoming an expert in a domain is learning to recognize useful information and to ignore or discount information that is misleading or proscribed by some normative system (law, ethics, probability theory, etc.). By interviewing and observing experts, we can often identify rules and principles that should be taught to novices, and we can develop explicit checklists to ensure that those capable of expert judgment actually perform at a consistently high level.[12] Too much introspection almost certainly has the potential to complicate or otherwise raise the cost of a decision.

Our argument is not that interpretability is impossible, and certainly not that it is undesirable. Rather, we are cautioning against two assumptions – that non-AI decision-making is necessarily interpretable and transparent, and that interpretability can be obtained without any loss of performance.[13] Taking the more realistic approach to interpretability that we advocate means acknowledging trade-offs between interpretability and other goals, such as technical efficiency, ease of political coalition-building to support a decision, or candor in the presentation of relevant information – even if it doesn't facilitate the relevant decision-maker's capacity to grasp the underlying logic of the process at issue.

To be sure, playing down or outright screening out from a decision-making process certain goals can be valuable if the goals that get neglected are socially inappropriate (for example, pecuniary conflicts of interest), but it is a bad thing if it discourages the emergence of "wisdom" in Sternberg's sense. In a clever set of studies, Timothy Wilson and his collaborators have demonstrated that the process of listing one's reasons for a judgment can actually produce judgments that are poorer by a variety of criteria.[14] For example, they have shown that analyzing one's reasons:

- makes lay participants' judgments become less correlated with those of experts;
- makes people less satisfied with their choice at a later time;
- makes people more likely to later change their mind about the judgment they reached; and
- produces greater overconfidence and greater reliance on confirmatory bias, and reduces the correlation between one's announced judgment and one's subsequent behavior.

---

[12] D. L. Hepner, A. F. Arriaga, J. B. Cooper, *et al.*, Operating Room Crisis Checklists and Emergency Manuals (2017) 127 *Anesthesiology* 384.

[13] R. J. MacCoun, Psychological Constraints on Transparency in Legal and Government Decision Making, in A. Gosseries (ed.), Symposium on Publicity and Accountability in Governance (2006) 12 *Swiss Political Sci. Rev.* 112.

[14] Wilson, above note 3.

What Wilson therefore concludes is that analyzing reasons can lead people to "give disproportionate weight to those factors that are salient or easily brought to mind, relative to other factors that otherwise would have (and often should have) weighed heavily in their judgment process."[15]

These costs must be balanced against the value of reason-giving as a means of rendering an opaque decision compatible with social expectations – often embodied in the legal system – that our policymakers and institutions avoid arbitrary decisions. What should non-arbitrariness require to justify government decisions? Is it enough to know that trustworthy experts validate the use of an algorithm? Probably not. Instead, we should ask why non-arbitrariness is an important principle, at least in a democracy. The answer is twofold: first, we rarely if ever allow important decisions to be made by a single person – instead, we force deliberation, and some justification that others will accept. How the Court works that the first author is associated with is one example: a person writing an opinion must garner three other votes at least. But agencies work that way, too: teams of people justify a decision, and they nearly always need to make the argument to some other entity such as a court or a legislator. Second, we expect informed laypeople to be able to deliberate about government decisions enough to decide whether they want to embrace or reject the justification. What this calls for, at least from public agencies, is what could be called "relational non-arbitrariness" – sufficient explanation for an informed layperson to deliberate about and critique the mix of data and algorithmic details that might drive a decision. This requires some disclosure of architecture and data, and perhaps some benchmarking. It probably also requires some possibility of audits to make sure the algorithm and data being discussed are actually the ones at the heart of a decision.

Juxtaposed against the "costs" of interpretability, the value of interpretation as an element of non-arbitrariness underscores that interpretability is neither an unalloyed good nor a mere inconsequential distraction. Whether in the context of a child being asked to show her work, a corporation or public organization being forced to account for its decision, or an AI system subject to a technical requirement to render an explanation intelligible by humans, the problem is largely one of managing decision costs: avoiding paralyzing, costly requirements that erode the benefits of fast, efficient decision-making while providing a means of deliberating about decisions that matter in the world. AI has neither a monopoly on this problem nor a fail-safe solution avoiding the resulting complexities.

"SOLUTIONS" TO THE LOOMING PROBLEM OF REGULATING AI

We suggest that there are essentially five distinct ways of managing the threat of unethical or hazardous conduct by AIs. We put "solutions" in scare quotes for two reasons. First, one class of approaches might solve the problems, but mostly by avoiding the challenge and forgoing the potentially enormous benefits of harnessing AI.

Ludditism is the view that we should ban AI because it will do more harm than good. Luddites have never been successful in the past, and we suspect most readers will share our view that even if such a ban were possible, it is based on an unwarranted degree of pessimism and a failure to seriously weigh the benefits we would forego.

---

[15]   See also J. McMackin and P. Slovic, When Does Explicit Justification Impair Decision Making? (2000) 14 *Appl. Cogn. Psychol.* 527.

Restricted AI is a less extreme possibility that we might demand that AI designers somehow handicap their programs in ways that minimize their potential for harm. In principle, this seems less objectionable than the Luddite position. It has precedents in the "governors" invented by Christiaan Huygens, and later James Watt, to control windmills and steam engines, respectively. To a considerable extent, this is already common in AI through the use of checksums, hashes, and other checks on the integrity of computations. But it seems unlikely to provide more than a partial solution given the complexity and multidimensionality of the domains where AI is being applied.

Sandboxing is a related option; rather than crippling the AI, we restrict its ability to interact with the world. Again, this has plenty of precedents, but if enforced too strictly it would forego many of the benefits of AI.

A second class of "solutions" earn scare quotes because, while promising and important, they are better thought of as tools for "managing" the hazards of AI on an ongoing basis. We see three approaches that work best in tandem: persuasion and socialization; *ex ante* rules and incentives; and *ex post* accountability. We suggest that these are the major tools we use to manage the challenges posed by the conduct of corporations and children, and they will be the major tools we use for AI, for much the same reasons. We discuss each in turn before reiterating why these tools – despite their value in a range of circumstances – tend to fall short of eliminating or meaningfully resolving value conflict in society.

PERSUASION AND SOCIALIZATION

A central task of parenting is to try to teach our children to behave in a pro-social manner, or at least not to behave in an antisocial manner. Anyone who has tried this – and all of us who were parented – understands full well both the importance of this parental duty, and the limits of parents to fulfill it.

If We Want to Socialize AIs, What Is It We Want to Instill in Them?

Values

Framing the problem as one of values seems promising because it maps cleanly onto the way economists, engineers, and computer scientists solve problems – they explicitly operationalize some criterion to be maximized or minimized subject to some constraints. But there are several drawbacks. One is that values like "beneficence" or "loyalty" are at a very high level of abstraction that is difficult to operationalize in a manner an algorithm might track. Indeed, the abstract nature of values makes them relatively weak predictors of human behavior unless aggregated across many people and many behaviors[16]. Another drawback is that there are inherent trade-offs among human values. For example, in the Schwartz psychometric taxonomy of human values, the value of "security" is negatively correlated with the value of "self-direction"; the value of "stimulation" (excitement, novelty, variety) is negatively correlated with the values of "tradition" and "conformity." These trade-offs lead to a third drawback; while most people endorse each of these values in isolation, there are large and robust differences across individuals and cultures in how these values are ranked. Directly acknowledging and confronting these trade-offs is psychologically aversive and politically abrasive, so humans learn a rich and nuanced set of skills for

---

[16]   I. Ajzen and M. Fishbein, *Understanding Attitudes and Predicting Social Behavior* (Prentice-Hall, 1980).

navigating these trade-offs,[17] including hypocrisy, denial, and rationalization. Indeed, one of the attractions of stating values at a very high level of abstraction is that it helps to obscure the trade-offs that would be involved in implementing them.

Ethics and Morality

There is a "rationalist" tradition of moral reasoning which argues for some sort of explicit set of rules or principles. Kohlberg's proposed stages of moral reasoning is an early example.[18] (Roughly, the claim is that over the life course, people transition through a series of different moral principles. At the lowest level, people judge the morality of an act by whether it gets rewarded or punished. At an intermediate level, people equate morality with conventionality – what others do and what others condone or condemn. At the highest level, people engage in abstract, rights-based reasoning to judge the morality of any given act in its context.) Mikhail argues that moral reasoning operates much like Noam Chomsky's theory of linguistic judgment.[19] Where Chomsky posits that people have an innate universal grammar that produces strong intuitions about grammaticality, Mikhail posits an innate universal moral code that produces strong intuitions about what is permissible, obligatory, or forbidden in a scenario.

As we alluded to earlier, there is an alternate tradition that argues that moral reasoning is strongly affective or even visceral.[20] That tradition is positive/descriptive, not normative; while many argue that we want AI to use rationalist principles of morality, far fewer would contend that we want AI to mimic human emotionality, at least not emotions like disgust, contempt, and spitefulness. But sympathy, empathy, compassion? Maybe. In contrast to the values literature, where values are easy to endorse in isolation, but difficult to rank relative to each other, the evidence suggests that there is considerable consensus about the relative ranking of the wrongfulness of acts, but less agreement about the absolute wrongness or blameworthiness of any particular act.[21] Also, many situations require an agent to choose "the lesser of two evils," as in triage situations where harm is inevitable, but the choice is whom to spare. This is illustrated by the now voluminous literature on "trolley dilemmas," and many have looked to that literature for guidance on the development and assessment of ethical AI algorithms. (The trolley dilemma represents the ethical approaches taken between two schools of moral thought: utilitarianism and deontological ethics. The general form of the problem is framed as follows: a person sees a runaway trolley moving toward five tied-up people lying on the main track. A person is standing next to a lever that controls a switch. If they pull the lever, the trolley will be redirected onto a side track, and the five people on the main track will be saved. However, there is a single person lying on the side track. Thus, there are two difficult options: (1) do nothing and allow the trolley to kill the five people on the main track; or (2) pull the lever, diverting the trolley onto the side track where it will kill one person.)

[17] A. P. Fiske and P. E. Tetlock, Taboo Trade-Offs: Reactions to Transactions that Transgress the Spheres of Justice (1997) 18 *Political Psychol.* 255; J. Robbennolt, J. Darley, and R. J. MacCoun, Constraint Satisfaction and Judging, in D. Klein and G. Mitchell (eds.), *The Psychology of Judicial Decision Making* (Oxford University Press, 2010).
[18] L. Kohlberg, *Essays on Moral Development*, Vol. I: *The Philosophy of Moral Development* (Harper & Row, 1981).
[19] J. Mikhail, *Elements of Moral Cognition: Rawls' Linguistic Analogy and the Cognitive Science of Moral and Legal Judgment* (Cambridge University Press, 2011).
[20] Haidt, above note 10.
[21] P. H. Robinson and R. Kurzban, Concordance and Conflict in Intuitions of Justice (2006) 91 *Minn. Law Rev.* 1829.

In any case, efforts to instill ethics or morality in others – or indeed in ourselves – have limits.[22] Just as the socialization of ethical values raises somewhat distinct problems in the context of children relative to corporations, it should come as no surprise that the machine-learning methods necessary to distill from behavior or other data the scope of a "fuzzy" conflict like morality may lack obvious similarity to the pathways for socialization one might plausibly expect to feature prominently in a child's socialization. Whether it will prove easier or harder to achieve such socialization with machines remains to be seen. What is difficult to accept at this point is the proposition that a concept like "socialization" has little or no place in the development of ethical competence for machine intelligence.

Fairness

Another literature frames the problem as one of "fairness" – particularly with regard to algorithms that make decisions (or at least support decisions) about the allocation of scarce goods and services – medical triage, hiring decisions, university enrollment decisions, etc. As with the values literature, appeals to fairness pose problems of abstractness (everyone is for fairness, but what exactly is it?), as well as conflicting criteria. For example, procedural fairness is distinct from distributive fairness. Within distributive fairness, there are many different criteria for assessing whether a given set of outcomes is fair, as debated in a very long conversation involving Aristotle, Bentham, Kant, Pareto, Rawls, and many others.

Recent advances in using machine learning to give meaning to "fuzzy" concepts will no doubt improve our understanding of concepts such as morality and fairness.[23] But such advances are unlikely to resolve definitively the most difficult and important arguments over algorithms, any more than a sophisticated understanding of aggregate child behavior or corporate compliance permits us, by itself, to derive a sensible normative standard for the conduct of children or corporations. The fundamental difficulty isn't just building a framework to induct from behavior, self-reported descriptions, or even physiological feedback some representation of a "fuzzy" concept like "reasonableness," or even "fairness" in a particular context. It's recognizing the likely distinction between any observed characteristic of the world, whether human behavior that some might call "revealed" preference or functional magnetic resonance imaging (fMRI) data on brain activity in response to a particular stimulus, and states of the world that some interpretive community aspires to treat as desirable. Because people can choose to act in a consistent manner even as they consider that course of conduct suboptimal, we're virtually always left to negotiate thorough institutions and the conversations they make possible not only about how much existing behavior embodies societal aspirations, but what the proper standards are to judge such aspirations.[24] As we explain below, similar foundational questions tend to persist despite our growing understanding of how to use *ex ante* rules and *ex post* sanctions to shape behavior.

[22]   See M. H. Bazerman and F. Gino, Behavioral Ethics: Toward a Deeper Understanding of Moral Judgment and Dishonesty (2012) 8 *Ann. Rev. Law Soc. Sci.* 85; Y. Feldman, *The Law of Good People: Challenging States' Ability to Regulate Human Behavior* (Cambridge University Press, 2018); N. Mazar and D. Ariely, Dishonesty in Everyday Life and Its Policy Implications (2006) 25 *J. Public Policy Mark.* 117.
[23]   P. S. Thomas, B. Castro da Silva, A. G. Barto, *et al.*, Preventing Undesirable Behavior of Intelligent Machines (2019) 366 *Science* 999.
[24]   M. F. Cuéllar and J. Mashaw, Regulatory Decision-Making and Economic Analysis, in F. Parisi (ed.), *The Oxford Handbook of Law and Economics* (Oxford University Press, 2017).

EX ANTE RULES, EX POST ACCOUNTABILITY

Ideally, we want our algorithms, like our corporations and our children, to internalize good values and a good moral compass. But when that fails, we set *ex ante* rules and enforce them with *ex post* consequences.[25] Garnering agreement about how to do that is rarely easy in practice. Even where the general public agrees broadly with a wide principle such as protecting free speech or preventing unjustified homicide, the devil is often in the details. Courts, legislatures, and public conversations often feature vigorous conflict about the extent to which a person or entity – such as a child, or a corporation – should be held accountable for the transgression of a norm, reflecting both practical and moral questions about the viability of doing so. Such debates may increasingly come to include the practical (and perhaps eventually, the moral and ethical) implications of singling out a particular algorithm or system for something like direct *ex post* accountability. It's not difficult, for example, to imagine an AI system benefiting from access to enormous computing power used to advance a reinforcement learning algorithm keyed to the goal of maximizing corporate revenue without violating the law. If the system works as designed, its performance would be affected by an *ex post* signal indicating that its behavior (or the behavior it recommends to a user) violations a legal norm.

As we consider how society may use *ex ante* rules and *ex post* accountability to shape the behavior of AI systems and the people who use them, it is worth remembering in the process that we already regulate robots and AI, however imperfectly.[26] We do so through the tort law that applies when a doctor is accused of malpractice and seeks to defend herself; through the contract law that guides whether agreements entered into between two autonomous systems are valid, and through the criminal laws that bear on whether people who relied on suspicious transaction detection systems that permitted money laundering or fraud to happen may be guilty of willful blindness; through intellectual property laws that guide our decisions about who owns the song or otherworldly picture produced by an AI system. Administrative and constitutional law defines how much public officials can delegate choices about how to police, how to allocate scarce benefits, and what counts as an acceptable reason to regulate; and through antitrust and consumer protection laws that make people and organizations liable for colluding when they develop robots or for allowing data breaches to happen without telling users.

As has long been the case with persons and corporations, a critical issue in deciding how to connect *ex ante* rules and *ex post* accountability to support socially desirable use of AI is how much to make use of "intentions" or any kind of representation of internal cognition versus behavior. Consider that employment discrimination litigation rarely hinges on "smoking gun" evidence that an employer has an explicit plan to act in a racist manner. Rather, plaintiffs first attempt to establish "disparate impact" – a statistically significant difference in hiring or other outcomes between a protected minority group and other groups. The plaintiff then attempts to establish that this difference in fact affected their selection outcome. The defendant then faces the burden of showing that the selection was based on factors that are relevant to job performance. At trial, evaluating these competing claims involves empirical evidence on the statistical validity of the variables used in the selection process. The

---

[25] For an insightful analysis of these issues, see B. Casey, Robot Ipsa Loquitur (2019) 108 *Georgetown Law Journal* 225, https://ssrn.com/abstract=3327673.

[26] M. F. Cuéllar, A Common Law for the Age of Artificial Intelligence: Incremental Adjudication, Institutions, and Relational Non-Arbitrariness (2019) 119 *Columbia Law Rev.* 1775.

predictive (or criterion) validity question is whether a variable in question statistically predicts (namely, is correlated with) performance outcomes. If so, the *internal validity* question is whether that correlation is spurious – that is, due solely to a correlation between some meaningful causal determinant of performance (for example, training, experience) and the protected category. There is also a *construct* validity question or whether ostensibly relevant screening variables (for example, intelligence test scores) are actually measuring what they are supposed to measure. In some ways, AI algorithms hide this issue to the extent that they operate atheoretically, using dozens of variables while ignoring their labels.

Indeed, one of the more persuasive ways of establishing patterns of discrimination has been the use of "correspondence tests" – survey or field experiments in which employers, lenders, and other actors in the marketplace are presented with applications from people who differ in race, gender, or some other ostensibly irrelevant characteristic, but are otherwise comparable in their qualifications and background characteristics.[27] This may in fact be the most effective way of testing AI algorithms, especially in the case of deep-learning systems, where direct inspection of the code may fail to resolve disputes about whether the algorithm is behaving in a discriminatory manner.

Our fears about AI are at least partly attributable to its alien "black box" nature, but we have suggested that ordinary humans and corporations also lack transparency, and are often less transparent and interpretable than folk psychology would imply. Does this mean we should stop worrying and learn to love AI? Perhaps, but vigilance and proactive engagement seem appropriate. It may be that the biggest threat posed by AI is not its impenetrability, but rather *its potential for correlated risk*. We routinely encounter acts of irresponsibility, recklessness, and even malice from other people (and corporations). But these incidents usually appear at a fairly random rate, one crisis at a time. The easy reproducibility of AI algorithms creates the potential for any error of judgment to be triggered pervasively as each copy is triggered by the same input conditions.

This kind of risk will almost certainly be an important part of society's deliberations about how to use existing or new legal arrangements to align the performance of AI systems as much as possible with what would be beneficial for society. That we can use not only some version of persuasion and socialization, but also *ex post* consequences to affect the performance and use of AI, however, leaves on the table at least two thorny questions: how to prioritize among competing values, and how to implement a given value in practical terms – even a relatively straightforward one firmly rooted in the legal system, such as recognition of the need to warn suspects subject to custodial police interrogation that they have a right to remain silent – when it must be applied to a specific set of facts.

THE PERSISTENCE OF VALUE CONFLICT

Given the various yet inherently imperfect legal mechanisms available to affect the performance of AI and range of human experiences and psychological process relevant to value questions, it is not surprising that even highly functional public institutions primarily channel value conflict instead of ever resolving it completely. When even well-meaning people describe governance challenges in terms that seem easily susceptible to some kind of optimization, easily enhanced by an unbiased AI system, they tend to misapprehend (or

---

[27]   E. Zschirnta and D. Ruedina, Ethnic Discrimination in Hiring Decisions: A Meta-Analysis of Correspondence Tests 1990–2015 (2016) 42 *J. Ethn. Migr. Stud.* 1115.

perhaps those of us writing on government have mis-explained) the nature of the choice our public institutions, or at least our courts of last resort, can face. The hard choices often have the political theory deeply entangled with doctrine, as with the dilemma of how police should question a 10-year-old child suspected of murdering his neo-Nazi father, for example. These choices are about channeling the understandable conflict among practical policing concerns, children, and constitutional norms, so we can – at least in a democracy – live with the results long enough for someone to have the chance to persuade other people or institutions that they have a better solution.

The persistence of value conflict in many societies and the role of institutions in mediating the resulting tensions offers good reason, in our view, to temper enthusiasm about any quest for a single set of ethical principles to govern the performance of AI. Indeed, governance tends to be an exercise in the channeling of value conflict. Examples of how government often prioritizes resolution of conflict over what is optimal abound. At key moments in the history of functioning nation-states, conflict that is actually or potentially violent must be channeled into institutions, as labor conflict in the United States was in the 1930s and 1940s, and civil rights conflict was in the late 1960s and 1970s.[28] That process doesn't necessarily focus on what's optimal or most efficient in a particular sector (for example, what's going to promote the most efficient industrial production), but what's going to hold together the political system. This is why it tends to be misleading to assess the efficacy of a particular government process purely on whether the status quo diverges from what an AI-based decision-making process might be able to provide, if the algorithm were designed to optimize just a specific government function, and had the right data and analytical elements. If we cared about social welfare for people in a given jurisdiction, we'd also want to know how greater efficiency within a sector (for example, pharmaceutical regulation or pre-trial detention decisions) might affect conflict and compromise across other sectors. This is why government activities are not all completely independent of some hierarchical structure – the presidency, for example, or a Supreme Court – that can be accountable or at least principled.

Here are some other examples of how governing is about managing conflict: in a constitutional democracy, legislative deals to facilitate passage of legislation introducing inefficiencies or drawbacks (delays in implementation, retention of loopholes, or difficulties); fierce compromises allowing government to exercise enormous power, but subject to administrative constraints that force public notice and comment and allow for judicial review, but slow down action; in various countries, a desire for "legitimacy" through hearings and adjudication even when this is costly; public employment provisions governing the public sector; and, of course, for some countries, an authoritarian system blatantly (and in some cases brutally) discouraging conflict. All of these methods have various costs for policymakers and stakeholders, ranging from accommodation of competing goals to the delays and risks of institutional paralysis that come from relying on procedures that disperse power.[29] Yet, societies aiming to use coercion to limit risk of conflict also run a secondary risk – that their coercion will galvanize sufficient backlash to be costly to the regime. If there's a way to use AI to zero in on discontent before it spurs rival organizational structures, or to tame political disagreement by subjecting it to an almost consumerist desire to maximize one's points, then it will be attractive to some regimes.

[28] M. F. Cuéllar, M. Levi, and B. R. Weingast, Twentieth-Century America as a Developing Country: Conflict, Institutional Change, and the Evolution of Public Law (2019) 57 *Harv. J. Leg. Legis.* 1.

[29] M. F. Cuéllar, From Doctrine to Safeguards in American Constitutional Democracy (2018) 65 *UCLA Law Rev.* 1398.

The alternative to either seeking to assuage conflict entirely through consensus, costly accommodation, or coercion is acceptance of some degree of friction, disagreement, and surprises in a unrulier political process. Assuming the risk of outright violence or institutional rupture is mitigated, such friction can conceivably serve useful purposes: by forcing groups of unequal stakeholders in society to consider the long-term impacts of existing practices on those who have less to gain from current arrangements, by upending appeals to tradition or order and leaving space for innovation in governance, and by reducing the risk that coalitions with existing power will endeavor to limit dissent or political challenges.[30] As we move from domain-specific AI systems serving as tools for social security adjudication or Securities Exchange Commission enforcement and toward more comprehensive systems to assist in social planning, the range of possible choices about how to balance the merits of different strategies for managing conflict may force more explicit conversations about the value of disagreement in society, and how to build it in.

Within the institutions that have a responsibility to justify their decisions, such as agencies, we have somewhat succeeded over the years in channeling conflict into discussions of whether institutions acted in an arbitrary manner. That inquiry is virtually always "relational," in the sense that it pivots on arguments that a community of stakeholders can understand enough about a problem to permit them to participate in conversations, debates, and decisions about how to resolve it, and at what cost.[31]

This means it is plausible to evaluate our institutions and their capacity to incorporate the values of relevant stakeholders by asking, first, if there is some basis for it in principle that we can defend as non-arbitrary; second, whether the relationship between the machine or analytical tool and the human conveys some of the complexity involved in the analysis and competing values at stake in the decision; and, third, whether the process for making decisions supports further deliberation about the decision among some members of the community of people involved in or affected by it.

CONCLUSION: PARALLEL COGNITION, INSTITUTIONAL DESIGN, AND OPERATIONALIZING "ETHICALLY ALIGNED" AI

We have argued that the opacity and parallel distributed nature of modern AI algorithms is actually shared to a considerable degree by corporations and ordinary people. But this should not be read as an argument against demands for greater transparency. Scholars in the neuro- and cognitive sciences have offered profound challenges to ordinary "folk" intuitions about consciousness, intention, and action, but there is still considerable disagreement about whether this entails any changes in our systems of accountability.[32] Indeed, some even contend that consciousness may have evolved for social reasons – as a way of communicating with others and explaining ourselves.[33] In turn, in judging and sanctioning the actions of others, we rely less on "but for" causation – what are the causal processes that produced this action? – and more on an assessment of "could this actor

---

[30]   See J. C. Scott, *Seeing Like a State: How Certain Schemes to Improve the Human Condition Have Failed* (Yale University Press, 1999).

[31]   M. F. Cuéllar, A Common Law for the Age of Artificial Intelligence: Incremental Adjudication, Institutions, and Relational Non-Arbitrariness (2019) 119 *Columbia Law Rev.* 1773.

[32]   J. Greene and J. Cohen, For the Law, Neuroscience Changes Nothing and Everything (2004) 359 *Phil. Trans. R. Soc. Lond. B* 1775; D. M. Wegner, *The Illusion of Conscious Will* (MIT Press, 2002).

[33]   Mercier and Sperber, above note 9; Hommel, above note 3.

have done otherwise?"[34] Thus, even if others' actions are produced by causal processes outside their awareness, people may assume that those actors are able to observe the consequences of their actions and take active steps to override inappropriate or undesirable conduct soon after it emerges.[35]

Indeed, despite our impressive technical achievements and elaborate legal and educational systems, humans tend to handle value conflict not by seeking to impose a single correct solution in any given context. Even in regimes that lack a full commitment to democracy, societies make extensive use of institutions that help us compromise, at least when they work reasonably well. The conflicts often tend to be between democratic responsiveness, individual fairness in how we treat someone who is accused or in need of special concern, and expert judgment about what is efficient for society. And we have competing, imperfect methods to capture "ethical values," none of which is devoid of trade-offs – including observing behavior, understanding what people say and write, and seeing how their behavior and professed beliefs change over time as they develop. To say we want to operationalize the concept of "ethical" AI is to invoke these debates.

Accordingly, we doubt that the most promising way forward in this domain is to assume we can always or even frequently capture consensus ethics – although some of that may be possible in some contexts. Instead, it is to work on building systems that can take account of the competing pressures and ideas reflected in the kind of vigorous debate you get in a well-argued court case, or when a group of well-informed doctors argue over a patient's treatment, or where a couple of different religious traditions discusses how to raise their child. Those systems can be designed not only to capture the nature of the debate, but also to apply a variety of principles to seek compromise and harmony regarding certain differing ethical and policy priorities, while defending others from arguments for compromise. Central to any such effort is an awareness that value conflicts among pivotal stakeholders, along with the underlying opacity of human decisions, have long given societies a reason to forge institutions capable of channeling conflict and arriving at imperfect, interim solutions while a measure of disagreement and innovation continues. This legacy of contending values and interests will keep most societies arguing over algorithms – and rightly so.

---

[34] V. L. Hamilton, Intuitive Psychologist or Intuitive Lawyer? Alternative Models of the Attribution Process (1980) 39 *J. Pers. Soc. Psychol.* 767; S. Nichols, The Folk Psychology of Free Will: Fits and Starts (2004) 19 *Mind Lang.* 473.

[35] B. Weiner, *Judgments of Responsibility: A Foundation for a Theory of Social Conduct* (Guilford Press, 1995).

34

Embodiment and Algorithms for Human–Robot Interaction

Yueh-Hsuan Weng and Chih-hsing Ho[*]

INTRODUCTION

To many people, there is a boundary which exists between artificial intelligence (AI), some-times referred to as an intelligent software agent, and the system which is controlled through AI primarily by the use of algorithms. One example of this dichotomy is robots which have a physical form, but whose behavior is highly dependent on the "AI algorithms" which direct their actions. More specifically, we can think of a software agent as an entity which is directed by algorithms that perform many intellectual activities currently done by humans. The software agent can exist in a virtual world (for example, a bot) or can be embedded in the software controlling a machine (for example, a robot). For many current robots controlled by algorithms, they represent semi-intelligent hardware that repetitively perform tasks in physi-cal environments. This observation is based on the fact that most robotic applications for industrial use since the middle of the last century have been driven by algorithms that support repetitive machine motions. In many cases, industrial robots which typically work in closed environments, say, for example, factory floors, do not need "advanced" techniques of AI to function because they perform daily routines with algorithms directing the repetitive motions of their end effectors. However, lately, there is an emerging technological trend which has resulted from the combination of AI and robots, which, by using sophisticated algorithms, allows robots to adapt complex work styles and to function socially in open environments. We may call these merged technological products "embodied AI," or in a more general sense, "embodied algorithms."

Embodied versions of systems operating with algorithms lead to new possibilities for human–robot interaction (HRI), such as allowing for a wider range of possibilities for the development of interactive interfaces. These new interfaces, made possible by the use of algorithmic-driven machines, are beginning to challenge established areas of law. For example, based on the pervasiveness of algorithms in different technologies (such as the Internet and robots), it is possible to design a networked humanoid robot to service human needs. Although such a system might, at first glance, look like a stand-alone system, in actuality its perception and decision-making abilities are tied to the networked smart envir-onment it occupies. We posit that such an intelligent and networked system will bring new challenges to established areas of law, and specifically to an emerging law of algorithms. As

[*] This work was mainly supported by JSPS KAKENHI Grant Number 19K13579, and partially supported by the Transatlantic Technology Law Forum, Stanford Law School regarding "Healthcare Robots: A Comparative EU-US Data Protection Analysis" and Academia Sinica's "Data Safety and Talent Cultivation Project – Subproject: Artificial Intelligence in the Field of Medicine." In addition, we would like to express our very great appreciation to Professor Woodrow Barfield for his kind suggestions regarding this chapter.

one example, a new threat to data protection and privacy will be possible when algorithmic-driven robots are connected to cloud computing,[1] and also when algorithms convert speech to text using remote servers[2] (especially in the access control of ubiquitous robots (Ubi-Bots)).[3] On this point, we note that current legislation for information privacy protection are data-driven, yet robots controlled by algorithms perform in various ways (that is, not always data-driven) – for example, when collecting personal information, or when interacting with humans. Thus, such systems are stretching the boundaries of current data protection and privacy law. Clearly, there is a legal gap between existing privacy and data collection law and the abilities of algorithmic-driven systems to collect data that is personal in nature – we explore that gap in this chapter.

In this chapter, we discuss the idea that the embodiment of an AI entity has particular significance for a law of algorithms because embodied forms of AI using algorithms may lead to the collection of personal information from users in social interactions. We note that "embodiment," as a feature of intelligent robots, has rarely been mentioned in the field of privacy and data protection law. Hence, in this chapter, we investigate the relationship between embodied forms of systems that are controlled by algorithms and their effect on privacy and data protection law. As a technology which highlights the points we wish to make, we will focus on healthcare robots because they have the ability to engage humans in multiple ways using different types of social interactions. The motivation for the chapter is to determine how the use of an algorithmic-driven system, such as a robot providing healthcare services and interacting socially with people, will influence privacy and data protection in HRIs.

APPLICATIONS OF ALGORITHMS

We start with general observations. Algorithms are not only used to direct the actions of robots, but are a critical feature of people's daily lives. For example, the algorithms directing e-commerce recommendation systems show users different products that consumers might be interested in by connecting records from other users who have similar interests. From a social science perspective, such systems are inspired by the idea of six degrees of separation and theory of social networks.[4] Additionally, targeted advertising also uses algorithms to determine suitable adverts for individuals based on specific users' online consumer behaviors. Further, encryption algorithms are used to ensure the security of e-commerce and digital financial transactions. And advances in algorithmic-driven systems have also shown success in games requiring high levels of human cognitive skill. For example, in 2016, DeepMind's AlphaGO AI software defeated Go legend Sedol Lee.[5]

---

[1] U. Pagallo, Robots in the Cloud with Privacy: A New Threat to Data Protection? (2013) 29 *Comput. Law Secur. Rep.* 501.

[2] J. F. Hoorn, Mechanical Empathy Seems Too Risky. Will Policymakers Transcend Inertia and Choose Robot Care? The World Needs It, in G. Dekoulis (ed.), *Robotics: Legal, Ethical and Socioeconomic Impacts* (IntechOpen, 2017).

[3] Y. H. Weng and S. T. H. Zhao, The Legal Challenges of Networked Robotics: From the Safety Intelligence Perspective, in M. Palmirani, U. Pagallo, P. Casanovas, and G. Sartor (eds.), *AI Approaches to the Complexity of Legal Systems: Models and Ethical Challenges for Legal Systems, Legal Language and Legal Ontologies, Argumentation and Software Agents* (Springer, 2012), Vol. 7639, pp. 61–72.

[4] D. J. Watts, *Six Degrees: The Science of a Connected Age* (W. W. Norton, 2004).

[5] Artificial intelligence: Google's AlphaGo Beats Go Master Lee Se-dol, *BBC* (March 12, 2016), www.bbc.com /news/technology-35785875.

Recent techniques in the design of algorithms are leading to systems with the capability to learn and thus become involved in numerous applications which require social interactions with humans. Based on advances in computing and Internet technology, for example, in cloud computing and the collection of big data, learning algorithms are now becoming more widely used in information technology fields. For example, the Chicago Police Department uses the Strategic Subject Algorithm developed by the Illinois Institute of Technology to create a risk assessment score called "Strategic Subject List (SSL)" which ranges from 1 to 500.[6] With the assistance provided by this algorithm, the Chicago police allocate resources with the goal to prevent future gun violence and to direct their limited policing resources into prioritizing high-risk areas. According to the data reflecting the use of the algorithm, the shooting rates in Chicago have decreased 39 percent after implementation of the program.[7] Finally, in the field of transportation, algorithms with the capability to learn have been utilized in improving self-driving cars' visual perception of the real world, and algorithms used in the medical field have improved recognition rates for certain diseases.

While the above examples of the use of algorithms have resulted in challenges to established areas of law, an evolving issue (which is the focus of this chapter) concerns potential legal consequences associated with using learning algorithms in society. As an example, COMPAS (Correctional Offender Management Profiling for Alternative Sanctions) represents software which uses machine-learning algorithms to assist judges in criminal cases to evaluate a defendant's risk of committing another crime. The algorithmic-based system has been used to assess more than 1 million offenders since its development in 1998.[8] And in the medical field, algorithms are being used to help doctors analyze complex data and to provide suggestions for suitable donors for kidney transplantation, in a program called "paired kidney donation" (more on this below). The short history of paired kidney donation started in 2000, and the program continues to handle more cases each year. For example, in 2018, 12 percent of living kidney donations came from paired donors,[9] based on matches between donor and patient suggested by algorithms.

Although algorithms used for decision support systems to assist human experts in many professional fields have shown great potential over the past two decades, recent trends in deep learning algorithms raise a potential concern about the accountability of using learning algorithms. One main criticism of deep learning algorithms is based on their "untransparency" or "black box" characteristics. After autonomous training (in the case of unsupervised deep learning), deep learning techniques generate new outputs from additional inputs fed into the algorithms, but the cause–effect relationships between inputs and outputs may be unclear to humans in the system or those affected by the algorithms' decisions. This unforeseeable situation may lead to an accountability gap among stakeholders resulting from the design and use of technology based on deep learning algorithms. For example, how can we ensure the COMPAS software, in the example above, isn't biased in the way that its algorithms calculate scores? On this point, consider again the example of paired kidney donation, which also raises ethical questions.

[6] Strategic Subject List (SSL), Chicago Data Portal, https://data.cityofchicago.org/Public-Safety/Strategic-Subject-List/4aki-r3np.

[7] J. Gunter, Chicago Goes High-Tech in Search of Answers to Gun Crime Surge, *BBC* (June 19, 2017), www.bbc.com/news/world-us-canada-40293666.

[8] J. Dressel and H. Farid, The Accuracy, Fairness, and Limits of Predicting Recidivism (2018) 4 *Sci. Adv.* eaao5580.

[9] C. Purtill, How AI Changed Organ Donation in the US, *QUARTZ* (September 10, 2018), https://qz.com/1383083/how-ai-changed-organ-donation-in-the-us/.

Suppose there are two patients, A and B, both experiencing an emergency medical crisis, who coincidentally match donor C's kidney. Further, suppose that only A or B can receive C's kidney donation, in which case, the patient not receiving the donation will suffer negative health consequences. From an ethics point of view, should an algorithm (mathematically) decide who receives a transplant and thus who may live or die? Now further consider that A is a retired national hero, but with many serious chronic diseases who is thought to have a short life span even if they receive the kidney transplantation. In contrast, B is known to be a habitual criminal, but a single parent with a 5-year-old daughter and a potential long life ahead with a successful transplant. In this example, should society entrust an algorithm with the power to decide who will live based on its calculation from the parameters it receives? Any bias or misjudgment, or lack of ethical clarity shown by the algorithm will have tragic consequences. This particular example, with its ethical ramifications, raises people's awareness about the issue of allowing algorithms to perform human decisions in areas involving moral and ethical questions and more generally the idea that perhaps algorithms should be regulated.

Among others, the above examples show that one key debate resulting from the use of algorithms concerns the accountability of algorithms to various stakeholders. Legal scholar Frank Pasquale and mathematician Cathy O'Neil have analyzed, using a macro perspective, how an accountability gap is formed when the operation of many social issues intersect and are taken over by big data and algorithms.[10] In addition to the accountability of algorithms, issues of importance for a law of algorithms also include the regulation of algorithmic-driven systems and the legal protection of AI-generated works, as well as the challenges to freedom of speech, privacy, and liability for damages when the use of algorithms leads to damages.

EMBODIED ALGORITHMS WITHIN ROBOTS

Another important issue for a law of algorithms, as mentioned above, is privacy and data protection for embodied AI (in this chapter, using healthcare robots as an example). In the context of an aging population, particularly in East Asia, Europe, and North America, it is evident that healthcare robots will be used to support the elderly in walking, climbing, and living independently, as well as providing non-physical support, such as daily communication and providing necessary information for day-to-day life, including social contact to alleviate loneliness. While healthcare robots will engage in important functions for society, especially in the background of an aging population, from the perspective of law, there is an important question which revolves around the issue of whether the embodiment of the social robot itself will lead to issues of privacy and data protection. On that point, this chapter discusses robot embodiment in a social context, an issue that, thus far, has been neglected in legal scholarship and specifically for a law of algorithms. We argue that healthcare robots are a prime example of embodied algorithmic-driven systems, due to their high contact levels with human beings in the form of embodied physical machines whose behavior is directed by algorithms. This raises a concern that data protection and privacy issues will result from the use of healthcare robots (controlled by algorithms) when they are deployed into society and interacting with humans in social settings.

---

[10] F. Pasquale, *The Black Box Society* (Harvard University Press, 2015); C. O'Neil, *Weapons of Math Destruction* (Broadway Books, 2016).

Based on recent advances in AI technologies, robots that are directed by algorithms are increasingly common within human society, and this has raised three important questions which relate to healthcare robotics: (1) How will the use of algorithmic-driven social robots that are in daily use (such as in the healthcare industry) influence privacy in HRIs? (2) How will the use of intelligent robots in healthcare impact current data protection laws? and (3) How can we apply the concept of "privacy by design" to the design process of healthcare robots, with the goal of covering the gap resulting from the use of embodied healthcare robots and data protection? To answer these questions, we will start by discussing the relevant philosophy and law which relate to algorithms and embodiment.

ALGORITHMS AND EMBODIMENT

We start with a historical perspective. René Descartes's Mind-Body Dualism discussion in the seventeenth century has had a huge influence on the thinking of modern Western societies. According to his theory, mind and body are two independent parts existing in one single person. To Descartes, the only connection between mind and body was the pineal gland, which is where he posited a person's soul exists.[11] Unlike traditional Chinese medicine, which focuses on a holistic view of the body to treat patients, Western medicine systematically developed many divisions of the body to provide patients with medical care in an efficient although system-by-system manner. However, under the Western medicine view, a psychophysical disorder may manifest itself as a combination of the mind and body which is thought to be suffering some malady. This type of disorder refers to physical symptoms which may manifest themselves due to psychological or social factors; for example, hypertension, a peptic ulcer, or a migraine headache. As a mind-body conundrum, also consider the phantom limb pain phenomena experienced by patients who lost their arm or leg – this represents another example of the inseparability of mind and body.[12] Clearly, the complex relationship between mind and body is not easily described by representing it as a dichotomy. The early stages of AI research have similarly experienced the conceptual difficulty associated with the mind-body duality, in that they focus on creating an artificial mind by imitating a human's high-level reasoning and problem-solving capabilities, but neglect the importance of a body in mediating an artificial agent's intellectual behaviors in the real world.

In the 1980s, the issue of embodiment became an important topic in AI research and development. We provide here a representative example from Rodney Brooks's proposal on a "subsumption architecture," which he explained used a "bottom-up" approach for intelligence without the use of symbolic knowledge representation. The subsumption architecture decomposes a machine's behaviors into several sub-behaviors and based on that division designs different reactive control layers in order to allow robots to respond to unstructured environments in real time.[13] One major difference between embodied intelligent robots and traditional applications of GOFAI (good old-fashioned AI)[14] is that behaviors of the former

---

[11] R. Descartes, *The Philosophical Writings of Descartes*, J. Cottingham, R. Stoothoff, D. Murdoch, and A. Kenny (trans.) (Cambridge University Press, 1984–91).

[12] Y. Oouchida and S. Izumi, Imitation Movement Reduces the Phantom Limb Pain Caused by the Abnormality of Body Schema, ICME International Conference on Complex Medical Engineering (CME), Kobe, Japan (July 1–4, 2012).

[13] R. A. Brooks, A Robust Layered Control System for a Mobile Robot (1986) 2 *IEEE J. Robot. Autom.* 14.

[14] J. Haugeland, *Artificial Intelligence: The Very Idea* (MIT Press, 1986).

have not been explicitly programmed into a system or an agent, such that "emergence" occurs.

Emergence can be described as a phenomenon which occurs when an entity taken as a whole is observed to have properties which its parts, if considered separately, do not have. Such properties or behaviors emerge when the parts of an entity interact as a combined or integrated object.[15] When this concept is applied to an embodied form of an algorithmic-driven object, the physical characteristics of the object, for example, a robot, may show new intelligent properties or behaviors separately that did not exist in the software controlling the individual parts.

According to another pioneer on intelligence and embodiment, Rolf Pfeifer, there are three different types of emergence, which include: (1) a global phenomenon arising from collective behavior; (2) individual behavior resulting from an agent's interactions with the environment; and (3) the emergence of behavior from one time scale to another.[16] From these three points we can see that the implications of embodiment for intelligence are more involved than people designing robots originally thought. Except for the well-known example of the passive dynamic walking robots created at Cornell University's Biorobotics and Locomotion Lab,[17] a multi-agent system's complex dynamic in artificial life, and a humanoid's embodied cognition in developmental robotics are examples of emergence from individual, collective, and time-crossing perspectives. The phenomenon of emergence also represents another aspect of AI that cannot be reproduced under a brain-centrism's viewpoint of creating intelligence via software agents or intelligent entities without a body. As discussed by law and robotics expert Ryan Calo, robots' emergence enables a particular embodied form of AI, to react in unstructured environments in ways beyond merely repetitive motions;[18] this complexity of behavior shown in the real world as directed by algorithms impacts the foreseeability of machine behaviors and therefore impacts its relationship with the law.

As mentioned before, the emerging field of the law of algorithms, in our view, mainly concerns the legal issues related to algorithmic accountability, and under this huge umbrella of AI governance it extends to many sub-issues which trigger the following questions: How can we make algorithmic decision-making more transparent? What kinds of machine-learning-based AI applications can be used for dealing with issues related to human rights and property protection, such as healthcare, public security, and national defense? Can we grant copyright to an AI art creator? Should governments regulate online "speech" generated by algorithms?[19] and What are the privacy and data protection issues resulting from information systems using autonomous functions produced by algorithms? As yet, there is no formal approach within law to the above-mentioned issues relating to embodiment. The authors believe this is not because embodiment itself is not an important topic for law; on the contrary, the reason can more likely be attributed to the lack of accountability between

---

[15] Emergence, *Wikipedia*, https://en.wikipedia.org/wiki/Emergence.

[16] R. Pfeifer and J. Bongard, *How the Body Shapes the Way We Think: A New View of Intelligence* (MIT Press, 2007), p. 85.

[17] Cornell University's Biorobotics and Locomotion Lab, http://ruina.tam.cornell.edu/research/; M., Hoffmann and R. Pfeifer, The Implications of Embodiment for Behavior and Cognition: Animal and Robotic Case Studies, in W. Tschacher and C. Bergomi (eds.), *The Implications of Embodiment: Cognition and Communication* (Imprint Academic, 2012), pp. 31–58.

[18] M. R. Calo, Robotics and the Lessons of Cyberlaw (2015) 103 *Calif. Law Rev.* 513.

[19] S. M. Benjamin, Algorithms and Speech (2013) 161 *Univ. Pa. Law Rev.* 6.

embodied AI and the accountability of algorithms. We argue that a law of algorithms should consider embodiment based on the reasons discussed above and presented below.

First, consider the difference between a software chatbot (digital embodiment) and an intelligent robot (physical embodiment) which has relevance for the cause and effect derived from the environment each operates in, which in turn influences their behaviors. A chatbot as a software agent exists in a digital, or virtual, environment, thus there is no gap between the words it speaks in VR and the decisions it makes in VR. On the other hand, the output actions of an intelligent robot may not be equivalent to its original plan of action due to the mediating effect of its physical environment, which is a feature of emergence. These factors influence the final output of a robot's decision-making, which is mediated by the physical environment; thus, a problem may result if a brain-centrism's viewpoint is used to judge legal liability for a tort action based on the conduct of a robot. In other words, to fully realize algorithmic accountability for human and machine, we should not merely consider the "black box"[20] and "Open-Texture"[21] aspects of robots, but, in addition, a third factor emerging from algorithmic processes: "emergence."

Second, although the method of computational simulation is used for many applications such as modeling the dynamics of infectious disease transmission, or to model the voter's behavior in democratic elections, computational simulation cannot be used to verify the safety of autonomous systems such as self-driving cars or intelligent service robots. This has implications for personal safety with embodied forms of AI, that is, for the design of "safety-critical systems." We posit that the reason why computational simulations cannot be used to verify the safety of autonomous systems is based on a human factor and a non-human factor.

From a human factor perspective, for algorithmic-driven entities we should consider adding more testing and certification processes to design safety-critical systems in order to ensure that they are reliable enough to resist cyberattack from human hackers.[22] As for the non-human factor, a threat to safety-critical systems concerns "modeling error," which refers to the inconsistency between software and the hardware comprising the same system. In other words, from a software perspective, the system may function normally, but the final performance of the system in the real world may not match how it should be performing according to its software instructions. There are many reasons which may cause system modeling error. For example, consider an accident involving a smart car which is equipped with an Eye-Sight autonomous braking system. Eye-Sight is an active safety system using cameras to evaluate ground conditions on the road and then decides whether or not to activate its brakes when the car is too close to front objects or other objects which would create an emergency. In this example, the accident was due to a misjudgment on whether to activate the brake when white snow on the ground reflected sunlight which then "confused" the car's sensors.[23]

To ensure the accountability of safety-critical systems, we have to run them through an empirical testing area like a regulatory sandbox for autonomous systems. Examples include

---

[20]   B. Waltl and R. Vogl, Explainable Artificial Intelligence – the New Frontier in Legal Informatics, International Legal Informatics Symposium (IRIS), Salzburg, Austria (February 2018).

[21]   Y. H. Weng, The Study of Safety Governance for Service Robots: On Open-Texture Risk, Peking University PhD Dissertation (2014).

[22]   S. O'Sullivan, N. Nevejans, C. Allen, *et al.*, Legal, Regulatory, and Ethical Frameworks for Development of Standards in Artificial Intelligence (AI) and Autonomous Robotic Surgery (2019) 15 *Int. J. Med. Robot.* e1968.

[23]   Y.-H. Weng and D. Hillenbrand, The Intelligentization of Automobiles: Smart-Cars, Robo-Cars and their Safety Governance (2014) 4 *J. Sci. Technol. Law* 632.

Japan's "Tokku" special zone[24] or the United States' "Faux Downtown."[25] When creating algorithmic-driven robotic technologies and introducing them into the real world, conflicts are unavoidable given current regulations.[26] However, if we can properly use special zones as a shock buffer via deregulation, it also helps lawmakers fill the accountability gap when developing a law for algorithms that relates to the design of safety-critical systems.

Third, embodiment brings new impacts to data governance and privacy to bear in HRI. As mentioned above, we see healthcare robots as the physical extension of an intelligent agent or "embodied AI." Suppose there are issues generated by the data used for the training process for machine learning and hackers are thus able to attack the system; this could result in healthcare robots behaving abnormally. In the worst-case scenario, the compromised system might physically injure a patient. In addition to security, another concern is the issue of privacy; in that regard, a key question is whether the body in which the AI finds itself influences the privacy protection which is necessary between HRIs.

Concerning robotic embodiment, Debora Zanatto and colleagues used two humanoid-appearing robots – iCub and Scitos G5 (the former having more of a human-like shape) to test whether there were differences in robot credibility when humans were interacting with the robots. They found that subjects were more likely to have social interactions with robots when they were more anthropomorphic in appearance.[27] In additional, Pavia and colleagues conducted a study that dealt with embodiment and empathy by comparing a virtual agent to a robotic agent. They found that it was more challenging for a robotic agent to perceive the user's affective state than for a virtual agent, because the human user sits in front of a screen which displayed a virtual agent; whereas, with a physical robot agent, the relative location between the user and robotic agent can be open-ended.[28]

To achieve a deeper model of artificial empathy, we might need to borrow the viewpoint developed from the field of "Cognitive Developmental Robotics," which refers to "new understandings of how humans' higher cognitive functions develop by means of a synthetic approach that developmentally constructs cognitive functions."[29] Based on these factors, we may infer that when robots are more anthropomorphic, there are risks that humans might disclose more personal and sensitive information during interactions with the robots. Another threat to privacy is that robots may require higher perception capabilities in order to utilize the complex interactions between humans and physical robots. But we are at the beginning stages of our study of privacy in HRI; in order to explore in more depth how the factor of embodiment influences a developing law of algorithms, especially from a privacy perspective, in the following section we will limit our discussion to healthcare robots, given their close social contact with humans.

[24] Y. H. Weng, Y. Sugahara, K. Hashimoto, and A. Takanishi, Intersection of "Tokku" Special Zone, Robots, and the Law: A Case Study on Legal Impacts to Humanoid Robots (2015) 7 *Int. J. Soc. Robot.* 841.

[25] W. Jones, University of Michigan to Open Robo Car Urban Test Track in the Fall, *IEEE Spectrum* (June 10, 2014), http://spectrum.ieee.org/cars-that-think/transportation/self-driving/university-of-michigan-to-open-robo-car-test-track-in-the-fall.

[26] Y. H. Weng, Robot Law 1.0: On Social System Design for Artificial Intelligence, in W. Barfield and U. Pagallo (eds.), *Research Handbook on the Law of Artificial Intelligence* (Edward Elgar, 2018).

[27] D. Zanatto, M. Patacchiola, J. Goslin, and A. Cangelosi, Priming Anthropomorphism: Can the Credibility of Humanlike Robots Be Transferred to Non-Humanlike Robots?, in Proceedings of the 11th ACM/IEEE International Conference on Human-Robot Interaction (HRI), Christchurch, New Zealand (March 7–10, 2016).

[28] A. Pavia, I. Leite, H. Boukricha, and I. Wachsmuth, Empathy in Virtual Agents and Robots: A Survey (2017) 7 *ACM Trans. Interact. Intell. Syst.* art. 11.

[29] M. Asada, Towards Artificial Empathy: How Can Artificial Empathy Follow the Developmental Pathway of Natural Empathy? (2015) 7 *Int. J. Soc. Rob.* 19.

HEALTHCARE ROBOTS AND ALGORITHMS

The growth of an aging population is a critical challenge to many developed nations and has been a topic of discussion in recent years. For example, in Japan, 35,152,000 people or 27.7 percent of the population are above 65 years of age,[30] and for that reason, many public policies have been discussed in Japan with regard to healthcare robots. For example, the "New Robot Strategy: Japan's Robot Strategy – Vision, Strategy, Action Plan" is a five-year mega-plan which aims to use robotics technology to create a new industrial revolution, and to expand its domestic industrial output of robotics. The application of robots in the healthcare industry has been mentioned among many strategic applications in Japanese policy guidelines.[31]

Not only in Japan, but many countries are considering the use of robot technology to alleviate the increased aging crisis, especially by developing robotic applications in health-care, or what is termed "healthcare robots." Because healthcare robots can perform many tasks designed to assist elderly people, they are proposed as a viable solution to addressing a nation's aging population. One example is using healthcare robots for people who suffer dementia. Denise Hebesberger and colleagues in 2016 used an autonomous humanoid robot, Scitos, to support people in physical therapy who suffered advanced dementia; they found that use of a robot enhanced the participants' motivation to participate in therapy.[32] In addition to using robots to assist training for specific groups who suffer dementia, healthcare robots can also be used for companionship, entertainment, monitoring, walk support, and navigation for the elderly. However, there is a question in the literature about the ambiguous-ness of the term "healthcare robots." As Woodrow Barfield has discussed, precisely defining the technology to be regulated is often a challenge to policymakers not trained in technology, especially when the technology is an emerging form of AI and robotics.[33]

However, there are many similar terms discussing healthcare robots found on the Internet; for example, personal care robots, medical robots, socially assistive robots, etc. Thus, it may be of value to review those terms here. Although they seem similar and even have some overlap, from a perspective of law, conflicts may arise if the terms are not carefully distinguished. The term "assistive robotics" as defined by Feil-Seifer and Mataric is a general description of robots with the capability to provide aid or support to a human user in a broad range of environments, such as care centers, hospitals, and homes.[34] Furthermore, Feil-Seifer and Mataric proposed a common term for the terms assistive robotics and socially interactive robotics, which they called "socially assistive robotics" that provide assistance to human users using methods of social interaction.[35] In addition, Armi Ariani and colleagues provided yet another different definition for assistive robotics. They divided assistive robotics into

---

[30] Statistics Bureau, Ministry of Internal Affairs and Communication (MIC), Population Statistics Report, Japan (2017), www.stat.go.jp/data/jinsui/2017np/pdf/2017np.pdf.

[31] Y. H. Weng and Y. Hirata, Ethically Aligned Design for Assistive Robotics, IEEE International Conference on Intelligence and Safety for Robotics (ISR) (2018), pp. 286–90.

[32] D. Hebesberger, T. Körtner, J. Pripfl, and C. Gisinger, Lessons Learned from the Deployment of a Long-Term Autonomous Robot as Companion in Physical Therapy for Older Adults with Dementia, in Proceedings of the 11th ACM/IEEE International Conference on Human–Robot Interaction (HRI), Christchurch, New Zealand (March 7–10, 2016).

[33] W. Barfield, Towards a Law of Artificial Intelligence, in W. Barfield and U. Pagallo (eds.), *Research Handbook on the Law of Artificial Intelligence* (Edward Elgar, 2018).

[34] D. Feil-Seifer and M. Mataric, Defining Socially Assistive Robotics, in Proceedings of the 9th IEEE International Conference on Rehabilitation Robotics, Chicago, IL, United States (June 28–July 1, 2005).

[35] T. Fong, I. Nourbakhsh, and K. Dautenhahn, A Survey of Socially Interactive Robots (2003) 42 *Rob. Auton. Syst.* 143.

"rehabilitation robotics" that can be used as treatment devices such as prostheses, tools for rehabilitation therapies, and/or physical and mobility supports; and "socially assistive robotics" that can be used for social interaction with people, including companionship and service.[36]

The Japanese government has also provided a guideline for classifying healthcare robots with a focus on daily assistive tasks and nursing care for the elderly. The guideline is offered by the Japanese Ministry of Economy, Trade, and Industry (METI) and the Ministry of Health, Labor, and Welfare (MHLW), and includes six applications such as "Bed-Transfer Assist," "Walking Assist," "Excretion that Assist," "Monitoring and Communication Assist," "Bath Assist," and "Nursing Care Business Assist."[37] Each of these has different algorithmic requirements. This classification has been used as a guideline for domestic manufacturers to develop robotic products used for healthcare, but most products currently operate with limited autonomy or only perform simple and repetitive healthcare functions.[38]

Considering that embodied AI operating in social environments is the subject of this chapter, we also discuss emerging healthcare robots that we expect to see operating in homes in the near future. Thus, our definition of "healthcare robots" includes autonomous service robots which have the goal of promoting or monitoring health, while assisting with the above six kinds of care tasks that are currently difficult to perform due to the health problems experienced by the elderly, or due to the difficulty of preventing the further health decline of the elderly.[39]

Note autonomy here refers to a "third existence" meaning that machines will resemble living beings in appearance and behavior, but they will not be self-aware.[40] In addition, some people may wonder if robotic surgery systems and other AI-based medical systems belong to the category of healthcare robots. We believe that such medical devices should meet higher regulation requirements, such as those provided by the Federal Drug Administration for medical devices;[41] therefore, they are not the focus of our discussion in this chapter. In the next section, we discuss embodiment and privacy in HRI by choosing three examples using the above six applications for healthcare robots.

EMBODIMENT AND PRIVACY IN HUMAN–ROBOT INTERACTION

The importance of HRI in a legal context will be apparent in the near future when the embodiment characteristics of AI connect with intelligent healthcare services. Wainer's (2006) research group, some time ago, started using an empirical research approach to investigate embodiment in HRI. By running experiments, they found that compared to virtual animation robots, people remain for a longer time period when interacting with

[36] A. Ariani, V. Kapadia, A. Talaei-Khoei, *et al.*, Challenges in Seniors Adopting Assistive Robots: A Systematic Review (2016) 6 *Int. Technol. Manag. Rev.* 25.

[37] METI and MHLW, Revision of the Four Priority Areas to Which Robot Technology Is to Be Introduced in Nursing Care of the Elderly, Japan (2014), www.meti.go.jp/english/press/2014/0203_02.html.

[38] Robotic Devices for Nursing Care Project, http://robotcare.jp.

[39] H. Robinson, B. MacDonald, and E. Broadbent, The Role of Healthcare Robots for Older People at Home: A Review (2014) 6 *Int. J. Soc. Rob.* 575.

[40] Y.-H. Weng, C.-H. Chen, and C.-T. Sun, Toward The Human-Robot Co-Existence Society: On Safety Intelligence for Next Generation Robots (2009) 1 *Int. J. Soc. Robot.* 267.

[41] K. Chinzei, A. Shimizu, K. Mori, *et al.*, Regulatory Science on AI-Based Medical Devices and Systems (2018) 7 *Adv. Biomed. Eng.* 118.

physical robots,[42] producing better results as well.[43] This difference between virtual and real robots also enables the applications of AI to be gradually entering physical human living spaces from virtual information spaces, and to provide people with healthcare services in various interactive ways. However, with robots in the home, users are unconsciously exposing themselves to higher-risk environments because their personal information is easily searched and collected by AI in the form of robots performing intelligent healthcare services. Considering that the impact of the embodiment of robots on the issue of privacy in HRIs is often overlooked, it is our view that it is necessary to rethink the relationship between embodied AI and privacy.

Ackerman has predicted that social robots could become humans' pets in the future due to two characteristics: affordability to consumers and similarity to real animals' affective interaction with humans.[44] If so, an important question would concern how robots' anthropometric or animal-like appearance would cause people to express their emotions when interacting with robots. Furthermore, would a user's personal information be "leaked unconsciously/unintentionally" when interacting with robots? Addressing this question, Tonkin's team at the University of Technology Sydney used two information interfaces, a humanoid robot and a tablet, for comparative research on human–computer interaction. The researchers found that humanoid robots were able to acquire personal information more easily from their users compared to tablets.[45] Mann and colleagues also pointed out that patients give more positive responses to instructions or messages provided by a humanoid robot compared to a tablet in some healthcare application scenarios.[46] The privacy concern associated with embodied AI in HRIs is not merely about the issue of similarity of human-like, or animal-like, physical appearances of the intelligent system in inducing a user to self-disclose their sensitive information. Another important concern is the risk that embodied AI systems might mislead users about their functionality. For example, Snackbot is an advanced service robot equipped with a 360-degree panorama lens to help it rapidly acquire environmental information from the real world. Because users are not knowledgeable of the full-frame vision perception of Snackbot, they often interact with the robot under the wrong premise; specifically, with the idea that the robot lacks the ability to see behind its back. This lack of knowledge of the robot's functionality generates other privacy risks.[47] Beyond the issue of embodied AI itself, in HRI other kinds of privacy risks emerge from the human side, or users' privacy perception, of their existing environment. This perception is related to their acceptance of emerging technology and shaped in various ways with factors including age,[48] gender, culture, health,

[42] J. Wainer, D. J. Feil-Seifer, D. A. Shell, and M. J. Mataric, The Role of Physical Embodiment in Human–Robot Interaction, in Proceedings of the 15th IEEE International Symposium on Robot and Human Interactive Communication, RO-MAN, Hatfield, Hertfordshire, United Kingdom (September 6–8, 2006), pp. 117–22.

[43] J. Wainer, D. J. Feil-Seifer, D. A. Shell, and M. J. Mataric, Embodiment and Human-Robot Interaction: A Task-Based Perspective, in Proceedings of the 16th IEEE International Symposium on Robot and Human Interactive Communication, RO-MAN, Jeju Island, Korea (August 26–9, 2007), pp. 872–7.

[44] E. Ackerman, Robots Might Be the Necessary Future of Urban Pet Ownership (2015), http://spectrum.ieee.org /automaton/robotics/home-robots/robots-might-be-the-necessary-future-of-urban-pet-ownership.

[45] M. Tonkin, J. Vitale, S. Ojha, et al., Embodiment, Privacy and Social Robots: May I Remember You?, in Proceedings of the 9th International Conference on Social Robotics, Tsukuba, Japan (November 22–24, 2017).

[46] J. A. Mann, B. A. MacDonald, I. H. Kuo, et al., People Respond Better to Robots than Computer Tablets Delivering Healthcare Instructions (2015) 43 *Comput. Hum. Behav.* 112.

[47] M. K. Lee, K. P. Tang, J. Forlizzi, and S. Kiesler, Understanding Users' Perception of Privacy in Human–Robot Interaction, in Proceedings of the 6th ACM/IEEE International Conference on Human–Robot Interaction (HRI), Lausanne, Switzerland (March 6–9, 2011).

[48] J. M. Beer, C. A. Smarr, A. D. Fisk, and W. A. Rogers, Younger and Older Users' Recognition of Virtual Agent Facial Expressions (2015) 1 *Int. J. Hum. Comput. Stud.* 1.

etc.[49] Consider again that Heerink commented that people who have a higher education usually have a less positive attitude toward robots as social entities.[50] Further, MacDorman and colleagues, from a culture perspective, analyzed the social acceptance of robots used within Japanese society based on Shinto religious beliefs and found that the religious perspective had value for social interactions with humanoid-appearing robots.[51] So, from the above discussion, the investigation of the embodiment of healthcare robots in relation to privacy in HRI relates to a host of variables as mentioned previously. Among them, we chose three variables which relate to privacy in HRI: proximity, deception, and safety. We present an analysis of these three variables below.

Proximity and Privacy

Personal space refers to the proper distance (which changes from culture to culture) that people try to maintain in relation to other people in order to ensure, among others, a given level of privacy. More specifically, personal space is the space that surrounds an individual, and any intrusion into this area of physical space without an invitation may lead to a feeling of unease and a response to back off or withdraw.[52] This invisible boundary between oneself and others creates a comfort zone. However, this boundary is not stable, but dynamic, and changes based on the circumstances. In an anthropological study, Edward Hall proposed four different spatial zones in his theory of proxemics to represent the way in which people use space when communicating with one another.[53] For Hall, the four spatial zones are categorized as follows: intimate distance, personal distance, social distance, and public distance. The intimate distance refers to a physical distance that results when one feels comfortable and protected, and it can range from 0 to 6 inches to 6 to 18 inches. Personal distance is the space within which intimate relationships can be built. Social distance (4 to 12 feet) refers to the space where business and general social contact occur. And "public distance" refers to the space associated with an occasion in which people communicate with one another. In fact, different cultures may have different distances for person-to-person communication, so the proximity associated with personal space and the satisfactory feeling of privacy could be different given various cultural contexts and scenarios.

For healthcare robots, their algorithmic understanding of appropriate proximity to humans (based on sensor information) is crucial in terms of maintaining a satisfactory level of privacy for people interacting with the robot. Therefore, in the design stage of creating healthcare robots, it is important to consider "privacy spheres" in terms of spatial distance that may exist between robots and people in order for the human to feel that their privacy is not being invaded. We believe that it is critically important for roboticists to "design-in" the feature of socially aware navigation systems for healthcare robots.[54] A robot's socially aware navigation

[49] W. Wilkowska, M. Ziefle, and S. Himmel, Perceptions of Personal Privacy in Smart Home Technologies: Do User Assessments Vary Depending on the Research Method?, in T. Tryfonas and I. Askoxylakis (eds.), *Human Aspects of Information Security, Privacy, and Trust: Third International Conference, HAS 2015* (Springer, 2015), pp. 592–603.

[50] M. Heerink, Exploring the Influence of Age, Gender, Education and Computer Experience on Robot Acceptance by Older Adults, in Proceedings of the 6th ACM/IEEE International Conference on Human-Robot Interaction (HRI), Lausanne, Switzerland (2011), pp. 147–8.

[51] K. F. MacDorman, S. K. Vasudevan, and C. C. Ho, Does Japan Really Have Robot Mania? Comparing Attitudes by Implicit and Explicit Measures (2009) 23 *AI Soc.* 485.

[52] I. Altman, *The Environment and Social Behavior: Privacy, Personal Space, Territory, and Crowding* (Brooks / Cole Publishing Co., 1975).

[53] E. T. Hall, *The Hidden Dimension* (Doubleday, 1910), Vol. 609.

[54] S. F. Chik, C. F. Yeong, E. L. M. Su, *et al.*, A Review of Social-Aware Navigation Frameworks for Service Robot in Dynamic Human Environments (2016) 8 *J. Telecommun. Electron. Comput. Eng.* 41.

framework should consider the interactions between persons and robots, which would be achieved by using algorithmic predictors to estimate the moving trajectory of robots in proximity to humans. In order to maximize the performance of tasks and improve skills, the robots usually need to collect and process large amounts of real-life environmental data. Japan's Advanced Telecommunications Research Institute International (ATR) conducted an experiment using a humanoid robot in a shopping mall which approached customers within Hall's estimate of social distance (4 to 12 feet) to have a conversation.[55] For those robots whose task is to guide people in shopping malls or an airport, there is a need for the robot to approach customers and passengers and occupy an appropriate social distance space to produce goodwill and encourage communication.[56] We propose that the default privacy setting for these robots should be based on previous experiences of robots when they were within testing areas investigating HRIs.

For healthcare robots providing services to the elderly or disabled persons in healthcare centers, we conclude that the proper proximity between humans and robots should be based on the personal distance estimate of 1.5 to 4 feet or even in some cases an intimate distance estimate (6 to 18 inches). However, the difference between the use of healthcare and shopping mall robots is more than the physical distance in HRI. The service of healthcare itself requires caregivers to have many close physical contacts with care receivers. How to solve the privacy challenge with embodied robots based on proximity is not only a crucial step in robot design, but also a potential concern when considering legal compliance.

One of the possible solutions to respond to the privacy challenge associated with embodied AI in the form of robots is to embed a so-called privacy filter in the early stage of design.[57] There are several factors to consider – such as locations, objects, and information – that we can use to evaluate a person's privacy concerns.[58] Different locations and objects may present different levels of privacy concerns, and the nature of the information also has relevance for privacy concerns with embodied AI – whether it is potentially sensitive information, like health and medical information, or not. These dimensions and their interactive complexity will have great impact on the design of privacy filters for limiting the information to be delivered to those who interact with social robots. Another solution can involve allowing users the opportunity to have explicit opt-outs from video surveillance or automatic video filtering for bystanders and objects.[59] With regard to what information a privacy filter ought to remove, there is a need to carry out further surveys of users' information requirements and then design a filter according to the results that are acceptable for end-users' privacy preferences and which have minimal impacts on interactions with social robots. In the case of healthcare robots, an appropriate filter should allow the robots to have the capability to evaluate environmental data collected from different locations and objects and then to distinguish whether they are situated in a public or private sphere. As a step further, a privacy filter can be designed such that it tailors different spatial zones according to the theory of proxemics for initiating a privacy-friendly communication.

[55] S. Satake, T. Kanda, D. F. Glas, *et al.*, A Robot that Approaches Pedestrians (2013) 29 *IEEE Trans. Robot.* 508.
[56] T. Kanda, M. Shiomi, Z. Miyashita, *et al.*, A Communication Robot in a Shopping Mall (2010) 26 *IEEE Trans. Robot.* 897.
[57] J. M. Janick, H. J. Locker, and R. A. Resnick, US Patent No. 6,765,550 (US Patent and Trademark Office, 2004).
[58] D. J. Butler, J. Huang, F. Roesner, and M. Cakmak, The Privacy-Utility Tradeoff for Remotely Teleoperated Robots, in Proceedings of the 10th ACM/IEEE International Conference on Human-Robot Interaction (HRI), Portland, OR, United States (March 2–5, 2015).
[59] *Ibid.*

Deception and Privacy

One aspect of deception comes from the expectation gap that users may experience when they interact with human-like, or anthropomorphic, robots. Taking ROBEAR as an example, this new experimental bear-shaped nursing care robot developed by scientists from RIKEN Japan is capable of performing basic tasks of care-giving, such as providing assistance to a patient to stand up or lifting him or her from a bed to a wheelchair.[60] The ROBEAR incorporates actuator units with a low gear ratio that allows its joints to move quickly. It is also equipped with three types of sensors, including the Smart Rubber capacitance-type tactile sensors that enable the ROBEAR to exert force in a gentle way, and it can perform power-intensive tasks without endangering patients.[61] Although the bear feature and the human-like features add to the acceptance and trust experienced by ROBEAR users, patients may still experience a gap in care compared to a professional human care-giver when they are lifted by the ROBEAR; this may be due to limitations of the algorithm controlling ROBEAR and the functionality of ROBEAR. As a worst-case scenario, this gap in care may influence the patient's human-dignity as a result of interacting with the care robot. That is, patients may feel humiliated if treated like an object due to the robot's awkward behavior.[62] We propose that this expectation gap in treatment may be reduced by adding more patients' biometric information to the robot's database and by improving robotic perception with advanced sensors. One example of this approach is called "Affective Touch," which allows humans' emotions to be conveyed via tactile interactions such as touch, light stroke, poke, press, squeeze, and grab.[63] However, at the same time, affective touch would lead to a trade-off for privacy protection because touch implies close proximity to the patient, which influences the privacy received by the patient.[64]

In addition to the loss of expectation, another example of deception concerns the oversight of privacy during daily HRI. Gender is a social cue for robots to consider and relates to a robot's social communication skills with humans. This is important especially in healthcare services, and thus robots need to know how to determine a person's gender. On this point, Arnaud Ramey and colleagues developed an algorithm for robots to judge user gender. The basic idea is to use robots' cameras to detect chest contours of humans' upper bodies and based on the data collected to decide whether their targeted person is male or female.[65] However, concerning this approach, some users have privacy concerns and regard this process as an "invasive" HRI. However, for autonomous mobile robots, acquiring people's location information is necessary for realizing robots' social navigation in tracking or guiding people in

---

[60] The Strong Robot with the Gentle Touch, Riken, ROBEAR (February 23, 2015), www.riken.jp/en/pr/press/2015/20150223_2/.

[61] *Ibid.*

[62] A. Sharkey, Robots and Human Dignity: A Consideration of the Effects of Robot Care on the Dignity of Older People (2014) 16 *Ethics Inf. Technol.* 63.

[63] R. Andreasson, B. Alenljung, E. Billing, and R. Lowe, Affective Touch in Human–Robot Interaction: Conveying Emotion to the Nao Robot (2018) 10 *Int. J. Soc. Rob.* 473; J. Sun, S. Redyuk, E. Billing, *et al.*, Tactile Interaction and Social Touch: Classifying Human Touch Using a Soft Tactile Sensor, in International Conference on Human–Agent Interaction (HAI), Bielefeld, Germany (October 17–20, 2017).

[64] M. Coeckelbergh, Health Care, Capabilities, and AI Assistive Technologies, and AI Assistive Technologies (2010) 13 *Ethical Theory Moral Pract.* 181.

[65] A. Ramey and M. A. Salichs, Morphological Gender Recognition by a Social Robot and Privacy Concerns, in Proceedings of the 9th ACM/IEEE International Conference on Human–Robot Interaction (HRI), Bielefeld, Germany (March 3–6, 2014).

real environments.[66] Still, most people don't know that they have been located in the environment by robots when they come close to them.

PARO is a well-known, seal-shaped social robot developed by AIST Japan with many different built-in sensors and hypoallergenic fur to support its social interaction with humans. It is thought to be an ideal social companion tool for elderly people in order to reduce their loneliness. As mentioned before, a privacy risk regarding deception in embodiment is that elderly people have a tendency to self-disclose to a perceivably cute and interactive social robot. One example of this phenomenon is from a "long period" experiment conducted by ATR in Japan. Researchers found that when they mixed hand gesture and conversation functions in a humanoid robot at a care center, elderly people were more willing to tell the robot many of their personal affairs, such as recent frustrations, happy moments, interpersonal relationships, health conditions, etc.[67]

It is also the case that discrimination is also relevant to privacy concerns regarding deception in embodiment. Suppose PARO robot's behavioral module is created by machine learning and its default settings allow it to learn and evolve specific ways of interaction with people. In other words, if person A spends more time interacting with PARO, then PARO will perform more intimate behaviors with him. This way of design thinking is reasonable because when robots spend more time with people in social situations, people experience the interaction as being more realistic and affective. On the other hand, when applied in a care center, a problem that may occur is that PARO will diligently interact and respond to users who have an interest in talking with the robot, but PARO may just keep repeating simple and monotonic behaviors when interacting with people who are shy or who may not spend much time interacting with it. In additional, some elderly people might "react" to this mode of interaction and may experience "discrimination" in their small group via their interaction with PARO, thus, they have to actively interact with robots. In the long run, a privacy concern is that PARO encourages people to engage in more self-disclosure to robots.

As studies have demonstrated, embodiment plays an important role for a trust relationship to be built upon and for the collaboration between a human and an AI agent.[68] A recent experiment showed that embodiment may increase risk tolerance and reduce users' privacy concerns when researchers measure the changes of behaviors for those interacting with an embodied robotic system and a disembodied one.[69] Based on the experiment, users tend to provide confidential information and are more willing to disclose private information to the embodied robots due to their level of trust and acceptance.[70] In the medical and healthcare context, it is crucial to assess the conditions for trust, which is essential for user engagement, especially when users tend to disclose sensitive information to social robots by treating them as friends rather than care providers or aids.

On the other hand, a confidential relationship between physicians and patients is one of the core duties in medical practice. Medical confidentiality limits access to information

---

[66] J. Pineau, M. Montemerlo, M. Pollack, *et al.*, Towards Robotic Assistants in Nursing Homes: Challenges and Results (2002) 42 *Rob. Auton. Syst.* 271.

[67] A. M. Sabelli, T. Kanda, and N. Hagita, A Conversational Robot in an Elderly Care Center: An Ethnographic Study, in Proceedings of the 6th ACM/IEEE International Conference on Human–Robot Interaction (HRI), Lausanne, Switzerland (March 6–9, 2011).

[68] S. Herse, J. Vitale, M. Tonkin, *et al.*, Do You Trust Me, Blindly? Factors Influencing Trust towards a Robot Recommender System, in Proceedings of the 27th IEEE International Symposium on Robot and Human Interactive Communication (RO-MAN), Nanjing, China (August 27–31, 2018), pp. 7–14.

[69] See Lee *et al.*, above note 47.

[70] *Ibid.*

shared between patients and their professional caregivers or anyone involved in care delivery. Outside of this circle of confidentiality, sharing confidential information requires a patient's explicit consent. In addition, data protection rules, such as the EU General Data Protection Regulation (GDPR), prohibit processing of data concerning health unless some exceptions are met; for example, necessary processing for the purposes of medical diagnosis or treatment.[71] When social robots play the role of care providers or assistants, they need to be compliant with the rules of confidentiality and data protection. In order to reduce the potential effect on trust and the disappointment experienced by individuals due to an unexpected use of personal information, a robot's functions affecting privacy should be constructed at the design stage and be communicated to users to make it transparent with regard to its operational capacities. For instance, in the programming stage of design, the interpersonal clues can be added to the robot's behavior system to make users more aware of the continuing activities of data processing.[72]

Except for direct care, explicit consent must be given in medical practice under a clear explanation of what data has been collected, the purpose of such collection, and who can access the data. It is important for users to be aware that healthcare robots function not only as caregivers, but also as devices of data processing, with the capability to capture large amounts of data. For the latter function, there is a possibility that those who are outside of the circle of medical confidentiality, such as cloud service providers and manufactures, can also access sensitive personal data processed by the robots. Under this scenario, proper consent needs to satisfy a two-facet requirement which includes: (1) consenting to the acceptance of the robotic assistance for medical and healthcare purposes; and (2) authorizing the collection and processing of personal data outside of the medical confidentiality, including but not limited to allowing additional parties to access the data for the purposes of the improvement of care.[73] Considering the vulnerability of many users of healthcare robots, such as elderly people, disabled people, or those with cognitive impairments, the consent mechanism needs to be designed carefully to ensure that the principles of autonomy, transparency, and account-ability can be respected.

Some common examples of healthcare robots are exoskeletons or lifting robots supported by AI and deep-learning technologies that rely on large amounts of data regarding the movement of users in order to optimize the performance of the device. Under the GDPR, a data protection impact assessment (article 35) is required to be carried out to evaluate on a contextual basis if robots have been designed in a privacy-friendly way and are able to comply with data protection rules and principles, such as purpose limitations and data minimization. Furthermore, the Guidelines issued by the Article 29 Working Party (WP29) emphasize employing the principle of privacy by design. The Guidelines' purpose is to make sure that privacy and data protection will be embedded within the entire life cycle of the development of robots. For example, thinking about the possible tasks the robots can perform during the design process may help reduce privacy invasion at the later stage, and through such design, an outcome is to make the robots' capacity for surveillance and data collection function only when it is permitted to do so.

---

[71] GDPR, art. 9.
[72] S. de Conca, E. Fosch Villaronga, R. Pierce, *et al.*, Nothing Comes between My Robot and Me: Privacy and Human–Robot Interaction in Robotised Healthcare, in R. Leenes, R. van Brakel, S. Gutwirth, and P. D. Hert (eds.), *Data Protection and Privacy: The Internet of Bodies* (Hart, 2018), p. 104.
[73] *Ibid.*, p. 107.

Safety and Privacy

Before comparing the two concepts of "privacy by design" and "security by design," it is first necessary to introduce these concepts separately. The term "privacy by design" refers to "data protection through previous technology design." Therefore, it is important to ensure that data protection in processing has already been integrated in the technology when created. A good example is the emphasis on the data protection impact assessment proposed under the GDPR. Nevertheless, how to implement "privacy by design" remains uncertain.[74] This is mainly due to EU Member States' incomplete implementation of the rule.

The principle of "Privacy by Design" requires defining technical and organizational measures at an early stage of design. In addition, the GDPR remains open to Member States' legislation to decide what exact protective measures are to be taken. As an example, "pseudonymization" is defined as one of the appropriate technical and organizational measures, but no more detail is given in the GDPR.[75] Further, article 25 of the GDPR does point out technical and organizational measures, which are designed to implement data-protection principles in an effective manner, and to integrate necessary safeguards into the processing of data in order to meet the requirements of the Regulation to protect the rights of data subjects.

It can be said that "privacy by design" tries to establish an appropriate regulation framework to prevent individual private information from being misused. However, with regard to thoroughly protecting individual private information, another concern is the coordination of the software and hardware, which falls under the concept of "security by design." The GDPR's focus on personal data also highlights how software is made and what components are used. It encourages enterprises to consider software security at the initial stage of design. Some scholars have also argued that GDPR obligations have extended to hardware choices.[76] According to their arguments, GDPR obligation should also include choosing and maintaining secure firmware and software for devices used for processing personal data. Therefore, the concept of "security by design" has become an emerging topic in the privacy area.[77]

Compared to privacy by design, security by design focuses more on the software and hardware development. In the general process of system development, it is difficult to address existing vulnerabilities or add in techniques and mechanisms to fix system problems at a later stage. However, in practice, it may also not be easy to design a comprehensive system at the very beginning. "Security by design" allows continuous testing and can be approached by complying with the best practice of programming.[78] On the other hand, making users aware of possible risks, namely to be more transparent in the overall process of system design, can help users make more explicit decisions when they plan to access particular devices or use their services. This consciousness of security can also help improve the design of the system.[79]

---

[74]   A&L Goodbody, The GDPR: A Guide for Businesses (2016), www.algoodbody.com/media/TheGDPR-AGuideforBusinesses1.pdf.

[75]   C. Kuner, L. A. Bygrave, and C. Docksey (eds.), *The EU General Data Protection Regulation: A Commentary* (Oxford University Press, 2018).

[76]   W. K. Hon, GDPR: Killing Cloud Quickly?, *Privacy Perspective* (March 17, 2016), https://iapp.org/news/a/gdpr-killing-cloud-quickly/.

[77]   D. Orlando, The Emerging Security by Design Principle in the EU Legal Framework, Master's thesis, University of Oslo (2018).

[78]   K. Yskout, K. Wuyts, D. Van Landuyt, *et al.*, Empirical Research on Security and Privacy by Design: What (Not) to Expect as a Researcher or a Reviewer, in L. ben Lothmane, M. G. Jaatun, and E. Weippl (eds.), *Empirical Research for Software Security* (CRC Press, 2017), pp. 1–46.

[79]   S. Wachter, Normative Challenges of Identification in the Internet of Things: Privacy, Profiling, Discrimination, and the GDPR (2018) 34 *Comput. Law Secur. Rev.* 436.

Therefore, the main difference between "privacy by design" and "security by design" is that the former emphasizes the previously discussed privacy assessment required by regulation, while the latter requires a continuous, dynamic facilities examination and improvement.[80] In addition, "privacy by design" controls the use of private information, ensures that the processing of private information is under the appropriate legal framework, and "security by design" keeps modifying the techniques to reassure that private information is always under comprehensive protection.

As mentioned above, embodied AI is also a safety-critical system. Its unwanted system behaviors from system integration will lead to consequences regarding physical safety and to human injury.[81] A difference between disembodied healthcare AI systems and healthcare robots concerns the system integration of software and hardware. Therefore, security by design is an important factor that healthcare robots should consider during the design and development stage.

An example of considering security by design for healthcare robots is a prototype standing-support machine with machine-learning capability that was developed by the Smart Robots Design Laboratory at Tohoku University in Japan.[82] In general, the main function of the standing-support machine is to assist patients in sit-to-stand and stand-to-sit motions via controlling the up and down function of a lift table on the top of the machine. Although current machines in use are controlled by human caregivers, in this application, a technical trend is to use AI to replace the caregivers' duty in order to save costs. Hence, the team from Tohoku University uses Support Vector Machine (SVM) to train their prototype in order to let the machine itself decide how to lift the patient in the right time and the right place. However, a difficulty in system design is keeping a balance between safety and privacy. To avoid privacy disputes, the team tried to suppress machine perception capability in numerous ways. They proposed a user state estimation method utilizing just a few inexpensive and simple sensors and also used the SVM learning algorithm to train the machine to distinguish different user motion states, so that the machine could autonomously support patients using data collected from machine pressure force sensors and distance detection sensors. Although this procedure doesn't need too much in terms of human biometrics, the gap of coordination between hardware and software is also reduced due to the simple design. The drawback, however, is its limited perception of human motions. The prototype machine can only understand three motion states, "standing, getting up, sitting," three conditions to infer the user's current state, and based on this knowledge decides how to adjust the countertop height. Here, an issue of security by design involves personal safety, such as the result of a fall or injury when the user rises too fast or the timing is wrong. At this stage, the machine infers the user's state mainly by relying on the pressure information of the user's hand grip and the distance information of the relative position of the user and the machine to assist in estimating the user's state. Considering alternatives to centroid calculations that allow machine learning to infer the user's state, while potentially improving the security of HRIs, it is likely to increase the user's information dimension and pose a challenge to privacy protection.

[80] S. Jacques, Safety and Security by Design (2016) 2 *Seek* 8.
[81] Y. H. Weng and D. Hillenbrand, The Intelligentization of Automobiles: Smart-Cars, Robo-Cars and Their Safety Governance (2014) 110 *J. Sci. Technol. Law* 632.
[82] M. Takeda, Y. Hirata, T. Katayama, *et al.*, State Estimation Using the Cog Candidates for Sit-to-Stand Support System User (2018) 3 *IEEE Robot. Autom. Lett.* 3011.

Discussion

Privacy is generally recognized as a fundamental human right today; however, there is no universal definition of privacy, and it changes according to different times and space, along with the influence of technological developments. In Japan, the definition of privacy rights is not only limited to Brandeis and Warren's classic definition as "the right to be let alone,"[83] it also includes many facets like the right to autonomy, the right to informational self-determination, the right to personal identity, etc.[84] Along this line, the aspect of a right to informational self-determination is especially important for data protection in healthcare robots since it deals with determining the governance of someone's personal information through daily HRIs. Hence, we are going to use this aspect of privacy to discuss how the factor of embodiment can be used by regulators to properly inspect the insufficiency of applying embodied AI healthcare robots into current data protection laws such as GDPR.

First, in terms of a data subject's rights, users as the data subject shall be protected under proper consent to the data processing of robots. In a previous section of this chapter, we mentioned two requirements for proper consent, including the acceptance of the robotic application for healthcare-related purposes, and the collection and processing of personal data outside of medical confidentiality. Such a consent mechanism might be revisited to ensure that the principles of autonomy, transparency, and accountability can be respected.

In addition, when individuals use robots in the processing of personal data, a common theme in data protection is to clearly convey to robots which data can be collected and also to require robots to make sure data is anonymous.[85] However, such an "informed consent" attitude is strongly influenced by embodiment in some use contexts of healthcare robots, and it will cause a gap in data collection. Hedaoo and colleagues conducted an experiment with a service robot using customer data in conversation in order to find out how people expected their data to be used. In their experiment, they divided robot data use into four categories: body language analysis, conversation analysis, database search, and ecological analysis for a Robot Barista which spoke to human testers. The researchers found that participants disliked being searched in databases, followed by being analyzed in conversation, but were most open to having their body language analyzed.[86] The outcome of the research showed that people have lower privacy expectations when a robot processes data from their body language.

Body language refers to a human's non-verbal gestures, movements, or social cues which have specific cultural meanings for people in communication. As Cabibihan and colleagues (2012) stated, applying gesture and body language into the design of a robot is an efficient way to enhance human–robot communication.[87] Although most people believe that robots' data processing of human body language is not likely to infringe privacy to a great extent, a major concern stems from the perception capability of robots in collecting human biometrics. With healthcare robots, collecting body language data from patients is inevitable, and also that

[83] S. D. Warren and L. D. Brandeis, The Right to Privacy (1890) 4 *Harvard Law Rev.* 193.

[84] M. Sogabe, S. Hayashi, and M. Kurita, *Information Law: An Introduction* (Koubundou, 2016).

[85] E. Fosch Villaronga, A. Tamò-Larrieux, and C. Lutz, Did I Tell You My New Therapist Is a Robot? Ethical, Legal, and Societal Issues of Healthcare and Therapeutic Robots (October 17, 2018), https://ssrn.com/abstract=3267832.

[86] S. Hedaoo, A. Williams, A. Fallatah, *et al.*, A Robot Barista Comments on Its Clients: Social Attitudes toward Robot Data Use, in Proceedings of the 14th ACM/IEEE International Conference on Human-Robot Interaction (HRI), Daegu, Korea (March 11–14, 2019).

[87] J. J. Cabibihan, W. C. So, and S. Pramanik, Human-Recognizable Robotic Gestures (2012) 4 *IEEE Trans. Auto. Mental Dev.* 305.

personal data will be collected as well. For example, say a patient waves his hand to tell the robot to stop its service, some inseparable personal data like his palm print, or face contour, can also be collected by the robot. Furthermore, another concern is that robot perception in social cues will sometimes infringe a higher level of sensitive personal data. An example is the case where an algorithm operating a robot is able to discern human gender differences by using its cameras to analyze human chest contour. Apparently, current users' attitudes concerning a robot collecting body language and biometrics will cause a gap of informed consent in data protection. This is not favorable considering that robots are gradually enhancing their perceptual capability and adapting to human living spaces. We propose that a solution to this problem is an education program designed to enhance people's understanding of the possible risks associated with emerging technology.

Second is the issue of privacy by design. The omnipresence of smart home technologies leads people to feel a loss of control over their personal data.[88] However, a concern beyond loss of data control could be the embodiment in deception and proximity from healthcare robots. From a study in evaluating elderly people's privacy-enhancing behaviors (PEBs) in home environments between a camera, a stationary robot, and a mobile robot, the results showed that elderly people changed their behaviors more when monitored by a camera.[89] In other words, elderly people may underestimate the risks of privacy violations from embodied robots. Consider that design strategies as discussed in this chapter might help to reduce the gap of PEBs regarding embodiment. Except for the idea of a privacy filter mentioned above, a self-explanatory user-menu might assist users in anticipating what tasks they can expect the robot to perform.[90]

As we have discussed, it is important to distinguish the concept of security by design from privacy by design. In May 2018, the International Organization of Standardization (ISO) established a new committee ISO PC/317 to draft the standard ISO/AWI 31700 on embedding privacy by design into consumer goods and services.[91] This proposal may support and encompass the privacy by design concept, but when it is applied to the concept of security by design, such as for healthcare robots, the concern exists that there will be a gap in risk assessment between data privacy and robot safety. Further, ISO 13482 (a robot safety standard)[92] adopts ISO 12100 for risk assessment with a three-step method in machinery risk reduction.[93] It is very different from PIMS's (privacy information management system) Privacy Impact Assessment for data protection. For safety-critical systems like healthcare robots, security by design needs to be seriously placed into the machinery risk assessment process in order to ensure system integration between software and hardware.

---

[88] W. Wilkowska, M. Ziefle, and S. Himmel, Perceptions of Personal Privacy in Smart Home Technologies: Do User Assessments Vary Depending on the Research Method? in T. Tryfonas and I. Askoxylakis (eds.), *Human Aspects of Information Security, Privacy, and Trust, HAS 2015, Lecture Notes in Computer Science* (Springer, 2015), Vol. 9190.

[89] K. Caine, S. Sabanovic, and M. J. Carter, The Effect of Monitoring by Cameras and Robots on the Privacy Enhancing Behaviors of Older Adults, in Proceedings of the 7th ACM/IEEE International Conference on Human–Robot Interaction (HRI), Boston, MA, United States (March 5–8, 2012), pp. 343–50.

[90] D. Hebesberger, T. Koertner, C. Gisinger, and J. Pripfl, A Long-Term Autonomous Robot at a Care Hospital: A Mixed Methods Study on Social Acceptance and Experiences of Staff and Older Adults (2017) 9 *Int. J. Soc. Rob.* 417.

[91] ISO/AWI 31700: Consumer Protection – Privacy by Design for Consumer Goods and Services.

[92] ISO 13482:2014: Robots and Robotic Devices – Safety Requirements for Personal Care Robots.

[93] ISO 12100:2010: Safety of Machinery – General Principles for Design – Risk Assessment and Risk Reduction.

CONCLUSION

In this chapter, we discussed the impacts of embodied AI for privacy in HRI from observations we noted in many use scenarios with three concerns consisting of embodiment in proximity, deception, and safety. We concluded that the embodiment factor of healthcare robots brings into focus new privacy risks in some applications of HRI. Although it is still difficult to predict how the outcome of our analysis in embodied AI will reshape the definition of future privacy rights at this time, the analysis shows that current data protection laws may need revisions in order to encompass the use of intelligent robots in healthcare, especially in aspects of data subject rights and privacy by design. As for the impacts of embodied AI on privacy in HRI and the law for algorithms, an overlap is the transparency for creating a trustworthy relationship between users and machines, and for the transparency of the circulation of personal data.[94] In addition, a straightforward way to look at the study of law and robotics through the viewpoint of embodiment is usually from the perspective of torts. However, the importance of privacy and data protection has been overlooked for a long period of time and thus provided motivation for the discussion we provided in this chapter. Finally, our analysis focusing on embodiment and privacy in HRI will not only benefit a law of algorithms, but also the development of privacy-friendly interfaces for healthcare robots.

[94] J. Günther, F. Münch, S. Beck, *et al.*, Issues of Privacy and Electronic Personhood in Robotics, in 2012 IEEE RO-MAN: The 21st IEEE International Symposium on Robot and Human Interactive Communication, Paris, France (September 9–13, 2012).

35

On Being Trans-Human: Commercial BCIs and the Quest for Autonomy

Argyro P. Karanasiou

The hope is that, in not too many years, human brains and computing machines will be coupled together very tightly, and that the resulting partnership will think as no human brain has ever thought and process data in a way not approached by the information-handling machines we know today.

J. C. R. Licklider, Man–Machine Symbiosis (1960)[1]

INTRODUCTION: MORE THAN A PENNY FOR YOUR THOUGHTS

In July 2014, Facebook ran a social experiment on emotional contagion[2] by monitoring the emotional responses of 689,003 users to the omission of certain content containing positive and negative words. The project was severely criticized[3] for manipulating emotions without the informed consent of the subjects, and raised concerns for users' privacy. Most importantly, it brought about the question of respect toward the user's autonomy in the era of automation.

Facebook's catchphrase "What's on your mind?" – prompting the user to share thoughts with their digital social circles – has gained a new, literal meaning in recent years: targeted advertising, fake news, and computational propaganda all being examples of mental manipulation exerted for profit or for power through harnessing AI at scale for the purposes of online profiling. In most cases, this involves an elaborate interpretation of one's digital footprint: the huge amount of data that is generated by our daily online and offline interactions and which defines our behavior. This chapter takes a slightly different approach and seeks to explore the use of AI to retrieve, analyze, and predict data that has not been externalized, yet which most defines us: brain data.

In fact, there has never been a more promising time in history for delineating the contours of human thoughts: public and privately funded projects studying the human brain have produced a high volume of scientific papers and findings in the last few decades, which more often than not are sensationalized in the news. The ambitious plan to explain the mysteries of the human brain has not fully materialized; however, ambition drives profit, and therefore the idea of using AI to decode the human brain

---

[*] I wish to thank the editor, Professor Woodrow Barfield, for all the support shown, as well as Professor Roger Brownsword for all the invaluable comments provided on earlier drafts of this chapter. Any omissions or mistakes remain the sole responsibility of the author, who is human and therefore errs.

[1] J. C. R. Licklider, Man–Machine Symbiosis (1960) HFE-1 *IRE Trans. Hum. Factors Electron.* 4.

[2] A. D. Kramer, J. E. Guillory, and J. T. Hancock, Experimental Evidence of Massive-Scale Emotional Contagion through Social Networks (2014) 111 *Proc. Nat. Acad. Sci.* 8788.

[3] J. Grimmelmann, The Law and Ethics of Experiments on Social Media Users (2015) 13 *Colo. Technol. Law J.* 219; J. R. Bambauer, All Life Is an Experiment. (Sometimes It's a Controlled Experiment) (2015) 47 *Loy. Univ. Chi. Law J.* 487.

has been a fast-growing commercial venture for many tech giants, which have been investing heavily in corporate R&D neurotech-related projects. It therefore comes as no surprise that 2019 has been described as the year of wearable consumer IoT; a nascent market that is expected to increase from 66.5 million units in 2019 to 105.3 million units in 2023. Among the top emerging wearable tech are a number of EEG (NeuroSky, Emotiv, Mindwave) or tDCS (Thync) products that monitor the user's brain activity, process and store all relevant data, and even alter state of mind. Unlike the Facebook experiment, such practices are able to bypass the user's voluntary involvement, relying purely on biometrical data. This would further support the aim of determining one's future choices through inferences yielded by sophisticated AI methods analyzing brain activity data, such as deep learning.

The chapter proceeds in four sections: the first section, "What's on Your Mind?," offers a historical overview of "mind-reading" techniques, building up some context as to how the neurotech market boomed and started employing AI to unravel the mysteries of the human brain beyond the clinical sphere. This is then followed by a techno-legal evaluation of the monitoring, collection, and analysis of brain imaging data from the use of commercial brain–computer interfaces (BCIs) in the second section, "The BCI Mechanics." Building further on this, the third section "Legal Considerations" explores the scope for user empowerment and agency in commercial BCI. This further supports the view that runs through the remainder of the chapter, namely that commercial BCIs constitute a special case of processed data that appear to be falling through the cracks of robust data protection laws, such as the General Data Protection Regulation (GDPR). The chapter seeks to highlight the need for data protection laws that reflect the conceptual redefinition of autonomy in the light of AI-driven pervasive neurotechnologies.

WHAT'S ON YOUR MIND? A SHORT HISTORY OF MIND READING

The year is 1896, the place: San Francisco. Long before it became part of the place that is affectionately called Silicon Valley, a local newspaper publishes an article about "the most wonderful of discoveries,"[4] a mind-reading machine able to register and convey thoughts through vibrations recorded by a motor-operated coated cylinder. The machine's inventor, Julius Emner, had drawn inspiration from another invention of that time, the phonogram,[5] in the hope that thought recording and transference could be achieved in a similar manner. The newspaper article reporting on the invention is certainly an entertaining read nowadays, mainly due to its enthusiastic tone when recounting the various uses such a machine could be put to, allowing us:

> ... to be able to preserve the record of our own thoughts, which we can read off at will; to be able to take down the thoughts of another when they may be unconscious of the operation; to fathom the brain of the poet; to examine the minds of the insane; to discern the secret thoughts of our friends, and to trace the workings of crime in the brain of the criminal are all fields of unlimited boundaries, operations of which science has as yet scarcely dreamed.

The lack of information thereafter suggests that this did not materialize successfully; however, it is an indicative example of the long-standing fascination and experimentation with capturing one's mind. In the quest to unravel the mysteries of the human brain, pseudo-science often thrived in science's shadow, which promised less thrills yet was able to deliver more. It soon became clear though, that the ability to study human physiology could potentially explain intent and to a certain extent further account for one's actions.

---

4   The San Francisco Call (April 12, 1895), https://juxtintime.wordpress.com/2014/04/12/the-mind-reading-machine/.
5   See https://chroniclingamerica.loc.gov/lccn/sn84024442/185–08-16/ed-1/seq-6.pdf.

Enter the polygraph: John Augustus Larson's 1921 invention that could detect abnormal behavior by measuring physiological functions, which were attributed to stress when lying under oath.[6] Identified as a method of detecting deception, the polygraph was greeted with skepticism as to the accuracy of its results and its admissibility in legal proceedings was deferred to a moment in time where the technique "has gained general acceptance in the particular field in which it belongs";[7] also known as the Frye standard. In short, the demand was there, the technology was not.[8] In the years to come, the use of lie detecting techniques would be a contested matter,[9] not only due to their debatable accuracy,[10] but also due to the numerous legal and ethical challenges they posed.[11]

At the same time though, as technology and science progressed, cognitive neuroscience led to new ways of identifying mental states through measuring brain functions. Lie detection techniques became more sophisticated, using functional neuroimaging methods such as fMRI (functional magnetic resonance imaging) that could measure neural activity through changes in blood flow.[12] Unlike the polygraph, which focused on the peripheral nervous system, fMRI was a method that measured the central nervous system. Namely, whereas the polygraph relied on inferring deception from fluctuations in one's breathing, blood pressure, and sweat gland activity, fMRI was able to generate a brain map by associating blood oxygenation to neuronal activity in a non-invasive manner: in short, fMRI-based methods in lie detection interpreted high neural activity in the prefrontal brain – an area responsible for behavioral control – as deception.[13] Closer to a "brain-reading" rather than a "mind-reading" method, fMRI still lacked translational accuracy in lie detection[14] and as such it did not satisfy the high threshold set in Frye[15] and reaffirmed in

[6] Known also as the Keeler polygraph, named after Leonard Keeler, who made the machine portable and testified as an expert at court for admitting evidence obtained through the polygraph. For more details on the mechanics of the Keeler polygraph, see L. Keeler, A Method for Detecting Deception (1930) 1 *Am. J. Police Sci.* 38; and F. Inbau, The "Lie-Detector" (1935) 40 *Scientific Mon.* 81.

[7] *Frye* v. *United States*, 293 F. 1013, 1014, 34 ALR 145, 146 (DC Cir. 1923). For more, see F. Inbau, Scientific Evidence in Criminal Cases: 11 Methods of Detecting Deception (1934) 24 *J. Crim. Law* 1140, 1148–50.

[8] The Polygraph and Lie Detection, Report of the Committee to Review the Scientific Evidence on the Polygraph of the National Academies of the U.S., National Academies Press, Washington, DC (2003).

[9] For a good historical overview, see Marion Oswald's Technologies in the Twilight Zone: Early Lie Detectors, Machine Learning and Reformist Legal Realism (April 7, 2019), https://ssrn.com/abstract=3369586 or http://dx.doi.org/10.2139/ssrn.3369586.

[10] E. H. Meijer, and B. Verschuere, The Polygraph: Current Practice and New Approaches, in P. A. Granhag, A. Vrij, and B. Verschuere (eds.), *Detecting Deception: Current Challenges and Cognitive Approaches* (Wiley-Blackwell, 2015), pp. 59–80.

[11] There are a large number of scholars who discuss the legal issues surrounding the use of lie detectors in court (e.g. N. A. Farahany, Incriminating Thoughts (2012) 64 *Stan. Law Rev.* 351), and by the police (e.g. G. Ben-Shakhar, M. Bar-Hillel, and I. Lieblich, Trial by Polygraph: Scientific and Juridical Issues in Lie Detection (1986) 4 *Behav. Sci. Law* 459) or in employment settings. As these matters fall beyond the scope of this chapter, they are only discussed here in passing.

[12] S. Ogawa, T. M. Lee, A. S. Nayak, and P. Glynn, Oxygenation-Sensitive Contrast in Magnetic Resonance Image of Rodent Brain at High Magnetic Fields (1990) 14 *Magn. Reson. Med.* 68; K. K. Kwong, J. W. Belliveau, D. A. Chesler, *et al.*, Dynamic Magnetic Resonance Imaging of Human Brain Activity During Primary Sensory Stimulation (1992) 89 *Proc. Nat. Acad. Sci.* 5675.

[13] J. D. Greene and J. M. Paxton, Patterns of Neural Activity Associated with Honest and Dishonest Moral Decisions (2009) 106 *Proc. Nat. Acad. Sci.* 12506. See also D. D. Langleben, J. W. Loughead, W. Bilker, *et al.*, Imaging Deception with fMRI: The Effects of Salience and Ecological Relevance, in 34th Annual Meeting of the Society for Neuroscience, San Diego, CA, Society for Neuroscience, Washington, DC (2004); S. A. Spence, The Deceptive Brain (2004) 97 *JR Soc. Med.* 6.

[14] M. J. Farah, J. B. Hutchinson, E. A. Phelps, and A. D. Wagner, Functional MRI-Based Lie Detection: Scientific and Societal Challenges (2014) 15 *Nat. Rev. Neurosci.* 123; R. Robinson, fMRI beyond the Clinic: Will It Ever Be Ready for Prime Time? (2004) 2 *PLoS Biol.* e150.

[15] G. Miller, fMRI Lie Detection Fails a Legal Test (2010) 328 *Science* 1336.

Daubert;[16] namely, that judges should act as gatekeepers and have the discretion to exclude scientific evidence determined to be unreliable.[17] The literature often refers to a triad of 2010 to 2012 cases,[18] where parties sought to admit results of fMRI lie detectors as evidence to prove the validity of a witness's or the defendant's testimonies. The judges ruled such evidence inadmissible on the basis that the relevant techniques had not yet gained acceptance by the scientific community for use in the real world. In short, the demand was there, the technology was slowly catching up, yet its adoption required more scientific evidence and a lower risk threshold for false positives.

No doubt the criticisms on the use of such methods beyond the confines of a lab make several valid ethical[19] and legal arguments,[20] which will be reviewed in the remainder of this chapter; yet, at the same time, it is interesting to note that fMRI lie detection highlighted a "strong and growing demand"[21] from governmental bodies and corporate businesses that translated into a profitable opportunity and the emergence of a new market focusing on commercial neuro-tech: since 2006, Cephos and No-Lie MRI have been marketing fMRI lie detectors "that objectively and reliably measure[s] intent, prior knowledge, and deception with proprietary fMRI human brain mapping techniques developed from recent advances in neuroscience." With a shared past as start-ups in medical diagnostics, both companies boast a broad application base and promise good investment returns as the emergent emotion detection and recognition market size is estimated to reach $56 billion by 2024.[22]

The demand was still there; the technology was catching up quickly and cognitive neuroscience started to become heavily commercialized in the absence of either clear premarket approval regulations[23] or general social and legal considerations.[24] Most importantly, a heightened governmental interest translated into funding research that would ensure better and more reliable results: grants from DARPA (Defense Advanced Research Projects Agency), DoDPI (Department of Defense Polygraph Institute), and the US Department of

---

[16]   J. C. Moriarty, Flickering Admissibility: Neuroimaging Evidence in the US Courts (2008) 26 *Behav. Sci. Law* 29.
[17]   *Daubert* v. *Merrell Dow Pharm., Inc.*, 509 US 579 (1993). For an excellent analysis on the *Daubert* standard and relevant legal and epistemological concerns see J. R. Law, Cherry-Picking Memories: Why Neuroimaging-Based Lie Detection Requires a New Framework for the Admissibility of Scientific Evidence under FRE 702 and *Daubert* (2011) 14 *Yale J. Law Technol.* 1.
[18]   *United States* v. *Semrau*, 693 F.3d 510, 516 (2012); *Wilson* v. *Corestaff Servs. LP*, 28 Misc.3d 425, 426 (2010); and *Smith* v. *Maryland*, 442 US 735 (1979).
[19]   F. Schauer, Lie-Detection, Neuroscience, and the Law of Evidence, in D. Patterson and M. S. Pardo (eds.), *Philosophical Foundations of Law and Neuroscience* (Oxford University Press, 2016). Note, however, that Schauer does not oppose the admissibility of elaborate scientific methods to inform the law, as posited in F. Schauer, Can Bad Science Be Good Evidence? Neuroscience, Lie Detection, and Beyond (2009) 95 *Cornell Law Rev.* 1191.
[20]   For a good account on primarily conceptual issues, see M. S. Pardo, Lying, Deception, and fMRI: A Critical Update, in B. Donnelly-Lazarov (ed.), *Neurolaw and Responsibility for Action: Concepts, Crimes and Courts* (Cambridge University Press, 2018).
[21]   D. D. Langleben, Detection of Deception with fMRI: Are We There Yet? (2008) 13 *Leg. Criminol. Psychol.* 9.
[22]   See www.reportlinker.com/p04458257/Emotion-Detection-and-Recognition-Market-by-Technology-Software-Tool-Service-Application-Area-End-User-and-Region-Global-Forecast-to.html?utm_source=GNW.
[23]   H. T. Greely and J. Illes, Neuroscience-Based Lie Detection: The Urgent Need for Regulation (2007) 33 *Am. J. Law Med.* 377.
[24]   J. Illes and M. L. Eaton, Commercializing Cognitive Neurotechnology – the Ethical Terrain (2007) 25 *Nat. Biotechnol.* 393.

Homeland Security have funded the neuroscientific studies[25] that yielded techniques used by Cephos[26] and NoLie MRI.[27]

In fact, the fast-moving pace of cognitive neuroscience, holding a promising potential to unravel the mysteries of the human brain, paired with the technological advancements in brain-inspired computing, ushered in an era of ambitious public-funded projects. In 2013, the Obama administration pledged \$5 billion to Brain Research through Advancing Innovative Neurotechnologies® (BRAIN)[28] to discover, inter alia, "how dynamic patterns of neural activity are transformed into cognition, emotion, perception, and action,"[29] with a view to create a "single, integrated science of cells, circuits, brain, and behaviour."[30] In a similar manner and almost simultaneously, 2013 was also the year the European Union announced the Human Brain Project,[31] a flagship ten-year project focused on neuroinformatics, brain simulation, neurorobotics, and neuromorphic computing.[32] Demand was there, technology was there, and money was there too. The time for neurotech to become commercially available seemed ripe.

Fast forward to today. In July 2019, Elon Musk's start-up "Neuralink" held a public event in California to give an update on its progress since 2016 when it was first announced. The start-up aims to develop the use of high-bandwidth machine interfaces to enhance human intelligence and there has often been skepticism as to whether it can deliver on its promised goals.[33] At the event, Neuralink unveiled its latest work: a robot supervised by a neurosurgeon, able to implant ultra-fine flexible electrodes into a brain to monitor neural activity.[34] Currently tested on animals, it was announced that – pending FDA approval – testing on human volunteers is planned to begin by mid-2020.

The ability to record many neurons at once certainly carries the promise of bringing us one step closer to understanding human cognition. While the corporate world has been interested fairly recently in neurotechnologies, for the past eighteen years DARPA has been actively

[25] J. T. Cohen, Merchants of Deception: The Deceptive Advertising of fMRI Lie Detection Technology (2010) 35 *Seton Hall Legis. J.* 158 (esp. n. 43). See also S. Silberman, Don't Even Think about Lying, *Wired* (January 1, 2006), www.wired.com/2006/01/lying/.

[26] F. A. Kozel, L. J. Revell, J. P. Lorberbaum, *et al.*, A Pilot Study of Functional Magnetic Resonance Imaging Brain Correlates of Deception in Healthy Young Men (2004) 16 *J. Neuropsychiatry Clin. Neurosci.* 295; F. A. Kozel, K. A. Johnson, Q. Mu, *et al.*, Detecting Deception Using Functional Magnetic Resonance Imaging (2005) 58 *Biol. Psychiatry* 605.

[27] D. Langleben, L. Schroeder, J. Maldjian, *et al.*, Brain Activity During Simulated Deception: An Event-Related Functional Magnetic Resonance Study (2002) 15 *Neuroimage* 727; D. D. Langleben, J. W. Loughead, W. B. Bilker, *et al.*, Telling Truth from Lie in Individual Subjects with Fast Event-Related fMRI (2005) 26 *Hum. Brain Mapp.* 262.

[28] See https://braininitiative.nih.gov/.

[29] Brain 2025: A Scientific Vision, Brain Research through Advancing Innovative Neurotechnologies (BRAIN) Working Group Report to the Advisory Committee to the Director, NIH (June 2014), https://braininitiative .nih.gov/sites/default/files/pdfs/brain2025_508c.pdf.

[30] *Ibid.*

[31] See Human Brain Project (HBP) Flagship, European Commission, https://ec.europa.eu/digital-single-market /en/human-brain-project.

[32] The HBP structure includes the following areas: Neuroinformatics (access to shared brain data), Brain Simulation (replication of brain architecture and activity on computers), High Performance Analytics and Computing (providing the required computing and analytics capabilities), Medical Informatics (access to patient data, identification of disease signatures), Neuromorphic Computing (development of brain-inspired computing) and Neurorobotics (use of robots to test brain simulations). For more, see Short Overview of the Human Brain Project, www.humanbrainproject.eu/en/about/overview/.

[33] See C. Towers-Clark, Neuralink Needs Careful Consideration, Not Hasty Commercialization, *Forbes* (July 25, 2019), www.forbes.com/sites/charlestowersclark/2019/07/25/neuralink-needs-careful-consideration-not-hasty-commercialization/.

[34] For Neuralink's white paper, see www.documentcloud.org/documents/6204648-Neuralink-White-Paper.html.

supporting projects that involve brain–computer interfaces (BCIs), namely bi-directional wearable (or implanted) devices that externalize brain communication and enable "diverse national security applications such as control of active cyber defense systems and swarms of unmanned aerial vehicles, or teaming up with computer systems to multitask during complex missions."[35] DARPA's latest N3 funding awards show the current focus on non-invasive BCI methods, as this will bring neurotech outside the narrow confines of clinical use and will enable applications on the able-bodied population. This perhaps explains why Neuralink's announcement has made such an impact: we are currently witnessing the first steps of commercial BCIs. Whether they will actually deliver on all promises regarding the applications of neurotech remains to be seen, but it cannot be denied that since the days of Emner's "mind reading" machine, we have come a long way.

There is one common thread in the cases presented thus far in this section: portability. The more portable devices have become, the easier it has been to integrate these into social fabric and commerce. The use of novel sensing and machine-learning techniques carried the promise of what once seemed unthinkable: to read one's mind. The next section offers some much-needed insights on how this is actually delivered and will explain how such devices came to be portable and thus commercially exploitable. Most importantly, though, it will offer a typology of key BCI traits, which will serve as a point of reference for the analysis in the remainder of the chapter.

THE BCI MECHANICS: A PRIMER AND A TYPOLOGY OF KEY TRAITS

The industrial appetite for brain-reading methods and applications has risen steeply in the past decade: indicative of this is that relevant patents for neurotechnologies decoding brain activity have risen from 400 in 2012 to 1,600 in 2014.[36] This hardly comes as a surprise given that the neurotech market[37] is expected to reach $13.3 billion in 2022, covering a wide range of applications in neuroprosthetics, neuromodulation, neurorehabilitation, and neurosensing.[38] For the purposes of this chapter, our spotlight is on a particular segment of this market that focuses on non-clinical applications: "pervasive neurotechnology." This is an emerging field in neuroscience developing brain-reading methods that due to their relatively low cost and limited safety risks allow for multiple industrial/commercial applications: Microsoft and IBM are among the key patent holders in pervasive neurotechnology.[39] Take, for example, Microsoft's recent patent[40] filing for a device that measures brain activity to allow users to launch and control applications hands-free, or Nissan's new concept vehicle debuting at the 2018 Geneva motor show and set to reach production in 2020, the IMs KURO car that uses

[35] See Six Paths to the Nonsurgical Future of Brain-Machine Interfaces, DARPA, www.darpa.mil/news-events/2019-05-20.

[36] See Market Report on Pervasive Neurotechnology: A Groundbreaking Analysis of 10,000+ Patent Filings Transforming Medicine, Health, Entertainment and Business, SharpBrains, https://sharpbrains.com/pervasive-neurotechnology/.

[37] For a roadmap predicting the neurotech state of the art in 2040, see C. Cinel, D. Valeriani, and R. Poli, Neurotechnologies for Human Cognitive Augmentation: Current State of the Art and Future Prospects (2019) 13 *Front. Hum. Neurosci.* 13.

[38] The Market for Neurotechnology 2018–2022, a market research report from Neurotech Reports, www.neurotechreports.com/pages/execsum.html.

[39] Market Report on Pervasive Neurotechnology: A Groundbreaking Analysis of 10,000+ Patent Filings Transforming Medicine, Health, Entertainment and Business, https://sharpbrains.com/pervasive-neurotechnology/.

[40] WO2017196618 – Changing an Application State Using Neurological Data, WIPO IP Portal, https://patentscope.wipo.int/search/en/detail.jsf?docId=WO2017196618.

a pioneering brain-vehicle (B2 V) interface to aid the driver's execution of evasive maneuvering.[41] Strictly speaking, both are examples of BCIs that do not read one's mind *per se*; rather, the instructions sent from one's brain are decoded by algorithms to reveal intent.

No doubt the implications for one's autonomy are tremendous, given the pervasive nature of such methods paired with wearable devices. To properly assess them though, it is important to first understand the mechanics of wearable BCIs and the breadth of their potential applications beyond the clinical terrain. To this end, we shall next review (1) the recording methods, (2) the targeted cognitive areas, and (3) the commercial applications. This is by no means a detailed technical analysis, but it will suffice to help us build a typology for evaluating the legal risks posed for the consumer in the coming sections. Moreover, it will build some much-needed context as it will help explain how merging BCI and wearables together with deep-learning algorithms has resulted in a booming industry of portable neurotech.

Recording Methods: Sensors and Hardware

The main principle behind BCIs is that observable brain signals can act as information carriers in a bilateral communication between a computer and a person:[42] the computing system *records* brain signals that are produced in the central nervous system (CNS), *analyzes and decodes* intention, and then *translates* this further into action-generating outputs.[43] Ultimately, a brain–computer interface suggests a machine acting as an exocortex that picks up electrical neuronal signals, uploads them on to a hard drive that algorithmically translates them into intent, and rewrites this code to an output device, either to enhance cognition or to enable action. Through such computer-based systems, functions that have been traditionally muscle based can now be performed through observation and analysis of brain signals.

In essence, neural signals correlating to mental processes are picked up by sensors (hardware) to be further algorithmically processed (software) for feature extraction and classification.[44] There are three types of sensors used for brain signal recording: (1) invasive, which require surgical implantation of a chip or array of electrodes into the cortex; (2) semi-invasive, which are also surgically implanted, but not directly on the grey matter of the brain; and (3) non-invasive – namely, arrays of metal electrodes placed as a cap atop one's skull. Given the limited health risks, especially when compared to surgically implanted sensors, it comes as no surprise that non-invasive sensors are extremely popular in commercial BCI and are thus at the fore and center of our analysis here. The most common sensing monitor in this category – and an industry favorite – is electroencephalography (EEG),[45] with others including magnetoencephalography (MEG), positron emission topography (PET), functional magnetic resonance imaging (fMRI), and functional near infrared spectroscopy (fNIRS). The limited accuracy of the results yielded by non-invasive sensors like EEG, especially when attached by the untrained consumer, is a downside

---

[41] See Nissan IMx Kuro Mind-Reading Concept Presented in Geneva, Auto Evolution, www.autoevolution.com /news/nissan-imx-kuro-mind-reading-concept-presented-in-geneva-124157.html.

[42] Vidal, one of the first neuroscientists to pioneer this field, defines BCI as "a collaboration between a brain and a device that enables signals from the brain to direct some external activity, such as control of a cursor or a prosthetic limb. The interface enables a direct communications pathway between the brain and the object to be controlled" (J. J. Vidal, Toward Direct Brain-Computer Communication (1973) 2 *Ann. Rev. Biophys. Bioeng.* 157).

[43] J. Wolpaw and E. W. Wolpaw (eds.), *Brain-Computer Interfaces: Principles and Practice* (Oxford University Press, 2012).

[44] For more, see R. A. Ramadan, S. Refat, M. A. Elshahed, and R. A. Ali, Basics of Brain Computer Interface, in A. E. Hassanien and A. T. Azar (eds.), *Brain–Computer Interfaces* (Springer, 2015), pp. 31–50.

[45] For a detailed overview of EEG's basic principles and applications, see J. C. Henry, Electroencephalography: Basic Principles, Clinical Applications, and Related Fields (2006) 67 *Neurology* 2092.

most companies are willing to accept when marketing such products: the low cost of developing portable headsets and the low health risk that in turn lowers the bar for product evaluation and approval by the regulative authorities for consumer protection explain why such methods are commercially attractive.

Targeted Cognitive Areas: Processing and Software

Moving on to review the targeted cognitive areas, let's consider Emotiv's EPOC+. Emotiv is a bio-informatics company developing and marketing neuro-headsets for consumers who wish to monitor their thoughts and emotions.[46] Its flagship product, EPOC+, is a wireless EEG headset currently retailing at $799 that offers access to raw brain data to enhance performance and wellness. According to the company's website, the headset collects data that can be analyzed using a number of proprietary apps for various purposes: enhancing performance and wellness, enabling thought control technologies, aiding academic research, or even offering consumer insights on emotions driving behavior and decision-making.[47] In essence, Emotiv is using a wireless non-invasive sensory hardware (for example, EPOC+), which collects neural signals that are then analyzed over six key cognitive metrics: interest, excitement, relaxation, engagement, attention, and stress. This is made possible through the use of three machine-learning algorithms that classify and grade the intensity of the captured brain data. The experience of accessing and understanding one's own brain activity is further complemented by several applications whereby consumers can provide this data as neuro-feedback to train a system to act on their mental commands or respond to their facial expressions. According to Emotiv's website, its technology focuses on retrieving brain data from the neomammalian cortex and the limbic system, the regions responsible for "planning, modeling of your surroundings, interpretation of sensory inputs up to and including your perception of reality, memory processing and storage and [are] the basic drivers of your moods and emotions."[48] Yet, what exactly can brain activity from these areas reveal and to what extent can cognitive activity translate into thought, emotion, or intent?

To address this question, we would first need to consider the complexity of the human brain. When reading this sentence, you are using your reptilian brain to control involuntary eye movement across the page, your limbic system to retrieve past knowledge on how to read, and your neomammalian brain to understand the argument being made. In other words, whereas the reptilian brain controls functions for instinctual and involuntary movements, the other two regions of the brain, the limbic system and the neomammalian brain, are responsible for more elaborate cognitive tasks, such as memory and decision-making.[49] Brain data from these parts of the brain provide an insight into what counts as memorable information, our ability to recall faces and associate these to social interactions determining trust, as well as reasoning, decision-making, and task execution. The emotional[50] and cognitive responses to

---

[46] T. D. Pham and D. Tran, Emotion Recognition Using the Emotiv EPOC Device, in International Conference on Neural Information Processing (Springer, 2012), pp.394–9.

[47] See Consumer Insights, Emotiv, www.emotiv.com/consumer-insights-solutions/#.

[48] See The Science behind Our Technology, Emotiv, www.emotiv.com/our-technology/.

[49] P. D. MacLean, *The Triune Brain in Evolution: Role in Paleocerebral Functions* (Springer, 1990).

[50] For an informative analysis on how emotion and cognition relate to each another, see J. LeDoux, *The Emotional Brain: The Mysterious Underpinnings of Emotional Life* (Simon & Schuster, 1998).

stimuli, when measured and analyzed, can localize and explain mental processes, revealing one's subconscious intent, free will, social preferences, or even cognitive bias.[51] As such, brain data are not equally valuable for neurotech and activity from certain regions holds greater potential for explaining behavior.

Clinical and Commercial Applications – a Typology

Having reviewed the cognitive areas targeted and the methods used to collect brain activity data, we shall now turn to the various applications these may have in a quest to assess their potential for commercial exploitation. In doing so, the chapter offers a much-needed typology, which will further underpin the legal assessment in the following section. Moreover, it will place it all into perspective to demonstrate how pairing AI and neuroscience is the BCI's formula for success. As seen in Table 35.1, the invasiveness of the sensory methods used in BCIs is in inverse proportion to their commercial applications: Highly invasive methods (for example, Deep Brain Stimulation) are mainly supporting therapy for brain-related disorders, such as Parkinson's; semi-invasive methods (for example, ECoG), which find applications in neuroprosthetics and implants, are primarily for restoration (but also for self-experimentation to a lesser extent); and non-invasive methods (for example, EEG, fMRI, fNIRS) are preferred in commercial products marketed as wearables for well-being and self-enhancement ("brain-hacking").[52] Nowadays, there are a good number of start-ups developing non-invasive brain–machine interfaces for self-enhancement – for example, by working on memory prostheses (Kernel), monitoring sleep neural activity (Dreem), and detecting stress-related mental states (Emotiv).

The available details on the operational and technical aspects of such commercially available products are limited and do not reveal much about their potential applications or future configurations: in their latest study,[53] McCall and colleagues surveyed all marketed EEG-enabled wearable "neurodevices," to find that there was little scientific evidence available on these projects (for example, peer-reviewed research or otherwise). This is not to say that such devices are not reliable, but rather to highlight the fact that there is a high degree of opacity due to trade secrecy. To understand their potential, one should further explore the findings of academic projects using similar non-invasive methods. Take, for example, the reconstruction of visual experiences from brain activity; a fascinating area of research that has already yielded several outputs: to name but a few, Nishimoto and colleagues[54] used fMRI to decode brain signals generated by movie trailers, while Nemrodov and colleagues[55] used EEG to reconstruct facial images that the subjects were seeing from their brain activity. Further to this, several projects benefit from using AI to build artificial systems to reproduce captured brain data: this is an approach that allows scientists to successfully reconstruct subjective images by capturing and decoding visual cortical activity in a deep neural network (DNN), namely a pre-trained

---

[51] M. G. Haselton, G. A. Bryant, A. Wilke, *et al.*, Adaptive Rationality: An Evolutionary Perspective on Cognitive Bias (2009) 27 *Soc. Cogn.* 733.

[52] J. Savulescu and N. Bostrom (eds.), *Human Enhancement* (Oxford University Press, 2009).

[53] I. C. McCall, C. Lau, N. Minielly, and J. Illes, Owning Ethical Innovation: Claims about Commercial Wearable Brain Technologies (2019) 102 *Neuron* 728. For an excellent legal analysis on cognitive enhancement, see also M. J. Blitz, Freedom of Thought for the Extended Mind: Cognitive Enhancement and the Constitution (2010) *Wis. Law Rev.* 1049.

[54] S. Nishimoto, A. T. Vu, T. Naselaris, *et al.*, Reconstructing Visual Experiences from Brain Activity Evoked by Natural Movies (2011) 21 *Curr. Biol.* 1641.

[55] D. Nemrodov, M. Niemeier, A. Patel, and A. Nestor, The Neural Dynamics of Facial Identity Processing: Insights from EEG-Based Pattern Analysis and Image Reconstruction (2018) 5 *Eneuro*.

TABLE 35.1 *A typology of traits, methods, and applications in BCIs*

Sensors/ methods	Key advantages/ disadvantages[58]	Health risk	Commercial value – applications	Legal and ethical risks – remedies
Invasive DBS	High-risk surgical requirements/ signal quality	High	Therapy for brain-related disorders (e.g. Parkinson's, Dystonia, etc.) Examples: Boston Scientific, Abbott, Medtronic (companies offering DBS system products for clinical use)	High/Direct – Consent from patients (clinical/ lab application)
Semi-invasive ECoG USEA	Surgical requirement – limitations from approved methods/signal quality	High	Restorative (neuro-prosthetics, implants) Examples: Boston Retinal Implant project, HAPTIX (DARPA-funded program for robotic prosthetics), Paradromics (DARPA-funded company developing prosthetics for speech decoding), speech restoration through ECoG and deep neural networks (Akbari *et al.* 2019,[i] Anumancipalli *et al.* 2019[ii]) Self-experimentation and self-enhancement to a lesser extent	High/Direct – Strict FDA/EMA approval
Non-invasive EEG, fMRI PET, MEG fNIRS	Portability/ limited spatial, temporal resolution	Low	Well-being (sleep/concentration/ stress/mood) Enhancement (cognition, mood, memory)[iii] Examples: MindWave (NeuroSky), Mindset (Mindset), Muse (InteraXon)	Low/ Indirect – Discretionary regulation for low-risk devices marketed for well-being

Notes:
(i) H. Akbari, B. Khalighinejad, J. L. Herrero, *et al.*, Towards Reconstructing Intelligible Speech from the Human Auditory Cortex (2019) 9 *Sci. Rep.* 874.
(ii) G. K. Anumanchipalli, J. Chartier, and E. F. Chang, Speech Synthesis from Neural Decoding of Spoken Sentences (2019) 568 *Nature* 493.
(iii) Wexler and Thibault provide a detailed list of consumer EEG devices marketed for wellbeing purposes A. Wexler and R. Thibault, Mind-Reading or Misleading? Assessing Direct-to-Consumer Electroencephalography (EEG) Devices Marketed for Wellness and Their Ethical and Regulatory Implications (2019) 3 *J. Cogn. Enhanc.* 131.

[58] B. I. Morshed and A. Khan, A Brief Review of Brain Signal Monitoring Technologies for BCI Applications: Challenges and Prospects (2014) 4 *J. Bioeng. Biomed. Sci.* 128.

algorithmic system analogous to neurons, producing artificial results for the same input image.[56] The growing interaction of AI and neuroscience has contributed toward greater accuracy, quicker processing of complex neural data, and better structure;[57] at the same time, neurotech demonstrates great potential for revolutionizing the burgeoning wearables market by incorporating elements of machine learning and clinical research in an attractive commercial packaging. The low cost of methods such as EEG and the plethora of scientific research are key factors in the clear preference for non-invasive methods for commercial BCIs.

Having considered the potential non-invasive BCI hold for research and commerce alike, a final – somewhat paradoxical – observation is in order: in spite of their low health risks and limited medical applications, non-invasive commercial BCIs still qualify as pervasive neurotech. In fact, the use of the term "non-invasive," especially when paired with a product marketed for non-clinical purposes, seems to imply trivial risks for the consumer; this, however, is not fully supported, as they still invade brain physiology.[59] Moreover, this does not correlate with the regulatory threshold being substantially lowered when compared to invasive and semi-invasive BCIs. The following section explains how this appears to be a major oversight and pinpoints key legal considerations.

LEGAL CONSIDERATIONS: BCIS, MULTI-MODAL DATA-FUSED DECISIONS, AND AUTONOMY

On turning the page, you have decided to carry on reading the next sentence: this is one of the 35,000 decisions we make daily.[60] This is a complex process that has been at the fore and center of several disciplines, ranging from cognitive psychology to neuroeconomics and philosophy. To perform a trivial task, such as to choose a soft drink to buy, we employ our memory,[61] heuristics,[62] and prior knowledge or information on the product.[63] Whether we further decide to take this soft drink to the cashier, or to place it in our bag and walk away, involves further moral reasoning that clothes the decision met in a social and ethical setting. The latter is where the law and neuroscience cross paths.[64]

To understand the ways in which neuroscience can inform – and at the same time disrupt – legal thinking, one must think of the scenario whereby we could obtain snapshots of the brain activity when taking these decisions: even though it would not be enough to explain moral

---

[56] G. Shen, T. Horikawa, K. Majima, and Y. Kamitani, Deep Image Reconstruction from Human Brain Activity (2019) 15 *PLoS Comput. Biol.* e1006633.

[57] N. Savage, How AI and Neuroscience Drive Each Other Forwards (2019) 571 *Nature* S15.

[59] N. J. Davis and M. V. Koningsbruggen, "Non-Invasive" Brain Stimulation Is Not Non-Invasive (2013) 7 *Front. Syst. Neurosci.* 76.

[60] The number comes from a Microsoft advertisement (www.youtube.com/watch?v=6k3_T84z5Ds) and is not corroborated in literature – as such, it is purely used here to add emphasis to employing cognition for decision-making on a daily basis.

[61] J. G. Lynch, Jr. and T. K. Srull, Memory and Attentional Factors in Consumer Choice: Concepts and Research Methods (1982) 9 *J. Consum. Res.* 18.

[62] J. A. Howard and J. N. Sheth, *The Theory of Buyer Behaviour* (John Wiley, 1969).

[63] H. A. Simon, *Models of Bounded Rationality: Empirically Grounded Economic Reason* (MIT Press, 1997), Vol. 3.

[64] Greely has grouped the main legal challenges posed by neuroscience into five categories: prediction, mind-reading, responsibility, treatment, and enhancement. Whereas these areas are by no means separate from one another, the focal point for this chapter is mind reading. H. T. Greely, Law and the Revolution in Neuroscience: An Early Look at the Field (2009) 42 *Akron Law Rev.* 687.

reasoning, it could provide links between physiological patterns and behavior/reasoning.[65] Yet, to claim that by reading one's brain we can also read one's mind would be a glaring reductionism that would in fact make no difference to legal thinking: after all, law's mission is not to uncover the scientific truth, but to restore social welfare.[66] As such, the elusive concepts of mind, intent, free will, and causation, although frequently evoked in jurisprudence (for example, liability), are only considered alongside evidence for basing a judgment on social inferences.[67] There is, however, a good chance that in reducing from brain to mind, science can be hijacked to validate half-baked inferences based on physiological data. This phenomenon in turn can trigger *ex post* legal responses in the form of a social/ethical stabilizer; it is the latter that is of interest here, rather than how neuroscience generally might disrupt or inform legal thinking. As such, the focus on autonomy rather than liability maintained here is easily understood.

Taking this a step further, BCIs present more complex legal challenges than neuroscience as they can go beyond merely monitoring: often credited as the key building blocks for neuro-engineering, BCIs have promised the consumer the ability to modify one's behavior, perception, memory, even emotion. Nowadays, the average consumer seems to rely on algorithmically driven technologies to optimize decision-making: from virtual private assistants to driverless vehicles, a great number of cognitive tasks are being outsourced to yield the best decision through a number of educated guesses. Commercial BCIs are no different in this aspect, given that they mostly analyze personal data to make inferences. There is, however, one critical aspect of BCIs that sets them apart: the fact that they are hardwired on to our bodies, and are able to instigate action or suggest changes by peeking inside the black box of the human processor: the brain. This means that: (1) neural activity data are biometric data and thus constitute a special category of personal data[68] that can be used in various contexts (versatility) while being located in diverse settings (brain plasticity); and (2) the level of agency is higher than usual, effectively translating mental state into action. This in essence constitutes a truly symbiotic relationship between the operator (man) and the artificial agent (machine); an idea as old as Wiener's theories

---

65   There are a great number of neuroimaging studies on reasoning and decision-making processes, including problem solving (V. Goel and J. Grafman, Are the Frontal Lobes Implicated in "Planning" Functions? Interpreting Data from the Tower of Hanoi (1995) 33 *Neuropsychologia* 623), analogical reasoning (J. K. Kroger, F. W. Sabb, C. L. Fales, *et al.*, Recruitment of Anterior Dorsolateral Prefrontal Cortex in Human Reasoning: A Parametric Study of Relational Complexity (2002) 12 *Cereb. Cortex* 477), inductive reasoning (V. Goel and R. J. Dolan, Anatomical Segregation of Component Processes in an Inductive Inference Task (2000) 12 *J. Cogn. Neurosci.* 110), and deductive reasoning (D. Osherson, D. Perani, S. Cappa, *et al.*, Distinct Brain Loci in Deductive versus Probabilistic Reasoning (1998) 36 *Neuropsychologia* 369; V. Goel and R. J. Dolan, Explaining Modulation of Reasoning by Belief (2003) 87 *Cognition* B11).

66   B. Cardozo, *The Nature of Judicial Process* (Yale University Press, 1921).

67   "Judges and juries do not, as a precondition to finding that a killing was intentional, peer into the defendant's mind in quest of the required intent. They look at the evidence of what the defendant did and try to infer from it whether the deed involved advance planning or other indicia of high probability of success, whether there was concealment of evidence or other indicia of likely escape, and whether the circumstances of the crime argue a likelihood of repetition – all considerations that go to dangerousness rather than to intent or free will. The legal factfinder follows this approach because the social concern behind criminal punishment is a concern with dangerousness rather than with mental states (evil or otherwise), and because the methods of litigation do not enable the factfinder to probe beneath dangerousness into mental or spiritual strata so elusive they may not even exist. Similarly, while interested in consequences and therefore implicitly in causality, the law does not make a fetish of 'causation'. It does not commit itself to any side of the age-old philosophical controversy over causation, but instead elides the issue by basing judgments of liability on social, rather than philosophical, considerations" (R. A. Posner, What Has Pragmatism to Offer Law? (1990) 63 *SC Law Rev.* 1653).

68   GDPR, art. 9 is applicable here, which reads as follows: "Processing of personal data revealing racial or ethnic origin, political opinions, religious or philosophical beliefs, or trade union membership, and the processing of genetic data, biometric data for the purpose of uniquely identifying a natural person, data concerning health or data concerning a natural person's sex life or sexual orientation shall be prohibited."

TABLE 35.2 *A typology of artificial agency in AI-supported decision-making*

Case Study	Procedural Stages and Interaction for ADM	Level of Automation	Operator Status	Role of Agent
Smart Streaming/Purchasing Services	Suggestion	Partly-automated	Active	Facilitator
Virtual Private Assistants	Advice	Partly-automated (requires trigger)	Active	Assistant
Driverless Vehicles	Nudge (road safety, low carbon emissions)	AI – Knowledge-based system	Stand-by	Expert Advisor
Commercial BCI	Micro-Directive	AI – Heuristics/Optimization Models	Passive (cognitive limitations of choice)	Enabler

on cybernetics[69] or Licklider's notes on Man–Computer symbiosis.[70] Consider the following cases of AI supported decision-making: a Netflix suggestion, Amazon's Alexa personalized music playlists, a driverless vehicle mode for low carbon emissions, and Emotiv's EPOC, an EEG headset that allows the user to play games using thought control.[71] As seen in Table 35.2, the pervasiveness of the agent correlates to various roles in the decision-making: from mere adviser (for example, Alexa) to full enabler (for example, EPOC+).

Following the same reductionist line of thought as earlier, if the human brain is to be reduced to a causal machine[72] – stripped away from any social, moral, and ethical considerations – this would mean that it could operate regardless of one's volition and free will.[73] As noted above, this is not a likely scenario from a jurisprudential viewpoint.[74] It does, however, affect a key bulwark of the Anglo-Saxon legal system:[75] autonomy.

To demonstrate the challenges posed by commercial BCIs for autonomy, we shall address three key manifestations of this concept: autonomy as communication, autonomy as self-control, and autonomy as selfhood. This will allow us to understand the promises and perils of

[69] N. Wiener, *Cybernetics or Control and Communication in the Animal and the Machine* (MIT Press, 1965), Vol. 25.

[70] J. C. R. Licklider, Man-Computer Symbiosis (1960) 1 *IRE Trans. Hum. Factors Electron.* 4.

[71] B. Zhang, J. Wang, and T. Fuhlbrigge, A Review of the Commercial Brain–Computer Interface Technology from Perspective of Industrial Robotics, in 2010 IEEE International Conference on Automation and Logistics, IEEE (August 2010), pp. 379–84.

[72] For a detailed account on the conceptual and empirical limitations of neuro-reductionism, see M. S. Pardo and D. Patterson, *Minds, Brains, and Law: The Conceptual Foundations of Law and Neuroscience* (Oxford University Press, 2015).

[73] M. S. Gazzaniga, *The Ethical Brain* (Dana Press, 2005); M. S. Gazzaniga, *Who's in Charge? Free Will and the Science of the Brain* (Robinson, 2012); A. Noe, *Out of Our Heads: Why You Are Not Your Brain, and Other Lessons from the Biology of the Consciousness* (Hill & Wang, 2010).

[74] This is further posited in *Zeki et al.*, below, as well as Morse, below: the law is interested in rationality and acknowledges its boundaries by requiring general minimal rationality. It is therefore unlikely that neuroscience will alter such legal assumptions determining, for example, liability: see S. J. Morse, New Neuroscience, Old Problems: Legal Implications of Brain Science (2004) 6 *Cerebrum* 81; S. Zeki, O. R. Goodenough, J. Greene, and J. Cohen, For the Law, Neuroscience Changes Nothing and Everything (2004) 359 *Philos. TR Soc. B: Biol. Sci.* 1775, 1778.

[75] Further to this, autonomy also seems to be at the heart of medical ethics. Yet, as already noted in the "Introduction" above, commercial BCIs are not considered medical devices and as such these considerations are not taken into account by the regulators. See also J. Saunders, Autonomy, Consent and the Law (2011) 11 *Clin. Med.* 94.

BCIs for the consumer and underline the main theme of this chapter: once again, the market, science, and technology are there, but the law is still lagging behind.

Autonomy as Communication: Toward the Internet of Minds

Recently, researchers from Cornell University unveiled BrainNet: a brain-to-brain interface (BTBI) that is "the first multi-person non-invasive direct interface for collaborative problem solving." Such interfaces offer a direct pathway between the brains of two animals/humans and enable communication/collaboration on specific tasks. Another successful project along the same lines is DARPA's Silent Talk, a user-to-user communication on the battlefield with vocalized speech substituted by BTBIs.[76] Neither of these projects are commercial, yet they clearly show strong potential for future commercialization. Interestingly enough, both operate on EEG, which would place them in the same category as less elaborate BCIs: non-invasive, low-risk communication methods that have not received much regulative attention to date. The concerns raised here are similar to those regarding BCIs in general and focus on privacy,[77] agency,[78] and even intellectual property rights concerning neural activity.[79] To date, however, the scholarship is limited[80] and seems to overlook communication:[81] a key area of law that finds its theoretical underpinnings in autonomy.

The option to communicate information about ourselves in a social setting has been the result of a delicate balancing exercise between privacy and free speech. Yet, the Lochnerization of the First Amendment in the United States[82] as opposed to the over-claiming approach of the GDPR in Europe[83] also suggests their limitations in offering a balanced solution. As Cohen posits, "invoking Platonic ideals of ownership, speech, truth, and choice just avoids the hard policy questions and inscribes in the guise of liberty a politics and practice of objectification."[84] In essence, we would effectively be oversimplifying the challenges posed to autonomy as communication to a mere trade-off for better services. In turn, this would treat consumers as datafied objects, without further considerations of their autonomy.

This objectification is already exacerbated in the wearables market: Matwyshyn's concept of the Internet of Bodies,[85] an emerging network of technologies attached to or implanted in humans, demonstrates this well. Commercial BCIs, being at the crossroads of neurotech and AI, launch the era of the "Internet of Minds" (IoM)[86] – namely, a platform merging smart

---

[76] B. Denby, T. Schultz, K. Honda, *et al.*, Silent Speech Interfaces (2010) 52 *Speech Commun.* 270.

[77] N. A. Farahany, Incriminating Thoughts (2012) 64 *Stan. Law Rev.* 351; S. Alpert, Brain Privacy: How Can We Protect It? (2007) 7 *Am. J. Bioeth.* 70; J. C. Bublitz, Privacy Concerns in Brain–Computer Interfaces (2019) 10 *AJOB Neuroscience* 30.

[78] A. K. Demetriades, C. K. Demetriades, C. Watts, and K. Ashkan, Brain–Machine Interface: The Challenge of Neuroethics (2010) 8 *Surgeon* 267.

[79] J. B. Trimper, P. Root Wolpe, and K. S. Rommelfanger, When "I" Becomes "We": Ethical Implications of Emerging Brain-to-Brain Interfacing Technologies (2014) 7 *Front. Neuroeng.* 4.

[80] S. Kiel-Chisholm and J. Devereux, The Ghost in the Machine: Legal Challenges of Neural Interface Devices (2015) 23 *Tort Law Rev.* 32.

[81] See also Shen, where mobile consumer neuroscience is discussed in passing, highlighting potential legal and ethical issues: F. X. Shen, Law and Neuroscience 2.0 (2016) 48 *Ariz. St. Law J.* 1043.

[82] R. Post and A. Shanor, Adam Smith's First Amendment (2015) 128 *Harv. Law Rev. Forum* 165, 167.

[83] J. E. Cohen, Turning Privacy Inside Out (2019) 20 *Theor. Inq. Law* 1, 6.

[84] J. E. Cohen, Examined Lives: Informational Privacy and the Subject as Object (1999) 52 *Stan. Law Rev.* 1436.

[85] A. Matwyshyn, The Internet of Bodies Is Here. Are Courts and Regulators Ready? (2018), www.wsj.com/articles/the-internet-of-bodies-is-here-are-courts-and-regulators-ready-1542039566.

[86] The term "Internet of Minds" was first presented in talks I gave at the 2017 Internet Law WIP Conference in Santa Clara and subsequently at the 2018 Algorithms in Society and The Law in Herzliya, Israel. Since then, the phrase has been used in various settings, including a global report (J. Woodhuysen and M. Birbeck, Internet of Things,

apparatuses, mental states, and bodily functions together in a true cybernetic fashion.[87] This augments the challenges posed already by the IoT to one's privacy. Following the taxonomy suggested by Peppet,[88] these include: (1) the issue of "sensor fusion" – namely, the value of the raw data collected by sensors can be multiplied in various settings and contexts, especially when combined with other datasets; (2) the operational difficulty to de-identify sensor data, given that IoT enables linkage of data to other third-party services; (3) the IoT's vulnerability to security flaws; and (4) the difficulty of meaningful consent. The IoM multiplies these concerns: as shown in "The BCI Mechanics," above, the BCIs employ a multi-modal fused approach to map and monitor brain data, decipher these into code, and use them in algorithmic training for adaptive systems. When this is further combined with the plasticity of the data, the safety vulnerabilities in neural engineering,[89] and the interlinked, seamless manner in which IoT operates, it is easy to understand that the law[90] is unprepared to tackle these challenges.

Autonomy as Self-Control: Mental Manipulation and Consumer Frailty

The functional significance that EEG bears for marketing research is certainly not a recent discovery: Krugman's pioneering study on using EEG to explain consumer engagement in 1971[91] set the tone for the years to come and was followed by a number of studies on what time-specific neural activity might reveal for the consumer's decisions. Take, for example, the "event-related potential" (ERP), a technique used in EEG-based methods in consumer neuroscience to capture time-specific neural responses to triggering stimuli. Certain patterns and frequencies generated by brain activity can translate to particular mental states (for example, dreaming, relaxing, being alert).[92] When these are studied as responses elicited before or during decision-making, they can yield valuable information as to sensory and psychological processes: P300, one of the most widely studied ERPs, is focused on attention and memory; N200 indicates inhibition and cognitive control; and P200 targets selective attention (for example, responses to threat).[93]

No doubt such methods exacerbate information asymmetries and add to consumer frailty, as they enable an *a fortiori* data-leveraging that ultimately weakens the consumer's bargaining power.[94] In this sense, these pervasive methods constitute a soft yet opaque method of control: a "hypernudge," as Yeung puts it, that suggests a subtle manipulation by "deliberately

Internet of Apprehension (2017), www.woudhuysen.com/wp-content/uploads/2017/01/internet-of-things.pdf) and a self-published essay (I. C. Lomovasky, *The Internet of Minds (IOM): An Essay* (independently published, 2018)). To the best of my knowledge, this is the first time the term is included in a legal peer-reviewed scholarly article.

[87] To the point that this arguably constitutes a paradigmatic shift in human evolution of cognition: W. Barfield, The Process of Evolution, Human Enhancement Technology, and Cyborgs (2019) 4 *Philosophies* 10.

[88] S. R. Peppet, Regulating the Internet of Things: First Steps toward Managing Discrimination, Privacy, Security and Consent (2014) 93 *Tex. Law Rev.* 85.

[89] T. Bonaci, R. Calo, and H. J. Chizeck, App Stores for the Brain: Privacy and Security in Brain–Computer Interfaces (2015) 34 *IEEE Technol. Soc. Mag.* 32.

[90] Peppet discusses privacy, data security, and consumer law, addressing the IoT's privacy concerns from a US standpoint. For an EU account along the same lines, see S. Wachter, The GDPR and the Internet of Things: A Three-Step Transparency Model (2018) 10 *Law Innov. Technol.* 266.

[91] H. E. Krugman, Brain Wave Measures of Media Involvement (1971) 11 *J. Advert. Res.* 3.

[92] For a general synopsis, see B. Zhang, J. Wang, and T. Fuhlbrigge, A Review of the Commercial Brain–Computer Interface Technology from Perspective of Industrial Robotics, in 2010 IEEE International Conference on Automation and Logistics, IEEE (August 2010), pp. 381–2.

[93] Lin *et al.* offer an excellent overview of ERPs used in consumer neuroscience, including details on their observing data and functional significance: see M. H. Lin, S. N. Cross, W. J. Jones, and T. L. Childers, Applying EEG in Consumer Neuroscience (2018) 52 *Eur. J. Mark.* 66, 72–3.

[94] R. Calo, Digital Market Manipulation (2013) 82 *Geo. Wash. Law Rev.* 995, 1034.

exploiting systematic cognitive weaknesses which pervade human decision-making to chan-nel behaviour in directions preferred by the choice architect."[95] The systematic failure of data protection to address "hypernudges" by reliance on informed consent[96] shows well the need for crafting better regulatory tools to shield one's conscious choices and cognitive liberty. While data protection provides some answers toward empowering the user, it does not tread a fine line between the individual and the markets, creating exuberant transactional costs for businesses to secure compliance.[97] Moreover, considering that commercial neuro-tech is nowadays also being used in clinical research as a cheaper alternative, a myopic consent-based approach would act as hindrance to scientific innovation, disregarding the economic value of big data.[98]

Autonomy as Selfhood: Selective-Opacity and the Black Box Conundrum

Having dissected the BCI's inherent limitations to communicating and controlling one's data, we now turn to the conceptual core of autonomy: the perception of one's data as identity. Consider the following series of studies on memory manipulation. In a series of papers published in 2012 and 2013, Ramirez and Lieu detailed their experiments on the fear memory of mice and made history by successfully implanting and reactivating false mem-ories.[99] Even though this involved highly invasive methods (optogenetics) in a lab setting and is therefore beyond the scope of what is discussed here, it nonetheless serves as a great example to explain the impact neuroscience has on one's selfhood.

What is unsettling about this use of neurotech is not only that certain cognitive abilities are externalized to third parties without our conscious involvement (communication) or that our mental states can be externally re-engineered (selective opacity), but rather that our self-consciousness is being compromised. We are defining ourselves through our interactions with others in a given social setting – who we are is not reduced to a genetic or physiological predisposition, but is formed through a discursive and social process with our environment.[100] The fusion of neuroscience and AI brought together in the shape of a wearable commercially available device holds great promise for opening the black box of human thought. Greene and Cohen have described this as a process that turns the mind into a "transparent bottleneck":

> There are many causes that impinge on behaviour, but all of them – from the genes you inherited, to the pain in your lower back, to the advice your grandmother gave you when you were six – must exert their influence through the brain. Thus, your brain serves as a bottleneck for all the forces spread throughout the universe of your past that affect who you are and what you do.[101]

At the same time, though, this method enables interaction with an array of automated logical systems, limiting our self-formation through human social interaction.[102] This reveals

95 K. Yeung, "Hypernudge": Big Data as a Mode of Regulation by Design (2017) 20 *Inf. Commun. Soc.* 118, 134.
96 F. Z. Borgesius, Informed Consent: We Can Do Better to Defend Privacy (2015) 13 *IEEE Secur. Priv.* 103.
97 F. J. Zuiderveen Borgesius, *Improving Privacy Protection in the Area of Behavioural Targeting* (Kluwer Law International, 2015), p. 33.
98 A. Acquisti, From the Economics of Privacy to the Economics of Big Data, in J. Lane, V. Stodden, S. Bender, and H. Nissenbaum (eds.), *Privacy, Big Data, and the Public Good: Frameworks for Engagement* (Cambridge University Press, 2014), pp. 76, 97.
99 X. Liu, S. Ramirez, P. P. Pang, C. Puryear, A. Govindarajan, K. Deisseroth, and S. Tonegawa. "Optogenetic Stimulation of a Hippocampal Engram Activates Fear Memory Recall." (2012) 484 *Nature* 381.
100 Cohen, above note 84, p. 10.
101 S. Zeki, O. R. Goodenough, J. Greene, and J. Cohen, For the Law, Neuroscience Changes Nothing and Everything (2004) 359 *Philos. TR Soc. B: Biol. Sci.* 1775, 1781.
102 Cohen, above note 84, p. 10.

a paradox, whereby BCIs rely, inter alia, on past social interactions, yet they do not reinforce them. In turn, we are faced with the complexities of the algorithmic "black box"[103] that support automated decision-making in an opaque and inscrutable manner.[104] Therein lies the dilemma as to whether the law should strive to either make the algorithmic black box transparent or to provide the mind with added opacity to restore selfhood. It seems that for now the regulatory approach is on the former, which – as Cohen notes[105] – only adds to a vicious circle of re-optimizing machine-learning systems to comply with the detailed legal provisions. She describes this as the "privacy as control paradigm," which is doomed to failure as it will "entail rapid proliferation of internal surveillance functionality" to catch up with exponential complexities in machine-learning systems.

CONCLUSION: THE QUEST FOR AUTONOMY

The technological and scientific advances in neurotechnologies, paired with an unprecedented sophistication in AI, have taken us a long way since the days when mind reading was considered a deceptive act of charlatanism. Working with inferences and rough consensus,[106] commercial BCIs promise to explain, enhance, or even alter human behavior with minimum involvement from the user. This is indicative of a shift from economies of scope, namely commercial entities focusing on the range and scalability of data gathered, to economies of action – commercial entities now profiting from derivatives of behavioral surplus. Zuboff calls this a new age of surveillance capitalism: an era in which digital commerce is driven from monitoring to actuation, exceeding the limits of our perception and awareness.[107] The emotion contagion experiment by Facebook, mentioned at the beginning of this chapter, demonstrates well this intended evasion of individual awareness, or as Zuboff puts it, "an effective form of telestimulation at scale."[108] The case of commercial BCIs offers another dimension to the same narrative: a physiological *in vivo* experiment for the consumer.

This chapter has placed particular emphasis on this commercial thirst for mind-reading machines, when discussing the uses of neurotechnologies beyond the laboratory confines of clinical research. The pervasiveness of these technologies, although understandably alarming, is not what is of primary interest here, nor is it what sets them apart from behavioral data processing, as seen in the agency typology presented in the first part of this chapter. What makes them an elusive category for the regulator is the fact that they operate on a number of levels (sensory, algorithmic, invocative) and perform a symbiotic, data-fused man-machine approach. The chapter discussed the BCI mechanics and outlined their key operational stages of (1) sensors monitoring neural activity (hardware), (2) algorithmic analysis/training based on obtained data using elaborate methods such as Deep Neural Networks (software), and (3) brain–machine interaction, able to direct some external activity. The final part of this chapter sought to further explore how this applies in decision-making optimization and

---

[103] F. Pasquale, *The Black Box Society* (Harvard University Press, 2015).
[104] A. D. Selbst and S. Barocas, The Intuitive Appeal of Explainable Machines (2018) 87 *Fordham Law Rev.* 1085.
[105] Cohen, above note 84, p. 7.
[106] Paraphrasing David Clark's famous phrase "we work on running code and rough consensus," when referring to the development of technical standards in the early days of Internet Governance. See D. D. Clark, A Cloudy Crystal Ball: Visions of the Future, in Proceedings of the Twenty-Fourth Internet Engineering Task Force (1992), pp. 539–45.
[107] S. Zuboff, *The Age of Surveillance Capitalism: The Fight for a Human Future at the New Frontier of Power* (Profile Books, 2019), pp. 130–8, 159 ff.
[108] *Ibid.*, p. 307.

outlined the challenges for autonomy. It appears that the transition from the IoT (Internet of Things) to the IoM (Internet of Minds) has found the law unprepared to tackle the challenges posed beyond the narrow confines of consent-based data protection mechanisms, mostly prevalent in Europe.

Looking beyond a data protection framework, scholars on both sides of the Atlantic have sought to expand privacy claims:[109] US-based scholars explore privacy as ownership[110] and EU-based scholars adopt the public/private dichotomy and the concept of identity.[111] Other scholars have suggested a rights-based approach that is premised on neuro-exceptionalism, ultimately calling for a new set of "neuro-rights": Bublitz and Merkel[112] introduce the concept of "mental self-determination" to protect against indirect interventions in one's mental state. Building on this further, Ienca and Andorno[113] suggest a triad of rights supporting cognitive liberty as a human right meriting special protection: the right to mental privacy (namely to determine the information that is externalized to others), the right to mental integrity (affording protection against "malicious brain-hacking"[114]), and the right to psychological continuity (allowing one to perceive and be aware of one's personal identity). We argue that the truth is neither here, nor there. Instead of steering away from privacy, what is required is a normative reconfiguration of informational privacy[115] that ensures and nurtures[116] autonomy[117] as communication, control, and identity.

---

[109]   For an initial discussion on key points in the relevant debate, see M. Scheinman, Protecting Your Brain Waves and Other Biometric Data in a Global Economy (2013), https://papers.ssrn.com/sol3/papers.cfm? abstract_id=2382951.

[110]   See, e.g., Farahany, who suggests a copyright-based interpretation of the Fourth Amendment to explain its application regarding emerging technologies: N. A. Farahany, Searching Secrets (2011) 160 *Univ. Pa. Law Rev.* 1239.

[111]   A. Etzioni, The Privacy Merchants: What Is to Be Done? (2011) 14 *Univ. Pa. J. Const. Law* 929.

[112]   J. C. Bublitz and R. Merkel, Crimes against Minds: On Mental Manipulations, Harms and a Human Right to Mental Self-Determination (2014) 8 *Crim. Law Philos.* 51, 65–73.

[113]   M. Ienca and R. Andorno, Towards New Human Rights in the Age of Neuroscience and Neurotechnology (2017) 13 *Life Sci. Soc. Policy* 5.

[114]   M. Ienca and P. Haselager, Hacking the Brain: Brain–Computer Interfacing Technology and the Ethics of Neurosecurity (2016) 18 *Ethics Inf. Technol.* 117.

[115]   Consider the valuable guidance offered by Brownsword here, seeing informational privacy as two concentric circles: the inner part constitutes the "inner sanctum" and remains a fixed concept, whereas the outer circle is flexible, subject to adjustment following convention, custom, and practice. R. Brownsword, Regulating Brain Imaging: Questions of Privacy, Informed Consent, and Human Dignity, in S. D. Richmond, G. Rees, and S. J. L. Edwards (eds.), *I Know What You're Thinking: Brain Imaging and Mental Privacy* (Oxford University Press, 2012), pp. 223–44, 232.

[116]   "Autonomous individuals do not spring full-blown from the womb. We must learn to process information and to draw our own conclusions about the world around us. We must learn to choose, and must learn something before we can choose anything. Here, though, information theory suggests a paradox: 'Autonomy' connotes an essential independence of critical faculty and an imperviousness to influence. But to the extent that information shapes behavior, autonomy is radically contingent upon environment and circumstance. The only tenable resolution – if 'autonomy' is not to degenerate into the simple, stimulus-response behavior sought by direct marketers – is to under determine environment. Autonomy in a contingent world requires a zone of relative insulation from outside scrutiny and interference – a field of operation within which to engage in the conscious construction of self. The solution to the paradox of contingent autonomy, in other words, lies in a second paradox: To exist in fact as well as in theory, autonomy must be nurtured" (J. E. Cohen, Examined Lives: Informational Privacy and the Subject as Object (2000) 52 *Stan. Law Rev.* 1373, 1424).

[117]   Schachter's notion of "decisional privacy" could arguably be an excellent application in this aspect: M. Schachter, *Informational and Decisional Privacy* (Carolina Academic Press, 2003).

Index

administrative law 162–163, 166–168, 176
  fishbowl transparency 176, 178
  governance 179
  transparency 176
admitting machine opinions 34
agency law 153, 157–161
  authority 161, 178
  legal agent 156–157
  legal agreement 154
  Restatement (Third) of Agency 157, 160
  unsuitability of 156
algorithm 3, 32–33
  accountability 49, 51, 85–87, 731, 737, 742
  assigning liability 4, 8, 483
  black box 29, 51, 90, 112, 125–126, 148, 163, 192, 233, 245, 296, 419, 521, 672
  computer science 13, 125, 276, 301, 366, 374, 391–392, 693, 721
  criminal law 60–61, 65
    PredPol 61–71, 255, 408
  cross examination 35, 41, 414, 419
  definition of 4, 51, 122, 141, 142, 306, 374, 519, 563
  embodiment 736, 740
  fairness 83, 107, 282, 427
  functioning of 20–22, 52, 216
  human bias 3, 49, 54–55, 142
  human impact statement 88–89
  legality 661
  legitimacy 108
    The Federalist No. 22 109
  Limited Liability Company (LLC) 156
  probabilities 111, 435–436, 439, 478, 483–484, 654, 715, 726
  public administration 210, 215, 221, 273, 301
  regulation of 3, 123–124, 271
  rule of law 219–221, 299
  specialized court 7
  statutory construction 5–7, 256–257, 267
  statutory penalty 248
  use of 3, 47, 122, 233
algorithmic bias 45, 51, 110, 674
  predictive models 282
algorithmic competition 199, 201
algorithmic contract 141, 146
  applications 144

contract terms 144
  gap-filler 147
  negotiator contract 148
algorithmic decision making 251, 265, 301, 501
  ADS (algorithmic decision system) 273–275
algorithmic discrimination 49, 182
algorithmic governance 162, 209, 213–214, 251, 702
  administrative decision making 253–255
  ambient law 229
  decision making 257, 259
  definition of governance 210, 212
  Digital Era Governance (DEG) 211, 231
  New Public Management (NPM) 211, 231
  regulation 701
  role of algorithms 223
algorithmic speech 543, 606
  authorship 593
  computer code 547, 553
  Charter of Rights and Freedoms.5 Section 2(b) 568, 573, 578
  Cyber-Plato 580–581, 585, 594, 600
  Digital Millennium Copyright Act (DMCA) 550, 584, 586–587
  First Amendment 543–546, 552, 579, 613–617
    O'Brien test 586–597, 602
    jurisprudence 612
    Spence test 602
  Free Speech Clause 609, 611–612, 623, 627, 631
  freedom of expression 466, 469, 558, 561, 564–565, 570, 684
  functionality doctrine 552, 575
  Google 595–596
  natural language expression 548
  Siri and Alexa 597
  speech and conduct 582
  strict scrutiny 550
  Turing 545, 630
  Wu and *Benjamin* theories 575–576
algorithmic transparency 112, 121, 123, 246, 259, 266, 521
  opacity 521
  taxonomy of 127–138
Alibaba 255, 642, 644
AlphaGo 16, 22, 39, 42, 354, 358
Amazon 41, 57, 148, 193, 201, 204, 499
American Civil Liberties Union (ACLU) 47, 112

antitrust 75
  elasticity of demand 75
  enforcement 199–200
  collusion 200, 202–205
  parallel pricing 199
  price fixing/discrimination 201, 203–204
artificial intelligence (AI) 107, 121, 162, 167, 187, 210, 342,
    403, 407, 517, 523–524, 579, 590
  AI speaker 590–591
  Artificial Intelligence Ethics Framework 272, 734–735
  Artificial General Intelligence (AGI) 340, 358
  Artificial Super Intelligence (ASI) 358
  authoritarian 659
  automation bias 65
  Berkman Klein Center 518
  civil rights 47–48, 50
  connectionist 724
  definition 690
  embodiment 736
  ethical 722, 729
  Partnership on AI to Benefit People and Society 272
  regulation 727
  socializing with 728
  speech 581, 583, 599–600
  trustworthy 667–668, 682, 686–687
Association for Computing Machinery (ACM) 84
  algorithm transparency and accountability 84
autocomplete 73, 450–455, 460–461, 464–470
automated decision making 81, 191, 303, 308
  Court of Australia 270
automated systems 115
  decision making 269–270, 326–327, 494
  equality 262
  legitimacy 115
  spectrum of automation 252
autonomy 474–476
  OODA ("Observe"; "Orient"; "Decide"; "Act") 475

behavioral targeting 71
  Fair Housing Act 71
bias 55, 57–59, 61–63, 280
  cognitive 65
  statistical and historical 55
big data 44, 47, 53, 72, 209, 224, 675, 679
  bias and 55
  privacy 173
  surveillance 60, 71, 113, 236–238, 250, 523, 679
  training bias 55
Biometric Information Privacy Act (BIPA) 9
blockchain 149–150, 156, 556, 707, 718
brain-computer interface (BCI) 758, 761,
    763–765, 768
  autonomy 769–772
British Computer Society 85

Cambridge Analytica 48, 683
CAPTCHA 674
Civil Rights 76–78, 106
  US Consumer Financial Protection Bureau 77
code as law 309, 704

Communications Decency Act (CDA) 457–460
computational social science 710
computer bias 69–71
Computer Fraud and Abuse Act (CFAA) 92–93, 269
computer-generated evidence (CGE) 24–25, 28
COMPASS 66–69, 94, 240–241, 256, 262–263, 271, 436–
    438, 440, 442, 445, 522
Computer Software Act of 1980 384
Consumer Financial Protection Bureau (CFPB) 634
Consumer Privacy Bill of Rights 91
contract law 154
  offer 155
  machine learning 179
copyright 94, 269, 370, 392–395
  infringement 201, 209, 269
criminal adjudication 407, 418
  bias and errors 408
  criminal law 242
  judicial decision making 255
  recidivism rate 242
cyberspace law 429

data 60, 239, 325
  and algorithms 693
  criminal activity 239, 249–250
  GPS 326, 588
  over selection 60
  protection 110
  reuse 239
data driven lending 634
data mining 55, 57
deep learning 9, 16, 20
DeepMind 353–354, 365, 366, 564, 672, 737
Defend Trade Secrets Act (DTSA) 92, 98–105
digital information and communications technology
    (ICT) 209, 213
disparate impact 79, 107
  Title VII (Civil Rights Act) 71, 79, 102
Digital Autonomous Organization (DAO) 148–151
digital government 303
discrimination 183, 187, 193, 234, 522
  New Zealand Human Rights Commission 234
  disparate impact 186
  disproportionally adverse outcomes 194
  lending 189
DNA and algorithms 8, 10–11, 38, 103, 238, 407, 411–413,
    421, 423, 425, 427, 557
Double click 451
due process 168–170
  Due Process Clause 81, 119, 416

electronic agent 153
  definition 146
Electronic Signatures in Global and National
    Commerce Act (E-Sign Act) 145
electronic-persons 472
electronically stored information 409
embodiment 736–737, 739, 740–743, 745
  proximity and privacy 747
emergence 741

algorithmic society 273
surveillance capitalism 677
European Commission on Human Rights 80
European Court of Human Rights 293
evidence 18, 34, 409–410
  admissibility 29
  Brady doctrine 416–417, 423
  California *Sargon* test 35
  Federal Rules of Evidence 411, 418, 420
  Frye or *Daubert* tests 411–412, 415, 418, 421–422,
    759–760
  hearsay 419–420
Equal Credit Opportunity Act (ECOA) 183–184,
    198, 633
Equal Employment Opportunity Commission (EEOC)
    47–48
equal protection 170–172
  Fifth Amendment 170
expert system 19, 188, 252

Facebook 54, 237, 263, 281–282, 554, 645–646, 676
facial recognition 412
Fair Credit Reporting Act (FCRA) 125, 633
Fair Housing Act 182
Fairness, Accountability, and Transparency in Machine
    Learning (FATML) 526, 528, 730
Federal Drug Agency (FDA) 15, 53, 430
Federal Trade Commission (FTC) 74, 101
  price discrimination 74
Financial Industry Regulatory Authority (FINRA) 248
  civic sanctions 640
FinTech 182, 193
  banking 188
  case law 185
  Equal Credit Opportunity Act 182
  FICO score 189, 632, 635
First Amendment 4, 7, 591–592, 609
FISA Court 662
fMRI data 415, 730, 759 F
Fourteenth Amendment 6
Fourth Amendment 663
French Code of Higher Education 284
French National Data Protection Agency 284
French Data Protection Law 286
Future of Humanity Institute 95

General Data Protection Regulation (GDPR) 82–83,
    87–88, 114, 121, 127, 267, 271, 297, 322, 329, 335,
    427–428, 462, 465, 467, 527, 654, 680–681,
    686, 751
  Article 4(1) 311
  Article 8 293, 317
  Article 22 129, 197, 271, 294, 297, 307
  Article 25 330
  Chapter III 328
  Data Protection Officer 88
  Data Protection Impact Assessment 540
  digital legal framework 304
  evidence 423
  government regulation 271

human rights 536
machine learning 279
privacy 174, 292
Google 52, 272, 281, 340, 450, 453, 460–462, 465–466, 560,
    569–570, 577, 588
  censorship 468
  DeepMind 353–354, 359, 365
  First Amendment 621–622
  Google Earth 409
  liability 469
  PageRank 607
  transparency 462–463

hearsay 26–28
HLEG 688–689
human-centered design 244–245
human rights 235, 285, 517, 520, 533
  European Commission High-Level Group on
    Ethics 518
  human right based approach (HRBA) 518, 529–533,
    535, 537–539, 541–542
  international Covenant on Economic, Social, and
    Cultural Rights (ICESCR) 533–534
  right to be forgotten 466, 559, 577
  UN Committee on Economic, Cultural, and Social
    Rights (CESRC) 533, 537
human-robot interaction (HRI) 736, 743, 745, 748, 756

IBM 353, 499
  Deep Blue 353
  Deep Thought 353
Institute of Electrical and Electronics Engineers (IEEE)
    84, 271
  ethically aligned design 84
inference engine 31
informational privacy 80
intellectual property 50, 391–392
  authorship 401
  Commission on New Technological Uses of
    Copyright Works (CONTU) 394
  copyright protection for software 393–394
  trademark law 393, 400
Internal Revenue Service (IRS) 637–638

legal decision-making system 305, 307–308, 315
legal person status 6
liability 247–248
LGBT 57–58, 116

machine learning 16, 54–56, 142, 162, 188, 217, 241, 247,
    266, 426, 519, 660
  accuracy 241
  definition 163
  introduction 275
  legal domain 279
  online child protection 704
  reinforcement learning 278–279, 519
  supervised learning 56, 277
  unsupervised learning 277
  working of 163–167

machine opinion evidence 17
  admissibility 27, 30
  heuristics 30
  Kelly hearing 46
  simulation versus animation 29
  validation 42–43
moral machines 667
  MIT 671

national security decision making 266
  legal exceptionalism 266
neural nets (neural networks) 16, 18, 39, 143, 159,
      192
  back propositional 21
  disadvantage 144
  functioning of 20–22
  juries 17
  supervised 21
  use of 22–24
  validation 40, 43–44
Norwegian Public Administration 301

Office of Data Analytics (New York City)
      165
Oxford Risk of Recidivism Tool (OxRec)
      443

parallel cognitive system 723
parole board 53
patent law 4, 10–11, 18, 339
  claim construction 380
  Federal Drug Administration (FDA) 37
  future predictions 373
  Inventive Algorithm Standard 341–343
  level of ordinary skill 350
  new machine principle 376
  non-obviousness inquiry 347, 348, 361, 379
  obviousness 339, 344–346
  Patent Act of 1793 345
  Patent Act of 1952 347
  person with ordinary skill in the art 349, 361–363
  prior art 351
  public policy 344
  35 U.S.C. Section 101 (subject matter) 374, 377,
      381, 386
  35 U.S.C. Section 103 (non-obvious subject matter)
      103, 377, 379
  35 U.S.C. Section 112 (skilled in the art) 390
  skilled person 341
  software inventions 375, 387
  subject matter 376–377
Patriot Act 655–656
persuasion profiling 71
predictive analytics/coding 19, 53, 64
  policing 61
  prosecution 416
privacy 173, 236, 523
  Privacy Act 173
  Data analysis 654
  Driver's Privacy Protection Act 174

E-Government Act 174
  GDPR (see separate listing) 174
  HIPPA 174
products liability 471, 473, 476, 493
  thinking algorithms 478–479

regulation 50, 196
reputational harm 449, 454
  defamation 454
  false light 455
  Internet 449, 455
  libel and slander 454
risk assessment 408, 432
  fairness 440
  risk assessment instruments (RAI) 432–435, 438–439,
      442, 444–448
  sentencing 436
robots 7, 13, 472–473, 495, 670, 678, 737
  civil law rules 667
  human-robot interaction 736
  merger with humans 580
  prison guards 221, 414
robo-doctor 480–482, 490–491 496, 501, 506–509,
      512, 514
robo-selling 199–202

search engines 62, 73–74, 107, 449–452, 461, 463,470, 559,
      563, 594–599, 608, 620, 670, 675
  case law 464
  functionality 452
  liability 466
  search engine optimization (SEO) 452–453
sensor facts 324
smart contract xx 148–149, 156, 707
Snowden revelations 209, 655, 663
Social Credit System (SCS) 253. 255, 260, 632, 635,
      640–644
  Sesame Credit 643
  opaqueness 652
  privacy 645, 649
Social Network Analysis (SNA) 699
Social Security Disability Insurance (SSDI)
      638–639
social segregation 651

tacit expertise 35–36
technology-assisted review (TAR) 18–19, 21, 40
testimony 31
Title VII (Civil Rights Act) 79, 85, 102,
      118, 186
tort law 454, 476, 493, 742
  design defect 499
  foreseeability 504
  horizontal equality 497
  liability 159–160, 495, 673
  reasonableness standard 493, 509, 510, 513
  thinking algorithm 496, 501, 504, 507, 510
Trade Secret 90–92, 95, 98–106
tragedy of the commons 715–718
transformation of legal sources 313

Turing 519, 545, 630, 669, 691
  Turing's Cathedral 691

Uniform Commercial Code (UCC) (product or service)
  7, 146
Uniform Computer Information Transactions Act
  (UCITA} 147

Uniform Electronic Transactions Act (UETA)
  145–147, 151

Watson 352–355, 358–360, 364, 367, 414, 417
Weapons of Math Destruction (Cathy O'Neil) 243
Whistleblower Protection Act (WPA)
  96–97

For EU product safety concerns, contact us at Calle de José Abascal, 56–1°,
28003 Madrid, Spain or eugpsr@cambridge.org.

www.ingramcontent.com/pod-product-compliance
Ingram Content Group UK Ltd.
Pitfield, Milton Keynes, MK11 3LW, UK
UKHW030903150625
459647UK00022B/2845